THE DIDACHE

Faith, Hope, & Life of the Earliest
Christian Communities, 50–70 C.E.

The Newman Press
SIGNIFICANT SCHOLARLY STUDIES

The Newman Press imprint offers scholarly studies in historical theology. It provides a forum for professional academics to address significant issues in the areas of biblical interpretation, patristics, and medieval and modern theology. This imprint also includes commentaries on major claassical works in these fields, such as the acclaimed Ancient Christian Writers series, in order to contribute to a better understanding of critical questions raised in writings of enduring importance.

THE DIDACHE

Faith, Hope, & Life of
the Earliest Christian Communities, 50–70 C.E.

Aaron Milavec

THE NEWMAN PRESS
NEW YORK/MAHWAH, N.J.

The publication of this book was greatly assisted by a generous gift from Dr. Colm Luibheid of the National University of Ireland, Galway.

Grateful acknowledgment is made to the following for the permission to incorporate revised versions of the following previously published works: "Distinguishing True and False Prophets: The Protective Wisdom of the Didache," *Journal of Early Christian Studies* 2/2 (1994) 117–36. Permission granted by Johns Hopkins University Press. "The Social Setting of 'Turning the Other Cheek,' and 'Loving One's Enemies' in the Light of the *Didache*," *BTB* 25/2 (1995) 131–43. Permission granted by the *Biblical Theological Bulletin*. "Saving Efficacy of the Burning Process in Didache 16.5," *The Didache in Context: Essays on Its Text, History and Transmission*, ed. Clayton N. Jefford. Leiden: E.J. Brill, 1995, pp. 131–55. Permission granted by E.J. Brill Publishers.

Jacket design by Valerie Petro
Illustrations by Ann Bain
Composition by The HK Scriptorium

The Newman Press is a trademark of Paulist Press, Inc.

Library of Congress Cataloging-in-Publication Data

Milavec, Aaron, 1938-
    The Didache : faith, hope, & life of the earliest Christian
communities, 50-70 C.E. / by Aaron Milavec.
        p. cm.
Includes bibliographical references and indexes.
    ISBN 0-8091-0537-3 (alk. paper)
    1. Didache. 2. Christian ethics—History—Early church, ca. 30-600.
3. Church polity—History—Early church, ca. 30-600. 4. Christian
ethics—Early works to 1800. 5. Church polity—Early works to 1800.
I. Didache. English and Greek. II. Title.
    BS2940 .T5 M55 2003
    270.1—dc21
                                                        2003003659

Published by
THE NEWMAN PRESS
An imprint of Paulist Press
997 Macarthur Boulevard
Mahwah, New Jersey 07430

www.paulistpress.com

Printed and bound in the
United States of America

CONTENTS

Part III: Special Issues

Epilogue

Flowcharts

PREFACE

T hose using this commentary are about to embark on a voyage of discovery. The *Didache* represents the preserved oral tradition detailing
the step-by-step training of gentile converts being prepared for full, active
participation in the house churches committed to the Way of Life. As an
oral tradition, the *Didache* encapsulated the lived practice whereby non-
Jews were being initiated into those altered habits of perceiving, of judging, and of acting characteristic of one branch of the Jesus movement
flourishing during the mid-first century.

The *Didache* is a "pastoral manual" that reveals more about how Jewish-
Christians saw themselves and how they adapted their Judaism for gentiles
than any other book in the Christian Scriptures. It is not a gospel, and,
accordingly, it does not attempt to offer guidance by narrating a life of
Jesus. In fact, it is older than the canonical Gospels and was written in the
generation following the death of Jesus, when the message of Jesus was not
yet encapsulated in stories about Jesus. Nor is the *Didache* a letter as in the
case of the letters of Paul. In fact, the *Didache* was created at the time of
Paul's mission to the gentiles but shows not the slightest awareness of this
mission or of the theology that undergirded it.

The *Didache* is an anonymous document. Like so many other books in
the Christian Scriptures, it did not belong to or originate with a single individual. It belonged to various communities of householders who had
received a Way of Life revealed to them by the Father through his servant
Jesus. Given the manifest clues of orality within the *Didache* itself, one can
be quite certain that it was originally composed orally and that it circulated
on the lips of the members of this community for a good many years before
any occasion arose that called for a scribe to prepare a textual version.

The *Didache* did not originally have any title. When it was used, everyone knew what it was and how it was to be applied. When the written copy
finally did get a title, it was called "The Training of the Lord Through the
Twelve Apostles to the Gentiles." Scholars today have abbreviated this long

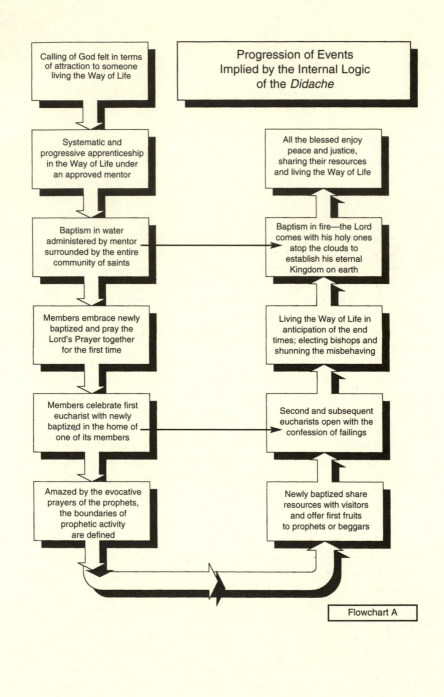

Progression of Events
Implied by the Internal Logic
of the *Didache*

Calling of God felt in terms of attraction to someone living the Way of Life

Systematic and progressive apprenticeship in the Way of Life under an approved mentor

Baptism in water administered by mentor surrounded by the entire community of saints

Members embrace newly baptized and pray the Lord's Prayer together for the first time

Members celebrate first eucharist with newly baptized in the home of one of its members

Amazed by the evocative prayers of the prophets, the boundaries of prophetic activity are defined

All the blessed enjoy peace and justice, sharing their resources and living the Way of Life

Baptism in fire—the Lord comes with his holy ones atop the clouds to establish his eternal Kingdom on earth

Living the Way of Life in anticipation of the end times; electing bishops and shunning the misbehaving

Second and subsequent eucharists open with the confession of failings

Newly baptized share resources with visitors and offer first fruits to prophets or beggars

Flowchart A

title as *Didache* (usually pronounced "Did-ah-Kay")—the Greek word for the systematic training that a mentor (or a master craftsman) would give to an understudy (apprentice). This was a remarkably fitting working title even though, as the commentary will show, it has not been adequately appreciated or understood.

The *Didache* represents the first concerted attempt by householders (Crossan 1998) to adapt the way of Jesus to the exigencies of family, of occupation, of home—the very things that Jesus and his wandering apostles had left behind (Theissen 1977). Paul did this for the communities he founded. The twelve apostles undoubtedly did this for the community in Jerusalem. From Paul, however, we have only occasional letters. From the Twelve, we have nothing. The Acts of the Apostles only gives passing details regarding community life in the Jerusalem church and in the churches founded by Paul. The *Didache*, in contrast, offers a full-blown description of nearly every aspect of community life:

> One overhears a candidate being trained from scratch by a mentor who becomes his beloved "father" or "mother." One witnesses the fasting and the solemn rite of baptism, preferably by immersion in flowing water. One overhears the daily prayers and the weekly Eucharist—both of which are sketched out in full detail. One learns how visiting prophets were a blessing and a danger at the same time. One comes to understand how manual work, the sharing of resources, and the cultivation of gratitude worked together to provide a mainstay for individual well being within a community. One learns how the confession of failings, the correction of backsliders, and the shunning of recalcitrant members worked to maintain the community's standards of excellence. Finally, one discovers how a community poised on the threshold of the Kingdom of God could fashion its daily life sharing the same passionate expectation of God's future that Jesus had formerly preached to the Jewish peasants and fishermen of Galilee.

All in all, therefore, the *Didache* represents the comprehensive and detailed schema used to train gentiles for full and active inclusion within the Didache communities of the mid-first century. The framers of the *Didache*, however, insofar as they were pastors poised on the threshold of the end time, may be suitably understood as passing on their cherished secrets of surviving and thriving until the Lord comes atop the clouds of heaven.

Christians have come to regard the books of the Christian Scriptures (New Testament) as including all the authentic writings produced by the Jesus movement during the first century. Sad to say, this judgment is not true. The *Gospel of Thomas* and the Q Gospel represent two instances of first-century productions not found in the canon. Now, after being lost for fifteen hundred years, the *Didache* has also been recovered. It was accidentally discovered bound within other early Christian documents in a manuscript library in Istanbul in 1873. Only one complete copy of the *Didache* survived the ravages of time.

The very existence of the *Didache* may cause puzzlement because nowhere in the Christian Scriptures does one find any mention of Didache communities. Nor, for that matter, do the Christian Scriptures say anything of the thriving community at Qumran or of the books in the fabulous two-thousand-year-old library nearby which was discovered in 1943 and has come to be known as the Dead Sea Scrolls. But think again. Even the Acts of the Apostles does not draw attention to, much less cite, any of the letters of Paul, even though Luke was writing at a time when the letters of Paul had been in circulation for roughly twenty years. This is all the more surprising since Luke claims, in typical Hellenistic fashion, to have given special attention to gathered primary sources (Lk 1:1–4). The modern reader, consequently, need not be puzzled or dismayed that the Christian Scriptures make no reference to the *Didache*.

THE ANALYTIC, GENDER-INCLUSIVE TRANSLATION AND COMMENTARY

Only one copy of the *Didache* has been recovered from the ravages of time. Given its practical character, it was inevitable that any first-century pastoral manual would be revised, updated, and expanded to reflect new developments taking place in the larger church. Thus, by the fourth century, use of the *Didache* had severely declined, and it had been replaced by updated church manuals. Furthermore, when the *Didache* failed to gain the necessary support for inclusion in the universal canon of scriptures being drawn up in this same period, it was destined for oblivion. During the Middle Ages, the *Didache* seems to have had some limited use within a few monasteries; yet none of the medieval theologians functioning within the new university centers appears to have given it any attention whatsoever. When the great revival of interest in the early church flourished during the sixteenth century, the *Didache* was nowhere to be found. Even in modern times, when ancient libraries were being meticulously catalogued, the disappearance of the *Didache* seems to have been complete. Then in 1873, Archbishop Bryennios finally discovered what has been hailed as the only known manuscript of the *Didache*, after it had been overlooked by first-rate scholars on at least three occasions when it was right under their noses.

Details regarding the manuscript itself and its discovery can be found after the translation in this commentary under the heading, "How the

Greek Manuscript Was Discovered, Transcribed, and Translated." In this same place, one can discover how the Greek transcription of the text in this volume was produced and what guidelines were used in translating it. For the moment, however, it suffices to formulate, in a nutshell, the special features of this commentary:

> An analytic, Greek-English, gender-inclusive translation allows one to glimpse the flow of topics and the oral structure upon first reading.
> An origination hypothesis is developed and tested to account for the implied logic and progression of topics found in the received text. Flow charts are used to visualize easily the overarching structure.
> The clues of the text are systematically probed in order to reconstruct, as far as possible, the practical operations, the rites, and the system of values exemplified by the senior mentors who created the *Didache*.
> Technical material has been placed in boxes throughout. For the non-expert, these boxes provide background information covering hundreds of aspects of the first-century environment. For the scholar, these boxes address scholarly concerns that may not be of interest to all. Thus all readers can enjoy the running commentary while electing to read only those boxes that they find important to their interests.

The object of my commentary is to reconstruct the pastoral genius of the framers of the *Didache* through a systematic examination of the clues of the text. Once examined, the *Didache* will reveal a comprehensive, step-by-step program of formation intended to transform the settled habits of perceiving and of judging of non-Jewish candidates seeking perfection in, what for them, was a new religious movement. As a pastoral guide, the *Didache* gives detailed norms and practical descriptions of how things are to be done. Behind these particulars, however, lie the concerns and the anxieties, the experience and the successes of senior mentors who, over a period of time, worked with candidates and fashioned a training program that transmitted, in measured and gradual steps, the operative values and theological underpinnings that knit together their individual and collective lives.

Undoubtedly the framers of the *Didache* were well aware that any community that did not effectively pass on its values, its rites, and its way of life would flounder and eventually perish from the face of the earth. Thus, while the *Didache* ostensively focuses on the transformation of an outsider into an insider, at every point one learns much more of the insiders themselves—what they cherished, what they expected of themselves, and what they expected of God. All in all, therefore, this commentary intends to embrace the *Didache* as a unified document that opens up the communal reality and theological vision undergirding its creation and use.

THE UNITY AND THE INDEPENDENCE
OF THE *DIDACHE*

In the course of the last fifteen years, my ideas regarding the *Didache* have changed many times. During this period, however, two convictions have emerged that have supreme importance for shaping my methodology for investigating the text:

1. *Unity of the Didache.* Up to this point, a unified reading of the *Didache* has been impossible because the prevailing assumption has been that the *Didache* was created in stages, with the compiler splicing together preexisting documents with only a minimum of editing. The end result, therefore, was a complex (or even a haphazard) collage that joined bits and pieces of traditional material coming from unidentified communities and/ or unknown authors (details given below). The conviction undergirding my commentary, however, is that the *Didache* has a marvelous unity from beginning to end that, up to this point, has gone unnoticed.

I began my study of the *Didache* fifteen years ago with only a glimpse of its holistic unity. In the end, however, I was persuaded that I had discovered the hidden key that accounts for how it was constructed. This is the same key that those who recited the *Didache* used to order their recitation. Accordingly, the present study of the *Didache* will expend only passing energy on issues of source and redaction criticism and will concentrate on hearing the text as a whole and endeavoring to discern the organizational thread that guided the framers in the ordering of their material.

2. *Independence of the Didache from the Gospels.* The *Didache* has been widely understood as citing either Matthew's Gospel or some combination of the Matthean or Lucan traditions. From this vantage point, it followed that the date of composition had to be set beyond the 80s and that the Synoptic material could be used to help interpret and understand the *Didache*. Thanks to my work with Willy Rordorf (see "How My Mind Was Changed"), I came to an early appreciation of the possibility that the *Didache* might have been created without any dependence on a known Gospel. My extensive study of this issue in chapter 11 of this volume demonstrates that the internal logic, theological orientation, and pastoral practice of the *Didache* run decisively counter to what one finds in the received Gospels. The repercussions of this conclusion are enormous.

Up to this point, the supposition of Gospel dependence has blocked most scholars from seriously entertaining the possibility of a mid-first-century origin of the *Didache*. It has also served to encourage what I regard as an "inappropriate" interpretation of the text. If one supposes, for example, that the *Didache* made use of Matthew's Gospel, then one could justifiably make use of Matthew's theology and church practice in clarifying the intent and background of the *Didache*. On the other hand, if one supposes that the *Didache* is independent of Matthew, then it would be unwarranted to use the Gospel of Matthew to clarify obscure segments of a text created outside of its influence (see, for example, chapter 13 below). My conviction that the *Didache* was composed independent of any known Gospel thus means that the Gospels can provide studies in contrast and comparison but they cannot be used to fill in the intent of the framers of the *Didache*. In this volume, consequently, great importance is placed on allowing the internal evidence of the text to speak for itself, free of the influence of what was believed and what was done elsewhere. The case of the *Didache* is thus comparable to that of the Letter to the Hebrews. As soon as it was discovered that Paul was not the author, it was likewise required that Hebrews be interpreted based on its own internal logic and rhetoric quite independent of the theology of the authentic Pauline letters.

SOME DISCOVERIES ANTICIPATED IN THIS COMMENTARY

Given the early dating of the *Didache*, the way is open to viewing the *Didache* as capturing an early moment in the formation of Christianity when wandering prophets were an everyday experience and when the frequent failure of gentiles to consistently live the Way of Life was an abiding issue. Along the way, there will be surprises. Among these are the following:

> The Way of Life found in the *Didache* cannot be traced back to a Jewish catechetical manual used in the synagogues. In effect, my commentary will demonstrate (a) that the Way of Life represents a clear and careful adaptation to the needs and weaknesses of gentiles, (b) that training in the Way of Life has an ordered progression, and (c) that the Way of Life has been fashioned so as to address the specific skills necessary for taking part in this community.
> The extensive attention given to the practice of the sharing of resources in the *Didache* will be shown to have little to do with performing a pious act of charity. Rather, when examined against the background of the brutal economic conditions governing artisans and merchants in the first-century Roman Empire, these practices will be discovered to form an economic safety net against debt servitude and slavery.

My commentary will reveal how the rule of abstaining from "food offered to idols" (*Did.* 6:3) was introduced at precisely the proper point in the formation sequence and that it would have been out of place either earlier or later. Furthermore, this rule will be shown to demonstrate no awareness of the so-called Jerusalem Council detailed in Acts 15 or of the Noachian Covenant.

The hopes and expectations of a community are sometimes best revealed in their prayers. Thus, my commentary will give a detailed analysis of the Lord's Prayer and the eucharistic prayers so as to reveal their consistent eschatological orientation. The members of the Didache communities lived on the threshold of the last days. This eschatological orientation allowed them to let go of their past and to cling to their beloved community and to the Way of Life that the Lord God will vindicate when he comes upon the clouds of heaven.

Prayers in the Didache communities were dynamic, evocative, and passionate events. My commentary will disclose how it can be shown that none of the prayers given in the *Didache* was ever read or recited word for word from memory. Prayer leaders were expected to be entirely familiar with the prayer synopsis that guided the opening phrases, the thematic flow, and the concluding refrain(s). The prayer leaders were thus expected to create the prayer anew in each new circumstance and to weave together the cares and concerns of those present into a harmonious tapestry sanctioned by their prayer tradition.

My commentary will show the marvelous symmetry and unity of the eucharistic prayers and demonstrate that these prayers did not originate as a variation of the *Birkat Ha-Mazon* (as the current scholarly consensus holds). Moreover, my commentary will discern the "hidden" institutional narrative within the Eucharist of the *Didache* and explore how this Eucharist belonged to Jesus.

Wandering prophets were both the blessing and the bane of the Didache communities. On the one hand, the wandering prophets spoke "in the Spirit," climaxing the eucharistic prayers and providing a passionate expectation that the Lord God would come soon. On the other hand, these same wandering prophets practiced a radical style of life that conflicted with and sometimes disrupted or exploited the Didache communities.

It is a curious thing that the Didache communities never created or sent out wandering prophets. Rather, they attracted and absorbed them. My commentary will provide the first systematic analysis of the creation and the disappearance of prophetic passion within the context of the Didache communities. The reader will discover how the pastoral genius of the *Didache* found a way to safeguard community interests at the same time that it provided the concrete means whereby prophets were healed of the tragic events that scarred their lives.

Scholars have been puzzled by the end-times scenario presented at the end of the *Didache*. My commentary will provide the first systematic analysis of the end-times scenario and show how this schema was used to correct and to guide wandering prophets. More than anything else, the end-times scenario gave concrete guidance to the members of the Didache communities as to what was to be done while awaiting the coming of the Lord God.

Readers who have only a passing familiarity with the *Didache* might do well to leave off here and go immediately to examine the analytical translation in order to gain a first hand experience of the document itself. Experts who are concerned (a) about the use of source criticism to investigate the *Didache* and (b) about the process for the creation and verification of an origination hypothesis are invited to read on.

How Source Criticism Obscured the Unity of the *Didache*

Source criticism consistently portrays the *Didache* as a clumsy collage constructed by gathering, trimming, and pasting together preexisting sources. From this vantage point, the framers of the *Didache* were expected to provide an artificial and precarious unity out of prefabricated traditions that could be snipped and arranged but not rewritten or reformulated so as to ensure a uniform style and predefined progression from beginning to end.

Once the *Didache* was broken down into its prefabricated pieces (its disjointed voices), it was useless to try to decide why each section was included. Were sections included, for example, because they represented what was authoritatively practiced somewhere in the past but, because of altered circumstances, no longer had any applicability? Inclusion, at this point, served only to celebrate or honor the past. Were other sections included because they described what was being done currently? If this was the case, then one might be curious whether this practice was universal or local, whether it was uncontested, or whether it needed to be maintained against a minority who favored altering or suppressing the current practice. Finally, were some sections included because the compiler wished his intended audience to undertake practices authoritatively observed elsewhere or even to recommit themselves to practices formerly observed by his audience? If so, then these sections of the *Didache* could be said to support a utopian or a reforming agenda of the compiler.

In practice, source criticism expends so much energy in hypothesizing, on the basis of shifts in the logic and rhetoric of the text, where one source ends and another begins, that any unity found in the original can be obscured in the analysis. Furthermore, since the hypothesized sources, in the form that the compiler knew them, could not be independently known and verified, scholarly debates have been unable to arrive at any working consensus, since every major author relied on his own "reconstruction" of the stages through which the document passed.

Thus, three contemporary German commentaries offer three divergent divisions of the text. According to Klaus Wengst (1984), the author of the *Didache* set down, in the initial ten chapters, the existing traditions of the community and then inserted 7:2f. and created 11–15 to offer rules to protect those traditions. According to Kurt Niederwimmer, the compiler of the *Didache* was most probably "a respected and influential bishop" who "quotes existing, sometimes archaic rules and seeks both to preserve what has been inherited and at the same time to accommodate that heritage to his own time [turn of the first century]" (Niederwimmer 1998: 228). Unlike Wengst, Niederwimmer finds traditional material scattered throughout: 1:1–3a; 2:2–5:2; 7:1; 8:1–11:2; 11:3–13:2; 14:1–16:8. Georg Schöllgen, for his part, fails to find any ordering principle in the *Didache*; rather, for him, the author "simply provides an authoritative regulation on controversial points" (1996: 63) set out at random. Schöllgen, consequently, finds breaks in the text as the normal indicators of the abrupt transition from one controversial point to the next. In settling such controversies, the author, according to Schöllgen, only made use of traditional material at four points: (1) 7:2–3, 4b; (2) 8:2; (3) 9:2–4; 10:2–6; (4) 13:3a, 5–7. All in all, one can glimpse how the three most recent German commentators fail to agree on where the sources end and the composition of the author begins.

Meanwhile, all three German commentators refuse to accept the thesis of Stanislas Giet and Willy Rordorf calling for two stages of composition by different editors (esp. Schöllgen 1996: 67–70). With even greater force, they reject Jean-Paul Audet and Clayton N. Jefford, who reconstruct three distinct, temporally separated stages of composition (Niederwimmer 1998: 42f.). Schöllgen, for his part, summarizes the results of source and redaction criticism as follows:

> It is significant that there is neither a consensus nor even only a limited number of types of solution between these some extraordinarily complex theories of origin. Nearly every attempt to solve the problem stands by itself, and forms its own criteria for the supposed division of sources. So one cannot avoid the impression

of arbitrariness, especially if even the smallest stylistic differences
must serve as signs of a change of author. (1996: 65)

Given the evident disarray, this present study of the *Didache* will expend
only passing energy on issues of source and redaction criticism and will
concentrate on hearing the text as a whole.

When I began my study of the *Didache* fifteen years ago, I could only
glimpse the organizational thread that guided the framers in the ordering
of their material. In the end, however, I am persuaded that I have discovered the hidden key that explains how it was constructed. This is the same
key that those who recited the *Didache* used as a means of ordering their
recitation. The key is this: the *Didache* was the comprehensive, step-by-
step program used for the formation of a gentile converting to Christianity. By adhering to the order of the *Didache*, mentors training novices were
assured of following the progressive, ordered, and comprehensive path that
master trainers in the community had effectively culled from their own successful practice in apprenticing novices. For an overview, see Flowchart A.

THE CREATION AND VERIFICATION
OF AN ORIGINATION HYPOTHESIS

The examination of any text continuously results in the formation of
hypotheses, theories, and interpretative matrices that enable the researcher
to integrate the clues of the text into meaningful wholes. In effect, there is
no neutral starting point in research. Everyone coming to a text, even if for
the first time, is already predisposed by what he/she expects to find and
what he/she already knows about the text. As a scholar dwells within the
clues of a text for a prolonged period, he/she eventually comes to define
an origination hypothesis that endeavors to account for the peculiarities of
the text and to provide an overall understanding of its origin, use, and content. The formulation of this origination hypothesis and its verification (or
falsification) are much more complex than is normally supposed.

Consider, for example, the origination hypothesis undergirding this
work, namely, that the framers of the *Didache* defined the progression of
topics and experiences that a novice might be expected to undergo when
being trained for full inclusion in the movement. How was such a hypothesis arrived at? How can it be verified or falsified? How does the community of discourse enter into this process? We call attention to five
considerations:

1. The first task of any reader is to decide whether the *Didache* is a unified production or whether it is the haphazard collage of preexisting doc-

uments. If the *Didache* is a collage assembled by a compiler who can only edit around the edges of preexisting sources, then, it is improbable that one will be able to identify an integrative thread that knits together the progression of topics. On the other hand, if the *Didache* is a deliberate and highly crafted composition, then the author must have had some guiding organizational plan and functional purpose whereby the topics unfold progressively from start to finish.

2. In this commentary I make the claim to have discovered an origination hypothesis that serves as a highly sophisticated "paradigm," "explanatory matrix," or "key" unlocking the secret of the *Didache*'s composition. Since this origination hypothesis is not explicitly stated at any point in the *Didache*, the validity of the "key" cannot be directly verified by referring to some (in this case nonexistent) "preface" or "topic paragraph" whereby the framers self-consciously defined the purpose and ordering of their text. Likewise, a "key" cannot be immediately falsified by showing that it accounts for some of the progressions in the text but fails to explain them all. This is so for two reasons:

(a) Every satisfactory origination hypothesis has a limit to its explanatory power. When it fails to account for some aspects of the text, this may be due to a limitation of the theory itself, but it might also be due to a corruption in the received text itself or to an inconsistency on the part of the framers themselves. When a manuscript is suspected of being corrupt, scholars normally revise the original text under the rubric that the copyist made an error in transcribing the text. This occurs a few times in our received text and is discussed in "How the Greek Manuscript Was Discovered, Transcribed, and Translated."

(b) When an origination hypothesis largely succeeds while failing in some particulars, this can be regarded as an anomaly. Faced with an anomaly, a researcher normally would be expected to press forward, to strain repeatedly at the clues in the expectation that some alternative way of viewing the clues or some alternate way of applying the theory will yield more satisfactory results. Only by holding on rather than immediately abandoning a theory can "inconsistencies" be noticed for what they are (Kuhn 1970: 77f.).

When a text can be plausibly "corrected" or when a theory can be modified so as to embrace perceived "inconsistencies," then its explanatory power grows and its users justifiably feel a greater confidence in its correctness because of the enlarged intellectual satisfaction experienced in its use. On the other hand, when inconsistencies remain unresolved and anomalies multiply, then the users of the text gradually lose faith in their theory and begin shifting about looking for a superior theory (Kuhn 1970: 82–89).

NOT ALL THEORIES ARE CREATED EQUAL

When contending origination hypotheses examine the peculiarities of the *Didache*, they necessarily act like lenses that force their users to see things quite differently. Consider, for example, an easily recognized peculiarity of the text: *Did.* 9–10 presents what the text calls "the Eucharist" (*Did.* 9:1), and, four chapters later, the confession of failings is described as taking place *prior to* the Eucharist (*Did.* 14:1). One may wonder why the compiler did not place *Did.* 14 just prior to *Did.* 9–10 and thereby retain a topical and chronological unity to his finished text. Jean-Paul Audet takes this problem up as follows:

> The author returns to the subject [in *Did.* 14] not because he is a bad writer, or because he had, oddly enough, forgotten something, or because he is compiling his materials at random, or because someone else had created a subsequent interpolation of 14:1–3, but simply because experience has demonstrated, in the meantime, the inadequacy of the instructions in 9–10. (1958: 460).

Now consider how Niederwimmer, Schöllgen, and Milavec each understand this disjunction in the text of the *Didache* quite differently.

Niederwimmer, as noted above, thought that the compiler of the *Didache* was most probably "a respected and influential bishop" who "quotes existing, sometimes archaic, rules and seeks both to preserve what has been inherited and at the same time to accommodate that heritage to his own time [turn of the second century]" (Niederwimmer 1998: 228). This origination hypothesis provides no explanatory matrix for understanding why *Did.* 14 was not placed just prior to *Did.* 9–10. When it comes to examining *Did.* 14, however, Niederwimmer put forward a supplemental explanation to account for the flow of topics chosen by the writer. Niederwimmer is clearly uneasy with the hypothesis that *Did.* 14 was added later by a second compiler (Rordorf 1978a: 49f., 1998: 226–28) or that the original writer might return at a later time to supplement what he had earlier written (Audet above). Rather, Niederwimmer discerns what he judges to be the internal logic of the text: "in chaps. 11–13, the Didachist had, in a sense, looked outward (toward the arriving guests of the community), in chaps. 14–15 he looks inward (at the relationships within the community itself)" (Niederwimmer 1998: 199). Thus, according to Niederwimmer, the framer of the *Didache* grouped his materials into suitable categories that decided their placement. Chronological order had nothing to do with it. The eucharistic prayers (*Did.* 9–10) come early because they are grouped with the prayer section (*Did.* 8:1–10:7); the con-

fession of failings comes later because it is grouped with "internal relationships" (*Did*. 14–15). Beyond the grouping of materials into different
chapters, Niederwimmer's theories do not either look for or expect to find
any logic as to why one grouping should come before or after another. In
a word, given the lenses used by Niederwimmer, he does not see or look
for any sequential plan in the *Didache*.

Schöllgen has an origination hypothesis much different from that of
Niederwimmer. For him, the author "simply provides an authoritative regulation on controversial points" (1996: 63). Thus, *Did*. 9–10 responds to
the problem of communities having for their eucharist "no fixed formula"
(1996: 50). *Did*. 14, on the other hand, is directed toward resolving the
author's concern for "the purity" at the eucharistic meal (1996: 59). Two
topics; two places. Here again, the origination hypothesis of Schöllgen
does not lead him to anticipate finding any special progression or grouping of topics; hence, Schöllgen is not surprised or disappointed when he
does not find any. Theories teach us how to look and what to look for.
Schöllgen, more especially, embraces an origination hypothesis that is
entirely blind to any ordering of the topics.

My own origination hypothesis, on the contrary, leads me to discover a
progression of topics that closely follows the training and the experiences
given to new members. In part, I reason as follows:

> Under ordinary circumstances, the *Didache* informs us that a
> confession of failings would have taken place in order to prepare
> the members to offer "a pure sacrifice" (*Did*. 14:1). The candi-
> date preparing for baptism is informed of this confession near the
> end of his/her training (*Did*. 3:14). When one encounters the
> eucharistic prayers (*Did*. 9f.), the confession of failings is curi-
> ously omitted. Many scholars read this as an indication of the fact
> that the *Didache* is a collage of preexisting documents assembled
> over a period of time and never attaining anywhere near a full
> integration.
>
> My surmise, on the contrary, is that this omission of the con-
> fession of failings is deliberate and signals what everyone knew—
> namely, that the order of events within the *Didache* follows the
> order in which a candidate comes to experience these events.
> Thus, if my surmise is correct, the Eucharist in the *Didache* rep-
> resents the "the first Eucharist," and the omission of the confes-
> sion of failings at this point deliberately points to the fact that this
> public confession was suppressed whenever new candidates were
> baptized just prior to the Eucharist. Many reasons could be put
> forward to sustain suppressing a public confession of failings at

"the first Eucharist." Foremost among them would be the fittingness of welcoming the new "brothers" and "sisters" who had
just been baptized without confronting them with a recital of the
failings of permanent members. . . . (chapter 3).

For the moment, the question is not whether my origination hypothesis is
correct or whether I have supplied probable reasons for suppressing the
confession of failings at "the first Eucharist." What is important is to notice
how my origination hypothesis forces one to probe the text more deeply
in order to find out just how far the evidence supplied by the text can be
understood to support the explanatory matrix being tested. The origination hypothesis of Schöllgen expects an unorganized movement from
topic to topic. Even Niederwimmer only expects categories of topics to be
grouped together. Neither of them expects to find, therefore, a hidden
logic that guides the narrator from topic to topic from beginning to end.

Not all theories, therefore, are created equal. Some force us to notice
more about the text. Superior theories have a greater fruitfulness—they are
"fraught with further intimations of an indeterminate range" (Polanyi
1966: 23) that reveal themselves, from time to time, in "as yet undisclosed,
perhaps as yet unthinkable, consequences" (ibid.). Such theories also provide a greater intellectual satisfaction—they say more about what is the
hidden depth of meaning within the text. As part of their greater fruitfulness and greater intellectual satisfaction, however, they also have a con-
comitant vulnerability to being falsified.

3. An origination hypothesis cannot be directly falsified. In most cases,
one must wait until one discovers an alternative hypothesis that provides
superior intellectual satisfaction when confronted with the clues of the text.
"The decision to reject one paradigm is always simultaneously the decision
to accept another" (Kuhn 1970: 77). Following upon what was noted
above, even new theories have to be tried out by those committed to them,
because, under the lens of a new theory, the entire text appears differently.
In the end, it is the superior explanatory matrix and superior fruitfulness of
a new theory that enables one to abandon an earlier theory as inferior.
Should the new theory fail to meet up with its anticipated expectations, the
researcher naturally inclines toward modifying the theory so as to make it
better fit the evidence. Should this fail to be satisfying, the researcher then
gropes around for yet another fresh alternative.

4. An individual faced with the superior intellectual satisfaction of a new
theory takes responsibility for sharing it with those working on similar
problems and having similar training. That is what this book is all about. It
would be ludicrous, however, for me to expect that all my professional

readers would, upon first reading, immediately abandon earlier theories and unanimously cling to my paradigm. Rather, a book like the present can only modestly expect to gain some adherence while, at the same time, gaining critics as well.

Capable and insightful critics can be a blessing. They press forward the weaknesses of an origination hypothesis and force the adherents to wrestle with anomalies that may not have been evident earlier. Critics worth their salt do not stop at articulating the soft spots or anomalies within an existing theory; rather, they go on to espouse an alternative that, for them, has a superior intellectual satisfaction and fruitfulness. In the end, therefore, a community engaged in authentic dialogue and facing shared problems of interpretation has much to gain by the exchange between passionately committed intellectual adversaries.

5. Even between fierce opponents there exists a conviviality based on shared tradition, shared problems, and commitment to a shared quest for truth. In the history of the development of any intellectual tradition, sometimes an issue will divide a community for some time before a new consensus is formed (Kuhn 1970: 144–54). In such instances, care must be taken that the majority does not use its influence to curtail the rights and standing of the minority. The history of science as well as the history of theology demonstrates many instances in which the judgment of the majority was ultimately overturned by the persistence and superior stand of the minority. When mutual respect breaks down and gives way to name calling, authoritarian appeals, and bullying, however, dialogue flounders. When one side of the argument feels justified in threatening the reputation, the livelihood, and/or the personal safety of an opponent or opponents, the winners do not thereby demonstrate the superiority of their claims; they merely demonstrate that raw power can effectively trample and silence opponents. The abuse of power, sad to say, takes place far too often within ecclesial and academic circles. Personal lives are downtrodden, and the community loses the innovative spirit required for its continued renewal and uplift.

PERSONAL AND PROFESSIONAL JUDGMENT IN SECONDARY MATTERS

Everything said above applies not only to the overall origination hypothesis but also to the multiple explanatory matrices every scholar brings to every line of the *Didache*. At every turn of the text, a scholar puzzles over the clues provided by the text. More often than not, an explanatory matrix spontaneously emerges to integrate the clues into a meaningful and satisfying whole. Not all scholars agree, however. Different scholars—owing to differences in their training, differences in their familiarity with the text, differences in their tacit assumptions—often latch onto different explanations for the same text.

Consider, for example, the various explanatory matrices brought forward by different scholars when explaining the norms regarding water suitable for baptism. The *Didache* contains a curious instruction: "If you are not able [to baptize] in cold, immerse in warm water" (*Did.* 7:2). Some early interpreters understood this text as making provisions for the warming of water when sick persons were to be baptized (Benoit: 8 n.15; Dölger: 175–83; Harnack 1886: 23). Other scholars objected to this, seeing that the text makes no mention of sick candidates, and preferred to understand the reference to warm water as a clue that the *Didache* must have been used in a cold climate: "It seems evident to me that one is speaking here of water being heated for the situation. This is a precaution that would be called for if the baptism took place in a climate too rigorous [for river baptisms]" (Rordorf 1972a: 506). Both of these hypotheses are inherently interesting because they hold out the hope of discovering the implied context that originated the discussion of the various different kinds of suitable water. Both of these hypotheses are misleading, however, because they fail to give sufficient attention to the internal logic of the text.

When read as a unit, the overriding norm was to give preference to "living" water (*Did.* 7:1)—flowing and cold in natural streams. When this was lacking, then non-flowing cold water (*Did.* 7:2)—as in a pond or lake—was permitted. Such cold water had the natural temperature of "living" water but was inferior since it was not flowing (Niederwimmer 1998: 127). Finally, when cold water was lacking, warm water was permitted. Vööbus surmises that "warm water" refers to "the kind to be found in cisterns, pools and reservoirs" exposed to the Mediterranean sun (Vööbus 1968: 24).

The language of the text says nothing about artificially heating the water. Accordingly, the logic of the text is far removed from making accommodations for a sick candidate or for a cold climate; rather, the issue was directed toward accommodating a situation where both cold-running and cold-standing water were not available. If the framers of the *Didache* had wanted to make adaptations for a cold climate, as Rordorf surmises, then one would have expected "warm water" to be preferred over "cold"—exactly the opposite of the norm supplied by the text (see ch. 3 below).

In sum, therefore, every segment of the *Didache* can be suspected of having an origination hypothesis or explanatory matrix that endeavors to unravel the hidden meanings of the text. Not all such mini-theories are created equal, however. Each contributes to the richness of the exchange, but, in the end, that theory that best takes into account the evidence of the text and reads it against a plausible context will be preferred. Needless to say, there are no living representatives of the *Didache* communities that can be consulted. The community of scholars is thus left with the necessity of entering into a dialogue with the text, with the context, with the pretext. In the process of moving toward a consensus, the five observations made above are always operative.

What I quickly discovered is that any book attempting to spell out and refute all known alternatives would soon be bogged down in trivialities. Hence, in every instance, I tried to distinguish those alternatives that had genuine merit and to represent them (leaving all the others to be subordinated or even buried in silence). Moreover, I was everywhere conscious that the framers of the *Didache* were responding to problems and contingencies that emerged out of their cultural and religious heritage. Thus, for example, when it came to grades of water, it seemed far more important to investigate how grades of water functioned within the Judaisms of the early centuries (as in Niederwimmer 1998: 127–29) in order to identify a probable context for the question in the first place. Within rabbinic Judaism, for example, the quantity and source of water used in purification rites were discussed in great detail (*m. Negaim* 14:1–3; *m. Miqvaot* 1:1–8). John the Baptizer, on the other hand, seemingly required "living" water for his baptisms. The Jewish context, therefore, provided a surer point of departure than surmising that a sick person may need "warmed water" or that the *Didache* itself was created in a cold climate. At every point, consequently, the act of deciding what to consider emerges out of my personal and professional judgment. Others would have done it differently. Every scholar, however, is forced to make selections or else to risk getting bogged down in trivialities.

All in all, the preparation of this book has resulted in nearly an encyclopedic review of all aspects of first-century life touched on by the *Didache*. In each instance, needless to say, I was limited by the sources known and available to me. In the case of grades of water, for instance, I carefully investigated a wide range of Jewish sources. One author suggested that Romans also classified water used for ritual purposes, yet I could find no primary source that testified to this idea. All in all, therefore, I am sure some resourceful scholar will someday come forward with more evidence and maybe even point me to a monograph on a topic that I entirely overlooked.

Be that as it may, it stands to reason that every scholar reading this book will quickly find particular areas where his or her specialty is neglected or his or her favorite sources are overlooked. In a word, everyone can be expected to find places where this study could have been improved. I will be grateful for every suggestion as to how particular topics in this book could have been more adequately treated. Meanwhile, I'm sure that most readers will patiently overlook my limitations and quietly substitute their superior understanding in those areas where they are better informed. On the other hand, I do believe that scholars with only a passing interest in the *Didache* will find my efforts to read the text as a whole and to reconstitute the community life that lies behind the text to be insightful and refreshing. In many cases I have had to push the evidence and sometimes to reconstruct intangibles (such as problems and motives standing behind the text) that cannot, in every instance, be positively verified. These secondary explanatory matrices may sometimes be wrong or misleading without calling into question the major origination matrix undergirding the construction of the whole text. For example, I may be dead wrong when it comes to my understanding of the implied logic regarding grades and quantities of water used for baptism (*Did.* 7:1–3); yet this might not touch my overall thesis regarding the progression and treatment of topics in the *Didache*.

No document in the Christian Scriptures is as descriptive, as organized, and as comprehensive as the *Didache* when it comes to offering evidence about the community that lies behind the text. The *Didache* provides not only the outline of training necessary for gentiles prior to their baptism, but, following baptism, one glimpses how the newly baptized enter into the semiweekly fasting, the rhythms of daily prayer, the first and subsequent Eucharists, the interaction with prophets and other visitors, the offering of first fruits, the election of bishops, the shunning of misbehaving members—all the while anticipating the coming of the Lord God on the clouds. By following the training of candidates through their prebaptismal training all the way to their final admonitions regarding the last days, one stands to gain a comprehensive overview of the way of life lived within a set of mid-first-century Christian communities poised at the threshold of the anticipated coming of the Lord. It is to this task that my commentary is dedicated.

How My Mind Was Changed

I have always been fascinated with beginnings. My graduate school professors made reference to the *Didache* as a gold mine of information regarding "the beginnings" of various aspects of church life in Syria-Palestine or in Egypt dating between 50 and 150 C.E. My church history professor, for example, made me aware that the *Didache* illustrated how the charismatic leadership of wandering prophets gave way to settled institutional offices. My course in the sacraments made me aware that the *Didache* offered unique data regarding the emergence of the catechumenate, baptism by pouring, and the development of eucharistic prayers. From the vantage point of dogmatics, the "very Jewish and very primitive" modes of presenting Jesus and the last days were points of fascination.

In each of these instances, however, the *Didache* was cut up and laid open in order to answer pressing questions other than those for which it was originally designed. No one seemed to notice that the *Didache* had its own agenda, its own logic, its own passionate concerns. No one wanted to talk about the "community life" of those who framed the *Didache* and to describe its unique joys and sorrows, triumphs and failures. Thus, there was no one attempting to read the document as a whole with the goal of reconstructing the practices and beliefs of those who lived out their lives according to its norms.

The Importance of Meeting Neusner

Then my surprise came. In 1988 I received an NEH Faculty Fellowship to participate in a research seminar entitled "The Analysis of Religious Systems: The Case of Judaism," under the direction of Professor Rabbi Jacob Neusner. Initially, I expected that the seminar was going to unravel the "system" hidden within rabbinic sources. But no! Neusner was aware that deep learning for adults can take place only when they discover things for

themselves. Neusner was also aware that, as Christians, most of us had neither the language skills nor the personal commitments necessary to work
successfully with rabbinic materials. Thus, he wisely invited each of us to
identify "an anonymous Christian text" that had some personal meaning
and that would form the focus of our application of the method he had
refined for Jewish texts.

I decided to select the *Didache* largely because of my fascination with
beginnings. Neusner promised me that he would train me "to learn how
to read [these] scriptures in such a way as to uncover the religious system
expressed therein" (Neusner 1989: ix). Within a few days, I realized that,
even though I had been routinely using the *Didache* in my seminary
courses, I understood nothing about the *Didache* that enabled me to apply
the methodology Neusner had perfected in his pioneering work with the
texts of formative Judaism.

In order to get started, Neusner emphasized the importance of ferreting
out the internal logic of the text so as to distinguish whether one is dealing with a collage of disparate materials spliced together by an editor or
whether one has a unified product shaped by a single-minded author. This
was tough. The literature occupied with the *Didache* was replete with
dozens of competing systems for parceling out the *Didache* to different
sources and different times of composition. This practice effectively
silenced any discussion of whether the *Didache* had a unified "voice," since
the overriding question was always what different "voices" coming from its
different sources and different times of composition were combined to
produce the text that came down to us. Encouraged by Neusner, I suspected that just maybe the experts had been wrong. Maybe there was a
simple, muffled, unified voice looming within the clues of the *Didache*.

After fifteen years of persistent and sensitive listening to the *Didache*, I
can finally offer Neusner a resounding roar of gratitude:

> You put me on a road that no one had traveled. You taught me
> to stay with the clues of the text until I discovered the unified
> worldview and the unique way of life that stood behind the text.
> You pointed me toward something that no one expected to be
> able to find.

The *Didache*, of course, did not yield its secret to me all at once. My pilot
essay (1989a), "The Pastoral Genius of the *Didache*: An Analytical Translation and Commentary," written at the end of the seminar, was my first
concerted attempt to identify the central question that every line of the
Didache was attempting to answer. Not bad for a first try. My method,
however, needed refinement. My conclusions were sometimes faulty. Two
years later, I changed my mind about what I had earlier identified as the

"overall purpose of the text" (Milavec 1988: 125). Ten years later, I discovered how tragically wrong I had been in allowing that the section dealing with bishops and deacons (*Did.* 15:1f.) was a turn-of-the-first-century addition by a "scribe wishing to update the *Didache* and to extend its usefulness" (1988: 119 n. 27).

HOW MY MIND WAS CHANGED

Don't get me wrong. My mind changed not only about some big things but, with great regularity, about small things as well. In fact, I realized that changing my mind was an integral part of *my* method. By listening intently for "the voice" of the *Didache*, by puzzling again and again over problematic aspects of the text, by pushing the evidence toward the reconstruction of the social and religious context presupposed by the *Didache* communities, it was inevitable that I would make frequent discoveries that changed my mind. Throughout, however, there was an abiding faith that I was being led forward by tacit intuitions that have a bearing upon hidden meanings buried in the clues surrounding me. In this aspect, Michael Polanyi, a gentle giant in the arena of correct methodology and an early mentor, was very dear to me:

> The pursuit of discovery is conducted from the start in these terms; all the time we are guided by sensing the presence of a hidden reality toward which our clues are pointing; and the discovery which terminates and satisfies this pursuit is still sustained by this same vision. It claims to have made contact with reality: a reality which, being real, may yet reveal itself to future eyes in an indefinite range of unexpected manifestations. (Polanyi 1966: 24)

Here, now, I have a confession to make. After publishing my pilot article in 1988, I was secretly convinced that I really understood the *Didache*. In 1992, however, having changed my mind often, I wrote in my journal, "Alas, now I can see that my pilot essay in 1988 was only dealing with the tip of the iceberg." In early 1996, when I had a rough draft of this book ready for Paulist, I again wrote confidently, "Now I know what the *Didache* is about!" I could have published then—but what a disappointment that would have been!

Then disaster struck. I fell into a prolonged depression. Over the months, I was gradually healed by devoting forty to fifty hours each week listening to "my companions" in the *Didache*. Indeed, I gradually came to realize that everything in the rough draft of my book was "fraught with further intimations of an indeterminate range" (Polanyi 1966: 23). The scope and depth of my work expanded. Thus, in late 2002, as this volume goes to press, it is immeasurably more intellectually satisfying than my rough draft of 1996.

EARLY CHRISTIANITY: THE EVIDENCE OF THE *DIDACHE*

Neusner made another major contribution to my methodology. He eloquently sustained the thesis that many scholars have gone awry because they overlooked the fact that, in every age, there are many Judaisms. Accordingly, in Neusner's major volume *Judaism: The Evidence of the Mishnah* (1988a), he allows from the very beginning that his study has a very limited and well-defined scope of application:

> The subtitle, "evidence of the Mishnah," is meant to be severely limiting and restrictive. The kind of Judaism under historical analysis in this book is that attested to by a single important document, produced in what appears to have been a continuous and fairly coherent movement of men (there were no women) who knew one another and who claimed to have studied with the same great masters. The Mishnah fully expressed the worldview and way of life of these men. That is not to suggest that the Mishnah exhausts the evidence about the group behind the Mishnah. But the Mishnah does exhaustively express a complete system— the fit of worldview and way of life—fantasized by its framers. (1988a: 24)

Because of his conviction of the many Judaisms, Neusner does not imagine, for example, that the Mishnah (200 C.E.) offers information about how the temple operated during the first century. Neusner demonstrates that the sections of the Mishnah devoted to the temple are "utopian" in character; that is, they portray temple worship as the rabbis intended to reconstruct it should the temple be rebuilt and should the rabbis be put in charge of directing the priests. Furthermore, Neusner rightly contends that the Mishnah could not have represented the Judaism that was practiced by the majority of Jews during the first two centuries, for "in its wars against Rome, the Jewish nation rejected" the worldview defined by the Mishnah (1988a: 24).

There were many Christianities during the first century just as there were many Judaisms. Diversity prevailed. The Letter to the Hebrews, for example, is an anonymous treatise, usually dated between 70 and 96 C.E. Like the *Didache*, Hebrews demonstrates no dependence on the letters of Paul or the known Gospels. Meanwhile, no book of the canon written after

Hebrews even hints at the order of Melchizedek which enables the framers of Hebrews to argue that Jesus, despite the fact that God calls only members of the tribe of Levi to be priests, can authentically lay claim to being God's high priest in the heavenly sanctuary not made with human hands. One has here, therefore, the blossoming of a form of first-century Christianity that stands distinctly apart from all the others. Readers unacquainted with the diversity of early Christian beliefs and practices might do well to have James D. G. Dunn's volume *Unity and Diversity in the New Testament* (1977) on hand during the reading of this volume.

Following upon this understanding, the title of this volume might have been *Early Christianity: The Evidence of the Didache*. As an explanation of this title, I adapt the words of Neusner cited above:

> The subtitle, "Evidence of the Didache," is meant to be severely limiting and restrictive. The kind of Jewish-inspired Christianity under historical analysis in this book is that attested to by a single important document, produced in what appears to have been a fairly coherent movement of women (the majority) and men who knew one another and who claimed to be living the Way of Life revealed to them by God through Jesus, his servant. The *Didache* fully expressed the worldview and way of life of these women and men. This is not to suggest that the *Didache* exhausts the evidence about the group behind the *Didache*. But the *Didache* does exhaustively express a complete system—the fit of worldview and way of life—fantasized and practiced by its framers.

The purpose of this volume accordingly is to push the evidence of the *Didache* so as to reconstruct the stubborn habits of perceiving and the committed modes of acting that shaped the adherents of this way of life. To the degree that I am successful, the reader will be able to discern the joys and sorrows, the hopes and disappointments, that marked a significant branch of the Jesus movement that has gone largely unnoticed and uncelebrated to this day.

THE ENDURING IMPACT OF RORDORF

Just as every rabbinic student needs a partner, so every fruitful scholar needs a learning partner. The 1983 movie *Yentl* gives a humorous presentation of what is involved. Even before I knew to look around and find such a learning partner, I inadvertently found one. This came about in late 1989 when I undertook to contact Professor Willy Rordorf, who, at that time, held the Chair of Patristic Studies at the University of Neuchâtel and was, hands down, the most-informed and best-published European scholar on the *Didache*. Rordorf's response to my letter was altogether astonishing. My earlier studies in Switzerland had made me aware that European scholars were generally more formal and reserved than their American counterparts and made it a point of honor to maintain the correctness of their published positions. Rordorf, in contrast, was totally disarming. He wrote, quite simply, that his own volume (1978a) was already ten years old and, therefore, ten years out of date; hence, it would be "exciting to 'resee' this writing with your eyes" (letter of 24 April 1989). Furthermore, he immediately proposed that I join him in Neuchâtel the following year and help him present his senior seminar, which, if I was able to come, would certainly be on the topic of the *Didache*. I was overjoyed!

Willy Rordorf turned out to be a kindred spirit. His teaching style was warm, engaging, pastoral—just the very things that my students prized in me. During the summer of 1990 and again in 1992, I received grants that enabled me to spend the entire summer working with my learning partner. We quickly became friends, and he opened up his home and family to me. He once summarized our collaboration saying: "Sometimes you convince me; sometimes I convince you." Together, however, we both entered into new depths of the *Didache*.

Rordorf's most significant contribution to me was his notion that the framers of the *Didache* did not use any known written Gospel. For a hundred years, nearly everyone supposed that the framers of the *Didache* made use of Matthew or Luke or both. A few scholars even proposed that smatterings of nearly every book in the Christian Scriptures could be found paraphrased in the *Didache*. Only a handful of French-speaking scholars held out against this consensus: Paul Sabatier in 1885, Jean-Paul Audet in 1958, Stanaslas Giet in 1970, and Rordorf in 1978 and 1998. Rordorf pressed forward new evidence and, to my satisfaction, was able to demonstrate the total independence of the *Didache* from any known written Gospel. If I have learned anything, it is the repercussions of this proposition.

The dating and the interpretation of the *Didache* have, for 120 years, been intimately tied to the supposed sources used in its composition. During the first eighty years, nearly everyone was debating whether the *Didache* made use of the *Epistle of Barnabas,* which was then dated around 130 C.E. Audet, making use of the scrolls discovered near Qumran in 1945, effectively terminated that debate. With the *Epistle of Barnabas* out of the picture, renewed interest flared up in linking the *Didache* with a known Gospel—Matthew being the favorite. By releasing scholars from this mistaken legacy, Rordorf sets the stage for a possible dating of the *Didache* before the composition of Matthew (70–80 C.E.). With even more importance, Rordorf made it illegitimate to suppose that the theology and structure of the *Didache* community could be illuminated by reference to what one finds in the Gospel of Matthew. In a word, Rordorf took the first step to ensure that future scholars would consider the necessity of discovering the uniqueness of the *Didache* independent of what is found in Matthew's Gospel. I have carried Rordorf's insights even further by arguing that the theology and structures of Matthew's community are incompatible with those of the *Didache*.

The Oral Character of the *Didache*

One unfinished and unnoticed dimension of the *Didache* is its oral character. Like most scholars, I began my studies looking at the *Didache* as a printed text. I now realize that I should have been hearing it spoken, since the text is the transcription of an oral production. The clues of this orality are found in the text itself. For example, the one being trained in the Way of Life is asked to "remember night and day" his/her mentor, "the one *speaking* to you the *word* of God" (*Did.* 4:1a, as also 4:1b, 1:3). Prior to the baptism itself, it appears that the one baptizing *recites* the Way of Life (7:1) as part of the rite. After the Eucharist, the *Didache* directs attention to "whoever should train you in all these things *said* beforehand" (11:1). Faced with approaching coming of the Lord God, members are told to "frequently be gathered together" (16:2) with the saints "in order that you may rest upon their *words*" (4:2).

The character of an oral production is significantly different from that of a written text. My style of speaking in the classroom, for example, is shot through with short snappy sentences, colloquialisms, humor. My style of writing for publication is very much more deliberate, sober, long-winded. I notice this most when I transcribe an oral lecture I have recorded. I can immediately "hear" that it is a transcription of an oral performance. You, the reader, may have had similar experiences.

To test this "orality" on the part of the *Didache*, I decided to memorize chapters 7 to 10 in the anticipation of presenting it orally at the opening of my class devoted to the *Didache*. Linda Bartholomew and other members of the National Organization of Biblical Storytellers gave me some practical hints on how to easily memorize Gospel texts. For my part, I was skeptical. The *Didache* did not have the narrative flow of a Gospel story. Furthermore, I had not memorized any sustained production since I was an amateur actor thirty-five years ago. Let's face it, I had become thoroughly habituated to making, consulting, and relying upon written records—in everything from analyzing texts to shopping for groceries. Once I put my mind to it, however, I was amazed. I fully memorized the four chapters in two one-hour sessions supplemented by two fifteen minute oral productions the following day to assure myself that I had everything down pat. I did!

How was this possible? For starters, submitting a text in translation to oral memory forced me to ferret out the oral patterns structuring chapter 7: topic sentence + threefold elaboration (7:1–3). Then I discovered the subtle way oral transitions work. Key words and key associations served to provide "oral links" which popped up when needed and never allowed me, the narrator, to be left hanging for the next line (see details in ch. 3 below). All in all, by abandoning the norms of linear logic that structure written texts, I found that I was able to intuit the oral logic that structured the *Didache*. Once this happened, I memorized the *Didache* with the same ease that members of the National Organization of Biblical Storytellers enable whole groups of people to memorize and reproduce Gospel stories in a half-hour at their public meetings. Everything that Walter Ong and Werner Kelber had been saying about the primacy of the oral and the uniqueness of oral logic suddenly took hold within me.

Once the whole of the *Didache* was in my bones, I took every opportunity to perform it—before my students, before my faculty, at regional meetings of learned societies. As word got around, I was even invited to perform it before a Jewish audience. Hearing the *Didache* is like hearing the Gospel of Mark performed orally for the first time. With written texts, the reader can visually stop, go backwards, compare lines. With oral productions, the listener is forced to follow the rate, the inflections, and the interpretation of the narrator. An oral performance is guided by the interpretation of the narrator. Silent reading, on the other hand, is guided by the interpretation projected onto the text by the reader—quite a different thing. Upon first hearing the entire Gospel of Mark performed orally, I was amazed how individual stories (pericopes) rubbed against each other and together created a unified impression of Jesus. In textual analysis, the micro-structures of Mark dominate. One cannot "see" (or analyze) how stories rub against each other. In oral narration, on the other hand, the macro-structures sound through. Individual "words" flash on the screen of the mind in rapid succession. No longer does one have a slide show (as in textual analysis) but a moving picture (as in linguistic or rhetorical analysis). The very same thing holds true for an oral performance of the *Didache*.

If the *Didache* is fundamentally oral in character, then it ought to be heard. In my seminars, consequently, I perform segments of the *Didache* so that participants can take in the oral feel before they read the text. I furthermore invite participants to make a tape of the *Didache* which they can listen to in their car as they travel back and forth. Accordingly, you, the reader of this volume, are invited to do the same. If you would like to own a sample "student tape" or to make use of my "electronic version" of the *Didache*, consult the final page of this volume for details.

THE SECOND VOYAGE OF COLUMBUS

Listening to NPR this morning, I learn that today is the anniversary commemorating the beginning of Columbus's second voyage (25 September 1493). He had outfitted sixteen ships and was ready to retrace the route to the new and strange world that he had discovered the year before.

You, the reader of this volume, can be compared to a shipmate signing on for such a second voyage. You are spared the terror and the uncertainty that accompanied the first passage. I faced them practically alone and returned alive to tell about it. Strange stories, strange experiences, and strange people returned with me. Now you, my reader, are signed on to retrace the route back in time whereby I discovered the "new world" of the *Didache*.

Reading this volume, you will encounter *strange stories*—for example, that, contrary to the current scholarly consensus, the *Didache* has a clearly defined order and purpose and logic from beginning to end. You will encounter *strange experiences*—for example, that the economic rules of sharing resources in the *Didache* are not centered on detachment, asceticism, or voluntary poverty but are part of the pragmatic skills of a working-class group bent upon securing their well-being in a hostile economic environment. You will encounter *strange people*—for example, those wandering prophets whose carefree existence and passionate prayers dazzled their hearers and evoked expectations that the Lord God would momentarily step into history. Yet, despite their inspired and inspiring words, these prophets were sent packing after one or two days and, as often as not, proved themselves to be troublemakers during the course of their short visits.

Needless to say, a shipmate making the second crossing will not credit all the stories of those who made the first passage. In fact, while reading this volume, you will even have experiences of your own which never showed up in the first passage. Finally, the strangeness of the people met will gradually wear on you, and, as the *Didache* notes, "some [of its members] you will reprove, and concerning others you will pray, and some you will love more than your own soul" (2:7).

So, as shipmates, let us pull up anchor and begin.

25 September 2002

ACKNOWLEDGMENTS

The writing of this book over a period of fifteen years would have been impossible without the generous help of many persons.

Jacob Neusner, Michael Polanyi, and Willy Rordorf contributed of themselves and of their special know-how in my quest to understand the *Didache*. The character of each of their contributions was profound and enduring and has already been detailed in How My Mind Was Changed. Without these giants, I would not have had the shoulders to stand on so as to see far.

Carol Andreini, Associate Professor of Classics at Northern Dakota State University, provided me with a fresh translation of the Greek text at the very onset of this project in 1988. During the following year, thanks to a Lilly Endowment grant, we were able to work side by side over a period of weeks sorting out the nuances of the Koine Greek of the *Didache* and identifying classical parallels. While the final form of the translation is my responsibility, its content and consistency reflect her expertise and linguistic insights.

Richard Arthur, a close personal friend going back to our graduate study days in Berkeley, prepared for me a fresh translation of the Coptic fragment of the *Didache* and patiently worked with me in examining various claims made on its behalf. Without his assistance, I would not have been able to negotiate these confusing and conflictual claims.

Dozens of colleagues offered me feedback and insights on the many academic papers and public presentations I offered on various topics of the *Didache*. Among these, John Dominic Crossan, codirector of the Jesus Seminar, Phil Culbertson of St. John's College (New Zealand), and Jonathan Draper of the University of Natal (South Africa) deserve special recognition for our stimulating hours of exchange and our shared concern to unearth the social questions which created the *Didache*. I am also thankful to Dennis C. Duling, Deirdre Good, Rabbi Simchah Roth, Richard

Sarason, and Eileen Schuller for offering me feedback on key questions along the way. The students in my *Didache* seminars, both in Cincinnati and in Neuchâtel, are also to be recognized for their sustained attention to the internal structure of the text and their creative efforts to draw out its pastoral genius. All in all, I frequently came away from class knowing I had learned more than I had taught.

During the course of my research, I was grateful to have received financial assistance and public recognition in the form of grants and faculty fellowships from the Association of Theological Schools, the National Endowment for the Humanities, and the Lilly Foundation (twice). I also want to warmly thank the library staff of United Theological Seminary (Dayton) for offering me full access to their academic collection and James Christy, pastor of the Greene Street Methodist Church (Piqua), for providing me with urgently needed office space.

Nancy Pardee, a doctoral candidate at the University of Chicago, took time out from the preparation of her dissertation on the *Didache* to offer me a careful and critical reading of the early chapters of my manuscript. Nancy knows the particulars of working with ancient manuscripts better than I do, and this volume is greatly improved because of her insights.

During the last five years, Dennis McManus has been assigned to me by Paulist Press to prepare the manuscript and guide it through the publishing process. Never in my life have I received such sensitive collaboration and personal support during times when the weight of preparing such a large and extensive work threatened to overwhelm me. Dennis acted not only as a capable editor and informed scholar but, in the end, as an advocate and a friend. The aesthetic quality of the layout is due to his dedication and the diligent work of The HK Scriptorium, Inc.

Deborah Rose-Milavec encouraged me to write not only for scholars, pastors, and students but for ordinary people as well. Deb has done insightful work on the role of women in the *Didache*. Currently, however, she is director of a women's shelter in Sidney. Even the victims of domestic violence, Deb continually reminded me, might well have a spiritual hunger for the *Didache*. Ordinary people, moreover, need to be engaged by their religious affiliations without being tyrannized, nourished without being force-fed, listened to without being patronized. The majority of boxes in this volume and, most especially, the epilogue, are dedicated, thanks to Deb, to the well-being of ordinary people who, in their own way, may find their personal spiritual hunger addressed in the *Didache*.

I give thanks to my family who walked with me during the long, arduous journey that the writing of this book entailed. I especially acknowledge my beloved spouse who held me up at times when the weight of this book seemed too much to bear.

I acknowledge "the four winds" (*Did.* 10:5) who alternately carried quiet layers of fog, fierce thunderstorms, and dancing snowflakes—each of which refreshed my soul again and again while writing this book. I give thanks to those living trees whose lives were extinguished in order that this book might be published. Moreover, I would be remiss if I did not acknowledge the excessive suffering inflicted on birds, animals, and fish as a byproduct of the many phases of forestry/paper/book production. Nearly all pulp mills in Europe recycle the staggering amounts of water necessary for paper production. In the United States and Canada, however, even while mills have taken some measures to reduce their toxic emissions, every mill hourly discharges thousands of gallons of contaminated water into the natural environment. Wildlife downstream without access to bottled water and the children of poorer families without access to a swimming pool are at risk. In places like the state of Washington, a full third of the total industrial toxic discharge comes from local mills. Bald eagles, the proud icons of American freedom, now helplessly watch their young die even though they are nesting miles from the contaminated waters. The tragedy, therefore, is that, here in "the land of the free, the home of the brave," the very words heralding the Way of Life are printed on the inexpensive paper made possible by an industry practicing the Way of Death.

Finally, I want to acknowledge those capable pastors of the mid-first century who collaboratively created the *Didache* as the summation of their successful practice in training gentiles to walk in the Way of Life. May this volume serve to honor their pastoral genius in addressing the need artfully and effectively to pass on their cherished secrets of surviving and thriving in the end time.

To my beloved daughter,
Jessica Elva Milavec

My daughter was born during the 1988 NEH Seminar in which I first learned from Jacob Neusner how to study the *Didache*. While my work was in progress, I learned how to gently rub her earlobe during her eight o'clock feeding in order to insure that she would be able to drink enough milk to sleep throughout the night. For countless hours, I carried her in a kangaroo pouch, which allowed her to hear my heart and feel my warmth as I searched through library stacks, typed out my findings, and washed the dishes. As she grew, she watched me at work, and I watched her at "her work." On many days, she was making designs with crayons while I was designing words at her side. Now she has turned fifteen and is well on her way to becoming an intelligent, dedicated, resourceful woman. She loves the "little ones" (from wasps to whales) who share this wonderous yet endangered earth with us. Grateful am I for her love and for her presence in my life. She is just the daughter that I always dreamed of. I dedicate this book, therefore, to my beloved Jessy.

Part I

Text

How the Greek Manuscript
Was Discovered, Transcribed,
and Translated

Archbishop Philotheos Bryennios was browsing in the library of the Greek Convent of the Holy Sepulchre in Istanbul in 1873 when, by chance, he discovered the only known copy of the *Didache* that has come down to us. Bryennios was forty at the time and had spent his early years teaching church history before being advanced to various administrative and pastoral posts in the Greek Orthodox Church. In fact, Bryennios had been appointed bishop a year earlier and was actively committed to church reform. Thus, even with his increased responsibilities, he deliberately made time for his scholarship because he wished actively to foster "a piety built upon a clear understanding of the transformations that modern society requires of the ancient churches" (cited in Sabatier 1885: 1). Given the wide range of interests and occupations calling for Bryennios's attention, another ten years passed before Bryennios fully recognized and finally published his extraordinary find.

No One Could See It
for What It Was

That Bryennios should have discovered the *Didache* during his first year as a reforming bishop contains an element of mystery. It is also mysterious that the three Western scholars who had combed through the contents of the Library of the Greek Convent of the Holy Sepulchre in 1845, 1856, and 1876 and published catalogues of their findings had entirely overlooked the *Didache* (Hitchcock and Brown: xii). The codex Bryennios discovered comprises 120 sheets of parchment measuring 7.4 by 5.8 inches bound under a leather cover. The *Didache* escaped the notice of early

researchers because it was sandwiched between other early church documents as follows:

1. Pseudo-Chrysostom *Synopsis of the Old and New Testament* (manuscript folios 1a–32b)
2. *Epistle of Barnabas* (folios 33a–51b)
3. *1* and *2 Clement* (folios 51b–70a and 70a–76a)
4. *Names of the Books of the Hebrews* (12 lines in the middle of folio 76a)
5. *Didache* (last four lines of folio 76a to end of 80b)
6. Letter of Maria of Cassoboloi to Ignatius followed by twelve letters of
   Ignatius (folios 81a–82a and 82a–120a)
7. Explanation of Jesus' genealogy (folio 120a–120b).

Plato noted in the *Meno* that one cannot begin to look for something
unless one has some premonition of what it is that one is looking for. This
applies very much to the discovery of the *Didache*. Everyone knew that
Origen and Athanasius had made early reference to the *Didache* by way of
naming ancient works whose reputation was too local to allow inclusion in
the universal canon. Nineteenth-century scholars had become resigned to
the fact that no extant copy of the *Didache* had survived. Some few scholars identified the *Ecclesiastical Canons of the Holy Apostles* as "the lost
Didache" after it was first discovered by Beckell in 1848, but this opinion
did not gain wide support (Hitchcock and Brown: lxv). Even in 1873,
what initially caught Bryennios's eye was not the *Didache* but a very old
version of the *Epistle of Barnabas*. In 1875 Bryennios published the *Epistle
of Barnabas* (folios 33a–51b), and in his publication he listed the other
titles in the discovered codex. No one immediately gave any attention to
the *Didache*, which was listed among the discovered texts (Hitchcock and
Brown: lxvi). Bishop Lightfoot, in 1877, was enthusiastic about the discovery of a new manuscript of the *Epistle of Barnabas* but doubted the
value of the *Didache* (Hitchcock and Brown: lxvi). A year later, Oscar von
Gebhardt and Adolf von Harnack, leading German experts in the early
church, published a treatise on Barnabas making use of Bryennios's find,
yet both failed at that point to give any importance to his reference to the
Didache. Thus, the *Didache* was there, right under the noses of the world's
experts, yet everyone failed to notice it for what it was because they weren't
looking for it and were distracted by seeing other things.

In 1882, Adam Krawutzeky turned this around. He used the new methods of textual criticism to reconstruct the Greek source that he speculated
stood as the foundation for the Two Way sections of the *Ecclesiastical
Canons of the Holy Apostles* and the *Apostolic Constitutions*. Krawutzeky
thus inadvertently reconstructed from derivative texts the first 45 percent

of the *Didache* with great accuracy. In 1883, when Bryennios finally published the text of the *Didache*, scholars hailed this as a vindication of Krawutzeky's "analytical skill," for the very source he had reconstructed had been found (Hitchcock and Brown: lxviii).

Almost overnight, everyone in Europe, England, and America was astonished that such an ancient and important work had gotten lost but, after nearly fifteen centuries, a single copy had surfaced. When the first English translation prepared by Hitchcock and Brown was released on 20 March 1884 in the New York bookstores, five thousand copies were sold on the first day (Sabatier: 5). Nonetheless, during the first years after its publication, some scholars dismissed Bryennios's find on the grounds that it was "a modern forgery" (see Hitchcock and Brown: v). It was almost as though a document (a) lost for nearly fifteen hundred years and (b) overlooked repeatedly by scholars cataloguing the library was not allowed to show up so unexpectedly. After a few years, however, the judgment of authenticity prevailed.

The *Didache* is approximately one-third the length of Mark's Gospel. After 1887, it was transferred to the library of the Orthodox patriarch of Jerusalem, where it has been catalogued as *Codex Hierosolymitanus 54.* The vocabulary and grammar are typical of popular Greek writings of the first century. "The style is simple, natural, terse, sententious, and popular" (Schaff: 96). As to its vocabulary:

> The *Didache* contains 2190 words. Its vocabulary comprises 552 words. . . . 504 are New Testament words, 497 are classical, and 479 occur in the Septuagint. 15 [words] occur for the first time in the *Didache*, but are found in later writers. 1 [word, *prosezomologein* found in 14:1] occurs only in the *Didache* [but its meaning can be easily surmised by combining known words]. (Schaff: 97)

The Greek manuscript is well preserved and carefully written, and it employs a score of tachygraphic signs or abbreviations in common use during the Middle Ages, when it was copied. The scribe who made the copy identifies himself as "Leon, scribe and sinner" and dates the completion of his work as 11 June 1056.

NORMS FOR ESTABLISHING A WORKING GREEK TEXT

J. Rendel Harris (1887: 1–10) produced a careful transcription of the manuscript in which he expanded the medieval tachygraphic signs. The

Greek text found in this book follows the transcription made by Harris with the following corrections made on the basis of a careful examination of a reproduction of the original:

1. The original manuscript has no upper-case letters save the first letter of the longer title. Accordingly, I have returned the upper-case delta, which Harris used in the shorter title along with his capitalization of references to David and to Jesus to their original lower case letters. Throughout the codex, "capitals are found only at the beginning of books, even proper names being written without them" (Hitchcock and Brown: cii).

2. At one point Harris joins words that ought to be separated (*dia-pantos* in 3:9). At one point, he separates words that ought to be joined (*hōs anna* in 10:6). I have corrected these minor errors in Harris's transcription.

3. At many points Harris placed a Greek period in his transcription where the original clearly has a colon: after *thlibomenon* and after *hapantōn* in 5:2, after *didaskei* in 6:1, after *hypokritōn* in 8:1, after *potēriou* in 9:2, after *kysi* in 9:5, after *poiēsate* in 11:3, after *kyrios* in 11:4, after *peirasete* in 11:7, after *estin* in 12:5, after *autou* in 13:2, after *ptōchois* in 13:4, after *autou* in 16:4. I detect a faint colon after *eleēmōn* in 3:8 where one would expect it; hence, I have included it. Harris overlooked a clear colon after *prophētēs* in 11:8. After *theou* in 16:4 the manuscript has a raised dot somewhere between a period and a colon. Willy Rordorf, after examining the original text, judges this to be clearly a colon. I accept his judgment.

Caution must be exercised in using Greek punctuation to interpret the text. To begin with, we cannot know whether such punctuation was in the original or whether it was added by a scribe later (as in the case of the short and long titles). Beyond this, one needs to take into account that, save for the final period at the end of the entire text, those six periods that do exist in the original manuscript (1:4; 1:5; 4:7; 5:2; 14:3; 15:3) all appear at the end of a line in the parchment. While Leon clearly has traced faint lines on the parchment to guide his hand, it appears suspicious that the six periods embedded into the text always appear at the end of line. Furthermore, while the use of punctuation is otherwise consistent, no rhyme or reason can be given why periods as opposed to colons should have been used at these six points. The strong possibility remains, therefore, that Leon inadvertently lowered the dot at the end of these lines and produced a period where he intended a colon. Since Greek grammar does not strongly distinguish between the colon and the period (as in English), the possibility remains that Leon intended all the dots at the end of lines to be colons. In sum, with some justification, I might have transcribed all the periods as colons. In order to retain an accurate transcription, however, I have placed periods, colons, and commas as they are found in the original.

4. Harris detected a half-dozen minor errors found in Leon's manuscript (1887: 12). Harris corrects these errors on the ground that a scribe often fails to hear or to copy a word correctly and introduces a sound-alike substitution. I, along with other scholars, accept these minor corrections of Harris.

Unknown to Harris, someone had already made four corrections of single letters using a violet ink written over the black ink of the original. Rordorf believes that Bryennios made these obvious corrections himself when he prepared the first transcription of the manuscript for publication (1998: 233). The facsimile copies used by Harris, however, were unable to distinguish between the violet and black ink. Harris, consequently, had been, without his knowing it, using a copy of the *Didache* that had already been corrected. Rordorf lists these four changes in his most recent edition of his book (1998: 263). They have no bearing on the meaning and the interpretation of the manuscript.

5. There are three places where colons were carelessly omitted (10:2, 4; 14:3) and three places where short words were omitted (9:4; 10:4; 11:5). These changes have been widely accepted by current scholars. For the sake of fidelity to the original, however, these minor additions are presented in angle brackets (<>) to indicate that they were added to the Greek text (details on p. 10f.).

Going beyond this, many scholars have tried to improve the intelligibility of the text by substituting near equivalents for unclear words or phrases. Harris himself gave much attention to a number of substitutions brought forward by Adolf von Harnack and Adolf Hilgenfeld. In the end, however, he preferred not to alter the original text on the following grounds:

> Indeed it must be admitted that with slight exceptions the attempts to emend the text have not been very successful. The most difficult passages have yielded to interpretative skill . . . , and this should assure us that any alterations in the text must not be more than moderate if they are to be in any degree acceptable. (Harris 1887: 14)

This then is the rule guiding this commentary—*lectio difficilior potior* ("The more difficult reading is preferable").

Once one begins to justify altering the original on the basis of known texts, customs, or theologies outside the *Didache*, one adulterates the *Didache* itself. One disguises from the reader the fact that the framers of the *Didache* had in mind routine meanings that were well known to them and seemingly unknown to us. The task of the scholar is best served by allowing the singularity of the text to stand out and refraining from harmonizing the text on the basis of what was said or done elsewhere.

Scholars such as Aelred Cody, Rordorf, and Georg Schöllgen have followed this approach to the text very successfully. Jean-Paul Audet, Kurt Niederwimmer, and Klaus Wengst, on the other hand, allow corrections on the basis of comparison with the Latin or Coptic fragments or the *Apostolic Constitutions*. Wengst, in his Greek reconstruction, introduces fifty alterations to the received text (see Dehandschutter). In the end, this creates a hypothetical hybrid that can never be known to have ever existed or ever been used.

Even seemingly moderate alterations are suspect. Niederwimmer, for instance, suggests that, for the unusual word *klasma* ("fragment") in *Did*. 9:3f., the more usual word *artos* ("loaf") be substituted. Peterson (1959: 168f.), Vööbus (1968: 89, 146–48), and Wengst (1984: 97f.) agree with him. He explains himself as follows:

> Verse 3 gives the second benediction, the blessing of the bread, introduced by the rubric *peri de tou klasmatos* ["And concerning the fragment"]. This suggests that we should understand *klasma* ["fragment"] to mean the bread broken at the meal celebration. In that case, the plural *peri de tōn klasmatōn* ["And concerning the fragments"] would seem more appropriate. . . . The parallels from later liturgies have *artos* in the analogous location. Peterson has pointed out that *klasma* is a technical term in the eucharistic language of Egypt; it refers to the particle of the host. The expression could then have entered the text at a secondary stage. (Niederwimmer 1998: 148)

If the technical term *klasma* goes back to the Egyptian liturgy and accordingly hints at a late origin of the *Didache* (Bigg 1905: 414), then one might be willing to drop the tainted "late word" in favor of the supposed earlier term, namely, *artos*. This substitution in *Did*. 9:3, however, would require that *Did*. 9:5 be altered such that "fragments of bread," or better, "grains of bread," would be scattered over the hills. It makes no sense to scatter a loaf (*artos*). The substitution allowed by Niederwimmer (as well as by Wengst, Peterson, and Vööbus) thus resolves one difficulty by creating another one.

Going deeper, however, what if it could be shown that the term "fragment" goes back to an ancient Jewish usage whereby the loaf was broken prior to being blessed and thus, only a "fragment" was held up as representing the whole? In this case, *klasma* would offer a hint of the Hebraic idioms that might have once flourished in the archaic form of the eucharistic liturgy found in the *Didache*. Hence, by retaining the more difficult reading of the original, one retains the necessity of finding a suitable answer to the question why this (*klasma*) and not that (*artos*). Those who would substitute *artos* gain a "quick fix" in terms of intelligibility but lose the precious fact that the *Didache* may contain archaic idioms that were part of its foundation and which, with a little prying, might reveal untold mysteries of its true origins and pastoral genius. I have elected, in every case, therefore, to stay with the original.

The Usefulness of Preparing an Analytical Side-by-Side Translation

The Greek transcription and the English translation on the following pages have been set out so as to facilitate the reading and analysis of the received text. The Greek manuscript prepared by Leon was presented on continuous lines with little or no spaces left to indicate the ends of words, of sentences, and of sections. In order to make the Greek text and its English translation more accessible, the following pages group and organize the material such that, upon first reading, the internal logic begins to make itself evident. Thus, one can identify units of thought, repetitious patterns, and key transitions which ordinarily only a studied examination of the text would reveal. This is what is meant here by an analytic translation. This is also something that I learned from Jacob Neusner.

The English translation produced here retains the literal Greek meaning, but without slavishly following the Greek word order and usage. Idioms in the Greek are rendered into English with only small adaptations being made in order to achieve a close, dynamic equivalence without becoming stilted English. Words or phrases placed in brackets ([ ]) are not represented in the Greek text but serve to clarify the elliptical intent of the Greek. English words linked together by underlined spaces signal instances where a single Greek word needs to be rendered by a phrase in English. In sum, the English translation in this volume is conservatively constructed such that, in principle, it could be retranslated back into the original Greek.

Since the English language has lost its ability to differentiate between the singular and plural "you," this translation allows one to see the second person plural pronoun by printing "ÿou." Furthermore, an umlaut is sometimes introduced over one of the vowels of an English verb when the context fails to make evident that it has a plural subject. Thus, for example, "Präy for ÿour enemies" (*Did.* 1:3) allows the English reader to know that the Greek has a plural imperative ("Präy") matched by a plural pronoun ("ÿour").

The post-positive particle *de* is frequently used in Greek to signal a continuation of the foregoing topic. An English-speaking storyteller who begins all his sentences with "And" or "And then" is effectively doing the same thing as a Greek speaker would do. Accordingly, when *de* appears in the Greek, the English translation will render this *de* as "(And)." Placing the "And" in parentheses at the beginning of the sentence indicates that current English style normally avoids saying it. Where *kai* ("and") is found in the Greek, it is consistently rendered as "and" without parentheses. The post-positive particle *de* can sometimes have an adversative sense. In these cases, it is rendered into English as "(but)" or "on the other hand." Where *alla* ("but") is found, it is consistently rendered as "but" without any parentheses.

Finally, the Greek language assigns gender to nouns and to pronouns somewhat differently than does English. Nouns in English designating "things" are neuter, while nouns designating "living beings" are either masculine or feminine. In Greek, nouns designating things may be masculine, feminine, or neuter (as in the case for all European languages). When Greek verbs allow for either a male or female subject or a female or male object, this will be appropriately signaled by using an inclusive English translation. Overall, the entire *Didache* is 99 percent inclusive; yet every modern English translation I have examined leaves the mistaken impression that "men" were addressing "men" about "manly things" throughout. This translation will demonstrate that "women" were also addressing "women" about "womanly things." This commentary will thus rectify a gender distortion that has misrepresented the intent and the use of the *Didache* by both women and men in the Didache communities of the mid-first century.

Notes regarding Additions to the Original Text

1:3 The Greek has a colon and comma where one might expect a question mark. In the Bryennios codex, the question mark (;) occurs only once (*1 Clem.* 1:17) (Hitchcock and Brown: ciii).

9:4 The addition of *to* only serves to clarify that this, the broken loaf, was scattered (Bihlmeyer, Funk, Gebhardt, Harnack, Rordorf). Otherwise, the Greek could be open to meaning, "This is the broken loaf scattered."

10:4 A scribal omission occurs here as a result of a faulty reading of the original (Bryennios, Harnack, Harris). The presumption is that the doxology would be repetitive; thus the close of 10:4 parallels 9:3, 9:4, and 10:2. Furthermore, the Coptic fragment presents a uniform doxology in all four places. Niederwimmer holds that the original presents no problem (1982: 126), yet he alters the beginning of 10:4 to read *peri pantōn* to bring it into alignment with the Coptic (1998: 159).

11:5 The original, as it stands, is confusing, for it says, "(And) he/she will not remain one day," and then goes on to speak of "another [day]" in cases of necessity. Thus, Harnack first conjectured that *ei mē* ("except/only") needs to be added to avoid contradicting itself (also Audet, Bihlmeyer, Niederwimmer, Rordorf, Wengst). The Coptic fragment confirms this reading of the text.

διδαχὴ τῶν δώδεκα ἀποστόλων

Διδαχὴ κυρίου διὰ τῶν δώδεκα ἀποστόλων τοῖς ἔθνεσιν·

1:1 ὁδοὶ δύο εἰσί· μία τῆς ζωῆς· καὶ μία τοῦ θανάτου·
διαφορὰ δὲ πολλὴ μεταξὺ τῶν ὁδῶν·

1:2 ἡ μὲν οὖν ὁδὸς τῆς ζωῆς ἐστιν αὕτη·
πρῶτον· ἀγαπήσεις τὸν θεὸν τὸν ποιήσαντά σε·
δεύτερον· τὸν πλησίον σου ὡς σεαυτόν·

πάντα δὲ ὅσα ἐὰν θελήσῃς μὴ γίνεσθαὶ σοι·
καὶ σὺ ἄλλω μὴ ποίει·

1:3 τούτων δὲ τῶν λόγων ἡ διδαχὴ ἐστιν αὕτη·

εὐλογεῖτε τοὺς καταρωμένους ὑμῖν·
καὶ προσεύχεσθε ὑπὲρ τῶν ἐχθρῶν ὑμῶν·
νηστεύετε δὲ ὑπὲρ τῶν διωκόντων ὑμᾶς·
ποία γὰρ χάρις ἐὰν ἀγαπᾶτε τοὺς ἀγαπῶντας ὑμᾶς;
οὐχὶ καὶ τὰ ἔθνητο αὐτὸ ποιοῦσιν‹;›
ὑμεῖς δὲ ἀγαπᾶτο τοὺς μισοῦντας ὑμᾶς·
καὶ οὐχ ἕξετε ἐχθρόν·

1:4 ἀπέχου τῶν σαρκικῶν καὶ σωματικῶν ἐπιθυμιῶν.

ἐὰν τις σοι δῷ ῥάπισμα εἰς τὴν δεξιὰν σιαγόνα
στρέψον αὐτῷ καὶ τὴν ἄλλην καὶ ἔσῃ τέλειος·
ἐὰν ἀγγαρεύσῃ σέ τις μίλιον ἕν
ὕπαγε μετ᾽ αὐτοῦ δύο·
ἐὰν ἄρῃ τις τὸ ἱμάτιόν σου
δὸς αὐτῷ καὶ τὸν χιτῶνα·
ἐὰν λάβῃ τις ἀπὸ σοῦ τὸ σὸν
μὴ ἀπαίτει·
οὐδὲ γὰρ δύνασαι·

Training of the Twelve Apostles

Training of [the] Lord Through the Twelve Apostles to the Gentiles

1:1   There are two ways: one of life and one of death—
       (and) [there is] a great difference between the two ways.

1:2   [A] On_the_one_hand, then, the way of life is this:
           [1] first: you will love the God who made you;
           [2] second: [you will love] your neighbor as yourself.
       [B] On_the_other_hand [the way of life is this]:
           as many [things] as you might wish not to happen to you,
           likewise, do not do to another.

1:3   (And) [for an assimilation] of these words, the training is this:

       [A] spëak_well of the ones speaking_badly of ÿou,
       [B] and präy for ÿour enemies,
       [C] (and) fäst for the ones persecuting ÿou;
           For what merit [is there] if ÿou löve the ones loving ÿou?
           Do not even the gentiles do the same thing?
       [D] ÿou, on_the_other_hand, löve the ones hating ÿou,
           and ÿou will not have an enemy.

1:4   Abstain from fleshly and bodily desires. [How so?]

       [A] if anyone should strike you on the right cheek,
           turn to him/her also the other, and you will be perfect;
       [B] if anyone should press_you_into_service for one mile,
           go with him/her two;
       [C] if anyone should take away your cloak,
           give to him/her also your tunic;
       [D] if anyone should take from you [what is] yours,
               do not ask_for_it_back;
                   for you are not even able [to do so].

1:5 παντὶ τῷ αἰτοῦντί σε δίδου
καὶ μὴ ἀπαίτει·
   πᾶσι γὰρ θέλει δίδοσθαι ὁ πατὴρ
   ἐκ τῶν ἰδίων χαρισμάτων·

   μακάριος ὁ διδοὺς κατὰ τὴν ἐντολήν·
      ἀθῷος γάρ ἐστιν·
   οὐαὶ τῷ λαμβάνοντι·
      εἰ μὲν γὰρ χρείαν ἔχων λαμβάνει τις
      ἀθῷος ἔσται·
      ὁ δὲ μὴ χρείαν ἔχων·
         δώσει δίκην·
         ἵναντί ἔλαβε καὶ εἰς τί·
         ἐν συνοχῇ δὲ γενόμενος ἐξετασθήσεται

      περὶ ὧν ἔπραξε·
      καὶ οὐκ ἐξελεύσεται ἐκεῖθεν·
         μέχρις οὗ ἀποδῷ τὸν ἔσχατον κοδράντην.

1:6 ἀλλὰ καὶ περὶ τούτου δὲ εἴρηται·
   ἱδρωτάτω ἡ ἐλεημοσύνη σου εἰς τὰς χεῖράς σου
   μέχρις ἂν γνῷς τινι δῷς·

2:1 δευτέρα δὲ ἐντολὴ τῆς διδαχῆς·

2:2 οὐ φονεύσεις·
οὐ μοιχεύσεις·
οὐ παιδοφθορήσεις·
οὐ πορνεύσεις·
οὐ κλέψεις·
οὐ μαγεύσεις·
οὐ φαρμακεύσεις·
οὐ φονεύσεις τέκνον ἐν φθορᾷ·
οὐδὲ γεννηθέντα ἀποκτενεῖς·
οὐκ ἐπιθυμήσεις τὰ τοῦ πλησίον·

1:5 To everyone asking you [for anything], give [it]
     and do not ask_for_it_back;
          for, to all, the Father wishes to give
          [these things] from his_own free_gifts.

          [A] Blessed is the one_giving according to the rule;
               for s/he is blameless.
          [B] Woe to the one_taking;
               [1] for, on_the_one_hand, if anyone having need takes,
                    s/he will be blameless;
               [2] on_the_other_hand, the one not having need
                    [a] will stand trial [on the day of judgment]
                         [as to] why s/he took and for what [use];
                    [b] (and) being in prison, s/he will be examined_thor-
                         oughly
                         concerning [the things] s/he has done,
                    [c] and s/he will not come_out from there
                         until s/he gives_back the last quadrans.

1:6 [C] But also, concerning this [rule], it has been said:
          "Let your alms sweat in your hands,
          until you know to whom you might give [it]."

2:1 (And) the second rule of the training [is this]:

2:2 [A1] You will not murder,
     [A2] you will not commit_adultery,
     [A3] you will not corrupt_boys,
     [A4] you will not have_illicit_sex,
     [A5] you will not steal,
     [A6] you will not practice_magic,
     [A7] you will not make_potions,
     [A8] you will not murder offspring by_means_of abortion,
     [A9] (and) you will not kill [him/her] having_been_born,
     [A10] you will not desire the things of [your] neighbor.

2:3   οὐκ ἐπιορκήσεις·
      οὐ ψευδομαρτυρήσεις·
      οὐ κακολογήσεις·
      οὐ μνησικακήσεις·
2:4   οὐκ ἔσῃ διγνώμων· οὐδὲ δίγλωσσος·
      παγὶς γὰρ θανάτου ἡ διγλωσσία·

2:5   οὐκ ἔσται ὁ λόγος σου ψευδής οὐ κενός·
      ἀλλὰ μεμεστωμένος πράξει·

2:6   οὐκ ἔσῃ πλεονέκτης·
      οὐδὲ ἅρπαξ·
      οὐδὲ ὑποκριτής·
      οὐδὲ κακοήθης·
      οὐδὲ ὑπερήφανος·

      οὐ λήψῃ βουλὴν πονηρὰν κατὰ τοῦ πλησίον σου·

2:7   οὐ μισήσεις πάντα ἄνθρωπον·
      ἀλλὰ οὓς μὲν ἐλέγξεις·
      περὶ δὲ ὧν προσεύξῃ·
      οὓς δὲ ἀγαπήσεις ὑπὲρ τὴν ψυχήν σου·

2:3 [B1] you will not swear_falsely,
    [B2] you will not bear_false_witness,
    [B3] you will not speak_badly [of anyone],
    [B4] you will not hold_grudges.
2:4 [B5] You will not be double-minded nor double-tongued,
      for being double-tongued is a snare of death.

2:5 [In sum] your word will not be false nor empty,
    but [will be] fulfilled by action.

2:6 [C1] You will not be covetous,
    [C2] (and) not greedy,
    [C3] (and) not a hypocrite,
    [C4] (and) not bad-mannered,
    [C5] (and) not arrogant.

[In sum] you will not take an evil plan against your neighbor.

2:7 You will not hate any person,
    [1] but some you will reprove,
    [2] and concerning others you will pray,
    [3] and some you will love more than your soul.

3:1 τέκνον μου φεῦγε ἀπὸ παντὸς πονηροῦ·
καὶ ἀπὸ παντὸς ὁμοίου αὐτοῦ·

3:2 μὴ γίνου ὀργίλος·
ὁδηγεῖ γὰρ ἡ ὀργὴ πρὸς τὸν φόνον·
μηδὲ ζηλωτής·
μηδὲ ἐριστικός·
μηδὲ θυμικός·
ἐκ γὰρ τούτων ἁπάντων φόνοι γεννῶνται·

3:3 τέκνον μου· μὴ γίνου ἐπιθυμητής·
ὁδηγεῖ γὰρ ἡ ἐπιθυμία πρὸς τὴν πορνείαν·
μηδὲ αἰσχρολόγος·
μηδὲ ὑψηλόφθαλμος·
ἐκ γὰρ τούτων ἁπάντων μοιχεῖαι γεννῶνται·

3:4 τέκνον μου μὴ γίνου οἰωνοσκόπος·
ἐπειδὴ ὁδηγεῖ εἰς τὴν εἰδωλολατρίαν·
μηδὲ ἐπαοιδός·
μηδὲ μαθηματικός·
μηδὲ περικαθαίρων·
μηδὲ θέλε αὐτὰ βλέπειν·
ἐκ γὰρ τούτων ἁπάντων εἰδωλολατρία γεννᾶται·

3:5 τέκνον μου μὴ γίνου ψεύστης·
ἐπειδὴ ὁδηγεῖ τὸ ψεῦσμα εἰς τὴν κλοπήν·
μηδὲ φιλάργυρος·
μηδὲ κενόδοξος·
ἐκ γὰρ τούτων ἁπάντων κλοπαὶ γεννῶνται·

3:6 τέκνον μου μὴ γίνου γόγγυσος·
ἐπειδὴ ὁδηγεῖ εἰς τὴν βλασφημίαν·
μηδὲ αὐθάδης·
μηδὲ πονηρόφρων·
ἐκ γὰρ τούτων ἁπάντων βλασφημίαι γεννῶνται·

3:1 My child, flee from every evil
     and from everything like it.

3:2 [A] Do not become angry,
          for anger is_the_path_leading to murder;
          nor envious,
          nor contentious,
          nor hot-headed,
          for, from all these, murders are begotten.

3:3 [B] My child, do not become lustful,
          for lust is_the_path_leading to illicit_sex;
          nor one_using_foul_speech,
          nor one_looking_up [into the face of a woman],
          for, from all these, adulteries are begotten.

3:4 [C] My child, do not become a diviner,
          since [this] is_the_path_leading to idolatry;
          nor an enchanter,
          nor an astrologer,
          nor a purifier,
          nor [even] wish to see these things,
          for, from all these, idolatry is begotten.

3:5 [D] My child, do not become false,
          since falsehood is_the_path_leading to theft;
          nor a lover_of_money,
          nor a_seeker_of_glory,
          for, from all these, thefts are begotten.

3:6 [E] My child, do not become a grumbler,
          since [this] is_the_path_leading to blasphemy;
          nor self-pleasing,
          nor evil-minded,
          for, from all these, blasphemies are begotten.

3:7 ἴσθι δὲ πραΰς·
      ἐπεὶ οἱ πραεῖς κληρονομήσουσι τὴν γῆν·

3:8 γίνου μακρόθυμος·
      καὶ ἐλεήμων·
      καὶ ἄκακος·
      καὶ ἡσύχιος·
      καὶ ἀγαθός·
      καὶ τρέμων τοὺς λόγους διαπαντός·
        οὓς ἤκουσας·

3:9 οὐχ ὑψώσεις σεαυτόν·
      οὐδὲ δώσεις τῇ ψυχῇ σου θράσος·
      οὐ κολληθήσεται ἡ ψυχή σου μετὰ ὑψηλῶν·
      ἀλλὰ μετὰ δικαίων καὶ ταπεινῶν ἀναστραφήσῃ·

3:10 τὰ συμβαίνοντά σοι ἐνεργήματα ὡς ἀγαθὰ προσδέξῃ·
      εἰδὼς ὅτι ἄτερ θεοῦ οὐδὲν γίνεται·

4:1 τέκνον μου τοῦ λαλοῦντός σοι τὸν λόγον τοῦ θεοῦ·
      μνησθήσῃ νυκτὸς καὶ ἡμέρας·
      τιμήσεις δὲ αὐτὸν ὡς κύριον·
        ὅθεν γὰρ ἡ κυριότης λαλεῖται
        ἐκεῖ κύριός ἐστιν·
4:2 ἐκζητήσεις δὲ καθ᾿ ἡμέραν τὰ πρόσωπα τῶν ἁγίων·
      ἵνα ἐπαναπαῇς τοῖς λόγοις αὐτῶν·

4:3 οὐ ποιήσεις σχίσμα·
      εἰρηνεύσεις δὲ μαχομένους·
      κρινεῖς δικαίως·
      οὐ λήψῃ πρόσωπον
        ἐλέγξαι ἐπὶ παραπτώμασιν·

4:4 οὐ διψυχήσεις πότερον ἔσται ἢ οὔ·

3:7 But be gentle,
   since the gentle will inherit the earth.

3:8 [A] Become long-suffering
       and merciful
       and harmless
       and calm
       and good
       and trembling through all [time] at the words
          that you have heard.

3:9 [B] You will not exalt yourself,
          (and) you will not give boldness to your soul.
          Your soul will not be joined with [the] lofty,
          but with [the] just and [the] lowly you will dwell.

3:10 [C] You will accept the experiences befalling you as good
          things,
          knowing that, apart from God, nothing happens.

4:1 [A] My child, the one speaking to you the word of God,
          [1] you will remember night and day,
          [2] (and) you will honor him/her as [the] Lord,
             for where [the] dominion [of the Lord] is spoken of,
             there [the] Lord is.
4:2   [3] (And) you will seek every day the presence of the
          saints
             in order that you may rest upon their words.

4:3 [B] You will not cause dissension:
          [1] (And) you will reconcile those fighting;
          [2] you will judge justly;
          [3] you will not take [into account] social status
             [when it comes time] to reprove against failings.

4:4 [C] You will not be double-minded whether it [God's
          future?] will be or not.

4:5   μὴ γίνου
      πρὸς μὲν τὸ λαβεῖν ἐκτείνων τὰς χεῖρας·

      πρὸς δὲ τὸ δοῦναι συσπῶν·

4:6   ἐὰν ἔχῃς διὰ τῶν χειρῶν σου

      δώσεις λύτρωσιν ἁμαρτιῶν σου·
4:7   οὐ διστάσεις δοῦναι·
      οὐδὲ διδοὺς γογγύσεις·
         γνώσῃ γὰρ τίς ἐστιν ὁ τοῦ μισθοῦ
         καλὸς ἀνταποδότης.

4:8   οὐκ ἀποστραφήσῃ τὸν ἐνδεόμενον·
      συγκοινωνήσεις δὲ
         πάντα τῷ ἀδελφῷ σου·
      καὶ οὐκ ἐρεῖς ἴδια εἶναι·
         εἰ γὰρ ἐν τῷ ἀθανάτῳ κοινωνοί ἐστε,
         πόσῳ μᾶλλον ἐν τοῖς θνητοῖς·

4:9   οὐκ ἀρεῖς τὴν χεῖρά σου
         ἀπὸ τοῦ υἱοῦ σου ἢ ἀπὸ τῆς θυγατρός σου·
         ἀλλὰ ἀπὸ νεότητος διδάξεις τὸν φόβον τοῦ θεοῦ·

4:10 οὐκ ἐπιτάξεις δούλῳ σου ἢ παιδίσκῃ
         τοῖς ἐπὶ τὸν αὐτὸν θεὸν ἐλπίζουσιν
      ἐν πικρίᾳ σου·
         μήποτε οὐ μὴ φοβηθήσονται τὸν ἐπ᾽ ἀμφοτέροις θεόν·

      οὐ γὰρ ἔρχεται κατὰ πρόσωπον καλέσαι·

      ἀλλ᾽ ἐφ᾽ οὓς τὸ πνεῦμα ἡτοίμασεν·

4:11 ὑμεῖς δὲ οἱ δοῦλοι ὑποταγήσεσθε τοῖς κυρίοις ὑμῶν·
      ὡς τύπῳ θεοῦ ἐν αἰσχύνῃ καὶ φόβῳ·

4:5 [A] Do not become [someone],

    [1] on_the_one_hand, stretching out your hands for_the_pur-
pose_of taking,

    [2] on_the_other_hand, withdrawing [them] for_the_pur-
pose_of giving.

4:6 [B] If you should have [something as the] through [the work
of] your hands,

    you will give [something] ransoming of your sins.

4:7   [1] You will not hesitate to give,

    [2] nor, giving, will you grumble;

      for you will know [the Lord God] who will be giving
back
excellent recompense [when he comes].

4:8 [C] You will not turn_away the one_being_in_need;

    [1] you will partner-together, on_the_other_hand,
[sharing] all [things] with your brother [sister],

    [2] and you will not say [such things] are your own.
For, if ÿou are partners in the immortal [things],
by_how_much more [are you partners] in the mortal
[things].

4:9 [A] You will not take away your hand

    from your son or from your daughter,

    but from youth you will train [them] in the fear of God.

4:10   [B] You will not command your male or female_slave

    (the ones hoping in the same God [as you])

    in your bitterness,

      lest they should ever not fear the God [who is] over
both [of ÿou],

    for [God] does not come to call [anyone] according_to
[his/her] social_status,

    but [God calls] those whom the Spirit has made ready.

4:11 [C] And ÿou, the slaves, will be_subject_to ÿour lords

    as to the image of God in shame and fear.

4:12 μισήσεις πᾶσαν ὑπόκρισιν
καὶ πᾶν ὃ μὴ ἀρεστὸν τῷ κυρίῳ·

4:13 οὐ μὴ ἐγκαταλίπῃς ἐντολὰς κυρίου·
φυλάξεις δὲ ἃ παρέλαβες·
μήτε προστιθεὶς· μήτε ἀφαιρῶν·

4:14 ἐν ἐκκλησίᾳ ἐξομολογήσῃ τὰ παραπτώματά σου·
καὶ οὐ προσελεύσῃ ἐπὶ προσευχήν σου ἐν συνειδήσει
πονηρᾷ·

αὕτη ἐστὶν ἡ ὁδὸς τῆς ζωῆς·

5:1 ἡ δὲ τοῦ θανάτου ὁδός ἐστιν αὕτη·

πρῶτον πάντων πονηρά ἐστι καὶ κατάρας μεστή·

φόνοι·	διπλοκαρδία·
μοιχεῖαι·	δόλος·
ἐπιθυμίαι·	ὑπερηφανία·
πορνεῖαι·	κακία·
κλοπαί·	αὐθάδεια·
εἰδωλολατρίαι·	πλεονεξία·
μαγεῖαι·	αἰσχρολογία·
φαρμακίαι·	ζηλοτυπία·
ἁρπαγαί·	θρασύτης·
ψευδομαρτυρίαι·	ὕψος·
ὑποκρίσεις·	ἀλαζονεία·

4:12 [A] You will hate every hypocrisy,
         and everything that is not pleasing to the Lord.

4:13 [B] You will not at all leave_behind the rules of [the] Lord,
         (but) you will guard the things that you have received,
         neither adding nor taking [anything] away.

4:14 [C] In church, you will confess your failings,
         and you will not go to your prayer with a bad conscience.

         This is the Way of Life!

5:1 The way of death, on_the_other_hand, is this:

     first of all, it is evil and full of accursedness:

[A1] murders,
[A2] adulteries,
[A3] lusts,
[A4] illicit_sexual_acts,
[A5] thefts,
[A6] idolatries,
[A7] mägic,
[A8] potions,
[A9] sorceries,
[A10] perjuries,
[A11] hypocrisies,

[A12] double-heartednesses,
[A13] trickery,
[A14] arrogance,
[A15] malice,
[A16] self-pleasing,
[A17] greed,
[A18] foul-speech,
[A19] jealousy,
[A20] audacity,
[A21] haughtiness,
[A22] false-pretension;

5:2

διῶκται ἀγαθῶν·   οὐκ ἐλεοῦντες πτωχόν·

μισοῦντες ἀλήθειαν·   οὐ πονοῦντες ἐπὶ καταπονουμένῳ·
ἀγαπῶντες ψεῦδος·
οὐ γινώσκοντες   οὐ γινώσκοντες
   μισθὸν δικαιοσύνης·   τὸν ποιήσαντα αὐτούς·
οὐ κολλώμενοι ἀγαθῷ·

οὐδὲ κρίσει δικαίᾳ·   φονεῖς τέκνων·
                         φθορεῖς
                         πλάσματος θεοῦ·
ἀγρυπνοῦντες
   οὐκ εἰς τὸ ἀγαθόν·
   ἀλλ᾽ εἰς τὸ πονηρόν·   ἀποστρεφόμενοι τὸν ἐνδεόμενον·

ὧν μακρὰν πραΰτης   καταπονοῦντες τὸν
   καὶ ὑπομονή·   θλιβόμενον·
μάταια ἀγαπῶντες·   πλουσίων παράκλητοι·

διώκοντες ἀνταπόδομα· πενήτων ἄνομοι κριταί·
                         πανθαμαρτητοί·

ῥυσθείητε τέκνα ἀπὸ τούτων ἁπάντων.

6:1 ὅρα μή τις σε πλανήσῃ
ἀπὸ ταύτης τῆς ὁδοῦ τῆς διδαχῆς·
ἐπεὶ παρεκτὸς θεοῦ σε διδάσκει·

6:2 εἰ μὲν γὰρ δύνασαι βαστάσαι ὅλον τὸν
    ζυγὸν τοῦ κυρίου τέλειος ἔσῃ·
εἰ δ᾽ οὐ δύνασαι
    ὃ δύνῃ τοῦτο ποίει·

6:3 περὶ δὲ τῆς βρώσεως·
    ὃ δύνασαι βάστασον·
    ἀπὸ δὲ τοῦ εἰδωλοθύτου
       λίαν πρόσεχε·
          λατρεία γάρ ἐστι θεῶν νεκρῶν·

5:2

[B1] [those] persecutors of
[the] good,

[B2] [those] hating [the] truth,

[B3] [those] loving lies,

[B4] [those] not knowing
[the] wages of justice,

[B5] not associating with
[the] good,

[B6] nor with just judgment,

[B7] [those] lying_awake
[at night] not for good,
but for wicked [things],

[B8] [those] far from being
gentle and patient,

[B9] [those] loving frivolous
[things],

[B10] [those] pursuing
recompense [for everything
they do],

[B11] [those] not showing_
mercy to the poor,

[B12] not toiling for the one_
weighed_down_by_toil,

[B13] [those] not knowing the
one_having_made them,

[B14] [those] murderers of
children

[B15] [those] corrupters
of God's workmanship

[B16] [those] turning away the
needy

[B17] [those] weighing_down_
with_toil the oppressed.

[B18] [those] advocates of the
rich,

[B19] lawless judges of [the]
poor,

[B20] [those] totally_sinful.

May ÿou be saved, [O] children, from all of these!

6:1 Look_out, lest anyone make you wander
from this way of training,
since without God s/he trains you.

6:2 [1] For, on_the_one_hand, if you are able to bear
the whole yoke of the Lord, you will be perfect;
[2] but if, on_the_other_hand, you are not able,
that which you are able, do this.

6:3 (And) concerning eating,
[1] bear that which you are able,
[2] from the food, on_the_other_hand, sacrificed to idols,
very_much keep_away
for it is worship of dead gods.

7:1   περὶ δὲ τοῦ βαπτίσματος οὕτω βαπτίσατε·

       ταῦτα πάντα προειπόντες βαπτίσατε·
       εἰς τὸ ὄνομα τοῦ πατρὸς
          καὶ τοῦ υἱοῦ
          καὶ τοῦ ἁγίου πνεύματος
       ἐν ὕδατι ζῶντι·

7:2   ἐὰν δὲ μὴ ἔχῃς ὕδωρ ζῶν·
          εἰς ἄλλο ὕδωρ βάπτισον·
       εἰ δ' οὐ δύνασαι ἐν ψυχρῷ·
          ἐν θερμῷ·
7:3   ἐὰν δὲ ἀμφότερα μὴ ἔχῃς·
          ἔκχεον εἰς τὴν κεφαλὴν τρὶς ὕδωρ
             εἰς ὄνομα πατρὸς
                καὶ υἱοῦ
                καὶ ἁγίου πνεύματος·

7:4   πρὸ δὲ τοῦ βαπτίσματος
       προνηστευσάτω ὁ βαπτίζων
       καὶ ὁ βαπτιζόμενος·
       καὶ εἴ τινες ἄλλοι δύνανται·

       κελεύεις δὲ νηστεῦσαι τὸν βαπτιζόμενον
       πρὸ μιᾶς ἢ δύο·

8:1   αἱ δὲ νηστεῖαι ὑμῶν·
       μὴ ἔστωσαν μετὰ τῶν ὑποκριτῶν·
          νηστεύουσι γὰρ δευτέρᾳ σαββάτων
             καὶ πέμπτῃ·
          ὑμεῖς δὲ νηστεύσατε τετράδα
             καὶ παρασκευήν·

7:1 (And) concerning baptism, bäptize thus:

Having said all these things beforehand,
ïmmerse in the name of the Father
        and of the Son
        and of the Holy Spirit
in flowing water—

7:2 [1] if, on_the_other_hand, you should not have flowing water,
        immerse in other water [that is available];
     [2] (and) if you are not able in cold,
        [immerse] in warm [water];
7:3 [3] (and) if you should not have either,
        pour out water onto the head three times
            in the name of [the] Father
                and [the] Son
                and [the] Holy Spirit.

7:4 (And) prior to the baptism,
     [1] let the one_baptizing fast;
     [2] and [let the] one_being_baptized;
     [3] and if any others have_the_strength,
        [let them fast also].
     Order, on_the_other_hand, the one_being_baptized to fast
     during one or two [days] prior [to the baptism].

8:1 (And) lët ÿour fasts
     not stand with the hypocrites,
        for they fast on the second [day] of the week
            and on the fifth
        ÿou fast, on_the_other_hand, during the fourth
            and during the [Sabbath] preparation [day].

8:2 μηδὲ προσεύχεσθε ὡς οἱ ὑποκριταί·
ἀλλ᾽ ὡς ἐκέλευσεν ὁ κύριος ἐν τῷ εὐαγγελίῳ αὐτοῦ·

οὕτως προσεύχεσθε·

πάτερ ὑμῶν ὁ ἐν τῷ οὐρανῷ·
ἁγιασθήτω τὸ ὄνομά σου·
ἐλθέτω ἡ βασιλεία σου·
γενηθήτω τὸ θέλημά σου·
   ὡς ἐν οὐρανῷ καὶ ἐπὶ γῆς·
τὸν ἄρτον ἡμῶν τὸν ἐπιούσιον δὸς ἡμῖν σήμερον·
καὶ ἄφες ἡμῖν τὴν ὀφειλὴν ἡμῶν·
   ὡς καὶ ἡμεῖς ἀφίεμεν τοῖς ὀφειλέταις ἡμῶν·
καὶ μὴ εἰσενέγκῃς ἡμᾶς εἰς πειρασμόν·
   ἀλλὰ ῥῦσαι ἡμᾶς ἀπὸ τοῦ πονηροῦ·
ὅτι σοῦ ἐστιν ἡ δύναμις καὶ ἡ δόξα εἰς τοὺς αἰῶνας·

8:3 τρὶς τῆς ἡμέρας οὕτω προσεύχεσθε·

9:1 περὶ δὲ τῆς εὐχαριστίας οὕτως εὐχαριστήσατε·

9:2 πρῶτον περὶ τοῦ ποτηρίου·

εὐχαριστοῦμέν σοι πάτερ ἡμῶν
ὑπὲρ τῆς ἁγίας ἀμπέλου δαϋὶδ τοῦ παιδός σου·
ἧς ἐγνώρισας ἡμῖν διὰ ἰησοῦ τοῦ παιδός σου·
σοὶ ἡ δόξα εἰς τοὺς αἰῶνας·

9:3 περὶ δὲ τοῦ κλάσματος·

εὐχαριστοῦμέν σοι πάτερ ἡμῶν
ὑπὲρ τῆς ζωῆς καὶ γνώσεως
ἧς ἐγνώρισας ἡμῖν διὰ ἰησοῦ τοῦ παιδός σου·
σοὶ ἡ δόξα εἰς τοὺς αἰῶνας·

8:2 (And) dö not pray as the hypocrites
but as the Lord ordered in his good news.

Präy thus:

> Our Father, the [one] in heaven,
> your name be_made_holy,
> your kingdom come,
> your will be born
> > upon earth as in heaven,
>
> give us this_day our loaf [that is] coming,
> and forgive us our debt [at the final judgment]
> > as we likewise [now] forgive our debtors,
>
> and do not lead us into the trial [of the last days]
> > but deliver us from [that] evil
>
> because yours is the power and the glory forever.

8:3 Three times within the day präy thus.

9:1 (And) concerning the eucharist, ëucharistize thus:

9:2 First, concerning the cup:

> We give you thanks, our Father,
> for the holy vine of your servant David
> which you revealed to us through your servant Jesus.
> To you [is] the glory forever.

9:3 And concerning the broken [loaf]:

> We give you thanks, our Father,
> for the life and knowledge
> which you revealed to us through your servant Jesus.
> To you [is] the glory forever.

9:4　ὥσπερ ἦν τοῦτο ‹τὸ› κλάσμα διεσκορπισμένον
　　　ἐπάνω τῶν ὀρέων
　　　καὶ συναχθὲν ἐγένετο ἕν·
　　　οὕτω συναχθήτω σου ἡ ἐκκλησία
　　　ἀπὸ τῶν περάτων τῆς εἰς τὴν σὴν βασιλείαν·
　　　ὅτι σοῦ ἐστιν ἡ δόξα καὶ ἡ δύναμις
　　　διὰ ἰησοῦ χριστοῦ εἰς τοὺς αἰῶνας·

9:5　μηδεὶς δὲ φαγέτω μηδὲ πιέτω ἀπὸ τῆς εὐχαριστίας ὑμῶν·
　　　ἀλλ᾽ οἱ βαπτισθέντες εἰς ὄνομα κυρίου·
　　　καὶ γὰρ περὶ τούτου εἴρηκεν ὁ κύριος·
　　　μὴ δῶτε τὸ ἅγιον τοῖς κυσί·

10:1　μετὰ δὲ τὸ ἐμπλησθῆναι οὕτως εὐχαριστήσατε·

10:2　εὐχαριστοῦμέν σοι πάτερ ἅγιε
　　　ὑπὲρ του ἁγίου ὀνόματός σου
　　　οὗ κατεσκήνωσας ἐν ταῖς καρδίαις ἡμῶν·
　　　καὶ ὑπὲρ τῆς γνώσεως καὶ πίστεως καὶ ἀθανασίας·
　　　ἧς ἐγνώρισας ἡμῖν διὰ ἰησοῦ τοῦ παιδός σου‹ ›
　　　σοὶ ἡ δόξα εἰς τοὺς αἰῶνας·

10:3　σύ δέσποτα παντοκράτορ ἔκτισας τὰ πάντα
　　　ἕνεκεν τοῦ ὀνόματός σου·
　　　τροφήν τε καὶ ποτὸν ἔδωκας τοῖς ἀνθρώπων εἰς ἀπόλαυσιν·

　　　ἵνα σοι εὐχαριστήσωσιν·
　　　ἡμῖν δὲ ἐχαρίσω
　　　πνευματικὴν τροφὴν καὶ ποτὸν καὶ ζωὴν αἰώνιον
　　　διὰ του παιδός σου·

10:4　πρὸ πάντων εὐχαριστοῦμέν σοι
　　　ὅτι δυνατὸς εἶ σύ‹ ›
　　　‹σοὶ› ἡ δόξα εἰς τοὺς αἰῶνας·

9:4   Just as this broken [loaf] was scattered
           over the hills [as grain],
      and, having_been_gathered_together, became one;
      in_like_fashion, may your church be_gathered_together
      from the ends of the earth into your kingdom.
      Because yours is the glory and the power
           through Jesus Christ forever.

9:5   (And) lët no one eat or drink from ÿour eucharist
      except those baptized in the name of [the] Lord,
           for the Lord has likewise said concerning this:
           "Do not give what is holy to the dogs."

10:1   And after being filled [by the meal], eücharistize thus:

10:2   We give you thanks, holy Father,
       for your holy name,
       which you tabernacle in our hearts,
       and for the knowledge and faith and immortality
       which you revealed to us through your servant Jesus.
       To you [is] the glory forever.

10:3   You, almighty Master, created all things
       for the sake of your name,
       both food and drink you have given to people for
           enjoyment
       in order that they might give thanks;
       to us, on_the_other_hand, you have graciously_bestowed
       Spirit-sent food and drink for life forever
           through your servant [Jesus].

10:4   Before all [these] things, we give you thanks
       because you are powerful [on our behalf].
       To you [is] the glory forever.

10:5 μνήσθητι κύριε τῆς ἐκκλησίας σου
        τοῦ ῥύσασθαι αὐτὴν ἀπὸ παντὸς πονηροῦ·
        καὶ τελειῶσαι αὐτὴν ἐν τῇ ἀγάπῃ σου·
        καὶ σύναξον αὐτὴν ἀπὸ τῶν τεσσάρων ἀνέμων·
     τὴν ἁγιασθεῖσαν εἰς τὴν σὴν βασιλείαν·
     ἣν ἡτοίμασας αὐτῇ·
     ὅτι σοῦ ἐστιν ἡ δύναμις καὶ ἡ δόξα εἰς τοὺς αἰῶνας·

10:6 ἐλθέτω χάρις
        καὶ παρελθέτω ὁ κόσμος οὗτος·
     ὡσαννὰ τῷ θεῷ δαυΐδ·
     εἴ τις ἅγιός ἐστιν ἐρχέσθω·
        εἴ τις οὐκ ἐστι μετανοείτω·
     μαραναθά ἀμήν·

10:7 τοῖς δὲ προφήταις ἐπιτρέπετε
     εὐχαριστεῖν ὅσα θέλουσιν·

11:1 ὅς ἂν οὖν ἐλθὼν διδάξῃ ὑμᾶς ταῦτα πάντα τὰ προειρημένα
        δέξασθε αὐτόν·
11:2 ἐὰν δὲ αὐτὸς ὁ διδάσκων
           στραφεὶς
              διδάσκῃ ἄλλην διδαχήν
        εἰς τὸ καταλῦσαι·
           μὴ αὐτοῦ ἀκούσητε·
        εἰς δὲ τὸ προσθεῖναι δικαιοσύνην
           καὶ γνῶσιν κυρίου·
              δέξασθε αὐτὸν ὡς κύριον·

10:5   Remember, Lord, your church,
              to save [her] from every evil
              and to perfect [her] in your love
              and to gather [her] together from the four winds
        [as] the sanctified into your kingdom
        which you have prepared for her,
        because yours is the power and the glory forever.

10:6   [A] Come, grace [of the kingdom]!
              and pass_away, [O] this world!
        [B] Hosanna to the God of David!
        [C] If anyone is holy, come!
              If anyone is not, convert!
        [D] Come Lord [*marana tha*]! Amen!

10:7   (And) türn towards the prophets [allowing them]
        to eucharistize as much as they wish.

11:1   [A] Whoever, then, should train ÿou in all these things said
              beforehand, rëceive him/her.
11:2   [B] If, on_the_other_hand, the one training,
              him/herself having been turned around,
              should train [ÿou] in another tradition
           [1] for the destroying [of things said beforehand],
                 dö not listen to him/her;
           [2] but, [if it is] for the supplementing of justice
                 and knowledge of [the] Lord,
                 rëceive him/her as [the] Lord!

11:3   περὶ δὲ τῶν ἀποστόλων καὶ προφητῶν
       κατὰ τὸ δόγμα τοῦ εὐαγγελίου·
       οὕτως ποιήσατε·

11:4   πᾶς δὲ ἀπόστολος ἐρχόμενος πρὸς
       ὑμᾶς δεχθήτω ὡς κύριος·
11:5   οὐ μενεῖ δὲ ‹εἰ μὴ› ἡμέραν μίαν·

       ἐὰν δὲ ᾖ χρεία καὶ τὴν ἄλλην·
       τρεῖς δὲ ἐὰν μείνῃ
       ψευδοπροφήτης ἐστίν·
11:6   ἐξερχόμενος δὲ
         ὁ ἀπόστολος μηδὲν λαμβανέτω·
           εἰ μὴ ἄρτον
           ἕως οὗ αὐλισθῇ·
         ἐὰν δὲ ἀργύριον αἰτῇ
           ψευδοπροφήτης ἐστί·

11:7   καὶ πάντα προφήτην λαλοῦντα ἐν πνεύματι,
         οὐ πειράσετε· οὐδὲ διακρινεῖτε·
       πᾶσα γὰρ ἁμαρτία ἀφεθήσεται·
       αὕτη δὲ ἡ ἁμαρτία οὐκ ἀφεθήσεται·
11:8   οὐ πᾶς δὲ ὁ λαλῶν ἐν πνεύματι προφήτης ἐστίν·
       ἀλλ᾽ ἐὰν ἔχῃ τοὺς τρόπους κυρίου·
       ἀπὸ οὖν τῶν τρόπων γνωσθήσεται
       ὁ ψευδοφροφήτης καὶ ὁ προφήτης·

11:9   καὶ πᾶς προφήτης ὁρίζων τράπεζαν ἐν πνεύματι,

         οὐ φάγεται ἀπ᾽ αὐτῆς·
         εἰ δὲ μήγε ψευδοπροφήτης ἐστίν·
11:10 πᾶς δὲ προφήτης διδάσκων τὴν ἀλήθειαν
         εἰ ἃ διδάσκει οὐ ποιεῖ
         ψευδοπροφήτης ἐστίν·

11:3   And concerning the apostle-prophets,
        in_accordance_with the decree of the good news,
        äct thus:

11:4   [A] (And) every apostle coming to ÿou,
             lët [him/her] be received as [the] Lord:
11:5   [1] s/he will not remain, on_the_other_hand, except one
                 day;
             [2] (and) if ever there be need, also another [day];
             [3] (but) if ever s/he should remain three [days],
                 s/he is a false prophet.
11:6   [B] (And), going_out,
             [1] lët the apostle take nothing
                 except a loaf [to sustain him/her]
                 until s/he might lodge [elsewhere],
             [2] if, on_the_other_hand, s/he should ask for silver,
                 s/he is a false prophet.

11:7   [A] And every prophet speaking in Spirit
             ÿou should not put_on_trial and not judge;
                 for every sin will be forgiven
                 but this sin will not be forgiven.
11:8   [B] (But) not everyone speaking in Spirit is a prophet,
             but if [s/he is], s/he should have the habits of [the] Lord.
             Therefore, from these habits should be known
             the false_prophet and the [true] prophet.

11:9   [A] And every prophet ordering a dining-table [to be set] in
             Spirit
             will not eat from it, (and) if [s/he acts] otherwise,
             s/he is really a false_prophet.
11:10 [B] (And) every prophet teaching the truth,
             if s/he does not do what s/he teaches,
             s/he is a false prophet.

11:11 πᾶς δὲ προφήτης δεδοκιμασμένος ἀληθινός

  ποιῶν εἰς μυστήριον κοσμικὸν ἐκκλησίας·
  μὴ διδάσκων δὲ ποιεῖν ὅσα αὐτὸς ποιεῖ

  οὐ κριθήσεται ἐφ᾽ ὑμῶν·
  μετὰ θεοῦ γὰρ ἔχει τὴν κρίσιν·
  ὡσαύτως γὰρ ἐποίησαν καὶ οἱ ἀρχαῖοι προφῆται·
11:12 ὅς δ᾽ ἂν εἴπῃ ἐν πνεύματι
  δός μοι ἀργύρια ἢ ἕτερά τινα
  οὐκ ἀκούσεσθε αὐτοῦ·
  ἐὰν δὲ περὶ ἄλλων ὑστερούντων
  εἴπῃ δοῦναι
  μηδεὶς αὐτὸν κρινέτω·

12:1 πᾶς δὲ ὁ ἐρχόμενος ἐν ὀνόματι κυρίου·
  δεχθήτω·
  ἔπειτα δὲ δοκιμάσαντες αὐτὸν·
  γνώσεσθε·
  σύνεσιν γὰρ ἕξετε δεξιὰν καὶ ἀριστεράν·

12:2 εἰ μὲν παρόδιός ἐστιν ὁ ἐρχόμενος
  βοηθεῖτε αὐτῷ ὅσον δύνασθε·
  οὐ μενεῖ δὲ πρὸς ὑμᾶς
  εἰ μὴ δύο ἢ τρεῖς ἡμέρας·
  ἐὰν ᾖ ἀνάγκη·
12:3 εἰ δὲ θέλει πρὸς ὑμᾶς καθῆσθαι

  τεχνίτης ὢν ἐργαζέσθω καὶ φαγέτω·
12:4 εἰ δὲ οὐκ ἔχει τέχνην·
  κατὰ τὴν σύνεσιν ὑμῶν προνοήσατε·
  πῶς μὴ ἀργὸς μεθ᾽ ὑμῶν ζήσεται χριστιανός·
12:5 εἰ δ᾽ οὐ θέλει οὕτω ποιεῖν
  χριστέμπορός ἐστιν·
  προσέχετε ἀπὸ τῶν τοιούτων·

11:11 [C] (And) every prophet having been put to the test [and
found to be] true,
doing a worldly mystery of the church,
(but) not training [ÿou] to do what s/he [her/him-
self] does,
s/he will not be judged by ÿou;
for with God s/he has his/her judgment;
for just so acted also the ancient prophets.

11:12 [D] (But) whoever [in this category] should say in Spirit,
[1] "Give me silver or any_other thing,"
ÿou will not listen to him/her;
[2] (but) if, concerning others being in want,
s/he should say to give,
lët no one judge him/her.

12:1 (And), everyone coming in [the] name of [the] Lord,
lët [him] be received;
(and) thereafter, having put him/her to the test,
ÿou will know,
for ÿou will have understanding [of] right and left.

12:2 [A] If, on_the_one_hand, the one coming is a traveler,
[1] hëlp him/her, as much as ÿou are able;
[2] s/he will not remain, on_the_other_hand, among ÿou,
except for two or three days,
if ever there should be a necessity.

12:3 [B] If, on_the_other_hand, s/he wishes to settle down
among ÿou,
being a craftsman, let him/her work and let him/her eat.

12:4 [C] If, on_the_other_hand, s/he does not have a craft,
according to ÿour understanding, plän beforehand
how a Christian will live among ÿou, not [being] idle.

12:5 [D] If, on_the_other_hand, s/he does not wish to act thus
s/he is a Christ-peddler.
Bëware of such ones!

13:1   πᾶς δὲ προφήτης ἀληθινός θέλων καθῆσθαι πρὸς ὑμᾶς·
        ἄξιός ἐστιν τῆς τροφῆς αὐτοῦ
13:2   ὡσαύτως διδάσκαλος ἀληθινός ἐστιν ἄξιος καὶ αὐτὸς
        ὥσπερ ὁ ἐργάτης τῆς τροφῆς αὐτοῦ·

13:3   πᾶσαν οὖν ἀπαρχὴν γεννημάτων
            ληνοῦ καὶ ἄλωνος·
            βοῶν τε καὶ προβάτων λαβών·
                δώσεις τὴν ἀπαρχὴν τοῖς προφήταις·
                    αὐτοὶ γάρ εἰσιν οἱ ἀρχιερεῖς ὑμῶν·
13:4   ἐὰν δὲ μὴ ἔχητε προφήτην
                δότε τοῖς πτωχοῖς·

13:5   ἐὰν σιτίαν ποιῇς
            τὴν ἀπαρχὴν λαβὼν δὸς κατὰ τὴν ἐντολήν·
13:6   ὡσαύτως κεράμιον οἴνου ἢ ἐλαίου ἀνοίξας
            τὴν ἀπαρχὴν λαβὼν δὸς τοῖς προφήταις·
13:7   ἀργυρίου δὲ καὶ ἱματισμοῦ καὶ παντὸς
            κτήματος λαβὼν τὴν ἀπαρχήν·
            ὡς ἂν σοι δόξῃ
            δὸς κατὰ τὴν ἐντολήν·

14:1   κατὰ κυριακὴν δὲ κυρίου

        συναχθέντες κλάσατε ἄρτον·
        καὶ εὐχαριστήσατε προςεξομολογησάμενοι
        τὰ παραπτώματα ὑμῶν·
            ὅπως καθαρὰ ἡ θυσία ὑμῶν ᾖ·
14:2   πᾶς δὲ ἔχων τὴν ἀμφιβολίαν
        μετὰ τοῦ ἑταίρου αὐτοῦ
            μὴ συνελθέτω ὑμῖν
            ἕως οὗ διαλλαγῶσιν·
                ἵνα μὴ κοινωθῇ ἡ θυσία ὑμῶν·
14:3   αὕτη γάρ ἐστιν ἡ ῥηθεῖσα ὑπὸ κυρίου ‹·›
            ἐν παντὶ τόπῳ καὶ χρόνῳ προσφέρειν μοι θυσίαν καθαράν·
            ὅτι βασιλεὺς μέγας εἰμί λέγει κύριος·
            καὶ τὸ ὄνομά μου θαυμαστὸν ἐν τοῖς ἔθνεσει.

13:1   [A] (And) every true prophet wishing to settle down
           among ÿou is worthy of his/her food;
13:2   [B] a true teacher is worthy likewise,
           just as the laborer, of his/her food.

13:3   [A] So, every first_fruits of the products
           of the wine_vat and threshing_floor,
           of both cattle and sheep,
           [1] you will give the first_fruits to the prophets;
               for they themselves are your high_priests.
13:4   [2] (But) if ÿou should not have a prophet,
               give [it] to the beggars.
13:5   [B] If you should make bread-dough,
           taking the first_fruits, give according to the rule.
13:6   [C] Similarly, having opened a jar of wine or of oil,
           taking the first_fruits, give to the prophets.
13:7   [D] (And) of silver and of clothing and of every possession,
           taking the first fruits,
           as it might seem appropriate to you,
           give according to the rule.

14:1   (And) according to [the] divinely_instituted [day/rule] of
       [the] Lord,
       having_been_gathered_together, bräak a loaf.
       [A] And ëucharistize, having_beforehand_confessed
           ÿour failings,
               so_that ÿour sacrifice may be pure.
14:2   [B] Everyone, on_the_other_hand, having a conflict
           with a companion,
               dö not let [him/her] come_together with ÿou
               until they_have_been_reconciled,
                   in_order_that ÿour sacrifice may not be defiled.
14:3   For this is [the thing] having_been_said by [the] Lord:
           "In every place and time, offer to me a pure sacrifice.
           "Because a great king am I," says [the] Lord,
           "and my name [is] wondrous among the gentiles."

15:1 χειροτονήσατε οὖν ἑαυτοῖς
        ἐπισκόπους καὶ διακόνους ἀξίους τοῦ κυρίου
        ἄνδρας πραεῖς
        καὶ ἀφιλαργύρους
        καὶ ἀληθεῖς
        καὶ δεδοκιμασμένους·
            ὑμῖν γὰρ λειτουργοῦσι καὶ αὐτοὶ
            τὴν λειτουργίαν τῶν προφητῶν καὶ διδασκάλων·
15:2 μὴ οὖν ὑπερίδητε αὐτούς·
        αὐτοὶ γάρ εἰσιν οἱ τετιμημένοι ὑμῶν·
        μετὰ τῶν προφητῶν καὶ διδασκάλων·

15:3 ἐλέγχετε δὲ ἀλλήλους· μὴ ἐν ὀργῇ· ἀλλ᾽ ἐν εἰρήνῃ·
        ὡς ἔχετε ἐν τῷ εὐαγγελίῳ
        καὶ παντὶ ἀστοχοῦντι κατὰ τοῦ ἑτέρου
        μηδεὶς λαλείτω·
        μηδὲ παρ᾽ ὑμῶν ἀκουέτω
            ἕως οὗ μετανοήσῃ·
15:4 τὰς δὲ εὐχὰς ὑμῶν καὶ τὰς ἐλεημοσύνας
        καὶ πάσας τὰς πράξεις·
        οὕτως ποιήσατε ὡς ἔχετε ἐν τῷ εὐαγγελίῳ τοῦ κυρίου ἡμῶν·

16:1 γρηγορεῖτε ὑπὲρ τῆς ζωῆς ὑμῶν·
        οἱ λύχνοι ὑμῶν μὴ σβεσθήτωσαν·
        καὶ αἱ ὀσφύες ὑμῶν μὴ ἐκλυέσθωσαν·
        ἀλλὰ γίνεσθε ἕτοιμοι·
            οὐ γὰρ οἴδατε τὴν ὥραν ἐν ᾗ ὁ κύριος ἡμῶν ἔρχεται·

16:2 πυκνῶς δὲ συναχθήσεσθε
        ζητοῦντες τὰ ἀνήκοντα ταῖς ψυχαῖς ὑμῶν·
        οὐ γὰρ ὠφελήσει ὑμᾶς ὁ πᾶς χρόνος τῆς πίστεως ὑμῶν
        ἐὰν μὴ ἐν τῷ ἐσχάτῳ καιρῷ τελειωθῆτε·

15:1 [A] Appöint, then, for ÿourselves,
            bishops and deacons worthy of the Lord,
        [1] men gentle
        [2] and not_money-loving
        [3] and truthful
        [4] and tested;
                for to ÿou they likewise gratuitously_serve
                the unpaid_public_service of the prophet-teachers.
15:2 [B] Dö not, then, look down upon them;
            for they themselves are your honored ones
            in_company_with the prophet-teachers.

15:3 [A] (And) rëprove each other, not in anger, but in peace!
            as ÿou have [it] in the good news.
        [B] And to everyone misbehaving against the other,
        [1] lët no one speak [to him/her]
        [2] nor hear from ÿou [about him/her]
            until s/he should repent.
15:4 (And) ÿour prayers and alms
        and all [ÿour] actions
        dö thus as ÿou have [it] in the good news of our Lord.

16:1 [A] Bë_watchful over ÿour life;
        [1] do not let ÿour lamps be_quenched,
        [2] and do not let ÿour loins be_let_loose.
        [B] But bë prepared;
            for you do not know the hour in which our Lord is
                coming.
16:2 [C] (And) frequently bë_gathered_together,
            seeking the things pertaining to ÿour souls;
            for the whole time of ÿour faith will not be of use to ÿou
            if in the end time ÿou should not have been perfected.

16:3   ἐν γὰρ ταῖς ἐσχάταις ἡμέραις
        πληθυνθήσονται οἱ ψευδοπροφῆται καὶ οἱ φθορεῖς·
        καὶ στραφήσονται τὰ πρόβατα εἰς λύκους·
        καὶ ἡ ἀγάπη στραφήσεται εἰς μῖσος·
16:4   αὐξανούσης γὰρ τῆς ἀνομίας,
            μισήσουσιν ἀλλήλους
            καὶ διώξουσιν
            καὶ παραδώσουσι·
        καὶ τότε φανήσεται ὁ κοσμοπλανὴς ὡς υἱὸς θεοῦ·
        καὶ ποιήσει σημεῖα καὶ τέρατα·
        καὶ ἡ γῆ παραδοθήσεται εἰς χεῖρας αὐτοῦ·
        καὶ ποιήσει ἀθέμιτα
            ἃ οὐδέποτε γέγονεν ἐξ αἰῶνος·

16:5   τότε ἥξει ἡ κτίσις τῶν ἀνθρώπων
            εἰς τὴν πύρωσιν τῆς δοκιμασίας·
        καὶ σκανδαλισθήσονται πολλοὶ καὶ ἀπολοῦνται·

        οἱ δὲ ὑπομείναντες ἐν τῇ πίστει αὐτῶν

            σωθήσονται ὑπ᾽ αὐτοῦ τοῦ καταθέματος·
16:6   καὶ τότε φανήσεται τὰ σημεῖα τῆς ἀληθείας·
        πρῶτον· σημεῖον ἐκπετάσεως ἐν οὐρανῷ·

        εἶτα σημεῖον φωνῆς σάλπιγγος·
        καὶ τὸ τρίτον ἀνάστασις νεκρῶν·

16:7   οὐ πάντων δέ·
        ἀλλ᾽ ὡς ἐρρέθη·
        ἥξει ὁ κύριος καὶ πάντες οἱ ἅγιοι μετ᾽ αὐτοῦ·
16:8   τότε ὄψεται ὁ κόσμος τὸν κύριον ἐρχόμενον
        ἐπάνω τῶν νεφελῶν τοῦ οὐρανοῦ.

16:3   [1] For, in the last days,

        [a] the false_prophets and corrupters will be multiplied,

        [b] and the sheep will be turned into wolves,

        [c] and the love will be turned into hate.

16:4   For, with lawlessness increasing,

        [a] they will hate each other

        [b] and they will persecute

        [c] and they will betray.

     [2] And then will appear the world-deceiver as a son of God,

      [a] and he will do signs and wonders,

      [b] and the earth will be betrayed into his hands,

      [c] and he will do unlawful things

        that never have happened from the beginning of time.

16:5   [3] Then the creation of humans will come

      into the burning-process of testing,

      [a] and many will be entrapped and will be utterly_
        destroyed,

      [b] the ones having remained firm in their faith, on_the_
        other_hand,

        will be saved by the accursed [burning-process] itself.

16:6   [4] And then will appear the signs of the truth:

      [a] [the] first sign [will be the] unfurling [banner] in
        heaven,

      [b] next [the] sign of [the] sound of [the] trumpet,

      [c] and the third [sign will be the] resurrection of [the]
        dead—

16:7   not [the resurrection] of all, on_the_other_hand,

     but as it has been said:

     "The Lord will come and all the holy_ones with him."

16:8   [5] Then the world will see the Lord coming

      atop the clouds of heaven.

Part II

Commentary

1
THE LIFE-TRANSFORMING
TRAINING PROGRAM

The Training Program

MY CHILD, THE ONE SPEAKING TO YOU THE WORD OF GOD, YOU WILL REMEMBER NIGHT AND DAY AND YOU WILL HONOR HIM/HER AS THE LORD, FOR WHERE THE DOMINION OF THE LORD IS SPOKEN OF, THERE THE LORD IS. MOREOVER, YOU WILL SEEK EVERY DAY THE PRESENCE OF THE SAINTS IN ORDER THAT YOU MAY REST UPON THEIR WORDS. YOU WILL NOT CAUSE DISSENSION; YOU WILL RECONCILE THOSE FIGHTING; YOU WILL JUDGE JUSTLY; YOU WILL NOT TAKE INTO ACCOUNT SOCIAL STATUS WHEN IT COMES TIME TO REPROVE AGAINST FAILINGS. YOU WILL NOT BE DOUBLE-MINDED WHETHER GOD'S FUTURE WILL BE OR NOT.

Contents

Any community that cannot artfully and effectively pass on its cherished way of life as a program for graced existence cannot long endure. Any way of life that cannot be clearly specified, exhibited, and differentiated from the alternative modes operative within the surrounding culture is doomed to growing insignificance and to gradual assimilation. Faced with these harsh realities, the first six chapters of the *Didache* unfold the training program calculated to alter irreversibly the habits of perception and standards of judgment of novices coming out of a pagan lifestyle. The content and the modality of this process of human transformation can be gleaned from the verbal clues conveyed within the text itself. The task of this chapter is to unravel these clues and to recover the passion, the content, and the methodology whereby those proponents of the Jesus movement associated with the *Didache* set about to form and transform the lives of gentiles into that graced perfection demanded for ready inclusion into the anticipated Kingdom of God on earth.

SECTION I: THE TWO TITLES AND THE WAY OF LIFE DEFINED

Pass on Your Way of Life or Perish

Within the Roman Empire of the first century, religious tolerance abounded—as long as the underlying Roman political and economic order was not disrupted. Within this milieu, all sorts of religious and philosophical programs of redemption, salvation, and healing were being promoted by zealous adherents. Each religious system served to bring strangers into a united "family" sharing the same gods, the same discipline, the same way of life, the same rites, the same resources, the same honor, the same hopes. Within this swirling and confusing arena of contending claims and alternate ways of being in the world, the "way" proposed by the disciples of Jesus emerged as a growing movement bent on bringing the grace and honor of God's program of living and hope of salvation into the lives of persons who were willing to abandon their ancestral religion in favor of throwing in their lot in with those who were increasingly becoming known as "Christians" (*Did.* 12:4).

The *Didache* holds the secret as to how and why Jesus of Nazareth, a seemingly insignificant Galilean Jew executed as a Roman criminal, went on to attract and to convert the world. Sure enough, the members of the Jesus movement regarded him as both "Son of God" and "Son of David" who had been sent by the Father to prepare the world for his coming kingdom. In fairness, however, such exalted claims were a commonplace within the religious flux of the Roman Empire (e.g., Crossan 1994: 1–28) and, at first glance, barely caused a ripple in the day-to-day business of deciding which of the many religious systems were worthy of personal adherence. In truth, potential members assessed the movement not so much on the basis of claims made on behalf of Jesus, who was absent, as on the basis of their experience of the way of life of members who were very much present to them. It is no surprise, therefore, that the entire system of the *Didache* displays little taste for negotiating, defining, and defending the exalted titles of Jesus and of the true God whom he revealed. Rather, the *Didache* is taken up with the business of passing on the Way of Life after converts had come forward ready to transform their lives under the direction of a tried and tested member of the movement.

Whether "the Twelve" Authored the Didache

The sole complete manuscript of the *Didache* that has come down to us was discovered in 1873 by Archbishop Bryennios in the library of the Monastery of the Most Holy Sepulchre located in Istanbul. The codex discovered contains twenty writings from the patristic period transcribed on 120 pages of parchment measuring 7.4 by 5.8 inches. The *Didache* occupies leaves 76 to 80. The scribe transcribed all twenty writings in a clear and even hand and identified himself as "Leon, scribe and sinner," and gave the date for the completion of his work as 11 June 1056 (according to our calendar). The codex was well preserved at the time of its discovery and, since 1887, has been carefully preserved in the Greek patriarchate library in Jerusalem and officially catalogued as *Codex Hierosolymitanus 54.*

While contemporary scholars routinely refer to leaves 76 to 80 as "the *Didache*," the manuscript itself has two titles. The first and short title is *Training of the Twelve Disciples.* The second and long title is *Training of the Lord through the Twelve Apostles to the Gentiles.* Since both the short and long title begin with the Greek word *didachē* ("training"), this explains why scholars use the first word of both titles as a shorthand reference to the entire work. Moreover, in English translation, scholars have rendered *didachē* as "teaching" rather than "training." My preference for "training" will be explained in section II of this chapter.

Opinions vary as to whether the *Didache* originally had a title at all. Greek texts often did not bear titles, and, only in the course of time, did scribes give them titles as a way of referring to or cataloguing texts they were copying. Scholars, for example, believe this was even true of the Synoptic Gospels—they were called "Gospels" and attributed to known "apostles" or to their immediate disciples only in the second century when apostolic origins became a necessary criterion for attesting to the "reliability" of an already revered text (R. Brown 1990: 60). The "Gospel According to Matthew," therefore, may have very little to do with historical authorship (as we understand "authorship" today) and much more to do with the general sense that the contents of the book in question derived from an apostolic community that had a special attachment to Matthew. Thus, in a parallel way, those communities where the *Didache* was being used and being appropriately regarded as "The Training of the Lord" may have found it necessary, as an afterthought, to claim the "authorship" of the twelve apostles in order to attest to the "reliability" of their way of life.

Both the short and long titles credit the "twelve apostles" as the framers of the *Didache*. Internal evidence from the *Didache* itself, however, makes this reference to the "twelve apostles" problematic and points in the direction of seeing "twelve apostles" as a later scribal addition. Two considerations:

1. The *Didache* itself has no internal reference to "twelve" apostles. Moreover, given the fact that minor inconsistencies pop up whenever the Twelve are listed (Mt 10:2–4; Mk 6:16–19; Lk 6:14–16; Acts 1:13) and given the fact that Paul only mentions the "twelve" once (1 Cor 15:5), many scholars today believe that the number "twelve" may have originated two or three decades after the time of Jesus in order to correspond to the twelve tribes of Israel, whom they would judge/guide in the world to come (Mt 19:28; Lk 22:30) (R. Brown 1990: 116f.; F. S. Fiorenza: 84–87; opposed by Meier 1997). Furthermore, only "later tradition began attributing to the Twelve careers of wide-ranging apostolates in various parts of the world" (R. Brown 1990: 117). If these surmises are correct, then presuming the early origins of the *Didache* (mid-first century), it seems unlikely that "twelve apostles" would have been originally used as part of the title for the *Didache*.

2. When the *Didache* does treat the subject of "apostles," it applies this title to wandering charismatics passing through the community (*Did.* 11:3–6). If these "apostles" were indeed the Twelve or even the founders of the *Didache* communities, then it remains difficult to understand why their stay would be limited to one or two days (*Did.* 11:5) and why some of them would be inappropriately asking for silver (*Did.* 11:6). The "apostles" familiar to the framers of the *Didache*, therefore, were clearly neither the Twelve nor the founding apostles of the communities. If the *Didache* originally was attributed to the "twelve apostles" as the titles suggest, then one would have expected some distinctions to be made when "apostles" were required to limit their stay to one or two days (*Did.* 11:5).

On the basis of these considerations, it remains doubtful whether the *Didache* originally had either of the two titles that have come down to us in *Codex Hierosolymitanus 54*. Hence, the reference to "twelve apostles" in the manuscript titles ought not be used in deciding who authored the *Didache*. [Commentary continues on p. 58.]

#1a How the *Didache* Got Two Titles

In the early centuries of the common era, the scroll was the normal format for a text. According to Jewish practice, the first line *at the start* of the text functioned as its title. According to Greek practice, however, "titles were not always given, but when they were used they were [short and] placed *at the end* of the scroll" (Pardee 1989: 27). In cases when the previous user neglected to rewind the scroll after reading it to the end, this short title at the end served to reveal the contents of the scroll *before rewinding*.

According to Nancy Pardee, some ancient biblical manuscripts reveal a combination of both the Jewish and Greek practice. For example, the opening line of Ecclesiastes (second century B.C.E.) reads: "The words of the Teacher (*ekklēsiastou*), the son of David, king of Jerusalem" (Eccl 1:1). This is the first line of the text, which functions as the title following the Jewish tradition. At the end of the manuscript, however, one finds a shortened title, namely, *ekklēsiastēs* (transcribed as "Ecclesiastes" in English), which represents the Greek word for "teacher" in the context of an assembly. Following the Greek tradition, the entire work was referred to by this single word taken out of the long title—a practice that has continued down to the present day. In effect, therefore, manuscripts of Ecclesiastes had two titles: a long title (following the Jewish tradition) at the beginning and a short title (following the Greek tradition) at the end.

Many manuscript copies of the Book of Revelation also demonstrate this placement of a long and short title. Revelation begins with a long descriptive first sentence that constitutes its long title:

> The revelation of Jesus Christ, which God gave him to show his servants what must soon take place; he made it known by sending his angel to his servant John, who testified to the word of God and to the testimony of Jesus Christ, even to all that he saw (Rev 1:1f.).

At the end of some early manuscripts, one finds the short title at the end which reads: "The Revelation of John." In this case, one can appreciate the value of the short title as a way of making it easy to refer to the entire scroll. Thus, using the manuscript versions of various texts known to us, Pardee provides half a dozen examples where, following the Jewish tradition, a long title stands as the first sentence and, following the Greek tradition, a short title stands at the end (Pardee 1989: 28f.).

With time, however, the codex consisting of uniform sheets of papyrus or parchment bound at one edge came to replace the scroll as the preferred format for manuscripts. As scribes copied the content of scrolls onto the pages of a codex, the short title no longer had any significant function at the end. As a result, "Gradually, [the short] titles came to be placed also at the beginning so that by the early fifth century C.E. a title was expected to be in the front position" (Pardee 1989: 28). With this development, now a work could have a short title for easy reference to the whole work immediately followed by the opening line that served as a long title. "Thus, with respect to the question of the co-existence of the [short and long] titles, both the *Didache* and the Revelation of John represent the transition in the early church from scroll to codex" (Pardee 1989: 30).

Given the residual oral-aural clues in the manuscript (see #11d = ch. 11, box d), it can be surmised that what we now know as the *Didache* was initially used and recited from memory. In effect, therefore, the Didache communities had many "living books," and its members were accustomed to hearing "audio productions" of the *Didache*. For reasons unknown to us, someone eventually went to the time, trouble, and expense of having a trained scribe produce the first of many hand-written copies. In greater probability, these early manuscripts had no title whatsoever. Hearing the first line ("There are two ways . . .") immediately struck a responsive cord in community members just as, in our day, anyone hearing, "Once upon a time, there lived seven dwarfs . . . ," knows immediately what is coming without any reference to a title. It is telling that no general introduction (as in Lk 1:1–4) or descriptive first line (as in Eccl 1:1 or Rv 1:1f.) was provided—thereby implying that it was used by insiders in the know and not by outsiders. These insiders probably contented themselves with references to "our Way of Life" or "the training of the Lord" to refer to either the aural or written productions of the *Didache*.

With time, as hand-printed scrolls of the *Didache* were commissioned, scribes were probably the first ones to suggest that their work ought to have a functional long title at the front and/or a short title at the end. The work clearly presented a "training" (*Did.* 1:3) given by "the Lord" (*Did.* 9:3) that was used for "gentiles." Given the absence of any internal reference to the "twelve apostles," however, it is difficult to decide on what grounds this manuscript was called "Training of the Twelve Apostles." Maybe the fact that no single name of any apostle was found in the text and yet the manuscript was recognized and honored as having apostolic origins inclined some scribe to attribute the "training" in a general way to "the twelve apostles." On the other hand, perhaps "the Twelve" was deliberately introduced into a preexisting title during the third or fourth centuries when "apostolic authorship" was recognized as an absolute necessity for any book seeking inclusion in the canon of approved books used in the universal church. In fact, the scribe who first produced the *Ecclesiastical Canons of the Holy Apostles* was so taken up with the necessity of authoritatively associating the Way of Life with the Twelve that he literally parceled out the opening chapters of the *Didache* between them. Thus, he artificially introduced *Did.* 1:1–2a with "John said," 1:2b with "Matthew said," 2:2–7 with "Peter said," 3:2 with "Andrew said," etc., ending with 4:3–8 introduced as "Cephas said" (Peter and Cephas being, in his eyes, distinct apostles).

When the *Didache* was transcribed onto a scroll, it may well have developed an initial long title as the first line and the short title at the end (as noted above). This would help to explain how and why, as the codex with double titles came into vogue, a scribe followed the new norms of his profession by writing the short title *Training of the Twelve Apostles* at the beginning instead of the end, immediately followed by the long title *Training of [the] Lord Through the Twelve Apostles to the Gentiles*. This represents the condition of the manuscript that Leon transcribed in 1056 and that has been preserved as *Codex Hierosolymitanus 54*.

Overall, therefore, building on Nancy Pardee's expansion of the earlier work of David Hellholm, one arrives at a plausible account of how the *Didache* was initially orally produced without any titles whatsoever but then, during the course of time, how it picked up a short and long title, which were placed, from the fifth century onward, at the head of the manuscript. For a long time the dual titles and the explicit reference to the Twelve have puzzled scholars. Now a tentative but sophisticated solution is forthcoming.

The Didache *as a Unified Production in Five Parts*

The *Didache* does not have a topic paragraph serving to specify the overall purpose of the text and to name the progression of topics to be treated. Nonetheless, the framers of the *Didache* did make ample use of topic sentences (or phrases) in order to signal the beginning of new sections. In addition, the author used summary statements (4:14b; 13:1f.; 15:4) and final cautions (4:12–14a; 6:1f.; 11:1f.) in order to bring closure to blocks of material before passing on to the next topic. When attention is given to these linguistic clues, the *Didache* breaks down into five topical divisions. Each of these divisions occupies progressively smaller fractions of the entire text as shown by the numbers in parentheses:

I. Training Program in the Way of Life (44%) *Did.* 1:1–6:2
II. Regulations for Eating, Baptizing, Fasting, Praying (22%) *Did.* 6:3–11:2
III. Regulations for Hospitality/Testing Various Classes of Visitors (15%) *Did.* 11:3–13:2

IV. Regulations for First Fruits and for Offering a Pure Sacrifice (10%)
     Did. 13:3–15:4
V. Closing Apocalyptic Forewarnings and Hope (9%) *Did.* 16:1–8

Each of these five subdivisions has enough internal coherence to stand alone. When placed together in their given order, however, they reveal a deliberate progression. Part I provides a detailed outline of how new members are to be initiated into the Way of Life prior to their baptism, while part II details the regulations for eating, fasting, and praying following baptism. Part II functions to look backward to part I and to look forward to part III. Thus, early in part II baptism includes "having said all these things beforehand" (*Did.* 7:1)—a looking backward to the training (1:3) that occupies part I. Part II ends with a caution to preserve "all these things said beforehand" against unnamed visitors who might "train you in another tradition" (11:2)—a looking forward to the potentially troublesome classes of visitors treated in part III. Part III, in its turn, ends with the note that tested and true prophets "wishing to settle down among you" are "worthy of food" (13:1)—thereby looking forward to part IV, which treats of the rules regarding first fruits. Part IV looks backward to part III insofar as first fruits are preferentially given to approved "prophets" (13:3). Then regulations treating the pure sacrifice are given that look backward to the eucharist (9:1ff.) in part II and the training to confess one's failings (4:14) in part I. Part IV, in sum, looks backward to the first three parts of the *Didache*.

Part V, at first glance, might appear to be an apocalyptic discourse that was tacked on to a unified instruction in four parts. When examined in detail, however, this discourse evokes a sense of urgency to "frequently be gathered together" (16:2)—a theme implied in the first three parts (4:2; 9:1ff.; 14:1f.). Likewise the scenario of the end times gives first place to the ungodly work of "false prophets and corrupters" (16:3)—an echo of warnings already given in the first three parts (6:1; 11:1f.; 11:3–12:1). Finally, the closing discourse warns that "the whole time of your faith will not be of use to you if in the last time you should not have been perfected" (16:2)—a looking backward to the training in the Way of Life in part I that closes saying, "If you are able to bear the whole yoke of the Lord [as just detailed], you will be perfect" (6:2). In effect, part V is not a chance appendix but would appear to be deliberately crafted to advance the agenda of the first three parts of the *Didache*.

Overall, therefore, the *Didache* can be shown to have an overall internal coherence that might escape the casual reader. Under no circumstances can the *Didache* be regarded as having been produced by the mere pasting together of units of disparate preexisting material. As will be shown more clearly as the genius of the *Didache* unfolds, even where and when preexisting material might have been used, the authorship of the *Didache* crafts its sources to fit the needs and to represent the practice of the communities wherein it was effective.

The Opening Definitions of the Way of Life

The opening line of the *Didache* serves as a topic sentence: "There are two ways: one of life, the other of death" (1:1). The Way of Life is defined immediately (1:2), but one has to pass through four chapters before the Way of Death is finally defined (5:1f.). The framers did not use these definitions in order to confront their hearers/readers with an existential choice between the Way of Life and the Way of Death. Rather, they pulled these two definitions apart in order to linguistically frame their main attraction, that is, the training program that occupies the central eight-tenths of part I. The training program itself is introduced with a fresh topic sentence (1:3a) and is closed with a summary statement (4:14b). This second framing device reinforces the centrality of the training program and again demonstrates that the definitions of the Two Ways have only a subsidiary interest for the author.

The rhetorical shifts in part I of the *Didache* confirm this emphasis. The text opens with the Way of Life being described in the present indicative. The tone is descriptive. As soon as "the training" begins, however, the text shifts into the imperative. Concrete demands are being made. The one being trained is directly addressed by his spiritual father or her spiritual mother. Given the oral character of the *Didache* (see #11d = ch. 11, box d) and the prevalence of mnemonic aids, one can surmise that the spiritual guide had the entire Two Ways committed to memory. Within this section, therefore, one "overhears" the authoritative "word of God" (*Did.* 4:1) that is being spoken by the spiritual master. As soon as "the training" is finished, the text returns to the indicative in order to take up the description of the Way of Death (5:1f.). Seen as a whole, part I may be visualized as follows: the two definitions (in the present indicative) frame the central training program (in the present imperative and future indicative):

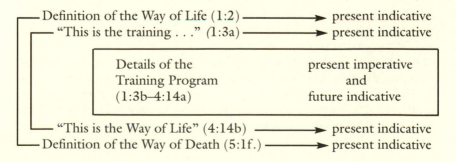

— Definition of the Way of Life (1:2) ⟶ present indicative
— "This is the training . . ." (1:3a) ⟶ present indicative

Details of the	present imperative
Training Program	and
(1:3b–4:14a)	future indicative

— "This is the Way of Life" (4:14b) ⟶ present indicative
— Definition of the Way of Death (5:1f.) ⟶ present indicative

The opening section of the *Didache* deals with the "two paths" (*hodoi dyo*). Within a Jewish horizon of understanding, each person is understood metaphorically as traveling either on the Way of Life (i.e., the footpath leading to life) or on the Way of Death. The Greek language has two general terms for "life": *zōē* refers to quality of life, while *bios* refers to the duration of life. The *Didache* uses the first of these terms. Similarly, Greek has two terms for "death": *thanatos* refers to the act of dying or the state of being dead, whether physically or spiritually, while *nekros* generally refers to death as lacking life, vitality, well-being. Here, again, the *Didache* uses the first of these terms. Thus, the "Way of Life" (*hodos tēs zōēs*) leads to quality of life; the "Way of Death" (*hodos tou thanatou*) extinguishes this life.

The notion that there are two well-defined paths would have been familiar to a Jewish audience. Psalm 1, for instance, contrasts "the way of the righteous" with "the way of the wicked." The first-named are defined as those who "delight . . . in the law [Torah] of the Lord" (Ps 1:2). The blessings of this path follow:

He is like a tree planted by streams of water,
that yields its fruit in its [due] season,
and its leaf does not wither.
In all that he does he prospers (Ps 1:3).

Standing in this tradition, the Jesus movement was, not surprisingly, known in some circles as "the Way" (Acts 9:2; 19:9, 23; 22:4; 24:14, 22). This was undoubtedly due to the fact that its members were trained in "the way of salvation" (Acts 16:17), "the way of the Lord" (Acts 18:25), or "the way of God" (Acts 18:26)—terms that are used hundreds of times in the Septuagint. In 2 Peter, false teachers are spoken of as having left "the way of truth" (2:2), "the right way" (2:15), "the way of righteousness" (2:21) in order to follow "the way of Balaam" (2:15). According to the Q Gospel, Jesus contrasts "the narrow gate" with "the wide gate" (Mt 7:13f.; Lk 13:23f.). The former "way is hard" but "leads to life" while the latter "way is easy" but "leads to destruction." In each of these cases, the two-way mentality is evident; yet in none of these cases is there the suggestion that the *Didache* was known or used to flesh out the exact meaning of the Way of Life.

In the Hebrew Scriptures, Jeremiah was sent by the Lord to say to the people: "Behold I set before you the Way of Life and the Way of Death" (Jer 21:8). In the *Apocalypse of Baruch* (c. 100 C.E.), the Jewish author writes that the Lord "established a covenant for them at that time and said, 'Behold I have set before you life and death'" (19:1). Similar passages can be found in Dt 11:26–28; Prv 2:1–22; 4:18f.; *Sibylline Oracles* 8:399. All in all, the Way of Life and the Way of Death served as evocative metaphors for giving voice to the challenge the Lord God made to Israel.

#1b The Two-Ways Mentality
in Other Jewish and Christian Sources

The character of the two-ways mentality in the *Didache* can be appreciated by virtue of the parallels and contrasts that exist between it and various other Jewish and Christian sources. Two Jewish and two Christian sources will be considered.

1. Thirteen copies of the *Manual of Discipline* were found among the Dead Sea Scrolls discovered near Qumran (see "Qumran" in the list of "Abbreviations" at the end of this book). The *Manual of Discipline* outlines the systematic training program whereby novices were prepared for entrance into the *yaḥad* ("community," literally, "the unity"). As such, therefore, the *Manual of Discipline* is akin to the *Didache* insofar as both define a rule of formation and discipline that applied to members preparing for full participation in their respective communities.

In the *Manual of Discipline*, the novice is trained in "the ways of light" and prepared for a cosmic end-time battle with those who walk in "the ways of darkness." These two ways, in their turn, are ruled over by the two angelic powers—"the prince of light" and "the angel of darkness":

> He [the God of knowledge] created man for the domination of the world and assigned him two spirits by which to walk until the season of his visitation: they are the spirits of truth and iniquity. From the fountain of truth (issue) the generations of truth and from the fountain of darkness (issue) the generations of iniquity. Within the hands of the prince of light is the rule over all the sons of righteousness: they shall walk in the ways of light. Within the hands of the angel of darkness is all the rule over the sons of iniquity: they shall walk in the ways of darkness (1QS 3:17–21).

2. The *Testaments of the Twelve Patriarchs* represents a Jewish ethical treatise wherein each of the twelve patriarchs reflects upon his life and draws appropriate guidance for his sons. Within this treatise, two diametrically opposed ways of life are described. Unlike the *Manual of Discipline*, however, these ways are associated not with two opposing angels but with two diametrically opposed internal dispositions. Here is a key passage:

> There are two ways, of good and evil, and along with these are the two impulses in the breasts that make the distinctions between them. So, if the soul is disposed to what is good, its

> every action is [done] in righteousness, and, if it sins, it repents at once. . . . But if the soul inclines [toward] the impulse toward wickedness, its every action is [done] in wickedness . . . , since the treasure-house of the impulse is filled with the poison of an evil spirit (*Testament of Asher* 1:6–8).

While the text here may represent nothing more than what later comes into the rabbinic material as the *yetzer hatov* ("good impulse") and *yetzer hara* ("evil impulse") that struggle within every individual (see *Testament of Judah* 20:1–2), nonetheless, the authors of the text clearly wanted to account for the existence of two ways by reference to some preexisting dualism. According to the *Testaments of the Twelve Patriarchs,* this dualism is internal (two opposed impulses in the human heart), while in the *Manual of Discipline* this dualism is external (two opposed angelic camps in the cosmos).

The Greek *Epistle of Barnabas* and the Latin *Teaching of the Apostles* (*De doctrina apostolorum*) represent two second-century Christian documents that not only embrace a two-ways mentality but offer substantial portions of the material found in *Did.* 1–5 as well. While both of these documents retain a flow of topics much like that found in the *Didache,* both of them demonstrate significant omissions and variations that have prompted most scholars to rule out a direct textual dependence upon the *Didache* or upon each other (Goodspeed: 233–35; Kloppenborg 1995: 90, 93).

1. The description of the Two Ways found in the *Epistle of Barnabas* evokes an angelic dualism:

> There are two ways of training and of power, the one of light and the other of darkness; and there is a great difference between the two ways. For on the one are stationed the life-giving angels of God, on the other the angels of Satan. And the one is Lord from all eternity and unto all eternity, whereas the other is Lord of the season of iniquity that now is. (18:1f.)

Here the contrasting metaphors of light and darkness are played out in ways similar to that seen earlier in the *Manual of Discipline.* So, too, *Barnabas* assigns dominion over the contrasting ways to either "the angels of God" or "the angels of Satan"—another approximation with the *Manual of Discipline.* No one, to my knowledge, supposes that there was direct dependence of *Barnabas* on the *Manual of Discipline.* However, even without direct dependence, the parallels attest to shared tendencies that were clearly displayed in both, yet at the same time were significantly absent in the formation of the *Didache*. Something can be learned about the *Didache* here. More on this later.

2. In 1900, a Latin version of the Two Ways was discovered bearing the title *Teaching of the Apostles* (*De doctrina apostolorum*). Despite the fact that the Latin title is equivalent to the shorter Greek title of the *Didache*, the *Teaching of the Apostles* represents an independent version of the Two Ways with a formal conclusion. Ninety percent of the material found therein is closely paralleled in *Did.* 1–5; sixty percent is found reordered in the Greek *Epistle of Barnabas*. But, here again, the opening of the document portrays an angelic dualism not found in the *Didache* and noticeably different from what one finds in the *Epistle of Barnabas*. Setting the texts side by side helps make this clear:

Epistle of Barnabas	*Teaching of the Apostles*	*Didache*
There are two ways of training and of power,	There are two ways in the world,	There are two ways
the one of light and the other of darkness;	[one] of life and [one] of death, [one] of light and [one] of darkness. In these [ways] have been set up two angels, one of fairness, the other of unfairness.	one of life and one of death,
and there is a great difference between the two ways. For on the one are stationed the life-giving angels of God, on the other, the angels of Satan. And the one is Lord from eternity to eternity, whereas the other is Lord of the present season of iniquity (18:1f.).	Moreover, there is a great difference between the two ways.	and there is a great difference between the two ways (1:1)

The *Teaching of the Apostles* begins by contrasting the Two Ways with the metaphors of life and death (human qualities) but then immediately associates these with light and darkness (cosmic qualities). Each way is then assigned an "angel." One can now note that the Greek *Epistle of Barnabas,* the Latin *Teaching of the Apostles,* and the Hebrew *Manual of Discipline* clearly embrace an angelic dualism when defining the Two Ways, while the framers of the *Didache* clearly avoid it. The full story behind this choice cannot be known. Nonetheless, a possible hint toward telling that story can be glimpsed from the fact that the framers of the *Didache* referred to idols as "dead gods" (6:3), thereby refusing to allow any support for the notion that the gods left behind by the novices had any power whatsoever. Equating the power of the gods (or the idols) with demonic power would have meant that new recruits would have risked the wrath of abandoned demon-gods and may have been terrorized by their imagined wrath and have been tempted to appease them. By training novices to regard their former gods as "dead," therefore, mentors may have deliberately crafted a pastoral position designed to assure their new recruits that they could turn their backs on their former gods without the slightest fear. Later it will be discovered that novices were trained to regard the God of Israel as the source of all things, both good and bad, that might happen to them (*Did.* 3:10). From this, it might be surmised that the blessings formerly attributed to their gods were now understood to be gifts of the Lord of Israel. A similar observation can be made regarding the end-times scenario. Chapter 10 will reveal that the events associated with the Lord's coming unfold without any angelic or demonic forces playing any role whatsoever. Thus, there is an inherent consistency within the *Didache.* Since the gods are "dead," they play no role either now or in the future. Thus, with some circumspection, the *Didache* embraces the metaphors of life and death but deliberately avoids associating these with cosmic/angelic dualism.

The Way of Life Defined by the Negative Golden Rule

The *Didache* defines the Way of Life using two functional definitions. The first definition summarizes positively what must be done; the second definition summarizes negatively what must be avoided. The first definition summarizes one's relationship with God; the second, with one's neighbor.

From other sources, one learns that both the first and the second definition would have been widely accepted and used among Jews. Twice each day, in the morning and the evening, Jews recited the *Shema* (Bradshaw 1992: 19). The first line begins, "Hear, O Israel: The Lord is our God," and the second continues, "You shall love the Lord your God . . ." (Deut 6:4f.). In Mark's Gospel, accordingly, when a scribe asks Jesus what is the "greatest commandment," Jesus responds by reciting these very same lines

(Mk 12:29ff.), and the scribe commends him for so doing. In Luke's Gospel, the scribe is described as "a lawyer" who asks not for the "greatest commandment" but, "What must I do *to inherit* eternal life?" (Lk 10:25). Jesus turns the question back to his inquirer, "What is written in the law [Torah]? How do you read?" (10:26). In this portrait, the inquirer delivers the second line of the *Shema* and the positive golden rule, and Jesus commends him saying, "You have answered right; do this and you will live" (10:28). Thus, whether on the lips of Jesus or on the lips of a Jewish lawyer, the *Shema* served to specify the "greatest commandment" and the route to "eternal life." This naturally shows up in the *Didache* as the first functional definition of the Way of Life.

The joining of loving God and loving neighbor would also be foundational within Judaism. According to the Mishnah, the priests in the temple recited the Decalogue prior to the *Shema* (*m. Tamid* 5:1). In the first-century *Testaments of the Twelve Patriarchs,* Dan teaches his sons, "Love the Lord throughout your life and one another with a true heart" (*Testament of Dan* 5:3), and Issachar teaches his sons, "Love the Lord and your neighbor" (*Testament of Issachar* 5:2). Philo (d. 50 C.E.), when describing the special commandments given to the Jews by God, notes that everything can be divided into two categories: (1) "the regulating of one's conduct towards God by the rules of piety and holiness" and (2) "[the regulating of] one's conduct towards men [women] by the rules of humanity and justice" (*Special Laws* 2.63). Matthew, in like fashion, has Jesus say, "On these two commandments hang all the law [Torah] and the prophets" (Mt 22:39).

The golden rule is found in Lev 19:18, where, after reciting numerous deeds to be avoided (19:11–18), it forms a kind of conclusion: "But [on the contrary], you shall love your neighbor as yourself." In Mt 22:39, these words are found on the lips of Jesus and, as a result, many well-meaning Christian scholars have attempted to demonstrate the superiority of the positive golden rule over the negative formulation which appears to be more common in Jewish sources and in the *Didache*. E. P. Sanders, however, notes that the negative formulation has a distinctively stronger force:

> The negative version follows naturally from Lv 19, where "love your neighbor" summarizes prohibitions, such as: do not deal fraudulently with your neighbor, do not rob him. . . . Even the commandment to be charitable to the poor is mostly phrased negatively: "do not reap your field to its border," etc. (19:9–10a). . . . Negative commandments are stronger in Jewish law (and in law generally) than are positive commandments: transgression of a prohibition is more serious than is failure to give effect to a positive commandment. Thus the epigrams which raise Lv 19:18 to a negative form ("do not do to others what you

would not like") make it a stronger and more specific commandment. (1990: 71)

The negative formulation of the golden rule has a special place in rabbinic Judaism because, according to the first-century school of Hillel, it
served as a comprehensive summary of the Torah that a convert needed to
know when approaching Judaism. As situated within the rabbinic material,
an unnamed proselyte approaches Hillel (d. 20 C.E.) and challenges him to
teach him the whole of Judaism while standing on one foot. Hillel, who is
not put off by this brash proposal, responds: "What is hateful to you, do
not do to your neighbor. This is the *whole* Torah while the rest is commentary" (*b. Shabbat* 31a).

The framers of the *Didache*, of course, would not be expected to know
this story. Nor can we be certain that Hillel acted in this fashion or that this
story circulated during the first century. Nonetheless, it is not unthinkable
that mentors in the Didache communities who were immersed in Judaism
might have been accustomed to the negative formulation of the golden
rule as a synthesis of the whole of the Way of Life.

The dual definitions offer a basic orientation. What it means to love,
however, has to be spelled out in its pragmatic details. In our own day,
some Christians, motivated by the love ethic, open up health clinics for the
underprivileged which offer, among other services, abortions; other Christians, meanwhile, are intent on closing these clinics down. In like fashion,
some Christians today are designing and building nuclear submarines as a
mark of their love for God and country; other Christians, meanwhile, "for
the sake of God and country," are protesting their production by pouring
their blood on them. The *Didache*—given its Jewish roots—was bent on
defining correct practice rather than hammering out correct belief.
Accordingly, it was imperative to specify what it meant to love God and
neighbor rightly. The training in the Way of Life, therefore, would be
devoted to "these words" (*Did.* 1:3).

#1c Filial Piety According to the Stoic Masters

In the ancient world, piety naturally flowed first to the gods, next to the
fatherland, and then to one's parents. Hierocles, in writing a handbook for
Stoics in the early second century, found it natural to link filial piety and
patriotism intimately with the love of God:

> Our fatherland [*patris*] is as it were some second god, and our
> first and greatest parent. Hence he who gave it a name did not
> do so inappropriately; he formed a derivative [from *patēr* =

"father"], but gave it a feminine ending so that it might be a sort of mixture of "father" and "mother." This word also dictates that we honor our one fatherland equally with our two parents . . . and more than our wives, children, and friends, in short, more than all other things. (*On Duties* 3.39.34)

Here the hierarchy of honor and of influence is drawn out. The gods first, fatherland and parents next, then wife, children, friends. One's fatherland, it will here be noted, is revered as that "first and greatest parent" who preserved the way of life and the blessings of its citizens. Thus, "the person who conducts himself well toward his fatherland" should preserve it with his/her life, if necessary, and "should also observe the laws of the fatherland as [coming from] secondary gods of a kind and be guided by them . . ." (*On Duties* 3.39.36). Hierocles then goes on to consider parents:

After discussing the gods and the fatherland, what person should be mentioned before our parents? We must then speak about them [these parents]. We won't err in saying that they are secondary and earthly gods of a sort and, if it is lawful to say so, we honor them on account of their nearness to us *more highly than the gods*. But we must begin with the assumption that the only measure of our gratitude to them is perpetual and unyielding eagerness to repay their beneficence, since, even if we were to do a great deal for them, that would still be far too inadequate. Yet even these deeds are almost theirs, since they made us who perform them. (*On Duties* 4.25.53, emphasis added and slightly modified)

Note here that Hierocles places gratitude as the fitting measure whereby the thoughtful individual bestows honor. God is honored and loved first because he has blessed each of us more than we can ever understand and repay. Fatherland and parents follow, under the same rubric, as lesser benefactors and gods, deserving our inexhaustible love and honor.

Ben Sira (c. 250 B.C.E.) has been identified as offering the "first hint" (Blidstein: 2) of an attempt to knit love of God and love of parents into a common fabric. He frames his argument as follows:

Those who honor their father atone for sins and those who respect their mother are like those who lay up treasure [in heaven]. Those who honor their father will have joy in their own children, and when they pray they will be heard. Those who respect their father will have long life, and those who honor their mother obey the Lord. . . . (Sir 3:3–6)

Ben Sira shares the perspective that filial piety carries with it the promise of a "long life" (Exod 20:12; Deut 5:16)—but he does not give it focal importance. In his eyes, filial piety, first and foremost, moves God to forgive sins, to give blessings, to hear prayers. The implied logic is that honoring one's parents tacitly functions to honor the Lord, who is addressed as "Father and Master of my life" (Sir 23:1, 4; 51:10). Thus, Ben Sira can be so bold as to say that "whoever forsakes a father is like a blasphemer" (Sir 3:16).

Josephus, a Pharisee writing in the first century, follows the link provided by Ben Sira, and even more emphatically demonstrates that love of God and love of parents are woven out of the same cloth:

> The law [Torah] ordains, also, that parents should be honored immediately after God himself, and delivers that son who does not requite them for the benefits that he has received from them . . . to be stoned. It also says, that the young men should pay due respect to every elder, since God is the eldest of all beings. (*Ag. Ap.* 2.206)

Into this world, the orientation of the *Didache* seems dangerously misguided. According to *Did.* 1:2, both fatherland and parents are silently passed over and, at best, are given no honor and no love beyond that of a "neighbor." Even the Decalogue (*Did.* 2:2), which will be considered shortly, entirely omits the commandment to "honor your father and mother." The sense of *Did.* 1:3, moreover, specifically downplays any "merit" in loving "the ones loving you"—namely, in the ancient world, parents, wife, children, friends. In what is to follow, the internal logic of the *Didache* will be examined in order to understand why the Way of Life deliberately omits "fatherland" and "filial piety"—a fact that would have immediately registered with pious pagans and Jews. On the other hand, reasons will be offered as to why the spiritual mentor assigned to the novice is "honor[ed] as the Lord" (*Did.* 4:1)—thereby assigning him/her the place normally given to one's biological parents. Thus, the *Didache* does embrace a notion of "filial piety," but it is a far cry from anything Hierocles or Ben Sira would sanction.

The Christian Scriptures, for their part, do not have any uniform tradition of honoring the fatherland and civil authorities. Paul, at one point, goes so far as to equate obedience to the Roman authorities as obedience to God "for there is no authority except from God" (Rom 13:1f.). The Book of Revelation, on the other hand, takes a diametrically opposite position by equating Roman power with the power of the Devil (Rv 12:7–13:10). By and large, however, the early churches honored the Father in heaven but dismissed both fatherland and biological fatherhood—as has just been noted in the *Didache*. The *Epistle to Diognetus* (c. 150 C.E.) expresses this perspective well when it says, "They [Christians] dwell in their own countries, but only as sojourners. . . . Every foreign country is a fatherland to them, and every fatherland is foreign" (6).

Once Christianity had established itself as the dominant culture, however, it would be only a matter of time before this glaring absence of the fourth commandment from the whole of the New Testament would be rectified. As for the *Didache*, the fourth-century *Apostolic Constitutions* takes over and modifies the content of the *Didache*. Now that Christianity was on its way to becoming the state religion, the *Didache* could be safely revamped to include special mandates requiring not only the honoring of one's parents but the honoring of one's siblings, civil officials, and tax collectors as well (7.15f.).

> You will care for *your father and your mother*
> as [those who are] responsible for your begetting
>   in order that you might become long-lived upon the earth
>   which the Lord your God has given to you [see Exod 20:12].
> Do not look down upon *your brothers and sisters:*
>   "For, the relatives of your seed, you will not look down upon"
>   [Isa 58:7].
> You will fear *the king,*
>   knowing that [his] appointment is the Lord's (choice);
> you will honor his rulers as ministers of God [see Rom 13:1],
>   for they are avengers of every injustice;
> to whom [it is due], pay in full the tax, tribute,
>   and every property-tax fairly. (*Apostolic Constitutions* 7.15.1–7.16.1)

SECTION II: APPRENTICESHIP
IN THE WAY OF LIFE

The Way of Life as Implying an Apprenticeship

After defining the Way of Life using the dual definitions, the *Didache* turns its attention to "the training" required for the assimilation of these words (1:3). As explained above, the definitions of the Way of Life and the Way of Death served to frame the main attraction, that is, "the training" itself given prior to baptism. Since much, if not all, of the *Didache* is devoted to this "training," it is not surprising that the entire manuscript was, at some point in time, given the title *didachē*.

The Greek word *didachē* makes reference to the training that a master-trainer (didaskalos) imparts to apprentices or disciples. In classical Greek, basket weaving, hunting with a bow, and pottery making represent typical skills transmitted under the term *didachē* (*TDNT* 3:135). For our purposes here, it is significant to note that the verb *didaskein*—customarily translated as "to teach"—was normally used to refer to a prolonged apprenticeship under the direction of a master: "Thus, *didaskein* is the word used more especially for the imparting of practical or theoretical knowledge when there is a continued activity with a view to a gradual, systematic, and therefore all the more fundamental assimilation" (*TDNT* 3:135).

When one examines the particulars of the training outline, it is apparent that one does not arrive at the skills necessary to "love those who hate you" (1:3c) or to "judge with justice" (4:3) merely by being told to do so on one or two occasions. Accordingly, while all the English translations prepared to date have been content to translate *didachē* as "teaching," it is evident that the force of *didachē* is better rendered as "training" or "apprenticing." Moreover, in our contemporary society, "teaching" is associated with classroom instruction, and, in the popular mind, this often evokes the passing on of information from professor to student. The word "training," on the contrary, has the advantage of suggesting the dynamics of an apprenticeship wherein novices gradually and progressively assimilate the performance skills of a master-trainer (*didaskalos*). In what is to follow, the terms "master-trainer," "mentor," and "spiritual parent" will accordingly be used in preference to "teacher" to identify the one who trains.

In the ancient world, in-depth training for a life-long profession was not provided through a system of technical schools. Someone aspiring to be a potter, a weaver, or a smith, for instance, had to find a recognized practitioner who would accept the would-be novice as an understudy. Normally this meant leaving one's home in order to live with the master. In cases where a son or daughter was learning the craft exemplified by one's father (or mother) who happened to be a master craftsman, then there was no need to leave home. One simply joined the other apprentices and became an understudy bent on learning the craft that constituted the family business. In a world in which slave labor was utilized in all the crafts, an artisan might buy a slave for the purpose of training him/her to work alongside his/her own children in the family business. Slaves were often purchased by managers who had them trained with the purpose of farming out their services in order to gain their salary (Nardo: 54–56).

Whatever their social status, the novice was expected to be a keen observer and imitator of the master's practice. A weaver's apprentice (often young girls being trained by their mothers), for example, had to learn how to judge the quality and quantity of various kinds of wool sold in the open market. Different natural fibers handle differently and produce significant variations in the end product. An apprentice needed to learn how to judge whether to wash and comb the fibers or to proceed directly to spinning the yarn. The novice needed to learn how to select a proper drop spindle and to pass through the painstaking trial and error of mastering the art of producing a uniform yarn. The prepared spindle was suspended by a single strand of yarn held between the left thumb and forefinger and, when ready, was given a sharp twist with the right hand. Then the mistress explains:

> The space between your two hands, where the unspun fibers are drawn, is the drafting area. The length of this space depends on the length of the fibers. . . . The drafting area allows the fibers to slide past each other as the right hand draws them down. Your right hand must grasp the fibers firmly to prevent the twist from running up too soon, because when the fibers are twisted they will not draft. . . . The weight of the spindle stretches the fibers and maintains the tension so they twist evenly up the forming thread. As your right hand is drawing down, the thumb and fingers of the left hand rub back and forth to spread the fibers, so a triangle of fibers is formed in the drafting zone. . . . This triangle spread prevents the twist from moving too high as the right hand releases the drafting fibers, allowing the twist to move up, spinning the fiber into yarn. The right hand drafts—a large number of fibers for a heavy yarn, and a few for a fine yarn—and then turns the spindle (Crockett: 25).

This description reveals only an intellectual grasp of the complexity involved in the actual practice of spinning yarn. At a craft show, I had the occasion to admire a woman twisting yarn on a spinning wheel. She was able to do this even while carrying on a conversation with onlookers. As an experiment, I asked her to let me have a try at it. She agreed. It took me only a half-minute to master how to set the wheel in motion using the pedal, but when it came to spreading the wool fibers in my fingers and releasing them in precise response to the gentle pull and rate of twisting of the spindle, I was entirely befuddled. Either I released the fibers too gingerly and the yarn developed ugly nodes or I restrained them too heavily and the yarn thinned and broke. After two or three minutes of abortive attempts, I quickly learned that this was an art akin to the playing of a musical instrument or to the throwing of pots on a wheel. Long periods of trial and error were required to gain even an initial mastery of the craft. One has not only to train the fingers and hands and foot to work in new ways; one has to establish habits of mindfulness that bring the action of the spindle into a measured synchronicity with the tactile feel of the fibers and their movement through one's fingers.

Thus, in practice, only gradually over a period of months, would an apprentice painstakingly learn to spin uniform yarns of various thicknesses and of various tightness. Once the yarn was prepared, the novice then needed to learn, under the watchful eye of the mistress, how to prepare dyes and how to apply them successfully to the yarn. Finally, with the yarn dyed and dried, the novice then began the still more complex process of learning how to select and operate a loom for weaving the yarn into cloth.

At the onset of an apprenticeship, the novice stood behind her mistress and observed her practice. Quite soon, however, the novice would be expected to directly assist and then to gradually take over the doing of simple procedures. And so the training would take place in small steps, which, over a period of months, showed great promise. Near the end of an apprenticeship, the mistress would stand behind her understudy observing her in every phase of her practice and discussing the fine points of what she was doing. At this point, the novice was expected to develop refinements of method and aesthetic sensibilities that enabled her to rival the quality and the beauty of the cloth produced by the mistress. Then and only then would the products of the understudy gain the same praise and price as the products produced by the mistress.

In the Synoptic Gospels, this same scenario was operative relative to Jesus. The habitual term for designating Jesus in the Synoptics is *didaskalos*. In Matthew's Gospel, for instance, Jesus is presented as *didaskalos* (translated as "master" or "teacher") eleven times, while he is named as *prophētēs* ("prophet") only three times. Luke uses *didaskalos* sixteen times for Jesus. Unlike Matthew, who reserves this term alone for Jesus, Luke uses this term for John the Baptizer (Lk 3:12) and for those teaching Torah in the temple (Lk 2:46). Meanwhile, the Synoptic Gospels habitually name the twelve who are intimately associated with Jesus as "disciples." The term *mathētēs* ("disciple") refers to a person who is undergoing training by a master. Matthew uses this term seventy-two times for Jesus' understudies. Only once does he refer to "the disciples of John" (Mt 9:14) and "the disciples of the Pharisees" (Mt 22:16). And lest the reader confuse the import of this relational term, Matthew and Luke present the disciples as being sent out in pairs to do on their own those feats Jesus exemplified in his own ministry, namely, preaching the kingdom, healing, and exorcising. Since Jesus judged that his disciples were, by virtue of their apprenticeship, ready to do what he did, it made perfect sense to have Jesus say, "He who receives you receives me" (Mt 10:40). Those in the ancient world, accustomed as they were to the transformative power of the master–disciple relationship, would have had no difficulty in understanding such a claim. Traditional theology, on the other hand, has entirely obscured the character of religious empowerment by insisting that these must be understood as Cinderella-like transformations (Milavec 1982: 15–38).

#1D The Mystery of Conversion and the Ties That Bind

Modern psychological studies endeavor to account for the human factors operative when a religious conversion happens. The human makeup is so complex that any given individual is largely incapable of accounting for why, in a given set of circumstances, he or she abandoned former religious ties in order to zealously affirm a new religious commitment. In every case, however, new converts report that they experience an overwhelming emotional and intellectual satisfaction that confirms the worth of their new lifestyle with its attendant rites and beliefs.

What Michael Polanyi says about the presence of guiding intuitions leading toward and anticipating a scientific discovery can be aptly transposed to describe the journey of a religious seeker approaching conversion:

> The pursuit of discovery is conducted from the start in these terms; all the time we are guided by sensing the presence of a hidden reality toward which our clues are pointing; and the discovery which terminates and satisfies this pursuit is still sustained by the same vision. . . . It [the pursuit of discovery] is personal, in the sense of involving the personality of him who holds it, and also in the sense of being, as a rule, solitary; but there is no trace in it of self-indulgence. The discoverer is filled with a compelling sense of responsibility for the pursuit of a hidden truth, which demands his services for revealing it. . . . The anticipation of discovery, like the discovery itself, may turn out to be a delusion. But it is futile to seek for strictly impersonal criteria of its validity. . . . You cannot formalize the act of commitment, for you cannot express your commitments non-committally. To attempt this is to exercise the kind of lucidity which destroys its subject matter. (Polanyi 1966: 24f.)

Polanyi notes that every instance of discovery has an inexplicable quality, since the guiding intuitions leading to a conversion operate tacitly throughout the search. The satisfaction that greets the final discovery, however, has the effect of dissolving the strains that accompanied the early period of searching and emerges as an unexpected "grace." Thus, in the case of a religious conversion, it is normal to hear converts saying that they experienced themselves as having been guided by an "amazing grace" that led them into the safe harbor where they found a peace that surpasses human understanding (#1h and #1w provide illustrations).

The *Didache* warrants this perception of things when it notes that slaves are not to be reluctantly forced to embrace the Way of Life just because their masters think of themselves as owning them. Rather, even masters must wait patiently, for the Lord "calls those whom the Spirit has made-ready" (*Did.* 4:10). In this instance, "the spirit" most probably refers to the Holy Spirit, but it could also refer to the living spirit within each individual. In either case, it is "the spirit" that inclines the heart to admire and to move toward a Way of Life that holds a great and unexpected fulfillment. Thus, whether one points to the agency of God who marginally shapes the yearnings of every human heart or whether one fingers the longings of the human heart themselves, one is confronted by the mutually penetrating factors in every act of conversion (Milavec 1982: 213–38).

Lewis R. Rambo, in his book *Understanding Religious Conversion,* concludes that "relationships are important to most but not all conversions" (108). Rambo notes that a special close personal relationship, along with a general group acceptance, functions to promote confirmation and consolidation of the converts new lifestyle:

> Some scholars have theorized that formation of close personal relationships during conversion enables converts to feel accepted at a deep level, and that such personal affirmation releases energy that gives vitality to the new orientation. Others have theorized that an experience of group acceptance enables people to transcend conflict, enhances self-esteem, and offers a new perspective on life. (Rambo: 108)

Psychologist Chana Ullman studied forty converts and thirty life-long members of four different groups (Bahai, Judaism, Roman Catholicism, and Hare Krishna) with a special focus upon relationships. She was startled by her results:

> Converts, to a statistically significant level, had absent, weak, or abusive fathers. This serious psychological deprivation and abuse appeared to motivate and inform the person's conversion. In many cases, the convert established a powerful relationship with a guru, rabbi, priest, or other person in the group to which they were converting, and these relationships were . . . absolutely central to their conversion. (Rambo: 111)

While these studies of conversion apply to the groups tested, it is difficult to know to what degree they also characterize converts to the Didache communities. In any case, the linguistic evidence of the *Didache* demonstrates that the spiritual mentor becomes a "father" or "mother" for the convert. This implies that their biological parents were not able to nurture them into the Way of Life and that "adoptive" parents had to be assigned to perform this vital task. Thus, just at the moment when their biological family and kin were exerting pressure against their conversion (and, by implication, against their spiritual well-being), each neophyte found him/herself in the care of a new parent and on the way to entering a new family. One can surmise, therefore, that the close personal relationship with a spiritual mentor (which will be discussed momentarily) flowered into an intimate, mutual, and lifelong support that Rambo reports. Moreover, if Ullman's study applies to some or many of the converts joining the Didache communities, then it makes even more sense to imagine that "powerful relationship" with their spiritual parent was "absolutely central to their conversion" of life.

Whether Each Novice Had a Single Spiritual Mentor

The *Didache* offers evidence suggesting that each novice was paired off with a single spiritual master. The principal clue for this is the fact that the entire training program (save for *Did.* 1:3) addresses a single novice using the second person singular. If, under normal circumstances, a single spiritual master was assigned the training of many or all the novices within a community, one would have expected that the second person plural would have been used throughout. Furthermore, within the Way of Life training program, the novice is instructed to actively remember and mull over the life and the training of "the one speaking to you the word of God" (4:1). This use of the singular here points in the direction of each novice having a single master. So, too, when regulations are put forward for choosing the water for baptism (7:2f.) and for ordering "the one being baptized to fast beforehand" (7:4), in each case the singular is used—again confirming the expectation that each candidate was baptized individually by a single individual—presumably the one who was their spiritual mentor and parent.

The *Didache* does not tell us how someone attracted to the Way of Life would come to have a spiritual mistress or master. One can surmise that the one coming forward to request admission would do so because of a keen admiration for the Way of Life of one or more members. Since the community gatherings were closed to outsiders (9:5), this limited personal attraction would be the basis for seeking admittance (4:10). If the community member to whom the potential candidate was initially attracted did not have the time, the temperament, or the skill to train a novice, one can further imagine that the community would have discussed among themselves who would be best fitted, by virtue of their sex, age, availability, temperament, state of life, and spiritual advancement to serve as spiritual master in the case of a particular candidate coming forward.

Whether Women Were Formally Trained

Since women in the ancient world were accustomed to be trained by other women, and since it would have been a source of scandal for a man to be alone for prolonged periods with a woman unrelated to him, it would be presumed that, save for special circumstances, women were appointed to train female candidates and men were appointed to train male candidates.

Deborah Rose-Gaier (1996) has investigated the roles of women in the *Didache*. In part, she concludes that the agenda for training includes material specifically addressed to women and other material specifically addressed to men (see Crossan 1998: 370). There is no attempt, on the part of the *Didache*, however, to create separate-but-equal training manuals—one for women and one for men. Within the household churches of the *Didache*, therefore, there was a pragmatic discipleship of equals. Women and men were trained to strive for the same perfection and to exercise the same responsibilities.

Deborah Rose-Gaier notes that the Way of Life itself provides clues that the training program was specifically intended for women as well as men. Three illustrations deserving special attention are the following:

1. In the decalogue (*Did.* 2:2), sexually corrupting young boys and murdering offspring through abortion are proscribed. The first applies especially to men while the second applies especially to women. If men alone were being addressed, one might have expected them to be advised to prohibit their wives and concubines from aborting their children.

2. At a certain point in the training program, the spiritual trainer begins addressing the novice as "my child" (*teknon mou*)—a term that applies equally to a son or a daughter without any regard for age. In Jewish training material found in the wisdom literature and the *Testaments of the Twelve Patriarchs,* the one being trained is habitually addressed as "my son" (*pais mou*), indicating that the training therein was intended for males alone. The term chosen by the *Didache* thus deliberately includes women being trained.

3. Since the *Didache* says, "You will not take away your hand from your son or from your daughter, but from youth you will train them in the fear of God" (*Did.* 4:9), this implies that ordinarily the novice might be expected to have children—thereby again dispelling the notion that the term "my child" (*teknon mou*) applied to a youth. Furthermore, since the training of daughters in the ancient world was principally given over to their mothers, the reference to "your daughter" would imply that the mother was being addressed.

In sum, one can note that internal evidence points in the direction of showing that apprenticeship in the Way of Life was intended for both women and men. This conclusion will become stronger as this study proceeds.

#1E SOCIAL INEQUALITY BETWEEN WOMEN AND MEN

In the ancient world, there was a marked social inequality between men and women. Women were the property of their fathers and, after marriage, of their husbands. While patriarchal structures dominated the ancient world, there was a surprising degree of diversity evident when this was put into practice:

> For example, in Rome women could at most be the power behind the throne, whereas in Egypt women could openly rule. Or again, in Athens married citizen-women seem to have been confined to domestic activities, whereas women in Asia Minor, Macedonia, and Egypt engaged in their own private businesses, served in public offices, and had prominent roles in various religious cults. (*ABD* 6:958)

Philo of Alexandria, an educated Jew who lived in the second largest city of the Roman Empire, wrote that women and men were functionally different insofar as women remained at home to oversee the household while men went to the marketplaces and courts of justice to oversee the affairs of the city. Thus, for the first century, there was not only a well-defined division of labor but an equally well-defined division of place:

> Market places, and council chambers, and courts of justice, and . . . a life in the open air full of arguments and actions relating to war and peace, are suited to men; but taking care of the house and remaining at home are the proper duties of women; the virgins [i.e., unmarried girls] having their apartments in the center of the house within the innermost doors, and the full-grown women not going beyond the vestibule and outer courts; for there are two kinds of states, the greater and the smaller. And the larger ones are really called cities; but the smaller ones are called houses. And the superintendence and management of these is allotted to the two sexes separately. . . (*Special Laws* 3.169).

To be sure, Philo's description is idealized. Poor women, for example, were often required to work in shops or in fields located some distance from their homes. Furthermore, in households sustained by a family trade, women and men would normally work side by side in the family-owned workshop. Slaves, meanwhile, were required to do any work in any place demanded by their masters. Moreover, both male and female slaves who had marketable skills were frequently hired out in order to bring their masters more income.

The division of labor and of place was driven home to me during the time I lived in Sidi Boulbaba, a remote village in southern Tunisia. The marketplaces and cafes were filled with men—women were conspicuously absent. The courtyards, meanwhile, were filled with women and children occupied with drying spices, with processing couscous, with washing laundry, with preparing meals, and with caring for children. Even during family meals, the sons over twelve ate first with their father while the mother and girls served the men. When the men were finished, then the mother ate at the same low table with the other women and children of the household. At the age of twelve, girls and boys stopped playing together, stopped walking together, stopped sharing secrets together, since they were being prepared to enter their separate spheres. At the mosque, at the cinema, and even at weddings, a man would never socialize side by side with women, not even his own wife, but both sexes took their separate places—men dancing with men, and women dancing with women. Within this social arrangement, I witnessed mutual affection and caring (esp. between fathers and their sons, mothers and their children) even though the ideal of romantic love and interpersonal intimacy dominating social customs in the West was nowhere in evidence.

In the ancient world, as in Sidi Boulbaba today, girls had no way to meet boys outside their immediate family circle much less to assess their qualities as potential mates. For this, therefore, they were entirely dependent on the discernment of their fathers and older brothers, who, in reality, alone had the socially sanctioned possibility of finding and evaluating suitable men. Marriage, moreover, was a social arrangement bringing together the persons and the resources of two different extended families; hence, parents had every reason to take a leading role in deciding whom their children were to marry.

On the basis of a careful study by Keith Hopkins, it was discovered that 63 percent of Roman girls married before the age of seventeen and that 20 percent married at the age of twelve—"very often before puberty" (Stark: 105). Thus, with husbands generally ten to fifteen years their senior, it was not surprising that most wives deferred to the superior skills and experience of their own husbands. Marriages of equality were unlikely and all but impossible given the social, legal, and religious advantages of the men. Nonetheless, history does provide us with instances in which some wives overreached their husbands in terms of public achievements and civic honors.

Given the traditional inequality that everywhere existed between men and women (see #1e), it was exceedingly unusual to find both women and men being trained to strive for the same perfection and to exercise the same responsibilities within the Didache communities. Even a child bride, therefore, would seemingly have been trained to "reconcile those fighting" and to "judge justly" (*Did.* 4:3). Even if social custom may have tacitly determined that women exercised these skills among their social equals and inferiors (it being unfitting for women to reconcile or judge men), nonetheless, in a world in which a child bride would pass from under the dominion of her parents to that of her husband and his mother, it was indeed important to note that women in the Didache communities were expected to learn to reconcile and to judge. When it came to reproving, women would have been expressly taught "not [to] take into account social status" (*Did.* 4:3). This implies that women (as well as men) were expected to reprove their social superiors.

This practice forms a sharp contrast to the separate and unequal training give to women in those communities represented by the Pastoral Epistles:

> Bid the older women . . . train the young women to love their husbands and children, to be sensible, chaste, domestic, kind, and submissive to their husbands, that the word of God may not be discredited (Ti 2:3f.).

The women of the *Didache* undoubtedly received training in these strictly "domestic virtues" from their mothers at home. In the common training manual of the Didache communities, however, Rose-Gaier (1996) correctly notes that no such list of "domestic virtues" was earmarked for female novices so as to ensure that they would continue to be "domestic, kind, and submissive to their husbands." The fact that the Pastoral Epistles assign the "older women" in the community to the training of "the young women" in these domestic virtues is an indication that these women may have, owing to the climate within the early Pauline church, departed from these virtues and, in the mind of the pseudo-Pauline author of the Pastoral Epistles, tried to bring back a separate and unequal training in virtue directed specifically at "the young women."

In the ancient world, women were normally expected to take charge of home life and of children and, accordingly, were routinely trained by their mothers in the "domestic virtues." The content of these "domestic virtues" can be surmised from the traits named in surviving funerary epitaphs: "chastity, obedience, pleasantness, hard working, bearing children, piety, staying at home, thrift" (Fant: 16–23). These funerary epitaphs, it must be remembered, represented the views of their surviving husbands. Yet, even among the men, there are exceptional instances when the "domestic virtues" were deliberately abandoned. The heroine in Sophocles' play *Antigone*, for example, displayed male heroic values and supported community values. The same thing, of course, could be said for Judith (second century B.C.E.)—the Jewish folktale in which the saintly heroine must, at least for a short time, become a shameless flatterer, a bold-faced liar, and a ruthless assassin in order to release her people from the menace of Holofernes. So, too, when the Greek philosopher Plato described the utopian city, the *Republic*, he advanced the novel thesis that young women were to be trained following a curriculum similar to that being used for young men. Plutarch (45–125 C.E.), going even further, argued that the virtues conducive to the well-being of women were precisely the virtues cultivated by men (*Moralia* 243e–263c). For the most part, however, it must be remembered that these were exceptional and idealistic positions held by a few men who could see beyond the limitations imposed by their historical and cultural circumstances. Within society at large, women were prized for their "domestic virtues" and their "usefulness" to men. Even Plutarch, in his "Advice on Marriage," thought it expedient for a wife to submit to her husband when it came to making sexual advances, to choosing suitable friends, and to making family decisions (*Moralia* 138a–146a).

Learning as Liberating

Care should to taken not to underestimate the significance of offering women training in the Way of Life. Having been so trained, a woman was not required to depend on her husband in order to learn from him whatever he thinks it is important for her to know. Trained by a competent woman, the female novice was on her way to becoming competent to discern for herself and for others what it meant to serve the Lord. Learning was liberating. Once a woman began to acquire the art of guiding her own life and trusting her own judgment in spiritual matters, she established herself as a disciple equal with the men. She could never go back to her former position of trusting that the men in her life entirely knew and understood all those things that were formerly beyond her grasp. More importantly, she could never go back to thinking that she need only obediently submit to masculine direction (as in Ti 2:3f.) to assure herself that she was entirely in harmony with what God would have her be and have her do. If every man gained his independence and his stature before men and before God by virtue of learning to interpret and to apply the Way of Life for himself, why should this same rule not also give independence and stature to women? The *Didache*, therefore, was offering a quiet revolution when it came to training women along with the men to become active agents within the household churches.

From the vantage point of rabbinic Judaism that obligated fathers to train their sons but discouraged them from training their daughters in Torah (*b. Qiddushin* 29b), the practice of the *Didache* was undoubtedly quite revolutionary. On the other hand, Philo speaks of the Jewish Therapeutae, wherein both women and men equally but separately strove for perfection by listening to lectures and by performing rites (*On the Contemplative Life* 68f., 83f.). In the Roman world, meanwhile, the prospects of a woman gaining an education were highly prized:

> It is notable that in Roman society, unlike some parts of Greece, the education of woman was considered important and desirable. Even among poorer families both daughters and sons received at least a rudimentary education, while in wealthier families all children regularly had tutors. Yet this did not lead Romans, even during the age of the Empire, to allow women to vote or hold public office. . . . (*ABD* 6:958)

More study is needed, consequently, before one can conclude to what degree the practice of the *Didache* was in harmony with or an advance upon the culture in which it thrived. In any case, since the *Didache* finds no need to defend the training of women or to prescribe a two-tiered agenda for training, it can be presupposed that the practice of the *Didache* was not far removed from expectations gained prior to their entrance into the community.

#1F TRAINING WOMEN IN THE SYNOPTIC COMMUNITIES

Nowhere in the Gospel accounts do we come across Jesus making general pronouncements about women: "Women ought to do this. . . . Women ought not to do that. . . ." Even in the case of the tension between Martha and Mary, Jesus does not fall into the trap of supposing that he ought to impose one solution upon all women for all time. Instead, Martha is allowed to continue, with honor, in the traditional role she has cut out for herself; yet she has to learn to do this, at least for the moment, without Mary, her "sister." As for Mary, one cannot help but note that Jesus is not presented as having invited Mary to sit at his feet in the first place. She does this by herself. He simply accepts her initiative.

If this narrative offers some insight into the internal affairs of Luke's community, it would have to be in the direction of signaling that the men in charge do not have a pastoral plan that covers all cases and all contingencies. Part of the "good news" is that women are free to take the initiative without seeking prior approval from the men who are in charge. Madonna Kolbenschlag admirably develops this same theme on the basis of Luke's portrait of another Mary, the mother of Jesus (Kolbenschlag: 82–88). On the other hand, the Martha and Mary narrative offers every reason for the men in charge to continue to honor those women who are quite content to retain their culturally determined roles.

As already mentioned, learning is liberating. Once Mary begins to hear Torah for herself "at the feet of Jesus" and then begins to acquire the art of applying it to her own life, she establishes herself as a disciple equal with the men. She can never go back to her former position of trusting that the men in her life entirely know and understand all those things that were formerly beyond her grasp. More importantly, she can never go back to thinking that she need only obediently submit to masculine direction to assure herself that she is entirely in harmony with what God would have her be and have her do.

Each of the Synoptic Gospels presents Jesus as meeting with Jews in local synagogues in order to preach the good news of the kingdom of God. Mark, for instance, summarizes the early years of Jesus' ministry as follows: "And he went throughout Galilee, preaching in their synagogues" (Mk 1:39). During this period, are we to imagine that Jesus met primarily or even exclusively with men (as might be the case if he had visited an Orthodox synagogue today)? Or, on the contrary, did Jesus sometimes preach the good news to the women who sat behind the men?

How could one even respond to such a question? Given the scarcity of written records that have come down to us, scholars today have difficulty even establishing how synagogues functioned in the time of Jesus. On the basis of indirect evidence, however, much can be learned. Consider the parables of the kingdom. Some of them directly speak to the experiences of men:

The Wicked Husbandman (Mk 12:1–11; Mt 21:33–44; Lk 20:9–18)
The Doorkeeper (Mk 13:33–37; Lk 12:35–38)
The Fisherman's Net (Mt 13:47–50)
The Lost Sheep (Mt 18:12–14; Lk 15:4–7)

These four parables appeal to the tasks and experiences traditionally associated with men. Women could observe men doing these things; but, by and large, they would not be expected to relate to these tasks since, in the normal course of events, they would rarely, if ever, have a chance to perform them.

On the other hand, another set of parables specifically focuses upon the experience proper to women:

The Yeast (Mt 13:33; Lk 13:20f.)
The Ten Maidens (Mt 25:1–13)
The Lost Coin (Lk 15:5–10)
The Unjust Judge (Lk 18:1–8)

Here again, men would have been expected to have observed women kneading yeast into dough, and so on. Men, however, would not be expected to relate to these roles, since they would never have had an occasion to assume them themselves. In contemporary society, some men do take pride in making loaves of bread from scratch. In the world of Jesus, however, the grinding of grain, the kneading of dough, and the baking of bread were the daily chores of women.

The same holds true for the other three parables. In contemporary society, men and women usually arrive together at the church for a wedding. After the wedding, they go together to the reception. No one has to wait. In traditional societies, on the contrary, the bride-to-be and her female attendants would wait for hours until the men, who gathered at the groom's home, finished their "bachelor's party" and processed together to the bride's house where the wedding would take place. As for the parable of the lost coin, one might expect that any man, either ancient or modern, would be ashamed to let neighbors know that he had carelessly lost his money—he would have pocketed the coin and not said a word to anyone. Only a women with little social status would be given to spontaneously inviting in her female (as understood by the social context) neighbors and sharing with them her good news. So, too, in the case of the unjust judge, the widow appears to have no man (husband or son or brother) who will use his influence to ensure justice. She does what only a woman without honor and without influence, yet driven by necessity, might be expected to do—she pesters the judge until he relents.

The Gospel writers implicitly recognize that Jesus told Kingdom parables addressing experiences sometimes proper to women and sometimes proper to men. This evidence indirectly testifies that Jesus wished the Kingdom to be intelligible to both women and men. In the synagogue, therefore, it can be presumed that Jesus occasionally directly addressed those women who sat behind the men and who were, in most cases, entirely hidden from the view of the men who sat around Jesus. Jesus, however, did not lose sight of them—even if he was not able to actually see them.

Furthermore, since women's experiences continued to show up in the Gospel parables collected by and for the Jesus movement, this provides indirect evidence about the audience to which the apostles and the communities that they left behind directed their message. What can be concluded from this evidence? What does it say about Matthew's portrait of Jesus that the Parable of the Ten Maidens would not only notice that the women were kept waiting but, following the terms of the parable itself, kept waiting for such a long time that many fell asleep and their lamps (actually "torches"; Gundry 1994: 498) went out? The men, it must be remembered, were having a "bachelor's party" and, in their merrymaking, were not expected to be attentive to the women who were waiting with the bride. The focus of the parable, on the other hand, is not the implied insensitivity of men. Rather, the parable takes the culturally given anticipation that women knew firsthand because of their repeated experience with weddings and holds it up as a powerful message for those wise virgins who are prepared to remain alert and ready to welcome the bridegroom ("the final coming of the Lord"; Gundry 1994: 499) even though his arrival has been postponed far into the night.

What is of special interest here is not so much the exact intent of the parable but the realization of how awkward it might have been for Jesus to expect that men would learn the mystery of the Kingdom by taking note of experiences proper to women. The very existence of such a parable, consequently, implies that it was designed to honor the experience of women and to relate that experience to the central expectation of the Jesus movement. Going further, the fact that Matthew does not hesitate to place such a parable on the lips of Jesus is a tacit recognition that he deliberately crafted such a parable because he wanted to bring directly to women's attention aspects of the Kingdom using experiences proper to themselves. Were all the Jesus parables crafted within the horizon of women's experience, one would have to imagine that Jesus either wanted to address women exclusively or that, when addressing men, Jesus had the bad taste of forcing men to enter into the experiential world of women. The opposite could be said if all the parables placed on the lips of Jesus were configured within the experiential world of men.

In conclusion, the Synoptic Gospels themselves provide indirect evidence that, within the communities of Matthew and Luke, women's experiences were honored and that, accordingly, women were accustomed to hearing the good news of the Kingdom being preached with attention to their own proper experiences. The initiative of Mary "who sat at the Lord's feet and listened to what he was saying" (Lk 10:39) may now not seem so audacious, since, in effect, the very content of Jesus' parables makes clear that he was accustomed to speaking over the heads of the men gathered around him in order to address the women in metaphors taken directly from their experience. This conclusion is not weakened if and when one remembers that the Synoptics were crafting a presentation of Jesus appropriate to the needs of their communities and not necessarily writing critical history in our modern sense of the term. Since the parables honoring women's experience were placed on the lips of Jesus, one is forced to surmise that Matthew and, more especially, Luke favored a Jesus (and a church leadership following his style) who addressed women by honoring their own proper experiences.

When it came to training in the Way of Life, however, women seemingly did not find an easy acceptance. In Luke's Gospel, where special attention is given to women's voices (Lk 1:24–58; 2:6–20, 33–38; 23:27–31), we are faced with a conflict narrative surrounding a woman named Mary, who neglected her kitchen duty in favor of taking a place along with the men sitting "at the Lord's feet and listened to what he was saying" (Lk 10:39). Assuming, for a moment, that this was a narrative designed to address a current problem in Luke's community, reconstructing the problem based on the internal logic of the text might go as follows:

> When conflict arose, women, who were tied to their culturally defined roles (in the kitchen), appear to have been the first to approach the leading men (Jesus) demanding that their "sisters" (a familiar term for a female religious associate) be ordered back into their proper roles (i.e., sent back into the kitchen). The voices of the "brothers" is not heard—suggesting that this dispute did not originate with them. The words found on Jesus' lips (Lk 10:42) represent the resolution of this crisis among the women. The resolution offered reveals that nothing would be gained in trying to force all of the women out of the kitchen or all of the men into the kitchen. Meanwhile, respecting the free initiative of those women who have joined the men, there is little desire to send them back into the kitchen. Thus, Jesus' words, "The good portion . . . shall not be taken from her" (Lk 10:42), served to secure the innovative role of women learning to interpret Torah, while at the same time it tacitly honored the contribution of women who retained their traditional service of waiting on the men. (see Milavec 1994a: 87)

In sum, the ruling principle placed on Jesus' lips provided sound pastoral genius at its best. Women coming forward for training were to be received (even encouraged) by the men. Women who wished to rely upon the directives of their husbands or fathers in matters bearing upon the Way of Life were likewise to be accommodated.

#1G How Women Flourished on Account of Their Disproportionate Numbers

Rodney Stark draws attention to the curious fact that, in the population at large, men outnumbered women by 40 percent, while in the Christian communities this sexual imbalance was reversed (97, 99f.; Pomeroy: 164–66). This reverse imbalance, Stark notes, greatly increased the prospects of Christian women and gave the Christian movement a foothold to outpropagate the pagans.

In the general population, men outnumbered women for identifiable social reasons: (a) fathers preferred sons; hence, a disproportionate number of female infants were exposed following birth in all social classes (Madden: 6; Pomeroy: 69–70, 164–68, 192); (b) women married early and bore many children, creating a situation whereby a disproportionate number of women died in childbirth or because of defective abortions (Stark: 98; Demand: 58); and (c) men customarily ate first and the women fed their children and themselves last, thereby exposing them to chronic malnutrition when resources were scarce (Demand: 8).

In the Christian communities, on the other hand, Stark's study of ancient sources allows him to conclude that the women outnumbered the men. Why might this be so? Stark suggests three aspects of Christianity that might have accounted for the disproportionate number of female converts: (a) "Like pagans, early Christians prized female chastity, but unlike pagans, they rejected the double standard that gave pagan men so much sexual license" (104). (b) Extensive studies by Keith Hopkins demonstrate that Christians "were married at a substantially older age and had more choice about whom they married" (105). (c) In the case of pubescent brides, Plutarch refers to "the hatred and fear of girls forced contrary to nature" (cited in Stark: 107)—a situation that occurred three times more often among pagans than among Christians (107). Finally, Christians were prohibited from practicing abortion and infanticide (as the *Didache* demonstrates); thus, Christian couples, in contrast to their pagan counterparts, were prone to bring more daughters into the faith.

Stark then goes on to show how sexual imbalance worked in favor of women's equality within Christianity while, in the society at large, it favored greater confinement and restrictions. In large part, Stark relied on the sociological and historical studies of Guttentag and Secord:

> To the extent that males outnumber females, women will be enclosed in repressive sex roles as men treat them as "scarce goods." Conversely, to the extent that females outnumber males, the Guttentag and Secord theory predicts that women will enjoy relatively greater power and freedom. (102)

To these considerations, I would like to reflect upon the observations of Nancy Demand, who noted that women spent the greater part of their lives in their courtyards, and "religious activities . . . offered women the most socially acceptable opportunities to venture outside the home" (24).

In this regard, the *Didache* must have offered a special attraction to women: (a) Women, according to the *Didache*, were given socially sanctioned weekly (*Did.* 14:1), if not daily (*Did.* 4:2), opportunities to visit the homes of other Christians for the purpose of sharing their life experiences and offering religious rites. (b) Since the members of each household church were considered "brothers" and "sisters," women had the possibility of socializing with an extended set of biologically unrelated persons whom, in the normal course of events, they could never hope even to address in public much less to engage in familiar conversation during shared meals. And (c) placing the locus of the eucharist within the "woman's natural place" gave Christian women a sense of ease and of belonging which enabled them to have an extended experience of "mixed company" within an "extended family" where they "felt safe" (see also #8i). All of these conditions taken together allowed for the relaxation of the safeguards that normally governed and restricted women's conduct, especially when they moved in public spaces.

As a result, Stark's discovery that women (more so than men) found certain natural inducements to become Christians would seem to apply with even greater importance to the Didache household churches. Given the disproportionate number of women and given the possibility of socialization within an "extended family," it is not so surprising that the Way of Life described in the *Didache* reflects a uniform code for both men and women and, by that fact alone, tends to honor the status and well-being of women.

Whether Private Reading or Studying Could Replace an Apprenticeship

The *Didache* describes the training necessary for the Way of Life. It would be deceptive to imagine that the spiritual master recited the "Way of Life" in one sitting or that the novice was handed a written copy of the "Way of Life" for home study. In the ancient world, everyone knew that you could discover the price of wheat by asking a vendor in the marketplace but, when it came to deep learning, this could only be achieved by virtue of a prolonged contact with a master.

Even as late as the Middle Ages, scholars like Thomas Aquinas were still aware that Jesus, Pythagoras, and Socrates could not rely on mere transmission of words (whether orally or in writing) to communicate their religious orientation:

> The more excellent the teacher, the more excellent should be his manner of teaching. Consequently it was fitting that Christ, as

the most excellent of teachers, should adopt that manner of teaching whereby his doctrine is imprinted on the hearts of his hearers. . . . And so it was among the gentiles, Pythagoras and Socrates, who were teachers of great excellence, were unwilling to write anything. . . . (*Summa Theologica* III.42.4)

According to Thomas, Jesus preferred personal associations rather than the solitary life because "he came into the world, first, that he might publish the truth" (III.40.1). To accomplish this, "the efficacy of his persuasion" and "the force of his righteousness" go hand in hand (III.42.1 ad 2). Within this horizon of understanding, Thomas finds it natural to identify the chief miracles of Christ to be those wherein "he tames the minds of thousands" (III.44.3 ad 1). When it comes to the mission to the gentiles, however, Thomas gave weight to the historical fact that this was accomplished not by Jesus but by his disciples:

> It is the sign, not of lesser but of greater [persuasive] power, to do something by means of another rather than by oneself. And thus the divine power of Christ was specially shown in this: that he bestowed on the teaching of his disciples such a [persuasive] power that they converted the gentiles (III.42.2 ad 2).

No complex human skill can be learned through the mere telling in words. Anyone who intends to become a potter, a carpenter, or a physician, for example, must learn from skilled practitioners. Someone who wants to begin to throw a pot, for example, might be told in words or given a set of printed instructions. In the book *Pottery Making: A Complete Guide,* for example, fifteen steps are photographed and described. The first five are as follows:

1. Place the clay in the exact center of the bat. With the wheel revolving very slowly beat the clay into a cone with simultaneous blows from the palms of both hands.
2. Consolidating the cone with gentle pressure from both hands locked together.
3. Closing the hands around the clay to cone up.
4. Taking the cone down into a disk.
5. Opening up the center of the disk. (Dickerson: 62)

Anyone trying to throw a pot based solely upon these words would become entirely frustrated. To begin with, these instructions presuppose that the beginner knows the correct consistency of the clay such that it can be successfully slapped onto the center of the bat. Merely "placing" the clay "in the exact center" will result in its flying off as soon as the wheel begins to revolve. Furthermore, actions described as "consolidating the cone" and "taking the cone down" can have little meaning apart from the performance of a skilled practitioner. In point of fact, the very words used by a practitioner "ring true" only because, at every point, the words are tacitly supplemented by his/her successful practice. Even misleading words, as in the case of step 1, are tacitly corrected by the successful practice of the skilled practitioner. For the beginner, however, step-by-step instructions taken by themselves, no matter how detailed, invariably lead to disastrous or mediocre results. A student of pottery can only properly learn to understand and to perform such words by submitting to an apprenticeship under the direction of a living master who, over a period of time, trains the student to enlarge his/her performance skills so as to replicate those of the master. While visiting Ireland recently, I looked into the matter and discovered that a two- to five-year apprenticeship is required to train a master potter. Once trained, the student then takes his/her stand with the master, and the words of instruction that were nearly incomprehensible initially now have a well-defined sense determined by their shared practice.

Consider another example. The grand masters of chess, such as Bobby Fisher, have published books wherein they offer rules of strategy and even make running commentaries on their tournament games. Any chess enthusiast could memorize such rules and exhaustively study the tournament games of the masters that supposedly illustrate their rules of strategy. No one should expect, however, that mastering the rules of strategy would instantly transform a chess enthusiast into someone able to rival the grand masters. Here again, any rules of strategy that a master might give "ring true" only because the master projects his powers of discernment into the application of that rule. For someone who has just mastered how the pieces move on the board, any such rules would be largely unintelligible. For example, a typical rule of strategy for beginners is that "the opening moves are meant to gain control of the center" (Roberts: 25). Only during the course of an apprenticeship does a novice in chess gradually learn the depth of meaning in these words and, once any rule has been mastered, the rule itself becomes largely unnecessary because the very habits of judgment exercised by such a player tacitly exemplify the content of the rule even when it is never mentioned.

Consider a religious example. The sacred texts of India have been translated into English and studied in the West for nearly two hundred years without producing any known converts. Once gurus began to migrate to the United States and to establish ashrams, however, zealous converts have been able to claim for themselves the feats of spirituality that had, until that time, remained entirely veiled to the "eyes" of Westerners reading the text. The same thing can be said for those missionary societies who pass out free copies of the New Testament printed in the local dialects of persons living in mainland China.

Michael Polanyi notes that all deep knowing implies a way of being in one's body and a way of being in the world that cannot be transmitted by a mere telling in words. Nor can such knowledge be entirely analyzed, dissected, and made plain such that a detached observer could discern the foundational principles involved and, through progressive steps in clear logic, arrive at the same affirmations as the teller. Polanyi repudiates the ideal of critical, detached knowing as unrealized and unrealizable (both in science and in religion), and Polanyi explains that this is so by virtue of the fact that all knowledge is embodied knowledge relying on tacit skills:

> If we know a great deal that we cannot tell, and if even that which we know and can tell is accepted by us as true only in view of its bearing on a reality beyond it . . . ; if indeed we recognize a great discovery, or else a great personality, as most real, owing to the wide range of its yet unknown future manifestations: then the idea of knowledge based on wholly identifiable grounds collapse, and we must conclude that the transmission of knowledge from one generation to the other must be predominantly tacit. (Polanyi 1966: 61)

In the end, for an adult to learn the ways of a master, he/she has to submit to a prolonged apprenticeship. Polanyi notes that, even in an apprenticeship, learning depends on a certain sympathy that exists between the novice and master. This sympathy begins in the spontaneous admiration that prompts the novice to establish a master–apprentice relationship in the first place. This sympathy operates throughout the apprenticeship itself, giving the novice the means to enter into and to assimilate the performance skills and words of his/her trusted master.

> The pupil must presume that a teaching which appears meaningless to start with has in fact a meaning which can be discovered by hitting on the same kind of indwelling as the teacher is practicing. Such an effort is based upon accepting the teacher's authority. (Polanyi 1966: 61)

Authority within the context of an apprenticeship is not to be confused with authoritarianism. The master of a craft does not intend to accept the compliance and admiration of disciples in order to rule over them but rather to transform them into skilled performers. The authority of a master, consequently, is directed toward progressively enlarging the performance skills of novices such that they, in the end, demonstrate that they understand his/her words in so far as they share the ways of seeing and doing prized by the community to which they aspire to belong.

When this is applied to the *Didache*, it becomes clear that novices were not intent upon entering an authoritarian system where they were simply told what to do and what not to do. Rather, novices came forward intent on achieving for themselves the way of being and of doing exemplified by those mentors whom they admired. This demanded an interior transformation that could be achieved only through trusting, person-to-person contacts over an extended period of time in what Polanyi would call an apprenticeship. When a novice first came to his/her spiritual mentor filled with enthusiasm and with admiration, the tacit powers of the novice were far removed from those of his/her mentor, due to long years habituated to pagan ways of thinking and of being in the world. During the opening sessions, more especially, novices undoubtedly found the words of their mentors open to confusion and misunderstanding. What sense, for instance, can someone previously trained to assert oneself and to defend one's honor make of the rule: "Speak well of the one speaking badly of you" (*Did.* 1:3)? Only by virtue of sustained empathy and interior effort did the novice progressively learn to replicate the ways of knowing and the ways of being exemplified by the master. Words that may initially have appeared foolhardy or dangerous became, in the end, filled with divine wisdom.

The same line of development would surround the exposition and assimilation of the training to "be gentle" (*Did.* 3:7) or to "judge justly" (*Did.* 4:3). At every point, the novice would have initially understood the words within his/her own horizon of understanding. Then, by virtue of sustained empathy and interior effort, the novice would gradually pass through an interior conversion whereby, in the end, the words of the master were properly understood within the horizon of understanding that the novice had assimilated during the time of his/her apprenticeship. This horizon of understanding operates in an atmosphere of commitment which, as Polanyi explains, is tantamount to relying on it and dwelling within the manifold emergent meanings and feeling tones that one has assimilated from one's respected master-trainer (Polanyi 1966: 17).

If one accepts the Way of Life spelled out in the *Didache* as implying a prolonged apprenticeship as outlined above, then this suggests certain consequences in how the "training" (*Did.* 1:3) mandated by the *Didache* functioned. Consider, at this point, the following three points:

1. The "training" program set forth in the *Didache* cannot be imagined as something that a mentor would merely recite a few times with the expectation that the novice would somehow immediately discover the depth of meaning intended and spontaneously readjust his/her life accordingly. The Way of Life was merely a bare-bones *training outline*. At every point, the spiritual mentor might have begun by reciting from the Way of Life, but then the mentor and novice would have moved immediately to an exchange bearing on the hidden meanings and spiritual transformation implied in the rule just recited. Only when the spiritual master judged that the novice had sufficiently assimilated for him/herself the horizon of

understanding implied by the rule under consideration would they move on to the next topic.

2. A spiritual mentor undoubtedly knew the entire training outline by heart, and, given the importance of orality in societies habituated to oral traditions, the novice most probably ended up memorizing the Way of Life as the training progressed. It is even possible that mentor and novice together publicly recited the Way of Life as part of the baptismal rite (*Did.* 7:1). Such a recitation would have served as a profession of intent and would have served to celebrate the Way of Life revealed to them by the Father (*Did.* 9:3). The details will be examined in chapter 3. For the moment, however, it suffices to note that since the training outline not only governed the initiation period but mapped out the standards of perfection expected by the Lord on the Last Day (*Did.* 6:2, 16:2), the Way of Life served a lifelong need, and, almost certainly, was progressively memorized during the initiation period.

3. The framing of topics and their sequence within the Way of Life must be suspected, from the onset, as exhibiting a deliberate design and progression. In the course of this chapter, this progression will be investigated and confirmed. For the moment, however, it must be suspected that the internal design and progression of topics within the Way of Life hint at the successful practice of senior mentors who, over a period of time, designed the Way of Life to impart a complete training program while responding to the existential needs of the novices in their care. Thus, minimally, the very existence of the Way of Life must mean that the Didache communities placed a great importance upon training and that spiritual mentors did not create from scratch their own lesson plans but relied upon the outlined Way of Life offered to them. This had the advantage, on the one hand, of making use of the pedagogical experience of senior mentors; on the other hand, it ensured that novices being trained in isolation would each receive a systematic initiation into all essential aspects of the life upon which they were embarking.

Remembering One's Mentor, the Presence of the Lord, and "Trembling"

Those who trained novices were not transmitting something of their own creation. Rather, such masters were "speaking to you the word of God" (*Did.* 4:1); hence, something that they themselves had received. When one explores the eucharistic prayers in chapter 5, it will become apparent that Jesus is identified as "the servant who revealed the Way of Life." The master, in consequence, was also understood as a servant of the Father revealing to the novice the Father's wisdom for living. Where his "dominion" was addressed and taking effect in the life of the novice, there and then the *Didache* speaks of the presence of the Lord being felt—"there the Lord is" (*Did.* 4:1).

At no other point in the *Didache* is there any mention of "presence of the Lord"—not even in the context of the confession of failings or in the celebration of the eucharistic meal. In this community, the presence of the Lord was felt when there was "trembling at the words" and "remember[ing] night and day" the persons who trained their inner dispositions and habits of judgment such that they can walk in the Way of Life revealed by the Father.

The *Didache* notes in passing that the novice becomes one "trembling through all time at the words that you have heard" (*Did.* 3:8). Here again, the internal clues of the *Didache* demonstrate that the Way of Life was not received as mere information. Having been set upon the path of life by "the God who made you" (*Did.* 1:2), the novice trembled with excited anticipation and reverential fear. This was the way that Israel originally experienced the word of the Lord from Mt. Sinai (Ex 19:16) and the way that others after them came to discover the transforming power of God's word (e.g., Ezr 9:4; Is 66:2; Hb 3:16). Thus, among the rabbis, it was a commonplace to remember that every master taught his disciples "with awe and fear, with trembling and trepidation":

> We have been taught: "Make them [the Lord's statutes] known to your children and your children's children" (Dt 4:9). Directly after that it is said, "How you once stood before the Lord your God at Horeb" (Dt 4:10). Even as at Sinai it was with awe and fear, with trembling and trepidation, so in teaching, it should be with awe and fear, with trembling and trepidation. (*b. Berakhot* 22a).

#1H REFLECTIONS ON THE TRIVIALIZATION OF TREMBLING

Many of us today might be tempted to trivialize "trembling" and to imagine that it is only a pious metaphor. On the other hand, readers who have known deeply transformative moments at the hands of significant persons in their own lives might inquire whether this is the stuff of which the *Didache* speaks.

Consider the case of Malcolm X. The *Autobiography of Malcolm X* makes it evident that Malcolm trembled at Elijah Mohammed's words and remembered him night and day during his time in prison (170). This was so, not because someone had told him to do so but because his soul was entirely gripped by the words he had read. These words were liberating him from his way of death and opening him up to embrace his true destiny and calling as a Muslim.

> I still marvel at how swiftly my previous life's thinking patterns slid away from me, like snow off a roof. It is as though someone else I knew of had lived by hustling and crime. I would be startled to catch myself thinking in a remote way of my earlier self as another person. (170)

Malcolm X was entirely "resurrected" through the teachings of the Nation of Islam received from his family and through the personal letters of Elijah Mohammed written to him in prison. In Malcolm's words:

> Every letter I received from them added something to my knowledge of the teachings of Mr. Muhammad. I would sit for long periods and study his photographs. (170)

While he was still in prison, his self-identity as a successful pimp and dope peddler "died" as he trembled during all that time at the words of Elijah Mohammed. When released, Malcolm immersed himself in every aspect of Muslim daily living and visited Chicago repeatedly in order to hear the message of Allah directly from the lips of Elijah Mohammed:

> I have sat at our Messenger's feet, hearing the truth from his own mouth. . . ! I went to bed every night ever more awed. If not Allah, who else could have put such wisdom into that little humble lamb of a man from the Georgia fourth grade and sawmills and cotton patches. . . . My adoration of Mr. Muhammad grew. . . . My worship of him was so awesome that he was the first man whom I had ever feared—not fear such as of a man with a gun, but the fear such as one has of the power of the sun. (210, 211, 212; Clegg: 106)

Elijah Mohammed represented a way of life that powerfully attracted Malcolm. Through letters and later through interpersonal contacts, Malcolm gradually discovered his own calling "to remove the blinders from the eyes of the black man [woman] in the wilderness of North America" (210). This calling emerged for Malcolm within the experience of awe and fear that he spontaneously felt for his teacher:

> To contemplate a person as an ideal is to submit to his authority. The admirer of Elijah Mohammed does not judge him by inde-

pendent previously established standards, but accepts, on the contrary, the figure of Elijah Mohammed as a standard for judging himself. Such an admirer may be mistaken in the choice of a hero, but his relation to greatness is correct. We need reverence to perceive greatness, even as we need a telescope to observe spiral nebulae. (Polanyi 1958: 96, with "Elijah Mohammed" substituted for "Napoleon")

Consider likewise the transformation of a woman. Sue Monk Kidd narrates in *The Dance of the Dissident Daughter* her traumatic journey toward recovering her lost feminine spirituality as she gradually freed herself from the constraints of the deadening patriarchal world view that had dominated her youth. Her journey did not have any single mentor or any single moment of realization; nonetheless, she thought of herself as undergoing an "initiation" that refashioned her identity and purpose in life. Here are her own words:

> Initiation is a rite of passage, a crossing over, a movement between two worlds. For women on a journey such as this one, initiation is the Great Transition. Making this transition into Sacred Feminine experience can be beautiful and deeply moving, even cataclysmic in its effect on our lives. But it also means a time of ordeal, descent, darkness, pain. . . .
>
> Initiation is a sacred disintegration. Despite its pain, we carry the conviction (often very faintly) that even though we don't know where we'll end up, we're following a soul-path of immense richness, that we're supposed to be on this path, that it's required of us somehow. We move in a sense of rightness, of lure, of following a flute that pipes irresistible music. (88)

Every deep initiation involves "a sacred disintegration." The one being transformed is being lured into a new way of being in the world and, at the same time, old habits of thinking and of being in the world are being challenged and are falling away. Thus awe and fear come together as the psychodynamics of deep interior transformation.

My suspicion is that this is the stuff of what the framers of the *Didache* were getting at when they spoke of "trembling through all time at the words that you have heard" (3:8) and of "remember[ing] night and day the one speaking to you the word of God" (4:1). The very use of these phrases in the *Didache* would have been a source of embarrassment and contradiction if novices had never experienced anything resembling them. Minimally, therefore, it would seem safe to conclude that the *Didache* is signaling that novices were not receiving a cool, detached rule of life (as when joining a garden or hiking club). Maximally, it would also seem safe to conclude that the *Didache* is expressing that the deepest longings of the human heart were being addressed and that "trembling" and "remembering" were apt ways of designating the existential response felt in various degrees by each of the novices.

Michael Polanyi has aptly taken note of the fact that novices cannot deeply assimilate for themselves the tacit powers of seeing, judging, and doing exhibited by a master unless they are bound to their mentor by a spontaneous admiration. This spontaneous admiration has a necessary propaedeutic function—the disciple must maintain and enlarge a disposition to self-surrender or else he/she cannot continue to assimilate those habits of mind and those performance skills exhibited by the master. Furthermore, Michael Polanyi has endeavored to demonstrate that this act of submission applies to both someone training to be a practicing physicist as well as someone training to be a practicing Christian (1958: 133, 264–68, 279–88):

> To learn by example is to submit to authority. You follow your master because you trust his manner of doing things even when you cannot analyze and account in detail for its effectiveness. By watching the master and emulating his efforts in the presence of his example, the apprentice unconsciously picks up the rules of the art, including those which are not [explicitly] known [or referred to] by the master himself. These hidden rules can be assimilated only by a person who surrenders himself to that extent uncritically to the imitation of another. (Polanyi 1958: 53)

The reverence undergirding every apprenticeship is not infallible. Novices cannot judge the true worth of the skills of any given master because, for the moment, they are excluded from participating in the very skills by which such an adequate judgment can be made. Masters, for their part, sometimes turn out to be pedantic in their methods and give themselves over to fits of jealousy when a novice begins to rival or surpass their own level of performance. Under the best of circumstances, however, masters have the skill to progressively enlarge the performance skills of their disciples until they become colleagues and, in some instances, rivals. Secular commitments to art, music, science, and medicine advance through the cultivation of shared skills pursued under the stimulus of overarching ideals. Religious societies dedicated to the discovery, transmission, and bold implementation of God's Way of Life within the concrete conditions here on earth cannot do otherwise.

The Progression within the Training Program

For the most part, the various topics taken up in the training in the Way of Life have been exhaustively studied from the vantage point of trying to discern how the author of the *Didache* functioned as an editor who, here or there, may have deliberately altered his sources or who, here or there, may have been influenced by parallel sentiments expressed in texts that may or may not have been known to him. When this process becomes very sophisticated, it makes it appear as though the *Didache* was composed using a cut-and-paste method whereby successive editors, each with her or his own particular theology and purposes, each representing a particular time and place in the life of the community, were constrained to splice together a document that had the character of a montage rather than a unified whole. This method of viewing a document obscures the fact that the document was created in order to express and transform a living community of action and thought standing behind the text. This method of viewing a document also derails the quest for examining how the given progression of topics may be meticulously set out to reflect the actual or the intended practice of skilled and successful practitioners in the community.

When the text is closely examined over a period of time, one gradually discovers a certain progression of topics that gives the Way of Life a pastorally sophisticated movement from beginning to end. Consider, for example, three illustrative cases:

1. The opening of the training program brings the candidate face to face with how to love "enemies." Since Matthew and Luke place words like this on the lips of Jesus, most scholars have been prone to imagine that these words of Jesus were placed up front in order to "christianize" a preexisting Two-Way tradition that originated in the Jewish synagogue (see #1j). The problem with this hypothesis is that it skews our reading of the text: (a) It blocks us from noticing that the Way of Life says nothing about making idols, honoring parents, keeping the Sabbath—agenda central to synagogue practice. (b) By assigning only a few opening sayings to Jesus, we are blocked from imagining that Jesus would have endorsed and lived the entire content of the Way of Life since he was a practicing Jew. (c) Given the large scope of sayings attributed to Jesus in the Gospels, we are blocked from asking how and why certain sayings and not others would have been selected at the beginning of the training program.

Seen from the vantage point of an orderly progression of topics, however, the initial section dealing with praying for enemies and turning the other cheek would appear to be placed at the head of the training program because new recruits had to be immediately prepared to respond to the abusive treatment by outsiders (*Did.* 1:3f.). When examined in detail (as will be done in ch. 12), the "enemies" in this case were not highway robbers or Roman soldiers but relatives and friends who had become "enemies" as a result of the candidate's new religious convictions. Thus, praying and fasting for such "enemies" functioned to provide the necessary orientation for sustaining a comprehensive nonviolent surrender to the abusive family situation hinted at in *Did.* 1:4. Among other things, the abusive family situation envisioned the forcible seizure of the novice's goods (1:4[D]), and the candidate was instructed to yield completely to such hostile acts and at the same time to surrender his goods to beggars (1:5), not because of any compulsion but simply because his/her "Father" wished it. Implicit here is the contrast between a natural father who may be authorizing the tight-fisted seizure of his daughter's or son's assets with that "new Father" who generously gives to all and invites imitation. The possibility of understanding the text as addressing such existential needs at the beginning of the training process cannot be sought unless it is presumed that the *Didache* reflects a training process fashioned and modified over a period of time to address the situation of real candidates.

2. Within the training program, the issue of giving is taken up at the beginning and again near the end. The first giving (*Did.* 1:4) is presented in the present imperative and represents the kind of giving the candidate was expected to practice immediately upon entering upon his/her apprenticeship. The second section on giving (4:5–8), however, is much more than a reinforcement of the earlier giving. Now everything (save 4:5) is presented in the future tense, and the focus is on the routine "taking and giving" and the much more extensive "partnering" of all one's resources "with your brother" (4:8). The future tense used here could function as a mild imperative (as in English), but this would leave the awkward situation whereby two diverse rules of giving are provided and no attempt is made to harmonize them. On the other hand, if one examines the second set of rules for giving, one discovers that this later giving involves sharing one's resources with members of the community—a situation that would prevail only after the time the candidate had gained admittance as a full member of the movement through baptism. These two sections dealing with giving, far from being a senseless repetition occasioned by the mindless combining of preexistent sources, represent a thoughtful progression wherein the giving of the first kind aptly develops habits of mind and of practice that prepare for and ensure the kind of giving necessitated following baptism. Since the first rule of giving is intended for immediate implementation, it is presented as an imperative. The second section on giving, being in the future tense, then accurately reflects preparing for what is to come

and is not yet. Here again, by allowing that the *Didache* is more than a wooden collage of sources and by allowing that it reflects a training program in action, one can gain hints as to the pastoral genius underlying its composition.

3. The absolute prohibition against eating "the food sacrificed to idols" (*Did.* 6:3) occurs after the conclusion of the training program and just prior to baptism. One could imagine that the sources used by the editor of the *Didache* placed them outside the Way of Life instruction and, as a result, the editor was constrained to make an awkward addition after the close of the Two Ways section. On the other hand, the placement of this important and absolute injunction may have evolved in order to address a practical purpose. As long as candidates were in training, they were obliged to refrain from attending the sacred community meals (9:5). Of necessity, therefore, most candidates would have been constrained to take part in family meals wherein, either regularly or periodically, some offering was made to the household gods as part of the meal or some portion of the meats served had been previously offered at a public altar. Only with baptism a few days away, therefore, could the candidate be expected to be bound by this new rule. During these few days, it is no accident that the candidate was told to fast (7:4). The one baptizing and able members of the community fasted in solidarity with the candidate (7:4). During this period, all "the food sacrificed to idols" eaten by the candidates was expelled, and they were prepared for eating only the pure and sacred food at the homes of "brothers and sisters," since the former communion meals binding them to ancestral gods would now be forever forbidden to them. When the *Didache* is expected to yield an orderly progression of topics, the rule of eating (6:3) no longer appears out of the blue as the opening to the so-called liturgical section; rather, the prohibition against eating foods sacrificed to idols comes at precisely the time when it would have been pastorally prudent to have it implemented. Thus, here again the placement of topics in the *Didache* is seen as deliberate and as reflecting a sound pastoral practice.

Section III: Particular Aspects of This Apprenticeship

An Overview of the Training Program

Within the text of the *Didache*, there are linguistic clues that delineate particular lists and that signal beginnings and endings. Using these linguistic clues, one could outline the Two Ways section of the *Didache* as follows:

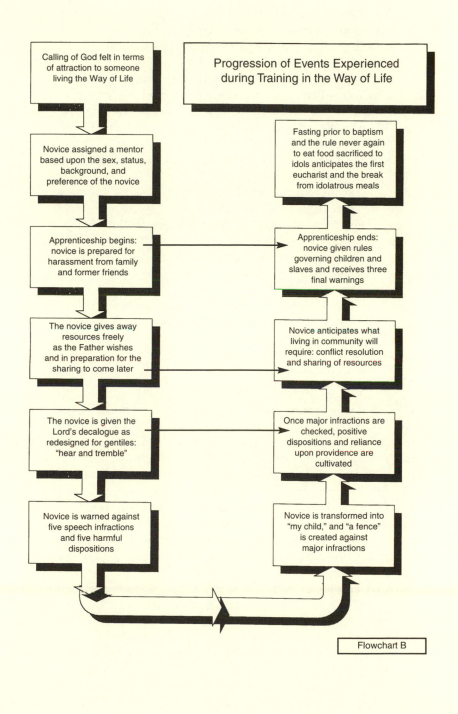

Calling of God felt in terms of attraction to someone living the Way of Life

Progression of Events Experienced during Training in the Way of Life

Novice assigned a mentor based upon the sex, status, background, and preference of the novice

Fasting prior to baptism and the rule never again to eat food sacrificed to idols anticipates the first eucharist and the break from idolatrous meals

Apprenticeship begins: novice is prepared for harassment from family and former friends

Apprenticeship ends: novice given rules governing children and slaves and receives three final warnings

The novice gives away resources freely as the Father wishes and in preparation for the sharing to come later

Novice anticipates what living in community will require: conflict resolution and sharing of resources

The novice is given the Lord's decalogue as redesigned for gentiles: "hear and tremble"

Once major infractions are checked, positive dispositions and reliance upon providence are cultivated

Novice is warned against five speech infractions and five harmful dispositions

Novice is transformed into "my child," and "a fence" is created against major infractions

Flowchart B

A. The Way of Life defined (1:2)
    1. Defined positively (two great commandments)
    2. Defined negatively (negative golden rule)
B. Training for the Way of Life (1:3–4:14)
    1. How to love outsiders (preparing for abuse)
        a. Four admonitions regarding enemies (1:3)
        b. Four case studies of yielding to enemies (1:4)
        c. Special case of yielding to those in need (1:5f.)
    2. Prohibitions (the secondary rule) (2:1–7)
        a. Decalogue (5 x 2) of action prohibitions for gentiles (2:2)
        b. Five speech prohibitions (2:3–5)
        c. Five proscribed dispositions (2:6)
        d. Three degrees of love (2:7)
        e. Five "fences"—wisdom from a father/mother (3:2–6)
    3. How to love insiders (once you have joined us)
        a. Three rules for cultivating "gentleness" (3:7–10)
        b. Three rules for community relations (4:1–4)
        c. Three rules for sharing internally (4:5–8)
        d. Three rules for household management (4:9–11)
        e. Three concluding cautions (4:12–14)
C. The Way of Death illustrated (5:1f.)
    1. Twenty-two accursed acts
    2. Twenty accursed persons
D. Closing blessing and curse (6:1f.)

The training program opens with pragmatic instructions for how to love abusive outsiders (B1); the program closes with pragmatic rules on how one will love insiders (B3). Since the abusive outsiders are members of one's biological family (see ch. 12 below), B1 equips novices to neutralize the hostility of their biological families, while B3 equips novices to take part in the lovingkindness of their soon-to-be-experienced spiritual family. Accordingly, the instructions of B1 are in the present imperative, implying that they demand immediate implementation; the instructions of B3, on the other hand, are almost entirely framed in the future tense, implying that they anticipate implementation once one has become a member of the community at baptism.

Both B1 and B3 are largely preoccupied with positive prescriptions for action. Sandwiched in the middle (B2) are the negative prohibitions, which apply with equal force to outsiders as well as insiders. Everything here is framed in the simple future, which, in Greek as in English, functions as a mild imperative and imitates the language of the Decalogue found in the Septuagint.

Almost exactly midway in the training program, one discovers a marked transition in the relationship existing between the one training and the one being trained. Here, for the first time, the novice is addressed as "my child" (*Did.* 3:1–6). This verbal clue signals that the master at this point becomes, by implication, the "mother" or "father" transmitting to his beloved offspring wisdom for living. One is prepared for this transition by 2:7, which starts out by saying, "you will not hate any person," and ends by noting that "some you will love more than your own soul." First among those in the latter category will be the spiritual father or mother whom the novice "will remember night and day" and "honor as the Lord" (4:1). One will soon discover that the *Didache* deliberately leaves out the commandment in the Decalogue calling for honoring father and mother; hence, by implication, the spiritual mentor becomes the new "father" or "mother" who will be honored. The acquisition of a new "mother" or "father" has deep roots in rabbinic tradition (see #1t) and serves as the transition point toward preparing to embrace a new "family" of brothers and sisters (as taken up in B3).

The third segment of training (B3) quickly drops the imperative and moves into the future tense, which will be uniformly used after *Did.* 3:9 to the very end (with the sole exception of 4:5). While this use of the future could be interpreted as a mild imperative (as in the previous section), the training in this section clearly looks forward to a situation that will prevail only after baptism. For example, the novice is told that he/she will no longer "be joined with the lofty" but "will dwell" with the "lowly" (3:9) and "every day" he/she will seek out "the presence of the saints" (4:2)— persons whom, for the moment, the novice cannot be expected to recognize. Furthermore, this section deals with training on how to "reprove against failings" (4:3), how to "partner-together all things with your brother [sister]" (4:8), and how to "confess your failings" (4:14) before the eucharist—all actions presupposing prior acceptance into the community. Since novices are expressly barred from admission to the community assemblies prior to baptism (9:5), the whole content of B3 must be understood as preparing for participation in their new "family."

As suggested above, training in the Way of Life follows a pragmatic, pastoral progression. The novice begins by being prepared to withstand the hostility of family and friends—the first thing that the novice can be expected to encounter. Next, the decalogue and its extensions are considered as the rules for living revealed by the Father. Finally, just prior to baptism, the novice is equipped with the skills necessary to live in the new "family" that will embrace him or her following baptism. Meanwhile, the novice has, in mid-course, gained a new "father" or "mother" who already is honored in place of biological parents and who prepares to bring forth the new member into the life of the community at the time of baptism.

B1 includes linguistic groupings of four; B2 favors groupings of five (or ten); B3 relies upon groupings of three. These groupings undoubtedly aided easy oral memorization. The significance of sets of four, five, and three, however, are not evident to us; yet my suspicion would be that the framers of the *Didache* gave some significance to these numbers. In any case, the set of twenty-two accursed acts illustrating the Way of Death appears to be rooted in the Yom Kippur tradition of confessing twenty-two failings in alphabetical order following the twenty-two letters of the Hebrew alphabet (Harris: 82).

#11 THE APPEAL OF PAGAN RELIGIONS

The term *pagani* ("pagan") originally meant "the inhabitants of the Italian countryside." Since Christianity during the fourth century came to dominate urban centers, "pagan" came to mean those backwater and ignorant holdouts refusing to accept the truth of Christianity. As the church fathers began to see the impious and immoral practices of pagans as the direct result of their false gods, a term of superiority gradually became a term of contempt. Only in the modern world, when dialogue has replaced slander, has it become possible to regard pagan religions as cultivating honorable ways of life deserving of our respect and understanding. Thomas M. Finn, following upon his study of paganism in the ancient world, accordingly observed:

> A steady stream of invective caused people, ancient and modern, to equate Paganism with false religion and immorality and to see it as a mixture of magic, superstition, and primitive depravity. As a result, it is hard to imagine sincere Pagans who lived devout, selfless, and reflective lives. Nor is it easy for people to concede vitality to the Pagan religions, in spite of the fact that ancient literature and inscriptions abound with testimonies to the devout Pagan in the Greco-Roman world. (Finn: 46)

The god Asclepius, for example, was widely worshiped with hymns, processions, and sacrifices. As a divine healer, Asclepius was imitated by his followers, who exercised a gentle and watchful care of the sick that resulted in healing the spirit along with the body. The following temple inscription depicts the devotee as being drawn to his shrine, where he expects to be blessed by Asclepius, who "alone" among all the gods proves a worthy Savior and Refuge and Healer:

> Asclepius, child of Apollo, these words come from your devoted servant. Blessed one, God whom I yearn for, how shall I enter

your golden house unless your heart incline towards me and you will to heal me and restore me to your shrine again, so that I may look on my God, who is brighter than earth in springtime? Divine, Blessed One, you alone have power. With your loving kindness, you are a great gift from the supreme gods to mankind, a refuge from trouble. (cited in Finn: 49)

Pilgrims would come to the temples of Asclepius (the most famous being in Epidaurus, Greece) with something of the pious expectation associated with those coming to Lourdes. After preliminary purification and sacrifices, the priests of the sanctuary would endeavor to discern which pilgrims were being invited "to incubate" (that is, sleep) within the inner courts during the night when the God roamed about (Finn: 55). The following testimonial is telling:

Ambrosia of Athens, blind of one eye. She came as a suppliant to the God. As she walked about in the temple, she laughed at some of the cures as incredible and impossible. . . . In her sleep she had a vision. It seemed to her that the God stood by her and said that he would cure her. . . . After saying this, he cut the diseased eyeball and poured in some drug. When day came she walked out sound. (cited in Finn: 55)

The worship of Asclepius was an old cult. In contrast, the veneration of Isis was a new religion of Egyptian origin, which, during the first two centuries, flourished throughout the empire. The worship of Isis involved a process of initiation involving awe-inspiring rites. In the eyes of the initiate, Isis was queen of heaven and of the underworld, and the life of the devotee was "wholly governed by her providence" (cited in Finn: 72) and thereby preserved from the practitioners of magic and from the indifference of the Fates. Isis, for example, proclaimed to one of her followers:

I will favor you and you will constantly worship me. But if by assiduous obedience, worshipful service, and determined celibacy you win the favor of my godhead, you will know that I— and I alone—can even prolong your life beyond the limits determined by your fate. (cited in Finn: 73)

The Romans, for their part, practiced traditional rites associated with major undertakings. For example, the Elder Cato prepared a manual on agriculture and, as was to be expected, he provided the appropriate religious rites necessitated in this domain. Before cutting down a stand of trees, for example, Cato prescribed the necessity of sacrificing a pig (a favorite offering to lesser gods; *ABD* 6:1131f.) while invoking the pardon of any gods disturbed by this action:

> Whatever god or goddess you are to whom this is sacred, you have the right to the sacrifice of a pig in return for cutting of this sacred copse. May it be right to do it, whether I do it or anyone acting on my orders. Therefore by sacrificing this pig in expiation I make this prayer, that you may be willing to be propitious towards me, my household, my servants, and my children. (*Agriculture* 139)

The boundaries between two farms were instinctively recognized as a dangerous place, and, accordingly, the god Terminus was invoked annually by the two households concerned. In a shared religious ceremony, the two families assembled at the boundary stone or stump and celebrated the following rites at dawn:

> Terminus, whether you are a stone or a wooden stump buried in the field, your power also has been respected since antiquity. Two landowners crown you from different sides, they bring you two garlands and two sacrificial cakes. There is an altar [prepared] to which the peasant woman herself brings fire taken from the warm hearth in a piece of pottery. An old man chops up firewood. . . . Next he feeds the incipient flames with pieces of dry bark. A boy stands by holding a flat basket in his hands. Then when he has thrown three handfuls of corn into the flames, a little girl offers the sliced honeycombs. Others hold the wine; some of each is dedicated to the flames. They look on, and, dressed in white, keep sacred silence. (Ovid *Fasti* 640–52)

Roman parents, meanwhile, were accustomed to performing many rites as a way of ensuring the blessings of a multitude of gods and goddesses associated with bearing and raising children. In this segment, Augustine rattles off the gods known to him and asks whether these are the activities of various individual gods or whether they all can be attributed to a single supreme god?

> Should we also suppose that this ultimate godhead [Jupiter] is visible in that multitude of [events attributed to the] so-called plebeian gods? [If so,] let him be in charge of men's seed in the person of Liber, and of that of women as Libera. Let him be Diespater to bring children [conceived in the womb] into the light of day; Mena, whom the Romans put in charge of women's monthly periods; Lucina, who is called on for help in childbirth.

> Let him be called Ops for helping the new-born by placing them on the surface of the earth; when he opens the infant's mouth for the first time to let him cry, let him be called Vaticanus; as Levana, let him look after the new-born child from the ground; as Cunina let him be said to guard the child's cradle. . . . When supervising children's drinking, they call him Potina, where supervising their eating, Educa. When children are scared, he overcomes them as Paventia. When hope comes, let him be Venilia. . . . When they learn to count, call him Numeria; when they learn to sing, Camena. . . . Let him appear as the goddess Juventas when a young man lays aside his child's toga, and as Fortuna Barbata when he first grows a beard. Let him be the god Jugatinus when joining man and wife in marriage. . . . If it cause no embarrassment, let Jupiter appear in all these aspects, and many that I have not listed here. (*City of God* 4.11)

While many Romans were gravitating toward one or the other form of monotheism during the opening centuries of the common era, Augustine's recital still indicates how traditional Roman believers had effectively compartmentalized the domain of the lesser gods. Aside from the great gods worshiped by the state, therefore, a multitude of gods held sway over various aspects of domestic life.

When one travels to modern India, one quickly discovers that parallel notions of polytheism hold sway there as well. Similarly, in the Catholicism of my youth, various saints specialized in bringing aid to certain difficulties. There was undoubtedly a certain comfort and guidance in imagining that the assistance of specialized holy ones with divine influence would be forthcoming when handling troublesome aspects of daily life.

All in all, the allure of ancient pagan religious practices should not be doubted or shortchanged. Persons in all walks of life believed in the efficacy of the gods and took care to secure the protection/blessings of these gods. Furthermore, many pagan cults were occasions for civic celebrations and offered public rites, oratory, drama, athletic contests, and the like. "To measure paganism by expressions of educated skepticism is to concentrate on a very small fraction of the cities' upper classes" (Fox: 64).

Learning to Serve God Within a Pragmatic Theology

The opening agenda of the *Didache* is clearly consumed with spelling out the solemn commitments of the community. The author of the *Didache* does not argue for the wisdom, for the pragmatism, for the ratio-

nal superiority of the Way of Life over the Way of Death. Rather, this superiority is presumed. With a calm assurance, the opening lines simply declare
what is evident, namely, that every individual is walking upon a life path
and that essentially only two exist: the path of life and the path of death.

Didache 1–6 is directed toward defining how a novice ought to be
trained (1:3). The framers of the *Didache* were not content to present
either a rationally compelling nor a divinely revealed set of propositions
about the nature of God. Moreover, they were consumed with "how to
live" and only secondarily with "how to believe." Given this leaning, references to God come in only as a way of enforcing praxis. Consider, for
example, the first and second references to God:

1. The first reference to God comes in when the Way of Life is defined:
"you will love the God who made you" (1:2). God, in the first instance, is
specified quite simply and pragmatically as the fashioner of the individual
being addressed. Quite clearly, the focus is not the universe as a whole.

The implied theology here follows from the Jewish understanding that
the man implants the seed (*semen* in Latin) in the fertile womb of a woman,
but then he goes away in ignorance while God takes over and sees to it
growth and development:

> For it was you [O Lord] who formed my inward parts;
>   you knit me together in my mother's womb.
> I praise you, for I am fearfully and wonderfully made.
> . . . .
> My [skeletal] frame was not hidden from you
>   when I was being made in secret, intricately woven. . . .
> Your eyes beheld my unformed [embryonic] substance. (Ps 139:13–16)

The notion that DNA molecules contain the entire blueprint of the living
being was entirely foreign to the ancient Hebrews. If the seed grew into an
embryo, it was molded by the Lord God who worked unobtrusively and
secretly within the human womb (Jer 31:7–9; Is 44:1–3, 21–24, 66:5–13;
Jb 31:15; Wis 7:1f.; Sir 1:14; Gal 1:15). In the face of this mysterious and
majestic activity during nine months, a spontaneous response was forthcoming: "I praise you, for I am fearfully and wonderfully made" (Ps
139:14). As a pragmatic theology, therefore, the framers of the *Didache*
combined "the God who made you" with the one "you will love" (1:2).
The love of God, by implication, emerged out of a sense of gratitude and
awe for having been so marvelously fashioned in the womb.

2. The second reference to God shows up in *Did.* 1:5. At issue is the
practice of yielding to the requests of those in need. The response is "to
give" precisely because God, now identified as "the Father," wishes it. The
love of one's neighbor in need, as seen here, is not primarily directed
toward cultivating feelings of compassion or developing an ideology of dis-

tributive justice. Feelings and ideology may be there or they may be absent. For the moment, the praxis of yielding is motivated by a yielding to the Father's wish in this matter. Three aspects of this giving stand out:

a. The *Didache* is the oldest known Christian document that makes it clear that, in the act of giving, what is given has been freely received from the Father. In effect, therefore, the one giving acts as a faithful steward or broker who dispenses "his own [the Father's] free gifts" to those making their requests known. This evaluation of personal possessions finds clear expression in other Christian and Jewish documents as well (see #2d).

b. The implied theology here is *imitatio dei* ("the imitation of God")— "loving him, you will be an imitator of his goodness" (*Diognetus* 10). God gives freely; hence, in imitation of the one who has blessed the novice with the necessities of life, the novice acts in a parallel fashion as a faithful steward of God's possessions.

c. The novice is prohibited from feeling proud or generous in the act of giving since whatever he or she gives belonged to the Father to begin with. The one receiving, meanwhile, need not feel humiliated or indebted to the one giving, since, in point of fact, the recipient is receiving what the Father intends. The *Derek Eres Zuta,* a third-century training manual for rabbinic students, echoes the same theology:

> If you did a great favor [for someone], regard it as small,
>   and do not say, "I did this good act with my own [money]."
> Rather it was [from what God] had graciously given you,
>   and you should offer thanks to Heaven. (2:10)

This illustration aptly captures how a pragmatic theology functions. The doctrine of God is introduced in order to orient correct action. The novice is never faced with some abstract notion of God or simply urged "to believe in God." Rather, at every point, the novice is trained to arrange his/her life such that the free gifts and the wishes of God are taken into account.

#1j WHETHER THE WAY OF LIFE ORIGINATED IN THE SYNAGOGUE

For the greater part of this century, nearly all the major commentators have come to the conclusion that the Two Ways existed as an independent text (a kind of Jewish handbook for proselytes) that was superficially "christianized" by the addition of sayings of Jesus (*Did.* 1:3b–5a). According to J. Rendel Harris, this idea "was proposed originally by Taylor [1886: 18–23] and has since been elaborated by Harnack" (Harris: 40).

Jean-Paul Audet, a French Canadian, gave concrete expression to this hypothesis in his massive 700-page commentary on the *Didache* published in 1958. Audet brought to his commentary his rich familiarity with Jewish sources and, at nearly every point in the text, Audet discovered Jewish parallels. Audet identified the Two Ways (*Did.* 1–5) accordingly as "belonging to the genre of an 'instruction on the commandments' . . . as it was being practiced by the contemporary synagogue" (Audet 1958: 284). Willy Rordorf, twenty years later, regarded the first five chapters of the *Didache* as "essentially Jewish, but the Christian community was able to use it as such" (1978a: 28) with the addition of the "evangelical section" (1:3b–5a). Nearly twenty years after him, John S. Kloppenborg even goes so far as to affirm that "in the final form of the *Didache*, of course, the presence of sayings of Jesus, which the reader presumably is intended to recognize as such, amounts to a 'Christianization' of the document" (1995: 98).

One has to be cautious when suggesting that the Way of Life exhibits a superficial christianization of a preexisting Jewish document. This is so for three reasons:

1. At no point does the *Didache* itself participate in this mentality, for example, by assigning an early section to Jesus and a latter section to Moses. According to the internal logic of the text, the entire Way of Life constitutes "the word of God" (*Did.* 4:1) "revealed to us" by the Father "through your servant Jesus" (9:2). Furthermore, the absence of any known Gospel (see ch. 11 below) would have meant that there may have been no known reason, outside of the *Didache* itself, for recognizing (as Kloppenborg suggested above) just certain sayings as belonging to Jesus.

2. The *Didache* presupposes that Jesus is rooted in Judaism and, as a consequence, his message ought not to be narrowly localized in those places where he can be shown to stand apart from Judaism. The Jewish scholar H.G. Enelow has rightly noted that both Jews and Christians have brought to the message of Jesus a considerable bias:

> Jewish writers have tried to prove that anything taught by Jesus may be found in the Jewish literature, and that therefore he could not be called original; while Christians have deemed it necessary to defend Jesus against the charge of borrowing or reproducing from Jewish sources, lest his originality be impugned (14).

Another instance of this bias is the "criterion of dissimilarity" commonly used by critical scholars bent upon recovering the historical Jesus. This criterion was first formulated by Rudolph Bultmann, popularized by Norman Perrin as "the strongest criterion for authenticity that contemporary research has found" (Perrin: 38), and routinely used by the Jesus Seminar. According to Perrin, a saying attributed to Jesus in the Synoptic Gospels can be deemed "authentic if it can be shown to be dissimilar to characteristic emphases both of ancient Judaism and of the early Church" (Perrin: 39). The use of this principle has the effect of singling out as "authentic" those sayings wherein Jesus diverges from what we know of the first-century Judaisms and of disparaging those sayings of Jesus wherein there is common ground within Judaism.

Over and against this either-or mentality, it must be allowed that the early church embraced a Jesus who was both Jewish and original at the same time. Hence the entire content of the Way of Life can be thought of as both Jewish and original at the same time. No one need suppose, therefore, that *Did.* 1:3b–5a provides an original Christian "addition" to a preexistent Jewish formation program. Nor can it be presupposed that Jesus and his disciples never taught or endorsed Jewish beliefs and practices beyond those expressly cited in the Synoptic Gospels.

3. Finally, no Jewish source has come down to us that specifically makes use of the Way of Life as found in the *Didache*. In fact, all the variations of the Way of Life that have come down to us find inclusion only in Christian sources. This opens up the possibility that the Way of Life was crafted expressly by the disciples of Jesus for use in a gentile environment.

The upshot of this whole discussion is the recognition that the whole of the Way of Life was seen, by the framers of the *Didache*, as having originated from Jesus. Since Jesus was a committed Jew and so were all his early disciples, one has to be careful when drawing a firm line between what originated in the synagogue and what originated in the church. The scholars cited above, therefore, have to be challenged not to introduce into our understanding of the *Didache* what the text itself would have found "foreign." More positively, the possibility has to be allowed that the Way of Life was first crafted by Jewish Christians precisely to address the need for a systematic formation for gentiles prior to their baptism.

Furthermore, the variant forms of the Way of Life that have come down to us make it evident that such a formation took hold both within the Didache communities and outside of them. No single text, however, has been established as "the source" used by the framers of the *Didache*. Even if, therefore, it is assumed that the framers of the *Didache* made use of a preexisting oral tradition or manual (whether Jewish or Christian), it must nevertheless be allowed that the framers of the *Didache* modified that tradition in order to address the specific pastoral circumstances encountered in their communities. This strategy undergirds the present study of the *Didache*. Accordingly, the presence of sayings regarding "loving your enemies" and "turning the other cheek" (1:3b–5a) will be interpreted as clues revealing the nature of the abusive treatment experienced by novices and the program for countering such harassment. Likewise, the material in the third section of the training (B3) will be carefully correlated with what can be learned of community life in the latter chapters of the text. Thus, for example, the preparation for "reprov[ing] against failings" (4:3) finds its fulfillment in 15:3. Similarly, the early warning given to a novice that "you will confess your failings in church" (4:14) finds its fulfillment in 14:1–3. This is what is required if one wishes to respect the unity and integrity of the received text.

Preparing Novices for Abusive Treatment

The training of novices begins with a practical preparation for bad words and for bad treatment. Since Matthew and Luke include variations on *Did.* 1:3b–4 in their Gospels, these texts have received extensive commentary. In most instances, these texts have been used to demonstrate that Christians are required not to retaliate in the face of abusive treatment. Gerd Theissen, on the other hand, has distinguished himself by endeavoring to discover the deeper significance of these texts by reconstructing the social setting in which these sayings originated. In so doing, Theissen's origination hypothesis enables him to observe that these sayings could not have applied to "Christians in general" but only to those "wandering charismatics" who functioned as itinerant prophets (as did Jesus) and received public scorn analogous to that heaped upon Cynics within Roman society during this same period (1992: 146–48). Chapter 12 takes up Theissen's arguments in detail. For our purposes here, however, the following conclusions deserve attention:

1. The members of the *Didache* were not suffering from any generalized persecution. Nor, more specifically, were the sayings regarding praying for enemies and turning the other cheek being used to address "experiences of the Jewish War and the postwar era" (Theissen 1992: 136). By examining the four conditional clauses in *Did.* 1:4, one notes that they contain nothing that even approximates the realities followed the Jewish War, namely, mass crucifixions of thousands of men, rape and enslavement of thousands of women, forced-labor (such as the building of the ramp at Masada), which drove untold thousands of undernourished and overworked captives to their death.

2. Nor, following the analysis of Theissen, can it be imagined that someone giving "you a blow on the cheek" and taking "away your cloak" (*Did.* 1:4 and Lk 6:29f.) is in the midst of "a holdup" which "generally took place on the open highway" (Theissen 1992: 142).

> The loss of clothing is not the first concern of victims of a mugging (wherever this might take place). Even in Luke's parable, the Samaritan who fell among robbers on the Jerusalem-Jerico road was stripped, beaten, and left half-dead (Lk 10:30). Nothing in the parable suggests that this was excessive or unusual treatment (e.g., because he foolishly put up a struggle). Rather, the narrative is told as though this was the usual treatment that highway robbers afforded to victims. . . . (Milavec 1995a: 134)

Thus, whatever Luke 6:29 had in mind, it seems doubtful that Luke's hearers would have been thinking of highway robbers. With even greater force, it seems doubtful that new recruits to the Didache communities would be given preparation for a holdup as their first lesson.

3. According to my reconstruction, the abusive treatment suggested in *Did.* 1:4 is expressly directed toward new members, who, it might be surmised, would ordinarily be expected to meet resistance to their new religious commitments on the part of family and friends. Thus, one is dealing here with the kind of harassment that a socially powerful group imposes upon "deviants" within its own boundaries who have gone over to a "socially unacceptable" way of life (details in ch. 12).

The first abusive behavior, for example, envisions "a blow on the right cheek" (*Did.* 1:4). Scholars have widely accepted this as designating an insult. Walter Wink, who is solidly attentive to first-century traditions, expresses this as follows:

> A blow by the right fist [or open hand] in that right-handed world would land on the *left* cheek of the opponent. An open-handed slap would also strike the left cheek. To hit the right cheek with a fist would require using the left hand, but in that society the left hand was used only for unclean tasks [e.g., toilet cleansing]. . . . The only way one could naturally strike the right cheek with the right hand would be with the back of the hand. The intention is clearly not to injure but to humiliate, to put someone in his or her place. (Wink 1992: 176)

Wink further surmises that "one normally does not strike a peer thus" (1992: 176). The Mishnah would support this when it decrees that, if a man smacks an equal "with the back of his hand, he pays him four hundred zuz" (*m. Baba Qamma* 8:6). If a man so treats his slave, however, "slaves are not subject to compensation for indignity" (ibid., 8:3). Here the governing principle is: "Everything is in accord with one's station" (ibid., 8:6). Thus, masters backhanding slaves, husbands backhanding their wives, and parents backhanding their children would seem to constitute "excusable conduct" within rabbinic circles.

Interesting enough, the cases of dyadic strife detailed in Mt 10:34–36 would all constitute instances wherein backhanding by the second person in the dyad would be permitted:

> Do not think that I have come to bring peace on earth: I have not come to bring peace, but a sword. For I have come to set a man against his father, and a daughter against her mother, and a daughter-in-law against her mother-in-law; and a man's enemies will be those of his own household.

Note that the son-in-law is not mentioned relative to the father-in-law for the very reason that they do not live and work together. Nor is husband–wife, brother–brother, or sister–sister strife mentioned. John Dominic Crossan is correct when he perceptively calls attention to the fact that all the divisions are cross-generational:

> Jesus says that he will tear it [the family] apart. The usual explanation is that families will become divided as some accept and others refuse faith in Jesus. But notice where and how emphatically the axis of separation is located. It is precisely *between the generations*. (1994: 60)

Putting this all together, one can imagine that the "blow on the right cheek" might signal the outcome of an altercation between father and son (or between mother and daughter). The father demands that his son withdraw his sympathies from the Christians. The son, for his part, defends the Jesus movement and reveals to his father his determination to join them. The father first tries to dissuade his son using reasonable arguments. When these arguments repeatedly fail, the father feels (rightly) that his son's filial piety has been eroded by this "sect"; he becomes totally frustrated, and, in exasperation, he backhands his son on the right cheek (to bring him to his senses). The son, prepared for this confrontation by prayer and fasting (as specified in *Did.* 1:3, with Jewish parallels found in the *Testament of Joseph* 18:2 and the *Testament of Benjamin* 5:4–5), might be expected to attempt to defuse the situation by reaffirming his love for his father while at the same time reaffirming his choice of the Christian way of life. "Turning the other cheek" should not be interpreted as a son bating his father "to strike him" in addition to insulting him. Rather, the sense is that the son takes no measure to defend himself or to retaliate. The son, it must be remembered, might in some or most instances be physically stronger than his father.

The remaining abuses can also be accounted for as illustrating the kind of harassment that a socially powerful group imposes upon "deviants" within its own boundaries who have gone over to a "socially unacceptable" way of life. The "enemies" of *Did.* 1:3, therefore, are not Roman soldiers or highway robbers but parents and relatives who openly oppose the new religious commitments of the novice. The details are worked out in ch. 12 below.

#1k Savage Attack on Filial Piety in the Synoptic Tradition

While many authors have noted that the Jesus tradition has some hard sayings regarding family ties, Crossan situates the earliest layers of the Jesus tradition as portraying "an almost savage attack on family values" (1994: 58). The first sign of this is found among the 108 sayings of Jesus listed in the *Gospel of Thomas:*

> Jesus said: "Whoever does not hate father and mother cannot be a follower of me, and whoever does not hate brothers and sisters . . . will not be worthy of me." (*Gos. Thom.* 55)

The attack on family bonds continues in Mk 3:31–35, where Jesus receives word that "his mother and his brothers" are standing outside— they refuse to sit and to take their place among Jesus' disciples. As a result, Jesus shames and disowns his family by looking at those sitting around him and saying, "Here are my mother and brothers! Whoever does the will of God is my brother and sister and mother" (Mk 3:35). Why does Jesus treat his own family members so harshly? According to Mark's Gospel, his own family is not coming to hear God's word but "to seize him" because, in their judgment, "he is beside himself" (Mk 3:21). This could mean that they thought he had gone berserk and was an embarrassment to them; hence, they wanted to seize him, take him home, and keep him out of the public eye. Mark thus demonstrates that even Jesus had to choose between his love for "his mother and his brothers" and his public calling to antici- pate and proclaim the kingdom of God.

Anyone who would be his disciple also would have to make this same choice. A disciple said to him, "Lord, let me first go bury my father" (Mt 8:21). Here is an expression of filial piety at its best: the son wants to live in his father's house according to his father's traditions and then, after his father has been properly buried, to come and follow Jesus. One might even suppose that this obligation falls upon him insofar as he is the firstborn or even the only son. Jesus, far from praising his filial piety and assuring him that he is not far from the kingdom of God, trashes his whole value system: "Follow me [now], and leave the dead to bury their dead" (Mt 8:22). Jesus is not speaking of zombies here. Rather he is implying that the way of his father is the way of death and that, if he would live, he must break himself away from his father and trust that those who follow the way of death will take care of their own. Thus, when Matthew carries forward the tradition that Jesus said, "Call no man your father on earth" (Mt 23:9), he did so with the acute awareness that the "fathers" of many or most of his community did not approve of the way of Jesus and that the rule of filial piety would have forced them to abandon the calling of their "one Father, who is in heaven" (Mt 23:9).

In a parallel light, this may be the primary reason why Matthew presents Jesus as having dual origins: on the one hand, he stands in the lineage of Abraham and David and, as such, has three times fourteen "fathers"; yet, on the other hand, he can be rightly understood only when he is perceived as entirely "fatherless," since he was "conceived of the Holy Spirit" (Mt 1:21). Accordingly, Joseph may stand for the new type of "father," who, "being a just man" (Mt 1:19), acts outside the Torah in order to bring under his own care and protection those who have been conceived by the Holy Spirit and thereby rendered "fatherless" by the curses stemming from their own biological parents (Milavec 1978: 114f.).

Luke mutes the tradition of family rejection. According to his Gospel, Jesus' parents (esp. his mother) are models of traditional Jewish piety. Luke cuts out of Mark's Gospel, therefore, any notion that "his mother and brothers" are out "to seize him." When they finally do arrive at the house where he is teaching, Luke twists the words in Jesus' mouth such that he implies that those seated must look to "his mother and brothers" as models of true piety, for they "are those who hear the word of God and do it" (Lk 8:21). Nonetheless, even Luke retains the Q Gospel tradition in radically placing the choice of Jesus over family: "If any one comes to me and does not hate his own father and mother and wife and children and brothers and sisters, yes, even his own life, he cannot be my disciple" (Lk 14:26). Luke is unique here in anticipating that a man might have to reject his wife in order to cling to Jesus (see Mt 10:37; *Gos. Thom.* 55, 101).

The *Didache*, while it fails to present the frontal assault on filial piety found in the Synoptics, does, nonetheless, share in some of its aspects. The interpretation of *Did.* 1:3f. offered above illustrates this. In what follows, one will discover that the commandment to honor father and mother was deliberately dropped from the Decalogue.

How the Jewish Decalogue Was Adapted for Gentiles

The negative golden rule concerns itself with avoiding "as many things as you might wish not to happen to you" (*Did.* 1:2). *Didache* 2:2–6 proceeds to spell these things out in detail. First a decalogue adapted to gentiles is offered. Then five speech failings and five evil dispositions are prohibited. All of this is then brought to closure by naming three classes of persons (2:7): (a) those whom one is bound to lovingly reprove—misbehaving members (looking ahead to 4:3 and 15:3); (b) those whom one cannot reprove who can only be prayed for—outside "enemies" (1:3) and insiders who are "shunned" (15:3); and (c) those whom one loves unreservedly and generally need no correction—"mentors" and "saints" (4:1f.).

The framers of the decalogue (2:2) retained the linguistic structure whereby the Lord delivered his Torah to his people on Mt. Sinai (Ex 20:1–17; Dt 5:6–21). Thus, one finds here the tenfold repetition of *ou/ouk* followed by a verb in the second person singular future tense. The use of the future tense works well here insofar as it indicates what the Lord will expect of those intent upon loving him.

Since the novice could not have known what the Lord wanted him/her to be and to do prior to this moment, the decalogue would not have been presented to the novice as a rebuke. This harmonizes with Jewish practice in training proselytes—no gentile was blamed for not having been raised as a Jew (Novak 1983: 110–15; 1989: 38). On the other hand, it can be presumed that the novice asked questions about the scope of each of the terms of the decalogue and that the novice reflected on his/her own life in contrast to the Way of Life. These periods of clarification and self-examination might have passed over into feelings of regret or repentance. In cases where this repentance spilled over into fits of depression or of self-negation, the spiritual mentor must have been quick to remind the candidate that their Father in heaven was formerly unknown to them and that they were naturally misled by well-meaning parents and household gods. From this point onward, however, the candidate would be expected to honor and to "love the God who made you" (1:2).

Philo of Alexandria (c. 20 B.C.E.–50 C.E.) was a Jewish contemporary of Jesus who left behind extensive Greek commentaries on the Jewish way of life. His treatise *The Decalogue* is important in this context because it represents the earliest Jewish source in which the Decalogue is regarded not simply as the opening discourse of God to Israel but as a summary of the entire Torah: "The ten commandments are the heads of all the particular and special laws which are recorded throughout all history of the giving of the law [Torah] related in the sacred scriptures" (*Decalogue* 154). Thus, it would be natural to ask whether *Did.* 2:2 represented a "decalogue" intending to summarize the entire revelation which "the Father of the universe . . . delivered . . . to the whole assembled nation of men and women" (*Decalogue* 32). When the "decalogue" of *Did.* 2:2 is compared with Ex 20:1–17, the following correlation appears:

A1 = seventh commandment (Ex 20:13)
A2 = sixth commandment (Ex 20:14)
A3 unlisted (pederasty)
A4 unlisted (illicit sex)
A5 = eighth commandment (Ex 20:15)
A6 unlisted (magic)
A7 unlisted (sorcery)
A8 unlisted (abortion)
A9 unlisted (infanticide)
A10 = tenth commandment (Ex 20:17)

The ninth commandment (Ex 20:16) may be omitted from this decalogue because five speech prohibitions are presented immediately following, and "you will not bear false witness" (*Did.* 2:3) is found among them. Even allowing for this, however, what is evident is the complete absence of the first five commandments. This omission could be partially explained if the "second rule" (*Did.* 2:1) were to be interpreted as referring to the "second tablet" (*Decalogue* 50) containing the sixth to the tenth commandments.

Scholars have been uncertain why the *Didache* speaks of this new section as the "second rule of the training" (*Did.* 2:1) and have offered various mutually exclusive explanations (Niederwimmer 1998: 86f.). Most probably, the *Didache* wants to identify the giving "to everyone asking you" as the "[first] rule" (*Did.* 1:5[A])—the addition of "first" only becoming evident once one arrives at a "second rule" (*Did.* 2:1) defined immediately thereafter. Within the progression of a training program, however, it would have been natural for the spiritual master to give the "rule" of *Did.* 1:5 first and to discuss it at length without making any reference to their even being a "second rule"—a topic that would be taken up at the next training session.

According to Exodus, the "ten commandments" (Ex 20:1–17) were spoken directly by the Lord to all the people. They, however, "were afraid and trembled" (Ex 20:18) and pressed Moses to approach God on their behalf: "You speak to us, and we will listen; but do not let God speak to us, or we will die" (Ex 20:19). Thus, after the ten commandments were delivered directly to the people, the remainder of God's ordinances, which comprise ten chapters in Exodus (20:22–31:18), was delivered to Moses alone. Deuteronomy confirms this double mode of revelation (Dt 4:12–13; 5:1–22; 6:1–30:20). Both of these narrative accounts have the effect of giving priority to the Decalogue without supposing (as Philo did) that the ten are summary headings under which all the ordinances given to Israel can be grouped. Thus Philo provides no help for understanding why the decalogue of the *Didache* presents the second set of five commandments while entirely omitting any mention of the first five.

#1M WHETHER EARLY JEWISH CHRISTIANS USED THE DECALOGUE

According to a rabbinic tradition, Jews of the first century recited the Decalogue each morning along with the *Shema*, but then, when Christians adopted the Ten Commandments for themselves as the whole of Jewish Torah, the Decalogue was dropped. The tradition reads as follows:

> Rav Mattana and Rabbi Shemuel bar Nachman both say that by rights the Ten Commandments should be recited every day. The reason why we do not do so is because of the claim of the heretics [*minim*] so that people should not think that these [commandments] alone were given to Moses on Sinai. (*y. Berakhot* 3c, Soncino ed.)

Jewish scholars who judge this sixth-century text as a valid historical recollection wherein the names and dates are correctly attributed and who identify the *minim* as "Christians," give credence to this story. Jacob Neusner and others (e.g., Crossan 1998: 47–101), however, demonstrate that it is hazardous to attribute our modern standards of historicity to Jewish documents that were created using entirely different standards of composition. New evidence, however, points in the direction of suggesting that the Decalogue was recited by members of the Qumran *yaḥad* each morning after the Shema (Falk 1998) and/or along with the blessings after meals (Weinfeld: 428). This issue thus merits further study.

Does the New Testament provide any evidence that Christians used the Decalogue? Upon examining Paul's letters, one finds many occasions when he puts forward lists of virtues and vices, yet not once does he presume to make reference to the "ten commandments" as a summary of what it means to be a faithful servant of God. On the contrary, Paul appears to regard the golden rule as his preferential summary of Torah:

> The one who loves another has fulfilled the law [Torah]. The commandments, You shall not commit adultery [Ex 20:14], You shall not murder [Ex 20:13], You shall not steal [Ex 20:15]; You shall not covet [Ex 20:17]; and any other commandments, are summarized up in this word, "Love you neighbor as yourself" [Lv 19:18b]. Love does no wrong to a neighbor; therefore, love is the fulfilling of the law [Torah]. (Rom 13:8f.)

Note that Paul, like the *Didache*, omits the first five commandments entirely and recites only four of the remaining five with only marginal reference to the order in which they are found in Exodus. If Paul had been reciting the Decalogue during his formative years in the synagogue, one would expect that he would have gotten the order correct and not omitted the ninth commandment. In any case, Paul clearly regards the golden rule (Lv 19:18b), whether positively (Rom 3:8a) or negatively (Rom 3:9b) stated, as summarizing the substance of the entire Torah. The Decalogue, therefore, cannot be supposed to function in this capacity.

Jesus, for his part, is presented in the Synoptics as calling Jews to a conversion of heart in anticipation of the nearness of the kingdom of God (Mk 1:15 and par.), yet he also fails to put forward or to make reference to the Decalogue. The closest Jesus gets to this is in his response to the man who runs up to him asking, "What must I do to inherit eternal life?" (Mk 10:17 and par.) According to Mark, Jesus responds:

> You know the commandments: "You shall not murder [Ex 20:13]; You shall not commit adultery [Ex 20:14]; You shall not steal [Ex 20:15]; You shall not bear false witness [Ex 20:16]; You shall not defraud ["a variant on stealing" Gundry 1993: 553]; Honor your father and mother [Ex 20:12]. (Mk 10:19)

One notices here that Jesus recites four out of the Ten Commandments in the order given in Ex 20 but then places the fifth commandment last. The first four commandments along with the ninth and tenth (according to Philo's reckoning) are entirely omitted.

Matthew edited Mark's narrative in three important ways: (1) Matthew dropped the aorist subjunctive of Mark and substituted the linguistic construction of the Septuagint (*ou* followed by a verb in the future tense); (2) Matthew omitted "Do not defraud" from Jesus' response "probably because he could not find it among the Ten Commandments" (Beare: 395); and (3) Matthew adds "You shall love your neighbor as yourself" (Lv 19:18b). Matthew, therefore, has Jesus respond as follows:

> If you wish to enter into life, keep the commandments. . . . "You will not murder [Ex 20:13]; You will not commit adultery [Ex

20:14]; You will not steal [Ex 20:15]; You will not bear false witness [Ex 20:16]; Honor your father and mother [Ex 20:12];
also, You will love your neighbor as yourself [Lv 19:18b]. (Mt
19:17–19 NRSV corrected to represent the future tense)

According to Matthew, Jesus also passes over the first four commandments. He then recites the fifth to the eighth and comes back to the
fourth. Then he uses Lv 19:18b probably because Matthew regarded this
as a summary of the Torah.

   From this evidence, one would be inclined to conclude the following:
(1) Nowhere in the Christian Scriptures nor in the *Didache* is there evidence that the Decalogue was used to summarize the entire Torah; rather,
the golden rule appears to function as the summary. (2) When the ordinances of the Lord are named, there does not appear to be any felt need
to recite word for word and in order what one finds in Ex 20:1–17. Thus
the freedom that the *Didache* projects respecting the ordering and expansion of the commandments would appear to be normal and expected
within first-century Jewish circles. The Synoptic authors confirm this.
Mark, for example, seemingly adds "Do not defraud" among the commandments because Jesus is addressing a rich man who, because of his possessions, would not be given over to coveting (the omitted tenth
commandment) but might be prone to enrich himself through economic
exploitation (Gundry 1993: 553; Ched Myers: 272).

Why the Way of Life Omits the First Five Commandments

   If the *Didache* deliberately omitted each of the first five commandments,
what might this say about the social situation of novices preparing to enter
the community?

   1. The first commandment prohibits honoring any gods other than or
alongside the one Lord. At the beginning of the *Didache*, the Way of Life
is defined as meaning "you will love the God who made you" (1:2)—
thereby affirming, from the start, a positive form of the first commandment. So, too, the *Didache* warns against becoming a diviner, an
enchanter, or an astrologer, for these things lead to "idolatry" (3:4). After
the close of the Two Ways, the novice is told that eating "the food sacrificed to idols . . . is worship of dead gods" (6:3). Hence, one might conclude that the first commandment might have been omitted because it was
redundant.

#1n Pastoral Reasons for Suppressing the First Commandment

Going beyond this, however, there may be even more subtle issues afoot. The first commandment, in its entirety, reads as follows:

> I am the Lord your God, who brought you out of the land of Egypt, out of the house of slavery; you shall have no other gods before me. (Ex 20:2)

The initial affirmation is not true for gentiles who, only now, are embracing the God of Israel. Furthermore, anyone who had witnessed or celebrated (at Passover) the marvels of the Lord during the Exodus, would have been expected to "have no other gods before me." The gentiles, on the other hand, were ignorant of the God of Israel and, therefore, were not blameworthy when they practiced idolatry. Thus, "it is important to note that when the prophets did condemn the gentiles for their sins, they did not condemn them for idolatry" (Novak 1989: 38). Yehezkel Kaufmann, reflecting upon this, explains:

> YHWH is the one and only God, but he has chosen Israel alone of all the nations to be his people. He governs the entire world, but he has revealed his name and his Torah only to Israel; therefore, only Israel is obliged to worship him. The nations are judged for violations of the moral law, but never for idolatry. . . . The idolatry of Israel is sin, but not that of the nations. (163–64)

In effect, since ways of living are passed down from parents to children, gentiles cannot be held blameworthy just because they had non-Jewish parents and were not raised as Jews (Novak 1983: 110–15; 1989: 38). Jews, on the other hand, know the Lord and are very much culpable when they cleave to other gods.

In the case of training gentiles in the Way of Life, therefore, the positive mandate, "You will love the God who made you" (1:2), is pastorally appropriate. How so? First, because gentiles meet the Lord of Israel not as the God "who brought you out of the land of Egypt" (Ex 20:2), but as "the God who made you." Second, because the gentile is not to be blamed or shamed for what was done in ignorance in the past. Third, because a complete abstinence from idolatry may have been an impossibility during the time of training.

This last point needs more development. During the time of training, a complete monotheism was probably impossible in those cases where novices were required to eat their meals in family circles where their parents occasionally or habitually worshiped other gods. Thus, a prohibition against "food . . . sacrificed to idols" (*Did.* 6:3) would have been premature and disruptive (as will be explained more fully in ch. 3). Hence, novices were deliberately not held to the negative command to "have no other gods before me" (Ex 20:2) until such time as their training in the Way of Life was complete and they had entered upon the prebaptismal fast (7:4) that prepared them for baptism and eating at the eucharistic table of the Lord for the first time (9:5). Then and only then could they be expected to be members of the Lord's family and to be fed on pure food from that point onward. The perfect practice of the first commandment, therefore, had to be postponed, and thus it was suppressed from the Decalogue for pastoral reasons.

2. The second commandment prohibits making or using a "graven image" (Ex 20:4). For a gentile whose public buildings, private homes, and even the money used in the marketplace were routinely decorated with such images, it would have been entirely unworkable to imagine that all of this could somehow be discarded, effaced, or replaced. For gentiles, the second commandment would have been nearly impossible to maintain unless they entirely abandoned their homes and cities. Hence, one might conclude that the second commandment was omitted because not even God could demand the impossible.

3. The third commandment prohibits swearing a false oath while calling upon God to witness to the truth of what one is saying. The *Didache* has five speech infractions after its "decalogue." Among these, swearing falsely is named first (*Did.* 2:3). Hence, one might conclude that restating the third commandment in *Did.* 2:2 would have seemed redundant.

4. The fourth commandment prohibits profaning the seventh day with work. For gentiles, the Sabbath rest (Ex 20:8f.) would have imposed an unworkable expectation, since the Roman lunar calendar governing public life made absolutely no provisions for a cessation of work every seventh day (see #4a). The "days of rest" named in the Roman calendar only occasionally coincided with the Jewish Sabbath and, even then, such days were ordinarily devoted to public festivals in honor of this or that god. Since the members of the *Didache* depended on the work of their hands, the fourth commandment would have imposed severe economic hardships. Hence, in order to safeguard a higher good, one might conclude that the Sabbath rest was suppressed.

#10 THE ABSENCE OF SABBATH AND FOOD REGULATIONS FOR GENTILES

Given the importance of the Sabbath rest, it is curious that nowhere in the *Didache* does one find any discussion of the Sabbath rest or any encouragement to keep it. The same things can be said of the entire Christian church during the first three centuries. Even when "Sunday" was taken over as the day when Christians met to celebrate the eucharist, this day remained an ordinary workday unless it accidentally fell on a civil holiday in the Roman calendar. One has to wait until 321 C.E. before one finds the emperor Constantine declaring "the day of the sun" to be commemorated by the closing of the civil courts. Later emperors prohibited slaves from working on that day, and the Germanic kings later banned hard labor by everyone. In sum, the origins of the gentile church completely disregarded the Lord's command to "remember the Sabbath day and keep it holy" (Ex 20:8) and only gradually in the early Middle Ages did the observance of a day of rest come to prevail among Christians. Jewish Christians and Jews generally, however, faithfully observed the Sabbath rest during this entire period. When the Synoptic Gospels came to be written, Jesus was remembered to have disturbed many of his contemporaries regarding how he kept the Sabbath (Mk 2:23–3:6 and par.). There was never any doubt, however, that Jesus regarded the Sabbath as the day of rest mandated by the Lord God.

The keeping of the Sabbath rest was a very old and very distinctive part of Jewish self-understanding. Gentiles may not have recognized their new neighbors as Jews by their language or dress. When they refrained from work every seventh day, however, their Jewish identity became perfectly evident. Furthermore, any gentile who was employed by a Jew or who had business dealings with Jews had to take into account the Jewish observance of the Sabbath.

The Roman calendar was divided into twelve months but made no provision for a weekly cycle of seven days. Jews, however, understood their seven-day week as rooted in creation (Gn 2:2–3) and divinely sanctioned in the Lord's Decalogue (Ex 20:8–11). Keeping the Sabbath was consequently a visible sign of adherence to the covenant (Ex 31:16–17; Dt 5:15; Is 56:6). Deliberately violating the Sabbath, on the other hand, was a visible sign of abandoning the covenant (1 Mc 1:43; Josephus, *Ant.* 2.346; Philo, *Life of Moses* 2.213–20) and was ordinarily punished by stoning (15:32–36). Even an inadvertent violation of the Sabbath required a sin offering in the temple (Lv 4:27–35).

E. P. Sanders, when posing the question of whether the Sabbath was a "very important part of first-century Judaism," responded as follows:

> On the most basic and general grounds: (1) It is one of the ten commandments. (2) It is one of the two that require positive action (the other is honor of father and mother). (3) Non-observance of it is, in a Jewish community, highly visible. (1990: 16)

So important was this observance that Jews living outside of Palestine had petitioned and received a special dispensation to gather together on the Sabbath even when other clubs and associations were prohibited (Philo, *Embassy to Gaius* 155–59; Josephus, *Ant.* 14.241–46, 258, 263–64). Furthermore, Jews had gained a special exemption from military service on the grounds that the Sabbath rendered them incapable from serving in the imperial armies (Josephus, *Ant.* 13.252; 14.237).

According to Paul, baptized gentiles were not required to keep the Sabbath. In fact, Paul vehemently discourages those gentiles who have begun to observe "special days, and months, and seasons" (Gal 4:10; Col 2:16) from continuing to do so. In his Letter to the Romans, Paul takes a more moderate position (probably since he is hoping to be well received in a community he is about to visit for the first time) and discourages quarreling (14:1) over matters where a lawful diversity ought to prevail:

> Some judge one day [the Sabbath] to be better than another, while others judge all days to be alike. Let all be fully convicted in their own minds. Those who observe the day [of the Lord], observe it in honor of the Lord. Also those who eat [on a day of fasting], eat in honor of the Lord . . . while those who abstain, abstain in the honor of the Lord. (Rom 14:5–6)

While Paul maintained that holiness of life for gentiles does not require them to take over the least part of Jewish religious observance, the *Didache*, in contrast, developed the practice of retaining two days of fasting each week but changed the days to differentiate themselves from the practice of the "hypocrites" (*Did.* 8:1). The eucharist, in like fashion, was celebrated on the "day of the Lord" (14:1), which was calculated using the Jewish cycle of weeks. This "Lord's day" was not celebrated as a Sabbath (a day of rest), yet the *Didache* offers the earliest evidence of a weekly celebration of the eucharist—probably on Sunday evening (see "When and How Often the Eucharist Was Celebrated" in ch. 5 below).

If the Sabbath was such a manifest aspect of Jewish life and since the keeping of the Sabbath was expressly mandated by the Lord, why did the gentiles not keep the Sabbath? Various reasons have been put forward in order to explain why the Sabbath observance never took root among gentile Christians while Jewish-born Christians presumably continued to observe the Jewish feasts as did Jesus. The most convincing explanation has been offered by Paula Fredriksen. Her solution might be summarized as follows:

1. The early Jewish Jesus movement set aside the expectation that all gentiles would be destroyed along with their idols (e.g., Mi 5:9, 15) and that their cities would be either devastated or repopulated by Israel (e.g., Is 54:3; Zep 2:1–3, 8) during the end times. Rather, the Jesus movement embraced "the positive extreme" (Fredriksen: 544)—gentiles in the last days would abandon idolatry and attach themselves to exiled Jews in their midst and join them in worshiping the God of Jacob (Is 2:2–4; Mi 4:1–3) and together eat the feast that the Lord would prepare for them in Jerusalem (Is 25:6).

2. In the Jewish synagogues, gentiles could learn the folly of depending on idols and could pray and fast with Jews. Unless such gentiles completely converted to Judaism, however, they could not be classed with the people of God and assured a place in the world to come. Within the Jesus movement, however, both Jews and gentiles shared a common faith in Jesus and a common expectation in the imminent coming of the Lord. Jews prepared for his coming by turning in faith to a heartfelt observance of the Torah; gentiles, on the other hand, "*turn from* idolatry (and the sins associated with it) and *turn to* the living God" (Fredriksen: 547). Thus, circumcision, Sabbath keeping, and kosher foods were required of Jews but not of gentiles since "gentiles are saved as gentiles: they do not, eschatologically, become Jews" (Fredriksen: 547).

3. This situation prevailed during the 30s and 40s and allowed Jews and gentiles to be joined in faith and fellowship bound together in the same hope. Then a critical stress point emerged:

> By mid-century, surely all these Christians must have realized that their expectations [of the imminent coming of the Lord] had not been fulfilled. . . . Gentiles continued to join the movement in numbers; the mission to Israel, however, had foundered. (Fredriksen: 560)

In response to this crisis, some Jewish Christians began to advocate that, given the delay in the Lord's coming, gentiles ought to completely convert to Judaism so as to ensure their place in the world to come. Others, like Paul, strenuously insisted that the old policy of admitting gentiles "with only the requirement of moral, not halakhic, conversion" be maintained: "This meant no idols. It also meant no circumcision" (Fredriksen: 561).

The value of Fredriksen's reconstruction is that she is able to explain how and why the early church was of one mind when it came to regarding circumcision, Sabbath observance, and kosher foods as unnecessary and inappropriate for those gentiles who waited upon the Lord. Then, as the feverish expectation of the coming of the Lord cooled and the mission to the Jews was drying up, there was an internal drive to bring gentiles into a full Jewish identity and practice. In part, this could be motivated by anxiety regarding the salvation of those who died prior to the coming of the Lord (as reflected in 1 Thes 4:13–18). In part, this could also be motivated by fear on the part of some that the Jewish identity of the church was in danger of being lost as the influx of gentile adherents increased while the influx of Jewish members nearly dried up. Whatever the complex motivations (see, e.g., Dunn 1991: 126–27), the early 50s marks the emergence of bitter internal quarrels regarding the status of gentile adherents who anticipated an eschatological salvation, that is, inclusion among the people of God when the Lord comes to establish his kingdom on earth.

In the Way of Life, the all-embracing anticipation of the end times only makes brief appearances (*Did.* 1:5; 3:7; 4:4, 7). Later chapters will make clear how completely the members of the Didache communities anticipated the coming of the Kingdom (see esp. chs. 4, 5, and 10 below). Nonetheless, Fredriksen's reconstruction allows some tentative insights regarding the overall character of the *Didache*:

1. The silence of the *Didache* regarding Sabbath observance, circumcision, and kosher foods might be easily explained if the Way of Life emerged during the period when the early church was in agreement that the Lord would only require a moral conversion of gentiles in the last days. The end-time expectation so profoundly present in the community eucharist (*Did.* 9–10) and in the final end-times scenario (*Did.* 16) might also be a testimony that these were formulated at a time when there was no doubt that the Lord was coming soon. All in all, therefore, not withstanding the use of "hypocrites" (*Did.* 8:1–2), one might surmise that the *Didache* was either created prior to the troubled period of the 50s or that, standing squarely in the threshold of God's future, the Didache communities were not tempted to circumcise gentiles.

2. The *Didache* clearly advocates extensive training in a way of life (*Did.* 1–5), daily prayer (8:2–3), bi-weekly community fasting (8:1), a weekly eucharist (9–10), and the offering of first fruits (13:3–7)—all practices that were unique to the *Didache* and not found in Paul or anywhere else in the Christian Scriptures. Later chapters will make evident how each of these practices has Jewish roots and embraces a pastoral genius designed to create and enforce an identity among gentile adherents that would have been honored and clearly recognizable by Jewish

members. This being the case, Jewish zealots would have been less prone to try to enforce a complete Jewish identity upon gentile adherents, as was the case in other churches during the 50s.

3. The silence of the *Didache* regarding Sabbath observance, circumcision, and kosher foods also further confirms the judgment made earlier regarding the grave improbability that the Way of Life was originally used in the synagogue for training would-be converts (see #1m). In the light of Fredricksen's reconstruction, only a Jewish movement bent on including gentiles without imagining that they ought to become Jews would have created the Way of Life.

5. The fifth commandment requires children to honor their parents. Gentiles could hardly be trained to honor their parents (Ex 20:12) when that "filial piety" so highly prized by Romans would have made the desertion of ancestral gods and the abandonment of their parental upbringing unthinkable save in those instances where an entire patriarchal household converted to the Lord as a group (e.g., as in the case of the household of Cornelius in Acts 10). In the Synoptic Gospels, one finds what Crossan refers to as "an almost savage attack on family values" (1994: 58). Sayings such as "I have come to set a man against his father" (Mt 10:35f.) and "Call no one your father on earth" (Mt 23:9) serve to illustrate how intergenerational strife (Crossan 1994: 60) arose as parents endeavored to use their authority to block the conversion of their adult children. Given the implication of *Did.* 1:3f. (namely, that many or most novices were encountering hostile resistance to their conversion from parents and siblings), it became impossible for most novices to honor their parents and at the same time honor the God of Israel. Accordingly, using a pattern of social displacement, novices preparing to enter the community are wisely directed to honor God as their true Father (1:5; 9:2f.; 10:2) and the members of the community as their true siblings (4:8). Hence, in order to safeguard a higher good, one might conclude that the obligation to honor parents was suppressed. Not even God could demand two contradictory commitments.

In retrospect, the above discussion makes it evident that the omission of the second, fourth, and fifth commandments was not accidental. The framers of the *Didache* deliberately modified the Jewish Decalogue in order to enable gentlies to walk in the Way of Life while continuing to live in Roman society. This, in itself, makes clear that the Way of Life was not designed for use in the synagogue (see #1j).

#1p Adultery Understood Within Different Social Contexts

When the *Didache* speaks of "adultery," we may be inclined to imagine that we know what is meant by this term because the prohibition against "adultery" continues down to our present day. Within different social structures, however, "adultery" is perceived differently. For example, Marco Polo, when traveling though Asia visited certain communities where the men generously welcomed visitors and gave them accommodations in their private homes with the intent of encouraging them to be sexually intimate with their wives (Polo: 118). In the mountains of Tibet, he encountered yet another form of sexual morality:

> No man [here] will marry a virgin on the grounds that if a woman has not had several lovers she must be undesirable to man and unloved by the gods. So when foreigners or strangers pitch their tents in the area, as many as forty young girls may be brought by their mothers from the village and offered to them. The more attractive girls are welcomed and the others go sadly home. A traveler many keep a girl with him as long as he stays in the village, and when he leaves he must give the girl a jewel to prove she has had a lover. If a girl has twenty jewels, she has had as many lovers. The girls with the most jewels are then chosen as wives because, by common accord, they must be the loveliest. Once they are married, their husbands cherish them and regard it as a great sin to touch another man's wife. (Polo: 116)

When socially sanctioned, therefore, what appears as "fornication" or "adultery" to an outsider may, from the vantage point of the insider, be cherished as a form of "hospitality."

L. William Countryman has carefully studied the social character of first-century Christianity against its Jewish background and concludes as follows:

> Among us, sexual activity outside the marriage on the part of either partner is understood as adultery; in antiquity, only such activity on the part of the wife (or the betrothed woman) qualified as adultery. The husband could commit adultery only by having intercourse with the wife (or betrothed) of another man; if he had sexual relations with a slave, a prostitute, a concubine,

> or a divorced or widowed woman, this did not constitute adultery. . . . Again, our own explanations of what is wrong in adultery usually focus on the betrayal of trust and of formal commitments between spouses, whereas the ancient understanding of adultery assumes rather that it is a violation of another's property. What for us is analogous to betrayal was for them a species of theft. (Countryman: 159)

Adultery, consequently, was interpreted according to a double standard and functioned in order to protect the property rights of men. Countryman poignantly illustrates this by making reference to the Book of Job. According to Job, a fitting calamity should follow upon every sin. Should he close his hands against the poor or raise his hand to strike the orphan, then "let my arm be broken from its socket" (Jb 31:22).

> Yet, in the case of adultery, he [Job] suggests that an appropriate punishment would be for his wife to become another man's household servant and be used sexually, like a prostitute, by a number of men [Jb 31:9f.]. This curse becomes intelligible only when we note that it is parallel to others in the chapter which deal with property offenses: if Job has practiced deceit, let his won crops be rooted out (31:5–8); if he has taken another's land, let his own grow weeds instead of good crops (31:38–40). If he has taken another man's wife, let another take his. The wife was a form of property; adultery was violation of the property of another and should therefore be punished with violation of one's own. (Countryman: 149)

All in all, therefore, adultery had to do with property rights held by men. A man could be thus assured that his seed and his seed alone would grow within the fertile womb of his wife.

With this in mind, it made sense that the Lord God required that a violation of these rights be punished. It also made sense that men were reluctant to marry a woman who was not a virgin (Countryman: 157) and that, in the case of young girls, they were expected to be able to demonstrate their virginity on their wedding night by the blood of the broken hymen on the sheets or else to be stoned to death (Dt 22:13–21). It is for this reason that, in rural areas of North Africa today, I discovered that certain women are charged with carrying the blood-stained sheets through the village in the name of the bride after her wedding night as a badge of honor. The fact that I along with most Westerners instinctively reacted to this gesture with anything from mild discomfort to revulsion only indicates how far our socially sanctioned instincts surrounding sexuality have changed.

In the Roman tradition, a similar double standard prevailed when it came to adultery: "Augustus declared adultery a public offense only in women" (Pomeroy 1995: 159). Fathers had the right to kill a promiscuous daughter. The husband, on the other hand, had more limited powers: "the husband was obliged to divorce his wife, and he or someone else was to bring her to trial" (Pomeroy 1995: 159). If convicted, the woman lost half of her dowry and both parties to the adultery were forced into exile. Jerome describes in detail the inhumane tortures inflicted by officials of the Roman state upon a woman refusing to disclose the name of her suspected lover (*Letter* 1.3–8). By these means, an injured father or husband was able to recapture his lost honor. Meanwhile, one fails to find fathers taking any action against sons visiting a prostitute or wives divorcing their husbands for their sexual liaisons (Pomeroy 1995: 159). Among Stoics, on the other hand, every form of sexual intercourse was suspect because their ideal was to act without passion. Hence, for Roman Stoics, marital intercourse alone was permitted, not for pleasure but exclusively for procreation (*TDNT* 6:583).

As for the *Didache*, it can be supposed that mentors trained novices to understand sexuality generally and adultery in particular within roughly the same framework practiced by their Jewish contemporaries. The Jesus movement was not a "sexual revolution" that came forward with a platform to do away with the double standard and to promote equal rights (or even equal pleasure) for women in the state of marriage. On the other hand, given the fact that the *Didache* did not openly advocate domestic subordination and gave equal training to women (see details in the Epilogue), a social environment was fostered in which men were undoubtedly more inclined to take the interests, the prohibitions, and the pleasure of their women into account when it came to sexual conduct.

Why the Way of Life Adds Six New Commandments

If the deliberate omissions from the Decalogue of Exodus 20 constituted pastoral adaptations, then one might suspect that the six prohibitions added to the *Didache*'s decalogue were also equally purposeful. Properly speaking, the six break down into three pairs.

1. The first pair (A3 and A4) prohibits pedophilia and illicit sex (*porneia*). A3 might be literally translated as "you will not corrupt boys" (*ou paidophthorēseis*). The term *pais/paidos* used here refers to either the relative age ("youth"), descent ("son/daughter"), or social position ("slave") (Bauer: 604c). The placement of this phrase between A2 and A4 clearly indicates that the corruption implied is "sexual" in nature. Audet

notes that the term itself "implies a [negative] judgment" (1958: 286). Classical Greek has the much more neutral term *paidophilein* (lit. "to love boys") from which our English term "pedophilia" is derived with all its modern negative connotations.

#1Q PEDOPHILIA IN THE ANCIENT WORLD

In contemporary society, pedophilia normally refers to an adult taking advantage of underage youths for his/her sexual pleasure. Pedophilia in the ancient Greek world, however, appears to have originated as the honorable means whereby upper-class parents entrusted their son to an older, respected male for the purpose of advancing his initiation into manhood. During the first twelve years, a boy was almost exclusively under the care and training of female nurses and mothers. Upon turning twelve, therefore, an initiation into the world of male values and of male virtues was desired:

> Traditionally it [pederastic homosexuality] played a central role in the introduction of young males into the value system of the dominant male culture. Whether it arose from military practices, as a means of inculcating courage in warriors, or from initiatory practices, by the classical period pederasty had developed into an institution that acculturated young males to their social roles. In essence, it was the means by which the society's dominant (i.e., male) values were passed on from one generation to the next (Demand: 138).

Given the fact that the Hellenistic training in manhood included a sexual initiation as well, it might have been important for those who were being trained in the Way of Life to realize that no sexual bond was to be awakened or cultivated during the course of an apprenticeship.

Jewish sources written in the first century emphasized the abhorrent nature of homosexuality as such without any reference to the special circumstances surrounding pederastic homosexuality. According to Josephus, "nature . . . abhors the mixture of a male with a male" (*Ag. Ap.* 1.199) since sexuality was uniquely fashioned for procreation. Philo, in his turn, deals specifically with "the love of boys" (pedophilia) as having the effect of "changing their manly character into an effeminate one" (*Special Laws* 3.37; *Contemplative Life* 52, 57–61)—presumably because, in the man– boy relationship, the boy plays the subservient role, which was associated with a woman's role. Philo, like his contemporary Josephus, decries pedophilia as "contrary to nature" insofar as the dominant male ends up "wasting his power of propagating the species" (*Special Laws* 3.39). Borrowing the Stoic perception that all sexuality is justified only by virtue of the offspring for which it is intended, both Josephus and Philo end up condemning pederastic homosexuality as contrary to nature and, by implication, as contrary to the ordinances of the Lord of Nature. In a similar vein, the *Sentences of Pseudo-Phocylides* (c. 150) admonished the reader: "Commit not adultery nor rouse homosexual passion" (3). Later this is expanded as follows:

> Transgress not for unlawful sex the natural limits of sexuality,
> For even animals are not pleased by intercourse of male with male. . . .
> Guard the youthful beauty of a comely boy;
> Because many rage for intercourse with a [young] man. (190f., 213f.)

The *Didache* does not expressly identify its abhorrence to pedophilia. Unlike Josephus and Philo, however, the *Didache* does not appear to take any interest in developing a reasoned approach based on the purposes of sexuality in nature. For the *Didache*, it suffices to prohibit pederasty with the same simple certainty whereby the Lord abhors adultery and murder.

Pedophilia was practically unknown among Jews (see *Testament of Levi* 17:11); hence it is not surprising that the Torah given to Moses contains no mention of it. Outside of Judaism, however, pedophilia was widely practiced and, within limits, was socially acceptable within the hellenized world:

> In civic life, homosexuality between young men, or an older and younger partner, was socially acceptable. Among many examples, the most telling is Apuleius's speech of self-defense, written in the Greek- and Latin-speaking milieu of high civic culture of North Africa. Like an orator in classical Athens, he cited his youthful poems to boy-lovers as a point in his favor. . . . Among Romans, the most acceptable homosexuality was an act conducted by citizens on slaves or foreigners. In early Rome, an obscurely attested law does seem to have punished all homosexual activity between citizens themselves. (Fox: 342)

When the *Didache* proscribes sexually corrupting "boys" (2:2), it is specifically singling out a practice that many male neophytes had experienced firsthand as part of their early sexual initiation (as shown in #1q). One should not imagine that the *Didache* was an innovator here, however, since ancient Jewish authors amply demonstrated their repugnance for this socially sanctioned pedophilia when writing to gentiles (#1q).

Along with pedophilia, the decalogue introduces *ou porneuseis*—a prohibition against *porneia* ("illicit sex"). The term *porneia* effectively embraces "every kind of unlawful intercourse" (Bauer: 693b). The commandments regarding adultery (#1p) and pedophilia, consequently, appear to prohibit specific kinds of illicit sex. Why then does the *Didache* insert a special prohibition against *porneia?* The original Ten Commandments contain no such prohibition. However, entire chapters of the Torah (Lv 18; 20) are devoted to spelling out a wide range of prohibited sexual relations. Thus, the framers of the *Didache* must have added this commandment against *porneia* in order to alert gentiles to the following:

1. *Incest.* Jews as well as Romans proscribed both sexual relations and marriage between those related to each other by blood ties. This is spelled out in detail in Leviticus (18:6–18; 20:9–12, 17, 19–21) and carried with it the penalty of death. These norms, however, were by no means universal: "In Egypt and much of the Near East, brothers married their sisters. Whatever its origin, this custom helped family property to cohere under a system of inheritance which recognized both male and female shares" (Fox: 341). Paul, in his first letter to the Corinthians, specifically names as *porneia* (1 Cor 5:1) an instance where "someone has his father's wife":

> The verb "has" suggests something more than casual intercourse, perhaps the creation of a full household. The woman in question could be the man's mother, but there seems no reason for Paul to have avoided saying so if that were in fact the case. More likely, she was a subsequent [perhaps very young] wife of his father, now either divorced or widowed. According to Leviticus, this would be incest [*porneia*] just as much as intercourse with his own mother [Lv 20:11]. . . . (Countryman: 197)

Thus, in this case, a socially sanctioned union according to the traditions of Corinth runs up against Paul's own firm views of what he, guided by the Lord, would regard as *porneia.*

2. *Menstruating Women.* Menstrual blood was regarded by Jews (and others) as imparting an "unclean" condition that made social intercourse and cultic worship impossible (*ABD* 5:1145). No Jewish husband, consequently, was permitted to approach his wife and "to uncover her nakedness while she is in her menstrual uncleanness" (Lv 18:19; 20:18) or both were to be "cut off from their people" (Lv 20:18). To the degree that the *Didache* emerged out of Jewish instincts, therefore, one can be certain that

"you will not have illicit sex" (*Did.* 2:2) would have prohibited sex with a menstruating woman. Since menstrual blood was widely regarded as abhorrent in the ancient world (Pomeroy 1990: 136), one can surmise that not much emphasis needed to be given to this prohibition.

3. *Prostitution.* The Hebrew Scriptures have strong admonitions against cultic prostitution and next to nothing regarding secular prostitution (Countryman: 164). In the ancient world, a double standard prevailed regarding prostitution. Consider, for example, the story of the patriarch Judah, who, following the death of his wife, propositioned his own daughter-in-law Tamar, mistaking her for "a temple prostitute" (Gn 38:15, 23). Temple prostitutes were, most commonly, slaves forced into prostitution in order to finance a temple operation (Pomeroy 1990: 147). The biblical narrative makes clear that the greatest risk for Judah is "being laughed at" (Gn 38:23), while Tamar risks being "burned [alive]" (Gn 38:24; also Lv 21:9).

#1R THE DOUBLE STANDARD REGARDING PROSTITUTION

Both cultic and secular prostitution were prevalent in the urban centers of the Roman Empire (Countryman: 157–67; Fox: 342f.; Pomeroy 1995: 88–92, 139–41). The Greek term for a brothel (*porneion*) was a derivative of *porneia*—but without any stigma involved as far as the men were concerned (*TDNT* 6:588). Men ordinarily did not hesitate to find sexual relief and gratification in the arms of a prostitute—unless, of course, they were athletes who regarded sexual abstention as guaranteeing a better performance (Fox: 349). Overindulgence might be frowned upon (Fox: 342) but, beyond this, there was no moral stigma associated with men visiting prostitutes.

Young girls, on the other hand, were never permitted the liberties given their brothers. They were expected to be virgins at the time of their marriage and to refrain from having sex with prostitutes or with slaves for the whole of their lives (Pomeroy 1995: 86–88, 150–55):

> Like the Augustan rule on adultery, the regulation on criminal fornication (*stuprum*) perpetuated a double standard. No man was allowed to have sexual relations with an unmarried or widowed upper-class woman, but he could have relations with prostitutes, whereas upper-class women were not allowed to have any relations outside of marriage. (Pomeroy 1995: 160)

Female slaves, more especially, were understood to be "sexually available without restriction" (*ABD* 6:69) to their masters and to those to whom their masters offered them. Obedience rather than chastity was mandated for these women, since their bodies were owned by men for their use. In addition to their assigned work in the shop or the home, female slaves were frequently hired out to provide entertainment (sexual and otherwise) during the dinner parties of men and to serve clients in brothels. "Employment in the sex trade brought great profit to the owners of female slaves" (Pomeroy 1995: 192).

Roman and Greek wives were expected to turn a blind eye when their men visited prostitutes, kept a concubine/mistress (Pomeroy 1995: 197), or sexually exploited the slaves within their own household. While some wives gave their explicit approval (Pomeroy 1995: 192), others objected to this practice (Pomeroy 1995: 90). Even in the household of the patriarch Abraham, Sarai initially approved of her husband's having sexual relations with Hagar, one of her slaves, but later changed her mind and expelled Hagar once she became puffed up with her own importance in the household (Gn 16:1–6). Slaves were not to be heedlessly injured or killed (Ex 21:20–27); yet nothing in the rules of Moses expressly prohibited a master from sowing his seed in the fertile womb that he owned (Countryman: 159). Paul, in coming up against prostitution practiced by Christians in Corinth, clearly went beyond the Jewish tradition as it then stood by condemning prostitution on the ground that "every sexual act between a man and woman established a union of flesh like that of marriage (1 Cor 6:16), though not, apparently, indissoluble" (Countryman: 204).

Taking the *Didache* as it stands, it is difficult to assess whether the prohibition of *porneia* was interpreted by mentors to apply to men having sexual relations with female slaves or prostitutes (*ABD* 1:83a). Such encounters were clearly off limits for women. While the *Didache* seems to have taken significant strides in enhancing the dignity and the roles of women within the community (see ch. 16 below), there is no evidence that the double standard regarding adultery and illicit sex was openly addressed and corrected. Nor can any argument be made on the basis of the prohibition against pederasty, since Jews widely regarded pederasty as a "gentile vice"; for this reason, it gained entrance into the decalogue. In sum, the *Didache* provides no compelling evidence to help one decide whether the prohibition of *porneia* was interpreted as obligating men not to enjoy unrestricted sexual relations with female slaves and prostitutes.

It should be remembered that the double standard was the stubborn prevailing tradition both inside and outside the Christian churches and that even well-meaning pastors were routinely ignored when they tried to change these ingrained habits. John Chrysostom, for example, installed a wooden partition separating the men from the women in his Antioch congregation, thereby "making plain the dangers of mixed company" (P. Brown 1988: 317). Chrysostom (d. 407 C.E.) used his gift for oratory to press his congregation to leave aside their secular ways and to conduct themselves with the single purpose of forming ideal Christian households. In so doing, Chrysostom lamented the double standard:

> I realize that many people [here] think it is adultery only when one corrupts a married woman. But I say that if a married man treats wickedly and wantonly an unmarried woman, even a prostitute or a servant girl, this act is adultery. . . . Do not tell me about the laws of the unbelievers which drag the woman caught in adultery into court and exact a penalty but do not demand a penalty from the married men who have corrupted servant girls. I will read to you the law of God which is equally severe with the woman and with the man. . . . (*Homily 20*)

The very terms in which Chrysostom put forth his argument reveal just how far the judgment of the members of his congregation differed from his own. Regarding the double standard, therefore, Chrysostom was hard pressed to enforce the notion that the husband could not continue to have sexual relations with a prostitute or slave girl without being guilty of "adultery." When it came to raising young boys, Chrysostom did not even try to persuade parents or their children that sexual relations with both their sons and their daughters were equally forbidden. Even when early church pastors endeavored to challenge the double standard, therefore, they made little headway (P. Brown 1988: 23f.). On this basis alone, one would have to be suspicious of any interpretation of the Decalogue in the *Didache* that upsets the double standard.

In pastoral practice, scarcity of details regarding the first pair of added commandments undoubtedly necessitated that each mentor would add details suitable to each candidate's sex and prior experiences. While sexual addictions undoubtedly needed to be rooted out, nothing in the *Didache* indicates the least disposition toward degrading sexuality as such nor toward proposing the virginal state as a permanent calling. The spiritual guides undoubtedly understood the Lord's mandate, "Be fruitful and multiply" (Gn 1:28), as the tacit backdrop authorizing and guiding the Father's will when it came to sexuality. Over and beyond this, one must also surmise that spiritual guides kept in mind the principle of gradualism (*Did.* 6:2) and the necessity of retaining a balanced orientation such that perfection was never narrowly focused on sexual restraint. Thus it seems that sexual asceticism and the ideal of virginity were entirely absent from the *Didache*.

2. The second pair of added commandments prohibits magic and *pharmakeuein*, a term that literally meant "to give drugs" but could also apply to the preparation of medicines using incantations to ensure their supernatural efficacy (Kohlenberger: 1065). The term *pharmakeuein* can refer to "compounding poisons" (Niederwimmer 1998: 89), yet in this context, the term is linked not with murder but with magic, as in the case of Pseudo-Phocylides: "Make no potions, keep away from magical books" (149). Magic and potions did not compete with the respectable religious rites of the established religions but provided "the illegal insider dealing of people who were overambitious to achieve a personal end" (Fox: 37).

Even though classical Judaism strongly and repeatedly condemned practicing magic and preparing potions (e.g., Ex 22:17; Lv 19:26, 31; 20:6, 27; Dt 18:10f.; *m. Sanhedrin* 6:6; 7:7, 11; 10:1), these pagan arts continued to flourish even among Jews (Schürer: 3.342f.). In Acts, for example, Paul, in his journeys, was confronted by two Jewish magicians: the first tried to purchase the secret to his spiritual powers (Acts 8:19); the second tried to prevent the conversion of his master and was himself struck blind by the "incantation" of Paul (Acts 13:11). Even in Christian circles, therefore, Luke was not averse to showing that Paul could counter Jewish magic with a divine spell of his own.

In Hellenistic society, magic flourished as a result of Greek contact with Near Eastern magical practices, especially those prevalent in Egypt (Fox: 36). Magic functioned in two ways:

> [1] Most of its spells can be defined as a type of sorcery used for competitive ends. They enlisted a personal spirit and deployed the power of words and symbols in order to advance a suit in love or in the law courts, to win at the games, to prosper in business, or to silence envious rivals.
> [2] In the Imperial period, Greek magical texts also catered to clients who had more spiritual aspirations. They served their wish to win immortality for their soul, to escape the confines of fate and necessity, and to confront a Supreme god alone, in a personal "introduction." (Fox: 37)

The *Didache* does not persuade the novice of the uselessness of magic or of the danger of entanglements with false gods; rather, the norm is spelled out with authoritative brevity. Later, the novice will be trained to "accept the experiences befalling you as good things, knowing that, apart from God, nothing happens" (*Did*. 3:10). In the end, therefore, the setting aside of a reliance on magic opens the novice up to a complete surrender to the providence of God. If one entirely trusts God, magic becomes unnecessary. Here too, however, one suspects that spiritual masters used the principle of gradualism (*Did.* 6:2) to induce anxious candidates to withdraw entirely from the use of magic arts prior to baptism.

3. The third pair of added commandments pertains to abortion and infanticide. These two prohibitions are closely linked, and the addition of the post-positive conjunction *de* ("and") signals this close connection. Since most abortions were induced by drugs, Noonan interprets A7 as specifically proscribing the giving of abortifacients (Noonan: 10). This interpretation seems too narrow: (a) It overlooks the pairing of the additional commandments, and (b) it overlooks many other reasons to secure potions, for example, for increased sexual potency or to secure a lover. However, Noonan might be correct in seeing A7 as including abortifacients and serving as an oral link to A8 and A9 that follow.

Although deliberate abortion and infanticide were not considered to be options in Jewish circles, they were widely regarded within Hellenistic culture as a normal mode of family limitation (*ABD* 1:34; Fox: 343). Thus, these two infractions were repeatedly underscored in the Jewish sources created for gentile instruction. The three examples below illustrate how the dual prohibitions of abortion and infanticide were routinely placed one after the other within Jewish sources:

Do not let
[a] a woman destroy the unborn babe in her belly,
[b] nor after its birth throw it before the dogs
     and the vultures as a prey. (*Pseudo-Phocylides* 184f.)

The law [Torah] . . .
[a] forbids woman to cause abortion of what is begotten,
[b] or to destroy it afterward. (Josephus, *Ag. Ap.* 2.202)

[a] [W]omen who slay the burden of the womb,
[b] and all who lawlessly cast off their offspring;
     wizards and witches with them; them also
     the wrath of the heavenly and incorruptible God
     shall bring to the pillory. (*Sibylline Oracles* 2.281–85).

The *Didache*, consequently, stands solidly within the Jewish tradition in proscribing abortion and infanticide. What one can conclude, therefore, is that the framers of the *Didache* deliberately modified the Jewish Decalogue so as to exclude precisely those injunctions that would have been impossible to maintain within a gentile cultural milieu and, on the other hand, to include those three pairs of infractions that were particularly odious to Jewish sensibilities. Since all three pairs would have been condoned by most gentiles, the insertion of these pairs clearly implies that the novice was expected to alter his/her moral sensibilities during the time of his/her training. When it came time "to reprove against failings" (*Did.* 4:3) or to "confess in full your failings" (4:14), the novice would be ready to judge and to be judged by standards remarkably different from those prevailing in popular culture. The countercultural force of the *Didache* thus becomes apparent.

#1s ABORTION AND INFANTICIDE IN THE ANCIENT WORLD

Rodney Stark has noted that infanticide and botched abortions contributed to the situation that in the Roman population men outnumbered women by 40 percent. In the Christian communities, however, this ratio was reversed. In a climate where abortion and infanticide were prohibited, Stark concludes that "the abundance of Christian women resulted in higher birthrates" (see #1g) and this "superior fertility contributed to the rise of Christianity" (128).

Abortion and infanticide were widely practiced and legally sanctioned within the empire (Pomeroy 1995: 166–70). When fertility rates no longer sufficed to replenish the Roman population even during times of comparative prosperity and peace, imperial legislation endeavored to mandate marriage and childbearing for all Roman citizens. According to the *Lex Julia de maritandis ordinibus* (18 B.C.E.) and the *Lex Papia-Poppaea* (9 C.E.), men still unmarried at twenty-five years of age and women unmarried at twenty forfeited their right to receive inheritances or legacies from nonrelatives. Those married without children forfeited half of their inheritance. Husbands with three children, on the other hand, were given preference in filling public offices. Their wives, meanwhile, were released from the perpetual legal "guardianship of women" and were able to enter into legal and financial transactions in their own name. Even though this legislation was "unpopular and not particularly effective," it remained in force until the fourth century (Grubbs: 381).

The scope of medical attention given to contraceptives and abortions testifies to the importance of these measures, especially among those who could afford medical attention:

> According to [the Greek physician] Soranus, there were only two reasons for a doctor to refuse to help a woman abort: (a) when the child was the product of adultery and (b) when the woman's

only reason for wanting an abortion was to preserve her beauty. The one case in which abortion was considered essential on medical grounds was when the woman was so young that her uterus was too small. (Rousselle: 44f.)

Regarding the last point, it is helpful to remember the study of Keith Hopkins revealing that pagans were three times as likely to be married before the age of thirteen as Christians (Stark: 106). Child brides, therefore, found themselves pregnant before the onset of their first menstrual flow. Hopkins notes that "Roman physicians suggested that it might be wise to defer intercourse until menarche, but did not stress the matter" (Stark: 107). These early pregnancies, consequently, invited complications which required medical intervention. Celsus (not the one writing against Christianity), writing in the first century, warned physicians that an abortion "requires extreme caution and neatness, and entails great risk" (cited in Stark: 120). As a result of the total unawareness of microbes and the crudeness of medical procedures, even therapeutic abortions frequently resulted in either permanent sterility or death. On the other hand, since Christian women married later, they were normally spared the necessity of requiring an abortion. Thus, Christian mothers fared better, and the birth rate of Christians outpaced that of the pagan population.

According to custom, an infant was placed at the feet of the father after the birth. If he picked it up, this symbolized that he accepted the child as his own, and the child was given a name, nurture, and protection. If the father refused to pick the child up, the infant was disposed of as unwanted and unneeded. Philo notes that while Jewish parents bless every infant born to them, pagans sometimes "slay them with their own hands, and stifle the first breath of their children" (*Special Laws* 3.114). Still others, Philo continues, are carried into a deserted place and exposed to the elements "in the hope that they may be saved by some one" before wild beasts and birds "attack them and feast on the delicate banquet" (*Special Laws* 3.115). From his Jewish vantage point, Philo judged parents who exposed their newborn babes as guilty of "homicide" (*Special Laws* 3.118)—a judgment which the *Didache* clearly endorsed.

Regarding the penalties following upon abortions, Philo clearly distinguished between the "unformed" and the "formed" fetus. When aborting an unformed fetus, Philo noted that a fine sufficed, while, in the cases where the aborted fetus has "a distinct [human] shape in all its parts, having received all its proper connective and distinctive qualities, he shall die" (*Special Laws* 3.108). Following this line of thought, which finds a resonance in the literature of the period, it would follow that the *Didache*'s prohibition not to "murder offspring by means of abortion" (2:2) probably implied that one is dealing here with a formed fetus. While we cannot know to what degree the *Didache* would sanction the use of herbs or withdrawal to prevent conception, it would be safe to conclude that the prohibition against abortion as murder did not rely on any notion of "ensoulment from the first moment of conception" but dealt with the much more tangible reality of the formed fetus being "like a statue lying in a sculptor's workshop, requiring nothing more than to be released and sent out into the world" (*Special Laws* 3.109).

Justin Martyr, writing an open letter to the emperor and to the Roman people in 150 C.E., described the training practiced by Christians as follows:

> [W]e have been taught that to expose newly-born children is the part of wicked men; and this we have been taught lest we should do any one an injury, and lest we should sin against God, first, because we see that almost all so exposed (not only the girls, but also the males) are brought up in prostitution. . . . And again [we refrain from exposing our new-born] lest some of them be not picked up, but die, and we become murderers. (*First Apology* 27, 29)

Presumably Justin did not exaggerate the truth when he invited his Roman audience to recall that exposed children were normally rescued by calloused individuals expecting to gain a profit by raising them for use in the sex trade (*ABD* 6:67; Pomeroy 1995: 140f.). Justin, like Philo, notes that those who do not get rescued die and thus turn their parents into "murderers"—a judgment the *Didache* clearly endorses.

All in all, therefore, the *Didache* represents the first Christian statement opposing abortion and infanticide. In so doing, however, the *Didache* (along with Justin Martyr) does not rely on any new teaching of Jesus. Rather, the Christian sources merely embrace the prevailing Jewish reverence for human life: (a) anyone deliberately aborting a formed fetus (using drugs or surgery) extinguishes a human life; (b) anyone exposing a newborn infant risks becoming a murderer.

Implications of Variations in Decalogues for Gentiles

As instruction in the Way of Life was transmitted, one might expect that local variations would emerge. In the table below, the decalogue of the *Didache* is presented along with three variants:

Teaching of the Apostles	Didache—	Ecclesiastic Canons of the Apostles	Apostolic Constitutions
You will . . .	You will . . .	You will . . .	You will . .
not commit adultery	not murder	not murder	not murder
not murder	not commit adultery	not commit adultery	not commit adultery
not bear false witness	not corrupt boys	not corrupt a boy	not corrupt boys
not violate boys	not have illicit sex	not steal	not have illicit sex
not have illicit sex	not steal	not be a diviner (Did. 3:4)	not steal
not make magic	not practice magic	not be an astrologer (Did. 3:4)	not practice magic
not make evil medicines	not make potions	not be a sorcerer	not make potions
not kill your son in abortion	not murder offspring by means of abortion	not cause abortion	not murder offspring by means of abortion
not cut down one having been born	not kill one having been born	not kill it after it is born	not kill one having been born
not desire anything from the things of your neighbor	not desire the things of your neighbor	not desire anything of your neighbor	not desire the things of your neighbor

Each of these decalogues begins with the prohibition against murder and/or adultery (sixth/seventh commandments) and ends with the prohibition against coveting (the tenth commandment). Pederasty, abortion, and the exposure of infants are included in each list in roughly the same place. Each list, however, has prohibitions unique to itself. On the basis of this evidence, I am inclined to draw three conclusions:

1. If the Decalogue of Ex 20:1–17 had been pivotal in the training of novices, one would have expected that the decalogues within these various training manuals would have been gradually rearranged (in either oral or written reproductions) with an eye to bring them into harmony with the text of Exodus. As it is, however, the variety of decalogues assures us that local tradition was more decisive in stabilizing the list of commandments than reference to Ex 20:1–17 (*ABD* 6:386). One can surmise that spiritual guides within local churches relied on their own intuitions and their own prior training to devise commandments suitable for those being trained. Thus, in each case, the authority of the spiritual guides shines forth as the determining factor and not conformity to a written Bible or harmonization with the universal church. Thus, a legitimate diversity and freedom existed even though everyone appealed to the revelation by Jesus though the apostles of the will of the Father respecting what we are to be and to do to enter into the kingdom of God.

2. In most instances, the Way of Life training material was transmitted orally for quite some time before and even after it was written down. Oral transmission in a community setting is remarkably faithful and conservative because the multiplicity of oral reciters and aural hearers has the effect of repeatedly correcting chance variations (Ong 1982: 40f., 67). Thus, when one encounters variants in the decalogue, this more assuredly represents local adaptations frozen because of repetition rather than instances of faulty recall. "Knowledge is hard to come by and precious, and [a primary oral] society regards highly those wise old men and women who specialize in conserving it" (Ong 1982: 41). On the other hand, minor variants, such as inversions in the ordering of the commandments, could easily be accepted as "faithful" since a given community might embrace repeaters who enforced such variations.

3. Quite clearly there was no master text being copied or master teacher being consulted by all. If and when such a thing takes place, one can be certain that the prohibitions and their order would remain intact. The *Apostolic Constitutions* provide an illustrative case. These were compiled in Greek in 380 C.E. Within this larger church manual, the *Didache* is presented in its entirety but with frequent expansions (being 50 percent longer) and some significant alterations as well. When it comes to the decalogue, however, the wordings for the commandments are identical and in order. In the *Apostolic Constitutions,* however, each of the prohibitions is supported by a citation from Scripture—an addition designed to give it

greater weight. It is unlikely, though not impossible, that the oral transmission of a list would remain unchanged after three hundred years of repetition. Thus, the framers of the *Apostolic Constitutions* most probably made use of a written text, which, as it turns out, demonstrates an historical continuity with the *Didache*.

The Five Speech Infractions

After the decalogue, five speech-infractions are proscribed using the same linguistic structure as found in the decalogue. First, the novice is trained not to swear falsely (*ouk epiorkēseis*). This clearly refers to the third commandment (Ex 20:7). Philo notes that this commandment requires that one tell the truth even when not invoking God as a witness (*Decalogue* 84). If one must swear an oath, however, Philo explains that this is tantamount to "calling on God to give his testimony concerning the matters which are in doubt" (*Decalogue* 86). Then the novice is warned against bearing false witness. This clearly refers to the eighth commandment: "You will not bear false witness against your neighbor" (Ex 20:16). Next, the novice is warned against speaking badly of anyone. The Torah specifically prohibits speaking badly of "father or mother" (Ex 21:16); next, against holding grudges (Zech 7:10; *Barn.* 2:8, *1 Clem.* 2:5). Finally, against being "double-minded or double-tongued" (*Did.* 2:4)—a reference to the person "who says one thing and thinks another" (Niederwimmer 1998: 91).

The final admonition is reinforced by an aphorism: "Being double-tongued is a snare of death" (*Did.* 2:4). The idea that an unruly tongue brings on death is widely attested in Jewish sources (Prv 13:14; 14:27; 21:6; Ps 17:6; Tb 14:10; Sir 28:13–26; *b. Arakhin* 15a–b). In the *Targum Neofiti*, moreover, the prohibition against being "double-tongued" is changed to "triple-tongued" and is related to giving evidence "when you know that he is innocent in the trial" (*Tg. Lev.* 19:16). Thus, if the explanatory additions of the targum are reliable, the implication is that false evidence is a death-dealing snare—for, on the one hand, if the false evidence goes undetected, then the innocent are entrapped; on the other hand, if the false evidence is exposed, then the one lying is entrapped.

Jonathan A. Draper (1983: 56–59) offers the ingenious suggestion that *Did.* 2:3–4 was designed to recall and paraphrase the kind of speech infractions that Jews were accustomed to hearing in association with "love your neighbor as yourself" (Lv 19:18) in Lv 19:11–18. The parallels with the Septuagint would be as follows:

B1 not swear falsely = opening words of Lv 19:12
B2 not bear false witness = paraphrase of Lv 19:15a

B3 not speak badly [of anyone] = opening words of Lv 19:14
B4 not hold grudges = paraphrase of Lv 19:18a
B5 not be double-minded nor double-tongued = free re-creation of
    Lv 19:16

The fact that the *Didache* does not follow the order given in Leviticus 19 and omits some of its material weighs against Draper's suggestion. On the other hand, a case could be made for the *Didache* improving on Leviticus 19 by arranging the first four speech infractions in the order of their gravity. Further, the omission of Lv 19:13, which deals with stealing, and Lv 19:17, which deals with hating, could be allowed on the grounds that these failings are treated elsewhere (*Did.* 2:2 and 2:7). Nonetheless, this seems too contrived. It seems safer to allow that the framers of the *Didache* relied on their own intuitions of holiness and their own prior training to devise commandments suitable for those being trained. Rather than looking for a written source that stabilized the composition of the *Didache*, therefore, one must allow that "oral societies live very much in a present which keeps itself in equilibrium or homeostasis by sloughing off memories which no longer have present relevance" (Ong 1982: 46).

After the five speech infractions, a positive mandate is used to summarize: "Your word will not be false nor empty, but will be fulfilled by action" (*Did.* 2:5). A "false" word implies a deception; an "empty" word implies an unfulfilled promise. The novice, in every situation, is trained to have his/her words match his/her deeds. In today's street language: "Walk your talk."

Five Prohibited Dispositions

Following the decalogue and the five speech infractions, five injurious dispositions are proscribed (*Did.* 2:6):

[C1] You will not be covetous,
[C2] (and) not greedy,
[C3] (and) not a hypocrite,
[C4] (and) not bad-mannered,
[C5] (and) not arrogant.

The first two dispositions are related—both pertain to an inordinate attachment to goods. The last two dispositions may also be related—both pertain to an inordinate attachment to one's self-importance. These pairs frame the term "hypocrite," and one can imagine that the hypocrisy referred to is intimately linked with the attachment to goods and to one's self-importance—a hint that will be taken up again in chapter 4 below, when "hypocrites" are again encountered in fasting and praying (*Did.* 8:1f.).

For the sake of argument, let's imagine that the five bad dispositions are so named because they represent those very traits that have caused much suffering and ruin among the members of the Didache community. Who are the covetous, greedy, bad-mannered, arrogant hypocrites? Are they currently members of the community? Are they former members? Are they outsiders causing many of the community to suffer? These questions will be left unanswered here and will be taken up afresh in chapter 2 when the entire emphasis on greed and generosity, which occupies 36 percent of the Way of Life (1:4b–1:6; 2:6; 3:5, 7–9; 4:5–8) will be fully considered.

Spiritual Parenthood and the Presence of the Lord

Once the negative prohibitions are accounted for, the training moves on to delineate how one must cultivate the discipline to act and think in such a way as to remain far from any of the grievous infractions named. At the same time, there is a transition in mood signaled by the fact that the novice is now, for the first time, to be routinely addressed as "my child." This verbal clue signals that the master at this point becomes, by implication, a "mother" or "father" transmitting to his beloved offspring wisdom for living. One is prepared for this transition by *Did.* 2:7, which begins by saying, "you will not hate any person," and ends by noting that "some you will love more than your own soul." First among those in the latter category will be one's spiritual father or mother whom the novice "will remember night and day" and "honor as the Lord" (*Did.* 4:1).

The Greek expression *teknon mou* literally signifies "my offspring" without regard for age or sex. In this context, however, it cannot be supposed that the master trainer is the biological father or mother of the novice. In the Septuagint, *teknon mou* is already used metaphorically as an intimate form of address (Gn 43:29) or to denote a novice in relationship to his trainer and mentor (1 Sm 3:16; 26:17). In the wisdom tradition, the one being nurtured to walk in the path of wisdom is repeatedly called "my son" (e.g., Prv 1:8, 10, 15; 2:1; 3:1, 11, 12, 21, etc.). The habitual use of *pais* ("son") instead of *teknon* ("child") in this literature may be significant, since *pais* literally refers to a male child between seven and fourteen years.

In the *Didache*, *teknon* may be used precisely because initiation into this community pertains to both women and men equally (as suggested above). While some aspects of the training itself may be oriented toward men (e.g., corrupting boys [2:2], emphasizing gentleness [3:7], disposing of business profits [4:6]), one could make a case that everything in the Two Ways could be appropriately applied to women as well. In the Pauline tradition, Paul does not hesitate to liken himself to either "a [female] nurse taking care of her children (*tekna*)" or "a father with his children (*tekna*)" (1 Thes 2:7, 11). Meanwhile, in the Pastoral Epistles, Timothy and Titus, church leaders trained by Paul (1 Cor 4:17; Phil 2:22), are uniformly greeted with the term *teknon* rather than *pais* (1 Tm 1:2; 2 Tm 1:2; Ti 1:4).

When the novice is addressed as "my child," this clearly signals that the mentor has come to take responsibility for the novice. Thus, novices are being fathered and mothered by their mentors (see #1t). If one extrapolates the evidence even further, one might imagine that the appearance of "my child" at the midpoint of the training program may signal the tragic case of many novices who, by this point, have despaired of winning over their biological fathers and/or mothers by prayer and fasting (*Did.* 1:3). In the face of this loss, such persons would have the need to bear their grief and to share their struggles with another "father" or "mother" who stands for them and with them in their new commitments.

#1T SPIRITUAL FATHERHOOD IN THE RABBINIC TRADITION

The rabbinic tradition is permeated with the notion of spiritual fatherhood. Put quite succinctly: "Anyone who teaches Torah to the son of his fellow is considered as if he made [fathered] him" (*b. Sanhedrin* 99b). It follows from this that masters routinely addressed their disciples as "my sons" (e.g., *Avot de Rabbi Nathan* 24a; *b. Baba Batra* 10b). When it came to deciding whether to seek a lost article belonging to one's father or one's master, the rule developed that one was to give precedence to the need of one's master's over that of one's natural father. The Mishnah explains:

> For his father brought him into the world,
> But his master, who taught him wisdom, will bring him
>   into the life of the world to come. (*m. Baba Mesia* 2:11)

The sage, therefore, who gives wisdom which opens up "the life of the world to come" is to be prized over one's father who brought him into this world.

The notion of spiritual fatherhood extended to God as well. In the Jewish tradition, God was honored as the "Father" of Israel (e.g., Dt 32:6; Is 63:16; Jer 31:9) and as "Father" of the king of Israel (e.g., 2 Sm 7:14; 1 Chr 17:13; 22:10; 28:6; Ps 89:26). This "fatherhood" was based not upon God's activity in creating—a trait shared with gentiles—but upon his election, his caring for them, his training them in Torah. According to the Jewish tradition, consequently, functional fatherhood took precedence over biological fatherhood.

Applying this to the *Didache*, it is no surprise that the "one speaking to you the word of God" is honored "as the Lord" (4:1), since the mentor was effectively God-fathering and God-mothering the novice. Nor is it a surprise that the mentor related to the one being trained as "my child" for indeed, the "spiritual father" or "spiritual mother" was doing for the novice what their own parents were unable to do, namely, nurturing them into the life of the world to come.

The Five Fences Examined More Closely

Didache 3:1 serves as a fitting opening to the five illustrations of how to avoid major infractions by keeping guard against minor infractions that might not be serious in themselves but which form a slippery slope toward great infractions. In each case, the linguistic repetition is apparent, and, quite evidently, *Did.* 3:1–6 formed an oral unit bound together by a single logic.

The progression of the five topics, however, remains puzzling. In the Sermon on the Mount, Jesus offers five illustrations of how the righteousness of his disciples must exceed "that of the scribes and the Pharisees" (Mt 5:20), but only murder and adultery are treated in common with those topics named in the *Didache*. The flow of topics, meanwhile, does not parallel what one finds in the decalogue, save again for murder and adultery. Murder and adultery were the gravest sins against one's neighbor; hence, it is no surprise to find them treated first by the framers of the *Didache*. Idolatry comes next, and one must suppose that the framers of the *Didache* were acutely aware that gentile converts had to be warned against seemingly innocent practices that formed the path leading to idolatry. The same holds true for thefts and blasphemies.

The first sequence warns against yielding to anger, since "anger is the path leading to murder" (*Did.* 3:2). This seems evident enough and finds Jewish and Christian parallels (e.g., *Testament of Simeon* 2:6–7; 3:1–6; *b. Yoma* 75a; Mt 5:21f.). If one reads *zēlōtēs* as "envious," then a graded progression exists from envious to contentious to hot-headed to murderous. The implied message is clear: "Check the beginnings lest you proceed any further down this path." In the Gospel of Matthew, Jesus begins by warning against anger but then passes on to consider insults and name calling—issues that find no parallel here.

The second sequence warns against yielding to lust, since "lust (*epithymia*) is the path leading to illicit sex (*porneia*)" (*Did.* 3:3). The term *porneia* here harks back to the decalogue (*Did.* 2:2), where it is paired with "pederasty." More to the point, "lust" and "illicit sex" are listed side by side when describing the Way of Death (*Did.* 5:1).

The literal translation of *hypsēlophthalmos* as "one-looking-up" makes no sense here unless it is correctly situated. In traditional societies in the

Middle East, clothing usually covered everything but the upper face, the hands, and the feet of a woman. Female slaves, of course, were deliberately displayed naked in the marketplaces and outside brothels. Free women, however, preserved their honor and their social standing by covering nearly all parts of their body in public places. In traditional societies, men habitually associated with men in public and never had occasion for either addressing or socializing with women. Such acts, properly speaking, normally took place in the family courtyard away from prying eyes. In the public sphere, virtuous men were trained not "to look up" into the eyes or "to look down" at the feet of passing women, who were off limits to them. These two areas represent the places where female skin was exposed. Naked slaves and half-naked prostitutes were available to men (#1q, #1r); hence, the *Didache* should not be interpreted as concerned about examining these sort of women.

On occasion, Jewish sources give attention to the dangers of "looking up." Two such instances are the offered here:

> He who gazes [lit., looks up] at a woman [to see her face] eventually comes to sin, and he who looks [down] at a woman's heel [by way of following her?] will beget degenerate children. (*Derek Erez Rabbah* 56a)

> The simple-hearted man . . . averts his eyes from a woman's beauty, so as not to mislead or corrupt his mind. . . . I [the patriarch Issachar] have not had intercourse with any other woman but my wife: I have not committed fornication through a lustful eye [lit., by the uplifting of the eyes]. (*Testament of Issachar* 4:4; 7:2–3)

The *Didache*, at first glance, may appear to parallel Jesus' judgment that "everyone who looks at a woman with lust has already committed adultery with her in his heart" (Mt 5:28). Jesus, however, "is saying that disciples are to regard looking lustfully at a woman as an offense no less serious than an act of adulterer" (Gundry 1994: 87). In contrast, the logic of the *Didache* and of the *Derek Erez Rabbah* cited above is that one must check even the innocent gesture of "looking up" into the face of another man's wife, lest this lead to "lust," and lust lead to adultery. Thus, even when the Sermon on the Mount and the *Didache* treat common topics, each does so using a guiding logic distinct unto itself.

The third sequence warns against engaging in divination, since "it is the path leading to idolatry" (*Did.* 3:4). This is the first and only mention of idolatry in the training program. Divination is specified as the leading inducement to idolatry. The Greek term *oiōnoskonos* ("divination") has the root *oiōnos* ("omen-bird") and represents the most typical Homeric method of divination. This method required some training and insight but was by no means restricted to professionals. Homer, for instance, presents Odysseus, the favorite warrior of the goddess Athena, as receiving an omen sent from heaven that he readily and correctly interprets as a sign of Athena's protection in his adventure:

> Pallas Athena sent a heron to them, on the right, near their path; they saw it, not with their eyes through the murky night, but they heard its cry. And Odysseus rejoiced at that omen and made prayer to Athena. (*Iliad* 10:274)

In the opening centuries of the Christian era, there existed a "maze of techniques and oracular practice" (Fox: 215), and the author of the *Didache* undoubtedly wished to warn novices against any practice calculated to gain privileged information regarding the future through omens attributed to this or that pagan god. Later on, the novice will be trained to yield to the future assured that "apart from God, nothing happens" (3:10). In the *Didache*, consequently, providence replaces Fate, and the practice of righteousness replaces the practice of divination.

Besides divination, the novice is warned against three other kinds of activities designed to alter or determine one's fate. An enchanter (*epaoidos*) typically made use of incantations and spells, generally invoking the power of some god or angel for either beneficial or harmful ends. Even in Jewish circles, such practices might be found. Josephus, for instance, when commenting on the wisdom of Solomon (cf. Wis 7:16–21), noted that God had bestowed upon this wise king such surpassing knowledge that he could make use of "incantations" by which distempers could be alleviated and demons dispelled (*Ant.* 2.45). To demonstrate his point, Josephus told the story of how one of his contemporaries, a certain Jew named Eleazar, "reciting the incantation which he [Solomon] composed" (*Ant.* 2.47) for the purpose of publicly removing a demon and thereby healing an afflicted man in the presence of the Roman general Vespasian (d. 79 C.E.) and his soldiers. While some Jewish writers would have been too ashamed to recount the story of a Jew making use of spells that, according to Enoch, were revealed by "Semyasa, the leader of the fallen angels" (*1 Enoch* 8:3), other Jewish writers, such as Josephus, deliberately tried to maintain Jewish superiority in this pagan field by claiming that Jews possessed superior spells that had venerable roots going back to Noah, Moses, or Solomon (Hengel 1974: 1.240f.; Schürer 3.342–57). The *Didache* offered no ground for this latter view and strongly warned novices away from either practicing spells or from even looking on as others did so.

Astrology is also set forth as categorically dangerous. While some Jewish circles halfheartedly embraced the legitimacy of astrology (see #1u), the framers of the *Didache* did not quibble with half measures. No matter how "innocent" and "useful" astrology may have seemed, the framers of the *Didache* regarded it as leaning toward idolatry and, accordingly, warned novices to avoid it entirely.

#1u THE PREVALENCE AND MARGINAL ACCEPTABILITY OF ASTROLOGY

Alexander, as a result of his conquests, introduced a Greek modification of Chaldaeo-Egyptian astrology throughout the Mediterranean world. With the collapse of belief in traditional Greek religion, astrology served to bind together the universal belief in Fate with a "scientific" method for unlocking the workings of Fate as they affected individual lives (Hengel 1974: 1.236). Astrology "pervaded the whole of Western thought, and became the principal form of divination" (Rose: 799).

> With the emergence of the astrological perspective, it was widely believed that human life was ruled not by capricious chance, but by an ordered and humanly knowable destiny defined by the celestial deities according to the movements of the planets. Through such knowledge it was thought that man could understand his fate and act with a new sense of cosmic destiny. . . . Belief in astrology pervaded the Hellenistic world and was embraced by Stoic, Platonic and Aristotelian philosophers, by mathematical astronomers and medical physicians, by Hermetic esotericists and members of the various mystical religions. (Tarnas: 82f.)

A practice so widely acclaimed and so beneficial for aligning one's life with the heavenly spheres could hardly be easily ignored or entirely uprooted by any alternative religious movement. The community of Qumran, for example, championed a complete segregation from both pagan and corrupt Jewish influences. Yet this segregation did not prevent its members from making use of astrological speculation (Hengel 1974: 1:237f.). Even the rabbinic synthesis provides clear testimony that the rabbis had adapted astrological signs for their own purposes. For example, regarding those born under the signs of the zodiac where Jupiter and Mars were the ruling planets, some rabbis had this to say:

> "He who is born under Jupiter [called 'righteous'] will be a person who habitually does righteousness." R. Nahman bar Isaac said, "Doing righteousness in good deeds."

"He who is born under Mars will shed blood." R. Ashi said, "That means he'll be a surgeon, thief, slaughterer, or circumciser."

Rabbah said, "I was born under Mars [and am none of these]." Said Abbayye, "Yeah, and you inflict punishment [as an elder] and kill [with words]." (*b. Shabbat* 156a)

While the Babylonian Talmud clearly signals that some rabbis approved the use of astrology for divining the destiny of individuals, the major rabbis held that the destiny of Israel was an exception:

R. Hanina says, "One's [birth] star is what makes one smart, one's star is what gives wealth, and Israel is subject to the stars."

R. Yohanan said, "Israel is not subject to the stars. . . . As it is said: 'Thus says the Lord, Do not learn the way of the gentiles, nor be dismayed at the signs of the heavens, for the nations are dismayed at them' (Jer 10:2). They are dismayed, but the Israelites are not dismayed." (*b. Shabbat* 156a)

Here one can see that Rabban Yohanan ben Zakkai (1–80 C.E.) was presented as having refuted those rabbis who sanctioned astrology. According to Yohanan, astrology might have some usefulness for divining the destiny of individuals, but when it came to Israel, he insisted that the Lord and not the constellations determined her future. Even when it came to individuals, however, the Talmud allowed that astrology could divine a person's future, but, at the same time, case examples were multiplied to show that acts of charity done by an individual served to modify their fate (*b. Shabbat* 156b). Thus, the rabbis were seemingly forced to allow that the ever-present and ever-popular use of astrology had some social sanction; yet, when it came to maintaining the destiny of Israel and of individuals doing acts of charity, the rabbis forced astrologers to back down and to acknowledge the preeminence of divine providence.

The *Didache* warns against becoming "a purifier." The meaning here is obscure. André Tuilier suggests that the term *perikathairein* ("to purify or to make purifications") might refer to something like Dt 18:10, where one secures divine assistance by "making his son or daughter pass through fire" (Rordorf 1978a: 153 n. 7). Tuilier also makes reference to an article by Knox in which this obscure Greek term refers to "circumcision" (cf. Jos 5:4). This provides little assistance, since it would seem unprecedented to regard circumcision as leading to idolatry. The reference to Dt 18:10 is also obscure. More to the point is the observation by Josephus that the Jewish sect of Essenes made use of "purifications" as part of their own divinations:

> There are also those among them [the Essenes] who undertake to foretell things to come, [1] by reading the holy books, and [2] using several sorts of purifications, and [3] being perpetually conversant in the discourses of the prophets; and it is but seldom that they miss in their predictions. (*J.W.* 2.159)

Various "purifications" were widely known and practiced by the Greek oracles at Delphi, Claros, and Didyma as preparation for revelatory dreams or visions that would disclose the future (see #6q). Josephus, in the text just cited, appears to suggest that the Essenes practiced purifications that gave them access to the secrets of the "holy books" and the "prophets." If this is the case, then Josephus clearly testifies that some Jews were very successful at divining the future and that they used religiously sanctioned purifications in the process. The *Didache*, in contrast, knows nothing of such legitimate purifications. In its purview, all purifications led to idolatry.

The fourth sequence warns against becoming false since "falsehood is the path leading to theft" (*Did.* 3:5). The causal relationship here is not immediately evident. One could surmise that falsely representing one's needs so as to receive alms or communal assistance amounted to a kind of theft that would, in the end days, have to be paid back to "the last quadrans" (1:5). More to the point, however, the intent here might be parallel to what one finds in the *Shepherd of Hermas,* where being false in business transactions is identified as leading to robbery (*Man.* 3.2, 5). From this vantage point, it can be understood how the "lover of money" would be prone to taking the path whereby one would defraud one's neighbor. Furthermore, if the amount of social esteem is thought of as limited in quantity, it could also be understood how the "glory seeker" would be prone to grabbing more than one's merited share. In the end, each of these characteristics is put forward as leading to the breaking of the fifth commandment (*Did.* 2:2[A5]).

The fifth and final sequence warns against grumbling since "it is the path leading to blasphemy" (*Did.* 3:6). The Greek term *blasphēmia* derives from *blaptō* + *phēmē* ("to injure" + "speech") and, hence, could be rendered as "slander." In the Septuagint, however, this term is used almost exclusively to denote injurious speech against the Lord, what is commonly called "blasphemy." Since the verb *goggyzein* ("to murmur") is used repeatedly to describe the grumbling of the Israelite people in the desert (Ex 16:2, 7[2x], 8[2x], 9, 12), some scholars believe this is the implied case history that stands behind the warning against murmuring (Ross: 218). While an individual mentor might have used this case history to illustrate the meaning of *Did.* 3:6, the text itself does not give any hint in this direction (Niederwimmer 1998: 99).

Even pagans could easily understand that, in the face of bad times, a devotee could complain that God should have arranged things differently.

Epictetus, a first-century Cynic philosopher, made this point by calling his disciples to take an oath "never to distrust, nor accuse, nor murmur at any of the things appointed by God" (*Discourses* 1.14). He illustrated this with the following case:

> How do we act in a voyage? What is in my power? To choose the pilot, the sailors, the day, the hour [to cast off]. Afterwards comes a storm. What have I to care for? My part is [already] performed. This matter belongs to another, to the pilot. But [suppose] the ship is sinking; what then have I to do? That which alone I can do; I submit to being drowned, without fear, *without crying out, accusing God,* but as one who knows that what is born must likewise die. (*Discourses* 2.5, emphasis mine)

In brief, Epictetus advised his disciples "to make the best of what is in our power and take the rest as it occurs" (*Discourses* 1.1). "And how does it occur?" Epictetus responded: "As God wills" (*Discourses* 1.1). Thus, many pagans would easily have grasped how murmuring or grumbling regarding one's lot could lead to blasphemy ("cursing God").

The *Didache* affirmed the necessity of seeing everything as happening providentially: "You will accept the experiences befalling you as good things, knowing that, apart from God, nothing happens" (*Did*. 3:10). In the face of sickness, poverty, failure, and misunderstanding, therefore, the novice had to learn to reinterpret such "misfortunes" as "good things" ordained by God. Those grumbling in the face of misfortunes failed to see the "good" hidden therein. Within this framework, being "self-pleasing" (*authadēs* = *autos* "self" + *hēdomai* "pleasing") (*Did*. 3:6 and 5:1[A16]) led to blasphemy insofar as attachment to one's own interests blocked one's ability to see events as promoting God's enterprise. Likewise, being "evil-minded" or "badly disposed" (*ponērophrōn* = *ponēros* "evil" + *phronein* "to be minded or disposed") led to blasphemy insofar as someone with a bad disposition was unable to see the good in anything and thus instinctively blamed others—God included—for every misfortune.

#1v THE FENCE AROUND THE TORAH

In rabbinic materials, *Did*. 3:2–6 would be metaphorically referred to as "making a fence around Torah [infractions]." And how was this "fence" constructed? The rabbis would go beyond what was strictly forbidden by the written Torah and construct a "fence" of minor prohibitions to ensure that one was protected from getting near the commission of a greater sin.

The rabbis explained that Adam was the first person to "make a fence":

> What fence did Adam, the first man, make. . . ? It is stated:
>> And the Lord God commanded the man saying: "Of every tree of the garden, you may freely eat; but of the tree of the knowledge of good and evil, you shall not eat of it . . . ." [Gen 2:16f.]
>
> Adam was unwilling to tell this to Eve exactly as the Holy One, blessed be he, had spoken to him. He therefore made a fence to his words, over and about the words which the Holy One, blessed be he, had spoken to him. And this is what he said to her:
>> "But of the fruit of the tree which is in the midst of the garden, God has said, "You shall not eat of it, *neither shall you touch it . . .*" [Gen 3:2].
>
> By so doing he meant to keep both himself and Eve away from the tree, even to the extent of not touching it. (*ARN* 17a, emphasis added)

One cannot but marvel at how carefully and perceptively the rabbis used the details of the text for their own purposes. The rabbis noted that Adam went beyond the mandate of the Lord and made the tree off limits not only for eating but for touching as well. The "fence" Adam constructed failed. Nonetheless, the prohibition against touching was the "fence" designed to make the serious failing of eating more remote.

Regarding the *Didache*, one can acknowledge that a young man checking out the young women on a street corner (3:3), dabbling in astrology (3:4), and entertaining fantasies of being rich (3:5) is not evil in himself. Yet such seemingly innocent activities can lead to illicit sex, idolatry, and theft; hence, they were to be avoided.

In the *Derek Erez Zuta*, a manual for training rabbinic disciples, the novice was trained as follows: "Keep aloof from anything that may lead to sin, from anything hideous and from whatever seems hideous" (1:12). This corresponds to *Did*. 3:1 and introduces a series of rabbinic principles:

> Keep aloof from anything which may bring you to sin. [How so?]
>> [A] Recoil from [even] a minor sin
>>> that it may not lead you to a major sin.
>> [B] Hasten to [perform] a light precept
>>> and flee from [even] a trivial transgression
>>>> lest it will lead you to commit
>>>> a grave transgression. (*DEZ* 2:7)

At a later point, these principles were given concrete form as a short series of "fences":

[1] The first stage of vowing
   leads to folly;
[2] the first stage of ritual uncleanliness
   leads to idolatry;
[3] the first state of levity with women
   leads to unchastity. (*DEZ* 3:6)

From these examples, one can discern that the logic portrayed in *Did.* 3:2–6 finds ample parallels in rabbinic Judaism.

One can also wonder that the Christian Scriptures do not offer anything like this, not even in the Sermon on the Mount. When Jesus warns against getting angry or hurling insults at "a brother," it is not because these things might lead to murder but because, in Jesus' eyes, God judges these things with the same severity with which he judges murder (Mt 5:21f.). When Jesus warns men against looking at a woman lustfully, it is not because lusty desires might lead to adultery; rather, "everyone who looks at a woman with lust *has already committed adultery*" (Mt 5:28). If this is the case, gouging out an eye or cutting off a right hand may be the radical measures required to prevent "your whole body from going into hell" (Mt 5:30). Notice that it does not occur to Jesus that severing a penis would suffice, since, in his view, the lustful eye "has already committed adultery" (Mt 5:28). Here one has the logic of hyperbole—but no "fences."

The Rewards of Being Gentle

The themes found in *Did.* 3:8–10 are rephrased and repeated in *Did.* 4:1–4. The correspondence is as follows:

A. *Did.* 3:8 and 4:1 both deal with respect for the master's words.
B. *Did.* 3:9 and 4:2f. both deal with bonding to the community.
C. *Did.* 3:10 and 4:4 both deal with trust in providence.

Didache 3:8 takes its starting point from the mandate to be "gentle" (3:7). Six dispositions are named. The terms "long-suffering" (12x) and "good" (77x) find frequent use in the Christian Scriptures. The four remaining terms are found twice each. Draper finds that four of the six dispositions have equivalents in 1QS 4:2–4, where three are listed in the same order in the training material for novices at Qumran. It is doubtful, however, that this suffices to identify an "underlying common schema" (Draper 1983: 78). In *1 Clement*, for example, the writer advocates "lowly-minded" virtues such as "forbearance," "long-suffering," "walking in obedience to his words" (13:1–3). This section closes with an exact citation of Is 66:2 from the Septuagint: "Upon whom will I [the Lord] have respect, but to the gentle (*praun*) and calm (*hēsychion*) and [the one] trembling (*tremonta*) at my words" (*1 Clem.* 13:4). Thus, it is possible that Is 66:2 might have formed the rudimentary oral and mental template whereby being "gentle" (*Did.* 3:7) and "calm" (3:8) culminated in "trembling (*tremōn*) at the words" (3:8). The significance of this trembling has already been considered above.

Didache 3:9a continues the theme of 3:8 by naming two dispositions to be avoided. The economic significance of these dispositions will be developed in the next chapter. For the moment, however, one can note that 3:9b promises that the novice will soon discover that the members of the community he/she will be joining are the "just" and the "lowly" (3:9). In 4:2, the novice learns that members of the community are worthy to be called "saints" and that daily contact with them can be anticipated as satisfying their souls. Two details are of importance here:

1. Even though the eucharist was celebrated weekly (*Did.* 14:1), subsequent chapters will show that "the saints" met daily for work, for prayer, and for mutual encouragement and support. Since the novice is told that he/she "will seek" (4:2) them out, this implied that, once baptized, he/she would visit them in their homes and workshops. Quite possibly, in many cases, the newly baptized were forced by circumstances to reside and to eat all their meals in a Christian home (ch. 3 below). In the end, the text leaves multiple possibilities of interpretation.

2. The text, translated literally, signifies that the novice will seek "the faces (*prosōpa*) of the holy [ones]." Internal evidence coming later indicates that, while members are traveling on "the path of life," most have not been perfected. Hence, they are "saints" not so much by reference to their achieved sanctity as to their having been called by the Lord as "those whom the Spirit has made ready" (4:10b). A close parallel in the Christian Scriptures is 2 Tim 1:9.

The novice is presented with a paradoxical situation: by renouncing the "lofty" (the socially well-connected and the financially well-off) and binding one's soul to the "lowly" (*Did.* 3:9), he/she "may rest" or "find refreshment" (4:2) in their words. Such a suggestion runs counter to popular wisdom:

> Among pagan authors, "humility" had almost never been a term of commendation. It belonged to ignoble and abject characters. Men were born "sons of God," said the Stoics, and thus they should cherish no "humble or ignoble" thoughts about their nature. The humble belonged with the abject, the mean, the unworthy. (Fox: 324)

In analyzing the abusive treatment of *Did.* 1:3f., it was already clear that joining a community observing the *Didache* meant joining those who were "lowly" and "socially powerless." Ostracized by the "lofty" and by members of his/her own family, the novice was assured of a hellish existence. However, in the face of this, the mentor assures the novice that, in the future, he/she "will seek every day the presence of the saints in order that you may rest upon their words" (4:2). The metaphor of finding "rest" in someone's words in this context signified, negatively, the cessation of the fear/turmoil/anxiety surrounding the conversion process (as hinted at in 1:3f.). Positively, finding "rest" signified the future "comfort or support" (Bauer: 283a) that the novice would experience once he/she had established a new social identity (see ch. 3 below) and gained a new economic security (see ch. 2 below) within their new religious family of true believers.

#1w THE SIGNIFICANCE OF "REST"

The *Didache* does not give much direct attention to interior experiences. The reference to the novice seeking out the faces of the holy ones "in order that you may rest upon their words" (4:2), however, clearly points in this direction. "Rest" refers literally to the cessation of work, as in the phrase "day of rest" describing the Sabbath (Ex 16:23, 25; 20:10). Since having a trade was the normal requirement for members of the Didache communities (*Did.* 12:3f.), the promise of "rest" cannot be understood literally. Consequently, "rest" in this context might have served as a metaphor for the cessation of that fear/turmoil/anxiety resulting from the random acts of harassment at home and the breaking down of long-standing familial, religious, and social ties. Positively, "rest" might also have signified the "comfort or support" (Bauer: 283a) of finding oneself understood and embraced by caring and dedicated persons who shared one's life values and way of being in the world.

A recent issue of *Newsweek* tells the story of two deeply religious women who struggled to find God's will for them after hesitantly setting aside the traditional judgment on homosexuality that marked their religious upbringing. "We knew we loved one another but we also loved the Lord. We prayed and prayed for an answer" (20 March 2000, p. 60). When the answer gradually came, they set up house together and, with fear and trepidation, informed their trusted pastor. He told them categorically not to return. Their response: "It was the final rejection. It broke our hearts and our souls" (ibid.). There followed a period of despair. Then they found a religious community that advertised itself as "a diverse and welcoming church." Their story continues:

The congregation consisted of mostly older, button-down and carefully coifed married couples and widows. But the pastor wore a rainbow stole, a symbol of diversity. And members seemed genuinely friendly. After church Kunst put them to the test. She nervously introduced Meeker as her "partner" and steadied herself for the rebuff. Instead, the strangers responded with warm hugs and offers of coffee and bagels. The two women broke down and cried. (ibid.)

While the social and economic ties involved in joining a Christian church today are much weaker than that experienced in the first century, this story nonetheless portrays how two wounded women ultimately came to discover "the presence of saints" with whom they might "rest upon their words" (*Did.* 4:2).

In the ancient world, the notion of finding "rest" was associated also with the satisfaction of finding true wisdom. In Ben Sira, for example, the quest for wisdom is spoken of in terms of a man searching for his true mate:

Search her out, discover her, seek her and you will find her. Then when you have her, do not let her go; thus you will afterward find rest (*anapausis*) and she will become your joy. (Sir 6:28f.)

Matthew applies this language to Jesus:

Take my yoke upon you, and learn from me; for I am gentle and humble of heart, and you will find rest (*anapausin*) for your souls. For my yoke is easy and my burden light. (Mt 11:29f.)

Philo of Alexandria (20 B.C.E.–50 C.E.) harmonizes with the thought of the above in working out his three stages of acquiring wisdom through the "way of virtue." In the first phase, beginners purge themselves of passion and of false opinions by attaching themselves to a master: "If you meet with anyone of the initiated, press him closely, cling to him . . . , stay till you have learnt his full lesson" (*Cherubim* 48). Having learned the basic disciplines, one progresses to the second stage, that of the proficient (*askētos*). At this stage, one passes beyond listening to instruction and "fixes his attention, not on what is said, but on those who say it and imitates their life as shown in the blamelessness of their actions" (*Mating* 69). This shift in focus might be precisely what the *Didache* had in mind when it specifically points to "the one speaking" (4:1) as being remembered and honored and not "what he/she said." In any case, in Philo's third stage, the proficient move toward the perfection of wisdom, where they ultimately find their rest:

> With the acquisition of wisdom, a person is brought to stability and rest. All forms of study and toil cease. This is because the mind is "released from the working out of its own projects, and is . . . emancipated from self-chosen tasks by reason of the abundance of the rain and ceaseless shower of blessings" (*Migration* 32). Rest is a metaphor for the "toil-free and trouble-free character of perfection. . ." [*Flight* 172f.]. (Deutsch: 124)

What one has here in Philo is a description of the personal strain experienced by the restless seeker in search for a truly wise and worthy way of life. Such a seeker eventually finds a community or a person who is able to satisfy the thirst for a richer life. By clinging to the adept, learning from him/her, and imitating his/her example, the seeker gradually enters into their "hidden" world. In the end, the strains and turmoil that characterized the quest finally fall away and give rise to the situation of rest. Earlier details on this point were presented in #1d.

The *Didache* was not familiar with or endorsing the system of Philo. However, parallel to what one finds in Philo, one can recognize that the metaphor, "rest (*epanapaēs*) upon their words" (4:2) might be an apt way to evoke the peace of mind and of heart that comes once a person has secured the way of life for which his/her soul thirsts. Both ancient and modern persons would have understood this, albeit in different ways and using different metaphors. In sum, therefore, finding "rest" in the company and in the words of a community living the Way of Life might have been the solemn promise that every mentor made to a novice. Such a promise would have come from the prior experience of the mentor and, with good reason, would have been anticipated by the novice as well.

The Art of Reconciliation

Being a realistic program, the *Didache* no sooner holds out the future promise of finding "rest" among the "saints" (4:2) than it turns to the darker side: "dissension" and "fighting" (4:3). The novice will be given an active role in preventing or in defusing the harmful effects of such community-splitting conduct. The actual practice of reconciliation and judging will be taken up in chapter 8 below, where the material of *Did.* 4:5–14 will be treated in detail.

The Significance of Not Being Double-Minded

Didache 4:4 has been puzzling to scholars. Its doublet, *Did.* 3:10, deals with surrender to providence; hence, "whether it will be or not" (4:4) might pertain to something in the future that God will cause to happen. What might that be? Barnabas employs the same phrase at a different point in his version of the Two Ways (19:5) but offers no hints as to its meaning. Hence, with Niederwimmer, we can say that what this phrase means "can no longer be determined with precision" (1998: 106). Yet consider the following:

1. The *Apostolic Constitutions* expands the *Didache* at this point to read:

Do not become double-minded in your prayer,
    whether it will be [answered] or not (7.11.1; also Hermas *Man.* 9:1).

In this context, however, "your prayer" most probably refers to the Lord's Prayer for the coming of the Kingdom (7.24.1 = *Did.* 8:2). If this expansion is to be trusted, therefore, it can be surmised that *Did.* 4:4 warns the novice not to be double-minded whether the Father will establish his Kingdom on earth.

2. Niederwimmer also makes use of the Georgian version, which at this point says:

In this also you shall not doubt: whether the judgment of God
    will come upon all human beings according to their works. (cited
    in Niederwimmer 1998: 107)

Since only a so-called "German translation" of the Georgian version of the *Didache* exists and since the original was either destroyed (or may never have existed), no conclusions can be securely grounded on this source. Rordorf entirely omits this as a reliable source, and the present volume does the same. Even Niederwimmer admits that "in light of its late and dubious tradition, the Georgian version is not to be regarded as an equal witness" (1998: 27).

3. In *1 Clement,* the author launches into an extended warning against being "double-minded" (*dipsychōmen*) and ends up making it quite clear that this hesitant or divided mind pertains to whether "he [the Lord] shall come quickly" (*1 Clem.* 23:3). Given the eschatological emphasis found in the Lord's Prayer (*Did.* 8:2), in the eucharistic prayers (*Did.* 9–10), and in the final exhortation which culminates in the Lord's coming (*Did.* 16:8), it is quite possible that *Did.* 4:4 has a meaning parallel to that of *1 Clement.*

In sum, *Did.* 4:4 does warn novices against being hesitant or doubtful regarding some future providential event. Probably the phrasing is deliberately vague, and mentors were expected to assure novices that the future was in God's hands—without entering into unnecessary details. Once they are baptized, however, the full import of God's coming, of his raising the dead, and of his gathering the elect into his Kingdom would be spelled out.

This will be fully detailed in chapters 4, 5, 6, and 10 below. In the end, therefore, the three suggestions made above do not need to be negotiated or relied on to give a definitive meaning to what was being expected. The *Didache* would provide the details in due course.

Three Special Household Rules

After dealing with the sharing of resources (a topic reserved for ch. 2 below), the *Didache* puts forward three household rules. Taken together, the three rules imply that the typical candidate had children and slaves. It will be discovered in the next chapter that the owning of slaves was not something reserved for the very rich; craftsmen of ordinary means frequently purchased one or more slaves to work with them in the family shop. Thus, the presence of slaves does not narrowly define the social status of candidates.

In the case of children, they were to be trained from their earliest years "in the fear (*phobon*) of God" (*Did.* 4:9). The *Didache* does not give any guidelines as to when and how such children were to be introduced into the community. Clearly, the framers of the *Didache* did not imagine that parents trained their children "in the Way of Life." Presumably, since the choice for the community was an adult decision prompted by the Spirit (4:10b), parents were expected to train their underage children in appropriate ways until such time as they came forward, in early adulthood, and asked for admittance (see #3g). In any case, parents were not to withdraw their guiding and protecting hand from their children.

In the case of slaves, the issues were more complex. In pagan households, it was taken for granted that slaves served the same deities to which their masters were attached. In a Christian household, it could hardly have been different, since, in effect, slaves expected their superiors to orchestrate the religious and social rites that transpired in the household. On the other hand, the master and mistress were directed not to issue commands "in your bitterness lest they [the slaves] should ever not fear the God who is over you both" (4:10). The implied logic here is that both masters and slaves owed a common service to their heavenly Master (also Eph 6:9); hence, masters, despite their social status, were not to command their slaves in *pikria* ("bitterness, animosity, anger, harshness" [Bauer: 657d]). For more details, see #1x.

The second half of *Did.* 4:10 is difficult to unravel. The intent of the *gar*-clause is to clarify the mandate that masters are not to be harsh in ordering their slaves. The meaning appears to be that "God does not come to call [anyone] according to [his/her] social status but [God calls] those

whom the Spirit has made ready." Niederwimmer believes that "the coming" referred to points to either the first or final coming of Jesus (1998:
111). This is unlikely, since "God" and not "Jesus" is the subject. Furthermore, if the past or future coming of Jesus was implied, then one
would have expected the framers of the *Didache* to have used the past or
future tense. As it stands, the present tense suggests that God calls to himself those whom the Spirit even now is making ready. The point of the *gar*-
clause is that this divine calling is not *kata prosōpon,* "according to
[his/her] face/countenance"—a metaphor for signaling "without regard
for social status" (Niederwimmer 1998: 111 n. 89). The earlier mandate
not to take into account "outward appearance" or "social status"
(*prosōpon*) when offering correction (4:3) makes use of this same term.

The overall sense of *Did.* 4:10 thus appears to be that God calls masters
and slaves alike without regard to their social status; hence, masters must
not despise or harshly treat their slaves, for they clearly are "the ones hoping in the same God as you" (4:10a). In view of what follows (4:11), it
would appear that the slaves in this case were neither Christians nor in formation to become Christians; hence, they rely on the same God someday
to call them just as their masters have already been called. From this perspective, therefore, the warning not to command slaves harshly has to do
with creating a climate in which slaves might be able to hear the Lord's call
and not have this voice hindered by the conduct of the master or mistress
(the Lord's disciple).

At this point, the spiritual mentor addressed the slaves directly. This
might be a hint that the training itself took place in the home of the candidate where household slaves were naturally present. Such a rule comes in
the wake of *Did.* 4:10, where it was stated that masters were not to treat
their slaves harshly. The central thrust appears to be that slaves' hearing
that their masters have limitations ought not to serve as an excuse to lose
respect or take advantage of them. Just as in the case of children, slaves
were expected to "fear the God who is over both of you" (4:10) until such
time as they were moved, under the impulse of the Spirit, to ask to be initiated into the Way of Life. Thus, the mentor (and not the master or mistress) admonished the household slaves then present to be subject to their
"lords" (masters) and to obey them as representatives of God with the
same "shame and fear" (4:11).

In the Christian Scriptures, shame (*aischynē*) is used only in the negative
sense. In classical Greek, however, it can be used positively as the disposition preventing someone from acting shamefully. The same can be said for
the disposition of fear. Here, both these inner dispositions are being recommended to slaves as the practical guides for maintaining order within
the household. This again enforces the notion that slaves have no interior
rule of life whereby to be self-possessed and self-directed; rather, they were

directed to fulfill the wishes and commands of their lords. When acting upon the orders of a master, for example, a slave would not be held accountable for having committed or collaborated in the commission of a criminal act. In such cases, the slave acted in the name of his master and, if punishment or honor was due, it belonged to the master and not to the slave. Thus, in this setting, it was important that the Christian master or mistress be a worthy "image of God" (4:11).

The directives of *Did.* 4:10f. are undoubtedly just the tip of the iceberg, since, once a candidate was baptized, he or she would discover that both slaves and free, both high and low, would come forward to embrace them as "brother" or "sister" and to eat with them as social equals at the eucharistic banquet (see ch. 5 below). Thus, the notion that "God does not come to call anyone according to his/her social status" (4:10b) might have been a weighty issue that challenged ingrained social prejudices for many of the candidates. Perhaps, for this reason, it was pastorally appropriate to reserve this topic for later in the training program.

#1x SOCIAL PREJUDICE RESPECTING SLAVES

The following chapter will have much to say respecting the source, status, and employment of slaves. At this point, however, it must be remembered that, in many instances, slaves had superior education and superior skills to their masters. Epictetus of Hierapolis (d. 30 C.E.), for instance, was brought up as a slave in the home of a freedman of Nero. His slavery was the result of the accidents of war. As a cultivated Greek, his master rewarded him with continued education and gave him extensive responsibilities. Eventually he became a revered tutor, and, when granted his freedom, went on to become a popular teacher of philosophy—Marcus Aurelius being his most illustrious student. It is not surprising, consequently, that Epictetus was not hesitant to challenge those Romans who regarded their conduct toward slaves as something not bearing close examination. Here is a case example from Epictetus's teaching:

> If you call for hot water, and your slave does not hear you, or, if he does, brings it only warm . . . , then to abstain from anger or petulance, is this not to the divine acceptance [i.e., acceptable to God]?
> [Response:] "But how is it possible to bear such things?"
> O slavish man! Will you not bear with *your own brother, who has God for his Father . . .* ? But if you chance to be placed in some superior station, will you presently set yourself up for a tyrant?

Will you not remember what you are and over whom you bear
rule—that they are by nature your relations, *your brothers*, that
they are the *offspring of God?*

[Response:] "But I have them by right of purchase, and not
they me."

Do you see what it is you regard? You bend your gaze downward towards the earth . . . towards the unjust laws of men long
dead; but up towards the divine laws, you never turn your eyes.
(*Discourses* 1.13)

This exchange is very revealing. It undoubtedly reveals the social prejudices that many of the candidates coming forward for baptism must have
felt. The response of Epictetus is also revealing. The social inequality associated with slavery is reduced to "the unjust laws of men long dead." The
higher, truer, divine perspective, however, is that we are all brothers and
sisters, and God is our common Father. The presenting problem, interestingly enough, is the self-righteous display of "anger or petulance" toward
one's slaves—precisely parallel to the starting point used by the framers of
the *Didache*. All in all, therefore, Epictetus and the *Didache* allows us to
gauge that the troublesome social issue of slavery was being wrestled with
by various detached persons who independently arrived at remarkably parallel lines of revisionist thought (also Col 4:1 and Eph 6:9).

Among Jews, the Mosaic Torah was upheld as divinely sanctioning slavery at the same time that it mitigated its effects (*ABD* 6:64f.; C. Brown
3.593). Nonetheless, there were those Jews who reflected on the condition of slavery more deeply and came to disagree with its underpinnings.
Already in the fifth century B.C.E., for example, one finds a moderate
protest in the Book of Job:

If I [Job] have rejected the cause of my male or female slaves,
when they brought a complaint against me, what then shall I do
when God rises up [and hears their complaint]? When he makes
inquiry, what shall I answer him? Did not he who made me in the
womb make them? And did not one fashion us in the womb? (Jb
31:13–15)

While this text does not openly challenge the institution of slavery, it does
put forward the principle that God shaped them in the womb just as he
does those born free. As a result, their complaint deserves to be heard. If
it goes unheeded, then God himself will take their side.

Philo, when describing the Jewish Therapeutae in the mid-first century,
noted approvingly that their shared meals were served by their own children without the use of slaves. In households where slaves were found,

they were assigned tasks in serving at table (*ABD* 6:65). Philo, in contrast, shows that the Therapeutae were categorically opposed to this practice:

> And they do not use the ministrations of slaves, looking upon the possession of servants or slaves to be a thing absolutely and wholly contrary to nature, for nature has created all men free, but the injustice and covetousness of some men . . . , having subdued some [others], has given to the more powerful authority [as masters] over those who are weaker. (*Contemplative Life* 70)

The phrase "absolutely and wholly contrary to nature" brings with it the judgment that slavery is absolutely and wholly contrary to the wishes of God who designed nature. Thus, among some Jews and pagans, there was a stiff resistance to the practice of slavery on both philosophical and religious grounds. These voices, however, were in the minority.

The Solemn Final Admonitions

Following immediately upon *Did.* 4:11, the novice is told to "hate every hypocrisy and everything that is not pleasing to the Lord" (4:12). This generalized rule would appear to stand in for all the cases not considered during the time of the training. This rule would appear to follow on what went immediately before: the novice is bound to please his Lord in the same way that household slaves were bound to please their masters.

The second admonition recalls that everything received must be "guarded" as "the rules of the Lord"—again emphasizing the source and character of the training received (recall 4:1). Furthermore, 4:13 appears to imply that what has been received and memorized is the totality of the training program, no more nor less. This final admonition must also signal that some have endeavored to alter what has been put forward. This issue will come up again in 11:1f., and the prophets will be named as the expected troublemakers in this realm. Hence, the full application of this rule will be taken up in chapter 6 below.

The final admonition points to the future: "in church [i.e., in the assembly], you will confess your failings" (4:14). The framers of the *Didache* thereby ensured that the particulars of the Way of Life would be the weekly matter for an examination of conscience and of public admission of failure. For the moment the candidate is unfamiliar with the eucharist; hence the details of *Did.* 14:1–3 are not presented. A full examination of this practice will be considered in chapter 8. For the moment, it suffices that the novice be forewarned that a regular confession will take place in the assembly and that this confession would ensure that "you will not go to your prayer with a bad conscience" (4:14).

Conclusion

All in all, the opening chapters of the *Didache* are devoted to a training program calculated to pass on and to preserve a way of life. Here one finds the repeated use of the imperative mood, systematic attention to details, and, most especially, sober warnings against those who might water down, change, or undercut what he has put forward (4:13; 6:1; 11:2). Taken together, these traits signify that the framers of the *Didache* had a personal investment in preserving a training program that, to some degree, might not have been consistently and completely operative in the preparation of new members for baptism.

In what has already been considered, something of the utopian aspirations of the Way of Life have been spelled out. In what is to come, one will discover that the Way of Life was the revealed way of perfection, not only for individuals preparing for baptism but, with even greater force, for entire communities committed to the Way of Life. But this is getting beyond our current agenda. For the moment, it suffices to note that the Way of Life offered a deliberately ordered, balanced, and progressive program for the transformation of gentiles who, in the end, were preparing to love God and their neighbor in the context of a community feverishly anticipating the coming of the Lord to establish a new world order.

This program was effective and graced by virtue of the interpersonal bonds whereby novices surrender themselves to be transformed by mentors who cherished them and revealed the Lord's ways. Quite naturally, therefore, these mentors came to be "honor[ed] as the Lord" (4:1). Thus, at the very time when the novice was being abusively treated by his/her biological parents, the novice was falling under the spell and the protection of a new "father" or "mother" who was progressively transforming settled instincts and nurturing ways of being in the world that would enable him/her to live among the saints and, in the end times, to be gathered with the elect into the Kingdom of God.

#1y WHETHER THE *DIDACHE* EMBRACED THE APOSTOLIC DECREE OF ACTS 15

According to Acts 15, the apostles and elders of the Jerusalem community deliberated and decided the issue of foods permitted to Christians in

49 C.E. Since the *Didache* takes its own unique stand on this issue without any knowledge and without any reference to the Jerusalem agreement, it must be surmised that the *Didache* was formed either prior to or in ignorance of the food laws. Since Paul himself makes no reference to the Jerusalem Council in formulating his own position (e.g., Gal 2), it can be surmised that Luke is presenting an idealized picture of what later developed in order to accommodate gentile Christians (Haenchen: 468–72). As a result, nothing certain can be known regarding the dating of the *Didache* on the basis of its ignorance of the events of Acts 15.

Some scholars think that *Did.* 6:3 presupposes a familiarity with the "apostolic decree" of the Jerusalem church (Acts 15:28f.; 21:25). This, however, fails to recognize adequately that the *Didache* knows nothing of the particulars of this decree (Rordorf 1978a: 33f.; Niederwimmer 1998: 123). Acts formulates this as follows:

> For it has seemed good to the Holy Spirit and to us to impose on you no further burden than these essentials: that (1) you abstain from what has been sacrificed to idols and (2) from blood and (3) from what is strangled and (4) from fornication. If you keep yourselves from these, you will do well. (Acts 15:28f.)

James initially argues for these four on the grounds that, wherever Moses is read, these prohibitions have been specifically imposed upon gentiles by the Lord (Acts 15:21). Each can be considered in turn:

1. *Abstaining from food sacrificed to idols.* Leviticus 17:3–7 first requires that all Israelites bring their offerings before the Lord "so that they may no longer offer their sacrifices for goat-demons" (Lv 17:7). Then attention turns to making the rule more inclusive:

> Anyone of the house of Israel or of the aliens who reside among them who offers a burnt offering or sacrifice, and does not bring it to the entrance of the tent of meeting, to sacrifice it to the Lord, shall be cut off from the people. (Lv 17:8f.)

This rule finds a place not only in *Did.* 6:3 but also in 1 Cor 8:1–13; 10:19–33; Aristides, *Apol.* 15.5; Justin, *Dial.* 34.8; Pseudo-Clement, *Hom.* 8.4.2; 8.19.1.

2. *Abstaining from blood.* Leviticus 17:10–12 prohibits the eating of meat with blood in it: "No person among you shall eat blood, nor shall any alien who resides among you eat blood" (Lv 17:12). Some segments of

Christianity took this prohibition seriously. Minucius Felix (36.6 [161 C.E.]) refutes the claim that Christians ate children by pointing out that they could never do this for they entirely abstain from drinking blood. Biblis, the woman martyr of 177 C.E. says the same thing: "How could they eat children who are not even allowed to eat the blood of irrational animals?" (Eusebius, *Ecclesiastical History* 5.1.26). Tertullian indicates that "Christians . . . have not even the blood of animals at their meals . . . [and] abstain from things strangled and that die a natural death, for no other reason than that they may not contract pollution" (*Apol.* 9.13).

3. *Abstaining from strangled animals.* As seen from the citation of Tertullian, the flesh of strangled animals contains blood and, by extension, is prohibited. Leviticus 17:15 extends this also to "what dies of itself or what has been torn by wild animals."

4. *Abstaining from illicit sex.* Leviticus 18:7–23 names a long list of prohibited sexual unions, which can be summarized under the heading of *porneia* (Acts 21:25). In this list, relations with a woman "while she is in her menstrual uncleanness" (Lv 18:19) is clearly prohibited. All these prohibitions apply to Israelites and to resident gentiles as well (Lv 18:26). It is quite probable that the *Didache* wished to include all these prohibited unions when it communicates to gentiles that the Lord commands, "do not have illicit sex" (*ou porneuseis*) (*Did.* 2:2).

All in all, the *Didache* embraces only two of the four prohibitions of the Jerusalem decree. The supposition of Acts 15 is that, "whereas in other respects the law [Torah] applies solely to the Jews, it imposes these four prohibitions on gentiles also!" (Haenchen: 469). The *Didache*, for its part, requires gentiles to live the Way of Life that exceeds the four prohibitions of the Jerusalem decree. The framers of the *Didache* accommodate even the Mosaic Decalogue so as to fit the gentile situation. If this is so, it is not surprising that the prohibition against eating blood and strangled animals was set aside as secondary. On the other hand, if the framers of the *Didache* had known that the mother church in Jerusalem had decreed these prohibitions upon gentile converts, then it might be supposed that they would have complied. Furthermore, since Paul does not embrace such prohibitions, one has to agree with Ernst Haenchen in allowing that the so-called Jerusalem decree did not take place as early and under the circumstances that Luke narrates (Haenchen: 462–72). Thus, it is not surprising that the *Didache* would appear to be ignorant of the existence of the Jerusalem decree of Acts 15.

#1z MODERN INSIGHT ON WHY CHURCHES FLOURISH

In the early 1970s, Dean M. Kelly was puzzled by the fact that, beginning in the 1960s, new conservative denominations in the United States were growing by leaps and bounds while the older, more established churches were slowly declining in membership. As a result, he visited scores of these growing denominations for the purpose of determining for himself what contributed to their outreach and retention of new members. He published his findings under the title *Why Conservative Churches Are Growing*. In part, he found that the growing denominations exhibited a "seriousness about their faith" that was absent from or diluted in liberal mainline denominations. He characterized this "seriousness" as follows:

1. Those who are serious about their faith do not confuse it with other beliefs, loyalties, or practices, or mingle them together indiscriminately. . . .
2. Those who are serious about their faith make high demands of those admitted to the organization. . . .
3. Those who are serious about their faith do not consent to, encourage, or indulge any violations of its standards of belief or behavior by its professed members. (121)

Kelly's discovery provides an excellent initial assessment of the kind of "seriousness" that one finds in the *Didache*. Scholars have become so accustomed to classifying the *Didache* as a church order or church manual (the first of many) that they forget that the document conceals the pastoral genius of a movement that, not unlike the Assemblies of God (116% growth, 1965–1985) or Jehovah's Witnesses (121% growth, 1965–1985), had a "seriousness" that attracted and retained new members even when the social order was indifferent or sometimes openly hostile to its existence.

Kelly also went back to study the formative years of the Anabaptists and Wesleyans. Stepping back, he tried to distill how, given their vulnerable status as new religious movements, they sought to preserve the identity and character of their adherents:

a. They were in no haste to take anyone into membership. A long period of training and preparation preceded admission, during which the rigors and privations of discipleship . . . were vividly described. . . .
b. The tests of membership were attitudinal and behavioral rather than solely or chiefly doctrinal. . . .

c. Membership was conditional upon continuing faithfulness. Spiritual discipline was vigorously applied among the Anabaptists: any member found walking contrary was admonished, and if he did not reform was charged in the congregation, which could impose the ban. . . .

d. Members made their life pilgrimage together in small groups, aiding and encouraging one another. No one worked out his salvation in isolation; each was surrounded and sustained by the brethren. (125f.)

Kelly is by no means an expert in analyzing new religious movements. Nonetheless, he points out some key factors that enable known religious movements permanently to alter the identity of their adherents such that neither antagonism from outside nor failures within would serve to water down the identity and purposes of the members. It is no surprise then that the *Didache*'s communities would exemplify features that can be easily recognized as functioning in ways parallel to the movements Kelly studied. The *Didache* is more than merely a "church order," and Kelly provides a much larger palate for examining the dynamic color and hues present in the clues of the *Didache*.

2

THE ECONOMIC SAFETY NET
IN THE ROMAN WORLD OF
SYSTEMATIC EXPLOITATION

The Economic Partnership

IF YOU SHOULD HAVE
SOMETHING THROUGH THE WORK OF
YOUR HANDS, YOU WILL GIVE
SOMETHING FOR THE RANSOMING
OF YOUR SINS. YOU WILL NOT
HESITATE TO GIVE NOR, GIVING, WILL
YOU GRUMBLE; FOR YOU WILL KNOW
WHO WILL BE GIVING BACK EXCEL-
LENT RECOMPENSE WHEN HE
COMES. YOU WILL NOT TURN AWAY
THE ONE BEING IN NEED; YOU WILL
PARTNER-TOGETHER, ON THE OTHER
HAND, SHARING ALL THINGS WITH
YOUR BROTHER OR SISTER, AND YOU
WILL NOT SAY SUCH THINGS ARE
YOUR OWN. FOR, IF YOU ARE PARTNERS
IN THE IMMORTAL THINGS, BY
HOW MUCH MORE ARE YOU PARTNERS
IN THE MORTAL THINGS.

Contents

Background Discussion Found in Boxes

No movement composed of peasants, fishermen, and artisans could thrive and be indifferent to the savage exploitation that would yearly destroy the economic well-being of some of its members drawing them and their families into destitution. It is not surprising, therefore, that economic training occupies over one-third of the Way of Life (*Did*. 1:4b–1:6; 2:6; 3:5, 7–9; 4:5–8). The previous chapter passed over these texts lightly. Now however, the impact of these economic rules of training will be systematically examined against the backdrop of the threatening economic conditions prevailing in the Roman Empire.

In this chapter the reader will discover how the sharing of resources in business cooperatives practiced by the Didache communities functioned as an economic safety net that safeguarded the small family-owned and operated businesses from the menacing economic conditions prevailing in first-century society. The reader will also come to understand how the seemingly unimportant rule of giving "to everyone asking of you" (*Did*. 1:5) had the effect of transforming the settled instincts and habits of judgment of novices such that they were prepared to abandon all former economic alliances in order to rely on collective workshops operated by members of the Didache communities. Furthermore, in a world in which most businesses prospered through patron–client relationships, the reader will discover why someone entering into a new religious movement might urgently need a new set of commercial alliances to replace those that would inevitably be ruptured by his or her new religious commitments. The community of the *Didache*, therefore, offered not only access to "the life and knowledge" (*Did*. 9:3) of the Father and the hope of entering into his "kingdom" (*Did*. 9:4; 10:5f.), it offered an alternative way of doing business. This alternative roundly condemned the exploitation and aggressive aspects of Roman commercialism as unacceptable to God (Crossan 1998: 200–205, 281f., 330–37) and, at the same time, provided an economic safety net protecting its own members against debt servitude, against commercial exploitation, and against compromising the "way of life" (*Did*. 1:1) in the name of economic survival. While the members of the Didache community looked for the redemption that was to come, they grasped the hands of their brothers and sisters and pledged to use their resources to safeguard each other from the ravages of exploitation and of poverty which threatened them while they awaited the promised kingdom.

Economic Exploitation in the Ancient World

The Roman world sanctioned the extremes of wealth and of poverty. Wealth in the Roman Empire was generally secured through inheritance and included agricultural lands worked by large numbers of slaves or by indentured farmers (de Sainte Croix: 112–14; Gonzalez: 15). Owners, generally operating through middlemen who are unequivocally loyal to their patrons, amassed enormous wealth through the sale (much of it in foreign markets) of their agricultural products and through land rents. This wealth served to promote the honor, the interests, and the life of leisure that characterized the privileged class. In gross terms, the economy of the Roman Empire ensured that "1 to 2 percent of the population took 50 to 65 percent of the agricultural productivity" (Crossan 1989: 154) and left the remainder to be divided by the masses, who scrambled to make ends meet according to their own devices.

By the first century, Rome had colonized the whole Mediterranean world and had distributed prime farm land everywhere to the benefit of Roman aristocrats and retired soldiers. These tax-free Roman estates had an edge over farmland held by indigenous peoples, where crops were grown in poorer soil and were taxed.

> The taxation of free citizens was traditionally considered tyranny and eventually came to be accepted only as an evil necessity. It would never have occurred to a Roman that taxation could or should be used as a means to redistribute wealth or to promote social policy, although it is clear to us now that the Roman system of taxation did promote the concentration of wealth in ever fewer hands. (Gonzalez: 19)

This concentration of wealth allowed the rich to organize larger and larger agricultural estates (*latifundia* and *magna latifundia*), stiffening the competition with modest family farms, which had been the backbone of the earlier economy (Gonzalez: 32f.; Hamel: 159). These huge agricultural estates (agri-businesses) were made possible by the large numbers (a) of *coloni* (farmers who worked the land owned by others in exchange for part of the crop) and (b) of *servi* (slaves, usually the victims of Roman wars or hard times, who were required to do menial labor of all kinds).

> In the long run, market fluctuations favored the rich, who could afford a smaller margin of profit or even some losses. The peasants, on the other hand, often found that a drop in the price of their produce forced them to sell their land to meet expenses and especially to pay taxes. In such cases, the land would be sold to a larger landholder, and the peasant would continue to till it [as a *colonus*], although now under new conditions. (Gonzalez: 73)

#2A THE PLACE OF ARTISANS IN THE ANCIENT ECONOMY

G. E. M. de Sainte Croix provides a systematic overview of the economic conditions prevailing in the ancient world. His study is filled with illustrative case studies culled from the primary sources coming from this period. Overall, de Sainte Croix makes the following points:

1. "In the Hellenistic and Roman periods the leading families of the cities of Asia enjoyed greater wealth than ever and were among the strongest supporters of the Roman rule" (119). The wealth and leisure of these leading families, in almost every instance, depended on the inherited ownership of huge expanses of agricultural lands that were cultivated by tenant farmers and/or unfree cultivators (slaves, serfs, etc.). "The Greek [and Roman] propertied class, then, consisted essentially of those who were able to have themselves set *free* to live a civilized life by their command over the labor of others, who bore the burden of providing them with the necessities (and the luxuries) of the good life" (116).

2. "Peasants and other free men such as artisans and shopkeepers, *working on their own account,* without much property of their own . . . , would normally have to spend most of their time working for their livelihood, with their families, at somewhere near the subsistence level . . ." (115). Beyond this, there were those who were moderately well off owing to their ability to exploit the labor of others: for example, "the owner of a large or medium-sized farm, worked by slaves under a slave bailiff" or "the proprietor of a workshop of, say, 20–50 slaves, supervised by a slave manager" or "the lessee of mines . . . , worked by slaves, similarly supervised by a manager who would himself be a slave" (116).

3. De Sainte Croix prefers to avoid any rigid classification among the various classes of workers. Solon, by contrast, did not hesitate to name farmers as better off than merchants, merchants than wage laborers, and wage laborers than artisans (de Sainte Croix: 130)—thereby placing artisans in a much more precarious position than farmers. Gerhard E. Lenski, a modern scholar who has studied social and economic inequality on a cross-cultural basis, represents the great divide and the ranking within each side of the divide as follows:

Ruler	
Governing Class	Peasant Class
Retainer Class	Artisan Class
Merchant Class	Unclean and Degraded Class
Priestly Class	Expendable Class

Lenski notes that artisans were "originally recruited from the ranks of the dispossessed peasantry" and "the medium income of artisans apparently was not so great as that of peasants" (Lenski 1970: 278). Such ahistorical categories are deceptive, for, as de Sainte Croix has noted, "the condition of the peasantry . . . deteriorated markedly during the first three centuries of the Christian era" and, by the end of the third century, resulted in "the enserfment of most of the free working agricultural population of the Roman empire" (1981: 243). Meanwhile, given the expansion of urban populations and the increased pressure of barbarian invasions, the army was expanded and city walls were built or rebuilt—projects that required the continued employment of a large class of stonecutters, transporters, builders, carpenters, ironworkers, spinners, weavers, uniform makers, bakers—all artisans. In general, therefore, skilled craftsmen whose talents were in demand prospered. The comparatively unskilled, meanwhile, lived a precarious existence dependent on market conditions—not unlike that of the tenant farmer, who could easily slip into debt bondage if climatic conditions did not favor his annual harvest (Lenski 1970: 269–71).

Helmut Koester makes the point that artisans "were not paid well for their work, hardly more than unskilled laborers" (1995: 80). De Sainte Croix would distinguish here between the level of skill exercised by a given artisan and whether products were being produced for daily use by the masses or whether they were high-quality products sold to the upper classes. In any case, Koester is quite correct in noting that "there was a chronic shortage of skilled craftsmen" due to "the many years of training required" (1995: 80) for such work:

> The artisan was the backbone of Hellenistic and Roman culture. All ancient art media, from architecture to metallurgy, from pottery and painting to weaving and dying, required an intimate knowledge of materials and highly developed skills that could be acquired only with years of training. The knowledge of a craft was handed down, usually in small workshops, from father to son and from master to apprentice; the secrets were family traditions. (1995: 79; Burford: 82–87)

Within this perspective, Lenski's remark that artisans were "originally recruited from the ranks of the dispossessed peasantry" (Lenski 1970: 278) must be taken with a grain of salt. Dispossessed farmers, most probably, became tenant farmers, wage laborers, or army recruits. Crossan presents a more balanced perspective when he suggests that farming families would have engaged in small crafts (woodworking, pottery, weaving) in order to supplement their income (1998: 223–30). When the need presented itself and sufficient skills were harnessed, such farming families might gradually move toward becoming full-time artisans, especially during the early centuries, when land rents, compulsory service, and taxation were increasingly crushing the peasant family farm (de Sainte Croix: 243; Crossan 1998: 230).

The Social Situation of Didache Members

The *Didache* gives ample testimony that the members of its community were recruited from the class of artisans, craftsmen, builders, shopkeepers, traders, and various low-level functionaries who earned their livelihood through their personal skills. Let three illustrations suffice:

1. Early in their training, novices were asked to give "to everyone asking you for anything" (*Did.* 1:5) and later, after joining the community, the rule was that "if you should have something through the work of your hands, you will give something . . ." (*Did.* 4:6). In the first instance, the presumption is that the novice was numbered among those who had an excess of the goods of this world such that he/she could give. They were not numbered among those asking (*Did.* 1:5). In the second instance, the presumption is that the average member is characterized by "the work of your hands" and, further, that when such manual labor produces an excess, one can immediately think of giving to those in need.

2. When it comes to the rule of giving the Lord gratitude by offering first fruits, the same set of values shows through. After mentioning the traditional Jewish agricultural first fruits ("the wine vat and threshing floor," *Did.* 13:3), the *Didache* moves beyond this by directing that first fruits should be offered when one "should make bread," "open a jar of wine or oil," or, more generally, gain an increase "of silver and of clothing and of any possession" (*Did.* 13:5–7). In each case, it seems that members of the Didache communities were grateful not only in those traditional instances when harvesting grapes or grain, but also when a housewife baked bread for her family or when the master of the household opened a stoneware jar of wine or oil purchased with funds derived from the family business. Since the *Didache* presumes that its members *did these things,* it testifies indirectly to their being employed and their having prospered *through the work of their hands.*

3. When it came to persons visiting the community, the *Didache* allowed for limited hospitality ("two or three days" *Did.* 12:2) and then immediately made provisions that the one who "wishes to settle down among you, being a craftsman, let him/her work and let him/her eat" (*Did.* 12:3). Here the community undoubtedly reflected its own values and its own way of life. Visitors were not permitted to be freeloaders (*Did.* 12:4f.), nor were they classed among the idle rich.

The members of the Didache communities, therefore, existed in a social world wherein they were numbered neither among the exploiters nor among the exploited. They were not the aristocracy, which considered it demeaning to work with their hands (de Sainte Croix: 116f., 121). Nor were they numbered among those who lived a life of leisure based on earnings from commercial agriculture, manufacturing enterprises, or civic contracts, which, in due course, guaranteed their elevated standard of living through the exploitation of hundreds of slaves, indentured laborers, and menial workers. The members of the Didache communities were not, for the most part, "the poor who had no special skills [and] had to sell their labor on the open market, at low pay, on farms and vineyards, or in construction" (Stambaugh: 71). They were not living a hand-to-mouth existence that opened them to random acts of exploitation.

#2B FEMALE WOOL WORKERS AS TEACHERS OF CHRISTIAN PERFECTION

Celsus, a Greek philosopher, wrote a tract against the Christians in the late second century. This tract has survived nearly intact because it was exhaustively cited and refuted by the church father Origen. Celsus despised Christianity in large part because it was a movement composed of manual laborers. Celsus informed his readers that Jesus, their founder, "gathered around him ten or eleven persons of notorious characters, the very wickedest of tax-gatherers and sailors" (cited in Origen, *Against Celsus* 1.62). Celsus declared that Christian teachers "are able to convince only the foolish, dishonorable and stupid, and only slaves, women and little children" (3.49). These teachers circulated, according to Celsus, as artisans and domestics who had access to the slaves, women, and children within private homes:

> Wherever one finds a crowd of adolescent boys, or a bunch of slaves, or a company of fools [women?], there will the Christian teachers be also—showing off their fine new philosophy [Christianity]. In private homes one can see [them as] wool workers, cobblers, laundry workers, and the most illiterate country bumpkins, who would not venture to voice their opinions in front of their intellectual betters. But let them get hold of children in private houses—let them find some gullible wives—and you will hear some preposterous statements: You will hear them say, for instance, that they should not pay any attention to their fathers or teachers, but must obey them. They say that their elders and teachers are fools. . . . These Christians claim that they alone know the right way to live. . . . These Christians also tell the children that they should leave their fathers and teachers and follow the women and their little chums to the wooldresser's shop, or to the cobbler's or to the washerwoman's shop, so that they might learn how to be perfect. (3.55)

In the ancient world, wool workers and laundry workers were undoubtedly women. The cobblers were men. What so provoked Celsus was that persons with only modest manual skills should presume to have the philosophical training to know and to teach "the right way to live." Having snared unsuspecting women and youths in private homes, then, these Christian teachers lured them to "follow the women and their little chums" to the various shops where they will meet others who supposedly have the art of training them "how to be perfect." According to Celsus, only a philosopher could have been an adequate guide in such a serious endeavor. Laborers and domestics doubling as Christian teachers were, by definition, incapable and incompetent. In sum, Celsus asserted that "Christian teachers are only happy with stupid pupils" (3.74)—persons like themselves who know little or nothing about how truth was to be discovered.

Origen responded to Celsus by noting that he resorts to slandering common laborers and domestics who, if they were carefully examined, would be discovered to be living lives exemplifying true wisdom—something that their fathers and teachers at home could not generally claim for themselves (3.56–58). Celsus, Origen noted, applied a double standard for he himself advocated shielding sons who learned true philosophy from "worthless parents" (3.58).

While Celsus was intent on vilifying the recruitment practices of Christian teachers, he inadvertently retained for us the observation that entire shops served as centers for disseminating the Christian way of life. Potential recruits were drawn to these shops, for here they could "seek every day the presence of the saints" (*Did.* 4:2). Later in this chapter, the business partnerships formed within the Didache communities will be considered as the principal means to forestall the ravages of economic disaster. For the moment, however, these same business partnerships can be seen as providing the ordinary means whereby the Christian movement recruited and nurtured new members.

The early Christian communities were predominantly situated in small towns or urban centers. Thus they would not have ordinarily been expected to include field slaves or their overseers. In towns and cities, however, slaves were routinely employed in domestic chores, in urban maintenance and construction, and in the various trades (e.g., making pottery, running shops, hauling merchandise). In significant ways, slavery in the first century was distinguishable from that practiced in the Old South of the United States:

> Racial factors played no role; education was greatly encouraged
> (some slaves were better educated than their owners) and

enhanced a slave's value; many slaves carried out sensitive and highly responsible [economic and] social functions; slaves could own property (including other slaves!); their religious and cultural traditions were the same as those of the freeborn; no laws prohibited the public assembly of slaves; and (perhaps above all) the majority of urban and domestic slaves could legitimately anticipate being emancipated by the age of 30. (*ABD* 6:66)

Slaves employed in the trades had a greater degree of opportunity and independence than agricultural slaves. Most of them were allowed to save a portion of their earnings as an incentive to work hard, and they could eventually save money to buy their freedom (*ABD* 6:70f.). In many cases, slaves who purchased their freedom did so on the condition that they continue to remain employed with their former master (Reimer: 107). The fact that the *Didache* presupposed that many of its members owned slaves (4:10f.) does not negate the "working-class" feel of the document, for, in the ancient world, it was common for craftsmen and shopkeepers to have purchased or rented one or more slaves for the purpose of training them and employing them alongside one's sons and daughters working in the family business (de Sainte Croix: 271; Burford: 87–91). In urban centers in Italy, for example, one in every three persons was a slave (Madden: 1f.).

Giving Motivated by Submission to the Father's Will

Having sketched something of the harsh economic realities operating in the ancient world and the urban working-class background presupposed by the membership of the Didache communities, our attention can now turn to the economic orientation that was given to novices aspiring to join the community. Training in this arena is concentrated in two sections:

Did. 1:5f.: the rule for giving to needy outsiders
Did. 4:5–8: the rule for reciprocal assistance to insiders

Immediately after giving the training regarding how to deal with the aggressive abuse of family members (1:3f.), the *Didache* moves on to consider the rule for giving. The last-named abuse begins, "if anyone should take from you" (1:4[D]), and this forms an oral link to the milder alternative, "To everyone asking you" (1:5). Both the former and the latter carry the refrain "do not ask for it back" (1:4[D]; 1:5). The former is framed in the conditional—perhaps as a hint that not every recruit suffers having a father or brother seize his/her goods. The latter, however, is framed as a general statement—thereby sending the message that no one can escape being approached by someone—beggars in town, for instance. Seen visually side by side, one has the following:

Forced Taking by Outsiders (*Did.* 1:4)	Free Giving to Outsiders (*Did.* 1:5)
If anyone should take from you what is yours, do not ask for it back; for you are not even able to do so.	To everyone asking you for anything, give it to him/her and do not ask for it back; for, to all, the Father wishes that there be given from his own free gifts.

The motive for responding to requests from outsiders is single-minded: "For, to all, the Father wishes to give these things from his own free gifts" (*Did.* 1:5). The elaboration on this point deals with the necessity of implementing this "rule" without calculating the merit or the need of the one asking. The dissimulator "will be examined thoroughly concerning the things he/she has done" (*Did.* 1:5) at the final judgment. No limit is set on the value of the thing being requested. Presumably, it could be something as small as a neighbor needing a needle or a pinch of salt; on the other hand, it could be something quite substantial—a craftsman facing foreclosure unless a large debt was paid in three days. The value of the item needed and the motive of the one asking were seemingly not to be taken into account. The novice's only concern was to respond to the expressed need as "the Father wishes" (*Did.* 1:5).

Roman society placed great emphasis on the inviolability of private ownership and upon economizing; hence, Romans felt no moral or civic obligation to come to the aid of the poor or destitute (de Sainte Croix: 194–97; Hamel: 219; Reid: 391f.). There were public benefactors, to be sure, who erected monuments, subsidized festivals, and provided for the poor. Such persons, however, did so with the motive of promoting themselves and their families as "benefactors." At the same time, the rich and the powerful were expected to provide banquets including lavish gifts and exotic entertainment for their friends and clients. To be sure, such activities were normally prompted by self-interest and were never designed to serve those who had neither influence nor wealth with which to reciprocate the favor received (Hamel: 219). Hesiod, for example, advised his readers, "Give to one who gives, but do not give to one who does not give" (*Works and Days* 254).

The *Didache* is the oldest known Christian document that makes it clear that, in the act of giving, the one giving is handing over what belongs *to the Father.* In effect, therefore, the one giving acts as a faithful steward or broker who dispenses the Father's resources to those making their requests known (see #2d). The unseen "benefactor" in every instance is the Father. The Roman notion of gaining public honor or influence as a "benefactor" is thus thwarted. Likewise, the framers of the *Didache*, in contrast to Roman benefactors, sought to promote giving to those in need without expecting anything in return—"do not ask for it back" (*Did.* 1:5). This stance finds ample parallels in both Jewish (e.g., Dt 15:11; Prv 3:27f.; Sir 4:8–10; Tb 4:7–11; *Ps.-Phocy.* 22–24) and Christian sources (e.g., Lk 6:30; Acts 20:35).

The emphasis on the rule of not examining the worthiness or honesty of the one asking (*Did.* 1:5) is startling and finds no ready equivalent in other sources except Hermas (Crossan 1998: 394f.; Jefford 1989a: 50f.; Niederwimmer 1998: 81–83). The radical character of this rule can be glimpsed by examining how, in the rabbinic materials, the same debate seems to have taken place with an entirely different resolution. The two sides of the argument are placed side by side so as to better appreciate the parallels involved:

[A] Rabbi Huna said:
 "Applicants for food are
    examined,
    but not applicants for clothes.
 This rule can be based, if you
    like on Scripture,
    or if you prefer, on common sense:
	[B] Rab Judah, however, said:
	 "Applicants for clothes are
	    examined,
	    but not applicants for food."
	 This rule can be based if you like on
	    common sense,
	    or if you prefer on Scripture:

[1] It can be based if you like on
    common sense,
    because the one [who has no
    clothing] is exposed to contempt,
 but not the other.
	[1] [It can be based] If you like on
	    common sense,
	    because the one [without food] is
	 actually suffering
	 but not the other.

[2] Or if you prefer, on Scripture—
    on the verse:
    "[The fast the Lord desires] Is it
    not to examine [*paros*] the hungry
    giving him your bread" [Is 58:7a].
    The word *poros* is written with a sin,
    as much as to say, "Examine and
    then give to him."
 Whereas later it is written:
 "[The fast the Lord desires,
    is it not that]
 When you see the naked,
 that you cover him" [Is 58:7b],
 that is to say, immediately.
	[2] Or if you prefer, on Scripture—
	    because it says:
	    "[The fast the Lord desires] Is it not
	    to deal [*pososh*] your bread to the
	    hungry," that is, at once.
	
	 Whereas later it is written:
	
	 "When you see the naked" [Is 58:7b],
	 that is to say,
	 "When you shall have seen [that he is
	 deserving]." (*b. Baba Batra* 9a,
	 Soncino ed.)

These parallel arguments make it evident that the rabbis were divided as to when the "expressed need" of the petitioner overrides the right of the giver to examine the worthiness and honesty of the one asking. Both sides of the argument appealed to common sense and to scripture. Furthermore, both sides cited Is 58:7, and each side interpreted it differently depending on how each vocalized the Hebrew text.

The absence of any grounds for inquiry in the *Didache* suggests that the "expressed need" of the petitioner overrides the right of the giver to examine the one asking in cases involving food or clothing. In cases of fraudulent requests, the *Didache* makes it clear that the receiver is in peril, since, at the final judgment, "he/she will be examined thoroughly " (*Did.* 1:5b). The Mishnah, in contrast, believed that God's judgment would overtake such a person before departing from this world (*m. Peah* 8:9).

#2C WHETHER *DID.* 1:6 MODERATED THE RULE OF GIVING

Some scholars have argued that "the rule" of giving proved unworkable and that *Did.* 1:6 was added later in order to indicate that "a certain discretion" was required and that one ought to hold onto one's alms until one found a "worthy recipient" (Audet 1958: 280; Vokes 1938: 21f.). Rordorf goes so far to say that *Did.* 1:6 "contradicts 1:5a" and "proves that the literary unity of *Did.* 1:5–6 is not the fruit of a single editing" (1981: 509). Thus, when the rule of unexamined giving gives way under abuses or when "one does not any more believe in the efficacy of the simple threat of divine punishment, one takes the problem in hand oneself" (ibid.) by testing the worthiness of those asking. Niederwimmer agrees with Rordorf, saying that "one receives the impression that the Didachist wanted, by quoting this aphorism, to restrict the appeal to unconditional giving that existed in his tradition" (1998: 86). I find this interpretation to be misleading for the following reasons:

1. The opening *alla* ("but") indicates "a difference with or contrast to what precedes" (Bauer: 38). While the sense could be understood as restricting the rule for giving, it could also be seen as expanding it. For example, in three instances Augustine cites the rule for giving (*Did.* 1:5) along with the present citation (*Did.* 1:6) as defining two distinct types of almsgiving:

My brethren, it is both said and read,
  [A] "To everyone who asks, give,"
and in another place Scripture says,

[B] "Let alms sweat in your hand
   until you find a righteous [*justum*] person to whom to give [it]."
One person begs of you, another you ought to seek out.
But do not leave empty the person who begs of you,
   [Rule A] "To everyone who asks, give,"
but there is another you ought to seek out:
   [Rule B] "Let alms sweat in your hand
   until you find a righteous [*justum*] person to whom to give [it]."
(*Commentary on the Psalms* 146:17, also 102:12, 103)

Augustine is important because he habitually juxtaposes rule A and rule B
(as in the *Didache*). In each case, Augustine does not use rule B to limit or
repeal rule A. On the contrary, rule A applies to the case of someone in
need coming and asking, while rule B applies to the one giving going out
to find a worthy receiver.

While Augustine cannot be upheld as providing a definitive interpretation of the intention of the *Didache*, he does, nonetheless, provide an illustration of how *alla* might be used in the Greek, not limiting rule A but
expanding it. Thus, the *Didache* can be understood as saying that giving
to those who ask of you (*Did.* 1:5) does not suffice; at times one must let
the alms sweat in your hands until one finds someone in need of it.

2. Niederwimmer cites fifteen instances in which *Did.* 1:6 shows up in
the Latin patristic literature (Niederwimmer 1998: 84f.). In some
instances, as illustrated by the case of Augustine just cited, the text of *Did.*
1:6 is quoted as "scripture." Rule B, however, differs from *Did.* 1:6 insofar as Augustine consistently writes "in your hand (singular)" and specifies
that the recipient is "a righteous/just person." The Greek text of the
Didache, on the other hand, makes no provision regarding the moral qualities of the recipient, either in *Did.* 1:5 or 1:6. If the framers of the *Didache*
had the intention of "warn[ing] against too hasty squandering alms on the
unworthy" (Niederwimmer 1998: 86), then it is curious that they did not
cite a text that expressly emphasized the moral qualities of the recipient.

3. Audet regarded the introduction "it has been said" as leading to "a
personal reaction" coming from "some apocryphal source, today lost to
us" (1958: 276). Audet's conjecture was not far from the mark. In 1963,
five years later, Patrick W. Skehan spotted a corrupt Hebrew rendering of
Sir 12:1, which he conjectured that "a man of courage, but of doubtful
prudence, translated . . . into Greek" in order to produce *Did.* 1:6 (335).
If Skehan is correct in identifying *Did.* 1:6 as having it source in Sir 12:1,
then it will quickly be noted that the context clearly mandates that alms be
given to the devout but withheld from sinners:

If you do good, know to whom you do it,
   and you will be thanked for your good deeds.

Do good to the devout, and you will be repaid—
    if not by them, certainly by the Most High. . . .
Give to the devout, but do not help the sinner.
    Do good to the humble, but do not give to the ungodly . . .
For the Most High also hates sinners
    and will inflict punishment on the ungodly. (Sir 12:1f., 4–6)

Skehan's argument is based on a corruption that entered into a Hebrew manuscript resulting in what he describes as an "unbelievable" (355) transformation of the opening phrase "if you do good" into "if you sweat good." Then he further presupposes that this corruption was translated into an equally corrupt Greek rendering of Sir 12:1. To be consistent, he would have to suppose that the corruption passed unnoticed and that it was expanded from "if you sweat good" to "let your alms sweat into your hands." All in all, while Skehan shows how small corruptions in the Hebrew (as found in a manuscript from the Cairo Geniza) could lead to significant changes in meaning, in the end he fails to supply a Greek manuscript of Sir 12:1 that reads anything like *Did*. 1:6. All in all, therefore, Skehan fails to prove his case.

Niederwimmer, on the other hand, suggests that the linking of Sir 12:1 and *Did*. 1:6 was already in the works long before Skehan's investigation. In fact, Niederwimmer postulates that Augustine might well have been the source of the problem:

> With the authority of the African church father, people quoted the saying [rule B] received from him as Scripture and ultimately sought a source for it in the Bible; Innocent III is demonstrably the first to have connected the aphorism with Sir 12:1 (although only dubiously), and Hugh of St. Cher's "Postille" then fabricated the idea that our aphorism stems from the *alia translatio* ["alternate translation"] of Sir 12:1. (1998: 86)

The upshot, for me and for Niederwimmer, is that the origin of *Did*. 1:6 is "uncertain" (Niederwimmer 1998: 86). Contrary to Niederwimmer, however, I find that the absence of any certain link between *Did*. 1:6 and Sir 12:1 is an indirect confirmation that the framers of the *Didache* did not want to restrict the giving of alms to the righteous alone. Had they intended this (as Niederwimmer and others contend), they would have cited Sir 12:1 properly and made their point. As the text now stands, it does not support limiting almsgiving to those deemed pious or just.

4. The *Apostolic Constitutions* might be examined to see whether it sheds any light on the interplay of *Did*. 1:5 and 1:6. The key section (7.2.6f.) reads as follows:

To everyone asking you [for anything], give [it to him]
and from the one wishing to borrow from you,
   do not close your hand [par. *Did.* 4:5],
[1] for a just man feels pity and lends.
[2] *For the Father wishes to give* to all,
   the One causing his sun to rise upon [the] wicked and [the] good,
and sending his rain upon [the] just and [the] unjust.
Therefore [it is] just to give to all from one's own labors [par. *Did.* 4:6]:
      "For," he says, "honor the Lord
      from your just labors" [Prv 3:9].
   (But) the saints must be preferred [in this giving] [par. *Did.* 4:8].

One immediately notes that the radical character of giving without expectation of return found in *Did.* 1:4 has been replaced by an admonition to lend. Since, in the case of lending, deception is no grave concern, the whole of *Did.* 1:5 was accordingly dropped. The insertion of Mt 5:45, however, serves to declare that, like the Father, one must be willing to lend to the "wicked" and the "unjust." Thus, even in the case of lending, the rule put forward demonstrates that the expressed need of the petitioner suffices and that one "feels pity" and responds as "the Father wishes" (*Apostolic Constitutions* 7.2.6). Thus, whatever might have been the force of *Did.* 1:6 in the past, it did not have the effect of modifying the rule of giving/lending in order to examine the moral worth and trustworthiness of the petitioner.

One also notes that *Did.* 1:6 has disappeared, and in its place one finds a direct appeal to give alms as a way of "honoring the Lord." The only restriction, in the end, is that "the saints must be preferred." Thus, even when treating almsgiving, the *Apostolic Constitutions* inherited no sense that persons asking for alms need be examined prior to responding to their need.

While the *Apostolic Constitutions* cannot be directly appealed to in order to interpret the *Didache*, the absence of any rule for refusing to lend does provide indirect testimony that *Did.* 1:6 most likely dropped out entirely when the issue was no longer one of giving.

5. Finally, many scholars interpret *Did.* 1:6 as they do because they suppose that the "eschatological place of punishment" (Niederwimmer 1998: 83) would not suffice to deter wicked persons from taking advantage of the generosity of the one who gave blamelessly "according to the rule" (*Did.* 1:5). In so doing, however, they forget that "the gifts given by the rich to the poor are really God's gifts" (Niederwimmer 1998: 83) and that, under this aspect, the novice acts as an obedient steward of the Father and neither suffers shame nor receives honor by giving—whether deservedly or undeservedly. Furthermore, when the rule of giving is seen as primarily

formative in character and when the value of the formative elements is weighed in the balance, instances of false or exaggerated requests pale in significance. It is to these formative elements that our attention must now turn.

If novices were not to protect themselves against deception (*Did.* 1:5), clearly the *Didache* had in mind allowing the petitioner to be exploited by false or exaggerated requests. Seemingly, the *Didache* allowed such aberrations in view of protecting a greater value. What was this greater value? I would surmise that the practice of training new candidates in this rule of giving had a key propaedeutic role embracing the following eight values:

1. *Preparing for a lifetime of sharing everything with one's brothers.* Candidates were being prepared to enter a community where they "will share all things" (*Did.* 4:8). In a culture in which "private possessions" and "family belongings" were emphasized, it was not an easy transition to reimagine the Didache community as one's "family" and to share accordingly. Consequently, mentors may have devised this rule to prepare the heart and mind of the candidate for lifelong responsiveness to the needs of "brothers" and "sisters" once they became full members.

2. *Breaking addiction to increased economic productivity.* Candidates were being prepared to enter a community in which they "will not be joined with the lofty but with the just and the lowly" (*Did.* 3:9). Later in this chapter, it will become clear that joining a Didache community meant, in many instances, diminished demands for one's skills and one's products. Thus, a candidate had to be prepared to lose business contacts and to lose income. Accordingly, mentors may have devised this rule for giving in order to prepare the hearts and the minds of candidates to detach themselves from the accumulation of wealth. Better to have the goodwill of beggars ("the lowly") than the applause of social and economic climbers ("the lofty").

3. *Developing the habit of acting in imitation of God.* Candidates were being prepared to enter a community in which they would love and serve God as their true Father. Accordingly, novices were trained to surrender to the requests of petitioners solely because "*the Father wishes* to give these things from his own free gifts" (*Did.* 1:5). The novice is accordingly reoriented to regard all personal possessions (gained by employment, by inheritance, by chance) as possessions of "the Father" (see #2d), who provided for his children from "his own free gifts." Unlike those biological fathers who may be seizing the possessions of their offspring (*Did.* 1:4[D]) and hording them against the needy, the pastoral genius of the mentors who

devised *Did.* 1:5 was directed toward preparing the heart and mind of the candidate for *welcoming the needy as the Lord wishes*. Thus, in *imitatio dei* (imitation of God), the candidates reorient their mode of being in the world by entering into a new way of acting and a new way of seeing the Father.

#2D THE NOTION THAT THE EARTH BELONGS TO THE LORD

The *Didache* is the oldest known Christian document that makes it clear that, in the act of giving, the one giving hands over what belongs *to the Father*. In effect, therefore, the one giving acts as a faithful steward or broker who dispenses the Father's resources to those making their requests known. This reevaluation of personal possessions is not unique to the *Didache* and finds clear expression in other Christian and Jewish documents. Three examples deserve our attention.

1. Carolyn Osiek carefully analyzes the *Shepherd of Hermas* (early second century) and finds that, in nearly every section of the treatise, "the ethical and theological implications of wealth go far beyond the traditional responsibility of giving to the poor and the traditional danger of being too intent on the things of this world to notice those in need" (47). More especially, in the first allegory, the rich Christians are being asked to live as though they were transients in a foreign country where, at any moment, they might be expelled as foreigners. Under these conditions, Christians would be anxious not to invest in houses or fields but, in their place, to "buy yourselves souls that are in [financial] trouble, as each is able, and visit widows and orphans, and neglect them not . . . *for to this end the Master enriched you,* that you might perform these ministrations for him" (Hermas *Sim.* 1:8f.). The rich Christian, therefore, acts on behalf of the Lord of his homeland when the financially afflicted, especially the widow and orphan, receive the good things of this world. Far from considering possessions as "personal property," the rich Christian lives without any major real estate (ready to take flight) and uses the resulting surplus to make it possible for those whom the Lord loves to receive the care he intends for them. As in the case of the *Didache*, therefore, the Christian who is rich functions only as a faithful steward of his Lord's possessions.

2. The *Testaments of the Twelve Patriarchs* (100 C.E.) present the deathbed exhortations of each of the twelve sons of Jacob. Each of the patriarchs reflects upon his life experience and encourages the cultivation of an associated virtue. Zebulon concentrates on compassion for the needy:

> I was the first to make a boat to sail on the sea, for the Lord gave me the necessary knowledge and skill. . . . And I sailed it along

the shores and caught fish for my father's household until we came to Egypt. . . . And if there was anyone who was foreign, or ailing, or aged, I boiled and dressed the fish and offered it to all men, as each had need, making them my guests out of a fellow-feeling for them. And so the Lord gave me a rich catch of fish; for he who shares what he has with his neighbor is repaid many times over by the Lord. (*Testament of Zebulon* 6:2–6)

This narrative makes clear that Zebulon shared with those in need from the resources that the Lord had given him. The Lord not only gave him "a rich catch of fish" but enabled him to gain "the necessary knowledge and skill" to be an excellent fisherman. This extended also to sharing his clothing:

I saw a man who was in distress because he had nothing warm to put on in winter, and I had compassion on him; and I took a garment from my house . . . and gave it to the man that was in distress. So you too, my children, must show compassion and mercy to all men without partiality, and *give to every man with a good heart from the things that God has given you.* And if you have nothing at the time to give a man in need, have a fellow-feeling for him, and show him compassion and mercy. I remember I had nothing ready to hand on one occasion to give a needy man, so I accompanied him on his journey for seven furlongs [= approx. one mile] in tears, and my heart went out to him in sympathy. (*Testament of Zebulon* 7:1–4, emphasis added)

The italicized portion of this text is practically a paraphrase of *Did.* 1:5. The notion put forward is that the Lord has generously blessed him; hence, it is incumbent upon him to share his goods with others. The *Testament* enforces this action both as a response to the Lord and in anticipation of future benefits: "Be compassionate and merciful to every man that the Lord may be compassionate and merciful to you" (*Testament of Zebulon* 8:1). The *Didache*, in contrast, promotes this line of activity on the grounds that this is what "the Father wishes" (*Did.* 1:5).

3. Finally, the *Sentences of Phocylides* (first century B.C.E.) portray an urgent concern that the poor not be neglected when it comes to dispensing justice and wages (10, 19). The *Didache* picks up similar themes in its depiction of the Way of Death (*Did.* 5:2[B10–12, 16–20]). The *Sentences,* moreover, make a strong plea for sharing resources with the poor:

Give to the poor man at once, and do not tell him to come
    tomorrow.
You should fill your hand. Give alms to the needy.

> Receive the homeless in your house, and lead the blind man. . . .
> When you have wealth, stretch out your hand to the poor.
> Of that which God has given you, give of it to the needy. (22–24,
>   28–29)

The last sentence, in particular, makes it clear that all resources belong to God and that the one giving offers "that which God has given." All in all, therefore, the perspective of *Did.* 1:5 finds significant parallels in Jewish and Christian manuals. For further insights, see #7b.

#2E CHRISTIANS AS AGENTS OF GOD IN THE CHURCH FATHERS

Gildas Hamel in her study *Poverty and Charity in Roman Palestine* concludes that the church fathers "did not [generally] depart from the [moral] feelings and conceptions common to their culture" (236). When it came to the response demanded by the poor, however, the church fathers embraced a Jewish perspective alien to their culture: "What is remarkable is that the poor became a very important part of Christian thought and practice, in a world having little or nor concern for them" (236). Hamel points out that the church fathers embraced "the shocking revelation of a God who was not only close to the poor . . . , but who even lived a life of poverty, the Son in the flesh" (237). As a consequence of this message, rich Christians were reoriented toward seeing their wealth as a positive danger to their spiritual well-being if they did not become "agents of God, who was presented as the only true philanthropist" (237):

> In becoming Christians, Greeks and Romans accepted to be taught the Jewish views on poverty and to practice charity as understood by Jewish Christianity. This they did with such enthusiasm that their contemporaries found it necessary to react with expressions of disgust or wonder. (240)

The *Didache*, consequently, represents the first steps of a countercultural stance that would play itself out in the instructions and deeds of the church fathers. In every case, pagans, who had a general disdain for poverty and who were inclined to assist only those of their own social class, were given a reorientation and a mission that set them at odds with the settled values of their culture. The initial rule of giving (*Did.* 1:5), therefore, as practiced by novices in the *Didache* shows the central importance of this reorientation. No sooner would a novice show up for instruction than they were given a rule of life apt to elicit expressions of "disgust or wonder" that set them apart from their peers. Those in their intimate circles initially saw them as "different" or "dangerous" because of the way they responded to those in need.

4. *Relieving the debt of gratitude for the knowledge and life received*. Candidates were not accustomed to receiving something for nothing. The Jewish notion of refusing to accept gifts or money for teaching Torah may also have been operative here. In Matthew, for instance, one hears Jesus say, "You received without payment; give without payment" (Mt 10:8). In the rabbinic tradition, a similar rule prevailed: "Take no compensation whatever for her [Torah] since the Omnipotent gave her [Torah] to you gratuitously" (*Derek Erez Zuta* 4.58b). The Didache community supported trainers (*Did*. 13:2); hence, they had no need to receive honorariums or gifts from the novices. Nonetheless, gentile candidates must have often felt a debt of honor that needed to be satisfied. Accordingly, mentors may have devised this rule for giving in order to enable candidates to save face and to relieve their debt of gratitude to their trainers and, more especially, to the Father who gave them "life and knowledge" (*Did*. 9:3).

5. *Tasting the benefit of almsgiving as ransoming one's sins*. Candidates were being prepared to enter a community in which alms would be understood as "ransoming your sins" (*Did*. 4:6). During the training process, novices were brought face to face with the new standards of morality that constituted the Way of Life. The revelation of such new standards undoubtedly led to moments of shame and regret regarding the mode of life that had hitherto occupied the candidates. In the Jewish framework of thought, temple sacrifices were required even in those instances when inadvertent failures or sins of omission were committed. In some Jewish circles, the giving of alms was considered to be an appropriate substitute "ransoming your sins" (see #2h). Accordingly, since the *Didache* accepts such a practice (4:6), the almsgiving required of novices during the period of training might have been a teaching moment for allowing candidates to feel the link between such almsgiving and the atonement for failures that would be operative following baptism.

6. *Beginning a prophetic witness to God's future designs*. It would be a mistake to read the almsgiving required of novices and full members alike as being tacitly motivated by some utopian vision whereby the prophetic stance of a few would become contagious and somehow fan out throughout society in order to eliminate poverty and homelessness in society at large. With even greater force, it would be a mistake to imagine that Christians had some pragmatic plan of social transformation whereby the

systemic evils in Roman society would be addressed and turned around. Christians of this period had neither the social standing nor the practical means to transform society. In effect, Christians of this period regarded themselves as capable only of "lighting a small candle rather than cursing the darkness." In the not-too-distant future, however, they expected that God himself would take action and bring to earth the kingdom of God. Thus, even now, the tokens of relief had a prophetic edge—they proclaimed a God who was responsive to the cries of the lowly and the poor. In a social world determined by Fate and hardened to the incessant demands of the poor, such an unusual and prophetic act as almsgiving may have been the occasion for the novice to begin to account for his/her faith and hope. Accordingly, mentors may have devised this rule for giving in order to prepare the heart and mind of the candidate to prophetically witness to God's future designs in this world.

7. *Preparing to account publicly for one's new commitments.* The rites of the community were private in nature, and the members of the Didache communities wore no distinctive garb. Hence, becoming a Christian could go largely unnoticed outside of one's intimate circle of family and friends. But now the novice began to act with an unusual sense of responsiveness to requests that were formerly turned down. Consider, for instance, the case of beggars. Initially, beggars receiving what they asked for might have felt themselves lucky. They might have run offf with the loaf they received in order to satisfy the hunger of those dependent on them. Later, however, beggars would have identified novices as "easy marks." After repeatedly receiving charity a few days in a row, some beggars might well have had the courage to engage their benefactors in conversation in order to discover *why* they have been so generous *to them*. At this point, the novice would be forced to account for his/her Way of Life. Accordingly, mentors may have devised this rule for giving as a way of providing the candidate with a benevolent but socially deviant act (that of almsgiving) that would have functioned to draw attention and to force him/her to account publicly for his/her new commitments. Thus, even while being trained in the Way of Life, the candidate was prompted from the beginning to witness to the transformation and new commitments entailed.

8. *Breaking down the bond between the candidate and the biological family.* The practice of unreciprocated giving would also be noted immediately by one's family. Those who did not share the new convictions of the novice might have been shocked, perhaps even angry, that their son or daughter, brother or sister was squandering resources on riffraff or diluting the cumulative family resources on strangers. While beggars might be inclined to ask sympathetically, "Why?" hostile members of one's own family would be more prone to demand to know why, and, upon receiving a

very unconvincing answer, would do all in their power to dissuade or stop the practice before it got out of hand. What sense, for instance, does it make to imagine that "your Christian God wants everyone to benefit from his own free gifts" when the traditional family gods have routinely displayed great favoritism by giving an abundance of blessings to us and not to them? "Why," a father might challenge his son, "does your new God not take care of the poor whom you claim he champions by feeding and clothing them himself?" (*b. Baba Batra* 10a cited in #2h). "And why," a mother might challenge her daughter-in-law, "do you suddenly claim that the Christian God is 'the one and only' and show such ingratitude to the *Lares* (Roman household gods) who have protected and blessed you for twenty years?" As persuasion fails to stop the insanity of the one doing the almsgiving, escalating frustration leads (as shown in *Did.* 1:4) to blows on the cheek, to giving servile orders, to seizing outer garments, and finally to the seizing of the novice's assets before "they are all shamefully squandered."

In the end, everything else in the Way of Life might be expected to have only minor or delayed repercussions. A younger brother might find it puzzling that his older brother no longer calls any of the slave girls to his bed at night. His father might even approve of his son's new-found restraint. A younger sister might find it puzzling that her older sister no longer consults soothsayers. Her mother-in-law might even approve of her new-found self-reliance. No one, however, neither brother or sister, father or mother would openly sanction the distribution of goods and of honor to total strangers without any hope of any return. Thus, the novices' "irresponsible almsgiving" had the explosive effect of creating a rift of antagonism within his/her own family. This antagonism slowly eroded those bonds of attachment to one's origins and to the way of life sanctioned by one's parents. As the antagonism grew, the victimized novice must have fled more and more frequently into the arms of his/her new spiritual "father" or "mother." Jonathan Draper, borrowing the terms of sociology, accordingly wrote that a "social dislocation" occurred forcing novices "to die socially to their kinship":

> Such unreciprocated giving and such loss of honor as would be entailed by following the instructions in 1:3–5 would have a heavy social cost. . . . If they allowed the alienation of their property and gave to everyone who asked without seeking repayment, they could only expect penury and social ruin. They would "drop out of society," would die socially to their kinship and social group. (Draper 1997b: 58)

Accordingly, mentors may have devised this rule for giving in order to accelerate the breaking off of attachments to family members who were unable to approve of the novice's new way of life.

All in all, therefore, at least eight different propaedeutic patterns can be detected whereby novices had much to gain and much to learn through the practice of giving "to everyone asking you for anything" (*Did.* 1:5). In each case, one can surmise that a particular trainer may have had in mind one aspect more than another or, in the case of a given novice, he/she may have experienced one aspect more than another. In every case, however, one cannot doubt that the novice was being introduced into the Way of Life by living its obligations.

As has already been suggested, when the novice gave freely without expecting any return, this giving was an *imitatio dei* (imitation of God). Like Father, like son, like daughter. This mentality removed the temptation on the part of the one giving to feel superior or to feel generous in the face of the neediness of the petitioner. Rather, the implied reality was that the needs of the one giving had already been provided for by the Father so that the present giving would only be a kind of gratitude/recognition that one had already received enough of the goods of this world so as to be able to comply with what "the Father wished" in this instance. The one receiving, on the other hand, was relieved of any necessity to feel inferior or indebted to the one giving since, in effect, what was received came from the Father. Both the one giving and the one receiving, therefore, escaped the usual entrapment implied in every case of unilateral giving, and both ended up giving thanks to God. The wisdom of such a mentality and its practical consequences were thus evident for both the one giving and the one receiving.

Did the application of the rule of unrestrained giving have the effect of driving the novice and those depending on him/her below the poverty line? Most scholars do not even think of asking this question. Draper, on the other hand, finding that no limitation was set upon this giving, supposed that novices "would run a grave risk of actual physical need or even starvation" and that "the [*Didache*] community had to provide financial or material assistance to many novices ruined by their conversion" (Draper 1997b: 58). I doubt whether Draper is presenting an accurate picture here. If novices were systematically dispossessed by the rule of giving, as Draper suggests, this would have placed an enormous strain upon the community resources each time new members were admitted. Furthermore, one would have expected some rule regarding the frequency with which new members were to be admitted or some provision for staving off starvation in the case of destitute novices. The absence of such provisions leads me to believe that there was a natural limit to the unrestrained giving of *Did.* 1:5. How so? Let's consider some hypothetical cases:

1. A young novice would normally be part of an extended patriarchal family. As such, he could give away that food, that clothing, that money to which he habitually had access. The moment he began to give away the products produced in his family's workshop or the excess household furni-

ture stored in a shed, he would have been challenged by his siblings and stopped cold by his father. Then, discovering that his son had gained some absurd notion of what "the Father wishes" (*Did* 1:5), the head of the household would have limited his access to family property—even to the extent of taking away his cloak and his spending money (as suggested in *Did.* 1:4[C and D]) (see ch. 12 below). Thus a young novice would quickly reach a point in which he had no more to give. Even at this point, however, since his home, his trade, and his meals were still intact, he did not "run a grave risk of actual physical need or even starvation" (Draper 1997b: 58). Furthermore, since the son was still subservient to his father (as implied by *Did.* 1:4), there would be no reason for disowning or disinheriting him—contingencies addressed later in the chapter.

2. If a novice were head of a household, however, then the rule of unrestrained giving could seemingly find no limit short of financial ruin. Hence, in practice, the spiritual mentor undoubtedly intervened in order to moderate or entirely set aside the first rule. At what point? We can't know for certain. Giving the reorientation and learning that were expected to result from the application of the rule, one can only suspect that each spiritual mentor was expected to judge when the rule had produced its required effects. At that point, the first rule would be moderated or entirely suspended, since the heart and mind of the novice would have been quite ready to embrace the permanent rules for sharing governing the conduct of full members (*Did.* 4:5–8). It is to these rules that our attention can now turn.

#2F CONTEMPORARY GIVING AS BREAKING THE ADDICTION TO BEING STYLISH

In the fall of 1958, I was walking to an early class along Euclid Avenue, just north of the University of California (Berkeley) campus. I noticed a slim, neatly groomed woman in her mid-twenties who was taking five shopping bags of neatly pressed clothes out of the trunk of her car and placing them in the "poor box" that stood outside the tobacco shop (which, in those days, sold roach clips). The "poor box" was well frequented by those who lived in the area. It carried a simple sign, "Take what you need; give what you don't need." Curious at the quantity and quality of her donation, I stopped and said, "You must have been collecting clothes for a long time to have so many to contribute to the poor box."

She responded, "Yes, my whole life has been spent working hard so that I could collect the best and most fashionable clothes available; but, now, this is going to stop!" She then went into detail to tell me how empty and stifling her addiction to "looking great" had become. The upshot was that now, "in order to free myself from this addiction," she explained, "I have set aside just those few clothes that I really need and have turned my surplus over to others in need."

Feeling the impact of this "giving" upon this young woman, one can imagine that, for candidates preparing to enter a Didache community, the giving "to everyone asking you" (*Did*. 1:5) must also have had the effect of breaking any addiction to wealth or to success that might possess the novice. Unless this drive was broken, a novice could not hope to be anything but someone "stretching out your hands for the purpose of taking" and "withdrawing them for the purpose of giving" (*Did*. 4:5)—which the *Didache* warns against.

Meanwhile, on the south side of campus, twelve members of the Hare Krishna movement were dancing joyously to the sound of the tambourine and drum and singing at the top of their lungs, "Hare Krishna, Hare Krishna," as they whirled around in their circle. Public dancing in this way was greeted as a curiosity by many University of California students; others regarded their dance as pure lunacy and made caustic remarks. In any case, one didn't have to be a psychologist to notice that such religious dancing had the effect of distancing members of the Hare Krishna movement from their onlookers. One can imagine that novices who were being trained to participate in "honoring the sacred name of Krishna through praising his name in dance" experienced their "scandalous conduct" as publicly affirming their commitments and of binding themselves to the sacred ways of the dancers. Needless to say, a novice could not continue dancing without being entirely submerged in the sacred dance and without entirely disregarding the caustic remarks of onlookers.

The unreciprocated giving by novices bent on embracing the Way of Life must have had a comparable effect on their contemporaries. What the novice was trained to honor as a religious act, onlookers were prone to scorn as "scandalous conduct" bent on squandering family resources on riffraff. The act of giving, therefore, had the effect of socially distancing the novices from their critics. Here, as in the Hare Krishna movement, a novice could not continue such unreciprocated giving without becoming entirely submerged in the sacred act of giving as "the Father wishes" (*Did*. 1:5) while ignoring the caustic remarks of outsiders.

From time to time, those who danced joyously for Krishna were met by an admiring student. Such an admirer was encouraged to come with them and to eat together the "sacred meal" consecrated to Krishna. Questions were asked, answers given. In the end, some of these admirers were led by the spirit of the dance to embrace a movement that others scorned. One cannot help but imagine that giving "to everyone asking" met with similar results in its day.

The Measure and Motives for Sharing
Resources with Insiders

Near the end of the training cycle, the novice was made aware that a new set of economic guidelines would come into play once they were members. *Didache* 4:5–8 presents an oral unit in three parts. The simple future tense aptly signals that these new guidelines would not be implemented immediately but only following baptism, when one took one's place at the eucharistic table (9:5) and enjoyed the company of the saints (4:2). Two possible objections might be considered:

1. Someone might object that the future tense does not always indicate future action, since, both in Greek and in English, the future can be used to express a mild imperative as, for example, in the decalogue of *Did.* 2:1. This objection can be examined by noting that *Did.* 4:5–8 is framed by two triads that refer to actions that can apply only after baptism. For example, the novice is instructed: "You will reconcile those fighting" and "you will . . . reprove against failings" (*Did.* 4:3) while at the same time, 9:5 makes it clear that no unbaptized person can be present at the weekly formal gatherings when the confession of failings and the exclusion of those fighting specifically takes place in order to ensure the purity of their eucharistic meal (14:1–4). Novices who were excluded from these gatherings could hardly have been expected to know who was fighting and who was failing, thereby rendering the mandate to "reconcile" and "reprove" as having no application. Moreover, no organization would expect novices still wet behind the ears and still without a complete grasp of the community bylaws and procedures to be in a social position to reconcile or reprove longtime members. Thus, while some ambiguity may surround the use of the future tense, the clear intent to frame *Did.* 4:5–8 by triads that clearly envision conduct after baptism puts the economic guidelines into the same category.

2. Someone may object that the content of *Did.* 4:5–8 demands immediate implementation by virtue of the fact that the novice has already gained a "spiritual father" or a "spiritual mother" (as detailed in ch. 1) and is thereby required to "partner all things" with his/her spiritual "brothers" and "sisters" (*Did.* 4:8). True, the novice does gain, half-way through his/her training, a "spiritual father" or "spiritual mother" but, for the time being, they do not meet as a family (*Did.* 9:5) and do not become business partners (as will be explained shortly). Once baptized, however, all this will change, and the reciprocal giving and receiving will begin (4:5). Thus, while a mentor does train a novice "like a nurse tenderly caring for her own children" (1 Thes 2:7) or "like a father with his children" (1 Thes 2:11),

the novice is not formally adopted into the family circle prior to baptism. Furthermore, the very notion of a progressive training program carries with it the hint that the novice does not become a "son" or "daughter" all at once; hence, even after becoming a faithful "son" or "daughter," the novice is not yet prepared to be a "brother" or "sister" to those within God's family. When the novice is ready, the mentor will know this and proceed to welcome him/her into "the family" through the status-changing rite of baptism (see ch. 3 below).

The linguistic structure of *Did.* 4:5–8 is triadic and fits comfortably within the triads of 3:8–10 and 4:1–4 which precede and follow it. When outlined, it might look like this:

[A] A call for reciprocity—giving and receiving
[B] Two motives for giving surplus resources:
   [1] For the "ransoming of sins"
   [2] For you will know him who will repay you
[C] Why one cannot avoid practicing *koinōnia* with a "brother" or "sister"

A. The first guideline (4:5) calls for reciprocity and balance. Members will be expected to show the same openhandedness in giving that they employ in receiving. The initial rule for giving was decidedly unreciprocal. Once a novice has mastered this art of giving, however, then he/she would be ready for the reciprocity called for by community living. *Didache* 4:5, consequently, offers the general principle that forms the foundation for economic life in the Didache communities.

B. The second guideline (*Did.* 4:6) implies that members are manual workers who from time to time enjoy a surplus. Such surplus is now given to (or received by) those in need—community members and outsiders alike. At this point, one can see that a modified rule of unreciprocated giving continues for the whole lifetime of the member. The long haul is now emphasized. The implied danger here is that one would continue to give but, after many years, end up doing it grudgingly with much "grumbling" (4:7).

The two motives supplied would appear to be introduced in order to encourage cheerful giving over the long haul. This will be examined in detail shortly.

C. The third guideline (4:7f.) deals not with surplus goods but with absolutely "everything" owned. A member cannot claim tools, or monies, or products produced as "personal property" in order to defend blindness or deafness to the need of a "brother" or "sister." The logic for this unrestrained internal sharing is an argument from the greater to the lesser. If members of the community were "sharers in the immortal things" (the greater good), then "how much more" ought they to be characterized as "sharers in the mortal things" (4:8) (the lesser good). This will be explored more fully in what follows.

#2G THE COMMON TREASURY IN THE *MANUAL OF DISCIPLINE*

The Dead Sea Scrolls illustrate how a Jewish association might regulate its internal affairs with a sophisticated set of rules comparable to what one finds in the *Didache*. More importantly, among the scrolls were found thirteen copies of the *Manual of Discipline*—an indicator of the importance of this community rule among those who copied and used the scrolls. Following the early studies of Roland de Vaux, most scholars assumed that the scrolls represented the community library of the Jewish sect of Essenes that had its "mother house" at Qumran for a period of two centuries before it was destroyed by the Romans in 68 C.E. Today, however, careful archaeological studies of the Qumran site appear to indicate that the scrolls were neither created nor used by the occupants at Qumran (Wise: 20–24, 123). Accordingly, the *Manual of Discipline* of "Qumran" now appears to be more of a charter document regulating the life of many scattered communities sharing the same rule of life:

> Each chapter of the association has a leader known as the Instructor, probably the foremost priest, who guides deliberations about the rules of the group's government, association funds, and biblical interpretation. . . . Decisions are by majority rule. The local chapters comprise at least ten men [with their families] who met for meals and for Bible study. Each year they conducted a full review of the membership. At that time a man's rank can change, for better or worse, according to his behavior and biblical understanding. (Wise: 124)

The *Manual of Discipline* prescribed a formal two-year training and testing period prior to full inclusion within the community life with its shared meals, shared work, shared resources, and shared rituals. During the first year of training, the candidate "must not touch the pure food of the general membership" or "admix his property with that of the general membership" (1QS 6.16f.). After being examined on "the details of his understanding and works of the Law [Torah]" and receiving a favorable vote of the membership, the candidate then proceeded to put "his property . . . under the authority of the Overseer" (1QS 6.18f.). Most probably, this was the intermediate step that prepared the candidate for full membership, when both the control and ownership of his property would pass over to the community. Should he leave during the second year or fail to receive a favorable vote during the deliberations at the end of the second year, then control of his property would be returned to him. During the second year, he was sustained by the community food but excluded from the community drink. Once a full member, all rights of property ownership were relinquished, and members who were subsequently excluded for serious infractions of the rule went away empty-handed.

The Essenes described by Josephus had branches for celibate men and for families. While Josephus does say that "every one's possessions are intermingled" (*J.W.* 2.122), he later explains that private possessions continued but that reciprocal giving and receiving were practiced:

> Nor do they buy or sell anything to one another; but every one of them gives what he has to him that wants it, and receives from him again in lieu of it what may be convenient for himself; and although there be no requital [tally] made, they are fully allowed to take what they want of whomsoever they please. (*J.W.* 2.127)

This practice of giving and receiving in response to requests would appear to be very close to what was practiced by members of the Didache communities (*Did.* 4:5–8). Where it differs is that the Essenes were required to have the permission of an elder when giving anything to another member (*J.W.* 2.134). This was undoubtedly understood as a safeguard. All in all, while the Essenes did not relinquish personal ownership, their practice of sharing their resources served the purpose of providing an economic safety net against the hardships and the threats associated with taking out loans, going into debt, and risking the degradations of debt slavery. Here again, this practice was not just a pious notion based on some romantic ideal of sharing; rather, it was the time-honored way by which members of a like-minded association could protect their colleagues from the ravages of an economic order in which "the rich became even richer" (Theissen 1977: 41) and the poor, more and more frequently, slipped into destitution (Crossan 1998: 330). For further details, see Murphy (2002).

Giving Motivated by Ransoming of Sins and Expectation of Reward

The motive for the first rule, giving to outsiders, was "your Father wishes" (*Did.* 1:5). The motives for reciprocal sharing among members are "ransoming your sins" (4:6) and receiving "an excellent recompense"

(4:7) when the Lord comes on the last day. Both of these motives have deep roots in the Judaisms known to us (#2b), and both imply some degree of self-interest. Here the pastoral genius of the *Didache* again becomes apparent: self-interest was acknowledged and even encouraged, but it was subordinated to the larger values and hopes of the kingdom of God.

The guideline for giving in *Did.* 4:6f. implies that something was accumulated "through your hands" (*dia tōn cheirōn sou*). This Greek phrase derives from "the tendency to speak of a person's activity as the work of his hand" (Bauer: 880c). In this instance, the metaphor signals that small surpluses were accumulated through manual labor—again pointing to the working-class membership of this community. But even here, a small degree of economic prosperity was not, in and of itself, an occasion to praise the worker, for, in accordance with 1:5, such prosperity came from God and the one having amassed the goods of this earth acted only as a go-between for executing the will of his/her Patron in heaven. Thus, "you will give something as the ransoming of your sins" (4:6) and "you will not hesitate to give . . . for you will know [the Lord God] who will give back an excellent recompense [when he comes]" (4:7). The message is clear. Those who serve the Lord's interests and take on his values relative to sharing their resources with the lowly will be forgiven their failings and given a just repayment in the world to come. These themes would not find any resonance in Roman society. Judaism, however, offers abundant parallels (#2b).

#2H RANSOMING SINS THROUGH ALMSGIVING

The legal codes of Israel provided a large measure of protection for the poor and many of the prophetic attacks deal with the abusive treatment of the poor by the rich. The following are examples:

Interest may not be charged and a mantle may not be kept as a guarantee on a loan (Ex 22:25–27; Dt 24:10–13); gleanings from the harvest must be left for the poor and the alien (Lv 19:9–10; 23:22; Dt 24:19–21); the wages of day laborers may not be withheld (Lv 19:13; Dt 24:14–15; cf. Tb 4:14; Sir 34:22); no partiality may be shown in judgment on the basis of economic status (Lv 1915; Amos 5:12; Is 10:1–2, 32:7). Above all, widows and orphans, the classical symbols of the poor and oppressed, must be protected rather than exploited (Ex 22:21; Dt 10:18; Is 1:17; Jer 5:28; Ez 22:7, etc.) by members of the covenant community even as they are defended by God (Ps 68:5). The ideal of the sabbatical year calls for the cancellation of debts from fellow Jews . . . and the release of Jewish slaves unless they wish to remain (Ex 21:1–6; Lv 25:39–43; Dt 15:12–18). (Osiek: 18)

In rabbinic literature, great care was taken to enforce and to expand the operation of each of these safety measures. Since the rabbinic materials have a utopian character, it cannot be known at every point to what degree these safety measures were applied in day-to-day living. Overall, however, the tone of encouraging assistance to the poor is very high. According to Rabbi Assi, "Charity is equivalent to all other religious duties combined" (*b. Baba Batra* 9a).

Since atonement for sins was formerly granted by God in association with a sacrifice in the temple, it was only a matter of time after the destruction of the temple before almsgiving was regarded as a suitable substitute for that sacrifice. Here are multiple expressions of this substitution:

And said Rabbi Eleazar, "When the Temple stood, someone would pay off his shekel-offering [the annual tax for the maintenance of sacrifices] and achieve atonement [for sins]. Now that the Temple is not standing, if people give to charity, well and good [atonement is made], but if not, the gentiles [Romans] will come and take it [the annual temple tax] by force. And even so, that is still regarded for them as an act of righteousness: 'I will make your extractors righteousness' (Is 60:17)." (*b. Baba Batra* 9a)

Said [also] Rabbi Eleazar, "Greater is he who discreetly carries out an act of charity than was our lord, Moses, for of Moses it is written, 'For I was afraid because of the anger and the wrath [of God]" (Dt 9:19), but of one who gives charity in such a manner [secretly] it is written, 'A gift in secret subdues [God's] anger [against the sinner]' (Prv 21:14)." (*b. Baba Batra* 9b)

Rabbi Meir would say, "Someone arguing with you [on the efficacy of almsgiving] may reply to you saying, 'If your God loves the poor [as you suggest], why does he not provide for them [himself]?' And say to him, 'It is so that through them [the poor] we ourselves may be saved from the judgment of Gehenna [the destroying fire at the final judgment]." (*b. Baba Batra* 10a)

Rabbi Meir intimates that God allows some to be poor so that the almsgiving of others will atone for their sins and thereby save them from the destroying fire of Gehenna (see ch. 10 below). But when R. Aqiba proposed this teaching, a critic of almsgiving refuted him with a parable calculated to demonstrate that almsgiving produces a greater burden of sin:

> To what is the matter [of almsgiving] to be likened? To the case of a mortal king who was angry with his *servant* and put him in prison and gave orders not to feed him or give him drink. But someone came along and gave him food and drink. When the king heard, will he not be angry with him? And you people are called *servants:* "For to me the children of Israel are servants" (Lv 25:55). (*b. Baba Batra* 10a)

The implied argument is well crafted: (a) If the Lord wanted food and drink given to his servants, the poor, he would have done it himself. (b) Since he does not, the poor are likened to those whom a king places in prison to punish them. (c) Anyone bringing assistance to those punished by the Lord, therefore, should expect to earn God's anger.

R. Aqiba, however, was not daunted. He countered with his own parable that artfully altered the one supplied by his opponent:

> To what is the matter [of almsgiving] to be compared? To the case of a mortal king who was angry with his *son* and put him in prison and gave orders not to feed him or give him drink. But someone came along and gave him food and drink. When the king heard, will he not send him a gift to him [in gratitude]? And we are called *sons:* "Sons are you to the Lord your God" (Dt 14:1). (*b. Baba Batra* 10a)

The implied logic in R. Aqiba's refutation is ingenious: (a) For the sake of argument, let's assume that the king punishes the poor by not providing them with food and drink. (b) They are nevertheless like "a son" to him rather than "a servant." (c) Accordingly, anyone who would lighten the punishment of "his son," the king would be inclined to bless (by the atonement of their sins).

Regarding the almsgiving of gentiles, the rabbis put forward two contradictory judgments. To emphasize the contradiction, both judgments were framed as derived from the same verse:

> Rabban Yohanan ben Zakkai said to his disciples: "My sons, what is the meaning of Scripture: 'Righteousness exalts a nation, but the kindness of the peoples [gentiles] is sin' (Prv 14:34)?" (*b. Baba Batra* 10b)

In response to this question, each of the five disciples of Rabban Yohanan gave their opinion in turn. The first four concluded that "a nation" refers to Israel, while the almsgiving of gentiles was "a sin" because they do it for base reasons: "to magnify themselves," "to prolong their dominion," "to display haughtiness," or "to reproach us" (*b. Baba Batra* 10b). The fifth disciple, Rabbi Nehuniah, answered by showing that the contradiction is only apparent because "sin" and "sin offering" are identical words in Hebrew; thus, Prv 14:34 wanted to declare that "the kindness of the peoples [gentiles] is a sin-offering." Rabban Yohanan confirms the superiority of Rabbi Nehuniah's response saying, "Just as the sin-offering [in the Temple] atones for Israel, so an act of charity [almsgiving] atones for the nations of the world." (*b. Baba Batra* 10b)

All these examples illustrate how the notion of almsgiving was associated with sacrifice in that, following the destruction of the Temple, almsgiving effected the atonement for sins. The last illustration is especially important because Rabban Yohanan ben Zakkai associates almsgiving by gentiles with atonement just as does the *Didache*.

The Babylonian Talmud, however, was compiled in the sixth century and, even though Rabban Yohanan ben Zakkai was a contemporary of Jesus, it is hazardous to use a composition of such late date to decide on rabbinic practice during the first century. The Book of Tobit (c. 200 B.C.E.), on the other hand, illustrates how Jews in exile could think of almsgiving as functioning to atone for sins long before the second destruction of the temple. Tobit is shot through with references to almsgiving. In a touching scene, the blind father, Tobit, hands over to his young son, Tobit, his final instruction as he prepares to travel a long distance, and father and son may never see each other again. Among his instructions, one hears this:

> Give alms from your possessions, and do not let your eye begrudge the gift when you make it. Do not turn your face away from anyone who is poor, and the face of God will not be turned away from you. If you have many possessions, make your gift from them in proportion; if few, do not be afraid to give according to the little you have. So you will be laying up a good treasure for yourself against the day of necessity [when the Lord will repay you]. For almsgiving delivers from death and keeps you from going into the Darkness [Hades?]. Indeed, almsgiving, for all who practice it, is *an excellent offering* in the presence of the Most High. (Tb 4:7–11)

The extended text demonstrates multiple reasons to give alms: (a) to ensure that God will hear your plea, (b) especially in the day of trial, (c) when you are facing death. All in all, almsgiving functions as "an excellent offering/sacrifice" (Tb 4:11). This later is expanded when Raphael, the angel of the Lord, says this to Tobias and his wife, Rachel:

Prayer with fasting is good, but better than both is almsgiving with righteousness. . . . It is better to give alms than to lay up gold. For almsgiving saves from death and purges away every sin. (Tb 12:8f.)

The Book of Sirach (c. 180 B.C.E.) also gives vast amount of attention to aiding those in economic distress. The section on almsgiving (Sir 3:30–4:10) begins as follows:

As water extinguishes a blazing fire,
so almsgiving atones for sin. (Sir 3:30)

Here again, the notion of fire is probably suggested because of the widespread notion that the Lord will use fire to purify the elect on the Last Day (see ch. 8 below). If such be the case, almsgiving acts like water, extinguishing the fire, atoning for sin.

All in all, therefore, the notion found in the *Didache* regarding the efficacy of almsgiving "as the ransoming of your sins" (*Did.* 4:6) would have been a commonplace within many Jewish circles. *Lytrōsis* has the primary sense of paying a ransom (*lytron*) for the release of a captive. If the judgment to come is perceived as repaying one's "debts" (a euphemism for "sin") to the Lord (1:5; 8:2), then almsgiving carries with it the notion of giving one's wages as payment of the "debt" due to one's sins.

#21 RECEIVING AN EXCELLENT RECOMPENSE FROM THE LORD

Regarding the recompense that faithful brokers will receive when the Lord comes, one has only to think of the images in Luke's Gospel. Consider the following:

"Be dressed for action and have your lamps lit; be like those who are waiting for their master to return from the wedding banquet, so that they may open the door for him as soon as he comes and knocks. Blessed are those slaves whom the master finds alert when he comes; truly I tell you, he will fasten his belt and have them sit down to eat, and he will come and serve them. If he comes during the middle of the night, or near dawn, and finds them so, blessed are those slaves. But know this: if the owner of the house had known at what hour the thief was coming, he would not have let his house be broken into. You also must be ready, for the Son of Man is coming at an unexpected hour."

Peter said, "Lord, are you telling this parable for us or for everyone?"

And the Lord said, "Who then is the faithful and prudent manager whom his master will put in charge of his slaves, to give them their allowance of food at the proper time? Blessed is that slave whom his master will find at work when he arrives. Truly I tell you, he will put that one in charge of all his possessions. But if that slave says to himself, 'My master is delayed in coming,' and if he begins to beat the other slaves, men and women, and to eat and drink and get drunk, the master of that slave will come on a day when he does not expect him and at an hour that he does not know, and will cut him in pieces, and put him with the unfaithful. That slave who knew what his master wanted, but did not prepare himself or do what was wanted, will receive a severe beating. But the one who did not know and did what deserved a beating will receive a light beating. From everyone to whom much has been given, much will be required; and from the one to whom much has been entrusted, even more will be demanded." (Lk 12:35–48)

The term "slave" is the familiar metaphor for someone who hears and does the Lord's wishes (*ABD* 6:72). In this instance, the servant is put in charge of his household while the Lord is gone. The servant is expected to function as God's broker and to serve his interests. His interest, needless to say, is the well-being of his household. Thus, when the master returns, he expects to find his servants busy about the tasks he has assigned to them. And when he does, what does he do? He sets a banquet *for them* and *waits upon them*. In practice, no human master could be expected to do this for his servants (see Lk 17:7)! The parable, therefore, at this point breaks through the strategies of human patronage and allows a vision of God's patronage to sound through. Unlike earthly patrons, who, in the end, exploit their clients in their own self-interest, our Father in heaven promises to come and to serve his servants.

This expectation of the Lord does not allow for complacency, for immediately Jesus turns his attention to the worst-case scenario, namely, the case of the servant who abused his position and exploited the other servants (quite unlike the master of the household). This unworthy servant, the Lord "will cut in pieces" or he will "receive a severe beating" (Lk 12:46f.). Here, again, one is reminded of the cruel punishments that masters sometimes inflicted on disobedient servants in the ancient world. Neither Luke nor the *Didache* would have flinched from allowing such corporal punishments.

Even though we cannot expect that the members of the Didache communities knew of Luke's Gospel (see ch. 11 below), we can say that the admonition to "be watchful over your life . . . for you do not know the hour in which our Lord is coming" (*Did.* 16:1) does point in the direction of being either rewarded or chastised by the Great Patron who expects his servants to act at all times in favor of his fellow servants whom he cherishes.

Giving Motivated by the Business Partnership with One's Brother

Didache 4:8 begins by telling the novice, "You will not turn away the one being in need." This clearly establishes a link with 4:7f. and 1:5, where the "expressed need" of the petitioner take precedence. The next line, however, points to the social relations within the community wherein the petitioner was now not a stranger but "your brother" or "your sister"— those who belong to you. For spiritual kin, the response anticipated knows no limit: "You will share all" (*Did.* 4:8).

The Greek term *koinōnia* (Acts 4:32) is used in Acts and twice in *Did.* 4:8. The force of this term may be much more than what standard English translators allow:

> The Revised Standard Version and the New American Standard Bible translate it [*koinōnia*] as "fellowship," and the Jerusalem Bible as "brotherhood." This is the common understanding of this word. . . . Yet, *koinōnia* means much more than that. It also means partnership, as in a common business venture. In this way Luke uses the related term *koinōnos*, member of a *koinōnia*, for in Luke 5:10 we are told that the sons of Zebedee were *koinōnoi* with Peter, meaning they were business partners. (Gonzalez: 83)

This would open up the meaning of "sharing" found in *Did.* 4:8 to include the notion of a "business partnership." Thus, straining the English language, the novice was being prepared to "partner together (*syn* + *koinōnēseis*) all things with your brother or sister" under the implied logic that since they will be "partners (*koinōnoi*) in the immortal things" it follows, with greater force, that they should be partners "in the mortal things" (4:8).

In the ancient world, an entire family normally practiced a trade together working side by side in the same workshop. Under these conditions, if the head of the family embraced Christianity, there would be no difficulty. If the head of the family judged that his son and daughter-in-law had "betrayed the family" by giving away scarce resources and by repudiating their guardian deities, one might expect such "deviants" to be expelled from the family business and disinherited. Those expelled were effectively "dead" both socially and economically, for in that moment they would be cut off from their biological family and from their family livelihood as well. With baptism, such persons were reborn as children of their Father in heaven and gained a new family. Accordingly, novices who were ousted from their family's business joined with a new family and thereby maintained themselves and their dependents by working at their craft. It was in these "new" families that everything was shared just as it had been in their former biological families. Even in the case of visitors who decided to settle into a Didache community, the operative rule was "let him/her work and let him/her eat" (12:3)—the presupposition being that any Christians could be immediately employed in the "family" businesses within the local community.

The "partnership" of workers in a common trade was neither a romantic notion of "charity" nor a form of ancient "communism." John Dominic Crossan aptly notes: "Patronal sharing (alms) is an act of power. Communal sharing is an act of resistance" (1998: 472). Survival at a trade in the ancient world meant having access to the needed licenses from the authorities as well as contracts with local distributors (Hanson: 104f.). Those who were discharged from their family business risked financial ruin and permanent exclusion from the only trade they knew. Thus it was no small thing for dispossessed novices to join collectives in which they shared their craft, their fortunes, and their incomes with their "brothers" and "sisters." One may see these as the collectivization necessary for economic survival. Any religious movement that would destroy the earning power of its new members without finding ways of restoring it would have otherwise been doomed to ruination.

In the end, therefore, the *Didache* opens up the image of a community that is firmly fixed upon living the Way of Life revealed to them by the Father "through [his] servant Jesus" (9:2). This way of life, however, serves to cut members off from banquets, festivals, and associations that might have been conducive for promoting their commercial interests. In joining together with a new family, however, new bonds of responsibility and service are born that place the resources of each at the disposal of all. The logic is strong: "If you are sharers in the immortal things, by how much more should you be sharers in the mortal things? (4:8). Thus, this association pushed forward the notion of Jew and gentile, slave and free, men and women binding themselves together for the common good of all. Much more than a funeral society or a workingmen's club, the *Didache* purported to provide an all-encompassing social and economic safety net for its members. The members thought of their own resources as a gift of the Great Patron who willed that these things be distributed to the needy through them as his brokers. Using the Lord's resources well, they expected to be called faithful servants when he came at the end of this age. While they were waiting, therefore, they were far from being idle.

#2J THE SURRENDER OF GOODS INTO A COMMON TREASURY IN ACTS

The situation among the disciples of Jesus in Jerusalem as reported in Acts suggests that members surrendered their goods into a common treasury:

> All who believed were together and *had all things in common;* they would sell their possessions and goods and distribute the proceeds to all, as any had need. (Acts 2:44f.)

> Now the whole group (*koinōnia*) of those who believed were of one heart and one soul, and no one claimed private ownership of any possessions, but everything they owned was held in common. . . . There was not a needy person among them, for *as many as owned lands or houses sold them* and brought the proceeds of what was sold. They laid it at the apostles' feet, and it was distributed to each as any had need. (Acts 4:32–35)

At first glance, the italicized phrases suggest a complete liquidation of assets followed by the complete mingling of the proceeds in a community treasury as mandated by the Qumran *Manual of Discipline.* Upon closer inspection, however, various interpretations are possible:

1. Ivoni Richter Reimer speculates that members retained ownership but "agreed to be ready at a moment's notice to relinquish the property declared to belong to the community by putting it up for sale, in order that the community . . . might survive [financially]" (12).

2. Justo L. Gonzalez reconstructs the practice of the community by placing special emphasis on the point that "Peter clearly tells Ananias (Acts 5:4) that he was under no obligation to sell his property" (82). Hence, Gonzalez concludes that members of the Jerusalem church were free to sell their surplus property *if they so wished* and to donate the monies received to the community treasury, which offered relief to those in economic distress.

3. Capper differs from both Reimer and Gonzalez. When Peter said to Ananias, "After it [the property] was sold, was it [the proceeds of the sale] not at your disposal?" (Acts 5:4), Capper understands this to mean that, should Ananias leave the community during the time of his training, he might have regained full possession of everything that he had laid "at the apostles' feet" (Acts 5:2) (339f.). As a consequence, Capper finds in Acts the same two-stage surrender of property as is operative in the *Manual of Discipline.* Initially, the novice liquidated all assets except those needed for day-to-day living and placed the sums gained into the safekeeping of the

apostles (acting as overseers). Then, once baptized, the novice would enter into the full fellowship and transfer everything over to the community, which "had all things in common" (Acts 2:44).

No matter how the property relations within the Jerusalem church are to be understood, it is quite clear that the framers of the *Didache* had none of these models in mind. The economic framework of the *Didache* is therefore distinctive.

Business Partnering as a Buffer Against Debt Slavery

G. E. M. de Sainte Croix concludes that the ancient world provided only a small margin of upward mobility for those who were naturally gifted, enterprising, and well connected (115). The dangers of downward mobility, however, were all too real and formed the everyday events threatening the small family business within the empire. A craftsman making pottery or weaving baskets in his family shop might, for instance, be forced to take out a loan in order to tide his family over in a lean year. Such a person would probably be inclined to ask his immediate acquaintances for the needed funds. Since the owners of small family businesses normally had little surplus, such loans were undoubtedly hard to come by. The necessary alternative, therefore, was to approach a wealthy client or a large-scale landowner for the assistance necessary to keep one's business going and one's family intact. The terms of such a loan always favored the lender and, depending on the degree of need, the borrower was sometimes not in a position to hold out for more favorable terms.

In the ancient world, there were no banks or bankers practicing an "equal lending policy" as we know it today. All loans were personal, and all loans were inherently risky. Social inequalities, moreover, ensured that those who urgently needed loans were in the worst condition to receive them while those who had ample resources had no difficulty finding a lender. The very existence of a loan meant that the borrower became a client to the lender and that he or she often had to provide personal services to the lender in addition to feeling the weight of the obligation due. Anyone defaulting on a private loan was at the mercy of the lender. When the collateral for a loan was the family farm or the family business (which was normally part of one's home), a debtor might face a foreclosure that would put him and his family out on the street. A compassionate lender might agree to allow him to take on the new status of renting the family farm or business. In this case, however, the family was forced not only to make a living but to sustain the additional burden of paying the new owner the rents due. With one's collateral diminished, the need to make ends meet would normally force family members to work extended hours. In severe cases, a man was forced to hire out his wife and children as domestic servants or to sell them into outright slavery (*ABD* 6:63). In the end, any further loan could be secured only by offering oneself as collateral. Now any default would lead the husband himself to be powerless to redeem his wife and children, for he himself would, most probably, be sold into slavery abroad to satisfy his creditors. In still other cases, his creditors could place him in prison (hoping to receive a ransom from relatives) or, if they chose, could torture or kill him (de Sainte Croix: 162–65). No one, especially those in the lower classes, had the option of declaring bankruptcy and thereby shielding his home and his family from creditors.

#2κ Money Lending and Debt Bondage in Roman Law

The famous Roman statesman Cicero (106–43 B.C.E.) regarded money-lenders as a "sordid lot" to be ranked with manual laborers and tax collectors. In effect, Cicero thought of money lending as slightly dishonest and incurring ill will (*Agriculture,* intro.). Nonetheless, Cicero himself borrowed from moneylenders and acted as a moneylender himself. For most wealthy Romans, "even though they may have engaged in lending money at interest on a large scale, they felt no contradiction or embarrassment about it" (Osiek: 74).

During the lending crisis of 33 C.E., the mortgaged properties of the aristocracy were endangered by creditors demanding payment on their loans. Cicero vigorously objected to legislation directed toward loan cancellation, yet he had no objection to the use of the imperial treasury to provide "a floating fund of one hundred million sesterces [= five billion U.S. dollars today] for interest-free loans to save those whose *dignitas* [dignity] and *fama* [fame] as well as their fortunes were at stake" (Osiek: 74).

Interest on loans between citizens was limited to twelve percent, "the legal limit throughout the history of Roman legislation" (Gonzalez: 19). In practice, however, interest rates for non-Romans fluctuated widely according to the borrower's social class, collateral, and risk. Even among Romans, "when the lender could claim that significant risk was involved, such as in shipping enterprises or in agriculture, interest rates could exceed the established limit, sometimes rising as high as 50 percent" (Gonzalez: 19).

Roman debt laws, meanwhile, had evolved toward protecting the well-being of upper-class Roman borrowers:

> The original right of a creditor to seize and even kill a debtor was modified and restricted as early as the Law of the Twelve Tables (c. 450 B.C.E.), which specified a procedure of imprisonment and public notification over a period of sixty days before capital punishment or, more likely, the sale of the debtor [was imposed]. . . .

> According to Livy (8.28) a *Lex Poetelia Papiria* of 326 B.C.E.
> abolished the formal legal power . . . of the creditor to exercise
> the right of personal seizure as security. However, the right of
> *addiction* or temporary bondage of the debtor or a dependent
> continued to be exercised with the consent of magistrates."
> (Osiek: 75)

When it came to non-Romans, however, none of these protections existed. Likewise, for the poor with Roman citizenship, "compulsory labor, the sale of children, and the seizure of property were the usual results of insolvency" (*ABD* 6:71; Osiek: 76).

In Jewish law, one also finds a double standard. A fellow Hebrew who was reduced to slavery was to be released at the end of six years (Ex 21:2–4), while a foreigner could be subject to perpetual enslavement (Lv 25:45f.). Nonetheless, all slaves were to be granted the Sabbath day of rest (Ex 20:8; Dt 5:14f.), and slaves were guaranteed some degree of protection. For example, masters who injured or beat their slaves to death were to be punished (Ex 21:20f.). With the Deutronomic reform, the Lord commanded "open[ing] your hand, willingly lending enough to meet the need of the poor" (Dt 15:8), and, every seven years, there was to be a complete remission of all debts in order that "there will be no one in need among you" (Dt 15:3). Presumably this lending to the poor was not widely practiced for the prophets regularly spoke out against the oppression of the poor and against debt slavery. Nonetheless, with the coming of the Lord, the prophet Isaiah proclaimed that all slaves and captives would be set free and would enjoy the prosperity that the Lord would take back from the nations and give to them (Is 29:19; 61:1–4).

One has only to listen to the parables of Jesus to capture something of the brutalities surrounding debt bondage for non-Romans in the ancient world. Matthew's parable of the unmerciful servant is an illustrative case in point. According to the parable, a king "who wishes to settle accounts" (Mt 18:23) with his debtors, has a man "who owed him ten thousand talents" (Mt 18:24) brought forward. This is an enormous sum—fifty times the annual revenues of King Herod Antipas—and one can be sure that a Jewish audience of the first century would have gasped when they heard the sum. One can also speculate that someone borrowing this much must have had the supreme confidence of the king at the point that the loan was made. Nonetheless, since "he could not pay, his lord ordered him to be sold, together with his wife and children and all his possessions, and payment to be made" (Mt 18:25). Thus, the very terms of the story indicate how the lender regards it as within his rights to sell everything the man owns, beginning with himself, his wife, and his children, in order to regain part of the defaulted loan.

The wretched man in the story understands this and, therefore, does not plead against the "injustice" of the system. Anyone borrowing such huge sums engaged in a huge risk. Thus, the miserable debtor can only plead for an extension of time on his loan: "Have patience with me, and I will pay you everything" (Mt 18:26). The tone of this remark is to reassure the king that he can still be trusted to come through. One must be surprised, there-fore, that the king entirely ignores the terms of the debtor's plea and decides, "out of pity" (Mt 18:27), to go so far as to cancel the debt itself. This reported act of mercy on the part of a king would have sounded entirely fantastic to the ears of first-century listeners, who knew that real kings incessantly schemed to increase their revenues by any means, foul or fair. Such an act of mercy, therefore, would have signaled that the King of the Universe was being spoken of in parabolic terms.

As the parable continues, the former debtor who was just a moment ear-lier facing certain ruin goes out and comes upon a fellow servant "who owed him a hundred denarii" (Mt 18:28). A hundred denarii is equivalent to one-sixtieth of a talent, thus, the fellow servant owes only a very small fraction (0.0000016) of what the former debtor owed. Since a denarius represents a two-day's wage for an unskilled laborer, the sum owed is roughly equivalent to $10,000 U.S. dollars. The debtor pleads for more time, yet the lender (unlike the king) shows no mercy and manhandles him and has him thrown into prison—presumably so that he can seize his assets. The king, hearing of the conduct of his servant, turns upon the man whom he had so generously treated and "in anger his lord handed him over to be tortured until he would pay his entire [original] debt" (Mt 18:34).

Throughout this parable, the brutal realities of indebtedness are rou-tinely presented. The king, it will be remembered, was initially disposed to have his debtor "sold, together with his wife and children" (Mt 18:25). When he fails to show "mercy" to his fellow debtor, the king "handed him over to be tortured" (Mt 18:34). Today, we would regard such conduct as barbaric and would be squeamish to imagine that the King of the Universe might be presented as acting this way; yet, as Philo noted, such conduct was acceptable in his day:

> Not long ago a certain man who had been appointed a collector
> of taxes in our country, when some of those who appeared to owe
> such tribute fled out of poverty . . . , [he] carried off their wives,
> and their children, and their parents. . . . But this tax collector did
> not let them go till he had tortured their bodies with racks and
> wheels, so as to kill them with newly invented kinds of death . . .

in the open air in the middle of the market place. (*Special Laws* 3.159)

In sum, the sharing of resources within the community was much more than a pious spiritual exercise. Sharing constituted a veritable safety net whereby a man or woman might be secure in knowing that his parents and children would not be tortured, would not be sold into debt slavery, would not be forced into prostitution should the family business begin to fail under the relentless pressure from the growing commercialization in the empire. In the face of the realities of the ancient world, the Didache communities never imagined that they could change the structures of society. The best they could hope for was to provide a measure of safety to their own members. Thus, in the end, the initial training in giving was a life-or-death proposition that ensured, in the long run, that "you will not turn away the one being in need" (*Did.* 4:8). This was a bond and promise that members made to each other.

#2M CHRISTIANITY SEEN BY THE ROMANS AS A MUTUAL AID SOCIETY

Robert Wilken has investigated how the Romans saw the early Jesus movement. To begin with, Wilken makes the point that, during the late first and early second century, the Jesus movement was quite small, insignificant, and urban—therefore invisible to most Romans:

> By the early part of the second century, when Pliny was living in Asia Minor, Christian groups could be found in perhaps forty or fifty cities within the Roman Empire. Most of these groups were quite small, some numbering several dozen persons, others as many as several hundred. The total number of Christians within the empire was probably less than fifty thousand, an infinitesimal number in a society comprising sixty million. . . . Most inhabitants of the Roman Empire had never heard of Christianity, and very few had any firsthand contact with Christians. (Wilken: 31)

Every Roman, meanwhile, would have had ample contact with the various "clubs" or "associations" (*hetaeria* in Greek; *collegium* in Latin) that offered fellowship, religious worship, and practical advantages to its members:

> The Greek clubs were more varied than the Roman—some organized around trades and occupations, some explicitly religious . . . , some named after their founders, and others simply groups

of people who came together for fun and fellowship. . . . All combined religious worship and social intercourse, and they sometimes offered commercial advantages and education. Almost all of these societies were local. . . . They were generally small, with an average membership under fifty; a few had memberships of several hundred. (Wilken: 34f.)

#2N BYLAWS OF A ROMAN FUNERAL SOCIETY IN LANUVIUM

One such society that left behind a public monument upon which was inscribed its bylaws was the funeral society of Lanuvium, a town in southern Italy. This particular society was dedicated to the goddess Diana and had an official permit from the Roman senate. The goal of the society was to offer the assurance that proper burial rites would be provided for members when they died. Undoubtedly this society appealed to persons who, for various reasons, did not live in the heart of an extended family and consequently felt anxious lest they should die without an appropriate burial.

Those desiring entrance into this funeral association were cautioned to "first read the bylaws carefully before entering, so as not to find cause for complaint later" (Wilken: 37). In this fellowship of equals comprising working-class individuals, the bylaws made it clear that their authoritative force derived from the open deliberations and voting of the membership:

> It was voted unanimously that whoever desires to enter this society shall pay an initiation fee of 100 sesterces [approx. $2500, a month's salary for a skilled worker] and an *amphora* [approx. a gallon] of good wine, and shall pay monthly dues of 5 copper coins [approx. $31]. . . . It was voted further that upon the decease of a paid-up member of our body there will be due him from the treasury 300 sesterces [approx. $7500 today], from which sum will be deducted a funeral fee of 50 sesterces [approx. $1250 today] to be distributed at the pyre [among those of the society attending]. . . . (Wilken: 37)

Once a month, members of the society convened for a simple dinner to celebrate either the "birthday of Diana and of the society" (Wilken: 38) or the birthday of one of the prominent members of the society. Four members of the society (in rotation) were charged with providing "an *amphora* of good wine each" to be shared by all and, for each one attending, a place setting, a loaf of bread, and four sardines (ibid.). Given the quantity of wine, one can surmise that the society comprised twenty to thirty members. Given the modest menu, one can further surmise that the working-class members of this society were willing to settle for simple meals. During the gatherings, the bylaws make clear that each of the four hosts was charged with conducting "worship with incense and wine" while "clothed in white" (Wilken: 39).

Given the fact that one of the monthly meals was held in the honor of the mother of a leading member of the society, one can surmise that women were members, took their turns at hosting and officiating at the monthly meals, and took part in the funeral rites. In addition, given passing references to members of the society who were slaves, one can surmise that slaves also entered into this society on a basis of equality and paid the fees out of surplus monies that masters allowed skilled slaves to retain in order to coax them to be enterprising on behalf of their masters. The bylaws even made provisions for the "unreasonable" possibility that a master or mistress of a slave might "refuse to relinquish his [her] body for burial" (Wilken: 38). If a slave should achieve his or her freedom while a member of the society, they were "required to donate an *amphora* of good wine" (ibid.). Thus, on festive occasions, members of the society could be relied on to honor one's good fortune. In sum:

> The burial society at Lanuvium provided far more than insurance against burial expenses [and the insurance of burial rites]. The regular meetings were occasions for eating and drinking, conversation, recreation. Their meetings not only provided relief from the daily round of work; they also provided friends and associates for mutual support, an opportunity for recognition and honor, a vehicle by which ordinary men [and women, whether free or enslaved] could feel a sense of worth. The society also gave people an opportunity for religious worship in a setting that was supportive, personal, and familiar. (Wilken: 39)

#20 SECOND-CENTURY CHURCHES AS MUTUAL AID SOCIETIES

While the Christians repeatedly thought of themselves as gathered in local churches (*ekklēsia*), Romans such as Pliny felt constrained to classify the "Christians" he had interrogated in the year 112 as forming local "associations" (*hetaeriae*) which "met regularly before dawn on a fixed day to chant verses alternately among themselves in honor of Christ as if to a god" and "reassemble[d] later [on that day] to take food of an ordinary, harmless kind" (*Letters* 10.97).

When one examines the apologies of Justin Martyr, which were written as open letters to the emperor and the Roman people, one finds a remark-

ably similar portrait. In 155 C.E., Justin Martyr described the meetings of
the Christians' pious association as follows:

> On the day called Sunday, all . . . gather together to one place,
> and the memoirs of the apostles or the writings of the prophets
> are read. . . . The president [presider] verbally instructs, and
> exhorts to the imitation of these good things [read]. Then we all
> rise together and pray, and . . . when our prayer is ended, bread
> and wine and water are brought, and the president in like man-
> ner offers prayers and thanksgivings, according to his ability, and
> the people assent, saying Amen; and there is a distribution to
> each . . . and to those who are absent a portion is sent by the dea-
> cons. (*1 Apol.* 47)

But, even beyond this, Justin Martyr was quick to show that this association functioned as a safety net that provided for those who, due to their
condition or their misfortune, had fallen victim to some hardship:

> And they who are well to do, and willing, give what each thinks
> fit; and what is collected is deposited with the president, who
> succors the orphans and widows, and those who, through sick-
> ness or any other cause, are in want, and those who are in bonds,
> and the strangers sojourning among us, and in a word takes care
> of all who are in need. (*1 Apol.* 47)

In a society without unemployment compensation and social security, widows had little prospect of being gainfully employed either inside or outside
of their home. Since tradition had it that a woman married a man ten to
fifteen years her senior, there were thus a multitude of widows who had
completely lost their source of incomes when their husbands died. Sickness, work-related accidents, and foul play could also quickly transform a
breadwinner into a dependent and bring a household closer to the borders
of poverty. As for those "in bonds," Justin Martyr has in mind not only
those who were, from time to time, imprisoned due to false accusations
(e.g., as during the persecution of Christians for the burning of Rome during the reign of Nero) but those who were incarcerated because of debts
as well. For all these cases of hardship, Justin Martyr explained how Christians collected money to protect their own.

Tertullian, writing in the following generation, addressed another open
letter to the Roman rulers calling for toleration. He described the Christian association as "a body (*corpus*) knit together as such by a common religious profession, by unity of discipline, and by the bond of a common

hope" (*Apology* 39). After discussing the role that prayer and sacred readings play in their common assemblies, Tertullian draws attention to the "treasure chest" (*arca*) formed out of the monthly collection:

> On the monthly day, if he like, each puts in a small donation. . . .
> These gifts are, as it were, piety's deposit fund. For they are not
> taken thence and spent on feasts, and drinking-bouts, and eating-
> houses, but to support and bury poor people, to supply the wants
> of boys and girls destitute of means and parents, and of old per-
> sons confined now to the house; such, too, as have suffered [lit-
> eral or economic] shipwreck; and if there happens to be any in
> the mines, or banished to the islands, or shut up in the prisons,
> for nothing but their fidelity to the cause of God's Church, they
> become the nurslings of their confession. But it is mainly the
> deeds of a love so noble that lead many to put a brand upon us.
> "See," they say, "how they love one another" . . . how they are
> ready to die for one another. (*Apology* 39)

Here again, Tertullian lists the vulnerable and the unjustly accused as being those who most deserve the financial support of the community. The "treasure chest" of the community, therefore, is indeed "piety's deposit fund." Tertullian even makes a point to say that "the family possessions which generally destroy brotherhood among you [Romans], create fraternal bonds among us" (*Apology* 39). Tertullian thus notes that the "associations" of Christians function in ways that families ought to function but, often enough, fail to do so. Unlike today, therefore, when the term "brother" or "sister in Christ" has come to take on largely a pietistic meaning, this same term had the effect of signaling the obligation to share one's resources and to come to the assistance of those within the community who were suffering and in need of help.

Justin Martyr makes the point that donations are "deposited with the president, who succors the orphans and widows, and those who, through sickness or any other cause, are in want" (*1 Apol.* 47). Tertullian, in the next generation, supports the same practice. The *Didache*, in contrast, has no collection of funds or centralized person for distributing them. The *Didache*, therefore, reveals a situation in which everyone responded to cases of need as they arose and "bishops and deacons" (*Did.* 15:1) played no central role in community finances (nor in liturgy or reconciliation, as will be seen in ch. 9). More importantly, however, the *Didache*'s notion of reciprocal giving and of partnering together (4:6, 8) finds no representation in Justin Martyr and Tertullian. The scope of the sharing of resources in the *Didache*, consequently, went far beyond that of a mutual aid society.

Surviving the Patronage System
with One's Soul Intact

When one comes to view the system of patronage in the ancient world, an even greater danger loomed. The craftsmen and merchants in the Didache community undoubtedly needed regular suppliers and guaranteed markets if they were to prosper. In the ancient world, small-time craftsmen and merchants had to survive by closely fitting their commercial enterprise within the local economy. John E. Stambaugh describes this as follows:

> People engaged in manufacturing, distributing, and service occupations on a small scale to meet local needs. Such trade was mostly a phenomenon of towns and cities, where there was a market for a variety of goods (James 4:13). Potters made dishes and vases for everyday use, fullers and weavers produced cloth, workers in leather sewed shoes and awnings, blacksmiths made farm implements and artisans' tools, carpenters made furniture and wagons, sculptors made statues and decorative reliefs. They ordinarily used raw materials that were produced near at hand and sold their finished wares in their own workshops, either on a free market or to fill some specific contract. . . . The men and women who operated these businesses generally did most of the work themselves, helped by spouse and children and by a few slaves or hired hands. (70)

On the other hand, if a potter could arrange to have his family business operate as a subsidiary under the direction of a rich patron, he would have a guaranteed outlet for his goods at a fixed price. Alternately, if this same potter could ingratiate himself with an aristocratic supplier, he might be able to devote himself to producing luxury items rather than the common fare for working-class people.

> To be lucky in one's patron was all-important to the ambitious craftsman; as Vitruvius rather feelingly remarked, many excellent craftsmen languished in obscurity because they had never chanced upon rich and influential patrons. (Burford: 124)

The ancient world abounded in middlemen who had business savvy. These middlemen had connections with rich and influential patrons and were only too ready to do anything it took to ensure that the enterprises placed under their direction would amass great wealth and the privileges that attended such wealth. Here are some examples:

> Detailed studies show that the pottery [at Arretium in central Italy] was produced in nearly a hundred small factories. A small number of skilled slave artisans (fewer than ten in most of them; about sixty in the three larger firms) produced the bowls, assisted by a larger but unknown number of others who dug and cleaned the clay, applied slip, and tended the kilns. As the market for these wares spread, new factories were established. . . . (Stambaugh: 70)

The hidden costs of getting involved with the rich, however, had also to be taken into account. To begin with, one now had to be willing to modify one's designs and one's standards of quality in order to meet those demanded by the rich patron and his go-betweens. Then, too, one would be expected to receive and to accept invitations to dinner that might compromise one's religious affiliation or one's moral standards. During the course of a meal at the home of one's patron, therefore, one would be expected to accept with some enthusiasm the patron's claim that a particular god or goddess protected his firm and that he ought to join him in an offering to give thanks for their shared prosperity. Or, again, household slaves in the homes of the rich were employed not only in serving the meals but for entertaining the guests as well. Not to participate in such amusements nor to revel in the sexual favors of a slave graciously offered by one's host would brand one as prudish and endanger one's social standing with the patron who, to some degree, one was bound to serve. Thus, while the patronage system promised to ensure and to increase one's wealth, one's influence, and one's honor as a client of a well-established patron, it also clearly required accommodating one's artistic, religious, and moral standards.

From this vantage point, the particulars of the *Didache* take on a heightened meaning. Near the end of the training period, the novice was instructed as follows:

> You will not exalt yourself,
>   (and) you will not give boldness to your soul.
> Your soul will not be joined with [the] lofty,
>   but with [the] just and [the] lowly you will dwell. (*Did.* 3:9)

Cultivating a patron in order to advance one's profession would have been a recognizable instance of "joining [your soul] with [the] lofty." On the other hand, by confining one's commercial interests within the local commerce served by the Didache communities, one took one's place among those who were "just" and "lowly" but offered little prospect for commercial advancement. Yet, with such as these, the "way of life" promises that novice that he/she will find "rest" (4:2).

The next line, however, has produced much puzzlement.

You will accept the experiences befalling you as good things,
   knowing that, apart from God, nothing happens. (3:10)

Why make an appeal to divine providence just at this point? Perhaps the
surmise was that, by abandoning the "lofty" in favor of working out one's
profession among the "lowly," the Lord himself would become the patron
guiding one's advancement. One may lose out on many business opportunities, but, in so doing, one has the assurance that God was taking this into
account and that God was in charge. This does not necessarily mean that
every bad thing that happens to good people has to somehow be construed
as having some mysterious good effect (see, e.g., Philo, *Providence* 2.2,
41–55). Rather, one might accept one's talents, one's social setting, one's
financial resources as arriving from God's free gifts, hence, with the peace
of mind that everything is as it should be under the patronage of God.
Thus, one is freed from the patronage of men. This, most probably, is the
first and central reason why the membership of the Didache community
has reinstated and expanded the practice of offering "first fruits" (13:3–7)
as a concrete measure to thank the Lord for the good deeds befalling them
rather than thanking some patron who would exploit them in the process.
Chapter 7 will examine the sentiment of gratitude surrounding first fruits
in detail. For the moment, it suffices to note that having God as one's
patron was perceived as preferable to patronage "with the lofty" (3:9).

The system of patronage functioned as a beneficent enslavement. A
client had to render specific services, which, when loyally completed,
would be gratefully rewarded. In most cases, however, one had to sell one's
soul to one's patron as well. One must love what he loves and hate what
he hates. Furthermore, a successful client would be expected to become
covetous, greedy, bad-mannered, arrogant, and avaricious for the well-
being of his/her patron—the very "virtues" that the *Didache* condemns
(2:6). Thus, for patron and client alike, it becomes bad business to be gentle, long-suffering, merciful, harmless, and good (3:7f.). The recitation of
the accursed persons named in the Way of Death in 5:2 emphasizes this:

[B13] *not showing mercy to the poor,*
[B14] *not toiling for the one weighed down by toil,*
[B15] not knowing the one having made them,
[B16] murderers of children,
[B17] corrupters of the creation of God,
[B18] *turning away the needy,*
[B19] *weighing down with toil the oppressed,*
[B20] *advocates of the rich,*
[B21] *despisers of [the] poor,*
[B22] totally sinful.

In contrast, members of the Didache communities were instructed to serve a Patron who has sympathy that extends even to the so-called worthless and expendable elements in society. Accordingly, right from the start, the novice was oriented to prefer the "foolishness" of God to the "success" offered by powerful clients.

Doing Business Without Exploitation

In the first chapter, attention was given to the five "fences" found in the *Didache*. Against the background of the Roman world, wherein the rich and powerful maintained and enlarged their standing in society by exploitation of natural resources, exploitation of human labor, and exploitation of the have-nots, the fourth "fence" can now be reexamined.

> My child, do not become a liar,
>   since lying is the path leading to theft;
>   nor a lover of money,
>   nor a seeker of glory,
>   for from all these things thefts are begotten. (*Did.* 3:5)

Clearly the "lover of money" and the "seeker of glory" are closely related. In the ancient world, wealth brought public recognition (as it does today), but, since great wealth ordinarily meant great exploitation, the "thefts" referred to might indeed be the wages robbed from slaves and from laborers who must work for nothing or for an unjustly low price. It is not equally clear how lying leads to thefts, however. One could surmise that this lying referred to those who falsely represented their need (in *Did.* 1:5 or 4:8) when asking for something. Since the members of the community were normally those giving, however, this would not appear to be the first meaning. It seems more plausible, therefore, that, in association with a "lover of money," the *Didache* has in mind "lying" or "deception" in business matters. Accordingly, the Lord spoke to the sons of Israel through Moses saying:

> You must not deal deceitfully or fraudulently with your neighbor. . . . You must not exploit or rob your neighbor. You must not keep back the laborer's wage until next morning. . . . Your measures—length, weight, and capacity—must all be just. Your scales and your weights must be just. . . . (Lv 19:11, 13, 35f.)

On the other hand, the framers of the *Didache* might also have had in mind the grand thefts that the rich have always been able to accomplish by falsifying documents, bribing judges, and seizing land from the poor. One has only to think of the string of broken promises and ignored treaties perpetrated by the U.S. government against Native American tribes to imagine that the Roman government acted with impunity when it came time for its own land grabs. Or, again, one can think of the multinational corporations who today have made great profits "legally" exploiting the natural and human resources within Third World countries as their "clients" within these countries line their pockets and hush up the ways they have betrayed their own people. Powerful patrons in the Roman world acted in the same fashion. Today as in the past, those who can be aptly characterized as "lovers of money" and "seekers of glory" are those who have robbed the poor of their land, of their labor, of their honor, of their culture, and (should they object) of their lives.

#2P RABBINIC WARNINGS AGAINST FRAUDULENT BUSINESS PRACTICES

The rabbinic materials greatly amplify how one must avoid fraudulent business practices. Regarding Lv 19:35 just cited, for instance, one finds the following expansion:

> "lineal measure"—This refers to surveying land, indicating that one should not survey for one party in the summer and for the other in the rainy season [when the measuring cord is longer].

> "weight"—This means that one should not salt his [wooden] weights [by soaking them in brine].

> "liquid measure"—This means that one should not cause the liquid to foam [when pouring it into the measuring vessel]. (*b. Baba Metzia* 61b)

Unfair business practices were therefore strongly proscribed. Even when giving financial advice, the rabbis cautioned that one must not cause a gullible man to stumble in order to secure one's own advantage:

> If a man seeks your counsel, do not give him counsel that is not right. . . . Do not say to him, "Sell your field and buy a donkey," so that you may circumvent him and take the field away from him. If you protest, "But it is sensible counsel I am giving him," remember that . . . the verse ends by saying, "You shall fear your God. I am the Lord" [Lv 19:14]. (*Sifra Leviticus,* Weiss ed., p. 88d)

Conclusion

In the end, the *Didache* opens up the image of a community firmly fixed on living the Way of Life revealed to them by the Father "through [his] servant Jesus" (*Did.* 9:2). This Way of Life cut members off from banquets, festivals, and associations calculated to serve their commercial interests. Having partnered together in defense against the economic exploitation and expansion in their society, they fashioned new bonds of reciprocal aid and service that effectively placed the resources of each at the disposal of all. The logic for their stand was compelling: "if you are partners in the immortal things, by how much more should you be partners in the mortal things? (4:8). Thus, this association pushed forward the notion that Jew and gentile, slave and free, men and women ought to bind themselves together for the common good of all. The impulse here was not so much social egalitarianism or a discipleship of equals as the "companionship of empowerment" (Crossan 1998: 137). Much more than a funeral society or a workingmen's club, the *Didache* purported to provide a social and economic restructuring by which the members would align themselves with God's ways in opposition to Roman commercialism and imperialism. In so doing, members thought of their resources as a gift of the Great Patron who willed to distribute his gifts through them as his broker. Using the Lord's resources accordingly, they expected to be called "faithful" servants when he came at the end of time. While they were awaiting the Lord who would complete their revolution, however, they were far from idle.

3
FASTING, FEASTING, AND
THE PRACTICE OF BAPTIZING ADULTS

Practice of Adult Baptism

CONCERNING BAPTISM,
BAPTIZE THUS: HAVING SAID ALL THESE
THINGS BEFOREHAND, IMMERSE IN
THE NAME OF THE FATHER AND OF THE
SON AND OF THE HOLY SPIRIT IN
FLOWING WATER· IF, ON THE OTHER
HAND, YOU SHOULD NOT HAVE FLOW-
ING WATER, IMMERSE IN OTHER WATER
THAT IS AVAILABLE; IF YOU ARE NOT
ABLE IN COLD, IMMERSE IN WARM
WATER; IF YOU SHOULD NOT HAVE
EITHER, POUR OUT WATER ONTO THE
HEAD THREE TIMES· PRIOR TO THE
BAPTISM, LET THE ONE BAPTIZING FAST;
AND LET THE ONE BEING BAPTIZED;
AND IF ANY OTHERS HAVE THE STRENGTH,
LET THEM FAST ALSO · · · DURING ONE
OR TWO DAYS·

Contents

Background Discussion Found in Boxes

Any community that wishes not only to survive but to thrive must have soulful rites that address the deepest desires of the human heart. Effective community rites do not spring from nowhere. They must be publicly authorized and deeply rooted within the experience of the community. Otherwise, they cannot be relied on to have a well-defined effect that promotes the identity and well-being of those participating. Furthermore, such rites must be sufficiently uncluttered and sufficiently transparent as to evoke soulful forms of feeling and of judging on the part of those who experience them for the first time. When these factors are examined, here too one might expect to find the pastoral genius of the *Didache*.

The Didache community had two evocative and transformative rites: baptism and the eucharist. The *Didache* speaks in passing of honoring spiritual mentors (4:1), fasting (7:4–8:1), praying three times daily (8:3), speaking in the Spirit (11:7–12), giving first fruits (13:3–7), confessing failings (14:1–3), appointing bishop-deacons (15:1), and reproving and shunning (15:3). One might expect that the community had appropriate gestures and words whereby each of these events was routinely practiced. Given this fact, therefore, one can perhaps dignify these practices as constituting mini-rites. Nonetheless, the fact remains that baptism and the eucharist formed the central and most highly elaborated rites of this community.

Training in the Way of Life came to a natural fulfillment in the rite of baptism. The rite itself, it will be discovered, may have taken a solid half-hour and flowed imperceptively into the feasting of a community eucharist. Thus baptism did not stand alone as an isolated rite (as it sometimes does today) but was a defining and awe-inspiring transition that permanently and irreversibly transformed the public identity of the candidate. What was done in baptism was immediately celebrated in the eucharist.

In parallel fashion, the weekly eucharist was no ordinary meal. Herein the mission of God and the role of Jesus were made present and celebrated as they affected the present and the future. On the basis of the attention given to the eucharistic meal, one can surmise that this rite was the source and summit of the community's spirituality. A full examination of the practice and theology implied by this eucharist will be undertaken in chapters 5 and 8 below.

Those who would take their place at the eucharist had to have been baptized beforehand (*Did.* 9:5). The act of being immersed in flowing water was no ordinary act of bathing prior to a religious function. This rite had the awesome effect of transforming an individual from outsider to insider, from pagan to saint, from stranger to brother or sister. Furthermore, the rite of baptism took place only once. An individual was forever transformed. The character of this transformation, along with the fasting and selective eating that preceded baptism, will be examined in this chapter.

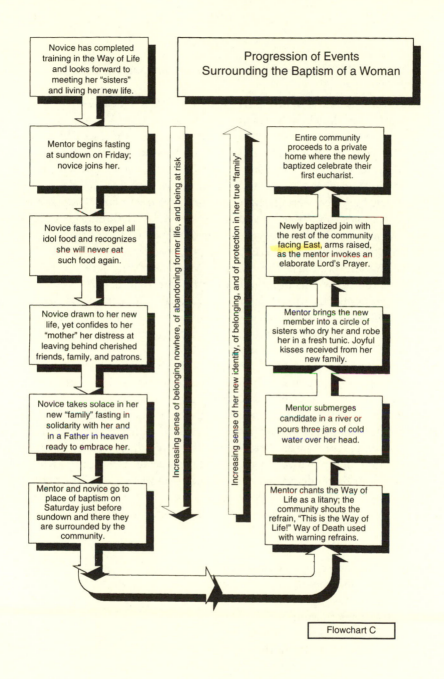

Progression of Events Surrounding the Baptism of a Woman

Novice has completed training in the Way of Life and looks forward to meeting her "sisters" and living her new life.

Mentor begins fasting at sundown on Friday; novice joins her.

Novice fasts to expel all idol food and recognizes she will never eat such food again.

Novice drawn to her new life, yet confides to her "mother" her distress at leaving behind cherished friends, family, and patrons.

Novice takes solace in her new "family" fasting in solidarity with her and in a Father in heaven ready to embrace her.

Mentor and novice go to place of baptism on Saturday just before sundown and there they are surrounded by the community.

Increasing sense of belonging nowhere, of abandoning former life, and being at risk

Increasing sense of her new identity, of belonging, and of protection in her true "family"

Entire community proceeds to a private home where the newly baptized celebrate their first eucharist.

Newly baptized join with the rest of the community facing East, arms raised, as the mentor invokes an elaborate Lord's Prayer.

Mentor brings the new member into a circle of sisters who dry her and robe her in a fresh tunic. Joyful kisses received from her new family.

Mentor submerges candidate in a river or pours three jars of cold water over her head.

Mentor chants the Way of Life as a litany; the community shouts the refrain, "This is the Way of Life!" Way of Death used with warning refrains.

Flowchart C

The Linguistic Structure of this Section

The careful attention to progression and to details that characterized the opening third of the *Didache* dealing with training in the Way of Life continues in the following section as well. After bringing the Two Ways to a close, the *Didache* turns to the treatment of assorted topics: eating, baptizing, fasting, praying. In treating these topics, the framers' penchant for detailed illustrations as opposed to abstract principles is again evident. The four topics, however, were given a very unequal treatment. The issue of praying occupies three times as much text as the other three topics combined. Moreover, the mood surrounding the first two topics (eating and baptizing) is significantly different from the mood surrounding the last two (fasting and praying). The first two welcome a variety of acceptable behaviors; the last two hammer out conformity to rigid details.

The present chapter will be devoted to an analysis of eating and baptizing. Fasting will be considered only insofar as it is linked to baptism. The rule for semiweekly fasting (*Did.* 8:1) and for daily praying (8:2f.) will be considered in the following chapter.

There is no topic sentence that structures the second part of the *Didache*. Moreover, upon first hearing, the topics treated do not exhibit any logical or linear sequence. The stylistic trait that serves to introduce each new topic is the Greek phrase *peri de* ("And concerning . . ."). The postpositive conjunction *de* ordinarily serves to signal that the speaker intends to amplify what went before either by adding more information or by presenting an alternative view. Thus, setting aside the rules of stylistic English, it can be rendered as either "(And) concerning . . ." or "(But) concerning . . ." This construction appears five times. In all five instances, it serves to introduce a topic not yet touched upon. These five instances are as follows:

> 6:3 (And) concerning (the) eating
> 7:1 (And) concerning (the) baptism
> > 7:4–8:1 fasting
> > 8:2f. daily praying
> 9:1 (And) concerning the eucharist
> > 9:2 First, concerning the cup
> > 9:3 (And) concerning the broken loaf
> 11:3 (And) concerning the apostle-prophets

The use of *peri de* in *Did.* 6:3 and 7:1 serves to introduce practical rules regarding eating and baptizing—both topics not yet mentioned. In the

treatment of baptism, the presentation passes from baptism to the prepara-
tory practice of fasting. Fasting, in turn, brings the topic around to considering prayer, which, in the Jewish world, was intimately linked to
fasting.

The Implied Audience, the Progression of Topics, the Use of the Plural

Nearly all scholars have attempted to demonstrate that the *Didache* was
composed by an editor who slightly altered and connected preexisting documents. The *Didache* thus appears as a kind of literary collage that was
composed by cutting and pasting together literary units that were already
at hand and which served purposes foreign to the *Didache*. Willy Rordorf,
for instance, characterizes the *Didache* as follows: "Such as it presents itself
in the Jerusalem manuscript, the *Didache* is devoid of literary unity. . . . In
effect, it is composed of many parts of unequal length which belong to different genres" (1978b: 17). From this vantage point, it is impossible to
imagine that the progression of topics flows from one section to the next
following a deliberate plan. Thus, in what Rordorf calls the "liturgical section" (1978b: 18) of the *Didache* (7:1–10:7), he does not anticipate that
there is any reason why this section should go from baptism to fasting,
from fasting to daily prayer, from daily prayer to the eucharist. Nor does it
appear strange that the repeated use of *peri de* in the "liturgical section"
actually begins with the instruction regarding permitted foods (6:3).
Because this instruction is in the singular and because "eating" is not considered "liturgical," this instruction is relegated to the Two-Way section
(Rordorf 1978b: 17) and said to form, along with 6:2, "a transition
between the first and second part of the book" (Rordorf 1978b: 17 n. 2).
From this point of view, there is no cause to wonder why the instruction
regarding permitted foods forms an awkward appendix to the Two-Way
section and does not take its rightful place as part and parcel of the training in the Way of Life.

In contrast to the prevailing consensus among scholars, I have come to
believe that the progression of topics within the *Didache* is very deliberate and that it follows the ordinary progression whereby a candidate
would be ushered step by step into community norms and practices. In
chapter 1, I spelled out in detail the intricate movement within the Way
of Life itself. In the Way of Life, for instance, what is most immediate—
namely, conflict within the candidate's circle of family and friends—is
framed in the present imperative and dealt with first. What is most
remote—namely the ways of relating that will prevail following entrance
into the community—is framed in the future tense and dealt with last.

Now it remains to suggest that the following sections also follow a natural progression (overview in #16b) and that the seemingly incoherent fluctuation between the use of the singular and the plural can be entirely accounted for within this natural progression.

The *Didache* presents the following progression:

1. Training in the Way of Life (second person singular after 1:3 in plural)
2. Training concerning permitted foods (second person singular in 6:3)
3. Baptizing rightly (second person plural with occasional use of singular in 7:1–4)
4. Weekly fasting (second person plural)
5. Daily praying (second person plural)
6. Sunday eucharist (second person plural)

Following the completion of the one-on-one training in the Way of Life, the candidate is ready for baptism. Baptism, however, will transform the candidate from an outsider to an insider, from an idolater to a servant of God, from a stranger to a "brother/sister." This change of identity will mean that the resources and shops of the community will be open to the new member (as explained in ch. 2). It will also mean that the new member "will seek every day the presence of the saints" (4:2)—sharing their homes, their fellowship, their tables, their prayers, their fasts. This identity change effected by baptism will also mean that the new member entirely withdraws from all pagan fellowship—a rule enforced by the requirement to abstain entirely "from the food sacrificed to idols" (6:3).

#3A CONVERSION AND RELIGIOUS INTOLERANCE

A. D. Nock notes that, in most instances, those in the ancient world who accepted a new god did not undergo a conversion. This was so, explains Nock, because those who accepted the worship and protection of a new god regarded these as "useful supplements and not as substitutes" (7) for the gods previously worshiped. Greek and Roman cults were quite tolerant; allegiance to one god did not preclude devotion to another.

> While some foreign habits in religion, as for instance animal worship [among the Egyptians], appeared strange to Greeks, there was among them no prejudice against alien worship, and a Greek in a strange country ordinarily paid homage to its [local] gods. (Nock: 19)

Judaism and Christianity, on the other hand, took the stance that all pagan cults were an abomination and that embracing the God of Abraham and Sarah meant to cast away the images, the rites, and the promises associated with any and all pagan cults. Thus, according to Nock, religious "conversions," as such, only occurred when an idolater turned from idolatry to accept Judaism or Christianity.

> By conversion we mean the reorientation of the soul of an individual, his deliberate turning from indifference or from an earlier form of piety to another, a turning which implies a consciousness that a great change is involved, that the old was wrong and the new is right. (Nock: 7)

In a word, Judaism and its offshoot, Christianity, were intolerant. For them, "true" religion had to replace "false" religion. In the course of time, Christianity and Judaism turned this instinct of intolerance against each other. Only in recent times has the tragedy of this excessive and unjustified intolerance been taken note of and partially corrected. Similar observations could be made regarding Islam.

The norm regarding permitted foods (6:3) was not given earlier, since, in many cases, the candidate could not regulate what was served at table. For example, a son who was converting would normally reside within his father's home and, while doing so, would have to tolerate his father's pious habit of dedicating every principal meal to the household gods. If the norm of abstaining "from the food sacrificed to idols" had been given earlier, it would have created an unnecessary hardship, since, prior to baptism, the candidate could not presume to share the table, much less the eucharist, of the community he/she intended to join. Thus, the instruction regarding permitted foods is neither misplaced (outside of the Way of Life) nor is it an accidental "transition" to the "liturgical section," which has a fixed order determined by a preexisting document. What will soon become clear is that the candidate for baptism fasted from all food "during one or two days prior to the baptism" (7:4). This fasting had the effect of expelling all "food sacrificed to idols" and, once baptized, authorized the one baptized to spend the rest of his/her days eating the holy food from the table and the eucharist of community members. *The norm regarding permitted foods, therefore, was situated in the oral enactment of the Didache in just that place where it would be expected to be introduced to the candidates for baptism—not earlier and not later.*

When Baptism Was Celebrated

The *Didache* specifies no special time of day, no day of the week, and no liturgical season when baptisms ought to be performed. This is especially clear from what the *Didache* says regarding solidarity in fasting with the candidate for baptism: "If any others have the strength, let them fast also" (7:4). Clearly, no attempt was made to coordinate this prebaptismal fasting even with the semiweekly days of fasting—Wednesday and Friday (8:1). In practice, however, some educated guesses can be made regarding when baptisms might be discouraged and when they might be preferred.

1. *Times when baptism would be discouraged.* Baptism had the effect of transforming the identity of the one being baptized from an outsider to an insider. As such, the gathered community would undoubtedly have desired to welcome the newly baptized "brother" or "sister" who joined their family with a festive sharing of food. One would think that this would discourage baptizing anyone early in the day or at midday since too many hours would elapse between the baptism and the feasting that would customarily take place in the evening when the full meal was taken (Willis: 39–42). Furthermore, most of the members worked during the day, and anything but an evening celebration would have been impractical.

The practice of community fasting "during the fourth day and during the Sabbath-preparation day" (8:1), which, according to Jewish reckoning, began at sunset, would militate against baptizing late the previous day, since, after baptism, the feasting would be cut short or entirely eliminated by the onset of a day of fasting. Similarly, since the community had to be informed regarding a fast of solidarity with a candidate just prior to baptism (7:4), one can surmise that the baptismal fasts were not scheduled to coincide with either of the semiweekly days of fasting. Thus, the third, fourth, fifth, and sixth day of the week would be days when baptisms would probably be discouraged.

2. *Times when baptism would be preferred.* Given the central importance of the eucharist in the Didache community, one might expect that, under normal circumstances, the community would have preferred that the meal breaking the fast would be the eucharistic meal. If the weekly eucharist was celebrated on "the Lord's day" (14:1), which will be shown in chapter 5 to begin with sundown on Saturday—following the Jewish reckoning of the end of the Sabbath (8:1)—then it might be expected that baptism would be preferentially celebrated Saturday evening just prior to the weekly eucharist. Such an arrangement would also have the advantage of ensuring that most or all the members of the community would be present.

3. *Further evidence based on the confession of failings.* Under ordinary circumstances, the *Didache* informs us that a confession of failings was

necessary in order to offer "a pure sacrifice" (14:1). The candidate preparing for baptism is informed of this confession near the end of his/her training (3:14). When one hears of the eucharistic prayers (9–10), however, the confession of failings is curiously omitted, only to show up four chapters later. Most scholars accept this as an indication that the *Didache* was a collage of preexisting documents assembled over a period of time that never attained anywhere near a full integration. My surmise, on the contrary, is that this omission of the confession of failings was deliberate and signaled what everyone knew—namely, that the order of events in the *Didache* followed the order in which a candidate experienced these events. Thus, if my supposition is correct, the eucharist in the *Didache* represents the "the first eucharist" and the omission of the confession of failings at this point deliberately points to the fact that this public confession was suppressed whenever new candidates were baptized just prior to the eucharist.

Many reasons could be put forward to sustain suppressing a public confession of failings at "the first eucharist." Foremost among them would be the fittingness of welcoming the new "brothers" and "sisters" who had just been baptized without confronting them with a recital of the failings of permanent members Thus, the linguistic clues of the *Didache* itself incline me to believe that baptism was preferentially celebrated immediately prior to the "first eucharist" and that, on these occasions, the confession of failings was supplanted by the baptism itself. This final scenario brings together all the above considerations and integrates them within a progression that, at every point, purposefully followed the experience of the newly initiated members (overview in #16b).

#3B BAPTISM ON SUNDAY MORNINGS DURING THE SECOND CENTURY

Justin Martyr, writing in 150 C.E., described the practice of the Roman church. Since the Roman calendar had been modified in the late first century to include a seven-day week (see #4a), Justin Martyr was able to use the term "Sunday" and to identify it as "the day on which we [Christians] all hold our common assembly" (*1 Apol.* 47). Justin Martyr further noted that "after we have washed [immersed/baptized] him [/her] who has been convicted and has assented to our teaching" (*1 Apol.* 45), then the eucharistic meal consisting of bread and wine was immediately celebrated. The Roman church of the mid-second century thus appears to have baptized candidates only on Sunday mornings prior to the weekly eucharist.

Scholars are persuaded that first-century eucharists were celebrated after sunset on the first day of the week (*ABD* 6:979f.). According to the Jewish reckoning, the first day of the week began on Saturday evening (following the Roman reckoning) after sundown. In chapter 5, this issue will be taken up in detail, and it will be concluded that the Didache communities celebrated their weekly eucharist on Saturday evening. As seen in Justin Martyr, however, the eucharist of the mid-second century was celebrated Sunday before sunset. Scholars are undecided as to precisely why, during the late first or early second century, the eucharist ceased being a full "supper" and became a "breakfast" (*ABD* 6:980; Bacchiocchi 1977; Rordorf 1968). Nonetheless, this change affected how baptism and the eucharist following was experienced.

Since Sunday was, in most instances, an ordinary workday until the early fourth century, this meant that the Sunday gatherings just referred to by Justin Martyr had to take place before sunrise. Even at this early hour, baptisms took place prior to the eucharist. Justin Martyr further tells us that baptism was preceded by communal fasting "for the remission of sin" (*1 Apol.* 41) without any duration of time being mentioned. Baptism itself was conferred in the name of the Trinity, and the one baptized was understood as "born again," "illuminated," and "washed of sins." Justin Martyr remarked that the brothers/sisters, once baptized, "offer hearty prayers in common for ourselves and for the baptized" (*1 Apol.* 45). Prior to the eucharist, the "kiss of peace" (*1 Apol.* 45) was exchanged.

From these details, one can glimpse how, in the century following the *Didache*, the ritual and theology of baptism developed. Nowhere in the Christian Scriptures does one find prebaptismal fasting or baptisms leading into the eucharist. These two practices appear, however, to take definite form within the *Didache*. A century later, these same practices show up in the Roman church. This is especially significant, since it meant that baptisms had to be celebrated in the proverbial coldest and darkest part of the day—just prior to sunrise. It also meant that the festive aspect of leisurely community "suppers" had to be surrendered in favor of short "breakfast" eucharists. For these reasons, it seems hard to imagine that Sunday morning somehow became the preferred and voluntary choice of the community (*ABD* 6:980). Rather, it seems safer to surmise that this decision was imposed upon Christians—perhaps by a Roman curfew prohibiting all groups from convening after sunset, as Joachim Jeremias has suggested.

Whatever the case, one cannot help but notice that the community of Rome assembled for predawn baptisms followed immediately by their weekly eucharist. This could only be the case if there had already been a strong and prevailing tradition of having baptisms prior to the eucharist during the period when supper eucharists were the norm. Late afternoon baptisms in a river or a pond might have actually been refreshing following the heat of the day. More importantly, however, the assembled community welcoming the newly baptized into their "family" had the yearning to break their arduous fast and to celebrate the eucharistic feast together. Thus the baptism–eucharistic link was born and, even when the shift was made to a predawn baptism, it was difficult to imagine breaking this tradition. Thus, it could be argued that the baptism–eucharist link to which Justin Martyr directs our attention was formed, even in Rome, during a period when these things took place at the end of a workday. Our reconstruction of the probable order of events in the *Didache*, therefore, finds a faint echo in the supposed practice of the Roman church.

Similar observations could be made respecting the water used for baptisms. As mentioned above, late afternoon baptisms in a river or a pond might have actually been quite refreshing following the heat of the day. On the other hand, a predawn dunking would most likely be quite miserable. With predawn sky lighting, one can even imagine some candidates becoming terrified at the prospect of stepping on some slimy toad or encountering a snake. No wonder, therefore, that the preferred choices of water prescribed in the *Didache* (7:1–3) find no reference whatsoever in Justin Martyr. At a later point, in the *Apostolic Tradition* (c. 220 C.E.), which is reputed to contain the liturgical traditions of the Roman church, one finds the following:

> And at the time when the cock crows, first let prayer be made over the water. Let the water be flowing in the font [sunken bath] or poured over it. Let it be thus unless there is some necessity; if the necessity is permanent and urgent, use what water you can find. (21.1)

Thus the norm of preferring flowing water was reinvented and reapplied to an entirely new situation. Baptisms were no longer held outside but inside. Cold water was no longer preferred as approaching the natural condition of rivers and ponds. Now the warm water of a Roman bathhouse was perfectly acceptable as long as a conduit or jar brought some "living water" into it. Then, too, one finds a curious exception clause remarkably like the one in *Did.* 7:3. This topic merits further study. For the moment, however, it suffices to note that changes took place in the time, the place, and the experience of baptism.

Tertullian, writing from Carthage in the late second century, proposed that Passover and Pentecost represented the most fitting days for baptism (*On Baptism* 19). After supplying many reasons to support his claim, Tertullian concluded:

> However, every day is the Lord's; every hour, every time [season], is apt for baptism: if there is a difference [it must be found]

in the solemnity, [for relative to] distinction, there is none in the grace. (*On Baptism* 19)

Thus, Tertullian knows of no fixed rule why any day or any season might be absolutely disallowed. Nonetheless, his preference for Passover and Pentecost signaled that particular feasts of historical commemoration were naturally regarded as having a solemnity that made them more suitable choices for the day of baptism.

According to Justin Martyr, every Sunday was a reminder of the resurrection and therefore well suited for baptisms. Thus, in the third century, once Easter came to be celebrated on the Sunday following the Passover, it was natural that the day of the resurrection would gradually become the preferred day for all baptisms. According to the *Apostolic Tradition* (c. 220 C.E.), consequently, an elaborate catechumenate was arranged such that all suitable candidates would come to the end of their training period at the Easter vigil. Now the entire community was to "spend all the night in vigil, reading the scriptures [to candidates] and instructing them" (20.1). This all-night vigil culminated in baptisms beginning "when the cock crows" (20.1). Now only menstruating women (20.6) and those in danger of death would be baptized on a different day. But, even here, alternate local traditions remained alive. The fifth-century *Testamentum Domini*, for example, prescribed that water baptisms should take place in the middle of the night during the Easter vigil (2.8).

In sum, in the case of the baptismal liturgy, the tendency was to move from the simple to the complex, from the indefinite to the definite; yet, on the other hand, "the movement toward uniformity was constantly being interrupted by a tendency toward local variation; that towards prolixity by a tendency toward abbreviation" (Anton Baumstark cited in Bradshaw 1992: 59).

Given the placement of the Lord's Prayer in the *Didache*, it was to be expected that the new member of the community would come to learn and to pray the Lord's Prayer at the appointed hours three times each day *only after baptism* (8:2f.). Joachim Jeremias has shown that the Lord's Prayer was memorized by novices and used by them for the first time at their baptism (1967: 82–85). The *Didache*, for its part, does not directly confirm this. Indirectly, however, two points are in its favor:

1. *Argument from placement*. The Lord's Prayer is introduced in the *Didache* immediately after baptism. If the order of events follows the experience of the candidate (as has been surmised) then the order implies that the practice of praying the Lord's Prayer three times daily was open to the candidate only *after* baptism. In the case of a baptism late Saturday after-

noon (as surmised above), the new candidate would pray the Lord's Prayer with the assembled community for the first time at sundown. Presumably this prayer would have been offered at the site where the baptism was performed and would form a fitting conclusion to the rite itself prior to going to the private home where the eucharist would be celebrated. This latter detail, however, is not specified in the *Didache*.

2. *Argument from God-talk*. Initially the candidate hears of "the God who made you" (1:2). Thereafter, during the entire training in the Way of Life, the term "God" is repeated. But this runs counter to the very usage of the community wherein "Father" or "Lord" is preferred. The implied meaning is that "Father" and, more especially, addressing God as "our Father" is only possible after the change of identity effected by the baptism itself. If this is the case, then it follows that the candidate would be capable of participating in the community prayer (9:5) and of praying the "Our Father" only after baptism.

When the Semiweekly Fasting Was Introduced

It remains to explain why the rule for the weekly rhythm of fasting is presented immediately after baptism and prior to the rule for praying:

1. On the one hand, it is possible that the rule regarding the days of fasting was introduced here merely because of an association of topics—the topic of fasting prior to baptism naturally led to considering the semiweekly fasting. The chronological order was thus dropped, for it cannot be supposed that the first semiweekly fast came before the first use of the Lord's Prayer. Even if the Lord's Prayer was not recited for the first time at the close of the candidate's baptism, this prayer would have been recited the very next morning—hence, prior to the upcoming semiweekly fast.

2. On the other hand, the experience of fasting prior to baptism constituted the first experience of communal fasting known to the candidate (note *Did*. 1:3). Undoubtedly, the mentor fasted with the novice and, in so doing, taught by example what it meant to fast and what impact fasting had on the life of a servant of the Lord. The fact that the *Didache* names the mentor first, saying, "Let the one baptizing fast; and let the one being baptized" (7:4), may signal that mentors began their fast first and then invited their novices to join them. While fasting together, this would be the natural moment to introduce and to prepare the novice for the semiweekly tradition of community fasting—something wisely passed over in silence during the training in the Way of Life. The once-in-a-lifetime fast thus became the teachable moment for orienting the lifelong rhythm of fasting. The placement of the semiweekly communal fasting would not indicate when this fasting actually began but rather when the rule for this fasting was first introduced.

Even more may be implied here. Baptism, as will be shortly noted, would mark the rite of passage into a new family. Fasting, meanwhile, marked the final breaking off of all table fellowship with those eating food sacrificed to idols (6:2). For many novices, therefore, there might have been intense grieving just prior to baptism. Fasting and grief go together. The tradition of fasting prior to baptism, for example, might have arisen out of the spontaneous and physiological revulsion to eating occasioned by the intense grief suffered by the candidates. Conversely, the practice of fasting may have served to intensify the sentiments of grief already present. These would be the experiences, consequently, that would spill over into the semiweekly fasting. Grief work cannot be completed in a few days. Hence, the semiweekly rhythm of fasting may have allowed the grief work that erupted during the prebaptismal fast to be completed weeks and months after the candidate's baptism. Fasting, of course, is not exclusively preoccupied with grief work (as the later part of this chapter will show). Nonetheless, the grief work erupting during the prebaptismal fasting and flowing over into the semiweekly fasting constitutes a deep emotional link that provides yet another reason why the topic of the semiweekly fasting comes immediately after the topic of prebaptismal fasting.

The oral logic of the *Didache* is important here. Clearly the instructions regarding fasting prior to baptism were deliberately placed outside their chronological order. When it came to baptism, the permitted kinds of water and the required threefold names were emphasized. Had the chronological order been strictly maintained, the norm for prebaptismal fasting would have been placed prior to the mention of the kinds of water, and the rule of semiweekly fasting would have been placed after the first eucharist (*Did.* 9–10). This would leave a considerable gap between the first experience of communal fasting and the giving of the rule regarding the semiweekly fasting. Alternately, the framers of the *Didache* could have introduced the instruction on both fasts (7:4 and 8:1) side by side prior to 7:1. They did not do so, however, because of the intimate link between fasting and praying (which will be explored later in this chapter). In sum, therefore, the exceptional order for introducing the prebaptismal fasting confirms the rule that the ordering of the *Didache* faithfully follows the training of the new member. This ordering, moreover, respects the propaedeutic and psychological links which pass through the experiences of fasting. The oral logic of the *Didache*, consequently, is not woodenly bound to chronological description but flexibly crafted to serve pastoral purposes.

The Puzzling Transitions
from Singular to Plural

One last task remains. How does one explain the movement from second person singular to second person plural? Jean-Paul Audet, mesmerized by his fixation upon source documents, postulated that the original author wrote the *Didache* in two stages and that an interpolator later made clumsy additions in the second person singular (6:2–3; 7:2–4; 13:3, 5–7) within sections written in the second person plural (Audet 1958: 104–20). Current scholars have entirely moved away from such a hypothesis, and one need no longer imagine that ancient interpolators made such a wooden use of their sources. How then explain the transitions?

The use of the singular for the food regulations fits, since, in effect, Christians were prepared for baptism by their individual mentors, who, after everything else, introduced them to the method and spirit of fasting. Hence, the one-to-one character of training in the Way of Life continues.

Immediately thereafter, however, the plural is used: "And concerning baptism, baptize thus:" (7:1). Here, it must be noted, the novice is not being addressed. Who is the implied audience? It is the same audience that has been addressed throughout, namely, those responsible for the training of new members. The training in the Way of Life is offered in the second person singular because the trainers need to hear the specific rules in the form in which they will use them to train their novices. The novices themselves are not immediately addressed by the *Didache*, as shown by the transition in 1:3. The same thing can be said for the use of the plural in "pray thus" (8:2) and "eucharistize thus" (9:1)—instructions that are likewise being addressed to the mentors in the community. Just as the novice does not and cannot baptize, so too, the newly baptized member cannot be expected to eucharistize at his/her first eucharist.

Why then does 7:2–4 lapse back into the second person singular? My hunch here is that the *Didache* has only one person—the mentor—doing the baptism. The rule to "pour out water onto the head" (7:3), for example, would most probably mean, in practice, that one person—the mentor—did the pouring. It would be difficult to envision a group doing the pouring. If this is correct, then the lapse into the second person singular makes perfect sense. First the spiritual fathers and mothers are told to immerse (plural) in flowing water in the name of the three. The decision regarding the kind of water (7:2f.) and the giving of instructions regarding fasting (7:4), however, must be carried out by the one person responsible for the candidate being baptized, namely, his/her personal mentor.

Stepping back, the following schema prevails:

1. The whole of the *Didache* is addressed to the spiritual fathers and mothers. Hence, the second person plural is used.

2. The second person singular prevails in the Way of Life and in 6:1–3 because here the mentor overhears the specifics of the training program where he/she will address an individual novice.

3. The further use of the singular in 7:2–4 points to the usage of the Didache community whereby a single person baptizes, namely, the mentor, who makes the choice of the kind of water, introduces the candidate

into the prebaptismal fasting, and alerts the believers to fast in solidarity prior to attending the anticipated baptism.

The persuasive power of this schema is that it allows the one who recites the *Didache* to anticipate the order based on remembered practice. Otherwise, the sheer power of memory has to decide everything. For example, does the rule of eating go before or after the instruction on baptism? . . . before or after the instruction on eucharist? Once the *Didache* is understood as following the normative practice of the community, however, everything falls into place. Our hypothesis here is that mentors who memorized the *Didache* did so with the knowledge that they were mastering an ordered process from beginning to end. The seemingly inconsequential shifts from topic to topic, from second person plural to singular, accordingly, must be looked to as potentially revealing the order of the training program itself. The recited order thus captured the observed order, and the observed order followed the recited order. As of this time, I am not aware of any other scholar who has so satisfactorily explained the progression of topics or the puzzling alternation between the singular and plural in the *Didache*. Jonathan Draper (1989: 3–5), to my knowledge, is the only scholar who postulates that the structure of the *Didache* follows the initiatory practice of the community.

#3C WHY THE CIRCUMCISION CONTROVERSY AROSE ONLY IN THE 50S

The Jesus movement was initially composed entirely of Jews. Under these circumstances, the issue of circumcision never arose, for all the men were circumcised. Baptism, therefore, was administered by John the Baptizer and by Peter (Acts 2) without any reference to circumcision. Once gentiles began to enter the movement, then one might have expected the issue of circumcision to be posed. However, the practice of administering baptism alone was continued. Peter affirmed to the household of Cornelius, "I [now] truly understand that God shows no partiality, but in every nation anyone who fears him and does what is right is acceptable to him" (Acts 10:34f.). Thus, gentiles became disciples of Jesus and beloved children of God *by baptism alone*—just as had been the case with Jews.

Circumcision was a divinely ordained rule that was a sign of the covenant between God and Abraham, for God had said to Abraham:

> You shall circumcise the flesh of your foreskins, and it shall be a sign of the covenant between me and you. . . . Any uncircumcised male who is not circumcised in the flesh of his foreskin shall be cut off from his people; he has broken my covenant. (Gn 17:11, 14)

The rule seems perfectly clear. Why then did Peter and others assume, at first, that baptism alone sufficed for gentiles just as it did for Jews? And what happened in the early 50s that served to bring the issue of circumcision to a racing boil within the Jesus movement (Gal 2:1–6; Acts 15:1–5)?

James D. G. Dunn has studied this issue and come up with a very attractive solution. According to Dunn (1991: 124–27), Cornelius and other early converts were effectively already monotheists and were practicing many of the traditions of Israel (Acts 10:2). Josephus and Philo amplify this picture when they note that, in every city in the empire, non-Jews were to be found who honored and adopted Jewish traditions for themselves, including the Sabbath rest and food laws (Josephus, *Ag.Ap.* 2.123, 209f., 280, 282; Philo, *Moses* 2.17–20). Thus, Dunn postulates that, in the beginning, baptism marked the commitment of both Jews and gentiles to follow the way of Jesus and "even the more traditional Jerusalem believers might also have been content for the time being to allow such gentiles to remain in an anomalous status" (1991: 126) since they were en route toward full inclusion, which would eventually be marked by circumcision (for the men).

But then something changed. Dunn points to "the deteriorating political situation in Judea" (1991: 126) beginning with Emperor Caligula's attempt to have a statue of himself set up in the temple (40 C.E.). A succession of power struggles followed (1991: 127), edging toward hostilities, which broke out in 66 C.E. During this period, "since religious identity and national identity were so inextricably intertwined in Jewish self-understanding, any factors perceived as a threat to national identity would make it necessary for both national and religious boundaries to be defended with vigor" (1991: 127). Thus, in the early 50s, it became necessary for Jews to know "who is for us," and, it followed that zealous Christians from Jerusalem went about challenging the relaxed boundaries surrounding gentile converts: "It is necessary for them to be circumcised and ordered to keep the [entire] law of Moses" (Acts 15:5).

We know the results. The Jerusalem community met and reached the decision "that we should not trouble those gentiles who are turning toward God" (Acts 15:19). Paul, in his own missionary journeys, went so far as even to oppose circumcision for gentiles. When Titus, who visited Jerusalem with Paul, "was not compelled to be circumcised" (Gal 2:3), Paul regarded this as a confirmation that he "was not running . . . in vain" (Gal 2:2). Later, Paul would create a theological fortress to justify his stance by affirming that "a person is a Jew who is one inwardly, and real circumcision is a matter of the heart" (Rom 2:29) and by showing that Abraham was pronounced righteous before he was circumcised (Rom 4:1–12). The practice of delayed circumcision for gentile males was thus slowly turned toward a practice of requiring only a circumcision of the heart.

Paul was not somehow un-Jewish when he spoke of circumcision as "a matter of the heart" (Rom 2:29). The symbolic understanding of circumcision was already part of his Jewish heritage (e.g., Lv 26:41; Dt 10:16; 30:6; Jer 4:4; 9:25; Ez 44:7, 9). Philo, a contemporary of Paul in Alexandria, argued that "in reality the proselyte is one who circumcises not his uncircumcision but his desires and sensual pleasures and the other passions of the soul for, in Egypt, the Hebrew nation was not circumcised" (*Questions and Answers on Exodus* 2.2). Josephus, another contemporary, recounts the history of Izates, the crown prince of the house of Adiabene, who, upon embracing Judaism, was persuaded not to be circumcised lest it cause political unrest. Ananias, his Jewish mentor, responded that "he might worship God without being circumcised" and that "God would forgive him . . . while it was omitted out of necessity and for fear of his subjects" (*Ant.* 20.41f.). While Philo gives circumcision a spiritual meaning and while Josephus records an exceptional case of conversion without circumcision, neither of these authors would have gone so far as Paul did when he taught all gentile converts to avoid circumcision. Nonetheless, Philo, Josephus, and others (Collins 1985: 164–79) demonstrate that Jewish contemporaries of Paul did join him to the extent that the inner reality and extraordinary circumstances were given precedence over mere legal conformity.

Where did the *Didache* stand? Did its framers presume that baptized gentiles would be expected eventually to embrace circumcision as well? Or did its framers affirm that baptism alone sufficed? This issue is very complex and is argued in detail in chapter 13 below. For the moment, however, it suffices to note that the *Didache* puts forward the Way of Life without at any time implying that there was any further rule necessary for perfection. In fact, the completeness of the rules given is maintained: "You will guard the things you have received, neither adding anything nor taking anything away" (*Did.* 4:13).

Moreover, the *Didache* betrays no interest in circumcision—which suggests, most probably, that the issue had been settled. Meanwhile, the eucharistic prayers leave no doubt that baptized gentiles drink of "the holy vine of your servant David" (9:2) and that they eat of the broken loaf that ensures them that they will be gathered "from the ends of the earth into your kingdom" (*Did.* 9:4). Baptized gentiles, consequently, were fully incorporated into the election and promise formerly reserved to Jews. They called upon God as "our Father" (8:2; 9:2, 3; 10:2). While the *Didache* betrays no influence of Paul and no awareness of the decisions of the Jerusalem Council (Acts 15), it does, nonetheless, assume that baptized gentiles were fully incorporated into the election and promises made to Israel. Thus, once again, it would appear as though the *Didache* had wrestled with a deep and universal problem and had arrived at a satisfactory solution. This solution, however, is not explicitly formulated; hence, we are forced to grope in the dark for what might have been their solution.

Dunn's account of why circumcision was a moot issue prior to the 50s has one glaring soft spot. He presupposes that baptized gentiles would eventually be circumcised and thus become fully Jewish and fully Christian. This is doubtful (see ch. 13 below). Dunn fails to take into account a critical difference within the Jesus movement due to its eschatological posture. Dunn's account, accordingly, needs to be corrected and supplemented with Paula Fredriksen's insights (repeated here from #1o):

> Within the Jewish synagogues, gentiles could learn the folly of depending upon idols and could pray and fast with Jews. Unless such gentiles completely converted to Judaism, however, they could not be classed with the people of God and assured a place in the world to come. Within the Jesus movement, however, both Jews and gentiles shared a common faith in Jesus and a common expectation in the imminent coming of the Lord. Jews prepared for his coming by turning in faith to a heartfelt observance of the Torah; gentiles, on the other hand, "*turn from* idolatry (and the sins associated with it) and *turn to* the living God." (Fredriksen: 547). Thus, circumcision, Sabbath keeping, and kosher foods were required of Jews but not of gentiles since "gentiles are saved as gentiles: they do not, eschatologically, become Jews." (Fredriksen: 547)

Dunn focuses on "the deteriorating political situation in Judea" in the early 50s (1991: 126). Well and good. This most probably needs to be supplemented, however, with Fredriksen's awareness of the strain caused by the delay of the coming of the Lord (560). This complex issue deserves further study.

The Rule Regarding Food Sacrificed to Idols

Now that the overall progression of pre- and postbaptismal training has been sketched out, attention can be given to the details. The rule regarding foods given to novices is as follows:

(And) concerning eating,
    [1] bear that which you are able,
    [2] (but), from the food sacrificed to idols,
      very much keep away
      for it is worship of dead gods (*Did.* 6:3).

In chapter 1, it was already noted that the novice was not instructed to remove images of idols from his/her environment. Such a task would be, in many cases, nearly impossible. Floor designs and architectural ornamentation routinely depicted images of the gods. The very coins used in buying and selling bore such images. Hence, the Christian had to bear that which he/she was able and to remove or plaster over household images he/she was unable to tolerate.

When it came to "food sacrificed to idols," however, the situation was different. Needless to say, no Christian would imagine that he/she could offer sacrifices to the gods or to participate in such sacrifices. But that is not the focal concern here. Rather, the rule against eating "food sacrificed to idols" had to do with the cultic meals that were a routine part of pagan life. Wendell Willis notes that such meals already routinely show up in Homer's epics:

> There is evidence already in Homer that the meal which followed sacrifice was characterized by merriment and joyous association. A sacrifice of the hecatomb [literally, a hundred oxen] by Odysseus when his warriors began the Trojan war is a good example. [The god] Apollo receives a prayer; [then] his share of the meat (thighs and fat) and a libation are immolated. But the focus in Homer's account is upon the fraternal meal which follows and stresses the abundant supply of meat and drink followed by joyful singing. Similarly, when Odysseus returns, a swineherd kills a pig for a feast to celebrate and to share dinner with friends. Homer's accounts illustrate Aristotle's statement that sacrifices and festivals were celebrated for "both paying honor to the gods and providing pleasant holidays" for the participants. (52f.)

Accordingly, a novice would be expected to receive invitations from friends and extended family members to give thanks to the gods on the occasion of important moments in their lives: the birth, coming of age, or marriage of a child; success in business; returning safely from a long voyage; and so on. Such meals were not in themselves pagan rites, nor was there necessarily any notion that eating the food constituted some sort of sacramental union with a god (Willis: 21–62; see 1 Cor 10:20). The *Didache*, after all, regarded the gods as "dead" (6:3). Nonetheless, those who joined in the meal would be expected tacitly to acknowledge that the feast was being celebrated in thanksgiving for a particular blessing received from a particular god (Willis: 39–42). Thus, eating any meal offered to idols constituted a denial that "apart from [the true] God, nothing happens" (3:10). Hence, such food was off limits.

This rule regarding eating undoubtedly needed clarification. Some novices might be imagined to ask, "What if a guest at such a dinner party receives some of the food to take home (Willis: 64) and later wants to share this with me?" Others might ask, "My meat market sometimes sells off excessive meat from temple sacrifices (Willis: 64; 1 Cor 10:25). Am I permitted to buy and eat meats from this market?" Note that the novice is not given detailed rules to cover all cases. For the cases just named, the general rule was to "bear that which you are able" (6:3). Thus it was left to the novice to discern whether he/she could or would eat. In effect, the novice was not even compelled to inquire. When it came to "the food [publicly acknowledged as] sacrificed to idols," however, the line had been crossed, and eating would be tantamount to the "worship of dead gods" (6:3). This the Christian could not do.

#3D WHETHER THE *DIDACHE* FOLLOWS PAUL'S RULE REGARDING IDOL MEATS

How does the Pauline tradition regarding permissible foods in 1 Corinthians 8 and 10 agree or disagree with the *Didache*? Wendell Willis, after having conducted a thorough investigation of the Pauline texts, came to the following conclusions:

> The first case Paul considers in 10:25 is whether Christians need to investigate the origin and history of meat sold in public markets. The second case is whether Christians must refuse invitations from pagan friends or, if they accept them, scrutinize the menu. In both of these instances Paul's principle is the same, "No investigation is called for, this is not a matter which involves conscience. Eat!" (260)

Thus Paul allows for a "don't know, don't tell" attitude when it comes to meat in the market (1 Cor 10:25) or food served by a nonbeliever during a noncultic meal (1 Cor 10:27). When it comes to a cultic banquet wherein the food has been expressly sacrificed to an idol, Paul draws an uncompromising line: "You cannot partake of the table of the Lord and the table of demons" (1 Cor 10:21). Willis explains:

> The Corinthians may consider the pagan cult meals as social, non-worshipful occasions, but Paul insists their choice is clear: the Lord or demons. . . . Paul takes both meal occasions to be religiously significant. (212)

Paul enforces this prohibition not on the grounds that demons really exist (1 Cor 10:19) but on the grounds that (a) such eating creates bonds of fellowship with idols (1 Cor 10:17f.) and (b) that such eating provokes "the

Lord to jealousy" (1 Cor 10:22 with such examples as Dt 32:17; 1 Kgs 14:22f.; Ps 78:58).

One has no way of knowing whether the *Didache* would invoke the same line of thinking. It is interesting, nonetheless, that both Paul and the *Didache* take a flexible approach save when it comes to eating food sacrificed to idols. Paul makes use of the phrase "table of demons" (1 Cor 10:21). In parallel fashion, the Pseudo-Clementines state, "We keep away from the table of devils" (7.4.2). The *Didache*, in contrast, makes no reference to "demons" or "devils" in this or in any other context.

The phrase *theōn nekrōn* found in the *Didache* can be read "of dead gods" or "of gods of the dead." In the Greek language, *nekros* has the root *nek-* and carries with it the basic meaning of trouble or misfortune. This ambiguity works well here, since the phrase can be understood to mean "gods of [spiritually] dead/unfortunate [persons]" or "dead [i.e., powerless or unfortunate] gods" (cf. Wis 15:17). Needless to say, the *Didache* has no intention of expressing any theological claim that the pagan gods are "nonexistent." Here, as elsewhere, the *Didache* contents itself with pragmatic rules of conduct and shows no interest in settling conflicting theological claims.

#3E WHY NO PROHIBITION AGAINST EATING BLOOD?

Jews understood the life force to be in the blood (Gn 9:4; Lv 17:11, 14; Dt 12:23). Even in the case of animal life, the blood was to be drained out prior to eating the flesh, under penalty of death (Lv 3:17; 7:26; 17:10; Dt 12:23; 1 Sm 14:32–35). This rule was considered so important that it was imposed on gentiles who elected to live in the towns of the Israelites (Lv 17:8, 12, 13, 15). Accordingly, one reads that the Jerusalem Council decided that, while gentiles were not to be bound by the entire Torah, they were, nonetheless, to "abstain from what has been sacrificed to idols and from blood" (Acts 15:29). In parallel fashion, the earlier *Sentences of Phocylides* (first century B.C.E.) put forward a similar rule: "Do not eat blood; abstain from the food offered to idols" (31). Philo even goes so far as to suggest that eating meat with the blood in it "is injurious and like[ly] to cause disease" (*Special Laws* 4.119).

This being the case, it is curious that the *Didache* gives no importance to warning gentiles regarding the Lord's mandate not to eat animal blood. One could argue that the prohibition of the eating of blood was set aside for the gentiles in the same way as Sabbath rest and the multitude of dietary rules. The case of the eating of blood was different, however, since it was required even of gentiles (as shown above) and formed part of what is regarded as the Lord's covenant with Noah. The reason for dropping this prohibition, therefore, seems unclear.

The Significance of Fasting Prior to Baptism

Nowhere in the Christian Scriptures does fasting figure into the preparation for baptism. Here, in the *Didache*, consequently, one finds the first known reference (Vööbus 1968: 20) to a practice of this kind. Then one must wait a hundred years before the next reference to fasting prior to baptism (Justin Martyr, *1 Apol.* 61.2).

It cannot be supposed that the practice of fasting prior to baptism originated with the *Didache*. The presentation is so low-key, so matter of fact, that it must be surmised that the *Didache* is merely giving voice to a tradition already practiced (although it is impossible to gauge how widespread this practice might have been).

No motive for this fast is offered, yet some educated guesses can be made:

1. *Fasting as intensifying prayer.* According to the Jewish tradition, fasting functions to intensify prayer. This instinctive association of prayer with fasting was earlier evident in *Did.* 1:3, where the novice is told: "Pray for your enemies and fast for the ones persecuting you." Just as there is an implied intensification between having enemies and suffering persecution at the hands of one's enemies, so too there is an intensification between prayer and prayer with fasting. Fasting promotes a sense of urgency that anxiously awaits God's response to one's need.

2. *Fasting as intensifying conversion.* Baptism is a rite of passage from one way of life to another. The entire training prior to baptism deals with altering the habits of the mind and the judgments of the heart in the anticipation of attaining the perfection in the Way of Life to which one is called. After baptism, there would be no turning back. One could not claim any longer to be an ignorant pagan who knew nothing of the ways of the Lord. On the contrary, from the time of baptism forward, one was to be held accountable (4:13f.); one was to "seek every day the presence of the saints" (4:2); one was to "share all things with your brother [and sister]" (4:8). Fasting and prayer might help one come to grips with all the hopes and dreams that conversion to a new way of life demanded. Fasting, therefore, had the effect of intensifying an already existing state of being clear-minded, focused, urgent.

3. *Fasting as a natural response to a momentous event.* Just prior to a long-distance race, runners lose their appetites entirely as soon as they mentally

rehearse what they are about to undertake. Marriage partners, just prior to their wedding, usually entirely give up eating, sleep fitfully, and may even have diarrhea. Paul, following his unsettling experience on the road to Damascus, "was without sight, and neither ate nor drank" (Acts 9:9) for three days. Thecla, a would-be disciple of Paul, was mesmerized listening to Paul's words "for three days and three nights" and did not rise from her window sill "either to eat or to drink" (*Acts of Paul* 7:6).

In parallel fashion, one can imagine that candidates for baptism generally felt a similar inner turmoil that made them naturally incapable of eating anything. Some may have felt a sweet anticipation of being accepted as a servant of the Lord, the Father of All, the Maker of Heaven and Earth. Others may have felt a dull fear of irreversibly abandoning familiar gods and their devotees. Still others may have experienced intense grief in the face of the anticipated or already finalized rejection of father, mother, brothers, and sisters. Still others may have wondered how well or how poorly they would relate to persons in the movement whom they had never met and with whom they would be expected to be spiritual kin for the rest of their lives. Such physiological and psychological aspects of involuntary fasting need not be neglected when it comes time to explain the hidden logic of the *Didache* in this matter.

4. *Fasting as due to the traumatic loss of identity prior to baptism.* Mary Douglas, an anthropologist who has studied initiation rites, reports the following:

> Danger lies in transitional states, simply because transition is neither one state nor the next, it is undefinable. The person who must pass from one to another is himself in danger and emanates danger to others. The danger is controlled by ritual which precisely separates him from this old status, segregates him for a time and then publicly declares his entry to his new status. Not only is transition itself dangerous, but also the rituals of segregation are the most dangerous phase of the rites. (97)

The rule of not eating "food sacrificed to idols" (*Did.* 6:3) separates the candidate from the protection of former gods and their devotees. The rule of not eating at all (fasting) enforces the separation of the candidate even from the table of those with whom he/she intends to bond. The candidate, therefore, is both cut off from an earlier identity and not yet participating in a new identity. Thus, as Mary Douglas notes, the candidate experiences the terror of being in an undefined transitional state—abandoned by former gods yet not belonging to the new God, shunned by former family members and friends yet not belonging to the new family. The candidate knows the state of being without protection, without support, without a future. Those entering rites of initiation, therefore, "risk their lives" and, according to Douglas, are "exposed to power that is enough to kill them" (97).

5. *Fasting as cleansing the system from food sacrificed to idols.* As noted above, the candidate for baptism was instructed a few days prior to baptism not to take "food sacrificed to idols" (6:3) and, once this rule was given, it would become the rule for the whole of the life of the Christian. As a consequence, the prebaptismal fasting functioned to cleanse the body so that all "food sacrificed to idols" (6:3) was entirely expelled. At the same time, the fasting might have stimulated hunger for the "holy vine" (9:2), the "broken loaf" (9:3f.), and "the life and knowledge which you [the Father] revealed to us through your servant Jesus" (9:3). (See the last paragraph in #3f.) While one cannot be certain of this implied meaning, one must be careful not to reject it out of hand since many of the most important things about the training itself cannot and were not directly said.

6. *Fasting as training for the semiweekly fast.* The recitation of the *Didache* subverts the natural order of things: baptism is described and then the prebaptismal fast is named immediately followed by the postbaptismal fast twice a week (8:1). The oral transition from one fasting to another may hint at the fact that the training and experience that a candidate receives in the prebaptismal fast will be put to use in the semiweekly fast of solidarity that the community undertakes. The importance of this semiweekly fasting and its association with the Lord's Prayer will be explored in the following chapter.

#3f FASTING AND WEEPING IN THE CONVERSION OF ASENETH

The book of *Joseph and Aseneth* narrates how Aseneth, the beautiful and virtuous daughter of an Egyptian priest, converts to Judaism and goes on to become the fitting bride of Joseph, who has gained great favor with the pharaoh in Egypt. While *Joseph and Aseneth* is a fictional romance and conversion story, it provides insights as to how almsgiving, fasting, weeping, and praying were popularly understood in Jewish circles as the appropriate signs of a true conversion. In what follows, version d (the "shorter recension") of the text will be used, because it provides an "unquestionably Jewish" document written in Egypt around 100 B.C.E. (M. Philonenko cited in M. F. D. Sparks: 468–70).

The narrative opens in the household of the Egyptian priest Pentephres. The narrator anticipates the drama to unfold when he introduces

Pentephres' eighteen-year-old daughter "as tall as Sarah, and as beautiful
as Rebecca, and as fair as Rachel" (1:8). As such, she was much sought after
by men. Yet "Aseneth despised all men and regarded them with contempt"
(2:1). Upon first meeting Joseph, however, Aseneth encountered a truly
exceptional man, and when she heard his virtuous words, "her eyes were
filled with tears" (8:8). When Joseph blesses her invoking the "the God of
my father Israel" (8:10), Aseneth abruptly leaves Joseph in haste.

When alone, "she wept bitterly, and she repented of her gods she used
to worship" (9:2). During the first evening, for example, "she was listless
and wept until sunset: she ate no bread and drank no water" (10:2). The
entire night, she passed alone "groaning and weeping" (10:7).

The next morning, Aseneth "took all her innumerable gold and silver
gods and broke them up into little pieces and threw them out of the window for the poor and needy" (10:13). Later, she took her royal dinner
"and all the sacrifices for her gods and the wine-vessels for their libations;
and she threw them all out of the window as food for the dogs" (10:14).
Aseneth then put on mourning clothes and covered herself with ashes. For
seven nights and days, she remained alone, without food or drink, weeping
bitterly and groaning.

On the eighth day, "she stretched her hands out toward the east, and her
eyes looked up to the heaven" (12:1) and she expressed for the first time
her prayer of repentance and conversion imploring God "like a child
[speaking] to her father and her mother" (12:7). In response, a heavenly
messenger (angel) arrived promising that she would "be made new, and
refashioned, and given new life" (15:4). Aseneth, aspiring only to become
the "slave" of Joseph, was then given the special revelation that the heavenly messenger has communicated everything to Joseph and that "he shall
be your bridegroom" (15:9). Her prayers having been answered beyond
her expectation, the narrator then recounts numerous narrow escapes
wherein Aseneth avoids the murderous plots of the jealous son of the
Pharaoh.

From beginning to end, *Joseph and Aseneth* has a narrative quality that
takes the reader deep into the life of Aseneth. The author achieves a balance between dramatic conflict and natural dialogue that even modern
short-story writers might emulate. In the end, the reader learns to care
about Aseneth and to applaud her heroism in the face of the many trials
attendant upon her conversion.

For our purposes here, it is important to note that the author of the narrative goes to great length to describe the mixture of wonder, of fear, of
regret that overwhelms Aseneth during the time of her conversion. No one
has to tell Aseneth to fast, just as no one has to tell her to weep. The author
of the narrative powerfully portrays the symptoms of a woman undergoing
a profound personal reorientation. While alone after her first meeting with

Joseph, for example, Aseneth "fell on her couch exhausted, because she felt not only happy, but also disturbed and very frightened; and she had been bathed in perspiration from the moment she heard Joseph speaking" (9:1f.). Likewise, after Aseneth's seven days of fasting and weeping, we hear the terror gripping the soul of a would-be convert:

> To you, O Lord . . . , will I cry:
> Deliver me from my persecutors, for to you I have fled,
> Like a child to her father and her mother.
> O Lord, stretch forth your hands over me,
> As a father who loves his children and is tenderly affectionate,
> And snatch me from the hands of the enemy. . . .
> The gods of the Egyptians whom I have abandoned and destroyed
> And their father the Devil are trying to destroy me. . . .
> Save me, O Lord, deserted as I am,
> For my father and mother denied me,
> Because I destroyed and shattered their gods;
> And now I am an orphan and deserted,
> And I have no other hope save in you, O Lord.
> (12:8f., 11 slightly altered).

This prayer vividly portrays the distress of a convert who is abandoned by her parents and remains defenseless against the gods whom she has abandoned. Aseneth's fasting and weeping, consequently, are partially the result of her being terrorized regarding the woeful consequences following upon her conversion. On the other hand, her fasting and weeping have purified her, and her prayer anticipates that the God of Joseph (as well as Joseph himself) will father and mother her and protect her from the displeasure of her former gods.

As in the case of conversions in the *Didache*, food and fasting play key roles. According to the narrative, Joseph always ate separately "because he would not eat with the Egyptians, for this was an abomination to him" (7:2). Meanwhile Aseneth, following her conversion, acknowledges that her "mouth . . . has been defiled by things offered to idols" (12:5); hence, she gives her royal food to the dogs. After her seven days of complete fasting, Joseph returns to her home and, for the first time, invites her to eat with him (20:5). The reader thus learns that fasting acts to purify Aseneth and to prepare her for feasting on the holy food eaten by Joseph. Fasting from the unclean food offered to idols, therefore, forms the necessary preparation for feasting on the gifts of the true God.

Not only does the candidate fast, but also "the one baptizing" and "others [in the community who] have the strength" (*Did.* 7:4). The fasting on the part of the one baptizing (7:4) receives no explanation. As noted above, it is undoubtedly significant that the fasting of the spiritual parent was mentioned first. Perhaps this reflects the existential reality that the mentor began fasting and then asked the candidate to join him/her. If so, this would provide an unexpected confirmation of the hypothesis spelled out above relative to the preferred time of baptism—namely, Saturday evening. Thus, the mentor would have begun fasting on the "Sabbath preparation day" (8:1) and continued his fast during the Sabbath—two days in all. The candidate, for his/her part, would fast "during one or two days prior to the baptism" (7:4). Thus, the fast of the mentor would invariably begin first or (in the case of two days) at the same time as that of the candidate.

In solidarity, many within the community who had "the [necesssary] strength" (7:4) joined in this fasting and praying. Their fasting also served to prepare their hearts and minds to be ready to receive new members into their "family" at the forthcoming baptism and eucharist. Then fasting would give way to feasting!

The duration, but not the rigor of this fasting, is defined. Presumably, members of the Didache community knew this and acted accordingly. In the next chapter, this issue will be taken up in depth. For the moment, however, it suffices to assume that the reference to those who "have the strength" probably means that the fast implied here represents a complete renunciation of all food and drink for "one or two [complete days]" (7:4). Furthermore, since my conjecture regarding the preferred time of baptism appears to be confirmed, then the first day of fasting would have been the semiweekly fast on the "Sabbath preparation day" (8:1) and the second day of fasting would have fallen on the Sabbath day itself. Two continuous days of fasting would have been very demanding and, furthermore, for gentiles, these would normally have been normal workdays (following the Roman calendar). With complete understanding, therefore, the *Didache* speaks of those who "have the strength" as extending their fast for the additional day. In the Book of Esther, for example, the Jewish queen advised her people to fast and pray for the success of her mission for three full days: "neither eat nor drink for three days, night or day" (Est 4:16)—night being mentioned first since in the Jewish reckoning of a full day, night always comes first and so it is mentioned first (as in *Did.* 4:1; Dt 28:66; 1 Sm 25:16; 2 Sm 2:32; 1 Kgs 8:29; Is 27:3; 34:10; Jer 14:17; Mk 4:27; 5:5; Lk 2:37; 2 Cor 11:25; 1 Thes 2:9; 3:10; 2 Thes 3:8; 1 Tm 5:5; 2 Tim 1:3). This fast of three full days, however, was a one-time emergency measure in favor of a mission designed to save the entire people. The fast of solidarity with a new candidate preparing to become one of them would hardly merit three days. Two continuous days of fasting, however, was a fast of unusual rigor.

#3G WHETHER THE DIDACHE COMMUNITIES BAPTIZED INFANTS

Scholars continue to be divided as to whether the early church baptized infants. The renowned German scholar Joachim Jeremias (1960; 1963), investigated the topic and concluded that infant baptism was implied in every instance where entire households were baptized (e.g., as in the case of the household of Cornelius in Acts 10). In response to the objections of Kurt Aland, however, Jeremias acknowledged that he did not find any explicit reference to infant baptism prior to Tertullian (d. 225 C.E.). Tertullian, however, opposed the practice and argued that baptism should be reserved for mature persons lest its benefits be lost by sin or lest the sponsors be brought into danger (*On Baptism* 18). One has to wait until the mid-third century to find the first texts endorsing the practice (e.g., Origen, *Commentary on Romans* 5.9; *Apostolic Tradition* 21.3f.).

Let us examine the evidence of the *Didache* regarding the baptism of infants or children. No direct evidence is forthcoming, but some indirect evidence is worthy of consideration:

1. The *Didache* requires that candidates for baptism be trained in the Way of Life (1:3; 7:1). The terms of this training (e.g., not corrupting boys [2:2], reproving against failings [4:3]) clearly demonstrate that a mature person is being addressed and not a child. The fact that the *Didache* offers no Way of Life for children, therefore, indicates that only adult candidates for baptism were expected.

2. Parents preparing for baptism were instructed to train their children "in the fear of God" (4:9). Christian parents, accordingly, were to give their children a rule of life appropriate to their age, but this rule was to be based on fear and not on the "love" (1:2) implied in the Way of Life. Furthermore, the Way of Life has nothing to say to parents regarding the baptism of future children born to them. If the *Didache* failed to instruct parents to do these things, it can be assumed that parents did not have their children baptized.

3. Household slaves were normally constrained to worship the gods of their masters. The *Didache*, however, appears to oppose this practice on the grounds that the Lord "does not come to call anyone according to his/her social status, but God calls those whom the Spirit has made ready" (4:10). This rule would cut both ways. It would prohibit Christian masters from imagining that God called them because of their social status; hence, slaves could never be called by God. It would also prohibit a master from commanding his slave to convert, since "God calls [only] those who the Spirit has made ready" (4:10). This would imply that slaves were required only to obey their masters (4:11) until such time as they were called by the Lord-God to pursue the Way of Life. Since children had a subordinate sta-

tus within a household akin to that of slaves, it would follow that parents were prohibited from commanding their children to convert or, in the case of infants, from having them baptized on parental authority.

4. The *Didache* made no provisions for infants or children who might be candidates for baptism. Can one suppose, for example, that infants or young children would have fasted "during one or two days" (7:4)? If not, and if no provisions were made for exceptions (as in the case of the different kinds of water), then it must be supposed that infants or young children were not admitted to baptism.

5. Similarly, the *Didache* made no provisions for infants or children at the eucharist. Everyone drank wine and ate bread at the eucharist. If baptized infants were present, it would be expected that there would be provisions for them (as in the case of Orthodox Christians today) or that communion would be delayed (as in the case of most Western churches today). Similarly, the necessity of "having confessed beforehand your failings" (14:1) also made no provisions for infants or young children. For these and other reasons, therefore, it seems doubtful whether the *Didache* would have baptized either infants or children.

In arriving at this negative conclusion, it must also be remembered that parents in the Didache community did not have any compelling reason to rush the children born to them into baptism. The notion of "original sin" was not developed prior to the third century, and one has to wait until Augustine (d. 430) to find a pastor threatening infants with eternal hellfire should they die without being baptized. Thus, one can suppose that parents in the Didache community felt assured that their children were loved and cared for by the Father and that no grievous harm would come to them should they die or should the Lord come before they were baptized. Any candidate for baptism anxious about such things would be told (a) that sins committed under the spell of false gods were done in ignorance and (b) that the very act of turning to the Lord (*teshuvah*) brought with it the Lord's forgiveness (see #3n). Not even adults, therefore, were rushed toward baptism.

The writings of Tertullian demonstrate that, even at the opening of the third century, the baptism of infants or young children was still being treated as an unwelcome novelty. Tertullian firmly believed in the necessity of baptism for salvation (*On Baptism* 13), yet even he advised that "if any understand the weighty import of baptism, they will fear its reception more than its delay" (*On Baptism* 18). Accordingly, "in the case of little children," Tertullian advised that "the delay of baptism was preferable" because this was "the innocent period of life" (*On Baptism* 18). The one approaching baptism in Tertullian's day was expected to fast and pray—as in the case of the *Didache*. To this, however, has been added all night vigils "with the confession of all bygone sins" (*On Baptism* 18)—a practice based on the "confession of sins" (Mt 3:6) preceding John's baptism and the Lord's admonition, "Stay awake and pray that you may not come into the time of trial" (Mt 26:41). Thus, even as the preoccupation with sin was overtaking baptism and baptism itself was understood as "the washing away of the sins of our early blindness" (*On Baptism* 1), the traditional practice of the church of baptizing only adults held sway.

#3H WHETHER THE DIDACHE COMMUNITIES PRACTICED BAPTISM FOR THE DEAD

Baptism for the dead finds a single passing reference in 1 Cor 15:29. The remainder of the Christian Scriptures, the *Didache*, and the entire works of the church fathers never espouse such a practice. It is possible, therefore, that some Corinthians had developed the practice of supporting "a vicarious baptism whereby the baptism of one as thought to secure the salvation of another already dead" (Dunn 1977: 157) or "to aid the deceased as they made the transition from life to death" (DeMaris: 671). Paul refers to this practice in arguing for the resurrection of the dead—he neither favors nor discourages the practice (DeMaris: 681; J. R. White: 488–92). Marcionites (second century) practiced baptism for the dead, and in our own day the Latter-day Saints (Mormons) have revived it (L. P. Wilson).

The Rite of Immersion in Water

The *Didache* puts forward the general rule that the immersion should take place "in living water" (*en hydati zōnti*)—an expression that could be rendered as "in flowing/moving water." Three reflections are in order here:

1. *John's practice.* The rule for using flowing water may hark back to an early period wherein natural rivers were used for baptizing—a trait distinctive of the baptisms of John in the Jordan River (Mt 3:6 and par.).

2. *Jewish tradition.* The Jewish tradition was always attentive to different grades of water. Flowing water, the highest grade of water, was required for the cleansing of former lepers (Lv 14) or the removal of corpse defilement (Nm 19:1–13). The rabbinic tradition reflected in the Mishnah dis-

tinguishes six different grades of water, with "living water" being the highest grade (*m. Miqvaot* 1:8). With the emergence of the Jewish practice of proselyte baptism during the first two centuries, it is not surprising that the rabbis required "flowing water" for the baptism of gentile converts. The rabbis argued that "the uncleanliness of idols" was analogous to leprosy (*y. Pesahim* 9:36c) or corpse defilement (*b. Abodah Zarah* 32b; *b. Hullin* 13b). Hence, even if proselyte baptism was not practiced within the Judaism that gave rise to the *Didache*, it is still possible to understand how and why "flowing water" would be preferred for Christian baptisms. In fact, the whole discussion of water preferences must have originated as part of an internal debate in which Jewish tradition, on the one side, was wrestling with accommodation to gentiles.

3. *Hellenistic preference.* This preference for natural sources of flowing water would have also had some appeal in Hellenistic culture as well (Klauser: 177–83). The ancient world did not have to deal with water purification plants or with bacterial/chemical contamination of water sources; hence, clear, cold water was naturally preferred for drinking, washing, bathing. This kind of water, however, was ordinarily the "living water" found bubbling out of subterranean springs or flowing in rivers.

The Greek term *baptizein* means to immerse or to dip in water. The verb, therefore, does not necessarily imply complete immersion. Furthermore, since the depth or quantity of water is not specified, the *Didache* seems more intent on specifying the kind of water rather than paying attention to whether the depth or quantity of water is sufficient for complete immersion. Even in the case of the Jordan River, John the Baptizer would have had to search hard to find sections where the depth of water was over four feet, and this would vary according to seasonal conditions. Thus, for those being baptized by John, it can be assumed that the candidate being baptized stood in the water and was immersed (or dunked) by crouching under the water.

Once the *Didache* declared its preference for flowing water, it immediately provided exceptions for instances where flowing water was not available (*Did.* 7:2f.). The "other water" allowed in exceptional circumstances is still or standing water (Rordorf 1972a: 506). Nothing is said regarding any emergency on the part of the person being baptized; hence, following the logic of the text itself, the *Didache* must be read as implying that some places did not have the preferred water and thus alternatives were being set forth. In the case of still water, however, cold water was to be given preference over warm, undoubtedly because it was closer to natural, flowing water. If neither cold nor warm standing water was available in sufficient quantity, then the one baptizing might, as a last resort, douse the person by pouring water over the head three times.

#31 THE SIGNIFICANCE OF "WARM WATER" (*DID.* 7:2)

Some early interpreters understood this text as making provisions for the warming of water when sick persons were to be baptized (Benoit: 8 n. 15; Dölger: 175–83; Harnack 1886: 23). Other scholars objected to this, seeing that the text makes no mention of sick candidates, and preferred to understand the reference to "warm water" (7:2) as pointing in the direction of water being deliberately warmed for baptisms in a cold climate:

> It seems evident to me that one is speaking here of water being heated for the situation. This is a precaution that would be called for if the baptism took place in a climate too rigorous [for river baptisms]. It would not be necessary here to think only of sick persons and, certainly, even less of the baptism of infants. (Rordorf 1972a: 506)

Rordorf appeals to baptisteries wherein water could be warmed (e.g., at Zurzach in Switzerland) and to the Mandaean critique of Christian baptism in warmed water (Hippolytus, *Ref.* 9.16.1) (Rordorf 1972a: 506 n. 38). Both of these testimonies, however, come from the third century and give no reliable evidence regarding the first century.

When read as a unit, the overriding norm was to give preference to "living" water (7:1)—flowing and cold in natural streams. When this was lacking, then non-flowing cold water (7:2)—as in a pond or lake—was permitted. Such cold water had the natural temperature of "living" water but was inferior since it was not flowing (Niederwimmer 1998: 127). Finally, when cold water was lacking, warm water was permitted. A. Vööbus surmises that "warm water" refers to "the kind to be found in cisterns, pools and reservoirs" exposed to the Mediterranean sun (Vööbus 1968: 24).

The language of the text says nothing about artificially heating the water. Accordingly, the logic of the text is far removed from making accommodations for a sick candidate or for a cold climate; rather, the issue was directed toward accommodating a situation where both cold-running and cold-standing water were not available. If the framers of the *Didache* had wanted to make adaptations for a cold climate, as Rordorf surmises, then one would have expected "warm water" to be preferred over "cold"—exactly opposite of the norm supplied by the text.

The trinity of names is repeated at the point where it is said that the one baptizing can "pour out water onto the head three times in the name of

Father and Son and Holy Spirit" (7:3). Three reflections are in order here:

1. Since immersion is preferred, it can hardly be expected that so little water would have been used as to interpret this instruction as allowing for mere sprinkling with water or pouring only a token quantity—practices that appear to have emerged no earlier that the mid-third century. Rather, one should expect sufficient quantity of water to be used so that the person being baptized would be entirely drenched.

2. When the *Didache* says "pour out water onto the head" (7:3), it must be assumed that the normal standing posture was used and that this ensured that the water continued down the whole length of the body. In fact, the very notion of "pouring" must have been perceived as approximating "flowing water" (7:1f.). Thus, here again the action of pouring would militate against any notion that only a token amount of water was used. The presumption would be in the direction of assuming that as much water was poured as possible—taking due account of the availability of water and the strength of the one baptizing.

3. Finally, the specific reference to "pouring three times" again weighs in the direction of ensuring a complete soaking. Parts of the body still dry would become the natural target of the second and third pouring of jars of water. However, the mention of the threefold pouring along with the repetition of the threefold names might be a clue that would incline some to find here the first step toward the practice of threefold immersion (e.g., as found in the *Apostolic Tradition* of 220 C.E.). As far as the *Didache* is concerned, however, one must be cautious. In fact, one must surmise that the one baptizing immersed the candidate only once, since it would have been very easy for the framers to have said "immerse three times" if such had been the prevailing practice.

#3J WHETHER PREBAPTISMAL ANOINTING WAS PRACTICED

Sometime during the second century, an anointing of the head with oil was introduced prior to baptism in Syria, the region where the *Didache* was quite possibly in use (Niederwimmer 1998: 53). According to the careful studies of Gabriele Winkler, this prebaptismal anointing involved the pouring of oil over the head (in the way that the kings of Israel were anointed) and was regarded as the central feature of baptism (1978: 36). Later, an anointing of the whole body with oil was introduced along with a prayer for the blessing of the oil (as shown in the third-century *Acts of Thomas*). Thus, when the *Apostolic Constitutions* was compiled in 380 C.E., the *Didache* was expanded to include the following additional instruction:

> You will anoint first with holy oil, then you will baptize with water, and finally you will seal with the balsam. . . . And if there is neither oil nor balsam, water is sufficient. (7.21.2f.)

From the available evidence, one can conclude that, in the course of time, the rite and theology of baptism expanded in Syria so as to include a royal/messianic pouring of oil on the head before and a bodily anointing following the water immersion. Some scholars, however, have not been content to allow this to represent second- and third-century developments and have been intent on finding some sort of pre- or postbaptismal anointing in the practice of the *Didache*.

Wirgman (1899), for example, argued that the *Didache* was a manual intended for use by presbyters and deacons and that the anointing assigned to the bishop was practiced but deliberately left out. Dix (1948), in his turn, argued that the *Didache* was intended to present rites that the laity could perform in the absence of the clergy and that this explained the omission of a rite of anointing.

Each of these arguments assumes a lay-clerical mentality absent from the *Didache* (see ch. 9 below). Furthermore, an argument based on textual silence is open to unrestrained flights of the imagination. What cannot be demonstrated cannot be known.

2. Others have argued that the Coptic fragment (British Museum Oriental Manuscript 9271), which closely follows *Did.* 10:3–12:2, has concrete textual evidence showing that some versions of the *Didache* did make provisions for blessing oil after the first eucharist (for use in a postbaptismal anointing). At the end of the eucharistic prayers (*Did.* 10:7), the Coptic fragment adds this:

> But concerning the saying for the ointment (*stinoufi*), give thanks just as you say, "We give thanks to you Father concerning the ointment (*stinoufi*) which you showed us, through Jesus your Son. Yours is the glory forever! Amen." (trans. from Stanley: 53)

This argument falls short because the Coptic word *stinoufi* refers to "incense" and not to "ointment" (Lefort: 32–34; Gero: 68). Thus, the Coptic fragment indicates that incense was burned during the solemn eucharistic meals—a practice common during the first century (Gero: 70). Even in the *Apostolic Constitutions* where pre- and postbaptismal anointings are clearly evident, the prayer over the *myron* after the eucharistic prayers speaks of its "sweet smell" (7.27.1) and makes no mention of its use for anointing.

All in all, there are no reasons to believe that the Didache community practiced any anointing in connection with baptism. The origins and theology of these anointings came later. Relative to development in the West, Justin Martyr described baptism in the mid-second century but makes no reference to anointing. By the time of the *Apostolic Tradition* (c. 250), however, both a pre- and a postbaptismal anointing were being practiced. These, however, differ markedly from the developments in Syria. Prior to immersion, the candidate stripped naked, renounced Satan, and was anointed by a presbyter from head to toe "with the Oil of Exorcism" (21.10). Following the triple immersion, each with its own profession of faith, another presbyter anointed those coming out of the water "with the Oil of Thanksgiving" (21.19). The candidates then dried themselves and put on clothes and went to the place where the community had assembled with the bishop. The bishop laid his hand upon them invoking the Holy Spirit. Then "pouring the oil [of Thanksgiving into his hand] and laying [his hand]" (22.2) on the head, he anointed each of them reciting a short prayer. The kiss of peace followed. All in all, therefore, three anointings were practiced: one prebaptismal anointing of the body as a form of exorcism and two postbaptismal anointings—one of the entire body and one of the head alone as an act of thanksgiving.

The Words Used during the Rite of Baptism

The *Didache*, using the aorist imperative, instructs those baptizing: "Immerse in the name of the Father and of the Son and of the Holy Spirit" (7:1). It would be misleading here to imagine that one has here a "baptismal formula" (as suggested by Kavanaugh 1978: 38; Rordorf 1972: 504f.; Niederwimmer 1998: 126) and that baptisms were performed, as today, with the minister saying, "I baptize you in the name of the Father, etc." Had such a formula been used, one would have expected some such entire formula to be spelled out as in the case of the eucharistic prayers. Furthermore, the Hebraic expression of acting "in the name of x" has to do with the way that a disciple or a servant is authorized *to act* as the result of the training or mandate received from his master. According to the Christian Scriptures, for example, the Twelve heralded the kingdom of God and apprenticed disciples "in the name of Jesus" (Acts 4:18; 5:28; 9:27, 29). At other times, they are presented as baptizing (Mt 28:19; Acts 2:38; 8:16; 10:48; 19:5; 22:16), healing (Acts 3:6, 16; 4:7), and exorcising demons (Acts 19:13–16) in this same name. Contrary to a widespread misunderstanding, "there is in the New Testament no belief in the magically [or even supernaturally] potent names; in fact, there are no mysteriously dreadful words or names at all" (*TDNT* 5:278).

Once it becomes clear that the trinity of names did not constitute a liturgical formula, then one has to ask whether the action of immersing constituted the entire rite. This seems improbable. In fact, the *Didache* specifically points to the words of the rite when it says, "having said all these things beforehand" (7:1). In chapter 1, it was explained that no one could expect that the candidate for baptism was hearing these words for the first time and that, in all probability, the candidate memorized the Way of Life as he/she was being trained. Now, however, just prior to baptism, the entire first six chapters of the *Didache* were most probably recited as a fitting "liturgical formula" prior to the baptism itself.

Every baptism was an affirmation of the Way of Life and a warning against the Way of Death. Accordingly, the first six chapters of the *Didache* come alive as they might be used in an oral enactment prior to baptism:

1. The opening line, "There are two ways, one of life and one of death" (1:1), defines the entire revelation received by the community from the Father through his servant Jesus. Now this life-giving treasure is being spelled out as defining the way in which the candidate for baptism will act. Most probably, the candidate and the one who trained him/her move into the pool of water where the baptism will be performed. One can imagine that most of the believers then form a circle around the two. The trainer would then be in a position to face the candidate and to address him/her with the words of life. Thus, what the *Didache* calls the "word of God" (4:1) is addressed to the candidate in the second person singular and the candidate would already know how to find the presence of the Lord in these words.

2. The closing line, "This is the Way of Life!" (4:14b), may have served as a liturgical refrain during the recitation. The mentor reciting the Way of Life might have chosen to inflect the ending of certain lines (e.g., the last line of 1:3; 1:4; 1:6; 2:2; etc.)—immediately signaling that the entire community should come in, chanting in unison, "This is the Way of Life!" Alternately, the mentor may have used this line as the signal that all were to chant together the refrain after him/her. Thus, at one and the same time, the candidate would recapture the warm feelings associated with hearing the words of the Lord voiced by his/her spiritual parent, and at the same time the chanted refrain would bring home to the candidates that their spiritual "family" affirmed their identity within this same Way of Life.

3. Then, once the Way of Life was finished, the Way of Death would be defined and repudiated. Here again the closing line, "May you be saved, O children, from all of these things" (5:2b), may have served as the liturgical refrain. Since the candidates are being directly addressed as "children" (recall the analysis of *teknon* from the first chapter), this points in the direction of having only the mentors recite this refrain. The use of the plural most probably signals that, under ordinary circumstances, more than one candidate was being baptized. Assuming this to be the case, the mentors quite possibly took turns reciting short segments of the Way of Life and short segments of the Way of Death. As for the candidates, this might have

been the first time that they would have heard the entirety of the Way of Death being spelled out.

When this dark litany was finished, the refrain, "May you be saved, O children, from all of these things!" (5:2), would be ringing in their ears. In the former section, "This is the Way of Life!" (4:14b), would be ringing in their ears. The clues whereby these two phrases could or would be used as refrains in the public enactment of the first 40 percent of the *Didache* are admittedly ambiguous at this point. In chapter 5 below, when refrains are discovered in the eucharistic liturgy and when such refrains are seen as a common dimension in Jewish prayer settings, then the evidence will become more clear. For the time being, however, we shall proceed as though the rite of baptism was preceded by an evocative and haunting litany that invariably made a strong impression on the candidates and on the community members as well. To expect that immersion in water standing by itself would suffice as an evocative rite would be to suggest that the framers of the *Didache* were liturgical dolts and had not the slightest inclination toward designing rites that profoundly moved the participants. Here again, once the liturgical genius of the eucharist is unpacked, it will become more evident that the baptismal liturgy was something to behold.

The water baptism immediately followed. In each case, one can expect that the spiritual father or mother of each candidate would ease their "child" down into the water. Quite possibly, if the mentor had the gift of prophecy (as in *Did.* 10:7), he/she might break forth in spontaneous prayers just prior to, during, and immediately after the immersion. If prophets were accustomed to offering spontaneous prayers at the end of each eucharist (as will be examined in ch. 5), then it might also be expected that such a possibility might have formed the tradition during baptism as well. The silence of the *Didache* on this point indicates only that such prayers were not a necessity and that, when they did occur, they did not disrupt or impede the proper administration of baptism.

Baptism was a rite of passage that irreversibly altered the public identity of those baptized. Each candidate entered the water as an outsider and emerged from the water as an insider. The community gathered must have greeted each of those emerging from the water as a "brother" or "sister" whom they were meeting and greeting for the first time. It might be expected (on the basis of Jewish parallels and of later liturgical practice) that, beginning with the mentor, the newly baptized might have received a sign of acknowledgment as a member of their new family (perhaps through a kiss of peace) and words of welcome, hope, encouragement (see boxes below).

One can speculate as to whether candidates for baptism stripped off their clothes in order to be immersed entirely naked. Consider the following:

1. *In favor of nude baptisms.* Nudity in the Roman baths was commonplace and, in many instances, men and women bathed together. Even Jews,

who normally abhorred nudity, made use of public baths and participated in athletic contests (Satlow: 437). Furthermore, in order to remove impediments to ritual purity, Jewish men and women immersed themselves in the purifying baths (*miqvaot*) only after removing not only all their clothes but all bodily ornaments as well. In these baths, both men and women had to take care to comb out "matted hair of the head, and of the armpits, and of the privy parts" (*m. Miqvaot* 9:3). If Jewish proselyte baptism was practiced in the mid-first century, the rules of the *miqvaot* undoubtedly applied (Satlow: 446f.).

2. *In opposition to nude baptisms.* The *Didache* shows no interest in the rubrics of the *miqvaot*. In fact, by allowing that, in case of necessity, one could "pour out water onto the head three times" (7:3), the framers of the *Didache* clearly established that they have abandoned any requirement that the water touch all parts of the body. Furthermore, the *Didache* says nothing about the privacy of the place of baptism nor are special considerations made to protect the modesty of women candidates.

3. *Resolution.* If flowing water was to be preferred, then an open-air setting would be supposed. "Nakedness was taboo in Judaism, and shame fell less on the naked party than on the person viewing or causing the nakedness" (Wink 1992: 179; Satlow: 431–47). Those presenting themselves to John the Baptist for immersion in the Jordan River would surely not have removed their clothing. In sum, therefore, one can judge with some certainty that candidates for baptism wore clothing. Where Roman customs prevailed, this would have consisted of the linen tunic customarily worn by both men and women.

After the baptism, it would have been very easy for the mentor of a female candidate to lead her charge out of the water, to introduce her to her new "sisters," and, surrounded by them, to quickly remove her wet tunic, dry her body with towels, and substitute a fresh, dry tunic. The men would have looked away "to avoid 'shaming' the woman" (Satlow: 447). A woman being baptized would not have experienced any acute shame or embarrassment at this. In fact, quite to the contrary, the woman being baptized might have considered it a sisterly gesture, since women relished caring for each other's bodies when they were alone in the public baths. These same procedures would also apply, due consideration being made for their sex, for male candidates. Consequently, if something like this were being practiced, there would be no need to make mention of it in the *Didache* since it would seem a simple and natural "family" gesture under the circumstances.

Following the baptism, the newly baptized almost assuredly joined the community in praying together the Lord's Prayer (Draper 2000: 129). Details as to how this was done three times each day will be taken up in the next chapter. For the moment, it is enough to allow that one of the mentors served as the prayer leader and provided an eloquent elaboration of the themes in the Lord's Prayer, to which the entire group responded in unison after the final refrain.

This would be immediately followed by a shared meal—most probably a shared feast—in which the fast of one or two days was broken in the midst of the new family circle. In those cases where the baptism took place on the Lord's day (*Did.* 14:1), it would be expected that this feast would be celebrated in the context of the evening eucharist on that day. In every other case, it might be expected that the bread and wine would be blessed, since, following Jewish tradition and following the logic of the eucharist, it might be expected that prayers of thanksgiving would grace every community meal. The logic of this will be spelled out in chapter 5 below.

The awesome rite of baptism here suggested may have overstepped the evidence of the *Didache*. Nonetheless, it seems better to err in the direction of adding excessive detail and color in order to flesh out the transformative power of the rite that joins the culmination of the initiation period. Most studies of the *Didache* end up using so little imaginative reconstruction that the rite of baptism becomes distorted because it is presented as having little or no evocative power. In any case, the rite of the *Didache* as I have reconstructed it would take place according to the following schema:

1. Community gathers in the place of baptism (most have been fasting for two days).
2. Candidates are led in by their spiritual mentors (all grow silent).
3. Mentors recite the Way of Life and Way of Death with the appropriate refrains.
4. Each candidate is immersed, dried off, and reclothed in a dry tunic.
5. New members are warmly embraced and kissed (same sex only) by new family.
6. Lord's Prayer is prayed together for the first time.
7. All retire to a home for a fast-breaking feast (the eucharist).

#3K BAPTISM "IN THE NAME OF THE LORD" (*DID.* 9:5)

The *Didache* appears to have an inconsistency. When it comes to describing baptism, the text initially speaks of baptism "in the name of the Father, the Son, and the Holy Spirit" (7:1, 3). Later, however, in the context of discussing the eucharist, the text makes reference to "those baptized in the name of the Lord" (9:5). What significance should one give to this shorter variant?

Within the context of the *Didache*, "Lord" is normally reserved for "Lord God" (see in #10n). Given the identification of Jesus as "the servant" of the Father (9:2f.; 10:2f.), one would not be astonished that *Did.* 9:5 retains the notion that baptism was, at one time, practiced "in the name of the Father." Given the ambiguity surrounding the term "Lord," however, it is possible that 9:5 makes reference to "in the name of the Lord Jesus"—although this choice bends in the direction of harmonizing *Didache* usage with that of the Christian Scriptures. In either case, scholars generally agree that 9:5 represents an earlier tradition that was gradually replaced by the trinity of names (Dunn 1977: 155f.). This would allow for a transition period when both the single name and the trinity of names were used during the same period (Rordorf 1972a: 504).

The tradition of acting "in the name of the Father, the Son, and the Holy Spirit" (7:1, 3) should not be thought of as reflecting early evidence of the doctrine of the Trinity (Mitchell: 254). Christianity took over from Judaism an instinct for monotheism that made it impossible for Galilean Jews to imagine any physical person being confounded with the invisible and all-powerful Lord of the Universe. The church fathers, however, came out of a different mind-set. Nurtured within Hellenistic philosophical speculation, they first linked Jesus with the power of the universal Logos and, in the end, developed the mental framework whereby a trinity of names proved to be a trinity of persons sharing the one, all-embracing divinity. This took time. Only in the early fourth century did the divinity of the Logos get hammered out in satisfactory terms at the Council of Nicaea (325 C.E.). One has to wait for the latter part of this same century before the divinity of the Holy Spirit is likewise made a binding doctrine.

In the Christian Scriptures, baptism was usually performed "in the name of Jesus Christ" (Acts 2:38; 8:16; 10:48; 19:5; 1 Cor 1:13; Gal 3:27). Matthew alone reads, "in the name of the Father and of the Son and of the Holy Spirit" (28:19). Vööbus points out, however, that Eusebius cites the great commission of Matthew more than two dozen times as "teach all nations in my name" (1968: 36). It is quite possible, consequently, that Eusebius's text of Matthew's Gospel did not have a trinitarian formula and that this was later edited into copies of Matthew's Gospel. Accordingly, the discovery of the simple formula, "baptized in the name of the Lord" (*Did.* 9:5) may also be a remnant of how 7:1b and 7:3 were expressed in early editions of the *Didache*. Hence, some weight must be given to the possibility that the trinitarian formula was introduced into the *Didache* in just the way that a copyist emended Mt 28:19 to conform to the liturgical practice of his day (Vööbus 1968: 37–39; Draper 1983: 146f.).

Rordorf has tried to maintain the integrity of the received text by suggesting that the gentile milieu required an expanded nomenclature, while the older formula continued to work in Jewish circles since "the Father"

and "the Spirit" were firmly tied into the identity of Jesus as the eschatological prophet and messiah sent by the Father and endowed with the
Spirit. Gentiles, meanwhile, "had to confess, first of all, the one God,
Father of Jesus Christ, in order to be able to be baptized" (Rordorf 1972a:
506). Thus, according to Rordorf, the trinity of names initially served as a
pastoral adaptation allowing gentiles to rightly affirm the absolute
monotheism undergirding their new identity as Christians. Thus two different pastoral situations existed side by side, each taking on a vocabulary
of its own:

> I would like to say that *Did.* 9,5 reflects, more or less, the situa-
> tion of the Jewish-Christian communities which is now being
> adapted, in Did 7,1 and 3, to the new situation of the pagan-
> Christian mission. One finds the same change of view in the
> works of Justin: in *Dial.* 39,2, addressing himself to Jews, he
> speaks of baptism in the name of Jesus alone; in *Apol.* I,61,
> 3.10.13, addressing himself to pagans, he employs the trinitarian
> formula. (Rordorf 1972a: 505 n. 28)

Without being forced to assume that the received text had been tampered
with by a scribal editor, therefore, Rordorf makes intelligible the appearance of two traditions existing side by side in the *Didache*. To this ingenious solution, I would add the possibility that "baptized in the name of
the Lord" (9:5), might be heard as "in the name of the Lord God" by gentiles and "in the name of the Lord Jesus" by Jews. Either way, the hearer
would approve the formulation and embrace it as his/her own.

What Rordorf does not address is why the pattern of *Did.* 9:5 should
have been retained if the entire *Didache* was meant to be heard by gentiles.
Furthermore, he does not address the unusual appearance of "the Son"
exclusively in 7:1 and 7:3 while "servant" is the habitual formula used for
Jesus elsewhere (9:2f.; 10:2f.). Not withstanding these unresolved difficulties, the advantages of Rordorf's point of departure are very attractive.
Further study is necessary on this point.

#3M THE PRACTICE OF JEWISH PROSELYTE BAPTISM

Sometime during the first century, converts to Judaism were baptized,
that is, immersed in water. Since women were not circumcised, baptism
constituted for them the only rite whereby a gentile was transformed into
a Jew (Daube: 112). The rabbinic tractate *Gerim* offers information
regarding the rite of proselyte baptism. While the date of composition is

quite late (sixth century), *Gerim* does paint a picture of water immersion that allows one to reflect upon the *Didache*.

According to the rabbis, candidates who presented themselves for conversion were to be discouraged: "Do you not see that this people [the Jews] are debased, oppressed, and degraded . . . ?" (1.1). For those who accept this and acknowledge their unworthiness "to place my neck under the yoke of him who spoke and the world came into being" (1.2), the rite of baptism was to be performed as follows:

> They take him down to the place of immersion, cover him in water up to his middle, and tell him some of the details of the precepts. [He is informed that he is accepted only] on condition that he give gleanings, forgotten sheaves, the corner of the field, and tithes. . . . They say to a woman that [she is accepted] on condition that she will be particular in regard to *niddah* [menstrual impurity], *hallah* [dough offering], and the kindling of the Sabbath lamp. (1.3f.)

One can hardly expect that candidates were hearing these things for the first time. Perhaps some of the more difficult and unusual aspects of the Jewish way were to be emphasized at the time of the baptism. In the case of men, all the categories centered on sharing of the produce of the land with the poor and with the Levites. In the case of women, three rules peculiar to women were offered.

As for the actual baptism, *Gerim* later notes that "a man gives immersion to a man, and a woman to a woman but not to a man" (1.8). One can surmise that modesty and social custom dictated this (as noted in ch. 1). Moreover, given the suggested topics for men and for women, one can also surmise that a man instructed a man and a woman instructed a woman both prior to and during the immersion itself. These are the very same conclusions arrived at relative to the practice of the *Didache*.

After the immersion, words of comfort were offered the convert:

> When he has bathed [immersed] and come up [out of the water], they speak to him words of kindness and comfort [saying], "To whom are you cleaving? Happy are you! [You are cleaving] to him who spoke and the world was created only for the sake of Israel; only [the children of] Israel are called 'sons of God,' and only [the children of] Israel are [described as] 'beloved of God.' All the things we have said to you we have said only to increase your reward." (1.5)

Thus, while words of warning were initially offered in order to discourage a potential convert, once the convert was accepted, corresponding words of comfort were offered. The convert was especially expected to find comfort in the realization that he/she had a powerful patron and that the altered identity of becoming "a beloved son/daughter of God" assured the convert of the Lord's unfailing care.

The rabbinic manual says nothing regarding a period of fasting prior to baptism. Following baptism, however, "vessels of wine" were opened (for a celebration or a meal?), but only if the convert was able to testify, "I am positive that none of it has been poured out as a libation [to the gods]" (*Gerim* 1.9). This implied that food offered to idols could not be used following baptism and that proselytes were informed regarding restrictions on what may not be eaten or drunk following baptism. The *Didache*, of course, is remarkably parallel at this point.

From the vantage point of an outsider, the Roman historian Tacitus (d. 120 C.E.) noted that converts to Judaism offended the rules of traditional filial piety (toward the gods, toward the fatherland, and toward parents):

> Those who are converted to their ways follow the same practice [of cutting themselves off from other peoples], and the earliest lesson they receive is to despise the gods, to disown their country, and to regard their parents, children, and brothers as of little account. (*Histories* 5.5.1–2)

While *Gerim* does not directly call for such things, it is apparent that the Jewish way of life cut a convert off from everything and everyone who was incompatible with his/her new commitments. The narrative of Aseneth's conversion (see #3f) amply illustrates the particulars of the multiple estrangements brought on by conversion. Members of the Didache communities, needless to say, experienced the same estrangements following their conversions.

The Experience and Theology of Baptism

Theology grows out of graced experience. As such, therefore, the theology of baptism originates in the experience of baptism. In turn, the theology of baptism serves to fashion expectations and to shape the experience of those who witness and those who undergo baptism. In effect, therefore, changes in experience serve to exert pressure for redefining theology. On the other hand, changes in theology serve to exert pressure in terms of redefining the lived experience evoked by the rite.

Those who were undergoing baptism in the Didache communities were adults who were in the throes of redefining their identity, their associates, their orientation to life. The essentially social nature of human identity, especially in non-Western cultures, has been identified by Geertz (1976) and Pitt-Rivers (1977) and applied to the ancient Mediterranean context of early Christianity by Bruce Malina (1991, 1995) and others. As a result, when pagans who had been socialized into some specific form of religious orientation with its implied ethics came over to Christianity, it caused a major social upheaval. Friends and family became antagonists overnight (N. H. Taylor: 133f.). In its place, the new religious community provided an alternative set of kinship bonds that served to replace those that were being shattered. According to social scientists, therefore, baptism was "a rite of status transformation" (Ascough: 205):

> It is focused on the individual and his or her entry into the larger group. As such, it involves a transformation of the status from "non-baptized" to "baptized" and places new obligations on the individual. Even if the individual should fall out of favor with the group or reject the group, his or her status as "baptized" cannot be changed. (Ascough: 203)

When applying this to the *Didache*, the following considerations come to the fore:

1. The immersion in water at the hands of a recognized mentor had the effect of permanently and irreversibly transforming the identity of the one being baptized. The outsider became an insider. The stranger became a "brother" or "sister" (4:8). The pagan (e.g., the false worshiper devoted to Isis) became a true worshiper walking in the Way of Life. A gentile became a "servant" of the almighty Father who would soon come and gather his own into the kingdom (9:2f.).

2. When the candidate for baptism entered into the place where the community had assembled, in most instances, professed members were seeing the candidate for the first time. They had no immediate acquaintance with his/her calling (4:10) or with the transformation effected during the training period. Likewise no public inquiries were to be made into these matters prior to the rite. The mentor of the candidate, consequently, acted as a public guarantor trusted by the community and trusted by the candidate. The guarantor was trusted by the community as one who would only bring forward someone called by the Spirit and suitably trained in the Way of Life. The guarantor was trusted by the candidate as affirming "readiness" to become one with the community.

The sheer social fact of bringing the novice forward into the midst of the community had the effect of conferring honor upon the candidate. It would be to the mentor's shame if the candidate turned out to be only superficially trained or only marginally committed. Thus, in the eyes of the *Didache*, it was no accident that the mentor was understood as the one who presented "his spiritual son" or "her spiritual daughter" (3:1–6) for baptism. The transformation of social identity that occurred during the time of the apprenticeship in the Way of Life was thus the existential ground whereby the transformation of social identity in baptism could be conferred. No one came forward spontaneously asking for baptism. In every case, the candidate was led forward by his/her mentor saying, in effect, "Those of you who accept me as belonging to your family must now accept this candidate who has become my beloved son/daughter as part of your family also." In a certain sense, the mentor also stood as a guarantor before God: "You who have accepted me as your servant must now accept this child of mine as your servant also." Without a mentor acting as guarantor and sponsor, there could never be a valid baptism in any of the Didache communities (Dujarier: 298f.).

3. Since the *Didache* does not assign baptism to any specific person or class of persons, the very character of the rite as the instrument of a social transformation suggests that the mentor or spiritual parent would recite the formula (1–6) and would immerse the candidate (7:1–3). The mentor, consequently, stood for and with the candidate and ensured that the members of the community would recognize the altered status of the candidate within the rite he/she performed. The mentor, therefore, may be seen as the guarantor of the authenticity of the rite and a perpetual witness—there being no registry of baptisms. The community, in its own right, was also a perpetual witness—not so much in what it remembered as having taken place as in its full and ongoing acceptance of the one who emerged from the water as belonging to God and to them as "brother" or "sister." One can see from this, that it would be ludicrous and irresponsible for a mentor to presume to baptize someone in private. In the Didache communities, there were no "private" believers or "secret" Christians. Being a Christian meant, first and foremost, belonging to a community. The community, therefore, was present not just as a passive witness but as an active agent conferring and sanctioning the new identity that the rite effected. Without a community engagement, there could be no valid baptism.

4. By virtue of the change in social status, the newly baptized had rights that did not exist previously. The baptized would be expected to join in the community at prayer and to participate fully in the eucharistic meal. During this eucharist (as will be shown in ch. 5) the newly baptized would drink the cup of wine, which bound them to "the holy vine" (9:2, i.e., the messianic covenant), and would eat "the broken loaf" (9:4), which ensured that they would be gathered together with the elect into the kingdom of the Father on the last day (9:4). The newly baptized, moreover, could call upon the resources of the community in case of every need and, reciprocally, the members of the community could now call upon the resources of the newly baptized (4:5–8). Additionally, the newly baptized had the right to reprove wayward members (4:3) and to receive the support and admonishment of the community (4:2). And so it continued through all other aspects of community life. In sum, therefore, baptism was not the instru-

ment of a private, spiritual transformation without, at the same time, being the instrument of a permanent social transformation that implied rights and duties binding upon every member of the movement—God included.

5. Baptism effected an irreversible transformation. The newly baptized could not fall back into the status of being strangers. Even in those instances where members acted unworthy of their calling (as in cases of conflict [14:2] or of shunning [15:3]), their new identity remained. This irreversible aspect of baptism eventually gave rise to the judgment that baptism was unrepeatable and, given the Neoplatonic tendencies of Augustine, led him to speculate that the rite conferred a "spiritual character" permanently marking the soul. Even in the first century, however, no one would ever have imagined an instance when the rite of social transformation had to be repeated. Its social effects were irreversible even when its spiritual effects were largely absent.

#3N VARIOUS BAPTISMS, CONFESSION/ CONVERSION, AND FORGIVENESS

Jesus was not remembered for having performed any baptisms (Jn 4:2) or for giving his disciples any instructions as to the proper rite and theology to be assigned to baptism. In any case, Acts makes clear that the Jesus movement did practice baptism from an early period (Acts 2:37) but without any specific reference to Jesus as having originated or commissioned the rite. The postresurrection commission to baptize found on the lips of Jesus after his resurrection (Mt 28:19) is unique to Matthew's Gospel and seemingly unknown within every other stratum of the Christian Scriptures. This makes it difficult to conclude that one has here a directive that goes all the way back to the historical Jesus. Raymond Brown puts it this way:

> If that statement (Mt 28:19) were made immediately after the resurrection in precisely those words, the Book of Acts would become almost unintelligible, for then there would be no reason why Jesus' followers should have had any doubt that he wanted disciples made among the gentiles. . . . Similarly if, as suggested by the Matthean text, such a developed baptismal form as "in the name of the Father and of the Son and of the Holy Spirit" was known from the immediate days after the resurrection, the common expression that we find elsewhere in the New Testament of baptizing in the name of Jesus becomes very hard to understand. (1990: 108)

As in the case of Mt 18:15–18, the commission to baptize given by the risen Lord most probably represents the inspired author's ahistorical mode of accrediting the practice of his community at the time when the Gospel was written (70–80 C.E.). When examined carefully, therefore, the evidence does not force one to conclude that Jesus performed baptisms himself or that he commissioned others to do so.

The emergence of baptism within the early church would seem to have its historical origins in the impact that the baptism of John had upon Jesus and the early disciples of Jesus—some of whom may have been disciples of John (Jn 1:35–42). Some scholars have tried to demonstrate that the Jewish use of proselyte baptism or the Qumran use of repeated baptisms had an influence on the decision of the early church to adapt this rite for their own purposes. The greater probability, however, is that the baptism of John found in all four of the Gospel accounts represents what the evangelists regarded as the immediate antecedent of Christian baptism (Dunn 1977: 152).

John's prophetic message appears to have been a call directed toward Jews to return to the ways of the Lord in preparation for his coming—along the lines of Isaiah 40. "The baptism of John was thoroughly eschatological" (Davies: 35; Dunn 1977: 152f.). Those Jews whose hearts were rent by his call for repentance "were baptized by him in the river Jordan, confessing their sins" (Mt 3:6). Thus John's baptism appears to have entailed an actual confession of sins followed by the immersion in the flowing water. Luke, accordingly, describes it as "a baptism of repentance for the forgiveness of sins" (Lk 3:3; Acts 13:24). Thus John's baptism served to bring to full expression what his preaching evoked: (a) repentance for their wayward lives, (b) commitment to return to the ways of their Father, and (c) anticipation of the coming of the Lord who would submerge them in the Holy Spirit and/or in fire (Mt 4:11). In brief, one might say that John's baptism was an adult conversion rite that accompanied John's prophetic warnings and expectations. Those baptized went back into their local Jewish communities to bear witness to their altered lives and to await the kingdom of God.

Luke presents Peter as following much the same formula as John. Prophetic preaching (Acts 2:14–36) results in some being "cut to the heart" (Acts 2:37). They ask, "What should we do?" (Acts 2:37 = Lk 3:10) Peter's response: "Repent, and be baptized . . . so that your sins will be forgiven" (Acts 2:37). Here, again, repentance and forgiveness come together. The repentance, at this point, appears to focus on the sin of failing to recognize that "God has made him both Lord and Christ, this Jesus whom you crucified" (Acts 2:36). Peter's baptism, moreover, introduced new elements: baptism is "in the name of Jesus" (2:38), and "they devoted themselves to the apostles' teaching and fellowship, to the breaking of bread and the prayers" (2:42).

Luke later presents Peter as baptizing the household of Cornelius. This time, however, the prophetic preaching (Acts 10:34–43) leads to the out-pouring of the Holy Spirit. On the basis of this divine initiative, Peter argues that they ought to be baptized (Acts 10:47). In this context, the theme of repentance is absent. The gentiles were not bound by Torah. Nor were they expected to recognize "the message . . . sent to the people Israel" (Acts 10:36). Nonetheless, they accepted Jesus and, with ecstatic utterances, praised God (Acts 10:42f.). And while "forgiveness of sins" is mentioned in passing, it appears now to be associated with the fact that "he is the one ordained by God as judge of the living and the dead" (Acts 10:42) and that "everyone who believes in him" (Acts 10:43) and walks in his way is assured of forgiveness at the last judgment. For gentiles, there-fore, no actual confession of failings was either implied or needed.

Thus, in brief, it would seem that while the confession of sins and their forgiveness figured centrally in John's baptism of Jews, this same confes-sion fell out completely when it came to the Christian baptism of gentiles. When gentiles were baptized in Acts 10 and in the *Didache*, no confession of sins was either implied or needed prior to these baptisms. Perhaps, how-ever, there was the implied forgiveness associated with the intended con-version of life that was a prerequisite for baptism. This needs to be examined.

Within the Jewish horizon of understanding, when someone turns back to the ways of the Lord, this act of turning (designated as *teshuvah* in Hebrew) sufficed for God to forgive and, in the much stronger sense, to forget a person's sins. *The Gospel accounts never supposed that Jesus somehow brought a forgiveness to the Jewish people that was not already available to them.* If anything, the ministry of Jesus served to reawaken Jews to the incredible experience of turning back that was already part of their rich tra-dition:

> When I declared not my sin, my body wasted away
>   through my groaning all day long. . . .
> [Later] I acknowledged my sin to thee,
>   and I did not hide my iniquity;
> I said, "I will confess my transgressions to the Lord";
>   then thou didst forgive the guilt of my sin. (Ps 32:3, 5)

Jesus' parable of the prodigal son (uniquely found in Luke's Gospel) even goes to the extreme of suggesting that God pines away at home wait-ing for the sinner's return. Then, when the sinner is in sight, God sets aside his dignity and his disappointment and rushes headlong through the street in order to throw his arms around the one whom he loves. According to the parable, the son on his way home is obsessed with the notion that he has acted so shamefully as to foreclose the possibility of pardon: "Father, I have sinned against heaven and before you; I am no longer worthy to be called your son" (Lk 15:18f.). What the son fails to take into account, however, is the compassion of this father, who races out to embrace his son even before he has a chance to confess his unworthiness! The very fact of the son's turning back is enough for the father to conclude "my son was dead, and is alive again; he was lost, and is found" (Lk 15:24). In all of this there is not the slightest hint of any act of atonement or restitution being needed before forgiveness of sins can take place. In fact, the father's undignified racing to his son and kissing him on the cheek prevents the son from abasing himself by kissing the feet of his father and confessing his unworthiness.

> He [the prodigal] is shattered by his father's demonstration of love in humiliation. In his state of apprehension and fear he would naturally experience this unexpected deliverance as an utterly overwhelming event. Now he knows that he cannot offer any solution to their ongoing relationship. He sees that the point is not the lost money, but rather the broken relationship which he cannot heal. Now he understands that any new relationship must be a pure gift from his father. He can offer no solution. (Bailey: 183)

The various Christian theories of atonement whereby sins against God cannot be forgiven unless there is some prior act of restitution or atonement do not find support in Luke's Gospel and Acts. G. Voss concludes: "In Luke the death of Jesus neither has the character of a sacrifice nor is it understood as an atoning death" (cited in Fitzmyer 1979: 22). Chapter 8 will conclude that the same proposition would hold true for the *Didache* as well.

Does this mean that the forgiveness of sins is not available? Hardly. Within the Jewish horizon of understanding underlying Luke, the forgiveness of sins (even when they are not confessed) was a consequence of the turning back (*teshuvah*) that was the prerequisite for baptism: "Return to me, and I will return to you, says the Lord of Hosts" (Mal 3:7). The rite of baptism, therefore, need not be assigned an inherent power to forgive by virtue of the atoning death of Jesus; rather, baptism confirmed and celebrated the forgiveness already given by the Father due to the person's conversion (*teshuvah*) prior to the rite.

Each of the baptisms considered above can be seen as requiring a prior conversion. Those coming forward for John's baptism may not have come forward "confessing their sins" (Mt 5:6) as Matthew suggests, but, as in the case of the prodigal son, their coming forward testified to their intent to return to the ways of their Father. In Acts 2, those coming forward dissociated themselves from those who killed Jesus and embraced God's endorsement of the crucified one as "both Lord and Christ" (Acts 2:36). In Acts 10, Cornelius and his household moved from ignorance of Jesus and his role in God's plan to acceptance of him as "the one ordained by God as judge of the living and the dead" (Acts 10:42).

In the *Didache*, the candidate goes through an extensive process of learning to walk in the Way of Life prior to baptism. Thus, conversion of life rather than confession of sins is seen as the necessary prerequisite to baptism. Consider the following points:

1. The *Didache* knows full well the importance of the confession of failings before its ordinary Sunday eucharist (14:1–3). Nonetheless, at no time in the training of candidates nor prior to the rite itself does the candidate reflect upon his/her past life for the purpose of acknowledging and confessing his/her failings either to God or to a representative of the community acting in the name of the Lord.

2. The *Didache* provides no link between the mission and/or death of Jesus and the forgiveness of sins. When forgiveness of sins is spoken of, the concern is the final judgment wherein the Father will judge the living and the dead (see chs. 4 and 10). Even when anticipating the last days, members of the community were focused upon the perfection required of them for entrance into the kingdom (6:2; 16:2) and seemingly confident that God would purify them of their past sins (16:5 as will be explained in ch. 10).

3. The *Didache* knows full well that sharing resources has the effect of "ransoming your sins" (4:6), yet the giving of alms prior to baptism (1:5) is never situated within this horizon of understanding. The *Didache*, therefore, must tacitly accept the position that sins committed prior to baptism were forgiven either because of ignorance of the true God and the Way of Life he has revealed or because of the *teshuvah* ("turning toward" the Lord) implied in embracing the Way of Life (as noted above).

In rabbinic Judaism, opinion was divided as to how God regarded sins committed prior to conversion:

> Proselytes are punished [for their sins before conversion] in the opinion of Rabbi Jose; [but, on the contrary] Rabbi Judah said: He is not punished but is like a new-born child. (*Gerim* 2.60b–61a)

Presumably the opinion of Rabbi Judah was to be preferred. In any case, even in formative Judaism, very little attention was given to the issue, and it was settled by a metaphor. A gentile who converted and was baptized was regarded as someone who died and was reborn as a Jew (Daube: 111–13). "Abraham" was assigned to the "newborn," as father, and

"Sarah" as mother. All former debts and obligations were canceled—even those before the Lord. Even a former marriage was dissolved and had to be reconstituted. Consequently, like a "newborn child," the convert was entirely without history and without sin—thereby offering another insight into why no confession of sins was required nor any forgiveness of sins necessary. One might be tempted to assign this as the perspective of the *Didache*, yet this would be hazardous, for nothing in the text inclines one toward it and the rabbinic theology here is admittedly late.

Outside of Luke-Acts, various Christian modalities were put forward metaphorically describing baptism. For example, in Jn 3:3–5 and Ti 3:5–7, baptism is likened to a rebirthing process accomplished by the Spirit. In Rom 6:1–11 and Col 3:11f., baptism is likened to a dying in Christ within a funeral bath. In Eph 5:26f., baptism is likened to a bride's prenuptial bath. Here, as in 1 Cor 6:11, water's power to cleanse the body is applied to the soul as well, and the path is open to later formulations in which the waters of baptism will be spoken of as "washing away sins." The *Didache* shows no influence of Paul or John; hence, it would be inappropriate to project these notions upon those baptisms practiced within the Didache communities.

Conclusion

When treating baptism, the *Didache* placed its emphasis on right conduct. In offering practical guidance regarding baptism, the *Didache* exhibited the same penchant for specific and practical detail that we noted earlier. There is no explicit theology of baptism proposed. It is almost as though the framers of the *Didache* relied on establishing right practice with the confidence that right practice would lead to right experience, and right experience would lead to right theology. Today, of course, it is largely the other way around; hence, some sustained effort is needed if one would recapture the horizon of understanding that captivated the original framers of the *Didache*.

In terms of the specifics, the text and context allowed us to deduce that the one baptizing was the mentor and spiritual father/mother of the candidate. Having foreseen what water was to be used, the mentor began the prebaptismal fast of two days and instructed the candidate to join in solidarity with him/her. Other members of the community who had the strength to forgo eating and drinking during this period joined them. At the same time, the candidate was given the rule that would bind his/her eating for the remainder of his/her life. Effectively this rule bypassed all the particulars of the Jewish dietary regulations and settled for advising the candidate to put up with as much suspect food as he/she was able but, as the bottom line, never to eat foods known to have been sacrificed to idols (6:3). Withdrawing, then, from the table of idolaters, the candidate fasted in anticipation of joining the table of the saints.

Baptism marked a turning point. Social bonds were broken, and new ones were forged. Following baptism, every day would be spent visiting the saints and "rest[ing] upon their words" (4:2). Prior to baptism, however, most candidates probably felt the keen anticipation of entering into their new way of life along with the anxiety attendant upon such an irreversible step that would cut them off from most of their family and friends. Anticipation and anxiety dulled the desire to eat. The fast, therefore, hardly needed a theology. It was an experience looking forward to a promised future: more immediately, inclusion in the community of saints but then, more importantly, inclusion in the final gathering from the four winds into the kingdom that the Lord God would establish when he came (10:5, 16:6f.).

The clues of the *Didache* reveal the ordering of events. What is concealed from us, however, is the impact of such a life-transforming rite. One can be sure that some went down into the baptismal waters with an overwhelming joy in their hearts—they were finally coming into the spiritual family that they had always wanted, always needed, always hoped for. Others, on the other hand, might have came out of the water filled with tears of regret—they had wasted so much of their life in superstition and fear and only recently did they discover that the God who made them is a Father. Still others must have felt the heavy loss of father and mother, brothers and sisters, since they had been emotionally, religiously, and financially bound to their natural families and to their gods and now all this was "dead" to them. All in all, identities and lives were permanently changed. No matter what their age, the newly baptized were starting over in life. Everything that they hoped for and dreamed about lay before them. Their old lives died in the water and they were born into a new existence.

Any community that would thrive and survive must have soulful experiences that speak to the deepest desires of the human heart. Undoubtedly, the yearning of the soul was first recognized in the life and words of the one who was to become a spiritual parent. Many, it must be suspected, felt that their whole lives were being pulled apart and that they were receiving the Way of Life that they always yearned for and of which their own biological parents were ignorant. Fasting with one's mentor, on the other hand, was a rite that allowed for enormous amounts of introspection (esp. after the initial hunger pangs fell away). One can imagine tears and laughter, fear and anticipation, joys and sorrows racing through the hollow spaces of each candidate's heart.

Finally, there was the public rite itself. The candidate was not preoccupied with prior theological explanations of how the rite would be efficacious. Such preoccupations have the tendency to block the soul from the immediate and subliminal grace of the rite itself. Powerful rites have lasting effects that go way beyond the designs of liturgists and the analysis of theologians. And so it is that the framers of the *Didache*, in their pastoral wisdom, designated just enough to shape the rite while they allowed for that virginal openness that the Spirit might fill according to its own designs. No better rite could be hoped for. No more lasting grace could be anticipated.

4
RHYTHMS OF FASTING AND PRAYING UNTIL THE KINGDOM COMES

Rhythms of Praying

DO NOT PRAY AS THE
HYPOCRITES BUT AS THE LORD
ORDERED IN HIS GOOD NEWS. PRAY
THUS: OUR FATHER,
THE ONE IN HEAVEN, YOUR NAME
BE MADE HOLY, YOUR KINGDOM
COME, YOUR WILL BE BORN UPON
EARTH AS IN HEAVEN, GIVE US THIS
DAY OUR LOAF THAT IS COMING,
AND FORGIVE US OUR DEBT AT THE
FINAL JUDGMENT AS WE LIKEWISE
NOW FORGIVE OUR DEBTORS, AND DO
NOT LEAD US INTO THE TRIAL OF
THE LAST DAYS BUT DELIVER US FROM
THAT EVIL BECAUSE YOURS IS THE
POWER AND THE GLORY FOREVER.
THREE TIMES WITHIN THE DAY
PRAY THUS.

Contents

Section I: Analysis of Fasting

Section II: Analysis of the Daily Prayer

Section III: Analysis of the Act of Praying

Background Discussion Found in Boxes

Every religious community expresses its hopes and its aspirations through its prayers. Official prayers arise out of the hidden depths of a religious tradition and flow over the participants refreshing them with insights into the heart of their God. Caught up in the heart of God, the believer cries out, "Lord, I want to love what you love, to see what you see, to be as you are!" The believer comes away from prayer refreshed, enlightened, transformed—ready to spontaneously act in sympathy with God's way of being in the world.

On the one hand, prayer is sometimes understood as our way of kicking God into action. It is as though God somehow does not know what is needed and requires our words (and sometimes our tears) in order to spring into action. On the other hand, for those adept believers immersed in the heart of their God, the mystery is that they always pray in harmony with what God is already prepared to do. Their prayers, therefore, reveal the pathos of God. Public prayers shaped through many generations thus serve to reveal the heart of God to a new generation hungry to know what God loves and what God is prepared to do. Anyone who would understand the joys and sorrows, the hopes and concerns of a religious movement, therefore, needs to listen deeply to their prayers.

This then is the agenda of this chapter—to listen deeply to the daily public prayer shared within the Didache communities. Before doing this, however, the semiweekly practice of fasting will be considered as a community defined and community sanctioned way of intensifying their prayer.

SECTION I: ANALYSIS OF FASTING

The Rhythm of Fasting Within the Jewish Week

The *Didache* presents the practice of community fasting as follows:

(And) let ÿour fasts not stand with the hypocrites,
    for they fast on the second
        and on the fifth day of the week,
    but ÿou fast during the fourth day
        and during the Sabbath preparation day (*Did.* 8:1).

What is immediately evident is that the *Didache* used a Jewish calendar. According to this calendar, the days of the week do not have names but are numbered. In Genesis 1, for example, one hears "on the first day," "on the second day," and so forth. Nowhere in the Hebrew or Christian Scriptures does one find names for the days of the week, and, when these do appear in translations, it is only because translators decided to substitute our modern terms for the days of the week. In my translation, I have purposely retained the literal rendering of the Greek so that those depending on the English translation could immediately understand that those who followed the *Didache* were using a Jewish calendar.

The seventh day of the week is "the day of rest" or "the Sabbath" (from the Hebrew term *shabbat* meaning "to cease or desist [from work]"). The first-century Romans had a calendar of months, each consisting of twenty-eight to thirty-one days, and the days in each month were consecutively numbered. Neither the Romans nor the Greeks had a Sabbath day of rest or a seven-day week; accordingly, neither Latin nor Greek has terms for these things. Thus, the Greeks transliterated the Hebrew term *shabbat* and gave it a Greek ending (*sabbaton*) and the Romans did likewise (*sabbata*). These loanwords were used to designate the "Sabbath" (the seventh day of the week), and Greek speakers used the genitive (either the singular *sabbatou* as in Mk 16:9 or plural *sabbatōn* as in Mt 28:1) to designate the Jewish "week" of seven days (Bauer: 739).

The *Didache* indicates that semiweekly fasting was to take place on the fourth and sixth days of the week. Instead of saying, "the sixth day," however, the *Didache* uses the familiar Jewish equivalent, "the preparation [day]" (*paraskeuē* in Greek):

> It is evident that the "Preparation" had become a technical term for "the Preparation for the Sabbath." At the time of the giving of the manna, the Israelites were instructed to prepare their food for the Sabbath on the sixth day of the week (Ex 16:5, 23). By New Testament times, *paraskeuē* had become the technical term for Friday [the sixth day of the week]. (Specht: 103)

In each of the Synoptic Gospels, the day Jesus died is designated as *paraskeuē*. Mark, aware that some of his gentile readers might not be familiar with the term, wrote this: "since it was the day of preparation, that is, the day before the Sabbath" (Mk 15:42). Luke's Gospel reads: "It was the day of preparation, and the Sabbath was beginning (Lk 23:54). Thus, in both instances, "the day of preparation" (*paraskeuē*) needed explanation for Greek readers. Matthew, presuming that his readers had sufficient familiarity with Jewish usage, used the term without any explanation (Mt 27:62).

Not only did first-century Romans not have "a week"; they also calculated the beginning of each new day differently than did the Jews. According to the Romans, a new day began at midnight. According to the Jews, a new day began at sundown. Gentiles who joined the Didache community, therefore, had to recognize that the semiweekly days of fasting followed the Jewish calendar of seven-day weeks (something not noted on Roman calendars) and that any given fast day began at sundown (rather than at midnight). The fast of "the Sabbath preparation day," therefore, began at sundown on what we call Thursday and it extended to sundown of the following day.

Every gentile joining the Didache community had to become acquainted with the Jewish calendar. On the one hand, the Roman calendar continued to be important in order to know to know what civic events to expect. On the other hand, the Jewish calendar had to be consulted in order to become attuned to the seven-day cycle that governed when to fast and when to assemble for the eucharist. Thus a gentile convert had to adopt a foreign (i.e., Jewish) set of habits for ordering time in order to function as a Christian. Thus, even though the *Didache* had deliberately dropped the observance of the Jewish Sabbath (since the seventh day normally fell on a work day), the rhythms of fasting and praying of the Jesus movement were, nonetheless, maintained using the Jewish reckoning of time.

#4A KEY CHANGES IN THE ROMAN CALENDAR

Since the length of the solar year was not precisely known, it was notoriously difficult to design an adequate calendar. As the Romans were on their way to becoming a world power, Julius Caesar ordered in 45 B.C.E. a sweeping reform of the Roman calendar based on the calculations of the astronomer Sosigenes. The result was the Julian calendar, which moved the beginning of the year back to the first day of January, as opposed to the vernal equinox in later March where it had been. This new calendar consisted of twelve months, each with thirty or thirty-one days, save for February which had twenty-eight days. An extra day was added to the month of February every fourth year so as to keep pace with the solar year. Romans consulted this calendar not only in order to help determine when to begin planting but to know when the open markets were to be held (every eighth day), when the courts were to be in session, when various civic and/or religious festivals were to be held. The Julian calendar, therefore, helped to regulate society by giving everyone advanced notice as to how many days from now some anticipated event was to take place.

The Julian calendar had days and months but no weeks. In the late first century, however, the Romans adapted the cyclic seven-day week (due, in part, to Jewish influence) and divided the Roman year into fifty-two weeks. At first, the days in the weekly cycle had no special names. By the beginning of the third century, however, the familiar names of the seven heavenly bodies were used to designate the days of the week: Saturn, Sun, Moon, Mars, Mercury, Jupiter, Venus (Rordorf 1968: 24–29). The first day of the week was initially named "the day of Saturn" (= Satur + day). This day happened to fall on the Jewish Sabbath. Thus, at this point, the first day of the Roman week was the seventh day of the Jewish week. Romans were cautious to go out or to begin any new enterprise on this day. This may in part be due to Jewish custom and, in part, due to the astrological interpretation of Saturn as a "maleficent planet" (Rordorf 1968: 29). Sometime in the second century, however, "the primacy and the prestige of the day of Saturn was transferred to that of the Sun" (Bacchiocchi 1982: 140) thereby giving us the familiar notion that "the day of the sun" (Sunday) was the first day of the week. This also had the effect of aligning the beginning of each Roman week with the long-established Jewish week.

When the Julian calendar was modified to include the seven-day week, no special day within this week was designated as a festival day or as a day of rest. In the fourth century, however, this began to change. The emperor Constantine, eight years following his conversion, declared that every Sunday was to be commemorated by the closing of the civil courts. Since the "day celebrated by the veneration of the sun" (Sunday) was chosen, many Christians interpreted Constantine's decree as honoring "the Son" who rose on this day and the Father who was worshiped in the sunrise eucharist held by Christians on this day. Furthermore, Christians were already referring to the "Day of the Sun" as the "eighth day," and by this they meant the first day of the dawning of the new age when Christ would return in all his glory to establish the kingdom of God on earth. Meanwhile, the soldiers in Constantine's army understood this choice as honoring the sun god (Mithras), whom they worshiped as the supreme god. As for Constantine himself, "he did not abandon his allegiance to the Sun god, even though he regarded himself as a servant of the Christian God [after 313]" (Frend: 484). On his deathbed, Constantine was finally baptized, yet Sunday continued to be, in most instances, a regular workday. Later emperors prohibited slaves from working on that day, and the Germanic kings finally banned hard labor by everyone. Thus, one has to wait until the sixth century before the Sunday within the Roman calendar became the official day of rest.

As these innovations were introduced into the Roman calendar, Christians found themselves in a position wherein they had less need to use the Jewish calendar. Gentile converts from the second century onward, for example, had no need to master the use of the Jewish calendar, since the official Roman calendar served very well to mark the worship and fasting cycle of Christians. Only the calculation of Easter as the first Sunday following Passover required the use of the Jewish calendar. As Christians began openly to express distrust and hatred for all things Jewish, however, even this was eventually to change.

#4B SIGNIFICANCE OF THE CHOSEN DAYS FOR FASTING

The *Didache* makes clear that fasting on the second and fifth days was to be avoided in favor of the fourth and sixth days. Why did the Didache community not choose other alternative days? What significance did the fourth day have? . . . the sixth? Jean-Paul Audet rightly notes that "the precise motives which inspired the choice of these days escapes us" and that "it would be hazardous to invoke later interpretations" (1958: 368). Nonetheless, something can be gleaned by probing the logic behind the choice of certain days.

The rabbinic tradition chose the second and fifth days if and when a public fast should become necessary. No special reasons are ever given. The Mishnah, however, notes in passing that a sequence of three fasts should not begin on the fifth day "so as not to disturb market prices" (*m. Taanit* 2:9)—a very pragmatic reason. The second and fifth days are also the days when the Torah was read in the synagogue morning service (*m. Megillah* 3:6; 4:1); hence, it would follow that these would be the days when most male Jews would attend, thus providing additional pragmatic reasons for the choice of the second and fifth days.

The Mishnah notes that "members of a delegation" (*m. Taanit* 4:3) fasted on the second, third, fourth, and fifth days. Why so? The Babylonian Talmud supplies a reason:

> On the 2nd day [they fasted] for those that go down to the sea; on the 3rd day, for those who travel in the deserts; on the 4th day, that croup may not attack children; on the 5th day, for pregnant women and nursing mothers . . . ; on the 6th day they did not fast out of respect for the Sabbath. (*b. Taanit* 27b)

Here one can discover that the motive for each day of fasting changes. The presumption is that members of the delegation would change their prayer to reflect the urgent need particular to that day. It would be a mistake to imagine, however, that those fasting only on the second and fifth days cared for sea voyagers but not so much for overland travelers or that they cared for nursing mothers and not so much for sick children. All in all, the earlier tradition provides no motive as to why the second and fifth days were chosen, and, as Audet noted above, "it would be hazardous to invoke later interpretations" (1958: 368).

The Mishnah, however, does make it quite clear why the first and sixth days were not chosen. The Mishnah states: "But they do not fast on the eve of the Sabbath, because of the honor owing the Sabbath, nor on the 1st day, so as not to go forth from resting and enjoyment to travail and fasting, and so perish" (*m. Taanit* 4:3; see also Jdt 8:6). The logic here appears to be that the Sabbath needs to be cushioned on both sides by a day of ordinary eating in order that one does not suffer the ill effects that can result from moving from arduous fasting to feasting or from feasting to fasting. The assumption here is that "feasting" (or at least better than ordinary meals) took place on the Sabbath.

Since the *Didache* has chosen the sixth day for fasting, does this signal the tacit intention to "deliberately flout the Sabbath" (Draper 1983: 172)? Hardly. Members of the Didache community were not required to keep the Sabbath (see #1o). Thus, for most members of the Didache community, the seventh day would have been an ordinary workday. Not to observe the Jewish Sabbath, therefore, cannot be confused with despising the Jewish Sabbath.

In the *Apostolic Constitutions* (380 C.E.) the *Didache* is expanded by way of explaining why the fourth and the sixth day have been chosen for fasting. As in the case of the Babylonian Talmud, the later tradition supplied reasons for things which, in the earlier tradition, were left unexplained.

> On the 4th day, the condemnation of the Lord came with Judas promising the betrayal for money; . . . on the Sabbath preparation [day], the Lord suffered his passion through a cross at the hands of Pontius Pilate. (7.23.2)

These later developments could not have existed in the first century. Gentile Christians in the Didache communities would have had no awareness as to what day of the week Judas and Pilate played a role in the life of Jesus. Only after passion narratives were created and Christian feast days were instituted commemorating key events in the life of Jesus could such motivations be added to the preexisting semiweekly fast.

Must one then suppose that the framers of the *Didache* chose the alternate days at random? Not entirely. We have already established the rule of not choosing a day before or after a feast. In Chapter Eight, it will be concluded that the eucharist was a feast celebrated Saturday evenings (see #8j)—the first day of the week according to the Jewish reckoning. This being the case, days before and after would fall out as unsuitable days for fasting. This leaves only the third, fourth, fifth, and sixth days. Since the fifth corresponds to the "hypocrites," this day is also unsuitable. Meanwhile, the choice of two consecutive days would have required a fast too arduous for most members of the Didache communities. When all factors are considered, therefore, the choice would be narrowed down to either the third and sixth or the fourth and sixth. Were these two possibilities of equal weight?

Annie Jaubert believes that the choice of the fourth day may have been prompted by the importance given to that day in the solar calendar devised by the Jewish community whose library was deposited at Qumran. The calendar of these communities was as follows:

> Each year consisted of twelve months of thirty days each, plus four additional days, one of which is intercalated at the end of each three-month period. . . . New Year's Day and the first day of each three-month period always fall on a Wednesday. Wednesday is the day mandated as the first day by the creation order, since the heavenly lights—sun, moon and stars, the basis of any calendar—were created on the fourth day (Gn 1:14–19). (Eisenman and Wise: 107)

The weakness of Jaubert's hypothesis is that the fourth day was not associated with fasting and that the Qumran communities have not been demonstrated to have influenced the Didache communities. Nonetheless, Jaubert does draw attention to the fact that a segment of Judaism might well create an independent calendar for its own use. In so doing, the communities using the Scrolls retained the same cycle of Sabbaths but all other feasts fell on alternate days. Given the fact that the Qumran communities felt themselves at odds with the rest of Judaism, the choice of an alternate calendar served to demonstrate and emphasize their separation.

In the end, Jean-Paul Audet's judgment is vindicated: "The precise motives which inspired the choice of these days escapes us and . . . it would be hazardous to invoke later interpretations" (1958: 368). Given the fact that the rabbinic tradition did not assign motives for designating its days, one must be content with the *Didache* acting in like fashion. The discussion above sheds light on why certain choices were passed over, yet the precise choice of the third and sixth days over the fourth and sixth eludes us.

The Rigor and Duration of the Fast

While the *Didache* prescribes when to fast, it says nothing about how to fast. In what did this fast consist? Did it entail a complete or partial abstinence from solid food? If partial, what foods in what quantity were permitted. In the case of a complete abstinence, did this also include refraining from drinking liquids, water included? Did the fast preclude natural enjoyments such as playing games, having sexual relations, and bathing? Did the fast begin at sundown and run for twenty-four hours, or did one fast only during the daylight hours?

Given the Jewish roots of the *Didache*, it can safely be assumed that members of the *Didache* observed their fasts in the same way as did the Jews of their day. Let us then examine traditional Jewish practice. The moment that one begins to do so, however, one encounters a variety of circumstances. When fasts were called in connection with the pursuit of war, it appears as though they entailed abstaining from all food and drink from the time they were called (e.g., early morning) until sunset (Jgs 20:26; 1 Sm 14:24; 2 Sm 1:12). The solemn annual fast on the Day of Atonement, on the other hand, appears to have lasted "during the entire day," that is, sunset to sunset, since the abstaining from work and the abstaining from eating and drinking are described in the same words (Lv 23:29 and 30). In the Book of Esther, the Jewish queen advised her people to fast and pray for the success of her mission for three full days: "neither eat nor drink for three days, night or day" (Est 4:16)—night being mentioned first since in the Jewish reckoning of a full day, night comes first. Needless to say, this was a very rigorous fast, and one can presume that it was mitigated for children, nursing mothers, the sick, etc. When facing horrendous disasters, however, there were even instances in which children were forced to fast (Jdt 4:9–11; Pseudo-Philo, *Biblical Antiquities* 30:4f.). In sum:

> The overall impression is that fasting mostly consisted of abstinence from food and drink, either entire or partial, but it might also include further signs of self-abasement, such as wearing sackcloth, putting ashes on the head, not washing, not anointing, and not engaging in sexual relations. (Sanders 1990: 83)

The Mishnah, for example, prohibited bathing, body oils, sandals, and sexual relations when fasting (*m. Yoma* 8:1). In so doing, the Mishnah went beyond the normal requirement of scripture. On the other hand, the Mishnah made exceptions, even when it came to eating and drinking, when children, pregnant women, or sick persons were involved. Even someone "seized by a ravenous hunger" was permitted to break his/her fast before sundown (*m. Yoma* 8:6). Thus, the Mishnah extended the scope of fasting for some, while at the same time diminishing it for others.

The Mishnah gave special and detailed attention to those fasts associated with securing the rains needed for a successful harvest. Rain was necessary for crops, and crops were necessary for survival. When the seasonal rains failed to arrive, the first strategy was to proclaim days of public prayer. During these days of prayer, the Mishnah makes it clear that "[some] individuals began to fast" (*m. Taanit* 1:4) but that this was entirely left to an individual's discretion. Should the prayer cycle be completed and the rains still not arrive, then public fasts were specified "on Monday and Thursday and Monday" (*m. Taanit* 1:4; 2:9). The fasting served to intensify the praying. This fasting was no longer optional but was required of all able-bodied adults. If the rains still did arrive, then another cycle of three fast days was decreed, then another, then (in desperation) a cycle of seven. As the delay in the rains becomes more menacing, therefore, one discovers that the rigor of the fasting was incrementally increased:

First cycle of three days of prayer	Fasting optional—"They eat and drink once it gets dark. And they are permitted to work, bathe, anoint, put on a sandal, and have sexual relations" (*m. Taanit* 1:4).
Second cycle of three days of prayer with fasting	Fasting required of all—rigor as above (*m. Taanit* 1:5).
Third cycle of three days of prayer with fasting	Fasting required with increased rigor — "They eat and drink [only] while it is still day [on the day prior to the fast]. And they are forbidden [on the fast day] to work, bathe, anoint, put on a sandal, and have sexual relations. And they lock the bathhouses" (*m. Taanit* 1:6).
Fourth cycle of seven days of prayer with fasting	Fasting required with still more increased increased rigor —"Lo, these [days of fasting] are still more stringent than the first ones, for on these they sound the *shofar* [ram's horn], and they lock up the stores . . ." (*m. Taanit* 1:6).

One notices that, during the first and second cycles, those who are fasting abstain from food and from drink from sunrise to sunset. Before sunrise and after sunset, as practiced within the Muslim tradition, they eat. In the third and fourth cycles, however, the complete abstinence is extended throughout the night thereby extending the fast from sunset to sunset. At this point, the fast includes a prohibition to work, bathe, anoint, put on a sandal, and have sexual relations. Since, in the ancient world, the vast majority of the population bathed in public bathhouses, the practice of "lock[ing] the bathhouses" ensured that no one was able to bathe— including the minority of gentiles who lived in Jewish towns. Thus, as the delay of the seasonal rains continued, even resident foreigners were required to enter into solidarity with the Jewish population. From the Mishnah we learn that the rabbinic tradition altered the rigor of a fast according to the urgency of the situation, one must suspect that there was no hard and fast tradition as to how one should fast on all occasions.

Given the fact that no uniform standard of severity of fasting can be discovered in either the biblical traditions or in the Mishnah, it seems safe to conclude that the *Didache* also envisioned the use of discretion when it came to fasting. This can be learned not only from the fact that no rules were given defining the rigor of the fasting but, in addition, when it came to fasting in solidarity with novices, the *Didache* suggests that "if any others have the strength, let them fast also" (7:4). Presumably, individual members decided whether they had "the strength" and acted accordingly. The same thing holds true for the prebaptismal fast: "Order the one being baptized to fast during one or two days" (7:4). In this case, the mentor was to use his/her discretion in deciding the length of the fast to be imposed on the novice. From this it would follow that the mentor also used discretion in stipulating the rigor of the fast. Someone of frail health or someone required to cut stone ten hours a day, therefore, might be given a rule for fasting that would vary considerably from someone of robust constitution who decorated pottery or wove cloth for a living. One can further surmise that the fasting performed after baptism followed the same standards of performance that were set for the novice in their prebaptismal fast. If this was indeed the case, then it would be most natural for no hard and fast rule governing the severity of the fast to be defined, since each one had a personal rule that took into account different circumstances.

#4c THE INTIMATE LINK BETWEEN FASTING AND PRAYING IN JUDAISM

Within the Jewish horizon of understanding, fasting and praying are intimately linked. There are numerous illustrations of this link in the Hebrew Scriptures (e.g., Jer 14:11–12; Neh 1:4; Ezra 8:21–23). Two cases close to the time of the *Didache* serve to illustrate this link:

1. The fictional story of the conversion of Aseneth (c. 100 B.C.E.) considered in the last chapter (#3f), provides a particularly striking example of how fasting during the time of distress leads to prayer. Aseneth, following the onset of her deep conversion upon hearing the words of Joseph, is so unsettled that she cannot eat or sleep. Furthermore, she removes all her adornments, dresses in black mourning clothes, wraps sackcloth around her waist, and sprinkles herself with ashes (*Joseph and Aseneth* 10:9–17)— all images signaling to the Jewish reader familiar aspects of the rite of fasting. During the complete fast over seven days, she does not and cannot

pray. After sunset, however, at the beginning of "the eighth day" (11:1), "she stretched out her hands toward the east, and her eyes looked up to heaven" (12:1)—more images signaling to the reader that here one has a "Jewish" woman praying to God in her extreme distress.

The experience of Aseneth finds a fitting parallel in the *Didache*. The prebaptismal fasting signals the final withdrawing from the protection of the novice's traditional gods (*Did.* 6:3). Meanwhile, the novice is effectively forlorn—without identity, without family, without protectors save his/her mentor. During this time, one will note that the novice is not particularly urged to pray. In fact, the novice cannot pray, for, as yet, he/she is a stranger to the true God. Only after the identity transformation of baptism, can the newly baptized pray "Our Father"—and this is precisely the first prayer that he/she will pray surrounded by his/her new "family." Thus, as in the case of Aseneth, the distress of conversion leads to fasting, and the rite of fasting leads to praying.

2. Within the Mishnah (c. 200 C.E.), the section on fasting is almost entirely occupied with how fasting and praying are to be handled in the case when the seasonal rains do not begin at the expected time. In this chapter, it was shown how, when "near [the time of] rain" (*m. Taanit* 1:2), prayer for rain was first allowed. If the rains fail to materialize, then the community undertook a cycle of official prayers with optional fasting (Monday, Thursday, Monday) (1:4). Then, if two weeks pass and no rain comes, "the court decrees a sequence of three fasts for the whole community" (1:5). The table above showed how, with each new sequence of fasts, the rigor of the fast was increased.

When the Mishnah describes the rite of beginning a fast, the intimate link between fasting and praying again becomes evident:

> They [the elders] bring forth the ark [containing the scrolls of Torah] into the street of the town and put wood ashes on (1) the ark, (2) the head of the patriarch, and (3) the head of the court. And [then] each person puts ashes on his head. [Then] the eldest among them makes a speech of admonition . . . (based on Jon 3:10 and Jl 2:13). [Then] *they arise for prayer.* . . . (*m. Taanit* 2:1f.)

The rites that accompany the onset of a public fast (as just cited) presuppose that the ashes (associated with the beginning of fasting) lead to admonitions to seek the Lord's help which erupts into prayer. The prayer leader—"an experienced elder, who has children, and whose cupboard is empty, so that his heart should be wholly in the prayer" (*m. Taanit* 2:2)—is deliberately chosen with this in mind. The man is someone adept in prayer whose children cry to him in their hunger and, since his cupboard is empty, he has nothing to offer them. Such a one would surely have "his heart wholly in the prayer." The act of community fasting ensures that everyone (even those who have sufficient supplies stored away) would enable everyone to put heart wholly into his/her prayer.

Fasting in Judaism has no association with self-mastery or with the ascetic disciplining of bodily appetites. Nor does one find many instances in which fasting is undertaken by Jews in order to evoke prophetic experiences (as will be explained in ch. 6). Fasting in Judaism, therefore, is most commonly associated with preparing for and intensifying prayer, especially in times of distress.

Solidarity in Fasting and Praying

Solidarity in fasting was of much greater significance in the ancient world than the rigor of the fast itself. When the troops of Nebuchadnezzar surrounded Jerusalem, for instance, the author of the Book of Judith wrote as follows:

> And every man of Israel cried out to God with great fervor, and they humbled themselves *with much fasting*. . . . They even draped the altar with sackcloth and cried out in unison, praying fervently to the God of Israel not to allow their infants to be carried off and their wives to be taken as booty, and the towns that they had inherited to be destroyed, and the sanctuary to be profaned and desecrated to the malicious joy of the gentiles. (4:9, 12)

Not to have taken part in this fast would have been tantamount to signaling that one had no solidarity with this hope and with this prayer.

The same thing could be said with the various fasts described in the Mishnah relative to the delay of the seasonal rains. During the first cycle of prayers, it was noted that fasting was undertaken at each individual's discretion (*m. Taanit* 1:4). If no rain came, however, then "the court [of town elders] decrees a cycle of three fasts" (*m. Taanit* 1:5). Participation, at this point, was required by all able-bodied adults irrespective of whether one was directly involved in agriculture or not. Solidarity in fasting and solidarity in prayer were expected of the entire community. For someone not to participate in the public fasts (made visible by the ashes on their heads) would be tantamount to declaring oneself cut off from this people.

Even when a public threat was not perceived, community fasting was generally required by virtue of solidarity. On the Day of Atonement (Yom

Kippur), for instance, no public danger was normally identified since it arrived at a fixed day each year. Nonetheless, nonparticipation was intolerable:

> For anyone who does not fast during the entire day shall be cut off from the people. And anyone who does any work during the entire day, such a one I [the Lord] will destroy from the midst of the people. (Lv 23:29f.)

This can be directly applied to the *Didache*. Solidarity in fasting was much more imperative than defining a uniform rigor to be used in this fasting. Furthermore, the act of changing the days of the semiweekly fast had the effect of saying to those named as the "hypocrites" that "we have no solidarity with your hopes and your prayers." What then? Our semiweekly fast stands in solidarity with "our hopes and prayers," which we define apart from you (*Did.* 8:3). Once one discovers the heart of the matter, it becomes even clearer why the rigor of the fast is quite secondary to the days chosen and the prayers used.

Whether the Didache's "Hypocrites" Are Matthew's Pharisees

Fasting and praying in the *Didache* are immediately addressed in the context of avoiding solidarity with the "hypocrites" (8:1f.). No attention whatsoever was given to spelling out either a higher motive or a tougher standard (cf. 1:3) when it came to fasting. The sole emphasis was that "our" fasts on the fourth and sixth day of the week served to dissociate us from the "hypocrites" who fasted on the second and fifth. Who were these "hypocrites"?

Most scholars equate these "hypocrites" with the Pharisees. Why so?

1. The Pharisees and scribes are repeatedly branded as "hypocrites" in Matthew's Gospel (Mt 6:2, 5, 16; 15:7; 22:18; 23:13, 15, 23, 25, 27, 29; 24:51). Most scholars, assuming that the Didache community used Matthew's Gospel, therefore conclude that the "hypocrites" named in the *Didache* relative to fasting and praying are the same group named by Matthew.

2. The Pharisee, in the parable found uniquely in Luke's Gospel, takes pride in saying, "I fast twice a week" (Lk 18:12). The *Didache*, for its part, suggests that the "hypocrites" fasted twice a week—on the second and fifth days. The Mishnah, curious enough, does not specify a tradition of fasting twice a week. When it comes to the failure of rains to arrive in due season, however, the days of public prayer and fasting were "on the 2nd and 5th

and 2nd day of the week" (*m. Taanit* 1:4; 2:9)—the same days as noted in the *Didache*. Since many scholars assume that the Pharisees gave rise to the rabbinic tradition of the Mishnah, they presume that the Pharisees of the first century fasted on the second and fifth days and, consequently, were to be identified as the "hypocrites" with whom the Didache community wishes to dissociate itself.

I am indebted to Willy Rordorf for consistently and perceptively demonstrating that the "hypocrites" of the *Didache* cannot be equated with the "hypocrites" of Matthew's Gospel. Rordorf, in his latest study says: "Assuredly this term designates the Jews in the Gospel of Matthew, but it has a sense radically different in the *Didache*" (1998: 224). I would elaborate and extend Rordorf's argument as follows:

1. The Pharisees in Matthew's Gospel are called "hypocrites" because of the way they exhibited their fasting in public:

> And whenever you fast, do not look dismal, like the hypocrites, for they disfigure their faces so as to show others that they are fasting. Truly I tell you, they have received their reward. But when you fast, put oil on your head and wash your face, so that your fasting may be seen not by others but by your Father who is in secret; and your Father who sees in secret will reward you. (Mt 6:16–18)

The complaint of Matthew is that the Pharisees are "hypocrites" because they show off their fasting and thereby receive their reward (public acclamation) immediately. Matthew's community, on the other hand, is instructed to fast in secret (by washing and grooming as on other days) and thereby receive their reward in heaven.

Matthew's critique and solution have nothing to do with the *Didache*. The *Didache* says nothing of fasting to gain public acclaim. Nor does the *Didache* propose that the Christian ought to fast in secret. Rather, the solution was to publicly fast on different days—thereby dissociating themselves from the prayer and the hope of the "hypocrites."

Furthermore, as will be shown in chapter 11, the *Didache* does not share or make use of any of the known Gospels; hence, it cannot be supposed that the name calling in the Synoptics is any indication whatsoever of the name calling of the *Didache*. Just because magician James Randi has been able to expose some faith healers as "fakes" and a jeweler refers to my gemstone as a "fake" does not mean that some faith healers are gemstones.

2. Nothing in the Gospels or the Mishnah includes any hint that the Pharisees distinguished themselves by fasting, whereas the rest of the Jewish population failed to fast or fasted on different days. Furthermore, from the evidence of the Mishnah, it would appear that public fasts began on the

second day of the week because this was a day on which Jews normally assembled in town for the public reading of the scriptures (*m. Megillah* 3:6–4:1) and that public fasts normally began with a procession of "the ark into the streets of the town" (*m. Taanit* 2:1). The fifth day was a market day. The Mishnah advises that public fasts ought not to begin on the fifth day "so as not to disturb market prices" (*m. Taanit* 2:9). Since the fifth day, being a market day, relieved many people from a full day of hard work, and since it was a day when Jews assembled in town, not only for the market but also for the reading of the scriptures, this was a natural choice for the second day of the semiweekly fasting. When a public fast was in effect, therefore, it was evident that the Jews who assembled fasted in solidarity, irrespective of whether they were Pharisees or not.

The practice of placing "ashes on his/her head" (*m. Taanit* 2:1) undoubtedly had the effect of broadcasting the beginning of a cycle of fasts, since those who were not present (e.g., women occupied with children in the home) would immediately learn of the public fast upon seeing the ashes. Nonetheless, all of these traditions of fasting named in the Mishnah appear to have evolved from the common practice of Jews over a period of time and cannot be limited as particular practices employed exclusively by the Pharisees.

Quite possibly, Matthew is referring to ashes placed on the head (*m. Taanit* 2:1) when he speaks of Pharisees as "disfiguring their faces so as to show others that they are fasting" (Mt 6:16). Even supposing that Pharisees and other Jews used ashes in order to herald the beginning of a public fast, it cannot be determined that this practice was necessarily always to be branded as hypocritical and that every Pharisee was motivated by the desire to "be seen by men" (Mt 6:17).

In any case, the solution of Matthew's Jesus is that the disciples of Jesus should "put oil on your head and wash your face" (Mt 6:17) so as to not to signal one's fasting. In saying this, Matthew seemingly allows and encourages solidarity in fasting on the days ordained (most probably the second and fifth). The *Didache*, in contrast, says nothing about ashes or oil, but affirms two distinct days for fasting—thereby breaking solidarity with the remainder of the fasting community, which must have included more than just Pharisees.

All in all, therefore, when *Did.* 8:1 is compared with Matthew, one quickly detects that the *Didache* has an agenda and an internal logic quite distinct from that of Matthew's Gospel. The objection of Jesus to the "hypocrites" in the Gospel of Matthew is directed toward "the how" of fasting. In the *Didache*, one finds nothing of this. The *Didache* objects to "the when" of fasting. How "the hypocrites" fast is presumed to be equivalent to how "the saints" fast. In sum, the identity of the "hypocrites" in the *Didache* cannot be revealed by an examination of Matthew's Gospel.

#4D WORD STUDY: "HYPOCRITE"

The word translated as "hypocrite" (*hypokritēs*) has a variety of meanings in Greek. The term can refer to an "interpreter" or "expounder," yet most often it refers to an "actor" on stage who makes his audience believe he is someone else, namely, the character he is portraying in the drama. The term "hypocrite," therefore, can have positive connotations.

In the Septuagint, on the other hand, *hypocritēs* is normally used to render the Hebrew term *hanef*, which brands an opponent as committing "every impiety" (Rordorf 1978a: 164 n. 2; Draper 1996c: 232) or as being "a deviant" (Niederwimmer 1998: 131). Thus, leaving aside positive meanings, the Greek term *hypocritēs* began to take on strong negative connotations among Greek-speaking Jews. In the case of Matthew, therefore, it is not surprising that he uses the word habitually with a negative connotation. Actors or interpreters are no longer involved. Rather, the term refers to non-actors who represent themselves publicly as being pious whereas, in actual fact, they are frauds. Thus, in Matthew's Gospel, for example, the Pharisees "disfigure their faces that their fasting may be seen by men" (Mt 6:16). Fasting, if it is intended to intensify one's prayer to God, needs not have any external display. Jesus, therefore, requires his disciples to pray and fast in secret that "your Father who sees in secret will reward you" (Mt 6:18).

The offensive conduct of the "hypocrites" in the *Didache* is not specified. Are they pious frauds? Possibly. In chapter 13, this topic will be taken up in detail, and it will be concluded that the "hypocrites" in the *Didache* were Jewish Christians bent on introducing gentile converts to their temple piety out of dangerously mixed motives.

Whether "Hypocrites" Promoted Temple Piety

The *Didache* does not offer any plausible reason why those fasting on the second and the fifth days can be judged "hypocrites" (8:2f.). Rordorf, after carefully setting aside misleading evidence from Matthew, conjectures that the *Didache*'s "hypocrites" are "Jewish-Christians who remain attached to the ritual practices of Judaism" (Rordorf 1998: 224, 1978b: 37). But one has to be careful here, for, as Rordorf correctly notes, semiweekly fasting and praying three times each day are "ritual practices of Judaism" (1998: 224). Thus, this explanation has not found much acceptance (Draper 1996c: 233), and most scholars retain the notion that "hypocrites" refers to pious Jews generally who have refused to accept the Gospel (Audet 1958: 367f.; Harnack 1884: 24f.). Niederwimmer, in like fashion, believes the term "is probably a general reference to the pious of Israel" without

referring to "Pharisees in particular" (1998: 131f.). Others, cit
dence that the semiweekly fasting and praying three times each
characteristic of all Jews, believe that "hypocrites" must "mo
refer to Pharisees in particular" (Draper 1996c: 233). None of
jectures, however, takes note of the fact that the *Didache* nowh ͜ ͜ ͜ ͜ws
any sharp hostility toward the Jews in general or toward the Pharisees in
particular. All of these conjectures, therefore, fall flat.

Chapter 13 endeavors to analyze the clues of the *Didache* within a historical context in order to discover the identity of the "hypocrites." At the
end of this study, it will be concluded that the *Didache*'s "hypocrites" were
Jews (many of them Christians) who promoted temple piety among gentile converts for mixed motives. Temple sacrifices were a traditional,
divinely approved, evocative aspect of Jewish piety. During the 40s and
50s, when troubles periodically erupted that pitted the Romans against the
temple traditions, the prospect of gentiles endorsing and/or participating
in these rites served to legitimate and to lend support to the Jewish cause
vis-à-vis the Romans. The *Didache*, consequently, branded those Jews and
Jewish Christians who encouraged gentile converts to pray and fast for the
temple as "hypocrites" insofar as they mixed the worship of God with
political and social advantage.

The framers of the *Didache* wished to remove entirely the name of Jesus
from any and every attachment to temple sacrifices. In so doing, they
hoped to free gentile converts from the dangerous mixture of politics and
piety that surrounded the Jerusalem temple. To effect this change, the
framers of the *Didache* deliberately removed the temple from their vision
of God's future (8:3; 9:4; 10:3–6; 13:3f.; 16:3–8) and altered the days of
fasting and words of praying so as to promote anticipation of "your kingdom come" devoid of any expectations for the temple or for Jerusalem.
When the clues are fleshed out against the backdrop of the *Didache*, one
can see that the term "hypocrite" in the *Didache* emerged out of a set of
concerns quite different from those issues named in Matthew's Gospel.

The framers of the *Didache* blotted out the historical importance of the
temple sacrifices and the temple establishment from God's future. This
bold revision had the effect of deeply disturbing the links between the
Jesus movement and Judaism. In many ways this bold revision was comparable to what the Protestant reformers did when they reverted to a New
Testament image of Christianity in order to erase the historical importance
of the papacy. One might even be tempted to say that the framers of the
Didache foresaw the bloody clash with the Romans that was sure to come
and that they rendered the Didache communities religiously indifferent to
the fate of Jerusalem.

Once the temple was actually destroyed by the Romans in 70 C.E.,
priestly power and divinely authorized sacrifices became moot issues. At
this point, it was possible to present Jesus as countering his own disciples'

admiration for the temple buildings with the dire prediction that "there will not be left here one stone upon another; all will be thrown down" (Mk 13:2; Mt 24:2; Lk 21:6). It is telling that neither the Pharisees nor the priests but Jesus' own disciples who spontaneously gave voice to their admiration of the temple (Mk 13:1 and par.). It was to them, therefore, that Jesus predicted "not one stone will be left here upon another" (Mk 13:2 and par.). This may be a recollection of the fact that the voices of temple admiration came out strong among those who called themselves "disciples." Also significant is Mark's portrait of Jesus as unwilling to offer sacrifice in the temple and as bent on preventing others from doing so as well (Mk 11:15f.). Only after the temple was destroyed could Luke edit Mark with a striking pro-temple introduction to his Gospel. It would appear that Jesus could now be positively associated with the temple because the Romans had once for all eliminated the danger and intrigue mixed into temple piety. John's Gospel, of course, completes this cycle by having Jesus go up to the Jerusalem temple to participate in all of the major Jewish feasts. All in all, therefore, the Gospels, when read against their historical background, may provide a way of understanding how the *Didache*'s bold revision against temple piety and its "hypocrites" continued to play itself out in the anti-temple portrait of Jesus in Mark—a portrait that was softened by Matthew and Luke and practically turned on its head by John. Needless to say, more study is imperative on this issue and there is insufficient time and space to pursue it here.

#4E WHETHER THE *DIDACHE* REVEALS AN ANTI-JEWISH BIAS

Does the *Didache* betray early signs of anti-Judaism? Some scholars believe so. For example, Clayton Jefford writes that "one already detects the presence of a fervent anti-Jewish element" in the *Didache*. He explains himself as follows:

> Thus, in 7.2 the ritual laws of Baptism concerning "running water" are emended. Also, in 8.1 the reader is exhorted not to fast "with the hypocrites" on Mondays and Thursdays. . . . Apart from these two pericopae, the *Didache* does not seem concerned to attack Judaism or Jewish Christianity. (Jefford 1989a: 133)

This judgment of Jefford is misleading. The issue of "running water" need not be interpreted as anti-Jewish; on the contrary, as suggested earlier, with the advent of proselyte baptism, Jews themselves might have engaged in discussion as to what sort of water suffices (since nothing of this is touched on in the Hebrew Scriptures). As for the "hypocrites," Jefford is unable to distinguish between the "hypocrites" of Matthew's Gospel and those of the *Didache* (as spelled out in this chapter) since he presumes that the *Didache* was created for use by the community that had the Gospel of Matthew. This viewpoint has been amply refuted by the text.

Even if the *Didache* did use Matthew's Gospel, Jefford fails to allow for the possibility of intra-Jewish conflict without presuming that either side is "attacking Judaism" as such. Jefford, therefore, not only fails to recognize the Jewish character of Matthew's community, but he finds "anti-Jewish element[s]" in areas where he ought to suspect that rival interpretations of Judaism were at play. Anthony Saldarini captures a corrected understanding of Matthew when he writes as follows:

> In order to judge where Matthew stands in relation to Judaism, an accurate description of the diversity within the first-century Jewish community in the Roman Empire must be developed. . . . Only then will the further explorations of the text show in detail that the teaching of the Gospel of Matthew fits within the compass of first-century Judaism. Though the author affirms the centrality of Jesus Christ as Son of God and Savior, this affirmation does not in his eyes contradict an authentic Jewish interpretation of the bible or the Jewish way of life. . . . The author is well aware of the tensions and conflicts which have plagued his group's relationship with the larger Jewish community, but he does not yet consider his to be a different religion from Judaism. (11f.)

These words could equally be applied to the *Didache*. The Jewish framers of the *Didache* clearly thought of themselves as offering a divinely sanctioned program whereby gentiles could walk in the Way of Life and find full inclusion when God comes to establish his kingdom on earth. When one reads the explanation in #1o, for instance, one discovers how informed Jews could sanction a gentile inclusion into the heritage of Israel without imposing Sabbath and food regulations. Future chapters will continue to demonstrate how positively the *Didache* is oriented toward Judaism, its election, and its hopes.

If I were to search for an arena in which the framers of the *Didache* appear to forfeit their Jewish identity, I would begin by noting the radicalness with which the Jerusalem temple and temple sacrifice have been effaced from God's future. Curiously Jefford does not even appear to recognize how radical a step the *Didache* was making on this point. Like it or not, the temple was the social, historical, political, and divinely sanctioned center of Judaism, and nearly every Jewish eschatology gave this temple (reconstructed) a key role in God's future. For the moment, however, I leave this aside. A fuller treatment of the topic will be taken up in chapter 13. For the moment, however, it suffices to recognize that the Christianity of the *Didache* would have been formulated by and endorsed by many (but not all) Jews as God's revealed plan through his servant Jesus for the salvation of the gentiles. Jefford is misinformed when he "detects the presence of a fervent anti-Jewish element" in the *Didache*.

SECTION II: ANALYSIS OF THE DAILY PRAYER

The Rule of Daily Praying the Lord's Prayer

When it came to praying, the framers of the *Didache* took great pains to offer an alternative prayer to that used by "the hypocrites. Three times a day, the prayer "the Lord commanded" (8:2) was to be recited. The use of the plural in both the instruction and the prayer itself probably indicates that a group recitation was implied. This would not mean that the entire community would gather three times each day; two or three members would suffice. The framers of the *Didache* found no need to define those times during the day when these prayers were to take place. The silence of the *Didache* on this point suggests that everyone was familiar with those times owing to the practice of the community. Following Bradshaw, "the times were traditional and unchanged, and so need not explicit mention" (1982: 26). Here again, one can presume that the rhythms of prayer were taken over from Judaism, and one can accordingly learn something of the practice of the *Didache* by examining first-century Judaism.

In chapter 1, the training anticipated in the Way of Life was shown to have been crafted for both men and women. The same observation can now be applied to the fasting and the daily praying. Unlike in the case in formative Judaism where only men were obliged to pray three times each day, the *Didache* makes no provisions for dispensing women from the obligation and the privilege of standing before the Lord and addressing him directly as "Father."

One can presume that children were encouraged to pray with their parents when the occasion brought them together during the time of prayer. Children, it will be remembered, were not admitted to baptism; hence, there would have been no obligation for them to pray three times each day. Children both then and now enjoy imitating and participating in those skills exhibited by their parents. Hence, when their mother would pray, her children would undoubtedly participate according to their ability. Nothing in the *Didache* suggests that children would not be allowed to observe or participate in such prayers. In fact, such shared prayers would undoubtedly have formed part of the occasion of "train[ing] them in the fear of God" (4:9).

#4F DAILY PRAYER IN FIRST-CENTURY JUDAISM

The revolution brought about by the Pharisees offered Jews a new framework for worship. When the temple was rebuilt (520 B.C.E.) following the Babylonian deportation, the Aaronide priesthood became the political and religious leaders of Israel. The sacrificial system within the temple served to centralize Jewish worship under the direction of the Jewish priests. When these same priests later capitulated to Hellenism, the Maccabean revolt occurred (167 B.C.E.). Following in the footsteps of this revolt, the Pharisees challenged the leadership of the temple priests by taking steps to decentralize Jewish worship. According to the Pharisees, each and every Jew had the right, even the obligation, to directly contact God in their homes, in their shops, in their synagogues.

> This was truly a revolutionary step, for nowhere in the Pentateuch is prayer obligatory. Although prayer may indeed have been as old as Israel, it had never been required by law. The Pharisees were therefore once again going off on a highly original tack when they made mandatory the saying of the *Shema*—"Hear O Israel, the Lord is our God, the Lord is one"—in the morning and evening, and when they introduced the recitation of the prayer now called the *Amidah* or *Shemoneh Esreh* as the prayer par excellence, when they required each individual to utter benedictions before meals, after meals, and on other occasions. (Rivkin 1971: 58)

Both the rabbinic tradition and the early church were born out of the Pharisaic revolution. It is no surprise, therefore, that the rabbis required all male Jews to recite the Eighteen Benedictions or an "abstract thereof" (*m. Berakhot* 4:3) three times a day (4:1, 7). The *Didache*, in its own turn, requires all members to recite the Lord's Prayer "three times within the day" (8:3).

The *Manual of Discipline* found at Qumran, in turn, prescribed that new members were to be trained to . . .

> . . . speak of [God] and bless him [with an offering] of the lips during the times that he ordained:
> [a] at the beginning of light
> during it coming round;

> [b] when it withdraws itself
> to its own dwelling. (1QS 9.26–10.2)

While some scholars interpret "during its coming round" as referring to the noonday prayer ("the middle of its course") given three times (Jan van der Ploeg), most scholars agree that the *Manual of Discipline* intended only two times for daily prayer (André Dupont-Sommer, Millar Burrows). Even in the rabbinic tradition, it appears as though the obligatory prayers were recited only twice each day, as in the case of *Shema* (Dt 6:4–9), which was recited "when you lie down and when you rise" (Dt 6:7) (Beckwith: 73).

The origins of the third time for prayer—the noonday prayer—are not clear. According to some, the times of prayer originated so as to allow the daily prayers to correspond to the times when sacrifices on behalf of the entire people were being offered in the Jerusalem temple (Beckwith: 72f.). Quite early, moreover, one finds in Ps. 55:17 allusions to praying at "evening, morning, and at noon," and Daniel testifies to praying "three times a day" (Dn 6:10, 13). Even before the Mishnah was written down (c. 200 C.E.), therefore, it would appear that some Jews were in the habit of praying, despite the evidence of Qumran, three times each day: at sunrise, at noon, and at sunset. The *Didache* probably presumes that the local Jewish tradition known to its framers sanctioned praying three times each day. Otherwise, there would have been some indication that a third time of prayer was being added and that it would take place at noon.

Prayer traditions, in both Jewish and Christian settings, were perfected in practice and passed on orally. Thus, in both the Mishnah and in the *Didache*, the specific details regarding the posture, the direction, and the modality of innovating on prayer themes are not discussed. In each case, one finds only passing references to schematic outlines that guided the free-flowing and innovative powers of the prayer leader (more on this later). By the time of the Mishnah, for example, rabbinic Judaism habitually used Eighteen Benedictions (*m. Berakhot* 4:3; *m. Taanit.* 2:2) in its daily prayer; however, one finds written statements defining the names (but not the full set of words) for the first three, the last three, and three others (*m. Berakhot* 5:2; *m. Yoma* 7:1; *m. Rosh Hashanah* 4:5; *m. Sotah* 7:7; *m. Tamid* 5:1). Furthermore, while these are referred to as benedictions, they include petitions (just as does the second half of the Lord's Prayer):

> The first three and penultimate benedictions do, in fact, consist of praise and thanksgiving, and not of petition, but the remaining benedictions are petitionary, and only justify their title because they close with a sentence blessing God that he does in fact give the benefits (forgiveness, the fruits of the earth, the restoration of Israel, or whatever it might be) for which the benediction was asked. (Beckwith: 77)

While it cannot be presumed that the Mishnah presents the universal practice of all Jews during the first century, the appeal to oral prayers known by all would incline one to imagine that a tradition of prayer existed in the synagogues that was not the exclusive preserve of the rabbinic tradition. Thus, it might be more proper to imagine that the rabbis gradually regulated those prayers that, for the most part, they did not necessarily originate.

The *Didache*, in contrast, would appear to want to remove its adherents from prayers of the "hypocrites" and to bind its members to use the Lord's Prayer. Even this prayer is not the creation of the framers of the *Didache*. They, too, call forward a prayer tradition that flourished among segments of the Jesus movement. The character of this prayer vis-à-vis the Eighteen Benedictions will be examined shortly.

The Various Versions of the Lord's Prayer

The Lord's Prayer in the *Didache* has a structure very close to that of the prayer found in Matthew's Gospel (Mt 6:9–13). There are only three small variations. Luke's version of the prayer (Lk 11:2–4) is shorter and manifests adaptations in harmony with the themes in his Gospel. Using the NRSV translation as a guide, one has the following:

Matthew	*Didache*	Luke
Our Father in heaven,	Our Father in heaven,	Father
hallowed be your name. Your kingdom come. Your will be done, on earth as it is in heaven.	hallowed be your name. Your kingdom come. Your will be done, on earth as it is in heaven.	hallowed be your name Your kingdom come.
Give us this day our daily bread. And forgive us our debts, as we also have forgiven our debtors. And do not bring us to the time of trial, but rescue us from the evil one.	Give us this day our daily bread And forgive us our debt, as we also forgive our debtors. And do not bring us to the time of trial, but rescue us from the evil one because yours is the power and the glory forever.	Give us each day our daily bread And forgive us our sins, for we ourselves forgive everyone indebted to us. And do not bring us to the time of trial.

Raymond E. Brown correctly notes that "the standard English form of the Lord's Prayer scarcely renders justice to the Greek" (1961: 179); hence, the translation I prefer in order to take note of the consistent end-times orientation of the prayer is as follows:

Our Father, the [one] in heaven,
your name be made holy,
your kingdom come,
your will be done on earth as in heaven,
give us this day our futuristic loaf,
and forgive us our debt [at the final judgment]
 as we likewise [now] forgive our debtors,
and let us not fail in the trial [of the last days]
 but deliver us from evil
because yours is the power and the glory forever.

#4G WHETHER THE *DIDACHE*'S LORD'S PRAYER WAS A VARIATION OF MATTHEW'S

Prayers recited by the entire community, even if they are not written down, are effectively established and known by all. Nonetheless, it is interesting to note that the Gospel of Matthew presents Jesus as training his disciple in words (Mt 6:9–13) that closely approximate *Did.* 8:2. The two versions diverge in four places: (a) the *Didache* identifies the Father as "in (the) heaven" instead of "in the heavens"; (b) the *Didache* petitions that "our debt" be forgiven and not "our debts"; (c) the *Didache* has *aphiemen* (as "we forgive" in the present tense instead of the aorist *aphēkamen* (as "we forgave"); and, finally, (d) the *Didache* omits "the kingdom" in the closing doxology. Some ancient manuscripts present the Gospel of Matthew without this doxology. This probably means that the doxology was added during the time of its liturgical usage and that such usage prompted copyists to complete Matthew's text with the well-known doxology.

How significant are these variants? Variant (a) merely represents an alternative way to designate "heaven." Helmut Koester has identified Matthew's preference for "heavens" as a mark of editorial activity (Mt 5:12 = Lk 6:23; Mt 7:11 = Lk 11:13; Mt 19:21 = Mk 10:21) (Koester 1990: 206). The next two variants fit well the context of the *Didache*. *Didache* 1:5 speaks of a debt (singular) which must be repaid to the Lord in the end times. According to the *Didache*, forgiveness of that "debt" is petitioned according to the measure that we "forgive our debtors." The present tense implies repeated action. The plural "debtors" makes reference to the many persons who request our forgiveness. Jonathan Draper rightly notes that the tendency would be "to envision a progression from the singular to the plural" and not the other way around (1983: 174). The use of the aorist in Matthew, "as we forgave," would normally imply a single act of forgiveness localized in the past—a situation that does not usually prevail. Finally, with respect to variant (d), the absence of "the kingdom" is evident also in the eucharistic doxologies of 9:5 and 10:4. This addition hardly seems necessary, since the kingdom was previously acknowledged as belonging to the Father in the body of the prayer. All in all, the *Didache*'s version of the Lord's Prayer is linguistically superior and better suited to the internal logic of the *Didache* itself.

The close approximation between Matthew and the *Didache* ought not to be interpreted as pointing to some literary dependence of one upon the other:

> According to *Did*. 8:3, the [Lord's] Prayer is repeated three times a day by every Christian, and it is absurd to imagine that [the framers of the] *Didache* would need a written source for a prayer so familiar to the community. The Prayer would already have had a fixed and tenacious liturgical form such that even minor variations would be significant. (Draper 1983: 174f.)

Following this logic, it would seem that any community that already had and used the Gospel of Matthew could hardly be expected to receive a "*Didache*" in which its own version of the Our Father was not operative. In effect, therefore, the small variations between the Gospel of Matthew and the *Didache* would argue forcefully against the possibility that any community embracing Matthew's Gospel could have created the *Didache*. Further details are found in chapter 11.

#4H WHETHER THE LORD'S PRAYER WAS AN ADAPTATION OF A SYNAGOGUE PRAYER

All scholars acknowledge that the Lord's Prayer fits comfortably within a Jewish horizon of understanding. After all, Jesus and his early disciples were profoundly influenced by their Judaism. Going beyond this, however, is it possible to know whether elements of the Lord's Prayer were borrowed from popular prayers already in use during the time of Jesus?

In the last half of the twentieth century, most scholars were persuaded that the Lord's Prayer had close counterparts in the synagogue service. Joachim Jeremias, for example, surmised that the first two petitions in the Lord's Prayer were not "newly constructed by Jesus, but come from the Jewish liturgy, namely from the *Kaddish*, the 'Holy' prayer with which the synagogue liturgy ended and which was familiar to Jesus from childhood" (1971: 198). James D. G. Dunn, writing twenty years later, came to the same conclusion when he noted how "striking" it was that the Lord's Prayer "was so closely modeled on Jewish prayers of the time—particularly the *Kaddish*" (1991: 38). The *Kaddish* used in the synagogue during the time of Jesus was surmised to be as follows:

> Exalted and *hallowed be his* great *name*
>   in the world which he created according to his will.
> *May he establish his kingdom* in your lifetime
>   and in the lifetime of the whole household of Israel,
>   speedily and at a near time. (Cited in Dunn 1991: 38)

The entire prayer expresses the hope that God's kingdom will break into the world soon. The highlighted phrases, more especially, demonstrate a remarkable affinity with the two opening petitions of the Lord's Prayer. Are we then to say that these elements of the Lord's Prayer emerged out of the *Kaddish* used by Jesus and his disciples?

Paul F. Bradshaw, in his *Search for the Origins of Christian Worship*, makes the point that most scholars in the last century had "a considerable degree of assurance what Jewish worship was like in the first century" (1991: 1) but that this assurance had almost entirely evaporated by the turn of the century. To begin with, Bradshaw draws attention to the fact that no surviving synagogue prayer book goes back earlier than the ninth century (1991: 1). Moreover, instead of assuming that the rabbis shaped daily prayers thereby ensuring a degree of uniformity, Bradshaw demonstrates that recent scholars have concluded that "diversity and variety" characterized this development and that the rabbis, by the end of the second century, had only partially succeeded in bringing a degree of standardization to the prayer life of their followers (1991: 6). In brief, Bradshaw concludes that a survey of all the relevant documents leads to the conclusion that three regular prayers were used by many ordinary Jews during the first century: the *Shema*, the *Tefillah*, and grace at meals. The *Kaddish* developed only later, hence, there is no certainty that the Lord's Prayer was shaped by first-century prayers used in the synagogue as scholars such as Joachim Jeremias and James D. G. Dunn have supposed.

The Eighteen Benedictions (*Tefillah*) are important for our consideration because, according to the Mishnah, it was said three times each day—in the morning, the afternoon, and the evening (*m. Berakhot* 4:1)—thereby providing a parallel to the Lord's Prayer, which was used "three times within the day" (*Did*. 8:3) in the Didache community. According to Bradshaw,

> the custom of threefold daily prayer was well established in earlier Judaism. It is mentioned in Dan 6:10; the afternoon times of prayer is referred to in the New Testament (Acts 3:1; 10:3, 30); and prayer three times a day may even have been the practice at Qumran. (1991: 19)

As for the content of the daily prayer, the sources demonstrate the following:

> Only at the end of the first century C.E. was the number of *berakot* ["blessings"] fixed at eighteen, together with the general theme of each and the order in which they were to be said. . . . The precise wording was not yet established, and on Sabbaths and festivals a different order of only seven *berakot* was substituted. (Bradshaw 1991: 19f.)

Here again, Bradshaw demonstrates a scholarly reserve. Furthermore, Bradshaw reminds us that the influence of the rabbis was not universally accepted; hence, "we should not single out any one Jewish tradition as normative and treat others as deviations" (1991: 14) when reconstructing those influences which shaped Christian prayers.

In conclusion, therefore, it would appear the daily prayers during the mid-first century were normally said three times each day but that existing rabbinic sources do not allow us to know precisely what these prayers were or how uniform they were from place to place. After all, the variant forms of the Lord's Prayer that have come down to us (Mt 6:9–13; Lk 11:2–4; *Did*. 8:2) testify that even Christians prayed differently from community to community, and that some communities (for example, those founded by Paul) may not even have known that there was a Lord's Prayer. On this basis, it seems safe to surmise that the prayers used by other Jewish groups would have had a similar range of fluidity.

Linguistic Structure of the Lord's Prayer

The Lord's Prayer consists of six petitions, grouped in two sets of three. The first set of three petitions begin with verbs in the third person singular imperative. The first and third verbs are passive. The verbs are followed by their subjects. The overall force is as follows:

be made holy (passive imperative)	your name . . .
come (active imperative)	your kingdom . . .
be done on earth (passive imperative)	your will . . .

The use of the passive is deliberate and traditional. If the active had been used, one would have: "Make holy your name" and "Do your will on earth." The active imperative would have the effect of commanding the Father to do these things. Occasionally Jewish prayers use the active imperative (as in *Did.* 9:4; 10:6; Heinemann: 64), but more often the passive form is used with the implied understanding that God is the unseen agent bringing about the effects described. Raymond Brown explains this as follows:

> This peculiar passive form in New Testament Greek does not necessarily convey a passive meaning, for it is frequently used as a surrogate for the divine name. . . . In the NT, instead of "May God do something to somebody," we often find "May something be done to somebody." This seems to be especially common in sayings dealing with divine eschatological activity. (1961: 185)

The second set of three petitions continues with the use of imperatives but now they are all in the active voice. The verbs continue to lead off the petitions save for the one dealing with "our loaf." Now, in contrast with the first three petitions, the pronoun "your" disappears, and "us" and "our" dominate. The brevity of the earlier petitions is broken by the use of subordinate clauses for the fifth and sixth petitions, which are presented with an opening *kai* ("and"). The overall schema is as follows:

be made holy (passive imperative)	your name . . .
come (active imperative)	your kingdom . . .
be done on earth (passive imperative)	your will . . .
our futuristic loaf	give [it to us] this day
and forgive us (active imperative)	our debt (+ subordinate clause)
and not let us fail (active imperative)	in the trial (+ subordinate clause)

"Your name be made holy" = "Your kingdom come"

The first two petitions are intimately connected: God's name will be made holy precisely when he brings his kingdom on earth. All in all, the notion of God's name being sanctified or made holy is rare in the Christian Scriptures. John's Gospel approximates this, for example, when Jesus addresses his prayer to the Father, saying, "Father, glorify your name" (Jn 12:28). The Hebrew Scriptures and liturgy, on the other hand, show frequent use of this notion (see the *Kaddish* cited in #4h). In Hellenistic religion, however, the sanctification of God's name would have been almost unintelligible, "for in pagan Greek the word 'holy' applied to places, but not to people" (Fox: 253).

John P. Meier (1994: 295–300) and Joseph A. Fitzmyer (1983: 898) identify instances wherein the sanctification of God's name is effected by some dramatic intervention in history. These instances provide a parallel to the motif in the Lord's Prayer wherein God's name will be made holy *just when and just because* he makes his kingdom come on earth. The clearest illustrative case comes from the prophet Ezekiel. Following the conquest and deportation of the people in 587 B.C.E., the Lord spoke through the prophet of how these events had profaned his holy name:

> I [the Lord] scattered them [the people of Israel] among the nations, and they were dispersed. . . . Wherever they came, they [the gentiles] profaned *my name,* in that it was said of them [the Israelites], "These are the people of the Lord, and yet they had to go out of his land." But I had concern for *my holy name.* (Ez 36:19–21)

In effect, this is a counterexample. Because the Lord did not take the field and defend his people, they have been enslaved by their enemies. As a result, the gentiles jeer at the people of Israel saying, in effect, "You claim to have the Lord as your God, yet, get real! He wasn't strong enough to prevent you from being taken captive *out of his land.* If he can't protect you in his own land, how much less so when you are removed from his territory." Thus, God's name was profaned; his power was ridiculed. But then the Lord spoke through the prophet of the future:

> It is not for your sake, O house of Israel, that I am about to act, but for the sake of *my holy name.* . . . I will *sanctify my great name,* which has been profaned among the nations, and which you have profaned among them; and the nations shall know that I am the Lord. . . . [How so?] I will take you from among the nations . . . and bring you into your own land. (Ez 36:22–24)

Meier comments on this text as follows:

> Ezekiel . . . stresses the theme of God sanctifying himself [his name] by a powerful intervention that will bring the scattered people Israel out from among the gentile nations and back home to their own land—through no merit of their own. This manifestation of God's power in saving and judging will make him known to friend and foe alike. While God has manifested holiness in various events of Israel's history, Ezekiel seems to envision a complete and definitive (in this sense, eschatological) manifestation of God's holiness in this gathering of Israel (see especially Ez 36:16–38 and 38:18–23). (1994: 296)

This understanding finds support in the eucharistic prayers of the *Didache,* where eschatological hope repeatedly centers on the ingathering. Unlike the case of Ezekiel, however, it is not the exiles who are gathered but "your church" (*Did.* 9:4; 10:5), and they are not returned to land of their forefathers but "into your kingdom" (*Did.* 9:4; 10:5). The force of these substitutions will become clear in the following chapter. For the moment, however, it is sufficient to note that the name of the Lord will be sanctified precisely when his kingdom is established on earth. Here, again, the eucharistic prayers make clear that just as the whole of creation was accomplished "for the sake of your name" (*Did.* 10:3), so too the final kingdom will be accomplished "because yours is the power and the glory forever" (*Did.* 9:4; 10:5). The first petition of the Lord's Prayer, consequently, receives clarification in the second petition.

The second petition, "your kingdom come," is a summary of the message and the hope of the Didache community. As just noted, the eucharistic prayers harmonize with this message—the scattered children of God will be gathered by their Father "into your kingdom" (9:4; 10:5). Chapters 5 and 10 below will develop this in detail.

While the *Didache* was crafted without the use of any known Gospel (see ch. 11 below), it is nonetheless noteworthy that, according to the Synoptics, the coming kingdom was also the central metaphor dominating Jesus' teaching:

> The central aspect of the teaching of Jesus was that concerning the Kingdom of God. Of this there can be no doubt and today no scholar does, in fact, doubt it. Jesus appeared as one who proclaimed the Kingdom; all else in his message and ministry serves a function in relation to that proclamation and derives its meaning from it. (Perrin: 54)

In Matthew's Gospel, for instance, Jesus' public ministry is summarized by saying that "he went about all Galilee, teaching in their synagogues and preaching the gospel of the *kingdom* . . ." (Mt 4:23 and par.). And again, when Jesus is presented as anticipating the future, it is summarized in these terms: "This gospel of the *kingdom* will be preached throughout the whole world, as a testimony to all nations; and then the end will come" (Mt 24:14). All in all, therefore, while Matthew and the *Didache* are quite divergent when it comes to the particulars surrounding the end times, both agree that "the kingdom" of the Father was the central message and profound hope of Jesus.

The Acts of the Apostles makes it clear that the proclamation of the kingdom continued to form the central agenda of the early church. Philip, one of the seven ordained by the Twelve, is presented as reaching out to the Samaritans in these terms: "he preached good news about the *kingdom* of

God and the name of Jesus Christ" (Acts 8:12). Likewise, Luke characterized the mission of Paul in these same terms: "he entered the synagogue and for three months spoke boldly, arguing and pleading about the *kingdom* of God" (Acts 19:8). The whole of Acts closes with this summary of Paul's final mission to the Romans: "he [Paul] lived there [in Rome] for two whole years . . . preaching the *kingdom* of God and teaching about the Lord Jesus Christ quite openly and unhindered (Acts 28:31).

According to the Synoptics, Jesus never specifically defined the kingdom of God. Nor does the *Didache*. Nor do the evangelists. Given the centrality of this concept, it must be presupposed that, in each of these cases, hearers would have been familiar with "the kingdom." Jews, more especially, were familiar with the notion that their Lord and God acted powerfully in history in order to promote the cause of justice and righteousness. "Kingdom," therefore, was not a place, not a title, not an office. Rudolph Schnackenburg explains:

> Israel experienced Yahweh's kingship in the historical action of its God. There is no "kingdom" and no "sphere of dominion" but a kingly leadership and reign which develops from Yahweh's absolute power and shows itself in the guidance of Israel. This original meaning, namely that Yahweh as king actively "rules", must be kept in mind through the whole growth of the *basileia* ["kingdom"] theme. God's kingship in the Bible is characterized not by latent authority but by the exercise of power, not by an office but a function; it is not a title but a deed. (Schnackenburg: 13)

Meier notes that "the kingdom" is "merely an abstract way of speaking of God ruling powerfully as king." What is troublesome, according to Meier, is the fact that the Father is petitioned to have his kingdom "come":

> It does indeed sound strange to speak of a kingdom or kingly rule coming. It makes perfect sense [on the other hand]—given the OT prophecies and eschatological expectations of first-century Judaism—to speak of God coming or, as in the case here, to pray that he comes. That God *comes* to save is a common affirmation in the OT, and . . . it carries special weight in eschatological prophecy. For example, Is 35:4 proclaims: "Say to the fainthearted, 'Be strong, fear not; behold, your God will come with vengeance and his own recompense; he will come and save you'. . . ." Zec 14:5–9 is of special interest, since there the promise that Yahweh will *come* is closely connected with the eschatological battle. . . . After winning the battle, "Yahweh will

become king over all the earth. On that day Yahweh will be one
and his *name* [will be] one" (Zec 14:9). (1994: 298)

This expectation finds expression in the *Didache* in the ecstatic outburst of
expectation at the culmination of the eucharistic prayers:

Come, grace [of the kingdom]!
and pass away, [O] this world!
Hosanna to the God of David. (*Did.* 10:6)

The *Didache*, it will later be discovered, is not intent on the coming of the
Son of Man or the return of Jesus but awaits the "God of David" (10:6)
who, after all the failures of fleshly kings, will finally come himself and rule
the world. The closing lines of the *Didache* return to this expectation, citing Zechariah:

"The Lord will come and all the holy ones with him."
Then the world will see the Lord coming atop the clouds of
heaven. (*Did.* 16:7–8)

Here again, therefore, Meier's explanation of the second petition fits very
well into the context of the *Didache*. The calling upon the Father to have
his kingdom come is tantamount to pleading with God that he himself
would come to gather the exiles and to rule the earth.

"Your kingdom come" = "Your will be done on earth"

The third petition, "your will be done on earth as in heaven," serves to
enforce and further specify the first two. The Father is "in heaven." His
absence is sorely felt "on earth." Thus, the third petition asks that his "will
be done on earth as [it is already done] in heaven."

Often this third petition is understood as expressing the hope that the
servants of the Lord would do "his will" on earth. Here again, one must
remember that the prayer is not addressed to his servants but to the Lord;
hence, as in the case of the first two petitions, it is the Father who is the
implied actor. When he comes, he will ensure that his project, his plan, his
justice is done on the face of the earth.

Addressing God as "Father"

Addressing God as "Father" in prayer has come to be understood by
Joachim Jeremias and his followers as the "unique and special" (1967: 53)

feature of Jesus' piety which exhibited his divine sonship and expressed the familiarity and warmth with which children today use "daddy." Today, however, Jeremias has strong critics (see #4i) who have shown that "Father" was very much a welcome metaphor in Jewish piety; hence, Jesus' use of this term was hardly unique, as Jeremias claimed. Furthermore, the term "father" combined the notion of power with benevolence and had none of the sentimentality with which Jeremias tried to associate the word.

When correctly understood within its context, addressing God as "Father" in the Lord's Prayer made full use of the rich history of this term in Jewish piety whereby the one who saves and forgives is also the one who universally provides for the whole of creation. Even for gentiles, the term had a rich scope of meaning. Worthy emperors and the god Zeus were designated as "father" insofar as they used their power for the welfare of the people (see #4i). Thus, while the petitions of the Lord's Prayer look entirely to the future kingdom (as will be shown momentarily), they do not lose sight of the present benefactions whereby God nurtures and feeds his people (as in *Did.* 10:2f.). Contrary to Jeremias, therefore, neither the Jewish nor gentile use of the term "Father" submerges itself in the realm of sentimentality. Those who suffered abuse and persecution at the hands of the powers of this world needed a powerful protector, a Father who would come with power and save them.

#4I SOFT SPOTS IN JEREMIAS'S INTERPRETATION OF "FATHER"

Joachim Jeremias popularized the notion that Jesus' use of "Father" was the "unique and special" (1967: 53) feature of Jesus' piety which exhibited his divine sonship. Jeremias interpreted the Greek term *patēr* ("father") as reflecting the Aramaic *abba*—the familiar word used by Jewish children to address their fathers, much as "daddy" functions in modern English today. I remember vividly the first time I heard this term being used when I visited Israel. On a typical hot and dry day in a crowded bus station, a boy of ten cried out "Abba! Abba!" as he spotted his father descending from a dusty bus. He quickly wedged his way through the crowd and his father promptly took him up into his arms. The child's eyes were filled with sheer delight. The use of such a familiar term to address God stood, in the mind of Jeremias, as a reflection of the unique and intimate relationship Jesus had with his Father. For Protestants as well as Catholics (e.g., Schillebeeckx 1974), therefore, Jesus addressing God as "Father" came to be understood as expressing his spontaneous intimacy with God which formed the foundation of all later dogmatic formulations of his unique sonship.

While some scholars have expressed reservations regarding Jeremias's conclusions (e.g., Meier 1994: 358 n. 20), Mary Rose D'Angelo has gone on to show the depth and breath of the soft spots in Jeremias's scholarship. In part, she concluded:

> Attempts to attribute "abba! father!" to Jesus have overemphasized . . . that Jesus' usage must be [uniquely] his because it would be unheard of or even impossible in early Judaism. This claim was built on a problematic use of evidence that was limited not only by the constraints of history but also by an unsympathetic reading of the Jewish materials. Much of this lack of sympathy can be attributed to the desire to establish the uniqueness of Jesus and especially of Jesus' teaching. (612)

Once the Jewish evidence is more expansively and sympathetically handled, Jesus' use of "father" in addressing his prayers to God is seen as within rather than against the stream of Jewish piety (e.g., Fitzmyer 1983: 902f.). Indeed, the prayer of Aseneth cited in the last chapter provides an instance in which God is implored "as a father that loves his children and is tenderly affectionate" (*Joseph and Aseneth* 12:8). Furthermore, when the Christian sources are more rigorously examined, even "Jeremias's claim that Jesus always addressed God as father cannot be supported" (D'Angelo: 417).

After examining approximately fifty instances where "father" is used to address God in Jewish prayers, D'Angelo summarizes her findings as follows:

> Three functions of "father" seem to have been particularly important in early Jewish literature. First, "father" functions to designate God as the refuge of the afflicted and persecuted. . . . Second, "father" frequently accompanies a petition for or an assurance of forgiveness. These two functions are grounded by a third: "father" evokes the power and providence that governs the world. (621)

In none of these three functions is there any sentimentality. In the ancient world, the "father" was the undisputed head of the family. A good father was one who used his power for the welfare and protection of those entrusted to his care (wife, children, servants).

With time, the term "father" was extended into the political realm. Benevolent emperors such as Augustus were awarded the title of *pater patriae* ("father of the nation") as a mark of their benefactions and military victories (D'Angelo: 623f.). During the first century, this term became popular. The Stoic philosopher Dio Chrysostom (d. 112) wrote four discourses on imperial leadership in which he explored this theme. D'Angelo summarizes his discussion of "father" as follows:

> He describes the good king, commenting that he is "more fond of toil [for the welfare of the citizens] than many others are of pleasure and wealth," and that "only such a one . . . can be called 'father' of his citizens and subjects not only in word, but also be manifested as such in deeds." Such a ruler prefers the title "father," rejecting such titles as *despotēs*. At the close of his description of the good king, Dio turns to a discussion of "the greatest and first king and ruler . . . for Zeus alone of the gods is named 'father' and 'king'. . . . He is named 'king' according to rule and power, 'father,' I think, according to providence and mildness." For Dio, the rule or kingship of Zeus the father is the model for true rule. . . . It is Zeus, as the common provider and father of gods and human beings, who nurtures the good ruler and ousts the bad. (624)

Thus, whether "father" was used to designate the head of the family or the head of the state, the term carried the sense that the worthy father combined power, justice, and benevolence.

As a case in point, the eucharistic prayers of the *Didache* never use the term "Father" in the sentimental modality with which Jeremias invested the term. In these prayers, the term "Father" combines power with benevolence. Thus, the "Father" is the "almighty Master [who] created all things" who is honored as the universal benefactor giving "food and drink . . . to people for enjoyment" while "to us, you have graciously bestowed spirit-sent food and drink for life forever" (*Did.* 10:3). Thus, God's power is associated with the welfare of his family—a notion that would have found resonance within the Roman world. Moreover, in the future, this same "Lord" would "save . . . perfect . . . and gather your church . . . from the four winds into your kingdom which you have prepared for her" (10:5). Thus, both now and in the future, Roman participants in the Didache community would have agreed that the term "Father" was aptly applied to the Lord Creator, the Lord Sustainer, and the Lord Redeemer.

Within the Lord's Prayer, one finds another case in point. The one addressed as "Father" is first and foremost the one coming in power to bring his kingdom "on earth as in heaven" (8:2). Even in the Book of Revelation, the warm image of God taking his throne in order to "wipe every tear from their [his children's] eyes" (Rv 21:4) stands up as credible only because, in earlier chapters, this same God had previously commanded his seven angels to "pour out on the earth the seven bowls of the wrath of God" (Rv 16:1). Fuzzy hugs without power to subdue evil were useless. Raw power immune to fuzzy hugs was diabolical.

#4J WHETHER THE KINGDOM WAS EXPECTED AS A FUTURE EVENT

Popular piety has become accustomed to making sense out of the Lord's Prayer without any reference to that future day when God himself or Jesus, acting for God, will return to establish the kingdom of God on earth. Thus, in many church circles, it has become fashionable to imagine that "your kingdom come" refers to the sovereign grace of God redeeming sinners or to the supernatural efficacy of the church mediating salvation through the sacraments. In these scenarios, the kingdom has already arrived with the mission of Christ or with the gift of the Spirit, and it only remains to be completed in the future. Should "your kingdom come" be given an entirely futuristic cast, then Christians usually have to imaginatively transpose the metaphor into a petition to "go to heaven"—an event that takes place when the souls of the elect separated from their bodies at death go to reside blissfully with their Lord. In this later interpretation, however, the one-time "coming" of God and his kingdom to earth on the last day has been transposed into the one-by-one "departure" of souls from the body in order to find God in an extraterrestrial realm (the kingdom in heaven).

In 1892, Johannes Weiss published *Jesus' Proclamation of the Kingdom of God*. Weiss had avidly participated in the German Lutheran Quest for the Historical Jesus because he hoped to demonstrate that historical-critical methods applied to the Gospels would be able to demonstrate that the faith and message of the Lutheran Church were the faith and message of Jesus of Nazareth. In the end, however, Weiss became convinced that neither his church nor any other church believed and taught what Jesus presented to the people of Galilee. His research convinced him that Jesus' central metaphor of the "kingdom of God" had nothing to do with justification by faith, with the growth of a church, or with going to heaven. Weiss, in part, summarized his findings as follows:

1. Jesus' activity is governed by the strong and unwavering feeling that the messianic time is imminent. . . .
2. The actualization of the Kingdom of God has yet to take place. In particular, Jesus recognized no preliminary actualization of the rule of God in the form of the new piety of his circle of disciples, as if there were somehow two stages, a preliminary one, and the Kingdom of Completion. In fact, Jesus made no such distinction. The disciples were to pray for the coming of the kingdom, but men could do nothing to establish it.
3. Not even Jesus can bring, establish, or found the Kingdom of God; only God can do so. God himself must take control. In

the meantime, Jesus can only battle against the devil with the power imparted to him by the divine Spirit, and gather a band of followers who, with a new righteousness, with repentance, humility, and renunciation, await the Kingdom of God. (129f.)

In brief, therefore, Weiss interpreted the "kingdom of God" within its original Jewish setting and, in so doing, discovered that "the Kingdom of God as Jesus thought of it is never something subjective, inward, or spiritual, but [it] is always the objective messianic Kingdom" (133).

In the century after Weiss, both scholars and pastors became aware that the petitions of the Lord's Prayer evoked a future kingdom which the Father would establish on earth at the end of this age. Such an expectation, however, was an embarrassment to many. The two principal reasons for this are as follows:

1. *The scientific worldview.* The expectation of a complete and sudden divine intervention that would massively alter the existing social, geological, and cosmic ordering of things runs counter to the scientific notion that geological, biological, and social evolution are limited by the laws of nature and by the slow process of evolution. Shirley Jackson Case, for example, represents the turn-of-the-century faith in human progress when he wrote as follows:

Today, in all circles dominated by the modern scientific spirit . . . the course of world-history is interpreted in terms of carefully observed facts revealing an evolutionary development, and in the light of this new knowledge premillennial pessimism is no longer tenable. . . . Instead of growing worse, the world is found to be growing constantly better. (237–38)

Here one has a clash of cultures. All the documents of the early church (including the teachings of Jesus himself) were formulated in a prescientific horizon of understanding.

2. *The failure of the kingdom to materialize.* Modern biblical scholars are embarrassed by the future expectation of Jesus precisely because, for the last two thousand years, the kingdom has not materialized. This is especially acute in view of the fact that the early church placed on the lips of Jesus sayings that presented a very limited time frame for the appearance of the kingdom. For example: "There are some standing here who will not taste death before they see the Kingdom of God come with power" (Mk 9:1 and par.).

There are various ways of dealing with this. The most common strategy worked out by biblical scholars has been to demonstrate that sayings like Mk 9:1 did not originate with Jesus. Norman Perrin, for example, in his classical volume *Rediscovering the Teaching of Jesus* (1967), noted that "no part of the teaching of Jesus is more difficult to reconstruct and interpret than that relating to the future" (154). When examining Jesus' time frame, however, Perrin discovered that "sayings which express an imminent expectation fail to stand up to serious investigation" (203). After reconsidering all the evidence thirty years later, John P. Meier came to the same conclusion:

> In sum, the three sayings that are the most promising candidates for logia [sayings] in which Jesus sets a time limit for the kingdom's arrival (Mt 10:23; Mk 9:1 and par.; Mk 13:30 and par.) all appear, on closer examination, to be creations of the early church. (1994: 347)

In sum, therefore, critical scholarship has been able to demonstrate that "almost all the elements in the tradition which give a definite *form* to the future expectation in the teaching of Jesus fail the test of authenticity" (Perrin: 203). Consequently, Jesus is vindicated as entirely reliable while the early prophets take the rap for overstepping their bounds by putting a time frame on the expectation of Jesus (as in Mk 9:1).

Fundamentalist churches have been able to sustain their prescientific belief in the imminent return of Jesus at the price of refuting the methods and the findings of both critical biblical exegesis and of modern science.

1. According to Christian fundamentalists, Perrin's distinction between the "authentic sayings of Jesus" and the "creations of the early church" only demonstrates to what degree critical biblical exegesis has become the willing tool of the devil in eroding confidence in God's word. The Holy Spirit, according to fundamentalists, guarantees the infallibility of the whole Bible, not just the so-called authentic sayings.

2. According to fundamentalists, when one explores the origins of the earth and of human life, one has to decide whether God's infallible record (Gn 1–4) ought to be given precedence over the human theories ("speculations") of modern science. The same thing holds true when it comes to the imminent end of the world. Here, too, the believer has to decide whether God's prophetic word ought to be given precedence over the so-called scientific theories regarding the eventual destruction of the earth as we now know it.

Many modes have been worked out whereby one can retain the modern scientific worldview and still believe the message of the kingdom preached by Jesus (see, e.g., #10t). Among contemporary biblical scholars, however, there appears to be a significant rift. Some are willing to allow that "only contorted exegesis can remove the element of future eschatology from Jesus' proclamation, as mirrored in the only prayer he taught his disciples" (Meier 1994: 300). Still others, however, are more inclined to remove from Jesus' teachings all future expectation of divine intervention.

Markus Borg is a scholar who has moved from the first to the second position. In his early period, Borg was comfortable with finding Jesus as an eschatological prophet confronting Israel with destruction using the cosmic imagery sanctioned in the Jewish sources (1984: 196–221). In his recent works, however, he takes the position that Jesus was principally a wisdom teacher with a boundary-shattering and revolutionary message (1987; 1991). Borg relies on careful studies of Q which demonstrate that eschatological motifs show up only in the later layers of Q (Kloppenborg 1987a and 1987b; Allison 1998: 107, 122–23) thereby assuring him that such themes were absent from the proclamation of Jesus. Borg thus finds a credible identity and teaching for Jesus along noneschatological lines.

According to Borg, he is far from being alone. A growing number of scholars (half of those polled in the Jesus Seminar) are persuaded that Jesus never expected a massive divine intervention on the part of God which would culminate in the "end of the world" as we know it (1986). James G. Williams attributes this, in part, to the fact that "apocalyptic eschatology has become a burning issue in our time" and that "biblical scholars who either have a 'Bible Belt' background or who must deal professionally with fundamentalists and dispensationalists" find it more congenial to put forward a noneschatological Jesus (1989: 25).

This issue is much too complex to sort out in the present volume. Interested readers may want to examine the claims of Borg (1986) and then to read the study of Bruce Chilton, *Pure Kingdom: Jesus' Vision of God* (1996) in response to Borg. Chilton, somewhat like a modern-day Johannes Weiss, reviews all the key modern evidence for and against a future-oriented kingdom of God. He also reviews the work of the Jesus Seminar, to which he belongs, and in conclusion notes that "the attempt by some of its members (including Marcus Borg) to write eschatology out of the record [of the historical Jesus] is misleading, as well as unsuccessful" (1996: 20). The Catholic scholar John P. Meier arrives at much the same position when he concludes that "any reconstruction of the historical Jesus that does not do full justice to this eschatological future must be dismissed as hopelessly inadequate" (1994: 350). For the purposes of this volume, I embrace their conclusions even while I do not always agree with all the analysis that leads them to their conclusions.

Leaving the historical Jesus aside, the purpose of this volume is to explore what the framers of the *Didache* believed relative to the Lord's Prayer. On this point, it will become evident in this and in subsequent chapters (esp. chs. 5 and 10) that the framers of the *Didache* envisioned their lives within a future-oriented framework that awaited the coming of the Lord God to establish his kingdom on earth. While the *Didache* gave no specific time frame for the realization of this expectation, it will become clear (esp. in ch. 10 and in the Epilogue) that the coming of the Lord was imminent. The expression of this imminence was deliberately and pastorally crafted out of traditional prescientific images designed, at one and the same time (a) to powerfully move the imaginations of believers and (b) to safeguard them from the destructive expectations promoted by false prophets. Full details of this will be taken up in chapter 10.

It would also be beyond the scope of this book to review the arguments as to whether the Lord's Prayer originated with Jesus and, if so, what version should be deemed "his own." In fact, this may be a moot issue because, given the preference for oral creativity in Jewish prayer (which will be developed later in this chapter), it is highly probable that the historical Jesus never prayed using the same words twice. The three versions of the Lord's Prayer that have come down to us, therefore, might be better understood as representing three different summaries and adaptations of the favorite themes Jesus was remembered to have repeatedly touched on in prayer. Had Jesus settled into a word-for-word prayer formula and had he expected his disciples to use it repeatedly, it would seem to follow that this formula would have been orally preserved and would have shown up in all the Gospels in the same form. The entire discussion regarding the authenticity of the Lord's Prayer, consequently, needs to be reframed within a proper understanding of how oral creativity routinely functioned in Jewish prayers. Everything that will later be discussed regarding the origin of the eucharistic prayers (see #5v) could thus be applied to the origin of the Lord's Prayer.

"Give us this day our futuristic loaf"

The fourth petition is commonly translated as "Give us today our daily bread." The fifth and sixth petitions deal with forgiveness and temptations—seemingly the everyday stuff of life. Thus, while some scholars are willing to find a future-looking expectation in the first three petitions, they see the second set of three as shifting over to "daily needs" (e.g., Gundry 1994: 104–10). Linguistically, however, the request for bread is expressed in the aorist imperative, in which a single action is anticipated. So, too, with forgiveness. The use of "our debt" in the singular also suggests the total weight of the community's offenses, which will come to light in the one-time final judgment. Only with difficulty can this be understood as asking God to forgive individual sins on a daily basis. Finally, the "trial" (singular) to be overcome is not the daily "trials" or "temptations," but the tribulation of the last days. In the judgment of Raymond Brown:

> The sixth and final petition is certainly eschatological . . . , and the fifth is very likely eschatological. A noneschatological interpretation would leave the fourth [petition] isolated among the other petitions. But, in our opinion, a good case can be made for interpreting this petition eschatologically. (1961: 195)

The key to resolving the fourth petition is the adjective modifying loaf, namely, *epiousios*. This word is not used anywhere else in the Christian Scriptures and is not found in the secular Greek of the period. Therefore, one has to discover the meaning by breaking it down to its root. Here Brown names two possibilities:

> 1. To derive the word from *epi* plus *einai* (the verb "to be"). (a) This could mean bread for the existing day, therefore "daily" [as it is usually translated]. . . . (b) Or it could give the meaning of bread for being, for existence (*epi ousia*), i.e., the bread needed to live. . . .
> 2. To derive the word from *epi* plus *ienai* (the verb "to go, come"). This would mean the bread for the coming day, for the future. The phrase *hē epiousa* (*hēmera*) means "the morrow." (1961: 195f.)

Those favoring a nonfuturistic interpretation of the petition follow the first derivation, while those wishing to allow a consistent one-time future orientation to all six petitions favor the second. Brown follows the second route and finds various texts within the Christian Scriptures wherein "bread" and "eating" are clearly equated with the futuristic banquet in the kingdom (Lk 6:21; 14:15; 22:29f.; Mt 8:11; Rv 7:16). "This eschatological understanding of the petition for bread was the dominant one in the first centuries" (Jeremias 1971: 200).

A second key for resolving the intent of the fourth petition is to take note of the aorist imperative verb: "Give us." The Greek language differs from English in that Greek, by inflecting the ending of verbs, can distinguish whether an action is to be done once or many times. The aorist tense is reserved for "one-time" events. Linguistically, therefore, just as the calling for the sanctification of the name and the arrival of the kingdom are one-time events, so, too, asking for the loaf using the aorist imperative presupposes that it will be given only once (R. Brown 1961: 197 with a caution by Meier 1994: 362 n. 38). All six petitions of the Lord's Prayer are framed in the aorist imperative. All six, therefore, anticipate a one-time fulfillment. The kingdom comes once. The loaf is given once. Our debt is forgiven once. We are preserved from failing "in the trial" once.

The *Didache* provides the forceful image of the broken loaf "scattered [like seed] over the hills" in order that, at the time of harvest, the Father might "gather together . . . from the ends of the earth into your kingdom" (9:4). The broken loaf represents "the life and knowledge which you revealed to us through your servant Jesus" (9:3) and which now has been scattered. Those whose lives are nourished by *this loaf* are destined to be gathered by the Father on the last day into the kingdom. If the fourth petition is to be explained as out of the same fabric as the eucharistic prayers, then the request for "our loaf" is clearly metaphorical. The request that the Father give the "loaf that is coming" to us today then has two possible meanings:

1. *Petition for the sowing.* Feed us with the "loaf that is coming" now at our eucharist such that, on the last day, you will gather us "from the ends of the earth into your kingdom" (*Did.* 9:4).

2. *Petition for the reaping.* Give us the "loaf that is coming" now by gathering together the "fragments" which have been "scattered over the hills" awaiting to be reassembled together as the one loaf in the kingdom.

Since the petition asks that the loaf be given "this day," the first meaning would anticipate that the eucharist was held on the day the prayer was being said. Since the prayer is used daily (8:3) but the eucharist is celebrated weekly (14:1), the first meaning seems very implausible. The second meaning is thus to be preferred. During the eucharist the "fragments" of the loaf were scattered; at the end time, the "fragments" would be "gathered together" into the "loaf that is coming." This reading of the text will be more highly developed in chapter 5.

In sum, while the fourth petition for "our loaf" has been interpreted as asking for "daily bread," linguistically and contextually the request is for the one-time giving of the "loaf that is coming." When read in the context of the eucharistic prayers of the *Didache*, this "loaf" is understood as the ingathering and coming together into the kingdom of those who have been nourished on the "life and understanding" of the Father. The request for "our loaf" is thus finally a request that the Father would come and gather together the elect from the four winds into his kingdom.

"Forgive us our debt"

Within the Jewish horizon of understanding, a "sin" is frequently referred to as a "debt" (R. Brown 1961: 200). Here, therefore, one has an idiom taken over from the Aramaic or Hebrew which has no Greek equivalent. A clue to this is the fact that Luke renders this petition as "Forgive us our sins" (Lk 7:41), using the present imperative and substituting the term "sins" for "debt"—an opaque metaphor for non-Jews (Fitzmyer 1983: 906). Matthew and the *Didache*, however, retain the aorist imperative. They differ only insofar as the *Didache* speaks of the one-time future forgiving of "our debt" (8:2) while Matthew speaks of the forgiveness of "our debts" (Mt 6:12). Raymond Brown holds that both the singular and plural carry "the same meaning" (R. Brown 1961: 200 n. 101). This may be the case. I, however, find a nuanced difference, which will appear shortly.

Regarding the *Didache*, one remembers that anyone receiving alms under false pretenses "will stand trial . . . will be thoroughly examined . . . and will not come out of there [prison] until he/she gives back the last quadrans" (1:5). The *Didache* here makes reference to the final judgment wherein the Lord will examine one's entire life. Failings (in this case, deception) are metaphorically regarded as a debt which, as in the case of someone in a debtors' prison, has to be repaid before release is possible. So, too, the notion that giving to those in need effects "the ransoming of your sins" (4:6) can also be understood as reducing the "debt" owed to the Lord on the day of judgment. Nothing in the *Didache* suggests any system for gaining the forgiveness of sins such that there will be no accounting in the last judgment; hence, to be consistent, the forgiveness asked for is the one-time forgiveness at the end: "Forgive us our debt [at the final judgment]" is the implied sense.

To this petition for future forgiveness is added "as we likewise forgive our debtors" (8:2). The effect of this subordinate clause is to ask the Father to forgive us in the future in the measure that we now forgive the sins of others. Withholding forgiveness now, therefore, translates into petitioning God to withhold forgiveness on the last day. The verb "forgive" in the subordinate clause is in the present tense. Thus, our ongoing and daily pattern of forgiving others is to be used as God's measure in forgiving us our debt at the last judgment.

The reference to why one needs to forgive others is "something strange in the context of the Lord's Prayer" (Jeremias 1971: 201). Why is our forgiving now so decisively important for being forgiven on the last day? Is it merely the case that the measure of forgiveness offered by God will be determined by the measure with which those being judged forgave others during their lifetimes? Yes. But this is a scandalous proposition in itself. Jeremias, sensing this was a scandalous proposition, tried to find a linguistic loophole whereby he might rid the text of any suggestion that God's forgiveness is limited by our measure of forgiving (1971: 201). Nonetheless, Matthew's parable of the unforgiving servant drives home the point that the king reverses his initial pardon: "And in anger his lord handed him over to be tortured until he would pay his entire debt" (Mt 18:34). Matthew also makes it clear that "If you forgive others their trespasses, your heavenly Father will also forgive you; but if you do not forgive others, neither will your Father forgive your trespasses" (Mt 6:4f.). Thus, when seen in context, the second half of the petition cannot be reduced to "a declaration of readiness to pass on God's forgiveness" (Jeremias 1971: 201), and the scandal of God's unwillingness to forgive in some circumstances remains.

"Let us not fail in the trial [of the last days]"

According to Raymond Brown, when the sixth petition is translated as "Lead us not into temptation," this leaves the impression that one is dealing with "daily deliverance from temptation" and that "it is God who is responsible for temptation" (1961: 204). In the Greek text, the aorist imperative relieves one from imagining that "daily temptations" were being referred to. The ordinary English translation, however, does not have this safeguard. Moreover, the English translation of *peirasmos* as "temptation" is also troublesome:

> While this word can refer to ordinary temptation [e.g., Lk 4:13], it also has a specialized reference to the final onslaught of Satan. Rv 3:10 contains a promise of Christ: "Because you have kept my command and stood fast, I will keep you from the hour of trial (*peirasmos*) which is coming on the whole world. . . ." (R. Brown 1961: 205)

The end-times scenario of the *Didache* deliberately removes any reference to Satan, yet a final tribulation is provoked by "false prophets and corruptors" who "will persecute and betray" along with a "world-deceiver" who "will do signs and wonders" (16:4) endeavoring to mislead the elect. In other literature of this same kind, one also finds that "God's faithful people would be exposed to one last fearsome testing, and some would fall into apostasy under the pressure of the final crisis" (Meier 1994: 301). This then is the "trial" (*peirasmos*) with which the sixth petition of the Lord's Prayer is concerned. It sent the message that things would get very bad for God's elect just prior to his coming in accord with the folk saying, "The night is always darkest just prior to the dawn."

The difficulty with the petition "lead us not" is that it suggests that God will be responsible for bringing the elect into this final crisis. John Meier comments here that "many writers in the OT and the NT . . . frequently attributed all events directly to God, with no great concern about whether these events were good or bad" (Meier 1994: 302; Fitzmyer 1983: 906f.). This corresponds to the *Didache* saying, "You will accept the experiences befalling you as good things, knowing that, apart from God, nothing happens" (3:10). In fact, the term *peirasmos* can mean a trial or testing which anticipates a successful outcome. Nonetheless, C. C. Torrey has proposed that behind the Greek for "lead us not" is a "popular idiom of Palestinian Aramaic [the language used by Jesus]" (292), which should be rendered into English as "do not let us succumb/fail." Jeremias finds a Jewish prayer (*b. Berakhot* 60b) that uses this very idiom and, accordingly, renders the text as "do not let us fall victim" (1971: 202). This linguistic solution nicely avoids the difficulty of the literal Greek translation, yet it has been accepted by some while being ignored by most.

The clause "but deliver us from evil" again looks forward to a one-time event. When the entire world has been racked by the havoc of "false prophets" and the "world deceiver," then the Lord's judgment will come as a "burning process of testing" that will "destroy" all evil while "purifying" the elect (*Did.* 16:5 as will be explained in ch. 15). In the end, therefore, "the ones having remained firm in their faith will be saved" (16:5). Taken as a whole, the sixth petition has this sense: "Do not let us succumb in the trial [of the last days], but deliver us from [this/every/all] evil."

Stepping back now, one can see that the last three petitions have a topical unity and perspective just as do the first three.

1. *The first three.* "Your name be made holy" looks forward to God's final intervention in human history, which is specified by "Your kingdom come" and "Your will be done on earth." In each instance, the focus is on God and what God will do. From the vantage point of God, the overwhelmingly positive benefit of his rule on earth is that his name will be made holy.

2. *The last three.* In the final three petitions, the focus turns to the coming of the kingdom as it will affect us—those who pray the Lord's Prayer. First, one has the urgent petition that the "future loaf"—the ingathering of the elect—would take place today! Second, one has the petition for a measure of forgiveness equal to our own when the Lord judges those gathered. Third, one has the petition that we might not succumb in the final "trial" but God would arrive to speedily deliver us from evil.

SECTION III: ANALYSIS OF THE ACT OF PRAYING

The Group Orientation of the Lord's Prayer

The Lord's Prayer begins with "Our Father" (rather than "My Father") and continues throughout with the plural pronouns "us" and "our." The plural form of the prayer makes it likely that it was intended for group use. However, as in the case of rabbinic prayers, which can be used when one person is alone—the prayer in such circumstances unites itself with all those who share the same prayer and look forward to the same kingdom.

When used in a group, the prayer was not necessarily recited in unison. In the ancient world, one does not encounter the group recitation of memorized prayers. It was more aesthetically pleasing when one person offered the prayer and the others responded by their "Amen" (10:6) or "because yours is the power and the glory" (8:2).

In the Mishnah, this principle was clearly operative. In the case of the special prayers at the time when the seasonal rains were delayed, "an experienced elder who has children and whose cupboard is empty" was chosen to recite the Eighteen Benedictions (known to all) plus the additional six (*m. Taanit* 2:2) on behalf of all present. In the case of prayer before eating, two different situations were anticipated: "If they sit down [to eat], each one recites the blessing for himself. [If] they reclined, one recites the blessing for all of them" (*m. Berakhot* 6:6). The posture of "reclining" is reserved for formal meals. Hence, at formal meals, one person (the host or someone appointed by him) recites the blessing on the foods for all. In the case of grace after meals, when three or more eat together, one among them initiates the prayer (*m. Berakhot* 7:1; 7:3) and all those assembled "answer after him: 'Blessed is the Lord our God, God of Israel, God of the Hosts, who sits upon the Cherubim, for the food we have eaten'" (*m. Berakhot* 7:3).

This latter case is of special interest. Those assembled listen to the prayer, and whenever the prayer leader comes out with the "closing refrain," they recite this refrain together after him. This serves to indicate their affirmation of the entire prayer. With regard to the *Didache*, the Lord's Prayer ends with "because yours is the power and the glory" (8:2)—the very same refrain that is used to close the eucharistic prayers both before and after the meal (9:4; 10:5). Undoubtedly, therefore, this was the "closing refrain" recognized by the Didache community: when the prayer leader came out with this line, he/she signaled the end of the prayer, and everyone spontaneously repeated the line after him.

The use of the Mishnah for learning how group prayer was handled has its limitations. In part, the Mishnah is late (200 C.E.), and it is difficult to know where the Mishnah is merely blessing widespread existing practice or where it advocates a change in practice. Paul Bradshaw (following Joseph Heinemann) is undoubtedly correct when he affirms that diversity of traditions existed and the rabbis were only gradually able to reshape and standardize the content and the style of synagogue prayers (1991: 4–7). Nonetheless, the use of a "closing refrain" in the Lord's Prayer and the eucharistic prayers before and after meals is more than accidental. I would submit, therefore, that this is the clue that signals how the prayer leader ends his/her prayer and that, as illustrated in the case of rabbinic prayers after meals, those assembled most likely responded by repeating this refrain and thereby gave their "Amen" to the content of the prayer.

#4K WHETHER THE LORD'S PRAYER WAS USED DURING THE EUCHARIST

R. D. Richardson has argued that the themes of the Lord's Prayer were initially used as a eucharistic prayer and that the expanded eucharistic prayers in *Did.* 9–10 can be largely traced back to the petitions of the Lord's Prayer. Richardson is correct in noting that the Lord's Prayer and the eucharistic prayer are dominated by an expectation of the kingdom, yet there is nothing in the *Didache* that inclines one to believe that the daily prayer of the Didache community originally emerged out of a eucharistic meal. Moreover, given the penchant for detail in the *Didache*, at no point is there any hint that the Lord's Prayer was recited as part of the eucharist. Even when the *Didache* was expanded and included in the *Apostolic Constitutions,* one still fails to find any notion that the Lord's Prayer was used within the context of any eucharistic celebration.

The first clear evidence that the Lord's Prayer was prayed by the congregation during the eucharist (Cutrone: 93) comes from a postbaptismal instruction of Cyril of Jerusalem (d. 386 C.E.). Thus, on the basis of a thorough examination of the evidence, "there is no reason to propose its presence until the middle of the fourth century" (Cutrone: 104).

The Lord's Prayer as Inviting Innovative Expansion

While the rabbis tried to introduce some standardization into the prayer life of those who followed their lead, Jakob Petuchowski notes that "spontaneous expression of our deepest concerns" was always encouraged following the mandate of R. Eliezer: "He who makes his prayers a fixed task—his prayers are not [valid] supplications" (*m. Berakhot* 4:4) (1972: 3, 9; Neusner 1988a: 86; Sanders, 1990: 72). By "fixed task," the Babylonian Talmud understood either prayers recited "as a burden" or said by rote "in which one cannot say something new" (*b. Berakhot* 29b). The Mishnah also cites in the name of R. Aqiva: "If one's prayer is fluent, he prays the [full] Eighteen [Benedictions]. But if not, [he should pray] an abstract of the Eighteen" (*m. Berakhot* 4:3). Most probably, this means that someone capable of improvising his prayer on each of the fixed themes should do so (see *m. Berakhot* 5:5). Someone unable to improvise, however, should recite an "abstract"—which, quite possibly, is a memorized synopsis. Finally, in the name of R. Joshua, the Mishnah refers to the Eighteen Benedictions saying: "One who walks in a place of danger prays a short prayer" (*m. Berakhot* 4:4)—meaning that, in cases of necessity, one can shorten one's prayer. Each of these directives would make little sense if the Eighteen Benedictions were memorized word for word and deviations were not allowed. In fact, as late as the fourteenth century, a Jewish liturgist wrote, "You will not find a single place in the world where the Eighteen Benedictions are word for word identical with the way in which the Eighteen Benedictions are recited anywhere else" (cited in Petuchowski 1972: 9).

With this in mind, it is quite probable that the Lord's Prayer was an "abstract" of the six key themes which invited expansion by gifted prayer leaders and also served as a summary prayer for those who lacked the gift of being able to improvise. Given the group orientation of the Lord's Prayer just considered, it would be hard to imagine that members of the Didache community assembled together to recite or hear recited a prayer which lasted twenty seconds. Rather, in the presence of a gifted prayer leader, one can expect that the Lord's Prayer served to indicate the progression of themes that were expanded upon and added to in accordance with the specific circumstances and perceived needs of those present. Prayer books were not used prior to the early medieval period; accordingly, the oral giftedness of the prayer leader was always operative interweaving familiar patterns of prayer with fluid expansions spontaneously arrived at. To this "enriched" version of the Lord's Prayer, those present undoubtedly acknowledged the prayer by reciting with or reciting after the prayer leader the concluding phrase, "Because yours is the power and the glory forever" (*Did.* 8:2).

The character of the Lord's Prayer as an "abstract" of key themes can also be glimpsed when the much shorter version found in the Gospel of Luke is compared with the longer version found in Matthew. If a standard prayer (memorized word for word) was at the origin of Jesus' own practice of praying, then it would be difficult to understand how or why (especially in an oral culture) the disciples of Jesus were so dim-witted as not to be able to remember exactly the prayer used hundreds of times by Jesus and by themselves. On the other hand, if a highly variable prayer stands at the origins of what has come down to us as the Lord's Prayer, then it becomes quite understandable how and why the "abstract" itself would vary. Furthermore, since one finds in all the various ancient Judaisms no tradition of memorizing standard prayers (other than the *Shema* of Dt 6:4f.), it would have been a remarked and remarkable "departure from tradition" had Jesus imposed upon his disciples a prayer of fixed words ("recite after me"). We must take great care, therefore, not to allow our own memorization and use of the Lord's Prayer to substitute for a concerted effort to understand how this "abstract" functioned in the *Didache*.

Posture While Praying the Lord's Prayer

The *Didache* makes no reference to any prescribed posture or bodily orientation. Needless to say, however, any group that came together to pray was prone to develop specific expectations as to a shared bodily posture and (given the absence of pews) a shared direction to face. Here again, given the silence of the *Didache*, one might suppose that Jewish tradition was followed. In fact, the reason that nothing is said about posture may be a silent witness that these patterns were common and shared, and, as a result, they needed no notice and aroused no controversy.

On the basis of the evidence (see #4m), it would appear that a standing posture with hands outstretched would have been the preferred prayer posture for group prayer. The church fathers accepted this posture for their congregations, and there was never any attempt to claim it as unique to themselves or as distinct from the practice of the synagogues. It would even appear, judging from the novel of Petronius (d. C.E. 65), that even a Roman "lifts his arms to the gods of his prayer" (101).

As for the preferred orientation, given the anti-temple stance of the *Didache* (see ch. 14 below), this posture was probably toward the east. While some Jews in the first century undoubtedly did pray facing the temple, this practice might have been expected of those who visited the temple and sensed God's awesome presence in the Holy of Holies. Those who lived in Jerusalem and could visually see the temple might also have been inclined to pray facing the temple. However, first-century Essenes presumably faced east even when they were in Jerusalem (see #4m). Apparently the evocative image of the rising sun and the metaphoric quality of light were more conducive to prayer than facing the temple. As for the members of the *Didache*, the eschatological character of the Lord's Prayer would not, in itself, necessitate an easterly direction as opposed to facing the temple. In the Jewish apocalyptic writings, God was frequently presented as making his final appearance in history in Jerusalem (e.g., Is 33; Rv 21). Given the fact that the *Didache* has deliberately removed the temple and Jerusalem from its vision of God's future (see ch. 14 below), it would have been unlikely that a temple orientation would have been favored during the kingdom prayer. This surmise would also suggest that those named as "hypocrites" also favored an easterly direction in prayer; otherwise the *Didache* would have changed not only the days of fasting and the daily prayer but also the prayer orientation.

#4M WHETHER THE LORD'S PRAYER WAS PRAYED FACING EAST

Ancient Judaism had a variety of prayer postures. Psalm 28 presents the petitioner as *standing with raised hands* and facing "the Holy of Holies" (Ps 28:2). Psalm 138, in contrast, has the petitioner *bowing down* toward "the holy Temple" (Ps 138:2). Daniel, on the other hand, prays three times each day "*on his knees*" from the inside of his house "which had windows in its upper room open toward Jerusalem" (Dn 6:10). In these three texts, one has three postures (shown in italics) and seemingly three orientations as well. Upon reflection, however, only one orientation is present. Let me explain. Daniel is at a great distance from the temple; hence, it would make little sense to speak of him as facing the Holy of Holies (as though he could refine with such precision the direction to be faced). Since Babylon was roughly six hundred miles to the east, we can suppose that Daniel did not even see the city but knew that the trails leading to Jerusalem were to the west of him and thus he prayed before an open westerly window—a practice the rabbis later regarded as normative (*m. Berakhot* 24b). Psalm 138, meanwhile, is much more precise in locating the direction and would appear to suppose that the one creating the prayer (traditionally David) was already located in Jerusalem and could visually pinpoint where "the holy temple" stood. Psalm 28, on the other hand, would appear to suppose that the one praying is already in the temple courts, where it was natural to pray facing "the Holy of Holies" (28:2). Each of the prayer orientations, therefore, favors facing that place wherein God's presence was most keenly felt by Jews.

In contrast to this, some Jewish texts favor facing east during prayer. Philo (d. 50 C.E.), in describing the Therapeutae (a Jewish sect bound together by a common rule of life and devoted to the study of the Torah, the sharing of resources, and voluntary simplicity), notes that they prayed twice each day, precisely at sunrise and at sunset. According to Philo, they rose before dawn, dressed, and waited in silence facing east; "When they saw the sun rising, they raised their hands to heaven, imploring [God to give them] tranquility and truth" (*On the Contemplative Life* 89). In this case, the choice of facing east clearly had symbolic importance, for "when the sun is rising [they are] entreating God that the happiness of the coming day may be real happiness, so that their minds may be filled with heavenly light" (*On the Contemplative Life* 26). The rising of the sun, consequently, had the symbolic meaning of anticipating the divine enlightenment to which each of the Therapeutae was dedicated. It might be surmised that at sunset they faced the setting sun.

Josephus (d. C.E. 100), writing in the next generation, describes the Essenes as a Jewish sect with significant parallels to what Philo called the Therapeutae. What is especially significant is their prayer posture toward the rising sun:

> And as for their piety toward God, it is very extraordinary; for before sunrise they speak not a word about profane matters, but put up certain prayers which they have received from their forefathers, as if they made a supplication for its rising. (Josephus, *J.W.* 1.128)

Here again, the supplication takes place facing the rising sun, and the symbolic meaning is that some great blessing is expected to appear "like the rising of the sun."

According to the studies of W. H. Brownlee and Paul Bradshaw, the metaphor of the rising sun was not only directed toward divine enlightenment but was evocative of the expectation of the Lord's coming, which would produce that enlightenment:

> It would seem from the passages quoted from Josephus and Philo that in these communities the eastward prayer had acquired an eschatological dimension, the "fine bright day" for which the Therapeutae prayed being apparently the messianic age and the Essene prayer towards the sun "as though beseeching him to rise" being a petition for the coming of the priestly Messiah, this interpretation being confirmed by passages in the Qumran literature which speak of the Messiah as the "great luminary." (Bradshaw 1982: 11)

Bradshaw identifies the rabbinic custom of facing "the Holy of Holies" (*m. Berakhot* 4:5f.) as "an adaptation of an earlier orientation toward the east" (Bradshaw 1982: 11), but he gives no reasons to support his statement. Quite possibly the orientation toward "the Holy of Holies" was introduced or at least received a new emphasis only when the temple was destroyed (70 C.E.), and the Eighteen Benedictions were formulated to include petitions not only that the Lord come to gather the exiles and to destroy the wicked, but that he rebuild Jerusalem, reestablish the Davidic kingship, and restore the temple cult (Neusner 1984: 182f.). The psalms make sense out of facing the "the Holy of Holies" (Ps 28:2) because God's presence is existentially felt in the innermost sanctuary of the temple. After the destruction of the temple, however, the rabbinic tradition of facing "the Holy of Holies" was tantamount to addressing the place *where God was now quite absent*. The logic of the rabbinic prayer orientation was not "to make believe" that the temple was there—since it wasn't. Rather, the logic might have been that one faces the place of infamy, where the gentiles dishonored the name of God in the firm expectation that "in this place" God would arrive on the last day to destroy the gentiles and to restore everything: city, dynasty, and cult. If Bradshaw is correct, therefore, the turning from east to the absent Holy of Holies was not a concerted attempt to diminish the expectation of the Lord's coming; rather, it was the intensification of it.

In the conversion story of Aseneth (detailed in the last chapter), Aseneth passed seven days in tears and fasting. At the onset of the "eighth day" (*Joseph and Aseneth* 11:1), "she stretched her hands out towards the east, and her eyes looked up to heaven" (12:1) as she prayed earnestly that God would rescue her. Her prayers were quickly answered:

> And as Aseneth finished her confession to the Lord, lo, the morning star rose in the eastern sky. And Aseneth saw it and rejoiced and said, "The Lord God has indeed heard me, for this star is a messenger and herald of the light of the great day. And lo, the heaven was torn open near the morning star and an indescribable light appeared. And Aseneth fell on her face upon the ashes; and there came to her a man from heaven. (14:1–4)

The text makes clear that Aseneth offered her prayer right before dawn, standing and facing east. Judging from the overall presentation of Aseneth, one can surmise that the Jewish author of this romantic fiction presented Aseneth as taking the posture that his contemporaries would have understood as appropriate to Jewish prayer. The "morning star" is known to us as the planet Venus and, because of its orbit, it appears close to the sun. When trailing the sun, it appears as the bright "evening star" that appears just after sunset; when preceding the sun, it appears as the "morning star" that is near the eastern horizon just prior to sunrise, thereby becoming "a messenger and herald of the light of the day." As herald of the light of "the *great* day," however, the metaphor could easily refer to a prophet of the Lord's final coming, such as Elijah.

All in all, the Jewish sources indicate various prayer postures. The standing posture with arms raised appears to be the most common. When it came to orientation, however, some faced the Holy of Holies, other faced the rising sun in the east. Both of these orientations were seen to imply expectation of the Lord's coming at the end of time. The members of the Didache communities, given their deliberate strategy to downplay the holy city and the temple as the center of the expected coming of the Lord, most probably chose to pray "your kingdom come" facing east. This posture, however, would not differentiate them from other Jews of their time period. Rather, it showed solidarity in their Jewish expectation of God's future (even if and when this future remained entirely silent regarding the restored temple in Jerusalem). Chapter 14 will take this up in more detail.

#4n Daily Prayer in North Africa during the Late Second Century

Tertullian (d. 225) retains for us the prayer traditions of the Christians of North Africa in the late second century. According to his treatise *On Prayer*, Christians pray five times each day: at sunrise, at sunset, and at three additional times (25). These three times, Tertullian relates as "in accordance with Israel's discipline" and in recognition that Christians are "debtors . . . to three—Father, Son, and Holy Spirit." While the three additional times of prayer are not fixed, Tertullian remarks that "the extrinsic observance of certain hours [namely, the third, the sixth, the ninth hours of the day] will not be unprofitable."

Throughout this discussion, Tertullian gives the impression that each Christian is free to decide for him/herself precisely when and where to pray, yet when he treats of the "kiss of peace" (18) and of "women's dress" (20f.), he clearly supposes that, in many circumstances, the daily prayers were offered in small groups. He describes the "kiss of peace" as a "custom [that] has now become prevalent" of "sealing" every prayer "made with brethren" by this kiss. Only on days of community fasting is the kiss dropped (18). From this one can learn that the kiss of peace was not reserved for the eucharistic prayers, since the eucharist would never be celebrated on a day of fasting.

Tertullian cautions his readers to "think not that the Lord must be approached with a train [recitation?] of words" (1). Nonetheless, Tertullian notes that the Lord has given us a prayer for our use which is "an epitome of the whole Gospel" (1) and which is "the legitimate and customary prayer" (10)—namely, the Lord's Prayer. In the use of this prayer, however, Tertullian specifically advises every Christian to add "petitions which are made according to the circumstances of each individual" (10). This freedom to expand the prayer undoubtedly signals that the Lord's Prayer was not recited as "a train of words" but, as explained above, was regarded as a prayer outline that guided the free improvisation of the one praying.

Tertullian makes it clear that the Christian normally prays in a soft voice (27), standing (16), with hands moderately elevated (17). However, Tertullian also makes reference to a diversity of practice, and he himself recommends prostrating oneself during the sunrise prayer and kneeling (as a mark of humility) on days of fasting (23)—"the fourth and sixth days of the week" (*On Fasting* 14). Tertullian makes no reference to a preferred compass orientation; yet, it would be difficult to imagine that the sunrise prayer would not be offered toward the rising sun (*On Prayer* 29).

Prior to prayer, Tertullian emphasizes the necessity of setting aside all anger (11) but merely tolerates those who imagine that they need to wash their hands (even when not soiled) prior to praying (13). After prayer, Tertullian notes with some disapproval "the custom which some have of sitting" (16) based upon a passage in the *Shepherd of Hermas* (*Vis.* 5). On the other hand, Tertullian strongly recommends exchanging "the holy kiss" (18) among the brothers when praying together—even if it should happen to be a day of fasting (18). When women join their prayers with the men, Tertullian spends a long time explaining how modesty encourages virgins to be veiled but absolutely demands that "the betrothed . . . are to be veiled from that day forth on which they shuddered at the first bodily touch of a man" (23).

Beyond the required praying of the Lord's Prayer five times each day, Tertullian notes in passing that Christians customarily pray before taking a meal, before taking a bath, and before taking leave of a Brother or Sister when visiting them in their home (25f.). All in all, based upon the treatise of Tertullian, one can catch a glimpse of how, in North Africa, elements of the *Didache*'s prayer tradition was shared and was greatly expanded.

When the Lord's Prayer Was Prayed and By Whom

Since the Lord's Prayer was directed to be used three times each day (*Did.* 8:3), one can suspect that it was used "when you lie down [to sleep] and when you rise" (Dt 6:7) or at sunrise and sunset (which, in the absence of effective lighting and of wristwatches, roughly determined when some-one would lie down or rise). When the Lord's Prayer was prayed in the evening facing the eastern darkness, perhaps the one praying would feel the emotional weight of the potentially dangerous night, and the petition "Deliver us from evil" (*Did.* 8:2) would, more often than not, invite more attention and expansion. When the Lord's Prayer was prayed facing the dawning sun, perhaps the one praying would feel the emotional hope associated with the emergence of a new day (as did the Essenes) and these feelings would flood over into the first three petitions centering on "Your kingdom come" (8:2). In any case, there is no hint that rigid times were set for beginning any prayer. Even the rabbis allowed for great discretion in this matter (*m. Berakhot* 4:1).

When it came to days set aside for fasting, it might be suspected that members of the Didache community took special care to come together to pray together the morning prayer (along the lines of *m. Taanit* 2:1–4). On the other hand, since the *Didache* is silent on this matter, nothing can be reliably determined.

The Lord's Prayer was required of all those baptized—both men and women—without regard to their status of life. In contrast, the rabbis noted that "women, slaves, and minors are exempt from the recitation of the *Shema*" (*m. Berakhot* 3:3) said in the morning and evening, yet all were "obliged to the prayer [i.e. the Eighteen Benedictions] . . . and the bless-ing over a meal" (*m. Berakhot* 3:3; 2:4). Even men were sometimes exempt from reciting the Shema (*m. Berakhot* 2:5). The *Didache* appears to make no exceptions, yet, given the tenor of the whole document, it hardly seems appropriate to imagine that circumstances sometimes exempted members from the daily prayers.

"As the Lord commanded in his good news"

The *Didache* declares that members should pray "as the Lord com-manded" (8:2). The "Lord," in this case, need not refer to Jesus, for he is regarded as "the servant" who reveals "the life and understanding" of the Father (9:3). For early Christians, Jesus proclaimed "the good news of God" (Mk 1:14; Rom 1:1; 15:16; 2 Cor 2:7; 1 Thes 2:2, 9; 1 Pt 4:17)—never the good news of Jesus. Thus, in each of the four places where "good news" (*euaggelion*) is found (8:2; 11:3; 15:3; and 15:4), there is nothing to suggest that "Lord" refers to anyone but the Father (see #10n). The "good news," therefore is not a book or "a Gospel," but a message (Kelber 1983: 144–47). The Lord's Prayer, consequently, is the prayer delivered by the Lord God in the good news delivered through his servant Jesus. It would not suffice, in the eyes of the framers of the *Didache* merely to put forward a prayer used by Jesus. Rather, since the prayer itself specifies what God is ready to do for those who trust in him, only God could be trusted to know and reveal what he is ready to do. Thus, the Lord's Prayer is seen not so much as preoccupied with the expectations of Jesus but as revealing the promise of God to his people.

Not to pray "as the hypocrites," therefore, implies a lack of solidarity with their prayer. What might this be? Unfortunately we cannot reconstruct what prayers were being used three times each day by those characterized as "hypocrites." Given the overall significance of the *Didache*, however, one can perhaps make some intelligent guesses:

1. The Didache communities surely would have opposed any kingdom petition asking God to wreak vengeance upon the gentiles. While gentiles would have to answer before God at the final judgment, the Didache communities opposed any assured favoritism being extended to Jews and any assured condemnation being extended toward gentiles. Any prayer that would have softened this stand would have been considered unacceptable.

2. The Didache communities surely would have opposed any kingdom petition that assigned a special status to the land of Israel or to its inhabitants. For the gentiles of the *Didache*, there was no "promised land" given to their ancestors. In the future, therefore, God would not be expected to return them (along with the Jewish exiles) to the land of Israel. Any prayer that would have softened this stand would have been considered unacceptable.

3. The Didache communities surely would have opposed any kingdom prayer that assigned any favored status to the city of Jerusalem or to the temple when looking forward to what God would do or where he would be in the future. Chapter 14 will show in detail how the framers of the *Didache* systematically undercut the importance of the Jerusalem temple both at the present time and in the world to come. Any prayer that would have softened this stand would have been considered unacceptable.

At this point, the Eighteen Benedictions need to be considered since, quite possibly, this might have been the prayer of the "hypocrites" that was being opposed (Davies: 313). If the Eighteen Benedictions were prayed in their entirety once each day (*m. Berakhot* 4:3), divided into the three times of prayer, then six benedictions would have been recited at each prayer period. This number, it should be noted, corresponds to the number of petitions in the Lord's Prayer. The framers of the Lord's Prayer, therefore, might have designated six petitions in order to replace the same number used by the "hypocrites." This is hardly a proof, however, since "six" could be a purely incidental or coincidental aspect of the Lord's Prayer.

The problem with any surmises here is that the Eighteen Benedictions were not completely fixed until late in the first century. Paul F. Bradshaw summarizes the state of the question as follows:

> Only at the end of the first century C.E. was the number of *berakot* [blessings] fixed at eighteen, together with the general theme of each and the order in which they were to be said. Even then some variation still remained: the precise wording was not yet established. . . . Prior to this date it appears that a number of different forms of prayer were in use, of varying lengths and with a diversity of themes, according to local custom. (1992: 19f.)

Moreover, even in the Mishnah, the Eighteen Blessings are routinely referred to without any fixed summary of what they were. In the Babylonian Talmud (c. 600 C.E.), however, one does find "an abbreviation" of the eighteen in the form of the twelve petitions (within the Eighteen Benedictions):

> R. Joshua says, "Each day one says an abbreviation of the eighteen benedictions" [*m. Berakhot* 4:3].
> What is this abbreviation of the eighteen benedictions?
> Rab said: "[It is a] précis of each of the blessings."
> Samuel said:
> [1] "Make us, Lord our God, know your ways,
> [2] and circumcise our hearts to fear [hear] you,
> [3] and forgive us so that we may be redeemed,
> [4] and take us far away from our anguish [sufferings],
> [5] and give us prosperity in the pastures of your land,
> [6] and gather our scattered ones from the four corners of the earth,
> [7] and may those who err in knowledge of you be judged [punished],
> [8] and wave [lift up] your hand against the wicked,
> [9] and let the righteous rejoice in the building of your city [Jerusalem]
> [10] and [in] the restoration of your temple [services]
> [11] and in the growth [exaltation] of the horn of David, your servant,

[12] and [in] the kindling of a light for the son of Jesse, your
   Messiah.
Before we call you, may you answer us. Blessed are you, Lord,
who listens to [our] prayer." (*b. Berakhot* 29a; Soncino variations
in brackets)

On the positive side, some of these petitions would be very welcome to
members of the Didache communities. For example, nos. 3 and 4 associate forgiveness with the coming redemption and then immediately turn
attention to preservation from sufferings—themes approximating the fifth
and sixth petitions of the Lord's Prayer. Also petition 6 deals with the
ingathering, which, as will be seen in chapter 5, is a central theme running
through the eucharistic prayers (*Did.* 9:4; 10:5). Petition 7 was added late
in the first century and, for our purposes, can be omitted from the discussion. On the negative side, some of the petitions would be entirely unacceptable to the framers of the *Didache*. Petition 5 intimates that the
prosperity to come will first overtake those in the land of Israel and then
be extended to the exiles who will be gathered there (no. 6). Petition 8
foresees the destruction of the wicked gentiles—a theme entirely absent
from the *Didache*. Petitions 9 and 10 assign a central role to the rebuilding of Jerusalem and the restoration of the temple sacrifices—themes that
the *Didache* has expressly suppressed and replaced (see ch. 14 below).

Stepping back, it will be remembered that we made three intelligent
guesses regarding the themes that would have been odious to the framers
of the *Didache*. Then, in full recognition that many forms of Judaism
existed in the mid-first century for which we have little or no information,
we took the abbreviated Eighteen Benedictions of the rabbis as a possible
prayer to be examined. Even if the prayer of the "hypocrites" may not have
been the one cited in the Babylonian Talmud, one could at least say that
any prayer that had petitions 5, 8, 9, and 10 would be opposed by the
framers of the *Didache*. With some certainty, we can also say that the
framers of the *Didache* would have distanced themselves from those who
prayed in this fashion and would have appealed to what "the Lord ordered
in his good news" (*Did.* 8:2) to ground their alternative. Nonetheless, it
would be hazardous to imagine that the "hypocrites" were the forerunners
of the rabbis (the Pharisees?) using the Eighteen Benedictions unless they
were, for the most part, Christians as well. Why so? Gentiles would not
have to dissociate themselves strongly from a group praying and teaching
on the other side of town—no matter what they are praying and teaching.
If the framers of the *Didache* decided to dissociate themselves from the
"hypocrites" by mandating alternate fast days and alternative prayers, it
could only be because the threat and influence of the so-called "hypocrites" were close at hand. The "hypocrites," consequently, must have
included "insiders" (Jewish Christians) zealous for promoting the central-

ity of Jerusalem and of temple sacrifices among the gentile converts. For the moment, this should suffice. The details will be left to chapter 14.

Conclusion

What does the Lord's Prayer say about the people who implored their Father to come, to gather? These people must have been terribly dissatisfied with the way things were. They were the discontents who did not trust in the lords of this world and the lords of the pagan pantheon to give them a fair shake. As a result, they took as their own the prayer delivered over to them by a discontent Jew who, for his efforts, was crucified as a Roman insurrectionist. With him, they daily relied on God's promise to come himself and to bring justice and peace and a measure of prosperity. The rulers of this world, it will be remembered from chapter 2, were busy advancing their own economic and political interests, and the weak and the powerless were exploited in the process.

What does the Father—"the God who made you" (*Did.* 1:2)—promise to the weak and the powerless? The training in the Way of Life makes this clear:

> But be gentle, since the gentle will inherit the earth.
> Become long-suffering
>   and merciful
>   and harmless
>   and calm
>   and good
>   and trembling through all time at the words
>   that you have heard. (*Did.* 3:7f.)

How will "the gentle" inherit the earth when, in the present order of things, the ruthless and the powerful had been able to possess all the best earth and to turn it, by virtue of exploiting slaves or indentured farmers, into a great source of prosperity—for themselves and for their children who inherit the earth their fathers had seized and exploited? The Father of heaven and of earth must come and again take possession of what rightfully belongs to him and to distribute it to his true children. Only when God returns to set things right, therefore, will the "gentle inherit the earth." Until then, the members of the Didache community were not preparing for armed insurrection or guerrilla warfare, for they were fiercely committed to being "long-suffering, merciful, harmless, calm, good, and trembling through all time at the words that you have heard." And what were these words that set them to trembling? For the novice, the words were those defining the Way of Life. After baptism, however, "the words" would have included the prophetic promises made by the prophets to Israel—promises that, in the course of their daily prayers and of the eucharist, they claimed for themselves. The Lord's Prayer, therefore, incited hope in the hearts of the hopeless: "Father, give us today our futuristic loaf."

The revolutionary character of the Didache community at prayer will become clearer in forthcoming chapters. For the moment, however, it suffices to note that the petitions of the Lord's Prayer not only summarized the teaching and the hope of Jesus but they caused the members of the Didache community to tremble as they prayed to the Father that his name would be sanctified by his quick coming upon the face of the earth in order to rule with justice, to redistribute the resources of the earth, and to bring lasting peace.

Negatively, however, the Lord's Prayer signals that the Didache community distanced itself from those Christians and Jews who prayed for the kingdom in such a fashion that it embraced the wholesale destruction of the gentiles. According to the *Didache*, even the gentiles are to receive the scraps that fall from the table of Israel and to be transformed into children. Lastly, the Lord's Prayer distanced the Didache community from those who expected the ingathering to be centered in Jerusalem and the temple cult. According to the *Didache*, "in every place and time . . . a pure sacrifice" is already being offered "among the gentiles" (*Did.* 14:3)—thus, the Jerusalem temple was to have no significant role to play in God's future.

This chapter opened with the prospect that the fondest hopes and deepest aspirations of a community might be laid bare by sympathetically overhearing how they prayed and what their God was expected to do for them. Now, at the end, the daily prayer has been heard.

#40 WHETHER RETRIBUTION OR FORGIVENESS AWAITS THE GENTILES

Why is forgiveness so decisive in the Lord's Prayer? My hunch is that it leaves room for the inclusion of gentiles in the final gathering of the elect. Most scenarios of the end times feature an ingathering of the Jews and a bloody destruction of the gentiles. In studying this issue, E.P. Sanders (1985) noted six categories of texts:

1. The wealth of the gentiles will flow into Jerusalem: Is 45:14; cf. Is 60:5–16, 61:6; Micah 4:13; Zep 2:9; Tobit 13:11; 1QM 12:13f.
2. The kings of the gentiles will bow down, and the gentile nations will serve Israel: Is 49:23; cf. 45:14, 23; Micah 7:17 (like the dust); *1 Enoch* 90:30; 1QM 12:13f. (quoting Is 49:23).

3. Israel will be a light to the nations; her salvation will go forth
to the ends of the earth [embracing the gentiles]: Is 49:6; cf.
Is 51:4; 2:2f.; Micah 4:1. . . .

4. The gentiles will be destroyed. Their cities will be desolate and
will be occupied by Israel: Is 54:3; cf. Ben Sira 36:7, 9; *1 Enoch*
91:9; Baruch 4:25, 31, 35; 1QM 12:10.

5. As a supplement to the theme of destruction we may add predictions of vengeance and the defeat of the gentiles: Micah
5:10–15; Zep 2:10f; *As. Mos.* 10:7; *Jub.* 23:30; *Ps. Sol.*
17:25–27.

6. Foreigners will survive but will not dwell with Israel: Joel
3:17; *Ps. Sol.* 17:31.

Sanders allows that such a list "obscures nuances" (1985: 214). Some of
the categories overlap. Nonetheless, what is important is that both the
Christian Scriptures and the *Didache* have set aside all the categories save
for (3). Paul, for instance, confronts his own fellow Jews in the synagogue
explaining that they were commissioned to reach out to the gentiles when
the Lord said: "I have set you to be a light for the gentiles" (Acts 13:47
citing Is 49:6). The Gospels, meanwhile, never present Jesus as insulting
gentiles and threatening them with destruction or servitude in the end
times (as did other Jewish prophets). The *Didache*, in its turn, presents an
end-times scenario in which the beginning of the tribulations emerges out
of conflicts within the Jesus movement (*Did.* 16:3) and not from hostile
acts on the part of gentiles toward Jews.

The question confronted in the Lord's Prayer is, How one can pray for
the arrival of the Lord to rule on the earth while at the same time divorcing oneself from the notion that God intends to gather Jews into the kingdom and to destroy/punish gentiles? I believe that this "false expectation"
was handled by reminding Jews that they also have sinned and will be in
need of God's mercy while at the same time promoting the notion that
God can hardly be expected to be merciful to you if he is not merciful to
the gentiles as well. Now, in the context of prayer, one cannot make subtle arguments in favor of the gentiles. Thus, the kingdom prayer settled for
omitting all appeals to God to bring vengeance upon the gentiles, and in
its place it promoted the notion that the one seeking God's mercy at the
final judgment must be the one who is already offering a full measure of
forgiveness to "our debtors"—gentiles and Jews alike.

Forgiveness is also a strategy that breaks the cycle of violence. The religious and national literature of Jews is filled with narrative after narrative
of the tyranny of gentiles toward the Jews. If the end times are imagined
to be filled with God taking our side and wreaking upon the gentiles the
full vengeance that they deserve, then the law of retribution is held as

sacrosanct and God merely does for us what we are not able to complete by ourselves. The imagined end, therefore, must be the complete subjugation or even annihilation of all the gentiles. Listen, for instance, to the kingdom prayer in Ecclesiasticus (c. 180 B.C.E.):

> Master, the God of all . . .
> Lift up your hand against foreign nations
>   and let them see your might.
> As you have used us to show your holiness to them,
>   so use them to show your glory to us. . . .
> Rouse your anger and pour out your wrath;
>   destroy the adversary and wipe out the enemy.
> Hasten the day, and remember the appointed time [of your coming],
>   and let [your] people recount your might deeds. . . .
> Gather all the tribes of Judah,
>   and give them their inheritance as at the beginning.
> Have mercy, O Lord, on the people called by your name,
>   on Israel, whom you have named your firstborn,
> Have pity on the city of your sanctuary,
>   Jerusalem the place of your dwelling.
> Fill Zion with your majesty,
>   and your temple with your glory. . . .
> Hear, O Lord, the prayer of your servants. (Sir 36:1–4, 8–10, 13–19, 22)

Clearly this prayer grows out of affliction. The God of Israel is invoked to demonstrate his holiness by utterly destroying the gentiles. Meanwhile, this same Lord is invoked to gather his chosen people and to bring them securely to Jerusalem, where he will take his rightful place in the temple. The distinction is clear: mercy and forgiveness are sought for Israel; anger and vengeance are called down upon the gentiles.

The invoking of divine vengeance in prayer by Jesus ben Sirach, the author of Ecclesiasticus, may seem strange given the history of foreign domination that plagued Israel during this period. However, Jesus ben Sirach also puts forward the norm that one must forgive one's neighbor if one expects the Lord to forgive:

> The vengeful will face the Lord's vengeance
>   for he keeps a strict account of their sins.
> Forgive *your neighbor* the wrong he has done,
>   and then your sins will be pardoned when you pray.
> Does anyone harbor anger against another
>   and expect healing from the Lord?
> If one has no mercy toward another like himself,
>   can he then seek pardon for his own sins . . . ?

> Remember the commandments, and do not be angry with
> *your neighbor;*
> remember the covenant of the Most High, and overlook faults.
> (Sir 28:1–5, 7)

The logic here is parallel to that of the fifth petition of the Lord's Prayer: If one has no mercy, how can one expect mercy from the Lord? But how can this be reconciled with the determination never to forget the crimes of the gentiles and to pray for their destruction? Easily. Jesus ben Sirach insists that the commandments require one to reconcile with a "neighbor"—a euphemism for a fellow Jew (e.g., Fitzmyer 1983: 880f.)—but, for the gentile who has no place in the world to come, vengeance is not only allowed, it is encouraged.

In contrast, the *Didache* begins by proposing the standard formula, "Love your neighbor as yourself" (1:2) but then quickly advances to a much more rigorous rule: "Pray for [the well-being of] your enemies. . . . Love the one's hating you, and you will not have an enemy" (1:3). This rule undoubtedly applied to family and friends who turned their faces from the novice and hated the change he/she was making to a suspect way of life. For Jews, however, this rule undoubtedly applied also to the traditional distinction between loving a neighbor and hating an enemy. Thus, while the Way of Life is framed for gentiles, it is woven out of a fabric that was generated by Jews who had set aside their enmity for gentiles.

Can one imagine that the Lord's Prayer is so subtle and so finely crafted as to erode the Jewish enmity for gentiles at the same time that it wears away gentile enmity for family and friends who turned against them? Why not? The logic of forgiveness was found spelled out in Sir 28:1–5. Matthew's parable of the unforgiving servant (Mt 18:23–35) illustrates this logic. In both instances, however, insiders alone are under consideration. Ecclesiasticus refers repeatedly to "your neighbor" (Sir 28:2, 7). And, in Matthew's Gospel, Peter's question, "Lord, if my brother sins against me, how often should I forgive?" (Mt 18:21), served as the occasion for the parable. When Peter comes to the point of saying, "I truly understand that God shows no partiality, but in every nation anyone who fears him and does what is right is acceptable to him" (Acts 10:34) and Paul does likewise (Rom 2:6–11), then the way is open to applying the fifth petition of the Lord's Prayer not only to insiders but to the gentiles as well. From that day forward, there could be no blanket prayer for divine vengeance upon the gentiles nor any end-times scenario that envisions only disaster for the gentiles and only felicity for the Jews.

5
KINGDOM EXPECTATION CELEBRATED IN THE EUCHARISTIC MEALS

Kingdom Expectation in the Eucharist

JUST AS THIS BROKEN LOAF
WAS SCATTERED OVER THE HILLS AS
GRAIN, AND, HAVING BEEN GATHERED
TOGETHER, BECAME ONE; IN LIKE
FASHION, MAY YOUR CHURCH BE
GATHERED TOGETHER FROM THE ENDS
OF THE EARTH INTO YOUR KINGDOM,
BECAUSE YOURS IS THE GLORY AND THE
POWER. REMEMBER, LORD, YOUR
CHURCH, TO SAVE HER FROM EVERY
EVIL AND TO PERFECT HER IN YOUR
LOVE AND TO GATHER HER TOGETHER
FROM THE FOUR WINDS AS THE
SANCTIFIED INTO YOUR KINGDOM WHICH
YOU HAVE PREPARED FOR HER,
BECAUSE YOURS IS THE POWER AND
THE GLORY FOREVER.

Contents

Background Discussion Found in Boxes

The Didache community had two evocative and transformative rites: baptism and eucharist. Chapter 3 explored how, after a prolonged apprenticeship under the direction of a trusted mentor, baptism marked a momentous turning point. Lifelong social and religious bonds were broken, and new ones were affirmed. The immersion in flowing water had the effect of transforming an individual from outsider to insider, from pagan to saint, from stranger to brother or sister. Upon coming up out of the water, the newly baptized were embraced by their spiritual "father" or "mother" and, for the first time, introduced to the "brothers" and "sisters" who would become the lifelong center of their new identity. Then, for the first time, the newly baptized prayed the Lord's Prayer alongside their new family members, for now they knew that the one who created them was "our Father." Then all proceeded to a private home, where, for the first time, the newly baptized participated in the eucharist.

The *Didache* offers us the earliest full-blown description of the eucharist. The purpose of this chapter will be to use the clues of the text to reconstruct the rite itself along with its implied theology and impact upon participants. For starters, one will discover that the eucharistic rite takes place in the context of a full meal from which all outsiders (the nonbaptized) are excluded. The newly baptized and those fasting with them thus broke their fast drinking consecrated wine and eating consecrated bread within a fellowship meal that was a proleptic foretaste of the kingdom of God. Everything that has been said earlier regarding how one discovers the soul of a community by examining its prayers will now, consequently, be applied to the eucharist:

> Every community defines its hopes and its aspirations through its prayers. Official prayers arise out of the hidden depths of a religious tradition and flow over the participants refreshing them with valuable insights into what their God is prepared to do. To feel the heart of God, to know what God is concerned about, therefore, is to enter into the public prayers of a community. Here the pathos of the community merges with the pathos of their God and both are disposed to act together for shared purposes.

The eucharist of the *Didache* has its surprises. Centered on the "message" of the Father delivered through Jesus, this early eucharist gives scant attention to the "messenger." Some may be initially disappointed, for example, that the bread and wine did not signify the "body" and "blood" of Jesus, nor did an institutional narrative surmise that the rite originated on the night before he died. That kind of eucharist was in the making elsewhere, but it had not entered into the minds and hearts of those who gave thanks *as Jesus did* to allow the "messenger" to overshadow the "message." Jesus, according to the Synoptic records, focused his attention on heralding the kingdom of God and gave scant attention to the places he and his disciples would have in that kingdom. The Lord's Prayer, following this same perspective, focuses on the redemption to be effected by the Father and passes over in silence any part "the Son" might have in this work. The Didache community, in like fashion, celebrated a eucharist much closer to the mind and heart of the Lord's Prayer than the later (Pauline and Johannine) eucharists, in which the role of the messenger became a focal interest. In the end, therefore, this study will endeavor to discern the interiority of the Didache community as it presents itself without importing ways of believing and ways of ritualizing foreign to the *Didache*.

Structural Analysis

The eucharistic prayers of *Did.* 9 and 10 have been carefully crafted into a unified whole. The prayers before and after the meal embraced a well-defined tripartite structure combined with a set pattern of refrains:

" . . . To you is the glory forever"
" . . . To you is the glory forever"
" . . . Because yours is the power and the glory forever"

Both before and after the meal, one has two thanksgiving strophes followed by a petitionary prayer. The thanksgiving strophes always ended: "To you is the glory forever." The petitionary prayer always ended: "Because yours is the power and the glory forever." The daily petitionary prayer ends in precisely these same words (*Did.* 8:2). Thus, the oral refrain signaled not only the end of a strophe but the kind of strophe. The following table illustrates this:

Prayers Before Meal	*Prayers After Meal*
A1 Thanksgiving for the cup = holy vine of your servant David	**B1 Thanksgiving** for his name in our hearts and for knowledge, faith, immortality.
" . . . **through your servant Jesus**" "**To you is the glory forever.**"	" . . . **through your servant Jesus**" "**To you is the glory forever.**"
A2 Thanksgiving for the broken loaf = life and knowledge	**B2a Anamnesis (Words of Institution):** (a) to all: food and drink given (b) to us: spirit-sent food and drink and eternal life

" . . . through your servant Jesus"	" . . . through your servant Jesus"
	B2b Thanksgiving (recapitulation)
"To you is the glory forever."	"To you is the glory forever."
A3 Petition for the eschatological gathering "from the ends of the earth"	**B3 Petition** for saving and perfecting the church and for the eschatological gathering "from the four winds"
"Because yours is the glory and the power . . . forever"	Because yours is the glory and the power . . . forever"
[Full meal shared]	[Free-form prophetic prayers]

#5A WHETHER THE EUCHARIST WAS SUNG

Singing played a regular part in both Jewish and Christian worship. The Psalms were, as their name suggests, hymns (*psalmōn*). In the Jerusalem temple, these were sung by trained choirs (*m. Tamid* 7:4). Scholars are divided as to whether hymns were also sung in the synagogue assemblies during the first century (Bradshaw 1992: 22f.). Within the home setting, however, Jewish feast days were celebrated with participation in song by all those present. This was especially true of the Jewish celebration of Passover, where the five *hallel* psalms were sung at the end (*b. Shabbat* 118b). Philo notes in passing that the Therapeutae "do not occupy themselves solely in contemplation, but they likewise compose psalms and hymns to God in every kind of meter and melody imaginable" (*Contemplative Life* 29, 80, 83, 84). Such hymns were sung by choirs at their festive meals while "stretching up their hands to heaven" (*Flaccus* 121).

The early pastoral letters circulated by Christians provide repeated references to singing. James, in his letter, writes: "Is any[one] cheerful? Let him sing praise" (5:13). In a similar vein, Paul and Silas were remembered as "praying and singing praise to God" at midnight (Acts 16:25). When Christians in Paul's community came together (to celebrate the eucharist?), "each one has a hymn, a lesson, a revelation, a tongue, or an interpretation" (1 Cor 14:26). One notes here that "hymns" were given the first place and, it may be surmised, were a central part of each assembly. In still other places, Paul admonishes the Ephesians: "Do not get drunk with wine [to lift your spirits] . . . but be filled with the Spirit, addressing one another in psalms and hymns and spiritual songs, singing and making melody to the Lord with all our heart" (Eph 5:18f. and Col 3:16). In the Book of Revelation, accordingly, the saints and angels in heaven awaiting the triumphal return with Christ, break out in song (Rv

4:8–11; 5:9–14; 7:9–12; 11:15–18; 12:10–12; 15:3f.; 16:5–7; 19:1–4, 5–8). Scholars are divided as to whether these hymns represent selections from the Christian liturgy or whether the author composed them himself (*ABD* 6:982). In either case, these hymns indicate how singing was understood to have a habitual place in Christian gatherings.

To be consistent, one should suspect that members of the Didache communities composed and sung hymns on suitable occasions, for example, after a baptism or while preparing to celebrate the eucharist. It is even possible that gifted prayer leaders would sing the entire liturgy using a kind of plainchant that has been retained within the Orthodox liturgies. I myself have no significant voice training. Yet I find myself coming away from such Orthodox liturgies with their melodies in my heart. Thus, I am inclined to spontaneously use these melodies to sing hymns of praise using my own impromptu words. It does not seem hard to imagine, therefore, that every Didache community would have had individuals who had developed the talent to improvise prayers within a range of easily learned melodies and that such prayer leaders used this to their advantage during the eucharist.

Since the *Didache* is silent on this issue, one can only make conjectures on the basis of the known practice of like-minded communities in the first century. In a culture without recorded music, the propensity for spontaneous displays of music would have been much more pronounced than in our own. One has only to witness how, in central Africa, songs break out in the fields or in the busses and, within a short time, more talented singers spontaneously create two- and three-part harmonies. There was nothing doleful or penitential about the *Didache*'s eucharist. Hence, as a people blessed by divine election and eschatological hope, it would be expected that songs of praise and of promise marked their weekly assemblies.

The Cup and Loaf Were Not Ordinary Food

The *Didache* speaks "concerning the cup" (9:2) and "concerning the broken loaf" (9:3)—both terms being in the singular. From the beginning, it can be surmised that the *Didache* envisioned one eucharistic cup and one eucharistic loaf that were distinguished from the ordinary food served at other meals. Possibly many cups and loaves were already on the table, and the one singled out by the presider was raised and consecrated. On the other hand, it is equally possible that the table was set with only one cup and one loaf, and, once the consecration and sharing of these was completed, other cups and loaves (along with other dishes) would be brought forward to ensure that everyone would be "filled" (*Did.* 10:1) by this festive meal. Further support of this proposition can be surmised from the distinction in the prayers themselves between ordinary food and drink, which the Father provided "to people for enjoyment" (*Did.* 10:3), and the "spiritual food and drink" which he provided "for us." Hellenistic meals in honor of this or that deity were sometimes open to anyone who desired to come (Willis: 52–54). Here, however, the rubric of *Did.* 9:5 made it clear that no one "except those baptized in the name of the Lord" were welcome to eat "what is holy." All in all, the *Didache* clearly understood the food and drink of this eucharist to be distinguished from ordinary food.

While this is so, it would be mistaken to imagine that those drinking the consecrated cup and eating the consecrated bread would have been anxious lest some wine spill or some crumbs fall. In other words, it would be out of place to imagine that the eucharitic piety of the Middle Ages was already present in the eucharist of the Didache communities. Moreover, following upon Jewish practice, participants undoubtedly regarded the entire meal as the "holy" eucharist. When the first cup and the first loaf were consecrated and shared, this imparted a distinctive character to all the food present. Thus, there would be no thought that, once the first cup and first loaf were shared, non-Christian visitors or unbaptized members of host's household could then be brought forward and participate in the remainder of the meal because now only ordinary food was being eaten. The rubric, "Let no one eat or drink from your eucharist" (*Did.* 9:5), points to the whole meal and not just the first cup and the first loaf that were consecrated by the presider.

The wine and bread were "consecrated" (Latin: *con* [intensive] + *sacrare* [to make sacred]). They were entirely set aside from ordinary wine and bread by the prayer of thanksgiving that consecrated them:

> The importance of the prayer of thanksgiving is attested by the fact that it is used to designate the Lord's Supper from the beginning of the second century. This prayer of thankful praise must be considered the apostolic forms of "consecration." (Kilmartin 1974: 273)

Enrico Mazza makes the point that "the problem of the validity of the consecration is a problem which does not exist in the Jewish concept of the ritual meal" (287). In the ordinary blessing over a cup of wine and a loaf at a Jewish meal, the essential identity and function of the food were altered by virtue of the "word" (*dabar*):

> The word is action, interpersonal action. The ritual meal of Judaism is woven together with words: man [woman] blesses God, retelling and celebrating his "great works" undertaken to

redeem and build Israel, on the basis of whose accomplishment Israel lives. (Mazza: 287)

Jeremias expresses this in yet another way:

> When at the daily meal the *paterfamilias* [father of the household] recites the blessing over the bread . . . and breaks it and hands a piece to each member to eat, the meaning of the action is that each of the members *is made a recipient of the blessing by this eating.* . . . The same is true of the "cup of blessing," which is the cup of wine over which grace has been spoken, when it is in circulation among the members: *drinking from it mediates a share in the blessing.* (Jeremias 1977: 232)

In the case of someone being baptized, the rite had the effect of permanently transforming someone from outsider to insider, from pagan to saint, from stranger to brother or sister. The same irreversible transformation took place within each eucharist. The cup of wine, therefore, took on an identity that it did not formerly have—that of "the holy vine of David" (*Did.* 9:2). The loaf of bread, in like fashion, took on an identity that it did not formerly have—"the life and knowledge" (9:3) of the Father. It would be foreign to this context to try to distinguish a symbolic/metaphorical transformation from a real/ontological transformation (Deiss: 105), for the transformation was, at one and the same time, both symbolic and real in the experience of the participants.

One possible way to approach the character of eucharistic consecration is to draw an imaginative parallel to what the *Didache* regards as "the presence of the Lord" in the spiritual mentor:

Real Presence in the Mentor	*Real Presence in the Wine*
[A] My child, the one speaking to you the word of God, [1] you will remember night and day, [2] you will honor him as the Lord, for where the dominion of the Lord is spoken of, there the Lord is (*Did.* 4:1).	[A] My child, the consecrated cup of wine, [1] you will remember night and day, [2] you will honor it as the holy vine of David (*Did.* 9:2) for where the cup of the Lord is drunk there his election is.

The novice hears the human voice of his/her mentor. What is heard, however, are the gracious words of the Way of Life and of the promise of the kingdom which the Father offers to the novice. As noted in chapter 1, one greets these words with trembling (*Did.* 3:8) and one meditates on "the one speaking to you . . . night and day" (4:1)—receiving him/her "as the Lord" (4:1). In like fashion, the newly baptized drink the cup of conse-crated wine at the eucharist. What is tasted, however, is the gracious act of election whereby God chose Israel as his own son/daughter. The newly baptized might accordingly drink with trembling and be instructed to meditate, night and day, on how good the Father has been by extending this election to the gentiles as "revealed to us through your servant Jesus" (9:2). By modeling the "real presence" of the election of the Lord God in the drinking of the cup upon the "real presence" of the Lord God in the person of the mentor, one has a kind of functional theology of eucharist which, one suspects, would be much at home in the Didache community. Beyond this it is hazardous to go.

#5B SIGNIFICANCE OF THE ORDERING OF THE CONSECRATIONS

The cup–bread ordering of the consecrations is significant (McGowan: 551–55). In the six instances in the Christian Scriptures where the eucharist is described, only Luke has Jesus blessing the cup before the bread (Lk 22:17–19). Paul, in 1 Cor 10:16, mentions the cup before the bread, but this does not appear to represent the practice within his churches (1 Cor 11:23–25). Niederwimmer is persuaded that the prior-ity given to the cup is "probably connected with the fact that, at a Jewish meal with guests, the first cup was given before the meal" (1998: 144). The more probable explanation, however, is that, even within Judaism, diversity existed on this point. The Mishnah illustrates this diversity quite well:

> If wine is brought [to the table] after the food and there is but one cup, the [adherents of the] School of Shammai say: "The benediction is said over the wine and then over the food." And the [adherents of the] School of Hillel say: "The benediction is said over the food and then over the wine." (*m. Berakhot* 8:8)

It is entirely possible, therefore, that the Christian Scriptures and the *Didache* together reflect the fact that local preferences existed in this mat-ter and that it is impossible to imagine that Jesus' actual practice was known or had any bearing on this issue.

The Transformative Effect of Drinking the Cup

Assembled around the table, the newly baptized were undoubtedly being introduced to persons whom they were meeting for the first time. Other members might be giving last-minute instructions regarding the dishes that had been prepared in advance or that were steaming over hot coals in the courtyard. At a prearranged signal, perhaps when the celebrant poured wine into a single cup or when this cup was elevated, all grow quiet. The fact that wine was being used signaled the beginning of a festive meal. Water was the ordinary drink taken by rich and poor alike at ordinary meals. "Wine was drunk only on festive occasions" (Jeremias 1966: 50).

The opening prayer consisted in a benediction over the cup. The newly baptized could hardly be expected to entirely appreciate the metaphors and allusions expressed in the prayers upon first hearing. What follows, therefore, can only be thought to represent what seasoned members of the community might be able to say should they be asked.

The "holy vine" evoked God's enduring love and election of Israel (Vööbus 1968: 125). The Jewish prophets characterized the people of God as "a low spreading vine" planted and cared for by the Lord, with "its branches turned toward him [the Lord]" (Ez 17:6) or, again, as "a luxuriant vine that yields it fruit" (Hos 10:1). Even when unfaithful, Israel was described by Jeremiah as "a choice vine" that "turned degenerate and become a wild vine" (Jer 2:21). According to Isaiah, when Israel abandoned its Lord, it continued to be the "pleasant vineyard," but now it was called to return to "its keeper" who "guard[s] it night and day" (Is 27:2f.). All in all, therefore, the image of the "holy vine" evoked God's abiding and enduring love for his people. Vööbus summarizes the immense expanse of this metaphor as follows:

> The "vine" became a favorite metaphor, a popular way of describing Israel under the figure of the vine—with this allegory, the picture and its interpretation were intermingled. It developed into a symbol of salvation history, a standard emblem for the elect people. . . . Rabbinic sources reveal an extensive exploitation of this imagery [e.g., *b. Chullin* 92a]. It was familiar as a symbol for the people of God for anyone who visited the temple [where the enormous golden vines laden with grapes hung over the gate]. Its popularity can be seen in the light of numismatics, architectural ornamentation, and frescos. (Vööbus 1968: 125)

In the prayer over the cup, therefore, baptized gentiles joined with the chosen people in giving thanks to the Father for having revealed his choice and his cultivation of Israel. By partaking in this cup, the baptized gentile was gladdened by the fruit of this vine and nourished by Israel's election. Thus, both Jew and gentile together boldly addressed God as "Our Father" (*Did.* 9:2). By sharing in this cup, the one who formerly worshiped "dead gods" (6:3) now found inclusion in God's election of his chosen people and in Israel's call to holiness (as in Rom 11:17–21). In sum:

> The proselyte is brought near to Israel and blesses God through [and with] Israel. The image of the vine is called for by the context of the blessing of the wine, and the blessing is a reminder to the proselyte of the privileged position of Israel. (Draper 1983: 189)

Rordorf, following his close study of the use of wine and vine images, concluded that the "holy vine" also served Jews as an apt metaphor for capturing the messianic expectation of Israel. These images begin in the prophets (Hos 2:10, 14, 17, 23; Jl 2:19; 4:18; Am 9:13f.; Mi 4:4; Zec 3:10; 9:17), find their place in the decor of the temple and the oldest known synagogues, and end up in the apocalyptic material of *Syriac Baruch* (35–40) and the church fathers. Rordorf summarizes his findings as follows:

> We have thus completed an overview of the religious symbolism of the vine and of the wine within Jewish and Christian tradition. This symbolism is quite rich. Within Judaism, the vine and wine have already become the most profound expressions of messianic expectation. (Rordorf, 1971: 146)

When the opening eucharistic prayer associated the "holy vine" with "your servant David," no specific content was spelled out. Gifted prayer leaders, however, could be counted on to expand upon the election and loving care of Israel and to find parallels in the election and loving care of David. Called by God and consecrated by the holy oils of the prophet (1 Sm 16:1–13), David was preeminently the "blessed servant" who wildly succeeded in all his enterprises—from his stand against Goliath (1 Sm 17:32–47) to his equally daring strategy for taking Jerusalem (2 Sm 5:6–10). It was David who brought to fruition the promises long ago made to the patriarchs: "I will appoint a place for my people Israel . . . and evildoers shall afflict them no more" (2 Sm 7:10f.). Associations such as this would naturally have heightened the eschatological promise of the cup. In every case, with all the Davidic legends at their beck and call, a gifted prayer leader would have had no difficulty in properly expanding upon the role of David in connection with Israel's election.

#5C WHAT THE OPENING THANKSGIVING MIGHT HAVE SOUNDED LIKE

The prayers given in the *Didache* are not word-for-word records of what a prayer leader recited without fail at every eucharist. Rote prayers had no place in ancient Judaism or in the early church (see #5d).

Accordingly, as an imaginative exercise, I have taken the words David used in his own prayer and have adjusted them to illustrate what a competent prayer leader might spontaneously offer so as to enlarge upon "the holy vine of your servant David" (*Did.* 9:2):

> We give you thanks, our Father, for the holy vine of your servant David (*Did.* 9:2).
>
> You know your servant David, O Father! Because of your promise, and according to your own heart, you have wrought all this greatness [on behalf of your beloved Israel], so that your servant may know it. Therefore you are great, O Father; for there is no one like you, and there is no God beside you. . . . Who is like your people, like Israel? Is there another nation on earth whose God went to redeem it as a people, and to make a name for himself, doing great and awesome things for them, by driving out before his people [other] nations and their gods? And you established your people for yourself to be your people forever; and you, O Father, became their God (2 Sm 7:20–24, substituting "Father" for "Lord God"; *doulos* trans. as "servant").
>
> And, now, in recent times, because of your promise, and according to your own heart, you have marvelously called to yourself those who knew you not. You, O Father, have turned the hearts of "your enemies" toward you, and, having made them "your servants," you revealed to them your divine election through the marvelous ministry of your servant Jesus. Therefore you are great, O Father, for there is no one like you. . . . What other God could rescue those who walked in the Way of Death and bring them safely into the Way of Life? What other God would look among "his enemies" for those whom he wished to embrace as "his chosen servants" and "his holy household"? We thereby give you thanks, Our Father, for this holy cup. To you is the glory forever.

Following the consecration, the cup was passed and each one present drank from it. The mentor would naturally have drunk first and then passed the cup to his son or her daughter at his/her side. Drinking from this common "cup" (9:2) brought the newly baptized into a sense of the common election and shared hope with those present. A brief hour ago, they were transformed from strangers to family, from outsiders to insiders, from enemies of God to beloved children of a common Father. Now, on an empty stomach, they passed around the cup of "the holy vine of David" (9:2) and drank it with members of their new family. As gentiles, they did not know of or participate in those marvelous things the Father did for David and his contemporaries. Jesus revealed them. Drinking the cup of the holy vine, therefore, enabled gentiles to join in fellowship with Israel and to partake of their messianic expectations.

#5D WHETHER SPONTANEOUS EXPANSION WAS PRIZED DURING THE EUCHARIST

In the previous chapter, it was indicated that since one finds no tradition for a wooden recitation of memorized prayers in ancient Judaism (other than the *Shema* of Dt 6:4f.), it would have been a remarkable "departure from tradition" had Jesus imposed upon his disciples a prayer of fixed words ("recite after me"). The Lord's Prayer, as a result, was seen as a schematic summary or abstract that invited spontaneous expansion and adaptation to present circumstances on the part of the one chosen to pray on behalf of the assembled group.

This same line of reasoning applies to the eucharistic prayers. Here, as in the Lord's Prayer, the plural form ("we" and "our") indicates that one is dealing with a prayer normally used in a group setting. The one chosen to lead the prayer would be expected to know the thematic summary and to expand and adapt it to fit the special moods and concerns of the group assembled. In the case of delayed rains, for instance, the Mishnah goes so far as to suggest that the prayer leader chosen to lead the morning prayers on the day when the fast begins ought to be "an experienced elder who has children and whose cupboard is empty so that his heart should be wholly in the prayer" (*m. Taanit* 2:2). The choice of an "experienced elder" with hungry children surrounding him at home was clearly done with the expectation that his personal engagement combined with his mastery of the prayer form would allow him to weave together the standard themes with a heart–felt expansion that moved those present.

Prayer leaders in ancient Judaism or in the early church were not expected to memorize and recite fixed prayer formulas (Draper 2000: 130). Justin Martyr (150 C.E.), for example, spoke of "the presider" at the eucharist as giving thanks "at considerable length" and "according to his ability" (*1 Apol.* 65, 67). He surely was not thinking of a rote recitation of *Did.* 9, which would take less than one minute. The *Apostolic Tradition* (220 C.E.), in its turn, presented an elaborate set of eucharistic prayers for use by the presiding bishop on various occasions. After this set of prayers, however, the following telling rubric was offered:

> It is not at all necessary for him [the bishop] to utter the same words as we said [note oral emphasis] above, as though reciting them from memory, when giving thanks to God; but let each [bishop] pray according to his ability. If indeed anyone has the ability to pray at length and with a solemn prayer, it is good. But if anyone, when he prays, utters a brief prayer, do not prevent him. (9)

Here again, the prayer of the celebrant was characterized as being "at length" and "solemn"—terms that could not apply to a "canned" prayer, where the length and mood were fixed in advance. All in all, one does not find a movement to standardize public prayers prior to the mid-third century (Hanson: 173–76). Beyond this, the push to regiment prayer leaders and to require that they "read" standard prayers from a printed text came about only after the invention of the printing press.

The rubric, "Let each pray according to his ability," undoubtedly prevailed in the Didache community as well. The prophets, more especially, were prized for their ability to improvise dynamic prayers that nourished and healed the hearts of those who heard them. Concerning this, the *Didache* says: "Let the prophets eucharistize as much as they wish" (*Did.* 10:7). The following chapter will make clear that the free-flowing style of spontaneous prayer that characterized the prophets was cherished and seen as a necessary complement to the more stylized expansion of the eucharistic prayers offered by the celebrant (*Did.* 9–10).

#5E THE SERVANT ROLE ASSIGNED TO DAVID AND JESUS

The eucharistic prayers of the *Didache* repeatedly refer to Jesus as "servant" of the Father (9:2, 3; 10:2, 3). They do this, however, only after they have designated David as "servant" first in the blessing over the cup (9:2). To understand the weight of this dual designation as "my servant," one must situate them in the context of Jewish tradition.

Within the horizon of Jewish understanding, the Lord God does not ordinarily rule or teach his people directly, but he sends and empowers chosen men and women to do this in his name. The case of David is a Cinderella story in which the Lord took an insignificant shepherd and made him the national hero, the redeemer, and, finally, the king of Israel. When Nathan the prophet came to Jesse's house looking for a suitable king, the six stripling young men in his household were presented as the obvious candidates. David, the youngest, was out in the fields, and no one, even in his own household, imagined that he should be called in since he had the qualities to be the Lord's anointed. Even after being anointed, David has to overcome not only the rejection felt within his own family circle but also that official antagonism originating from King Saul and his court. Even on the battle field, the Jewish soldiers did not judge that David, being of small stature, had a ghost of a chance against the Goliath of the Philistines. But the Lord stood by David and progressively "the runt" in the family overcame all the obstacles confronting him.

At the height of his career as the uncontested hero, redeemer, and king of all Israel, the Lord addressed his prophet Nathan as follows:

> Go and tell *my servant* David, "Thus says the Lord: Are you the one to build me a house to live in . . . ?" Now therefore thus you [Nathan] shall say to *my servant* David, "Thus says the Lord of Hosts: I took you from the pasture, from following the sheep, to be prince over my people Israel. . . ." (2 Sm 7:5, 8)

These words of the prophet demonstrate that David, even at the height of his success, still remained a "servant" of the Lord, beholden to him and honor bound to fulfill his desires.

The prophets again and again invoked the word of the Lord against the enemies of Israel with repeated appeals to "my servant David" (e.g., 2 Kgs 19:34; 20:6; Is 37:35; Jer 33:21, 22, 26). In fairness, however, the Lord's designation of David as "my servant" must not obscure the fact that the prophets were also repeatedly designated as "servants" by the Lord (e.g., Jer 25:4; 26:5; 29:19; 35:15; Am 3:7; Zec 1:6). Among the prophets, Moses is most frequently singled out and remembered as "my servant" (e.g., Nm 12:7f.; Jos 1:2, 7; Neh 1:7f.; Dan 9:11; Mal 4:4). Thus, while the Lord called one to be a king and another to be a prophet, both the one and the other were regarded by the Lord as "his servants." In this context, therefore, the community of the *Didache* addressed the Lord and gave him thanks for David and Jesus who, before all else, were seen as the Lord sees them, namely, as *his servants*.

The Greek language distinguishes between *pais*, which is used in the eucharistic prayers, and *doulos*, which was used earlier (*Did.* 4:10) and which stands behind the Septuagint translation of all the references in the above paragraph. *Pais* defies any easy rendering into English because the term was equally used to designate "a youth" or "a slave" living in the master's house. The term directs attention to the insignificance or smallness of the one being referred to and their total subordination to the directives of the lord of the household. In addition, the vocative form of *pais* was almost always used to address household slaves, and, curiously, this parallels the usage of the term "boy" for referring to male slaves as well as to underage sons on Southern plantations in the United States. *Doulos*, on the other hand, most often referred to involuntary servitude. In the Greek literature mentioned in the above paragraph and in the literature of late Judaism, *doulos* came to dominate over *pais* as the term to express servitude to God (e.g., 2 Mc 7:33; *Jub.* 23:30; Josephus, *Ant.* 11.4.4). Hence, while being careful not to overdraw the distinction between the two terms, it does, nonetheless, remain significant that *pais* should show up in the *Didache* as the preferred term.

Part of the significance of *pais* in the developing Christology of the Christian Scriptures is that this term figures in the early sermons of Acts and then appears to be abandoned, probably in favor of designating Jesus as "son of God." *Huios* is the proper Greek term for reference to "a son" without regard to his age. *Pais*, as just explained, could equally designate "a son" when his status as a minor was to be emphasized. This, most probably, accounts for why *doulos* came to predominate over *pais* as the familiar term for the religious submission to God which lasts throughout ones life and not just during the time of ones youth.

John A. T. Robinson (1956) was the first to demonstrate that the two sermons in Acts 2 and 3 represent a very early and, most probably, very authentic presentation of the importance of Jesus shortly after his death. In Peter's sermon in Acts 2, the destiny of Jesus was tied in with the destiny of David; in Acts 3, the destiny of Jesus was tied in with Moses. Moreover, here one finds the term *pais* applied to Jesus (Acts 3:13, 26; 4:27, 30) and, a short time later, this same term is applied to David (4:25). Acts 3, according to Robinson, represents an even earlier Christology than Acts 2. According to Acts 3, neither the Messiah nor the messianic age has yet come. Rather, God has selected "his servant Jesus" (Acts 3:13) by raising him from the dead and holding him in heaven as *the future Messiah*. The crowds are told to "repent . . . and turn again, (a) that your sins may be blotted out, (b) that [the messianic] times of refreshing may come from the presence of the Lord, and (c) that he may send the Christ appointed for you, Jesus" (Acts 3:19). Repentance, here, is understood as *teshuvah*, that is, the "turning back" to God with the expectation of receiving his merciful forgiveness (see Ps 32). Repentance also functions to hasten the messianic age and the "sending" of the messiah, whom God has now "appointed for you" (Acts 3:20). Such language implies that Jesus was not the messiah earlier but, as the text makes clear, "a prophet" (Acts 3:22f.) who, as in the case of Moses, was sent "to bless you in turning every one of you from your wickedness" (Acts 3:26). Robinson comments:

> According to this conception [of Jesus in Acts 3], Jesus is still only the Christ-elect; the messianic age has yet to be inaugurated.

. . . We know who the Messiah will be; there is no need to look for another. The Messiah, to be sure, is still to come. But Jesus has already been sent, as the forerunner of the Christ he is to be, in the promised role of Servant and Prophet, with the offer of the covenanted blessing and a preaching of repentance. Accept that therefore, despite all that you [Jews] have done, that you may be able to receive him in due time as the Christ, the bringer of God's new age. (1979: 144f.)

If Robinson is correct "that no evidence is to be found that the *Parousia* [second coming] expectation formed part of the earliest strata of Apostolic Christianity" (1979: 29), then Acts 3 and *Did.* 9 share some common ground: (a) Both frame Jesus as the servant (*pais*) of God; (b) both perceive God the Father as central to the awaited salvation; and (c) both speak of the Jesus as the messiah without defining what functions he will perform alongside the Father at "the time of universal restoration" (Acts 3:21).

The eucharistic prayers of the *Didache* portray a community awaiting the kingdom from the Father as entirely a future event (*Did.* 9:4; 10:4; and 8:2). Furthermore, in contrast to Acts, the *Didache* offers Jesus no defined role in God's future.

1. The repeated use of the aorist imperative clearly indicates that petitions for the ingathering anticipate a one-time future event. The *Didache*, therefore, does not seem to encourage its members to find any partial presence of the kingdom now or to anticipate a progressive arrival of the kingdom in multiple stages. What was observed regarding the consistent eschatology of the Lord's Prayer in the last chapter finds a parallel here.

2. The link between David and Jesus as "servants" does not allow the Didache community to surmise that Jesus somehow succeeds David in establishing the kingdom of the Father on earth. Clearly David was the "servant" sent to rescue powerfully and protect "the holy vine" Israel in the name of the Father. Jesus, on the other hand, is not named as succeeding David but rather *as revealing* the election and care of Israel established through the agency of David. According to *Did.* 9:2, therefore, Jesus is not fingered as the messiah or even the forthcoming messiah; rather, he is the "servant" who "revealed to us" how God once established his kingdom on earth and how, in the future, God will do so again.

3. At the climax of the eucharist, it became quite clear that the one who was to come to establish the kingdom was "the God of David" (*Did.* 10:6) and not "the Son of David" as found in Mt 21:15. The *Apostolic Constitutions* transformed the closing words of *Did.* 10:6 to read, "Come Lord! Hosanna to the Son of David" (7.26.5). The early church took those prophetic texts in the Hebrew Scriptures that looked forward to the coming of the Lord God and reinterpreted them as messianic passages—look-

ing forward to the "second coming" of the Lord Jesus (Robinson 1979: 140). Thus, "Come Lord [*Marana tha*]" remains, but, in the *Apostolic Constitutions* the Lord Jesus, the Son of David, is expected and not the Lord God, the God of David. The *Didache* focuses on the "God of David" (10:6) and allows that the Father himself will gather the elect into "his" kingdom (9:4, 10:5).

4. While there are tangential references to Jesus as the Christ (see #5f), both the eucharistic prayers and the final end-times scenario (*Did.* 16) give no role whatsoever to this messiah. The work of gathering the elect "into his kingdom" (*Did.* 9:4; 10:5) is entirely identified as the work of the Father. According to the end-times scenario, the work of destroying evil, of purifying the elect, and of raising the righteous dead was entirely given to the Lord God (*Did.* 16:5–7). In the end, only the Lord God appears "coming atop the clouds of heaven" (*Did.* 16:8). Further details regarding this issue will be taken up in chapter 10.

#5F THE INTRODUCTION OF "THROUGH JESUS CHRIST"

5. Even within the *Didache*, on the other hand, there are intimations of a development of a Christology. While it is true that Jesus is the revealing servant and that he is given no role in the world to come, nonetheless, at one point, the refrain, "because yours is the power and the glory forever" (10:5) is unexpectedly changed to "because yours is the glory and the power through Jesus Christ forever" (9:4). The reversal of the terms "power and glory" and the insertion of "through Jesus Christ" in *Did.* 9:4 appear as a jarring alteration for three reasons: (a) It breaks the expected pattern of endings (8:2; 10:5); (b) it introduces a new christological orientation (Jesus = Christ) that deviates from the pattern whereby "through your servant Jesus" shows up with expected regularity throughout; and (c) the eschatological ingathering (8:2; 9:4; 10:5; 16:6f.) is assigned to the Father alone without any provision for Jesus to assist or to accompany him as the Christ (Messiah). Given these difficulties, the temptation would be to exclude this from the received text as a later scribal addition (e.g., Wengst 1984).

On the other hand, the use of the terms "Christian" (12:4) and "Christ-merchant" (12:5) were acceptable terms elsewhere in the *Didache*. It will be noted, however, that these terms were introduced into the *Didache* referring to travelers who decide to settle in the community from outside (12:3). This suggests an alternative explanation. Perhaps some or many of these travelers placed great stock in the identification of Jesus as the Christ, and, over a period of time, perhaps some of these travelers settled in the community. Since cases were known in Judaism in which disciples named their "master" as the future messiah (*b. Sanhedrin* 98a) and since even the early Gospels testified to a hesitation on the part of Jesus to be identified as "the Christ" (Mk 8:29f. and par.), there clearly were factors working both for and against such an identification. This whole issue is very complex and need not be spelled out here. Nonetheless, it does remain plausible that the eucharistic prayers might have been marginally altered in order to give a small nod in the direction of sanctioning a minority position. In so doing, the servant-revealer identity of Jesus remained intact, and the Father was assigned the principal role in bringing in the kingdom. This was the foundational identity of Jesus, and to this the eucharistic prayers continued to point. For the sake of the minority, however, a refrain honoring Jesus as the Christ (the future messiah to be appointed by the Father in the end times) might have been incorporated in order to give them a liturgical token of inclusion.

All in all, the *Didache* offers invaluable evidence regarding development in the christological identity of Jesus. Chapter 10 will explore in greater detail how, even in Judaism, there was a movement for insisting that God alone would save his people while, at the same time, others were enthusiastic in assigning more and more significant roles to the messiah. John A. T. Robinson does a splendid job in showing how both Jewish and Christian texts referring to the "coming of the Lord" at the end of time gave way to the notion of the "coming of the Lord-Messiah" or, alternately, to his "return" (1979). Furthermore, as noted above, Robinson named Acts 3 as "the most primitive Christology of all" (1956). Quite possibly, had Robinson examined the *Didache*, he would have concluded that the *Didache* deserved being named "most primitive." The end-times scenario of the *Didache* (16:3–8) does not make any expressed provisions for a messianic figure within its eschatological expectations (see ch. 10 below). This would serve to confirm that messianic speculation was not part of the foundational genius of the Didache community. Nonetheless, while we cannot know precisely why and how the identification of Jesus as the future Christ was introduced into the community, we can identify the position of the *Didache*'s framers and at the same time note that a certain diversity or development was acknowledged in practice. The *Didache*, consequently, represents the first steps whereby a community bent on preserving the kingdom message of Jesus gradually changed its focus from the message to the person of the messenger. This development extends beyond the scope of this study. Nonetheless, anyone interested in the development of doctrine will find in the *Didache* fascinating clues for christological development.

Let me close this discussion by offering a personal note of caution. Many persons imagine that christological development unfolds along a fixed trajectory and that "primitive forms" were somehow cast off as more advanced titles were embraced. This is clearly not the case. Once Jesus was affirmed as the messiah, he continued to be understood as the master of his disciples, the prophet of the end times, and the one who revealed "the life and knowledge" (*Did.* 9:3) of the Father to the gentiles. Nor is it unthinkable that, in the same community, some would honor Jesus as the future messiah while some would retain a "wait and see" attitude (as suggested above for the *Didache*). *One has only to investigate modern messianic movements to discover that a diversity of judgments regarding the identity of their founder flourished at one and the same time even among the most mature members* (as in the case of Elijah Mohammed, Sun Young Moon, David Koresh, R. Menachem M. Schneerson). The Gospels and the writings of the early church show this also to have been the case for Jesus.

The Transformative Effect of Eating the Loaf

Next, the "broken [loaf]" (*klasma*) is taken up by the celebrant. The Greek *klasma* (here used as a substantive) has the meaning of a "broken [thing]." The term would be apt for referring to a broken pot or a broken plate. Only in the context of a meal would one guess that the term refered to "the broken loaf," and, only in a Jewish context, would one recognize *klasma* as an attempt to capture the *peras* or *perusah* ("broken loaf") blessed at every Jewish meal. In the ancient Near East, bread was baked in the shape of flat, rounded loaves and one "broke" or "tore off" a portion of the loaf before passing it on to the next person. A loaf was not "cut" as is our custom today. The very use of the term *klasma* would thus seem to imply that the celebrant broke the loaf and held half in each hand prior to delivering the prayer of thanksgiving.

#5G SIGNIFICANCE OF THE ORDERING OF THE BREAKING AND BLESSING

None of the scriptural presentations of the Last Supper uses the term *klasma* ("broken [loaf]"); rather, the verb *klaein* ("to break") is used with *artos* ("loaf"). Mark, for example, has "he took bread [lit. "a loaf"], and blessed, and broke it" (14:22). This implies that the sequence is as follows: (1) taking, (2) blessing, (3) breaking. The fact that the *Didache* designated the loaf as broken prior to the thanksgiving might then be thought to mean that the loaf was broken/torn first. This implies that the sequence was as follows: (1) taking, (2) breaking, (3) blessing.

Neither the Marcan sequence nor the *Didache* sequence can be claimed to be closer to Judaism, since the Talmud testifies that some rabbis followed the cup–loaf tradition (*b. Berakhot* 39a; *y. Berakhot* 6:10) while others followed the loaf–cup tradition (*b. Berakhot* 39b). It is possible, therefore, that both Mark and the *Didache* simply absorbed the local Jewish custom.

In the course of time, the term *klasma* fell into disuse. In its original Jewish setting, it retained a manner of speaking familiar to all. Outside of this milieu, however, it created puzzlement. Thus, when the *Apostolic Constitutions* took over the *Didache*, the term *klasma* entirely disappeared (7.25.3). Indeed, an argument could be made to the effect that, even in Mark's Gospel, the term *klasma* was already regarded as obscure. Therefore, the existence of the term *klasma* in the *Didache* points to its Jewish roots and to its early origins.

At times liturgies are notoriously conservative. In the current Roman Catholic eucharist, for example, the celebrant breaks the host before the words of consecration. Five minutes of prayers elapse before he actually eats the consecrated bread wafer. Quite possibly, one has here a liturgical appendage that recreates an ancient practice. The "breaking" now has no relationship whatsoever to the distribution, while, in the *Didache*, the "breaking" anticipated the distribution immediately following the consecration.

As in the case of the cup, the loaf is "consecrated." In the first century, bread was the staple at every meal. Not to have bread was to go hungry or, in extreme cases, to starve. Bread, therefore, preserved life. The sharing of bread was the sharing of life. The prayer of *Did.* 9:3, however, does not suggest that one has here merely a thanksgiving for the "fruit of the earth." The loaf that was the staple for nourishment of the body was transformed into nourishment for the soul—specifically, "the life and knowledge which you revealed to us through your servant Jesus" (9:3). Furthermore, the "life" (singular) given by "our Father" was not just human life received from "the God who made you" (1:2) but, preeminently, the "Way of Life" which the Father offers to his children (see p. 61 above). In like fashion, the "knowledge" referred to here is not just the individual knowledge that each one has but the "knowledge revealed" to the community. This must at least include (a) knowing the true God, the Father; (b) knowing the Father's Way of Life; and (c) knowing the Father's future kingdom.

To this day, Hasidic Jews living in the Mea Shearim district of Jerusalem routinely gather for ritualized meals at the onset of every Sabbath. Chaim Potok's novel and movie *The Chosen* provides strangers to this world with an insight into how the men dressed, how they prayed, and how they ate together. When I visited Mea Shearim, I had occasion to observe such a ritualized Sabbath meal. In effect, the disciples of a master grouped around their master, who sat at the head of their table. During the meal, he was the host and the center of attention. The master offered his disciples Torah, which took the form of heart-warming stories, pointed questions, applications to daily living. While speaking, he took bread, broke it, and distributed it to his disciples. Those immediately next to him who were the first to receive it kissed his hand before taking it. In this context, I noted how the feeding with bread and the feeding with life and knowledge took place simultaneously. Within a rabbinic mind-set, one could even say that the master was in their midst as "living Torah." In a true sense, therefore, the disciples were being nourished on his body (which was Torah) and on his bread (which was Torah).

The Jewish tradition frequently associates "eating bread" with "giving Torah." *Torah* is the Hebrew word that denotes all the wisdom for living which a loving parent passes on to his/her children. According to Deuteronomy, the Lord did not give his Torah to Israel immediately upon their departure from Egypt. He had to train them by making them feel hunger first:

> He humbled you by letting you hunger, then by feeding you with manna . . . in order to make you understand that one does not live by bread alone, but by every word that comes from the mouth of the Lord. (Dt 8:3)

More especially, however, "eating bread" functioned to evoke "our loaf that is coming" (*Did.* 8:2), which will satisfy the human hunger for permanent justice and universal well-being.

> To Orientals the idea *that divine gifts are communicated by eating and drinking* is very familiar. Reference may be made to the *symbolic language of eschatology*. In apocalyptic and Talmudic literature as well as in the New Testament there are innumerable variations on the theme of the bread of life which satisfies all hunger [e.g., Mt 5:6; John 6:35, 50] . . . ; the wine of the world to come which is kept for the children of the kingdom [e.g., Mk 14:25 and par., *b. Pesahim* 119b]; the feast of salvation in the last days, which imparts salvation and life [e.g., Is 25:6f.; 65:13f.; *1 Enoch* 62:14f.; *Syr. Bar.* 29:3–8]. "Those who serve God unto death will eat of the bread of the world to come in plenty" [*Gen. R.* 82:8 on 35:17]. "Blessed is he [she] that shall eat bread in the kingdom of God" (Lk 14:15). "Blessed are they which are called unto the marriage supper of the Lamb" (Rv 19:9). The righteous will "be filled with the glory of the *Shekhinah*" [Midr. Ps. 45 par. 3]. It is well known that in the New Testament the idea of the

feast of salvation which imparts the gifts of redemption is very
common. Mt 5:6; 8:11 par.; 22:1–14 (par. Lk 14:15–24); 25:10,
21, 23 (*chara* means "meal of joy"); Lk 22:15–18 (par. Mk
14:25); 22:29f.; Rv 3:20; 19:7, 9 may be mentioned here. (Jeremias 1966: 233f.)

Just as the consecrated cup brings together both the past and future, so
too does the broken loaf. The following table endeavors to summarize this:

	Consecration of the Cup	*Consecration of the Loaf*
Past (already given) aspect	divine election	life and knowledge
Present (proleptic) aspect	Drinking the cup affirms the divine election received. Those drinking the "holy vine" have a foretaste of the joy of the Father's final banquet.	Eating affirms the life and knowledge received. Those eating a "fragment" already lay claim to the Father's reassembling of the loaf.
Future (anticipated) aspect	promise of the kingdom	gathering into the kingdom

On the one hand, the consecration of the loaf transforms it into the already
received "life and knowledge" of the Father. On the other hand, those eating a "fragment" of this loaf have within themselves what the Father
intends to "gather together . . . from the ends of the earth into his kingdom" (*Did.* 9:4). Eating of this loaf thus constituted a proleptic participation in God's future.

Something is wrong here. Anyone with a rudimentary knowledge of
agriculture would know that grains of wheat that have been ground and
baked are quite useless as "seed." So, too, no farmer could imagine harvesting "from the ends of the earth" (*Did.* 9:4). Here, as elsewhere in the
use of Jewish metaphors and parables, agricultural realism is deliberately
pushed beyond human limits so as to evoke the Divine Sower and the
Divine Harvester. The passive voice is regularly used to signal divine
agency. True, one could register the terms of the "scattering" and "gathering" as pertaining to the farmer/baker who provided the loaf for the
eucharistic meal. What is being "scattered," however, is the "broken" loaf
and not grain or seeds as one would expect. But this loaf, according to the

prayer of consecration said over it, is "the life and knowledge which you [our Father] revealed to us through your servant Jesus" (*Did*. 9:3). The evocative power of the symbols therefore points in the direction of God as sowing "the life and knowledge" which he has revealed through his servant Jesus and through all the spiritual mentors of the local community as well. These "fragments" take root and bear fruit within the lives of the members of the community (#5h) who are scattered over the hills. Then the mood shifts from description to petition. The Divine Sower is petitioned to come and to gather those who have been scattered "from the ends of the earth" into that one place which all desire—his kingdom.

This image of God as the Sower or as the future Gatherer (Harvester) finds clear and repeated expression in the parables of Jesus (Mk 4:3ff.; 4:26ff.; and par.) as well as in the vision of the end times (e.g., Rv 14:14–16). The hearer, therefore, would be presumed to understand how the thinly veiled images evoke the Lord who, in the last days, will gather his elect into his kingdom. In the rabbinic tradition, Jonathan Draper identifies the following metaphor as helping to illuminate the eucharistic prayers (1983: 195):

> R. Eleazar says, "The Holy One, blessed be He, exiled the Israelites among the nations only so that converts should join them: 'And I will sow her unto me in the land' (Hos 2:25). Certainly someone sows a seah of seed to harvest many kor of seed."
> (*b. Pesahim* 87b)

In effect, R. Eleazar suggests that the dispersion of the Jews was a deliberate ploy on the part of the Holy One, for he wished to sow his life and knowledge over the entire earth. The intended result (as seen from the last line) is not just the gathering of what has been scattered but the thirtyfold increase (1 kor = 30 seah). Given the conditions of Palestinian farming, a thirty-fold increase was nearly optimal. Both the eucharistic prayers of the *Didache* and the parable of R. Eleazar share the common horizon of perceiving the scattering of the present time as directed toward multiplying converts prior to the final day when the Lord will harvest his elect. The *Didache*, needless to say, does not expressly draw attention to the increased harvest; yet, in the context of the metaphor, every hearer would instinctively be repulsed by the notion that the Holy One would be such an inept "farmer" as to sow without intending to reap an abundant harvest. The terms of *Did*. 9:4, it must be remembered, functioned as a thematic summary that relied on the expansive innovation of the prayer leader to bring it to full life.

Finally, the prayer of *Did*. 9:4 reveals an intimate consciousness of togetherness. The "life and knowledge" (9:3) of the Father were eaten in view of the future ingathering wherein, no matter how far one traveled or how long one lived, their lives were bound together. Even in the present, the act of sharing bread enacted the sharing of resources—both the mortal and the immortal (*Did.* 4:8)—both of which had been received from the Father. For those who were "brothers" and "sisters," therefore, knew that they could count on each other, come hell or high water, come sickness or health, and not even death would be able to tear them apart.

> In conclusion, this prayer enabled the thoughts of the celebrating communities to coalesce in an awareness of belonging-together, to fan out reaching brothers [and sisters] in far-away places, to nourish the consciousness of the *ekklēsia* [see #5h] as the brotherhood [sisterhood] of that society upon which God has lavished his gifts. (Vööbus 1968: 132)

#5H Implications of "Your Church"

The term "church" (*ekklēsia*) is used twice in the eucharistic prayers. In each case, one finds "your church" (9:4, 10:5)—that is, the Father's church—and never the "Christian church" or the "church of Jesus Christ." The term is used only in the singular—and with good reason. In each instance, the Father is petitioned to "gather together your church from the ends of the earth" (9:4) or to "gather her together from the four winds" (*Did.* 10:5)—expressions that imply that the elect are "scattered to the four corners of the earth" (*Testament of Asher* 7:2). The term "church," therefore, refers to what we today would call the "global" ingathering of the elect. This fits well with the meaning of the term in secular Greek, where *ekklēsia* was essentially an event: the calling together (*ek + kaleō*) of free citizens for common deliberations directed toward the welfare of the *polis* (the democratic city-state). In the eucharistic prayers, "church" is also the event in which the Father summons and gathers together his elect. In the context of the eucharistic prayers, "church" should not be understood as referring to a place of worship, to a local community, or to a religious organization.

Paul, it should be noted, habitually applied the term "church" (*ekklēsia*) to particular, local communities: e.g., "the church which is in Corinth" (1 Cor 1:2). Following upon this, he used the plural "churches" to designate church in an extended geographical area such as Judea (Gal 1:22), Macedonia (2 Cor 8:1), Asia (1 Cor 16:19). This corresponds to the third usage of *ekklēsia* in the *Didache*: the novice is told that "in church, you will confess your failings" (4:14). Now, clearly, a local gathering is intended, and it has no association with the final ingathering, save for the curious fact, that the confession of failings makes possible the offering of a "pure [eucharistic] sacrifice" (*Did.* 14:1–3), which, as we have just seen, is a proleptic foretaste of the final gathering of the elect.

The fourth and final use of "church" in the *Didache* is the most puzzling. In regard to the testing of prophets, the rule put forward is that "every prophet having been put to the test and found to be true, acting for the worldly mystery of the church, but not training you to do as much as he/she does, he/she will not be judged by you" (*Did.* 11:11). At first glance, one cannot decide whether "church" in this context refers to the summons for the final gathering (9:4; 10:5) or to the local assembly (4:14). The complexities of "worldly mystery of the church" will be spelled out in the following chapter.

Those Excluded from the Eucharist

Once the character of the eucharistic consecrations is clear, it makes perfect sense that one should not permit the unbaptized to "eat or drink of your eucharist" (*Did.* 9:5). How can someone who is not committed to the Way of Life and who has no knowledge of the Father be a participant in the present or future reality of the "loaf"? Similarly, how can someone who knows nothing of "the holy vine of David" be expected to drink of the cup?

Now the problem begins. If what we just said was so evident, why do the framers of the *Didache* have to pound away at it, even to the point of supplying a mandate from "the Lord." This is a clue that here one has a trouble spot. Both the Greeks and Romans were accustomed to opening up the table of their lords to any who would come (Willis: 52–54). In fact, by their own admission, they thought of their sacrificial banquets as open celebrations of the power and worth of their gods. Not so with the Didache community. What has been consecrated at this table has been made "holy"; hence, not to be given "to the dogs" (*Did.* 9:5).

Many scholars immediately jump to the conclusion that "the Lord" refers to Jesus here since a word-for-word repetition of this saying is found in Mt 7:6. This seems doubtful for three reasons: (1) To begin with, the *Didache* is focused on the Father's revelation and never explicitly quotes "Jesus," "Moses," or anyone else. (2) When a similar formula is used in *Did.* 14:3, the citation is from Mal 11:1 and, consequently, the appeal to what was "said by the Lord-God." (3) Finally, the context of the saying about "holy things" in Matthew clearly pertains to Jesus' teaching and has no oblique reference to the eucharist. For these reasons, it seems more probable that the *Didache* imagines that the Lord-God is being cited in *Did.* 9:4.

The saying itself, when read in the context of the *Didache*, clearly describes the eucharistic bread and wine as "holy" and, therefore, not to be given to "the dogs." The reference to "dogs" was pejorative since, in the experience of the first-century hearer, the dog was not the beloved household pet but "the annoying and despised eastern dog of the streets" (*TDNT* 3:1101), essentially a wormy, uncared-for scavenger. In the New Testament, the term "dogs" is used on multiple occasions as a metaphor to designate the gap between "the children of God" and the gentiles (Mt 15:26f.; Mk 7:26f.; Phil 3:2; 2 Pt 2:22). In rabbinic literature, "it is the flesh of [temple] sacrifice that the much quoted saying refers: 'what is holy is not to be released to be eaten by dogs' (*b. Bekhorot* 15a interpreting Dt 12:15; *m. Temurah* 6:5; *b. Temurah* 117a & 130b [correction: 17a & 30b]; *b. Shabbat* 11b and *b. Pesahim* 29a)" (*TDNT* 3:1102). In pagan sacrifices, given the absence of refrigeration, sacrificial meat not consumed during a feast in the name of a god would be sent home with the guests, given as a prize, or sold off in the local meat market (Willis: 64). This helps to explain *Did*. 6:3. Among the Jews, however, the saying of *Did*. 9:5 implies that meats offered to the Lord were "holy" and therefore could not be sold off to "dogs" (gentiles). This sense works well here if and only if the eucharist is understood as being equivalent to a temple sacrifice. Later in the *Didache*, this very equation is evident: the eucharist is designated as "your sacrifice" (14:1f.). Thus, by extension, the outsider is the "dog" who is regarded as unworthy of partaking of that which is regarded as *to hagion* ("the holy [thing]") (*Did*. 9:5b).

#51 WHETHER *DID*. 9:5 WAS A LATER ADDITION

After the eucharistic prayers over the cup and the loaf are presented, the *Didache* breaks the flow by inserting a rubric: "(And) let no one eat or drink from your eucharist except those baptized in the name of the Lord" (9:5). This rubric has caused great puzzlement. To begin with, the order "eat or drink" seems to run contrary to the previous order whereby the cup was drunk before eating the bread. Then too, in *Did*. 9:1 and 10:1, the "eucharistizing" is the activity of "giving thanks," while, in 9:5, the eucharist points to the "eating." Finally, as treated in an earlier chapter, baptism "in the name of the Lord" appears to be an earlier designation that predated the trinity of names in *Did*. 7:1 and 7:3.

These three contrasts have led some scholars to consider this to be an editorial comment inserted later into the text (e.g., Niederwimmer 1998: 139). Even as an editorial addition, however, it would be extremely clumsy. It seems unlikely that a later editor would use an older, archaic designation for baptism while overlooking the trinity of names in 7:1 and 7:3. As for the order of eating and drinking in 9:5, this corresponds to what one finds in the eucharistic prayers themselves (10:4 [2x]); hence, too much weight should not be attached to the ordering of terms here. Finally, both 9:1 and 9:5 equally point in the direction to using "eucharist" as a noun. This finds an exact counterpart in 7:1 and 7:4, where "baptism" is also used as a noun.

In sum, therefore, it appears hazardous to dismiss *Did*. 9:5 too readily as a later, editorial addition based on its seeming incongruence with the remainder of the *Didache*.

#5J WHETHER THE PRAYERS OF *DID*. 9–10 CONSTITUTED THE EUCHARIST

Ever since the rediscovery of the *Didache*, not all scholars have agreed that the prayers found in *Did*. 9–10 represent what Christians have come to regard as the eucharist or the Lord's Supper. A significant group of scholars want to see in *Did*. 9–10 modified Jewish prayers designed for ordinary community meals or for a special meal that took place prior to the eucharist (Audet 1958: 372–98; Draper 1983: 185–88; Jeremias 1966: 118; Niederwimmer 1998: 161; Rordorf 1978a: 38–42). In their favor, the following points must be granted with regard to the eucharistic prayers of the *Didache*:

1. The bread and wine are not identified as the "body" and "blood" of Christ.
2. No "words of institution" link the *Didache*'s eucharist to the Last Supper.
3. Nowhere is there any memorial of the death of Jesus (as in 1 Cor 11:23–25).

In arriving at this judgment, however, these scholars have been guided by Pauline notions of what constitutes eucharist and have come to expect the institutional narrative of the Synoptics to be explicitly recited. The *Didache*, however, comes from an early sector of Christianity that shows no influence of Paul and that has no record of a Gospel (see ch. 11 below). Thus, "if primitive Christianity was as pluriform as contemporary New Testament scholarship suggests, then it should not be surprising to find a diversity of patterns" (Bradshaw 1991: 159). Thus, when it comes to deciding whether *Did*. 9–10 represents a "eucharist," one must examine the clues of the *Didache* and allow the text to speak for itself.

Arthur Vööbus has provided the most detailed examination of this question, and those interested ought to consult his work (1968: 68–101). Vööbus makes seven points, which might be summarized as follows:

1. The text itself introduces the prayers by calling them "the eucharist" (*Did.* 9:1), and, once the opening prayers are completed, the text says that the unbaptized are to be excluded "from your eucharist" (*Did.* 9:5). Nowhere does one hear that the cup and bread are only "blessed food" eaten "prior to the eucharist" as some suggest. When the *Didache* speaks of "the eucharist" and of "eucharistizing" (*Did.* 9:1; 9:5; 10:1), these words are to be taken at their face value (esp. Vööbus 1968: 55f., 68; also Connolly 1937a: 488f.; Kilmartin 1974: 276f.).

2. The prayers after the meal clearly distinguish ordinary food from "spirit-sent" or "pneumatic food" given "through your servant Jesus" (*Did.* 10:3) (Vööbus 1968: 68).

3. The exclusion of the baptized from eating is on the basis that "what is holy" (*Did.* 9:5) cannot be given to them. What has been given to those present, then, must be the "holy" eucharist (Vööbus 1968: 69).

4. The distinction between an *agapē* meal and a eucharistic meal is a much later (mid-second century) development that ought not to be read back into the *Didache* (Vööbus 1968: 69f.; Mazza 1996: 285–87). There is no suggestion in the text that *Did.* 9–10 refers to an *agapē* meal while *Did.* 14 refers to the eucharist.

5. The final acclamation, "If anyone is holy, be admitted!" is not an invitation for some to take communion. All present already took communion in 9:2–5. Here, in the context of the imagined end times, the holy are "admitted" into the kingdom (Vööbus 1968: 71–74).

6. The *Apostolic Constitutions* take over the eucharistic prayers of the *Didache* and, even though they still do not have an institutional narrative and still do not equate the cup and bread with the "blood" and "body" of Christ, they are clearly regarded as a eucharist (Vööbus 1968: 79).

7. Words of institution relating the eucharist to the Last Supper came into vogue only once the passion narratives began to identify an "institutional moment" on the night before Jesus died. Prior to that, the eucharistic community did what Jesus did (see #5o). "It is evident that a very archaic form of the eucharistic liturgy stands before us" (Vööbus 1968: 94).

The Social Dynamics of the Eucharist
as a Festive Meal

Didache 10:1 introduces the prayers "after being filled" by the eucharistic meal. The *Didache* makes clear that it is not dealing with just a token meal. Thus, the cup and the loaf which are blessed cannot presume to be the sum total of the nourishment provided. Vegetables and fruits of various kinds and, on rare occasions, even meat would be served. This festive meal provided a proleptic experience of the kingdom; hence, it does no good to imagine that it would have been just a light snack.

Sharing a meal in the Middle East implied social bonding and created social obligations:

> Table fellowship is synonymous with fellowship in all aspects of life (see, for example, Gn 14:18–20; 26:26–31; 29:22, 27–28; 31:44–46, 51–54; Jos 9:3–15; Jgs 9:26–28; 2 Sm 3:20; 9:7, 10–11; Prv 15:17; 17:1). A person who shares table fellowship with another "enjoys his salt" (Ez 4:14). . . .
> Refusal to eat together severs the relationship (1 Sm 20:34). Those who do not eat or drink together are without any obligation to one another, if not actually enemies. The worst kind of traitor is the traitor with whom one has shared food (Ps 41:9; Ob 1:7; Mt 26:21; Mk 14:17; Lk 22:21; Jn 13:18, 24–27). (Feeley-Harnik: 86)

In the case of the parable of the Prodigal Son, for instance, the father organizes a feast upon his son's return. This feast has the social force of reinstating the son who "was dead [to us] and is alive again" (Lk 15:24) as beloved of his father. More importantly, however, villagers who had seen the suffering of the father and who had built up a heavy resentment of the younger son were expected, in the context of the shared meal, to lay aside their antagonism and to take on the frame of mind exhibited by their host (the father). Conversely, the refusal of the older brother to enter into the meal constituted his declaration "that he had nothing in common with his lesser sibling who dishonored his father and himself" (Neyrey: 375). The father "came out and began to plead with him" (Lk 15:28). The elder son clearly signals his antagonism when he presses home the fact that "this son of *yours* . . . devoured *your* property with prostitutes" (Lk 15:30). The parable is open-ended—whether the elder son enters into the festivities or remains fuming outside is left up to the hearer to decide.

When the newly baptized were invited to the eucharistic feast, this implied that their Father in heaven as well as their new family acknowledged them as "one of us." In the context of the festive meal, therefore, "group identity is affirmed . . . ; status is confirmed" (Neyrey: 375). The newly baptized, by entering into the feast, acknowledged their new status as insiders and tacitly affirmed their intention to maintain those reciprocal religious, social, and economic obligations defined in the Way of Life (see ch. 1). Even aside from the sharing of a single consecrated cup of wine and a single loaf, the very act of eating a full meal together affirmed and reinforced the social ties that bound the members together. More especially, the shared cup affirmed that the election of Israel has been expanded to include those who drink the wine. Those who shared the loaf anticipated being gathered together from the four winds (if necessary) in order to enter into the kingdom of God together with those with whom the meal has been shared. Possible exclusion (whether voluntary or involuntary) from this meal had serious social implications that will be explored in chapter 8.

The Father as Host at Every Eucharist

In the eucharistic prayers, the members focused on the status of the Father. He was addressed directly. Thanks were given to him personally. Petitions were offered to him to do what he had graciously promised. In the ancient world, guests at a festive meal were expected to acknowledge the importance of their host and to thank him during the course of the meal for the benefits (past, present, and future) received from his hands. By implication, therefore, *the Father was the unseen but very much present host at every eucharistic meal.* The drink and food served were provided by him (*Did.* 10:3; 1:5). His "holy name" was dwelling within "our hearts" (*Did.* 10:2).

This presence of the Father as the unseen host at every eucharistic meal had the following implications:

1. The social hierarchy at the meal had to be established to honor the wishes of the host. The places of honor and the order of serving, therefore, would presumably have to follow the lines of thought of the Father, who expressly favored "the just and the lowly" (3:9). Presumably, since *Did.* 9–10 represents the first eucharist, the newly baptized themselves would have occupied the places of honor and have been served first. The spiritual father(s) or mother(s) might have been the prayer leader(s) or celebrant(s) in this setting, since they had the supreme confidence of the newly baptized and, at the same time, were held in high esteem by the community. As in the case of baptism, there was no class of persons to whom presiding at the eucharist was reserved. This will be examined in detail in chapter 9.

2. The baptized members of the Didache community were trained to experience the effective presence of the Father in the whole of their lives (*Did.* 3:10). The Father was the one who made them (1:2) and who, in the proper moment, called them to himself through his Spirit (4:10). During the time of their training, they heard an echo of his voice and his care sounding through their spiritual mentor (4:1). Once they were baptized, however, the experience of the eucharist opened up a fresh sense of the Father's presence: (a) in the past, as the one who cultivated and cared for the "holy vine of your servant David" (9:2); (b) in the present, as the one bringing Jews and gentiles alike into solidarity in this proleptic celebration of the kingdom; (c) in the future, as the one who is getting ready to gather his elect from the four winds into his kingdom (9:4). Having partaken of

the cup of election and the bread of promise, the baptized were ready—even at this very moment—to have the Father come and to greet him, "Hosanna to the God of David" (10:6). And the ecstatic prayers of the prophets (10:7) lent even greater poignancy to this expectation—a topic that will be examined in the following chapter.

3. All in all, anyone in the community who spoke of the "real presence" would undoubtedly have made reference to the honored presence of the Father in all the ways mentioned above. As noted, this presence would have been especially evident in the course of the eucharistic celebrations, when the Father was the honored host and, when addressed, came close to the mind and hearts of the participants.

In contrast to this "real presence," the Didache community would have been inclined to speak of the "real absence" of Jesus. True, Jesus was the revered servant of the Father who revealed, just a few decades earlier, the knowledge of the true God to the gentiles and the Way of Life championed by this Father. For the moment, however, Jesus was felt to be absent, and many or most of the Didache community might have seriously considered that he "must remain [absent] . . . until the time of universal restoration that God announced long ago through his holy prophets" (Acts 3:21). In this regard, interested persons ought to consult Brawley 1990.

#5k WHETHER CHILDREN RECEIVED COMMUNION

In chapter 3, it was concluded that infants and children were not candidates for baptism. From this, it would follow that the rubric of *Did.* 9:5 precludes such persons from drinking and eating of the consecrated cup and loaf. It remains to be considered, however, whether such persons were present during the time of the eucharist and were invited to participate in the eucharistic meal.

Nursing infants were probably present. Women engaged in family trades were not always in a position to have wet nurses (Nielson 66 n. 30); hence, it would have been normal for a nursing mother to take her infant with her wherever she went and to nurse her infant during the time of the eucharist. Since ancient women did not substitute the milk of animals and since breast-feeding might continue until a child's second or third year (Bradley 1986: 219), the sight of a nursing mother must have been fairly commonplace. Some mothers may have invited an older child or a slave to accompany them and to take charge of an infant during the time of the eucharist. These mothers would undoubtedly have followed this same practice when working at their trades or crafts.

In the ancient world, there was no equivalent to our modern extended period of adolescence, during which teens hover between childhood and adulthood and partake of their own unique teen culture. Girls entered into marriage near the onset of puberty (see #1s); boys passed an extended period apprenticing themselves in a trade. Hence, both sexes passed directly from childhood to adulthood.

In the Roman world, the extended family of adult freepersons (grandparents, parents, apprentices, visitors) usually ate at a common table while being served by household slaves and by their own underage children, whose service at table was frequently regarded as one of their chores (Dixon: 117). These children waited upon the adults and ate along with the kitchen slaves after the meal was finished. In households where no slaves were present, the mother would supervise her daughters and daughters-in-law in the preparation of the meal. Even in upper-class households where chores were not assigned to free children, their lower status usually required that they eat together at a place separated from the adults. "No matter how frequently they attended *cenae* [the main evening meal], children were never admitted as full and equal members of a family group, and never as the focal element of the proceedings" (Bradley 1998: 46). The point at which free youths were included at the adult table was variable, but most often it came with marriage in the case of girls and with the assumption of the *toga virilis* (the adult toga) in the case of boys—both were considered marks of adulthood and were celebrated with feasts (Dixon: 101f., 134f.).

Keith Bradley, in his study of the Roman family, reminds us of the following:

> The *cena* [the main evening meal] was not an affair that had anything of the familial about it in any modern sense. Rather, it was in essence an occasion for a man and his friends, his male friends about all, to pursue ease, well-being and conversational refinement while consuming food and drink. (Bradley 1998: 38)

Given this tradition, there would have been no cultivated sentiment on the part of a Roman husband always to have his wife dine with him (Bradley 1998: 38). With even greater force, however, underage children would not normally dine with their parents. "Until that crucial stage of adulthood had been reached, the child was in many ways kept at a social distance, a liminal being rather than a fully incorporated member" (Bradley 1998: 46). Hanne Neilson, in her study of Roman children at mealtimes, concurs:

> It is striking how far the Roman ideas of family life are from our concepts. Our concepts of the family, on the other hand, is [*sic*]

much more in accordance with the ideal presented by the early [fifth century] Christian writers. (Neilson 1998: 62)

To the degree that the Roman tradition prevailed within the households of the Didache community, there would have thus been little stimulus to have underage children join their parents during the time of the eucharist. Given the fact that the eucharist routinely took place in a household setting of a prominent member of the community, however, one can expect that nonbaptized slaves and children were occupied with the preparation of the food and the waiting on the table. In many instances, some of the baptized women joined them in this task and, when the eucharistic meal began, divided their attention between the meal preparation and the holy rite that was being enacted.

In the course of time, there were undoubtedly instances in which non-baptized members of the host family were invited to take part in the eucharistic feast. This, undoubtedly, had mixed results. On the one hand, the open eucharistic celebration served to exemplify the spirit and the bonds animating its members. On the other hand, the community was undoubtedly distracted from its own proper "family" agenda because it was endeavoring to be a gracious host and to cater to the level of understanding of its guests. Quite possibly the rule of allowing only the baptized to "eat and drink from your eucharist" (*Did.* 9:5) was set in place in order to prevent the recurrence of such compromising situations.

The Holy Name Dwelling in Our Hearts

Didache 10:2 gives thanks for the "holy name" that "you [the holy Father] tabernacle in our hearts." The framers of the *Didache* here used a familiar set of Jewish metaphors. The verb *kataskēnoō* literally means that the Father "pitches a tent" in which his "holy name" dwells. In the Hebrew Scriptures, "the place which the Lord your God will choose to make his name dwell" becomes a circumlocution for the Jerusalem temple (e.g., Dt 12:11; 14:23; 16:11; Ez 43:7). Nothing in the Hebrew Scriptures goes so far as to suggest that in lieu of or alongside of the Jerusalem temple, God had chosen to dwell "in our hearts." Draper comments:

> *Did.* 10:2 envisages the Name tabernacling in the hearts of believers as it had formerly done in the Temple. The community is the locus of God's presence, the place where the Shekhinah dwells. It is the equivalent of Paul's "Temple of the Holy Spirit" (1 Cor 3:16f.; cf. 6:19; 2 Cor 6:16; Rom 8:9). (Draper 1983: 216)

Draper is correct in identifying the Father's choice to dwell "in our hearts" as paralleling the tabernacling of his name in the Temple (also Vööbus 1968: 164). Moreover, while recognizing the independence of the *Didache* from Pauline influence, Paul's Jewish argument might nonetheless apply here: "For God's temple is holy, and that temple you are" (1 Cor 3:17). The *Didache* accordingly dropped "our Father" (9:2f.) in favor of "holy Father" (10:2) and made reference to "his holy name" (10:2). In rabbinic understanding, the Temple was the holiest place on earth (*m. Kelim* 1:6–9). The *Didache*, in contrast, regards its members as "saints" (4:2) such that the "holy Father" can pitch his tent in their hearts:

> We are permitted a glimpse into the inner life of these people, into that piety which moved them to gratitude and reverence. For these Christians felt themselves filled with the holiness of God who has chosen to make his dwelling place not just among them but in them. (Vööbus 1968: 119)

This indwelling of the "holy Father" is not to be reduced to a pious fiction or to sentimental feelings. "Holiness," for the framers of the *Didache* was firmly attached to knowing the Way of Life revealed by the Father and putting it into practice: "If you are able to bear the whole yoke of the Lord [the Father], you will be perfect" (6:2). Thus the servant of God living the Way of Life becomes the occasion for gentiles to marvel and to praise his holy name just as did many gentiles when they visited the temple in Jerusalem (Philo, *Embassy to Gaius* 295f.).

#5M WHETHER "THE NAME" (*DID.* 10:2) REFERRED TO JESUS

Some scholars have tried to see in the indwelling "holy name" an oblique reference to Jesus Christ, who is the image or "the Name" of God (Peterson 1944: 5; Kraft 1965a: 70). Vööbus comments:

> He [Peterson] believes that the term "Name" in this instance is a designation for "Christ." . . . This viewpoint has been given approval rather swiftly. Indeed, it has even been regarded [as] persuasive and decisive. What is more, it has been welcomed as a case excellently portraying the adaptation of an Old Testament formula referring to God by Jewish Christians who applied it to Christ. True enough, the word "Name" was used in primitive Christianity. . . . Nonetheless, instructive and interesting as all this may be, it is insufficient to carry conviction. As soon as this thesis is subject to closer scrutiny, this interpretation fails to hold

water—it proves to be nothing more than a theological construction. (Vööbus 1968: 115)

More accurately, one has here another case of a theological projection: a seemingly obscure term is given a definite meaning based on its use in a foreign context. Vööbus faithfully follows the inner logic of the text as his guide and rightly dismisses such imaginings as "nothing more than a theological construction" that "does violence to the role of Jesus clearly characterized as Servant" (1968: 115).

The Knowledge, Faith, and Immortality Revealed by Jesus

Along with his "holy name," the prayer after the meal offers thanks for "the knowledge, faith, and immortality" that has been revealed by the Father through his "servant Jesus" (*Did.* 10:2). Each of these three terms is significant:

1. *Knowledge.* In the eucharistic prayers before the meal, the broken loaf was consecrated as the "knowledge which you revealed to us through your servant Jesus" (*Did.* 9:3). Now that these fragments have been eaten, the "knowledge" revealed by the Father is associated with his "holy name" residing in "our hearts" (10:2). The heart, in Jewish anthropology, is not the center of "feeling" but of "discernment." The "knowledge" which is referred to here, therefore, must include (a) discerning the true God, the Father; (b) discerning the Father's Way of Life; and (c) discerning the Father's guarantee of his future kingdom. Those who have the "holy name" dwelling in their hearts can be said to have "knowledge" of these things.

2. *Faith.* In the context of the future-oriented eucharist, "faith" (*pistis*) does not have so much to do with accepting revealed truths that surpass rational discovery as with accepting God's promise of the future kingdom as trustworthy. The broken loaf was heralded earlier as evoking the eschatological ingathering of the scattered (9:3). Now those who have eaten these fragments have received a proleptic foretaste and promise of the kingdom. Thus "faith" here is primarily the "trust" that one can confidently adhere to the Way of Life and anticipate the future kingdom which the Father revealed through his servant Jesus.

3. *Immortality.* The term *athanasia* literally means the condition of "no-death" (*a-thanatos*). The *Didache* is not framed within a Greek anthropology wherein the soul, at the time of death, separates from

the body and enjoys "immortality." Hence, one cannot suspect that the Didache community suddenly left aside its anticipation of the resurrection of the dead (16:7) and substituted the immortality of the soul. The *Didache*, it will be remembered, opened by contrasting the Way of Life with the Way of Death (1:1) and the forty-two characteristics of the Way of Death (*hodos tou thanatou*) were enumerated with the final admonition: "May you be saved, my children, from all these things" (5:2). Therefore, in the context of the *Didache*, the "no-death" condition should be thought of as freedom from all these things. In 4:8, this same sense is again confirmed when the brothers and sisters are spoken of as being "sharers in the no-death things" (*en tō athanatō*). Thus, the eucharistic prayer would appear to give thanks for the "knowledge" and "faith" enabling them to experience freedom from "death" now and, in the future, to have that freedom confirmed by the resurrection of the righteous who have died (see ch. 10 below).

#5n Significance of "Almighty Master" (*Did.* 10:3)

The term "almighty Master" (*despotēs*) is only used once in the entire *Didache* and represents a shift away from "our Father" (*Did.* 8:2; 9:2f.), "holy Father" (10:2), "Lord" (10:5f.), and "God of David" (10:6). This term, however, was entirely at home in other Jewish and Christian prayers:

> God's omnipotence had usually been expressed by the title *despotēs*, "Master," in the Septuagint, especially in those books which did not form part of the Hebrew canon, in Philo, and in Josephus (where it was the most common form of address in prayer), either on its own or as part of a phrase such as "Master of all" (Jb 5:8; Wis. 6:7; 8:3), "Master of heaven and earth" (Jdt 9:12), "Master of every age" (Josephus, *Ant.* 1.272), while his creative activity is expressed in a relative clause, "who made heaven and earth" (Gn 14:19; 2 Chr 2:12). . . . The latter is continued in first-century Christianity (Acts 4:24; 14:15; Rev 10:6; 14:7), while the word *despotēs*, though rare in the New Testament, occurs frequently in *1 Clement*, once in the *Didache* (10:3), and occasionally in other early writings, but is short-lived and appears much less often after the middle of the second century. (Bradshaw 1982: 35)

For the intimate relation between acknowledging God as "Father" and as "almighty Master," see #4i.

The Institutional Narrative

Didache 10:3 represents the anamnesis or institutional narrative. According to the rabbinic tradition, prayers after a meal carry a divine mandate to "do this in memory of me." According to the Babylonian Talmud:

> How do we know that the invitation to recite the benediction after meals has a scriptural basis? It is as Scripture states, "And you shall eat and be full, and you shall bless [the Lord your God]" (Dt 8:10)—this [refers to] the blessing [after a meal], "Who feeds all." (*b. Berakhot* 48b)

Thus, within the prayers after meals (*Birkat Ha-Mazon*), one finds some reference to Dt 8:10—sometimes in the form of a direct quotation and sometimes as an allusion. The same holds true for the prayers after meals attributed to Abraham in the *Book of Jubilees* (150–100 B.C.E.):

> He [Abraham] blessed the Most High God, who created heaven and earth, who made all the good things on the earth, and gave them to the sons of men so that they might eat and drink and bless their creator. (*Jub.* 22:6)

The *Didache*'s institutional narrative acknowledges Dt 8:10 but then, knowing that the cup and loaf are consecrated, it makes reference to "spirit-sent food and drink" (*Did.* 10:3b). Thus, one has the following contrast:

Did. 10:2a— General Institutional Nar.	*Did.* 10:2b— Special Institutional Nar.
"to all people"	"to us"
"ordinary food and drink"	"spirit-sent food and drink"
"you have given"	"you have freely-given"
"for [*eis*] enjoyment"	"for [*eis*] life forever"
[through the fertile land]	"through your servant Jesus"

Didache 10:3a recites the mystery of creation whereby the Creator is remembered for having given to all peoples ordinary food and drink for their enjoyment. *Didache* 10:3b then immediately recites the mystery of redemption whereby the Father is remembered for having given "to us" that spirit-sent food and drink that is "for life forever" (*eis zōēn aiōnion*).

The *Didache* suggested earlier that slaves ought not to be compelled to embrace "the Father," for he calls only "those whom the Spirit has made ready" (4:10). Hence, the earlier universalism of 10:3a gives way here to a doctrine of election whereby those assembled know themselves as called by the spirit and as baptized "in the name of the holy Spirit" (7:1, 3). For this reason, the "spirit-sent" food and drink eaten at this meal cannot be offered to those estranged from the Spirit (9:5). Meanwhile, the alteration of verbs is significant: the "almighty monarch" merely "gives" (*didōmi*) ordinary food and drink to the masses while he "graciously bestows" (*charizomai*) the spirit-sent food and drink on us.

#50 WHY THE INSTITUTIONAL NARRATIVE OMITTED MENTION OF THE LAST SUPPER

In the past, the origins of the eucharist were approached by examining Jesus' deliberate intention voiced at the Last Supper to have his disciples "do this in memory of me." When these words were heard within a horizon of understanding that regarded the sacrament of the eucharist as absolutely unprecedented within Judaism and as absolutely unique to the Christian church, the mandate to "do this" was tantamount to establishing Jesus' direct intention of instituting a sacred rite that immediately and permanently sets the Christian church outside of Judaism. When these same words are heard within a Jewish horizon of understanding, however, the mandate to "do this" can be linked with the divine mandate of Dt 8:10—reestablishing the link whereby Jesus as a Jew would have been moved to bless God within the context of a meal. The former point of view takes great care to preserve the uniqueness of the eucharist (and the uniqueness of the church) by cutting Jesus off from his Jewish roots. The latter point of view takes care to preserve the uniqueness of Jesus' exemplary mode of table fellowship while allowing that the metaphors and intentionality with which he gave thanks were well within the understanding of the first-century Jewish disciples who carried on his tradition. The former point of view finds it imperative that the narrative of institution focuses exclusively on what Jesus did and said at the Last Supper. The latter point of view is content to allow that Jesus and his disciples came to the meal owing to a divine mandate to celebrate the Passover or, if multiple meals were involved, the divine mandate to give thanks as found in Dt 8:10.

Both points of view have a legitimate and historically sanctioned place within the Christian tradition. In the context of this work, where the Jesus movement is first and foremost honored as an enterprise within the boundaries of Judaism, the latter point of view is taken (see Talley 1976: 115f.). In so doing, it immediately becomes understandable how the eucharist of the *Didache* was what the early church understood as "doing" what Jesus did. In more specific terms, the very mandate to "do this" meant to give thanks to the Father as Jesus did. As such, the "do this" need not be interpreted to mean "tell what I did" as if to imagine that the "doing" was somehow deficient unless it included the "telling" of what Jesus did. Pierre Benoit was among the first Catholic scholars to allow that "do this" was not part of the rite itself but a rubric (i.e., a directive regarding the execution of the rite). If so, he insisted: "One does not recite a rubric. One executes it" (1939: 786).

Going further, Edward J. Kilmartin pointed out that many early Christian communities proceeded to "do this [i.e., to give thanks to the Father as Jesus did]" without narrating the events of the Last Supper (1974: 276f.; also Klein: 411–17; Mazza: 294–99). Thus, as far as the eucharist of the *Didache* was concerned, Kilmartin cautions that "it would be incorrect to conclude that this text does not represent a true eucharist because of the lack of an explicit reference to the Last Supper" (1974: 276). In fact, Kilmartin (also Mazza: 289–92) notes significant instances of the Christian eucharist from which the so-called "institutional narrative" was entirely absent:

> Another example of an early eucharist prayer which relates to [the] *Didache* can be found in the *Apocryphal Acts of the Apostles* (second/third century). One such prayer is that of *Acts of John* 85, where a breaking of bread is accompanied by a thanksgiving for faith and knowledge directed to Christ. The *Martyrdom of Polycarp* 14 also contains a simple thanksgiving prayer almost certainly derived from the Lord's Supper. It begins with an invocation of God, emphasizes the gifts of knowledge and election, and closes with a reference to the sharing of the cup of Christ unto eternal life. (Kilmartin 1974:277)

Norman Perrin was one of the early theologians to find a certain artificiality in the notion that Jesus, on the night before he died, enacted the one and only eucharist that he ever performed. Significant rites do not normally emerge out of a single instance of their performance. Moreover, the Synoptic Gospels share the perspective that Jesus was celebrating the Jewish Passover with his Jewish disciples on the night before he died; hence, even allowing that Jesus expanded and altered the Passover liturgy, it remains curious that the Lord's Supper did not remain a yearly event coinciding with the Jewish feast of Passover (Perrin: 104). Furthermore, it is also curious that the unblemished yearling that was killed and roasted just prior to every Passover played no part in the understanding of Jesus or of his disciples concerning what was taking place.

Faced with these difficulties, Perrin began with the notion that the eucharist emerged out of Jesus' habitual style of celebrating meals with his disciples (104f.). Every Jewish meal was hedged in by simple rituals before and after the meal. The *Didache*, consequently, presents precisely such a pattern: *Did.* 9 represents the prayers before the meal, while *Did.* 10 represents the prayers after the meal. Perrin had this to say:

> It is evident that the meals themselves were the important thing and not a theological purpose which they might be said to serve. The existence of such different theological emphases as those connected with the "Lord's Supper" in the New Testament (1 Cor 11) is an indication that the occasion has called forth the theologies, not the theologies the occasion. The practice of early Christian communal meals existed before there was a specifically Christian theology to give it meaning. (104)

Perrin asked himself why the habitual table fellowship of Jesus was so impressive and so central to his message. Was it because Jesus allowed religious and social outcasts ("tax collectors and sinners" [Mt 11:16–19 and par.]) to take their places with him and his disciples? Perrin allows that this might have given offense to pious Jews who could not imagine forgiveness being extended to persons such as this (107). Nonetheless, it cannot be imagined that Jesus' disciples all fell into this category or that table fellowship was continually about the challenge of forgiveness (107). What then? Perrin concluded that table fellowship with Jesus must have been a proleptic foretaste of the kingdom which formed the heart of Jesus' message (106f., 204f.). Bruce Chilton, using the same key texts as Perrin (Mt 8:11f.; 20:21; 22:1–14 and par.), expresses this integration of message and meal in this way:

> Meals in Jesus' fellowship became practical parables whose meaning was as evocative as his verbal parables. . . . To join in his meals consciously was, in effect, to anticipate the kingdom as it had been delineated by Jesus' teaching. Each meal was a proleptic celebration of God's kingdom. . . . There is, then, a certain inevitability in the saying, "I will not again drink of the fruit of the vine, until I drink it new in the kingdom of God" (cf. Mt 26:29, Mk 14:25 and Lk 22:16, 18). Quite outside the context of what came to be known as "the last supper," the practice of fellowship at meals in Jesus' movement in its formative period forged a link with the kingdom such that the promise of God's

final disclosure on behalf of his people was as ardently and carelessly anticipated as the next dinner. (1996: 86)

This is exactly what one finds in the eucharist of the *Didache*—those present drank of the cup of divine election and ate of the fragmented loaf which anticipated their inclusion in the final ingathering of the elect into the Father's kingdom. As a proleptic celebration of the kingdom, the eucharistic meal allowed those present to taste the future so vividly that some among them spontaneously cried out, "Hosanna to the God of David!" (*Did.* 10:6).

Today almost all scholars recognize that Jesus focused all his energies on the message of the kingdom, while, with the passage of time, the church gradually focused its energies on the messenger. Within the church of the second and subsequent centuries, consequently, the heralding of the kingdom (the prophetic message of Jesus) was forced to take a back seat to the heralding of the messenger. This transition showed up in the historical development of the eucharist. At first, the early church continued Jesus' practice of meal fellowship as a proleptic foretaste of the kingdom. Then, at a later point, the focal attention on the anticipated kingdom was forced to take a back seat to the experienced presence of the messenger in eating his "body" and drinking his "blood." With time, the "real presence" became such an awesome dynamic in the celebration of the eucharist that it gradually obscured the "absence" of Jesus (see Brawley: 142–45, Kilmartin 1974: 271f.) as the one who "would come again" (see John A. T. Robinson 1979: 118–39). In medieval practice, this naturally led to the desire on the part of the faithful to adore the eucharistic host and, because of their sense of being unworthy, never to eat thereof.

From the vantage point of this long historical trajectory, it is evident that the eucharist of the *Didache* stands near the beginning. Clearly the framers of the *Didache* were still doing what Jesus did when he took meals with his disciples as a proleptic particiation in the kingdom of God. The so-called primitive Christology of the *Didache* (see #5e) thus harmoniously takes its place within a primitive eucharistic theology of the anticipated coming of the Lord to gather the elect and to heal the terrible "absence"—absence of God, yes, but even more so, the absence of justice, peace, and righteousness on the face of the earth. I deliberately leave out the "absence" of Jesus because, true to the *Didache*, both David and Jesus have already played out their parts as "servants" of the Father and nothing more is expected of them. If the prophets called out, "Hosanna to the God of David!" (*Did.* 10:6), they might just as easily have called out, "Hosanna to the God of Jesus!" Quite simply, the framers of the *Didache* were expecting the Father to come (see ch. 10 below).

Various scholars have endeavored to reconstruct a trajectory bringing together the diverse strands of eucharistic development evident during the first century. One such trajectory would be as follows:

(1) The historical Jesus practiced an "open table fellowship" with disciples, tax collectors, sinners, and others.

(2) These meals continued after Jesus' death and began to be seen through a variety of allegorical, eschatological, and messianic lenses.

(3) With special emphasis on the soteriological significance of bread, the followers of Jesus in Hellenistic Judaism concentrated on the power of the elements at the meal. Pre-Pauline circles particularly exhibit pneumatic understanding of the meal. In certain circles, this pneumatic interpretation of the elements led to an identification of the elements with Christ's body and blood. . . .

(4) On these same Hellenistic grounds, christological interpretation developed the "words of institution," and associations with Hellenistic remembrances of the dead elaborated the connection of the community's cultic meal to Jesus' death. . . .

(5) Some pre-Marcan and pre-Lucan traditions joined the historicizing of the last supper to the Passover meal; others did not.

(6) By the latter quarter of the century three different cultic meal traditions were celebrated . . . :

   (a) a regular "eucharistic" meal with pneumatic interpretation of the elements . . . and testified to most thoroughly in the *Didache*;

   (b) a sacramental meal where the food and drink were identified with Jesus' flesh and blood . . . and testified to in the Johannine traditions; and

   (c) a combination of Hellenistic last/Lord's supper practices with Synoptic elaborations of a "sacramental last supper." (summary of Kollmann in Taussig: 733f.)

This synopsis is instructive from a number of vantage points. First, it enables us to appreciate that "a variety of allegorical, eschatological, and messianic lenses" were shaping the eucharist during the entire period of the first century. Second, it enables us to situate the eucharist of the *Didache* within an authentic trajectory even though it did not identify the elements with Christ's body and blood.

It is interesting to note that the *Apostolic Constitutions* (380 C.E.) retained the key elements of the eschatology of the *Didache* while importing new elements as well. While it is beyond the scope of this volume to trace the development of the eucharist during the first four centuries, it is instructive to discover some of the ways the eucharist of the *Didache* was expanded following the mid-first century. Let three points suffice:

1. The order of the consecrations (cup–fragment) was changed to harmonize with what became, in the course of the centuries, the preferred order (loaf–cup) (see #5g).

2. The thanksgiving over the loaf retained the significance of "the life which you revealed to us through your servant Jesus" (*Apostolic Constitutions* 7.25.2) but then was expanded in order to identify Jesus as the one "whom you also sent for our salvation to become a human being, whom you also assented to suffer and to die, whom you also seated at your right hand . . ." (7.25.2). Despite this expressed concentration on Jesus, the eucharist still retained the full eschatological import of the bread scattered over the hills (7.25.3 = *Did.* 9:3).

3. The thanksgiving over the cup was entirely silent about the "holy vine of David" for the cup was now to be associated with "the prized blood of Jesus Christ, the one poured out for us" (7.25.4), and at this point the bread is referred to as "the prized body" (7.25.4). Consistent with this new understanding, the rubric of *Did.* 9:5 continued to exclude those who have not been baptized, but the text read "baptized into the death of the Lord" (7.25.5) instead of the earlier "baptized in the name of the Lord" (*Did.* 9:5).

From this brief summary, one can appreciate that the *Apostolic Constitutions* reflect how the eucharist of the *Didache* changed over three hundred years and absorbed Pauline overtones (1 Cor 11:23–26). However, even in the *Apostolic Constitutions,* the loaf is not initially identified as "the body of Christ" and no institutional narrative drawn from the Synoptics is anywhere in sight—proof that, even in the fourth century, the eucharistic prayers of the *Didache* were still honored as valid without a recitation of the so-called "words of institution." For those interested, Enrico Mazza develops this argument in detail (293–99). For our purposes, enough has been said.

The Petitions for the Kingdom

The recitation of God's past accomplishments in *Did.* 10:3f. looked forward to God's future accomplishments in 10:5. Here again, the gathering together of "your church" at the end of time was the overriding concern. *Did.* 9:4 had this gathering take place "from the ends of the earth"; now, using an alternate metaphor, it was to be "from the four winds" (10:5). Those in whom his Name dwells, those who have drunk the "spirit-sent food and drink" of this eucharist, earnestly looked forward to being gathered into the kingdom. Members of the community already acknowledged that "apart from God, nothing happens" (3:10). At this point, therefore, it was the Lord of the Future who was called upon: "Remember, Lord, your church" (10:5). How so? To save her; to perfect her; to gather her. Each of these is decidedly eschatological:

1. *To save her.* The deliverance from evil also figured in the Our Father (8:2). There, the aorist imperative made clear that the one-time future deliverance was being envisioned. *Did.* 16:3f. makes it clear that the Didache community expected enormous evils to emerge "in the last days" (16:3).
2. *To perfect her.* The perfection of the church is an ongoing process (6:2), but it takes on a special urgency as the end times approach (10:6; 16:2). The perfecting of the church "in your love" was expected to take place through "the burning process of testing" whereby "the ones having remained firm in their faith will be saved by the accursed burning-process itself" (16:5). The meaning of these texts will be worked out in detail in chapters 10 and 15.
3. *To gather her.* After being delivered from every evil and perfected, then "the sanctified church" can be gathered together "into your kingdom which you have prepared for her" (10:5). In effect, the members of this community belong to him (Draper 1983: 213; Vööbus 1968: 119)—their "holy Father" (10:2) and, in the end, the community petitions that they will be holy just as he is holy.

One notes here a decidedly communitarian consciousness. Far from being an individual appeal for deliverance and holiness, the presumption is that all stand together. This is consistent with *Did.* 14:1–3 where the eucharist is regarded as "your sacrifice" and not as "your sacrifices." So, too, the apocalyptic ending warns: "Be watchful over your [singular] life" (16:1). The implications of this communitarian consciousness will be explored further in chapters 8 and 10.

The Final Ecstatic Anticipation

In the context of a prayer for the ingathering of the elect and the coming of the kingdom of God, anticipation grows hot. Four bold acclamations are shouted out:

1. *"Come, grace!"* The term "grace" (*charis*) refers to a "free gift." The celebrant has just called upon the Lord to save, to protect, and to gather his church "into your kingdom which you have prepared" (10:5). This is the "grace" that is now ecstatically called for (Niederwimmer 1998: 162; Vööbus 1968: 104). And, as the kingdom comes, "this world" will "pass away" (*Did.* 10:5). Both verbs are in the aorist imperative suggesting a once-and-for-all coming and a once-and-for-all passing away.

2. *"Hosanna to the God of David!"* The "God of David" is greeted as though he is already on his way to earth. As will be shown in chapter 10, it would be mistaken here to imagine that "the community rejoices in God who sends the Messiah, the son of David" (Niederwimmer 1998: 162f.). Later rabbinic evidence shows that while "the Kingdom of David" was an obligatory part of the prayer after meals in Babylon (*b. Berakhot* 48b), the Palestinian rabbis preferred to expect "the God of David" (*y. Berakhot* 4:5; *y. Rosh Hashanah* 4:6). The *"hosanna,"* meanwhile, is not a Greek word at all; rather, it is a transliteration of "a liturgical acclamation borrowed from the Jewish cult" (Vööbus 1968: 103; see, e.g., Ps 118:25). Here, in the *Didache*, one finds the first use of "hosanna" in a Christian rite (Niederwimmer 1998: 162).

3. *"If anyone is holy, be admitted!"* Following upon the mood and the context of what comes before, those who are holy (*Did.* 10:5, 16:2) are urged to enter into the kingdom that God has prepared for those who love him. Those not ready, meanwhile, are urged to use this final moment to repent (i.e., to turn toward God and God's ways).

4. *"Marana tha! Amen!* This ecstatic welcome to the Lord parallels no. 2 above. Here, however, one lapses entirely into Aramaic—the everyday language used by first-century Jews. *"Marana tha!"* means "Come Lord!" "Amen!" resists translation for it is the unique acclamation "found in the cult of the temple and in the worship of the synagogue" as the "response of the people to the blessings [just pronounced]" (Vööbus 1968: 103; also Niederwimmer 1998: 164).

The lines, "If someone is holy . . . ; if someone is not . . . ," clearly breaks the flow within these four acclamations. Those present were addressed and not the Father. Nonetheless, if it is remembered that we are dealing with thematic summaries, then it is easy to understand how the feverish anticipation of the Lord's coming would be a dream fulfilled for some and a terror for others. The phrases here do not differ markedly from the contrasting phrases used by the Son of Man in Matthew's end-times parable:

> "Come, you that are blessed . . . , inherit the kingdom. . . ." (Mt 25:34)
> "You that are accursed, depart from me. . . ." (Mt 25:41)

In the context of Matthew's parable, however, conversion of life is too late. In the case of the *Didache*, in contrast, these sober admonitions are heard at a time when they can be acted upon.

The evident stylistic unity of *Did.* 9:2 to 10:5 suggests that the complete thematic material for the celebrant ends at *Did.* 10:5 with the refrain,

"Because yours is the power and the glory forever." The four fragments of 10:6, therefore, must represent "other voices." In practice, once the final refrain was recited or sung in unison, perhaps various persons shouted out this or that acclamation (like those suggested in 10:6). Alternately, given the emotional pitch with which the eucharist climaxes, perhaps everyone, all at the same time, shouted out the acclamations following the lead of the celebrant or in dialogue with the celebrant (Lietzmann 1979: 193; Niederwimmer 1998: 161). Or, again, given the proximity of 10:7, perhaps 10:6 represents a sampling of the urgent themes taken up and expanded upon by the prophets—a suggestion that will be developed in the next chapter. In any case, the overlapping and randomness within 10:6 would be satisfactorily understood if they represented not the themes developed by the celebrant but the popular and spontaneous response that erupted within the congregation.

#5P VARIATIONS IN THE COPTIC FRAGMENT OF THE *DIDACHE*

The British Museum Oriental Manuscript 9271 represents a single sheet of papyrus written in Coptic that corresponds to *Did.* 10:3b–12:2a. In *Did.* 10:6, the Coptic fragment has variations deserving our attention because they may shed some light on the intent of the *Didache* itself. The Coptic fragment may be translated as follows:

. . . because yours is the power and the glory forever. *Amen!*
Come *Lord!* And pass away, this world! *Amen!*
Osanna to the *house* of David!
   He who is holy, *come!*
   He who is not holy, be converted!
Marana tha! Amen!
But allow the prophets to eucharistize in the manner. . . (1.10–15).

The Coptic has "Come Lord!" where the manuscript of the *Didache* reads "Come grace!" The Greek is admittedly more obscure to our ears, yet it would be a mistake to try to correct the *Didache* text by admitting the Coptic variant. This can be seen more clearly when the second acclamation is considered. The Coptic omits the initial "H" when transliterating *hosanna*. What is being hailed, however, is "the house of David" and not the "God of David" (*Did.* 10:6). The "house of David" leans toward referring to the expected messianic king who would fulfill the divine promises made to David. Thus, the "Lord" expected in the Coptic fragment might indeed refer to the Lord Messiah and not to the Lord God (as is the clear intent of the *Didache* in its use of "God of David").

When the end-time scenario of *Did.* 16 is examined in chapter 10, it will be shown that the *Didache* has (as yet) no notion that Jesus or some other messianic figure would come to establish the kingdom on behalf of the Lord God. In the eucharistic acclamations of the *Didache*, therefore, it is the "grace [of the kingdom]" and the "God of David" that are fervently expected. On these grounds alone, it would appear that the Coptic fragment represents a liturgical and theological development that the *Didache* did not yet embrace but which later users of the *Didache* would embrace. The *Apostolic Constitutions,* for example, reads, "Hosanna to *the son* of David; *blessed be the one coming in the name of the Lord, the Lord God, the one appearing in the flesh*" (7.26.5). Here, "the house of David" of the Coptic fragment has been replaced by "the son of David," and the text has been expanded based on Mt 21:9.

Ever since the Coptic fragment was first discovered in 1923, there has been considerable debate about whether the fragment represents an earlier version of the *Didache* (in translation) or whether the fragment represents a more developed and consequently later version of the *Didache* (Jones and Mirecki: 84–86). If the Coptic fragment could be shown to be earlier, then it would be legitimate to use it in order to reconstitute an earlier version of the *Didache* (Wengst 1984) or to correct the received text (Audet 1958: 62–67). If later, however, then the Coptic would be valuable only to signal one route by which the *Didache* was later expanded and edited to reflect subsequent liturgical and theological developments.

On the basis of the variant considered above, the Coptic fragment would appear to be later. The *Didache* embraces the Jewish message of Jesus that God was coming to establish his kingdom. In the course of time, Christians moved their eschatological focus from "the final coming of the Lord God" to "the return of the Lord Jesus" (see, e.g., John A. T. Robinson 1979: 140ff.). The Coptic variations lean in the direction of this shift.

C. Schmidt, writing only a few years after the discovery of the fragment, concluded that the Coptic reflects a liturgical reworking of the *Didache* (93). He made this judgment on the basis of the three additional "Amens," the expression "son of man," and the "ointment prayer." In the section translated above, one can see two of the three additional "Amens." The expression "son of man" need not concern us here. The "ointment prayer," however, is significant because, while it is entirely absent from the received text of the *Didache*, it appears in precisely the same place in the *Apostolic Constitutions*. The "ointment prayer" comes immediately after the section of the Coptic fragment translated above:

> But allow the prophets to eucharistize in the manner they wish. And concerning the word of *myron*, eucharistize in this way, saying this:

> We give you thanks, Father, for the *myron*
> which you have made known to us through Jesus, your Son.
> To you is the glory forever. Amen (1.14–20).

To begin with, it is not certain whether the Coptic word *myron* refers to "ointment [for the sick]" (e.g., Mk 6:13; Jas 5:14f.) or to "ointment [used for the newly baptized]" (see Vööbus 1968: 43–45; Niederwimmer 1998: 166). Or, again, perhaps Stephen Gero is correct when he tries to demonstrate that *myron* was used in this context to refer to "incense" that was traditionally blessed and burned at Roman dinners (Gero: 68ff.; see critique of Niederwimmer 1998: 166f.). Whatever the meaning, it is difficult to understand how the *myron* was, in any sense, "made known to us through Jesus." The *Apostolic Constitutions,* for example, entirely overcomes this difficulty by giving thanks "for the sweet smell of the balsam and for the immortality which you revealed to us through your servant Jesus" (7.27.1).

Without attempting to resolve these and other difficulties, the "ointment prayer" can at least be identified as a later addition "imitating the archaic language of the preceding prayers of the *Didache*" (Niederwimmer 1998: 167). Klaus Wengst, however, disagrees. Accordingly, with some hesitation, he adds the "ointment prayer" to the received text of the *Didache* on the grounds that it appears to have been removed by the medieval copyist (1984: 59). The logic of this "removal" is not evident. Nonetheless, Wengst places great stock in the authenticity and early character of the Coptic fragment. B. Dehandshutter, upon evaluating the nearly fifty changes that Wengst makes in the received text, notes that in seven instances, Wengst alters the received text to reflect what he finds in the Coptic fragment. Needless to say, after making so many alterations in the received text, it is difficult, if not impossible, to provide a coherent historic and linguistic analysis of the text because one never has the firm assurance that all the "corrections" made were heard and used at one time and in one place. With this in mind, the present commentary has joined hands with those who prefer to work with the received text of the *Didache* as far as possible. Furthermore, given the conviction that the Coptic fragment represents an alternative and later version of the *Didache*, there is no sound reason to use the Coptic fragment to either alter or interpret the received Greek text.

The variations in the Coptic fragment, however, do provide us with some marginal help in evaluating the *Didache*. In the first place, the ragged construction found in *Did.* 10:6 can be definitively seen as not resulting from errors on the part of the copyist. The Coptic fragment has the self-same ragged construction at this point; hence, the suspicion that *Did.* 10:6 lists various acclamations voiced by persons other than the celebrant tends to gain further support. Second, given the kind of alterations found in the

Coptic, one can surmise that it found its home in a community bent on welcoming the Lord Messiah rather than the Lord God. The Coptic fragment, therefore, gives testimony to how the expectation of "your kingdom come" gradually gave way to the expectation of the "the second coming." Third, the Coptic fragment illustrates how the *Didache* exercised an authority and an appeal outside the Greek-speaking world.

Beyond this, care must be taken not to allow the Coptic fragment to interpret the intent of the received Greek text even when the received text is not altered to conform to the Coptic fragment. The intent of the *Didache* must be primarily resolved on the basis of sustained attention to the internal clues within the *Didache* itself. The same thing, of course, can be said for the Coptic fragment, since it represents a time and a place, a liturgy and an eschatology, that is proper to itself. This exploration remains to be done and goes beyond the scope of this present book (see Jones and Mirecki: 86).

#5Q WHETHER THE "UNHOLY" EXITED BEFORE RECEIVING COMMUNION

Martin Dibelius (32ff.) and Hans Lietzmann (192) understand the words, "If anyone is holy, come! If anyone is not, convert!" (*Did.* 10:6), to be a rubric whereby "the holy" were called forward to receive communion while the unholy were called to depart from the assembly and to reform their lives. Such an interpretation either requires (a) that the earlier benedictions (9:2–4) were not immediately followed by passing the consecrated cup and broken loaf or (b) that the rubric found at 10:6 has to be reassigned to its "proper place" immediately after 9:4. Such a cut-and-paste methodology imposes upon the text the preunderstanding of the interpreter and violates the integrity of the text (Vööbus 1968: 71, 83). Furthermore, the very notion that the unholy were called on to depart from the assembly to reform their lives finds little support within the context of the *Didache* or elsewhere. In fact, the confession of failings (14:1) and the resolution of conflicts (14:2) already presume that those present were worthy; hence, a fresh barrier just before communion hardly seems to be what the text intends.

#5R LIVING IN THE EXPECTATION OF THE END TIMES

From our contemporary situation, it is difficult to enter emotionally and religiously into the eucharist of the *Didache*, since it is so patently directed toward the future expectation of God coming into history to gather his elect into the kingdom prepared for them. Some would be tempted to think of such persons as "having their heads in the clouds" or of "escaping reality into a fantasy world." The fact that God did not come and gather his elect into his kingdom during the last two thousand years lends further weight to seeing this way of being in the world as irresponsible. Furthermore, the fact that modern-day fundamentalists have revived a fervent expectation of the end times without satisfactorily explaining why God has waited for two thousand years has had the effect of further distancing many sober Christians from such a persuasion.

In the course of researching the *Didache*, my own perceptions on this score have been entirely turned around. I now understand that the members of the Didache communities were persuaded by their own experience that the social order they knew was rapidly becoming unstable and heading for certain destruction. In the meantime, God was getting ready to come to earth to establish an entirely new social order. The members of the Didache communities were dedicated to this new order. Their prayers gave voice to their experience of living on the threshold of God's future. In subsequent chapters (esp. ch. 10), the internal logic governing their eschatological vision will be explored. For the moment, however, it suffices to note that the anticipation of the kingdom of God was not a marginal or transitional aspect of the *Didache*—it was the heartfelt center of every eucharistic celebration and the social glue that lured and bound together those living the Way of Life revealed by the Father through his servant Jesus.

#5s The Jewish Character of the Eucharistic Prayers

While it cannot be established that the eucharistic prayers of the *Didache* represent an editing of known synagogue or meal prayers (see #5v), the Jewish character of the prayers in the *Didache* can be clearly established. Joseph Heinemann, when he discusses the character of the official Jewish prayers, singles out aspects such as the following:

> By comparison with other prayers of this type found among the peoples of the ancient Near East, the "praise of God" . . . is quite restrained; the Talmudic Sages strongly opposed its elaboration through the heaping-up of additional epithets of praise. (244)

> Nor does the style of the petitionary prayers express the same abject humility and self-abnegation of the petitioner who views

himself as a lowly, worthless creature in the presence of his Master, the Great King. Only rarely do such prayers use the supplicatory interjection *nā'* (= "we beseech thee") which expresses the humility and hesitation of the petitioner, while they frequently make use of the imperative . . . without any reservation as to its propriety. . . . This relationship is thus conceived as more closely akin to that of a son to his loving father. . . . (244, 245)

They [the official statutory prayers] are not the clamorous type of prayer in which the petitioner relies on his own merits and demands that which is legally due to him. He does not request a reward for his good deeds, but rather God's mercy and grace. There is not a single instance in any of the basic statutory prayers in which the petitioner will seek to justify the expectation that his request will be granted by citing his own merits. . . . (246)

There are no prayers from the Talmudic period which are addressed to intermediaries of any sort—neither to angels, nor to saints or Patriarchs. (249)

The confessional-type prayer (referring specifically to the confession of sins) does not occupy as central a position in the Jewish liturgy as it does, for example, in the [later] Christian liturgies. . . . The confessional prayer is not, then, to be regarded as a separate category of prayer. . . . (249f.)

We have not found a single instance of a separate or special prayer which the worshipper will recite "on behalf of someone else (although he is permitted, "if he has a sick person at home," to include a special request for his recovery . . .). It is not difficult to discover the reason for this since the statutory prayer, whether it is recited by an individual or by the congregation, is by its very definition a congregational prayer, i.e., one which is recited on behalf of the entire community and, for this reason, is phrased throughout in the first person plural, "we." (250)

Each of these characteristics of the official prayers in rabbinic Judaism finds a substantial resonance in the prayers of the *Didache*. The character of the prayers of the *Didache*, consequently, can be said to be profoundly shaped by the same currents that thrived in the synagogues.

When and How Often the Eucharist Was Celebrated

Initially, the Jesus movement does not appear to have had any fixed rule for when and how often the eucharist was celebrated. Since the eucharist involved a full meal, one can presume that early eucharists took place in the evening as did the Lord's Supper. The prevailing opinion of scholars is that "the eucharist appears to have been held on Saturday evening during the first century, . . . but on Sunday morning from the second century on" (*ABD* 6:983e). Various opinions have been offered as to why this switch became necessary, but this need not concern us here.

The Christian Scriptures say nothing about the frequency of the eucharist and offer no rule as to the preference of a fixed day. Thus, the *Didache* represents the first instance within Christian sources wherein a rule is offered to the effect that the eucharistic gatherings should take place "every divinely instituted Lord's Day" (*Did.* 14:1). "The Didachist orders that a eucharist be celebrated on every Lord's day when the community comes together" (Niederwimmer 1998: 195). Since a full meal is involved, a Saturday evening meal would be implied if it can be assumed that the "Lord's Day" begins at sundown after the Sabbath.

Justin Martyr, writing in 150 C.E., is the first church father to testify that "Sunday is the day on which we all hold our common assembly" (*1 Apol.* 47), and early morning assemblies were the rule. The use of the term "Sunday" here offers evidence that his readers, the Roman emperor and his subjects, have adopted the seven-day week and have named the days after the planets (see #4a). Since the Romans adopted the seven-day week into their calendar sometime during the first century, it is most probably the case that "Sunday" would have had no meaning for the mid-first-century audience of the *Didache*.

Niederwimmer follows Rordorf (1968: 179–205) in concluding that the *Didache* had a weekly eucharist on Sunday evening rather than Saturday. Niederwimmer even goes so far as to translate the awkward opening phrase of *Did.* 14:1 (*kata kyriakēn de kyriou*) as "the Sunday of the Lord" (1998: 195). This rendering of *Did.* 14:1, however, is not without its difficulties. A complete discussion of this complex issue is reserved for chapter 8 (see #8j).

#5T WHO PRESIDED OVER THE EUCHARISTIC CELEBRATION?

The issue of eucharistic presidency is a very tender one in many contemporary church circles. Moreover, massive amounts of energy have been used to support denominational apologetics whereby each confessional church has endeavored to demonstrate that the church order found in the Christian Scriptures authenticates key elements within their currently existing way of operating (F. Fiorenza: 67–71). When scholars enter into an ecumenical climate that frees them from the necessity of rigidly maintaining a narrow confessional rhetoric, they are free to acknowledge that

the first-century churches operated using diverse norms, many of which differ markedly from those prevailing today. The following represents the growing Catholic scholarly consensus governing this issue (Noll 1970, 1993;
Osborne 1988, 1993; Schillebeeckx 1981, 1985):

1. Jesus celebrated the Last Supper without any defined or implied priestly
identity. Nothing in his Jewish tradition necessitated that a priest would or
should "preside" over every Passover. The theological reconstruction
whereby Jesus was regarded as instituting the Holy Sacrifice of the Mass
which could be presided over only by "a validly ordained priest" derives legitimately from a medieval horizon of understanding and fails to represent the
perspective of the early church.

2. The Gospels and the Acts of the Apostles are silent about "priesthood"
precisely because no one who knew Jesus or who had joined the Jesus movement regarded "priesthood" as having anything to do with Jesus of with the
early rites of the church. The Twelve whom Jesus trained acted by virtue of
having been his disciples and having been commissioned to teach, to heal,
and to baptize in his name. "To presuppose that the twelve, the apostles, the
episkopoi or even others had to be ordained is a dogmatic presupposition,
which neither historical data nor scriptural data support" (Osborne 1993:
26). Even the author of the Letter to the Hebrews (90–120 C.E.) takes as his
starting point that "if he [Jesus] were *on earth,* he would not be a priest at
all" (Heb 8:4) before going on to argue that Christ was appointed priest by
God *in the heavenly sanctuary* to atone for sins (Heb 9:23f.).

3. The Acts of the Apostles speaks of baptisms, of ordinations, and of the
"breaking of bread" (which most scholars understand as designating
"eucharist"). None of these rites, however, is explicitly or implicitly tied to
any notion of priesthood, nor is there any suggestion that only the Twelve or
those ordained by them could preside at these rites. Presuming that the
eucharist was celebrated by the early church, the New Testament knows of
no class of persons by any title for whom "presidency" at the eucharist is
assigned or reserved. During the early second century, this situation will
change insofar as liturgical functions will be increasingly reserved to the bishops or those appointed by them, but this later situation should not be read
back into the first-century churches.

Relative to the *Didache,* conservative Catholic scholarship has taken the
directive regarding the appointment of "bishops and deacons" (*Did.* 15:1)
as the point of departure for assuming that the material regarding the
eucharist (9–10) was directed to them as "presiders." The additional fact that
their office is defined and defended as "the ministry (*leitourgian*) of the
prophets and teachers" (15:2 as traditionally translated) is used to further
confirm this perception. The Greek term *leitourgia* refers to the public service performed by a free citizen. This term was appropriately taken over by
the church to describe the ordained ministries in the church. Hence, the use
of this term seemed to imply that bishops were appointed for the "liturgical"

ministry—a position that even some Protestants are willing to confirm (e.g., Campenhausen: 73; see detailed illustrations in #9d and #9f).

The internal logic of the *Didache* itself fails to support such a contention. To begin with, nothing permits the hearer to deduce that the liturgical sections are somehow set aside from the rest of the document and addressed exclusively to the bishops. If this were the case, the framers would have done what the editors of the *Apostolic Constitutions* (380 C.E.) did when they revised the *Didache* to read, "(And) concerning baptism, *O bishop or elder . . . , thus will you baptize as the Lord appointed . . ."* (7.22.1; words added in italics). Furthermore, the *leitourgia* ("unremunerated public service") assigned to bishops and deacons is never equated with presiding at baptisms and eucharists but is specifically associated with "*the unpaid public service* [characteristic] of the prophet-teachers" (*Did.* 15:2). This will be examined in detail in chapter 9.

In Protestant circles, the tendency has been to see the *Didache* as exhibiting the first signs of an official ecclesial ministry as being set up to control and to replace an earlier reliance on a charismatic ministry. Thus, Protestants have been eager to designate the *Didache* as a document written after the close of the New Testament era and to emphasize church organization. The fact that the "bishop-deacons" are legitimated by virtue of pointing to the "prophet-teachers" (*Did.* 15:1f.) appeared to demonstrate that, in the early phase, only charismatic persons directed community affairs (see #6o). While this schema has some possible resonance within the text, it also has the danger of projecting problems coming from another period back into the framework of the *Didache* (details in #9f).

All in all, the *Didache* makes no mention of any special class of persons as administering baptism or presiding at the eucharist. In the last chapter, it was concluded that, in the case of baptism, the one who had trained the candidate and become his/her spiritual parent would have been the expected person to make the final arrangements regarding fasting and to handle the selection and use of appropriate water (7:2). Since both baptism and eucharist are introduced with the same introductory formula, it would seem that the first eucharist might normally be presided over (as suggested above) by the same mentor who oversaw the training and baptism of the candidate. In the case of a female candidate, therefore, it would be presumed that the "spiritual mother" of the newly baptized woman would preside over the first eucharist. No argument from silence based upon the patriarchal structures of the early church should be allowed to preclude, in principle, the action of women in presiding. Moreover, the fact that the *Didache*'s church is an extended family and that the eucharist is a shared meal in a private home would have given women a much greater freedom to act with and among men. Chapters 9 and 16 will consider arguments on both sides of this issue in greater depth.

The practice of Judaism is quite important as providing a background out of which the practice of the *Didache* emerged. The temple rites were largely in the hands of the officiating priests—"the people were merely onlookers and even the chanting of hymns was entrusted to the Levitical singers" (Heinemann: 145). In the synagogue, however, "the prayer . . . was recited by a Prayer Leader, an 'emissary' of the people themselves, rather than by a priestly officiant" (ibid.). Even though the local synagogue had a system of elders, it would seem that "any male [Jew] might be called upon to read the Hebrew Scriptures, supply the Aramaic translation, or recite the Shema or Tefillah [the Eighteen Benedictions]" (Beckwith: 80). According to the Mishnah, not even a minor, a blind man, or a man in rags could be wholly excluded from these liturgical roles (*m. Megillah* 4:4–8). In the rites celebrated within the home, the father of the household normally presided, yet even official Judaism designated certain roles as reserved to women (e.g., the lighting of the Sabbath lamp with the associated prayer [*m. Shabbat* 2:6]). Details regarding synagogue organization and the impact this might have had upon the *Didache* will be taken up in chapter 9.

Social Implication of Women and Slaves Eating with Freemen

Meals in the ancient world served to emphasize and maintain social status (Neyrey 1991: 363). Children, therefore, did not eat at the same table as adults, even in upper-class households where they were exempted from waiting on table owing to the number of slaves assigned to that duty (Dixon: 117). Free women, on the other hand, frequently ate with their men at a common table—a situation favored by Roman custom over and against the Greek (Bradley 1998: 38; Corley: 28). Especially in rural areas and in household shops where women worked alongside their men, it was even possible for men and women to work together in the preparation of a meal (Foss: 46). The case of slaves, however, is entirely different: "Slaves were not normally allowed to recline at dinner or eat during dinner because they were busy cooking and serving the meal, and were not of adequate rank to join the company [of free-persons] regardless" (Foss: 48).

Needless to say, these traditions were not allowed to prevail during the eucharist. The host at every eucharist was the Lord, and everyone invited was a "servant" of the Lord (as were Jesus and David). Men, women, and slaves were all equally trained to "not exalt yourself" or "give boldness to your soul" (*Did*. 3:9). Men, women, and slaves were all trained to "reconcile those fighting" and "not take into account social status when it comes time to reprove against failings" (4:3). Men, women, and slaves were all likewise trained in the rules of reciprocal giving and taking (4:5–8). At the eucharistic table, therefore, one can expect that issues of social rank and individual merit were sidestepped in order to anticipate the social situation—an equality of discipleship—that would prevail in the forthcoming kingdom of God.

The *Didache* has no need to draw attention to this aspect of their common meals because voluntary associations existed that brought together men, women, and slaves as equal participants in a common rule of life throughout the Roman Empire. The bylaws of the Roman Funeral Society in Lanuvium (see #2n), for example, provided women and men, slaves and free-persons, the shared benefit of a fitting burial. All members paid a uniform monthly fee and took their turn at presiding at the regular meetings, which involved worship, eating, and companionship. The by-laws even made provisions for the "unreasonable" possibility that a master or mistress of a slave might "refuse to relinquish his [her] body for burial" (Wilken: 38). In cases where a slave would achieve his/her freedom while a member of the society, they were "required to donate an *amphora* [approx. a gallon] of good wine" (ibid.) so that the members could drink to their good fortune. Thus, in the Didache community, it would be commonplace to expect that baptized slaves would have equal rights and responsibilities within the assemblies but that this did not alter their public and legal status outside the organization.

In the case of slaves, therefore, even their Christian owners were forced to regard them as free agents, even as "brothers" and "sisters," in the context of the eucharistic assembly. Outside of the assembly, however, "slaves will be subject to your lords as to the image of God in shame and fear" (*Did.* 4:11). Such an arrangement required that masters and slaves would live in a bifurcated world in which habits from one side would sometimes spill over to the other side. Consider the case of meals, for instance. During ordinary meals, even baptized slaves would be expected to keep their place and to serve at the table of their master and mistress and, when they had eaten, to receive from the mistress a share of the leftovers in the kitchen. When the eucharistic assembly met in this home, however, those baptized slaves might prepare the meal but, when the rites began, they would have their place "as equals" with all others at the table. Undoubtedly this caused some dissatisfaction in the kitchen since, even among slaves, there would have been the expectation that none of their number should attain a preferment that raised them above their station in life. This may even have caused some uneasiness among some of the Christians in attendance, since in their world, they were accustomed to eating among social equals. The Lord, however, "calls those whom the spirit has made ready," and it was not for them to call into question the preferments of the Lord who was "over both" (*Did.* 4:10).

The treatment of slaves in the ancient world was both more harsh and more lenient than in the Old South (*ABD* 6:66). Slaves, for instance, were often called upon to do dangerous and body-breaking work (e.g., mining, stone quarrying, bridge building), which meant dying at an early age. Based on Roman tombstones, the average life expectancy of a slave was little more than twenty years (Harris). On the other hand, slavery practiced by Romans most commonly extended the incentive of allowing slave pseudo-marriages to prosper and of allowing slaves to garner extra earnings that could eventually be used to purchase their freedom (*ABD* 6:68–72). In the case of the *Didache*, those in the trades would have naturally used slaves as part of their production teams, even in the case of household shops (de Sainte Croix: 271; Burford: 87–91). As members of such teams, however, skilled slaves took on a functional status that partially overcame their social status. One can expect, therefore, that, in many instances, slaves in the Didache community's households were appreciated and maintained like members of the family. The gap between slave and free-person, therefore, would have been blunted both inside and outside the eucharist because they worked their trade in order to be able to survive and thrive all together in a hostile economic world (see ch. 2). Slaves in the Didache community, moreover, received a share of respect that had been routinely denied them in the society at large, where slaves were subject to capricious whims and demeaning commands of their masters. Slaves bound to a Christian household, therefore, would have been quite zealous to use their labors to ensure its economic success, since the welfare of the household craft ensured the long-term welfare of the slave as well. All in all, this helps explain how and why there was no movement toward general emancipation within the Didache community or within the Christianity at large during the Roman period.

Petronius, in his first-century novel, narrates at great length the events transpiring at the Trimalchio's banquet. Trimalchio, aware of his own impoverished beginnings prior to his unprecedented success at trading, displays an uncommon humility in the face of his slaves. After an exquisite meal, he calls in the hordes of kitchen slaves responsible for the feast and has them sit among his guests even though they "stank of pickles and rank sauces" (54). One of the slaves began with a comic imitation of a well-known figure for the amusement of the guests. Then Trimalchio confesses "in a gush of emotion":

> Ah, my friends, even a slave's a human being and drank mother's milk like you and me, though fate played him [her] a dirty trick. Still, if nothing goes wrong with me, they'll soon be drinking with free men. To give you the plain fact, I'm freeing the whole bunch in my will with a stroke of the pen. And I'm leaving Philargyrus [his chief cook and comic] here a farm and his woman as well. . . . Fortunata [his wife] I have made my heir, and I commend her to the care of all my friends. . . . (54)

Even outside the *Didache*, therefore, there were individuals who broke with social convention within the private rooms of their own home—even to the extent of giving slaves recognition at the end of a formal banquet and promising to grant them their freedom. Such conduct, needless to say, was not an everyday event. Petronius, however, does not hesitate to portray such conduct as prone to capture the imaginations and admiration of many of his readers.

The case of women provides a nice parallel. By virtue of their sex, women were owned by their fathers and, at marriage, handed over to their husbands. In working-class households, however, the wife was not just a "baby machine"; she was, during the entirety of her life, a collaborator with her husband in his trade. In many instances, husband and wife worked together as collaborators in a shared craft—butchering, baking, tailoring, metalworking. In other instances, women and their children undertook crafts that supplemented the family income—spinning and weaving being favored. In most instances, therefore, child-rearing and household maintenance were only part of the daily concerns of a woman attached to a family of artisans. Women, consequently, were highly valued for their administrative roles, which often included supervising children and slaves in those industries attached to the home. For example, even the upper-class Pomponia, the wife of Cicero, was remembered as being out-of-sorts when the organizing of the family meals at one of the family estates was taken out of her hands. She protested this treatment by refusing to eat with her husband and brother-in-law, saying she felt "just like a guest" in her own household (Cicero, *ad Atticum* 5.1.3).

In the Didache community, therefore, women and men shared an "equality" at the eucharist that had been prepared for in their economic collaboration. It is no surprise then that women in the Didache community were given the same training in the Way of Life as the men, were initiated into the community using the same rite, and were assigned responsibilities for the well-being of the community alongside the men. Roman law gave the husband the right of life and death, within limits, over his wife and children and, as shown in chapter 1, Roman custom allowed men practically unrestricted sexual freedom while women were hedged in and threatened with severe (see #1P) punishments. Jerome, for instance, recounts in one of his letters the hideous tortures inflicted upon a Roman wife because her husband (whether rightly or wrongly) suspected her of being unfaithful with another man whose identity he was bent on discovering "by any means" (*Letter* 1.3–8). In the Didache community, however, an equal standard of faithfulness was expected for both husband and wife. No one in the Didache community would have imagined that a husband could cruelly beat or savagely torture his wife. Thus, all in all, the *Didache* had created religious sensibilities that promoted mutual esteem, mutual reliance, and mutual affection—traits indispensable for the common pursuit of a craft or profession.

In the Roman world, great attention was given to seating (reclining) arrangements. Even in the peasant household of Dio Chrysostom's *Euboean Discourse* (7.65–67), men reclined while their woman sat in order to distinguish the elevated social status of the men (Bradley 1998: 47). In Petronius's *Satyricon* (67.5), however, Scintilla, the wife of Habinnas, is presented as reclining at table, when Fortuna, the wife of the host, joins her—at the insistence of Habinnas. Trimalchio, the host, explains her absence during the meal saying, "Do you think she'd let even a sip of water wet her lips before she'd stowed all the silver safely away and divided all the scraps among the slaves" (50). Thus, in this rags-to-riches working-class household, the wife first supervised the preparation and serving of the meal and then distributed the leftovers to the slaves before joining the guests at table. When she does so, she reclines with Scintilla—and not with her husband. When women were members of collegia or other associations, Kathleen Corley concludes that the literary evidence suggests that the "women . . . would have been seated together as a group or perhaps in a separate room" (Corley: 31). This corresponds well to the overall social situation in which men habitually associated with men and women associated with women.

In the eucharistic assembly of the *Didache*, nothing is said regarding any social hierarchy. If David and Jesus are named as "servants" (*Did.* 9:2, 3; 10:2) in the ritual, then all the men and women present can be assumed to be "servants" of the Lord God, the implied host at every eucharist. The women, by virtue of their status as "children of God," were consequently "sisters" to each other and to the men as well. The same can be said for the men as being "brothers." Hence, one can imagine that both women and men ate together as "brothers" and "sisters" might do so in an extended family. In Roman society, however, where social mixing of the sexes was limited, the men, most probably, naturally clustered together and so did the women. While women and men often worked side by side in the household shops and may indeed have cooperatively prepared the meal together as well, the separation of the sexes during the meal did not so much serve to signal a social hierarchy as to acknowledge the socially nurtured inclination of both women and men to be more comfortable in the company of persons of the same sex. In such a setting, one can imagine that the elders (both women and men) were served first—following the order of service that prevailed in a well-regulated Roman family. Here again, however, the *Didache* found no reason to address this issue and, in so doing, presumed that the prevailing order during the eucharistic meals was acceptable and in harmony with the status of each as a child of God.

#5U Paul's Concerns Over Abuses in Table Fellowship

Paul, in his letters to congregations that he founded, cites abuses of table fellowship as failures to recognize the social status conferred by baptism. In Gal 2:11–14, Paul recounts his heated confrontation of Peter at Antioch when the latter desisted from dining with gentile Christians as soon as Jewish Christians came "from James" (Gal 2:11) in Jerusalem. At another point, Paul castigated the Christians at Corinth for continuing "to eat with" (1 Cor 5:11) a person engaging in immoral practices. In both of these instances, the inclusion or exclusion of persons from fellowship was tantamount to either honoring or denying their social status within the Jesus movement.

In society at large, it was perfectly acceptable to serve better portions, even a different menu, to those of higher social status gathered at a formal dinner. The quality and quantity of food and drink, therefore, served to enforce social distinctions. This, most probably is what Paul has in mind when he criticizes the eucharistic assemblies of the Corinthians wherein "one is hungry [for lack of sufficient food] and another is drunk [for surplus of wine]" (1 Cor 11:22).

> It shows that the house church meetings of the Pauline tradition were regularly organized around the communal meal located in the dining room of the house. The eucharist was part of the dinner. As is now well known, the concern over "abuses" at the dinner were primarily social in nature, but in Paul's view they threatened the religious character of the dining fellowship. . . . In each of these cases, the meal setting in the earliest setting of the Christian movement called forth key concerns about the communal nature of the group, its fellowship, and social dynamics. In the Pauline context, however, we see that communal dining was not yet the fully developed liturgical and sacramental ritual of an institutional church. (White: 179)

While the Pauline letters clearly indicate a trail of abuses, this should not be understood to mean that such abuses never existed in the Didache community. On the contrary, given the instincts that prevailed in society as a whole, the members of the Didache community must have had repeated occasions to struggle against patterns of table fellowship that would deny their status as "sisters" and "brothers" who were all "servants" of their Lord and their host.

Conclusion

Jerome Neyrey makes a strong point that baptism and eucharist have two entirely different sociological functions. Baptism functions as a "ritual" that effects a "status change and transformation" (Neyrey 1991: 362). Eucharist, on the other hand, Neyrey regards as a "ceremony":

> Ceremonies . . . do not focus on the crossing of lines and boundaries that define and structure a group, because that is the function of rituals. Nor are ceremonies concerned with status reversal or transformation. Rather they bolster the boundaries defining a group or institution. . . . Unlike rituals, which are concerned with the perimeter, ceremonies focus on the inside, the inward dimension of a social body and its structure. They attend, not to change, but to stability; they are concerned not with newness, but with continuity. Meals-as-ceremonies replicate the group's basic social system, its values, lines, classifications, and its symbolic world. (1991: 363)

Baptism, in the *Didache*, alters the social identity of the individual. Immersion in flowing water had the effect of transforming an individual from outsider to insider, from pagan to saint, from stranger to brother or sister. Once transformed, however, the newly baptized enter into the symbolic world of the eucharistic meal wherein their new identity is celebrated and their collective future hope become proleptically present.

It is difficult to know precisely how the newly baptized responded to their first eucharist. Many, in the process of embracing the Way of Life, created enemies among those who regarded them as shamelessly abandoning all piety—piety to the gods, piety to their father, piety to their ancestral "way of life." Having lost fathers and mothers, brothers and sisters, houses and workshops, the newly baptized were now embraced by a new family that restored all these abundantly. The act of eating together in their new family must have been an overwhelming joy. Now, at last, they had gained a true "father" among the fathers present or a true "mother" among the mothers present. It would be as though their whole lives were pointed in this direction: finding brothers and sisters with whom they would share everything—without jealously, without competition—with gentleness and truth. The mere act of eating together foreshadowed the rest of their lives, for here were the faces of their true family sharing, in the name of the Father of all, the wine and bread that were the foretaste of their unending future together.

It is difficult to know precisely how the newly baptized responded to the consecration of the cup and the loaf. Undoubtedly the spiritual father or mother who presided knew the candidate through and through and adapted the prayers to the understanding of the novice that he/she had trained. The consecrated cup evoked the holy vine of David; the consecrated broken loaf evoked the life and knowledge of the Father. The former indicates that the Father had elected Israel and established a kingdom of promise through David, his servant. The gentiles did not know what marvelous things the Father did for David and his contemporaries. Jesus revealed them. Drinking the cup of the holy vine, therefore, allowed newly baptized gentiles to solemnly affirm their divine calling and to join in fellowship with Israel and to share her eschatological expectations. Yet the promises were not enough. The Lord required fidelity to the Way of life that he revealed to the Israelites through Moses. In the case of the gentiles, however, they received the bread of God's Torah—the Way of life and knowledge of the Father—through Jesus, his servant. The newly baptized undoubtedly felt a great sense of gratitude for Jesus and for their "father" or "mother" who, being God's chosen servants, had personally revealed these things to them and who, during the eucharist, had extended to them the cup of election and the bread of life.

Above all, the eucharist of the *Didache* was profoundly forward looking: Those whose lives were nourished on the broken loaf were earmarked for the final ingathering—for just as the grains forming the loaf were once "scattered over the hills" (9:4) and only later kneaded and baked into one loaf, so too, those who ate the fragments of this loaf were assured that the Father would one day harvest them "from the ends of the earth" so as to gather them into his kingdom. Those who ate, therefore, tasted the future and collective promise which the "one loaf" signified.

It is impossible to know precisely how much the newly baptized had already tasted of the future promises of God. The Way of Life is silent regarding these things. One can imagine, however, that every spiritual mentor was so filled with these things by virtue of their lives being nourished on the daily prayers and the weekly eucharist that they could hardly have stopped themselves from tangentially describing some of these things during the training sessions.

It is difficult to know precisely how the newly baptized were drawn into the conversation during their first eucharistic meal. Undoubtedly the spiritual mentor who was the presider for this particular eucharist was also the one to touch off the dinner conversation. Perhaps the newly baptized were asked to recount the pain and the joys of the spiritual journey that brought them to this moment. Perhaps their mentors did this for them in order to introduce them to their new family. Others may have joined in adding snippets of their own dramas—all so as to allow the new "brother" or "sister" to recognize those who suffered as they had suffered and those who rejoiced as they had rejoiced. Having lost all honor within the family circle of their biological parents, telling their stories must have served to heal their woundedness and to recapture their lost honor. One can be certain that embraces were exchanged and tears were shed. So much had been lost, and so much promise and expectation had been gained.

Then, with the dishes and the tables taken away, the prayers after the meal began. Now the newly baptized encountered the "holy name" of the "holy Father" that was "tabernacle[d] in our hearts" (*Did.* 10:2). Then, themes of creation and redemption were recounted (10:3). Then, the Lord was called upon to remember his church (the assembly)—"to save her from every evil, to perfect her in your love, to gather her together from the four winds, sanctified, into your kingdom. . ." (10:5). Here the sentiments of the newly baptized might have found their most forceful stirring. "This new family to which you led me, this wonderful family which I always dreamed of, may my Father who created all things save her . . . , protect her . . . , gather her."

Just as the message of the *Didache* continued the message of Jesus of Nazareth, so too the eucharist of the *Didache* perpetuated the proleptic foretaste of the kingdom that marked the table fellowship of Jesus. Fed on the eucharist, therefore, those who shared the Way of Life of the Father were nourished in their altered social reality. They were not of this world. Each day of the week, they thought and acted in anticipation of the world that was to come. "Brothers" and "sisters" bound together under the direction of the same Father shared their resources, shared their Way of Life, shared their dreams. Each new eucharist, consequently, celebrated the group identity, the standards of excellence, and the habits of judgment that the community needed to champion in the name of the Lord. Together, then, these early Christians faced a world that, in so many ways, had betrayed their trust and shattered their hopes. With their eyes on the future, they altered long-standing social barriers between Jew and gentile, male and female, slave and free. In their personal commitment to the future of God, they fully expected that the Lord would honor their trust and fulfill their dreams. Clinging to each other, they clung to the promises of God, and, in Jewish fashion (Vööbus 1968: 164–68), they prayed: "Remember, Lord, your church . . ." (10:5).

Some never dream at all. Others dream wild and confusing dreams. The Didache participants, however, dreamed a dream inspired by the Lord who spoke to them through his servants, the prophets. To these prophets, our attention will turn in the next chapter.

#5v WHETHER THE EUCHARISTIC PRAYERS ORIGINATED IN THE *BIRKAT HA-MAZON*

How the Eucharistic Prayers Came Into Being

Almost all scholars today regard the eucharistic prayers of the *Didache* as christianized forms of known rabbinic after-meal prayers: the *Birkat Ha-Mazon* ("grace after meals"). As early as 1928, Louis Finkelstein used the newly fashionable form criticism to establish the "earliest form" or "original text" of the *Birkat Ha-Mazon*. He then placed the *Birkat Ha-Mazon* and the eucharistic prayers after the meal (*Did.* 10) in parallel columns and then noted those "deviations made intentionally . . . such as we might expect early Christian authors to introduce in a Jewish prayer" (213).

Over the next seventy years, Finkelstein's study was cited approvingly again and again by Christian scholars and gradually became a fixed point of departure for examining the eucharistic prayers of the *Didache*. Thus, Enrico Mazza, in his extended study *The Origins of the Eucharistic Prayer*, was able to declare that because of the studies of Finkelstein, M. Dibelius, and K. Hruby, "the connection between the *Birkat ha-mazon* and *Didache* 10 no longer requires demonstration" (Mazza 1995: 17). Paul Bradshaw, in his excellent survey "The Evolution of Eucharistic Rites" (1991: 131–60), also concluded that "even the few scholars who have acknowledged the possibility of fluidity in Jewish prayer-patterns in the first century have still seen the *Birkat ha-mazon* as the starting-point for comparison" (1991: 158). Other scholars make no reference to Finkelstein but to intermediaries. John Riggs, for example, claims that "Talley (1976: 120–25) has shown by structural analysis that the prayer in *Did.* 10 is a Christianization of the *Birkat Ha-Mazon*" (Riggs 1984: 95). When one examines Talley, however, one finds that Talley begins with "Finkelstein's magisterial essay" (1976: 125) and refines his analysis relying on Finkelstein's English translation of the "earliest form" of the *Birkat Ha-Mazon* as the basis for his work. The overwhelming consensus among liturgists and *Didache* scholars (Mazza 1995: 14 n. 7), therefore, is that the first-century *Birkat Ha-Mazon* has been reliably reconstructed by Finkelstein and that the *Didache*'s eucharistic prayers after meals (*Did.* 10) represents a Christian editing of this Jewish prayer (see Vööbus 1968: 159–69 for a rare dissenting voice).

In opposition to a near consensus on this point, I am persuaded by Joseph Heinemann's study of Jewish liturgical texts that it is impossible to reconstruct the after-meal prayers used in Jewish households in the mid-first century. Even more importantly, however, Heinemann has persuaded me that, given the fluid state of early rabbinic prayers, even the rabbis themselves had no standard or "original" text that formed a universal standard for prayer leaders. Heinemann, attentive to the oral culture that then predominated, concludes that the "origins" of Jewish prayers are to be found in a wide variety of everyday creations which, after the fact, the rabbis endeavored gradually to synthesize and order:

> The Jewish prayers were originally the creations of the common people. The characteristic idioms and forms of prayer, and indeed the statutory prayers of the synagogue themselves, were not in the first place products of the deliberations of the Rabbis in their academies, but were rather the spontaneous, on-the-spot improvisations of the people gathered on various occasions to pray in the synagogue. Since the occasions and places of worship were numerous, it was only natural that they should give rise to an abundance of prayers, displaying a wide variety of forms, styles, and patterns. Thus, the first stage in the development of the liturgy was characterized by diversity and variety—and the task of the Rabbis was to systematize and to impose order on this multiplicity of forms, patterns, structures. This task they undertook after the fact; only after the numerous prayers had come into being and were familiar to the masses did the Sages decide that the time had come to establish some measure of uniformity and standardization. (37)

If diversity and oral creativity were the normative modes prevailing during the formative years of rabbinic Judaism, then the works of Finkelstein and others to identify an "original" text is an enterprise that violates the very character of the period under study:

> The widely accepted goal of the philological method—viz., to discover or to reconstruct the one "original" text of a particular composition by examining and comparing the extant textual variants one with the other—is out of place in the field of [early] liturgical studies. We must not try to determine by philological methods the "original" text of any prayer without first determining whether or not such an "original" text ever existed. (Heinemann: 43)

Heinemann, as a consequence, would fault Finkelstein and others because they wrongly assume that an "original" text existed and that (unfortunately) no one bothered to write it down. It never entered their minds that no uniform text was written down because, should any of the rabbis have written down a given prayer formula, it would have been received merely as a local and occasional variant. In a word, no one was imposing a fixed prayer destined to be memorized and used by all persons on each and every occasion that the particular prayer was called for. The best that the rabbis could do was gradually to synthesize the best traditions and to promote given thematic outlines that would guide the fluid creativity of the prayer leader. Even when entire prayers were written out in the rabbinic materials, therefore, these functioned in order to guide the opening phrases, the thematic flow, and the concluding refrain of the one who prayed. No tradition of reciting memorized or printed prayers word-for-word yet existed. Quite to the contrary, the tradition prized "the necessity to 'create' the prayers anew each time they were recited" (Heinemann: 47).

If this was the case in Judaism, one would suspect that the formulation of the eucharistic prayers in the *Didache* might have parallel origins. Nonetheless, the vast majority of *Didache* scholars presume that the author of the *Didache* made use of some "authoritative source" that he faithfully cited, adding his own editorial remarks (usually identified as *Did*. 9:5 and 10:7; Niederwimmer 1998: 139). This "authoritative source," moreover, is almost always imagined to be a single written source—thereby imposing the bias of our own scholarship upon a culture that was overwhelmingly oral. The members of the Didache communities trusted what they heard! Following the reconstruction of Heinemann, therefore, the eucharistic prayers of the *Didache* might be better imagined as representing a thematic synopsis of what the superior prayer leaders were presenting before the community. The "authority" which the *Didache* carried was thus conducive to providing a standard set of phrases for formulating the introductory words, the progression of themes, and the final refrains. The "authoritative source," consequently, was not a single, written text but hundreds of weekly eucharistic celebrations. Thus, it went without saying that the framers of the *Didache* presented the eucharistic liturgy in a straightforward manner without the least hint that what was now being practiced was deficient and somehow needed replacing (as was the case in *Did*. 8:1f.). The designers of the *Didache*, therefore, presumed acceptance of what they put forward because they were merely bringing into focus what the prevailing tradition of freeform prayers already used during the eucharist. Once formulated, however, the thematic outline served to guide the weekly celebrants. Improvisation continued to be prized and to flourish but now the heartfelt expansions created on each new occasion borrowed the opening lines, the refrains, and the structured flow of topics outlined in the schema used by prayer leaders.

My contention is that Finkelstein's essay has promoted an identification of the "Jewish source" standing behind the eucharistic prayers that is both defective and misleading. Jonathan Draper (2000: 130–32), working independently of me, ended up by calling the whole enterprise "anachronistic." In addition to the corrective of Heinemann summarized above, the following five additional reasons account for my willingness to set aside Finkelstein's research:

1. *Problem of dating.* To begin with, Finkelstein details the evolution of the *Birkat Ha-Mazon* by relying on the story of origins given in the Babylonian Talmud. Thus, Finkelstein cites the text, "Moses formulated the first benediction when the manna came down from heaven; Joshua the second when Israel entered the Land . . ." (*b. Berakhot* 48b as cited in Finkelstein: 212), as "fixing the date of the benedictions" (211). Jacob Neusner has shown that these stories of origin cannot be taken at face value, for, in every instance, one has to suspect that deferential forms of authorization were in vogue that ignored the need for historical evidence (e.g., 1983: 99–146). Furthermore, if Finkelstein had more closely examined his own sources, he would have noted that the sources themselves presented divergent and incompatible statements regarding the origins of existing prayers. Heinemann concludes:

> Since almost every one of these dicta attributes the institution of fixed prayer to a different generation, public body, or personage, nothing can be deduced from their joint testimony with any degree of surety. . . . (13)

2. *Problem of sources.* Finkelstein notes at one point that the Babylonian Talmud presents diverse forms of the *Birkat Ha-Mazon* and comments that "apparently each author gave it the form which he knew from his own [local] rite" (217 n. 9). When it comes to establishing the "original form" of the prayers, however, Finkelstein mysteriously sets aside his sixth-century source and begins analyzing five versions of the *Birkat Ha-Mazon* used in the ninth century to discover "the part that is common to all" (224). This methodology might recommend itself if he imagined he was reconstructing the ninth-century form of the prayer. But no! He imagines that this suffices to reconstruct the "original form" used in the first century (224).

3. *Problem of method.* Finkelstein uses his own rules in an arbitrary fashion. For instance, he puts forward the rule that "the briefest form is very often the most akin to the original" (224)—a rule familiar to form critics. When the Babylonian Talmud is consulted, one finds the *Birkat Ha-Mazon* described thus:

> The first blessing is that of "The One who nourishes"; the second is the blessing for the land; the third is for "The One who rebuilds Jerusalem." (*b. Berakhot* 48b)

On the basis of this evidence alone, one would expect that the "briefest form" of the *Birkat Ha-Mazon* known and used by the rabbis of the sixth century was much simpler than the one offered by Finkelstein. For example, the Babylonian Talmud indicates that the first blessing honors "the One who nourishes"; yet, in effect, the *Birkat Ha-Mazon* reconstructed by Finkelstein is infected with a spiritualizing tendency—the nourishment named is not "food and drink" (as in *Did.* 10:3) but "goodness, grace, and mercy" (215). The Babylonian Talmud indicates that the second blessing pertains to "the land" (as Finkelstein himself notes: 230), yet the *Birkat Ha-Mazon* reconstructed by Finkelstein goes way beyond this to mention "the covenant, the Torah, life and food" (216f.). The upshot is that the *Birkat Ha-Mazon* reconstructed by Finkelstein puts forward "the briefest form" rule but then completely fails to apply this rule when searching for the earliest form of the prayers after meals.

If "the briefest form" rule were to be applied, then the Mishnah (c. 200 C.E.) would have to be consulted. The Mishnah explains that, as the number of persons present increases, the prayer after meals ought to be lengthened. In the case where ten thousand have eaten, however, the longest prayer is still a very short blessing: "Blessed is the Lord our God, God of Israel, God of the Hosts, who sits upon the Cherubim, for the food we have eaten" (*m. Berakhot* 7:3). If the Mishnah is to be trusted at face value, as Finkelstein would have it, then his reconstruction of the *Birkat Ha-Mazon* should have begun where the "briefest form" can be found, namely, in the Mishnah. Had he done so, however, his expectation of finding the source for the eucharistic prayers of the *Didache* would have entirely evaporated (as it should have).

4. *Problem of tampering.* Even using his ninth-century sources, Finkelstein has to invert the first two segments of the *Didache*'s after-meal prayers (*Did.* 10) in order to parallel the movement he discerns in his reconstruction of the three parts of the *Birkat Ha-Mazon*: blessing, thanksgiving, supplication. At no point does he give any justification for tampering with the received text.

5. *Problem of stylistic difference.* The structural morphology of the medieval sources for the *Birkat Ha-Mazon* is significantly different from that found in *Did.* 10. The *Birkat Ha-Mazon* begins with *Barukh attah adonay* ("Blessed are you Lord God"). The *berakhah* form addresses God in the second person but then shifts to third person descriptives ("who feedest . . .") and closes with the *chatimah* (the "seal") that recapitulates the entire prayer, "Blessed art Thou, O Lord, Who feedest all." If the content of *Did.* 10:3 were to be given this classical structural form, it would be formulated like this:

> Blessed are you, O Lord, our God, the Almighty, who has created all things for the sake of his name and who has given both food and drink to people for their enjoyment in order that they might give you thanks. . . .

> Blessed are you, O Lord, who has created all things for our enjoyment.

Thus, setting aside the misleading work of Audet and others who have tried to show the equivalence of the *berakhah* form with the prayers in *Did.* 9–10 (Talley 1976: 127), one can now see how the linguistic style of expressing prayer that was to surface as the hallmark of the late rabbinic tradition (Heinemann: 39–43, 88f.) finds no commonality with the style of the eucharistic prayers of the *Didache*. In order to sustain his conclusions, however, Finkelstein ignores this strong stylistic difference.

Heinemann, in contrast, carefully notes that both public and private prayers originally had a variety of forms, including the "we give you thanks" form found in the *Didache* (40). After the fifth century, however, these alternative forms gave way to a nearly exclusive use of the *berakhah* form (as defined above) (42). Heinemann points out that "we should not regard as accidental the preference shown for the formula, *Barukh attah adonay,* which is only found twice [Ps 19:12; 1 Chr 29:10] in the [Hebrew] Bible, over all of the other introductory formulae which appear in it more frequently" (89). Thus, as the synagogue and church began to separate, they each naturally specialized in oral styles of prayer that were favored in their congregations even when such styles were not necessarily the favored styles used in the scriptures. One can say, therefore, that the *Didache* served to "preserve old Jewish patterns which were subsequently discarded from the Jewish liturgy" (Heinemann: 42). Thus, while Finkelstein ignores the divergence in style, his reconstruction of the *Birkat Ha-Mazon* leaves the false impression that a uniformity of style might have existed from the time of origin.

All in all, ten years ago I was willing to cautiously allow for the use of the findings of Finkelstein (Milavec 1989a: 112f.). Now that I no longer consider that his reconstruction is credible, I find it misleading to use it as a possible "source" for the after-meal prayers of the *Didache* (also Vööbus 1968: 166f.). I take it as normative that Heinemann has demonstrated that the prayers of the *Didache* were created at a time when there was a diversity of style and content in Jewish prayers. Hence, it must be supposed that the eucharistic prayers of the *Didache* had Jewish origins that were refined and defined due to the patterns of preferred usage that gradually emerged among the freely improvised eucharistic prayers used in the Didache communities. The same anonymous and obscure origins, of course, stand behind the creation of the Jewish *Birkat Ha-Mazon*.

6

HOW AND WHY THE *DIDACHE* CHECKED MEDDLING PROPHETS

Honoring and Scrutinizing Apostle-Prophets

CONCERNING
THE APOSTLE-PROPHETS, IN ACCORDANCE
WITH THE DECREE OF THE GOOD
NEWS, ACT THUS:
LET EVERY APOSTLE COMING TO YOU,
BE RECEIVED AS THE LORD: HE/SHE
WILL NOT REMAIN, ON THE OTHER
HAND, EXCEPT FOR ONE DAY; AND, IF
EVER THERE BE NEED, ALSO AN-
OTHER DAY; BUT, IF EVER HE/SHE
SHOULD REMAIN THREE DAYS,
HE/SHE IS A FALSE PROPHET. GOING
OUT, LET THE APOSTLE TAKE
NOTHING EXCEPT A LOAF NEEDED TO
TIDE HIM/HER OVER UNTIL
HE/SHE MIGHT LODGE ELSEWHERE; IF,
ON THE OTHER HAND, HE/SHE
SHOULD ASK FOR SILVER, HE/SHE IS A
FALSE PROPHET.

Contents

Background Discussion Found in Boxes

The *Didache* was created for a community in which prophets were not vague memories from a past era but persons to be honored and reckoned with in their midst. Needless to say, such prophets were not the designated leaders of the community and, as a consequence, had no essential role in the training of candidates, in baptism, in eucharist, in the correction of backsliders. The first mention of prophets in the *Didache* has to do with their honored role during the eucharist. From this point onward, almost all one hears about prophets is cautionary. One gains the first impression that the community had more to be feared from abusive and wayward prophets than to receive from true ones. Upon closer examination, however, one discovers that the prophets were the true visionaries who already lived in the age to come and who incessantly called to their comrades to follow them. Here was their glory; here was their failure—like two sides of the same coin.

The task of this chapter is to reconstruct the impact of the prophets on the Didache community and to make sense out of the rules offered by the *Didache* whereby true prophets were to be honored and false prophets were to be checked. At the end of this chapter, the reader will come to understand how prophets originated, how they functioned, and how they disappeared—all from the vantage point of the clues provided by the *Didache*.

#6A THEISSEN'S WANDERING CHARISMATICS

Gerd Theissen has been very influential in changing the way scholars understand the beginnings of the church. With the appearance of *Soziologie der Jesusbewegung* (*Sociology of Early Palestinian Christianity*) in 1977, Theissen has been the single most important person to bring sociological analysis to bear on the examination of early Christianity. Theissen began his analysis by examining the texts relating the sending forth of the Twelve (Mk 6:6–56; Mt 10:1–11:1; Lk 9:1–11) and the seventy (Lk 10:1–20). Through a meticulous examination of these texts, Theissen was able to reconstruct the well-defined strategy whereby the first disciples of Jesus operated not as community organizers but as wandering charismatics. Their itinerant lifestyle and their message matched those of Jesus. Only later did householders (such as the framers of the *Didache*) organize persons who embraced the expectation of the kingdom of God into settled base communities ("home churches"). Wandering charismatics found only brief refuge in their essentially itinerant lifestyle within these communities. In a nutshell, Theissen has persuaded his contemporaries that neither Jesus nor his immediate disciples founded "churches" (as Acts seems to imply), but they operated as wandering prophets spreading the good news of the kingdom.

Theissen's methodology and conclusions have been widely embraced. They have also been widely critiqued (e.g., Crossan 1998; Gager 1983; Horsley 1989; Schottroff 1995: 6–11). Nonetheless, more than three decades later, Theissen continues to represent a strong current in early church studies. Theissen has a special importance for the readers of this volume insofar as he repeatedly uses the *Didache* in order to sustain and elaborate his thesis.

With unfair brevity, Theissen's foundational insight might be summarized as follows:

> Wandering charismatics were not a marginal phenomenon in the Jesus movement. They shaped the earliest traditions and provide the social background for a good deal of the synoptic tradition. . . . (1977: 10)

In particular, Theissen was able to show that many sayings in the Synoptics did not apply to the ordinary Christians (the householders) for they were formulated by and descriptive of the wandering charismatics. Theissen groups these under four headings:

1. *Homelessness*. Giving up a fixed abode was an essential part of discipleship. Those who were called left hearth and home (Mk 1:16; 10:28ff.), following Jesus, and like him became homeless. "Foxes have holes, and birds of the air have nests; but the Son of man has nowhere to lay his head" (Mt 8:20) is a saying that applied to them.

2. *Lack of family*. One marked feature of the wandering Christian charismatics is their lack of family: they had left this behind along with their hearth and home (Mk 10:29). The break with their family included disregard for the demands of piety: one disciple was forbidden to bury his dead father (Mt 8:22). Others abandoned their fathers at work (Mk 1:20). Indeed, hatred of all members of the family could be made a duty (Lk 14:26).

3. *Lack of possessions*. A third characteristic of the earliest Christian wandering charismatics was their criticism of riches and possessions. Someone who was manifestly poor, without money, shoes, staff, or provisions, and with only one garment, who traveled the roads of Palestine and Syria (Mt 10:10), could criticize riches and the possession of property (e.g., Lk 6:24f.) without losing credibility. This was especially true if he had given up his own possessions (Acts 4:36f. vs. Mk 10:17ff.).

4. *Lack of protection*. To relinquish all rights and all protection was a deliberate risk. Anyone who walked along ancient roads without a staff made it clear that he had absolutely nothing to defend himself with. This was the relevant situation for the command not to resist evil, to offer the left cheek if one is struck on the right (Mt 5:38f.). (Theissen 1977: 10–14).

The genius of Theissen's thesis is that it allows one to understand how a significant set of sayings honored in the Jesus tradition did not existentially fit the condition of the Christian householder. Theissen then takes these misfit sayings and uses them to construct the image of "those unknown persons" for whom the sayings would be entirely relevant. The result is the "wandering charismatics"—apostles and prophets who lived the same lifestyle of Jesus and had the four characteristics named above.

This volume on the *Didache* embraces the insights of Theissen and of Crossan (1998) in reconstructing the role of the wandering prophets in early Christianity. From time to time, I will disagree with them and, at other times, supplement them. Nonetheless, we all remain committed to reading the evidence of the past through the same lens.

Honoring Prophets Who Prayed Freely at the Eucharist

The Greek term *prophētēs* ("prophet") refers, generally, to "anyone who announces or proclaims something on behalf of another," and, specifically, to "one who speaks on behalf of a god" (Aune: 195; Callan: 128; *TDNT* 6:783–96). The Greek term was used to translate *navi* ("mouth-piece")— the graphic term found in the Hebrew Scriptures. In the Greco-Roman world, "the word was never laden with such connotations as 'one who predicts the future'" (Aune: 195), although, in both Christian and pagan contexts, prophets did speak of future events (e.g., Acts 11:27f.; 20:23; 21:10f.).

The term *prophētēs* ("prophet") occurs twenty-one times in the *Didache*. *Did.* 10:7 introduces "the prophets" for the first time at the end of the eucharistic prayers of the community (9:1–10:6). The community was instructed in the imperative voice as follows: "Turn towards (*epi + trepō*) the prophets" (10:7). This literal rendering of *epitrepete* works well here. It suggests that the framers of the *Didache* were again relying upon the order of events to guide the order of their telling. Thus, the text would literally suggest that the community moved its attention from the action and words of the celebrant (9:1–10:6) to the action and words of the prophets (10:7). Most probably, however, the figurative sense of *epitrepete* is also intended: "Entrust [yourselves] to the prophets" or "Permit the prophets"

(Kohlenberger: 349). Both the literal and figurative senses can be captured by saying: "Turn towards the prophets [allowing them] to eucharistize as much as they wish" (10:7).

The community was told to rely on the prophets "to eucharistize" or "to give thanks" (*eucharistein*). The *Didache* uses the same action verb to present prophetic prayer as it formerly used to present what the prayer leader did at the eucharist (9:1). Where this is the difference? Five points:

1. *Prophetic freedom.* To begin with, one notes that the community has received a specific prayer summary (*Did.* 9–10) for its thanksgiving while no such format was given to the prophet(s). This points in the direction of indicating what must have been unique about prophetic prayer, namely, that their prayer spontaneously flowed from the Spirit that inspired them on the occasion and not from a prearranged pattern that was set in advance (de Halleux: 9). The last chapter emphasized how every accomplished prayer leader was expected to improvise; hence, it should not be imagined that the prayer leader merely recited a memorized prayer while the prophets formulated their prayers spontaneously. Nonetheless, the improvisation of the prayer leader used well-worn phrases and followed a well-tried progression of themes (*Did.* 9–10) whereas, for the prophets, they were being counted on to "let loose" and take their prayer where the Spirit led them.

2. *Prophetic content.* While the *Didache* offers no themes or outline that guided prophetic eucharistizing, it should not be imagined that the prophets gave thanks for anything and everything under the sun. The prophetic voice, it must be remembered, takes place in the context of well-known and well-established eucharistic themes. In fact, while prophetic prayers might have inserted themselves during the natural breaks in the community's eucharist (e.g., after *Did.* 9:2, 9:3, 9:4, etc.), the placement of 10:7 might signal (as suggested above) that the prayers of the celebrant came to an end before the community turned toward the prophets, relying on them to bring the eucharistic prayer of the community to a dramatic close. Assuming this to be the case, special attention must be given to the four disjointed eucharistic acclamations in 10:6, which the last chapter suggested might represent the spontaneous shouts or chants of various members of the congregation who were caught up in the future expectation with which the prayer leader closed the official prayer (10:5). In light of *Did.* 10:7 which follows, it can now be suggested that these jubilant anticipations might have functioned in various ways: (a) in order to prime the prophets for their charismatic prayers of thanksgiving (see #6b); (b) in order to summarize typical prophetic themes that punctuated the closing prayers of the free-wheeling prophets; and/or (c) in order to indicate the spontaneous shouts/chants whereby the congregation affirmed the prayers of the prophets.

#6B Whether Prophets Functioned Principally during the Eucharist

Gifted prayer leaders improvised the eucharistic prayer of the community using the commonly accepted phrases and expertly crafted patterns established by *Did.* 9:1–10:6. Their speech and gestures were the result of their native talents refined by training and were under their control at all times. Prophets, in contrast, remained silent until the Spirit of God moved with such urgency within them that they were forced to speak.

Without evoking any extreme notion of prophetic inspiration, it must be allowed that, even today, most of us have known those special moments when we were driven to perform extraordinary deeds or to express ourselves powerfully in speech/poetry/song. When such moments of inspiration come, we experience them as not of our own making, as enlarging our normal powers, and as transitory (see #6q). Freedom is retained insofar as we can yield to them or to block them, but we feel powerless to create them. When they pass, we cannot voluntarily resurrect them. When one yields to a moment of inspiration, one feels swept along to think, act, and speak in ways that exceed our normal powers. Prophets, in parallel fashion, ought not be thought of as continually inspired or as inspired at will but as those persons who have gained a reputation for being more forcefully and more frequently inspired than the rest of the population.

Inspiration cannot be directly caused, yet there are ways in which a person can be disposed to receiving inspiration. Thus, in the ancient world, it was widely recognized that prophets could provoke or invite inspiration by performing certain rites, by prolonged fasting, by submitting to the energy/spirit inhabiting certain places. The Christian prophets, for their part, appear to have found their inspiration within the time and place where the eucharistic prayers were being enacted. Paul, for instance, speaks of prophets as functioning at the time when the community assembled for prayer and never speaks of them functioning in any other context (Aune: 196). This curious fact might suggest that prophetic inspiration was somehow evoked and helped along by the presence of the community and participation in the common prayers.

What is unclear in Paul comes to full clarity in the *Shepherd of Hermas*. According to Hermas (90–135 C.E.), the Spirit of true prophecy must always and everywhere be evoked in the assembly at prayer:

In the first place,
[A] he who has the Spirit proceeding from above
    [1] is meek
    [2] and peaceable
    [3] and humble

[4] and refrains from all iniquity and the vain desire of this world

[5] and contents himself with fewer wants than other men,

[B] and when asked [to prophesy]

[1] he makes no reply;

[2] nor does he speak [in the Spirit] privately;

[3] nor when man wishes the Spirit to speak does the Holy Spirit speak

but it speaks only when God wishes it to speak.

[C] When, then,

[1] a man having the Divine Spirit comes into an assembly of righteous men who have faith in the Divine Spirit,

[2] and [when] this assembly of men offers up prayer to God,

then

[1] the angel of the prophetic spirit who is destined for him fills the man [the prophet];

[2] and the man being filled with the Holy Spirit speaks to the multitude as the Lord wishes. (*Mand*. 11.8; orig. Greek is gender neutral)

According to Hermas, therefore, two things distinguish the true prophet: (a) he/she has the five appropriate habits/dispositions; and (b) he/she strictly refrains from prophesying on demand or in private. The Christian prophet, therefore, cannot be consulted in private and asked to invoke the Spirit for the benefit of this or that client—a practice widespread among the pagan prophets. On the contrary, Hermas tells us that, for true prophecy to exist, two conditions are required: (a) The prophet comes into the faith-filled assembly, and (b) this assembly offers up prayer. Then, and only then, does the Holy Spirit fill the one predestined to receive her so that he/she speaks "as the Lord wishes":

> The Spirit which is in the church becomes active when the church gathers in worship and fellowship, and breaks forth in the words of the prophet. The prophet needs the church, for it is through her [the assembly] that he [she] is filled with the Spirit. The church needs the prophet, for it is through him [her] that she hears what the Spirit says to the church. (Reiling: 148)

All in all, therefore, Hermas makes it clear that the prayers (eucharistic or otherwise) of the faith-filled community stimulated the prophets and created an ambiance conducive to prophecy.

While the *Didache* does not expressly restrict prophetic activity to the time of the eucharist as does Hermas, the placement of *Did*. 10:7 would seem to imply that the prophets needed to take in the eucharistic prayers before they began to give thanks to the Father as the Spirit directed them. On this point, therefore, both the *Didache* and Hermas appear to agree that Christian prayer was a stimulus for Christian prophecy.

Hermas makes this point even more clearly when he characterizes false prophets:

First,
[A] the man who seems to have the Spirit
    [1] exalts himself
    [2] and wishes to have the first seat,
    [3] and is bold and imprudent and talkative,
    [4] and lives in the midst of many luxuries and many other
        delusions,
    [5] and takes rewards for his prophecy;
        and if he does not receive rewards, he does not prophesy.
[B] Can, then, the Divine Spirit take rewards and prophesy?
    [1] It is not possible that the prophet of God should do this,
        but prophets of this character are possessed by an earthly spirit.
    [2] Then it never approaches an assembly of righteous men,
        but shuns them.
    [3] And it associates with doubters and the vain,
        and prophesies to them in a corner,
        and deceives them, speaking to them, according to their
        desires. . . . (*Mand.* 11.12; orig. Greek is gender inclusive)

In contrast to the five virtues of the true prophet (*Mand.* 11.8), Hermas here lists the five vices of the false prophet. The true prophet "contents himself with fewer wants" while, in contrast, the false prophet "takes rewards for his prophecy" (*Mand.* 11.12).

> The true prophet is subordinate to the assembly of righteous men *because he comes to them* and it is the prayer of the assembly that precedes the prophesying; the false prophet has comparatively greater status *since those who wish to make oracular inquiries come to him*. (Aune: 210f.)

Hermas makes it clear that a false prophet preys upon "doubters" (*Mand.* 11.2, 12) who come to him/her privately with money in hand "as to a soothsayer, and inquire of him what will happen to them" (*Mand.* 11.2). Having only "an earthly spirit," the prophet takes their money and "fills their souls with expectations according to their own wishes" (*Mand.* 11.2).

> That this false prophet was a Christian is indicated by the fact that he is depicted as coming to Christian assemblies but as being unable to prophesy in that setting (*Mandates* 11.14). The Christian mantic that Hermas describes is unique in early Christian literature, since he apparently stands more in the tradition of Greco-Roman magical divination than in the Jewish prophetic tradition. (Aune: 211)

The *Didache*, for its part, does not seem to have encountered Christian prophets who arranged for private consultations for individual Christians anxious to inquire whether a particular business venture will succeed or whether a proposed marriage will produce many sons. The fact, however, that novices were cautioned against divination (3:4) and trained to trust in God's loving providence (3:10) indicates that Christians were being recruited from among those who, either occasionally or habitually, made use of divination. Nonetheless, the *Didache* does come down hard on the practice of some Christian prophets of "ask[ing] for silver" (11:6, 12); however, unlike the case of Hermas, there is no indication that such requests are associated with private divination. A true prophet, however, who arouses a feverish anticipation of the future blessings of the church within his/her Spirit-led eucharistic prayers might be misunderstood by some as having the power to foresee the short-term future well-being of individuals. Thus, while one can imaginatively understand how some Christians might be inclined to hire a Christian prophet for their private purposes, the *Didache* does not give any direct evidence that this was a problem already encountered. In the case of Hermas, on the contrary, "Christian prophets for hire" were a decided menace instigated by "the devil . . . in the hope that he might be able to overcome some of the righteous" (*Mand.* 11.3).

While there are decided differences between the two, Hermas does agree with the *Didache* on some very fundamental points:

1. Prophecy takes place primarily in the praying assembly and, accordingly, is practiced in the presence of all and for the benefit of all.

2. Even though a prophet claims to be inspired by God, ordinary members of the community had the right to judge which inspiration was to be regarded as true.

3. While the content of the prophet's message could not be judged (*Did.* 11:7), a true prophet was expected to have certain traits (*Mand.* 11.8; *Did.* 11:8).

4. Prophets are expected to live simply and to depend entirely on the room and board provided by the community. Any prophet asking or receiving money (*Mand.* 11.8, 12; *Did.* 11:6, 12) beyond this allowance was to be rebuffed.

5. While the Jewish tradition sometimes made provisions to kill false prophets because they led to idolatry (Dt 13:6; *m. Sanhedrin* 11:5f.), false prophets within Christian circles, even though they were likewise regarded as bringing on idolatry (*Mand.* 11.4; *Did.* 3:4) were not officially menaced beyond that of ignoring their words (*Mand.* 11.21; *Did.* 11:12).

3. *Prophetic style.* The prophets were relied on "to eucharistize as much as they wish" (*Did.* 10:7). The Greek phrase *hosa thelousin* ("as much as they wish") could also be construed to mean "as often as they wish." Thus, given the nature of prophetic inspiration, this leaves open the possibility that this or that prophet would remain silent precisely because he or she was, at that moment, uninspired. A prayer leader was expected to function and, unless caught by a fever or struck by laryngitis, he/she would function according to skills at his/her command. The prophet, however, was understood to rely upon an inspiration from the Spirit that blows when and where she wills. When the Spirit was active, however, each inspired prophet gave thanks "as much as" he/she wished—a hint that, when the prophets got rolling, their combined ecstatic prayers might well run on over an hour. In the second-century *Martyrdom of Polycarp,* for example, one discovers that Polycarp "stood up and prayed, being so full of the grace of God, that for two hours he could not hold his peace" (7). Yet, for those present, such charismatic prayers might have been expected to so grip their souls that time stood still and an hour passed quickly. The prayers and the gestures of the eucharistic celebrant might have been engaging, true, profound—provoking deep longings and offering fervent hope. The prophets, on the other hand, began with the closing eucharistic petitions of saving, perfecting, and gathering of the church (*Did.* 10:5) and transformed these into living and breathing expectations that those present were able "to taste and see"—provoking tears and trembling and jubilation. The prophetic eucharistizing, therefore, was the sweet desert that culminated every eucharistic meal.

4. *Prophetic suffering.* If wandering prophets were largely drawn from the ranks of those who had been dispossessed of their homes, their livelihood, and their family due to the crushing economic system of Roman commercialization as Crossan suggests (details to come), then it could be surmised that the prophets had been broken in spirit and, perhaps, in body as well by an enormous amount of personal suffering. Women and men in this condition would be enormously hungry and thirsty for justice and prone to seize upon the promise of God to come to rectify the injustice and evil of this world with passionate vigor and urgency. The charismatic prayer of the prophets, then, must have derived from their enormous compassion for the victims of this world.

5. *Deeds before words.* Even before the passionate anticipation of the kingdom was heard in the prophet's prayer, members of the community must have felt it in their very style of living. Unlike the householders of the community who cherished their homes, their livelihood, their families, the prophets had seemingly set aside all these things in order to devote every day to announcing, to praying for, and to anticipating the kingdom of God. Thus, as Theissen has so artfully suggested, the prophets moved about with "no bread, no bag, no money in their belts" (Mk 6:8 and par.). They blissfully counted on God to take care of them even when they did not know, from day to day, where their next meal was coming from. The life of the prophet, therefore, must have made a deep impression on the community even before their words were heard.

#6C THE SIGNIFICANCE OF PROPHETS PRAYING AT THE EUCHARIST

David E. Aune's meticulous study *Prophecy in Early Christianity and the Ancient Mediterranean World* concludes that our sources do not permit synthesizing prophetic functions either diachronically or regionally (320f.). He settles, therefore, for offering a synchronic morphological description of the various types of prophetic speech, fully recognizing that they can occur alone or in combination. In sum, six types of prophetic speech are delineated (321–25):

1. Oracles of assurance
2. Prescriptive oracles
3. Announcements of salvation
4. Announcements of judgment
5. Legitimation oracles
6. Eschatological theophany oracles

What is evident here is that the author of the *Didache* appears to be prizing the prophets visiting his community for a contribution that was not, either then or now, regarded as central to the prophetic phenomenon. Moreover, since the *Didache* was entirely silent regarding any healings or exorcisms associated with these prophets, we can safely assume that they did not do such things in order to verify their prophetic calling. As for "eucharistizing," this was something that all, in principle, were capable of doing. Consequently, the prophets of the *Didache* were honored, first and foremost, for what they had in common with the rest of the community and not for what was absolutely distinctive. The difference was one of degree and not one of kind.

The Didache's *Role in Checking Meddling Prophets*

Didache 10:7 not only provides an oral bridge to a new topic, it also represents how the framers of the *Didache* artfully honored that very class of persons whom they were getting ready to challenge. Saving face was an important ingredient in traditional Middle Eastern societies. Before giving extensive rules for checking meddling prophets, therefore, the framers of the *Didache* forthrightly honored the prophets for their primary charism and gift to the local community, namely, their ability to evoke a passion for the world to come through their eucharistic prayers.

Didache 11:1–2 has a dual function. On the one hand, it accredits all those persons who faithfully pass on "all these things said beforehand" (*Did.* 11:1) as worthy to be received as the Lord. On the other hand, the rule presented here offers a general principle for judging all classes of visitors (apostle-prophets and teachers more especially) and serves as a jumping off point for defining the particular threat posed by the Spirit-led prophets in *Did.* 11:3–12:1. The framers of the *Didache* presented similar warnings against those who would "leave behind" (*Did.* 4:13) or "wander from" (*Did.* 6:1) the Way of Life. Now these warnings are being extended to cover everything within the first ten chapters.

Didache 11:2 does not merely repeat 11:1. *Did.* 11:1 specifies that those who "train you in all these things said beforehand"—namely, in everything found in the first ten chapters—are to be received "as the Lord." *Did.* 11:2 specifies that those who "train you in *another* tradition . . . for the supplementing of the justice and knowledge of the Lord" are also to be received. Training was expected to bring "knowledge of the Lord." In the eucharistic prayers before the meal, it will be recalled, the broken loaf was consecrated as the "knowledge which you [the Father] revealed to us through your servant Jesus" (9:3). The "knowledge" referred to here, therefore, must include (a) discerning the true God, the Father; (b) discerning the Father's Way of Life; and (c) discerning the Father's guarantee of his future kingdom. All in all, therefore, it follows that "knowledge of the Lord" referred to here was first and foremost "knowledge of the Lord God" and not "knowledge of Lord Jesus" as some (Niederwimmer 1998: 172) have wrongly supposed. Novices were previously trained to honor their mentors "as the Lord God" for "where the dominion of the Lord is spoken of, there the Lord is" (4:1). The same thing now applies to all those who would bring the newly baptized closer to the "justice and knowledge of the Lord" (11:2) after their baptism—they too are to be "received as the Lord" (11:2). No more significant recommendation can be offered, for in effect, it says, "Trust this new person to reveal the Lord's ways just as you trusted your first spiritual mentor!"

Going further, the second section of *Did.* 11:2 implies that the framers of the *Didache* knew full well that there were "alternate traditions" out there and that they couldn't all be scorned as incompatible with "the tradition" of the *Didache*. An elastic rule, therefore, was given. If the "alternate tradition" served for "the supplementing" and not "the destroying" of what the *Didache* set forth, then such a one was to be received "as the Lord" (11:2). If, however, the outsider presented an alternative "for the destroying" of the tradition of the *Didache*, "do not listen to him" (11:2). No further penalty was imposed. One does not find, for example, the *Didache* moving from "you shall not listen to the words of that prophet" (Dt 13:3) to the extreme penalty: "that prophet. . . shall be put to death" (Dt 13:5) as found in the code of Deuteronomy and, in a mitigated form, in the Mishnah as well (*m. Makkot* 11:5). The *Didache* settled for shunning of false teachers and prophets, just as it settled for shunning as the most extreme penalty in those instances where reproof and reconciliation were ineffective (*Did.* 4:3, 15:3).

The rules of *Did.* 11:1f. are fraught with unsuspecting consequences the moment that one takes into account that these rules are meant to be applied by the newly baptized. Consider the following:

1. Ordinarily new members might be expected to be shielded from outsiders. But this was not the case with the *Didache*. Even at their first eucharist, wandering prophets might show up and speak up (10:7). The very existence of the rules given in 11:1—12 thus clearly implies that not even the newly baptized of the community could be cut off from meeting with and listening to those who have been trained in other traditions. Had there been a mechanism in place whereby only preapproved prophets showed up at the weekly eucharist, then such cautions would be unnecessary. The radical lifestyle of the wandering prophets and their obsession with the future kingdom made them imposing figures. If they were not received in one place, they shook the dust off their feet and went to another (Q, Lk 9:5 and par.). Accordingly, these prophets had little patience or interest in applying for formal recognition before they were permitted to meet or to speak in the assembly. Furthermore, it will become quickly apparent that the requirements of hospitality (*Did.* 11:4) and the recognition of the Spirit (11:7) precluded any pretesting of prophets. Thus, from the time of their first eucharist, the newly baptized had to be prepared for meeting, for relishing, and for protecting themselves against wandering prophets.

2. Ordinarily new members would be expected to rely on their seniors (mentors and officers) and not to be entrusted with discerning who was to be received and who was to be shunned. The same thing, of course, could be said of the expectation that new members would reconcile and reprove other members, no matter what their social status in the organization (*Did.* 4:3). Quite clearly, mentors were not expected to cultivate a lifelong subservient mentality ("Father/mother knows best.") nor to reserve certain

decisions to the approved "bishops and deacons" (15:1). At first glance, therefore, the newly baptized were being expected to develop an informed, independent judgment on matters of great consequence. This, in itself, might suggest that seasoned mentors and elected bishops might not always be available or might not always be trustworthy when it came to these matters. The use of the plural imperatives in *Did.* 11:1f., on the other hand, suggested that the newly baptized did not necessarily make these decisions in isolation. For the moment, it suffices to note these things for it makes comprehensible the detailed examination of apostle-prophets that immediately follows. As for the bishops and deacons, their absence throughout this entire section dealing with the eucharistic liturgy and with troublesome apostle-prophets offers the first evidence of how limited a role they played in the Didache communities. The details of community organization will be reserved for chapter 9.

3. Ordinarily one does not make rules to protect against nonexistent threats. Thus, the guardedness of the *Didache* with regard to innovators must point to a real menace. In the apocalyptic scenario closing off the *Didache*, the community will be similarly warned that "false prophets and corruptors" will be "multiplied" in the last days and turn the sheep into wolves and the love into hate (16:3). The clear implication here is that the Way of Life and prayer tradition of the *Didache* were being opposed and torn down by powerful opponents. As soon as the general warning against outside innovators was delivered (11:1f.), therefore, it is no mystery that the framers of the *Didache* passed on immediately to the "apostle-prophets," for they were the ones whom the framers wished to single out as potentially the most dangerous corruptors due to their charismatic gift "for destroying" (11:2). Accordingly, the framers of the *Didache* felt the need to devote an extensive set of rules designed to expose and neutralize the potential menace of the apostle-prophets. To this, then, our attention now turns.

The Identity of the Apostle-Prophet

Didache 11:3 begins with *peri de tōn apostolōn kai prophētōn*. The *peri de* ("and concerning") is a familiar phrase that the framers of the *Didache* used repeatedly to open an associated topic (cf. 6:3; 7:1; 9:1, 3). The topic is *tōn apostolōn kai prophētōn*. Most scholars translate this as "apostles and prophets" (see Niederwimmer 1996: 329 n. 26) and consider these as two distinct classes of persons: (1) apostles, who are treated in *Did.* 11:5–6, and (2) prophets, who are treated in 11:7–12. The presence of the definite article before *apostolōn* and the absence of the definite article before *prophētōn*, however, would normally indicate that the second term is intended to function as an attributive modifier (cf. the same construction in *Did.* 15:1,

2). If the argument from grammar is indecisive, then the logic of the text can be seen to definitely favor this understanding (see #6d). Therefore, *Did.* 11:3 opens up a consideration of "apostle-prophets," that is, apostles who also are prophets.

#6D WHETHER *DID.* 11:3 REFERRED TO APOSTLES WHO WERE PROPHETS

Even if the Greek grammar did not make provisions for the attributive modifier (as noted above), the internal logic of the rules themselves would still favor regarding apostle-prophets as a single class of visitor and not two distinct classes. Consider, for instance, the following:

1. To begin with, those apostles who overstay the two-day limit or who ask for silver are designated as "false prophets" (11:5, 6)—a term that, on the face of it, would imply that these "apostles" were "received as the Lord" (11:4) precisely because they presented themselves as "prophets." The use of "false prophet" rather than the expected "false apostle" cannot be dismissed, as Jonathan Draper has done, by imagining that the author or redactor of the *Didache* confused the role of apostle and prophet (1983: 237). Nor can the language of the *Didache* be dismissed, as Willy Rordorf has done, by suggesting that *pseudapostoloi* ("false apostles") is very rare and that *pseudoprophētai* ("false prophets") has an equivalent meaning (1978a: 53). Finally, the disarming suggestion of Niederwimmer that the text "should say *pseudapostolos* ["false apostle"] . . . , but the one supplying the tradition is apparently unfamiliar with the word *pseudapostolos* and therefore chooses instead—out of sheer desperation—a word familiar from Old Testament and Jewish language" (1998: 176; 1996: 329 n. 26) is equally hypothetical. Each of these suggestions presupposes that *pseudoprophētai* ("false prophets") reflects the personal limitations of the author or editor of this section. The moment that one takes into account the widespread use of the *Didache* and its oral transmission (see #11d), however, it is impossible to imagine that its framers or its users would not have emended the text to overcome perceived errors or misunderstandings (Ong 1982: 45–57). Thus, the use of *pseudoprophētai* ("false prophets") should be taken at face value, and it should be allowed that those "apostles" on mission who overextended their stay or asked for silver were to be identified as "false prophets"—implying that members of the Didache community were to dismiss their message (11:2) and to cancel their hospitality. The reasons for this strong medicine for seemingly small infractions will be considered shortly.

2. Once limitations are set upon the coming and going of apostles, the *Didache* moves directly to prophets "speaking in Spirit" (11:7, 8, 9, 12).

If two different classes of persons were being considered here, then it remains hard to understand why the *Didache* omitted any instructions to the effect that visiting prophets were to be "received as the Lord" and that provisions were to be made for feeding and lodging them. If prophets wishing to settle merit free room and board (*Did.* 13:1), then it remains problematic that the reception and hospitality of visiting prophets were somehow left unaddressed until they decided to settle down. Needless to say, these problems entirely disappear as soon as one allows that "apostle-prophets" are a single class of persons being spoken of throughout.

3. *Didache* 13:1 makes provisions for prophets "wishing to settle down among you." Niederwimmer, noting that no parallel provisions were being made for apostles, suggests that "at the time of the Didachist, there was no longer any need to expect itinerant *apostles*" (1998: 188). If this were the case, then Niederwimmer needs also to explain why the framers of the *Didache* did not drop out the rules pertaining to apostles since such rules would have had no scope of application. Ong, notes, for example, that "oral societies live very much in a present which keeps itself in equilibrium or homeostasis by sloughing off memories which no longer have present relevance" (1982: 46). The need of Niederwimmer's hypothesis thus entirely disappears once one supposes that "apostle-prophets" were being spoken of during the entire time and that no separate provisions had to be made for apostles.

4. It might be objected that, if a single class of persons were being referred to, then the text would provide two separate and distinct instances where the rule against asking for silver is put forward. When carefully examined, however, the settings are quite distinct. The first setting deals with an apostle-prophet being given bread as he/she prepares to depart. Not satisfied with this, the prophet asks for silver (11:6). The second setting deals with a request for silver made "in Spirit" (11:12) by a prophet— whether he/she is passing through or is a resident prophet. This case needs to be addressed because the general rule is that a prophet speaking "in Spirit" cannot be judged (11:7). Thus, far from being redundant, the *Didache* portrays two quite distinct settings wherein different rules apply.

5. That a single person might be functioning as an apostle and as a prophet is not astonishing. The "apostle" in the Jewish tradition "was a representative vested with authority on some particular matter by the person or group who sent him [her]" (Draper 1983: 232; Agnew: 75–84). Unlike an "apostle" sent to arrange a betrothal (*m. Qiddushin* 2:1) or a divorce (*m. Gittin* 4:1) or to slaughter the Passover lamb (*m. Pesahim* 8:2) in the rabbinic tradition, the apostles functioning in early Christianity were, for the most part, commissioned and sent out *to accomplish a prophetic task*. Thus, while a soldier or a teacher or a rabbi might be given an apostolic charge, Christian sources, given their specialized interest, nor-

mally limited themselves to describing instances in which prophets were given the apostolic charge to follow the example and way of the prophet Jesus heralding the kingdom of God. In Matthew's Gospel, for instance, when the Twelve are sent out to preach the kingdom in the name of Jesus, the clear implication of the text is that they are received as "prophets" (Mt 10:41). Additionally, Acts 13 gives an illustrative case of how Barnabas and Saul, two resident "prophets and teachers" (13:1), came to receive an apostolic charge from the Holy Spirit (13:2) that took them out on mission to address those who had not yet heard the good news of the Lord (Acts 13:4–14:28). Here, as in the case of the *Didache*, one is dealing with prophets who, for a period of time, functioned as apostles.

While the Twelve are routinely called "the apostles," *Did*. 11:3 does not point directly or exclusively to the immediate disciples of Jesus. Nor can it be surmised that the apostles referred to were the original founders of the Didache community/communities, since clearly the text envisions apostles in transit from their originating community to another place. Accordingly, there is nearly universal agreement that the "apostles" referred to by the *Didache* are not the Twelve sent out by Jesus nor those who founded the Didache community itself (e.g., Niederwimmer 1998: 175). Rather, the terms of *Did*. 11:5–6 presuppose that these apostle-prophets have a mission elsewhere and that, from the vantage point of the Didache community, they are only passing through.

#6E THE ORIGIN OF THE WANDERING APOSTLE-PROPHETS

The *Didache*, needless to say, gives a lot of attention to apostle-prophets. Some scholars suggest that, at the time that the *Didache* was written, itinerant apostles (Aune: 208; Draper 1983: 232; Niederwimmer 1998: 169) no longer visited the Didache communities and that even prophets had taken to settling down (*Did*. 13:1). To this, Audet rightly responds: Why waste so many words on something that no longer exited? (1958: 443) The oral tradition of the *Didache* devoted so much attention to the apostle-prophets because it needed to (Ong 1982: 46–49). Thus, they were dealing not with just a rare visit but regular visits.

Where did all these apostle-prophets come from? Where were they going? And why were some of them making the decision to settle in a Didache community?

To begin with, one must ask whether apostle-prophets came from other Didache communities. The *Didache* itself makes no provisions for sending out its own prophets. Furthermore, those prophets coming to them are strangers to the ways of the *Didache* (an aspect that makes them danger-ous); hence, one can be doubly sure that these apostles are not the origi-nal founders of the community (see ch. 1 above) or prophets returning from an apostolic mission originating in another Didache community. The apostle-prophets are clearly outsiders.

Three theories of origin will be considered. The first theory comes from Acts and suggests that the apostle-prophets were missionaries sent out from Antioch to preach and to found new communities. The second theory comes from John Dominic Crossan and suggests that the apostle-prophets were peasants who had recently lost their source of livelihood and were consumed by bitterness and loss, on the one hand, and fired up with the hoped-for kingdom that would restore their dignity (*Did.* 3:7), on the other. The third theory comes from Steven J. Patterson, who reconstructs a two-phase theory based on a redactional analysis of the text that allows him to identify the settling prophets as refugees of the Jewish wars.

In what follows, each of these three theories will be tested in turn. Test-ing in this case involves careful attention to the clues provided by the *Didache* so as to discern to what degree the directives would suitably apply to each type of apostle-prophet.

#6F THEORY OF ACTS: THE APOSTLE-PROPHETS WERE MISSIONARIES SENT OUT

Acts 13:1–3 provides an illustrative case of how an originating commu-nity (in this case Antioch) acted under the impulse of the Spirit in order to designate two of its "prophets and teachers" to begin functioning as "apostles":

> Now in the church at Antioch there were prophets and teachers: Barnabas, Simeon . . . , Lucius of Cyrene, Manaen . . . , and Saul. While they were worshiping the Lord and fasting, the Holy Spirit said, "Set apart for me Barnabas and Saul for the work to which I have called them." Then after fasting and praying they laid their hands on them and sent them off. So, being sent by the Holy Spirit, they went down to Seleucia. . . . (Acts 13:1–4)

Acts initially notes that five named persons functioned as "prophets and teachers" in the Antioch community. While they are praying together, the Holy Spirit prompts them to undertake an apostolic mission to proclaim the Word to outsiders. Acts does not make it clear whether Barnabas and Saul were seized by the Spirit to earnestly desire such a mission for them-selves or whether the five felt the earnest need to send out missionaries and that, after prayer and fasting, Barnabas and Saul were selected. In any case, after the second period of fasting and praying, "the three prophets who will remain in Antioch lay their hands on the two departing and send them forth" (Haenchen: 396).

The laying on of hands in this instance does not function to confer an office to be exercised in the community (as in Acts 6:1–6); rather, the laying on of hands is here understood to confer an apostolic charge that is to be exercised in the name of all five:

> The idea was that the two should carry out their special duties on behalf of all. They were sent out as representatives of the whole group. The others [the three prophets] made them into their extended selves. (Daube: 239)

Acts 13, it will be noted, traces Saul's apostolic calling within the prayer, fasting, discernment, and laying on of hands of the Antioch community and not within the events on the road to Damascus, which, according to Acts 9, left him blinded. Saul had received "letters from the chief priests" (Acts 9:2) authorizing him to act in their name when arresting those who professed faith in Jesus and bringing them back to Jerusalem for trial. Saul, therefore, was initially an "apostle" acting on a mission from the chief priests. His encounter with Jesus on the road to Damascus blinds him, thereby canceling this mission. Contrary to popular opinion, however, one has to wait for quite a few years before Saul (Paul) receives his new apostolic charge to act in the name of the Holy Spirit.

If the above theory were to account for the apostle-prophets known by the *Didache*, it would be supposed that apostles like Barnabas and Saul would rightly "be received as the Lord" (*Did.* 11:4) and given hospitality. So far so good. But then three trouble spots appear:

1. The one- or two-day limitation on hospitality is puzzling. Would not the community naturally urge someone with the stature of a Barnabas or a Paul to stay on at least until the next eucharistic gathering? Would there not be the expectation that such an apostle-prophet would bless the community with charismatic prayers and by reporting of the marvels God worked in his missionary adventures? If the apostle-prophets were anxious to get on with finding new places where the word of God had not yet been heard, this could be allowed. The *Didache*, however, remains blind to all this and sets down a very impolite rule: "If ever he/she should remain three days, he/she is a false prophet" (*Did.* 11:5).

2. The rule welcoming a prophet "to settle down among you" (*Did.* 13:1) is not only puzzling; it runs directly counter to what Acts 13 would lead us to expect. Anyone sent out on an apostolic mission was naturally

expected to return to their place of origin and report their successes and failures. This is what Barnabas and Saul do (Acts 14:15–27). In Luke's Gospel, this is what the Twelve (9:10) and the seventy sent out by Jesus do (10:17–24). When the *Didache* invites wandering prophets to settle down permanently, consequently, this runs directly counter to Luke's expectation that prophets were to return to their community of origin.

3. The rules regarding the testing of apostle-prophets (*Did.* 11:7–12) presuppose that they arrive without any formal letters of authorization or recommendation from their originating community. Within Jewish circles, however, it was a common feature for those acting as an apostle to carry a letter of authorization. One finds this in Acts, for example, where Saul, on his mission from the high priest, bears with him "letters addressed to the synagogues of Damascus that would authorize him" (Acts 9:2) to make arrests in the name of the high priest. Similarly, after the Council of Jerusalem, Judas and Silas are chosen to accompany Paul and Barnabas back to Antioch and to communicate the decision made by the assembled apostles and elders. The chosen delegates (apostles) carried with them an official letter (Acts 15:22–29) that authorized them to confirm "by word of mouth" (Acts 15:27) the decision of the council. Accordingly, after the letter was read, Acts notes that "Judas and Silas, who were themselves prophets, said much to encourage and strengthen the believers" (Acts 15:32). Furthermore, when Barnabas and Paul were sent out on mission from Antioch, we can presuppose that, at every synagogue they visited, they presented their letter of authorization identifying them and their mission. Without any testing, therefore, they were given free access to preach to those assembled there (e.g., Acts 13:5). The *Didache*, however, makes no mention of any letters of authorization being used to accredit any visiting prophet. One must conclude, therefore, that the Didache community was receiving apostle-prophets who had little similarity to those described in Acts.

In conclusion, while Acts 13 provides an interesting instance of how apostle-prophets might be commissioned by an established community, clearly the rules of the *Didache* were not designed with the likes of Barnabas and Saul in mind.

Crossan's Theory: Dispossessed Peasants Become Wandering Prophets

Crossan takes seriously Theissen's thesis that wandering charismatics moved about without money, without knapsack, without a change of clothes (Mk 6:8–11 and par.). What Crossan adds to this, however, is that these persons did not embrace this harsh lifestyle willingly as a form of "voluntary renunciation of possessions" (Theissen cited in Crossan 1998: 281) or as a "temporary" abandonment "necessitated by their mission" (Horsley cited in Crossan 1998: 280), but that this condition came crashing down upon them because of the ruthless pressures of the Roman economic order, in which huge agricultural estates worked by slaves flooded the markets with inexpensive grains that squeezed the already marginal profits available from small family farms:

> What that process [rural commercialization] meant was a complete dislocation of peasant life, family support, and village security. Some peasants, of course, did quite well at the expense of others. But, for those others, it meant certain indebtedness, possible enslavement, and probable dispossession. It meant a move from subsistence on a small family farm to the status of tenant farmer, landless laborer, beggar, or bandit. . . . It is these *destitute landless one* and *poor landed ones* that the Kingdom-of-God movement brings together as *itinerants* and *householders.* (Crossan 1998: 330)

Persons accustomed to grinding poverty for many generations may continually object to their plight but they don't become revolutionaries. On the other hand, those who have lived by the work of their hands in comparative security for many generations become openly rebellious when economic conditions beyond their control reduce them to a landless situation where they are no longer able to protect either themselves or their children from a precarious hand-to-mouth existence menacing them with exposure to the elements and with slow starvation (Crossan 1998: 166–70; Theissen 1977:39–40). Such persons, Crossan notes, could have easily embraced "a God who stood on the side of the oppressed against the oppressor, a God who opposed systemic evil not because it was systemic but because it was evil" (1998: 282). Driven by a divinely inspired hope that healed their desperation, their humiliation, their homelessness, such landless peasants created a class of itinerant charismatics who visited the householders and delivered a powerful message of healing:

> The itinerants look at the householders, which is what they were yesterday or the day before, with envy and even hatred. The householders look at the itinerants, which is what they may be tomorrow or the day after, with fear and contempt. The Kingdom program [of Jesus] forces those two groups into conjunction with one another and starts to rebuild a peasant community ripped apart by commercialization and organization. (Crossan 1998: 331)

Going beyond Crossan, I would say that the itinerants received not only bread and lodging for a short time; they also received the healing that comes from having a divine calling and purpose in this world—that of being a prophet of the kingdom. Despairing of this world, they clung to the world to come; bereft of honor and dignity according to the standards of this world, they gained both honor and dignity in the eyes of those who awaited the world to come. The householders, meanwhile, received the healing provided by the itinerant prophet's "ideological, symbolic, and material resistance to oppression and exploitation" (Crossan 1998: 331). These prophets went into the dark pit of indigence and did not cut their wrists but came away with a fierce confidence in God and an unshakable hope in the future. Thus, both itinerant and householder found "healing" (Crossan 1998: 331) in their mutual exchanges created out of a dire necessity.

If the above theory were correct, then one might expect that apostle-prophets would "be received as the Lord" (*Did.* 11:4) and given hospitality. Unlike the apostles of Acts 13 (see #6f), however, these vagabond prophets were often smelly, with unkempt hair and ragged clothes—much like the condition of the homeless in our modern cities. Their life was their message, and their message was their life. They gave no thought to what they should put on or what they were to eat, and yet God took care of them. Once they delivered their message, however, they quietly left so that the householders would not feel that their hospitality had been overtaxed and so that, in a few weeks, they could be received again without any resentment. If they stayed "three days" or asked "for silver," they would have crossed over this delicate line.

The arrival of the kingdom absorbed the entire lives of the apostle-prophets. They were broken men and women who hungered and thirsted for justice. When it came time to pray, therefore, their entire souls let loose! Their frightful experience of being ground down by the Roman economic order and being made to suffer what no one ought to suffer fueled their prayer of yearning and hope that God would come soon. As they prayed, these apostle-prophets undoubtedly remembered the years of distress during which, crop after crop, they slipped deeper and deeper into debt despite the backbreaking work of their entire family. Defaulting on their loans, they forfeited their houses and lands. A merciful lender might have allowed them to remain as tenant farmers on their own land—but now one-fourth to one-third of each crop had to be set aside as land-rent. But if a farmer was unable to feed his family and pay the Roman taxes on his own land, how much more so was he handicapped by land-rents and new loans for seed. Inevitably, the farmer would be forced to sell off his children into slavery—an act of mercy—for he could no longer provide food or clothing for them. Finally, he would sell off his beloved wife or send her back to her father's house. Then, bereft of honor and resources, he would flee his moneylenders and take on the life of a fugitive rather than be sold by his creditors into debt-slavery himself.

The rabbinic tradition provides a parallel case of how deep suffering nurtures urgent prayer. According to the Mishnah, when the seasonal rains fail to arrive at the expected time, the people gather around the ark which has been brought forward "in the street of the town" and "they bring down before the ark an experienced elder who has children and whose cupboard is empty" (*m. Taanit* 2:2). Note that the prayer leader must be someone *respected*, someone *skilled* in improvising the daily prayers, and someone *suffering* at the cries of his own children for bread. This last qualification was very significant. The text explains why: "So that his heart should be wholly in the prayer" (2:2).

Crossan's theory does well in explaining why an apostle-prophet would be "received as the Lord" (*Did.* 11:4)—a high honor—but then strictly limited to "two days" (*Did.* 11:5) of hospitality. Yet the moment that a visiting prophet signaled that he/she wished "to settle down among you" (13:1), he/she was given access to free room and board. How does one explain this sudden switch from restricted to unrestricted hospitality? Seven considerations follow:

1. *Why the Didache sent out no prophets.* As explained above, Crossan theorizes that the prophets emerged from the ranks of those peasants who had recently fallen from poverty into indigence. In the Didache communities, however, the economic safety net (Milavec 1996) ensured that its own members would not fall into indigence because of the shared work and shared resources among them. Thus, none of its own members was ever forced or tempted to take up a vagabond existence as a beggar, bandit, or prophet. Hence, *Crossan inadvertently accounts for why the Didache community neither created nor sent out its own prophets.*

2. *Why prophets never went home again.* Many or most prophets would not have been inclined to return home, not only because there was no home to return to, since it had been repossessed as a result of loans defaulted on, but because they themselves risked being apprehended by their moneylenders to be sold into debt-slavery or to be publicly tortured. Thus, *Crossan accounts for why prophets did not return to their originating communities* (as they do in Luke-Acts).

3. *Why wandering prophets chose to settle down within the* Didache *communities.* If they were unable or unwilling to return home, why then would they abandon their vagabond existence in order to settle down? Crossan notes that the charismatic vagabonds received the honor and respect due to prophets, but he did not note that some of them evidently discovered that the economic safety net—the mark of pastoral genius in the Didache community—was a redeeming feature of the *Didache* evidently absent from their base communities. Had it been present, they would have been

saved from the suffering and the shame that accompanies the fall into indigence. It is understandable, therefore, that some prophets received a kind
of existential shock when they realized that *their loss of home, family, and
occupation could have been avoided had they initially been part of a Didache
community.* Hence, with good reason, some prophets asked "to settle
down among you" (*Did.* 4:8).

4. *Why settled prophets did not work.* For those prophets in this condition,
one can surmise that a long period of grief work would be in order. Like
those who have lost intimate members of their own family in times of war
or those who were the victims of sadistic torture, they needed a time to
heal. The *Didache*, in its pastoral genius, therefore allotted to them free
room and board. This is in sharp contrast to the case of other visitors wishing to settle, who fall immediately under the rule: "Let him/her work and
let him/her eat" (*Did.* 12:3). Moreover, *no time limit is given to this period
of grief work.* With time, however, such prophets found healing of hearts
and of spirits and felt ashamed that others had to work harder to maintain
their well-being.

5. *Why the first fruits were given to the prophets.* With real pastoral wisdom, the *Didache* assigned the prophets the role of giving thanks to God
for the first fruits of members of the community (*Did.* 13:3). The one
offering the first fruits gained an eloquent prayer from the prophet, yet the
prophet gained a sense that God could be thanked for the little daily successes in the fields and in the shops and that not everything had to stop
until the kingdom arrived. Hence, by degrees, the prophets who settled in
the Didache community began to laugh again and to work again. By and
by, their love of life returned. At the same time, one can surmise that the
edge gradually disappeared from their anticipation of the kingdom.
Accordingly, they were inspired to pray less at the community eucharist.
Finally, the prophetic fire left them entirely.

6. *Why provisions are made for a community without a prophet.* Relative
to first-fruits, the *Didache* has the curious rule of directing that they be
given "to the prophets . . . but if you should not have a prophet, give to
the beggars" (13:4). This provision for the absence of a prophet finds no
explanation in the text, yet here again, Crossan's theory supplies an unexpected solution. Given the allure of the Didache community, it would
hardly be likely that any community would not have a single prophet. And,
with even a single prophet, the community would have a resident prophet
for life. Why then make provisions for the case when a community had no
prophet? In view of the above, however, this exception clause would appear

to confirm the supposition above that *as the brokenness of settled prophets was healed, the prophetic fire left them.*

7. *Why the Didache likens prophets to beggars.* If first fruits were not given to an available prophet, then they were to be given to "the beggars" (13:4). This rule strongly suggests that the near equivalent of "a prophet" is "the beggars"—*thereby unexpectedly confirming Crossan's theory that visiting prophets were in many ways indistinguishable from beggars and vagabonds.*

All in all, Crossan's theory provides a rich and well-rounded explanatory matrix for the rules governing apostle-prophets in the *Didache*. This is an excellent example of how fruitful theories not only integrate the clues of the text but go on to provide unexpected insights that could not have been arrived at without seeing through the lens of the theory itself. Crossan's theory, for example, allowed me to notice for the first time that the *Didache* did not create or send out any of its own apostle-prophets because it had a safety net (see ch. 2 above). Crossan's theory also presents a marvelously compelling reason why the apostle-prophets never return home and why they have no letters of authorization. More unexpectedly, Crossan's theory can be expanded to provide an entirely unexpected reason why the first fruits were given to the prophets (13:3) and why, if such prophets were periodically attracted to settling down, any community had to make provisions for the absence of a prophet and give the first fruits to "the beggars" (13:4). The whole idea of realizing that "as the brokenness of settled prophets was healed, the prophetic fire went out," would seem like a flimsy fantasy if it were not linked to a fruitful theory that sees beyond the text because it so admirably, as its point of departure, sees the clues of the text for what they really are. Needless to say, even such a fruitful theory may, in the end, be proved wrong. Yet the intellectual satisfaction of such a theory is so persuasive and its range of unexpected manifestations so tantalizing that only a superior explanatory matrix could displace it. Until a more satisfactory theory is put forward, therefore, Crossan's ideas as expanded above will be used as the most probable ground for understanding the clues of the *Didache*. A third theory will be considered, yet as will become evident, it will be shown to be very unsatisfactory (see #6g).

One last point. The *Didache* makes it quite clear that apostle-prophets were sorely tempted to "ask for silver" (11:6, 12). The most common Roman coin minted in silver was the *denarius* (worth about $100 today). Thus, the request "for silver" signals the need for a quantity of *denarii*—a substantial amount but not so enormous as asking for "gold" (Roman *aureus* worth $2,500 today) and not so insignificant as asking for "copper" (Roman *ass* worth $6 today). Thus, the request "for silver" could easily signal that an itinerant prophet might have been collecting funds with the prospect of reversing his lost prosperity. Might it not be the case, therefore, that some visiting prophets, sensing the generosity of the community, might have suddenly had the vision of returning home with the silver, paying off their debtors, and buying one or more of their family members out of slavery as well.

But this was not to be. The limited resources of the Didache communities did not allow paying the bad debts of even a few of the wandering prophets. If one or the other wanted to settle down, to heal their brokenness, and to become contributing members in the workshops, well and good. They might be able, by these ordinary means, eventually to buy their children out of slavery. Giving out silver, however, in even one worthy case would have swamped the local community with a dozen more worthy cases in the month to come. How could they explain why they helped some and not others? Even in the case of those who had been helped secretly, would they not return in ninety percent of the cases and explain that they needed yet more silver to stay afloat? And what then?

Finally, the resources of the Didache communities were, at every point of time, limited. An economic safety net would be shredded in just a short time if resources were drained to outsiders instead of being given back and forth among insiders (*Did.* 4:8). The rule for charity "for the ransoming of your sins" (4:6) served to ensure that local pagans and traveling Christians falling on hard times were given some emergency help; there was no expectation, however, that any individual or the community as a whole could solve the economic difficulties of an entire village, town, or city. This is the unspoken reason, I believe, why the rule of the *Didache* made no provisions for the ransoming of slaves who had become members of the community (4:10).

In their wisdom, therefore, the householders turned the requirement among prophets of not carrying silver against them (Mt 10:9 and par.). Hence, the rule, "if he/she should ask for silver, he/she is a false prophet" (*Did.* 11:6b). To safeguard the future of the community itself, therefore, sentimental giving to outsiders had to be severely curtailed, especially when it came to the apostle-prophets, who could be very persuasive.

#6G PATTERSON'S THEORY: TROUBLESOME RADICALS RESETTLED AS WAR REFUGEES

Stephen J. Patterson (1995) has devised an alternate interpretation of prophetic origins based on an extension of Theissen's theory of wandering charismatics. Patterson distinguishes two distinct phases in the response of the *Didache* to incoming prophets: in phase 1, wandering radicals have become troublesome and the community takes measures to stop their abuses; in phase 2, these same wandering radicals have lost their base of support (due to the Jewish wars) and are being admitted for permanent residence along with other refugees.

Patterson grounds his study on the conviction that *Did.* 12:2b-13:7 represents a later addition to the *Didache*. This conviction is based in part on the redactional studies of Niederwimmer (1995) and in part on the fact that the Coptic fragment ends at *Did.* 12:2a (Patterson 1995: 319–24). If two phases are evident within the text itself, this could be construed to reveal two phases in the community's dealing with wandering prophets: "Thus 11:1–12:2a and 12:2b-13:7 represent two distinct moments within the history of the Didachist's confrontation with itinerants" (1995: 324, error in citation corrected).

Thus, in phase 1 (*Did.* 11:1–12:2a), three classes of itinerants (apostles, prophets, teachers) visit the community but none wish to settle. In phase 2 (12:2b–13:7), apostles disappear, and wandering prophets and teachers wish to settle in the community along with other travelers whom Patterson surmises are refugees from the Jewish wars with the Romans:

> One perhaps envisions the stream of refugees from Palestine which would have been produced by the Jewish Wars [66–70 c.e.], or later by the revolt of Simon bar Kochba [135 c.e.]. Both the settled communities [of Palestine] and the itinerants who depended upon them would have been displaced by such events. It perhaps is not surprising, therefore, that one finds among the refugees . . . both normal refugees who have no claim to any special status (12:3–5) and prophets and teachers who have lost their base of support (13:1–7). (1995: 326)

Patterson's theory imaginatively turns the clues of a supposed textual history into a reconstruction of social history. Leaving aside the question as to whether *Did.* 11:1–12:2a envisions three classes of charismatic itinerants or only one (namely, apostle-prophets who occasionally teach), Patterson's theory provides a seductive explanation as to why phase 1 has no settling of wandering prophets while phase 2 is preoccupied with the settling (of refugees) and the support of prophets and teachers as well.

To test this theory, let's assume for the moment that Patterson's reconstruction is correct and that *Did.* 12:2b–13:7 does represent a later addition. The moment that one does this, however, the rules of the *Didache* immediately appear ill-suited to address the needs of wartime refugees:

1. The limited assistance to travelers (12:2) and the conditions for possible settlement (12:3f.) do not adequately reflect wartime refugees. As

the Roman armies moved through Galilee, whole populations would have taken flight in advance of the armies; hence, in a few days, dozens of persons, maybe even hundreds, would have arrived all at once. The first to arrive would have been offered food and lodging; those coming later would most probably been given a loaf and sent to search out other towns.

2. Among war refugees, there would have been no way to sort out the so-called Christ-peddlers (12:5). Nor would there have been any conceivable way to "plan beforehand how a Christian will live among you not being idle" (12:4). The rules of the *Didache*, consequently, seem far removed from the crisis situation created by the arrival of masses of war refugees. Think, for instance, of the war refugees showing up at night in Luc Besson's film, *The Messenger: The Story of Joan of Arc*, and how Joan's father turned them all away.

3. If community resources were being taxed to the limit by arriving refugees, it would have been preposterous to imagine that "true prophets" and "true teachers" would be sorted out and given special treatment, namely, offered free room and board. Rather, one would have expected some sort of triage system whereby the ill and the wounded would have been given preferential treatment.

4. Similarly, the prescriptions for first fruits suggest relatively normal times. If the community was swamped with refugees, for example, "a jar of wine or of oil" (13:6) would not be opened but sold so as to provide the needed bread to sustain the influx of starving individuals. Drinking wine at such a time would be blasphemous. Furthermore, if *Did.* 13:4 was created during a period of massive settlement of wandering prophets as Patterson surmises, then it remains incomprehensible that any community would not have a single prophet to receive the first fruits.

5. Finally, if the Didache communities were inundated by prophets fleeing from the Roman wars, one might have expected these momentous events to have shown up in their scenario of the end times (*Did.* 16). Mark's Gospel, for instance, speaks of "wars and rumors of wars" (13:6) as signs of the approaching end and advises "those who are in Judea [to] flee to the mountains" (13:14). The end times in the *Didache*, on the other hand, makes no mention of these events.

In sum, the rules of phase 2 (12:2b–13:7) offer no solid evidence that they were designed to address a situation in which war refugees (prophets and teachers among them) were showing up from the Roman wars. In contrast, the rules of the *Didache* reflect settled times wherein itinerant charismatics, over an extended period of time, were creating both opportunities and problems for the Didache community. Thus, without going into the redactional analysis of the text, the internal logic of the text itself serves to demonstrate that Patterson's imaginative reconstruction of the social history of the *Didache* is off the mark.

#6H EXPANDING CROSSAN'S BREEDING GROUND FOR PROPHETS

Crossan (1998), based on his analysis of peasant society in the ancient world, focuses on poor peasant families as being those most vulnerable to the pressures of Roman commercialization. In so doing, Crossan overlooks two other classes of persons who would have often been reduced from self-sufficiency to indigence as a result of circumstances beyond their control, namely, small-scale artisans and merchants. The possibility is open that, among them also, there was a breeding ground for potential wandering charismatics.

Crossan rightly focuses on the plight of the small farmer (1998: 215–18). The economic squeeze on artisans and merchants, however, was sometimes equally brutal. John E. Stambaugh characterizes the small, family-centered workshops as follows:

> Potters made dishes and vases for everyday use, fullers and weavers produced cloth, workers in leather sewed shoes and awnings, blacksmiths made farm implements and artisans' tools, carpenters made furniture and wagons, sculptors made statues and decorative reliefs. They ordinarily used raw materials that were produced near at hand and sold their finished wares in their own workshops. . . . The men and women who operated these businesses generally did most of the work themselves, helped by spouse and children and by a few slaves or hired hands. (Stambaugh: 70)

Just as the large population of unfree labor led to the establishment of huge agricultural enterprises (ch. 2), so too in some cases commercial manufacturing enterprises were established that threatened the viability of family-owned and family-operated workshops. Consider, for instance, the impact of the commercialization of pottery at Arretium in central Italy:

> Detailed studies show that the pottery [at Arretium] was produced in nearly a hundred small factories. A small number of skilled slave artisans (fewer than ten in most of them, about sixty in the three larger firms) produced the bowls, assisted by a larger but unknown number of others who dug and cleaned the clay, applied slip, and tended the kilns. As the market for these wares spread, new factories were established. (Stambaugh: 70)

Where such mass manufacturing existed, the local markets and those cities earmarked by the distribution system were flooded with such goods for sale. Even while price wars most probably did not take place (de Sainte

Croix: 201), the family-owned workshops would have been severely hand-icapped and, in certain areas, quickly ruined by the influx of outside goods.

The commercial pottery works at Arretium could transport or ship its goods long distances. Crossan notes in detail the comparable situation in Galilee, where, for half a millennium, the archaeological evidence demon-strates that all the bowls and storage jugs were exclusively manufactured in two pottery-making centers (1998: 223–26), yet he fails to imagine how many local family workshops were closed down at the time that these two commercial centers were expanding their production and extending distri-bution routes more than twenty-five kilometers from the manufacturing centers. Family-owned businesses were limited in this prospect, since they lacked the time and the personnel to transport and to sell their goods at a distance.

Furthermore, when a large number of workers were mobilized in a man-ufacturing process, specialization permitted a more efficient production of quality goods, since each worker had to master only a small aspect of the total production. Adult laborers in family-operated shops, meanwhile, had to give time and attention to nearly every aspect of their craft, thereby diluting their energies. While manufacturing and commerce were looked down upon by the old aristocracy, who made their fortunes in agriculture (de Saint Croix: 123f.), such enterprises represented the second source of great wealth during the first two centuries of the common era (de Saint Croix: 124).

Against this backdrop, one can surmise that everything Crossan says regarding recently dispossessed peasants forming a pool of humiliated and desperate persons out of which prophets and bandits were spawned could also be applied, in those affected areas, to artisans and merchants as well. The Didache community, it will be remembered, was primarily a commu-nity of artisans and merchants which developed an economic safety net protecting its members against spiraling into destitution (ch. 2). Accord-ingly, it would seem likely that dispossessed artisans generally, as well as those turned into prophets, would have been attracted to and well received (*Did.* 12:2f.) by the Didache communities if and when they came across them. Like would be attracted to like. Thus, my hunch would be that peas-ants-turned-prophets would have been inclined to find shelter and share their charismatic message within peasant households. Accordingly, the artisans-turned-prophets would have been more inclined to show up at the family-run shops managed by the members of the Didache communities.

Limited Hospitality and Unacceptable Conduct

The *Didache* directed that every apostle-prophet was to be "received as the Lord" (11:4). No probing questions were to be asked. This corresponds to the warm reception accorded apostle-prophets elsewhere (Mt 10:40; Mk 9:37; Lk 9:48; Jn 5:23; 12:44–45; 13:20; 1 Thes 4:8; Ignatius *Eph.* 6:1). The *Didache* is unique, however, in the statute of limitations it placed upon its hospitality. Ordinarily one day of food and lodging was offered. Two days "if there be need"—which would be the sort of contingency required in cases of Jewish prophets being prohibited from traveling distances on the Sabbath (Draper 1983: 240), in cases of extreme fatigue, in cases of healing minor foot injuries. On the third day, if the apostle was not gone, however, he was to be rejected as a "false prophet," meaning that he was not to be listened to or offered any further hospitality. The harsh clarity of this judgment had nothing to do with the content of the message or with the kind of activity exhibited by the apostle-prophet. The sole criterion here was the self-presentation of the visitor as an "apostle" on mission to some other place. If such a one did not subject himself to his own divine calling, then he would be condemned out of his own mouth.

The same rule applied to both men and women prophets. Given Crossan's understanding of how prophets came into being, it would be expected that the preponderance of prophets were men. In the case of women prophets, however, given the vulnerability of women traveling alone, it would have been expected that female prophets moved about in the company of a male prophet. This will be examined shortly. For the moment, however, male pronouns will be used with the understanding that everything said will apply to female prophets as well.

#61 MISHNAIC RULES FOR ASSISTING PENNILESS TRAVELERS

The Mishnah has rules for assisting someone traveling without the resources to pay for lodging. These rules reflect concerns parallel to those addressed in the *Didache*, namely, "how long?" and "how much?" It reads as follows:

[A] They give to a poor man traveling from place to place
    no less than a loaf [of bread] worth a *dupondion*. . . .
[B] [If such a poor person] stayed overnight,
    they give him enough [to pay] for a night's lodging.
[C] [If such a poor person] spent the Sabbath,
    they give him food for three meals. (*m. Peah* 8:7; *b. Baba Batra* 9a).

While the material here is arranged differently, what is clear is how, practically speaking, wisdom lies in restricting the amount of assistance given to someone passing through lest (a) such a person begin to exploit the community resources or (b) such a community develop a reputation as "a soft sell" attracting vagabonds from a whole region. The particulars are remarkably like those of the *Didache*. The prophet, upon leaving, is given "nothing except a loaf" (11:6)—likening him to a poor man traveling from place to place. When the prophet stays, he is offered lodging for "one day" (11:5) save "if there be need [the Sabbath?], also another day" (11:5). Since no Jew would be expected to sell food on the Sabbath, the Talmud notes that a traveler staying over on the Sabbath has to be given "food for three meals." Since the Didache communities do not observe the Sabbath, this prescription was unnecessary for them. Allowing a prophet to stay implied offering him/her food and lodging.

The next concern is with the apostle departing. When he did go, he was emphatically given "nothing except bread." Any apostle asking "for silver" was immediately to be rejected as a false prophet. Here again, no attention was given to the virtue, wisdom, honesty, or charismatic powers of the apostle or any lack thereof. Furthermore, members of the community had been trained to give "to everyone asking you for anything" (1:5 and 4:8a) and to "share all things with your brother" (4:8), yet, understandably, this mandate did not apply to apostles. No reasons are given. Behind this forceful rejection, therefore, must lie a common understanding that "the decree of the good news" (11:3) expressly prohibited "apostles" from carrying "money in their purses" (Mk 6:8) and from "prophets" receiving remuneration for their services. The prophets themselves, therefore, would have been prone to knowing not to ask for money even if it had not been stated in the *Didache*. Consider the following three points:

1. In Matthew's Gospel, Jesus sent out the Twelve on their prophetic mission with the rule, "Take no gold, nor silver, nor copper in your purses" (Mt 10:41), just after putting forward the principle, "You received without pay, give without pay" (Mt 10:9). Luke appears to have had an even more rigorous code for traveling prophets, since they were prohibited from taking not only "money" but "bread" as well (Lk 9:3). This meant that they arrived at their next location hungry.

The latter rabbis also have parallel prohibitions. The *Kallah Rabbathi* condemns anyone who would flatter another in order to secure his food and drink "for such is the conduct of false prophets" (53b; also Mi 3:5; Jer 23:15). Similarly, those teaching Torah, the revelations made to Moses on Mt. Sinai, were not to accept any remuneration:

Teach others your understanding of Torah for free. Take no compensation whatever for her, since the Omnipotent gave her to you gratuitously. And it is forbidden to make compensation for [telling another] the words of the Torah. If you take compensation for the words of Torah, it is considered as though you had destroyed the whole world. Do not plead, "I have no money to live on." For all money is his [the Lord's], as it is written: "The silver is mine and the gold is mine! These are the words of the Lord of Hosts" [Hg 2:8]. (*Derek Erez Zuta* 58b; also *b. Bekhorot* 29a; *b. Nedarim* 37b)

2. Nothing in the *Didache* (or the Synoptics, for that matter) suggests that apostles renounced their possessions so as to be "radically poor for God's sake" (Niederwimmer 1998: 177). Rather, following the analysis of Crossan offered above, the apostles visiting the Didache community were indigent because of the crushing weight of the Roman economic order, and they responded to this not by romanticizing the condition of poverty but by turning their anger and resentment into a full-hearted expectation of the kingdom of God. While some may have been tempted to "ask for silver" to pay off their debtors and to resume their occupations and family life, such a move would have withdrawn them from their radical waiting upon the Lord. Being hungry and thirsty for justice, they were not interested in obtaining relief from their suffering through the temporary band-aid generosity of a Christian. Niederwimmer correctly notes that they "surrendered themselves completely to God's care" (1998: 177) while awaiting the coming of the Father to establish his kingdom.

3. Pagan prophets were accustomed to receiving payment in exchange for their services, which usually entailed divination (see #6q). Even the ancient prophets of Israel were sometimes handsomely paid for their divination (e.g., 1 Sm 9:8; 2 Kgs 8:9; Mi 3:11). The *Shepherd of Hermas* (see box, "Whether Prophets Got High on the Eucharistic Prayers") makes much to-do about Christian prophets conducting private consultations for money and complains bitterly that the false prophet "takes rewards for his prophecy and if he does not receive rewards, he does not prophesy" (*Mand.* 11.12). The *Didache*, in contrast, gives not the slightest hint that prophets were inclined to give private consultations in exchange for silver. Hermas, as a consequence, appears to be dealing with prophets who modeled themselves after their pagan counterparts. There is no reason, consequently, to believe that requests for silver on the part of the prophets of the *Didache* had to do with divination. The *Didache* opposed "becom[ing] a diviner" (*Did.* 3:4) but mentions nothing regarding seeking divination from Christian prophets. One can assume, therefore, that prophetic activity centered on the eucharist and that no one imagined that prophets practiced private divination or that those who did were so rare that there was no need to create a general rule prohibiting such a practice.

Given the tropical climate of the Middle East, one would expect a wandering charismatic to begin a journey around sunset. Under the one-day norm (11:9), a weary traveler arriving after a day of walking could be expected to arrive mid or late afternoon and leave again early the next morning. In the Middle East, however, an evening meal celebrated with an itinerant charismatic would be the natural occasion to invite friends and neighbors.

Even under the one-day rule (11:9), one might have imagined that the visiting prophet would not be around long enough to create much trouble. Such was evidently not the case, however. The host family would undoubtedly prepare a leisurely evening meal and would invite friends and neighbors to join them in welcoming the itinerant charismatic, in exchanging stories of mutual interest, and in praying together. Judging from the attention that the *Didache* gives to "speaking in Spirit," one can surmise that this was the potential trouble spot. To this (*Did.* 11:7–12), our attention now turns.

The Special Case of "Speaking in Spirit"

Didache 11:7–8 forms a doublet concerned with the special case of prophets "speaking in Spirit" (i.e., under the influence of the Holy Spirit). The exact nature of such speaking is not defined; hence, it can be assumed that this was well known to the hearers of the *Didache*. Presumably, one is not dealing here with glossolalia or with obscure poetic predictions of the future: forms of speech that would demand an interpreter. Nor should it be supposed that "speaking in Spirit" necessarily implied some paranormal ecstatic state wherein voluntary control was surrendered to "the Holy Spirit" who spoke through the prophet (see #6q). Rather, "speaking in Spirit" (*en pneumati*) must carry with it the notion of speech that is "inspired" and "inspiring."

Ordinary speech between equals leaves much room for critical thought and evaluation. The apostle-prophets, however, had a manifest dedication in their style of life and an urgency in their speech that was difficult or impossible to refute. Having lost their honor and having been broken on the wheel of unjust suffering, they set out as vagabonds bent on spending the rest of their days pouring all their grief and rage into their expectation of the coming of the Lord. Thus, as in the case of every engaged passionate speaker, the content of their inspired words was not to be contested. To do so would be commit the sin that "will not be forgiven" (*Did.* 11:7)—a rule that is applied to a wholly different context in the Synoptics (see Mk 3:28–30 and par.). The sense here would be that one cannot doubt their sincerity, their inspiration, and their dedication to God's future. To do so would be a grievous sin against God, which, in the language of the *Didache*, "will not be forgiven" (11:7).

Having acknowledged that prophetic speech was immune from human judgment, the *Didache* then adds a cautionary proviso: "but not everyone speaking in Spirit is a true prophet" (11:8). Alas! The passionate and urgent message was not enough. False prophets were also capable of speaking in Spirit (de Halleux: 16). Thus, the Spirit-filled prayer of the prophet was not to be objected to; however, outside of this, the prophet was open to judgment. And given the penchant of the *Didache* for orthopraxis, the test of the true prophet was spelled out: "he/she should have the habits of the Lord (*tropous kyriou*)" (*D*11:8).

The Greek term *tropos* refers to a "way of life, turn of mind, conduct, character" (Bauer: 827c; *Apostolic Constitutions* 8.32.2). Many scholars have been too quick to identify these "habits of the Lord" (*Did.* 11:8) with the lack of home, family, and possessions expected of Theissen's wandering charismatics (see details in #6j). The mere fact of living a homeless and penniless existence, however, would be a crude and misleading litmus test for distinguishing between true and false prophets. Many false prophets and even some pagans (the Cynic philosophers) would have displayed these same characteristics. Nor can "habits of the Lord" refer to "voluntary poverty" (Rordorf 1978a: 55) or to celibacy, for, here again, false prophets can renounce sex and possessions (see details below). When it came to the "habits of the Lord," therefore, the members of the Didache community must have had a litmus test in mind such that the true could be distinguished from the false. Otherwise, with impractical rules of discernment, the community would have been regularly victimized by charlatans.

#6J WHETHER "HABITS OF THE LORD" MEANT NO HOME OR POSSESSIONS

The phrase "habits of the Lord" has sometimes been interpreted to mean lack of possessions. Rordorf, for example, suggests that this obscure phrase might mean "voluntary poverty" (1978a: 55) on the basis of Eusebius's report that the successors of the apostles "had first fulfilled the Savior's precept by distributing their substance to the needy" (*Ecclesiastical History* 3.37). Draper expands "habits of the Lord" to include the renouncing of home, family, and income—traits that Theissen (see #6a) associates with the apostolic charge in the early church (1991: 18). Niederwimmer, influenced by Theissen, states that, with regard to "habits of the Lord (*kyriou*)" (*Did.* 11:8), the historical Lord Jesus was meant:

"*Kyrios*" means Jesus. Thus the true prophet is in continuity with the lifestyle and praxis of Jesus—the earthly Jesus! This reference

to the way of life of the earthly Jesus does not appear here by
accident—if there is really a social and tradition-historical connection between the discipleship movement of Jesus . . . and the
itinerant prophets of the *Didache* tradition. (Niederwimmer
1998: 179; see also Crossan 1998: 377)

Niederwimmer here presupposes that Jesus and his disciples moved about
without money, without knapsack, without a change of clothes (Mk
6:8–11 and par.), and that such traits were used by the Didache community to identify true prophets.

While "habits of the Lord" might have included the lack of home, family, and possessions and/or continual wandering, such external traits
would never have been sufficient, in and of themselves, to distinguish
between true and false prophets for the following reasons:

1. A visiting prophet would have been a stranger to the community. It
would have been futile, therefore, to try to determine whether an arriving
prophet was practicing "voluntary" as opposed to "circumstantial"
poverty. Even in the case of "voluntary poverty," it would have been
impossible to know whether the visitor had formerly distributed his/her
substance to the needy. Eusebius writes according to the mood of his generation. Nothing in the Gospels suggests that Jesus or his disciples received
their prophetic gifts in connection with distributing their belongings to
the poor. This ideal became fashionable in Christian circles only after the
mid-second century, and it would be misleading to project it back into the
beginnings.

2. The *Didache* makes clear that members of the community were to
"give the first fruits to the prophets" (13:3). Since the rule anticipates first
fruits "of silver and of clothing and of every possession" (13:7), this means
that such things would be presented to the prophets. If wandering
prophets were required not to have money or an extra garment as some
suppose, it would be problematic for someone to offer these things to any
prophet under the guise of offering him/her first fruits. Since the *Didache*
places no such restriction on these things, it follows that the "habits of the
Lord" could not be understood as meaning that prophets did not sometimes receive silver and clothing.

3. In parallel fashion, it would have been futile to try to determine
whether an arriving prophet had a home and a family in another village.
Furthermore, such external characteristics, even if they could be investigated and reliably known would be of little help in distinguishing between
"the false prophet and the true prophet" (11:8).

4. If every true prophet must be a wandering charismatic, then any "true
prophet wishing to settle down among you" (*Did.* 13:1) would seemingly
destroy his credibility since he/she would no longer have the "habits of
the Lord" (as Niederwimmer claims). The fact that settled prophets

receive full community support makes clear that the *Didache* did not regard "wandering" as a "habit of the Lord." Furthermore, since the *Didache* did not restrict a resident prophet from having a home, a family, or even "two tunics" (Mk 6:9 and par.), it is difficult to imagine that these things were being thought of as "habits of the Lord."

5. The use of *kyrios* most probably refers to the "habits of the Lord God" rather than to "habits of the Lord Jesus." Chapters 4 and 5 have already shown (a) that the *Didache* prefers to regard Jesus as "servant" as opposed to "Lord," and (b) that in the other uses of *kyrios,* the Lord God is clearly meant (e.g., 10:6; 16:7) (see #10n). The "habits of the Lord" could thus be more easily understood as being "long-suffering, merciful, harmless, calm, good" (*Did.* 3:8)—traits that are much more decisive than wandering about without money, without knapsack, and without a change of clothes.

Beyond this, three additional considerations can be put forward based on evidence outside of the *Didache*.

1. Luke, in his Gospel, has a rigorous instruction given to the seventy being sent out on mission: "Carry no purse, no bag, no sandals: and greet no one on the road" (10:4). Even after this instruction, however, Luke never makes a point of noting that Jesus in his wanderings or any of the traveling charismatics in his Acts of the Apostles were doing precisely these things. Even if Luke had been reading the *Didache*, therefore, it is doubtful that he would come to the conclusion that Luke 10:4 summarized the "habits of the Lord." Moreover, later in his Gospel, Luke has Jesus requiring his disciples to alter their game plan: "But now, the one who has a purse must take it, and likewise a bag. And the one who has no sword must sell his cloak and buy one" (22:37).

2. While David Aune acknowledges Theissen's contribution to understanding the early church (e.g., 214), he finds little evidence in Acts to support Theissen's conclusions. In his study of Acts, Aune finds only three instances in which a trip is undertaken by a prophet for the purpose of exercising his/her prophetic gift. He concludes his study as follows:

> The last two examples [Acts 15:22–35; 21:8–11], and probably the first as well [Acts 11:27–30; see also 21:10–14], are not instances of aimless wandering, but each trip is apparently undertaken for a specific purpose. All such traveling is done in the region of Syria-Palestine, and it is at least implied that such prophets returned to their home communities as soon as their mission had been completed. (212)

Thus, according to Acts, homelessness and wandering were not part of the habits of true prophets. Only in the Book of Revelation does Aune find an instance of a sustained itinerant ministry:

In Rv 2–3, John addresses seven local churches in the western regions of Asia Minor. If John was personally known to each of the congregations he addresses, a conclusion which seems inescapable, he must have exercised an itinerant prophetic ministry. . . . John appears to have had a circuit of congregations which he visited from time to time and over which he tried to exert an authority based on his prophetic role. (212f.)

Even in this latter case, however, nothing is said respecting a prophetic lifestyle comparable to that of Theissen's reconstruction of the wandering charismatic.

3. The analysis of Theissen assumes that the wandering charismatics of the first century were without a home (Mt 8:20; Lk 9:59; *Gos. Thom.* 86), traveling without money (Mk 10:17–31 and par.; *Gos. Thom.* 95), and eating whatever was offered to them by those receptive to their message (Lk 10:5–8 and par.; *Gos. Thom.* 14). So far so good. When examined in detail, however, the Synoptic picture shows variations. Mark, for example, makes provisions for a staff and sandals (Mk 6:8f.); Matthew and Luke expressly forbid these (Mt 10:9; Lk 9:3; 10:4). Luke is unique among the Synoptics in prohibiting the taking of "bread" (9:3)—something that the *Didache* positively allows (*Did.* 11:6).

Going beyond these variations, the Synoptics also recognize (a) that, despite Mt 8:20 ("nowhere to lay his head"), Jesus had "his home" (Mt 4:13; 9:1, 10, 28; 13:1, 36; 17:25 and par.) in Capernaum, which seemingly formed his center of operations when he was not on the move (Milavec 1984; Waetjen 77f.); (b) that Jesus was, in the eyes of some, "a glutton and a drunkard" (Mt 11:19 and par.)—a clear indication that he was not always living life close to the bone; and (c) that certain named women "provided for them [Jesus and his disciples] out of their own resources" (Lk 8:3 and par.)—thereby revealing that Jesus had known benefactors who gave him money and clothes (Milavec 1982: 116f.; Jn 12:6).

In sum, Theissen and his supporters press too hard when they try to portray Jesus himself as living without home, without money, without possessions. Furthermore, when the evidence of the *Didache* is closely examined (as done above), it becomes impossible to maintain "that the Didache community members know the [itinerant] lifestyle of the Lord Jesus and can use it to judge the validity of itinerant prophets" (Crossan 1998: 377).

As this commentary shows, I strongly endorse Crossan's notion that the prophets of the *Didache* were drawn from the ranks of those who had recently fallen into destitution. The mere fact of living a homeless and penniless existence, however, does not credit one as having "the habits of the Lord" (*Did.* 11:8), for false prophets (and even ordinary vagabonds) would have these same characteristics. When it comes to the "habits of the Lord," therefore, the members of the *Didache* must have had a pragmatic litmus test in mind that could distinguish the true from the false prophet.

Habits of the Lord in the Shepherd of Hermas

In order to explore practical rules for judging prophets, the *Shepherd of Hermas* (90–135 C.E.) deserves attention. The question posed to the Shepherd is this: "How then, sir, will a man know which of them is a [true] prophet and which the false prophet?" (*Mand.* 11.7) The initial response comes: "Try the man who has the Divine Spirit *by his life* [*apo tēs zōēs*]" (11.7). What this means comes shortly, for the Shepherd supplies five characteristics of the true prophet and, further on, contrasts these with five characteristics of the false prophet. Placed side by side, one can immediately see how the characteristics of one mirror the five characteristics of the other:

True Prophets	False Prophets
[A] He who has the Spirit proceeding from above	[A] the man who seems to have the Spirit
[1] is meek	[1] exalts himself
[2] and peaceable	[2] and wishes to have the first seat,
[3] and humble	[3] and is bold and imprudent and talkative,
[4] and refrains from all iniquity and the vain desire of this world	[4] and lives in the midst of many luxuries and many other delusions,
[5] and contents himself with fewer wants than other men. . . (*Mand.* 11.8).	[5] and takes rewards for his prophecy. . . . (*Mand.* 11.12)

Since Hermas was created in a context divorced from the *Didache*, it cannot be supposed that these are the "habits of the Lord" that the *Didache* had in mind. On the other hand, both Hermas and the *Didache* share a common perception (a) that the prophets known to them were not evangelizers making converts and founding new communities and (b) that the prophets known to them did not go into states of ecstasy or frenzy in order to confirm possession by the Spirit. "Charismata are for Hermas not extraordinary endowments, but moral qualities" (Reiling: 126). In the end, therefore, Hermas convincingly puts forward lists of characteristics that could be employed in order to distinguish the true from the false prophet. Even granting that Hermas paints a sharp either-or picture that might become blurred when applied to actual cases, the overall contrast does have enough definition to enable ordinary Christians to make a first approximate discernment. One can decide quite easily whether someone "is meek and peaceable and humble" (*Mand.* 11.8) or whether he "exalts himself and wishes to have the first seat, and is bold" (*Mand.* 11.12).

The same thing, of course, could be said for the Didache community with its decided penchant for finding perfection in the Way of Life (*Did.* 6:2; 16:2) rather than in spectacular accomplishments or miraculous events. Outside of their Spirit-filled prayer, prophets were to be judged by their habits. Do they walk in the Way of Life or the Way of Death? The contrasts were there just as they were in Hermas. Moreover, it is clear that everyone knows what the terms mean because each has been trained to apply them to his/her own life. Thus, if ordinary members were trained to "become long-suffering and merciful and harmless and calm and good" (*Did.* 3:8) and to "accept the experiences befalling you [even financial ruin] as good things" (3:10), would it not be the case that these "habits of the Lord" would also have to be visible traits of the itinerant charismatics as well? On the other hand, would not those "loving frivolous things, pursuing revenge, not showing mercy on the poor" (5:2) be thereby exposing themselves as false prophets walking in the Way of Death? In sum, therefore, it seems safest to surmise that "habits of the Lord" refers to the characteristics in the Way of Life whereby the Father judges what is true and false.

When it came to prophets, Hermas had additional rules. Any prophet who failed to limit his speaking in Spirit to the praying assembly, for example, was automatically classed as a false prophet (see #6b). For Hermas, the rule limiting the speaking in Spirit within the praying assembly had the effect of absolutely obstructing visiting Christian prophets from becoming prophets-for-hire who "practiced soothsaying like the gentiles" (*Mand.* 11.4) for their special clients in private (Reiling: 171f.). The *Didache*, for its part, also had special rules (11:9–12), and it is to these that our attention must now turn.

Four Additional Test Cases Defining Prophetic Limitations

Following the overarching rule of *Did.* 11:7f., the *Didache* provides four illustrations of improper prophetic conduct (*Did.* 11:9–12). Undoubtedly the framers of the *Didache* felt that the general rule failed to suffice and that specific case illustrations were required in order to offset abuses that had (here or elsewhere) taken place in the past. Each of these illustrations begins with *pas prophētēs* ("every prophet"), thereby providing a linguistic unity to the four.

The first case deals with a prophet "ordering a table to be set in Spirit" (11:9). Scholars have understood this "ordering a table" to be "for the poor" (Draper 1983: 246) or "for the needy in the community" (Niederwimmer 1998: 179; Rordorf 1978a: 186 n. 3). These conjectures, however, fail to provide any suitable explanation as to why the prophet should be so rigorously excluded from partaking of these meals. Indeed, the wandering prophet would be counted among the very needy and among those spiritually hungry for the coming kingdom. Why then should he not eat? The traditional explanation of scholars leaves much to be desired on this score.

Didache 11:9 might find a solid explanation if it could, in some way, be tied to the "habits of the Lord" (11:8) which immediately precede it and/or to "the destroying" (11:2) that represents the threat of charismatic innovators. Along these lines it might be allowed that "the table" ordered by the prophet is "the common 'table' for which the rite of chapters 9–10 is intended" (Audet 1958: 450). Should a prophet convene a eucharistic meal, however, he would undoubtedly be looked to as the presider over that meal. Maybe here one touches upon the heart of the problem. Prophets may have tended to take over and even to dominate the eucharist with their charismatic gifts (as in 1 Cor 14). The *Didache*, by virtue of safeguarding the right of the appointed prayer leader, effectively determined that the community owned and presided over every eucharist. Thus, the pastoral genius of the *Didache* may have reached an ingenious solution: (a) One the one hand, the prophet initiative was to be honored; (b) on the other hand, the prophet was banned from presiding. This "fence" or safeguard was effected by prohibiting the prophet from partaking of this meal and, by implication, from offering the prayers of thanksgiving. This is so because, in the Jewish tradition, only one who eats could offer the blessing before and the thanksgiving after the meal (*b. Berakhot* 48a-b). The prohibition against eating, therefore, served to honor the prophetic mandate (*Did.* 11:7) without allowing the prophet to "tear down" (11:2) the tradition of having the community preside at its own eucharist.

The second special case presumes that, if and when a prophet should presume to give training to the community as to what the Lord expects of them, the prophet will, first and foremost, be a living example of what he/she promotes. The *Didache*, at this point, does not clearly specify that such training is given "in the Spirit." Nor does the *Didache* imply that prophets routinely functioned as teachers/trainers. On the other hand, since "teaching the truth" (*Did.* 11:10) is clearly stated, the prophet here would evidently be "received as the Lord" because he/she is promoting "these things said beforehand" (11:1). Note in passing that, here again, the norm of conduct is paramount. This rule enforces the traditional rabbinic notion that a rabbi is "living torah" and trains his disciples as much by what he does as by what he says. The Christian Scriptures are replete with similar suggestions. In Matthew's Gospel, for instance, prophets coming to Jesus saying, "Lord, Lord, did we not prophesy in your name, and cast out demons in your name, and do many mighty works in your name?"

(Mt 7:22) are entirely disowned ("I do not know you") precisely because they failed to do that torah that Jesus taught them. Thus, here again the pastoral delicacy of the *Didache* shines through. The training of a prophet is held up for honor, but, at the same time, it is required that the words of the training conform to the *Didache* and that the deeds of the prophet conform to his/her words.

The third special case is difficult to unwrap owing to our ignorance of what the *Didache* had in mind when it came to prophets "acting for the worldly mystery of the church" (*poiōn eis mystērion kosmikon ekklēsias*) (11:11). This obscure phrase finds no explanation within the *Didache* and no exact parallel in either the secular or religious literature; hence, it is impossible to know precisely what the phrase meant for the community of the *Didache*. One can surmise, however, that an entire range of evocative and/or disturbing prophetic gestures were anticipated that were not to be judged or imitated "for with God he has his judgment; for just so acted also the ancient prophets" (11:11). Note that the emphasis is expressly upon a prophet having been tested and found "true." Such tested prophets were effectively granted great liberty in "acting for the worldly mystery of the church" as long as they did not presume to train others that God required them to act likewise.

What might this include? Maybe a prophet undertook degrading tasks normally reserved for women or slaves—like cleaning toilets or washing the feet of visitors or dressing the wounds of a leper—with the idea of demonstrating that, when the Lord arrives, even the most demeaning acts of service will be understood rightly as cloaked with dignity and love. Then again maybe another prophet said that the Lord had trained him to despise money and thus he took up the practice of referring to money as "shit" and made a vow never to touch it again. Another prophet may have refused to eat anything one or two days prior to any eucharist in the expectation that, perhaps at this eucharist, the Lord might come. At still other times, a prophet might even hold up his own prophetic calling to leave all in order to undertake an itinerant lifestyle in service of the kingdom as an imitation of Jesus' way of "acting for the worldly mystery of the church." In any case, it is misleading to imagine that "the worldly mystery of the church" can be reduced merely to a "spiritual marriage" since, if this is what the framers of the *Didache* had in mind, they would have come out and said so (see #6k).

#6K THE MEANING OF "THE WORLDLY MYSTERY OF THE CHURCH" (*DID.* 11:11)

While *Did.* 11:11 has occasioned, from the very beginning, a wide variety of interpretations (Jacquier: 238–40), most living scholars have contented themselves with interpreting this "worldly (or cosmic) mystery" against the backdrop of Eph 5:32, in which Paul speaks of "the great mystery" (*to mystērion mega*) whereby a husband's self-sacrificing love for his wife images Christ's love for his church. Against this backdrop, most scholars speculate that the "worldly mystery of the church" represents "an allusion to women who accompanied the wandering prophets and whose relations to them were not unequivocal" (Theissen 1992: 41). Niederwimmer sees it as "a spiritual marriage" between a prophet and a sister, which, being a celibate union, "corresponds to its heavenly model, namely, the union of the *Kyrios* ["Lord"] with his bride, the church" (1998: 182; 1996: 329, 331 n. 34; Campenhausen: 73 n. 119; Harnack 1884: 121f.; Rordorf 1978a: 187). Draper remarks that such a "'spiritual marriage' caused offense to the local congregation, and the redactor [of the *Didache*] is concerned to justify it within limits (that others are not encouraged to do the same!)" (Draper 1983: 247; Niederwimmer 1996: 331 n. 31). Alternately, Crossan speculates that *Did.* 11:11 was wrestling with "spiritual marriage" more as a practical mode whereby female prophets could safely travel in the Mediterranean world:

> The only way a woman could have been involved in the earliest Jesus movement as an itinerant prophet, given the cultural situation of the day, was if she traveled with a male as his "wife" (or in some other acceptable female role). As long as she was with a male, nobody would have really cared about the relationship or bothered to ask about it. Such companionship did not threaten patriarchal domination in any way; a woman accompanying a man could be servant or slave, sister, mistress, or wife without male chauvinism caring enough even to ask for definition. This is how we should also understand Paul's mention of a "sister wife" in 1 Corinthians 9:5. . . . (1998: 379)

When one explores these meanings within the context of the *Didache*, Audet rightly concludes that one is left with only "a crash of thunder coming from a cloudless sky" (Audet 1958: 452). Nothing in the *Didache* points to any influence from Ephesians; hence, it would be hazardous to project meanings found in a foreign context upon the obscure clues of the *Didache*. Furthermore, if the "worldly mystery" referred to "spiritual marriage" or "celibacy," it remains to be seen why the writer of the *Didache*, with his penchant for precision, did not just come out and say so. It must be surmised, therefore, that the text anticipated an extended set of prophetic gestures that defied easy enumeration. This might include "spiritual marriage" but it cannot be limited to this. For example, the practice of "the ancient prophet" Hosea remaining faithful to his wife despite her repeated adulterous liaisons (Hos 1:2–9) must be allowed as a possible application of how a prophet might act "for the worldly mystery of the church" (*Did.* 11:11). The ancient prophets provide a variety of symbolic acts (e.g., 1 Sm 15:27f.; 1 Kgs 11:30–39; 2 Kgs 13:15–19; Jer 19:10f.; Ez 4:1–5:6). In sum, the imagination of most scholars has been entirely too restrictive on this point and overly wedded to Eph 5:23.

The Coptic fragment drops out "worldly mystery of the church" and, in its place, has the prophet enacting the "mystery of a tradition according to good order in the church" (Horner 1924: 225–31). G. Horner's translation at this point is cumbersome. Richard Arthur suggests that the Coptic text should be read as follows:

> Obviously, the passage marks a concession to visiting prophets. Don't judge them! God will judge. They are like the prophets of olden times and presumably should be respected. It is required that their teachings be inspected, but having passed inspection they are hereby licensed to "do mysteries," with the proviso that they are done "traditionally" and "in decorous order" (*kocmikon*). The Coptic rendering of "*kocmikon*" is flawed, as is so often the case with Greek words transcribed into Coptic where we presume some scribes could only trust their ear for the sound of the word, not knowing Greek vocabulary or phonetics. (letter of 16 Aug 93)

The upshot of this is that the Coptic fragment provides no help. According to Arthur, the corrupt *kocmikon* that was read by Horner and others as *kocmion* ("decorous" or "in an orderly manner") is merely a transliteration of *kosmikon* ("cosmic" or "worldly") found in the Greek. Thus, it would appear that the Coptic translator was confused by the Greek phrase *eis mystērion kosmikon ekklēsias* (lit., "for the mystery cosmic of the church") and settled for having the prophet acting out "a mystery *traditionally* cosmic *in* the church" (following the Coptic word order). Since *mystērion* in Greek commonly meant a "secret rite, secret teaching" (Bauer: 530b) and was especially applied to initiation rites performed in places where no outsiders were present, the Coptic translator may have understood the prophet as performing a baptism in the church. If so, this would make understandable why the translator added "traditionally" ("in a traditional manner") to emphasize the fact that the prophet had to perform the rite of the church. The translator was undoubtedly puzzled that a prophet was performing the rite in the first place. Not knowing what to make of the word *kosmikon* ("cosmic") modifying *mystērion*, the translator settled with leaving the word in its place and simply transliterating it into Coptic. Instead of settling the mystery, the translator thus only passed along his confusion.

John Dominic Crossan had this to say after he evaluated the attempt of Jones and Mirecki (1995: 68) to translate this difficult passage from the Coptic fragment:

> The Coptic translation either does not like or does not understand that "cosmic mystery" [of *Did*. 11:11] and replaces it with something both known and liked—namely, "orderly tradition." (Crossan 1998: 380)

In any case, the Coptic fragment offers no clarification whatsoever of what the prophets of the Didache community were doing that merited the rule of *Did*. 11:11.

What the Coptic fragment does confirm, however, is that the original Greek did have an obscure phrase ("the worldly mystery"). This is no accidental error of some distracted copyist. The Coptic fragment also reveals that the translator did not know what it meant, and he was much closer in time and in culture to the *Didache* than we are. This may be likened to that period during the 70s when the term "stonewalling" (a rarely used term going back as early as 1889) was reintroduced into the everyday language of Americans during the course of the Watergate investigations. Everyone who followed those investigations understood the term. College students prior to Watergate as well as college students today, however, readily admit to me that they have not heard the word, do not use the word, and have only vague hunches as to what the word might mean. Thus, in this instance, while everyone in the Didache communities knew very well what was meant by a "worldly mystery of the church," their everyday understanding has died with them and may never be recovered.

In addition to the Coptic fragment, the Ethiopian *Ecclesiastical Canons of the Apostles* includes a version of *Did*. 11:3–13:7. As for the difficult text of *Did*. 11:11, however, the Ethiopian text speaks of a prophet "who acts in the assembly of men and acts unlawfully" (Horner 1904: 230). Here again, no clues are given as to the meaning of the *Didache*. Both the Coptic and Ethiopian fragments do signal, however, that neither "spiritual marriage," nor "celibacy," nor any other single activity could be supplied as the evident meaning of a prophet "acting for the worldly mystery of the church" (*Did*. 11:11).

Finally, the *Didache* turns its attention to prophets who employ their divine inspiration for personal gain—"silver or any other thing" (*Did*. 11:12). While pagan prophets routinely accepted remuneration and gifts from those patrons whom they served by being mediums of the gods, the mandate here blocked any visiting prophet from falling into this practice. Hermas, for example, repeatedly blasts this practice and offsets it by declaring that any prophet using his/her gifts outside of the praying assembly is automatically to be branded a false prophet (see #6b). Nothing in the *Didache* suggests anything remotely like this practice, yet, given the prevalence of this practice in the pagan world, it could not be far away from the minds of some.

In the case of a prophet requesting contributions "concerning others being in want" (*Did*. 11:12), however, this was to be allowed. These "others" were supposedly persons known to the prophet due to his/her wandering and not local folks who would be expected to make their needs known personally. Furthermore, unlike the earlier case (*Did*. 11:6), the request was made speaking "in Spirit" (*Did*. 11:12), most likely at the end of the eucharistic assembly, and thereby carried with it the conviction that God himself suffered with those in need and that members of the Didache community were urged to enter into sympathy with God and bring relief "from his own free gifts" (*Did*. 1:5). Here again, one can surmise that "silver" (*Did*. 11:12) might be requested, thereby indicating that the need presented might involve substantial but not enormous sums.

The implied response to the prophetic alert of an urgent need was to allow individuals to give as much as they were willing and able to (as in *Did*. 4:6–8; 12:2). On the other hand, the rule of the *Didache* did not go so far as to say, "Let a collection be undertaken," thereby ensuring that the need would become a community priority (as in Acts 11:28–30). Rather, the response is decidedly muted: "let no one judge [the prophet]" (*Did*. 11:12). The implication here is that the prophet's report of the existence and extent of the need was not to be openly examined and verified, nor was the prophet's honesty in delivering the collected aid to be challenged. One can assume that, in the case of known and urgent cases of need, delegated members of the community would have been appointed to receive the collection and to carry it personally to those in need (as in Acts 11:28–30). Thus, here again, even in the face of passionately delivered pleas by known prophets to the effect that God urged them to bring massive aid to named groups or persons in distress, the *Didache* provides a delicate compromise: On the one hand, the prophet's message was not to be challenged; on the other hand, the community was not to be mobilized. The result was left up to a freewill offering for those who wished to participate.

#6M SIGNIFICANCE OF UNDERSTANDING OF RIGHT AND LEFT (*DID*. 12:1)

Given the openness with which outsiders were received, the average member of the community had to be trained and trusted to "have understanding of right and left" (12:1). This metaphor is only marginally operative in our present-day culture. We speak of "right and wrong," associating "the right direction" or "the right hand" with justice and truth. The older term "righteous" refers to someone deemed to be good. The left hand, however, is not normally associated with injustice and falsehood. In traditional Middle Eastern societies, however, one always takes food and passes gifts with the right hand. The left hand, associated with toilet cleansing, had the sense of being unclean or boding ill. Using the left hand to pass something to another would be taken as an insult. Our term "sinister," for example, comes from the Latin word *sinistra* meaning "left" or "left-handed." In the parable of the last judgment, therefore, ancient peoples would have found a deep significance in the fact that the elect were placed "at his right [hand]" and the damned on "the left" (Mt 26:33). Nineveh, meanwhile, was described as the city wherein most of its inhabitants "cannot discern between their right and their left [hand]" (Jon 4:11). See also Dt 17.20; 28.14. Accordingly, *Did.* 12:1 functions as a sort of summary statement concerning all outsiders. Any outsider "coming in the name of the Lord" was to be welcomed and, over a period of time, "put to the test" so that "you will [by this testing] have understanding of right and left [hands/deeds/persons]" (*Did.* 12:1). And this testing, as has been shown, was entrusted to the skills possessed by the average community member and was not reserved to a special class of persons or to a special process governed by the community rule.

Why the Didache Communities Absorbed But Never Created Prophets

From what has been discussed, the Didache community can now be seen as honoring the prophets yet taking care that they did not wear out or abuse their welcome. With delicacy and firmness, the *Didache* set limits. The divinely given passion of the prophets was never to be challenged as such, yet neither was everything a prophet said or did taken at face value. This guarded appreciation of the prophets becomes most evident when it is noticed that the Didache community made ample provisions for welcoming prophets but gave no attention whatsoever to creating them and sending them out. Furthermore, wandering prophets were welcome to settle down—an indication that some prophets liked what they saw and knew of the Didache community. But even with prophets settling in the community with regularity, the distribution of first fruits had to anticipate the case when a prophet would not be present and the first fruits would have to be given to their nearest equivalent, beggars. This is an unsettling clue. On the face of it, the Didache community appears to attract, absorb, and, in the end, dissolve the prophetic spirit itself.

Why is this? What was going on?

To begin with, one has to enter into Crossan's discovery that the prophetic character blossomed in great adversity. Crossan was able to find no special reason why, in and of itself, there was anything glorious about abandoning home, occupation, family. If the prophets were called to abandonment as such, then Christians would have had good cause to roundly criticize them for making the vulnerable members of their family even more vulnerable and for bringing an even greater heap of misery into the world. A family without a breadwinner is not a happy family—and no amount of clever theology or appeals to a divine calling can explain to hungry children why God wants their daddy or mommy to go off and do something more important than feeding, clothing, and protecting them.

Thus, I believe Crossan is correct. The prophets, along with the bandits and beggars, were drawn from the ranks of those who were entirely unsuccessful at protecting, feeding, and caring for their children because of savage economic forces beyond their control. The impersonal and voracious program of Roman commercialization forced everyone to work harder just to keep afloat. As debt increased and moneylenders came to collect their collateral on loans in default, fathers and mothers were crushed at their inability to satisfy the hungry cries of their children. Now their children were forced to beg in the streets or, as a last resort, were sold into slavery so as to be saved from starvation. To be sure, in the ancient world, where enlightened social programs did not exist, starvation was always a grim and real possibility.

Among the ranks of those recently broken on the wheel of harder and harder labor and deeper and deeper debt, the prophets emerged. Not everyone eaten up by the system, needless to say, automatically turned to God when they were at the end of their rope. For some men and women recently driven into desperation, however, the prospect of the kingdom of God opened up their last hope in this world. No one expected governments to do anything for the poor. Friends and family helped to the degree that they were able, yet in hard times even this had to be limited, lest all be exposed to the same fate. The prophets felt that God and God alone was their sure advocate and expected liberator (Pss 10:1–18; 34:16–22; 37:7–13; 70:5; Is 41:17–20; Jb 5:8–16; 29:11–17). Because they relied on God so completely, they prayed for the coming of the kingdom with a fierceness and rage that defied human understanding. Although they were broken in spirit, their confidence in the Lord took fire and enabled them to hold on and wait for the end times with the innocence of children waiting for their papa to come home with the groceries.

Prophets offered their urgent prayers to God and received, in exchange, a small measure of food and lodging from the Christians who received them. When the prophets arrived at the doors of a Didache community, these folks had something to offer to prophets that went beyond a short period of room and board. Other Christian communities could not protect their own members against the ravages of the debt cycle; the Didache community, in contrast, had worked out an elaborate way of life that made such a fate well-nigh impossible. One for all and all for one. Needless to say, the Didache community did what it did out of its own conviction that everything belonged to the Father and that each person was a steward using the good things of this world in such a way as to ensure that "to all, the Father wishes to give from his own free gifts" (*Did.* 1:5). Among themselves, moreover, they practiced a hard-won tradition of giving and receiving goods and services based on the conviction that they were *koinōnoi* ("business partners") in both material and spiritual goods (4:8). Thus, far from forming an emergency chest to handle emergency situations (as in Acts and in Justin Martyr), the people of the *Didache* pioneered a way of being in the world that obviated starvation and debt-servitude.

In like fashion, the members of the Didache community had developed new ways of seeing the poor. Indigence was not due to fate or to laziness, as some would believe (Prv 10:4; 13:18; 20:13; 28:19). Nor was it the will of God (remember *Did.* 4:12). Rather, the conviction grew that the Father in heaven cared for the poor, and, as a consequence, the Didache community was obliged to do the same (*Did.* 5:2[B13–21]; Prv 14:21; 31:21; 22:22f.; 28:27). Sympathy with God was at the heart of this movement. Here, however, was more than a sympathy that, in the face of hardship, prayed helplessly and waited for God to step in. Rather, *here was a sympathy that moved into action in anticipation of God's action.*

No wonder, then, that some prophets came "wishing to settle down" (*Did.* 13:1). The community extended to those broken by grief and sorrow a chance to receive free room and board. With time, however, such prophets found that their broken hearts began to mend and their depression began to lift. With real pastoral wisdom, the *Didache* assigned the prophets the role of giving thanks to God for the first fruits of members of the community (*Did.* 13:3). The one bringing the first fruits gained an eloquent prayer (see ch. 7 below), yet the prophet gained a renewed faith that God could be thanked for the little daily successes in the markets and in the shops and that life did not have to stop and remain breathless until the kingdom arrived. Hence, by degrees, the prophets who settled in the Didache community began to laugh again and began to work again. They returned to work because they felt ashamed (having worked all their lives) that others had to work harder to maintain their well-being. But, more than this, they returned to work because their love of life was returning. And as they worked and gained a degree of self-reliance again, their passion for the coming of God burned less feverishly. With time, the Spirit no longer provoked them with the same overriding obsession that they had known earlier when it came to praying after the eucharist. As they healed, therefore, they laughed and loved and worked more and found that the Spirit more and more passed them by. Finally, the prophetic urge left them entirely.

In effect, the Didache community knew that it could not change the world, where powerful men were trained to be resourceful and to stamp out their economic well-being on the backs of those less fortunate. It could, however, bring the hearts of men and women back into sympathy with their Father in heaven. The revealed way is the Way of the Father, and it does give life—not some pie in the sky kind of life—but the very day-to-day existence that rejoices in work, family, and play and expects God to bless and to sanction their Way of Living when he finally comes.

All good prayer leads to good action. The members of the Didache community knew that the God of Israel could not be bribed by sacrifices or buttered up by good deeds to do whatever the petitioner wanted. Rather, the whole focus in prayer was to draw close to the heart of the Father and to change one's heart so that one could sympathetically enter into God's heartfelt designs for the future. Only humans can dream dreams and fancy a future that is better, happier, and more secure than what currently exists. And God is the great guarantor of dreams and dreamers.

The genius of the Didache community, therefore, is that it took the world as it was handed to them and began to change those who were closest at hand whom they had the power to change, namely, themselves. Aided by love, by mentors, and by visionary leadership, therefore, they moved forward into the world anticipating here the conditions God would want in his kingdom. For them there was no need of extraordinary feats of asceticism and no need to escape the misery of this world in order to find happiness in another realm after death. No. They believed as they prayed: "Your kingdom come on earth as it is [already established] in heaven" (*Did.* 8:2). God was preparing to come to them, and they were getting ready here and now to greet him when he comes.

All in all, it was not so much prophetic visions as prophetic living that was prized by the community. Thus, the wandering prophets discovered something about prophecy that they had never quite understood—that prophecy is not the end but the beginning and that a spoonful of prophetic living is more valuable than a whole barrel of prophetic dreaming. The prophets had hoped to make way for the kingdom by the ardor of their words that burned red-hot as a result of the tormented rage and despair running through the wreckage of their lives. The members of the Didache community, in contrast, endeavored to savor the contentment of everyday holiness (the Way of Life) as they lived and worked and laughed among the saints. No wonder, then, that the Didache community honored the prophets but refused to give them even a small edge to pry up and destroy the least of what had "been said beforehand" (*Did.* 11:1). No wonder, then, that the Didache community ended up attracting, cooling down, and healing those charismatic wanderers whose minds and bellies had once blasted forth with prophetic fire.

Conclusion

In the end, one can step back and try to situate the above conclusions within the larger program of the *Didache*. To begin with, the *Didache* defined a way of life that enabled adherents to attain that "perfection" that would be expected of them by the Lord on the last day (*Did.* 6:2; 16:2). By gathering together "frequently" (16:2) and maintaining a community rhythm of daily prayer (8:2–3), semiweekly fasting (8:1), and the weekly confession of failings followed by the eucharist (4:14; 14:1), the adherents of this community found "rest/refreshment" for their souls (4:2; 16:2). Then apostle-prophets entered the picture. These were the ones whose lifestyle and charisma could just as easily tear down as build up "all these things said beforehand" (11:1). As for these vagabonds, therefore, the operative rule was that they ought to be "received as the Lord" (11:4) only as long as they adhered to their own self-definition as "passing through" and "having no possessions."

When they prayed in Spirit, the prophets' evident charisma would not be directly "put on trial nor judge[d]" (11:7; 11:11). They would, however, be expected to have the "habits of the Lord" (11:8) that were defined and understood by the community in their Way of Life. A prophet could "in Spirit" convene a eucharistic assembly but could not presume to preside and supplant the established patterns for community eucharist. Even when prophets might be present at the weekly eucharist, the evocative and spontaneous prayers of prophets were to be honored, but only to the degree that they added to and did not displace the community taking charge of its own rite. When it came to the way of the Lord, the prophets could freely act out the radical demands of their calling and feverishly anticipate God's future, yet they could not train others "to do as much" (11:11). The spirituality of everyday holiness was thereby secured against the excesses of apocalyptic fever.

Within the first-century world of conflicting spiritualities, the *Didache* affirmed the everyday holiness practiced by householders while resisting the eschatological extremes practiced by those charismatic wanderers who had tragically lost their homes, families, and occupations in order to promote this Gospel. The pastoral genius of the *Didache* is that it knew how to honor the heroic virtue and charismatic gifts of the prophets without imagining that perfection consisted in doing these things (11:11). The *Didache* celebrated the love of God and neighbor (1:2) in the daily little things: in short prayers (8:2), in sharing resources (4:8), in reconciling those who were fighting (4:3). Prolonged prayers, selling all one had in order to give it to the poor, and reconciling the whole world to Christ were left to others—the few and not the many. Here, then, was the moderate and delicate wisdom of the *Didache* that was so compelling. Thus, the unspectacular attraction of ordinary holiness supplanted and tamed the unmitigated excesses of the wandering apostle-prophets themselves. The God of the *Didache* was accordingly the one who wiped away all tears.

#6N WHETHER A SOULFUL EUCHARIST AROUSED THE PROPHETIC SPIRIT

Only a community with a dynamic tradition of effective and spontaneous prayer leaders would ever be blessed to have prophets. A prophet is not just born or created in some instantaneous extraterrestrial experience. A prophet has to be nurtured over a prolonged period of time by a eucharistic spirituality that engenders a longing for the things to come. Only by encountering the pathos of the heavenly Father bent on saving, perfecting, and gathering could or would anyone ever become capable of receiving a prophetic calling. "The prophet is stirred by an intimate concern for the divine concern" (Heschel: 88). Thus, a dull eucharist within a dull community would inevitably dull the Spirit such that either there would be no prophets or there would be no community willing to receive them.

On the other hand, even an evocative and deep eucharistic tradition does not automatically mean that prophets will be multiplied as though the prophetic calling could be created in a climate in which members were swept away by feeling:

> Nothing is further from the prophetic mind than to inculcate or to live out a life of feeling, a religion of sentimentality. Nor mere feeling, but action, will mitigate the world's misery, society's injustice or the people's alienation from God. Only action will relieve the tension between God and man. Both pathos and sympathy [which make for the prophetic calling] are . . . demands rather than fulfillments. Prophetic sympathy is no delight; unlike ecstasy, is not a goal, but a sense of challenge, a commitment, a state of tension, consternation, and dismay. (Heschel: 89)

All in all, the emergence of the prophetic soul remains a mystery. Even the one who will eventually be a prophet does not, at the beginning, know where his/her attachment to the pathos of God may be leading. On the other hand, prophets do not emerge out of a void and are not recognized as prophets unless there are communities ready to receive them. Thus, since prophecy is not an art acquired by a systematic apprenticeship at the hands of other prophets, *the eucharist of the community itself must have been the stimulus that aroused the prophetic soul.* It is no surprise, consequently, that the *Didache* had such an enormously developed liturgy and that the prophets, once they emerged, gravitated toward these communities to exercise their gifts within the context of the eucharist. Whatever has been our own experience of liturgy, therefore, this should not disguise the evidence that the eucharistic meal of the Didache communities was a marvelous door to the sacred and a mysterious means of grace.

While a soulful liturgy nurtured the prophetic spirit and fashioned the expectation of the world to come, not every person attending even the best of eucharistic liturgies became a prophet. One other ingredient was necessary—the suffering experienced by someone slipping into destitution. As shown above, the prophets emerged from the ranks of those whose spirits had been broken—persons no longer able to protect their parents, their children, and themselves from the ravages of increased debt and destitution. Such persons, should they survive, become beggars, bandits, or prophets. Bandits risk their lives and fall upon their victims because only by so doing can they survive the brutalization to which they have fallen victim. Prophets, on the other hand, risk their souls and fall upon their God because, in their eyes, God and God alone is their sure advocate and expected liberator (Pss 10:1–18; 34:16–22; 37:7–13; 70:5; Is 41:17–20; Jb 5:8–16; 29:11–17). Having no one to rely on, they rely on God, and thus they pray for the coming of the kingdom with a fierceness and a persistence that defy easy description. Although they are broken in spirit, their confidence in the Lord enables them to hold on and wait for tomorrow with renewed expectation. The same thing, with minor adjustments, could be said of those new converts who were disowned and disinherited by their parents (see #6h).

In conclusion, one might say that soulful liturgies provided a proximate climate while falling into destitution provided the immediate impulse that nurtured the prophetic spirit. Why this poor person and not another, however, is always shrouded in mystery. In the end, the Lord "calls those whom the Spirit has made ready" (4:10).

#60 WHETHER PROPHETS WERE THE NORMAL CELEBRANTS OF THE EUCHARIST

Rordorf and Niederwimmer are convinced that, because the prophets were given the first fruits traditionally reserved for the high priests (*Did.* 13:3), this implies that the *Didache* names them as the celebrants of the eucharist (Rordorf 1978a: 52f.; 1998: 228; Niederwimmer 1998: 192). Georg Schöllgen and Andre de Halleux, on the contrary, are persuaded that the acceptance of the prophets as "your high priests" (13:3) is limited to the domain of first fruits; hence, "one can conclude nothing from this passage concerning the specific liturgical function of the prophets" (Schöllgen: 58 n. 89; de Halleux: 19).

In my judgment, the evidence strongly favors this latter judgment:

1. When it came to first fruits, the *Didache* took care to make provisions for the case when a community might not have a prophet (13:4). No such provision settled the issue of who would be celebrant at the eucharist in the absence of a prophet. No one, to my knowledge, allows that "beggars" (13:4) would replace the prophets as celebrants just as they did in the case of receiving first fruits. This can only mean that prophets were not counted on to be the regular celebrants.

2. The existence of a schematic outline for the eucharistic prayers (*Did.* 9–10) implies that the celebrant was not a charismatic; hence, one would not have expected prophets to take on the role of prayer leaders even when they were present. Their Spirit-led prayers were welcomed after the completion of the prescribed prayers (10:7). Furthermore, the very notion of "speaking in Spirit" implies that prophets kept silent if and when the Spirit did not prompt them to speak. No regular celebrant could function within such a provisionary rubric.

3. Within the Christian Scriptures, "priests" were never presented as having any official function in the Jesus movement; hence, the term "high priests" would not have been associated with those "presiding" at the eucharist. Only in the late second century did the eucharist come to be understood as "a sacrifice" that was offered or presided over by "a priest." It would be anachronistic to project this development back into the *Didache* even though 14:1–3 (see ch. 8 below) presents the first steps toward that development.

4. The term "high priests" was applied metaphorically to the prophets *only in so far as* they received the first fruits. No one imagines, for example, that they were sons of Aaron or that they were ordained. If the *Didache* had in mind a complete identification of "the prophets" as "your high priests" (*Did.* 13:3), then it would follow (a) that the first fruits would have had to be carefully preserved until a prophet arrived or (b) that the first fruits would have had to be transported to a place where the prophets were to be found. When the *Didache* allows that "the beggars" (13:4) were alternate recipients of the first fruits, this confirms the mindset of the framers of the *Didache*.

5. When speaking of bishops and deacons, the *Didache* says that they deserve honor because they exercise the *leitourgia* of the prophet-teachers (15:1). Niederwimmer interprets *Did.* 15:1f. to mean "that the local officials, together with the prophets and teachers (or, to the extent that the last two groups are absent, they alone) lead the worship service that formerly was in the hands of the prophets and teachers alone" (1998: 202).

Rordorf, for his part, reads *Did*. 15:1f. in a more radical manner: "the bishops and deacons are charged to replace them [the prophets]" (1998: 228) as presiders at the eucharist. In chapter 9 I will establish these points: (a) The qualifications of the bishops gave no hint of a liturgical function. (b) The ministry they undertook was the "unremunerated public service" (*leitourgia*), as in the case of the prophet-teachers. (c) The bishops of the *Didache* were not eucharistic presiders; they would become so only in the second century (see #9f).

Despite these arguments, Rordorf's position has been widely accepted. Edward Schillebeeckx, for instance, carefully arrives at the conclusion that the New Testament never reserves to any class of persons the right to preside over the eucharist, and yet, when it comes to the *Didache*, he allows, without much discussion, that "in the earliest stratum of the *Didache* the 'prophets and teachers' preside at the eucharist; in a later stratum they are joined by presbyters and deacons who do so by virtue of their office" (1985: 20). Eduard Schweitzer, as part of a comprehensive study of ministry in the early church, came to a parallel conclusion based on his interpretation of *Did*. 15:1 as casting the elected "bishops and deacons" in the role of the "prophets and teachers." For Schweitzer, however, "they [the bishops and deacons] do not pray extempore as the prophets do, but they say [?] the prescribed liturgical prayers [namely, *Did*. 9–10]" (142).

The practice of Judaism is important in providing a background out of which the practice of the *Didache* emerged. The temple rites were largely in the hands of the officiating priests—"the people were merely onlookers and even the chanting of hymns was entrusted to the Levitical singers" (Heinemann: 145). In the synagogue, however, "the prayer . . . was recited by a Prayer Leader, an 'emissary' of the people themselves, rather than by a priestly officiant" (ibid.). Even though the local synagogue had a system of elders, it would seem that "any male [Jew] might be called upon to read the Hebrew Scriptures, supply the Aramaic translation, or recite the Shema or Tefillah [the Eighteen Benedictions]" (Beckwith: 80). This did not mean, of course, that anyone and everyone took their turn at presiding. As explained in chapter 4, presiding in the context of either rabbinic or Christian prayers required a knowledge of the thematic summary of the prayers and the ability to develop and contemporize these themes spontaneously in a public setting.

In conclusion, it would be misleading to suggest that the framers of the *Didache* implied that either "prophetic gifts" or "ecclesial ordination" was a prerequisite for presiding. This would come, to be sure. One has only to examine the *Apostolic Constitutions* (380 C.E.) to discover how church offices imparted by ordination came to be assigned to the liturgical rites named by the *Didache*. The rules for baptism (7:1–3), for example, were expressly assigned to the "bishop or elder" (*Apostolic Constitutions* 7.21.1) and, at the end of the eucharist, one finds *Did.* 10.7 altered to read: "(And) turn towards the elders also [allowing them] to eucharistize" (7.26.6). By way of safeguarding the integrity of the *Didache*, however, great care must be taken not to project into the text the concerns and the ministries proper to other times and other places. In this regard, Arthur Vööbus (1968) has been exemplary in consistently insisting that the evidence of the *Didache* ought to be allowed to speak for itself. This is what I have endeavored to do in my examination of this sensitive and knotty question.

#6P WHY RESIDENT PROPHETS WERE EXEMPT FROM WORKING

Didache 12:1 gives the general rule that "everyone coming in the name of the Lord" ought to be received as the Lord, and, only after being received warmly and generously, should a visitor be put "to the test." This rule serves to recapitulate the reception afforded apostle-prophets (11:3–11) and prepares for the reception of traveling Christians (12:2–5) which follows. Prophets have a two-day limit to their free room and board (11:5); visiting Christians, for reasons not explained, have a three-day limit (12:2).

The *Didache* treats of the special case of ordinary visitors who wish "to settle down among you" (12:3) and then goes on immediately to consider the case of prophets who wish "to settle down among you" (13:1). Settling visitors were expected to work at their trade and, accordingly, to be self-sufficient (12:3b). In the special case where they had no trade, the community was required to make arrangements so that no one was idle. Presumably, such a person was assigned tasks in one or more of the cooperative shops maintained by the community (see ch. 2 above) and was expected in the course of time to learn a trade. Settling prophets, however, were not expected to work—"the community is obliged to provide for their livelihood" (Niederwimmer 1998: 189).

What is the implied logic here? If the phrase "just as a laborer" (*Did.* 13:2) is meant to apply to true prophets as well as to true teachers, then the general rule "let him/her work and let him/her eat" (12:3) applied to settling prophets. The Didache community accordingly regarded the activities of the prophet as the "work" to which the Lord had called them. It followed that they were "worthy of their food" (13:1).

According to the Synoptic tradition, the rule that "laborers deserve their food" (Mt 10:10, Lk 10:7) served to justify the open hospitality given to wandering apostle-prophets. While this may be a saying of the Lord found in Q, it appears to have more of the character of a widely circulated folk saying (Koester 1990: 182 n. 3). In the Nag Hammadi codex, *Dialogue of the Savior* framed the rule in the singular: "The laborer is worthy of his food" (139.8–13). Paul, in his letters, spoke of those engaged in ministry as destined "to receive wages according to the labor of each" (1 Cor 3:8). Later in this same letter, Paul argued at length for his "right to food and drink" (1 Cor 9:3–14) but then went on to state that he declined to make use of "these rights" (1 Cor 9:15). Later, in the pseudo-Pauline *1 Timothy,* these same arguments were extended to apply to "elders" (1 Tm 5:17). Two texts from "the Scripture" were brought forward: (1) "You shall not muzzle an ox while it is treading out the grain" (Dt 25:4) and (2) "the laborer deserves to be paid"—a citation nowhere found in the Hebrew Scriptures but possibly a folk saying akin to Mt 10:10. All in all, the application of the metaphor "laborer" (*ergatēs*) to prophets and teachers seems very widespread (see also Mt 9:37 and the *Gos. Thom.* 73).

In the ancient world, it was common for prophets to expect payment in exchange for their prophecy (see #6q). Hermas noted that false prophets give private consultations when hired (see #6b). By offering prophets room and board at community expense, the Didache communities may have wished to discourage private consultations. More significantly, however, if Crossan's analysis is correct, then one might have expected that the prophets were entirely disenchanted with their former trades (something that entirely failed to protect them and their families) and threw their entire future into the hands of the living God. Offering prophets room and board in exchange for their "labor" was thus a way of preserving the honor of those whose lives had been utterly shattered by their former losses so that they were psychologically (and oftentimes physically as well) incapable of working.

That teachers (*didaskaloi*) should be given community resources is surprising in view of the fact that, within the Jewish setting, one was not to receive payment for giving another the word of the Lord:

"You received without payment, give without payment." (Mt 10:8)

What is the scriptural basis for this rule?
Said R. Judah [in the name of] Rab, "Scripture says, 'Behold I have taught you [even as God commanded me]' (Dt 4:5)—just as I [taught you Torah] at no fee, so you must do so at no fee." (*b. Bekhorot* 29a)

"Take no compensation whatever for her [Torah] since the Omnipotent gave her [Torah] to you gratuitously." (*DEZ* 58b)

These teachers do not appear to be visiting or wishing to settle down; rather, the reference here points backward to the trainers/mentors already established in the community. As a matter of justice, however, anyone functioning as a mentor would be taken away from his/her trade; thus, compensation was in order. The *Didache* does not tell us whether trainers in the Way of Life were customarily occupied full-time in this endeavor or whether they were compensated only when and to the degree that they were drawn away from their craft. Furthermore, the expression, "worthy of their food" (*Did.* 13:2) suggests that trainers could forgo compensation, and, only when they requested it, would it actually be given. Many mentors, it will later become apparent, offered their labors as a *leitourgia* ("unremunerated public service") (*Did.* 15:1f.). The details of this will be taken up in chapter 9 in the context of considering the *leitourgia* of bishops and deacons.

How Prophets Came into Being:
(a) Expectation of the kingdom;
(b) Experience of working harder but sinking deeper into a debt which culminated in the shameful selling of his own family into slavery;
(c) Flight to avoid capture and forced enslavement by money lenders.

How Some Prophets Disappeared:
(a) After becoming a permanent resident, regular eating and sleeping restored their health;
(b) As their grief and rage subsided, they began to laugh and to work again;
(c) As their healing progressed, their prophetic fire naturally cooled.

How Prophets Lived:
(a) Wandering as a vagabond without provisions;
(b) Receiving short-term hospitality within Didache communities;
(c) Obsessed with the expectation of the Kingdom; (fueled by their rage and longing and shame).

What Prophets Gave to Their Hosts:
(a) An example of how bad things could get;
(b) A burning longing for God's future;
(c) Gratitude for the modest prosperity of their hosts as expressed in the evocative prayers offered by the prophets for first fruits.

What Prophets Received:
(a) Honor that lessened their shame;
(b) Lament that they had no economic safety net;
(c) When praying over the first fruits; prophets recaptured the small joys of daily living that promised to bring them healing.

Flowchart D

#6Q WHETHER THE PROPHETS PRAYED IN ECSTASY

In the ancient world, pagan prophets spoke in ecstasy—thereby signaling that a god had taken over the faculties of his/her messenger. Contemporary studies of the Hebrew prophets have not yielded any agreement as to whether ecstasy was a normal part of the observable behavior of the prophets (R. Wilson: 324). The Christian Scriptures, for their part, do not offer any direct analysis of prophetic inspiration. Accordingly, some scholars have argued that prophecy emerges in a state of ecstasy; others, however, vigorously deny this (summary in Callan: 126–28). The *Didache*, for its part, allows that prophets "speaking in Spirit" utter things that are exempt from human judgment (11:7). This raises the question of whether these things were spoken in ecstasy.

At Delhi, Claros, and Didyma (all in Greece), the ancients had their celebrated lines of female prophets (beginning with Sibyl) who delivered oracles from the god Apollo. To some degree, this practice existed also in ancient Israel (e.g., 1 Sm 9:3–10; 14:41f.; 28:7f.; 1 Kgs 22:5f.; 2 Kgs 1:2; 8:7–15; 22:13; Aune: 85f.). Pagans who wished to consult the god would travel to one of the sacred sites with their formulated questions and take lodging and offer sacrifices. Meanwhile, the prophetess prepared herself:

> The prophetess followed "a rule of compete purity," presumably sexual purity. She bathed, and as at Claros, so at Didyma she prepared for the god by eating nothing. She fasted not for one day, but three, and "a multitude of sacrifices" preceded her work: famished, she lived meanwhile in the inner shrine and "was already possessed by the divine light, enjoying it for a long while," at least in Iamblichus's view. (Fox: 182)

Suitably prepared, the prophetess took her place on a cylindrical block in the inner court in the middle of the night holding a rod "handed down from the god" (Fox: 183). Water from the nearby sacred spring "wetted her feet or the hem or her prophetic robe and gave off a vapor that she 'breathed' when she received the god" (ibid.). A prophet was assigned to record the ecstatic message of the prophetess and, with help from the temple staff, to turn it into poetry, which in due course was recited or sung in the presence of the petitioners (ibid.).

Thomas W. Overholt, in his study of cross-cultural divination, concluded that all forms of divination assume that "the gods are responsible for the existence of, or otherwise stand behind, the system of divination" (1989: 133f.), yet since all divination requires rites of preparation and rules of manipulation, "divination is, therefore, both limited and subject to subjective manipulation by the diviner" (1989: 137). Even in the pagan world, therefore, prophecies sometimes failed, and stories circulated of instances in which prophetic seizures were deliberately staged or in which the results of legitimate prophecy were altered to fit the expectations of wealthy clients (Fox: 243–46, 254f.; Josephus, *Ant.* 18.65–80).

"The clients of oracles were people who wished to know and argue, to be reassured or guided through their many choices of thought and action" (Fox: 189). Since the oracular responses of the god were generally formulated in obscure or general phrases (akin to modern-day horoscopes found in the daily newspapers), the petitioners often needed time to decipher them. Petitioners left the shrine with a bound copy of the responses of Apollo which they could contemplate at their leisure.

In some cases, entire cities became regular clients and sent delegations to make inquiries about a major decision (Fox: 179). Even theological and philosophical inquiry was welcome. A delegation from Oenoanda, for example, asked, "What is the nature of God?" and inscribed the response received on their city walls (Fox: 176). The Greek philosopher Apollonius asked, "What do you consider to be the most complete and pure philosophy?" He returned with a book that he sent to Emperor Hadrian, patron of oracles and oddities, who displayed it to tourists (Fox: 189). The oracles in the archives at Delphi were copied into numerous volumes and sold to the Romans, who were already beginning to catch on to their importance. In a few generations, these oracles took on enormous significance:

> There is no possession of the Romans, sacred or profane, which they guard so carefully as they do the Sibylline oracles. They consult them, by order of the senate, when the state is in the grip of party strife or some great misfortune has happened to them. . . . (Dionysius of Halicarnassus *Roman Antiquities* 4.62.5 [late first century])

Since the results of these various consultations with Apollo were derived from a state of ecstasy, the notion developed that prophecy takes place when the spirit of a god enters into prophets and takes over their faculties completely such that they do and say only what the god wishes. Plato, for instance, endorsed such a theory and went so far as to allow that the inspiration received by the prophetess at Delhi produced a "divine madness [*mania*]" (*Timaeus* 71e) whereby her intellectual powers were fettered so that those who heard her might know that a god was speaking through her (*Ion* 534c). Plato's notion of prophetic inspiration was widely shared in the ancient world (Callan: 128–30; Heschel 2:104–46) and, even to this day, the origin of genius is often portrayed as a phenomenon bordering on madness. Even the term "ecstasy" endorses such a theory, for it comes from the Greek *ekstasis* (*ek* + *stasis* or "standing out [of one's mind]"), and *The American Heritage Dictionary* continues to define it as "a state of any emotion so intense that rational thought and self-control are obliterated." Plato, on the other hand, thought that the inspiration guiding the writing of poetry was also an instance of "divine madness" induced by the Muses (*Phaedrus* 245a).

Even in the ancient world, however, more moderate theories of prophetic inspiration were heard. Plutarch (d. 120 C.E.), for instance, perhaps noting the diverse stylistic peculiarities of various prophetesses, reflected on the Sibylline oracles as follows:

> The god supplies the origins of the incitement and then the prophetesses are moved each in accordance with her natural faculties. . . . The voice is not that of a god, nor the utterance of it, nor the diction, nor the meter, but all these are the woman's; he provides only the visions and puts a light in her soul in regard to the future. (*Moralia* 397c)

Philo of Alexandria (d. 50 C.E.), for his part, had a very ambiguous notion of Jewish prophecy. At times he wrote that the mind of the Hebrew prophet was "removed from its place at the arrival of the divine Spirit" by what he calls a "heaven-inflicted madness" and "in real truth the prophet, even when he appears to be speaking is silent, and another being is employing his vocal organs, his mouth and tongue" (*Who Is the Heir of Divine Things* 265f.). When coming to Moses, however, outside of eight rare instances of ecstatic prophecy (*Life of Moses* 2.246–92), Philo insisted that the Torah was "delivered by Moses in his own character as a divinely-prompted law-giver possessed by divine inspiration" (2.188). Thus, according to Philo, Moses delivered the Torah with complete control of his own faculties. Philo even goes so far as to say that his own ability to write down what he wants to say comes from a similar "divine inspiration" that guides his writing (*Migration* 35). In sum, therefore, Philo sometimes repeated what he had learned from Plato, but, when he thought about it more, he sometimes thought that Moses was inspired to create the Torah in much the same way that he was sometimes inspired to write.

Speaking in tongues (praising God in spontaneous gibberish or in unknown languages) is clearly an ecstatic phenomenon. Paul shames the Corinthians by suggesting to them that "if the whole church comes together and all speak in tongues, and outsiders or unbelievers enter, will they not say that you are out of your mind?" (1 Cor 14:23). As for prophecy, however, Paul insists that it must be "intelligible" (1 Cor 14:6–12) to those present and serve "for their upbuilding and encouragement and consolation" (14:3). Thus, prophetic delivery was not ecstatic:

"The spirits of the prophets are subject to the prophets" (14:32). Accordingly, Paul says that "if all prophesy, an unbeliever or outsider who enters is reproved by all and called to account" such that, in the end, "that person will bow down before God and worship him" (14:24f.). While ecstatic glossolalia is already the praise of God, Paul notes that prophetic speech leads to the praise of God.

In the *Didache*, prophetic speech is preeminently giving thanks to God within the context of the community eucharist (10:7). The prophet was speaking to God and not for God. The praise and thanksgiving offered, however, were seemingly delivered so spontaneously and so forcefully as to evoke the impression in those present that the prophet was speaking "in Spirit." While this can be credited as "ecstatic" in nature (e.g., Campenhausen: 72), it could also be recognized as "enthusiastic and bold speech" that manifestly differed from ordinary conversation (e.g., Callan: 139 n. 41).

At this point, I would like to risk telling something of my own experience. I have witnessed James Cone speak to African American audiences and have felt the palpable transition in pathos and mood as he goes from his teaching mode to his prophetic mode:

> Dr. Cone is an exceptional African American scholar and teacher. He begins his address by sketching out, in clear and distinct language, the issue or the problem which occupies him and his audience. After about ten minutes, however, he suddenly shifts from his teaching mode to his prophetic mode. He becomes visibly animated. The volume and pitch of his voice go up. His eyes burn with intensity and never leave the congregation. Now he is transformed into the Gospel preacher striking at the hearts of his listeners. Some respond with spontaneous outbursts: "Tell it like it is, Brother!" "Amen!" "God be praised!"

This transition is analogous to what might have been experienced in the Didache community. The eucharistic celebrant would improvise, would contemporize, and would animate the moods and rhythms of the eucharistic prayers (*Did.* 9–10). When the prophets got going, however, their speech was akin to James Cone shifting into his preaching mode. Prophets raised their voices and poured themselves into their prayers so completely that the hearts of their listeners shook and tears flooded their eyes. They felt the truth of it! Onlookers had no doubt that the Spirit of God animating them, since, as in the case of James Cone, their speech patterns were so manifestly altered.

Lest my personal experience seem to far-fetched to apply to prophetic inspiration, I call upon Philo as a testimony that he too reflected upon his own experience in his study when it came time to illustrate the character of the "divine inspiration" that illumined Abraham and Moses:

> I am not ashamed to relate what has happened to me myself. . . . Sometimes, when I have desired to come to my usual employment of writing on the doctrines of philosophy, though I have known accurately what it was proper to set down [in writing], I have found my mind barren and unproductive and have been completely unsuccessful in my object[ive], . . . and sometimes when I come to my work empty I have suddenly become full, ideas being, in an invisible manner, showered upon me and implanted in me from on high; so that, through the influence of divine inspiration, I have become greatly excited and have known neither the place in which I was nor those who were present . . . nor what I was writing; for then I have been conscious of a richness of interpretation, an enjoyment of light, a most penetrating sight. . . . (*Migration* 34f.)

For Philo, consequently, the experience of being carried forward in the conduct of his writing "under an influence of a divine inspiration" corresponded, in an analogous way, to the experiences of Abraham and Moses being carried forward in the conduct of their lives. In the ancient world, therefore, Philo demonstrates that these two instances were fabricated out of the same piece of cloth, whereas today, our familiarity with writer's block and our unfamiliarity with prophetic inspiration work to allow us to imagine that these processes are altogether different.

All in all, the issue of the interior experience of any prophet cannot be solved with any degree of satisfaction because the prophets never got into the business of drawing attention to their private experiences. As for the *Didache*, the rules governing the prophets do not hint that ecstasy was involved. The very fact that the *Didache* would have rules governing prophetic speech presupposes that such speech was seen as under the control of the one speaking. Furthermore, the fact that no one was assigned to interpret the prophets clearly indicates that praying in the Spirit did not come out in poetic riddles or in strange tongues but provided a forceful prayer in plain speech. The lifestyle of the prophets was idiosyncratic (*Did.* 11:11), but no one regarded them as mindless or deranged when hearing their charismatic style of praying at the eucharist.

Given the pagan association of ecstasy with true prophecy, it was almost inevitable that converted pagans would sooner or later make the presence of ecstasy felt in the churches. This happened in the last half of the second century when a movement known as the New Prophecy by its adherents and as Montanism by its opponents broke out in Asia Minor. The New

Prophecy aimed at the total renewal of the life of the church in the face of the imminent arrival of the kingdom of God. The outpouring of the Spirit, in the form of prophecy, was regarded as the hallmark foreshadowing the new age. Opponents of the movement agreed that "on questions of dogma, they were in entire agreement with the Catholic Church" (Campenhausen: 188). Nonetheless, they were disturbed by the novel shape of prophecy that pervaded the movement:

> The primitive Christian concept of prophecy had certainly not excluded the element of ecstasy; but equally it did not make use of this element to prove its superhuman, spiritual nature. For Paul prophecy always means the power of moving and convincing speech. . . . In the second century . . . prophetic enthusiasm was on the decline. For this very reason the "new Prophecy" stresses this aspect of the matter, and sees in the spasmodic ecstasy which suspends consciousness, and on occasion causes outbursts of strange, incomprehensible cries and sounds, the hallmark of genuine prophecy. (Campenhausen: 189)

When the New Prophecy spread to North Africa at the opening of the third century, the church father Tertullian became its strong supporter. Cecil Robeck summarizes Tertullian's analysis of the New Prophecy as follows:

> The concepts of prophecy and ecstasy are inextricably interwoven in Tertullian's mind. The Holy Spirit is the source of each. Ecstasy is understood to be the medium through which prophecy is made possible. In *On the Soul,* Tertullian calls ecstasy "the Holy Ghost's operative virtue of prophecy" [11.4]. He describes the medium of such activity with various phrases such as being "in the Spirit" [*in spiritu*], "in a rapture," or "in an ecstasy" [*in amentia*]." (104)

Disturbed by the reliance on "ecstasy" as the medium of prophecy, opponents in the church tried to suppress it by branding it as "false prophecy" precisely because it was ecstatic:

> The false prophet is carried away by a vehement ecstasy . . . beginning, indeed, with a designed ignorance, and terminating . . . in involuntary madness. They [Montanists] will never be able to show that any of the Old or any of the New Testament [prophets] were thus violently agitated and carried away in spirit. (Alcibiades, cited in Eusebius, *Ecclesiastical History* 5.17.2f.)

From this it would appear that, as prophecy within the church began to appear more and more like the pagan forms of prophetic phenomenon, leading voices within the church began to exclude any and every association of "ecstasy" with true prophecy. In the course of history, consequently, the phenomenon of prophecy has not had a uniform cast and, from time to time, prophecy within the churches has been vigorously resisted precisely because it was too closely associated with the ecstasy associated with pagan phenomenon known at the time.

One can wonder whether the pagan revival of prophecy during the second century (Fox: 201) might have had something to do with the emergence of ecstatic prophecy in the church. Or, conversely, should one imagine that history itself displays charismatic periods when prophetic phenomena show up across denominational lines and fashion new religious movements as they did in the 1960s? In any case, one can safely conclude that the *Didache* was formulated in an early era when the phenomenon of prophecy itself was not called into repute. Presumably, this was the case because prophecy in the church did not pretend to be an ecstatic phenomenon and was manifestly distinct from the prophecy practiced in the Greek shrines dedicated to Apollo. With time, however, the Greek horizon of understanding began to alter the imaginations of both Jews and Christians as to what they thought about "prophecy." Philo already shows such influence on the Jewish side. The New Prophecy shows this influence in Christian circles.

Owing to the massive reaction against the New Prophecy, prophecy of any kind in the church became suspect during the third century. In this climate, the *Didache* itself may have become suspect in many circles because it had been used to sustain the claims of the New Prophecy. Interestingly enough, this was the very time when church councils were endeavoring to hammer out a universal canon of inspired books. In this climate, needless to say, the *Didache* did not make it into the canon. One does not have to go so far as to imagine that the *Didache* itself was proto-Montanist as Connolly (1937d) and Vokes (1938) have done. The oldest and most time-honored document of the mid-first century was simply in the wrong hands at the wrong time. Had the New Prophecy not erupted in North Africa and had the backlash against it not been so vigorous, then we would surely have been reading the *Didache* in our bound versions of the Christian Scriptures today.

But all was not lost. In fact, we know that the massive overreaction to prophecy in the churches did not entirely suppress the *Didache* because it showed up in the so-called *Apostolic Constitutions* compiled in 380 C.E. What one quickly discovers, however, is why this version of the *Didache* was permitted to be included: *all the material pertaining to the prophets (Did. 11:3–11) has been eliminated. Did.* 10:7 is retained, but now it is the "elders" (7.26.6) who are named as eucharistizing after the celebrant and not the prophets. Only two of the original twenty-one references to "prophets" remained (7.28.5; 7.32.1 corresponding to *Did.* 13:1 and 16:3), and these are of little consequence. Thus, by the end of the fourth century, only a few vestiges remained of the *Didache*'s rich legacy of prophetic activity in local church life. Fortunate are we, therefore, that Archbishop Bryennios was able to discover an older version of the *Didache* that allowed us to see those sections that would be cut out a century later as a result of the backlash against the New Prophecy.

7
LEARNING GRATITUDE BY OFFERING FIRST FRUITS

The Rule Regarding First Fruits

YOU WILL GIVE THE
FIRST FRUITS TO THE PROPHETS, FOR
THEY ARE YOUR HIGH-PRIESTS. BUT
IF YOU SHOULD NOT HAVE A PROPHET,
GIVE IT TO THE BEGGARS. IF YOU
SHOULD MAKE BREAD-DOUGH, TAKING
THE FIRST FRUITS, GIVE ACCORDING
TO THE RULE. SIMILARLY, HAVING
OPENED A JAR OF WINE OR OF OIL,
TAKING THE FIRST FRUITS, GIVE TO THE
PROPHETS. AND TAKING THE FIRST
FRUITS, AS IT MIGHT SEEM APPROPRI-
ATE TO YOU, OF SILVER, OF CLOTHING,
AND OF EVERY POSSESSION, GIVE
ACCORDING TO THE RULE.

Contents

Background Discussion Found in Boxes

The *Didache* stands as a unique document in the first-century church, for it alone required that individuals set aside first fruits. The Christian Scriptures made occasional reference to "first fruits" (*aparchē*) (Rom 8:23; Jas 1:18; Rv 14:4), but in every instance a purely metaphorical meaning was intended (*ABD* 2.797). The framers of the *Didache*, however, not only took over the Jewish practice of offering first fruits; they deliberately modified and expanded its application to fit their own circumstances. Jews, for example, brought their first fruits to the temple priests in Jerusalem. In contrast, the *Didache* directs that first fruits were to be given to "the prophets for they themselves are your high priests" (13:3). Nothing in the many varieties of Judaism suggests the substitution of the prophet for the high priest, just as nothing in the Christian Scriptures prepares one literally to offer first fruits. Hence, one has here a mystery that has much to reveal about the way of life and the intuitions guiding the Didache communities.

The Origin and Character of First Fruits

First fruits in the Jewish tradition constituted an offering made to the Lord in gratitude for the agricultural blessings derived from the land that the Lord gave them (Lv 23:10–14; Nm 15:20f.; Dt 26:2–11).

> Two Hebrew words are rendered "first fruits." The first is *bikkûrim,* which specifically refers to first-ripe grain and fruit, which was harvested and offered to the Lord according to sacerdotal prescriptions. The term always appears in the masculine plural. . . . The second is *re᾽šît,* which is usually translated "first" or "beginning" of a series . . . with special reference to processed produce. This term specifically refers to dough (Nm 15:20f.; Ez 44:30; Neh 10:38 [37]), . . . to oil (Dt 18:4; 2 Chr 31:5), to honey (2 Chr 31:5), . . . and even to wool. (Dt 18:4) (*ABD* 2.796)

The Hebrew term *bikkûrim,* which is always in the plural form, was translated into the Vulgate as *primitiae,* a noun conjugated only in its plural forms. In Greek, however, both of these plural terms were sometimes rendered as *aparchē*—a singular noun (details in #7a). Thus, in the Septuagint and in the Christian Scriptures, *aparchē* is regularly rendered as "first fruits"—ignoring the fact that the Greek term is singular. Since "first fruits" functions as both a plural and a singular form, *aparchē* in the *Didache* has been consistently translated as "first fruits."

The *Didache* delineated a simple "rule" (*Did.* 13:5, 7) governing the selection of agricultural first fruits. This rule both parallels and diverges from what one finds in Exodus; hence, they are placed side by side as follows:

Did. 13:3	Ex 22:29f.

So, taking
    every *first fruits* of the products
    of the *wine vat and threshing floor,*
 	
of both cattle and *sheep,*
 	
you will give the first fruits to
the prophets; for they (themselves)
are your high priests
	You will not keep back
	    the *first fruits*
	    of your *threshing floor and wine vat.*
	The first-born of your sons,
	    you will give to me.
	So will you do
	    with your calf and with your *sheep*
	    and with your ass:
	seven days will it be under the mother,
	and the eighth day *you will give* it to
	me.

The progression of topics in the *Didache* roughly follows Exodus. The "wine vat and threshing floor" are named first, but in reverse order. First-born sons are passed over entirely. Then "cattle and sheep" are named instead of "your calf and your sheep." The term *moschos* denotes a "young calf," and, from what follows, one gathers that one is dealing with a new-born calf. The term *bous* denotes bulls and cows without any regard to their age (Bauer 146d).

The agricultural rule of the *Didache* reveals much in what it says. It reveals much more in what it fails to say:

1. According to Jewish practice, the farmer went into his fields and selected the first sheaf of grain ready for harvesting (Lv 23:10) and the first bunch of grapes ripening on the vine as his first fruits. The absence of such a rule might be another passing indication (see ch. 2 above) that the members of the Didache communities were not ordinarily the hands-on farmers tending the fields and the vineyards. The rule as it is given here could be construed to apply to those who owned and managed a wine press or a threshing floor.

2. According to Jewish practice, first fruits were set aside only from the land of Palestine: "When you enter the land that I am giving you and you reap its harvest" (Lv 23:10). According to the later rabbis, first fruits could be given only from Palestine (*m. Bikkurim* 3:2), and pious Jews who brought "first fruits" to the priests in Jerusalem from places outside Palestine were refused (*m. Hallah* 4:10f.). The *Didache*, needless to say, neither names nor implies any such geographical limitation. Hence, in the *Didache*, the offering of first fruits took on a universal character and, within

a Jewish horizon of understanding, served to acknowledge that all lands and all flocks equally belonged to the Lord. This is also consistent with what will be examined later (ch. 14), namely, that the *Didache* consistently refuses to give any preference or priority to the land of Israel.

3. In the case of "cattle and sheep" (*Did.* 13:3), one cannot subdivide offspring; hence, according to the Jewish tradition, the firstborn of domesticated animals were set aside as a thanksgiving offering for the Lord (Ex 13:2–16; Nm 3:12–16). In the case of the *Didache*, however, since these first fruits were going to be given "to the prophets" (13:3), it is difficult to imagine that offering a week-old sheep or calf to a wandering charismatic would be a welcome or suitable action, either for the animal or for the prophet. Juice from the wine vat could be tasted and grains from the threshing floor could be munched on (as in Mk 3:23), but a young animal would be an absolute encumbrance to a prophet moving about every day or two. Even if the prophet were to sell the animal, he would receive a few pieces of silver, which he was prohibited from carrying.

It might be with good reasons, therefore, that "cattle" rather than "calves" were spoken of in the *Didache* and that no reference whatsoever was made to the "firstborn" (see #7a). In the gentile world, the "first fruits" (*aparchē*) could refer to the first and best cut when a cow or sheep was being roasted (Sanders 1990: 291). Since meat in the ancient world was generally eaten at times of a celebration, the rule of the *Didache* would imply that the best portion of the meat would be given to the prophets during the celebration so that they could suitably give thanks to the Lord. Such a solution does away with the awkward situation of given the prophet an eight-day-old lamb.

4. According to the Jewish tradition, the firstborn child and the firstborn lamb were similarly situated: "Consecrate to me all the firstborn; whatever is the first to open the womb among the Israelites, of human beings and animals, is mine" (Ex 13:2). This, almost immediately, became the "firstborn males" (Ex 13:12f.) in all categories. But then a distinction was made: "I sacrifice to the Lord every male that first opens the womb, but every firstborn of my sons I redeem" (Ex 13:15). And this redemption takes place, as in the case of unclean animals, by substituting a suitable sacrifice in place of the firstborn. Later, the firstborn son is bought back from the Lord "at the price of five shekels" (Nm 18:16; approx. $2,000 today). Thus, in this case and in the case of impure animals, a monetary value was set that was reckoned as the value of the newborn son.

From the table above, one can judge that the *Didache* passed over in silence the first fruits of the human body. On the one hand, since the firstborn son was redeemed by offering five shekels to the temple priests, the *Didache* may have suppressed this practice because it would have created the situation whereby silver would be given to the prophets—a practice that was opposed to their calling (ch. 6). On the other hand, if the first fruits of cattle or sheep were chosen during the time of roasting, it may have been confusing or indelicate to imagine that firstborn sons had to be redeemed from the roasting pit. For multiple reasons, therefore, the whole notion of the "firstborn," which was so well established among Jews, was suppressed in the rules of the *Didache*.

5. Given the observations made, it becomes more and more evident that the *Didache* severely altered and abbreviated the Jewish tradition of offering agricultural first fruits. No mention is made, for instance, of offering first fruits of the olive or fruit trees. Nor does the *Didache* make clear whether the categories of "cattle and sheep" were illustrative or exhaustive. Granted that cattle and sheep represent the most common domestic animals (Philo, *Special Laws* 1.135), one should not lose sight that the Jewish Torah went beyond cattle and sheep in order to include the firstborn of goats, horses, asses, camels. Since the latter three named were considered "unclean" (not to be sacrificed, not to be eaten), suitable rules were developed whereby the firstborn of unclean animals were to be "redeemed." For example, Exodus provided the rule that "every firstborn donkey you shall redeem with a sheep" (13:13). The unclean donkey was thereby redeemed by offering a sheep. Among gentiles, moreover, pigs were raised for their meat, for their fat ("highly regarded for medicinal purposes" [Simoons: 29]), and for their value as a fitting sacrifice to the gods (Simoons: 29, 98). Pigs, within the Jewish horizon of understanding, were just the opposite: they were neither fit for eating nor fit for sacrificing. Curiously the *Didache* says absolutely nothing regarding all these things (recall *Did.* 6:3).

From what has just been said, one can conclude that the designation of agricultural first fruits was very sketchy and, from the vantage point of most Jews, would have been considered "severely flawed." The most probable explanation for this is that the vast majority of the members of the Didache community were engaged in the various crafts and trades and, consequently, the agricultural sector was not their focal interest. In fact, as one reads on and discovers how the framers of the *Didache* extended the application of first fruits to the commercial sector, one gains the impression that the framers of the *Didache* were content to sketch out the principal categories of first fruits that would have been recognized by Jew and gentile alike (13:3) and then to proceed quickly to extend these to address those categories relevant to the members of the community (13:5–7). The pastoral genius of the *Didache* shows through, however, insofar as the rule given for agricultural first fruits would have been perceived as having a Jewish flavor (assuming, of course, that a Jew would fill in the details from their knowledge of Torah), and, at the same time, the rule would have gained the assent of gentiles since they too were accustomed to offering agricultural first fruits to their guardian deities (MacCulloch: 1–47; Fox: 92).

Since the rules for first fruits were intended for gentiles, it would only make sense that the sensibilities that they cultivated as pagans would find an arena for action vis-à-vis the God of Israel.

First fruits were not to be confused with tithes. First fruits refer to "a token amount" (Sanders 1990: 289) of the agricultural harvest of grapes or grains grown on the land that the Lord gave to Israel. The first fruits belonged to the Lord—"Because God had given them the land, they were to return a portion of its produce in gratitude for God's benevolence" (Horsley 1985: 53). The tithe, on the other hand, refers to a precise amount: one-tenth of the harvest. The English term "tithe" is derived from the Middle English word for "tenth." "Tithe" is the only appropriate translation for the Hebrew *maaser* and the Greek *dekatē*, since, in each of these languages, the term popularly meant "tenth" (Sanders 1990: 290). The tithe belonged to the Levites and their families since they were restricted from owning or cultivating land for their task was to maintain and operate the Jerusalem temple. The distinction between "first fruits" and "tithes" cannot be missed within the Hebrew Scriptures themselves (e.g., Nm 18:12–32; Neh 10:35–38).

In the Mishnah, the distinction between first fruits and tithes becomes even more elaborate (*m. Bikkurim* 2:3f.). First fruits were offered from the seven kinds of produce for which the land of Israel was noted: wheat, barley, grapes, figs, pomegranates, olives used for oil, and dates for honey (*m. Bikkurim* 1:3). Unlike tithes, which were separated out after harvesting, the first fruits were designated by marking the sheaf of grain or the bunch of grapes as they matured in the field. The Mishnah noted that the particular fig or grape cluster or whatever was not only to be marked but also verbally designated: "he binds it with a reed and says, 'Lo, these are first fruits'" (*m. Bikkurim* 3:1). Here again it becomes clear that the first fruits of the soil involved a token quantity of high quality set aside as an offering to the Lord.

From this it can be surmised why first fruits would be embraced while tithes would be set aside. Tithing was designed to support the priests, the Levites, and their families. To be consistent, the *Didache* would have had to give tithes "to the prophets for they themselves are your high priests" (13:3). Since tithing involved a "tenth," the practice of tithing would have quickly destroyed the identity of prophets—their lack of possessions and their wandering. Even when prophets settled down in the Didache communities and were given free room and board, the *Didache* was never tempted to regard this as their "tithe." When one discovers, however, that first fruits and tithes were very different in the minds of Jews, it becomes possible to understand how the framers of the *Didache* could so strongly embrace one while flatly rejecting the other.

#7A WHETHER THE *DIDACHE* BLURRED THE JEWISH DISTINCTION BETWEEN "FIRST FRUITS" AND "FIRSTBORN"

At first glance, the rule of *Did.* 13:5 appears to make no clear distinction between the "first fruits" of the land and the "firstborn" of a living person/animal. In its inception, the "first fruits" consisted in taking the first and best portion of the produce of the land and setting it aside as a gift of gratitude to the unseen "owner" of the land:

> Early Israel . . . conceived of the land as belong to its God, Yahweh. Because God had given them the land, they were to return a portion of its produce [to the Lord] in gratitude for God's benevolence. (Horsley 1985: 53)

The same thing applied, in an analogous way, to the firstborn. The early Jewish tradition closely associated the "first fruits" with the "firstborn":

> You will not keep back the first fruits of your threshing floor and wine vat. The firstborn of your sons, you will give to me. So will you do with your calf and with your sheep and with your ass: seven days will it be under the mother, and the eighth day you will give it to me. (Ex 22:29f., my literal translation)

The Septuagint made a clear distinction between "first fruits" (*prōtogenēma* in Lv 23:17, 19; Nm 18:13; Neh 10:35; also Tb 1:6) and "firstborn" (*prōtokos* in Nm 18:15, 17; Neh 10:35f.). The *Didache*, however, sets aside these precise terms in favor of the more general term *aparchē*. After an extensive study, E. P. Sanders summarizes his findings as follows:

> In the pagan world, *aparchē* and *aparchomai* could refer to the first part of a sacrifice or to a gift of first fruits (in agreement with etymology), but the terms could also be used for an offering in general. . . . *Aparchē* in the Diaspora would have been taken as a very general agricultural offering. Its meaning expanded still more in LXX Exodus, where it was used for the offering of gold, silver and other precious stuff to build the tabernacle. (1990: 291)

At this point, the orientation of the framers of the *Didache* becomes clear. They refrained from using the specialized Greek terms found in the Septuagint, since, in effect, this would have cluttered *Did.* 13:3–7 with a group of specialized terms that would have required some extended explanation for a non-Jewish audience. The use of the general term, *aparchē*, however, enjoyed widespread use in the gentile world and had been used by Greek-speaking Jews to refer to the entire range of offerings enumerated in 13:3–7. The Alexandrian Jew Philo (d. 50 C.E.), for example, used the term *aparchē* to refer to the first fruits of produce, the firstborn of animals, and the dough offering (*Special Laws* 1.141, 132f.). Thus, the framers of the *Didache* not only accommodated their vocabulary to their hearers; they simplified and unified their instructions as well. In the end, a hellenized Jew hearing *Did*. 13:3–7 would tacitly fill in the details and the distinctions known to him/her, while the gentile would make general sense of the prescriptions in terms of what he/she understood as the offering of first fruits practiced in their pagan environment.

The Motive for Offering First Fruits

The *Didache* offers no explicit reason for setting aside and offering first fruits. Within the Jewish tradition, however, first fruits were offered to express gratitude for the use of the land that belonged to God:

> Early Israel . . . conceived of the land as belonging to its God, Yahweh. Because God had given them the land, they were to return a portion of its produce [to the Lord] in gratitude for God's benevolence. (Horsley 1985: 53)

As already noted, since the *Didache* made no provisions to restrict first fruits to the land of Israel, it must be concluded that the framers of the *Didache* wished to acknowledge that all lands and all flocks equally belonged to the Lord. The necessity of gratitude was thus extended to gentiles (and Jews) living everywhere.

Some scholars are convinced that the rule of first fruits served to provide the day-to-day food for the settled prophets (Draper 1983: 259; Schöllgen 1996: 58 n. 89). Their argument for this comes from the flow of topics in the *Didache*. Every settled prophet was declared to be "worthy of his/her food" (13:1), and then the categories of first fruits were taken up to be given "to the prophets" (13:3). It might appear, therefore, that first fruits constituted the means whereby the prophets were to be supplied with their needs. Such a conclusion would be misleading, however, for the following reasons:

1. It obscures the primary reason for bringing the first fruits—namely, to have the prophet offer them up to God. Even in Judaism, where the priests in the temple offered the first fruits to the Lord, the first fruits were never thought of as bringing any necessary benefit to the priests themselves.

2. It obscures the distinction between first fruits and tithes (as discussed above). The first fruits (a token portion) were set aside for the Lord; the tithes (a full tenth) were set aside for the Levites, who, in their turn, took a tithe of what they received and gave it to the priests.

3. It obscures the fact that resident prophets would be residing in a household where they would be, as a guest, invited to the family table. Hospitality would hardly be served if prophets were left to go hungry until such time as this or that person brought them their first fruits. Furthermore, it seems hard to imagine that resident prophets would always eat alone.

The Hebrew Scriptures do not dwell on the motives for offering first fruits. This is the case, most probably, because the motives were largely evident to farmers. In Leviticus, for example, the offering of first fruits to a priest in Jerusalem undoubtedly meant an outing for the family and a feast as well following the intensive and prolonged work of bringing in the harvest:

> When you enter the land that I [the Lord] am giving you and you reap its harvest, you shall bring the sheaf of the first fruits of your harvest to the priest. He shall raise the sheaf before the Lord, that you may find acceptance; on the day after the sabbath the priest shall raise it. On the day when you raise the sheaf, you shall offer a lamb a year old, without blemish, as a burnt offering to the Lord. And the grain offering with it shall be two-tenths of an ephah of choice flour mixed with oil, an offering by fire of pleasing odor to the Lord; and the drink offering with it shall be of wine, one-fourth of a hin. You shall eat no bread or parched grain or fresh ears until that very day, until you have brought the offering of your God. (Lv 23:10–14)

Here one intimates that the land belongs to the Lord and that one cannot use the fruits of the land until such time as the Lord has been recognized as its owner. In this case the priest takes the first fruits of the harvest (the first sheaf cut from the field) and raises or waves it before the Lord reciting a prayer of gratitude (which is not given). Then, once the Lord has been duly thanked, the entire harvest became available as food for consumption. Part of the gifts offered would be burned on the altar; part would be used for a family feast; and the rest would be used by the priests and their families.

Much later, in Deuteronomy, one finds a full-blown rite in which the one bringing the first fruits now takes an active role and makes a profession of faith to the priest which has for its purpose to extend the motives for offering first fruits:

When you have come into the land that the Lord your God is giving you as an inheritance to possess, and you possess it, and settle in it, you shall take some of the first of all the fruit of the
ground, which you harvest from the land that the Lord your God
is giving you, and you shall put it in a basket and go to the place
[the Jerusalem temple] that the Lord your God will choose as a
dwelling for his name. You shall go to the priest who is in office
at that time, and say to him, "Today I declare to the Lord your
God that I have come into the land that the Lord swore to our
ancestors to give us." When the priest takes the basket from your
hand and sets it down before the altar of the Lord your God, you
shall make this response before the Lord your God: "A wandering Aramean was my ancestor; he went down into Egypt and
lived there as an alien, few in number, and there he became a
great nation, mighty and populous. When the Egyptians treated
us harshly and afflicted us, by imposing hard labor on us, we cried
to the Lord, the God of our ancestors; the Lord heard our voice
and saw our affliction, our toil, and our oppression. The Lord
brought us out of Egypt with a mighty hand and an outstretched
arm, with a terrifying display of power, and with signs and wonders; and he brought us into this place and gave us this land, a
land flowing with milk and honey. So now I bring the first of the
fruit of the ground that you, O Lord, have given me." You shall
set it down before the Lord your God and bow down before the
Lord your God. Then you, together with the Levites and the
aliens who reside among you, shall celebrate with all the bounty
that the Lord your God has given to you and to your house. (Dt
26:1–11)

Deuteronomy understands the offering of first fruits to include a thanksgiving for deliverance from bondage along with thanksgiving for the fertile
land of Palestine. Here again, the intimation in the last line is that the produce of the harvest were off limits until the Lord of the harvest had been
recognized first. Following the offering of the first fruits, a harvest festival
took place to which Levites and gentiles (who had not land) were to be
invited.

The Mishnah, looking forward to an idyllic period of temple restoration,
described how the people of an entire town would make a pilgrimage
together toward Jerusalem with a decorated ox and a flute player leading
the procession of the first fruits (*m. Bikkurim* 3:3). Now, for the first time,
the rabbis supplied the rule that proselytes and women "bring [first fruits]
but do not recite" (*m. Bikkurim* 1:4f.). It went without saying that gentiles were also excluded from reciting.

#7B MOTIVES FOR OFFERING FIRST FRUITS IN THE TALMUD

The Tosephta (c. 250 C.E.) finds the rabbis formulating a general rule regarding those who benefit from the things of the earth:

> It is forbidden for someone to derive benefit from any thing in this world without reciting a blessing, and whoever derives benefit from this world without reciting a blessing thereby commits sacrilege. (*t. Berakhot* 4:1)

Thus, at this point, a universal outlook has taken place. The earth belongs to the Lord (see #2d). Everything received from the earth, accordingly, is received from the Lord. From this it follows that anyone taking without acknowledging this (in a blessing) commits a sacrilege.

This mode of logic becomes abundantly clear when the passage above is cited and explained in the Babylonian Talmud:

> Said R. Judah said Samuel, "Whoever derives benefit in this world without reciting a blessing is as if he derived benefit from Holy Things that belong to Heaven [and so has committed sacrilege]. For it is said, 'The earth belongs to the Lord, and everything that fills it' (Ps 24:1)"
>
> *R. Levi contrasted verses of Scripture:* "It is written, 'The earth belongs to the Lord, and everything that fills it' (Ps 24:1). And it is written, 'The heaven belongs to the Lord, but the earth he has given to men' (Ps 115:16).
>
> *But there is no contradiction.* The former verse refers to the case before one has recited a blessing, and the latter verse refers to the case after one has recited a blessing."
>
> Said R. Hanina bar Pappa, "Whoever derives benefit in this world without reciting a blessing is as if he mugged the Holy One blessed be he, and the community of Israel. (*b. Berakhot* 35a–b)

The discussion here shows how conflicting texts of Scripture may be harmonized. Ps 24 declares that the earth belongs to the Lord while Ps 115 declares that the earth was given by the Lord to humans. The act of acknowledging it as the Lord's in the blessing serves to move it from the first status to the second. Hence, R. Hanina might well declare that anyone deriving benefit from the earth without reciting a blessing acts as a thief.

According to the Talmud, this general schema applies whether the benefit from the earth implies first fruits that must be brought to the priests in the temple or whether one is dealing with prepared food brought to the table (*b. Berakhot* 35a). By the sixth century, therefore, acknowledgment of the Lord as the benefactor was the undergirding principle that mandated a blessing. The motive behind offering first fruits, therefore, was centered on acknowledging and giving thanks to the Lord for his gifts.

The probable reason that the practice of first fruits never showed up in any other gentile Christian community is that the Jewish founders of these communities instinctively felt that first fruits pertained only to those cultivating the land of Greater Palestine (see #7e). The pastoral genius of the *Didache* is demonstrated in its ability to reframe the character of first fruits such that they applied to the blessings of the Lord everywhere. The pastoral genius of the *Didache* is shown in its ability to provide occasions for expressions of thanksgiving for benefits received that allowed for some continuity with their past. Two considerations follow:

1. Pagans embracing the Way of Life came from a lifestyle wherein a calendar of religious festivals punctuated the seasons of their life: "Certain festivals were the business of women only. . . . Others concerned the prosperity of fields and crops and honors for the dead" (Fox: 92). The practice of offering first fruits to a god/goddess was not a distinctly Jewish practice (e.g., *Iliad* 9.529; Ovid, *Metamorphosis* 8.273; 10.431; Pliny, *Natural History* 4.26). Among the Romans, in particular, one finds the following:

> Roman husbandmen offered a sacrifice of first fruits of all the various crops to those divinities who were chiefly associated with their welfare: the first ears [of grain] to Ceres, the first vintage to Liber. Pliny says that neither new corn nor new wine was tasted until the priests had offered the *primitiae* ("first fruits"). (Mac-Culloch: 42)

Thus, the practice of offering first fruits would have been a settled instinct that new converts brought with them. The only question was how to suitably offer their first fruits to the "almighty Master" who "created all things" and who gave "both food and drink . . . to people for enjoyment in order that they might give thanks" (*Did.* 10:3). The *Didache* admirably responds to this need.

2. Piety figured predominantly in the Roman world: piety to the gods, piety to the fatherland, piety to the parents (see #1c). In order to embrace the Way of Life, most recruits had to abandon piety to their parents. Piety to the fatherland was also very thin within the Jesus movement. The only piety that was manifest and evident was piety to the Father. For gentile converts, this meant living the Way of Life in expectation of the coming

kingdom. This also meant daily prayers and the weekly eucharist, which, it will be remembered, specialized in giving thanks for joining in the election of Israel and for the ingathering when the Lord comes. Thus, thanksgiving for the past and for the future were well taken care of. What was neglected were the occasions to give thanks for the present blessings received from the Lord. The framers of the *Didache* address this need through the offering of first fruits. Gentiles were taught that "apart from God, nothing happens" (3:10); consequently, the offering of first fruits provided a concrete realization of this truth. Thus, with so much of their former world of piety having been disrupted, the practice of first fruits gave gentiles an abiding sense that "the God who made you" (1:2) was continually reaching out to them in their everyday affairs and that they were grateful.

Why Prophets Were Chosen to Receive the First Fruits

The rule of the *Didache* signals that first fruits were to be given "to the prophets for they themselves are your high priests" (13:3). Prior to the establishment of the temple, first fruits "were apparently used in religious festivals in which God was seen as sharing the bounty with those who brought them" (Horsley 1985: 53). With the establishment of the temple and the centralization of worship in the hands of the temple priests, the first fruits were brought to the temple priests. These priests offered the fruits of the fields to the Lord with a heartfelt prayer and then used the gifts for their own needs (Nm 18:17–19).

The internal clues in the *Didache* demonstrate a systematic attempt to displace and to demote the temple cult. This can be seen at five crucial points:

1. *Did.* 8:1 had the effect of removing gentiles from the prayer-and-fasting cycle of the "hypocrites" who favored the centrality of the Jerusalem temple.

2. *Did.* 8:2 had the effect of redefining the expectation of the kingdom using the Lord's Prayer, which provides no role for Jerusalem or the temple.

3. *Did.* 14:1–3 had the effect of establishing the eucharist as the "pure sacrifice," which, according to Mal 11:1, took place "in every place and time" and "among the gentiles," thereby making the temple sacrifices not only entirely unnecessary but contrary to "the divinely instituted rule of the Lord" (*Did.* 14:1).

4. *Did.* 13:3 had the effect of establishing that "first fruits" should be presented "to the prophets; for they themselves are your high priests," thereby bypassing the priests of the temple who ordinarily received first fruits.

5. *Did.* 16:3–8 had the effect of recasting the end-time expectations

such that Jerusalem and the temple had no role whatsoever in either the apostasy prior to the end or in the coming of the Lord God in the future.

When the anti-temple position of the *Didache* is appreciated within its social milieu (ch. 14 below), then the substitution of "the prophets" as the recipients of the first fruits becomes part of the unified program of the framers of the *Didache*. The choice of prophets was not accidental. With good reason this class of persons was singled out as the recipients of the first fruits. The pastoral genius standing behind this choice might be explained as follows:

1. *Gratitude was increased.* The prophets had a proven track record for pouring forth inspired and inspiring prayers (ch. 6). Coming to a prophet with first fruits, then, meant that the prophet took them in his/her hands, raised his/her eyes to heaven, and gave forth eloquent prayers of thanksgiving. Hearing this prayer, those coming forward with the first fruits would have gained an enlarged sense of how much the Father had reached into their daily life and blessed them with the material blessings they had received. Gratitude was increased.

2. *Pride of possessions was diminished.* The prophets had suffered great losses (ch. 6). But, more importantly, the prophets realized that God took care of them even when their business was failing and their family ties were coming apart. Furthermore, coming to a prophet with first fruits meant, in most instances, approaching a wretched and unkempt vagabond, and this set up a contradiction. Those coming to offer first fruits normally had a certain natural pride in their success at a trade or business. Thus, when the prophets gave all the glory to God and spoke of "the lilies of the field, how they grow; they neither toil nor spin" (Q, Mt 6:28; see Theissen 1977: 13) and demonstrated by their disregard for success that "life [is] more than food, and the body more than clothing!" (Q, Mt 6:25), the one offering first fruits glimpsed a deep lesson—namely, that wealth did not define the value of an individual in the sight of God and that, for those who experienced a measure of success, there was the danger of becoming "advocates of the rich, despisers of the poor" (*Did.* 5:2).

3. *Fear was decreased.* Besides offering a contradiction, the life of the prophet offered a remedy for fear. Those who were mildly rich and successful in the things of this world brought their first fruits to those who had lost everything. Despite their momentary success at a trade or business, therefore, the one coming realized that injustice and poverty might be just around the corner for them as well. At this, a cold fear might have gripped their hearts and made them sick with worry. Yet the very life of the prophet provided an antidote to this sickness. They knew they could survive poverty, should it come, with their dignity intact—just as did this prophet. They thus became capable of engaging in various forms of covert resis-

tance, and their consequent sense of empowerment contributed to their healing (Crossan 1998: 301). They also came to see that God's care did not end when someone sank into destitution. Quite to the contrary, the first fruits belonged to this Lord and, already in this world, he was exalting the lowly by decreeing that his best portion be given to them.

4. *Honor restored to the dispossessed.* The prophets were broken men and women who, owing to economic pressures, had suffered the loss of their families, their homes, and their shops (ch. 6). Since they had once been hard-working and self-sufficient, it was undoubtedly humiliating for them to receive handouts. But here the genius of the *Didache* steps in. The successful artisans and merchants come to them with the first fruits and press them to offer prayers to the Father thanking him for his blessings. In most cases, this reversed their roles. It is the prophets who are sought out. It is they who are in demand. Thus, their honor is restored. Sure, they were unkempt and unwashed vagabonds and considered by some to be leeches upon society, yet they provided a fury for the distributive justice of the coming kingdom and a passion for evocative prayer that was prized. Thus, having lost all their former honor in not being able to protect themselves and their families, they now received the new honor of being those chosen by God to speak of his suffering and his restlessness to bring in the kingdom.

Someone receiving handouts would normally settle for only a minimum both in quantity and quality. In the Didache communities, however, the prophets were being sought out in order to hand over to them the first and the best portion of things! Beggars in the ancient world generally had to content themselves with receiving spoiled or dried-out food and cast-off or ruined clothes. In the Didache communities, however, the Lord had honored them by singling them out to receive *his best gifts.* This illustrates one of the first lessons in the training manual: "To all, the Father wishes to give from his own free gifts" (1:5).

5. *Prophets received medicine for their grief.* When petitioners came forward requesting prayers of thanksgiving, the prophets' attention was distracted, at least for a brief moment, from their terrible past and from their feverish expectation of the future. More especially, those bringing first fruits with light and happy hearts brought something of their simple joy to the prophets, who, for the most part, had abandoned all joy and all expectation of joy in this world. Yet, in sampling the simple joys of a mother bringing a loaf of warm bread just out of the oven (13:5), perhaps the barefoot children giggling and hiding behind her skirts transported the prophet back to a happier time. Undoubtedly, on such occasions, many a prophet found him/herself spontaneously shedding quiet tears of postponed grief. As their tears flowed, the bottomless grief in their hearts lightened. In the end, therefore, bringing the first fruits to the prophets was calculated to bring a potent medicine for healing the grief of the prophets

and for reviving their spirit for entering into the simple joys of living (as explained at the end of the last chapter).

We do not have any way of knowing how well or how earnestly individual prophets functioned in their role of offering first fruits. Some undoubtedly were gruff and recited a perfunctory prayer that offered little satisfaction to themselves or to those offering. Others, however, must have offered a moving prayer experience that left a deep impression on all concerned. It is these latter prophets who earned the traditional role of "high priests" and who gained admission, by their practice, into the daily life and times of the Didache communities. Since the first fruits were given individually to the prophet of one's choosing, one can guess that those who were gruff were ordinarily passed over in favor of those who were outwardly broken but inwardly revered "high priests" among the people.

One can be sure of this—if the experience of having the prophets offer thanksgiving was a miserable failure, then it would have been given over to others—mentors or widows—or else it would have been dropped entirely. One can safely conjecture, therefore, that because the members of the Didache communities were deeply moved by the inspired and inspiring prayers of the prophets at the eucharist, they decided, probably on their own initiative, to bring gifts and first fruits to these prophets and were delighted by the prayers that they received for their efforts. Therefore, while the origins of bringing first fruits to the prophets will always be obscure, one can be sure that the practice emerged out of a felt need and was greeted with an unexpected success.

Our task in this section has been to reconstruct imaginatively the outlines of this success story keeping in mind the clues of the *Didache* and the cultural climate of their day. The hidden reasons named above for presenting first fruits to the prophets, therefore, may not be all precisely on the mark. Nonetheless, not to look for them and try to name them would be a much more serious failing since it would inadvertently make the *Didache* appear like a wooden rule designed by bureaucrats rather than the efforts of sympathetic pastors to listen deeply to the yearnings and watch carefully the spontaneous practices of their people such that all things might be arranged for the well-being of all concerned. The reasons offered above, therefore, may not be rigorously demonstrable, yet they are correct and appropriate insofar as they evoke the pastoral genius of the *Didache*.

The First Fruits When Baking Bread
or Opening a Jar of Wine

Once the agricultural first fruits were specified (*Did.* 13:3), the *Didache* went on to delineate other times when an offering of first fruits was appropriate: (1) when baking bread (13:5); (2) when opening a jar of wine or oil (13:6); and (3) when increasing possessions of any kind (13:7).

The term *aparchē* ("first fruits") is repeated five times in *Did.* 13:3–7 and was applied to all the various instances named. Consider, for instance, the first nonagricultural offering named by the *Didache*: "If you should make bread-dough . . ." (13:5). According to the Jewish tradition, the "dough offering" (Hebrew *hallah*) was set aside during the time that one was making bread-dough. A portion of the dough ("one loaf" according to Nm 15:20; "one twenty-fourth" according to *m. Hallah* 2:7) was designated as the "dough offering" and formed into loaves that, once baked, were set aside to be given to the high priests. E. P. Sanders judges that the "dough offering" was probably originally considered another instance of "first fruits," since it was compared to the setting aside of grain from the threshing floor (Nm 15:20) (1990: 290; Neusner 1988a: 173). In Nehemiah, however, it is designated as "a distinct offering" (Neh 10:37) (Sanders 1990: 290), and, accordingly, the rabbis classified it as an offering distinct from first fruits (ibid.). On the other hand, Philo of Alexandria, writing during the time the *Didache* was being created, classified it as the first category of "first fruits" (*aparchē*) to be set aside for the priests:

> In the first place, . . . God commands those who are making bread . . . to take [out] of all the fat and of all the dough a loaf as first fruits for the use of the priests. (*Special Laws* 1.132)

Sharing the practice of Philo, the framers of the *Didache* also described the "dough offering" as another instance of "first fruits" (*aparchē*). The same thing can be applied to all the other offerings as well. Both Philo and the framers of the *Didache* use *aparchē* to designate every form of offering and set aside the special vocabulary of the Septuagint (Sanders 1990: 289–303).

The extension of the meaning of *aparchē* to include an offering when "opening a jar of wine or oil" (*Did.* 13:6) or when receiving an augmentation "of silver and of clothing and of every possession" (13:7) finds no counterpart in ancient Judaism and might serve to suggest that craftsmen and merchants had as much cause to thank God for their prosperity as did the farmer and the baker. The novice, it will be remembered, was trained to regard everything he/she possessed as the Father's "free gifts" (1:5) and to "accept the experiences befalling you as good things, knowing that, apart from God, nothing happens" (3:10). In the light of this understanding, undoubtedly the first and best products of the kiln, of the loom, and of the forge were set aside for first fruits and given to the prophets so that they could give thanks to God.

The *Didache* even spoke of an increase "of silver" (13:7) and, in so doing, undoubtedly addressed the situation of day laborers who worked for others or merchants who retailed the products made by others. In such instances, the *Didache* made clear that the merchant might, "as it might seem appropriate to you, give according to the rule" (13:7). The window was thus open for a merchant to give "silver" to the prophets. This would be quite different from the prophets "asking for silver" (11:6; 11:12). On the other hand, a merchant might consider it more appropriate to offer something like a pair of sandals in lieu of money. In most instances, one can suspect that prophets, after receiving the first fruits and after warmly giving thanks to God, might be pleased to pass the first fruits on to the householder of their lodging place. After all, in many instances, the first fruits would have been an encumbrance to them and a distraction from their passionate calling; hence, they would have been only too willing to distribute their possessions and, at the same time, give thanks to those who so generously saw to their food and lodging.

In the Roman world, "first fruits" would, in most instances, have been burnt upon an altar dedicated to the god who was being thanked (MacCulloch: 42). The *Didache* makes no reference to the destruction of first fruits upon an altar; hence, one discovers how much the Jewish tradition was being followed in this regard. Philo, for example, makes it a point to note for his gentile readers that the *aparchē* was not burnt or otherwise destroyed but was assigned to the priests so "that the necessary food for their support shall at all times be provided for them without any labor or toil of their own" (*Special Laws* 1.132). Philo eloquently explained the double function of first fruits in this fashion:

> And to prevent anyone of those who give the offerings [of the first fruits] from reproaching those who receive them, he [God] commands that the first fruits should first of all be carried into the temple, and then orders that the priests shall take them out of the temple; for it was suitable . . . that those who had received kindness [from God] in all the circumstances of life, should bring the first fruits as [a] thank-offering, and then that he [God], as a being who was in want of nothing, should with all dignity and honor bestow them on his servants and ministers . . . for to appear to receive these things not from men, but from the great Benefactor of all men. (*Special Laws* 1.152)

The first fruits, then, were an *aparchē*—a thanksgiving offering to the Lord—and the priest or the prophet was expected to present it before the Lord and offer it up on behalf of the one bringing the first fruits. Once the offering was made, however, the first fruits were then at the disposal of the priest/prophet as a gift *from the Lord*—a sign of the dignity and honor that God wished to bestow on his servants.

#7C THE SO-CALLED ERRORS MADE BY THE FRAMERS OF THE *DIDACHE*

Kurt Niederwimmer faults the framers of the *Didache* for thinking that the prophets substitute for "high priests" (*Did.* 13:3). Georg Schöllgen faults the framers of the *Didache* for enforcing a "double offering" of first fruits: once at the time of the harvest itself, and again at the time when the products were being consumed. These will be treated in reverse order.

Schöllgen finds it problematic that first fruits of grain are set aside at the time of the harvesting (*Did.* 13:3) and again at the time of making dough (13:5). Schöllgen suggests that the members of the Didache communities were being offered the choice of one or the other time for offering first fruits, but not both:

> It is not very likely that . . . all the required *aparchē* are demanded of every member of the community; in that case, the *Didache* would have anticipated a twofold offering from the produce of the grain harvest: first at threshing (v. 3) and then again when bread is baked (v. 5); there is then a similar double offering of grapes and wine (vv. 3 and 6). Hence it is more likely that, as regards the individual *aparchē*, there were different possibilities for fulfilling one's obligation to support the prophets." (1985: 141)

Even though Schöllgen mistakenly sees the first fruits as primarily intended to support the prophets, his observation on the unseemly "double offering" needs to be considered.

The Mishnah casts an entirely different light on what Schöllgen calls a "double offering." According to the Mishnah, a farmer would carefully tie the first sheaf of grain to ripen in his field and declare it as the "first fruits" (Hebrew *bikkhurah*). After harvesting and winnowing, he would then set aside a "heave offering" (Hebrew *terumah*) for the priests and the "tithe" or "second tithe" (Hebrew *maaser*) would be set aside for the Levites. Later, when the farmer's wife made dough from the grain (now harvested, winnowed, and ground into flour), a "dough offering" (Hebrew *hallah*) would be set aside for the exclusive consumption by a priest or a member of his family (slaves included). The rabbis decided that a "dough offering" was required only if the flour used was more than 1¼ qab (approx. 3 cups) (*m. Hallah* 2:6). As to the quantity of each offering, the Mishnah notes that some discretion was possible. In the case of a "heave offering": "[If a man is] generous, [he separates] one-fortieth [of his produce]. . . . And [if he is] miserly, one-sixtieth" (*m. Terumot* 4:3). In the case of a "dough offering," "one twenty-fourth" was normally set aside (*m. Hallah* 2:7). Furthermore, in the case of untithed stored grains, a "heave offering" was to be set aside "three times [in the year]" (*m. Terumot* 4:6). Everything considered here in the case of grain/flour had its counterparts for grapes/wine and olives/oil. In sum, therefore, the Mishnah required what Schöllgen would call a "double offering" (and frequently even a "triple offering") on agricultural products.

One might be tempted, therefore, to apply the above to the *Didache* and claim that the "double offering" noted by Schöllgen was a matter of course and that 13:3–6 simply represented a short summary of the Mishnah. The problem, of course, is that the Mishnah developed these multiple offerings in order to secure the welfare of exiled priests between the two wars (70–135 C.E.) (Neusner 1988a: 173). It would be hazardous, therefore, to imagine that—even if the use of the general term *aparchē* in the *Didache* was understood to cover the "first fruits" (Hebrew *bikkhurah*), the "heave offering" (Hebrew *terumah*), and the "dough offering" (Hebrew *hallah*)—Jews in the mid-first century practiced all the first fruits offerings found in the Mishnah.

Accordingly, Philo (d. 50 C.E.) needs to be examined, since he wrote at the time that the *Didache* was being created. In his *Special Laws,* a treatise meant for both a gentile and a Jewish audience, Philo presented an account of the "first fruits" that shows a remarkable harmony with what one finds in the *Didache*. We can consider the following three points:

1. Philo uses the term *aparchē* with the same wide scope of application as does the *Didache* (Sanders 1990: 292). While the Hebrew Scriptures and their Greek translation (the Septuagint) provide specialized terms for each of the distinct offerings, Philo uses *aparchē* to designate the "dough offering" (*Special Laws* 1.132), the "first fruits" of the wine vat and threshing floor (1.134), and, in a summary statement, even the "firstborn males" are designated by this term. Philo also passes over in silence the fact that "first fruits" were due exclusively on the produce of the land of Israel—a characteristic that the *Didache* shares.

2. Philo spells out the first fruits in the following order:

> (a) In the first place, . . . God commands those who are *making* bread . . . to take [out] of all the fat and of all the *dough* [and make] *a loaf as first fruits* for the use of the priests. (1.132)
> (b) In the second place, he commands the nation also to given them the first fruits of their other possessions: *a portion of wine out of each winepress; and* of wheat and barley *from each threshing floor.* And in like manner they were to have *a share of oil* . . . and of eatable fruit. . . . (1.134)

(c) The third honor allotted to this is an assignment of all the firstborn males, of all kinds of land animals which are born for the service and use of mankind . . . ; the offspring of *oxen, and sheep, and goats*. . . . (1.135)

(d) Moreover the law, going beyond all these enactments in their favor, commands that people bring them the first fruits . . . of their own lives and bodies . . . their own firstborn male children after the fashion of other first fruits as a sort of thanks-offering for fertility. (1.137)

If one leaves out the notion of "firstborn males" and transposes some of the categories, one might find in *Did.* 13:3–7 a sort of miniature outline of the rule of *aparchē* similar to what Philo has set forth. The italicized text in the above citation helps to direct attention to those parts of the four categories represented in the *Didache*.

3. Philo, with his focus on different kinds of *aparchē*, makes no mention of tithes in regard to the priests. The *Didache*, in a parallel move, sets out its rule of *aparchē* without any mention of tithes. In point of fact, however, Philo is quite aware that tithes were made to the Levites, who, in turn, took a tenth of what they received and set it aside for the priests (1.157). Nonetheless, Philo treats of these tithes not in regard to the priests but as being destined for "the second rank of the priesthood . . . the [up]keepers of the temple" (1.156). Accommodating his gentile readers, Philo uses the term "second rank" to designate the Levites, who are not priests, and, following upon this designation, refers to those receiving the first fruits as "priests of the superior rank" (1.157).

Niederwimmer regards the reference to "the high priests" (*Did.* 13:3) as an "error" on the part of the framers of the *Didache*, since the Hebrew Scriptures have "no specific regulations for the income of the *high* priest" (Niederwimmer 1998: 192 n. 9).

Needless to say, if an "error" were present at this point, Jewish members of the Jesus movement would have been quick to spot and correct it. The use of "high priests," therefore, despite Niederwimmer's objection, must be deliberate. Based on Philo's distinction between "priests of the superior rank" (1.157) and "the second rank of the priesthood" (1.156), one might wonder whether the term *archiereis* (*archē* + *hiereis* "first" + "priests") was used by the framers of the *Didache* to designate "priests of the superior rank." If so, the use of *archiereis* ("first priests") could be seen as providing a more accurate impression to gentiles than would the term "priests," and Niederwimmer's "error" would become, in fact, a helpful clarification intended for gentiles.

All in all, therefore, when one sets aside the Mishnah (200 C.E.) and holds on to Philo (d. 50 C.E.), one gets a vision of the rule of first fruits that harmonizes quite well with what one finds in the *Didache* (due consideration being given to its character as a summary and its omission of "firstborn males"). It might be expected, accordingly, that a first-century Jew would have greeted the rule of *aparchē* found in the *Didache* as a first-approximation outline of the Jewish tradition. If taken as the complete rule, it is decidedly flawed (as noted earlier). As a first-approximation outline, however, it might pass muster.

How the Prophet Offered First Fruits to the Lord

When the members of the Didache community brought first fruits to the prophets, they did so at a time and place of their own choosing. The use of the second person singular throughout (*Did.* 13:3–7) indicates that each individual had to decide when and what quantity was to be set aside as first fruits for the Lord. One can imagine that a sense of gratitude guided and motivated Christians in the application of the rule. Then, at an appropriate time, these first fruits were brought to a prophet. If there was a resident prophet, most probably the first fruits would be taken and presented to the prophet where he/she was staying. If there was no resident prophet, the first fruits might have been carefully set aside and brought to the next eucharistic meal in the expectation that there might be wandering prophets who would show up and the first fruits could be presented to them at the end of the eucharist.

If not a single prophet showed up, then the first fruits would be given, following the rule, to beggars (13:4). At this point, the singular gives way to the plural, and the aorist imperative (*dote*) is used. This implies that many persons (namely, all those bringing their first fruits to the eucharist) were to engage in a one-time (namely, after the eucharist) giving to the beggars. Furthermore, the term *ptōchos* ("beggar") is "an adjective describing one who crouches and cowers" and "stresses his [her] poverty-stricken condition," since the Greek has another term (*prosaitēs*) that "stresses his [her] begging" (Kohlenberger: 101). The choice of *ptōchos* allows one to surmise that the entrance to the place of meeting was not crowded with beggars who had become accustomed to receive first fruits at the time that the congregation dispersed. Since the members of the community were protected by the economic safety net (ch. 2), one can further surmise that the beggars to be sought out were not members of the congregation. Those to receive the first fruits, therefore, would have been poverty stricken pagans living in the neighborhood or vagabonds gathering in the market square. The rule of *Did.* 1:6 might have applied to the first fruits in this instance.

We have no way of knowing what words or gestures were used by the prophets when they offered first fruits. From what has been said regarding posture in prayer (ch. 4), however, it can be presumed that a prophet prayed standing and facing east. Perhaps with hands raised, the prophet held up the loaf of bread or article of clothing that was being offered and spoke to the Father something like the following:

> We give you thanks, Our Father; before the nations we sing your praise. We give thanks to your name for your steadfast love and your faithfulness, for you have exalted your name in this season by giving to people both food and drink for their enjoyment. And now, with our hearts overflowing with gratitude, we offer this fine loaf of bread to you, which still carries with it the sweet aroma of the oven. Graciously bless those who have prepared it. Protect them in their rising up and in their lying down. Make the work of their hands prosper until that glorious day when you gather us into your kingdom because yours is the power and the glory forever.

Undoubtedly some prophets were more brief, others more verbose. In any case, while no two prayers would have been the same, one might have expected the prophets to follow the liturgical tradition of addressing the Father using "we" and "our" with a final refrain that would be repeated by all those present.

When it came to beggars, perhaps the one offering the first fruits would have said something like the following:

> This loaf [or whatever] is the first fruits that the Lord has directed us to give to you. In his eyes, you are precious, and he extends his care over you. Please be so kind as to give thanks to him on behalf of me and my family.

In most cases, the beggar would undoubtedly leave quickly and marvel later at what a fine gift he/she had received, since, for the most part, beggars had to make do with spoiled food and with cast-off clothing. In some instances, however, one might have expected a beggar to have the presence of mind to inquire as to "which god" they ought to express their thanks to. In a few instances, an exceptional beggar might even offer a prayer on the spot. In any case, the rule of the first fruits would have been completed (*Did.* 13:3), and the presenters would have returned home assured that God was gracious and that he had been good to them.

#7D JEWISH ECONOMIC PROTECTION
ABSENT FROM THE *DIDACHE*

The Roman view of the absolute rights of the property owner finds a fitting and sharp contrast in the Jewish tradition. To begin with, the land of Israel was understood as God's promise to his people, yet the land never ceases to belong to the Lord, who exercises his right to regulate its use. For instance, the Lord requires that "the land not be sold in perpetuity, for the land is mine" (Lv 25:23). Furthermore, the Lord gives permission to anyone hungry or thirsty (whether Jew or gentile) to go into a field or vineyard and take what grain or grapes were needed but without taking any excess out (Dt 23:24f.). Likewise, the poor, the widow, and the orphan had an inalienable right to a portion of every harvest derived from the land of Israel. According to the understanding of the rabbis this included the following: the corner (*peah*), the gleanings (*leget*), whatever was missed or forgotten by the harvesters (*shikhah*), grapes that fell to the ground (*peretl*), and small clusters that were passed over during the harvest (*olelot*).

Following the Deuteronomic reform during the reign of King Josiah (640–609 B.C.E.), an even more radical right to a portion of the harvest was extended to the poor. According to the rediscovered Deuteronomy, a full tenth (*maaser,* or "tithe") of the harvest was to be distributed "to the Levite, the sojourner, the fatherless, and the widow, that they might eat within your towns and be filled" (Dt 6:12) on the third and the sixth year of the seven-year agricultural cycle. In all of this God's own concern for those who had no means of sustenance stands out and those who received the land from the Lord were expected to respect these limitations placed upon their use of the land. In Jewish eyes this was not cultivating "generosity" or practicing "charity," rather it was *zedakah* ("righteousness")—the word habitually used in the rabbinic material to describe all those rights that the vulnerable had according to the Torah of the Lord.

While gleanings and tithes provided for those already poor, it did not massively improve their lot. Two other provisions in Jewish law, however, had the effect of limiting and even reversing the ravages produced when farmers were forced to sell their land and then, under the pressure of growing debt, to sell their families and themselves into slavery. These two provisions are as follows:

1. The first provision limited the duration of slavery for male Jews to six years (Ex 21:2). A Hebrew farmer or craftsman whose business failed, therefore, would be sold into slavery along with his family but, unlike in the Roman world, after the sixth year the farmer or craftsmen and his family would be released. According to the Deuteronomic reform, this rule was extended to include female slaves (Dt 15:12 in contrast to Ex 21:7), and the former owner was admonished not to send him/her out empty-

handed: "Provide liberally out of your flock, your threshing floor, and your wine press, thus giving to him [her] some of the bounty with which the Lord your God has blessed you" (Dt 15:14). This latter provision offered the prospect that the liberated slave would establish him/herself in a business and become self-sufficient.

2. The second provision was the Jubilee Year, which was calculated as the year following seven cycles of seven years (i.e., the fiftieth year). During that year, all agricultural land had to be returned to its original owner or to his kin (Lv 25:8–34). Meanwhile, the Jubilee Year obliged those families who had been sold into slavery to be released at the same time so that they could efficaciously begin to establish themselves as free persons on the land that had been returned to them. The provisions of the Jubilee Year also included the obligation to secure "the redemption" of any kin who might have been sold into slavery to gentiles and could not, consequently, hope to be released on the Jubilee Year (Lv 25:47–54).

With the advent of Roman occupation of the land of Israel, however, the provisions named above could not be practiced and, consequently, did not bring the relief intended. In Galilee, for instance, land tenure was gradually taken out of Jewish hands and given over to Roman colonists:

> The period of the Herodians (37 B.C.–A.D. 70) saw significant change in land tenure, accelerating the dispossession of the local peasantry as well as many of the former Hasmonean nobility. Many of the latter Herod executed and then either appropriated their lands or redistributed them among his own supporters. When Samaria was rebuilt and given the name of Sebaste, six thousand Roman veterans [of war] were settled in the area and given land to till. In Galilee itself, most of the better land belonged to large landholders, while the small properties seem to have concentrated on the less fertile hill country. (Gonzalez: 72)

With large portions of the land being owned by foreigners, one can be sure that this land was not turned back to its former owners during the Jubilee Year. Meanwhile, after the two Jewish uprisings against Rome (66–70 and 135 C.E.), hundreds of thousands of Jewish survivors were sold into slavery at the far-flung Roman slave markets in order to help pay for the military expenses of putting down the uprisings. Such slaves, for the most part, could not reasonably hope to be found much less to be redeemed by those kinsmen who remained free.

In practice, therefore, by the time that the *Didache* was being created, most of the safeguards found in the Jewish Torah were no longer operative even though pious Jews continued to regard them as the ideal condition that would again prevail once the Lord returned to take charge. Only at one point in the *Didache* does one hear voiced this promise: "Be gentle, since the gentle will inherit the earth" (3:7). Beyond this, even while either some or many of the members of the Didache community owned slaves (4:10f.), no provision was made for limiting the duration of slavery as Jewish law required. At the same time, none of the Jewish measures noted above designed to secure the welfare of the widows and orphans shows up. This could be because such provisions applied only to the land of Israel and hence were not even understood by Jews to apply to agricultural produce derived from the lands held by the nearly four million Jews living outside Israel. On the other hand, the tradition of first fruits did find a place of importance in the *Didache*. Such first fruits were given to the prophets (13:3) and, when no prophet was present, the rule was "give [the first fruits] to the beggars" (13:4). Accordingly the modified rule of first fruits demands some attention.

Conclusion

From the study of the *Didache*, what remains clear is that the tradition of setting aside first fruits for the Lord did not become an organized or widespread practice in any of the first-century churches outside of those following the rule of the *Didache*. Undoubtedly many pagans who embraced Christianity had the practice of offering first fruits prior to their conversion and, following their conversion, they wanted to know how they were to offer their first fruits to the true Lord of the harvest. Christianity had no shrines or temples and, more importantly, they had no priests ready to receive these first fruits. Accordingly, the *Didache* took a bold and innovative step when it designated "the prophets" as the honorary "priests" (13:3) to whom members of the Didache community were to bring their first fruits. Now there was not a place but a person to whom the faithful could be directed when it came time for them to express their gratitude to the Lord.

When explored carefully, the categories of first fruits appeared to be a sketchy synopsis of some of the traditions of first fruits practiced by Jews but artfully adopted for gentiles. Even such small details as the phrase, "make dough [*sitia*]" (Niederwimmer 1998: 191 n. 17), links the categories within a specifically Jewish mentality wherein the baked bread set aside for the priests later came to be referred to as the "dough offering" (Hebrew *hallah*). The only thing conspicuously absent was the specification of the "firstborn male," both of domestic animals and of humans. One might be tempted to suggest that this omission could be explained by reference to the deliberate refusal on the part of women and men in the *Didache* to support the gender preference rooted in patriarchal society. This point deserves more attention and research in the future.

The anti-temple stance of the *Didache* and the decided preference for the Spirit-led prayers of the prophets was shown to explain why the first fruits were to be given to "the prophets," who, when all was said and done, were regarded as the most fitting substitutes for the priests of the temple. When the evidence was pushed, moreover, the pastoral genius of the *Didache* was again revealed in the surprising honor and dignity that members of the community conferred on lowly vagabonds and beggars, who, in God's eyes, were chosen as those favored to receive the first and the best gifts of his creation. While the prophets were being honored, at the same time, their obsession with the future was being neutralized by a prayer focused on the marvels of God's present order of creation. For the moment, even the prophets' fixation on the future kingdom had to be set aside in favor of giving the Father thanks for present blessings.

Where prophets were absent, the first fruits were given "to beggars" (13:4). The previous chapter concluded that the need for an alternative suggested the fact that the Didache communities attracted, healed, and cooled prophetic fires and that the choice of alternates demonstrates that "the prophets" were indeed the near-equivalent of vagabonds. This chapter explored why a community that had seemingly already made ample provisions for beggars (*Did.* 1:5; 4:6f.) should give their first fruits to beggars. An indigent person could be expected to thank God mightily for his/her bounty. Yet could not an artisan or merchant do this for himself? Surely. But not as warmly and graciously and persistently as the one who was broken by suffering the loss of home, of family, of occupation.

According to the *Didache*, persons who had fallen on hard times were not to be turned away and shamed because of their condition. Now, however, the artisan or merchant in the community deliberately sought out the indigent and offered him/her the best of his/her increase in the name of God. Here again the offering of first fruits centers on giving thanks to God, who has been gracious and kind.

When the prophet or the beggar joined their thanksgiving with that of the artisan or the merchant, their prayer was intensified and multiplied. Reciprocal giving (4:5) did not figure in here, nor did the atonement for sins (4:6). Here the rule of the Lord surrounding gratitude decided that those who were of least account were deserving of the best things that the Lord could offer. As in the case of 1:5, this had absolutely nothing to do with charity. Rather it is what "the Father wishes" and was a proleptic foretaste of that new order that would prevail when his "will is born on earth as [it is now already operative] in heaven" (8:2). Ordinary members of the Didache communities, therefore, cultivated a present gratitude that was a prophetic action bearing on the future: "He has brought down the powerful from their thrones, and lifted up the lowly; he has filled the hungry with good things, and sent the rich away empty" (Lk 1:52f.).

The huge gap between rich and poor sanctioned by society stands as ample proof that God is not in charge. Those implementing the rule of first fruits lit a small candle in the darkness of their world that said, "God is committed to changing this. Get ready!" And those Christians everywhere, even today, who are, in their turn, lighting small candles in the darkness, join with God in getting ready.

#7E WHETHER THE RULE OF FIRST FRUITS REVEALS THE LOCATION OR DATE OF THE *DIDACHE*

In Judaism, the offering of first fruits was reserved to certain persons at certain times. Hence, it might be possible to specify the geographical, religious, or social location of the members of the Didache communities on the basis of the rule for first fruits (*Did.* 13:3–7). Furthermore, since first fruits were discontinued with the destruction of the Jerusalem temple in 70 C.E., it might be possible to say something about the date of composition of the *Didache*. Each of these possibilities will be examined.

First fruits were set aside only from the land of Palestine: "When you enter the land that I am giving you and you reap its harvest" (Lv 23:10). E. P. Sanders, after carefully investigating the rabbinic material, concludes: "They [first fruits] could be given only from Palestine (*m. Bikkurim* 3:2); supplementary gifts from beyond Palestine were not equivalent to first fruits" (1990: 299). The rabbis circulated stories whereby pious Jews who brought "first fruits" to the priests in Jerusalem from places outside Palestine were refused (*m. Hallah* 4:10f.). The only grey area was the northern boundary of Palestine, which, during the reign of King Solomon, had included a large segment of southern Syria. For the purpose of first fruits and tithes, land owned by Jews in this area was considered part of Greater Palestine (*m. Hallah* 4:7; *m. Maaserot* 5:5; *m. Ohalot* 18:7). Sanders finds no evidence that first fruits were actually brought in from Syria and regards the rabbis as having engaged in a "fanciful" projection (1990: 302); nonetheless, for the sake of argument, let us consider that southern Syria constituted part of Greater Palestine in the minds of the framers of the *Didache*.

With the geographical location of the land subject to first fruits defined, it could then be argued that the framers of the *Didache* enforced the rule of first fruits precisely because they were aware that some or all of the Didache communities fell within the area defined as Greater Palestine. In fact, since some scholars have concluded that the Didache communities were located in Syria (see discussion of Niederwimmer 1998: 53f.), it might even appear as though the rule of first fruits would serve to enforce that conclusion. On the other hand, there are weighty reasons for not insisting that the rule of first fruits can be used to make any clear determination of the geographical location of the Didache communities. Two points:

1. The obligation of first fruits applied to Jews who owned land in Palestine. According to the rabbis, Jews who did not actually own the land (e.g., sharecroppers or tenant farmers) did not bring first fruits (*m. Bikkurim* 1:2) because it is written: "You shall bring the first of the first fruits of *your* land" (Dt 26:2). The *Didache* finds no reason to mention much less to enforce this refinement on the rule; hence, it seems unlikely that the framers of the *Didache* thought of themselves as promoting the Jewish tradition of first fruits that was geographically limited.

2. Gentiles farming land in Greater Palestine were not required to bring first fruits to the Jerusalem priests. The affirmation that the one bringing first fruits made before the priests was the following: "A wandering Aramean was my ancestor [Abraham]; he went down into Egypt and lived there as an alien . . ." (Dt 26:5). This formula would hardly fit on the lips of a gentile. Thus, if the framers of the *Didache* were influenced by Jewish habits of mind, they would have resisted speaking of first fruits to gentiles even if they owned land in Greater Palestine.

All in all, therefore, one can say only that the framers of the *Didache* may have been influenced by the Jewish tradition of setting aside and offering first fruits to the Lord, yet they revised, simplified, and expanded the application of this rule. Accordingly, therefore, it would be hazardous to conclude that the rule of first fruits was applied to the members of the Didache communities precisely because some or all owned land in Greater Palestine.

A parallel argument could be made based on the understanding that first fruits were offered only if and when the temple was standing (*m. Bikkurim* 2:3f.). This being the case, one might be tempted to conclude that the rule of first fruits in the *Didache* must have been originally formulated at a time when the temple was still standing, that is, prior to 70 C.E. Alternately, one could argue from the fact that the first fruits were being given to the prophets as "your high priests" (13:3) rather favors the conclusion that the temple was destroyed and a substitute recipient thereby became necessary. On the other hand, given the anti-temple bias of the *Didache* (see ch. 14 below), one could argue that even while the temple was standing, the framers of the *Didache* would have deliberately designated a substitute. All in all, given the freedom with which the framers of the *Didache* revised, simplified, and expanded the application of Jewish rules, there is nothing to preclude that a substitute was created precisely when the temple was standing or that, even after the destruction of the temple, the *Didache* wished to maintain the rule of first fruits even when most pious Jews no longer practiced it. In sum, therefore, it would be hazardous to try to date the *Didache* on the grounds that the rule of first fruits implied that the Jerusalem temple was either standing or not standing at the time of its composition.

Finally, an argument could be made to the effect that the framers of the *Didache* originally envisioned the rule of first fruits since, by and large, most of the members were engaged in farming or herding (Schöllgen 1985: 140–43). If this were the case, however, one would have expected more definition to be given to the selection of agricultural products (as was evident in the commentary), and one would not have expected that first fruits would be extended to nonagricultural areas (opening a jar of wine, making clothing).

Accordingly, my hunch is that the *Didache* arranged a rule for first fruits that began in the agricultural sector but extended beyond it to cover the actual circumstances of the members of his community, namely, artisans and merchants (ch. 2). Thus, not being farmers or herders, the members of the Didache community could not bring the normal first fruits at the time of the harvest or the time of birthing. Thus, first fruits for grain were offered at the time of baking bread; first fruits for grapes or olives were offered at the time of opening a jar of wine or oil. In brief, we are not dealing here with a double offering but with a single offering specially designated to take into account the actual occupations of the community members. Contrary to what some scholars have said concerning the rule of first fruits pointing in the direction of farmers and herders, I judge that the extended rule (*Did.* 13:5–7) decidedly points in the direction of artisans and traders who buy farm products with their profits but do not produce these products themselves.

In the end, nothing conclusive can be decided regarding the geographical or chronological location of the framers of the *Didache* based on the rules for first fruits.

#7F FIRST FRUITS AFTER THE TIME OF THE *DIDACHE*

It is difficult to know the extent to which Christians continued to practice offering first fruits during the second and third centuries, since the church fathers gave so little time and attention to it. Irenaeus (bishop of Lyons, 178–200 C.E.), for example, followed the standard practice of the fathers by demonstrating that "God did not seek sacrifices and holocausts from them, but faith and obedience and righteousness" (*Against Heresies* 3.17.4). When it came to first fruits, however, Irenaeus claimed that Jesus gave "directions to his disciples to offer to God the first fruits of his own created things" (3.17.5) when he took "created things" and gave thanks at the Last Supper. Accordingly, Irenaeus advised Christians who insisted upon offering first fruits beyond those offered in the eucharist to settle for offering them to the Lord by handing them over to the poor, as suggested by Prv 19:17 (*Against Heresies* 3.17.6). Since Irenaeus makes use of Proverbs and since he never refers to the poor as "your high priests" (*Did.* 13:3), it seems doubtful that Irenaeus was aware of the rule of first fruits found in the *Didache*. That Irenaeus was constrained to take up this subject, however, can be taken as an indication that he knew that some Christians were accustomed to giving first fruits.

The practice of offering first fruits was practiced sporadically in various places even up to the time of the French Revolution (MacCulloch: 45). A few church fathers (Origen, Jerome, Gregory of Nazianzus) even spoke of the giving of first fruits as obligatory. Quite possibly, however, this may have been because first fruits were being confused with the obligatory tithe.

The *Apostolic Constitutions* (380 C.E.) are important for examining the ongoing development of first fruits because there we find an expanded and modified version of the *Didache* that has come down to us. In the *Apostolic Constitutions,* it is telling that all the material regarding the apostle-prophets has been taken out (see #6q). The rules for giving first fruits, on the other hand, were retained—a testimony that during the previous three centuries, a remnant of Christians (probably in Syria) continued to offer first fruits according to the *Didache*. The rule for doing so, however, was massively altered:

[A] *Every first fruit of the products*
    of the wine vat and threshing floor,
    of both cattle and sheep,
      you will give to the priests, in order that
    [a] the storehouses of your stewardship
      and the rents of your lands may be blessed,
    [b] and you may be supplied with grain and wine and oil,
    [c] and your herds of cattle may grow and your flocks of sheep.
[B] You will give every tenth part to the orphan and the widow,
    to the poor and the sojourner.
[C] *Every first fruit of* warm bread,
    of a jar of wine or oil,
    or of honey or of fruit trees,
    of a bunch of grapes or other things,
    you will give the first fruits to the priests;
[D] *and of silver and of clothing and of every possession,*
    [you will give these first fruits] to the orphan and the widow.
    (7.29.1–3).

The italics indicate where the original Greek of the *Didache* was retained. Needless to say, significant modifications have been inserted. Consider the following:

1. The first fruits of all agricultural products [A] and their derivatives [C] are now brought to the "priests." From the vantage point of the *Apostolic Constitutions,* these "priests" are neither the priests of the Jewish temple nor the prophets but the bishops who have come to be understood as functioning as "priests" when offering the eucharistic sacrifice. Nonetheless, one can note that first fruits of nonagricultural products [D] are given "to the orphan and widow, to the poor and the sojourner" (7.29.3).

2. The specification of first fruits has been clarified and expanded. The Hebraic term "make dough" has lost its meaning, and the easily understood category of "warm/fresh bread" has been substituted. Honey, fruits, grapes, and "other [agricultural] things" (e.g., figs, olives, vegetables) expand the category of agricultural offerings in harmony with the Jewish tradition.

3. Tithes have been introduced for the first time. We are now looking at a substantial amount (one-tenth) of the agricultural produce that was to be given not to the Levites but "to the orphan and widow, to the poor and the sojourner" (7.29.2). This rule shows the influence of the Deuteronomic reform that modified the practice of tithing (Sanders 1990: 43–45). Instead of the tithe being set aside from the fields and the flocks and given every year to the Levites as before (Lv 27:30–32), Deuteronomy substituted a tithe of the crops alone, every third and sixth year of the seven-year cycle, to be given to the Levites and to a new category of persons: "to the orphan and widow, to the poor and the sojourner" (Dt 10:18; 14:28; 16:11, 14; 24:17, 19, 20f.; 26:12f.; 17:19). When the *Didache* was altered, therefore, the Deuteronomic code was used to introduce the tithe, but, in this new church context, the tithe was offered *every year* and given exclusively "to the orphan and widow, to the poor and the sojourner" (*Apostolic Constitutions* 7.29.2)—the Levites having been dropped out. The emergence of the tithe in the church may signal that the economic safety net (*Did.* 4:5–8 expanded as *Apostolic Constitutions* 7.12.1–5) had broken down and that the practice of Jewish tithing had to be introduced to take care of the large class of vulnerable members who depended entirely upon the community for their support.

4. The first fruits "of silver and of clothing and of every possession" (*Did.* 13:7 = *Apostolic Constitutions* 7.29.3) are also set aside for the set of vulnerable persons named for the tithes.

5. First fruits in the *Didache* were given with the understanding that the Lord owned the land and the Lord oversaw fertility; hence, first fruits recognized his ownership and thanked him for his blessings. In the *Apostolic Constitutions,* on the contrary, motives of self-interest are now spelled out

in great detail. Those who gave first fruits were promised that they would prosper in this world to the degree that they contributed to the Lord's work (somewhat akin to what one often hears in fundamentalist churches today, where tithing is often zealously promoted).

After the fourth century, even in places where first fruits continued to be given, they gradually were replaced entirely by the tithe. During the early medieval period, therefore, the obligatory tithe served as the means to collect revenues for the construction and maintenance of churches and for the support of the clergy, widows, and orphans—persons with no source of income other than that coming from the church.

During the French Revolution and its aftermath, the obligatory tithe disappeared. Now state governments "of, for, and by the people" enacted legislation to collect taxes that permitted the state to care for its vulnerable citizens—a task that had formerly been done single-handedly by the churches. In countries like the United States, where a complete separation of church and state was mandated, taxes were never collected on behalf of a state religion (as continues in some European countries even today) and, as a result, each denominational church was left to secure revenues by soliciting freewill offerings during the Sunday worship. Some Protestant denominations practice tithing (either voluntary or mandatory), but, to my knowledge, no existing Christian community today trains it members to offer first fruits to the Lord in the fashion of the *Didache*.

8

THE CONFESSION OF FAILINGS
AND EUCHARISTIC SACRIFICE

Offering the Pure Sacrifice

HAVING BEEN GATHERED TOGETHER, BREAK A LOAF AND EUCHARISTIZE, HAVING BEFOREHAND CONFESSED YOUR FAILINGS, SO THAT YOUR SACRIFICE MAY BE PURE. EVERYONE, ON THE OTHER HAND, HAVING A CONFLICT WITH A COMPANION, DO NOT LET HIM/HER COME TOGETHER WITH YOU UNTIL THEY HAVE BEEN RECONCILED, IN ORDER THAT YOUR SACRIFICE MAY NOT BE DEFILED. FOR THIS IS THE THING HAVING BEEN SAID BY THE LORD: "IN EVERY PLACE AND TIME, OFFER TO ME A PURE SACRIFICE BECAUSE A GREAT KING AM I," SAYS THE LORD, "AND MY NAME IS WONDROUS AMONG THE GENTILES."

Contents

Background Discussion Found in Boxes

The fourteenth chapter of the *Didache* returns to the topic of the eucharist. In the earlier chapters, the prayers of the eucharistic celebrant and of the prophets were considered. Since this was the first eucharist following the baptism of new members, the confession of failings was deliberately omitted. Now, however, the framers of the *Didache* introduce the confession of failings and the discipline of reconciliation that will mark the experience of new members at their second and subsequent eucharists.

In the previous chapter, the offering of first fruits was shown to represent a unique rite of gratitude that finds no parallel in the whole of the Christian Scriptures. In this chapter, the *Didache* will be shown to expand its pioneering spirit in two domains:

1. The *Didache* presents the oldest explicit instance of the community understanding its eucharist as a sacrifice (Niederwimmer 1998: 196f.). One has to wait until the writings of Justin Martyr (150 C.E.) before one finds a second instance (see #3a). Furthermore, the *Didache* offers the first instance in which we hear that the eucharistic meal was held weekly on a day explicitly referred to as "the day of the Lord" (*Did.* 14:1).

2. The *Didache* also discloses that, prior to each eucharistic meal, members of the community were expected to have "confessed" (4:14; 14:1) their failings and resolved any interpersonal conflicts (14:2). Nowhere in the Christian Scriptures does one find any reference to a confession of failings in connection with the eucharist. Historically speaking, therefore, the *Didache* provides the first instance in which confession and reconciliation were established as the necessary conditions (in addition to baptism) for participation in the weekly eucharist.

In the context of the early churches, therefore, the *Didache* promises to offer insights into how the confession of failings and the notion of sacrifice came to be associated with eucharistic experience. The purpose of this chapter is to explore the character and implications of this groundbreaking vision.

The Confession of Failings and the Eucharistic Sacrifice

The confession of failings in *Did.* 14 does not come as a complete surprise. At the very end of the catechumenate, the novice was told, "You will not leave behind the rules of the Lord . . . (*Did.* 4:13), and, immediately thereafter, he/she was given the means to be used to sustain this attachment to the rules of the Lord:

> In the church,
>   [1] you will confess-in-full your failings,
>   [2] and you will not go to your prayer with a bad conscience.
>   (4:14)

Two processes were named. Few particulars were given. Both were described in the future tense since both processes took place in the context of the eucharist, of which the novice had no direct experience. Mentors, consequently, must have deliberately avoided excessive details at this point for they were well aware that there would be ample time, following the first eucharist, to prepare novices for the confession and reconciliation that would be part of every subsequent eucharistic meal.

When *Did.* 4:13 and 14:1–3 are placed side by side, one can see that the progression of topics in both cases is the same:

Did. 4:14	*Did.* 14:1–3
	(And) according to the divinely instituted day of the Lord
In the church,	having been gathered together,
[1] you will	break a loaf and eucharistize,
confess your failings,	having beforehand confessed ÿour failings,
	so that ÿour sacrifice may be pure.
[2] and you will not	Everyone, on the other hand, having a conflict with (his) companion,
go to your prayer	do not let him/her come together with ÿou
with a bad	until they have been reconciled,
conscience.	in order that ÿour sacrifice may not be defiled.
	For this is the thing having been said by the Lord:
	"In every place and time, offer to me a pure sacrifice
	because a great king am I," says the Lord,
	"and my name is wondrous among the gentiles."

According to the earlier formulation (*Did.* 4:14), one discovers that the confession of faults takes place "in the church" (en *ekklēsia*), that is, when the members are called together as an "assembly." While being trained in the Way of Life, the novice knew little or nothing of the eucharist; hence, it was fitting to omit any mention of it. Later, however, precise details would be given, namely, that this confession would take place when the community gathered on each Lord's day to break bread and eucharistize. Likewise, the earlier formulation provided no motivation for the confession. Later, however, the notion of "pure sacrifice" would be introduced in order to explain the necessity of this confession. The earlier formulation indicated that members would not go to pray (in the assembly) with a "bad conscience." No details are offered, however, to explain how this was to be avoided. The later formulation filled this gap: "You will not go to your prayer" (4:14b) if you have an unresolved "conflict" (14:2) with a "companion/associate/friend" (*hetairos*), and you will be prevented from doing so until you "be reconciled" (14:2). Finally, a motivation is provided: "that your sacrifice not be defiled" (14:2c).

A semantic parallel is evident. The positive activity of confessing has the positive effect of producing a pure sacrifice; the negation or absence of conflict has the effect of avoiding the negation of the pure sacrifice, namely, defilement. In both instances, the motivation is clearly drawn in the direction of assuring the community that its sacrifice is "pure." The citation from the Lord nails down the requirement that a "pure sacrifice" (14:3) was an absolute requirement, for the Lord is a great king whose name must be "wondrous among the gentiles" (14:3c).

#8A PROBLEMS IN TRANSLATION

Didache 14 contains some problematic words and phrases that have a strong bearing on the meaning of the text. Three, in particular, need to be considered:

1. *"Having a conflict"* (14:2). The Greek language has many words to signify a conflict, a quarrel, or a disagreement, but none of these common words is used here. *Amphibolia* is derived from *amphi* (around) + *bolē* (a throw [of a net], a hurling, in contrast to striking). Liddell and Scott define the noun as "a state of being attacked on both sides" (47). Niederwimmer comments as follows:

> *Amphibolia* really means "hemmed in on both sides, attacked," and then "ambiguity, doubt, confusion"; but these meanings of the word yield no sense in this passage. Here it must mean something like "quarrel." (1998: 197)

Niederwimmer's suggestion is problematic. It take a least two people to have a quarrel. One wonders, then, why the response is not "do not let *them* come together with you." Rather, the text reads: "Do not let him/her come together with you" (14:2). Thus, only one person is excluded.

If only one person is excluded, this must mean that the person excluded has somehow injured another by something said or done. *Did.* 15:3 may be associated with this. The one injured "reproves" the offender "not in anger but in peace." If the offender acknowledges his/her offense and apologizes/repents, all is well. If the offender, however, resists doing so: "Let no one speak to him/her nor hear from you about him/her until s/he should repent" (15:3). Mt 5:23 and 18:15–17 represent variants of this situation. All in all, therefore, rendering the text as "having a conflict" (*Did.* 14:2) leaves open the result that the community would embrace the offended party and exclude the offender: "Dö not let him/her come together with ÿou."

This meaning of the text also places a new emphasis on "having beforehand confessed your failings" (14:1). The offender, in this case, would seemingly be expected to confess before the community his failing against a particular member even if some sort of private reconciliation had already been achieved. The confession of failings, consequently, had the effect of signaling an achieved reconciliation in the eyes of the community that may have had a part in enforcing an earlier exclusion of the offending member. In effect, therefore, the earlier suggestion that the public confession was not primarily concerned with receiving the forgiveness of God gains renewed support here.

2. *"With his/her companion"* (14:2). Apparently the *hetairos* ("companion/associate/friend") could be an outsider, since the injured party is not specifically designated as a "brother" (as in 4:8) or "sister" as might be expected. Thus a child, a slave, or a co-worker who was not a member of the community also had just claims upon the members. The discipline of reconciliation, consequently, while it was primarily directed toward maintaining the unity of the community was also directed toward protecting the honor of the community respecting injured outsiders. Thus, in cases where a member had acted unfairly or injured an outsider, the community itself might indeed take the part of the offended party and exclude the member. A signal was thus given that the norms of the Way of Life applied to all persons, irrespective of their religious affiliation. The term *hetairos*, therefore, would appear to be deliberate.

3. *"And every divinely instituted day of the Lord"* (14:1). The translation of the Greek here is universally agreed to be problematic. *Kata* is a preposition that has a wide range of meanings (e.g., along/over, through, in, upon, at, during, according to), and the noun in the accusative case that would be its object is not supplied by the text. Two alternatives have been sustained:

(a) Most translators have judged that the implied noun is *hēmeran* ("day"), but even then the adjective in the accusative case, *kyriakēn* ("belonging to or instituted by the lord"), and the possessive genitive, *kyriou* ("of the lord"), appear as mildly redundant expressions. Audet speculates that *kyriakēn*, which is absent from one version of the *Apostolic Constitutions*, might have originated as "an intrusive gloss" intending to replace the "archaic *hēmera kyriou*" (1958: 460). Rordorf speculates that the redundant expression specifically served to urge "the Christian communities to assemble on Sunday to the exclusion of Saturday" (1978a: 65).

Neither of these resolutions has gained widespread acceptance. The translation above favors understanding *kyriakēn* as pointing to the "divinely instituted [day]," while the possessive genitive points to the day as being the "[day] of the Lord."

(b) Thibaut (1924: 33f.) and S. Bacchiocchi (1977: 114) have judged that the implied noun is "rule," since the line immediately preceding ends in "according to the rule" (*kata tēn entolēn*). The second *kata* beginning the new sentence (14:1), therefore, does not require that *tēn entolēn* be repeated. Thus the text should be rendered into English as follows: "And according to the sovereign [rule] of the Lord." The case made for this rendering hinges on three points:

(1) *Did.* 14:1–3 deals with confession of faults and mutual reconciliation as prerequisites for the eucharist; hence, the issue of the time or frequency of assembling does not arise: "*Kata* with the accusative establishes a relation of conformity and not of time" (Bacchiocchi 1977: 114 n. 13). The use of Malachi ("in every time and place"), the freedom of prophets to order a eucharistic meal without any reference to the "day of the Lord," and the exhortation to frequent gatherings found later (16:2) may even suggest that the community has not yet arrived at the practice of regular weekly gatherings on the "day of the Lord."

(2) Since the troublesome phrase opening 14:1 includes the postpositive conjunction *de* ("and"), which links it to what has come before, and since the phrase *kata tēn entolēn* ("according to the rule/commandment") at the end of 13:6 immediately precedes the *kata*-phrase opening 14:1, the repetition of *tēn entolēn* might have sounded redundant—especially when orally presented. Hence, it was omitted but understood.

(3) *Kata* is habitually used in the *Didache* to enforce exhortations to act "according to the rule/doctrine" (1:5; 2:1; 4:13; 6:1, 11; 13:6) and is never used for designating time or frequency. Meanwhile, the term *kyriakēn* ("belonging to the lord") could be construed as equivalent to *kyriou* ("of the lord") or could be rendered as "given by" or "instituted by the lord" (Stott: 73). Hence, *kyriakēn* and *kyriou* need not be perceived as redundant and could be rendered into fluid English as "(And) according to [another] divinely given [rule] of the Lord."

The reasons offered by Thibaut (1924: 33f.) and Bacchiocchi (1977: 114) are strong but do not preclude the generally accepted opinion that "[day] of the Lord" was intended. While the framers of the *Didache* might have indeed crafted their language so as to invite both interpretations, the *Apostolic Constitutions* testifies that "day of the Lord" (7.30.1) was the preferred and inferred meaning. Hence, in this study, I support the majority opinion but leave open the possibility that Thibaut and Bacchiocchi may not have missed the mark.

The Language of Sacrifice

The Greek language distinguished between "sacrifice" (*thysia*) and "holocaust" (*enagismos*). A "sacrifice" was "typically a festive daytime celebration with music and procession (*pompē*) toward the temple" (N. Jay: 22). A "holocaust" was "commonly a nighttime ritual" performed in silence, with the procession (*apopompē*) "leading away from the temple or city" (ibid.: 22–23). In both Roman and Greek circles, a "sacrifice" had the effect of "joining people together in an alimentary [meal-sharing] community; it was life-enhancing and life-maintaining" (Malina 1996: 33). On the other hand, the "holocaust" had the effect of "separating the person and group from defilement and danger; it was life-protecting" (ibid.). A "holocaust" was entirely burnt upon the altar and made no provisions for a fellowship meal to follow.

The sacrificial traditions of Israel differed from those of the Romans and Greeks, yet a clear demarcation was made between "sacrifice" (*zebach shelamim*, "sharing offerings," as in Lv 3) and "holocaust" (*olah*, "burnt offering," as in Lv 4) (Malina 1996: 36). In the case of a "sacrifice," Leviticus directs that the blood be poured out "on the borders of the altar" (Lv 3:13) and that the kidneys and the fat on the entrails be burnt (Lv 3:15f.). The rest was eaten in the context of a festive meal. In the case of a "holocaust," however, the "bull's skin, all its flesh, its head, legs, entrails and dung . . . must be carried outside the camp . . . and the bull must be burnt there" (Lv 4:11f.). Nothing was eaten. Malina summarizes as follows:

> Thus in terms of the sacrifices described in Leviticus there are two major triggers that require sacrifice. In the first case, when persons seek to celebrate life with their Lord God, to honor the Lord and share with friends. . . . On the other hand, sacrifice [the "holocaust"] is likewise required when somebody inadvertently offends the honor of the deity to such an extent that only death or equivalent seems reasonable (adequate for satisfaction of that honor). (1996: 36)

The language of the *Didache* is entirely centered on "sacrifice" (*thysia*); the term "holocaust" (*enagismos*) nowhere appears. This is entirely to be expected, since "sacrifice" in the ancient world was commonly associated with a fellowship meal (see #8i). Thus, both Jews and gentiles would have been disposed to regard the eucharistic meal as a kind of "sacrifice" even though (as will be explained later) no animal was ritualistically killed. The absence of the term "holocaust" (*enagismos*), meanwhile, signals that both Jews and gentiles would not have been inclined to regard the confession of failings or the discipline of reconciliation as being motivated by the need for the forgiveness of sins or for the atonement of guilt (see #8b). The key motive is offering a "pure sacrifice" (14:1f.)—a concept that will become clear as our investigation continues.

#8b THE CONFESSION OF FAILINGS AND THE FORGIVENESS OF SINS

When the confession of failings prior to the eucharist is explicitly said to ensure a "pure sacrifice" (14:1), one would be mistaken to understand this confession as a primitive form of the sacrament of Confession. The church of the early centuries practiced shunning and excommunication in order to deal with serious sins, and only in the sixth century did the confession of sins to a monk or priest emerge as a practice recommended to the laity—a practice that caught on so well that it eventually became established as a sacrament in the medieval church.

In early Judaism as well as in early Christianity, it was understood that the Lord forgives transgressions as soon as a person approaches him and confesses his/her failings (Sanders 1977: 175–82). This may at first glance look like a "Protestant approach" to the issue, yet it must be remembered that, regarding minor sins, even Catholics have always maintained the same understanding. Thus the psalmist prays:

> I acknowledged my sin to you,
> and I did not hide my iniquity;
> I said, "I will confess my transgressions to the Lord,"
> and you forgave the guilt of my sin. (Ps 32:5)

In early Judaism, therefore, public confession was neither implied nor necessitated. In actual practice, if someone was bringing a sin offering to the temple, he/she had to confess to the priest the sin involved so that sacrifice could be treated as a "holocaust" (Büchler: 417). In those cases involving fraud (Lv 5:21–26), the priest had to ascertain whether suitable restitution had been made. Bystanders had no way of discerning what kind of offering was being made until they saw how it was handled by the priest (Büchler: 417). In later rabbinic Judaism, "so long as the sins were committed in private, the repentance of them could be a private matter of the sinner's heart; but after sinning publicly, repentance would have to be accompanied by a public confession of sins" (Büchler: 423). Nothing of this, however, shows up in the *Didache*.

All in all, the *Didache* was concerned with perfection in the Way of Life (esp. *Did.* 6:2; 10:6; and 16:2, as explained in ch. 13 below). When the forgiveness of sins is considered, the Lord's Prayer makes clear that only a final (one-time only) forgiveness is sought when the Lord comes (as detailed in ch. 4). Outside of this, the sharing of one's resources is done "for the ransoming of your sins" (4:6)—a typical Jewish perspective. Beyond this, nothing is said. It would be a mistake, therefore, to try to read into the "confession of failings" anything of the penitential system that emerged in early monasticism.

With even greater force, one must be careful not to allow medieval theology to interpret the *Didache*. Medieval theology was built on the premise that the fall of Adam and Eve in the garden infected all their children in all generations making them enemies of God. Jesus and Jesus alone, among all those born of women, was just and holy and entirely without sin. Thus, within this horizon of understanding, Jesus and Jesus alone was capable of offering an acceptable sacrifice to God. The sacrifices offered by God's just and devoted servants (e.g., Abel, Noah, Abraham) were demoted in importance and given the status of "prefiguring" the one and only true sacrifice acceptable to God. Jesus' sacrificial death on Calvary was thus elevated as *the* sacrifice that gained *infinite* merits, which, over the course of time, secured the forgiveness of sins for those who were locked in darkness and unable to help themselves. According to medieval theology, the purpose of the eucharist was to apply the merits gained by Christ on Calvary to those sinners who unite themselves to him in faith.

Little or nothing of this is found in the *Didache*. The only assumption shared by these two systems is that a pure sacrifice can be offered only by the one who is holy. Beyond this, the *Didache* appears to know nothing of a catastrophic fall in the garden that spiritually doomed the whole of humankind. Quite to the contrary, the *Didache* presumed that ordinary holiness pursued along the paths revealed by the Father in the Way of Life was pleasing to God. Accordingly, when the community gathered, the *Didache* does not hesitate to acknowledge that here one has "the presence of the saints" (4:2). Not all who were assembled to offer the "sacrifice" of the eucharist, however, were fully perfected—otherwise there would be no need for fraternal correction (4:3), for the confession of failings (14:1), and, in severe cases, for shunning (15:3). One must surmise from this that the framers of the *Didache* regarded those who offered the eucharistic "sacrifice" as worthy due to their striving toward perfection and sustaining each other in that quest (6:2; 16:2). Only someone locked in "a conflict with a companion" (14:2) or maliciously "misbehaving against the other" (15:3) had to be excluded, lest their "sacrifice be defiled" (14:2). In contrast to the medieval synthesis, the *Didache* is entirely mute regarding the "sacrifice of Jesus Christ" and entirely vocal regarding the "pure sacrifice" (14:1, 3) that even gentiles on the Way of Life were capable of offering to the God of David.

Returning to the language of the *Didache*, recall again that the language is entirely centered on "sacrifice" (*thysia*) and that the term "holocaust" (*enagismos*) nowhere appears. When the term "sacrifice" is properly distinguished from "holocaust," it appears quite natural that the confession of failings was directed toward ensuring a "pure sacrifice" (as will be explained shortly). Nothing should be decided, therefore, on the mistaken assumption that the confession of failing was used by the framers of the *Didache* to secure the forgiveness of sins or to gain the merits of Christ.

#8C THE EXPERIENCE OF SACRIFICE IN THE ANCIENT WORLD

The *Didache* finds no need to define "sacrifice" (*thysia*) or "pure sacrifice" (*kathara thysia*). This is so because "sacrifice permeated the ancient world, and it was a fact of life" (Stevenson: 11); hence, both Jews and gentiles stood in a cultural milieu wherein such things were generally understood and taken for granted. Sacrifice made sense to them, although it does not entirely make sense to us (Malina 1996: 26f.). Similarly, those who approached God to offer a sacrifice would have been conscious of whether they had the requisite "purity" (*katharsis*). Here again, notions of purity associated with sacrifice were prevalent not only among the Jews (Cooke) but among all other ancient peoples as well (Farnell; Reid).

Going beyond the various anthropological, psychological, and sociological schools of thought as to how ancient sacrifices functioned (Beers; Bell; Girard; N. Jay; Levenson; V. Turner), Bruce Malina has endeavored to reconstruct, from the vantage point of a pragmatic sociology of religion, the shape of the ancient impulse to offer sacrifices. Malina writes as follows:

> Religion (*pietas, eusebeia*) was about respect for those who controlled one's existence, beginning with the gods and followed closely by the ancestors, emperors and other high-ranking human beings. This respect was shown in ritual (*cultus*) rather than in beliefs or theological ideas. Roman domestic religion looked to the customary rituals, undertaken by the *paterfamilias* ["father of the family"] (and others in the family) on behalf of the family. When necessary, an individual would promise a sacrifice in requital of favors received (*nuncupatio*) and fulfill the promise if the god did his part (*solutio*). The gods were to be shown respect, hence placated [when offended], given acknowledgment, even gratitude. (1996: 31)

Just as a person or family would be inclined to offer gifts to a social superior on fixed occasions (an anniversary) or spontaneously (on the occasion of a visit), Malina explains that this same range of sentiments applied when it came to offering sacrifices to the gods (see #1c).

The practice of offering sacrifice (animals, grains, incense) was the usual route for expressing piety toward the gods. Whether in the case of domestic or political worship, the Romans were guided by custom in both the elaborate preparation of and the participation in a sacrifice:

> It [Roman worship] consisted mainly in songs and dances followed by a sacrifice to the gods; and this really meant a feast to the worshippers, which would give them a welcome change from the usual vegetable diet. When those who were taking part in the worship had bathed themselves in a running stream, robed themselves in their snow-white togas, and placed on their heads garlands . . . , a crier bade all keep silence, that no word of ill omen might be heard. The piper (*tibicen*) . . . then blew a strain on his pipes: all present veiled their heads: the sacrificer repeated a prayer dictated by the priest or pontiff: the victim, adorned with garlands (*serta*) and ribbons (*vittae*), was gently led to the altar: wine, incense and salted meal were sprinkled on his head: and the attendant (*popa*) struck him down with a mallet and cut his throat with a knife. The blood was caught in a basin and poured upon the altar. The inside of the carcass (*exta*) was sprinkled again with incense, wine, and meal, and burnt in the flames. The flesh furnished a feast for the family [or the guests]. . . . (Wilkens: 117f.)

The festive meal that followed the sacrifice had the social effect of bonding the worshipers to each other. The roasted meat of the victim was considered "holy" for sacrifice (*sacri-ficium* in Latin literally meant to "make holy"). While the meal "took place before the god or gods," those celebrating together were "bound . . . to each other, not to the god" (Malina 1996: 31f.; Willis: 52–64). Livy describes the public conviviality associated with a day of public sacrifices as follows:

> They [the Romans] also observed the rite in their homes. All through the city, they say, doors stood wide open, all kinds of viands [meats] were set out for general consumption, all comers were welcomed, whether known or not, and men even exchanged kind and courteous words with personal enemies. (5.3.5f.)

Thus, the social character of sacrifice and its festive aftermath required a degree of reconciliation among the participants. Disorderly conduct or insulting language was not only popularly seen as unfitting; it was punished with fines (Willis: 54–56). When the *Didache* speaks of quarreling persons being excluded from the sacrificial meal, therefore, everyone would have easily agreed that such persons "defiled" (*Did*. 14:2) a sacrifice.   The notion of ritual impurity in connection with sacrifices extends far beyond the notions of moral or sexual purity that are familiar to us in segments of our society. In the ancient world, shedding blood, even when done accidently or juridically, rendered the individual "impure" and incapable of offering sacrifice (Farnell: 483f.). Similarly, anyone in the house where a corpse was laid out or anyone participating in a funeral ceremony was considered to be "impure" for a period of time and was excluded from worship (Farnell: 485). Sexual intercourse, even when entirely legitimate, was considered to render one "impure" in the cultic sense—the whole body had to be washed before approaching an altar or entering into a place of public worship lest the place itself be desecrated and the sacrifice defiled (Farnell: 486).

In sum, from the vantage point of the *Didache*, gentiles would have considered it unusual that nothing was said of shedding blood, corpse defilement, or sexual intercourse when discussing purity and defilement relative to the community's sacrifice. As noted above, given the convivial character of the festive meals that followed domestic and civic sacrifices, "everyone having a conflict with his companion" had to be excluded lest the "sacrifice . . . be defiled" (14:2). This would require no explanation. On the positive side, however, gentiles would have considered it unusual that nothing was said of bathing and putting on a fresh white toga as the necessary preparation for offering a "pure sacrifice." Yet the Roman and Greek gods did not put forward rules of living and demand progress toward perfection of their adherents (Malina 1996: 30). The *Didache*, on the other hand, made it clear that the Father had revealed "life and knowledge" (9:3) that guided the way of his "children." The eucharistic meal, meanwhile, looked forward to the arrival of the kingdom, wherein perfection of life would be expected of all (10:5; 16:2). Thus, while unusual, gentiles would have found the "confession of failings" to be a consistent, helpful, and supportive preparation for offering a "pure sacrifice" to this God whom they now knew as a loving Father preparing his "children" to enter the kingdom he has prepared for them. All in all, therefore, the system of the *Didache* would be received as reflecting the socially honored modes whereby a pure sacrifice might be offered and whereby a defiled sacrifice might be avoided.

Whether an Individual Confession of Failings Was Practiced

The *Didache* does not define which "failings" were to be publicly and communally confessed (Rordorf 1978b: 68). The Greek term found in both 4:14 and 14:1 is *parantomatos,* which literally means "a false step." Three considerations are in order here:

1. *Infractions against the Way of Life.* The term *parantomatos* harmonizes well with the notion that the members of the community were being trained to walk on "the path of life." A "false step," consequently, would include anything that deviated from the specifics given in *Did.* 1–4. In effect, this could include anything from murder (2:2; 3:2) to grumbling (3:6). One might even be tempted to say that the specifics drawn out in the "way of death" illustrate the kind of "faults" that might have been confessed at one time or another in the community. In any case, the following examination will suggest that the principal benefit gained when confessing such failings was to solicit the practical support necessary to aid individuals in their striving for perfection.

2. *Everyday infractions against another.* The term *parantomatos* also harmonizes well with the notion that the members of the community were preparing to share a festive meal (the eucharist) and were living in close proximity—sharing meals, work, and (in many cases) lodging. A "false step," consequently, might also include day-to-day matters that caused grief or injury, e.g., failing to comb wool properly for spinning or misplacing a tool through negligence. The *Didache* does not expressly list such matters; yet insofar as such matters could cause "a conflict" (14:2), such everyday matters might well be included. The following examination will indicate that the principal benefit gained when confessing such everyday failings was to renew the human bonding necessary for harmonious community living and the joyful celebration of the eucharist.

3. *Grave infractions that led to shunning.* Given the fact that "everyone having a conflict with his/her companion" had to be excluded "in order that your sacrifice may not be defiled" (14:2), one can surmise that, on these occasions, the confession of failings functioned as a way of publicly acknowledging the "false step" that had led to exclusion and to public shunning by the entire community (15:3). The examination that follows will indicate that the principal benefit gained from confessing such grave failings was the readmission of someone who had for a period of time been publicly shunned as a result of his/her bad conduct.

Rordorf maintains (1978b: 68) that the confession of failings consisted in a community prayer rather than an individual confession. This prayer, Rordorf continues, was designed to acknowledge the sinfulness of the community generally without enumerating specific failings. He even goes so far as to suggest a possible formula:

> Only one thing is certain: it [the confession of failings] does not consist in a penitential prayer, individual and detailed, but in a

prayer of the community. But this would not be the Our Father because it is already recited three times daily as we have seen. Now, *First Clement* has preserved for us a community prayer of the confession of sins which can give us an idea of the prayer of the *Didache:*

> [God], merciful and compassionate, pardon our iniquities and our unrighteousness, our faults and negligence. Do not take into account any sin of your servants [male] and servants [female], but cleanse us with the cleansing of your truth and guide us such that we might walk entirely in holiness of heart and might do that which is good and agreeable in your eyes [*1 Clem.* 60.1–2]. (1978b: 228; 1973: 287)

This interpretation on the part of Rordorf faces three difficulties:

1. Whenever community prayers were intended, the framers of the *Didache* provided a working schema detailing the prayer structure (8:1–2, 9–10). One can readily accept Rordorf's suggestion that, if the Our Father were the intended prayer, this would have been specified. It remains difficult to imagine, however, why the framers of the *Didache* would not have delineated the public prayer of confession if, as Rordorf assumes, such a prayer were used on a weekly basis. Finally, when the community prayer from *First Clement* is examined in its own context, one discovers that the author says nothing of its being a "confession of failings" or having anything to do with the "eucharist."

2. The *Didache* routinely introduces collective prayers using the plural imperative (8:2; 9:2ff.). *Did.* 14:1 uses the plural. Earlier, however, the singular is used: "you [singular] will confess your [singular] failings" (4:14). The verb here is *exomologein,* an intensive form of *homologein.* This verb could be rendered as "to acknowledge," but here it refers to publicly "confessing [personal] transgressions" (Bauer: 277a; as in Mt 3:6 and Acts 19:18). Why would the novice be alerted to this personal confession at the very end of training in the Way of Life if only a general prayer of collective sinfulness were being practiced? Such a confession would be of little consequence and not worth mentioning. However, if the mentor knew that a personal and specific acknowledgment of *paraptōmata* (literally, "false steps") was expected, then the mentor would have had good reason to prepare the novice to anticipate this. In effect, the novice would anticipate examining his/her conscience weekly regarding the norms of conduct revealed in the Way of Life.

3. Nothing in the *Didache* supports the assumption that the "confession of failings" takes the form of a prayer. Rordorf comes to this conclusion in part because he likewise assumes that the confession took place "before God" with the understanding that only those who had regained the "lost

holiness" (1978b: 229) of their baptism were to be permitted to come forward to receive communion after the meal (*Did.* 10:6).

In sum, therefore, it seems more prudent to set aside the untested assumptions of Rordorf and to return to the text itself, which, as shown above, favors an audible and individual confession of specific failings when assembling prior to celebrating the eucharist. From what follows, this conclusion will become all the more evident.

Spiritualization of Sacrifice in Judaism

In order to understand the pastoral genius of the *Didache*, one has to leave aside our modernity for the moment and enter into an ancient horizon of understanding that is quite foreign to our contemporary modes of seeing and reflecting. All in all, when this chapter is finished, we will have constructed a sturdy three-legged stool:

1. The first leg is already in place. This is the widespread experience in the ancient world that every "sacrifice" (*thysia*) involves and culminates in a festive meal. This pillar allows us to recapture how the framers of the *Didache* found it entirely natural to link "breaking bread" and "giving thanks" with their notion of "sacrifice" (14:1).

2. The second leg is the recognition that the confession of failings involves a verbal acknowledgment of particular failings that has little or nothing to do with obtaining forgiveness and very much to do with ensuring that the community can offer a "pure sacrifice" (14:1).

3. In just a moment, we will explore the spiritualization of sacrifice in the various Judaisms of the first century, and this will provide the background whereby the *Didache* intuitively makes a connection between the confession of failings and preparing to offer a "pure sacrifice." Then we will have the third leg and the interconnecting braces, which, when finished, will allow us to feel how the "confession of failings" and "fraternal/sororal correction" joined together with the eucharist in order to ensure a pragmatic stimulus to holiness within a caring community of like-minded individuals.

When our sturdy three-legged stool is finished, we can sit and contemplate or dance and celebrate the magnificent pastoral craftsmanship that went into the construction of the *Didache*. Let us go now and examine the second leg: the spiritualization of sacrifice.

In Judaism, one finds a long-established tradition of offering suitable sacrifice to God. The Torah delivered to Moses gave great attention to the when, where, and how of offering sacrifice. In the prophetic literature, however, a shockingly new voice was heard—for the first time, one heard stinging critiques of temple sacrifices based on the perception that God had no patience with traditional sacrifices. This new voice represented, according to Karl Jaspers, an illustration of the epochal shift that swept through the progressive world cultures at that time (2–10). Acting justly and virtuously began to assert itself as the normative preparation for offering true sacrifice. The prophet Isaiah stunned his contemporaries with graphic images such as these:

> "What are your endless sacrifices to me?" says the Lord. "I am sick of holocausts of rams and the fat of calves. The blood of bulls and of goats revolts me. . . . When you stretch out your hands [in prayer] I turn my eyes away. You may multiply your prayers, I shall not listen. Your hands are covered with blood, wash, make yourself clean. Take your wrong-doing out of my sight. Cease to do evil. Learn to do good, search for justice, help the oppressed, be just to the orphan, plead for the widow." (Is 1:11, 15–17)

One notes here that sacrifices were taken for granted. Isaiah, speaking for the Lord, intended not to abolish them but to drive home the fact that (whatever may have been the case earlier) God was no longer pleased with offering sacrifices unless the one approaching the altar was both ritually and morally pure and upright of heart.

Philo (d. 50 C.E.), an Alexandrian Jew, demonstrates quite well how deep and how widespread the epochal shift had become when he writes as follows:

> God is not pleased even though a man bring hecatombs [100 oxen] to his altar; for he possesses all things as his own and stands in need of nothing. But he delights in minds which love God and in men who practice holiness, from whom he gladly receives cakes and barley, the very cheapest things, as if they were the most valuable. . . . (*Special Laws* 1.270)

> God looks upon even the smallest offering of frankincense by a holy man as more valuable than ten thousand beasts which may be sacrificed by one who is not thoroughly virtuous. . . . In the eyes of God it is not the number of things sacrificed that is accounted valuable but the purity of the rational spirit of the sacrificer. (*Special Laws* 1.275, 277)

Nothing remotely like this can be found on the lips of Moses. Philo, speaking as though he knew the sentiments of God, uses great exaggeration in order to demonstrate again and again that the quantity means nothing to God and that the quality of a sacrifice increases in direct proportion to the holiness/purity of the one making the offering. In the same way as just judges refuse to receive gifts from those pleading a case before them, Philo argues, so the Judge of the whole world cannot be "corrupted by bribes" for he "rejects the gifts of the wicked" (*Special Laws* 1.277)—an argument that finds almost an exact parallel in Plato (*Republic* 364–66).

Taken to an extreme, Philo goes so far as to conclude that the just person who loves God can offer to God "the smallest thing." Indeed, such a one can even come into the temple empty-handed. At this point, Philo goes way beyond the prophets of Israel:

> And even if they [persons who practice holiness] bring nothing else, still when they bring themselves, *the most perfect completeness of virtue and excellence,* they are offering the most excellent of all sacrifices, honoring God, their Benefactor and Savior, with hymns and thanksgivings. (*Special Laws* 1.272)

In this fashion, holiness of life becomes "the most excellent of all sacrifices." Thus, "when they [the righteous] have no longer any materials left in which they can display their piety, they then consecrate and offer up themselves, displaying an unspeakable holiness and a most superabundant excess of a God-loving disposition" (*Special Laws* 1.248). The sacrificial language here is evident. Even when the temple still existed in Jerusalem, therefore, Philo represented how many diaspora Jews were entirely content to live their ordinary lives of holiness with the firm conviction that they were thereby offering true sacrifice to God without ever traveling to Jerusalem to offer an animal or grain sacrifice upon the altar.

Robert J. Daly carefully documents this "spiritualization of sacrifice" in his treatise *The Origins of the Christian Doctrine of Sacrifice.* He defines the broad scope of this movement as follows:

> We are using the word *spiritualization* in a much broader sense than simply antimaterialistic. This sense includes all those movements and tendencies within Judaism and Christianity which attempted to emphasize the true meaning of sacrifice, that is, the inner, spiritual, or ethical significance of the cult over against the merely material or merely external understanding of it. We include here such different things as: the effort among pious Jews to make their material sacrifice an expression of an ethically good life; the prophetic criticism of the sacrificial cult; the philosophically influenced doubts about the sense of offering material sacrifice to a spiritual God; the necessity of finding substitutes for material sacrifice when participation in the sacrificial cult of the Jerusalem temple was not possible, as in Qumran, or in the diaspora, or after the destruction of the temple. (7)

"Sacrifice permeated the ancient world, and it was a fact of life with which any new religions had to reckon" (Stevenson: 11). In like fashion, the spiritualization of sacrifice made firm inroads during the first century in both Jewish and gentile attitudes toward sacrifice. Paul, for instance, at one point urged Christians "to present your bodies as living sacrifice (*thysian*), holy and acceptable to God" (Rom 12:1) and, at a later point, he referred to his own "preaching the gospel" as his "sacrificial/priestly service" (Rom 15:15).

The strongest instance of this is found in the *Letter to the Hebrews*. Hebrews argues that, since Jesus was not a Levite, "if he were on earth, he would not be a priest at all" (Heb 8:4). In the heavenly sanctuary, however, Jesus is the eternal high priest, chosen by God as an exceptional case paralleling God's former choice of Melchizedek (Heb 7:1–17). In the end, the author of Hebrews brings this revolutionary framework home by specifying a novel understanding of sacrifice:

> Through him then let us continually offer up a sacrifice (*thysian*) of praise to God, that is, the fruit of lips that acknowledge his name. Do not neglect to do good and to share what you have, for such sacrifices (*thysiais*) are pleasing to God. (Heb 13:15f.)

The reference to a "sacrifice of praise" here can be interpreted as referring, among other things, to the eucharistic prayers, yet the text is far from clear on this point. What Hebrews does make plain, however, is that "brotherly love" (Heb 13:1), "hospitality to strangers" (Heb 13:2), and many other aspects of Christian living (Heb 13:3–15) constitute "acceptable worship" (Heb 12:28).

Unlike Paul and Hebrews, the framers of the *Didache* pioneered an alternative solution: the act of gathering together, taking a meal, and giving thanks (all named in *Did.* 14:1) was the true "sacrifice" pleasing to God. This meant that the festive eucharistic meal celebrating the election of Israel and anticipating the final ingathering constituted the "sacrifice" of the community. Hebrews focused on "doing good" and "sharing resources" as those moments in which God was pleased to receive their sacrifices. Philo, in his turn, focused on those moments when wisdom (knowing Torah) and holiness (doing Torah) came together in a person's life.

Each of these programs entirely revamped the character of the traditional animal sacrifices in such a way as to bypass the Jerusalem temple (see ch. 14 below). Each provided a way of spiritualizing sacrifice. Each program highlighted distinctive operative values. Note, for example, that both the framers of the *Didache* and Philo presume that the suitability of a person's sacrifice is directly proportional to his/her holiness of life. For the *Didache*, however, the focus is decidedly communal. Only "one sacrifice" is offered, and one would suspect that the suitability of this sacrifice might be directly proportional to the striving for perfection and the deepening of interpersonal bonding within the community. Philo, of course, would not exclude such elements, yet his metaphors betray his emphasis. Sacrifice, for Philo, is first and foremost an individual affair dependent on achieved perfection of life. Sacrifice, for the framers of the *Didache*, is first and foremost, a communal affair dependent on interdependent forms of mutual support and bonding. This contrast will be seen more clearly in what follows.

Confession and Reconciliation as Enlarging Holiness

In what has already been said, it is clear that striving toward holiness represents the key preparation for offering the eucharistic "sacrifice." Accordingly, the confession of failings and the discipline of reconciliation need to be explored in the perspective of sustaining and enlarging the interdependent holiness of individuals within community.

1. *Sustaining the quest for perfection after baptism.* According to the *Didache*, the initial lure toward the Way of Life begins as an impulse of the Spirit (4:10) that draws an outsider to know and admire one or more insiders. Yielding to this impulse, the community then assigns a mentor, possibly one of those whom the outsider already admires (see ch. 1 above). In the training period, the habits of feeling and of judging of the novice are gradually transformed by "the one speaking to you the word of God" (4:1) and, progressively, the novice assimilates for him/herself the ability to walk in the Way of Life revealed by the Father through his servant Jesus. Even at the end of the training period, however, the process is not complete:

[1] For, on the one hand, if you are able to bear
      the whole yoke of the Lord, you will be perfect;
[2] but if, one the other hand, you are not able,
      that which you are able, do this. (*Did.* 6:2)

Given this fact of life and given the decisive importance of growing in perfection until the Lord comes (16:2), the framers of the *Didache* undoubtedly designed the confession of failings in order to provide a weekly stimulus toward this perfection. The mention of specific failings by any individual reminded the entire community that such things were to be avoided. Thus, the scope of the Way of Life was renewed in the minds of those present and maybe even expanded. The mention of specific failings by each member also provided the occasion on which persons close to them came to a deepened awareness of how these persons needed support in particular ways. Finally, while humiliation or self-abasement was not the primary goal of the confession, one can easily understand how a person locked in a particular sin would, after repeatedly confessing the same failing, either reform his/her life or leave the community.

Those who have had experience with the Chapter of Faults practiced in religious orders or who have witnessed the truth telling practiced in Alcoholics Anonymous will quickly grasp the impact of mentioning specific failings. For these reasons, therefore, it seems preferable to imagine that members of the community took their turns to confess specific failings wherein they deviated from the Way of Life during the proceeding week. Remembering that the eucharist in the *Didache* community was a full evening meal, there is no necessity to imagine that the number of participants impeded such individual confession. Furthermore, since the forgiveness of God was not the primary objective, there would be no reason to limit the confession to sins against God, since, as one examines the Way of Life, one quickly discovers that it is nearly entirely occupied with how to love one's neighbor.

2. *Removing obstacles to a festive meal and to the final ingathering.* Given the nature of the eucharistic "sacrifice" as a festive meal that affirmed the election of the participants in the promises made to Israel and that anticipated the final ingathering into the kingdom, it becomes transparently clear that "everyone having a conflict with his/her companion" would be excluded "in order that your sacrifice may not be defiled" (14:2). As shown above, this exclusion had a practical aspect (see #8c). How could a festive meal proceed with a convivial spirit if one or more of the members were "misbehaving against the other" (15:3)? The very character of the eucharist, consequently, imposed the discipline of reconciliation.

In a community of strangers, the acknowledgment of specific deeds causing pain for others would be of no great consequence. In a community of intimates, the regular acknowledgment of small failures would become the vital means whereby resentments were defused, hidden conflicts were openly acknowledged (quieting down the rumor mill), and past hurts were smoothed over. In a word, no practice would be more conducive to restoring and to enlarging the bonds that keep an intentional community alive and growing. I myself have seen how unspoken problems, festering resentments, and backbiting can bring even an idealistic community to a standstill and destroy the dedication and joy of individuals therein.

The voluntary confession of failings had the effect of bringing closure to a painful incident that otherwise might have gone unattended. On the other side, however, those persons who were offended or hurt by another member of the community were urged to bring this to the attention of the offender (as will be seen in the next section). When the offender, however, took the initiative by acknowledging his/her fault, the one injured had no further cause for confrontation. On pragmatic grounds, therefore, it can be surmised that the confession of failings served, in many instances, as a means of avoiding the pain of being reproved (Sir 20:3).

3. *Publicly ending a period of shunning.* When someone being reproved failed to acknowledge his/her fault or when the fault was very grievous, then the discipline of shunning and of exclusion from the eucharist would have come into play (15:3). In the first case, shunning had the effect of forcing the offending party to take into account how they injured someone (even while not fully intending it). In the second case, grievous sins (like adultery) normally require an extended period in which the innocent party and his/her allies grieve for and with the person injured. In both of these cases, the readmission of the offending party after a period of public shunning (15:3) would normally have taken place through the public confession prior to a eucharist. The importance of this will be considered in what follows.

Reproving and Shunning as Complements to the Confession of Failings

When examined closely, the *Didache* provided its members with a very well considered program for maintaining the bonds of unity among its members. Such training began when a novice was prepared in the following terms for becoming an active arbitrator and a courageous critic:

You will not make dissension
[1] but will reconcile those fighting.
[2] You will judge justly;
[3] you will not take into account social status
when it comes time to reprove against failings. (*Did.* 4:3)

All three responsibilities are expressed in the second person singular—a sign that every member was expected to take the initiative for these community maintenance functions and not just a chosen few. The Didache community had the informality and lack of privacy that characterized an extended "family." No complex procedures were established for "reconciling those fighting" (4:3), for instance, and neither mentor-trainers nor bishop-deacons were assigned any role in the process. Anyone could arbitrate between quarreling Christians.

The same thing held true for "reproving against failings" (4:3). Here again, one finds the informality and the lack of privacy characteristic of a "family." While reproving had to do with infractions against the Way of Life, it surely was not reserved to such things. Reproving, for the most part, had to do with the everyday hurts and disappointments that arose whenever committed persons eat, work, and live together. One can imagine, therefore, that reproof had to do with carelessly misplacing shop tools or inadvertently failing to properly vent a kiln. So, too, reproof had to do with "speaking badly of someone" or "holding grudges" (2:2)—infractions against the Way of Life, to be sure, but also ways in which the bonds of unity were fragmented and the respect and support of a brother or sister was withdrawn.

#8D THE JOY AND EFFICACY OF CORRECTION

In Lv 19, a set of practical rules is given to illustrate how to "love your neighbor as yourself" (Lv 19:18). Among these one finds the admonition to "judge justly"—"You shall not be partial to the poor or defer to the great" (Lv 19:15). This corresponds closely to the rule of the *Didache* to "judge justly" and "not take into account social status" (4:3). Then, a moment later, Lv 19 continues: "You shall not hate in your heart anyone of your kin; you shall reprove your neighbor, or you will incur guilt yourself" (Lv 19:17). The order here follows that of *Did.* 2:7. The first admonition prohibits allowing hate to fester. The second admonition presents a practical way to relieve hatred: reproof. The motive, however, tends to make reproving an obligation: "Either reprove your neighbor or you are tainted by his/her sin." This is a theme widely enforced in rabbinic Judaism.

In the Jesus movement, sentiments parallel to Lv 19:17 find expression. The Letter of James, for example, closes with these words:

> My brothers and sisters, if anyone among you wanders from the truth and is brought back by [the gentle reproofs of] another, you should know that whoever brings back a sinner from wandering will save the sinner's soul from death and will cover a multitude of [his/her own] sins. (Jas 5:19)

The results of the reproving are here expressed in positive terms. First, the sinner is rescued "from death" (from the Way of Death) and the one reproving has his/her sins forgiven. Instead of the negative ("incur guilt" of Lv 19:17), an abundant positive outcome ("cover a multitude of sins") is specified.

In the *First Letter of Clement,* an even more positive approach to reproving is put forward. In this approach, praying accompanies reproving:

> Let us then also pray for those who have fallen into any sin, that meekness and humility may be given to them, so that they may submit, not unto us [who reproved them], but to the will of God. For in this way they shall secure a fruitful and perfect remem-

brance from us, with sympathy for them, both in our prayers to God and our mention of them to the saints. (*1 Clem.* 56)

One notes here that "sympathy" motivates the reproving and guides the prayers and the speaking about them "to the saints." Then moving on to admonitions:

> Let us receive correction, beloved, on account of which no one should feel displeased. Those exhortations by which we admonish one another are both good [in themselves] and highly profitable, for they tend to unite us to the will of God. For thus says the holy word: "The Lord has severely chastened me, yet has not given me over to death" [Ps 118:18]. "For whom the Lord loves, he chastens and scourges every son whom he receives" [Prv 3:12]. . . . You see, beloved, that protection is afforded to those that are chastened by the Lord; for since God is good, he corrects us, that we may be admonished by his holy chastisement. (*1 Clem.* 56)

The intimation here is that admonishing one another accomplishes the work of the Lord who corrects those whom he loves. Even upon receiving correction, therefore, "no one should feel displeased" since God is thereby correcting us for our own good. In sum, the one who admonishes a brother or sister enters into sympathy with God and accomplishes the work of God. Prayer, therefore, as the means of entering into God's sympathy is the fitting preparation for anyone who would admonish another "as the Lord."

In the *Testaments of the Twelve Patriarchs* one finds a Jewish rule for reproving that touches on the practical outcomes to be effected:

> If anyone sins against you, speak to him as a friend, having first gotten rid of the poison of hatred, and be frank with him.
> [A] And if he confesses and repents, forgive him.
> [B] But if he denies it,
> > [1] do not get involved in a dispute with him, in case he starts to swear and you become responsible for a double sin. . . .
> > [2] And if he denies it, and yet exhibits a sense of shame when reproved, desist: do not provoke him any further, for a man who denies something may repent [later] and not wrong you again: on the contrary, he may even do you honor and be afraid of you and live at peace with you.
> [C] But if he is shameless and persists in his wrong-doing, even so forgive him from the heart and leave vengeance to God. (*Testament of Gad* 6:3–7)

The *Testament*, like the *Didache*, takes note of the danger of reproving in anger (*Did*. 2:7; 15:3). The *Testament* also highlights the intimate connection between reproving and forgiving—an aspect that the *Didache* leaves undeveloped (see *Did*. 8:2). In the case of the repeat offender [C], the *Didache* offers the possibility of community shunning—an aspect that the *Testament* does not entertain.

All in all, therefore, while the practice of reproving was widely practiced in both Jewish and Christian circles, there were significant variations regarding the motives and the practice of giving correction. The *Didache*, therefore, promoted a form of correction advantageous to its own lived experience. A fruitful discussion of how different social settings favored certain variations would be interesting, but it goes beyond the scope of the present study.

The *Didache* empowered ordinary members with the tools for living in harmony most of the time and for living in joy much of the time. The overall interpersonal goal was stated as follows:

You will not hate any person,
[A] but some you will reprove,
[B] and concerning others you will pray,
[C] and some you will love more than your soul. (*Did*. 2:7)

The insistence that hate could be entirely quenched was earlier explained as the flip side of loving your neighbor (*Did*. 1:2, 3). At this point, however, the rule pertains to insiders (as also in Lv 19:17). Then reproving enters the picture as the loving service whereby each member sustains the others on the Way of Life. Praying for others undoubtedly had to do with supporting others in their efforts but also with forgiving others for the grief caused. The earlier praying "for your enemies" (1:3) had to do with outsiders; the focus here is primarily on insiders. Three times each day, members prayed that the Lord would ultimately forgive "our debt as we likewise forgive our debtors" (8:2)—hence, prayer clearly was intended to soften the hearts of those who were scandalized, disappointed, or inconvenienced by the failings of others. The last category, loving "some . . . more than your soul" (2:7) undoubtedly pertained to cherished mentors and others who shared the joys and the pains of their life journey. This category may also have included those who reproved others gently and forgave without any trace of vindictiveness.

The Way of Life defined the personal responsibility of reproving and reconciling. In *Did*. 14:1–3 and 15:3–4, the communal aspects were brought forward. In effect, *Did*. 15:1–2 is a "digression" (Niederwimmer 1998: 203) interrupting the flow of the text. *Did*. 14:1–3 deals with the confession of failings and the exclusion of "everyone having a conflict with his/her companion" (*Did.* 14:2) relative to the eucharistic sacrifice. *Did.* 15:3 expands this into a general rule for defining the discipline of reproving:

[B] And reprove each other, not in anger, but in peace,
    as ÿou have it in the good news.
[C] And to everyone misbehaving against the other,
    let no one speak to him/her
    nor hear from ÿou about him/her
    until s/he should repent. (*Did.* 15:3)

Again, for the third time, the importance of reproving is brought forward. Again, the clear note is that everyone does this and that no special class of persons is assigned this responsibility. Here, however, the personal aspect is hinted at. Each would reprove those who offended him/her. In such instances, where personal injuries were involved, the tendency was to allow anger and disappointment to drive the reproof. The *Didache* cautions against this. Even reproof is to be done "in peace" and out of love for one's "neighbor" (*Did.* 1:2). The reproof would thus be easier to receive and to implement.

When reproving was ineffective, then the community proceeded to shunning. Niederwimmer notes that "the next rule (*Did.* 15:3b) seems to apply to the cases of those who persist in sin despite brotherly or sisterly correction" (Niederwimmer 1998: 204). "Sin" may be too narrow a category here. Failings, as noted above, can refer to infractions against the Way of Life but also to the day-in, day-out grievances that arise among people living and working together. *Did.* 15:3b, therefore, might just as well signal the case of someone refusing to take responsibility for misplacing a shop tool—in a word—refusing correction. In any case, where the consequences were grave or the infraction persistent, then the whole community entered into the action: "let no one speak to him/her nor hear from ÿou about him/her until s/he should repent" (15:3b). Needless to say, there must have been some time and place in which the whole affair could be deliberated before the community (as in the parallel instance of Mt 18:15–17) so that the community could arrive at a collective decision to employ shunning.

Shunning was directed toward "reconciliation." Hence, it can be presumed that the community grieved the loss of one of its members at the next eucharist, and that the rule of *Did.* 14:2 was now operative. Likewise, in the case where public shunning had been invoked, one can suspect that its removal required a public confession prior to the eucharist in which reconciliation was to be publicly effected. In the case of persons excluded because of infractions that occasioned the rule for shunning, the open confession revealed to all that the offender was taking responsibility and acknowledging his/her misbehavior. In the case of grave injuries (e.g., adultery), the open confession after an extended period of exclusion served to reveal to the community that the offended party or parties had finished their time of grieving and were ready to embrace the offending member who was repentant. In both cases, the confession signaled an end to the publicly established and maintained period of shunning.

#8E WHETHER REPROVING AND SHUNNING CAN BE GENERATIVE

The emphasis on every member being ready to reprove, judge, and arbitrate might give the false impression that the *Didache* fostered a critical frame of mind wherein members picked each other apart. Such pickiness would lead to loss of honor, discouragement, and disputes. Such disputes would take up time and energy, create bad feelings, and require arbitration. Thus a cycle of negativity would infect the community, which, in the course of time, would exhaust its energies and destroy its creative powers.

In contrast to this, the skill of reproving can be understood as the time-honored means whereby a group of dedicated persons can improve their collective performance. One finds this today in the quality control meetings held each morning in Japanese shops, where managers and workers sit down together to discuss problems encountered in production and to work out provisional collective solutions. This is also evident in some team sports, when individual players intend not to become "stars" but to improve the overall performance of the team. Meanwhile, at meetings of Alcoholics Anonymous (and all those groups adapting their methods), confrontation generally serves as a therapeutic means directed toward enabling individuals realistically to acknowledge their "being out of control" such that support from recovering members and from "a higher Power" can come into play. Reproving, therefore, can be used for creating a cycle of generativity which, in the course of time, would enable individuals to receive needed support and direction without subverting the standards of excellence and the dreams of the community at large. This, then, represents the spirit of the *Didache* (see also #8d).

The Meaning of Malachi 1:11

The text of Malachi cited by the *Didache* is not easy to interpret even in its own context. Modern scholars have difficulty understanding precisely what the prophet had in mind when he indicated that the name of the Lord is honored "among the nations" while, among his own people (the "priests" in the Jerusalem temple according to Mal 1:6; 2:1), it is held in contempt. The text of the Septuagint reads as follows:

> I have no pleasure in you [priests], says the Lord Almighty, and I will not accept a sacrifice from your hands. For from the rising of the sun to the going down thereof, my name has been glorified among the gentiles; and in every place incense is offered to my name, and [everywhere] a pure sacrifice, for my name is great among the gentiles, says the Lord Almighty. But you [priests] you profane it. (Mal 1:10–12)

Both the Greek and the Hebrew text clearly indicate that the gentiles ("the nations") already offer an acceptable sacrifice in every place. Many scholars have tried to project a future intent on the verbs, but this "cannot be maintained on grammatical grounds" (Vriezen: 132). The intent of Malachi's oracle would then be something like the following:

> The oracle of Mal 1:11 delineates the glorification of Israel's God among the nations as already a reality in "every kind of place." . . . The precise situation in this regard in the time of Malachi (c. 475 B.C.E.) is unknown to us and probably will remain so. The prophet who more obviously than his predecessors lived in the expectation of the nearness of the revelation of God's kingdom, also, as appears from this oracle, lived in the certainty of the visible spread of the acknowledgment of Israel's Lord by the nations. Certainly there must have been reasons for this. . . .
>   A beginning of Yahweh worship among the nations may . . . be assumed, and not only in syncretistic form. Malachi in particular . . . acknowledged the earnestness with which the nations worshiped Yahweh through incense and offerings. In any case, what he knew . . . gave him the right to hold up the cult of the nations as an example to the priests of Jerusalem. (Vriezen: 133f.)

Needless to say, the framers of the *Didache* found Mal 1:11 riveting and were quick to bend it to suit their particular purposes. The Hebrew Scriptures offer a few other instances in which foreigners would be welcomed (e.g., 1 Kgs 8:41f.; Is 44:1–5; 56:1–8), but these instances may have been objectionable either (a) because they presumed gentiles would offer their sacrifices in the Jerusalem temple or (b) because they presumed the prior defeat and subjugation of the gentiles. Malachi, in contrast, allows that the gentiles honor the name of the Lord with incense and pure sacrifices "in every place"—thereby downplaying the centrality of the Jerusalem temple. The fact that the textual paraphrase of the *Didache* puts this idea first is therefore another confirmation of the intention held by the framers of the

Didache to displace the temple (see ch. 14 below) and a clear indication of why this text was so attractive.

When the Greek text of Mal 1:11 and 14b is placed side by side with the paraphrase of *Did.* 14:3, other aspects also become evident:

Septuagint	Didache
"For from the rising of the sun to the going down thereof, my name has been glorified among the gentiles; and *in every place* incense is offered to my name, and [everywhere] *a pure sacrifice* for my name is great among the gentiles," says the Lord Almighty. . . .	[. . . in every time . . .] "*In every place* and time, offer to me *a pure sacrifice.*
"For *a great king am I,*" *says [the] Lord* Almighty, "*and my name* [is] glorious *among the gentiles.*"	Because *a great king am I,*" *says [the] Lord,* "*and my name* [is] wondrous *among the gentiles.*"

1. Mal 1:11, in its original context, was intended to shame the Jewish priests by holding up the "pure sacrifice" offered by gentiles. By lifting out Mal 1:11 and 1:14b and omitting 1:12–14a, which consists of detailed attacks on the unfitting sacrifices offered by the Jerusalem priests, the framers of the *Didache* retained the pro-gentile stance of the oracle but entirely suppressed any overt criticism of Israel. The deliberate editing on the part of the framers of the *Didache* thus reinforces their affirmation of the election of Israel (see ch. 5) and their intention to demote the temple cult by displacing it (ch. 14).

2. The framers of the *Didache* reduce secondary aspects of Mal 1:11. The poetic phrase, "from the rising of the sun to the going down thereof" (Mal 1:11) is reduced to "and in every time" (*Did.* 14:3). The reference to "incense," a common ingredient in Jewish and gentile worship, is dropped out, since it distracts from *Did.* 14:1f. The phrase, "my name . . . among the gentiles," is repeated three times in Mal 1:11–14. The *Didache* retains only the last usage. The substitution of "wondrous" (*thaumaston*) for "glorious" (*epiphanēs*) does not appear to be significant (Niederwimmer 1998: 198 n. 35) and may be considered as a normal substitution when oral recall of the text is being depended upon.

3. Malachi's present-tense "is offered" (lit., "drawn near" *prosagetai*) is transformed into an infinitive functioning as an imperative, "offer [me]" (lit., "bring near" *prospherein*) (14:3). The framers of the *Didache* took Malachi's oracle describing what the gentiles of his day were doing and

understood it as a command incumbent upon the gentiles addressed by the *Didache*.

All in all, therefore, the framers of the *Didache* felt the liberty to take an oracle of Malachi out of its context and to apply it to a new situation. While the prophet Malachi is not directly cited, there is no hint that the prophets in the Didache community originated this command, and the parallel with Mal 1:11 and 14 is too obvious to be accidental. Thus, the framers of the *Didache* reached into their past and found an imperative that applied to their situation. Gentiles "in every place" were to offer "pure sacrifice." The "sacrifice," in this case, was the eucharistic meal, which, in order to be "pure," required the prior confession of failings.

No one suggests that Mal 1:11 was somehow used to originate and to justify the confession of failings and the discipline of reconciliation prior to the eucharist. Rather, it is the other way around. Once the sacrificial language was already at home in the community, the themes of Mal 1:11 stood out as addressing a situation that was already being played out. No doubt, the discovery of Mal 1:11 was greeted as an unexpected surprise and was pushed forward with religious passion: "See, this is what the Lord said through the prophet, and this is what we have been doing all along!"

#8f Mal 1:11 Interpreted within Rabbinic Judaism

The emergence of rabbinic Judaism provides an instructive illustration of still another alternative route not taken. After the destruction of the temple in 70 c.e., the rabbis needed to rethink the whole sacrificial system. When the disciple of Yohanan ben Zakkai came to him weeping over the fact that "the place where the iniquities of Israel were atoned for is laid waste," he responded as follows:

> "My son," Rabban Yohanan said to him, "be not grieved; we have another atonement [sacrifice] as effective as this. And what is it? It is acts of loving-kindness, as it is said, 'For I desire mercy and not sacrifice' (Hos 6:6)." (*ARN* 20a)

Later rabbis latched upon another hidden meaning of Mal 1:11. The rabbis found it strange that the Lord, speaking through the prophet, spoke of "pure sacrifice" at a time when they (wrongly) assumed that the first temple had been destroyed and the prophet had been taken into the Babylonian exile. What then were the "offerings" referred to by the Lord? Two solutions were forthcoming. According to Rabbi Huna, the "sacrifices" to which the Lord referred was the study of Mishnah: "Seeing that you are engaged in the study of Mishnah, it is as if you were offering up sacrifices" (*Lv. Rab.* 7.3). According to other rabbis, the "sacrifices" to which the Lord referred were the evening prayers in the synagogue:

> Offerings alludes to the evening prayer, as is born out by the text, "Let my prayer be set forth as incense before Thee, the lifting up of my hands [in prayer] as the evening sacrifice" (Ps 141:2). Thus the phrase, "My name is great among the nations," means in every place where Israel abides. (*Nm. Rab.* 13.4)

Both solutions were ingenious, and both illustrated how Malachi's oracle could again be taken out of its original context and applied to new situations. The rabbis, it will be noted, interpreted "among the gentiles" as referring to Israel in exile, and thus the "pure sacrifice" was offered by Jews—and not by gentiles as the framers of the *Didache* and modern Christian scholars surmise. Here again, one can be sure that the study of Mishnah and evening prayer in the synagogue existed first, and only later, under new circumstances, did the rabbis discover that the prophet's reference to "pure sacrifice" referred to them when he voiced the Lord's displeasure with the animal offerings of the priests.

Rabbinic Judaism at the time of the *Didache* had, as yet, no idea of directly substituting studying or praying for the sacrifices in the Temple. Neusner concludes, on the basis of his careful study of rabbinic development, that during the period between the wars (70–135 C.E.), "there is no surrogate for sacrifice" (1988a: 115). Nonetheless, the later rabbinic development does indicate how Mal 1:11 was being read in an exegetical climate that was eager to give an analogous application to "sacrifices" such that the words of the prophet would be fulfilled. Furthermore, in the prophetic literature, one finds the prophets attacking the abuse of sacrifices but never the centrality of the Jerusalem temple. Here, too, the phrase, "in every place," can be seen as providing a unique opportunity to legitimate the synagogue when used within the rabbinic context and the church when used in the *Didache*.

#8g WHETHER MAL 1:11 SUPPORTS ANTI-JUDAISM

While the *Didache* deliberately suppressed the intent of Malachi to shame the Jewish priests by holding up the "pure sacrifice" offered by gentiles, subsequent generations of Christians began to use Mal 1:11 as a point of departure not only for illustrating the corruption of Malachi's time, but for a wholesale condemnation of the sacrificial system of the Jews.

Justin Martyr (d. 165 C.E.), in his *Dialogue with Trypho,* carries on an imagined dialogue with a Jew who recently escaped from the Bar Kokhba War (135 C.E.). In this dialogue, Justin cites the Hebrew Scriptures copiously in order to demonstrate that the new covenant founded upon Christ replaces the old covenant founded upon Moses:

> For if there was no need of circumcision before Abraham, or of the observance of Sabbaths, of feasts and sacrifices, before Moses; no more need is there of them now, after that, according to the will of God, Jesus Christ the Son of God has been born without sin, of a virgin sprung from the stock of Abraham. (*Dialogue* 28)

Relative to sacrifices, Justin uses Mal 1:11 in order to maintain that "our sacrifices, he [the Lord] esteems more grateful than yours" (*Dialogue* 29). After citing the entire text of Mal 1:10–12, Justin concludes:

> So he [the Lord through the prophet] speaks of those gentiles, namely us, who in every place offer to him sacrifices, i.e., the bread of the eucharist and also the cup of the eucharist, affirming both that we glorify his name and that you [Jews] profane it. (*Dialogue* 41)

Justin demonstrates no acquaintance with the *Didache*—he knows nothing of how the framers of the *Didache* altered the text of Mal 1:11 and used it to enforce the need for the confession of failings and the discipline of reconciliation. Nonetheless, he does share common ground with the *Didache* insofar as he interprets the "pure sacrifice" of Mal 1:11 as pointing to the eucharist. He even goes so far as to claim that "we [Christians] are the true high priestly race of God, as even God himself bears witness, saying that in every place among the gentiles sacrifices are presented to him well-pleasing and pure" (*Dialogue* 116). In sum, therefore, Justin relies on Mal 1:11 to affirm the priestly character of all Christians and to discredit the sacrifices of the Jews.

In the earlier discussion of Mal 1:11, it was observed that this text was puzzled over and interpreted in rabbinic Judaism in order to affirm that either Mishnah study or synagogue prayers constituted the "pure sacrifice" offered to God by Jews living "among the gentiles" (see #8f). Justin appears to be well aware of this rabbinic argument:

> You assert that God does not accept the sacrifices of those who dwelt then [during the time of Malachi] in Jerusalem . . . ; but [God] says that he is pleased with the prayers of the individuals

of that nation then dispersed, and calls their prayers sacrifices. . . . When you interpret what the Scripture says as referring to those of your nation then in dispersion, and maintain that their prayers and sacrifices offered in every place are pure and well-pleasing, learn that you are speaking falsely . . . for, first of all, not even now does your nation extend from the rising to the setting of the sun, and there are nations among which none of your race ever dwelt. Yet there is not one single race of men . . . among whom prayers and giving of thanks are not offered through the name of the crucified Jesus. And then, as the Scriptures show, at the time when Malachi wrote this, your dispersion over all the earth, which now exists, had not [yet] taken place. (*Dialogue* 117)

Justin's refutation is tendentious. If he wished to prove that Mal 1:11 could not refer to Jews during the Babylonian deportation because they were not scattered over the whole earth, then he would have had to allow that, at that same time, there were no Christians at all; hence, the text could not refer to them. Despite the weaknesses in his argument, however, Justin does show a well-defined familiarity with a Jewish interpretation of Mal 1:11 which he feels compelled to refute in favor of his own interpretation, which identifies the Christian eucharist as the only "true sacrifice" acceptable to God.

In the next generation, Irenaeus of Lyons (d. 200), writing his treatise *Against Heresies*, again makes use of Mal 1:11, even though he demonstrates no explicit reliance on either the *Didache* or Justin Martyr. Again, the Septuagint text of Mal 1:11 is cited in full and then interpreted as . . .

. . . indicating in the plainest manner, by these words, that the former people [the Jews] shall indeed cease to make offerings to God, but that in every place sacrifice [the Christian eucharist] shall be offered to him, and that a pure one; and his name is glorified among the gentiles. (4.17.5)

Irenaeus takes the position that the Jewish sources (esp. Is 1:10–16 and Ps 51:17–19) demonstrate that God abhors material sacrifices (4.17; also *Barn.* 1:10; *1 Clem.* 18.17; 35.12; 52.3f.). Nonetheless, Irenaeus explains, "we are bound to offer to God the first fruits of his creation" (4.18.1) as Jesus instructed his disciples at the Last Supper "to offer to God the first fruits" (4.17.5) as he himself showed them. "But the Jews do not offer thus [the first fruits]; for their hands are full of blood." (4.18.4)

Irenaeus, therefore, uses Mal 1:11 quite differently from either the *Didache* or Justin. In fact, Irenaeus appears to be ignorant that Mal 1:11 was being used by some Jews to authorize the substitution of Mishnah study or synagogue prayers as the "pure sacrifice" required of God "among the gentiles." Irenaeus categorically affirms that the Lord has no need of sacrifice and then backs up to make allowances for the offering of first fruits. Christians, according to Irenaeus, offer first fruits with the required interior dispositions at their eucharist. The Jewish offering of first fruits, however, is unacceptable to God (as was the offering of Cain) because "their hands are full of blood" because "they [like Cain] slew the Just One [Jesus]" (4.18.3). Thus, with Irenaeus, the use of Mal 1:11 takes a back seat. Jewish "blood guilt" is now brought forward as the prime reason why the Jews can never again offer an acceptable sacrifice to God.

The critique of Jews and of Judaism cannot be understood as anti-Judaism. The Jewish prophets, for example, are filled with criticism. Likewise, Christian writers, from the earliest centuries, judged and condemned bad behavior among Christians. In each of these cases, however, Jews criticized Jews and Christians criticized Christians. When Christians (no longer in touch with or ever having practiced Judaism) began criticizing Jews, however, the climate changed. Particulars fell aside as polemics took over. Initially, as in the case of Justin, this polemic involved demonstrating that the practice of true religion and the understanding of the Hebrew Scriptures among Christians surpassed that practiced by the Jews. By the time of Irenaeus, however, this polemic had gone up a few notches. Now the aim was to demonstrate that Judaism was no longer even a legitimate religion and the ugly face of "blood guilt" began to dominate the interconfessional turf. It was no longer necessary to "dialogue" with Jews, to understand their religious passion and their religious hurts; rather, the goal now was to discredit Jews totally on the basis of *what Christians made them out to be*. Thus by the end of the second century, a systematic anti-Judaism began to drive the interfaith polemic. The persistence of a Judaism that did not accept Jesus was a thorn in the side of Christianity, and Christians began progressively to distort Judaism in order to intensify and to justify its rejection. Only in the last forty years has there been a concerted effort on the part of Christian pastors and theologians to reverse this smear campaign and to enter into dialogue with Jews. As a result of this dialogue, Christians have had to reassess what they thought they knew of Judaism. Jews, for their part, have likewise had to reassess what they thought they knew about Christianity. Jacob Neusner captures the climate of the break quite well when he writes as follows:

We have ample evidence for characterizing as a family quarrel the relationship between the two great religious traditions of the West. Only brothers can hate so deeply, yet accept and tolerate so impassively, as have Judaic and Christian brethren both hated, and yet taken for granted the presence of, one another. (Neusner 1986: 9)

The *Didache* represents a bridge to the past. In the *Didache*, the centrality of Jesus is affirmed, but so are the election of Israel and the promises made to David (ch. 5). In the *Didache* one finds the first steps of a Jewish movement to define itself at the boundaries of Judaism as a legitimate expression of true religion bent on the inclusion of gentiles in the promises made to Israel. Even the use of the term "Christian" does not set the movement against Judaism but merely marks out its turf as a kind of Judaism that set its store upon the Way of Life and the hoped-for kingdom which Jesus brought within reach of the gentiles. Thus, the *Didache* represents a Christianity free of anti-Judaism, and, for that reason, it bears an importance in our times to aid Christians to arrive at a self-definition that allows them to acknowledge that "Jews remain very dear to God, for the sake of the partriarchs, since God does not take back the gifts he bestowed or the choice he made [of Israel]" (Vatican II, *Nostra Aetate* sec. 4). Historically the pastors of the second and subsequent generations fostered a virulent anti-Judaism in order to distance themselves from their Jewish roots. Hopefully we are now in a position to distance ourselves from their errors, to acknowledge our lost roots going all the way back to our father Abraham (Rom 4), and to acknowledge our "brothers and sisters" who cling to the one, true God without making any claims for or against Jesus of Nazareth.

Whether Mal 1:11 Was Used
to Validate a Problematic Practice

When and why did the framers of the *Didache* cite Mal 1:11 in order to support the practice of the confession of failings? One cannot be sure. In three other instances, the *Didache* cites the Lord in order to authorize particular ways of conduct. In each instance, it is unclear to what degree the appeal to the Lord was introduced in order to shore up a practice that was being resisted or neglected by a segment of the community or being openly challenged by visiting outsiders. With regard to the confession of failings, one has to remember that no other form of first-century Judaism or Christianity known to us ever devised such a system for community maintenance. It may well be the case, therefore, that Mal 1:11 was used to provide a divine authorization for this innovative practice. On the other hand, since the focus of the text (as adapted by the framers of the *Didache*) is to affirm that the gentiles offer "pure sacrifice" in their eucharists, it is equally possible that this rare pro-gentile text of Malachi was originally used in order to spurn the notion that "pure sacrifice" was exclusively offered by Jews in the Jerusalem temple. This argument will be developed in detail in chapter 14. For the moment, however, it remains clear that Mal 1:11 had a vital role in the self-understanding of the Didache communities. It remains unclear, however, to what degree Mal 1:11 emerged historically out of a conflict situation.

In passing, it should be recognized that the framers of the *Didache* appear to be entirely unaware of the words of Jesus cited by Matthew:

> So when you are offering your gift at the altar, if you remember that your brother or sister has something against you, leave your gift there before the altar and go; first be reconciled to your brother or sister, and then come and offer your gift. (Mt 5:23f.)

This text has the effect of requiring reconciliation prior to offering a suitable sacrifice (see #8h). Therefore, it parallels *Did.* 14:2, in which "everyone having a conflict with a companion" is excluded from the eucharistic sacrifice "until they have been reconciled." Matthew's text, for its part, presumes that the sacrifice Jesus referred to was a traditional Jewish sacrifice in the Jerusalem temple. Nonetheless, had the framers of the *Didache* been aware of this saying, they would have immediately seen that it addressed their own concerns. Since they did not make use of it, this presents a strong indication that the framers of the *Didache* were unaware that Jesus had offered a teaching linking reconciliation with sacrifice. It also presents one of many arguments to the effect that either the framers of the *Didache* did not have use of Matthew's Gospel or, if they did, they refused to acknowledge it. The details of this issue will be taken up in chapter 11.

Whether "the Lord" Referred to the Lord God or the Lord Jesus

When the framers of the *Didache* cited Mal 1:11 as "having been said by the Lord" (*Did.* 14:3), they unambiguously understood themselves as referring to the Lord God and not to the Lord Jesus. Niederwimmer, at this point, allows that "*kyrios* here probably does not refer to Jesus" (1998: 198). Niederwimmer is hesitant on this point because he prefers to believe that most or all of the references to "the Lord" in the *Didache* might have referred to the Lord Jesus. At this point, readers of this study will have already noted that the previous references to "the Lord" have all been interpreted as referring to the Lord God. The whole of this argument will be taken up in chapter 10 (see #10n). For the moment, however, one can judge from the implied Christology of the *Didache* (ch. 5) that it would have been blatantly blasphemous for members of the Didache communities to even imagine that Jesus might somehow adopt Mal 1:11 as referring to himself and, accordingly, direct the gentiles offer pure sacrifices to him. Even as late as the early third century, Christian communities were still struggling with whether it was fitting to offer prayers to Jesus (e.g., Origen, *On Prayer*); thus, it would be ludicrous to imagine that the *Didache*, given its Jewish horizon of understanding, would have entertained anything but a strict monotheism. The words of Mal 1:11 thus could *only* be understood as "having been said by the Lord God" (*Did.* 14:3).

#8H RECONCILIATION, PRAYER, AND THE KISS OF PEACE

The church fathers used Mt 5:23f. in order to maintain the necessity of reconciliation prior to the eucharist. The *Apostolic Constitutions* (380 C.E.) cite Mt 5:23f. and explain that the text refers to Christians coming to offer the eucharistic sacrifice (2.53.3). There then follows a lengthy section in which unresolved conflicts are presented as making it impossible for God to hear either public or private prayers:

> If then you have something against your brother, or he has something against you, your prayer will neither be heard nor will your eucharist be accepted due to the anger which is within you. It is necessary to pray unceasingly, brothers; but because God does not hear those who unjustly hate their brothers, even if they pray three times each hour, it is necessary to put an end to all hate and to all malice in order that you might be able to pray with a heart, pure and without stain. (2.53.4–5)

Nothing is said here or elsewhere regarding the confession of faults. Accordingly, when it comes to *Did.* 4:14 and 14:1, the *Apostolic Constitutions* omit all references to "having confessed in full your failings" in favor of substituting "acknowledging in full the good things which God did for us through Christ" (7.30.1). Since the compilers of the *Apostolic Constitutions* altered the *Didache* to conform to their own practices, it becomes impossible to use this fourth-century compilation for interpreting the intent of the *Didache*.

While the *Apostolic Constitutions* dropped the confession of failings, it revised and expanded the rites surrounding the necessity for mutual reconciliation prior to the eucharist:

> This is why, O bishops, when you are at the point of beginning the [eucharistic] prayer . . . , let the deacon stand near you and call out in a loud voice, "Should any person hold anything

against another, let not that person be a hypocrite!" In this fashion, if there be found those who are in conflict, they will be disturbed in their conscience [and] they will pray to God and be reconciled with their brothers. (2.54.1)

Thus, those who are aware of having been offended are pressed to let their injury be known, right there and then, such that a forgiveness can be offered. Note that the injured party was expected to take the initiative (in contrast to Mt 5:23f.) for, as indicated earlier, anger and resentment were the impediments to having one's prayer received. Note also that anyone not taking the initiative was effectively called a "hypocrite" since he/she, by thinking of remaining silent, only pretended to be reconciled.

The "kiss of peace," which originated in the third-century churches, was no mere handshake and exchange of friendly greetings within the liturgy. Prior to the beginning of the eucharistic prayers, the deacon admonished everyone (as noted above), and then the kiss of peace was given. The exchange of this kiss of peace took some time since it would appear that all the men and all the women exchanged it among themselves in order to familiarly express that they were "at peace" with each other and ready to celebrate the eucharist together. The "kiss" was, in fact, given mouth-to-mouth among the men and among the women who inhabited separate sections of the assembly. In the ancient world, men who were close to each other felt no cultural bias against expressing their affection by a kiss. In northern Africa and in parts of Italy today, one can still discover men kissing men as a mark of mutual friendship and trust.

All in all, therefore, while the confession of failings as practiced in the *Didache* disappeared, the necessity of mutual reconciliation did not. It flourished and became a mainstay of eucharistic practice. The eucharist, therefore, insofar as it was understood as a "sacrifice" was also understood as requiring reconciliation as the prior condition for offering a "pure sacrifice."

It is important to note that the exclusion of the unbaptized from the eucharist is also upheld as directly due to a mandate from "the Lord":

(And) let no one eat or drink from your eucharist
except those baptized in the name of [the] Lord,
    for the Lord has likewise said concerning this:
    "Do not give what is holy to the dogs." (*Did.* 9:5)

Many scholars immediately jump to the conclusion that "the Lord" refers to Jesus here since a word-for-word repetition of this saying is found in Mt 7:6 (Niederwimmer 1998: 153). This seems doubtful for three reasons:

(1) To begin with, the *Didache* is centered on the Father's revelation and never explicitly quotes Jesus, Moses, or anyone else. (2) When a similar formula is used in 14:3, the citation is from Mal 1:11 and, consequently, the appeal to what was "said by [the] Lord" clearly refers to the Lord God. (3) Finally, the context of the saying about "holy things" in Matthew clearly pertains to Jesus' teaching and has no oblique reference to the eucharist. For these reasons, it seems safer to understand that the *Didache* thought of the Lord God when it cited "the Lord" in 9:4.

The saying itself, when read in the context of the *Didache*, clearly understands the eucharistic bread and wine as "holy" and, therefore, not to be given to "the dogs." The reference to "dogs" was pejorative since, in the experience of the first-century hearer, the dog was not a beloved household pet but "the annoying and despised eastern dog of the streets" (*TDNT* 3:1101), who is essentially a wormy, uncared-for, scavenger "commonly consuming flesh not acceptable for humans, such as animal carcasses and even human bodies" (Simoons: 247). In the Christian Scriptures, the term "dogs" is used on multiple occasions as a metaphor to designate the gap between "the children of God" and the gentiles (Mt 15:26f.; Mk 7:26f.; Phil 3:2; 2 Pt 2:22). In rabbinic literature, however, "it is [to] the flesh of [temple] sacrifice that the much quoted saying refers: 'what is holy is not to be released to be eaten by dogs' (*b. Bekhorot* 15a interpreting Dt 12:15; *m. Temurah* 6:5; *b. Temurah* 117a and 130b [actually 17a and 30b]; *b. Sheviit* 11b and *b. Pesahim* 29a)" (*TDNT* 3:1102). In pagan temples, given the absence of refrigeration, excessive numbers of flesh sacrifices resulted in the sacrificial meat being sold in the local meat market. This helps to explain *Did.* 6:3. Among the rabbis, therefore, the saying of *Did.* 9:5 seemed to say that meats offered to the Lord were "holy" and therefore ought not to be fed to dogs (literally) or sold off to "dogs" (metaphorically, the gentiles). The framers of the *Didache*, consequently, had only to redraw the lines between insiders and outsiders, between the children and the dogs, in order to discover that such a saying of the Lord applied to their eucharist. In order to do so, however, the eucharist had to be seen as the equivalent of a temple sacrifice. Thus, the framers of the *Didache* used both Mal 1:11 and this saying to signal their perception of the eucharist as a "sacrifice."

The Community Maintenance of Purity at Qumran

According to the *Manual of Discipline* found in the caves near Qumran, "walking" in the way of God's Torah constituted "an acceptable sacrifice" and "a pleasing freewill offering" (1QS 9:4f.). The sacrifices in the Jerusalem temple and rites of immersion were considered ineffectual: "Anyone who refuses to enter into the society of God . . . cannot be reckoned faultless. Ceremonies of atonement cannot restore his innocence, neither cultic waters his purity" (1QS 2:26; 3:3f.). The members of the community were told, therefore, that only through righteous living did they succeed in "offering the sweet savor of an atoning sacrifice":

> For only through the spirit pervading God's true society can there be atonement for a man's ways. . . . Let him order his steps to walk faultlessly in all the ways of God. . . . Let him turn aside neither to the right nor to the left. . . . Then indeed will he be accepted by God, offering the sweet savor of atoning sacrifice, and then only shall he be a party to the covenant of the eternal *yaḥad* [community]. (1QS 9:6, 9–12)

Since holiness of life in the community was seen as equivalent to offering atoning sacrifices, great care was taken to prepare members for entrance into the community. Novices who came forward were trained by instructors for an unspecified period. When candidates were deemed ready, an initiation ceremony was conducted which included a general confession of failings and a solemn blessing by the priests of the community (1QS 1:24–2:4). Upon entrance to the community, new members still retained a probationary status, and they were not admitted into full fellowship prior to being "initiated further into the secret teaching of the *yaḥad* [community]" (1QS 6:19) and demonstrating that they could live their lives in complete fidelity to the rule given them during a period of two full years. For those who received a positive recommendation of the general fellowship after two successive annual reviews, the full membership granted them meant (a) being enrolled "at the appropriate rank among his brothers for discussion of the Law [Torah]" (1QS 6:22), (b) being admitted to community meals eaten in ritual cleanliness, and (c) combining their assets (held apart by the overseer during the probationary period) into the general treasury.

A member who had been admitted, however, could still lose holiness. The *Manual of Discipline* lists infractions for which various periods of exclusion were warranted (1QS 6:24–7:25). Anyone committing a grave offense against the Torah of Moses "intentionally" was "to be expelled from the society of the *yaḥad* [community], never to return" (1QS 8:22f.). Minor infractions were taken up at community meetings and appropriate remedies were imposed. Some examples:

> Whoever nurses a grudge against his companion—in blatant disregard of the *yaḥad* statute about [offering] reproof on the selfsame day—is to be punished by reduced [namely, one-fourth] rations for six months. . . . Whoever speaks foolishness: three months. Anyone interrupting his companion while in session: ten

days. Anyone who lies down and sleeps in a session of the general membership: thirty days. (1QS 7:8–10)

Stiffer penalties were imposed for infractions that disrupted the well-being of the community:

> The man who gossips about his companion is to be barred for one year from the pure meals of the general membership and punished by reduced rations [as well]. But if a man gossips about the general membership, he is to be banished by them and may never return. (1QS 7:15–17)

By this means, those following the *Manual of Discipline* hoped to maintain a holiness of life that constituted the only acceptable sacrifice pleasing to the Lord. Furthermore, this community saw themselves as destined to become "a temple for Israel" and "true witnesses to justice, chosen by God's will to atone for the land and to recompense the wicked their due" (1QS 8:5f.).

While there is no suspicion that the framers of the *Didache* were influenced by the *Manual of Discipline,* it is, nonetheless, clear that both communities adopted parallel strategies for maintaining fidelity to their respective community rules and for envisioning holiness of life as necessary for offering a pleasing sacrifice. In each instance, both communities depended on an intensive initiation process to guarantee a transformation of life. Once admitted, however, new members were continually held accountable. Minor infractions were dealt with in diverse ways, but in both communities shunning and expulsion were used to remedy serious failings. In both communities, moreover, meal fellowship was regarded as the high point of community existence, and exclusion from meal fellowship was used in order to maintain the "pure sacrifice" of the community. Finally, both communities entirely rejected the animal sacrifices then being offered in the Jerusalem temple and envisioned themselves as offering the true sacrifices acceptable to God.

The Community Maintenance of Purity in the Didache

In the community of the *Didache,* a certain holiness of life and avoidance of broken relationships were required for participation in the eucharistic sacrifice. To begin with, no one was to be baptized until he/she had been trained in the Way of Life. And no one who had not been baptized could be admitted to the eucharistic meal. The reason given: "Do not give what is holy to dogs" (*Did.* 9:5). In rabbinic literature, this saying is repeatedly used as a euphemism for the prohibition against giving the meat sacrificed upon the altar in the temple to gentiles for food (*TDNT* 3:1102). Thus, some possibility exists that the community of the *Didache* embraced this as their own logic for accounting how the saying of the Lord applied to those to be excluded from their eucharist. Thus, one does not have to wait until *Did.* 14 to discover that the eucharistic meal was regarded as a "sacrifice" that must be offered and eaten by those who are morally pure. Furthermore, the strong directive expressed earlier about refraining in all circumstances "from the food sacrificed to idols" (6:3) also points in this direction. Should one buy and prepare such food or eat of it when served by one's host, the *Didache* regarded the mere eating as the "worship of dead gods" (6:3) even when one had no part in the prayers or the pagan sacrifice as such. If mere "eating" was regarded as participation in the worship of pagan gods, then it followed that the community of the *Didache* must be prepared to regard its own "eating" as worship of the living God.

Offering sacrifice was not enough. According to the *Didache*, the confession of failings was positively necessary in order to offer a "pure sacrifice," and the exclusion of unreconciled members was negatively necessary in order to prevent defilement (*Did.* 14:1f.). In those Jewish communities following the *Manual of Discipline*, every infraction required either a reduced participation in the community meals or a more or less extended period of exclusion from them entirely (as detailed above). In the case of the *Didache*, it would appear that the voluntary confession of failings served sufficiently to manifest the *teshuvah* that made a person capable of offering a "pure sacrifice" (14:1). In part, the contrast with the *Manual of Discipline* could be explained by noting that baptism and full inclusion in the community came not after two years of demonstrated fidelity but only after training in the way and beginning to bear "the yoke" of the Lord (*Did.* 6:2). Under these circumstances, failings were to be expected, since one was admitting persons still partially addicted to pagan ways. Thus, "confession in full" served not only to allow new members to examine their conduct and to freely acknowledge their errors; it also served as a reminder that, in the eyes of all, the Way of Life was being recognized and revered. Far from immediately excluding persons who had failed, therefore, the Didache community opted to embrace the broken and the fallen as fit subjects to offer "pure sacrifice" to God.

Even in the *Didache*, however, tolerance for progressive holiness had its limits. In one case, that of an unresolved interpersonal conflict, persons involved *had to be excluded,* for their inclusion was perceived as risking defilement of the community sacrifice (*Did.* 14:2). How so? First, one must try to imagine how a grave failing such as practicing divination, when confessed, offered no obstacle to a pure sacrifice while a petty quarreling, even should it be confessed, could not be tolerated unless reconciliation was effected. To begin with, one must call to mind my opening observation that we are dealing here with table fellowship wherein no anonymity was possible. When even one person at table was visibly upset or angry, everyone was immediately affected. Like it or not, in the face of any dispute, persons would be prompted to take sides—to favor one party over another. An unresolved dispute involving two persons, therefore, could potentially divide the entire community. Even beyond this, however, the very eucharistic prayers include petitioning the Father to gather them together into his kingdom at the end of time (*Did.* 9:4; 10:5). Such a prayer would have to stick in the throat of those who knew of someone whom they did not want to see or encounter, much less to eat with. Such persons could not properly join in this expectation of being united in the future; hence, they risked rendering the sacrifice of the community "unclean," because their hearts denied what their words expressed.

Conclusion

This study began by noting that "sacrifice" was a common phenomenon in the ancient world and that the "spiritualization" of sacrifice was a widespread response to the traditional piety of offering animal sacrifices. Along the way, we discovered that the Didache community was so bent on offering suitable worship to God that they set up two distinct safeguards: no unbaptized or unreconciled person was admitted (9:5) and the confession of failings was to be held prior to the eucharist on the Lord's Day (14:1). These practices had the effect of enforcing the divinely revealed standards of holiness cherished by the community members. No one could keep coming back week after week and repeatedly confess the same failing. Thus, in a community out of step with the rest of society, the confession of failings served to recall both backsliders and forgetters to those standards of conduct revealed to them during their preparation for baptism.

Rather than avoid conflict, the community of the *Didache* trained its members to judge supportively and to reconcile boldly (4:3 and 15:3). The Didache community was not leaderless (as the following chapter will show), yet those functions understood to be vital to all were wisely set out as incumbent upon all. Thus every novice being prepared for community living was trained to get ready: "You will judge justly; you will not take into account social status when it comes time to reprove against failings" (4:3).

Only a community that knows how to confront the evil in its own midst can be taken seriously. Only the community that knows how to stimulate and to enable its own members to be perfected in clearly defined standards of excellence can expect permanently to diminish evil without maintaining a police force. The eucharist of the *Didache*, therefore, served not only to evoke the hope of the future kingdom; it served to stimulate practical processes whereby the holiness necessary for entrance into the kingdom could be sustained and enlarged. The weight and the promise of the eucharistic meal thus overflowed into bringing the anticipated kingdom closer at hand. The practical wisdom of the framers of the *Didache* was that they knew how to light many small candles rather than curse the darkness.

#81 SACRIFICIAL MEALS IN FEMALE-DOMINATED RELIGIONS

Susan Starr Sered provides an analysis of "sacrifice" from the vantage point of her cross-cultural anthropological study of religions dominated by women. Sered discovered that "in women's religions food rituals rarely include animal sacrifice" (136), while in "male-dominated religions in patrilineal societies" animal sacrifice is almost universally practiced (137). Food rituals, Sered points out, are favored by women because this is the domain where they are in charge and where their preference for acting in solidarity can be best expressed:

> In most cultures, women prepare food. Thus it is not surprising that food rituals are important to women. Food is a resource that women control, and food rituals sacralize women's everyday activities of cooking and serving. By sharing food with the gods, profane work becomes elevated to sacred ritual. Even in male-dominated religions women are often responsible for preparing ritual foods (although the public food ceremony is typically conducted by men; e.g., Jewish women cook for the Sabbath and men recite the kiddush [the blessing over the food]). (136)

Sered also makes a telling point about the quantity and quality of sacred food:

> Food rituals in women's religions share several significant characteristics. To begin with, the foods used in female-dominated religions are not served in small symbolic portions. No Catholic Church style eucharist ceremonies have been reported here. Instead, we have seen large quantities of elaborately prepared food. (136)

Sered's study is important for the understanding of the *Didache*. Clearly the framers of the *Didache* could have elected to identify their "sacrifice" as their holiness of life (see #8f) or as their daily prayers (as does Heb 13:15) rather than the weekly eucharistic meal. Even if a meal was elected, the emphasis could have been on token amounts of sacred food rather than on a full, festive meal (*Did.* 10:1). Furthermore, the framers of the *Didache* could have elected to burn part of the meal so that it ascended upward to the Father:

> In women's religions food for the deity is eaten by human par-
> ticipants and not sent up as burnt offerings. I believe this is con-
> sistent with the interpersonal emphases of women's religions. . . .
> In women's religions neither people (shamans) nor offerings
> (food) ascend; rather, gods, spirits, and ancestors descend and
> join in the communal, human experience. (Sered: 138)

Here again, one can appreciate the stark difference between Jesus ascend-
ing to the heavenly sanctuary to offer "his own blood" (Heb 9:11) and his
"body" (Heb 10:10) as the once and for all time eternal sacrifice as
opposed to the *Didache* proposing that weekly meals here on earth with
the community become the locus of true sacrifice. The prayers of the
Didache, moreover, point in the direction of God coming to them to
gather the elect wherever they are found (8:2; 9:4; 10:5; 16:7f.) rather
than having the elect being caught up in rapture "in the clouds" (1 Thes
4:17). All these things taken together indicate that Sered would classify the
Didache as a religion shaped by women.

At an earlier point in this study (see #1g), the disproportionate number
of women in the Jesus movement was shown to provide conditions in
which "women will enjoy relatively greater power and freedom" (Stark:
102). This conclusion can now come together with the discoveries of
Sered suggesting that the very identification of the eucharistic meal as
"sacrifice" favored women's interests over and against the men's. This
would mean that the framers of the *Didache* were either men extraordi-
narily sensitive to the perspectives and interests of their sisters (who formed
60 percent of the membership) or that women's voices were well represented among the framers of the *Didache* themselves.

What Robert Daly has so marvelously classified as the "spiritualization
of sacrifice," therefore, may need to be corrected and nuanced by studies
such as those of Sered. Needless to say, such a study goes beyond the scope
of this present book. In the future, however, it might be possible to differentiate between the "spiritualization" going on in various communities
(e.g., in Hebrews, in the Pauline letters, in the *Didache*) by reference to
the degree of "feminization of sacrifice" that each exhibits.

#8J WHETHER THE EUCHARIST WAS CELEBRATED ON SATURDAY OR SUNDAY

While Paul was in Troas, Acts records the following:

> On the first day of the week, when we met to break bread, Paul
> was holding a discussion with them; since he intended to leave

the next day, he continued speaking until midnight. There were many lamps in the room upstairs where we were meeting. (Acts 20:7f.)

If one allows that "breaking bread" was the familiar euphemism for "celebrating the Lord's Supper [eucharist]," then it remains to be determined whether "the first [day] of the week" (Acts 20:7) meant Saturday or Sunday. Willy Rordorf, as part of his far-reaching study of the origins of Sunday as the day of worship, concludes that texts such as Acts 20:7 confirm that "Sunday evening" (1968: 247) was the designated time for the eucharistic meal. Thus, even before the seven-day week was adopted by the Romans and the days assigned names in their calendar (see #4a), what the second century would call "the day of the Sun" was the preferential day for celebrating the eucharist. Samuele Bacchiocchi, reviewing all the evidence of Rordorf, comes to a different conclusion. Following the Jewish reckoning, "the first day of the week" would have begun at sundown on Saturday and extended to sundown on Sunday. Thus, the evening eucharistic meal of Acts 20:7 would have taken place on Saturday evening. This latter judgment is to be preferred. However, "we must resist any temptation to use Luke's account as though it were a paradigm of 'first day' observance" (Turner 1982: 133).

As for the *Didache*, the significance of "divinely instituted (*kyriachēn*) day" (14:1) is also contested. Given that the Jewish calendar dominates the *Didache* (see ch. 4), the "divinely instituted day" could refer to either the Sabbath or the first day of the week. While Bacchiocchi overstates Sabbath observance in the early church (Turner 1982: 136f.), he is correct in noting that the use of *kyriachos* in Rv 1:10 does not allow one to decide that this refers to "the first day of the week, the day of Christian worship" (1977: 112f.; Stott: 70–75). Among the three uses of this term during the second century (which Bacchiocchi designates as *Did.* 14:1, Ignatius's *Epistle to the Magnesians* 9.1, and the *Gospel of Peter* 35.50) only the last allows the term to be unmistakably identified (Bacchiocchi 1977:113). In two different verses, the *Gospel of Peter* reads:

Now in the night in which the divinely instituted day (*hē kyriachē*) dawned, when the soldiers, two by two in every watch, were keeping guard, there rang out a loud voice in heaven. . . . (35)

Early in the morning of the divinely instituted day (*tēs kyriachēs*) Mary Magdalene . . . took with her women friends and came to the sepulcher where he was laid. (50f.)

Following the Jewish reckoning of days which typifies the entire *Gospel of Peter*, one must conclude that *kyriakos* ("divinely instituted" or "belonging to the Lord") is here used to designate the "first day of the week" and not the "Sunday" of the Roman solar week. Given the fact that the eucharistic meal was a full meal and that the day of worship more often than not fell on a work day (according to the Roman calendar), one can surmise that the Didache community celebrated the eucharist after sunset. Thus, according to *Did*. 14:1, the eucharist would be celebrated every Saturday evening (in the Roman reckoning). Passages such as *Did*. 11:9 and 16:2 leave open the possibility that the eucharist was celebrated at other times as well.

All in all, therefore, the opinion of scholars remains divided. Scholars such as Rordorf and Foerster (*TDNT* 3:1095f.) interpret *Did*. 14:1 as signaling Sunday evening, while scholars such as Bacchiocchi and Harald Riesenfeld (111–38) favor Saturday evening. In my judgment, the latter opinion is to be preferred.

I pass over the opinion of some that *Did*. 14:1 originally meant Easter Sunday, thereby making the confession of failings and the eucharist that followed an annual affair (Dugmore: 275–77; Strand 1982a: 348). Niederwimmer refers to this opinion as "highly questionable" (1998: 195 n. 8).

#8K WHETHER *DID*. 14 WAS ADDED LATER

Scholars have noted that *Did*. 9–10 deals with the eucharist and that, following a long digression regarding prophets and first fruits, *Did*. 14 takes up the topic of the confession of failings that ought to take place prior to the eucharist. This awkward chronological placement of *Did*. 14 has convinced many scholars that this section was a later addition by a second editor (see discussion of Rordorf 1998: 226–29) or, minimally, was an afterthought by the first editor "because experience has demonstrated, in the meantime, the inadequacy of the instructions of 9–10" (Audet 1958: 460; see discussion of Niederwimmer 1998: 194 n. 2). I believe that a strong case can be made for the unity of the *Didache*, which entirely overcomes the seemingly awkward placement of *Did*. 14:1–3.

Earlier in this volume, it was shown that the sequence of rules in the *Didache* can be very satisfactorily explained in view of the progression of experience of a new member (ch. 3). Thus, for example, the rule regarding food sacrificed to idols (6:2), the rule regarding fasting (8:1), and the rule regarding the daily rhythms of prayer (8:2) appear to be out of place or haphazardly spliced together until one discovers that the sequence, at each point, closely follows the progression of experiences proper to the newly admitted member of the community. This key to the internal logic also serves, I believe, to account for why *Did*. 14 was not presented just prior to *Did*. 9–10 where one might ordinarily expect it:

When one encounters the eucharistic prayers (*Did.* 9–10), the confession of failings is curiously omitted. Many scholars read this as an indication of the fact that the *Didache* is a collage of pre-existing documents assembled over a period of time and never attaining anywhere near a full integration. My surmise, on the contrary, is that this omission of this confession of failings is deliberate and signals what everyone knew, namely that the order of events within the *Didache* follows the order in which a candidate comes to experience these events. Thus, if my surmise is correct, the eucharist in the *Didache* represents the "the first eucharist" and the omission of the confession of failings at this point deliberately points to the fact that this public confession was suppressed if and when new candidates were baptized just prior to the eucharist. Many reasons could be put forward to sustain suppressing a public confession of failings at the time of a Baptism. Foremost among them would be the fittingness of welcoming the new "brothers" and "sisters" who had just been baptized without confronting them with a recital of the failings of members. Thus, the linguistic clues of the *Didache* itself incline me to believe that baptism was preferentially celebrated prior to the "first eucharist" (*Did.* 9–10) and that, on these occasions, the confession of failings was supplanted by the baptism itself (chapter 3).

The rules regarding the confession of failings and the exclusion of quarreling members, therefore, represent what new members would need in order to prepare themselves for the second and subsequent gatherings for the eucharist. It sufficed, therefore, to give the candidate an intimation of what was to come at the end of his/her training in the Way of Life (*Did.* 4:14), but then the details are set out only following the first eucharist (*Did.* 9–10).

One might be tempted to allow that the novices never had any experience of prophets in action prior to their first eucharist. Thus, the seemingly sudden and unexpected appearance of *Did.* 10:7 may not only follow the progression of the eucharist but also, and more importantly, the progression of experience of the new member(s). Once they had been bedazzled by prophets in action, it then became important to spell out the set of cautionary rules governing the stay of prophets within the community. Since, following the first eucharist, the new members mingled familiarly within their new family (including, in many instances, lodging and working with them as well), they would have ample occasion to encounter (and maybe even to be shocked by) apostle-prophets and other visitors (*Did.* 12:1–5). Then, for the first time, there would have been the occasion to enter into the spirit of gratitude represented by the offering of first fruits to the Lord through the prophets (*Did.* 13). All these things would take place prior to the second eucharist, when the instruction of *Did.* 14 would be applicable.

All in all, therefore, the progression from *Did.* 10:7 to *Did.* 14 makes eminent sense when one keeps in mind the postbaptismal training that new members would need in accord with the progressive unfolding of new experiences following baptism. Needless to say, other factors are also operative in the design and progression of the rules (e.g., the general rules regarding nonprophetic visitors fits nicely after the rules regarding prophetic visitors), but the underlying architecture appears to be designed to follow the experience and the associated training appropriate to new members.

The use of the second person singular in this section is also revelatory. The last use of the singular was in *Did.* 7:2–4 where it was a question of the mentor (the one baptizing) deciding on the most suitable form of water and instructing various persons to fast. The rules for fasting and praying that follow (8:1–10:6), however, are clearly formulated in the plural, since fasting and praying are here understood as communal activities (as shown in chs. 3 and 4). The same goes for the rules regarding visitors (*Did.* 11–13). An apostle-prophet or an ordinary Christian may lodge in the home of a particular individual; however, the understanding was that the whole community received, tested, and sustained him/her. Even the tested prophet is spoken of as settling down "among ÿou (plural)" (13:1) indicating the collective responsibility involved in such an arrangement. Immediately, however, when first fruits are spoken of, everything shifts to the second person singular (13:3–7). While some may be tempted to say that the source was formulated in the singular and the creator of the *Didache* was constrained to retain it as he found it, this presents a wooden use of sources and overlooks the essential oral character of the *Didache*. Rather, the use of the singular must be approached as deliberate and carefully crafted to fit the material itself as used by its membership.

Why, then, are the rules for first fruits given in the second person singular? My surmise is that the decision as to when and how much of a thanksgiving offering is to be set aside in gratitude for the Lord falls upon the individual. Baking bread and opening a jar of oil are actions carried out by individuals in the context of particular households. Furthermore, the use of the singular suggests that each individual decides how much to set aside and when to present this to the prophet. Even in the Hebrew Scriptures, the entire text implies that individuals bring their baskets of first fruits to the priest one by one and make an individual profession: "I bring the first of the fruit of the ground that you, O LORD, have given me" (Dt 26:10). Thus, following this tradition, the use of the singular in the *Didache* can be understood as sustaining this tradition. The prophet, consequently, would not receive the first fruits of the community collectively and offer a prayer of thanksgiving for them all; rather, each presented his/her first fruit and the prophet, as a consequence, said an individual prayer for each one coming.

All in all, therefore, transitions to the second person singular as well as transitions from one topic to the next provide valuable clues for unraveling the internal logic that guided the framers of the *Didache* in their composition. Those who ignore these clues or reduce them to "givens" depending on preexisting sources fail to appreciate something of the depth and deliberateness of the pastoral genius of the *Didache*. In the end, the tacit scheme underlying the progression of topics and the use of the second person singular may be more complex or simpler than the one I have discovered; nonetheless, that there is an underlying scheme cannot be doubted. The task is to discover what is there lying below the surface waiting to be brought into the light.

9
Community Organization in a Companionship of Empowerment

Honoring Bishops and Deacons

APPOINT FOR YOURSELVES
BISHOPS AND DEACONS WORTHY
OF THE LORD, MEN WHO ARE
GENTLE, NOT MONEY-LOVING, TRUTH-
FUL, AND TESTED; FOR TO YOU
THEY LIKEWISE GRATUITOUSLY SERVE
THE UNPAID PUBLIC SERVICE OF
THE PROPHET-TEACHERS. DO NOT,
THEN, LOOK DOWN UPON THEM
FOR THEY THEMSELVES ARE YOUR
HONORED ONES IN COMPANY WITH
THE PROPHET-TEACHERS.

Contents

Background Discussion Found in Boxes

At first glance, the *Didache* seems to be bereft of any formal community organization based upon privilege or patriarchy. Chapter 1 demonstrated that trainers/teachers were the heart and soul of the formation of novices; yet, when it came to baptism, daily prayers, and the eucharist, no special role was specifically assigned to any person or any class of persons in the administration of these rites. This, of course, does not mean that everyone *did* baptize or preside at the eucharist. In any given circumstance, it would have been recognized that this or that person was more suited to do these things. Thus, it was argued that the baptism of novices and their first eucharist would be presided over by the spiritual "mothers" and "fathers" who trained them. The logic of the rite itself allowed them to say, "You have accepted me as your sister, now you must accept this one whom I bring before you and baptize as your sister as well" (ch. 3). Hence they would have been chosen as the most appropriate presiders *at that time*. At other times, other choices would be made. At no time did the community exclude, in principle, potential presiders on the basis of gender, race, economic status, marital status, or social status. Thus, according to Elisabeth Schüssler Fiorenza, a certain "discipleship of equals" (1984: 147–51) did prevail, but not one that overlooked the presence of "mothers" and "fathers" and "prophets" having their appropriate functions at appropriate times. For this reason, it seems preferable to describe the community as a "companionship of empowerment" (Crossan 1998: 337).

In the last chapter, it was discovered that no one was assigned to lead or to exempt themselves from the public confession of faults and the responsibility of reproving backsliders. Everyone did it, and everyone was responsible for doing it. Yet this does mean that everyone did it with equal pastoral tact—knowing when to be tender or when to be stern, knowing when to reprove privately or when to do it in the presence of witnesses, knowing when to use few words or when to use many, and so on. Moreover, the one reproving generally is most effective when the one straying holds him/her dear. Even in the case of the traveling prophets, seemingly everyone in the community was obliged to keep prophets operating within the defined boundaries and to give them the silent treatment should they overstep their bounds. But this does not mean that everyone had the courage and the wisdom to challenge prophets. All in all, it would appear that, while a certain equality of membership was the order of the day, in a given circumstance, some would deliberately hold back and wait for others to exercise their special gifts as needed.

Just when all this seems evident, suddenly the *Didache* speaks of appointing "bishops and deacons worthy of the Lord" (15:1f.). Does this mean that the egalitarian image of the *Didache* bursts? Many scholars would think so. For them, the presiders at baptism and eucharist have at last appeared. Now the confession of failings and the reproving/shunning of deviants come into sure hands. Yet, upon a second look, maybe all of the egalitarian glow is not lost. The bishops and deacons were elected/ appointed by the community at large and were, accordingly, accountable to the community, even to the point of being open to censure and removal by the community. One does not find here any hint that somehow a founding apostle stands behind the appointment (as in Acts 14:23; 1 Tm 5:17– 22; *1 Clem.* 44.3) and that only this apostle could remove them. Neither does one find any hint that outside bishops were brought in for an episcopal consecration and that somehow the office was lifted beyond the reach of local evaluation. Going further, even if any given bishop did, on one occasion preside, the *Didache* would seemingly admonish even this bishop to confess "your failings, so that your sacrifice may be pure" (*Did.* 14:1). Apparently, such a public confession did not have the effect of degrading the dignity required by the episcopal office. And what is one to make of novices being trained to "not take into account social status when it comes time to reprove against failings" (*Did.* 4:3)? Does this give a "recent novice" the mandate to censure a "bishop" in cases of necessity when no one else comes forward or when no one else is even informed. Assuredly. When all is said and done, therefore, the appearance of "bishops and deacons" in the *Didache* ought not to be confused with the installation of an ecclesiastical hierarchy that suddenly takes over most of the roles and privileges that have been already assigned. This will have to be investigated.

Election of Local Overseers

Didache 15:1 instructs the congregation to "appoint . . . for yourselves" local overseers. Three observations seem to be in order:

1. The framers of the *Didache* present this rule without any fanfare or any injunction of the Lord (as in *Did.* 14:3); hence, one can presume that the communities had already been functioning according to this rule (Niederwimmer 1998: 200). Thus, this rule should not be read as having any more solemnity than if the framers had said, "Keep up your good work at appointing worthy officers for yourselves."

2. The term *episkopos* ("bishop") was at this time an entirely secular term for designating someone charged with oversight (see #9a). The term had nothing to do with power or presiding. The use of the term "bishops" therefore must be entirely divested of all the ecclesiastical trappings if one is to understand it within the context of the *Didache*.

3. The reason for this rule for appointing overseers appears to be directed toward supporting the honor of these local overseers in the face of charismatic prophets and teachers (15:2). In effect, therefore, "bishops"

were the underdogs who needed shoring up. More will be said regarding this shortly.

In the synagogues, Jews were accustomed to electing "elders," and free elections also took place in various Roman associations and clubs (see, e.g., #2n). Niederwimmer makes a point of insisting that *cheirotonein* here means "choose" or "elect," not "appoint" (Niederwimmer 1998: 200). This Greek term is ambiguous. In Acts 14:23, the term designates that Barnabas and Paul "appointed" elders for the churches they founded. In 2 Cor 8:19, however, entire congregations "choose" or "elect" Titus as a "fellow worker" to accompany Paul and as an "apostle" (*apostolos*) sent by their churches (2 Cor 8:23). Niederwimmer's point seems to be that in the *Didache* there is no superior authority (such as a founding apostle) to make local appointments; hence, "the Didachist calls on the community to choose their own officers or representatives from among themselves" (Niederwimmer 1998: 200).

#9A THE MEANING AND FUNCTION OF "BISHOPS"

In classical Greek, the term *episkopos* could be used "to describe a deity (e.g., Artemis in Elis) as the one who keeps watch over a country or people, and in particular over the keeping of treaties and the markets" (C. Brown: 1:189). In the plural, this term was often "given to men who had a responsible position in the state":

> The title was given to officials . . . sent from Athens to dependent states to ensure order or to fix their constitutions. In Rhodes they are mentioned together with councilors, treasurers, secretaries and military strategists. . . . Syrian records use the title for members of a committee of control for building or a board of trustees. (C. Brown: 1:189)

This term was not normally associated with any religious office or ministry—a fact that will become increasingly important as this chapter proceeds.

The term *episkopos* ("bishop") occurs only four times in the Christian Scriptures and thirteen times in the Septuagint. The Greek term points to someone who has oversight over a group of people, for example, someone in charge of a construction site or someone supervising grape harvesters. The Septuagint, for instance, uses this very term when it presents Joseph as advising the Pharaoh "to appoint overseers [lit., "bishops"] over the land, and take [and store] a fifth part of the produce of the land of Egypt during the seven plenteous years" (Gn 41:34).

The terms *episkopoi* ("bishops") and *presbyteroi* ("elders") were often used interchangeably (e.g., Acts 20:17, 28; Ti 1:5–7; 7:1; 1 Tm 3:1; 5:17; *1 Clem.* 44) (Burtchaell: 297; R. Brown 1980: 333f.). This is so because *zeqēnim* ("elders") was the widely used Hebrew term designating the members of a Jewish administrative council. The term *zeqēnim* ("elders") can be literally translated as *presbyteroi* ("elders"), but in Greek this term may be unclear because it focuses on the advanced age of the person. The preferred term in Greek, therefore, was *episkopoi* ("bishops"). Acts suggests this equivalence when, in Ephesus, Paul assembled the "elders of the church" and urged them to be watchful over "the flock in which the Holy Spirit has made you guardians [lit., 'bishops']" (Acts 20:28). This is the first instance in which "elders" were spoken of as functioning as "bishops/overseers"—terms that during the course of the next hundred years would be used interchangeably in many church contexts.

#9B ELECTION OF BISHOPS

The tradition of the local church designating an individual from its own ranks for a pastoral office has a long tradition. In Acts 6:1–6, for example, the twelve apostles do not select the seven whom they will ordain but wisely allow the Greek-speaking Christians to discern among themselves who is "full of the Spirit and of wisdom" (Acts 6:3). Even with the development of the monarchical bishop in the third century, the normal way of selecting a new bishop was to have the local clergy choose the best candidate among themselves and to see whether the entire congregation gathered in the cathedral church would endorse their choice. Pope Leo I (d. 461 C.E.) put the matter quite succinctly: "He who must preside over all must be chosen by all" (*Ad Anast. Patrologia Latina* 54, 634).

#9C THE MEANING AND FUNCTION OF "DEACONS"

The meaning of the noun *diakonos* in classical Greek reflects the various meanings associated with the verb *diakonein*:

(a) to wait at table; this is expanded to (b) care for household needs, and from this to the general meaning (c) to serve generally. The first meaning involves personal subjection which was considered unworthy and dishonoring for a free man. When used in the third sense it can be service for a cause, e.g. for the good of the community . . . or for a god. As such it is an honorable task and a fitting occupation for a free man. (C. Brown: 3:545)

Church tradition and popular piety have viewed the seven men ordained by the twelve apostles in Acts 6 as "deacons." Modern scholars, however, have been hesitant to credit these views as what Luke had in mind. Why so? In the first place, Luke never explicitly names the seven as "deacons." In the second place, while the term "deacon" (*diakonos*) occurs some thirty times in the Christian Scriptures, it almost never designates a specific office but rather points to "serving" as the special character of all Christian ministry. For example, Paul frequently designates himself as "a deacon" (1 Cor 3:5; 2 Cor 3:6; 6:4; Eph 3:7; Phil 1:1; Col 1:23, 25), and in two instances he does not hesitate to designate Jesus as "deacon" (Rom 13:4; 15:8). Finally, when it comes time for Luke to specify what the Seven do, Stephen and Philip are routinely characterized as doing public preaching, healing, and exorcism (Acts 6:8–10; 8:6–13)—the very same ministries Luke designates for the Twelve. As a result, a growing number of scholars would be more inclined to perceive the Seven as taking on the identity and ministry of the Twelve insofar as the Hellenists are concerned. Raymond Brown, for instance, concludes that "they [the Seven] seem to have been the top-level administrators for the Hellenistic Christians" (1980: 326). Nothing in Acts 6, therefore, ought to be used in order to determine what the *Didache* has in mind when it speaks of "deacons" (*diakonoi*).

Where Is the Rub Between Bishops and Prophets?

Didache 15:2 is aimed at reconciliation (Niederwimmer 1998: 200). On the one hand, one has prophets; on the other hand, one has bishops. The first are charismatics who have settled recently in the community (13:1f.); the latter are longtime members who have been elected to office. The mood of the framers of the *Didache* is defensive. When the members were told, "Do not look down upon them [the bishops]" (*Did.* 15:2), one can be sure that many had indeed *done just this*. Why? Three suggestions come to mind based on what has been discovered in earlier chapters:

1. *Contrasting styles of prayer.* Niederwimmer suggests that "the worship service . . . formerly was in the hands of the prophets and teachers alone" (1998: 202) and that now both groups shared it. The *Didache* does not support this hypothesis (see #60). Nonetheless, Niederwimmer may be touching the edge of the problem.

In chapter 5, it was noted how presiders were expected to improvise within the guidelines provided by *Did.* 9–10, whereas prophets were given the right to give thanks as the Spirit led them (*Did.* 10:7). The liturgy of the presiders was predictable and well ordered; the liturgy of the prophets was exciting and demanding. While the role of presider was not limited to bishops, one can surmise that the bishops did sometimes function as eucharistic celebrants or appoint others to do so.

The prophets, for their part, did none of these things. They were the charismatic zealots for the kingdom. When they arrived, they naturally drew attention to themselves. During the liturgy they may have closed their eyes or audibly groaned as they afflicted their spirits in order to join in sympathy with God's pathos. When it came to their part of the liturgy, they exploded into prayers of anguish and pain, prayers of delight and expectation, prayers of fire and blood. When it was all over, everyone was spellbound by the prophets and repeated their words for many days to come.

Here, then, is the principal arena wherein the charismatics completely outclassed the bishops and deacons. Hence the words: "Do not look down upon them; for they themselves are your honored ones in company with the prophet-teachers" (15:2).

2. *Contrasting spiritualities.* Another arena of tension is the contrast between the spirituality of the bishops and the spirituality of the prophets. The bishops' role was to uphold ordinary holiness in the prosaic ins and outs of the everyday affair of raising children, working in the shop, sharing "family" meals.

The charismatics, on the other hand, were given to extraordinary feats of holiness. To begin with, these were the ones who had slipped down into the depths of poverty and come up out of it with an unbounded confidence in God and his future. They were the ones who had abandoned home, family, and work in order to live as precarious vagabonds bent on heralding God's future.

Here, too, the charismatics outclassed the bishops and deacons. Hence the words: "Do not look down upon them; for they themselves are your honored ones in company with the prophet-teachers" (15:2).

3. *Contrasting senses of how soon.* A final arena that suggests itself is the contrast between how differently the bishops and the prophets awaited the kingdom. The bishops had to make practical preparations for the long haul. For example, they may have had to ensure that shops maintained production goals when key workers were sick or injured. At another point, they may have had to negotiate for buying a plot of land for the burial of members of the community.

The prophets, in contrast, woke each morning in the expectation that the Lord was lacing his sandals and getting ready to come. They did not wake up every hour of the night to feed and comfort a colicky baby. They did not make provisions for an elderly parent who was nearly blind and needed help to function almost on an hourly basis. They did not have to deal with depression and chronic fatigue. For the prophet, everything would be resolved as soon as the Lord arrived. His angels would rock fussy babies in their arms. He himself would give strength to the weak and sight to the blind. Weavers would sing his praise at their looms and smiths would keep time with their hammers. By and by the prophets fanned the flames of hope and, in so doing, made it possible for practical sorts (like the bishops and deacons) to keep things humming without the added burden of depression and hopelessness.

Here, then, is the final arena wherein the charismatics completely outclassed the bishops and deacons—in distributing the healing balm of hope. Hence the words: "Do not look down upon them; for they themselves are your honored ones in company with the prophet-teachers" (15:2) in this arena as well.

All in all, there was bound to be a conflict between the prophets and the bishops. They prayed differently. They lived differently. They hoped differently. Yet the framers of the *Didache* had the good sense to realize that all were blessed by having such polar opposites functioning in their midst. The pragmatic bishops and deacons, to be sure, did not have the same flare, the same exuberance, the same upbeat assurance as did the prophet-teachers, yet the framers of the *Didache* insisted that "to you they minister" (15:1) for "they themselves are your honored ones" (15:2) along with the romantic prophets.

Criteria for Selection

The framers of the *Didache* specified that candidates ought to be selected who were "worthy of the Lord" (15:1; also Ignatius *Ephesians* 2.1; 4.1; 15.1; *Magnesians* 12). This phrase indicates that candidates chosen ought to be men whom the Lord would endorse. Four specific qualifications are highlighted.

1. The requirement of being gentle (*praüs*) ("mild-tempered"; Niederwimmer 1998: 201) repeats the general admonition to all members (*Did.* 3:7) as part of the Way of Life. The following phrases bear something of the same sentiments: "do not lord it over those in your charge" (1 Pt 5:3); "not violent but gentle (*epieikē*)" (1 Tm 3:3), "not violent" (Ti 1:7). This requirement would presuppose that the candidates were expected not to push their weight around but to act collaboratively, consultatively, and sensitively.

2. The requirement of *aphilargyros* (lit., "not-loving-money") is repeated in 1 Tm 3:3 and finds close approximations in the two other lists:

"not for sordid gain (*aischrokerdōs*)" (1 Pt 5:2) and "not greedy for gain (*aischrokerdēs*)" (Ti 1:7). This common tradition suggests that the office holder exercised responsibility for collecting and dispensing community funds; hence, someone who was greedy would be prone to mismanage funds (Niederwimmer 1998: 201).

3. The requirement of being "truthful" finds no parallels in the texts considered. The term *alēthēs* (lit., "not-forgetting") can refer to acting "truthfully, righteously, honestly" or to being "real, genuine" (Bauer: 36) as in *Did.* 11:11; 13:1f. Matthew 22:16; Mk 12:14; and Jn 7:18 use this term in reference to Jesus. While one might be tempted to see this quality as applying to honesty in financial matters, yet most probably this signaled the requirement that an officer had to assess, report, and act upon the expressed needs of the community honestly and accurately.

4. The requirement of being "tested" points in the direction of ensuring reliability. Teachers and prophets were to be tested (*Did.* 11). The character of this testing undoubtedly changed according to the office to be filled. In the case of bishops, one would suspect that recent converts were to be excluded (as in 1 Tm 3:6; Niederwimmer 1998: 201). More especially, one would suspect that candidates were judged on the basis of how well they managed their own families (as in 1 Tm 3:4), for the community was nothing less than an extended "family."

Ordinary members of the community were expected to understand these qualifications and to apply them in choosing among the possible candidates. The selection or election process, therefore, was not to be based on popularity or on the personal aspirations of the candidate but upon a discernment process into the character of alternative candidates. More will be said about this later.

One is reminded here of the comparable texts found in 1 Tm 3:1–10; Ti 1:5–11; and 1 Pt 5:1–4. These texts, however, come from a period later than the *Didache* when the qualifications were multiplied and those pertaining to "bishops" were distinguished from those pertaining to "deacons." Moreover, 1 Tim 3:2 required a bishop to be "an apt teacher"—a function that "bishops" in the Pauline communities may have taken on at the beginning of the second century in order to meet new needs. In any case, the *Didache* says nothing of teaching or preaching or presiding as qualifications for the desired candidates, and care must be taken not to presume to allow the later "Paul" to fill in the silence. Thus, based on the qualifications sought, it would safe to conclude that bishops were not normally looked to for teaching, preaching, and presiding. In the third century, the term "bishop" was reserved for the chief pastor/teacher/celebrant in the urban churches. In the mid-first century, this same term, always used in the plural, does not yet include these functions.

If the bishop is designated by the ordinary term for an "overseer," then one must be careful not to presume that the bishop did everything of importance. When a "bishop" is in charge of a theater (as depicted in the 1999 film *Shakespeare in Love*), for instance, he does not thereby become writer, director, choreographer, costume designer, and leading actor. In fact, he is most probably neither trained nor temperamentally suited for these roles, and, for the success of the theater, he coordinates the particular skills of many others. Should he agree to take a part, it would be a minor one indeed. The same thing could be said of a "bishop" in charge of a construction crew. He does not presume thereby to become the chief architect, stonecutter, mason, or the like. In fact, if he attempts to do too much (by competing with the roles of others), he would neglect and fail at his role as "overseer." The same thing can be applied to the role of "bishop" within the Didache communities. The very choice of the term and the very qualifications named require one to think of someone with the talent of coordinating the skills of many others rather than trying to do too much himself.

The association of "bishops" with "deacons" is curious. If the deacons (*diakonoi*) are "table servants," as their name literally suggests, this might signal that they were assigned the tasks of arriving early, arranging the tables, preparing the foods, and serving the meal itself when the community gathered each week. Bishops, in association with such deacons, might then be fittingly named as those who acted like managers who brought together the needed provisions and assigned roles to each of the cooks/waiters. Such managers might conceivably be chosen from among those more prosperous members of the community who owned larger homes where the community could meet. Their oversight in this arena would be an extension of what large householders were accustomed to whenever a dinner party was being planned. This would also help to explain why they would preside at the meal itself and thus be in a position to lead the eucharistic prayers or assign others to do the same, and how and why they would be overlooked and not be given due honor as the *Didache* suggests.

On the other hand, it is also possible that the Greek text want us to see not two distinct offices ("bishops" and "deacons") but only one ("bishops who are deacons"). The fact that two sets of qualifications are not mentioned (as in 1 Tm 3), one for bishops and one for deacons, would argue in favor of seeing the *kai diakonous* as an attributive modifier that was meant to be read, "overseers who are also table servants." In any case, the twofold repetition of *tōn prophētōn kai didaskalōn* (15:1, 2) most probably also signals an attributive modifier since the second noun lacks the definite article (as in 11:3); thus: "prophets who are also teachers" or "prophet-teachers." On the other hand, the *Didache* is not rigorous in its use of definite articles; hence, the issue cannot be decided on the basis of Greek construction alone. The teachers were "mentors" (ch. 1), it must be remembered, and were "honor[ed] as the Lord" (4:1). The framers of the

Didache were not free to speak of the bishop-deacons in this fashion. They, after all, were not the ones "speaking to you the word of God" (4:1). "Waiters" (even "head waiters") were sometimes overlooked in an association bent on prizing spiritual food and prophetic fire. In the end, therefore, no wonder the framers of the *Didache* had to argue in favor of giving them at least a little honor in view of their *leitourgia,* "unremunerated public service"—to this we will return shortly.

#9D HOW PROTESTANT–CATHOLIC RIVALRY DISTORTED THE *DIDACHE*

Beginning with Adolph Harnack (1851–1930), the *Didache* has been used in order to support the thesis that the primitive church had a charismatic leadership (apostles, prophets, teachers) that was taken over by a noncharismatic, institutional leadership (the beginnings of a hierarchy). Harnack, writing at the beginning of the twentieth century, thus used the *Didache* to support the then-prevalent Protestant thesis that the early churches were responsive to the Spirit and emphasized charismatic leadership (the Protestant model) whereas the later churches substituted human tribunals and offices (the Catholic model).

> The *Didache* enabled Harnack to put forward a threefold order of apostles, prophets, and teachers against the Catholic order of bishops, priests, and deacons as the earliest order of ministry. The *Didache,* he argues on the basis of 4:1, knew only one class of dignitaries in the community, namely those who were ministers of the gospel, and this vindicated Article V of the Augsburg Confession. The Catholic order is the result of a two hundred year development, in which the "service of the Word" degenerated into the ministry of "Priester und Hierarchen" ["priest and hierarchy"]. (Draper 1996a: 5)

Protestant theology during Harnack's lifetime championed the prophetic and reforming movements in church history and took a critical stance toward the "church of officialdom" that squelched the Spirit. Thus, Harnack and his disciples welcomed the *Didache* as supplying clear evidence supporting the Protestant conviction that the Catholic hierarchy was an aberration imposed on the Spirit-led first-century churches.

Even when Protestant and Catholic apologetic positions softened as ecumenical exchanges emerged in the twentieth century, almost everything that Harnack and his disciples had set in motion continued unchallenged to the end of the second millennium. Willy Rordorf, the leading

French-language scholar, and Kurt Niederwimmer, the leading German-language scholar both agree (a) that *Did*. 10:7 and 13:3 testify that the worship service was formerly in the hands of the prophets and teachers alone (Niederwimmer 1998: 202; Rordorf 1978a: 63f.; 1998: 227f.) and (b) that *Did*. 15:1f. represents a later development in which local officials had taken over the leadership of the worship service, since, at this point in time, prophets were in short supply (Niederwimmer 1998: 202; Rordorf 1978a: 63f., 72). The Catholic scholar Georg Schöllgen takes a dissenting position. After summarizing Rordorf's two developmental stages, Schöllgen remarks that "the evidence for this is not very convincing" (1996: 68). I, on the contrary, would say that the evidence offered by Rordorf and Niederwimmer is very convincing if and only if certain assumptions are made. I would name three:

1. *That bishops received community support.* Rordorf notes that no provisions were made for the support of bishops (*Did*. 13:1f.) and that first fruits were given to the beggars if prophets were wanting (13:3). This allows Rordorf to conclude that the community did not have any elected local officials when these rules were being formulated. Schöllgen responds:

> It is implicitly assumed that local officials possessed the right to support from the beginning. A look at the sources shows, however, that this only happened from the turn of the second to the third century, mainly in large communities. (1996: 68)

This does not, however, entirely respond to Rordorf's observation that prophets and teachers did receive community support and that, at least in theory, this could have been applied to the bishops and deacons as well. It was not, because, as the *Didache* itself makes clear, they exercised a *leitourgia* ("unremunerated public service"). The commentary explains this in detail.

2. *That prophets declined in numbers or in integrity.* Niederwimmer emphasizes the decline in numbers (Niederwimmer 1998: 192, 202), while Rordorf emphasizes the decline in integrity (Rordorf 1998: 52–63, 228; Harnack 1908: 319–68). Schöllgen responds:

> The *Didache* does not attest a declining number, or a collapse, of the prophets and teachers either. *Did*. 13:4 simply specifies what to do when a community is without a resident prophet. The assumption that in a previous time all communities had resident prophets and teachers . . . is nowhere attested in the text or even suggested. Furthermore, while steps are taken against imposters,

. . . it is not permissible to conclude from this a general collapse of the "charismatic office." (1996: 69)

Both Niederwimmer and Rordorf continue to support Harnack's thesis that settled officers emerged as a result of the decline of the charismatics. Schöllgen's observations are valid to a point. My solution is to allow that prophets in the Didache communities did decline (as explained at the end of ch. 6), but that this did not occasion the election of bishops and deacons. The commentary takes this up in detail.

3. *That bishops presided at the eucharist.* Niederwimmer interprets *Did.* 15:1f. to mean "that the local officials, together with the prophets and teachers (or, to the extent that the last two groups are absent, they alone) lead the worship service that formerly was in the hands of the prophets and teachers alone" (1998: 202; also held by Catholic scholars, such as Schillebeeckx 1981: 23). Rordorf, for his part, reads *Did.* 15:1f. in a more radical manner: "the bishops and deacons are charged to replace them" (1998: 228; also held by Catholic scholars, such as R. Brown 1980: 336) as presiders at the eucharist. Schöllgen, in contrast, takes the position that "these matters remain in the dark" (1996: 59). Going beyond Schöllgen, I would argue that the *Didache* provides sufficient evidence to decide that neither the prophets nor the bishops presided at the eucharist (see #6o and #9f).

While the essential position of Harnack continues to influence Protestant scholarship, one can also detect a softening and a setting aside of anti-Catholic rhetoric surrounding the transition from charismatic to institutional leadership. Niederwimmer provides an excellent example of this. Consider the following:

1. Niederwimmer criticizes earlier Protestant scholars (notably Hans von Campenhausen and Gottfried Schille) for distinguishing too sharply the transition from "prophetic charisma" to "the charisma of office" (Niederwimmer 1996: 338 n. 60). Niederwimmer, accordingly, writes very positively and sympathetically regarding this transition:

> The charismatics are being integrated into the local community (without losing their exceptional status), while the local community is producing functionaries who are assuming the leadership functions of the charismatics. Incidentally, *all of this does not necessarily imply that the "officials" had come to restrict or even rob the community of its autonomy.* The warnings and instructions are still directed toward the entire community. It is the community that is called on to conduct itself properly toward the different groups of immigrants; it is considered capable of deciding for

itself (12:4) in cases which cannot be determined casuistically from the outset, and it is the community, finally, which must elect functionaries out of its ranks (15:1). (Niederwimmer 1996: 338, emphasis added)

The bold-faced caution of Niederwimmer signals that he has distanced himself from the anti-Catholic bias of Harnack wherein the *Didache* was portrayed as providing evidence of how charismatics were eclipsed by officialdom.

2. Then comparing Niederwimmer's 1977 pilot article (1996) with what he later produced in his book, one can detect a significant transition in vocabulary. Over a period of twelve years, Niederwimmer stopped using the negatively biased terms such as "functionaries" (1996: 338) to name bishops/deacons and adopted more neutral terms: "local clergy" (3x), "community officers" (4x), and "local officials" (5x) (Niederwimmer 1998: 200–202). Furthermore, he stopped using Harnack's potentially pejorative term "catholicization" (Niederwimmer 1996: 339) entirely.

Catholics, to be sure, had their own apologetic agenda when interpreting the *Didache*. The *Didache* was hailed by most Catholics, for example, as providing testimony that the apostolic tradition (a) embraced the sacrificial character of the eucharist (14:1–3) and (b) named bishops as the successors to the apostles and prophets (15:1). An example of this can be seen in the scholarship of Jacquier and Dean M. Kelly (see #9f). Happily, these points of Catholic interest are no longer used to decide the intent of the *Didache*. This present volume is a testimony in that direction.

How the Synagogue Model of Organization Flowed Over into the Church

For many years, I was persuaded that *Did.* 15:1f. represented a later development in the organizational life of the Didache communities (Milavec 1994b: 136 n. 30). In so doing, I shared part or all of the assumptions noted in #9d. I was also persuaded that 15:1–2 "destroys the natural continuity that exists between the confession of transgressions which preceded it and the practice of reproving and shunning (15:3) which follows it" (Milavec 1989a: 119f.). Upon reading James Tunstead Burtchaell's *From Synagogue to Church* (1992), however, my mind was changed. Let me explain why.

Burtchaell does three things: (a) he reviews the last five centuries of study on ministry in the early church; (b) he carefully details the synagogue structure that prevailed during the period when the church was being formed; and (c) he delineates those synagogue offices that were retained and modified by the early churches. With unfair brevity, Burtchaell's conclusions relative to our topic might be stated as follows:

1. Burtchaell demonstrates that, even though there were local variants, the Jewish synagogue was administered by a group of "elders" (*zeqênim* in Hebrew; *presbyteroi* in Greek) (228). In this, there is nothing new. But then Burtchaell goes on to show that dissident groups used this same system when they created alternatives to the local synagogue (270f.). In such cases, there was a tendency to shift titles.

2. Burtchaell finds that Christianity functioned in the same way as other dissident groups. When they broke away from the local synagogue, they created a system of governance making use of "elders," but the titles for this office were gradually changed. "Synagogue" was replaced by "church" (*ekklēsia*)—both terms originally referring to the assembly itself and only later being applied to the place of the assembly (225). "Elder" was replaced by "bishop." "Assistant" (*chazan*) was replaced by "deacon" (*diakonos*) (317).

The Issue of Community Support Revisited

With regard to community support, it is with good reason that prophets were specifically mentioned as receiving support but not the elders. The prophets, it will be remembered, were persons who had left family and occupation in order to move about, as did Jesus and his disciples, proclaiming the kingdom of God. The *Didache* received them "as the Lord" (*Did.* 11:4; 12:1) and gave them limited hospitality. Should one or the other "wish to settle down among you," however, "s/he is worthy of his/her food" (13:1). As for the elders, they had no need of community provisions; hence the omission of "bishops" or "elders" in 13:1f. *says nothing about their absence from the community;* rather, it affirms that they were not classed among those needing community support.

In the Jewish synagogue structure, "elders" were generally chosen from among the senior members of the most prosperous families in the community (Burtchaell: 231; Draper 1995a: 292). As such they did not need community support. Elders gave themselves over to administration as a *leitourgia* and not as a remunerated service. In the Roman world, this would be equivalent to the role of senator (*senator*), which was reserved for senior men of the notable families who filled the office out of a sense of civic duty (*leitourgia*) and because it brought honor to their family name. Thus, it is no mystery that both the verb and the noun show up in the *Didache*:

> *Leitourgeō* . . . means do[ing] public work at one's own expense. It is a political, almost legal, concept. The noun [*leitourgia*] means service for the people. In the later classical period it was as

common as "taxes" today [as brought together in Rom 13:6].
(C. Brown: 3:551; *TDNT* 4:217)

From this, it becomes clear that *leitourgia* has to do with "unpaid public service" and not with "liturgy." Only, in the third century, once bishops
became preoccupied with liturgy, would the Greek term take on this additional meaning (Burtchaell: 345). A possible confusion arises insofar as the
Septuagint uses *leitourgeō* nearly one hundred times and *leitourgia* nearly
forty times to describe the public service of priests in the temple (esp. in Ex
28–39 and Ez 40–46). These Greek terms work well in the Septuagint
because they point to the fact that priests were not paid but were supported
by tithes (even at those times when they performed no service). Moreover,
the terms "bishops" (*episkopoi*) and "deacons" (*diakonoi*) are not associated with cultic functionaries in secular Greek (C. Brown: 1:188–92,
3:544–49).

The *leitourgia* of the prophet-teachers was founded on the Jewish tradition discussed in chapter 6: "You received without pay, give without pay"
(Mt 10:8). Presumably this *leitourgia* was not compromised by their food
rations any more than was the *leitourgia* of the temple priest compromised
by tithes (13:1f.). Nowhere in the Christian Scriptures or in the *Didache* is
the least interest shown in establishing a new order of priests to replace
those of the Jerusalem temple. What then is the shared identity between
prophets and bishops? That they both perform unremunerated public service: the bishops as members of the administrative council of the community; the prophets as the harbingers of the kingdom of God. The force of
Did. 15:1b is not that bishops are replacing prophets (as Rordorf and
Niederwimmer suggest), but that the bishops deserve honor, just as do the
prophets, because of their unremunerated public service (*Did.* 15:2).

Needless to say, interpretation enters into every translation. One quickly
discovers this when the various translations of 15:1f. are compared. For our
purposes here, note the following two translations:

Milavec	Niederwimmer
Appoint, then, for yourselves, bishop and deacons worthy of the Lord,	Select, then, for yourselves bishops and deacons worthy of the Lord,
[1] men gentle	[1] mild-tempered men
[2] and not money-loving	[2] who are not greedy,
[3] and truthful	[3] who are honest
[4] and tested;	[4] and proven,
for to you they likewise gratuitously serve the unpaid public service of the prophet-teachers.	*for they too perform the services of prophets and teachers for you.*
Do not, then, look down upon them;	So, do not disregard them,

| for they themselves are
your honored ones in company
with the prophet-teachers. | for they are the persons
honored among you together
with the prophets and the teachers.
(1998: 200) |

Our translation is more literal; Niederwimmer's is more dynamic. The clause in italics deserves close attention. Both the noun *leitourgia* ("unpaid civil service") and the verb *leitourgein* ("to do unpaid civil service") appear together. This could be literally translated "they likewise perform unpaid (*leitourgousi*) the unpaid public service (*tēn leitourgian*)." For the sake of simplicity, this becomes: "they likewise gratuitously serve the unpaid public service of the prophet teachers" (15:1).

Niederwimmer use the verb "to perform" and the noun "the services" (which the English translator elected to make plural). This translation obscures the relationship of the verb with its object. Niederwimmer's German translation is better in this regard: "denn auch *sie dienen* euch mit *dem Dienst* der Propheten und Lehrer" (1989: 241). André Tuilier's translation, on which Rordorf depended, reads: "car *ils remplissent* eux aussie près de vous *l'office* des prophètes et des docteurs" (Rordorf 1998: 193). Tuilier entirely obscures the link between the verb *leitourgein* ("to do unpaid civil service") and the noun *leitourgia* ("unpaid civil service"). While "office" may do for *leitourgia,* translating the associated verb as "they replace" finds no support in the Greek whatsoever.

The framers of the *Didache* had a rich choice of verb-noun combinations when it came to comparing the bishops and prophets. For example, the verb *latreuein* with the corresponding noun *latreia* would have signaled "hired service" (as in Rom 1:25 and 9:4). The verb *hypēretein* with the corresponding noun *hypērtēs* would have signaled "service under someone's direction" (lit., "under + rower") (as in Acts 24:23 and 5:26). The verb *hierateuein* with the corresponding noun *hierateia/hiereus* would have signaled "priestly service" (as in Lk 1:8 and 1:5)—a combination that might have served well if "worship" or "offering sacrifice" had been their focal issue. The Greek language also has a general combination: the verb *diakonein* with the corresponding noun *diakonia* would have signaled "service" (as in Acts 1:17, 25; 6:4; 12:25; 21:19). This last choice might have been appealing since it corresponds to the name of the "servants" (*diakonoi*) used in *Did.* 15:1a. Niederwimmer's translation (given its general character) would best have translated this option.

The point I am trying to make here is that the Greek language has sophisticated nuances and that one learns something by noting what selections the framers of the *Didache* did not make. Finally, however, the selection of the verb *leitourgein* with the corresponding noun *leitourgia* clearly signals "unpaid civil service" (as in 2 Cor 9:12; Phil 2:30). Any translation that fails to capture this point misses the nuance of the Greek. The *gar-*

clause, consequently, explains why "bishops and deacons" were appointed/ elected by the community—"they likewise gratuitously serve the unpaid public service of the prophet-teachers" (15:1). The focal point is *leitourgia* ("unpaid public service")—not *diakonia* ("service," in general, or "waiting on tables," in particular) or *hierourgos* ("priestly service").

Once "bishops" in the *Didache* are seen as members of an administrative council performing a *leitourgia*, then the fact that they are not assigned community support falls into place. Once it is shown that the "bishops" were not the normal presiders at the eucharist (see #9f), then the fact that they are not called "your high priests" (*Did.* 13:3) and are not offered the first fruits (13:3–7) also falls into place.

Who Presided at Liturgies in the Synagogue?

According to Burtchaell, presiding at liturgical events in the synagogue was the role not of "elders" but of the *archisynagōgos* (lit., "first in the assembly"):

> The *archisynagōgos* was not simply a master of religious cere-
> monies. He was the executive of the local community, acting
> under the formal oversight of the elders. . . . He presided over the
> community, he convened it for its activities, he superintended its
> staff. It was a position of some permanency, and one in which
> fathers might hope to see their sons succeed them. . . . If he
> presided at worship, it was because he presided at all community
> functions. (Burtchaell: 244; also Draper 1995a: 298; Theissen
> 1982: 74)

This term appears five times in the New Testament in the context of the Jewish synagogue (Burtchaell: 243). The *archisynagōgos* did not make decisions for the community but convened the elders when matters of policy needed to be looked into and acted upon. When it came to worship, he saw to it that cantors, readers, and prayer leaders were all appointed and prepared for their tasks. In the Jewish synagogue, it must be remembered, every adult male was prepared to read and, to some degree, interpret the Torah and to lead the community in its prayers. Not every male could hold a tune, however, and not every adult male could equally improvise on the prayer themes so as to address the Lord appropriately within the existential mood required. The task of the *archisynagōgos* was to ensure sound and compelling liturgies and to chair the council of elders.

The early Christian churches do not appear to have taken over this title (save among the Ebionite Christians [Burtchaell: 306 n. 125]): "Like the word *synagōgē*, this is part of the synagogal vocabulary which the new group disliked" (Burtchaell: 306). In practice, however, James appears to have occupied this position in the Jerusalem church even though the title was not used (R. Brown 1980: 327):

> It is he whom both Peter and Paul report to at critical junctures. He is in several scenes depicted in the midst of the elders, and on the most decisive occasion, it is he who brings a strenuous debate to closure by saying simply: "I rule, then . . ." He is given no title other than "brother of the Lord." Even the letter that was later published in his name only calls him a *doulos* = slave of God and of the Lord Jesus Christ. (Burtchaell: 306)

With a few exceptions, this office is absent from other first-century communities but then appears c. 110 C.E. in the letters of Ignatius under the title of *episkopos* ("bishop"):

> In the face of these data, one could reasonably conjecture that the communities had gone through an early period of revolutionary populism, with no single presiding officer in the local assembly. On this view, Ignatius, with the vehemence of his personality and the credibility of his martyrdom, would have held up a pattern which, in the divisive and acrimonious days of the second century, eventually imposed itself as the universal church order. That order, with its single, authoritative overseer, has been called the monarchical episcopate. (Burtchaell: 308)

But these are later events. The *Didache*, for its part, knows nothing of this. It has an administrative council of *episkopoi* ("bishops"). The use of the plural "bishops" clearly suggests a group with a shared function. The monarchical "bishop" surrounded by a council of "elders" took shape only during the second century.

Responsibilities of the Council of Bishops

The term *episkopoi* was sometimes used interchangeably with *presbyteroi* in the first century (e.g., Acts 20:17, 28; Ti 1:5–7; 7:1; 1 Tm 3:1; 5:17; *1 Clem.* 44) (Burtchaell: 297; R. Brown 1980: 333f.). Burtchaell generalizes from the evidence as follows:

> The elders held authority in the assemblies. Their duties seem to have included preaching and teaching, as also *the control of community finances, admonition and rebuke* when unity was at risk, appointment of officers and endorsement of apostles, care for the

sick and for the community's dependents. Their rank deserved honor and . . . obedience. (Burtchaell: 298)

Only those functions in italics would appear operative in the Didache community, and even here one can make only educated guesses. For example, the rule regarding reproving and shunning (*Did.* 15:3) comes directly after 15:1f. Reproving was the responsibility of all; the act of shunning, however, normally required a common consent: "Let no one speak to him/her" (15:3). In practice, therefore, one can surmise that the council of bishops met to consider the case of someone "misbehaving against the other" even after being rebuked. Here their qualities of being "gentle" and "truthful" came to the fore. The bishops' pastoral sensitivities undoubtedly led them to take corrective action in the hope of achieving a reconciliation of the parties. If this failed, the decision to shun the offending member would have been made and the judgment of the council shared with the community.

Regarding visitors, undoubtedly one or more of the bishops was charged with greeting them and extending hospitality in the name of the community. At the right moment, discreet inquiries would be made as to how long they intended to stay and what they might hope to accomplish during their stay. The bishop would then outline any limitations that applied to their circumstances. Then the bishop might hand the guest over to one of the deacons, who would bring the guest to the household assigned for lodging and meals and introduce the guest to the hosts. Of all these things, however, one can only make intelligent conjectures.

Responsibilities of the Deacons

Burtchaell notes that the second distinct office in every synagogue was that of the *chazan* (or *chazzan*):

> The post of *hazan* was most likely the first one among the officers of a synagogue to become stipendiary. Even poorer communities unable to pay a full-time chief might find a salary for a *hazan,* who would then become a combination choir director, sacristan, master of ceremonies, janitor, Hebrew teacher, hostel manager, bailiff, caterer, plumber, clerk, scribe, welfare officer, penal officer, and gravedigger. Where Jews constituted the entire population of a village, . . . the synagogue was the community, and the *hazan* its basic municipal employee. (Burtchaell: 248f.)

In the Christian assembly, the task of the *chazan* was accomplished by the "deacons." Here again, as in the case of *episkopoi* ("bishops"), the term *diakonoi* was gathered from ordinary secular usage. The term *diakonoi* is derived from the verb *diakonein,* which means "to wait on someone at table" (Bauer: 184a). The *diakonoi* consequently were, first and foremost, "waiters." The term was widely extended to refer to any person caring for or helping someone. In its larger sense, therefore, the *diakonoi* were "helpers."

In the Lord's household, these *diakonoi* were neither slaves working under compulsion nor hired hands working for wages but volunteers appointed by the community and performing tasks as a *leitourgia* (*Did.* 15:1). Philo describes in great detail how the Therapeutae held periodic feasts peppered with exposition of Scripture and choral music which lasted all night and ended with a sunrise prayer (*On the Contemplative Life* 64–89). With regard to the table service during these meals, Philo gives expanded details:

> Free men minister to the guests, performing the office of servants (*diakonoi*), not under compulsion, nor in obedience to any imperious commands, but of their own voluntary free will, with all eagerness and promptitude anticipating all orders, for they are not any chance free men . . . appointed to perform these duties, but young men who are selected from their order with all possible care on account of their excellence. (71f.)

Following the tradition in Roman households, in which youths were trained to serve their parents and guests at table (Dixon: 117), Philo takes special pride in pointing out that this extended banquet was served by "young men" especially "selected" for this service. Going further, Philo makes a great point of noting that these waiters dress not like slaves who would ordinarily do this service but like free men "with their tunics let down" (72). In almost idyllic terms, he notes that they serve an intentional "family" and "with affectionate rivalry minister to their fathers and mothers, thinking their common parents more closely connected to them than those who are related by blood" (71). Later, Philo points out that these "young men who are standing around" after the meal are not bored or distracted but "attend to this explanation [of the Scriptures being presented] no less than the guests" (77). With this flourish of words, one suspects that Philo is taken up with defending the honor of these *diakonoi* because, in the ancient world, menial work of this kind was looked down upon as "slave work." Philo, accordingly, not only presents us with a well-ordered community meal suggestive of the eucharistic meals of the *Didache,* but he also gives us a glimpse of how he uses "appointment," "free service," and "tunics let down" to uphold the honor of those who are the unseen and unsung servants. What Philo does in one way, the framers of the *Didache* do in another. Their common concerns were good order and conferring honor.

From what has been said in earlier chapters, one can surmise that one or two deacons might have been responsible for coordinating the sharing of workers between shops and for finding work placements for members wishing to settle down among them. Another deacon might have been charged with selecting the music and the prayer leader. Another with rehearsing the singers and with instructing visiting prophets on what was expected of them during the liturgy. A set of deacons might have formed two teams such that, on alternate weeks, one team would secure adequate groceries, prepare the tables, cook the food, serve the community meal, and clean up afterward. Another set of deacons might have been responsible for hospitality for visitors and care of the sick or injured. Another set of deacons might have accompanied sisters to ensure that they would not be harassed when walking back and forth from the assemblies. Still another set of deacons might have been responsible for properly preparing the bodies of dead members and for providing a suitable place for viewing, grieving, and for mourning rituals. Finally, another deacon might have been charged with grave digging.

The German folk saying has it that "shared work is half the work" (*Geteilte Arbeit ist halbe Arbeit*). Accordingly, the multiplicity of deacons made it possible for a wide assortment of services to be provided to the community *at no cost*. Anyone who has ever been part of an intentional community, a religious order, or a commune knows how the voluntary and joyful service of individuals functions for the good of the whole.

#9E WHETHER WOMEN SERVED AS BISHOPS AND DEACONS

The first qualification for bishops and deacons is that they be "gentle/mild-tempered men" (*andras praeis*). Greek has a gender-neutral term *anthropos* ("man/woman") that it could have used if both genders were intended; hence, the use of *anēr* presumably excludes females (Kohlenberger: 706). It seems difficult to avoid the conclusion, therefore, that *men alone* were elected as bishops and deacons.

Such a conclusion does not diminish what has already been established regarding the necessary role of women as trainers, as baptizers (see chs. 1 and 3), and as prayer leaders (ch. 4) when other women were involved. Nowhere in the *Didache* is there the least hint that such roles were reserved to men, and the internal logic of the text argues for the inclusion of women in these roles. Regarding the appointment of bishops and deacons, however, there seems to be a strong reversion to patriarchy. How does one explain this? Three considerations:

1. In the ancient world, there were only very limited possibilities for unrelated men and women to have casual meetings or to engage in collaborative efforts together. Boys and girls did not date before marriage and, even after marriage, husbands and wives had very limited access to mixed groups. It is no mystery, therefore, that even while the Jewish Therapeutae included women at their banquets, Philo delicately mentions that the greater part of them were "old women" who "out of an admiration for and love of wisdom . . . are indifferent to the pleasures of the body" and, for all practical purposes, are "virgins" (*On the Contemplative Life* 68). Needless to say, Philo would never think of speaking of the men in this light; rather, being a gentleman, he is about the task of *saving the reputation of those women who would dine with men*. In brief, they were not "loose women." When they came to table, the men and women deliberately sat in separate sections assigned to them (69). One must understand from this that not even married couples sat together. The unspoken message is: "What honorable purpose could be served for a husband to introduce his wife to another man and to allow them to have free discourse together?" Philo emphasizes the fact that the choral performances among the Therapeutae were offered by the men and women arranged in separate choirs under separate directors (83) and, when they sing together, Philo goes into an elaborate contortion in order to justify this "mingling" of voices in the name of "piety" (88). Here again, since women present at the banquets of men frequently functioned to entertain and to provide sexual services for the men, Philo has to justify the mingling of male and female voices even in separate choirs.

If Philo correctly represents the situation of men and women in proper Jewish society, it becomes apparent how difficult it would have been for unrelated men and women to serve side by side as bishops on the community council. Given the cultural climate of the times, therefore, one can be fairly certain that the *Didache* made no mistake when it noted that men alone were to be elected as bishops (see also #1e).

2. On the other hand, Karen Jo Torjesen (1989) has rightly observed that, within the confines of a private home, relations between men and women were very much relaxed. Insofar as the early assemblies took place in private homes and insofar as those assembled regarded one another as "family," this transformed social consciousness made possible free and familiar association between women and men, between slaves and free. Parents, meanwhile, charged with protecting the virtue of their daughters, would have been much more relaxed and even "permissive" in a social setting wherein everyone was firmly committed to the Way of Life. Likewise, given the fact that men and women habitually worked together in the "family" shops, they were not strangers and everyone tended to feel quite "safe" in a mixed social environment. The social inhibitions inbred by

virtue of living in a divided society, however, would have acted as a natural point of restraint that not even the theological perspective of being "family" could entirely overcome.

3. Within the assemblies of the Didache community, therefore, there would have been a natural tension between the church as "family" and the church as "civic association." Insofar as the community was a family, women and men could eat, sing, pray, and work together as brothers and sisters. Here, again, therefore the language of family was not just a pious gesture but a pragmatic notion that permitted ways of relating appropriate to the family setting.

A Roman club might have women as patrons and might celebrate their birthdays. Women in the association might even be assigned their turns to preside and to lead prayers during the monthly meetings (see #2n). Yet, when it came to electing a council that would deliberate on matters of policy and that would represent the association to outsiders, one can be sure that men and only men would be regarded as suitable candidates. Women, of course, would have been socialized to accept such an arrangement without question. Going further, they would have felt "safe" in such an arrangement, just as did most of our great-grandmothers.

When it came to the *leitourgia* of deacons, however, my hunch is that the men could not manage without the women. Philo speaks for men of his own era when he writes as follows:

> To the man the public affairs of the state are committed, but the particular affairs of the house belong to the woman; and a want [i.e., the absence] of the woman will be the destruction of the house; but the actual presence of the woman shows [i.e., ensures] the regulation of the house. (*Questions and Answers on Genesis* 1.26)

Take, for instance, the weekly meal preparations, the visiting of sick widows, the lodging of female visitors/prophets—in these areas, a man would feel "out of sorts" to try to do much without the close collaboration of women. On the other hand, it undoubtedly took "gentle/mild-tempered men" to be able to perform routine and unremunerated services for which there was little or no public honor. One can be fairly certain that there were men who refused to bake bread, to cook vegetables, and to wash dishes precisely because they had been socialized to see these things as "beneath their dignity." One can also be fairly certain that some men were elected to a service position but then proceeded to boss women and slaves around and had to be rebuked or dismissed because of it. The Didache communities had a variety of members, and not all were equally up to the demands of the personal and social transformation necessitated by communal dining and working.

In sum, it would seem fairly certain that places on the administrative council of bishops were reserved to men. This conformed to the expectations of their culture, which the community was unable to change and unwilling to expend its energy in challenging. With regard to deacons, on the other hand, insofar as they were occupied with essential "household" services, the community was bound to elect both women and men. The countercultural stance of the Didache communities might have been in the fact that men served at providing routine services that were normally reserved to women and slaves. Moreover, given the "safe" environment of an extended "family," women and men were able to work creatively, collaboratively, and consultatively, side by side. The silence of the *Didache* on this point should be taken to mean that no cultural revolution was being deliberately undertaken; rather, whatever degree of collaboration existed would have been seen as the natural result of their having become, by baptism, members of one family with God as their Father.

The Removal of Unworthy Bishops and Deacons

The bishops and deacons were elected/appointed by the community at large and, accordingly, were accountable to the community. Such accountability meant that the bishops and deacons were open to censure and removal by the community. One does not find here any hint that somehow a founding apostle stands behind these appointments (as in Acts 14:23; 1 Tm 5:17–22; 1 Clem. 44.3) and shields officeholders from easy removal. Neither does the *Didache* assure us that outside bishops were brought in (as in the third century) for an episcopal consecration, which somehow also functioned to lift the office beyond the reach of ordinary community censure. Going further, bishops and deacons confessed their "failings" prior to the weekly eucharist (*Did.* 14:1). No one imagined that the obligation of a public confession would have the effect of degrading the dignity of an officeholder; rather, the implied perception is that all were striving for the same perfection in the Way of Life. Medicine good for the recently baptized would surely be the same medicine with proven efficacy for the advanced. Accordingly, the framers of the *Didache* made it a point to have novices trained "not [to] take into account social status when it comes time to reprove against failings" (*Did.* 4:3). In so doing, they imposed on the "newly baptized" the license to censure a "bishop."

Some might imagine that the bishops could hardly be expected to function since anyone and everyone had the right (even the obligation) to call into question their "defective" judgments and deeds. But it was just the reverse. History demonstrates that the abuse of episcopal power took place more or less in direct proportion to the absence of local accountability. In the case of the *Didache*, since the right to censure unworthy bishops existed, they ensured themselves that bishops "worthy of the Lord" (15:1) remained so. When a bishop was misbehaving and deaf to reproof by those he injured, the council of bishops would have been certain to give him the silent treatment, which had been discovered to be so salutary for ordinary members. If and when such a wayward "bishop" was readmitted to the community, one can be certain that he would return without any office and that no office would ever be given to him again until he was again "tested" and proved "worthy" (15:1). This might take a long time. In any case, for the first thousand years of the church, there was nothing so permanent about any office that the officeholder could not be removed from it (Schillebeeckx 1981: 41).

Conclusion

Stepping back, one can now see how the clues of the *Didache* form a coherence considerably different from what Rordorf and Niederwimmer would have us expect. For them, the key issue was bishops and deacons presiding at the community worship in place of the prophets and teachers. For me, the key issue is the unseen and unsung servants who perform a *leitourgia* and deserve to be honored "in company with the prophet-teachers" (*Did.* 15:2). Beyond this, one can only make conjectures based on the observation that breakaway groups tend to use the same modes of organization as the parent group, which, in this case, was the local synagogue. On this basis, one can surmise that the council of bishops coordinated community life, applied the rules of the community in disputed areas, and decided cases deserving shunning.

No body of regulations in the history of humankind, no matter how divinely approved or transmitted, has been so clear in its intent, so straightforward in its application, and so unambiguous when encountering new circumstances as to be able to create the same understanding in separate minds fashioned in diverse cultural and social experiences. The fact that the *Didache* is a practical document shaped within the life experience of those who set out to live by it must have meant that some forum for discussion and arbitration was already set up for the resolution of the inevitable disagreements that arose. I would submit that the council of bishops/elders was established and functioned in this role. Those who lived the Way of Life defined by the *Didache* knew much more than they were able to tell. Hence, they had only to mention "bishops" and their hearers filled in the practical details for themselves.

This same trajectory could be continued when it comes to the "deacons." No social group could have a meal once each week without, in the course of time, defining roles and responsibilities so as to arrange who does what and when and how. When everyone is equally responsible, people duplicate efforts needlessly and step on each other's toes. Then people's feelings are hurt and they withdraw, and key aspects of the planning and the execution are neglected until, at the last moment, some impetuous person steps forward to do a half-baked job. In the end, everyone is miserable. Discontent reigns. Accordingly, given the practical bent of the *Didache*, shaped within the life experience of those who set out to live by it, there must have been some apparatus whereby roles and responsibilities were parceled out in advance and routinely improved in their operation. I would submit that the "deacons" fulfilled this *leitourgia*. Here again those who lived in the community knew much more than they could tell. Hence, they had only to mention "deacons" and their hearers filled in the practical details for themselves. We have to stretch our imaginations and call upon our own experiences of community living to know how to fill in the silences.

All in all, the equality operative in the Didache communities was not severely compromised by the election of bishops and deacons. Thus, one can wonder whether this trait gave the Didache people a certain supreme advantage when it came time to spread the Way of Life revealed by the Father. When traveling in Africa, for example, I discovered that Islam was (and continues to be) the most rapidly expanding religion in that part of the world. I didn't need to ask why. An ordinary truck driver who was giving me a lift felt not the slightest embarrassment when pulling off the road and having me wait in the cab while he went off a hundred paces into the hot desert to recite his noonday prayers. Later, while living in an Islamic household, I discovered that the Islamic traditions governed all the moments of their lives. When meeting someone or sitting down next to someone, these Muslims spontaneously recited a blessing just as we do when someone sneezes. When killing a chicken for supper, a special ritual and prayer united the life force which flows out with the Author of all life. An ordinary worker with less than a primary education felt entirely at ease being the prayer leader in his home or in his mosque. He was surprisingly adept at discussing and explaining the complexities of the Islamic way of life to an outsider. In effect, I discovered that he and his family had no need for mosques or for imams. There was no need for ordained clergy or for specialized theologians. *An ordinary adherent was sufficiently apprenticed in his/her way of life that he/she could entirely train a convert and introduce him/her gradually into all aspects of the life.* As I experienced Islam in Africa, I understood how ordinary practitioners (not trained missionaries) were its greatest calling card and its spontaneous missionaries.

My experiences in the small towns of North Africa brought to mind the *Didache*. By leaving its prayers, its rites, and its functions open to everyone, it effectively ensured its survival and its increase in a world in which older, more established, and well-funded institutions were floundering. Simplicity was the bearer of truth. Ordinary members lived the Way of Life and were quite adept at leading or taking part in all its rites. As the assembly grew, bishops and deacons were called upon to keep pace with their needs. These bishops and deacons wore no special garb, were addressed with no special titles, and bore no special charism. They were simply its tried and true, older and wiser counselors and its unpaid servants, who ensured that the community retained its unity and purpose while leading the most important functions for everyday persons pursuing an everyday holiness. This simplicity blessed their lives, and, with time, attracted many to their doors.

#9F WHETHER BISHOPS WERE THE NORMAL PRESIDERS AT THE EUCHARIST

The *Didache* gives no indication that any class of persons was either the preferred or the necessary presiders at the weekly eucharist. In fact, since the prohibition of food sacrificed to idols, the conferring of baptism, and the celebration of the eucharist were framed using the same linguistic structure (*peri de*), the text itself wanted to indicate that, in principle, every member of the community, whether a man or a woman, whether young or old, was addressed by all these things and, thus, that every member was a potential celebrant of the eucharist.

Roman Catholic and Protestant believers alike affirm that, in case of some necessity, any baptized Christian could administer valid baptism. When it comes to the eucharist, however, Catholics have insisted along with most Protestants that only a validly ordained minister/priest can administer this sacrament. No exceptions were allowed.

When I was attending Holy Cross Grade School in Euclid, Ohio, my sixth grade teacher explained this to me in a riveting story that I remember to this very day. It ran something like the following:

> When the priest says, "This is my body," over the host (i.e., the small wafer of unleavened bread) at mass, it is changed. It continues to have the appearance of bread, but, in reality, it has become the sacred body of Christ. Only a priest has this power to consecrate. Anyone else could recite the words of institution a hundred times over a host and nothing would happen. The priest has only to say it once. In fact, if a priest would go into a bakery and quietly say the words of institution over all the loaves on the shelf and really mean it, all at once, every one of those loaves would become the body of Christ. No priest, of course, would do such a thing. But the truth remains that he could, by virtue of

his powers as a validly ordained priest, effect such a change if he really wanted to.

The hypothetical case of the priest in the bakery is clearly a pious exaggeration; however, in its original setting, this kind of narrative served to emphasize for a ten-year-old boy such as myself the supreme importance Catholics placed on the ordained priest at every mass. It also served to inforce an anti-Protestant bias. Even as a lad of ten, I could easily understand why the Protestant celebration of the Lord's Supper had nothing to do with the "true mass" that Jesus instituted during the Last Supper. In simplified terms, the argument would have been that the "defective intention" and "defective rites" used by Protestants in their ordinations could never have produced any "validly ordained priests." As a consequence, Protestant ministers were perceived by Catholics in the 1940s as merely "going through the motions" when they celebrated the Lord's Supper. True sacraments (save for the exceptional case of emergency baptism), Catholics wanted to insist, *always and everywhere required validly ordained priests.*

I make reference to these things because even conscientious scholars are influenced by their childhood training and because, within many church circles, there is often a tacit presupposition that anything valid today in the church *must have been there from the very beginning.* Robert Wilken, in his small volume *The Myth of Christian Beginnings* (1971), provides a brilliant exposition of this principle operating in all the major epochs of Christianity. In view of this myth and in view of the silence of the *Didache* respecting the presider at the eucharist, the Catholic imagination would thus be prone to supply what was wanting: Of course the bishops named in 15:1 were ordained by one of the apostles or their successors. How could the community have imagined that they could have had valid eucharists if they hadn't been certain that they have valid ordinations?

Let me provide a specific case documenting how the myth of Christian beginnings operates within scholarly circles. E. Jacquier was a French Catholic priest writing his doctorate on the *Didache* in 1891 at the University of Lyons. With regard to 15:1, Jacquier takes great care to demonstrate that the term *cheirotonein* ("to appoint/elect") was frequently used in connection with "the imposition of hands" in the Christian Scriptures (251). When considering the *Didache*, consequently, he easily concludes that *Did.* 15:1 "indicates the establishment of bishops and deacons by election, *without any prejudice being understood toward ordination that was done by the competent ministers*" (251, emphasis added). In the italicized text, Jacquier allowed his Catholic instincts to take flight and to discover episcopal ordinations hidden behind the silence of the text. Furthermore, since the creation of bishops follows closely upon the heals of the section on the "pure sacrifice" of the eucharist (14:1–3), Jacquier's Catholic instincts again led him through the darkness and allowed him to expose the critical link:

> There is not the least doubt, therefore, that the principal func-
> tion of the bishops and the deacons was the celebration of the
> eucharist. Here again our document is in agreement with church
> tradition and confirms it. (255)

Jacquier, in his attempt to message the text and to claim it as affirming Catholic realities, was clearly troubled by what the *Didache* says of prophets: (a) they have the right to eucharistize (*Did.* 10:7); (b) they receive first fruits as "your high priests" (13:3); and (c) they have "the ministry" that the bishops share (15:1f.). Jacquier says quite openly that the *Didache*, should it assign prophets a role in the "ecclesial hierarchy," it would then be "in contradiction with all the Christian literature of the first two centuries" (231). Having decided in advance that only validly ordained bishops have the right and the power to consecrate the eucharist, Jacquier then goes to work to remove the possibility that the *Didache* might embarrass him by assigning this role to prophets. His solutions are ingenious:

1. If prophets did have the right to eucharistize, Jacquier conjectures, then either (a) they did so only at the evening *agapē* meal that was not a sacrament and required no ordination, or (b) they were also ordained "members of the presbyterate" and had the right to eucharistize by virtue of that office (233).

2. If prophets did receive first fruits as "your high priests" (*Did.* 13:3), this could only be true as a sort of pious fiction maintained in order to establish their right to receive sustenance (231). If the *Didache* had intended a "complete identification," Jacquier assures his readers, "it would have also attributed to them tithes . . . and, above all, it would not have ordered to give these first fruits to the poor in the case of absent prophets" (231).

3. Finally, if prophets did perform a *leitourgia* as *Did.* 15:1 suggests, Jacquier clarifies that this term, in the Christian Scriptures, has "a restricted sense, save in a single passage (Lk 1:23)" and can simply mean "to fill an office." Thus, the *leitourgia* of the prophets is their teaching and preaching, and it is this office that the bishops were taking over and *not the office of celebrant at the eucharist that was always reserved to the church hier-archy* (233).

All in all, Jacquier operates as a sincere scholar investigating the clues offered by the text. At every point, however, he is informed by Catholic instincts that dominated French Catholic scholarship in the late nineteenth century. He does not suspect that the framers of the *Didache* thought differently and inhabited a religious horizon of understanding that differed from his own. Everything that Jacquier reads into the silence of the text (e.g., episcopal ordinations), he sincerely believes must be there by virtue of the Catholic character of the text. Everything that Jacquier dismisses from the text, he does so on the seemingly inescapable grounds that Catholics everywhere and at all time dismissed these things (e.g., that prophets presided at the eucharist).

Writing a century later, another Roman Catholic priest and scholar, Edward Schillebeeckx, comes to vastly different conclusions. In his volume *Ministry* (1981), Schillebeeckx endeavors to show how the notion of the absolute requirement of a valid ordination for a valid eucharist grew and became codified in the medieval church. Prior to this, the notion of "ordination" as the "sacred power necessary to transform the bread and wine into the body and blood of Christ" was not yet either a pressing concern or an operative idea. What Schillebeeckx knows is that, in order to recover the past, one has to enter into an imaginative and cognitive landscape where some of one's own operative and stubborn notions did not exist. Thus the faithful believer in the first century must be allowed to remain rooted in his/her first-century modes of feeling and thinking and not be forced to replicate those essential to another generation (entirely unknown and future). Accordingly, the faithful scholar in the twentieth century must enter into a listening dialogue with the text that allows him/her to sort out how the framers of the *Didache* wished to define ministry among themselves. In this, there is continuity and discontinuity.

As a living and confessing Catholic, Schillebeeckx is quite certain that the eucharist today can be celebrated only by a validly ordained priest. On the other hand, as a sensitive scholar, Schillebeeckx is also aware that this contemporary commitment had a beginning and that this beginning is entirely outside the first century. Here are some of the findings of Schillebeeckx on this matter:

> Nowhere in the New Testament is an explicit connection made between the ministry of the church and presiding at the eucharist (except to some degree in Acts 13:1f.). However, that does not mean that any believer whatsoever could preside at the eucharist. In the house churches at Corinth, it was the hosts who presided at the eucharistic meal, but these were at the same time leaders of the house churches. (1981: 30)

> Tertullian [d. 225 C.E.] . . . writes that in normal circumstances, presiding at the eucharist is by definition a role for the leader of the community. . . . However, he says, "But where no college of

ministers has been appointed, you, the laity, must celebrate the eucharist and baptize; in that case you are your own priests, for where two or three are gathered together, there is the church, even if these three are lay people" [*Exhortation to Chastity* 7.3]. (1981: 51)

Raymond Brown, the Catholic scholar who gained the applause of Catholic bishops and of Protestant scholars alike, harmonizes with Schillebeeckx's conclusions entirely. In a key article that he prepared at the request of the Catholic bishops, "*Episkopē* and *Episkopos:* The New Testament Evidence," these are some of the findings he reported:

> During the ministry of Jesus Mt 10:5–6 has the Twelve being sent to the lost sheep of the house of Israel, and after the Resurrection Mt 28:16–20 has them (minus Judas) being told to go and make disciples of all nations. . . . Nevertheless, we do not know that all or most of them did this, since all the references to the Twelve as a group . . . portray them in Jerusalem. . . . The image of them as carrying on missionary endeavors all over the world has no support in the New Testament or in other reliable historical sources. (1980: 324f.)

> As for exercising supervision, there is no New Testament evidence that any of the Twelve ever served as heads of local churches; and it is several centuries before they begin to be described as "bishops" of first-century Christian centers, which is surely an anachronism. In particular, D.W. O'Connor, *Peter in Rome* (New York: Columbia University, 1969) 207, contends that the idea that Peter served as the first bishop of Rome can be traced back no further than the third century. (1980: 325 and n. 7)

> No cultic or liturgical role is assigned to the presbyter-bishop in the Pastorals. The closest to that in the New Testament is James 5:14–15, where the presbyters of the church are called in to pray over the sick person and anoint him in the name of the Lord. . . . As for the eucharist, we know virtually nothing of who presided in New Testament times. (1980: 336)

The fact that the above conclusions are shared by the vast majority of Catholic and Protestant scholars should not disguise the fact that there exist today some believers and even some scholars who are profoundly troubled by these conclusions. As a case in point, consider George A. Kelly, a Catholic priest who devoted an entire book to faulting Raymond Brown for having abandoned Catholic dogmatics as the sure guide for interpreting the Scriptures. In part, Kelly writes as follows:

> Brown actually downgrades the priestly order, first by suggesting it is not intended by Christ or found in the New Testament, second, by alleging that the ordained priest is "commissioned by the whole Church, including the people." If either of these arguments are [*sic*] correct, then the Catholic priesthood is indeed a distortion of Christ's and/or New Testament [*sic*] original intent. (96)

Kelly is so captivated by the myth of Christian beginnings that he cannot allow that the first century would believe or practice anything essentially different from what Catholics believe and practice today. If Brown is correct, therefore, Kelly believes that he would have to concede to the Protestants that "the Catholic priesthood is indeed a distortion." For Kelly to be able to hear Brown, he would have to leave aside his wooden notion of history and to embrace an adequate notion of the development of doctrine as offered by such scholars as R. Brown (1985), Cooke (1976), Dulles (1992), Milavec (1994a; 1996a), Moran (1963), O'Collins (1993), Osborne (1988; 1993), Ratzinger (1987). This is a big order, and many believers like Fr. Kelly are not able to do this. For the moment, therefore, Kelly is constrained to remain deaf to Brown because he fails to find Brown asserting that Jesus' words at the Last Supper to the Twelve, "Do this in memory of me," established once and for all time the Catholic understanding of the ordained priesthood (G. Kelly: 96).

When one applies the studies of Brown and Schillebeeckx to the *Didache*, one can say something like this:

1. There is nothing in the *Didache* that remotely suggests either that a valid ordination was necessary for a valid eucharist or that a bishop presided in every instance. Accordingly, one might expect, as Schillebeeckx suggests, that the owner of the home in which the community assembled might have been invited to function as prayer leader him/herself or to appoint a gifted person to act in his behalf. It is quite possible that the householder was a "bishop," but no one in the Didache community would have regarded this fact as *the necessary and preexistent condition for celebrating the eucharist*.

2. While the *Didache* makes no mention of ordinations, one can allow that, given the Jewish roots of the framers of the *Didache*, the laying on of hands may have been used as the normal means whereby bishops admitted an elected candidate into their circle of bishops. While such an ordination would have irreversibly altered the public status of the one being ordained,

no one would have regarded the laying on of hands as conferring special supernatural powers absolutely required for there to be a eucharist (Milavec 1994a: 55–61).

3. The eucharist of the *Didache* clearly belonged to the entire community. The faith, the language, and the expectation of the eucharist were the faith, language, and expectation of those gathered. Undoubtedly, everyone in the community experienced various presiders as possessing various gifts (holiness, artistry, imagination) for this public service. As a matter of course, then, certain persons (men and women) were routinely called forward more than others. Some of these may have been "bishops." Others may have been former "prophets." All in all, however, nothing in the *Didache* points in the direction of fingering the bishops as the best or the only presiders, just as nothing points in the direction of fingering the prophets in this role. Bishops were honored for their gift of oversight; prophets were honored for their gift of Spirit-led prayer—neither was defined as "president" or "prayer-leader" either in the daily prayers or in the eucharistic meals. Stepping back from the *Didache*, therefore, it can be concluded, with a degree of historical assurance, that the framers of the *Didache* did not regard either prophets or bishops as the normal presiders at the eucharist.

What has been explained above does not imply that everything was frozen for subsequent centuries. With time, the function and theology of bishops changed for the very reason that the needs of the times required such changes and that the Holy Spirit guided the church successfully to meet new circumstances. Consider this example:

> Cyprian [d. 258] was one of the first [bishops] to have a clear predilection for the Old Testament priestly sacrificial terminology, to which he compared the Christian eucharist. In this way, the sacerdotalizing of the vocabulary of the church's ministry in fact developed gradually, though this was at first in an allegorical sense. . . . By contrast, Augustine continues to refuse to call bishops and presbyters *priests* in the real sense, in the sense of being mediators between Christ and the community. (Schillebeeckx 1981: 48)

Thus, during the third century, when the monarchical bishop (now always used in the singular) was increasingly portrayed as the "high priest" offering the "sacrifice" on the "altar," the term *episkopos* came to designate a cultic functionary. These two hundred years of development, however, should not be projected back into the *Didache*. It would be a disservice to the history of Christianity to force the first century to look like the third. Similarly, it would also be a disservice to force the third to look like the first and thereby subvert the fact that there was significant development in the function of "bishops" and a corresponding development in the theology surrounding the episcopal office during a period of two hundred years.

Standards and expectations of what constitutes appropriate community organization differ widely today, just as they differed widely during the first three centuries of Christianity. When the narration of church history breaks away from being a self-serving denominational propaganda and begins to wrestle with the evidence of sources caught up in the dynamics of history, then history itself will make it evident that there has never been any universally applicable rule whereby Christians at all times and in all places organized their worship and their decision making.

John Henry Newman was one of the first to detect this historical dynamic within authentic Christianity and to demonstrate that the old formula, *semper ubique eadem* ("always, everywhere, the same") was an ideological construct humanly unattainable as long as one is dealing with real people in real churches (1845: 148–52). For Newman, both our personal lives and our church histories exemplify a much deeper and richer rule of historical fidelity: "To live is to change, and to be perfect is to have changed often" (1845: 100). Care must be taken, accordingly, not to read back into the *Didache* elements of church life and church organization that are rightly and appropriately precious to us but entirely out of place in the cultural and religious sensibilities of the framers of the *Didache*.

#9G WHETHER THE *DIDACHE* WAS CREATED TO TRAIN ELDERS

In the late 1980s, Clayton Jefford put forward the argument that the *Didache* was a training manual designed specifically for the training of new elders (1989a: 123–29; 1989b). Up to this point, his thesis has not been seriously considered nor formerly refuted (Rordorf 1998: 230). This short appendix will endeavor to do both quite independently of the discussion within the chapter itself.

If Jefford's thesis were true, then one would have to read the *Didache* quite differently. Many troublesome elements would even be ironed out. Jefford notes, for example, that "it remains somewhat confusing to imagine. . . a community. . . which was devoid of an office whose roots were both early and primary in the Judeo-Christian tradition" (1989b: 123). By allowing that the *Didache* was addressed to elders, one then has the advantage of having the community organize itself using the model most familiar and most practical—namely, the organization of the synagogue.

How does one decide whether Jefford's hypothesis is correct? One must, first and foremost, examine the clues offered by the text itself. But what is the evidence of the text? Embarrassingly, the word "elder" never shows up in the *Didache*. This Jefford acknowledges (1989a: 123; 1989b: 125). On the other hand, if the entire *Didache* were addressing elders every time the imperative was used, then it would not be strictly necessary to ever find the word appearing. Those hearing the *Didache* (or reading it) would have known themselves to be elders, and, accordingly, it would have been entirely redundant to mention "elders" since the context provided this.

An argument from silence, however, is very difficult to sustain. Accordingly, let us assume for the moment that Jefford's hypothesis is correct and push the evidence of the text to see whether this creates more problems than it solves. Jefford assumes that those sections in the second person plural are addressed to the elders (1989a: 127). According to this rule, the following duties would be assigned to elders: administering baptism (7:1–4), fasting (8:1), daily prayers (8:2), presiding at the eucharist (9:1), accrediting true teachers and prophets (11:1–12), testing travelers (12:1–5), giving first fruits (13:1–7), confessing failings (14:1–3), appointing bishop-deacons (15:1f.), reproving and shunning (15:3). One immediately notes that the semiweekly rhythms of fasting and the daily praying of the Lord's Prayer would now be limited to elders. The same would hold true for the confession of failings prior to the eucharist. The reference to "your sacrifice" (14:1) and "offering" (14:3) would pertain to the elders and not to the community at large.

One can see from this that the overall character of the Didache communities changes radically and that nearly everything is placed in the hands of the elders. Upon close inspection, however, problematic areas appear. Three that are especially troublesome are the following:

1. The rationale for giving the first fruits to the "prophets" is that "they themselves are your high priests" (13:3). Some scholars take this as clear evidence that the "prophets" were the presiders of the eucharist. Jefford, from his vantage point, would reject this presupposition on the basis that the mandate to eucharistize was being given directly to the "elders" (9:1). If elders were the normal presiders at worship, as Jefford's hypothesis suggests, then it would appear that they most clearly approximated the role of "high-priests." Furthermore, since eucharist in the *Didache* was clearly being regarded as a "sacrifice" (14:1–3), the elders who confessed their failings before each eucharist should be regarded as "priests." It seems puzzling, therefore, that the elders were not receiving the first fruits but were being passed over in favor of the prophets.

The situation is even more puzzling when the text says, "But if you should not have a prophet, give [the first fruits] to the beggars" (13:4). Even if the first fruits were given to the prophets because of their charismatic gift for formulating spontaneous prayers (ch. 7), it still seems puzzling that the presiders at the community eucharist were bypassed in favor of "beggars." This double bypass may be indirect evidence that "elders" simply did not exist or that there is some overlooked reason why the elder-presiders were overlooked in the offering of first fruits.

2. Finally, *Did.* 15:1 addresses itself to appointing "bishops and deacons" but makes no mention of "elders." Given the careful thoroughness of the *Didache*, it would seem unusual for no directives to be given for the selection of elders. To respond to this, Jefford calls forth the first-century evidence that, in many churches, the terms "elder" and "bishop" were used interchangeably (1989a: 125; 1989b: 124). If this were the case in the *Didache*, then 15:2 would be tantamount to asking elders to honor themselves. One could try to escape this difficulty by interpreting this to mean that the newly appointed elders were being directed to honor those already appointed. If this were true, however, one would have expected that they would have been honored as "fellow presbyters" and not as "prophet-teachers" (15:1).

3. During the time of training novices, rank-and-file members were being trained to "judge justly" and "reconcile those fighting" (4:3). According to Jefford's hypothesis, however, the elders were being commissioned to do these things themselves (14:2–3 and 15:3). The same conflict holds true for the confession of failings. Rank-and-file members were told during their time of training that "in church, you (singular) will confess your failings" (4:14) while later, this confession was mandated in the plural and, according to Jefford, reserved for the elders. This double assignment of specified tasks finds no easy resolution within Jefford's hypothesis.

All in all, while Jefford's hypothesis initially resolves some difficulties, consistent application of his hypothesis creates more difficulties than it resolves. As such, therefore, Jefford's seemingly promising rereading of the *Didache* unfortunately turns out to be a wrong turn that leads nowhere.

10
PURIFYING FIRE, SELECTIVE RESURRECTION, AND GOD'S COMING

Events of the Last Days

THEN THE CREATION
OF HUMANS WILL COME INTO THE
BURNING-PROCESS OF TESTING.
MANY WILL BE ENTRAPPED AND WILL BE
UTTERLY DESTROYED; THE ONES
HAVING REMAINED FIRM IN THEIR FAITH,
ON THE OTHER HAND, WILL BE SAVED
BY THE ACCURSED BURNING-PROCESS
ITSELF. THEN WILL APPEAR THE
SIGNS OF THE TRUTH: THE FIRST SIGN
WILL BE THE UNFURLING BANNER
IN HEAVEN, NEXT THE SIGN OF THE SOUND
OF THE TRUMPET, AND THE THIRD SIGN
WILL BE THE RESURRECTION OF THE DEAD
- NOT THE RESURRECTION OF ALL, ON
THE OTHER HAND, BUT AS IT HAS
BEEN SAID: "THE LORD WILL COME
AND ALL THE HOLY ONES WITH HIM."
THEN THE WORLD WILL SEE THE LORD
COMING ATOP THE CLOUDS OF HEAVEN.

Contents

Background Discussion Found in Boxes

According to *Did.* 11:7, the content of a prophet's speech was not to be judged. This, in itself, requires some examination. Recall (from ch. 6) how the prophet delivered urgent prayers for the saving, the perfecting, and the gathering of the church into the anticipated kingdom (10:5f.). On occasion, a prophet might have been carried away when anticipating this future by offering too much detail, by naming the signs of the approaching end, or by saying that the last days had already begun. After all, an acclamation like "Hosanna to the God of David" (*Did.* 10:6), when chanted fervently at the end of a eucharist, could lead some to imagine that God was already on his way and that the congregation was welcoming his approach. Then, if God was indeed on his way, maintaining work schedules and saving for tomorrow would quickly appear, in the minds of many, as useless or even "faith-less" concerns. Should a whole community become infected with a frenzied assurance that the Lord was on his way, then many would be tempted to abandon occupation, home, and family just as the prophets did (ch. 6). This, of course, would have had disastrous consequences.

How were such consequences to be avoided? Some might have been tempted to silence unruly prophets. Such a solution would have risked dissension, for, in practice, it would have been almost impossible for everyone to agree that a particular prophet was to be silenced. Furthermore, how could a community, on the one hand, sanction prophetic speech as coming from the Spirit of God (*Did.* 11:7) and then, on the other hand, selectively silence prophets who did not follow the party line? In the end, therefore, the framers of the *Didache* had to beat the prophets at their own game. How so?

The purpose of this chapter is to examine in detail the content of *Did.* 16. In so doing, one will discover how an end-time scenario functions in a healthy community. One will also discover how the framers of the *Didache* managed to safeguard the values of the community and to counter misleading or dangerous visions of the future by putting forward a step-by-step unfolding of the last days bent on harnessing the enthusiasm of all concerned. In the end, therefore, even the modern skeptic might come to understand and to appreciate the gentle urgency and benevolent hope that sound eschatology provides. The ready believer in end-time prophecies, on the other hand, might come to appreciate that discernment is necessary especially when it comes to detailing the things that are to be hoped for.

#10A PROPHETIC VS. APOCALYPTIC ESCHATOLOGY

In Jewish and Christian sources, one finds various views of what will come to pass in the "last days" when this evil age filled with the suffering of the just will pass away and give rise to a golden age where goodness thrives. Consequently the "last days" do not refer to the end of history as such but to the end of this world and the beginning of God's new world order.

Jewish eschatology began in the prophetic movement surrounding the first destruction of the Jerusalem temple. This movement and the books it left behind understood the failure of Israel to resist her enemies as due to the fact that God had ceased to protect Israel as a result of her faithlessness. In the future, however, God would again hear their cries and come to rescue them as he did of old:

> They are a rebellious people, faithless children,
> children who do not hear the instruction of the Lord. . . .
> Therefore this iniquity shall become for you
> like a break in a high wall, bulging out . . .
> whose crash comes suddenly, in an instant. . . .
> Therefore the Lord waits to be gracious to you [again];
> therefore will he rise up to show mercy to you.
> For the Lord is a God of justice;
> blessed are all those who wait for him. (Is 30:9, 13, 18)

Distinct from this prophetic eschatology is the apocalyptic eschatology that emerged in full swing in the third century B.C.E. Both forms of eschatology share a common hope:

> Common to both is the belief that, in accordance with divine law, the adverse conditions of the present world would end in judgment of the wicked and vindication of the righteous, thereby ushering in a new era of prosperity and peace. (*ABD* 1:281a)

Apocalyptic eschatology begins in an *apokalypsis* ("revelation, disclosure"). Thus, for example in the Book of Revelation, "a revelation is given by God through an other worldly mediator to a human seer disclosing future events" (*ABD* 1:279c). In apocalyptic eschatology, God's coming to the rescue normally entails "destruction of this world and resurrection of the faithful" (*ABD* 1:281b). Such themes, however, are already present in "late prophecy" or "early apocalypticism" (e.g., Is 24–27; 56–60; Zec 9–14); hence, the roots of the later apocalyptic eschatology may lie in the late prophetic literature (*ABD* 1:281e):

> There is obvious continuity between the apocalyptic expectation of a final judgment and the prophetic "day of the Lord." The idea of a cosmic day of judgment is widely attested in the prophets and the psalms. (e.g., Pss 96, 98; Is 2:4). (*ABD* 1:284b)

While some scholars continue to make a clear-cut distinction between the character of prophetic and apocalyptic literature, other scholars tend to see points of contact and continuity (as suggested above). The work of Paul Hanson (1979) is especially noteworthy in this regard:

> Paul Hanson claims to find the perspective of apocalyptic eschatology already in the late sixth century B.C.E., especially in the oracles of Isaiah 55–56. On Hanson's reconstruction, the authors of these oracles belonged to a disenfranchised group which was excluded from power in the restored Jerusalem temple. As they despaired of rectifying this situation by human means, they called on their God to "rend the heavens and come down" (Is 64:1) and envisaged "a new heaven and a new earth" (Is 65:15). (*ABD* 1:284c)

Hanson's work is important for it demonstrates that the editing of prophetic and apocalyptic texts can function as social criticism. It did not take insufferable atrocities by gentiles to make the apocalyptic imagination flourish; in some instances, God's expected coming could be appealed to against failings within one's home religious community. This line of thinking will be pursued in our commentary on the *Didache* and will also show in our analysis of the *Ascension of Isaiah* (see #10g).

Possible Uses for a Synopsis of the Last Days

The framers of the *Didache* provided its community with a synopsis of the last days (*Did.* 16). This synopsis could have served a number of purposes:

1. *God's coming is "not yet."* First and foremost, *Did.* 16 served to challenge prophets tempted to cross the line between "coming soon" and "already arriving." Paul himself put forward a normative ordering of the events in the last days (see #10b) as the decisive point whereby the Thessalonians could safely dismiss false claims that "the day of the Lord is already here" (2 Thes 2:2). The framers of the *Didache*, having encountered a similar problem, did the same. The stages leading to the end as defined in *Did.* 16 thus function as an existential safeguard against those who would claim that God is already on his way.

2. *Ordinary holiness is what counts.* The introduction to the last days (*Did.* 16:1f.) clearly indicates that the framers of the *Didache* were not simply taking over ready-made materials crafted by others. Preparing for the last days meant turning aside from all forms of heroic spirituality (e.g., prolonged fasting and praying, giving away or selling all one's possessions) in favor of "frequently gathering together," "seeking the things pertaining to your souls," and remembering that "the whole time of your faith will not be of use to you if in the last time you should not have been perfected" (16:2). Thus, in the end, living the Way of Life is the common and most reliable road to perfection (6:2)—ordinary holiness is what counts. *Did.* 16 thus puts forward an existential safeguard against those who would claim that the last days call for radically new ways of being and serving God.

3. *Beware of false prophets.* The first century was plagued with a multiplicity of end-time scenarios. Many of these favored way of thinking and of acting that were antagonistic to the values of the *Didache*. By sanctioning a normative outline for eschatological expectations, the framers of the *Didache* ensured that its own members were preserved from what was of doubtful merit. At the same time, the *Didache* fingered "false prophets who are corruptors" as the opening phase of the last days. Unlike nearly all other eschatological scenarios, therefore, the first menacing wave of evil emerges squarely within the heart of the Didache communities.

#10B PAUL'S CHALLENGE TO THOSE WHO CROSS THE LINE FROM "COMING SOON" TO "ALREADY ARRIVING"

Paul, in his first letter to the Thessalonians, reacted strongly against those who "despise prophesying" while cautioning that one should "test everything" (1 Thes 5:19). In his second letter, however, Paul provided a particular warning against some who had gone over the thin line between "coming soon" and "already arriving":

> As to the coming of our Lord Jesus Christ and our being gathered together to him, we beg you brothers and sisters, not to be quickly shaken in mind or alarmed, either *by spirit* or by word or by letter, as though from us, to the effect that *the day of the Lord is already here*. Let no one deceive you in any way; for that day will not come unless the rebellion comes first and the lawless one is revealed. . . . He opposes and exalts himself above every so-called god . . . so that he takes his seat in the temple of God, declaring himself to be God. (2 Thes 2:1–4)

Apparently some members of the community have become alarmed because the word was circulating that "the day of the [arrival of] the Lord is already here" (2 Thes 2:2). The use of the phrase, "by spirit (*dia pneumatos*)" very probably "refers to the oracular utterance of a prophet" (Aune: 220). The source, on the other hand, could be a "letter" falsely attributed to Paul. In response, Paul did not pry into the nature of the source; rather, he assured his hearers that it is flatly wrong to say, "The day of the Lord is already here."

How so?

Paul negates the content of this message by affirming that "the rebellion comes first and the lawless one is revealed" (2 Thes 2:3). Thus, in effect, *Paul, who is himself a prophet, puts forward a normative ordering of the events in the last days as the decisive point whereby the Thessalonians can safely dismiss any claim that "the day of the Lord is already here"* (2 Thes 2:2).

This is an unusual strategy. To appreciate this, take note of the alternatives that Paul set aside in order to defuse the claim that the day of the Lord has arrived:

1. "About that day and hour no one knows, neither the angels of heaven, nor the Son, but only the Father" (Mt 24:36). If this is the case, then Paul could tell the Thessalonians that neither he nor any other prophet could expect to know that "the day of the Lord is already here" (2 Thes 2:2).

2. "So, if they say to you, 'Look! He is in the wilderness,' do not go out. If they say, 'Look! He is in the inner rooms,' do not believe it. For as the lightning comes from the east and flashes as far as the west, so will be the coming of the Son of Man" (Mt 24:26f.). If this is the case, then Paul could tell the Thessalonians that, since the Lord's arrival is not evident everywhere and to all, they can be assured that the day of the Lord has *not* already arrived.

3. Nor does Paul say, as do some modern theologians, that the "coming of the Lord" is a symbolic metaphor that must not be understood as having a literal realization in historical time. If this were the case, then Paul might have told the Thessalonians that it would be foolhardy to expect a historical realization of a promise that was meant to be taken metaphorically (see #10t). But no. Paul would not embrace this strategy because he believed in an extraordinary future: "We speak God's wisdom, secret and hidden, decreed before the ages for our glory . . . no eye has seen, nor ear heard, nor the human heart conceived what God has prepared for those who love him" (1 Cor 2:7, 9).

Thus, Paul abandoned each of these alternate strategies and appealed exclusively (with historical literalness) to a known *sequence of events* leading up to the day of the Lord: "that day will not come unless the rebellion comes first and the lawless one is revealed" (2 Thes 2:3). This argument, by the way, could be easily set aside by anyone who would bother to read Paul's earlier letter:

> Now concerning the times and the seasons . . . you yourselves know very well that the day of the Lord will come like a thief in the night. When they say, "There is peace and security," then suddenly destruction will come upon them, as labor pains come upon a pregnant woman, and there will be no escape! (1 Thes 5:1–3)

Someone among the Thessalonians might object:

> Think carefully upon these things, my brothers and sisters. Paul in his first letter told us that the day of the Lord would come suddenly and unexpectedly as a thief in the night or as the first labor pains of a pregnant woman. Now, in his latest letter, he tells us that the day of the Lord cannot be here because the rebellion and the enthronement of the lawless one in the Jerusalem temple must come first. Surely, my brothers and sisters, you can hear that Paul is very inconsistent here. Either the day of the Lord comes suddenly and unexpectedly *without any warning,* or it comes *only after certain prophetic events and signs* which are known to the elect. Paul cannot have it both ways.

No one, to our knowledge, offered Paul this insightful objection. We cannot know, consequently, how Paul would have addressed this inconsistency. If I were to double-think Paul, I would suggest that the inconsistency arose in the following manner.

1. *Tiptoe anticipation.* At first, new converts to the movement were introduced to the eschatological hope in its broadest terms: God is coming to gather the elect into a kingdom ruled by God (or his Messiah), where justice, mercy, and peace abound. At this phase, the imaginations of new converts were swept away by the vision of a God planning to disrupt history by stepping in and giving it a new direction. This great expectation loomed large and enabled new converts to suffer tribulations and to sever ties with those who did not share their hope. The Christian prophets at this phase served to foster this tiptoe expectancy—the conviction that the day of the Lord would arrive unexpectedly at any moment (1 Thes 5:1–11).

2. *Sure-footed expectancy.* As the years passed, however, the feverish expectation of the Lord's coming could not be psychologically maintained hour by hour, day by day. At this mature phase, growth in perfection and

the building up of the community replaced the earlier romantic notions associated with first conversion. Tiptoe expectancy was replaced by a sure-footed grounding in the Way of Life that integrated everyday concerns with the enterprise of hope. Now it was the details of the end-times scenario that provided a deep-seated confidence that everything has been determined beforehand and that the Lord of history was hidden off-stage directing history step by step toward its intended goal. At this phase, even the evident delay in the arrival of the day of the Lord was perceived as part of the master plan. Then the Christian teachers (more so than the prophets) would tend to concentrate on the perils of the last days (e.g., the rebellion and the enthronement of the lawless one in 2 Thes 2:1–12) in order to encourage believers to "stand firm and hold fast to the traditions" (2 Thes 2:15). At this phase, accordingly, advancement in perfection and community growth were better served by a moderated expectancy. Paul's second letter to the Thessalonians thus represents the maturing of his earlier tiptoe expectancy.

The observations made above have relevance for understanding the *Didache*. What is evident is that the framers of the *Didache* were not promoting a tiptoe expectancy of the kind found in 1 Thessalonians. Rather, their investment was solidly planted in a sure-footed expectancy calculated to promote the striving for perfection and the consolidation of community life (16:1–3). To defuse prophets bent on promoting the notion that "the day of the Lord has arrived," the *Didache* appears to have used the same strategy as did Paul in 2 Thes, namely, to recount the events that must come first. Thus, if the above analysis is correct, one can begin to see that the pastoral genius of *Did*. 16 included a powerful challenge to prophets who might be tempted to cross the line between "coming soon" and "already arriving."

#10c The Danger and the Promise of an Imminent Expectation

As excitement mounted in the camp revival meetings in the early 1840s, William Miller was pressed to refine his biblical computations so as to give a definitive date for the Lord's coming. Miller first came up with 21 March 1843. On that day, his enthusiastic followers donned their robes and took their places facing east. When the sun set that day, folks were disappointed but not disheartened. Miller soon found some errors in his method and fixed 21 October 1843 as the day of the Lord. When that day came and passed, Miller confessed his disappointment but did not lose heart that "the day of the Lord is at the door" (de Lys, cited in Walker: 252). Miller had always been opposed to "excesses of zeal" on the part of his followers.

Many, however, were quite certain that he had struck a gold mine of prophetic insight and that the Lord most certainly would return before the year 1843 was completed.

> As 1843 drew to its close, the dangers of such religious excite-ment and delusion became apparent. Suicides were attributed to despair over the necessity of facing the day of judgment. The state insane asylums reported the admission of several who had been crazed by fear of the end of the world. . . . A Massachusetts farmer cut his wife's throat because she refused to be converted to Millerism, and a despairing mother poisoned herself and all her children. . . . In Wilkes-Barre, Pennsylvania, a storekeeper requested the sheriff to give all his goods to anyone who would take them away . . . since "he had no further use for them." (Tyler: 60)

These unfortunate incidents illustrate how a seemingly innocent calcula-tion of the day of the Lord's coming can lead to disastrous consequences. Hope, however, has its own appeal and its own logic. The followers of William Miller noted the error of relying on biblical calculations, yet they held firm to their experience of living in the expectation that today the Lord may return. This living in expectation, in turn, gave rise to the mod-ern movements known as Jehovah's Witnesses and Seventh-Day Adventists.

From time to time, prophetic figures emerge at the fringes of these movements. Vernon Howell, the messianic figure who took the name David Koresh, spent most of his life enamored by the followers of Victor Houteff, who formed a religious community living in a deserted com-pound outside of Waco, Texas. Houteff himself was a Seventh-Day Adven-tist who was expelled in 1934 for his radical views. Koresh gradually gained respect in this community and sought to revive the original charism of its foundation:

> Koresh thought that the modern [Seventh-Day Adventist] church was in league with the "churches of Babylon"—the main-stream Christian churches that were now formal religious "insti-tutions"—rather than the true church of the select, who would ultimately serve at the right hand of God. Koresh came to see himself as the messiah of Revelation, symbolized as the slain lamb, the only one who is worthy to open the seven seals and interpret its contents to his followers and the world. . . . To open the book is not only to explain it, but also to orchestrate the events it sets forth, leading to the climax of history, the end of the world. (Lamy: 184)

This preparation for the end of the world was interrupted, however, when federal agents, impatient with the protracted negotiations surrounding Koresh's so-called willingness to surrender, created an atmosphere of siege. On 19 April 1993, the FBI used CS tear gas with the expectation that it would drive the seventy-four adults and forty-three children from their compound. Meanwhile, a fire broke out—the seventeen survivors of the fire claimed it was started by the FBI when they realized that the members had donned gas masks; the FBI, meanwhile, claimed it was begun by the members in order to precipitate a mass suicide. Either way, a hundred persons were burned alive.

If one goes to the web site of the Branch Davidians, one can receive, free of charge, a two-volume biblical study entitled *Seven Seals.* These books detail how the events of 19 April 1993 were anticipated by the prophetic books (Dn 8:10f. and Rv 6:10f.; 11:7; 13:7) and form only a small part of the end-time scenario that is unfolding (1:86–92). These books make no mention of the bombing of the federal building in Oklahoma City on 19 April 1995 (exactly two years after the Waco incident), even though the bomber(s) left a note explaining that their actions were motivated in response to the "conspiracy" on the part of the federal government to destroy the Davidians. Thus, while militant survivalist groups have championed the Waco cause, the Branch Davidians themselves do not appear to want to give any prophetic weight to these groups or to the Oklahoma City bombing.

Fundamentalist Christians, meanwhile, look not to David Koresh but to Hal Lindsey when it comes time to open the seals on the hidden meaning of biblical prophecy. Hal Lindsey, the so-called "father of the modern-day prophetic movement" (1994: back cover), has sold thirty-five million copies of his books, which purport to demonstrate that the signs of the end time found in the Bible are being fulfilled in our time. His first and most popular volume, *The Late Great Planet Earth,* appeared in 1970. In this volume, Lindsey simplified the diverse and contradictory aspects of prophetic literature and provided a unified, compelling end-time scenario capable of gripping the imaginations of his readers. On numerous occasions, I have been startled to discover that the message preached in fundamentalist churches comes directly from the pages of his book.

In his 1994 update, *Planet Earth—2000 A.D.,* Lindsey acknowledged that nearly every prediction in his earlier book had been on target and that he "felt an urgency to write about the flood of prophetically significant events that have happened in the last 25 years" (1994: 2). His bottom-line message was as follows: "Examined together, these signs lead inevitably to one conclusion: The long-awaited Messiah of the Bible is coming soon" (1994: 3). This comes, of course, with a proviso:

I am not a prophet. But I have studied the prophets. And I am certain that all of what they predict for mankind up to and including the Second Advent will occur in the next few years—probably in your lifetime. (1994: 3)

Lindsey and his readers track current events with the firm conviction that every banner headline in the *San Francisco Examiner* (especially those that proclaim catastrophic or tragic events) can be correlated (for those who have eyes to see) with the prophetic texts that point to some aspect of the last days. A sample of Lindsey's chapter titles provides a synopsis of some of the tragic signs heralding the Lord's return:

The Rise of Deceiving Spirits
Earthquakes and Berserk Weather
The Rush to Rebuild the Temple [in Jerusalem]
The New Islamic Threat
Asia's March to Armageddon
The Rise of the Roman Empire II [= the European Community]
The Final Conflagration
The Coming Persecution
Operation Evacuation [= the Rapture]

In his various books, Lindsey offers little or no guidance as to what Christians ought to be doing as the last days foretold in the prophets find their fulfillment in our daily newspapers. On the last page of his 1994 update, Lindsey even goes so far as to soberly caution his readers against taking any extraordinary measures or precautions:

Even though he may come today or tomorrow, we should plan our lives as though we will be here on Earth for our full life expectancy. Don't drop out of the world. Don't stop working for righteousness on this plane. Make the most of the time we have. . . . It's late, but there's still time to bring many others to salvation. And that is our final mission. (1994: 312)

Thus, according to Lindsey, even Christians who live each day in the anticipation of the Lord's return in glory are not to cancel their insurance policies or fail to plant their spring crops. Having given over one's life to Jesus, his/her personal Savior, the believer is assured that "as the world becomes more chaotic and troubled, . . . we can rest assured that Christ will protect us until his purpose is finished and then we will be taken up to be with him in heaven" (1994: 312). Thus, even though the time is growing short, one can rely on the Lord and effectively use the time remaining for evangelism and for recommitment to the Lord.

The *Didache*, for its part, shares some common ground with Hal Lindsey. Those waiting for the Lord were admonished to tend their "lamps" and gird their "loins" so as to attain the perfection that the Lord expected of them (16:2). The *Didache* says nothing about taking flight or gathering arms. The same thing holds true for members of the Nation of Islam (see #10s)—God alone will deal with the "white menace." Eschatology, therefore, when it is properly regulated, leads to increased commitment to one's way of life as the end approaches. Here again, ordinary holiness has priority over extraordinary measures (see end of ch. 6). Any eschatology promoting a "dropping out" or advocating a fight-or-flight response to the tribulations of the last day would constitute a false and dangerous eschatology. With good purpose, therefore, the framers of the *Didache* were on guard against end-time prophets (like William Miller) who failed to grasp the internal safeguards necessary for a well-tempered eschatology.

The Linguistic Patterns in Did. 16

Chapter 16 opens up by making repeated use of the imperative mood. This mood dominated the earlier parts of the *Didache* and, accordingly, it finds a natural continuity here. Once the apocalyptic scenario begins (16:3), the future indicative dominates, as would be expected in the case of a futuristic "end time."

The linguistic structure of 16:1f. manifests a certain symmetry. Three interconnected mandates are offered: [A] "be watchful," [B] "be prepared," [C] "be gathered together." The negative admonitions regarding lamps and loins form a couplet that defines the opening thematic statement [A] that functions as a topic sentence and sets the mood for everything that follows. This couplet, in turn, is linguistically framed by "be watchful" and "be prepared."

[A] Be watchful
  [a] "do not let lamps"
  [b] "do not let loins"
[B] Be prepared → *gar*-clause to explain why
[C] Be gathered together → *gar*-clause to explain why

The *gar*-clauses attached to [B] and [C] serve to explain the necessity of the conduct mandated: "for ÿou do not know the hour . . ." and "for the whole time of ÿour faith. . . ." The postpositive conjunction *gar* ("for") is "used to express cause, inference, continuation, or to explain" (Bauer: 151e) and is repeatedly used in the earlier part of the *Didache* (1:4, 5a, 5b, 5c; 2:4; 3:2a, 2b, 3a, 3b, 4b, 5b, 6b; 4:1, 8, etc.).

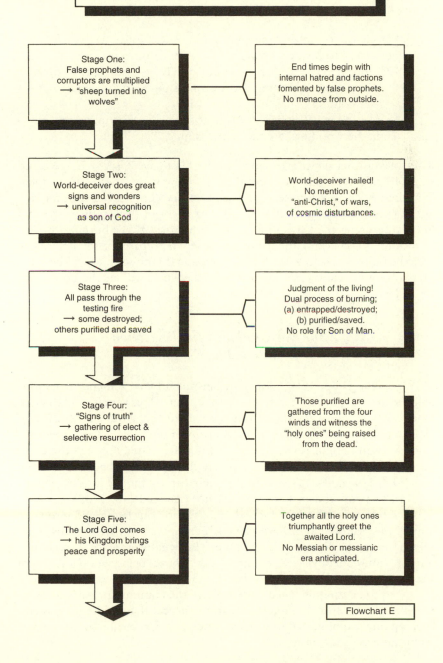

**Progression of Events
Anticipated during the End Times**

Stage One:
False prophets and corruptors are multiplied
⟶ "sheep turned into wolves"

End times begin with internal hatred and factions fomented by false prophets. No menace from outside.

Stage Two:
World-deceiver does great signs and wonders
⟶ universal recognition as son of God

World-deceiver hailed! No mention of "anti-Christ," of wars, of cosmic disturbances.

Stage Three:
All pass through the testing fire
⟶ some destroyed; others purified and saved

Judgment of the living! Dual process of burning; (a) entrapped/destroyed; (b) purified/saved. No role for Son of Man.

Stage Four:
"Signs of truth"
⟶ gathering of elect & selective resurrection

Those purified are gathered from the four winds and witness the "holy ones" being raised from the dead.

Stage Five:
The Lord God comes
⟶ his Kingdom brings peace and prosperity

Together all the holy ones triumphantly greet the awaited Lord. No Messiah or messianic era anticipated.

Flowchart E

The end-time scenario is introduced by a *gar*-clause and the first of four descriptive triplets. All the verbs, from this point onward, are in the future tense. *Kai tote* ("And then") and *tote* ("then") are used alternately to mark the progression from stage to stage in the apocalyptic scenario. This can be represented schematically as follows:

[1] *gar*-clause to explain "the end time" → descriptive triplet
 gar-clause to further explain above → descriptive triplet
  [2] And then will appear the world-deceiver → descriptive triplet
   [3] Then the burning-process of testing → two possible outcomes
  [4] And then will appear the signs of truth → descriptive triplet
[5] Then the world will see the Lord coming

Thus five distinct stages are defined in the "last days" (16:3). Stage 2 and stage 4 begin with *kai tote* ("and then") followed by a descriptive triplet. This linguistic parallelism serves to heighten the contrast between the ravages of the "world-deceiver" and the promises of "the signs of truth." Stage 3 separates the two and focuses on the role of "the burning-process of testing" for checking the former in order to prepare for the latter. The added citation in stage 4 breaks the linguistic rhythm but, as will be seen, prepares for the climax in stage 5, when "the world will see the Lord coming" (16:8).

Being Watchful and the Perfection
Demanded at the End

The opening imperative, *grēgoreite,* calls the implied audience to continually be in a state of being watchful/awake/alert. This verb is used to open or close eschatological exhortations elsewhere (e.g., Mt 24:42, 25:13). This watchfulness is directed "in behalf of ÿour life" (*hyper tēs zōēs hymōn*). The use of the singular here indicates either the shared "life" of the community or the Way of Life so assiduously defined at the beginning of the text (*Did.* 1–4) and celebrated in the eucharist as "the life . . . revealed to us through your servant, Jesus" (9:3; 10:3) (Audet 1958: 470; Ladd: 57).

If the framers of the *Didache* had said, "Tend your lamps and gird your loins," the hearers might have gained the impression that perhaps these things were to be done for the first time. The negative form of these admonitions, consequently, clearly signals that those being addressed were already doing these things. As the last days approach, therefore, these activities need to be carefully safeguarded. Since the community is not a group of lamplighters or ditch-diggers, one must suspect that tending lamps and keeping one's loins girded must have a metaphorical meaning. To this our attention must now turn.

Lamps are necessary at night. In our day, electric lamps can simply be turned on and left on without giving them any attention, In the first century, however, oil lamps had to be maintained by adding oil and adjusting the wick. Without timely maintenance, the light would go out and one would be overwhelmed by the darkness. The admonition not to let "your lamps be quenched" (16:1), therefore, presumes being vigilant and active so that one is not overtaken by the darkness (real and/or symbolic). Since the Didache communities were not groups of lamplighters or given to any special activities after dark, it must be assumed that the admonition is to be taken metaphorically, that it, when "darkness" falls as in 16:3f., one must give attention to the "lamps."

#10D LAMPS AS A METAPHOR FOR TEACHERS AND FOR THE WAY OF LIFE

In the *Syriac Apocalypse of Baruch* (c. 100 C.E.), "A gifted Jew, using old traditions, . . . struggled to assert that Judaism is a religion based on Torah—Law—and that the loss of the temple [in 70 C.E.] was due to the failure of the chosen nation to be obedient" (*ABD* 1:620e). According to this book, the prophet Baruch is given special revelations from the Lord about the last days and is commissioned to prepare the people. The metaphor of "lamps" is evident in the text:

1. In the first place, Adam is noted to have lived 930 years, yet he "transgressed" (*2 Apoc. Bar.* 17:2) and "brought death" (17:3) into the world. Moses, on the other hand, is noted to have lived only 120 years, yet he "obeyed his creator" and "brought the law [Torah] to the sons of Jacob and lit a lamp for the nation of Israel" (17:4). Here, "lit the lamp" is a metaphor for bringing Torah, for revealing the ways of the Lord. The text continues:

> He that lit the lamp took advantage of its light; but there are few who have done as he did. Many of those to whom he has given light have preferred Adam's darkness and have not rejoiced in the light of the lamp. (18:1f.; also 59:2)

In the next line, Moses is presented as saying: "Behold I have set before you life and death" (19:1). Thus, the contrasts are expanded: life or death, light or darkness, the way of Adam or the way of Moses (see also *Testament of Levi* 14:3–4; 18:2–5; 19:1). The lamp, here, is Torah—a metaphor that will be later taken up and expanded in the rabbinic literature (*TDNT* 4:324–26).

2. Later in the text, since teachers are understood to being living Torah,

"lamps" becomes the fitting metaphor for those who give "light," that is, training in the Torah. Thus, the elders ask:

> Does the Mighty One wish to chasten us so much that he is pre-pared to take you [Baruch] from us so soon? Then we shall really be in darkness, and there will be no light [lamp] at all for the peo-ple who are left. For where again shall we look for instruction in the law [Torah], or who will show us the difference between death and life? (*2 Apoc. Bar.* 46:1–3)

The prophet Baruch is later asked to write a letter before he departs so that those who do not have the good fortune to be able to hear his words may be prepared for the future:

> For the shepherds of Israel have perished,
> And the lamps that gave light have gone out . . .
> And we are left in darkness. (87:13f.)

In response, Baruch says:

> Shepherds and lamps and fountains come from the law [Torah];
> And though we depart, yet the law [Torah] remains.
> If then, you respect the law and turn your heart to wisdom,
> A lamp will not be wanting and a shepherd will not fail. (87:15f.)

Thus, even though the people lament the fact that the Roman wars (66–70 C.E.) have extinguished most of "the lamps" (teachers of Torah), if they respect Torah, "a lamp" (a teacher) will be given to them.

All in all, the *Syriac Apocalypse of Baruch* illustrates how some Jews used the metaphor of "lamps" in a period close to that of the *Didache*. While the *Didache* demonstrates no dependence on this text, it does, nonethe-less, hint at how the metaphor of "lamps" might have been used in *Did.* 16. It is even possible that the twin admonitions to keep lamps burning and keep loins girt refer to learning and doing Torah (the Way of Life). In any case, during "the night" (the dark times ahead), members of the Didache communities would appear to be admonished to gather around and attend to their teachers or, alternately, to their Way of Life. The initial admonition to "be watchful over your [way of] life" would then be under-stood as receiving an evocative expansion in the reference to "lamps."

In the Gospel of Luke (and nowhere else), one finds an eschatological admonition that associates both lamps and loins: "Let your loins be girded and your lamps be burning" (12:35). In contrast to the couplet found in the *Didache*, Luke's order is reversed and his verbs are expressed positively. Luke inserted this dual admonition within an eschatological parable taken over from Mark (13:34–36). According to the terms of this parable, an undisclosed number of servants are waiting "for their master to come home [lit., to break loose] from the wedding feast" (12:36). Reference to "the wedding feast" here does not evoke the eschatological banquet (as it does in Matthew's parables), but simply provides a plausible reason why the master would be delayed away from home after sunset. Thus, the internal setting of the parable accounts for the necessity of lighting and trimming lamps. Furthermore, since the parable notes that the master may return "in the second watch [9 P.M. to midnight], or in the third [midnight to 3 A.M.]" (12:38), the point is made that the lamps must be tended long after sunset.

When the master returns, those found faithful enter into the eschatological repose wherein the master serves (rewards) those prepared for his return: "he will gird himself and have them sit at table and come and serve them" (Lk 12:37). Such a role reversal clearly breaks the cultural expectations of the day. No master would come home dog tired in the predawn hours and undertake to serve his slaves who were occupied in his absence. Thus, the parable makes plain that only the Lord would be such a Master and that, when he arrives at the darkest hour, he will undertake to serve those ready to receive him.

Moreover, now that a meal (the messianic banquet?) is anticipated when the master arrives, it can be supposed that the servants were either too busy or under direct orders not to take a meal without the master. Now the emphasis on lamps and loins takes on an extended meaning—the "servants are expected to carry out their duties in the absence of their master, whose return can occur at any time" (Fitzmyer 1983: 985). The necessity of having the male servants gird their loins now becomes clear. Men do not gird their loins just so "they may open the door for him as soon as he comes and knocks" (Lk 12:36). From the terms of the judgment found in the next parable (12:42–48), it is clear that the master had assigned specific tasks to be accomplished in his absence and, from the anticipated meal, one must surmise that they did their work while fasting.

Fitzmyer suggests that "in the Lucan Gospel, the first set of sayings (vv. 35–38) urges disciples to eschatological vigilance and readiness, for in their present condition they are like servants who are expected to carry out their duties in the absence of their master, whose return can occur at any time" (1983: 985). What Fitzmyer fails to note is that the lamps here are functionally necessary, since the period of vigilance specifically takes place during the night. In this setting, therefore, there would be no need to imagine a metaphorical meaning being given to "the lamps" as such. On the other hand, why mention the lamps at all unless they had a significance beyond their pragmatic use in the context of the parable?

In contrast to Luke's sayings and parable, Matthew speaks of a master who goes away and puts servants in charge of his household (24:45–51). Matthew emphasizes the conduct of disorderly and abusive servants who, when the master returns at an unknown day and hour, cuts them to pieces (Mt 24:50). In this case, since there is no suggestion that the master is returning at night, lamps go unmentioned.

Immediately following this parable, however, Matthew places the parable of the ten maidens who "took their lamps and went to meet the bridegroom" (Mt 25:1). Robert H. Gundry is quick to point out that the Greek text here does not say "lamps" but "torches":

> *Lampas* ordinarily means "torch," and a lamp [*lychnos*] would not stay lighted in a breeze, would not provide enough light outdoors, and would not need an extra supply of oil. Torches resist a breeze, give a bright light, burn only about fifteen minutes, and then need to have the rags that are wrapped around the end of the stick soaked again in oil. . . . Here, a bridegroom comes to his wedding with the expectation that some virgins [friends waiting with the bride at her father's house] will have torches ready for a dance [or welcoming procession] as part of the festivities. (Gundry 1994: 498)

In this case, the torches are necessary because the groom, along with his male friends, arrives near midnight (Mt 25:6), and there are no street lamps. Then all ten bridesmaids shake off their sleep and light their torches for the first time (Gundry 1994: 500) in order to go out and meet the groom, his friends, and his family. On the way, the foolish virgins discover that their torches are going out, and, lest all the torches be extinguished, the wise virgins are unwilling to share their reserves of oil.

Clearly, in Matthew's parable, both the wise and the foolish girls have been waiting and expecting the arrival of the groom. When the five foolish girls discover that their torches have gone out, however, they are forced to leave the wedding procession and go buy more oil from the dealers—a nearly impossible task in the middle of the night (Gundry 1994: 501). When they do finally return, everyone has gone inside "into the wedding banquet; and the door was shut" (Mt 25:10). They call to the groom, "Lord, Lord," but he responds, "I do not know you" (Mt 25:12, see par. in 7:23). The key point of Matthew's parable, therefore, is that expectation does not suffice—the true disciple must have reserves of oil—a metaphor for "good works" (Gundry 1994: 499).

All in all, the indoor lamps of Luke's parable as well as the outdoor torches of Matthew's parable have a functional role in the narration itself. The lamps remaining lit in Luke's parable signify vigilance and readiness to "open the door for him as soon as he comes" (Lk 12:36) at night, but does not appear to have any clear metaphorical meaning beyond that. The torches, in Matthew's parable, go out, but the foolish virgins are not blamed for this. No one says, "Do not let your torches go out." Rather, it is because they did not have oil reserves that they are forced to miss the actual arrival of the groom. Thus, these reserves take on a metaphorical meaning quite apart from the torches. In neither case, therefore, does Matthew or Luke offer special insights as to the metaphorical meaning of "not let[ing] your lamps be quenched" (*Did*. 16:1).

What the parables in Matthew and Luke illustrate is how the theme of the "unexpected coming at night" served primitive Christians to evoke the arrival of the last days. The "night" was not taken literally, since "you do not know the hour" (*Did*. 16:1c; Mt 24:36, 44, 50; 25:13). Most probably "night" suggested the recurring theme in apocalyptic literature that the Lord comes when the forces of "darkness" are at their strongest (as will be seen in 16:3f.).

In a Jewish horizon of understanding, the final coming of the Lord was often associated with the first Passover meal in Egypt eaten with "loins girded" (Ex 12:11) in anticipation of the Lord's coming "that night" (Ex 12:12). It would be overextending the evidence, however, either here or in Lk 12:35–40 to suggest that one has "allusions to the Passover" (Deterding: 85). Furthermore, the time of eschatological salvation was frequently described as coming "like a thief in the night" (1 Thes 5:2, 4; Mt 24:32, 44; Lk 12:39; 2 Pt 3:10; Rv 3:3; 16:15; *Gos. Thom*. 21, 103) entirely free of Passover images. Quite aside from teachers and the Way, an admonition to maintain lamps might well have had the original meaning of signaling that the elect must "be prepared" (16:1) during the times of trial (i.e., "at night") for the coming of the Lord.

The associated saying about loins (lit. "genitals") implies that those waiting for the Lord are either already engaged in or are preparing for some strenuous activity. In the Middle East, one finds non-Westernized men traditionally wearing a cotton, ankle-length tunic without any underclothing. When preparing for strenuous activity, such men take a band of cloth about two yards in length and wrap it around their waist and between their legs in such a way as to bind their genitals to their body. Alternately, "girding consists in tucking the end of the long loose garment into the girdle, so that the garment did not hinder work or become soiled" (Jeremias 1972: 187 n. 66). In either case, the "girding of loins" represents the common expression for preparing for strenuous work or distant travel (e.g., 1 Kgs 18:46; 2 Kgs 4:29; 9:1; Jb 38:3; 40:7) or figuratively (e.g., Eph 6:14; 1 Pt 1:13). Here again, since the Didache communities were not especially given to working or traveling at night, it must be assumed that the admonition is to be taken metaphorically, that is, when "darkness" falls, as in *Did*. 16:3f., one must work strenuously at the everyday occupations that now circumscribe one's life.

The activity of "girding loins" does not apply to women. On the other hand, the activity of trimming lamp wicks and adding oil was ordinarily a household chore assigned to women or to household slaves. It is quite possible, therefore, that the framers of the *Didache* specifically used a metaphor drawn from women's experience followed by a metaphor drawn from men's experience. Outside of this, the whole of *Did.* 16 is gender inclusive save for the "world-deceiver," who is named as "a son of God" (16:4). Meanwhile the reference to lamps and loins is reversed in Lk 12:35 (as will be considered shortly). One might speculate that the metaphor of the lamps might have been used first because of the larger proportion of women in the Didache communities (see #1g), and the framers of the *Didache* might have wanted to honor them first. Nothing in the events that follow give the slightest hint that women were especially the troublemakers named in *Did.* 16:3f.; hence, it would seem difficult to conclude that the framers of the *Didache* wanted to address women first because, in their case, they had a greater need to maintain their vigilance.

Be Prepared for You Do Not Know the Hour

In addition to being watchful, members of the Didache communities were told: "Be prepared for you do not know the hour in which our Lord is coming" (16:1b). Both in Q (Mt 24:44/Lk 12:40) and in Mark (13:33, 35), one finds close parallels concerning "the unexpected hour" in which "the Son of Man is coming." Shortly I shall argue that the *Didache* expected the coming of the Lord God; hence, the Synoptic parallels pertain to a later time, when the return of the Lord Jesus (as "the Son of Man") began to supplant the coming of the Lord God (John A. T. Robinson 1979: 118–39).

In Luke's Gospel, the admonition regarding loins and lamps (Lk 12:35) is associated with being prepared: (a) Servants are to be prepared at all times to "open the door for him [the Master] as soon as he comes" (Lk 12:35). (b) A homeowner must be prepared at all times so as to not "let his house be broken into" (Lk 12:39) by a thief. In both case, the metaphors imply that it would be easy to be prepared if "the hour" was known: "If the owner of the house had known at what hour the thief was coming, he would not have let his house be broken into" (Lk 12:39). Since the hour is not known, however, one must be prepared continually. The same sentiment applies to the *Didache*. Not knowing "the hour in which our Lord is coming" (16:1b), one must be continually vigilant.

Didache 16:2 opens with a postpositive *de* and has the force of extending, in practical terms, the meaning of "be watchful" and "be prepared" in v. 1 (Audet 1958: 470). Frequently being "gathered together seeking the things pertaining to your souls" is emphasized (16:2). Now the plural "souls" is used, with *psychē* drawing attention to individual well-being. Such individual well-being, however, is sought within the interpersonal dynamics of the community. The novice was earlier forewarned that, following baptism, "you will seek out every day the companionship of the saints in order that you may rest upon their words" (4:2). The novice is further told that "in the church [assembly], you will confess your failings" (4:14), a practice that later in the *Didache* is clearly specified as taking place prior to every eucharist (14:1). The eucharistic prayers themselves make reference to the fragments "having been gathered together" into one loaf as a sign and symbol of the final gathering together "into the kingdom" (9:4). Fasting, following the Jewish tradition, is understood by the *Didache* as a community affair insofar as all members fast on the same days (8:1). Prayer, traditionally associated with such fasting, is specified as a variant on the "Our Father" and is prayed "three times within the day" (8:3)—preferably in a group setting (ch. 4). In sum, the *Didache* offers an ample overview of the forms this "seeking" may take in the community gatherings. Appeals to parallel admonitions in other early Christian literature to assemble frequently add little or nothing to what the *Didache* says for itself (cf. Heb 10:25; *Barn.* 19:10; Ignatius *Ephesians* 13.1; 20.2; Polycarp *Philippians* 4.2; Herm. *Vis.* 3.6.2; *Sim.* 8.9.1; 9.26.3f.; *1 Clem.* 46.2; *2 Clem.* 17.3).

#10E WHETHER THE "CORRUPTORS" WERE FALSE TEACHERS

Didache 16:3 indicates that the last days will erupt when "false prophets and corruptors will be multiplied." The *Didache* gives ample attention to false prophets, yet one is hard put to identify the "corruptors." The term used here, (*phthoreis*) usually designates "seducers in a moral sense" (Ladd: 66 n. 9). Some scholars, seeing that this term was associated with "false prophets," wanted to imagine that the framers of the *Didache* had "false teachers" (Ladd: 66; Niederwimmer 1998: 217) in mind. This surmise, however, is not very satisfying since, by implication, the "corruptors" would have been responsible for turning the sheep into wolves and the love into hate. Thus, the "corruptors" here would appear to be much more menacing than teachers proposing "another tradition" (*Did.* 11:2) of perfection since the rule here is that these can be combatted by simply ignoring them.

It would make more sense to imagine that the corruptors responsible for turning love to hate would be those who "cause dissension" (*Did.* 4:3) and those "misbehaving against the other" (*Did.* 15:3). Furthermore, it should be noted that, according to the Didache, "corruptors" precipitate acts of hatred, persecution, and betrayal—acts directly opposed to the three kinds of cherishing prized in the Way of Life (*Did.* 2:7). The Way of

Death, in its turn, is primarily associated with "persecutors of the good, those hating the truth, those loving lies" (*Did.* 5:2). In the end, therefore, one might be on firmer ground to understand "corruptors" as those who seduce the sheep into becoming wolves and acting out all the menacing and frightful forms of conduct named in the Way of Death. As this seduction takes place within the Didache communities, a seduction of another kind is taking place globally under the direction of the "world deceiver." The Epilogue will flesh out this global seduction in greater detail against the backdrop of aggressive capitalism.

The Beginning of the Last Days: Corruption Within

Didache 16:3 describes the "darkness" of the last days. Unlike other apocalyptic scenarios, the *Didache* is rather tame and unimaginative and has been rudely chastened as "studied, dull, and unreal" (Bigg 1905: 412). Here one finds neither mobilization of armies fighting world wars nor any cosmic upheaval in the seasons or the falling of the stars. Nor does one find demonic forces overwhelming and persecuting the children of God.

Didache 16:3 specifies the arrival of "the end time" in terms of what will happen to (a) the prophets, (b) the sheep, and (c) the love. The intimation here is that the "darkness" of the end time will begin quite modestly as a failure in the heart of the Jesus movement. The initial fingering of "false-prophets who are corruptors" signals the danger that the community feels in the face of visiting charismatic prophets who have, on more than one occasion, used their gifts to tear down and to mislead (11:1–12). The transformation of sheep into wolves represents the transformation of the tame/useful into the wild/destructive. The metaphor of "sheep" depends upon a Jewish tradition that frequently associates the people of God with sheep (*TDNT* 6:690). The parallel construction of [b] and [c] serves to allow one to explain the other. The use of the definite article before "love" (*agapē*) but not before "hate" (paralleling the article before "sheep" but not before "wolves" in the line before) indicates that what is meant is not an abstract quality but the particular love of God and neighbor (1:2) that characterizes "the saints" (4:2) of the community. In sum, the first wave of "darkness" prefacing the end of history will be large-scale sheep-to-wolf, love-to-hate transformations instigated by misguided prophets.

The *Didache* is striking in what it does and does not say about the menace of the last days. Consider the following summary of what occurs in other end-times scenarios:

> Among the Jewish traditions on eschatological adversity and antagonism, the expectation of a climax of evil is very prominent. The anticipated climax of evil is often depicted in terms denoting a general inversion of order. Descriptions of this kind are found in Daniel 7–8 and 11–12; *Jub.* 23:16–21; *1 Enoch* 80:2–7; 91:6–7; 93:9–10; 91:11; 99:4–8; 100:1–4; *Assumption of Moses* 7–8. . . . These passages all describe an inversion of the social, the natural, and the cosmic order, or a combination of two or three of these. (Peerbolte: 341)

What is unusual about the *Didache* is that it is entirely silent regarding both natural and cosmic disruptions (see #10j). Furthermore, when treating of the "inversion of order" in the social sphere, all of the instances point to disruptions originating in the community itself (*Did.* 16:3f.). This is a unique feature of the *Didache* (see #10g), and it undoubtedly adds greater confirmation to the repeated observations above that the framers of the *Didache* were much more attuned to the menace of false prophets in the communities than to any other social or political forms of harassment or danger coming from outside.

Didache 16:4a presents another *gar*-clause that further elaborates or explains this shocking state of affairs. The genitive absolute construction is used here (the only occurrence in the entire *Didache*) to enforce "lawlessness" as the cause of what was portrayed in 16:3. *Anomia* breaks down into *a + nomia* ("without" + "law") and, in a world in which "law" is instinctively thought of as divinely ordained, *anomia* designates the breakdown not of humanly designed conventional regulations but of the attempt to overthrow the guidance of "the God who made you" (1:2). As a result, *anomia* must here signal that those who have been trained in "the Way of Life" that the Father has "revealed to us through your servant Jesus" (9:3) have abandoned their calling and have taken up a lawless way of life. "Increasing lawlessness," in turn, will give rise to (a) hate, (b) persecution, (c) betrayal—all in an increasingly ugly crescendo.

#10F WHETHER *DID.* 16:4 POINTS TO ROMAN PERSECUTIONS

Niederwimmer imagines that the reference to members who will "persecute and betray (*paradōsousi*)" (*Did.* 16:4) refers to "apostate Christians . . . denouncing their former fellow believers to the authorities" (Niederwimmer 1998: 218). Earlier in the *Didache*, the novice was trained to pray "for your enemies" and fast "for the ones persecuting you" (1:3). Yet, when these phrases were examined in the context of *Did.* 1:4, they amounted only to insulting slaps on the cheek and the seizure of clothing and possessions (see ch. 12). Nothing worse. So, too, those walking in "the way of death" were earlier so characterized as "persecutors of the good, hating truth, loving lies" (*Did.* 5:2)—terms far removed from torturing or killing (see #15c). Niederwimmer appears to be influenced by Mt 24:9–14, where some threads of the *Didache* are seemingly mixed with violent abuse:

> Then they will hand you over (*paradōsousin*) to be tortured and will put you to death, and you will be hated by all nations [gentiles] because of my name. Then many will fall away, and they will betray (*paradōsousin*) one another and hate one another. And many false prophets will arise and lead many astray. And because of the increase of lawlessness, the love of many will grow cold. But the one who endures to the end will be saved. And this good news of the kingdom will be proclaimed throughout the world, as a testimony to all the nations; and then the end will come. (Mt 24:9–14)

According to Matthew, persecution from outside (the gentiles) leads to defections and treachery inside (Gundry 1994: 479). The *Didache*, however, studiously leaves out any reference to persecution from the outside—a very familiar theme in almost all Jewish eschatological literature. Not even the world-deceiver is identified as persecuting the righteous (see #15c). I would conjecture that this studious absence of gentile atrocities is a deliberate attempt on the part of the framers of the *Didache* to subvert and replace unacceptable eschatological themes.

In light of this, it could even be suggested that when the framers of the *Didache* studiously abandoned references to gentile atrocities and gentile persecution in their eschatological scenario, they were doing something that went against the grain. Many visiting prophets speaking in the Spirit may have been infected with anti-Roman sentiments and have been quick to portray gentile atrocities as calling to heaven for eschatological retribution (as in Rv 13). This theme, in itself, would allow one to explain how "false prophets" (16:3a) had the effect of turning "the sheep . . . into wolves and the love . . . into hate" (16:3b).

#10G INTERNAL STRIFE IN A SECOND-CENTURY APOCALYPSE

The *Ascension of Isaiah* (late second century) describes the events that led to the death of the Jewish prophet Isaiah along with visions he had prior to his death. Scholars normally regard this as a Jewish work that was heavily reworked by Christian editors. One can clearly discover Christian editing, for example, in the vision of Isaiah wherein the prophet was able to foresee " . . . the calling and instruction of his twelve disciples, and that before the Sabbath he would be crucified upon the tree, . . . and that he would be buried in the tomb, . . . and that Gabriel . . . and Michael . . . would on the third day open the tomb" (3:13–16). From there, Isaiah's vision allows him to foresee an ideal period in the life of the church that suddenly turns sour:

> And afterwards, before he [Jesus] comes again, his disciples will forsake the teaching of the twelve apostles and their faith and their love and their purity. And there will be much strife before he comes. In those days many there will be who love [to take] office [in the church] even though they are devoid of wisdom. And there will be many lawless elders and shepherds who oppress their flocks; and they will ravage them, because they are not holy shepherds. . . . And there will be much backbiting and empty ambition before the Lord comes. . . . Shepherds and elders will hate one another. For in the last days there will be great jealousies, because each one will proclaim what he thinks is right. (3:21–25)

As the commentary has pointed out, it is altogether rare to find an end-time scenario that begins with disruptions within the heart of the church. Here, in the *Ascension of Isaiah,* one has such a rare text. Instead of false prophets being multiplied, the *Ascension* laments the fact that there were "in those days only a few, whether prophets or any others, whose words can be trusted" (3:27). Instead of the sheep being turned into wolves, it is the shepherds and elders who have become lawless oppressors. Instead of the love of the average member being turned into hate, it is the leaders themselves who have become infected by "backbiting and empty ambition."

This study has noted repeatedly that the framers of the *Didache* deliberately cast their scenario of the last days in order to address the menacing forces confronting their community. The same thing could be said of the *Ascension of Isaiah.* The editor of this text fingers the shepherd/elders of his community as oppressing the people and tearing apart the church. The text thus stands as a trenchant indictment and as a social critique leveled at these persons in the church. When prophecy gave out and when reproving faded, then pastorally conscious editors appear to have revised revered texts in order to provide an authoritative appeal to the Lord to come and correct the ecclesiastic leadership menacing the flock. Texts such as this deserve further study.

Appearance of the God-Like World-Deceiver

The internal havoc within the Didache communities opens the way to the second stage of the end-time scenario, namely, the appearance of the "world-deceiver." While the *Didache* does not specifically say that the "world-deceiver" will set himself up in opposition to God, this is implied by the entire context. Thus, according to the *Didache*, in the last days, a final impostor will massively succeed in being recognized as "son of God" because of "signs and wonders" (*Did.* 16:4b) rather than because of raw power. The use of "signs and wonders" to effect a general apostasy is a frequent theme in apocalyptic literature (see #10i). As a result, the inhabitants of the earth will "be betrayed into his hands" (16:4b)—again focusing on the deceptive character of these "signs and wonders." Needless to say, a remnant faithful to the one true God (16:5) will refuse to accept "the world-deceiver."

One can only imagine what might be the "unlawful things that never have happened from the beginning of time" (16:4b). The Jewish imagination might be inclined to remember the so-called "desolating sacrilege" (Dn 11:31; 12:11; 1 Mc 1:54; 2 Mc 6:2; *Assumption of Moses* 8:5) consisting of statue of Olympian Zeus which Antiochus IV Epiphanes set up in the Jerusalem temple in 167 C.E. The Jewish imagination might also recall the persecution of the saints as in the case wherein Antiochus IV Epiphanes had seven sons subjected to excruciating and prolonged tortures in the sight of their mother, who encouraged them throughout to remain faithful to the true God (2 Mc 7). These things were known to have happened. It is left to the hearer, therefore, to imagine yet worse things.

#10H THE WORLD-DECEIVER AND THE UNIVERSAL APOSTASY

The Greek term *kosmoplanēs* ("world-deceiver") is not found in either biblical or secular Greek. The sole instance of this term is found in the *Apostolic Constitutions* 7.32.2, in which *Did.* 16:4 is reproduced and expanded. While the term itself is absent from other literature, however, alternate terms and metaphors abound.

In Jewish apocalyptic literature, it is quite usual to find the expectation of a general rebellion against God during the last days without associating this rebellion with a single evil figure (e.g., 1QpHab 2.1–10; *1 Enoch* 90:22–27; 91:7; 93:9; *Jub.* 23:14–16; *4 Ezra* 5:1–2).

In Christian apocalyptic writing, this powerful figure is usually termed "the Anti-Christ," but there are two instances of "the deceiving one (*ho planōn*)" (e.g., 2 Jn 7; Rv 12:9). The Synoptics, in contrast, always make reference to a plurality of figures: "false Christs and false prophets" (Mk 13:12; Mt 24:11, 24), thereby presenting the picture of widespread deception due to charismatic figures. In fact, the reference in the *Didache* to "a son of God" may not refer to divine attributes so much as to divine approval (e.g., as in Dt 14:1; 32:6 and 18; Ps 82:6; 89:26f.; Jer 31:9).

The Jewish people had already suffered in the past because of the ambitions of famous men intent on having themselves exalted as "god." Three instances especially stand out. In 605 B.C.E., the Babylonian king Nebuchadnezzar sent out his armies, according to pious fiction, under the direction of Holofernes "to destroy all gods of the land, so that all nations should worship Nebuchadnezzar alone, and that all their dialects and tribes should call upon him as a god" (Jdt 3:8; also 11:7f.). In 167 C.E., Antiochus IV Epiphanes suppressed temple sacrifices to the Lord of Israel and set up the "desolating sacrilege" (Dn 11:31; 12:11; 1 Mc 1:54; 2 Mc 6:2) consisting of a statue of Olympian Zeus and perhaps also a statue of himself in the Jerusalem temple. As recently as 40 C.E., the Roman emperor Caligula, "thinking that he was a god" (Philo, *Embassy to Gaius* 25 [162]) had "ordered a colossal statue of himself to be erected in the holy of holies" (29 [188]). In each of these instances, an ambitious human, puffed up with pride, undertook to secure divine adulation for himself.

In the Book of Revelation, one finds a close parallel to the "world-deceiver" in the second "beast" that looks "like a lamb" (13:11) and "makes the earth and its inhabitants worship the first beast" (13:12) by virtue of performing great signs:

> It performs great signs, even making fire come down from heaven to earth in the sight of all; and by the signs that it is allowed to perform on behalf of the beast, it deceives (*plana*) the inhabitants of earth, telling them to make an image of the beast; . . . and it was allowed to give breath to the image of the beast so that the image of the beast could even speak and cause those who would not worship the image of the beast to be killed. (Rv 13:13–15)

Here one can see that a universal deception accomplished through signs and wonders leads to idolatry. According to the Book of Revelation, both the first and the second beast receive their power from "the great dragon," which is to be understood as "the devil and Satan" (Rv 12:9). The fact that the "signs and wonders" in the *Didache* are not associated with demonic power is probably due to the overall hesitancy of the framers of the *Didache* to evoke the reality of demons under any circumstances (see chs. 1 and 3).

Paul provides a close parallel to what one finds in the *Didache*:

> That day [of the ingathering] will not come unless the rebellion comes first, and the lawless one is revealed, the one destined for destruction. He opposes and exalts himself above every so-called god or object of worship, so that he takes his seat in the temple of God, declaring himself to be God." (2 Thes 2:3–4)

A few lines later, Paul explains his power to deceive as follows:

> The coming of the lawless one is apparent in the working of Satan, who uses all power, signs, lying wonders, and every kind of wicked deception for those who are perishing. . . . (2 Thes 2:9f.)

Here again, the signs and wonders associated with "the lawless one" have Satan as their source—something that the *Didache* does not endorse (as noted above).

In sum, while there is no unified presentation of the forces opposing God, the general situation appears to be that, just prior to his coming, either a single person or many will perform signs and wonders (see #10i) and thereby effect a great apostasy.

#10i NAMING THE SIGNS AND WONDERS OF THE WORLD-DECEIVER

Various signs and wonders are attributed to the world-deceiver. The *Didache* does not go into detail on this point. Other works, however, do. The three illustrative texts below are significant insofar as they imagine signs and wonders that allow the one who is an impostor to gain the honor due to either "God" or "a son of God" (*Did.* 16:4b).

Lactantius's *Divine Institutes* (c. 313 C.E.) provides a richly detailed description of the last days gathered from both Christian and pagan sources (McGinn: 22–24). According to Lactantius, two "evil kings" will appear during the last days. His description of the second "evil king" (leaving aside the material borrowed from Rv 11) reads very much like an expansion of *Did.* 16:4b (parallel passages shown in italics):

> Another king, born of an evil spirit, *will arise* from Syria. He will be the *subverter* and destroyer *of the human race.* . . . He will set himself up and *call himself God. He will* be given the power to *do signs and wonders* in order thus *to ensnare men to worship him.* He

will command fire to come down from heaven, the sun to stand still outside its orbit, and a statue to speak. These will all happen at his word. By these miracles he will attract many of the wise to himself. Then he will destroy the temple of God and will persecute the just people; *there will be affliction* and sorrow *such as has never been seen from the beginning of the world.* (7.17)

One notes that both the "signs and wonders" (three in number) and the "unlawful things" (two in number) are detailed. None of these signs was ever associated with Jesus. The first two (commanding lightning to strike or the sun to stand still) would clearly constitute asronomical signs associated with divine power. The speaking statue is puzzling and may be associated with a popular legend known to Lactantius's audience (Bousset: 138–43).

The *Ascension of Isaiah* (late second century) identifies the world-deceiver as Beliar, the "angel of lawlessness" (2.4) who comes down from heaven in imitation of "the Beloved" (= Jesus) (compare 3.13 and 4.2f.). This angel incarnate gains universal recognition as "God" because of his signs and wonders:

> At his command the sun will rise during the night, and he will make the moon appear at mid-day. And he will have his own way in the world over everything: he will act and speak like the Beloved and will say, "It is I who am the Lord, and before me there has been no other." And all the people in the world will believe in him. And they will sacrifice to him and serve him, saying, "This is the Lord and beside him there is no other." And he will turn away the greater part of those who have been united to receive the [true] Beloved [coming] after him. And the effect of his miracles will be felt in every city and in every place. (4.5–10)

As in the first case, two astronomical signs serve to accredit his divine power. In addition, however, he is able to "act and speak like the Beloved"—thereby imitating Jesus and providing grounds for deceiving "the greater part" of the elect who await the return of Jesus. According to the *Ascension of Isaiah,* 1,332 days are given over to this apostasy; then "the [true] Lord with his angels and with the hosts of the holy ones [the saints] will come from the seventh heaven" (4.14)—the same place from which Jesus originally came (3.13). "He will take Beliar and his hosts away to Gehenna" (4.15). Then he will refresh the saints and clothe them "in their garments from on high" (4.17) before resurrecting the dead and "sending fire among them" so as to "burn up all the ungodly" (4.18) left on the face of the earth.

In the *Apocalypse of Esdras* (variously dated from second to ninth century) the one who now is clearly identified as the "Anti-Christ" is bound in hell and shown to the prophet, who inquires regarding him. The response received by the prophet is this:

> This is the man who says, "I am the son of God," and who made stones bread and water wine. . . . He has been exalted to heaven: to hell shall he descend. At one time he will become a child, at another an old man. (4.27f., 32f.)

In this instance, astronomical signs are absent. All the signs are associated with Jesus. According to Matthew's Gospel, Jesus was challenged by the tempter to demonstrate his true identity: "If you are the Son of God, command these stones to become loaves of bread" (4:3; Lk 4:3). Jesus demurs. According to the *Apocalypse of Esdras,* however, the Anti-Christ goes ahead and does this, along with turning water into wine (as in Jn 2:1–12). The reference to becoming a child and later becoming an old man is also a direct parallel to Jesus, since God complains to the prophet: "[H]e [Jesus] becomes both a child and an old man, and yet no one believes him, that he is my beloved Son" (3.35). The overall irony present in the *Apocalypse of Esdras* is that the signs and wonders performed by the Anti-Christ will deceive the whole world, while the parallel feats, when earlier performed by the true Christ, led to his rejection.

The *Didache* makes reference to "signs and wonders" performed by the world-deceiver in order to be received as "a son of God" (16:4b). One can suppose, therefore, that the framers of the *Didache* regarded Jesus as having performed signs and wonders as well so as to warrant his identity as the true "Son" (7:1, 3). If this is the case, then one must wonder why the framers of the *Didache* would imagine that the world-deceiver would gain a nearly universal acceptance as "a son of God" while Jesus failed to do so. Thus, here again, there is ample room for further work on the *Didache*.

Divine Judgment Arrives
like a Burning Process

The third phase of the apocalyptic scenario envisions all humans and their works passing through "the burning-process of testing" (*Did.* 16:5a). The term *pyrōsis* ("burning-process") is a derivative of *pyr* ("fire") and is found only once in the Christian Scriptures (1 Pt 4:12). *Dokimasia* normally has the sense of "testing," with the prospect of approving something, for example, a team of oxen or a piece of gold (Bauer: 202d). This is precisely the construction that one would expect if the "burning-process" functions both to approve and to destroy, as suggested by alternatives [a] and [b] that follow in the text.

The image of fire is frequently used in both the Hebrew and Christian Scriptures to evoke God's terrifying and mysterious presence (*TDNT* 6:936f., 942–46). More especially, fire functions as the preferred metaphor for evoking the fearsome and consuming judgment of the Lord.

> In the prophets fire is one of the most common means of divine judgment. It smites both the vain-glorious enemies of Israel (Am 1:4, 7, 10, 12, 14; 2:2; Jer 43:12; Na 3:13 etc.) and also the disobedient people of Israel itself (Am 2:5; Hos 8:14; Jer 11:16; 17:27; 21:14; 22:7; Ez 15:7; 16:41; 24:9 etc.). The close relation between images of judgment and theophany expresses the fact that fire is understood, not as a blindly raging natural force, but as an instrument of punishment in the hand of the divine Judge. (*TDNT* 6:936)

In the *Didache*, the burning-process envisions a dual functioning. The first function is to entrap and to destroy those whom the Lord judges as unfit for the kingdom. The Greek verb *skandalizein* comes from *skandalon* ("snare/trap") and literally means to cause someone to fall into a trap or snare (figuratively: "into sin"). The literal sense works well here, for, in the overall design of *Did.* 16, the framers of the *Didache* suggest that the world-deceiver had remarkable success in fooling many into imagining that he was "a son of God" (16:4a) and therefore following him in his ways. But the justice of God is not fooled; rather, it entraps and utterly destroys (*apollymi* being the emphatic form of *ollymi*) "the false prophets and the corruptors" (16:3a) along with the "world-deceiver" and his supporters.

The second function of the "burning-process" is that of saving those "having remained firm in their faith" (16:5b). One finds instances of this in the prophetic notion that God's judgment will destroy the wicked but purify the elect. Herein the image of the refiner's fire is employed to suggest that the elect are like metals being purified as they pass through the final judgment (Is 1:25f.; Jer 6:29; Ez 22:20; 24:11; Zec 13:9; Sir 2:5; Prv 17:3). The prophet Malachi provides the clearest images of this dual functioning of the burning-process when he explains that "the day of his [the Lord's] coming" will be like a "refiner's fire" (3:2). This fire "will purify the sons of Levi and refine them like gold and silver" (3:2f.) while "the arrogant and all evildoers" among God's people shall be like straw in the oven: "the day that comes shall burn them up" (4:1). Texts in the Christian Scriptures that suggest this same dual function are rare and somewhat obscure (1 Cor 4:13–15; 1 Pt 1:5–9). In apocalyptic literature, the

destroying and tormenting dimensions of fire were more and more emphasized after the second century. In a few instances, however, the dual functioning of the burning-process was retained (e.g., *Apocalypse of Peter* 5f.,
Lactantius, *Divine Institutes* 7:20f.). A succinct summary of this dual functioning is found in the Christian *Sibyllines* (second century):

> And then shall all pass through the burning river
> And unquenchable flame; and the righteous
> Shall all be saved, but the impious shall perish. (2.252–54)

The closing words, "saved by the accursed itself" (16:5b), have been
routinely interpreted as making a veiled reference to the crucified Christ.
The church fathers (Harris: 62–68; C. Taylor: 100f.) and even the letters
of Paul (Gal 3:3; 1 Cor 12:3) make reference to Jesus as "the accursed."
Recent critical commentators such as Rordorf (1978a: 198) and Niederwimmer (1989: 265) accordingly conclude that "the accursed itself"
evokes an appeal to the crucified Lord. This position, however, has three
significant soft spots:

1. The internal logic of the *Didache* contains nothing that points in the
direction of the soteriology of the cross. The death of Jesus is not even
mentioned in the entire text.

2. When addressing issues respecting the confession of transgressions
(*Did.* 4:14; 14:1) and the forgiveness of sins (*Did.* 4:6; 8:2), the framers of
the *Didache* provide Jewish-inspired forms of logic entirely outside the
context of the death of Jesus.

3. Even the eucharistic prayers have their own internal logic and symbolism without in any way making use of any Pauline appeal to "covenant,"
"remembrance," or "the Lord's death" (1 Cor 11:25f.).

In consequence, if the internal integrity of the *Didache* is to be allowed
to stand, "saved by the accursed itself" (16:5b) should not be interpreted
by a Pauline understanding foreign to the text itself. In chapter 15, this
phrase is given more careful scrutiny, and the superiority of the dual
process of testing by fire is developed.

The Final Signs of God's Truth

In the fourth phase, three "signs of the truth" are specified. The Greek
term *sēmeion* refers to "the sign or distinguishing mark by which something is known" (Bauer: 747d). Such "signs" are very common in apocalyptic tracts (see #10j) and ordinarily refer to momentous events that will
occur just prior to the Lord's final coming. According to the *Didache*, the
world-deceiver appeared offering "signs" (*sēmeia*) (16:4b) that pulled the
wool over the eyes of humankind. Now, with the likes of him destroyed,

the time is ripe for new "signs" (*sēmeia*) to appear—"signs of truth" (16:6). Both of these events are linked with identical opening words: "And then will appear . . ." (*Did.* 16:4b; 16:6).

Didache 16:6 specifies three signs: (1) the unfurling [what?] in heaven; (2) the sound of the trumpet; and (3) the resurrection of the dead. The first sign is the most difficult to comprehend. J. Rendel Harris, one of the first commentators to be puzzled by this, wrote as follows:

> The word *ekpetasis* is in its first idea [a] the spreading abroad of a bird's wings, then it is used of [b] the attitude of a man in prayer with his arms outstretched, and finally of [c] a human form stretched upon a cross. (1887: 74)

Overwhelmingly, the church fathers and early apocryphal material routinely interpreted "the sign of the Son of man in the heaven" (Mt 24:30) in terms of the third meaning (Harris: 75–77) and accordingly imagined that the crucified Christ or a cross carried by an angel would constitute the terrible sign of the final coming. C. Taylor, in his early commentary, thus rendered the obscure text as "the sign of a (cross) spreading out in heaven" (101–3).

This tradition of interpretation has continued down to the present day. Scholars such as Harris (75), Audet (1958: 473f.), and Giet (1970: 253 n. 38) have expressed hesitations in this regard. Rordorf, however, concluded that "the reservations of critics with regard to this interpretation are not convincing" (1978a: 198). Niederwimmer also cast his vote for the dominant tradition:

> The sign thus referred to would thus be as follows: the cross of the *Kyrios* appears in the heavens as precursor of his parousia. This cross (as we perhaps must suppose) was previously taken up with him into heaven; now the cross reappears and announces his [the *Kyrios'*] immediate appearance. (1998: 224)

The notion that the cross was taken up into heaven with Jesus was first related in the *Gospel of Peter* (mid-second century). According to this Gospel, a pair of Roman soldiers was assigned to guard the tomb in which Jesus had been laid. During the night, they witnessed the heavens being opened, and two men surrounded by a great light came down from heaven and removed the body of Jesus from the tomb and "a cross followed them" (10.39) into the heavens. The trouble with this legend is that it is late—much later than the canonical Gospels. It is further troubling that this legend presupposes that the cross was buried with Jesus in the tomb—a practice that would have been extremely unlikely.

If the *Didache* had been composed in the mid-second century as has been supposed for so long, then it would be possible to allow that the legend of the cross just noted may have been understood behind the obscure first sign of truth. Even though Rordorf and Niederwimmer both date the *Didache* as having been composed, at the latest, at the opening of the second century (Rordorf 1998: 245; Niederwimmer 1998: 43), neither of them appears to give much weight to the late evidence for the legend of the cross. Even in the commentaries on Matthew, the identification of the "sign of the Son of Man" with the cross can be dated no earlier than the opening decades of the second century (Dinkler: 77–87; Hill: 108–15). For me, however, the most pressing reason to abandon the idea that the *Didache* envisioned the cross coming from heaven is the recognition that the soteriology of the cross finds no confirmation in the internal logic of the text itself.

Jonathan Draper provides an attractive alternative reading of the first sign, taking his point of departure not from the church fathers but from the prophetic literature of Israel. Draper took note of the fact that repeatedly the setting up of a standard or flag accompanied by the sounding of a shofar or trumpet constituted the signal for the assembly of the nation of Israel (Is 5:26; 11:10–12; 13:2; 31:9; 62:10; Jer 51:27) and was very common in eschatological settings as well (Is 27:13; Jl 2:1; Zep 1:14–16; Zec 9:14; Mt 24:31; Rv 1:10; 4:1; 8:2, 6, 7, 8, 10, 12, 13; 9:1, 13, 14; 10:7; 11:15; *TDNT* 7:80–88). Draper summarizes his results as follows:

> It [the raising of a flag or totem] always involved the ingathering of peoples: either the ingathering of nations for war against Israel—for victory or for calamitous defeat—or the ingathering of the dispersed people of Israel and Judah from the four winds or corners of the earth. The raising of the totem is usually accompanied by the blowing of the shofar. Associated with these firm features of the symbol, other expectations surface in the Targum [of Isaiah]: the coming of the Davidic messiah, or a mighty king on, or like, a cloud, possibly accompanied by the righteous dead. . . . (1993: 7)

A fresh solution for the *Didache* thus emerges. The first sign is the *ekpetasis* ("the spreading out") of a flag in the heavens accompanied by the second sign, the sounding of a trumpet. The tenth benediction of the *Shemoneh ʿEsreh* interestingly retains this dual signal quite aptly:

> Sound the great trumpet to announce our freedom; set up a banner to collect our captives, and gather us together from the four

corners of the earth. Blessed art thou, O Lord, who gathers the dispersed of your people Israel.

This interpretation of the first two signs has the advantage of providing an unexpected solution to another puzzling problem. The eucharistic prayers of the *Didache*, in two places, make direct appeal to the Father that "your church be gathered together from the ends of the earth into your kingdom" (9:4; 10:5). It would be strange, accordingly, to find no reference to this ingathering in the apocalyptic vision of this same community. Thus, Draper not only supplies a satisfying alternative that is consistent with the internal logic of *Did.* 16, but, in addition, he supplies a link with the eucharistic expectation, namely, the ingathering of the elect. In effect, therefore, after passing through the burning-process, all the purified ones remaining will be signaled to assemble.

The interpretation of the first two signs as effecting the gathering of the elect also has the advantage of designating the *place* where the righteous will be raised to life (*Did.* 16:7) and where the Lord God will come to dwell among his people (16:8). In Jewish prophetic and apocalyptic literature, Jerusalem is the center of the world, where the Lord God will assemble his people in the eschatological kingdom. In the Christian Book of Revelation, the "new Jerusalem," where God "lives among men" (Rv 21:3), is not equated with the historical Jerusalem, for the "holy city" is seen "coming down from God out of heaven" (Rv 21:2). The theme of a "new Jerusalem" already established in heaven also finds its Jewish adherents (2 Esdras 8:52; 10:27; *2 Apoc. Bar.* 4:1–6). The *Didache*, for its part, silently passes over any mention of Jerusalem both in its eschatological scenario and in its eucharistic prayers (see #10q). The presumption must be, accordingly, that the Lord God will decide where the elect will be assembled and that the dual signs of the unfurling banner and sounding trumpet will signal to the elect God's choice.

At the very end, the Lord God will appear, like a triumphant monarch, arriving on the clouds (his chariot) with the "holy ones" forming a kind of reception committee or imperial guard (Gundry 1987: 163; P. D. Hanson: 375; Meyers: 430). In effect, however, the Lord God has already been actively present in the burning-process of testing (16:5), in the gathering of the elect, and in the raising of the righteous dead (16:6). This is a common feature in Jewish literature: "For his visitation, God uses underlying forces which form a second level, a level of efficacious powers" (Koch: 64, commenting on Amos). Thus, the signs of the unfurling banner and the sounding trumpet indicate that the Lord will gather his elect in the place he chooses, the place where the righteous dead will be raised to life (or, alternately, where they will congregate once raised from their sleep). Everything, then, will be in readiness for the Lord's arrival on the clouds of heaven to that place.

#10J THE IMPORTANCE OF KNOWING
THE SIGNS OF THE LAST DAYS

The notion of "last days" presupposes a linear conception of history in which there is a beginning and there is an end (Dunn 1977: 312). The "end" in apocalyptic literature, however, is not the end of historical time as such, but the end of a degenerate epoch filled with affliction and injustice that must pass away in order to give birth to a new age in which the blessings of God will prevail.

> A frequent feature of apocalyptic thought is that the ending of the old age and introduction of the new one will be marked by a period of severe distress such as the world has never known— sometimes thought of as a heightening of ordinary woes or under the figure of childbirth, sometimes in terms of military conflict and war, sometimes in terms of supernatural cosmic portents and catastrophes. . . . (Dunn 1977: 313)

Thus, when the faithful ask, "How long will this corrupt age endure?" "How long before the Lord comes to bring judgment on the old and to begin the new age?" (e.g., Dn 8:13; 12:6), various "signs" are usually given whereby one can know that this is the "real thing" and not just a passing tragedy in world history. In the Gospel of Matthew, for instance, one reads:

> When he [Jesus] was sitting on the Mount of Olives, the disciples came to him privately, saying, "Tell us, when will this [the destruction of the temple] be, and what will be the *sign* of your coming and of the end of the age?"
> Jesus answered them, "Beware that no one leads you astray. For many will come in my name, saying, 'I am the Messiah!' and they will lead many astray. And you will hear of wars and rumors of wars; see that you are not alarmed; for this must take place, but the end is not yet. For nation will rise against nation, and kingdom against kingdom, and there will be famines and earthquakes in various places: all this is but the beginning of the birthpangs. Then they will hand you over to be tortured and will put you to death, and you will be hated by all nations because of my name." (Mt 24:3–9)

In this Gospel, Jesus gives many "signs" of the end of this age: wars, famines, earthquakes, and a universal persecution of his disciples. Still other signs follow (Mt 24:10–29). Then the special "sign" of his coming will appear:

Immediately after the suffering of those days the sun will be darkened, and the moon will not give its light; the stars will fall from heaven, and the powers of heaven will be shaken. Then the *sign* of the Son of Man will appear in heaven, and then all the tribes of the earth will mourn, and they will see "the Son of Man coming on the clouds of heaven" with power and great glory. And he will send out his angels with a loud trumpet call, and they will gather his elect from the four winds, from one end of heaven to the other. (Mt 24:29–31)

In order to appreciate how signs functioned in non-Christian circles, the end-time inquiries of the prophet Ezra in 2 Esdras (late first century) are helpful. The angel Uriel refuses to disclose whether Ezra will still be living during the last days, yet, he does offer signs whereby the onset of the last days can be known:

Now concerning the signs: lo, the days are coming when those who inhabit the earth shall be seized with great terror, and the way of truth [Torah] shall be hidden, and the land shall be barren of faith. Unrighteousness shall be increased beyond what you yourself see. . . . There shall be chaos also in many places, fire shall often break out, the wild animals shall roam beyond their haunts, and menstruous women shall bring forth monsters. Salt waters shall be found in the sweet, and all friends shall conquer one another, then shall reason hide itself, and wisdom [Torah] shall withdraw into its chamber. . . . (2 Esdras 5:1f.; 8f.)

Here one does not find wars, famines, and earthquakes but another set of unnatural disturbances: wild fires, roaming animals, human monsters. The most emphasized sign is that unrighteousness and unfriendliness will increase beyond all former bounds.

In addition to the signs of the last days revealed by Uriel, the Lord God himself reveals to Ezra the signs of his "draw[ing] near to visit the inhabitants of the earth" (2 Esdras 6:18).

Then I will show these signs: the books [recording the deeds of all] shall be opened before the face of the firmament, and all shall see my judgment together. Children a year old shall speak with their voices, and pregnant women shall give birth to premature children at three and four months, and these shall live and leap about. . . . The trumpet shall sound aloud, and when all hear it, they shall suddenly be terrified. At that time friend shall make war on friends. . . . It shall be that whoever remains after all that I have foretold to you shall be saved and shall see my salvation. . . . For evil shall be blotted out, and deceit shall be quenched; faithfulness shall flourish, and corruption shall be overcome, and the truth which has been so long without fruit shall be revealed. (2 Esdras 6:20f., 23f., 25, 27f.)

At first, the books recording the deeds of all (see Rv 20:12, *1 Enoch* 89:61–64) are opened up in the heavens such that all can see them. Whereas women formerly suffered deformed births, now they give birth to child prodigies. Then the trumpet sounds. It would appear here that the trumpet functions at this point to gather the avenging angels who will strike down those who, according to the open books of judgment, were the persecutors of the just. This helps to explain the terror "they" experience and to account for how "evil shall be blotted out" and how "whoever remains . . . shall be saved and see my salvation" (as cited above). The signs come to a summation in the promise made to the elect by the Lord God to the effect that "the truth which has been so long without fruit shall be revealed" (2:28).

From these two instances, one can see how diverse the signs of the last days and the signs of the coming can be. In fact, if one would compare and contrast the various lists of signs found in the Jewish and Christian literature, one would find little or no coherence. Incompatible lists of signs can sometimes appear in the same book (2 Esdras 5:1–13; 6:20–28). Those who created these lists undoubtedly knew of the lists of others; nonetheless, since there was no standard list that everyone repeated, each author created his own list in order to address the popular traditions and the pastoral needs of those being addressed.

As for the *Didache*, there are effectively two sets of signs. The first set (16:3f.) does not use the term "signs," yet it is quite apparent that the things listed signal the terrible beginning of the end. The second set, "the signs of truth" (16:6), point to the wonderful events that will overtake the elect just prior to when they "will see the Lord coming" (16:8). This last event is not a "sign" but the reality to which the earlier "signs" were pointing. The elect who are struggling with the increase of "false prophets and are corruptors" and with "lawlessness" (16:3f.) were then "watchful," for they knew that things would get far worse before they got better.

#10ᴋ Tʜᴇ Iᴍᴘʟɪᴇᴅ Eꜱᴄʜᴀᴛᴏʟᴏɢʏ ᴏꜰ ᴛʜᴇ Eᴜᴄʜᴀʀɪꜱᴛɪᴄ Pʀᴀʏᴇʀꜱ

The very sequence of the apocalyptic scenario appears to have been inspired in part by the eschatological prayer used after the eucharistic meal. Consider the following:

> Remember, Lord,
> [a] to save your church from every evil
> [b] and to perfect it in your love
> [c] and to gather it together from the four winds into your
> kingdom. (*Did.* 10:5)
>
> Accordingly, in the face of the ravages of the "world-deceiver," who is
> made out to be a religious leader ("a son of God") doing "signs and won-
> ders" (16:4b), the "burning-process of testing" is calculated [a] to save the
> righteous from this deception and [b] to perfect those "having remained
> firm in their faith . . . by the accursed [burning-process] itself" (16:5)—
> which, as in the metaphor of the metallurgist's fire, purifies rather than
> destroys. Then, the three "signs of the truth" (16:6) bring about [c] the
> gathering together from the four winds of the living and the dead into the
> kingdom that arrives along with "the Lord coming atop the clouds of
> heaven" (16:8).
>
> In the Babylonian Talmud (*b. Megillah* 17b) one finds a stark apocalyp-
> tic scenario that is directly modeled after the Eighteen Benedictions used
> in the synagogue service (see #10q). This provides a fitting parallel to what
> one has in the *Didache. Lex orandi lex credendi* ("The rule of praying is the
> rule of believing").

The Resurrection of the Righteous Who Sleep in the Earth

The last sign, that of the resurrection of dead, frequently figures into
apocalyptic texts from the second century B.C.E. onward (Nickelsburg
1972: 174). Effectively, the first two signs suggest that all the just scattered
on the face of the earth will be gathered together in the place designated
by the Lord. With the resurrection, all of the just will be raised to life and
gathered together with the assembled elect.

For a resurrection to take place, there was no presumption that the
decomposed bodily parts had somehow to be gathered together again and
reanimated by the immortal soul (as if such a thing were possible in the vast
majority of cases). Rather, resurrection implied a new creation of persons
whose complete identity was kept intact by the loving memories of the
Lord:

> Resurrection is, therefore, a creation in the strictest sense of the
> word, a creation *ex nihilo,* not the reunion of the immortal soul
> with its corruptible but now reassembled body. The true miracle
> of the resurrection is not that we come to life, but that we come

to life as identifiably the person who once lived and wholly died [body and soul]. (Marrow: 585)

The sign of the resurrection of the dead, consequently, was not understood by Jews as a natural or predictable process (as in the case of reincarnation). It was understood as the Lord's way of vindicating those saints who had been victimized for their fidelity to God (2 Mc 7:9, 11, 14, 29; 12:39–45; Prusak: 477–80; Ratzinger: 181–214). As such, it would take place when and where the Lord God has chosen.

The *Didache* makes the point of asserting that only the just will be raised and offers Zec 14:5 as a divine testimony to this effect. The Septuagint version of Zechariah reads: "[The] Lord God (*kyrios ho theos*) will come and all the holy ones with him." The *Didache* omits *ho theos* and supplies *kyrios* with a definite article. Some scholars, influenced by Mt 24:30, have argued that the framers of the *Didache* deliberately modified Zec 14:5 so as to make room for the understanding that "the Lord" coming is Jesus rather than God (e.g., Giet 1970: 254). As explained earlier, however, I find no evidence in the larger text of the *Didache* which assigns any eschatological functions to Jesus; hence, I am inclined to believe that the framers of the *Didache* were intent on justifying the selective resurrection of the elect and supplied the text of Zec 14:5 from memory to support their contention. Hence, the variation on the Septuagint does not alter its meaning (see #10m and #15c).

#10M WHETHER THE LORD GOD COMES OR THE LORD JESUS RETURNS

Niederwimmer allows that *Did.* 16:7 makes use of Zec 14:5:

The quoted version follows the Septuagint, with a slight change at the beginning ["The Lord" instead of "The Lord my God"]. The same quotation is also found in Mt 15:31a [should be 25:31a], but the *Didache* passage does not come from Matthew; it is taken directly from Zechariah. (Niederwimmer 1998: 225)

Since the text of Zechariah makes it amply clear that it is the Lord God who comes and that no coming of a messianic figure or a Son of Man figure into the text, one might have expected Niederwimmer to conclude that "the Lord" in *Did.* 16:7 and 16:8 refers to the Lord God. But this is not the case:

The text of the *Didache* [16:8], in the sequence of its elements, is closer to Mark 13:26 par. than to the text of Daniel [7:13].

> Again, striking is the replacement of the title "Son of man" by
> *kyrios*. The text is especially close to Mt 24:30b. . . . This would
> speak more for a dependence on Matthew rather than Mark. . . .
> Literary dependence upon Matthew, however, cannot be
> demonstrated with assurance in this passage. (Niederwimmer
> 1998: 226)

Niederwimmer thus identifies "the Lord" with Jesus because (1) he
believes that the framers of the *Didache* began with a text like Mt 24:30b
or Mark 13:26, and (2) he presumes that the *Didache* embraces the second coming. Both of these assumptions, however, are doubtful:

1. Niederwimmer presumes that the *Didache* could have been written as
late as the beginning of the second century (1998: 43). Accordingly,
Niederwimmer cautiously flirts with the possibility of dependence on a
known Gospel, Matthew's more especially, throughout his volume. Given
the complexity of this issue, chapter 11 is entirely devoted to it, concluding that not only is dependence on Matthew not evident but, point after
point, Matthew's Gospel and the *Didache* evoke two independent religious systems addressing common problems in divergent ways. Niederwimmer, at one point in this volume, would appear to agree: "The *Didache*
lives in an entirely different linguistic universe, and that is true not only of
its sources but of its redactor as well" (Niederwimmer 1998: 48). In practice, however, he vacillates on this question (as seen from the citation
above).

2. The prayers of the *Didache* make clear that the Father was expected
to come to gather the elect into his kingdom (8:2; 9:4; 10:5f.). Nothing is
said regarding any role that Jesus or any other figure would play in this
drama. Thus, this is entirely in harmony with the end-time account of
Zechariah:

> The city shall be taken [by the gentiles] and the houses looted
> and the women raped. . . . Then the Lord will go forth and fight
> against those nations. . . . Then the Lord my God will come, and
> all the holy ones with him. . . . And the Lord will become king
> over all the earth; on that day the Lord will be one and his name
> one. . . . Then all who survive of the nations . . . shall go up year
> after year to worship the king, the Lord of hosts, and to keep the
> festival of booths. (Zec 14:2f., 5, 9, 16)

Here, as in the *Didache*, the God of David does everything; nothing is said
of the "Son of David" or of a messianic kingdom being established prior
to the arrival of the Lord God (see extended discussion in #10r).

While it is commonplace to regard the Second Coming or Parousia as representing the earliest expectation of the Jesus movement and as "firmly rooted in all strands of the New Testament" (*ABD* 5:166c), this claim does not stand up under close analysis. John A. T. Robinson (1979), for example, has demonstrated that the early church only made slow and hesitant steps toward formulating an expectation of the second coming and, even after doing so, retained fragments of earlier incompatible positions.

While some of Robinson's ideas are now dated, his overall program remains sound. Two points made from his book are especially important for our question:

1. Robinson takes his starting point from a study of T. F. Glasson:

> Glasson . . . proceeded to show with a wealth of illustration (162–179) how the language in which the *Parousia* expectation is couched derives, not from *messianic* passages of the Old Testament, but from its visions of the coming of *God* to his people in final and glorious theophany. "Broadly speaking," he wrote, "the Christians took over the Old Testament doctrine of the Advent of the Lord, making the single adjustment that the Lord was the Lord Jesus." (176) (Robinson 1979: 140)

In effect, with regard to the *Didache*, one might therefore begin with a healthy suspicion that Zec 14:5 might have been deliberately chosen precisely because (as shown above) the framers of the *Didache* expected the Lord God to come with his angels and establish his universal kingdom on the face of the earth. When Zec 14:5 is examined in connection with late texts such as Mt 24:30b, it is no wonder that Niederwimmer and others fall into the trap of reading "Lord" as referring to the "Lord Jesus" instead of the "Lord God."

2. Robinson shows that the Christian Scriptures show evidence of transitions. For example, consider the transition from Jesus as an advocate at God's side during the final judgment to Jesus as acting alone as the final judge:

> According to the earlier tradition, represented by the saying as we have it in "Q" (and indeed in the body of Mark 8:38), as well as in Mt 7:22f. = Lk 13:26f., Jesus pictures himself as occupying the Old Testament role of the figure who stands at the judgment before the throne of God to accuse or to plead for those he represents. . . . But the general position of the Church was that by virtue of the Resurrection Jesus was himself designated *judge* on God's behalf (Acts 10:42; 17:31). Consequently, in the later strands of the Gospel tradition, he is made to occupy the throne of judgment itself (Mt 19:28; 25:31). And, in this capacity as

judge, it is natural that he should also be represented as "com-ing" (as, again, in Mt 25:31); for in the biblical tradition God regularly "comes" to judge the world (e.g., Pss 96:13; 98:9; Dn 7:22; *1 Enoch* 3:9). (1979: 56)

The eschatological trajectory within Judaism was, in its early phases, without any messianic age, and then, in its late phases, the mighty works of God were given over to his Messiah (see #10r). Robinson's observations of the transition within the Christian Scriptures as to the identity of the final judge further strengthen this position. To the degree that this is true and to the degree that the *Didache* could have been created in the mid-first century, then it becomes necessary to suspect that *Did.* 16 presents an early and formative eschatology that is much closer to Zechariah than to the Synoptics. Furthermore, while the *Didache* does make a single passing reference to Jesus as the "Christ" (9:4), the *Didache* does not regard this as its central position, nor does it spell out the ramifications of this asser-tion for the last days (see #5e and #5f.). This may help explain why the "world-deceiver" in the *Didache* was never called the "Anti-Christ." Hence, the *Didache* witnesses to the life and hope of those who embraced Jesus without assigning him any expectations that the community was looking to be delivered by the Lord God himself. Indeed, further study is necessary in order to situate the *Didache* in the spectrum of Christologies that developed during the first two centuries. When this study finally emerges, my suspicion is that the *Didache* will be identified as represent-ing the "most primitive Christology of all" (see John A. T. Robinson 1956).

#10N THE RESTRICTED USE OF "LORD" IN THE *DIDACHE*

The *Didache* makes frequent use of *kyrios* ("lord"). In each instance, the context can be explored in order to discern whether the "Lord God" or the "Lord Jesus" is meant.

In the eucharistic prayers, Jesus is portrayed as "the servant" who reveals the life and understanding of the Father (*Did.* 9:3). This accords well with the understanding of the Christian Scriptures that Jesus proclaimed "the good news of God" (Mk 1:4; Rom 1:1; 2 Cor 2:7; 1 Thes 2:2, 9; 1 Pt 4:17)—never the "good news of Jesus." Thus, in the four places in the *Didache* wherein "good news" (*euaggelion*) (see #11e) is found (8:2; 11:3; 15:3; and 15:4), it must be supposed that this is the "good news of our Lord God" (15:4).

For the reasons just mentioned, it must also be supposed that when it comes to baptizing and receiving visitors "in the name of the Lord" (9:5;

12:1), this means, first and foremost, doing these things "in the name of the Father" (7:1). The members of the Didache community were pre-occupied with his "name" (8:2; 10:2) and not with the "name of Jesus."

On four occasions, the *Didache* makes reference to persons being hon-ored or received "as the Lord" (4:1; 11:2, 4; 12:1). The most elaborate of these is the following:

> [A] My child, the one speaking to you the word of God,
> [1] you will remember night and day,
> [2] and you will honor him/her as the Lord,
>   for where the dominion of the Lord is spoken of,
>   there the Lord is. (4:1)

Here the novice was being shown the appropriate posture to take toward his/her mentor: (a) remember him/her continually, that is, reflect on his/her life and words; and (b) honor him/her "as the Lord." Nieder-wimmer believes that "as the Lord God" would have been intended in its original Jewish context but that here, it refers to the "Lord Jesus" (1998: 105). In the context of the *Didache*, this does not make sense. The novice receives "the life and knowledge which you [our Father] revealed to us" (9:3). This is the "good news of the Lord God" (15:4). "Where the dominion of the Lord God is spoken of, there the Lord God is" (14:1). In the Synoptics, Jesus says to his disciples: "Whoever welcomes you wel-comes me, and whoever welcomes me welcomes the one who sent me" (Mt 10:40; par. Lk 9:48). These words fit because the disciples are on mis-sion, at this point, having been sent out by Jesus. Whoever welcomes them, accordingly, welcomes the one who sent them. The same is not true of mentors in the *Didache*. They are not trained and sent out by Jesus. They, then, would simply use Jesus' words: "Whoever welcomes me wel-comes the one [namely, the Lord God] who sent me" (Mt 10:40). Thus, the novice honors his/her mentor "as the Lord God" and not as the "Lord Jesus" for it is "the word of God" and the Way of Life revealed by the Father that were being transmitted. Thus, R. Eleazar ben Shammua said, "The reverence owing to your master [mentor] should be like the awe owing to Heaven [= God]" (*m. Avot* 4:12; *Kallah Rabbathi* 52b).

In four instances, words are received "from the Lord" (*Did.* 8:2; 9:5; 12:3; 16:7 implied). When passages from the Hebrew Scriptures are put forward with the indication that "the Lord says" (as in 12:3 and 16:7), no one would doubt that the Lord God is meant. When the passages cited, however, have an equivalent in the Christian Scriptures, then the reference is unclear. The *Didache* has two such cases:

1. When "pray as the Lord ordered in his good news" (8:2) stands before the Lord's Prayer, it is unclear whether this is what Jesus ordered or what God ordered. When it is remembered that Jesus proclaims the "good

news of God" and that those who hear him, hear the Lord God, then it does not seem strange to attribute to the Lord God a rule of praying. Only when the notion of "following Jesus" became the fixed point of reference does *Did.* 8:2 lose its sense as pointing to the Lord God.

2. The eucharistic meal contains a rubric regarding the exclusion of the nonbaptized. This rubric is enforced as being from "the Lord" (*Did.* 9:5) on the basis of the saying: "Do not give what is holy to dogs" (9:5). Earlier it was shown that this was a common saying used to prohibit the distribution or sale of meats sacrificed in Jerusalem to gentiles (see ch. 5). The framers of the *Didache* clearly thought that this saying was part of the words of the Lord God in the Hebrew Scriptures. They made the same innocent mistake that contemporary Christians sometimes make when they cite, "Money is the root of all evil," as a biblical saying. In rabbinic literature, "it is the flesh of [temple] sacrifice that the much quoted saying refers: 'what is holy is not to be released to be eaten by dogs' (*b. Bekhorot* 15a interpreting Dt 12:15; *m. Temurah* 6:5; *b. Temurah* 117a & 130b [correction: 17a & 30b]; *b. Shabuot* 11b; and *b. Pesahim* 29a)" (*TDNT* 3:1102)

Many scholars immediately jump to the conclusion that "the Lord" refers to Jesus here since a word-for-word repetition of this saying is found in Mt 7:6 (Niederwimmer 1998: 153). This seems doubtful for three reasons: (1) To begin with, the *Didache* is focally centered on the Father's revelation and never explicitly quotes "Jesus," "Moses," or anyone else. (2) When a similar formula is used in *Did.* 14:3, the citation is from Mal 1:11 and, consequently, the appeal to what was "said by the Lord God." (3) Finally, the context of the saying about "holy things" in Matthew clearly pertains to Jesus teaching and has no oblique reference to the eucharist. For these reasons, it seems more probable that the *Didache* imagines that the Lord God is being cited in *Did.* 9:4.

When the return of "the Lord" in *Did.* 16:8 is examined against the backdrop of Zec 14:5, which is cited in 16:7, it is quite clear that it is the Lord God who is awaited. In the eschatological battle envisioned by Zechariah, it is the Lord God who "will take the field" (Zec 14:3) in order to vanquish the enemies of Israel. Following the Lord's victory, it is also the Lord God who "will be king of the whole world" (Zec 14:9). The end-time in Deutero-Zechariah, therefore, accords well with Deutero-Isaiah and other postexilic prophets in order to insist that the final and eternal king will be God himself (Lindblom: 395). As a result, the apocalypse of the *Didache* appears to confirm the attachment of the community to Jesus without in any sense disturbing the eschatological roles assigned to the Father.

When everything is examined, it would appear that all of the instances of "Lord" in the *Didache* ought to be understood as referring to the "Lord God."

Jesus reveals the holiness of Israel to the gentiles, and for this the Father is given thanks. But more. Jesus reveals the "life and understanding" that give both Jew and gentile a share in the kingdom to come. Surely Jesus will have a part in this kingdom; he will be among "the holy ones" (*Did.* 16:7) coming with the Lord on the last day. But, in the end, the *Didache* joins with the expectation of Isaiah:

> Look down from heaven and see,
> from your holy and glorious habitation. . . .
> For you are our Father,
>   though Abraham does not know us
>   and Israel does not acknowledge us,
> you, O Lord, are our Father;
> our Redeemer from of old is your name. . . .
> O that you would tear open the heavens and come down,
>   so that the mountains would shake at your presence—
>   as when fire kindles brushwood and the fire causes water
>   to boil—
> to make your name known to your adversaries,
>   so that the nations might tremble at your presence!
>   (Is 63:15f.; 64:1f.)

A final note needs to be made regarding those who would jump to the conclusion that, since the *Didache* embraces a trinitarian formula (*Did.* 7:1), it would make no distinction between "Lord God" and "Lord Jesus" when it comes to *Did.* 16:7f. Those who wish to equate Jesus with "God" would do well to read Raymond Brown's essay "Does the New Testament Call Jesus God?" (1967: 1–38). For an in–depth study, I would recommend James D. G. Dunn (1991: 163–229). A key passage in his work is as follows:

> Paul in fact calls Jesus "Lord" as much as a means of distinguishing Jesus from God as of identifying him with God. We have already cited 1 Cor 8:6 more than once: "For us there is one God, the Father . . . and one Lord, Jesus Christ." Evidently Paul could confess Jesus as Lord, while *at the same time* confessing that God is one; the two claims were not seen to be in any kind of competition. Paul could acknowledge the lordship of Christ, without apparently diminishing his commitment to Jewish monotheism. . . . We should also note a phrase which recurs quite often in the Pauline corpus, "the God and Father of our Lord Jesus Christ" [Rom 15:6; 2 Cor 1:3; 11:31; Eph 1:3, 17; Col 1:3; also 1 Pt 1:3]. Even Jesus as *Lord* has God as *his* God. (1991: 190)

The Lord Coming atop the Clouds

Finally, at the end, the Lord appears like a triumphant monarch, arriving on the clouds (his "chariot" according to Ps 104:3) with the "holy ones" forming a kind of reception committee or imperial guard (Gundry 1987: 163; P. D. Hanson: 375; Meyers: 430). The elect, both living and dead, were gathered by the three signs; as yet, however, they are without the kingdom. The Lord himself, as their king, will meet with them and bring them into his kingdom (*Did.* 9:5; 10:5). Perhaps one would do better to say, along with the Lord's Prayer, that he is "their kingdom come" (*Did.* 8:1; see ch. 4).

The vision of the Lord riding on the clouds and coming from heaven down to earth offers a very anthropomorphic image of God. In reality, the God of Israel cannot be seen and had no need of clouds to transport him from the heavens. Yet, in both Jewish and Christian apocalyptic, it was standard practice to present God as coming in such anthropomorphic terms (see #10o).

#10o THE SIGNIFICANCE OF THE LORD GOD COMING ATOP THE CLOUDS

In the prophets, one finds many anthropomorphic images of the Lord God coming to earth. In one of the earliest visions, after Israel has been vanquished, the Lord says, "Now I will arise. . . . Now I will lift myself up" (Is 33:10) and, accordingly, he arrives in Jerusalem as a "devouring fire" (Is 33:12, 14; see ch. 15).

Zechariah 14, developing the same theme, gives greater detail: "The city shall be taken and the houses looted and the women raped" (14:2). "Then the Lord will go forth and fight against those nations as when he fights on a day of battle. On that day his feet shall stand on the Mount of Olives" (14:4). Zec 14 provides no detail on how the Lord God comes from heaven to earth. In this scenario, as in Is 33, the city is vanquished and then the Lord takes the field alone to oppose all the nations who have plundered and raped the children of Israel.

In the *Apocalypse of Peter* (early second century), the Day of the Lord begins with all the living "gathered before my Father," who then releases all the dead from Hades (4). Then "cataracts of fire shall be let loose" (5) and "an unquenchable fire shall drive them [the living and the dead]" (5) to the place of judgment. Then, the Lord Jesus will arrive to take his place at the right hand of the Father:

> And all will see how I [Jesus] come upon an eternal shining
> cloud, and the angels of God will sit with me on the throne of my
> glory at the right hand of my heavenly Father. He will set a crown
> upon my head. As soon as the nations [gentiles] see it, they will
> weep. . . . (6)

This image goes beyond the Synoptics (Mk 13:26 and par.). The text
begins with a variation on Zec 14:5 where the "holy ones" are angels.
Here one sees how the Messiah takes over divine functions. The Father
raises the dead, but then Jesus comes from heaven to receive the crown
that authorizes him to "judge the living and the dead" (*Apocalypse of Peter*
1, 6). This is in contrast to 2 Esdras (late first century) where "the Most
High shall be revealed [alone] on the seat of judgment" (7:33) after the
death of the Messiah (7:29).

The Christian *Sibyllines* (c. 150 C.E.) develop many of the themes found
in the *Apocalypse of Peter*. "The Almighty himself" (2.220) comes to earth,
takes his "judgment seat" and "raises the dead" (2.237f.). Then Christ and
his angels come to take their place on the right hand of God:

> There shall come on a cloud . . .
> Christ in glory with his blameless angels,
> And [he] shall sit on the right hand of Majesty, judging on his
>   throne
> The life of the pious and the ways of the impious men.
>   (2.241–45)

Here, as in the *Apocalypse of Peter* (c. 135 C.E.), the Father raises the dead,
but then Jesus Christ comes "on a cloud" (1:4; 6:1) with "glory" and takes
his place at the "right hand" of the Father in order to judge the living and
the dead.

In the *Apocalypse of Thomas* (date uncertain), there is a twofold coming
and, as in the *Didache*, only the elect are resurrected from the dead. The
"signs" of the end time are distributed—one on each of eight consecutive
days. On the sixth day, the Lord Jesus comes, the elect arise and return
with him to heaven—all on the same day. The Lord's coming is so
described: "They [those living] will see me as I [Jesus] come down from
above in the light of my Father with the power and the honor of the holy
angels." One will note that there is no mention of clouds serving to transport Jesus and his entourage, the angels. After the dear are raised "by the
power of my Father" and assembled "by the hands of the holy angels,"
then "they will be carried off in a cloud of light into the air, and rejoicing
go with me [Jesus] into the heavens." Thus, one can surmise that clouds
functioned on both legs of the transport.

On the eighth day, according to the *Apocalypse of Thomas,* the clouds function like "sky taxis" transporting the holy ones—the angels and the elect.

> And there will go forth . . . all the angels sitting on my holy Father's chariots of clouds, rejoicing and flying around in the air under heaven, to deliver the elect who believe in me [Jesus]; and they will rejoice that the destruction of the world has come.

Renaissance artists put wings on angels, making them self–propelled. The greater part of the Jewish tradition, on the other hand, saw angels as having the form of humans (without wings, e.g., Gn 18:2–19:29; Mk 16:5 and par.). The customary reference to the seraphim "with six wings" (Is 6:2; also 14:29; 30:6) refers to "serpents"—"a symbol in ancient Egypt of the royalty of the gods and of the pharaoh" (Mills: 810). Hence, there is no surprise that the angels of the *Apocalypse of Thomas* required clouds for their transportation.

In the Acts of the Apostles, the ascension of Jesus into heaven also makes use of cloud transport: "a cloud took him from their sight" (Acts 1:9). As for his return: "Jesus will come back in the same way as you have seen him go there" (Acts 1:11). The Book of Revelation takes this seriously when it says that Jesus "who is to come" (Rv 1:4) will arrive "on the clouds" (Rv 1:7). In this same book, "one like a son of man" (Rv 14:14; also Dn 7:13) gathers in the elect under the metaphor of reaping. This reaping takes place as the son of man sits "on a cloud" (Rv 14:14, 16).

In the Hebrew Scriptures, the Lord God sometimes appears "as a cloud" (e.g., Ex 16:10; 34:5). At still other times, the clouds function as the Lord's chariot:

> O Lord my God, you are very great. . . .
> You make the clouds your chariot,
> you ride on the wings of the wind. (Ps 104:1, 3; also
>   2 Sm 22:10f.)

The presumption here is that God dwells in heaven among the clouds (e.g., Pss 68:35; 89:7). Hence, the clouds are perceived as "chariots" for the Lord as he moves about surveying the world events. When he comes to earth in the final coming, therefore, it would have been quite natural to describe his arrival "atop/upon the clouds" (*Did.* 16:8).

The arrival of the Lord God presupposes the backdrop of Israelite faith that the Lord dwells in the heavens but, from time to time, he makes himself known by his marvelous rescuing and redemptive acts in history. In the Book of Revelation, following the final judgment, one even has the notion that God would not only come temporarily but permanently dwell among his people (see also *Testament of Dan* 5:12–13). After the final judgment, the "new Jerusalem" comes down from heaven and a voice "from the throne" says:

> See, the home of God is among mortals. He will dwell with them as their God; they will be his people, and God himself will be with them; he will wipe every tear from their eyes. (Rv 21:3)

No details are given as to how an entire city would come down "out of heaven" (Rv 21:2). The metaphor of God permanently dwelling among his people, however, conveys the notion of a permanent salvation: "Death will be no more; mourning and crying and pain will be no more" (Rv 21:4).

In this literature of expectation, one never finds philosophical reflection on the omnipresence of God or on the universality of divine Providence. Nor is there emphasis upon the supreme transcendence of God that prohibits him/her from being merely "here" or "there" since the whole world cannot contain him/her. This literature favors concreteness over the abstraction of metaphysics (Tillich: 1–20). Emil Fackenheim, in opposing the way that philosophical reflection works to remove the embarrassment and the contradiction of biblical history, says quite simply that "salvation at the Red Sea is real only because the prior threat of catastrophe is real" (18). Thus, sophisticated as we might become, the truth remains that those who hoped in God used concrete metaphors to convey their hope. Mourning and crying and pain happen in this historical moment because God is not "here." Thus, in the near future, the Lord God himself will come down from heaven together with his holy ones "atop the clouds" (*Did.* 16:8). Then and only then, can those with Jewish apocalyptic instincts trust that, when this happens, "mourning and crying and pain will be no more" (Rv 21:4).

Whether the Didache *Had a Lost Ending*

Even though there is some suspicion that Leon, the eleventh-century copyist, may have left seven blank lines because the end of the text before him was broken off or lost, we can say with some certainty that the so-called "lost ending" did not contain a judgment scene (see ch. 15 below):

1. The insistence in *Did.* 16:4b that resurrection is meant exclusively for "the holy ones" makes any separation or final judgment for those raised unnecessary. So, too, they need not pass through "the burning-process of

testing" with its dual effects serving to purify the elect and to utterly destroy the evil ones (16:5).

2. If a final judgment had been anticipated, *Did.* 16:8 would have read something like the text cited above: "[Then] the Most High shall be revealed on the seat of judgment . . ." (2 Esdras 7:32f.).

3. The purpose of the coming of the Lord is to bring the expected reign of God into the midst of his people as the Lord's Prayer suggests: "your kingdom come, your will be born upon earth as in heaven" (8:2).

Conclusion

From what has been said earlier, the prophets visiting the Didache communities were those who had lost their families, their homes, their occupations and had thrown themselves upon God as the one who safeguards the future. The eucharistic prayers of these prophets, accordingly, were filled with passionate and tiptoe expectancy of this kingdom. *Did.* 16 is too flat and too bereft of detail to have been the work of a prophet. Furthermore, one would hardly expect that the prophets would be so hard on themselves as *Did.* 16:3 presents. One must suspect, therefore, that the framers of *Did.* 16 were sympathetic to eschatology but wary of the prophets who imaginatively fashioned the future dangerously close to their own likings and their own inclinations.

Some might have been tempted to silence unruly prophets. Such a solution would have created dissension and division. A prophet whom the majority was bent on silencing would inevitably be the one favored by some minority. Furthermore, how could a community sanction prophetic speech as coming from the Spirit of God (*Did.* 11:7) and then turn it back on this understanding by authoritatively silencing prophets not following the party line. In the end, therefore, the framers of the *Didache* had to beat the prophets at their own game.

How so? They devised a sketch of the end time that was to be normatively taught to all new members. Visiting prophets, consequently, were forced to come to grips with the local tradition of the Didache communities and to adapt their materials to fit into this schema of things. Not to do so would be to risk censure as a "false prophet."

In the course of this chapter, there were three areas in which prophetic content was considered dangerous and invited the correction by members of the Didache communities. These are as follows:

1. Prophets who moved eschatological expectation beyond the bounds of "coming soon" to "already arriving."

2. Prophets who gave the temple and the holy city of Jerusalem a central role in God's future.

3. Prophets whose visions of the future focused on gentile atrocities and had the effect of fueling hatred against the gentiles.

The framers of the end-time scenario were so alert to the possible dele-terious effects of prophecy that they conjectured that "false prophets who are corruptors" would be the very ones to instigate the internal dissension that would initiate the end time. If this were the case, one can perhaps wonder why the Didache communities did not settle for a policy that excluded all prophets. This would be the time to recall, consequently, two manifest blessings that the prophets brought to the communities they vis-ited:

1. Someone contemplating the merits of a new religious movement had to weigh whether he/she could afford to break away from the tried and true realities of parents, friends, and gods in order to entrust themselves to an alternative set of realities that, for the time being, were largely untried and might be found to be untrue. Persons within ancient societies placed a great premium on tradition (Wilken: 46–51). For most would-be con-verts, therefore, it would have been "irresponsible" and "half-crazy" to surrender the certainty of their past on the basis of their infatuation with a Way of Life that might turn out to be just a pipe dream without any long-term future. Most potential recruits were accordingly psychologically frozen in place by the horrific vision of letting go of what was familiar to them—no matter how unsatisfactory it might be. In our modern society, we find bruised and abused women who return again and again to their abusive spouses on the grounds that there is more security in living with the known—no matter how ugly—than in letting go and believing that a better life is possible "on the other side." This same fear of letting go undoubtedly kept many potential recruits bound to their past—no matter how unsatisfactory.

At this point, the genius of eschatology enters in. The would-be recruit is assured, by those he/she has come to trust, that the seemingly stable society to which they are wedded is quickly approaching a cataclysmic destruction so that a new order can take its place. The passion for the future that drove the prophets to abandon family, occupation, and social identity so as to throw themselves upon God's future was thus a witness and a foretaste of what was soon destined to be the common experience of all humankind. The present realities were already beginning to be swept away in favor of what was to come. Eschatology as a lived vision, therefore, served to allow those "on the fence" to relax their fear of letting go in favor of abandoning themselves to a movement bent on anticipating a future that was not yet. See #10s below for a modern instance of this.

2. For long-term members committed to a new religious movement, some mechanism needs to be in place whereby the accumulated weight of disappointments with themselves and with their co-religionists does not erode the habits of seeing and believing that were formed during the idyl-lic period surrounding the initial conversion and apprenticeship. One such method is to "keep one eye on the prize." Here is where the eschatologi-

cal vision of the prophets which bubbled out of their passionate eucharistic prayers served to renew and refurbish personal commitments even in the face of insurmountable obstacles in the society at large and the everyday disappointments within.

The end-time scenario of the *Didache* confirmed the overall judgment that society at large was corrupted at its core and unredeemable save for a brief time when the world-deceiver would seduce it into a last-ditch revival based on deceptive signs and wonders. Members of the Didache communities were thus relieved of the necessity either to grieve or to correct this society that was headed for certain destruction. Their energies were thus harnessed in building up their alternative communities destined for the future.

The end-time scenario of the *Didache* urged vigilance and sustained effort to attain the perfection that the end time required. Especially pernicious, in these times, were corrupting prophets who turned the sheep into wolves and the love into hate. One can only imagine the havoc wreaked by these prophets. Maybe some pitted brother against brother on the issue of the importance of offering sacrifices in the Jerusalem temple or of the attitude one should have toward Roman rule. Maybe others pitted sister against sister on the issue of whether repentant sex offenders were to be readmitted or whether accumulated wealth was a crime against the poor. In all these cases, the prevailing wisdom was to "be gathered together seeking the things pertaining to your souls" (*Did.* 16:2).

All in all, the *Didache* had the pastoral wisdom of maintaining a moderate rule of holiness. Zealots and prophets may have lived by a stricter code, but they were not to act or speak so as to imply that all would be judged by their own exalted personal standards. Those who were too lenient were open to one-on-one correction which, in severe cases, could lead to a time of shunning. Even in the last days, the Lord had provided a burning-process of testing. The term *dokimasia* normally has the sense of "testing," with the prospect of approving something, for example, a team of oxen or a piece of gold (Bauer: 202d). Thus, even while "many" will be utterly destroyed in the Lord's judgment, those "having remained firm in their faith" (16:5) expected to be purified and approved. Maybe this notion carried over in the practice of the weekly confession of failings whereby those confessing anticipated being purified in that final fire. The Lord's process of burning would be a saving event for the faithful and, in anticipatory fashion, mutual correction, confession of failings, and even the practice of shunning might have been regarded as a merciful "fire" intending to purify and save the elect lest they be entrapped and destroyed in the last days.

Every social movement that captured the allegiance of the masses began as a small minority bent on letting go of the present in order to live for the future. Augustus Caesar (d. 14 C.E.) adopted the eschatological and prophetic expectations and refashioned them to gain public adherence to the Augustinian era (see #10p). Even the founding of America was shot through with prophetic energy that is now well concealed from public awareness and that causes embarrassment for most modern Americans (Bellah). It was no different for the movement that the Lord Jesus left behind. Jesus himself lived and died in the expectation of the kingdom of God. Jesus and his disciples were bent on letting go of much of their past in order to prepare for entrance into that kingdom. Most Christians do not have any accurate grasp of these beginnings, and, among those who do, there is often embarrassment that Jesus endorsed an eschatological arrival of the kingdom of God (see #4j).

Nonetheless, in the *Didache*, one finds a community riveted to the eschatological vision of our divine founder. Unlike other Christian communities that ended up glorifying the Son at the expense of his message, the members of the Didache communities were heaven-bent on glorifying his vision by walking in the Way of Life he revealed to them. In effect, they lived a simpler Jewish commitment to the Lord God than did those hellenized Christians who took the route of glorifying his Son. From our vantage point, we can only sympathetically enter into their world so as to understand and to reverence our roots. At some points, the *Didache* confirms what we now are. At still other points, it challenges who we now are because it witnesses to what we once were and have abandoned. In any case, reaching out to the Didache communities, one can expect to find a sister and brother in faith who share what we are and, at the same time, who challenge us by their difference. For this we can give thanks to the Father of us all!

#10p WHETHER GENTILES WERE KEEN ON ESCHATOLOGY

More often than not, eschatological expectations of a divinely ordained utopian future have been examined entirely within Jewish sources. The impression left is that gentiles, standing outside of Judaism, had little or no interest in apocalyptic eschatology. Of late, however, it has been demonstrated that themes running in Jewish sources find ample parallels in gentile sources as well.

John J. Collins, for example, in his *Apocalyptic Imagination,* draws attention to the fact that Babylonian, Persian, and Hellenistic sources feature utopian visions and end-time scenarios remarkably parallel to what one finds in Jewish sources (1989: 20–28; Hengel 1974: 1:181–218). Given these parallels, issues of origins and dependence are naturally raised:

It remains true that the [Jewish] apocalypses draw heavily on biblical traditions and that common Hellenistic motifs take on a dis-

tinctive appearance in a Jewish context. . . . It is equally true, however, that Jewish tradition is adapted in ways that are broadly typical of the Hellenistic age. It is important that several of the most prominent aspects of the apocalypses involve modifications of biblical traditions that are in accord with widespread ideas of the Hellenistic age: pseudepigraphy, periodization, *ex eventu* prophecy, heavenly journeys, interest in the heavenly world, judgment of the dead. (Collins 1989: 28)

Collins concludes that Jewish apocalyptic literature had its own originality and integrity even while it shared the atmosphere of ideas and attitudes—the "Hellenistic mood" (1989: 28)—which characterized its neighbors. Many or most of those who joined the Didache communities, therefore, would have breathed this "Hellenistic mood" and been ready to hear prophets divining the contours of the future and teachers spelling out the stages anticipated during the last days (*Did.* 16:3–8).

For Romans, more especially, the reign of peace that climaxed the period of civil wars ravaging the Roman populace during the first century B.C.E. was welcomed as an eschatological fulfillment. The poets of the age, Horace and Virgil, looked forward to this age:

> Horace [in his *16th Epode*] calls for the emigration by ship over the high seas, like the boat people who fled from the horrors of Vietnam, for all those who still have a vision of a blessed future and who have the courage of hope. They will return only after a cosmic catastrophe and not until the establishment of a new paradise will signal the beginning of an eschatological restitution. The Appenine Mountains will plunge into the ocean, and then the paradise will come when the tiger mates with the deer and the falcon with the dove. . . . (Koester 1992: 11)

When Augustus inaugurated, with public ceremonies, the new era of peace in 9 B.C.E., he "was not only aware of these prophetic eschatological poems; he consciously announced his new order of peace as their fulfillment" (Koester 1992: 11). Thus, for Romans who had suffered during the civil wars and who were caught up in a nostalgia for the past and alienation from the present, the *Pax Romana* ("Roman Peace," 9 B.C.E.–27 C.E.), the manifest destiny of the Augustinian era, represented a divinely ordained eschatological fulfillment.

> There are several characteristic features of this Roman imperial eschatology: (1) The new age is the fulfilment of prophecy. . . . (2) The new age includes this earth as well as the world of the

heavens: Apollo as Helios is the god of the new age; the zodiac sign of the month of Augustus' birth appears on the shields of the soldiers. (3) The new age is universal: it includes all nations. . . . (4) There is an enactment of the new age through the official celebrations of the empire. . . . (5) The new age has as a savior figure the greatest benefactor of all times, the *divi filius* ("son of god") . . . the victorious Augustus. (Koester 1992: 12–13)

In the face of this, the Didache communities chose to herald Jesus as "the Son" (*Did.* 7:1) and to anticipate being gathered together in the last days by "the Father" (7:1; 8:2; 9:2, 3; 10:2) into "his" kingdom (8:2; 9:4; 10:5). Thus, for Romans who embraced the Way of Life, they were keenly aware that the themes of Roman imperial eschatology were being deliberately ignored in favor of another vision of the future. Such persons, needless to say, were undoubtedly disenchanted with the eschatological claims of the empire and were attracted by the divinely authorized Way of Life of "the Father" who was yet to come.

In sum, divinely authorized utopian visions were the stuff of Jews and gentiles alike. Gentiles joining the Didache communities were thus embracing an alternate eschatology.

#10Q THE ABSENCE OF THE MESSIAH AND THE TEMPLE IN THE LAST DAYS

Judaism has many eschatologies. The Book of Tobit (third century B.C.E.), for example, centers on the rebuilding of the temple and the conversion of the gentiles but without the least hint of a Messiah:

Indeed, everything that was spoken by the prophets of Israel, whom God sent, will occur. . . . [1] God will bring them [the exiles] back into the land of Israel. . . . [2] After this they . . . will rebuild Jerusalem in splendor; and in it the temple of God will be rebuilt, just as the prophets of Israel have said concerning it. [3] Then the nations in the whole world will all be converted and worship God in truth. . . . [4] Those who sincerely love God will rejoice, but those who commit sin and injustice will vanish from all the earth. (Tb 14:4–7)

The eschatological scenario offered here claims that it represents a summation of the predictions of the prophets of Israel. The scenario begins with the ingathering of the exiles. Then these exiles rebuild Jerusalem and its temple. Once the temple is restored, Tobit anticipates a universal conversion of the gentiles (presumably, because of divine intervention) such that they too "will worship God in truth," presumably, by offering sacrifices to God in the Jerusalem temple. The Israelites will then "live in safety forever in the land of Abraham" and "those who commit sin and injustice will vanish" (Tb 14:7)—an apt description of the final reign of God on earth. This eschatological scenario distinguishes itself by having God act directly without any Messiah (son of David) and by having a universal conversion of gentiles without any of necessity of having them destroyed (see discussion of D. S. Russell: 297–303).

In the Babylonian Talmud (600 C.E.), one finds a well-crafted description of the last days based on a series of prophetic texts. The order of events, however, follows exactly the order of things prayed for each day in the Eighteen Benedictions (Neusner 1984: 182f.). The events flow as follows:

[1] And when the exiles are assembled, judgment will be visited upon the wicked, as it says, "And I will turn my hand upon you and purge away your dross as with lye" [Is 1:25]. . . .

[2] And when judgment is visited on the wicked, transgressors cease, and presumptuous sinners are included with them, as it is written, ". . . They that forsake the Lord shall be consumed." [Is 1:28]

[3] And when the transgressors have disappeared, the horn of the righteous is exalted, as it is written [Ps 75:11]. . . . And "proselytes of righteousness" are included with the righteous, as it says [Lv 19:32]. . . .

[4] And where is the horn of righteousness exalted? In Jerusalem, as it says [Ps 72:6]. . . .

[5] And when Jerusalem is built, David will come, as it says [Hos 3:5]. . . .

[6] And when David comes, [joyful] prayer will come, as it says [Is 156:7]. . . .

[7] And when prayer has come, [8] the Temple service will come, as it says, "Their burnt-offerings and their sacrifices shall be acceptable upon my altar" [Is 56:7]. (*b. Megillah* 17b as translated in Neusner 1984: 182f.)

In this scenario, as in Tobit, the ingathering of the exiles marks the beginning of God's final intervention in history. Once assembled, the Lord purifies Israel. Those "who forsake the Lord" (unrepentant Jews and gentiles) are neither converted, as in Tobit, nor purified but destroyed ("in the furnace" of Is 1:25) in stage 2. Then the righteous of Israel and proselytes from among the gentiles will be exalted, and Jerusalem will be rebuilt.

David (the Messiah) does not appear until Jerusalem is rebuilt—an indication that the rabbis here viewed the Messiah as having nothing to do with judging and destroying the wicked. Presumably the Messiah shows up only to provide a righteous king to lead them in the restored city of Jerusalem. So too, the rabbis asserted the priority of prayer over sacrifice when they allowed that joyful prayer would take place (presumably in the synagogues) as a prelude to the restoration of the temple sacrifices.

Neither of the above two scenarios of the last days speaks of the raising of the dead to life. In the case of Tobit, this might be due to the fact that the expectation of resurrection did not yet figure into the expectation of Jews at the time in which it was written. In the case of the Babylonian Talmud, on the other hand, the rabbis firmly anticipated the resurrection of the dead, not during the messianic age, but only in the "age to come" that followed (Neusner 1984: 180). Thus, only when the messianic age came to an end would there then be resurrection and final judgment and the opening of the world to come: "All the prophets prophesied only concerning the days of the Messiah, but as to the world that will come [thereafter], 'Eye has not seen, [O] God, beside you' [Is 54:3]" (*b. Berakhot* 34b).

Already in 2 Esdras (late first century), one finds a distinction between the messianic age and the world to come. When "the Messiah shall be revealed," the just rejoice in the rebuilt Jerusalem for four hundred years; when "the Most High shall be revealed," however, the dead are raised, judged, and sent either to the "paradise of delight" or the "furnace of hell" (7:36). The key passages are as follows:

> Everyone who has been delivered from the evils that I have foretold shall see my wonders. For my son *the Messiah shall be revealed* with those who are with him, and those who remain shall rejoice for four hundred years. After those years, my son the Messiah shall die, and all who draw human breath. Then the world shall be turned back to primeval silence. . . . After seven days . . . the earth shall give up those who are asleep in it . . . and the chambers shall give up the souls that have been committed to them. *The Most High shall be revealed* on the seat of judgment. . . . Only judgment shall remain, truth shall stand, and faithfulness shall grow strong. . . . The pit of torment shall appear, and opposite it shall be the place of rest. . . . (7:27–35)

The Messiah in 2 Esdras has nothing to do with destroying evil or with restoring Jerusalem. "His sole purpose is to create joy for them [the righteous survivors] during the messianic interval of four hundred years" (J. M. Myers: 127). Only following his death will the resurrection and judgment begin—activities entirely in the hands of the Most High.

#10R HOW THE MESSIAH WAS ASSIGNED INCREASING RESPONSIBILITIES

Later in 2 Esdras, larger responsibilities were assigned to the Messiah. At this point, it no longer suffices that the Messiah would be a gifted king who brings justice and joy to his people. Now he had to be a warrior with awesome supernatural powers:

> I saw that this man flew with the clouds of heaven; and wherever he turned his face to look, everything under his gaze trembled, and whenever his voice issued from his mouth, all who heard his voice melted as wax melts when it feels the fire. (13:3f.)

2 Esdras makes clear that "the Most High will deliver those who are on the face of the earth" (13:29)—not personally any longer—but through his son, the Messiah. First of all, the Messiah will bring back the captives of Israel (13:40) into the safety of the sanctuary (13:48f.). When all the gentile armies then mobilize and rush at him as he stands on Mount Zion defending God's people, he defeats them single-handedly, not by the force of arms, but by the fire of his mouth—a highly symbolic metaphor:

> I saw only how he sent forth from his mouth something like a stream of fire, from his tongue he shot forth a storm of sparks. All these were mingled together, the stream of fire and the flaming breath and the great storm, and fell on the onrushing multitude that was prepared to fight, and burned up all of them, so that suddenly nothing was seen of the innumerable multitude but only the dust of ashes and the smell of smoke. (13:10f.)

One suspects that the framers of 2 Esdras were uncomfortable with the enormity of the powers and responsibilities being assigned to the Messiah because, point for point, the commentary endeavors to offer an allegorical meaning (13:25–50) that so undercuts the powers of the Messiah as to make him practically useless. Nonetheless, in the pages of 2 Esdras, one can glimpse how end-time activities originally assigned exclusively to God are transferred to his Messiah. Thus while 2 Esdras 7 paints a Messiah who is revealed only after God has gathered the elect and vanquished the enemies of Israel, 2 Esdras 13 now has the Messiah doing all these things in the name of God.

The *Syriac Apocalypse of Baruch* (100 C.E.) reveals a remarkably similar pattern. The end-times scenario begins with twelve periods of destruction, when all the nations are destroyed as the Lord God shields Israel. "The Messiah shall then begin to be revealed" (29:3). "When the presence of the Messiah on earth has run its course" (30:1), then the resurrection of the dead and the final judgment take place because of God's direct power. The *Syriac Apocalypse of Baruch* thus follows the same sequence of end-time events found in 2 Esdras 7, with the Messiah having no functions prior to or following the messianic age. Later in this same book, however, the periods of destruction are again enumerated, but this time those who survive "will be delivered into the hands of my servant, the Messiah" (70:10) and "the Messiah . . . will call all the nations together, and some of them he will spare [namely, those who have not harmed Israel], and some of them he will destroy" (72:2). In this second recounting of the last days, the Messiah takes on supernatural roles hitherto entirely in the hands of the Lord God. This, as noted above, is precisely what one finds in 2 Esdras 13.

Stepping back from the materials discussed above, one could speculate that we may be in the presence of an eschatological trajectory that might be crudely summarized as follows:

1. Tobit (200 B.C.E.) and Deutero-Zechariah (to be discussed shortly) represent a stage in which the Lord God was being awaited as the sole savior of Israel. At this stage, one hears nothing regarding the Messiah, the messianic age, or the resurrection of the dead.

2. 2 Esdras 7, *Syriac Apocalypse of Baruch* 26–33, and *b. Megillah* 17b represent an interim phase. Now the messianic era under the direction of a Son of David has been introduced as a partial realization of the Lord's future. Once this has run its course, however, the Lord God will come for the final time and judge the living and the dead. The Messiah has no functions prior to or following the messianic era.

3. 2 Esdras 13 and *Syriac Apocalypse of Baruch* 67–72 demonstrate the further developments that undoubtedly took place during the first century and were included in the later chapters of our two sources. Now the messianic figure takes on supernatural powers and activities formerly assigned to God, especially the ingathering of the exiles, the destruction of sinners, and the protection of the faithful ones.

Our survey includes only a few sources. One might well suspect that the enlargement of activities assigned to the Messiah might have continued during subsequent centuries. Jacob Neusner's study of the flux in rabbinic eschatologies (1984: 216–18) and John A. T. Robinson's study of Christian eschatologies (1979: 16–35, 118–39) confirm the broad trajectory that has been described here.

Now, on the basis of this, something of the particular character of the *Didache* comes into better light. In contrast to the eschatological trajectory operative in this period, the *Didache* clearly runs against the grain by having no Messiah and no messianic age. Some scholars have tried to discover such a messianic age by having the Lord in *Did.* 16:8 refer to Jesus, the Messiah, and by postulating a lost ending. The thesis of this volume, however, is that such interpretations of the *Didache* are defective.

Furthermore, if the coming of the "holy ones" with the Lord "atop the clouds of heaven" (*Did.* 16:8) is the final triumphal procession of the Lord God coming to gather the elect and to establish his kingdom (see #10m), then all the events of the last days would be monopolized by the Lord God. This means that the *Didache* itself was not in flux and tentatively flirting with messianic images (see #5e and #5f). Nonetheless, its codified scenario of the last days assigns nothing to the Messiah.

Why does *Did.* 16 resist this larger Jewish trajectory?

I don't know, but I would like to hazard a guess. According to Paul D. Hanson, the early prophets looked forward to the return of the exiles and the rebuilding of Jerusalem as a fulfillment of the Lord's promise. When the postexilic leadership (king and priesthood) exploited the people, however, this effectively created pockets of discontent which judged that the fulfillment spoken by the prophets had been aborted. Thus, according to Hanson, Deutero-Zechariah (Zec 9–14) . . .

> . . . is directed against the Davidic governor and the heirocratic temple party with which he is associated. Together they are destroying Yahweh's people through their corruption. To this situation of cultic and community degeneration the visionary group . . . felt directed by Yahweh toward a new course of action, that of accepting the inevitability of the impending doom, hastening its advent, and looking for deliverance as a refining act of Yahweh on behalf of the faithful remnant on the other side of the judgment. (P. D. Hanson: 350)

Thus, because Deutero-Zechariah despaired of the "incompetent shepherd" (Zec 11:15, also 10:3; 13:7) and "the arrogance of the House of David" (Zec 12:7), the final salvation envisioned was deliberately restricted to the Lord God alone:

> Thus, the restoration hope of the visionaries, long deferred and yet so fervently longed for, would finally be realized, inaugurated by a pure act of Yahweh the Warrior, and guaranteed forever by the permanent elimination of the opponents [the House of David, the prophets, the priests] who repeatedly have frustrated the restoration efforts of the visionaries. (P. D. Hanson: 393)

The framers of the *Didache*, for their part, were deeply dissatisfied with the priestly temple party (see ch. 14 below). For parallel reasons, they might have been wary of a Davidic Messiah, for, when it came to eschatology, this would inevitably focus unwanted attention on the centrality of Jerusalem. Thus, the framers of the *Didache* may have found in Deutero-Zechariah a sympathetic voice and a perspective on the future that satisfied their passionate expectations. If this was the case, then it would follow that they spurned the tendencies illustrated by 2 Esdras and the *Syriac Apocalypse of Baruch* in favor of aligning themselves with the future envisioned by Deutero-Zechariah. Furthermore, since Deutero-Zechariah was openly antagonistic to prophets (Zec 13:2–6) and envisioned a universal salvation (Zec 14:16–21), the framers of the *Didache* might have found in Zec 9–14 a resolution to their own problems surrounding the future. In sum, the use of Zec 14:5 may have signaled a sympathy with an eschatology that deliberately eliminated all humans from playing any role whatsoever in the final restoration when "the Lord will become king over all the earth" (Zec 14:9). Further study is merited on this point.

Stepping back, the character of the *Didache* can now be better understood. In the first place, neither Jesus nor the Messiah was given any role in the end-time scenario whatsoever. The Lord God alone takes the field, destroys the world-deceiver and his supporters, purifies the elect, assembles the dispersed, raises the just, and comes in triumphal procession to establish *his kingdom* on earth. The eucharistic prayers do give a nod in the direction of naming Jesus as the Messiah; nonetheless, it is the kingdom of the Father that stands front and center in the consciousness of the faithful:

> Remember, Lord, *your church,*
> to save her from every evil
> and to perfect her in *your love*
> and to gather her together from the four winds
> into *your kingdom* which you have prepared for it,
> because *yours is the power and the glory* forever.
>
> Come, grace of the kingdom!
> and pass away, O this world!
> Hosanna to the *God of David.* (*Did.* 10:5f.)

For the framers of the *Didache*, the Father stood at the center of things. Believers praised and thanked him for saving "your church," for perfecting her in "your love," for gathering her into "your kingdom." Everything was in the hands of the "God of David." Nothing eschatological was left over for the "Son of David."

#10s The Liberating Eschatology of the Nation of Islam

The Nation of Islam erupted as a movement of consequence in the 1950s and 1960s. In 1952, Elijah Mohammed, the Messenger of Allah in the last days, had two hundred followers in a small mosque in Chicago. Ten years later, thirty-two mosques, concentrated in northern cities, routinely served the tens of thousands of adherents living a way of life founded on a mixture of black nationalism, Islamic revisionism, and the imminent final destruction of "the blond-haired, blue-eyed white devils" by Allah.

The Black Muslim movement indicates how eschatology serves to strengthen hope and to reorient the efforts of thousands of American blacks who were constantly plagued by racism, self-pity, and the allure of drug abuse, prostitution, and thievery. Even before black pride was popular, Black Muslims lived out lives dedicated to a mission and an identity that gave them pride in themselves, in their heritage, and in their racial identity.

> The significance of Elijah Muhammad is primarily ideological and secondarily programmatic, though the two themes are interrelated. In essence, his life was dedicated to equating blackness with power and initiative. No other historic personality has had the kind of prolonged impact on black consciousness that he has had, and no recent group in the African-American community has promoted—largely by example—economic self-help, cultural regeneration (or redefinition), and moral living more vigorously than his Nation of Islam. The Muslims were "black" before it became fashionable to be labeled as such, and the Black Power Movement and all subsequent African-American protest styles, from the rhymes of the nationalistic rap group Public Enemy to the raison d'être of the Million Man March, are undeniably offshoots of the legacy of Elijah Muhammad. (Clegg: 282)

Even though Elijah Mohammed and the Nation of Islam are separated from the *Didache* and its countercultural communities by nineteen hundred years, both movements have very much in common. Both groups were primarily ideological and secondarily programmatic. Both groups attracted the remnants of society and refashioned them into persons with a fresh personal identity and an overarching social future. Both groups fostered economic programs that enabled persons cut off from their families and their culture to be economically self-supporting while living harmoniously in an environment of like-minded individuals. Both groups fostered daily habits of prayer and believed that they were divinely revealed and that God was getting ready to come and secure a glorious future on earth in which their Way would be uniquely accredited. Finally, both groups found a sustaining hope and embraced a vision of nonviolent resistance in the expectation that God and God alone would bring about the destruction of those who oppose him and his servants.

The Nation of Islam indicates how the assurance of the Lord's coming need not have the effect of leading to foolishness or irresponsibility but, on the contrary, leads to taking new courage to act and to live counterculturally in expectation of the Lord's coming. Neither the Black Muslims nor the members of the Didache communities had the power or the resources to change the prevailing attitudes of their society. Moreover, they were despised and looked down upon by their society. It was enough, however, to know that the One who created them saw things differently and that they were living their lives submissive to his ways of seeing and of evaluating things. Eschatology, consequently, offered them a way out of the spiral of hopelessness and of powerlessness that overcomes those who live their lives on the fringes of their society.

The eschatology preached by the Messenger of Allah and embraced by the Nation of Islam is very complex. With unfair brevity, this eschatology begins with a creation story of a paradise that forms the foundation of what Allah originally had in mind and what will come to be in the future.

> The black people, the first and sole human residents of the planet, were organized into thirteen tribes, which formed a Nation united by skin color (black), religion (Islam), and natural disposition (righteousness). Since Allah, the first man and founder of the Black Nation, was born at the beginning of time and no written documents were kept until 6 trillion years later, the black people, or Nation of Islam, had no birth record or knowledge of any history prior to Allah's ascendancy. (Clegg: 42)

With time, the achievements of the original peoples grew, they became diversified, and their numbers (five million) covered the face of the earth. In 4600 B.C.E., however, a full-scale revolution took place:

> Yacub, charismatic and visionary, tapped into the discontent in Mecca and preached an Islam that stressed wealth and luxury. . . . The dispossessed, the frustrated, and the opportunistic flocked to him and made Yacub their champion against the government of Mecca. . . . To avoid bloodshed, . . . the monarch cut a deal with Yacub, which included passage by ship for the Yacubians to the island of Pelan [or Patmos as in Rv 1:9] in the Aegean Sea. The arrangement also provided for twenty years of assistance for the exiles to help them construct a civilization. (Clegg: 49)

On Pelan, a system of genetic selection was tyrannically imposed that resulted, over a period of many generations, in producing a brown-skinned population. "In six hundred years, Yacub and his servants had turned a completely black people into a population of 'white devils,' genetically programmed to oppose freedom, justice, and equality" (Clegg: 51). After a failed attempt to take over the government of Mecca, the white race was exiled to the hills of Europe. Here, given their inferior genetic makeup and their self-destructive cultural legacy, they nearly reverted to bestiality. Allah, the Compassionate One, sent them Musa (or Moses) and, some time later, Jesus and Muhammad. This enabled the "white devils" to recover a smattering of civilization that had been abandoned with the revolt of Yacub.

The white race, however, continued its program of expansion and domination and genocide. Allah, however, had decreed a limitation to their madness:

> The divinely decreed year for the end of the white man's rule was 1914, but Allah extended the time by fifty to seventy years so the black people in America could regain their knowledge of self and Islam. . . . The enslavement period had actually made the "so-called Negroes" in America no longer Original People, but instead, individuals "wrecked, robbed, and spoiled" by the slave master's brutality and useful only "as a tool for whatever purpose the white man sees fit." The black man partook of swine. . . . He fornicated, drank alcohol, swore, fought his brother over nonsense, mistreated his women, lived on credit and handouts (like the biblical Lazarus), forsook his God (Allah), and loved the devil. (Clegg: 58f.)

Since blacks had been brutalized and deceived by the white race, their first step toward liberation consisted in renouncing the ways of the white man (including his religion) and in promising fealty to Allah and his apostle Elijah Mohammed. Next, a would-be convert had to drop the names that the white man had given him/her and take on a temporary name until such time that Allah would reveal their true name on the Day of Judgment.

> In preparation for the destruction of the white world, the righteous "lost-founds" (or new converts) were required to keep their bodies physically fit and properly nourished. Observance of the major dietary rules of Islam was mandatory. (Clegg: 63)

In accordance with ancient Judaism, the *Didache*, and with Islam, "heaven and hell" were not places that were entered upon dying but were "conditions of life on earth" (Clegg: 63). Following the time of tribulation, judgment, and the destruction of America, Allah would enable a new beginning to take place according to his design in creating the Original People.

A new people, numbering a bit more than the 144,000 prophesied in Revelation, would build a new government "based upon
truth, freedom, justice, and equality," which would live forever
under the guidance of Allah. Sickness, fear, grief, and vices of the
old would be eliminated, as would the language and names of
Yacub's people. In twenty years time, even the memory of American civilization would be erased from the minds of the saved.
Amidst the new spawning of trees, vegetation, and sparkling
waters, the [reconstituted] Original People themselves would
look different, clearly better. . . . The new paradise, more than
anything else, would be a testament to God's omnipotence and
his new Islam. (Clegg: 67)

On the positive side, anyone gripped with this vision of the future was
freed from the necessity of taking white culture into account. No Black
Muslim had to wait until some new government program or some kind
Christian people from a white church came to save them. They already
knew that they were called and empowered by Allah to change their own
lives and their own futures. Moreover, no Black Muslims were tempted to
participate in the race riots of the late 1960s, which burned and looted
stores run by whites. On the other hand, no Black Muslims were tempted
to engage in voter registration or lunch-counter sit-ins—for they anticipated a future in which there would be no need to change or to negotiate
with white rules, white services, and white limitations. Black Muslims,
accordingly, maligned Martin Luther King and his movement (Clegg:
244) and likewise stayed away from the tactics of the Black Panthers—"the
burden of deliverance was left to God, who would act in his own good
time" (Clegg: 67).

All in all, the Nation of Islam provides a modern movement that demonstrates how necessary and how effective the right eschatology can be for
sustaining the ability of the remnants of a repressed society to establish an
identity, a mission, and a future that is independent of the existing powers.
The *Didache*, for its part, was involved in a similar adventure. Both movements must be evaluated, not on the failure of God to step into history as
they forecast, but on their ability to take a bold step to transform their history on the basis of God's promise.

#10T HOW AN END-TIME SCENARIO CAN BE JUDGED TO BE TRUE

Needless to say, there are many diverse and incompatible end-time scenarios. Modern fundamentalists agree among themselves that the elect

"will be caught up in the clouds . . . to meet the Lord" (1 Thes 4:17), but they disagree as to whether this rapture will take place before, during, or after the thousand-year reign of Christ on earth. Black Muslims agree among themselves that Allah will come soon to judge the living and the dead, but they disagree as to how few or how many whites will be judged fit for entrance into Paradise. First-century Christians agreed among themselves that the God of David would come to destroy the wicked and to reward the righteous, but they disagreed as to what role, if any, Jesus would play in this process. Nuclear scientists, meanwhile, agree among themselves that a nuclear exchange between the superpowers would sweep millions of tons of radioactive dust into the atmosphere and that this dust would be dispersed over the entire planet by the prevailing winds, but they disagree as to whether such gigantic dust storms would result in the creation of an artificial "nuclear winter" in which dropping temperatures would destroy all living crops and bring about the slow starvation of the vast majority of the human race.

If one would imagine, for just a moment, that some fundamentalists, some Black Muslims, some first-century Christians, and some nuclear scientists met to discuss the "human prospect" at the end of this world (as we know it), such a discussion would be immediately bogged down by confessional disagreements. Fundamentalists would want to speak of the "human prospect" in terms of the rapture of Christ's servants that would save them from the tribulations, wars, and "nuclear winters" to come. The other three groups, however, would be puzzled by this "expectation of rapture" and would acknowledge that they hold no such hope for themselves. Muslims, in their turn, would want to speak of Allah's coming to end the six-thousand-year reign of the "blond-haired, blue-eyed, white devils." The other three groups, however, would be angered or pleased by such a "racist" future based on the color of one's skin. The first-century Christians, in their turn, would want to speak of "the Spirit and the fire" (Mt 3:11) that the Lord God was preparing to send down upon the face of the earth. The other three groups would then each try to relate to these "metaphors" in terms of their own convictions regarding the last days. When the first-century Christians began to assign any special role to Jesus, however, immediate divisions would arise. The fundamentalists would object that "Jesus is God" and that there is no reason to have God the Father coming along with his Son to judge the living and the dead. Muslims would object that Allah alone is God and that Muhammad would be the first to be raised from the dead and that he would intercede with Allah to be merciful and gracious when it came time to judge those "servants" who, in life, had been Muslims. The nuclear scientists, meanwhile, would be puzzled that all the others seemingly accepted it as inevitable that the earth as we know it would be destroyed. These scientists, for their part, were committed to putting in place safeguards whereby a "nuclear winter" might be avoided.

Overhearing this discussion, most of us would take sides based on our own current religious/scientific persuasions. Most people think of themselves as well informed, and they rely on their settled convictions (those received from trusted parents and mentors) as true and beyond easy refutation. Yet, even among Christians, there is little or no consensus as to what the future will hold. So how does one grapple with the evident diversity of convictions regarding the "human prospect"? Does religious faith offer believers an unassailable, privileged position owing to the fact that they know something "true" about the future of which outsiders are ignorant? Yes. Does science, on the other hand, allow us to know something "true" about the "nuclear winter" which international rivalries combined with military might seem to make inevitable? Yes. But what are the limits, both religious and scientific, to our ability to know the future? This needs to be considered.

During the height of the Cold War, Karl Rahner wrote an essay entitled "The Hermeneutics of Eschatological Assertions" (1966). Three points are of special interest:

1. Rahner began with the sobering reminder that "the end [as the final human prospect] has for us a character of hiddenness which is essential and proper to it" (1966: 329). Next, Rahner noted that "because man [woman], by and in being orientated to the future, must know about his future" (1966: 332). What humans can know and can understand about the future, however, is always rooted in (limited by) what can be spoken of and envisioned in terms of culturally conditioned experiences. When aboriginal people first encounter an airplane or a television, they marvel at these things as forms of "magic," since, for them, the unusual and the unexplainable are always accounted for in this fashion (Polanyi 1964: 288–92). Their immediate impulse, therefore, is not to ask "how it works" (in terms of physics and/or electronics) but whether it represents a "good" or an "evil" form of magic.

2. According to Rahner, the future human prospect is not only shrouded in mystery; it also invites true freedom: either one rushes forward to embrace it or one pulls back in order to avoid it. According to Rahner, eschatological assertions about the future "must be something impenetrable and uncontrollable, since this alone leaves room for freedom—the true freedom of the creature, which must believe, hope, dare and trust, go out of itself, entrust and surrender itself to the uncontrollable" (1966: 333).

This can be clarified by an illustration. Fundamentalists feel in conflict with modern culture and judge that world events (wars, famines, plagues) are signs of the approaching last days. Nonetheless, they also trust that

God is pledged to protect them and to extricate them (the rapture) from the mess as soon as Jesus arrives on the clouds. Thus, their eschatology is "true" at least insofar as it quiets their anxiety regarding "the works of the devil" and releases their energies to create safe havens whereby those who love God can await being saved from the universal destruction that is to come. Black Muslims believe that their eschatology gives them the identity and the future that allows them to stand tall and, despite their history of slavery, to work together productively and peacefully for an anticipated future guaranteed to vindicate their race when Allah comes (see #10s). The eschatology of the Nation of Islam is therefore "true" at least insofar as it liberates God-given energies toward a future that includes Black Muslims as the apple of God's eye. The eschatology of the Nation of Islam may include "false" elements insofar as it paints the perpetrators of enslavement and their children in such demonic colors as to bar them and their religion from having any significant future. Yet, when one examines the correctives already introduced into the Black Muslim mainstream following the death of Elijah Mohammed, one catches a glimpse of how a community of dialogue finds the time and place to modify and to enhance the truth-bearing vision of its eschatology (Clegg: 271–81).

3. Rahner states quite boldly that "the imaginative portrayals of Scripture [regarding the last days] cannot be harmonized with one another" (1966: 335). And, further, they deliberately use fantastic metaphors in order to remind readers that the future as future remains forever known and unknowable: "Now we see in a mirror dimly, but then face to face" (1 Cor 13:12).

> Eschatology is therefore not a pre-view of events to come later. . . . It does not draw on future events, accessible [to the prophet or inspired seer] because God is "already" contemporary to them . . . and so can already speak of them. Eschatology is the view of the future which man needs for the spiritual dimension of his freedom and his faith. (1966: 334)

Rahner needs to be corrected here. He might have done better to say that eschatology is not a "literal" preview of events to come. Thus, it would be mistaken to imagine that "the sheep will be [literally] turned into wolves" (*Did*. 16:3) or that the elect "will be caught up [literally] in the clouds" (2 Thes 4:17). It would be mistaken, therefore, to study the behavior of wolves or take up skydiving in order to be more secure in the last days. It would be likewise mistaken to join with Jimmy Swaggart and to expect that the rapture would result in many vehicles on our highways running out of control because their drivers had suddenly been removed and caught up in the clouds (see also LaHaye 1995).

On the other hand, it would be equally mistaken to imagine that the "truth" of any end-time scenario consists only in the sum total of practical or existential effects in the lives of believers (Rahner 1966: 337). For example, when the *Didache* speaks of the "burning-process of testing" (16:5), the "truth" of this metaphor goes beyond giving hope to the underdog. Rather, this metaphor points to the historical aspect of God's future that remains hidden in the present and that assures believers that the current standards of justice in the family, in the state, and in the churches are not "all there is" of God's justice in this world. In some way, which only the future will disclose, the justice of God will overreach and overturn defective human tribunals. Thus, the eschatological reversal found on Mary's lips ("He has brought down the powerful from their thrones, and lifted up the lowly" [Lk 1:52]) represents a real dimension of God's system of values that will prevail when his kingdom comes and his will is done on earth as it is now already done in heaven.

In sum, the scriptures do not give us previews of coming attractions in the way that our local cinema does. Nor do scriptures engage in a form of "pious pretending" that functions to sustain hope for the downtrodden and mistreated in the way that Kevin Costner does in the 1998 eschatological film *The Postman*.

As for the revelation of the future, however, Rahner makes the following point:

> They do not reach us in a discourse about the future still to come, but in an action, in which God has already really begun them in us. And so we can only speak of this beginning by describing it as a beginning which wills to fulfill itself and therefore brings with it the knowledge of this fulfillment. (1996: 336)

The "burning-process of testing" (*Did.* 16:5), for example, might be construed today as the conviction of believers that God does not bestow his blessings now, nor will he judge humans as fit for inclusion in his future, using the standards of excellence whereby the editors of *Business Week, Sports Illustrated*, or *Playboy* decide upon inclusion in their next issue. The "world-deceiver" may judge according to these standards and, by so doing, might attract the entire world (*Did.* 16:4b), yet believers will retain "their faith" in the Father and his Way of Life. Thus, every revelation of God's future begins, as Rahner notes, with a present sympathy with God's standards of excellence. Every end-time scenario, therefore, is the imaginative extrapolation into the future of what is already known and already in operation in the hearts of those who sympathize with God.

Part III

Special Issues

11
WHETHER THE *DIDACHE* MADE USE OF ANY KNOWN GOSPEL

Contents

Background Discussion Found in Boxes

E ver since a complete copy of the *Didache* was first discovered in 1873, widespread efforts have been undertaken to demonstrate that the author or authors of the *Didache* depended on a known Gospel (usually Matthew, Luke, or both) and/or on an apostolic father (Barnabas, Hermas, Justin Martyr) as well. In more recent times, however, some scholars have pushed back the date of composition and called into question dependence on these known sources. In the late 1950s, Jean-Paul Audet (1958), R. Glover (1958–59), and Helmut Koester (1957) cautiously developed this stance independent of one another. More recently, John S. Kloppenborg (1979), Jonathan Draper (1984), and Willy Rordorf (1991, 1998) have argued quite persuasively for the independence of the *Didache* from all the Gospels known to us. As this book goes to press, Huub van der Sandt and David Flusser have just come out with a new volume that entirely enforces this position (2002: 39–50, 291–96, 352). Opposition voices are still heard, however. C. M. Tuckett (1989) of Oxford University, for example, reexamined all the evidence and came to the conclusion that parts of the *Didache* "presuppose the redactional activity of both evangelists" thereby resasserting an earlier position that "the *Didache* here presupposes the gospels of Matthew and Luke in their finished forms" (230). Clayton N. Jefford, writing in the same year independently of Tuckett, came to the conclusion that the *Didache* was produced in the same community that produced the Gospel of Matthew and that both works had common sources but divergent purposes (1989a: 18–19, 115–18). Vicky Balabanski, in a book-length treatment of the eschatologies of Mark, Matthew, and the *Didache*, likewise concludes that *Did.* 16 was written "to clarify and specify certain aspects of Matthew's eschatology" (201).

This chapter will weigh the evidence for and against dependence on the Gospel of Matthew—the most frequently identified "written source" for the *Didache*. My gratitude goes to Willy Rordorf, who first alerted me to the possibility that the *Didache* might have been created without dependence on any known Gospel and that this conclusion has a heavy bearing on the dating and the interpretation of the text. At the end of this chapter, I will join with Rordorf in his final conclusions, yet my analysis of the problem will take me in directions that he did not travel.

The Early History of Dating and Identifying Sources

During the first eighty years after Bryennios published the text of the *Didache* (1883), the burning question was not on whether the *Didache* made use of one or more of the Gospels but whether the *Didache* made use of the *Epistle of Barnabas*. Bryennios made the judgment that *Barnabas,* with its more primitive presentation of the Two Ways material, was the source for the Two Ways material (*Did.* 1–5) of the *Didache.* This single fact inclined him to date the composition of the *Didache* between 120 and 160 C.E.—depending on whether one takes an early or late date for the composition of the *Epistle of Barnabas.* Adolph Harnack, writing in the following year, wrote, "One must say without hesitation that it is the author of the *Didache* who used the *Epistle of Barnabas* and not the reverse" (1884: 82). Harnack, accordingly, dated the *Didache* between 135 and 165 C.E. and fixed the place of origin as Egypt, where *Barnabas* was thought to have been composed. Quite early, therefore, the dating of the *Didache* and its place of origin were fixed in the mid-second century so as to take into account its supposed dependence on the Greek *Epistle of Barnabas.*

While a few scholars (e.g., Sabatier 1885) held out for an earlier dating based on the textual independence of the *Didache* from *Barnabas,* the international influence of Harnack ensured that his judgment would prevail. In 1886, however, Harnack changed his mind after reading C. Taylor (1886) and began advocating that a Jewish catechetical manual designed for proselytes was the common source for the Two Ways section of both the *Didache* and *Barnabas.* This line of thinking was effectively strengthened in 1900 when Joseph Schlecht discovered the *Teaching of the Apostles* (*De Doctrina Apostolorum*). The Latin text of the *Teaching* made reference to "light and darkness" in its opening line and omitted *Did.* 1:3–6—characteristics evidenced in *Barnabas* but absent from the *Didache.* This evidence for the circulation of an independent version of the Two Ways effectively buried the notion that the framers of the *Didache* relied on *Barnabas.*

This burial, however, was not definitive. In 1912, J. Armitage Robinson conducted a new research into the literary construction of the *Epistle of Barnabas* and argued that the rhetoric and content of the entire manuscript were of one piece such that no compelling reasons existed to suppose that the Two Ways section was not immediately composed by Barnabas. Robinson thus revived Harnack's early thesis (1884) that *Barnabas* was the source for the Two Ways section of the *Didache.* From this vantage point, the *Teaching of the Apostles* (*De Doctrina Apostolorum*) was reinterpreted as a detached Latin translation of a small portion of *Barnabas.* The thesis of Robinson gained allegiance (R. H. Connolly, J. Muilenburg), and with it came an even firmer determination that the *Didache* could not have been composed earlier than 140–150 C.E. (see Audet 1958: 17).

In 1945, E. J. Goodspeed published a landmark article in which he was troubled by the Latin versions of *Barnabas* that had no Two Ways section. Goodspeed argued that "early Christian literature usually grew not by partition and reduction, but by combination and expansion" (228), and from this it can be deduced that the oldest version of *Barnabas* must have been prepared without any Two Ways section. Robinson was thus dead wrong (228, 231). In addition, Goodspeed laid the various Two Ways passages side by side and carefully tabulated the textual parallels (238–47). He concluded, on the force of numbers alone, that a Greek version of the *Teaching of the Apostles* stood as the source for all other versions:

> To recapitulate: of the 161 items in *Doctrina* [*Teaching of the Apostles*]; 77 can be recognized in the "Life of Schnudi"; 94 in both *Didache* and *Barnabas;* 104 in *Barnabas;* 145 in *Didache.* . . . The bearing of these figures is unmistakable; *Doctrina* closely approximates the source of all three of the other documents. . . . Nor can these relationships be reversed, so as to make *Barnabas* the source of *Didache* and *Doctrina,* or *Didache* the source of *Barnabas* and *Doctrina.* (237)

The upshot of this was that Harnack's later thesis (1886), which Robinson had discounted, was revived.

The discovery of the Dead Sea Scrolls in 1948 laid the foundation for further refutation of Robinson and company. Jean-Paul Audet (1952), a Canadian scholar writing in French, argued that the Two Ways motif clearly used in the *Manual of Discipline* conclusively demonstrated that its origin was Jewish and, consequently, that *Barnabas* repeated but did not originate the Two Ways motif (1952: 237–38). Working on the conviction that the Two Ways material was originally a Jewish catechetical manual designed for gentiles, Audet argued that both the *Didache* and the *Epistle of Barnabas* made use of this manual in their composition. Thus, when Audet's book-length commentary appeared in 1958, it consolidated the growing consensus that the *Didache* never made use of the *Epistle of Barnabas* and that both works had available to them a Jewish catechetical manual that each of them edited for their own purposes (1958: 121–63). While Audet's conjectures regarding the redactional history and textual reconstruction of the *Didache* have been widely questioned, his arguments regarding the hypothetical "Jewish catechetical manual" and the independence of the *Didache* from *Barnabas* have been solidly received (e.g., Draper 1996a: 13; Niederwimmer 1998: 30–40; Rordorf 1972b: 112).

Once the *Epistle of Barnabas* was no longer considered to be the source for the Way of Life section of the *Didache,* this had the effect of giving new impetus to the question of which, if any, of the known Gospels was used by the framers of the *Didache.* It is telling that, in 1958, Audet had devoted forty-two pages to the question of dependence on *Barnabas* (1958: 121–63) and only twenty pages to the question of dependence on the Gospels (1958: 166–86). Audet tried to show that, when the mind is set free of the presumed late dating (120+), then the parallel texts can be set side by side and some fair estimate can be made regarding a possible dependence on the basis of literary analysis and *not on the basis of dating* (1958: 166). Audet concluded that even the so-called evangelical addition of *Did.* 1:3b–5, when examined closely, cannot be explained as coming either from Matthew or from Luke and, given "the approximate date when the interpolator made these additions to the *Didache*, it is not even permitted to imagine a textual mixture coming from two Synoptics" (1958: 186). Thus, Audet himself was mildly biased in favor of removing the Gospels themselves as obstacles to the early dating of the *Didache*. Audet's enduring accomplishment was to demonstrate that the *Didache* can be best understood when it is interpreted within a Jewish horizon of understanding more or less independent of what one finds in the Gospels. Accordingly, in the end Audet was persuaded that the manifestly Jewish character of the *Didache* pointed to a completion date prior to 70 C.E. in a milieu (Antioch) *that did not yet have a written Gospel* (1958: 192, 210).

How the Identifying of Sources Is Skewed by Dating the Didache

Audet (1958: 166) and Rordorf (1991: 395) have wisely noted that the issue of dependence must be settled while bracketing the question of when and where the *Didache* was composed or else one is drawn into circular reasoning. If one supposes an early-second-century origin for the *Didache*, for example, then one is naturally disposed to find points where the *Didache* shows dependence on one or more known Gospels that were then in circulation. If one supposes a pre-Gospel date of origin, on the other hand, then one is naturally disposed to acknowledge that the framers of the *Didache* had access to a Jesus tradition that, in part, showed up in the *Didache* and, only later, showed up in the canonical Gospels. Thus, only after the issue of dependence is settled can a fair estimate be made of the date and place of origin of the *Didache*.

The issue of Gospel dependence also has a strong bearing on how one interprets the text. If one supposes, for example, that the *Didache* made use of Matthew's Gospel, then one could or should make use of Matthew's theology and church practice in order to clarify the intent and background of the *Didache*. On the other hand, if one supposes that the *Didache* is independent of Matthew, then it would be an unwarranted projection to expect that the Gospel of Matthew could be used to understand a text created outside of its influence.

The Questionable Use of Parallel Texts

The older methodology consisted in isolating parallel citations and then drawing conclusions based on an analysis of the degree of coincidence between the texts. John M. Court (1981), for example, provides the following table of parallel citations:

Didache	Matthew	
1:2	22:37ff.; 7:12	Two commandments and golden rule
1:3	5:44ff.	Pray for your enemies
1:4	5:39ff.	Turning the other cheek, etc.
1:5	5:26	The last farthing
2:1f.	19:18f.	Commandments
2:3	5:33	Commandments
3:7	5:5	The meek shall inherit the earth
5:1	15:19	List of vices
6:1	24:4	See no one leads you astray
7:1, 3	28:19	Baptismal formula
8:1	6:16	Fasting contrary to hypocrites
8:2	6:5	Prayer contrary to hypocrites
8:2	6:9–13	Lord's Prayer
9:5	7:6	Do not give what is holy to the dogs
10:5	24:31	From the four winds
10:6	21:9, 15	Hosanna
etc.	etc.	(15 additional entries omitted)

After briefly noting the degree of coincidence between the parallels, Court arrived at a sweeping conclusion:

> With such weight of evidence, where this particular gospel is cited as a distinctive authority, there can be little doubt that the *Didache* stands in the tradition of St. Matthew's Gospel. (1981: 112)

This, of course, is begging the question. The list of parallels makes it appear that Matthew is being cited, but, in effect, other explanations are also possible that preclude any reliance on a written Gospel. The following points will make this clear:

1. *Cases of exact verbal agreement.* Court presupposes that exact verbal agreement allows one to safely conclude that the *Didache* is citing Matthew, or, to be more exact, the distinctive material that Matthew adds to Mark's Gospel (Court 1981: 111). The gathering of the elect "from the four winds" (*Did.* 10:6 and Mt 24:31), for example, exhibits exact verbal agreement. In this case, however, Court does not seem interested in knowing whether "from the four winds" is unique to Matthew or whether, in contrast, it was an expression so common that unrelated authors would have been likely to use it.

Another case of exact verbal agreement is the saying of the Lord, "Do not give what is holy to dogs" (*Did.* 9:5 and Mt 7:6). Here again, Court moves uncritically from verbal agreement to the conclusion of dependence. In contrast, a committee of Oxford theologians noted as early as 1905 the problem with uncritically concluding that *Did.* 9:5 cites Mt 7:6:

> The verbal resemblance [with Mt 7:6] is exact, but the passage in Matthew contains no reference to the eucharist, and the proverbial character of the saying reduces the weight which must be attached to verbal similarity. (Bartlet 1905: 27)

In support of its proverbial character, one can note that the saying "Do not give what is holy to dogs," shows up in *Gospel of Thomas* 93 and in the sayings of Basilides (Epiphanius *Panarion* 24.5.2). Even when the exact origin of this saying cannot be determined, Court is mistaken when he does not allow that proverbs associated with the Lord can be freely cited without reference to Matthew as "the source" (Audet 1958: 174; Niederwimmer 1998: 153). Nonetheless, Court is not alone in judging that *Did.* 9:5 indicates dependence on Matthew (e.g., Jefford 1989a: 140; Massaux 1950: 618).

2. *Cases of variant sayings.* In most cases, exact verbal agreement is not found. If Matthew was the source for the *Didache*, therefore, the framers of the *Didache* clearly elected to alter their source. Court takes note, for example, that "the Golden Rule occurs in its negative form in *Didache*, and positive in Matthew" (1981: 111 n. 9), yet he gives no special relevance to this alteration (also Massaux 1950: 607f.; J. A. Robinson 1934:228–30). Jefford, in contrast, highlights the relevance of these two variations:

> The Golden Rule saying is found commonly throughout both Jewish and Hellenistic sources. The rare occurrence of the saying in its *positive* form in the Matthean and Lucan Gospels, however, argues that the redactors of those texts are dependent on a common source, which is most likely the Sayings Gospel of Q. The *Didache*, on the other hand, reveals the *negative* form of the saying, which is a form that is predominant throughout the tradition of the golden rule [Tb 4:15; *Ep. Arist.* 15:5; Irenaeus, *Against Heresies* 3.12.14; Clement, *Stromateis* 2:23; *b. Shabbat* 31a]. Though there is the possibility that the Didachist is dependent upon the Q tradition as it is reflected in the Synoptics and that s/he consciously has chosen to change the format into one that is negative, this hardly seems likely. Instead it would appear that the Didachist is dependent upon a form that was distinct

from the form which was derived from the Sayings Gospel Q.
(1989: 33)

Furthermore, the negative formulation of the golden rule harmonizes well
with the linguistic preference in the *Didache* for the weightier negative
prohibitions. This can also be seen, for example, when the framers of the
Didache concluded the decalogue (*Did.* 2:2) and its extensions (*Did.*
2:3–6) with "You will not take an evil plan against your neighbor" (*Did.*
2:6b)—a negative form of the golden rule. In conclusion, therefore, it can
be seen that scholars such as Court were so intent on finding parallel citations that demonstrated dependence that they gave only superficial attention to what might have been viewed as "significant differences" in content
and style.

F. E. Vokes tried to save the day by arguing that the framers of the
Didache deliberately altered Mt 7:12 to "conceal the borrowing" (1938:
92). This surmise on the part of Vokes, however, failed to gain a consensus, for (a) no systematic program of concealment has been demonstrated,
and (b) no adequate motive has been put forward to account for this concealment. Vokes, moreover, gave little weight to the widespread existence
of the negative golden rule outside of Matthew's Gospel. Thus, the simpler explanation is that the framers of the *Didache* were accustomed to
hearing the negative form of the golden rule and had no need to alter or
conceal what they read in Matthew.

3. *Case of the Lord's Prayer.* Even when extended passages show a
remarkable similarity, caution must be used. Court, for example, placed
great reliance on "the Lord's Prayer, where Matthew and the *Didache*
(apart from the doxology) are very closely parallel, while Luke's version is
radically different" (1981: 111). Court, in this instance, presupposed that,
based on form, Luke can be safely eliminated as the source. The close
agreement between the Lord's Prayer in Matthew and the *Didache* thus led
Court to feel entirely justified in concluding that one has here strong evidence of textual dependence on Matthew's Gospel alone. When dealing
with oft-repeated prayers, however, one might expect that the framers of
the *Didache* did not borrow from Matthew but made use of the concrete
prayer tradition within their own communities as source.

But even here, small variations can be significant. Audet, noting the
three small variations and the doxology distinguish the form of the Lord's
Prayer found in the *Didache* from that found in Matthew, appropriately
reflected on the import of these variations:

> If the Didachist had borrowed from Matthew, is it reasonable to
> assume that he would wish to modify it? . . . and touching upon
> details, in themselves, so insignificant! According to this hypoth-

esis, he would have gone contrary to received practice, and contrary to the most tenacious practice, [namely] liturgical practice. But for what end? A change which had touched a depth might well be understandable. But a purely formal alteration? In fact, one cannot regard the variations in the Lord's Prayer of the *Didache* as intentional modifications of the Lord's Prayer of Matthew without consigning the author of the *Didache* to the artificial and without placing him in contradiction with himself. . . . One returns, therefore, to our point of departure—the variations offered by the Lord's Prayer of the *Didache* constitute, even by their gratuity, a precious clue to its independence with regard to Matthew. (1958: 173)

Thus, in the end, the strong verbal parallelism in the form of the Lord's Prayer fails to support the dependence that scholars such as Court were eager to demonstrate. The truth is in the details. A community that put forward variant details of small significance (as Audet rightly notes) must have relied on its own unique practice and must not have gone about copying and slightly modifying the text of Matthew—even supposing that such a text was already in existence and available for use.

The Seductive Influence of Verbal Agreement

Christopher M. Tuckett aptly testifies to a newer and more discerning methodology that corrects the errors of scholars such as Court. Tuckett cautions against concluding that verbal parallelism points to textual dependence since, in most cases, alternate explanations are available:

The measure of verbal agreement between the *Didache* and Matthew cannot be used to determine whether that agreement is due to direct dependence of one on the other or to common dependence on a prior source [e.g., daily prayers]. Common dependence on a prior source does not necessarily involve less close verbal agreement. (1989: 207)

Clayton N. Jefford, working independently of Tuckett, produced a book-length inquiry into the source of the *Didache* (1989a). Jefford shared Tuckett's methodology insofar as, again and again, he acknowledged that one cannot easily distinguish between direct dependence and reliance on a common source. For example, he writes:

In most cases the relationship between the sayings collection in the *Didache* and the collection in the Matthew Gospel is best explained by the hypothesis that the Didachist and the Matthean redactor have shared a common sayings source. (1989a: 91)

Jefford, however, was quite uneven in applying this principle. When it came to the Lord's Prayer, for example, Jefford began by acknowledging that it was impossible to specify the source for the Lord's Prayer in the *Didache* (1989a: 138), yet he then promptly abandoned this position and concluded that "the literary structure of the piece reflects that of the Matthean Gospel to such an extent that one probably need go no further than the composition of the Matthean text for the source of the *Didache*'s reading" (1989a: 138). This conclusion ignores the rule that close verbal agreement *does not necessarily* indicate textual dependence, since it is possible to explain this agreement "by the hypothesis that the Didachist and the Matthean redactor have shared a common sayings source" (cited above). Moreover, Jefford, like Court before him, never seriously entertained the possibility that a prayer recited three times each day might constitute an "oral source" and that the multiple deviations from Matthew's text must signify, minimally, that the framers of the *Didache* were not citing from an open Gospel set out before him. This will be returned to momentarily.

Close verbal agreement will always be incapable of establishing dependence for yet another reason. Consider, for a moment, the fact that there are three instances in which Justin Martyr, writing in the mid-second century, offers sayings of Jesus that are in closer verbal agreement with the *Didache* than with any of the Synoptic parallels (Glover: 13–15). Even given these three instances, it is telling that no one today returns to the abandoned position whereby the *Didache* was conjectured to have been written using Justin Martyr as a source. Nor, for that matter, does any contemporary scholar, save for M. A. Smith (1966), conclude that Justin Martyr wrote with the *Didache* open before him as his source. The reason for this, as Paul Achtemeier explains, is that ancient writers did not, even when they were citing known and available sources, bother to open them, find the place, and copy them word for word:

> In such written texts [where they existed], the location of a given passage would be extraordinarily difficult: aside from the need to roll and re-roll, there would be no visible indication of where various parts of the composition began or ended. Nor would there be a way, once the passage was located, of referring to it by paragraph or page so that others could also find it. . . . Authors did not "check references" in the way modern scholars do (or ought to do!). In light of the pervasive orality of the environment, and the physical nature of written documents, references were much

more likely to be quoted from memory than to be copied from a source. (1990: 26–27)

In the case of Justin Martyr, consequently, one should not be surprised to find variations present no matter whether he is citing the Jewish prophets or culling sayings of Jesus from what he repeatedly identifies as the "memoirs of the apostles" (Koester 1990: 38). Furthermore, in those instances in which Justin Martyr has variations that strikingly agree with the *Didache*, this agreement was not necessarily due to his having read or heard the *Didache*; rather, this could be satisfactorily explained by noting his highly developed ability demonstrated throughout his writing for recalling from memory and reproducing sayings and narratives without clearly identifying when and where he came upon them. Helmut Koester thus concluded that Justin Martyr habitually paraphrased his "sources," often harmonizing elements from both Matthew and Luke, and even adding narrative details and complete sayings of Jesus that find no clear parallel in any written source known to us (1990: 360–402). In effect, therefore, Justin Martyr wrote and spoke like many ministers and religious people today who fill their speaking with biblical verses and allusions taken from memory. Their memories, needless to say, seem quite secure to them even while they are constantly paraphrasing, omitting unimportant elements, and substituting familiar for unfamiliar words. From time to time, they even create new material, as when I heard a preacher attribute to Jesus the saying, "Money is the root of all evil."

The upshot of this discussion is that no degree of verbal similarity can, in and of itself, be used to conclude that the framers of the *Didache* knew and/or cited the written Gospel. In every case, it is quite possible that both Matthew and the framers of the *Didache* relied on free-floating sayings that they both incorporated into their material in different ways.

Divergent Norms Supported by Appeals to the Lord

If the degree of verbal agreement cannot be used to decide definitively the issue of dependence, then other factors must be taken into account. One such method is to examine areas of common concern shared by the *Didache* and the Gospel of Matthew and to determine how the rhetoric and logic of one corresponds to or diverges from that of the other. Seven such cases will be considered:

1. The *Didache* puts forward "Do not give what is holy to dogs" (9:5) as a "saying of the Lord" that authoritatively supports the exclusion of the nonbaptized from the eucharistic meal of the community. The parallel saying in Mt 7:6 is preceded by a warning against hypocrites and followed by a warning against throwing "your pearls before swine." In this case of exact

verbal agreement (as noted above), one quickly notes that Matthew's context has nothing to do with either baptism or eucharist. Rather, Matthew, according to Robert Gundry, uses the dual sayings about dogs and pigs to warn "against easy conditions of entrance into the church" that create conditions where disciples "turn against other disciples in times of persecution" (1994: 122):

> "Dogs" and "pigs" are the only important words unaccounted for. But these stem from the typically Jewish vocabulary of derogation. Jewish-minded Matthew finds it easy to use them. In fact, he probably draws the figure of dogs from Ps 22:17(16), where it stands for those among God's people who turn on the righteous in persecution—exactly the implication here (cf. Phil 3:2; Rv 22:15). The figure of dogs naturally leads to that of pigs for the sake of parallelism. . . . Not only did Jews abhor pigs (cf. Lv 11:7; Lk 15:15–16), but also dogs were generally detested. They roamed the streets scavenging for food. (1994: 122–23)

The *Didache*, in contrast, knows only of the saying regarding "dogs" (*Did.* 9:5). The force of the saying can be gathered from its context: only those baptized may "eat or drink from your eucharist" (*Did.* 9:5). In the *Didache*, the eucharistic food was considered to be "a sacrifice" (*Did.* 14:1, 2); hence, in a Jewish context, it was "holy" (Ex 29:33–34; Lv 2:3; 22:10–16; Nm 18:8–19). The saying thus has the sense of warning that the meats offered in the temple sacrifices were not to be consumed by gentiles. The late rabbinic tradition used this saying with exactly this purpose: "What is holy is not to be released to be eaten by dogs" (*b. Bekhorot* 15a cited in *TDNT* 3:1102). The *Didache*, consequently, would appear to embrace the original application of this saying to temple sacrifices and to apply it to the "sacrifice" newly recognized by the Didache communities (Audet 1958: 173f.; ch. 5 above).

In brief, one has here a saying that has exact verbal correspondence but, when interpreted in two different contexts, evokes meanings markedly divergent. It would be improbable, therefore, that the framers of the *Didache* were aware of or in any way dependent on Matthew's Gospel in the use of this saying. Furthermore, since this saying was available as a saying of the Lord God within segments of the Jewish tradition as well as within sayings collections attributed to Jesus (*Gos. Thom.* 93), it would be difficult to maintain that Matthew's Gospel was the unique source, especially since Matthew deflects the meaning of the saying in a direction devoid of sacrificial overtones.

2. *Didache* 8:1 specifies that one should not fast "with the hypocrites"; hence, two alternate days of community fast are prescribed. *Did.* 8:2 goes on to say that one should not pray "as the hypocrites" but should use the

Lord's Prayer three times each day. Matthew, in contrast, prohibits praying "like the hypocrites" (6:5), who stand "that they might be seen by men." The solution, in Matthew's context, is not to change the prayer formula but to "go into your room and shut the door" (6:6). Likewise, in the case of fasting, "the hypocrites . . . disfigure their faces" (6:16). Matthew would have the followers of Jesus "anoint your head and wash your face" (6:17) thereby disguising their fast from public view. The *Didache*, in contrast, appears to presume a mode of fasting that was in common with that of the "hypocrites," yet since fasting together signals public solidarity in the reasons for fasting, the days of fasting are altered.

In brief, the functional descriptions of "hypocrites" surrounding fasting and praying and the corrective responses of the community found in Matthew appear to be entirely distinct from what is found in the *Didache*. It would appear that the common term "hypocrites" serves to describe two different classes of people, who are to be responded to by two different strategies in two distinct communities (Audet 1958:172; Rordorf 1978a: 36f.). Furthermore, the *Didache* appears to know nothing of the Jesus sayings in Matthew and, accordingly, designs altered norms with complete indifference to Matthew's. It would be highly improbable, therefore, that the framers of the *Didache* were aware of or in any way dependent on Matthew's Gospel in defining or resolving issues related to fasting and praying.

3. Both the *Didache* and Matthew had to deal with backsliders and with misbehaving members. To accomplish this, the *Didache* prescribes confessing personal transgressions before the weekly eucharist (14:1) and the shunning of members unwilling to amend their lives (15:3). For the former, the *Didache* cites Mal 1:11 in support—implying that the framers of the *Didache* know of no saying of Jesus nor any mandate from tradition that might be used in order to support such a practice.

Matthew's Gospel, meanwhile, endorses an entirely different procedure described in Mt 18:15–18. This procedure is seemingly normative, since Jesus is heard to endorse it in his own words. Had the author of the *Didache* known of this, it seems evident that he also would have made use of it and not had to stretch and strain Mal 1:11 (see details in ch. 8) to support a novel practice of using the eucharist as a gate for reconciliation: "Everyone having a conflict with his companion, do not let him come together with you [for the eucharist] until they be reconciled, in order that your sacrifice not be defiled" (*Did.* 14:2). Alternately, instead of citing Mal 1:11 to support this practice, it could be argued that he could have made easy use of Mt 5:23. But he didn't! It would be highly improbable, therefore, that the framers of the *Didache* were aware of or in any way dependent on Matthew's Gospel in defining or resolving issues dealing with backsliders and misbehaving members.

4. The *Didache* includes a well-defined and well-adapted (see ch. 1

above) decalogue but then goes on to suggest a system of "fences" (*Did.* 3:1–6) that give attention to forestalling minor infractions that might prove to be the slippery slope toward major infractions. Matthew, on the other hand, approaches the insufficiency of the Decalogue by developing a series of antitheses that are filled with hyperbolic language (e.g., Gundry 1994: 82–83). In the *Didache*, the system of "fences" is used to securely train gentiles. In Matthew, the series of antitheses are designed to ensure that "the righteousness" of Jesus' disciples "exceeds that of the scribes and the Pharisees" (Mt 5:20). Thus, one has two diverse religious systems appended to the Decalogue—each designed in response to differing existential needs. Neither system appears aware of the other (Kloppenborg 1995: 104–8). If the *Didache* had existed in a community that used Matthew's Gospel (as some suppose), one would have expected that there would have been some cross-fertilization of methods. It would be highly improbable, therefore, that the framers of the *Didache* were aware of or in any way dependent on Matthew's Gospel.

5. *Didache* 6:2 uses "yoke of the Lord [God]" in a way that harmonizes with Jewish tradition (e.g., Sir 51:25; *m. Berakhoth* 2:2; *b. Sotah* 47b) and makes no use of Matthew's having Jesus say, "Take my yoke upon you, and learn from me" (11:29). Chapter 13 will explore and contrast the context and meaning of these two sayings.

6. *Didache* 6:3 reflects an aversion to "the meat offered to idols" that finds no exact parallel in either Acts (10:14, 28; 11:3) or Paul (1 Cor 10:23–33; Rom 14:1–23). Meanwhile, the *Didache* appears to be unaware that "it is not what goes into the mouth that defiles a person" (Mt 15:10). It would be highly improbable, therefore, that the framers of the *Didache* were aware of or in any way dependent on Matthew's Gospel.

7. Matthew and the *Didache* provide two different interpretations of the "unforgivable sin." For Matthew, "whoever speaks against the Holy Spirit will not be forgiven" (12:32). Matthew develops this saying, which he finds in Mark 3:29, in order to retain Mark's defense of Jesus' power of exorcism against the verbal attacks of Pharisees (Mt 12:24 = Mk 3:22 ["scribes"]). For the *Didache*, the unforgivable sin is putting on trial or judging a "prophet speaking in the Spirit" (11:7). While some degree of overlap is present here, clearly the *Didache* and Matthew have distinct agendas. It would be improbable, therefore, that the framers of the *Didache* were aware of or in any way dependent on Matthew's Gospel for the development of their tradition on the unforgivable sin.

In brief, as particular texts and issues are examined, one finds the *Didache* defining and resolving common problems differently from Matthew. When parallel citations are used with strong or exact verbal agreement, the investigations above show that divergent religious systems were providing different contexts and meanings for these sayings. Overall, despite some verbal similarities, one is forced to conclude that the framers of the *Didache* operated independently of Matthew's Gospel even when addressing common issues. One could, of course, argue that the framers of the *Didache* were aware of Matthew's solutions but consciously chose neither to address them nor to make use of them. Such a position would have to supply a sufficient reason for each instance in which the *Didache* passed over the Matthean tradition in silence (e.g., as in the case where the confession of failings was upheld on the basis of the obscure Mal 1:11 while Mt 5:23 offers a ready-made support). Since no such reasons are forthcoming, the simpler and more satisfying route is to acknowledge that the framers of the *Didache* worked out solutions to their problems without any awareness of the practice of Matthew's communities or of Matthew's Gospel.

Whether the Double Love Commandments Demonstrate Dependence

Tuckett makes the point that each of the love commandments (Dt 6:5 and Lv 19:18b) finds ample testimony in Jewish sources but only rarely are they found together (see #11a below) and never are they enumerated ("first . . . second . . .") as in *Did.* 1:2a. As a result, Tuckett jumps to the conclusion that "the simplest solution is to postulate dependence on Matthew" (1989: 210).

#11A WHETHER THE DOUBLE LOVE COMMANDMENT IS UNIQUELY CHRISTIAN

Christopher M. Tuckett notes that the *Testaments of the Twelve Patriarchs* represent the Jewish source that notably juxtaposes the love commandments (Dt 6:5 and Lv 19:18b) (1989: 210; see fuller treatment of Kloppenborg 1995: 98 n. 41):

> If anyone were in distress, I joined my sighs with his: and with the poor have I joined my bread. I never ate alone. No boundary stone have I moved. I have been reverent and truthful all my days. *I have loved the Lord with all my strength;* and in the same way *I have loved all men as though they were my own children.* Do these things too, my children. . . . (*Testament of Issachar* 7:6, emphasis added; also 5:2; and *Testament of Dan* 5:3)

In examining this, one notes the following: (a) The double love commandment comes at the end of a list and may serve as a summation, but this aspect is not emphasized. (b) The allusion to Dt 6:5 drops "with all your heart and all your soul" and retains simply "with all your strength." (c) The reference to loving others "as though they were my children" clearly goes beyond Lv 19:18b ("as yourself").

Stepping back, one can suppose that Tuckett is on solid ground when he proposes that the association of Dt 6:5 and Lv 19:18b along with their numeration as "first" and "second" finds its unique place in Christian sources (Mk 12:28; Mt 22:40; *Did.* 1:2) (1989: 210). Since the Jewish traditions of the first century were diverse and largely dependent on oral communications, it does not follow that the silence of the Jewish sources on this point precludes a Jewish source. Jesus and his immediate disciples, it must be remembered, were presenting themselves to Jewish audiences; hence, if Mt 22:34–40 represents the views of the historical Jesus, then it must also be allowed that Jesus offered "an acceptable Jewish response" (Mk 12:22–23) to a Jewish question. Furthermore, even if the juxtaposing of the love commandments could be known to be uniquely a Christian tradition, this still leaves open the possibility that the framers of the *Didache* became aware of this tradition either before or independently of Matthew's Gospel (Kloppenborg 1995: 98–99).

Here, again, attention must be given to the particulars. The double love commandment in Matthew's Gospel emerges as a response to "a lawyer" who "asked him a question to test him" (Mt 22:35). Jesus recites a close variant of Dt 6:5: "You shall love the Lord your God with all your heart, and with all your soul, and with all your mind" (Mt 22:37). The *Didache*, in contrast, puts forward, "You will love the God who made you" (*Did.* 1:2a). This is an unexpected variation on Dt 6:5, and it serves here to define "the Way of Life" and not to define "the greatest commandment" (Mt 22:36) on which "hangs all the law [Torah] and the prophets" (Mt 22:40). Extending Audet's argument above, one could thus say the following to Tuckett:

> If the Didachist had borrowed Mt 23:37, is it reasonable to assume that he would wish to modify it? . . . and touching upon details, in themselves, so seemingly insignificant! According to this hypothesis, he would go contrary to received practice, and contrary to the most tenacious practice, the oral recitation of Dt 6:5 which immediately follows the Shema. But for what end? A change which had touched a depth might well be understandable. But a purely formal alteration? In fact, one cannot regard *Did.* 1:2a as an intentional modification of Mt 22:37 without consigning the author of the *Didache* to the artificial and without placing him in contradiction with himself. . . . One returns, there-

fore, to our point of departure—the variations offered in *Did.* 1:2 constitute, even by their gratuity, a precious clue to its independence with regards to Matthew. (Audet 1958: 173 imaginatively redone)

In sum, if the Didache communities put forward variant details of small significance, they must have relied on their own stubborn oral traditions and not gone to the trouble of consulting and deliberately modifying what Jesus "said" according to the Gospel of Matthew—even supposing that such a manuscript was already in existence and available at hand. Oral tradition is more stubborn to change and more authoritative within an oral culture than is commonly supposed (Ong 1967: 54–55, 231–36, 283–86). Even today, we ourselves tend to mentally correct public readers in the church whenever they misread the Sunday portion of the Bible or whenever they use an English translation unfamiliar to our ears. With even greater force, the *Didache*'s formulation of *Did.* 1:2a must have been quite deliberate and must have stood in a solidly received tradition for it to withstand being harmonized with Dt 6:5 or with Mt 23:37. It would be highly improbable, therefore, for the framers of the *Didache* to be aware of or in any way dependent on Matthew's Gospel in defining the Way of Life.

Whether "Turning the Other Cheek" Demonstrates Dependence

Nearly all the major commentators have come to the conclusion that the Two Ways existed as a Jewish catechetical document for gentiles that was superficially "christianized" by the addition of Jesus sayings (*Did.* 1:3b–5a). Audet gave concrete expression to this hypothesis in his massive seven-hundred-page commentary on the *Didache* published in 1958. Audet brought to his commentary his rich familiarity with Jewish sources and, at nearly every point within the text, Audet discovered Jewish parallels. Audet identified the Two Ways (*Did.* 1–5) accordingly as "belonging to the genre of an 'instruction on the commandments' . . . as it was being practiced by the contemporary synagogue" (Audet 1958: 284). Willy Rordorf, twenty years later, regarded the first five chapters of the *Didache* as "essentially Jewish, but the Christian community was able to use it as such" (1978b: 28) with the addition of the "evangelical section" (*Did.* 1:3b–5a). Nearly twenty years after him, John S. Kloppenborg even went so far as to affirm that "in the final form of the *Didache*, of course, the presence of sayings of Jesus that the reader presumably is intended to recognize as such, amounts to a 'Christianization' of the document" (1995: 98).

Earlier in this volume, caution was expressed regarding this hypothesis (see #1j). In part, the very act of recognizing "sayings of Jesus" has been prejudiced by the judgment that they are to be found in the Synoptic Gospels. Moreover, only gradually has there been a willingness to allow that sayings attributed to Jesus circulated orally outside the Synoptics and that these sayings showed up in written materials (e.g., the *Gospel of Thomas*) both before and after the creation of the Synoptics (Koester 1990: xxix–xxxi). The *Didache*, consequently, may contain a much larger section of Jesus sayings than is commonly admitted and even the so-called "evangelical section" (Rordorf 1978a; 1978b: 28; also Niederwimmer 1998: 68) of the Way of Life may owe its existence to this oral tradition circulating independently of written sources.

#11B WHETHER THE "EVANGELICAL SECTION" WAS PART OF THE ORIGINAL

Helmut Koester normally moves against the current by making due allowances for the oral circulation sayings of Jesus, yet he completely sets this alternative aside when examining *Did.* 1:3b–5a.

> This section [of the *Didache*] is a compilation of sayings from the Sermon on the Mount, but with distinct features of harmonization of the texts of Matthew and Luke. It is an interpolation that must have been made after the middle of the second century and cannot, therefore, be used as evidence for the original compiler's familiarity with written gospels. (1990: 17)

Koester cites B. Layton (1968: 343–83) and K. Wengst (1984: 18–20) and notes the reservations of Niederwimmer (1998: 68–87) to support his judgment that the "evangelical section" was not in the original *Didache* but was added later. Support for this conjecture comes from two observations: (1) We have in our possession second-century editions of the Way of Life that do not contain the so-called "evangelical section" (*Epistle of Barnabas* 18–20, *Teaching of the Apostles* (*De Doctrina Apostolorum*). (2) The introduction of the "evangelical section" leads to the rather clumsy creation of *Did.* 2:1 with its reference to a "second/secondary rule" (Niederwimmer 1998: 45; Rordorf 1978a: 32–33). Based on these observations, it is possible to conjecture that the original framers of the *Didache* omitted the "evangelical section," and that much later, when the Gospels were in wide circulation, a "final editor" took the initiative to insert the "evangelical section" into the *Didache* as a "harmonization of the texts of Matthew and Luke" (Koester cited above).

On the other hand, there are those who find no compelling evidence for allowing that the original framers of the *Didache* did not incorporate the "evangelical section" themselves (Niederwimmer 1998: 42–45; see ch. 12

below). The nuances of this debate are amply summarized by Niederwimmer (1998: 68–77) and need not detain us here.

The issue at hand is whether the text of the *Didache* as it now stands demonstrates a dependence on a known Gospel. Whether this edition was arrived at in one, two, or three stages of composition does not undercut the issue of Gospel dependence—it can only complicate or detain it. One can thus move directly to examining the evidence for dependence on Matthew or Luke.

Leaving this aside for the moment, let us proceed with a standard evaluation of the so-called "evangelical section" of the *Didache*. In order to make this study more manageable, only *Did.* 1:4–5a will be considered, relying on the careful textual study of Tuckett (1989). Tuckett's analysis needs to be carefully considered because it demonstrates that a cautious critical analysis of the parallel texts can result in the conclusion that the *Didache* depended on both Matthew and Luke for its composition. Tuckett's study, moreover, has been received by Rordorf as offering "the most careful and comprehensive study of the problem that I know [after Koester]" (Rordorf 1991: 400).

To begin with, Tuckett examines the parallel texts in Greek. These parallel texts are reproduced here in English translation in order to make this study accessible to a wider audience. Care has been taken to modify the NRSV translation where necessary to correspond to the *Didache* translation where exact Greek equivalence exists. To make these passages visually apparent, they are displayed in boldface type.

Matthew 5:38–42	*Didache* 1:4–5a
You have heard that it was said, "An eye for an eye and a tooth for a tooth." But I say to you, Do not resist an evildoer.	Abstain from fleshly and bodily desires. [How so?]
[A] But if anyone strikes you on the right cheek, **turn to him/her also the other;**	[A] if anyone should give you a strike on the right cheek, **turn to him/her also the other,** and you will be perfect;
	[B] if anyone should press you into service for **one mile, go with him/her two;**

[B] and if anyone wants to sue you and take your tunic, give (*dos*) **also** your cloak;	[C] if anyone should take away your cloak, give (*aphes*) to him/her **also** your tunic;
[C] and if anyone presses you into service **one mile,** *go with him/her two.*	
	[D] if anyone should take from you [what is] yours, do not ask for it back; for you are not even able [to do so].
[D] Give (*didou*) **to everyone asking you,** and do not refuse anyone who wants to borrow from you.	*To everyone asking you* [for anything], give (*dos*) and do not ask for it back; for, to all, the Father wishes to give [these things] from his own free gifts.

When Matthew and the *Didache* are compared in the table above, one notices that each has four sayings (A to D) but that they are used by each author to illustrate significantly different topics. Chapter 12 below develops this in detail. For purposes of brevity, I will point out some of the observations of Tuckett and then proceed to examine his conclusion, namely, "that this section of the *Didache* appears on a number of occasions to presuppose the redactional activity of both evangelists, perhaps Luke more clearly than Matthew" (1989: 230). The evidence will be reviewed, beginning with Matthew.

The two most significant instances that Tuckett finds to suggest dependence on Matthew are as follows:

> *Did.* 1:4 [A] agrees very closely with the Matthean form of the saying specifying the "right" cheek, using *didonai rapisma* ["give a strike"] . . . , and *strepson* ["turn"]. . . . (1989: 225)
>
> *Did.* 1:4b [B] is parallel to Mt 5:41 [C], which has no Lukan parallel. (1989: 226)

Thus, in the first instance, the *Didache* has "right" cheek whereas Luke fails to specify which cheek. The Greek terms are also closer to Matthew than to Luke. In the second instance, the situation of being pressed to go one mile is placed in a different order in Matthew but is entirely absent from

Luke. Tuckett, however, does not want to give excessive weight to the absence of this saying from Luke because it is possible that Luke found this in Q but, for reasons unknown to us, omitted it (1989: 226).

Luke 6:27–32	*Didache* 1:4–5
But I say to you that listen, Love your enemies, do good to those who hate you, bless those who curse you, pray for those who abuse you.	Abstain from fleshly and bodily desires. [How so?]
[A] If anyone strikes you on (*epi*) **the cheek,** offer **also the other;**	[A] if anyone should give you a strike on (*eis*) **the** right **cheek,** turn to him/her **also the other,** and you will be perfect.
	[B] if anyone should press you into service for one mile, go with him/her two;
[B] and from anyone who takes away **your cloak** do not withhold **also your tunic.**	[C] if anyone should take away **your cloak,** give to him/her **also your tunic.**
	[D] if anyone should take from you [what is] yours, do not ask for it back; for you are not even able [to do so].
[C] **To everyone asking you [for anything], give;**	**To everyone asking you [for anything] give.**
[D] and if anyone takes away your goods, **do not ask for it back;**	and **do not ask for it back;** for, to all, the Father wishes to give [these things] from his own free gifts.
Do to others as you would have them do to you.	
"If you love those who love you, what credit is that to you? For even sinners love those who love them."	

Tuckett also finds evidence suggesting that the framers of the *Didache* depended on Luke's version, of which the two most evident instances are as follows:

> The *Didache* here [C] reveals close affinities with the Lukan version. . . . Matthew's version presupposes the situation of a lawsuit where the person addressed is being sued for his shirt (*chitōn*) ["tunic"] and is told to surrender even his cloak (*himation*). . . . Luke's (and the *Didache*'s) version reverses the order of the *chitōn* and the *himation* and seems to presuppose a robbery situation: if a person is robed of his cloak (the first thing a robber would grab) he is to surrender his shirt [tunic] as well. (1989: 227)

> The *Didache* [D] agrees with Luke against Matthew in referring to someone who takes, rather than someone who wants to borrow; there is also agreement between the *Didache* and Luke in using *apaitei* ["ask back"] in the final part. (1989: 228)

The upshot of Tuckett's investigation is that the "*Didache* appears on a number of occasions to presuppose the redactional activity of both evangelists" (1989: 230). Tuckett is firm on this point:

> The evidence of the *Didache* seems to show that the text is primarily a witness to the post-redactional history of the synoptic tradition. It is not a witness to any pre-redactional developments. (1989: 230)

The Bias of Textuality and the Ignorance of Orality

Willy Rordorf attempted to analyze and refute Tuckett's conclusions regarding the "evangelical section" while sharing his methodology (1991: 401–12). His results are less than convincing. Rordorf's key argument appears to be that "with a canonical text [such as Matthew and Luke] it is impossible to chop and change [it] as the *Didache* does" (1991: 411). To this, Tuckett might well respond that it would be anachronistic to speak of "a canonical text" in the first two centuries. Moreover, not only do Matthew and Luke demonstrate the freedom to chop and change the material received from Mark, but the same can be said for the early church fathers citing them. In the mid-second-century writings of Justin Martyr, for example, "the vast majority of the sayings in Justin's writings are harmonizations of the texts of Matthew and Luke" (Koestev 1990: 365).

In my judgment, Tuckett's conclusions cannot be effectively refuted unless one calls into question the bias of textuality and the ignorance of orality that mark his methodology. This might proceed as follows:

1. *The bias of textuality.* Tuckett frames his inquiry entirely around which "source" or "sources" the *Didache* used. Since we live in a post-Gutenberg era, Tuckett is naturally disposed to think of ancient authors gravitating toward written sources. Thus, it is only natural that affinities with Matthew on some points vie with affinities with Luke on still other points, and, in the end, this quandary can be settled only by presupposing that the framers of the *Didache* knew both Gospels. Tuckett never takes into account the possibility that the *Didache* was created in "a culture of high residual orality" (Achtemeier 1990: 3), wherein "oral sources" (attached to respected persons) were routinely given greater weight and were immeasurably more serviceable than "written sources" (Achtemeier 1990: 9–11; Ong 1967: 52–53). Moreover, Tuckett does not seem to allow that "oral sources" had a certain measure of socially maintained stability but not the frozen rigidity of a written text (Achtemeier 1990: 27; Ong 1967: 231–34). Thus, Tuckett's methodology suffers from "the bias of textuality and the ignorance of orality":

> The form-critical search for the archetypal composition, and the compulsion to honor it as a first rung in the evolutionary ladder betray the bias of textuality and ignorance of oral behavior. The works of Milman Parry and Albert B. Lord have made it incontrovertibly plain that each oral performance is an irreducible unique creation. If, for example, Jesus spoke a saying more than once, the first utterance did not produce "the original," nor was the second one a "variant" thereof, because each moment of speech is wondrously fresh and new [since it is adapted to each different audience]. The concepts of *original form* and variants have no validity in oral life, nor does the one of *ipsissima vox,* if by that one means the authentic version over and against secondary ones. "In a sense each performance is 'an' original, if not 'the' original" [Lord: 101]. (Kelber 1983: 30; also Crossan 1998: 49–52)

#11c ORAL MEMORY AND Q

While considerable effort has been deployed to push the evidence of Matthew and Luke to reconstruct a written Q Gospel (Crossan 1998: 110; Koester 1990: 128–71), this entire post-Gutenberg project assumes that an "original source" did exist. The presumption of a written Q Gospel helps explain how both Matthew and Luke, writing independently, have so many shared Jesus sayings in their editing of Mark's Gospel distributed in the same order. Our purpose here is not to evaluate either the methods or the results of this project but to reflect on how the notion of an "original form" of the hypothetical written Q Gospel manifests a bias of textuality that ignores oral behavior.

While both Matthew and Luke enjoyed a great degree of freedom in inserting the so-called Q material into the framework of Mark's Gospel, it might be supposed that the communities that they served already had a rich oral tradition of sayings of Jesus which each evangelist was anxious to incorporate into the Gospel designed for their use. One must grant that the degree of diversity in both the ordering and the internal logic could be accounted for by supposing that each evangelist brought his own editorial preferences to bear upon identical Greek copies of the written Q Gospel. Against the backdrop of an oral culture, on the other hand, the degree of diversity might be more satisfactorily explained by supposing that variant written or oral productions of Q circulated and that each evangelist incorporated the version known to him and his would-be readers. Given the stubbornness inherent in localized traditions, it is even possible that Matthew and Luke did not have to choose between variant written or oral productions of Q, since each knew of only one version—the one that they had assimilated in their own period of training and of living the way of Jesus.

Even supposing that oral productions of Q came to be written down during the period when the *Didache* was being created, a problem arises. It is one thing to expect a degree of standardization when, for example, letters of Paul were copied and circulated since, in each instance, a single written letter began the process. In the case of the Q Gospel, however, no such "original" has become known to us and, given the normal fluctuations present in oral transmission, it would be more faithful to the first-century oral environment to suspect that various editions of written Q circulated in just the same way that variant oral sayings of Jesus were found in the mouths of the wandering prophets and local teachers (Koester 1990: 133, 137) and variant versions of the Serbo-Croatian epics are told today (Crossan 1998: 71–74).

Research on oral memory and on variations found in the Way of Life can provide an illustrative case. Let us suppose, for the moment, that the Way of Life was designed and used for a prolonged period as an oral production before it was ever committed to writing. As in the case of the hypothetical Q, one would not expect that it would have been committed to writing in only one place by one scribe but in multiple places by local scribes. Accordingly, there would be various versions of the Way of Life present in writing—a reflection of the various versions of the oral production in use. What has come down to us textually confirms this. All in all, we have various written versions of the Way of Life: *Did.* 1–5, *Teaching of the Apostles* (*De Doctrina Apostolorum*), *Epistle of Barnabas* 18–21, *Ecclesiastic Constitutions of the Holy Apostles* 4:1–13:4, Arabic *Life of Shenoute*. Each version reveals a clearly identifiable progression of topics, yet each incorporates noticeable omissions and additions. These written versions freeze moments of oral production and allow us to see that, in various local communities, oral traditions can be stubbornly upheld and maintained. In point of fact, given the oral studies of Albert B. Lord and Milman Parry, it could be supposed that the same teacher/mentor introduced small variations and pastoral expansions every time he/she recited the Way of Life (Crossan 1998: 69–78). If asked, "Is this the Way of Life just as you recited it last time?" The response would be, "Certainly. My memory didn't falter. I recited it for you from beginning to end just as I did last time." If a tape recorder had been present to freeze these moments, however, the variations would have shown up.

In this volume, there is neither the time nor the space to test each of these alternative hypotheses. It suffices, for the moment, to make room for the possibility of looking to oral transmission for clues as to how variant sayings show up in parallel texts (Crossan 1998: 103–8; Draper 1996e; Henderson 1992). It also makes room for acknowledging that local variations in oral production would inevitably lead to variations when making written copies. In sum, variations among the existing versions of the Way of Life and variations within the sayings of Jesus might be more simply and appropriately accounted for by examining the oral dynamics within traditional societies than by presuming an "original source" that gets edited by subsequent authors (Achtemeier 1990; Ong 1982).

2. *The* Didache *as an oral production*. When the residual clues of orality are again noted in the *Didache* (see #11d), it becomes possible to understand that its oral creation and oral recitation marked its internal structure long before it was ever a written text. The *Didache*, once it was first written down, would normally have been created as a scribal transcription listening to an oral production being recited by someone who had mastered it (Achtemeier 1990: 12–13). Those who received or used this written manuscript would have, in their turn, instinctively read it aloud even when alone, for it was in hearing it that it was recognized for what it was (Achtemeier 1990: 15–17; Ong 1967: 58). The text itself, lacking capitals, lacking paragraph indentations, lacking even spaces between words, *had to be heard to be recognized*. The creation of the *Didache*, therefore, never took place as a composite of written sources that the author produced in a study surrounded by source documents. It would be anachronistic, consequently, to imagine that the *Didache* was composed with the books of Matthew and Luke open. "All the quotations in the *Didache* are clearly made from memory" (Jefford 1989a: 314).

#11D THE MEDIUM OF ORALITY IN THE *DIDACHE*

In the *Didache*, the vocabulary and the linguistic structure display a one-sided preference for orality. Thus, the *Didache* defines the Way of Life and immediately goes on to specify the "training" required for the assimilation "of these *words*" (1:3). The novice is told to honor "the one *speaking* to you the *word* of God" (4:1) thereby signaling that oral training was presupposed. Moreover, the novice trembles "at the *words* that you have *heard*" (3:8).

In every instance where the *Didache* cites specific mandates from the Hebrew Scriptures, the oral aspect (as opposed to the written) is highlighted: "It has been *said*" (1:6); "The Lord has likewise *said*" (9:5); "This is the thing having been *said* by the Lord" (14:3); "As it has been *said*" (16:7). The same thing can be presumed to hold true when citing the "good news" (8:2; 11:3; 15:3, 4; see #11e). Accordingly, the *Didache* gives full attention to speaking rightly (1:3b; 2:3, 5; 4:8b, 14; 15:3b) and entirely neglects false or empty writing. At the baptism, the novice is immersed in water "having *said* all these things beforehand" (7:1). Thus, when the novice is warned to watch out for those who "might make you wander from this way of training" (6:1), one surmises that defective words rather than defective texts are implied. The same holds true, when later in the *Didache*, the baptized are warned only to receive him/her who "should train you in all the things *said* beforehand" (11:1) indicating that even the *Didache* was being heard. Finally, faced with the end time, each one is alerted to the importance of frequently being "gathered together" (16:2). This enforces an earlier admonition to "seek every day the presence of the saint in order that you may rest upon their *words*" (4:2)—thereby signaling once again how verbal exchange was paramount when "seeking the things pertaining to your souls" (16:2). The one misbehaving, accordingly, was reproved "not in anger [i.e., angry words], but in peace" (15:3). Those unable to abide by the reproof received were cut off from hearing or being discussed by community members: "Let no one *speak* to him/her, nor let anyone *hear* from you about him/her until he/she should repent" (15:3).

From beginning to end, therefore, the vocabulary and linguistic structure of the *Didache* reinforce oral performance. The literary actions of seeing, reading, writing, and editing are passed over in silence (Henderson 1992: 295–99). This feature has repercussions concerning how the *Didache* was accordingly created, transmitted, interpreted, and transformed in "a culture of high residual orality which nevertheless communicated significantly by means of literary creations" (Achtemeier 1990: 9–19, 26–27).

3. *The transmission of a Jesus tradition.* The formation of the *Didache* drew upon oral sources that were wedded together by virtue of reflecting what was already being heard and practiced in the Didache communities. The Way of Life, since the *Didache* attributes it to the Father revealing (i.e., speaking) through his servant Jesus (9:3; 10:2), must have had the community-approved resonance as being what the God of Israel would have required of gentiles in the last days. Even the Synoptic Gospels make it clear that Jesus himself did not train his own disciples using some progression of sayings that they repeated in unison after him. Rather, they signal that he apprenticed them in a way of life that enabled them to do what he did, to value what he valued, to expect what he hoped for (Milavec 1982: 1–24, 79–144). The Way of Life, on the other hand, exhibits a carefully crafted progression of sayings (see ch. 1) which was received as authoritative because it was used by community-recognized teachers/mentors to initiate gentiles into habits of mind and judgments of the heart required of them in preparation for the age to come proclaimed by Jesus. It seems mistaken, consequently, to imagine that the Way of Life required "Jesus sayings" to lend it authority and that these sayings were largely limited to the so-called "evangelical section." Rather, the whole of the Way of Life would have been understood as reflecting the values lived and taught by Jesus and his apostles. Only a misplaced bias of textuality would somehow imagine that the authority of Jesus somehow dissipates as soon as community-approved teachers/mentors are not repeating the historically verified sayings of Jesus.

4. *The term "Gospel" used by the Didache.* When the *Didache* itself uses the term *euaggelion* ("gospel"), it refers, first and foremost, to the "good news" preached by the Jesus movement, and not until the mid-second century does "gospel" receive the extended meaning of referring to written texts (see #11e). Christopher Tuckett, to his credit, appears to be aware of this because, unlike many other scholars, he never makes the mistake of imagining that the references to *euaggelion* in the *Didache* provide evidence for the existence of an authoritative written text used in the community.

#11E WHETHER "GOSPEL" REFERS TO A WRITTEN SOURCE

In four places, the framers of the *Didache* make reference to an authoritative source known as the "good news" or "gospel" (*euaggelion*). These are as follows:

And do not pray as the hypocrites
but as the Lord ordered in his *good news*. (8:2) [The Lord's
  Prayer follows.]

And concerning the apostle-prophets,
in accordance with the decree of the *good news*,
act thus. (11:3) [Rules for visiting prophets follow.]

And reprove each other! [Do it] not in anger, but in peace!
[Do it] as ÿou have [it] in the *good news*. (15:3)

And your prayers and alms and all [ÿour] actions
dö thus as ÿou have [it] in the *good news* of our Lord. (15:4)

Eduard Massaux initially argued strongly that, since in the first instance
the framers of the *Didache* referred to Matthew's Gospel as their source,
there is certainty that "in the three other places (11:3; 15:3; 15:4), the
Didachist returns again to the [same] Gospel" (1949: 40). The following
year, however, aware that the term *euaggelion* was not used to designate
any written Gospel prior to Justin Martyr (c. 150), Massaux wrote with
greater circumspection:

> If one judges that the *Didache* is a writing that is quite early, one
> will have the inclination to not see in the term *euaggelion* a ref-
> erence to a written gospel; but if, on the contrary, one thinks . . .
> that it [the *Didache*] can be dated around 150, *euaggelion* can
> then very easily signify a writing because Justin [writing in the
> same period] certainly gives to this term the sense of a written
> Gospel. (1950: 605)

Since Massaux was persuaded that he found in the *Didache* "the profound
literary influence of the Gospel of Matthew" (1950: 644), he was accordingly inclined to assign the *Didache* a date of composition after 150. Here
again, therefore, the supposed date of composition strongly interfaces
what one expects to find in the *Didache*.

R. Glover appears to be the first person to argue that *euaggelion*, as used
by the *Didache*, could not refer to any of the canonical Gospels because the
term was not used in this sense prior to the mid-second century (28).
Niederwimmer, after making a literary analysis of *euaggelion* in the context
of the *Didache*, concluded that this term refers not to "the Christological
kerygma" or "the epiphany, death, and resurrection of Jesus for our sake"
(Niederwimmer 1998: 50) but to a set of practical rules for living which
are seemingly known by the members of the Didache communities. These

rules include guidelines for praying (namely, the Lord's Prayer), guidelines for visiting prophets, guidelines for reproving, guidelines for almsgiving and "all your actions" (*Did.* 15:4). At no point does the *Didache* clarify whether such guidelines are oral or written (1998: 51).

In the Christian Scriptures, the term "good news" (*euaggelion*) customarily refers to an oral production. Jesus, for example, is remembered as having proclaimed "the good news of God" (Mk 1:14; Rom 1:1; 15:16; 2 Cor 2:7; 1 Thes 2:2, 9; 1 Pt 4:17)—an oral message. Paul, in addition, makes reference to "the good news of Christ" (1 Cor 9:12; 2 Cor 2:12; 9:13), to "my good news" (Rom 2:16; 16:25), and to "our good news" (1 Thes 1:5; 2 Cor 4:3). In each of these instances, it is clear that the "good news" (or "gospel" as it is sometimes translated) was not a writing, first and foremost, but a message (Kelber: 144–47; Koester 1990: 1–48).

Historically speaking, therefore, the term *euaggelion* referred to an oral production, and only in the latter third of the second century were books recording the "good news" designated by this name. Helmut Koester extensively studied the origin of the term "gospel" and carefully retraced when and how the term came to be applied to writings (Koester 1990: 1–48). In part, Koester concludes as follows:

> What *2 Clement* calls "gospel" is a collection of sayings of Jesus, not the story of Jesus' birth, life, death, and resurrection. Marcion and Justin Martyr come closer to such a kerygma concept of the written gospel. . . . But for most of the first two-thirds of the second century the best characterization of the meaning of the term "gospel" is that given by Hans von Campenhausen: "'The Gospel' to which appeal is normally made remains an elastic concept designating the preaching of Jesus as a whole in the form in which it lives on in church tradition." (1990: 29)

> Papias [100–150 C.E.] says about Matthew that he composed "the sayings" (*ta logia*). In neither statement does Papias use the term "gospel. Even in their written form, these traditions about Jesus and of Jesus' words do not carry any greater authority than that which was transmitted orally. (1990: 33)

Justin Martyr (150 C.E.) was the first Christian writer to self-consciously and repeatedly cite the written sources attributed to the apostles. In each instance, he does not name any single Gospel book but refers to the material he quotes as coming from the "memoirs of the apostles" (Koester 1990: 38). In three instances, he also uses the term "gospels" to refer to these sources:

> The apostles in the memoirs which have come from them, which are also called gospels (*euaggelia*), have transmitted what the Lord had commanded. (*1 Apol.* 66.3; also *Dial.* 10.2, 100.1)

One can see here that the notion of "memoirs" was dominant and that the term "gospels" was a secondary or even a suspect term due to its use by Marcion (Koester 1990: 36–38).

Justin Martyr also repeatedly quotes from the Torah and the prophets, not naming particular books, but preferring the all-embracing introductory formula, "it is written" (Koester 1990: 41). In contrast, Jesus is presented in Matthew's Gospel as citing the Torah with the introductory formula, "You have heard that it was said to the men of old" (5:21, 27, 31, 33, 38, 43)—thereby clearly signaling an oral transmission. Justin Martyr's use of "it is written," however, clearly focuses upon his own familiarity with Torah as coming through hearing what has been written. Clearly the Septuagint carries a weight of authority as "inspired writing"—something that Justin Martyr did not identify with the "memoirs of the apostles" (Koester 1990: 41).

When the *Didache* was dated as originating in the mid-second century, it was natural to assume that the internal references to *euaggelion* pointed to one of the written Gospels. Even here, however, this assumption was suspect, since, as already shown, the "good news" of the *Didache* was equated with practical guidelines on ways of acting approved by the Lord. The canonical Gospels included some such practical guidelines but always in the context of a narrative style. Thus, among the known Gospels, only the *Gospel of Thomas* or the hypothetical Q Gospel—both of which list sayings of Jesus outside any narrative structure—would have had the character of the *euaggelion* referred to four times by the *Didache*.

If the *Didache* was produced during the first century, then "good news" could have referred to the sayings of the Lord transmitted orally. Since the whole posture of the *Didache* is oriented toward oral production (see #11d), it would have been unlikely that the "good news" would have been a written source. On the other hand, since even written sources were habitually "heard," the question of the oral or written character of the "good news" is not decisive. The source, in either case, would have been more akin to the *Gospel of Thomas* than to the Gospel of Mark—practical sayings rather than narrative action (Glover: 28; Niederwimmer 1998: 50). Thus, while one cannot decide whether the framers of the *Didache* made use of oral or written/heard sources, one can decide that a narrative Gospel would have been a highly unlikely candidate for the *euaggelion* referred to by the *Didache*. In sum, therefore, the literary history of *euaggelion* plus the internal logic of the *Didache* itself combines to eliminate any of the canonical Gospels as providing rules for visiting prophets as found in the "decree of the good news" (*Did.* 11:3).

5. *Why so much passed over in silence?* If the *Gospel of Thomas* and a written copy of Q existed during the formative period of the *Didache*, there is no evidence that the framers of the *Didache* relied on either. Had they done so, it would have been difficult to understand why such a miniscule portion of the Jesus wisdom found therein was taken over into the *Didache* itself. When it comes to the written Gospels of Matthew and Luke, this same argument could be extended. Let us presume, for the moment, that the framers of the *Didache* did have and did acknowledge a Jesus tradition in a written Gospel of Matthew. How then, might one explain, why so much of the material in Matthew is passed over in complete silence—especially considering the fact that the framers of the *Didache* were treating common topics such as fasting, praying, almsgiving, reconciling, shunning, examining prophets? Put differently: If the framers of the *Didache* did borrow from Mt 5:38–42, why did they not borrow materials either before or after their slim borrowings?

Many scholars surmise, as explained above, that *Did.* 1:3–5a was introduced into the *Didache* at some late point when the Gospel of Matthew became available. If this were the case, then it remains puzzling why this and only this small portion of the Sermon on the Mount was borrowed? It remains doubly puzzling why the borrower, presuming (mistakenly as some do) that he wanted to give the *Didache* a decided push in the direction of being "from Jesus," did not take the time and the effort to reproduce more closely the order and wording that those accustomed to hearing Matthew's Gospel would have found familiar. E. E. Vokes, at least, honestly deals with this issue by suggesting that the *Didache* wished to disguise this borrowing, but then, as explained above, he does nothing by way of explaining what purpose would be served by this subterfuge. Finally, even if some sense could be made of why so little of the Sermon on the Mount was borrowed and why its form was so severely edited, it would still remain puzzling why the borrower would then go on to append an editorial expansion of such length (seventy-eight words). To my knowledge, neither Tuckett nor those who share his methodology ever seem interested in either asking or answering such questions.

From the vantage point of an oral environment, however, simple answers are forthcoming: The framers of the *Didache* did not have to make a slim selection from the wealth of Jesus material in the Sermon on the Mount because they were entirely unfamiliar with Matthew's written Gospel—and any other Gospel that has come down to us as well. In a milieu strongly wedded to oral traditions, the framers of the *Didache* undoubtedly embraced *Did.* 1:3–5 as part of the Jesus tradition that responded to an urgent set of needs felt by gentiles who presented themselves for membership. Matthew and Luke, each in their turn, were familiar with and adapted the saying in the Q Gospel in response to the social needs of their own readers. Chapter 12 will examine critically the various needs responded to by each of these bearers of the parallel tradition. Each wrote independently of the other. Matthew knew nothing of Luke. The *Didache* knew nothing of either. The strongest positive evidence is that each author molds detached sayings to speak to a different need(s) set within a different context. The strongest negative evidence is that none of the three documents demonstrates any awareness of the context wherein the parallel sayings show up in the others and, especially in the case of the *Didache*, common problems are addressed in complete ignorance of the others. This latter point would suggest that the *Didache* was created in an environment where the text of the Gospel of Matthew was either unknown or, if known, was disregarded. Given the diversity of defining and responding to pastoral issues, one must further conclude that even the formational influence of the Gospel of Matthew upon the community practice of the *Didache* is not evident. All in all, as the rhetoric, logic, and implied praxis are investigated, both Matthew and the *Didache* appear more and more to be working out of two divergent religious systems that have only a small degree of shared turf.

Eschatological Divergence: The Special Case of Didache *16*

The final chapter of the *Didache* offers an eschatological scenario that forms a complete unit. As a result, scholars have been keen to identify the source of this unit. The dominant view has been that *Did.* 16 depends on Matthew 24 (e.g., Balabanski: 183–205; Harnack 1886: 60; Jefford 1989a: 85–90; Ladd: 3, 99; Massaux 1950: 631–38; Vokes 1938: 111–15). When the elements of *Did.* 16 are set side by side with possible "source" material in Mt 24, the results are impressive (Niederwimmer 1998: 209 n. 5):

Didache	Matthew
16:3	24:11–12 (7:15)
16:4a	24:12 and 10
16:4b	24:24
16:4d	24:21
16:5b	24:10
16:5c	24:13 (10:22b)
16:6a	24:30a
16:6b	24:31
16:7	25:31
16:8	24:30b (26:64)

From this table, it would appear that the framers of the *Didache* freely altered the order of Matthew, but, on the whole, the material was gathered from the Gospel. When the actual text of Mt 24 is examined and the purported borrowings into the *Didache* are placed side by side, this impression changes markedly:

Matthew 24	Didache 16
When he was sitting on the Mount of Olives, the disciples came to him privately, saying, "Tell us, when will this be, and what will be the sign of your coming and of the end of the age?" [1] Jesus answered them, "Beware that no one leads you astray.	In the last days . . . (16:2)
[a] For many will come in my name, saying, 'I am the Messiah!' and they will lead many astray. [b] And you will hear of wars and rumors of wars; see that you are not alarmed; for this must take place, but the end is not yet. [c] For nation will rise against nation, and kingdom against kingdom, and there will be famines and earthquakes in various places: all this is but the beginning of the birthpangs. (24:3–8 = Mk 13:4–8)	And then will appear the world-deceiver as a son of God . . . (16:4b)
[2] Then they will hand you over to be tortured and will put you to death, and you will be hated by all nations because of my name. Then *many will be entrapped* [fall away],	*many will be entrapped* (16:5)
[1] and *they will betray* one another and *[they will] hate one another.*	[a] *they will hate each other* . . . [c] *and they will betray* (16:4)
[2] And many *false prophets* will arise and lead many astray.	*False prophets* . . . will be multiplied (16:3)
[3] And because of the increase of *lawlessness, the love* of many will grow cold.	*The love* will be turned into hate. For, with *lawlessness* increasing . . . (16:3–4)
But the one who *remains firm* [endures] to the end *will be saved.* (24:9–13 = sections of Mk 13:9–13)	The ones **having remained firm** in their faith *will be saved* . . . (16:5)

[3] And this good news of the kingdom will be proclaimed throughout the world, as a testimony to all the nations; and then the end will come. (24:14 = Mk 13:10)	

[4] So when you see the desolating sacrilege standing in the holy place, as was spoken of by the prophet Daniel (let the reader understand),
    [1] then those in Judea must flee to
    the mountains;
    [2] the one on the housetop must not
    go down to take what is in the house;
    [3] the one in the field must not turn
    back to get a coat.
Woe to those who are pregnant and to those who are nursing infants in those days!
Pray that your flight may not be in winter or on a sabbath.
For at that time there will be great suffering, such as *has not happened* [been] from the beginning of the world until now, no, and never will be.
And if those days had not been cut short, no one would be saved; but for the sake of the elect those days will be cut short. (24:15–22 = Mk 13:14–20)
	He [the world-deceiver] will do unlawful things which never *have happened* from the beginning of time. (16:4b)

[5] Then if anyone says to you, "Look! Here is the Messiah!" or "There he is!" — do not believe it.
    [a] For false messiahs and false
    prophets will appear and produce
    great *signs and wonders* [omens], to
    lead astray, if possible, even the elect.
    Take note, I have told you
    beforehand.
    [b] So, if they say to you, "Look! He
    is in the wilderness," do not go out.
    If they say, "Look! He is in the inner
    rooms," do not believe it.
    [c] For as the lightning comes from
    the east and flashes as far as the west,
    so will be the coming of the Son of
    Man. Wherever the corpse is, there
    the vultures will gather. (24:23–28 =
    Mk 13:21–23 + Lk 17:23–24, 37)
	He [the world-deceiver] will do *signs and wonders* and the earth will be betrayed into his hands. (16:4b)

[6] Immediately after the suffering of those days 　[a] the sun will be darkened, 　[b] and the moon will not give its light; 　[c] the stars will fall from heaven, 　[d] and the powers of heaven will be shaken. (24:29 = Mk 13:24)	
[7] Then the sign of the Son of Man will appear in heaven, and then all the tribes of the earth will mourn, and they will see "the Son of Man *coming on the clouds of heaven*" with power and great glory. (24:30 = Mk 13:26)	Then the world will see the Lord *coming atop the clouds of heaven.* (16:8)
[8] And he will send out his angels with a loud *trumpet call,* and they will gather his elect from the four winds, from one end of heaven to the other. (24:31 = Mk 13:27)	The sign of the *call of the trumpet.* (16:6)

Matthew 24 follows Mark 13 quite closely. Where Matthew has added new material, this is underlined. One can see that (save for Mt 10–12), Matthew takes over Mark's content and order quite faithfully adding only small phrases from time to time. In the first section, for example, one can see that the "sign" asked for pertains to the second coming of Jesus and the end of the age, whereas, in Mark, the disciples ask only for a "sign" pertaining to the destruction of the temple (Mk 13:1–4).

Now note how little material of Mt 24 is found in the *Didache*. Where the Greek of Matthew is exactly or nearly equivalent to the *Didache*, the parallel texts are displayed in bold type. The text of the NRSV has been modified where necessary so as not to disguise the Greek parallels. In the first section, for example, none of the expressions found in Mt 24 find any verbal equivalence in the *Didache*. Matthew prefers "end of the age" or "completion of the eon" (*synteleias tou aiōnos*), whereas the *Didache* uses only "in the last time" (*en tō eschatō kairō*) and "in the last days" (*en tais eschatais hēmerais*). Nowhere in Matthew's Gospel does one find either of these expressions used by the framers of the *Didache*.

If the framers of the *Didache* made use of Mt 24, the side-by-side texts indicate just how little of Matthew was carried over into the *Didache*. Matthew, and Mark before him, shows great interest in "false messiahs" (Mt 24:5, 23, 24 and par.) who will endeavor to lead the faithful astray. Matthew also refers to international wars, famines, and earthquakes, which some misinterpret as "the end" (Mt 24:3). Matthew's community, however, awaits the proclamation of the good news "throughout the world" as the "sign" of when "the end will come" (Mt 24:14). Then, "the desolating sacrilege . . . spoken of by the prophet Daniel" (Mt 24:15; Dan 9:27; 11:31; 12:11) will necessitate flight at a moment's notice and will result in great suffering. Then, "after the suffering," the sun, moon, and stars will "fall from heaven" (Mt 24:29). Then "the sign of the Son of Man" will appear ushering in the final judgment and the ingathering of the elect (Mt 24:31–32). None of these things are carried over into the *Didache*. It must be asked, therefore, what sense it makes to imagine that Mt 24 was the source that the framers of the *Didache* elected almost entirely to ignore.

Even in those instances where there is close verbal agreement, the logic and order of the *Didache* are openly in conflict with what one finds in Mt 24. Take, for instance, the "coming on the clouds" and the "trumpet call"—areas where there is close verbal agreement and no parallels in Mark 13. B. C. Butler speaks of *Did.* 16:6–8 as "practically a copy of Mt 24:30–31, with the omissions and rearrangements necessitated by the *Didache*'s decision to select and enumerate three signs" (1960: 277). The divergence, however, is much deeper than Butler acknowledges. Consider the following:

1. The "sign" of the Son of Man in Matthew's Gospel (borrowed from Dan 7:13–14) is directed toward alerting his readers to when and how Jesus will return (Mt 24:3). The emphasis is on universal "visibility" (Gundry 1994: 488)—much "as the lightning comes from the east and flashes as far as the west" (Mt 24:28). In contrast, "false messiahs . . . appear and produce signs" locally—in the wilderness or in the inner rooms (Mt 24:23–27).

The "signs" in the *Didache*, on the other hand, are principally the "signs of truth" (16:6) directed against the deceiving "signs and wonders" (16:4b) performed by the universally accepted world-deceiver, who is received as "a son of God." The issue, consequently, is not that Matthew has one while the *Didache* has three signs as Butler implies. Rather, the logic and function of "signs" in each writing are quite distinct.

2. The "coming on the clouds" and the "trumpet call" are reversed in the *Didache* and for good reasons. According to the *Didache*, "the burning-process of testing" will destroy the wicked and purify "the ones having remained firm in their faith" (*Did.* 16:5 as detailed in ch. 15 below). The unfurling banner and trumpet call thus serve to assemble the purified elect and the resurrected saints who together form an entourage to welcome the Lord when he comes atop the clouds (16:8). No further separation or judgment is necessary.

According to Matthew, on the other hand, the one coming as the "Son of Man" is the one who "sits on his glorious throne" (Mt 25:31) for the purpose of judging. This is signaled by the phrase: "and then all the tribes of the earth will mourn" (Mt 24:30; Gundry 1994: 488–89). The angels, therefore, along with the trumpet call come into play at this point for the purpose of gathering the elect on his right hand and, by implication, gathering those to be consigned to "the eternal fire" (Mt 25:41) on his left. Consequently, the ordering of the "coming on the clouds" and the "trumpet call" are distinctly different in Matthew and in the *Didache* because they hold different views of the resurrection and of the role of the one coming.

3. Following upon this, it is no surprise that Matthew and the *Didache* diverge respecting the identity and the mood surrounding the one coming. The "Son of Man" anticipated by Matthew, scholars agree (e.g., Gundry 1994: 488), is Jesus coming to judge the nations. At this "sign," "all the tribes of the earth will mourn" (Mt 24:30)—and "the context in Matthew favors a mourning of despair" (Gundry 1994: 488). In the case of the *Didache*, it is not Jesus but the Lord God (see #10m) who is anticipated "atop the clouds" (*Did.* 16:8). This Lord comes to bring the promised kingdom (*Did.* 8:2; 9:4; 10:5) to his elect who have assembled to meet him. The mood surrounding his coming is therefore triumphal and filled with unmitigated expectation. Here again, therefore, a significant divergence distinguishes the *Didache* from Mt 24.

#11F WHETHER MT 24:30 MADE USE OF RV 1:7

The Book of Revelation includes this telling vision of the end:

> Look! He [Jesus Christ] is coming with (*meta*) the clouds; every eye will see him, even those who pierced him; and on his account all the tribes of the earth will mourn (*kopsontai*). So it is to be. Amen. (Rv 1:7)

This text runs very close to what one finds in Matthew:

> Then *the sign of the Son of Man will appear in heaven, and then all the tribes of the earth will mourn* (kopsontai), *and* they will see "the Son of Man coming on (*epi*) the clouds of heaven" with power and great glory. (Mt 24:30)

No scholar, to my knowledge, claims that this material in Matthew is to be derived from the Book of Revelation. Nor, does anyone claim that the Book of Revelation made use of Matthew (e.g., Kloppenborg 1979: 60 n. 23). Rather, both are expected to have had access to traditions (whether oral or written) that guided them in their composition (e.g., Dn 1:7; Zec 12:10).

If this is the case, then it opens up the possibility that Mt 24 and *Did.* 16 could be acknowledged as having some verbal parallels without imagining that one is dependent on the other as a written source. In effect, given the divergent internal logic, it becomes almost impossible to imagine that the framers of the *Didache* relied on Mt 24. If there was reliance, one would have expected it to go the other way—from the *Didache* to Matthew—a proposition that does not have any adherents owing to the fact that nearly all scholars dated the *Didache* in the second century. Even if advocates were forthcoming, however, the divergent internal logic would argue against such a dependence. When the demonstrated dependence between two documents is so thin or so fragile as to be practically nonexistent, it seems best to acknowledge that it is nonexistent and that shared traditions would be able to account for similarities (as in the case of Mt 24:30 and Rv 1:7 just considered).

In the end, therefore, the "omissions and rearrangements" that are attributed to the framers of the *Didache* go much deeper than just the switch from one sign to three. "Signs" play a different function in the *Didache*. Events are rearranged because the framers of the *Didache* hold different expectations as to when judgment will take place and who will be raised. Furthermore, the identity of the one coming in the *Didache* is the Father and not Jesus. Needless to say, this sort of discussion could be extended to examine *Did.* 16:3–5 as well. If this were done, an even greater list of divergent views would surface that would demonstrate that Mt 24 and *Did.* 16 are not cut out of the same piece of cloth.

#11G EXAMINING AND REFUTING THE POSITION OF BALABANSKI

Vicky Balabanski, aware of seeming difference between the two eschatologies, prefers to maintain that *Did.* 16 was written "to clarify and specify certain aspects of Matthew's Gospel" (201; also Massaux 1993: 173). To begin, Balabanski takes for granted all the "omissions and rearrangements" noted above:

> *Didache* 16, like other Christian writings from this era, shows a remarkable freedom to rearrange, interpret, and omit material drawn from Matthew 24 and elsewhere in the Gospel, as well as the freedom to supplement it from other sources. (197)

Balabanski further insists that the *Didache* did not aspire to "comprehensiveness," as did Matthew and Luke in editing Mark (197). Why, we are not told; however, we are told that the "function of this chapter, and indeed of the *Didache* as a whole, was in no way to supplant the Gospel material" (197):

> *Didache* 16 was composed as an adjunct to Matthew's Gospel rather than as an attempt to supplant it, it seems intended to simplify, summarize and interpret certain aspects of Matthew's eschatological discourse, as well as to elaborate certain features. (202)

Balanbanski does not say how she arrived at this inside knowledge. Presumably, she was faced with the evident omissions and rearrangements that the framers of the *Didache* allowed themselves and had to explain how an editor could act in this way while still affirming Matthew's eschatological expectation. In so doing, however, Balanbanski presumed what she set out to prove. She presumed that the framers of the *Didache* did not aspire to "comprehensiveness" even when they appeared to bring a great measure of comprehensiveness to everything they treated. She presumed that the framers of the *Didache* were in essential agreement with Matthew even when this was based on the silence and the omissions of the *Didache* on this matter. In the end, therefore, Balanbanski bends over backward to find total agreement between the eschatological expectations undergirding both writings. Some examples:

1. *Sign of the Son of Man.* Balabanski implies that the "signs of the truth" (*Did.* 16:6) served to explicate the obscure "sign of the Son of Man" (Mt 24:30):

> The feature that is most strikingly specified and elaborated is the immediate prelude to the End, the signs of truth. The fact that this was felt to be necessary by the writer of *Didache* 16 may imply that the Matthean "sign of the Son of Man in the heavens" was not specific enough for the needs of the communities. Perhaps there were some enthusiasts whose imminent expectation of the End may have led to them seeking to identify the sign themselves, or more probably this simply reflects a midrashic tendency to explicate those points which remain intriguingly obscure. (202)

Balabanski glosses over the differences between the two authors with the hypothesis that the three signs of *Did.* 16:6 offer a midrashic elaboration of the one sign of Mt 24:30. If this were true, one would have expected that the *Didache* would have retained the phrase "Son of Man." Balabanski never explains why Matthew's Gospel has thirty-two occurrences of "Son of Man" while the *Didache* has none. Perhaps Balabanski understands the "signs of truth" to be an explication of "the sign of the Son of Man" (Mt 24:30)—but this is not clear. In any case, since the "call of the trumpet" is the second sign (*Did.* 16:6), Balabanski never explains how this is to be understood since Matthew deliberately inserts a "call of the trumpet" (Mt 24:31) after the arrival of the Son of Man. Does the *Didache* add a second trumpet call or want to transfer the trumpet call of Matthew to a new location? In either case, would not Balabanski have to concede that the framers of the *Didache* were modifying Matthew's eschatological scenario and not merely explicating it? The same unanswered questions holds true for the third sign, the resurrection of the righteous, something that finds no place in Mt 24.

2. *Universal or limited resurrection.* Balabanski acknowledges that the *Didache* envisions only the resurrection of the righteous. Matthew, on the other hand, is found to be ambivalent on this point:

> In Matthew's Gospel, the proleptic resurrection of the saints in the passion narrative, Mt 27:52–53, could indicate that the evangelist shared this view, but the picture of the great assize in Mt 25:31–46, if one takes it as a judgment of the dead as well as the living, gives the opposite view. (203)

Balabanski then goes through all the texts of Matthew pertaining to the resurrection (Mt 7:21–23; 11:20–24; 12:41–42; 22:23–33) and finds no clear evidence of a general resurrection of the dead (203–5). Even if this were the case, Balabanski fails to explain how the "proleptic resurrection of the saints" occurs at the time of Jesus' death in Mt 27:52–53, while, at the same time, the framers of the *Didache* place this event in the future following the trumpet call. Should we then understand that the framers of the *Didache* envisioned two periods of the resurrection of the righteous—one at the death of Jesus and one prior to the coming of the Lord upon the clouds? Or would it better to understand the framers of the *Didache* as correcting Matthew by silently passing over Mt 27:52–53 in favor of a universal resurrection of the righteous in the last days? Balabanski omits any reference to these problems, for, in the end, "*Did.* 16:7 . . . is not so much a contradiction of Matthew's doctrine as a particular clarification and concretization of it" (204).

3. *Trial by fire.* Balabanski acknowledges that "only . . . the trial by fire, can be claimed with some certainty to have no clear synoptic parallel" (196). Balabanski elaborates:

Although Matthew has a greater interest in eschatological fire than do Mark and Luke, it is primarily portrayed as the fire of Gehenna, into which evildoers will be thrown at the close of the age (cf. 3:10, 12; 5:22; 7:19; 13:40, 42, 50; 18:8, 9; 25:41). Only Mt 3:11 . . . has the notion that the faithful will be subject to fire. This saying may preserve a tradition of a fiery testing, presumably eschatological in nature, to which all will be subjected, but it is clear that the *Didache* did not draw 16:5a from here. Nevertheless, it is unnecessary to postulate a special source for this tradition, given its wide currency in Jewish and Christian texts. (196)

Balabanski rightly finds Mt 3:11 obscure, especially since Matthew 24 and 25 make no use of it. Balabanski's appeal to the "wide[spread] currency" of "trial by fire" is undoubtedly overstated (see ch. 15 below); yet here it functions to ensure that "traditions that have no direct parallel in the Synoptic Gospels do not require one to reject the theory that the *Didache* 16 knew and used the Gospel of Matthew" (196).

All in all, while Balabanski is quite imaginative, her theory fails to convince. She rightly rejects the gate of "direct literary dependence" (196–97) as being too narrow to decide literary dependency, but then proceeds to construct such a large gate that the *Didache* cannot fail but pass through. The moment that she allowed that the *Didache* "shows a remarkable freedom to rearrange, interpret, and omit material drawn from Matthew 24" (197), it became virtually impossible that any amount of rearrangement and omissions would disqualify the *Didache* from being a literary dependent of Matthew. The moment that she decided that all new materials inserted into *Did.* 16 functioned "to elaborate certain features" (202), it became virtually impossible for him to even notice that linguistic differences revealed divergent expectations framed within a different eschatological hope. In the end, therefore, while Balabanski includes many valuable insights along the way, her overall method, however, eroded her ability to detect how two religious systems might diverge and, in the end, address different issues and project different hopes.

John S. Kloppenborg has undertaken a careful investigation of *Did.* 16:6–8. He observed quite rightly along with George Eldon Ladd (22), R. Glover (25, 28–29), and B. C. Butler (1960: 283) that the *Didache* finds parallels to Matthew almost exclusively in those areas where he inserts distinctive traditions not found in Mark:

The presence of a disproportionately large amount of material in *Did.* 16:3–8 which has parallels only in special Matthean material and the corresponding lack of *distinctively* Marcan material as reproduced by Matthew suggest that *Did.* 16:3–8 drew not upon Matthew but upon a tradition to which Matthew also had access. This tradition must have contained the *Vorlage* ["prior source"] of Mt 24:10–12 (13?), a quotation from Zec 14:5, an adaptation of Dan 7:13 (using either *epi* or *epanō tōn nephelōn)*, a reference to a sign appearing in heaven prior to the Parousia, and the mention of a trumpet call. Matthew conflated this source with his Marcan source. . . . (Kloppenborg 1979: 66)

Kloppenborg should have said in his last line, "Matthew supplemented his Marcan source with this source," for the outline of Mark's eschatology is clearly retained while only smatterings of his source are included. Moreover, Kloppenborg is clearly on soft ground when he guesses at the contents of his special source. Nonetheless, Kloppenborg is on target when he observes that *Did.* 16:3–8 did not draw on the Gospel of Matthew:

> The *Didache* shows no dependence upon either Mark (or his source) or Matthew, but rather seems to represent a tradition upon which Matthew drew. Moreover, even a cursory glance at *Did.* 16:3–8 suggests the same conclusion. *Did.* 16:3–8 agrees with Matthew only when Matthew is using his special source. Agreements with Mark are registered only when Mark was quoting common and widely known apocalyptic sayings (e.g., Dan 7:12, 12:12). (1979: 66)

An examination of the side-by-side texts above, for example, shows how Mt 24:10–12, which is commonly regarded as part of Matthew's "special source" (Koester 1990: 325), finds ample representation in the *Didache*, while the material surrounding it (material taken over from Mark) finds no hint of representation. If such a "special source" existed, one could go beyond Kloppenborg by postulating that it was oral in nature (e.g., found in the habitual prayers of wandering prophets) and open to a wide variety of representation. Clearly this source was not the *Didache*, for, as shown above, *Did.* 16:3–8 has an entirely different set of end-time expectations.

#11H EXAMINING AND REFUTING THE POSITION OF TUCKETT

Tuckett, who is persuaded that the *Didache* "presupposes the finished form of the Synoptic Gospels, or at least that of Matthew" (1989: 198), faults Kloppenborg's argument on two points:

1. Tuckett's first objection relates to the small measure of verbal agreement between Mt 24 and *Did.* 16. On this ground alone, Tuckett insists

that one cannot draw any firm conclusions as to whether the *Didache* used Matthew or whether both had a common source:

> The measure of verbal agreement between the *Didache* and Matthew cannot be used to determine whether that agreement is due to direct dependence of one on the other or to common dependence on a prior source. Common dependence on a prior source does not necessarily involve less close verbal agreement. (1989: 207)

While Tuckett is correct in what he says, this does not advance the claim for one side or the other. What is at issue is that the material common to Matthew and Mark is almost entirely absent from the *Didache*, while the material special to Mt 24 finds partial inclusion. This observation of Tuckett thus misses the point.

2. Tuckett's second objection returns to this very point:

> If the question is whether the *Didache* depends upon Matthew's Gospel or on a pre-Matthean source, one cannot use the evidence of the *Didache* itself to solve the source problem of Matthew's text. Koester's [or Kloppenborg's] argument is thus dangerously circular. (1989: 207–8)

Here, again, Tuckett dodges the real issue. The *Didache* does supply information regarding the availability of certain end-time expectations not found in Mark. If they show up in the *Didache* and in the editorial additions of Matthew, then one can conclude (without being circular), that they both depended on a "pre-Matthean source." Otherwise, Tuckett would have to explain how and why the framers of the *Didache* could have had Matthew open before them and artfully avoided (without knowing it) 99 percent of the material taken over from Mark. This is the argument raised by Kloppenborg, reinforced by Koester and Rordorf, to which Tuckett has not given any adequate reply.

Again and again, Tuckett seems determined to show that no common "pre-Matthean source" exists. Matthew, for instance, alters Mark's Son of Man as coming "in (*en*) the clouds" (Mk 13:26) to read "on (*epi*) the clouds of heaven" (Mt 26:30). Kloppenborg argues that this seemingly small alteration serves "to make it clear that the clouds were the medium of movement and not merely the backdrop of the scene" (1979: 59–60) (see #10o). Kloppenborg also notes that this suggestion of causality is implied in the *Didache*'s "atop (*epanō*) the clouds of heaven" (*Did.* 16:8). He concludes:

> Far from suggesting that *Did.* 16:8 depends on Mt 24:30, the evidence indicates that *Did.* 16:8 represents an independent tradition under whose influence Matthew altered his Marcan source, namely by substituting *epi* ["on"] for *en* ["in"] and adding *tou ouranou* ["the clouds"]. (1979: 63)

Tuckett accepts this data but faults the conclusion:

> A much simpler explanation is available. Matthew's differences from Mark here serve to align his version of Dan 7:13 with that of the Septuagint. A tendency by Matthew to conform OT allusions to the form of the Septuagint is well-documented. The "tradition under whose influence Matthew altered his Marcan source" need only be the Septuagint text of Dan 7. There is no need at all to postulate a tradition very closely parallel to Mark 13, but independent of Mark and known only to Matthew. Such a theory is a totally unnecessary and complication. (1989: 205)

In like fashion Tuckett suggests alternatives for other changes as well. The call of the trumpet, for example, finds it inclusion as one of many "stock apocalyptic ideas" (1989: 208). Thus, when Matthew and the *Didache* include the call of the trumpet, they need not be relying on a special source unknown to Mark. The same holds true for the *Didache*'s substitution of "the Lord" for the "Son of Man"—Tuckett suggests this could be due to the force of citing Zec 14:5 rather than a special source (1989: 205).

I agree with everything Tuckett says. Kloppenborg does, at times, make it appear that a written source unknown to Mark and used by Matthew and the framers of the *Didache* is what he had in mind (see citation above). As already suggested, the widely dispersed end-time themes orally presented by the prophets and found dispersed in the scriptures could be all that is needed as the "special source." The very fact that Matthew and the *Didache* operate using their material to express divergent systems (as explained above) even favors imagining that the common source did not have a compelling logic of its own. Matthew, to be sure, does not move far from the Marcan source that he mildly edits to bring forth his own emphasis. The framers of the *Didache*, in like fashion, must have done the same even when we have no hard-copy evidence of what was their starting point.

The argument of Tuckett, while very ingenious, still fails to convince. How so?

1. Tuckett can cast doubt as to the existence of a specific written source to which Matthew and the *Didache* were privy, but he cannot undo the fact that certain metaphors shared by Matthew and the *Didache* are not found in Mark.

2. Not to acknowledge some shared tradition of "stock apocalyptic ideas" makes the weak linkage between Mt 24 and *Did.* 16 incomprehensible. The end-time possibilities as expressed in the existent literature are too large and too divergent to allow for mere "accidental" coherence to occur.

3. While Tuckett is correct in noting that verbal variations do not preclude the availability of written Gospels, the weak verbal linkage between Mt 24 and *Did.* 16 points in either of two directions: (a) The framers of the *Didache* knew Matthew but elected to ignore him on all points in favor of enforcing only those select areas where he diverged from Mark. Or (b) the framers of the *Didache* knew nothing of Matthew but they did share some nexus of end-time motifs that each independently used to enforce their own particular hope and expectation. Proposition (a) requires that the framers of the *Didache* blocked out large themes (e.g., wars, famines, earthquakes, the "Son of Man," proclamation of the good news to "all the nations") precisely because these were found in both Mark and Matthew. Tuckett's thesis, in the end, stumbles on this quaint and unacceptable exclusion. Proposition (b), therefore, provides a much more plausible explanation.

Conclusion

Stepping back, this chapter began with a brief history of the scholarly discussion regarding possible sources of the *Didache* and made some brief comments regarding the interplay between dating and identifying sources. When parallel texts are listed or even compared side by side, a plausible case can always be made for dependence on Matthew's Gospel. More recently, however, more rigorous criteria have been developed in order to establish dependence. Jefford and Tuckett, for example, make the point that verbal agreement, in and of itself, cannot establish literary dependence, since, in every case, one has to consider the possibility that the agreement present is due to both the *Didache* and Matthew having access to a common Jesus tradition. Thus, to establish dependence, one has to explore, even in cases of close or exact verbal agreement, to what degree the contexts and meanings overlap. Furthermore, one has to explore to what degree shared issues (fasting, praying, almsgiving, correcting, shunning) are defined and resolved along parallel lines. When these investigations were undertaken, however, they progressively revealed areas of wholesale divergence between Matthew and the *Didache*. In the end, consequently, this present study concludes that Matthew's Gospel and the *Didache* reveal independent religious systems reflecting two different modes of community existence. While they occasionally made use of parallel material in defining themselves, they shaped this in contexts that served their own distinctive ends. Hence, in the end, diversity marks even their common heritage.

Consequently, John M. Court's surmise that "the *Didache* stands in the tradition of St. Matthew's Gospel" (112), Jonathan Draper's surmise that "the *Didache* is the community rule of the Matthean community" (1991: 372; see ch. 13 below), and Edouard Massaux's surmise that the *Didache* was created "as a catechetical résumé of the first evangelist" (1950: 644) cannot stand up to close examination. The Gospel of Matthew and the *Didache*, point after point, evoked two independent religious systems addressing common problems in different ways. "The *Didache* lives in an entirely different linguistic universe, and that is true not only of its sources but of its redactor as well" (Niederwimmer 1998: 48).

In order to provide a basis for examining those like Tuckett who employ an elliptical methodology biased toward textuality and immune to the dynamics of oral transmission, this chapter made a foray into the social dynamics of orality in a tradition that has a marginal use of textuality. As long as one remains within Tuckett's presuppositions, it is difficult to fault his observations and his conclusions (as Rordorf amply demonstrates). By way of closing, therefore, I apply to Tuckett words borrowed from Paul J. Achtemeier:

> In these and other matters, one suspects, scholarly suppositions have prevailed that are simply anachronistic when applied to the actual environment within which documents were written and read. Many such suppositions need to be questioned, and much work remains to be done—and redone!—if we are to form a clear and probable picture of the way the New Testament documents [and the *Didache*] were produced and the way they functioned within the oral environment of late Western antiquity. (1990: 27)

My own conviction (shared by Rordorf, with whom I have worked) is that it can be demonstrated that the *Didache* does not depend on Matthew or any other Gospel that has come down to us. Should *Didache* scholars come to accept the thesis of this essay, the way would be open for an early dating of the *Didache* and for its interpretation as a well-integrated and self-contained religious system that must be allowed to speak for itself without any interference from Matthew's Gospel. This latter task I have endeavored to carry forward in the chapters of this volume.

12

WHETHER THE *DIDACHE* REVEALS THE SOCIAL SETTING FOR "TURNING THE OTHER CHEEK" AND "LOVING ONE'S ENEMIES

Contents

Background Discussion Found in Boxes

Throughout the course of history, "turning the other cheek" and "loving one's enemies" have meant different things to different people. In order to determine what this might have meant for the first-century wandering charismatics, one has to reconstruct the social setting in which homeless, penniless preachers of the gospel would have had occasion "to love their enemies" and "to turn the other cheek." The same thing holds true for the settled communities of Matthew, Luke, and the *Didache*. Each of these communities embraced some form of the mandate "to love enemies" and "to turn the other cheek" (Mt 5:38–48; Lk 6:27–38; *Did.* 1:3–4). When, how, and why such a rule might have been regarded as God's wisdom by each of these communities does not become clear until one identifies "the enemies" and the social situation where these rules would have been expected to apply. Gerd Theissen, who is a leading proponent and practitioner of this approach, enunciates this methodology as follows:

> It is impossible to determine what love of enemies and nonviolence meant apart from the social situation in which these demands are made and practiced. Now, it is clear from the outset that historically speaking the Matthean and Lukan [and *Didache*] traditions belong to different religious milieus. . . . (Theissen 1992: 130)

The purpose of this study is threefold: (1) to summarize Gerd Theissen's reconstruction of the various social settings wherein "turning the other cheek" and "loving ones enemies" functioned; (2) to identify the soft spots in Theissen's analysis; and (3) to provide a systematic and coherent reconstruction of the social setting of these same sayings in the social context implied by the *Didache*.

"Love of Enemies" as a Radical Saying of the Wandering Prophets

Gerd Theissen has made it commonplace to regard the radical sayings of Jesus about "selling all," "hating father and mother," and "having no place to lay one's head" as belonging to the lived experience of those charismatic wanderers who adapted for themselves both the words and the lifestyle of Jesus. Accordingly, it comes as no surprise that Theissen should insist that the gospel sayings about "turning the other cheek" (Mt 5:38–48; Lk 6:27–38) must have had an existential relevance within the lives of these charismatics quite distinct from those transposed reinterpretations that they took on among the settled householders embracing the gospels of Matthew and Luke. Theissen's reading of these texts as applying to the wandering charismatics brings forward three important points:

1. Theissen notes that "loving enemies was something for people who were persecuted and hated" and, as various texts in Matthew's Gospel make clear, these people were regarded as "prophets" (Theissen 1992: 144). Who were these persecuted prophets? According to Theissen, they cannot be "Christians in general" since "the reference to the prophets would be almost pointless" (Theissen 1992: 144). These sayings, save for the mandate to give (Mt 5:42; Lk 6:30a) and to lend money (which constitutes the particular emphasis of Luke's editorial additions of 6:34, 35a, 37b), Theissen regards as applying to the "wandering charismatics." These itinerant missionaries, Theissen is convinced, functioned as prophets and received a public scorn analogous to that heaped upon Cynics in Roman society in this same period (Theissen 1992: 146–48).

2. Based on the assumption that "nonresistance increases the likelihood that attacks will be repeated" (Theissen 1992: 149), Theissen conjectures that the material under consideration could hardly have been the operational principle of Christian householders. Why not? In Theissen's view, the requirement to give in to abusive behavior . . .

> . . . could be much more convincingly met by the wandering charismatic. He was really free. He could leave the place where he had been defeated and humiliated. He need never expect to meet his opponent again. (Theissen 1992: 149)

On the basis of functionality, therefore, Theissen is persuaded that only the transient charismatic could "turn the other cheek" without thereby "inviting cheating and slights to continue" (Theissen 1992: 149).

3. While Theissen acknowledges that the illustrative cases specified in Mt 5:39–42 and Lk 6:29–30 do not allow envisioning any specific application, he singles out Lk 6:29 as an exception:

> Lk 6:29 does point to a quite particular context: "To him who strikes you on the cheek, offer the other also; and from him who takes away your coat do not withhold even your shirt." Here, as we know, Luke is thinking of a holdup: the thieves seize the victim's coat first, and then reach out for his shirt. (Matthew is thinking of a court trial, and he reverses the order.) But an attack of this kind generally took place on the open highway. That is to say, Luke was thinking about the situation of wayfarers and travelers. (Theissen 1992: 142)

In sum, Theissen is persuaded that the case of Lk 6:29 applies most easily to wandering charismatics. Hence, the original context of "turning the other cheek" and "loving one's enemies" can be seen as representing the working rules governing the transient life of the wandering charismatic "prophets" within the Jesus movement.

Love of Enemies Transposed into the Ethic of Householders

When it came time to incorporate these same sayings into the lifestyle of settled householders, however, Theissen is persuaded that these radical norms had to be retooled for the new social setting. The "enemies" of the householders were surely not the hecklers and naysayers who jeered and challenged the wandering prophets addressing the crowd in the market-place. Who were they then? At this point, Theissen meticulously distinguishes the social climate of Matthew as distinct from Luke based on the unique material found in each Gospel. For our purposes here, we will begin by examining Theissen's overarching conclusions:

> [1] Jesus formulated the commandment that we should love our enemies and renounce violence at a time when his demands could fall on fruitful ground, since nonviolent conflict strategies proved effective against the Romans. But Jesus' demand goes far beyond every specific situation. It is general. It takes no account of effectiveness or noneffectiveness. . . . Just because it was formulated generally and apodictically, it could continually be brought up to date.
>
> [2] Jesus' disciples—roving, itinerant charismatics—were able to relate his commandment to their situation: the persecuted prophets were thus able to free themselves from hate for their persecutors.
>
> [3a] The congregations behind the Gospel of Matthew bring the commandment up to date in the period following the crushing of the Jewish revolt, in order—as people outwardly defeated—to meet the victors as inwardly sovereign.
>
> [3b] The Lukan congregations [meanwhile] associate love of enemies with conflicts between the people who lent money and their debtors. (Theissen 1992: 154, numbers added for clarity)

During the various stages of transmission, one can glimpse that the identification of "enemies" shifted as different audiences faced different conflictual situations. One might chart this as follows:

Rule for Whom?	Conflictual Situation?	Who Is the "Enemy"?
[1] Jesus and his Palestinian hearers	How to deal with Roman occupation?	Roman overlords and military
[2] Jesus' disciples: wandering charismatics	How to survive as an itinerant prophet?	highway robbers and disgruntled hearers
[3a] Matthew's community	How to deal with Roman aggression after 70?	Roman military
[3b] Luke's community	How to deal with economic disparity among the brethren?	the poor debtor unable to repay his/her loan

Luke: Loving Enemies in the Context of Economic Disparity

In Luke's community, Theissen identifies "a Western type of righteousness which insists on the establishment of symmetry and mutuality between equals" (Theissen 1992: 130). For our purposes here, it is important to sketch out what Theissen recognizes in Lk 6:27–38 that allows him to identify "enemies" from the vantage point of economic disparity and the lending of money. I summarize Theissen's analysis into three points:

1. In the first place, attention is given to how each evangelist frames the common Q material. Luke knows nothing of Matthew's repeated framing device: "You have heard it said . . . but I say to you. . . ." Rather, Luke situates Jesus' call for "love of enemies" just after he declares as blessed (or fortunate) those who are "poor" and "hungry" (Lk 6:20f.) while those who are "rich" and "filled" are expressly warned (Lk 6:24f.).

2. Furthermore, when Luke illustrates what "love your enemies" means in practice, his unique contribution is directed toward giving "to *everyone* who asks of you" (Lk 6:30) and "going beyond Matthew—he insists that one should not ask anything back" (Theissen 1992: 138). Then, further, Luke appeals to the golden rule (a tradition popular in Hellenistic circles) not as a summation of "the Torah and the prophets" (Mt 7:12) but as a call to the rich to put themselves in the place of the poor and "to lend to those from whom you [cannot] hope to receive" (Lk 6:34, 35). As an aside, Theissen notes that according to Eccl 29:6, "the debtor becomes an enemy (*echthros*) and pays back in curses and abuse" (Theissen 1992: 139).

3. Finally, attention is given to the unique closure offered by each evangelist. Luke ends with a call to the rich to "be merciful just as your Father is merciful" (Lk 6:36) while Matthew's appeal is to "be perfect as your

heavenly Father is perfect" (Mt 5:48). Within the Lucan framework, the final appeal to be divinely merciful is immediately specified in terms of not judging or condemning, and, positively, of forgiving debts. The ultimate promise is that "the measure you give [now] will be the measure you get back [later]" (Lk 6:38). Thus, "Luke passes from imminent to eschatological reciprocity without any pronounced breach" (Theissen 1992: 125).

In sum, therefore, Theissen concludes that Luke took the radical sayings of the wandering charismatics and restructured them to provide divine guidance toward "a greater social symmetry in the relationship between [rich and poor] Christians" (Theissen 1992: 141).

Matthew: Loving Enemies
in the Context of Postwar Experience

In contrast, Theissen finds that Matthew's use of the Q tradition "emerges from the buildup of the series of antitheses" (Theissen 1992: 132) in which "do not resist an evildoer" (Mt 5:39) and "love your enemies" (Mt 5:44) are put forward as the *higher righteousness* required by those who would "be perfect . . . as your heavenly Father is perfect" (Mt 5:48). The "evildoer" and "enemy," in the case of Matthew's community, do not emerge out of the experience of economic disparity between Christians but against the backdrop of "experiences of the Jewish War and the postwar era" (Theissen 1992: 136). The principal clues that Theissen singles out to support this reading are as follows:

1. Matthew distinguishes himself from Luke by making reference to the experience of "someone forcing [*aggareusei*] you to go one mile [*milion*]" (Mt 5:41). Theissen rightly points out that the vocabulary here signals that the Matthean community is dealing with the conscription by Roman soldiers of pack animals and baggage carriers from among the civilian population:

> *Aggareuein* is a technical term of Persian origin which was used for services to the state rendered under duress. The only parallel we have (Mk 15:21) is thinking of the soldiers who, meeting Simon as he comes back from the fields, force him to carry Jesus' cross. . . . The foreign word *milion* (translated mile) is a special pointer to Romans, for this is the only time the word occurs in the New Testament, the usual term [designating distances] being *stadion* (Theissen 1992: 133).

2. Next, Theissen notes that Matthew provides multiple instances of the violence of the "evildoer" followed immediately by the rule to "love your enemies" (Mt 5:43–45). This tacit link forces one to ask "whether this

does not reflect the situation of a subjugated people" (Theissen 1992: 134). Theissen considers that Josephus, writing in this same postwar climate, suggests to his fellow Jews something of the same nonviolent response to abuse when he advises that "nothing puts an end to [Roman] blows as quickly as patient endurance, and the submission of the victim makes the tormentor mend his ways" (*J.W.* 2.351).

3. Finally, Theissen notes that "loving enemies" in Matthew is motivated not by the pragmatic considerations of Josephus but by the intention of imitating God, who blesses both the righteous and the unrighteous (Mt 5:45). Earlier, in Mt 5:9, the peacemakers were termed "sons of God." Later, those who love their enemies are spoken of as "children of their Father in heaven" (Mt 5:45).

In sum, therefore, after examining the unique material of Matthew, Theissen concludes that Matthew's community took the radical sayings of the wandering charismatics and applied them to their own situation, which called for "peacemaking" and "loving enemies" in imitation of God "in the years after the Jewish war" (Theissen 1992: 136).

Soft Spots in Theissen's Analysis of Matthew and Luke

Theissen's methodology is sound. In each instance, he carefully distinguishes the unique material of Matthew and Luke and analyzes the clues therein as though they were the solution to a social problem that stands behind the texts. Even when Theissen's methodology is fully accepted, however, one can find fault with the application of this methodology. Consider, for instance, the following:

1. Theissen places a lot of weight on "if anyone forces you to go one mile" (Mt 5:41) as pointing to Roman abuse following the Jewish War. While the distinct vocabulary of Mt 5:41 clearly points to the right of the Roman forces of occupation to commandeer pack animals and humans for military transport (which is amply testified in Roman sources), it is curious that pack animals are not mentioned, since, in point of fact, these would be the preferred choice of the Roman occupiers. Furthermore, conscripting animals and persons for military transport would have represented a continuous situation in the occupied territories and would not distinctly identify a situation after the Jewish War. On the other hand, such conscription is benevolent compared to the actual realities that followed the Jewish War, namely, mass crucifixions of thousands of men, rape and enslavement of thousands of women, forced-labor details (like the building of the ramp at Masada) that drove untold thousands of undernourished and overworked captives to their death.

This same sort of observation could be extended to the illustration that precedes Mt 5:41. A blow of insult on the right cheek even when followed by being struck on the left does not suggest the kind of treatment that Jewish rebels or even innocent bystanders were likely to receive from military men. More to the point, nothing in the text implies that either blow produced any permanent injury or even death. Once again, as in the case of Mt 5:41, the text here seems to envision mild consequences that are far removed from the realities of the Jewish War and its aftermath.

The remaining instance, that of suing someone in court (Mt 5:40), is decidedly not what one would expect of a Roman soldier in peacetime or following hostilities. Once again, even if the plaintiff surrenders both cloak and tunic, this is far removed from any permanent or death-dealing injury.

The three illustrations of Matthew, when they are taken as a whole, therefore, do not appear to address the situation of a subjugated people following an abortive uprising against Roman rule.

Along parallel lines, even if one follows Theissen in discerning that Lk 6:29b reflects the situation of itinerant charismatics confronted by highway robbers (Theissen 1992: 140 n. 48), one has to admit that the loss of clothing [or of money] is not the first concern of victims of a holdup (wherever this might take place). According to Luke's parable, the Samaritan who fell among robbers on the Jerusalem–Jericho road was stripped, beaten, and left half-dead (Lk 10:30). Nothing in the parable suggests that this was excessive or unusual treatment (e.g., because he foolishly put up a struggle). Rather, the narrative is told as though this was the usual treatment highway robbers afforded to victims who might have connections and might be in a frame of mind to later identify and retaliate against them. In any case, whatever Lk 6:29 had in mind, it seems doubtful that Luke's hearers thought of highway robbers.

Even if Matthew's parallel (Mt 5:40) is taken as an instance of a Jewish court ruling against an impoverished peasant who has only the clothes on his back to give in repayment or to be held until making payment, this too would constitute a mild outcome. In juridical cases where a man was legally required to liquidate a large debt, a man was often forced not only to sell all he had, but to sell into slavery his children, his wife, and, last of all, himself as well. Here again, even in the Gospel of Matthew, the servant who is unable to pay his debt finds that "his lord ordered him to be sold, with his wife and children and all that he had, and payment to be made" (Mt 18:25). Faced with such brutal first-century realities, it hardly seems that Mt 5:40 would have been understood as having to do with the legal settling of a large debt where the person and the family of the debtor were at risk.

Taken as a whole, the intended applications for Mt 5:39–42 (as well as Luke's variants) would appear to have nothing to do with persons facing grave harm to themselves or to women and children under their protection.

Life-threatening Situations
Requiring Flight

In contrast to Mt 5:39–42, Matthew's Gospel does specifically address two situations in which the disciple's life is threatened. In the first case, "Brother will deliver up brother to death" (Mt 10:21). Here the threat comes from insiders—not from soldiers or from bandits. The mandate, at this point, is clear: "Flee to the next [town]" (Mt 10:23). So too, in the second case, where the death-dealing end-times hatred is depicted as coming from "all nations" (i.e., from outsiders, Mt 24:9), again the advice is that "those who are in Judea flee to the mountains" (Mt 24:16). These two instances illustrate that, when faced with death-threatening events, the pragmatic advice was to flee and not to offer any form of "demonstrative nonresistance."

Going even further, Jesus' own personal conduct in avoiding arrest by staying close to the supportive crowds and keeping a low presence at night would have to be used to nuance what it would mean "not to resist an evildoer" (Mt 5:39). The passion narrative according to John even goes so far as to present Jesus as openly rebuking a soldier who strikes him in the face when he offers what the soldier judges as an impertinent reply to the questioning of the high priest (Jn 18:23)—thus demonstrating that even Jesus did not "turn the other cheek" under these circumstances. Moreover, supposing that Jesus did have a premonition of his impending arrest, it is instructive to note that he failed to train his disciples in any form of nonviolent resistance that might have helped him or them in those circumstances. If "turn the other cheek" did have a scope of application in Jesus' own self-understanding, it would appear that it had no relevance for understanding his own actions surrounding his arrest. Some scholars posit that Jesus' injunction to Peter to "put away his sword" constitutes such an application. In point of fact, none of the Gospels makes any reference to "turning the other cheek" during the arrest. Rather, other lines of logic support Jesus' injunction. For example, in Matthew's Gospel, Jesus says to Peter:

> For all who take the sword will perish by the sword. Do you not think that I cannot appeal to my Father, and he will at once send me more than twelve legions of angels? But how then should the scriptures be fulfilled? (Mt 26:52–54)

Roman soldiers routinely pillaged, killed, enslaved, and raped those who resisted them in war. Under no circumstances could "turning the other cheek" be construed as meaning that a man whose wife was just raped by a band of marauding soldiers ought to hand over to them his virgin daughter as well. I make reference to such a shocking and insane application in order to immediately demonstrate that, whatever Jesus meant, it cannot, willy-nilly, have an application to every situation and, furthermore, some situations would have to be positively precluded from its meaning.

In sum, greater care must be exercised when reconstructing the social situation that lies behind Jesus' saying, "Do not resist the evildoer" (Mt 5:39). For the reasons given, it would seem very doubtful that Matthew had the hostile situation following the Jewish War in mind when he wrote these words.

#12a Loving One's Enemies and the Legitimacy of Rage

The gospel is sometimes distorted by well-meaning preachers and theologians who latch onto a few sayings of Jesus regarding "turning the other cheek" and "forgiveness of enemies" and overextend their application while ignoring the rest of the gospel in the process. The overall effect of such preaching is that solidarity with victims is eroded and the rage that victims sometime need to retain their dignity goes unsupported.

Luke's Gospel is a favorite of such preachers. Luke, alone, for instance, has Jesus being tortured to death by a Roman crucifixion designed to ensure the maximum of personal pain and public humiliation while saying, "Father, forgive them; for they do not know what they are doing" (Lk 23:34). The image thus presented is that of the Divine Messenger and Savior going to his death forgiving his enemies. His last testimony thus enacts in concrete circumstances what was the substance of his lifelong message to his disciples:

> Be merciful, just as your Father is merciful. Do not judge, and you will not be judged; do not condemn, and you will not be condemned. Forgive, and you will be forgiven; give, and it will be given to you. A good measure, pressed down, shaken together, running over, will be put into your lap; for the measure you give will be the measure you get back. (Lk 6:36–38)

In point of fact, however, victims of rape, victims of torture, victims of racial hatred need their rage to preserve their human dignity in the face of their dehumanizing suffering. Jeffrie Murphy puts forward the following sober considerations:

> If a total case is to be made against hatred, it must be made against examples where the hatred appears at its best and most

prima facie justified. . . . For example, when the victims in a recent series of vicious rapes in Phoenix testified that they wanted the "Camelback rapist," who had utterly trashed the lives of some of them, to be sentenced to the maximum term that the law allowed, many of them openly admitted that they were acting out of anger and hatred [and fear of further victimization]. These women were outraged at the thought that this vicious man, utterly unrepentant, could soon continue to lead a free life, given what he had done to their lives. I sympathized with their anger and hatred, having no inclination at all to call them petty or spiteful. I would have found it indecently insensitive and presumptuous had anyone charged them with the vice of failing to forgive and love their enemies. . . . (91f.)

With this, I expect that most Christians would agree. Jesus' mandate, "Do not judge. . . . Do not condemn. . . . Forgive. . ." (Lk 6:36f.) cannot be immediately applied to this case. And why not? For this reason:

The primary value defended by the passion of resentment is *self-respect* . . . , and a person who does not resent moral injuries done to him [her] . . . is almost necessarily a person lacking in self-respect. (Murphy: 16)

In truth, therefore, victims of rape, victims of torture, victims of racial hatred—crimes calculated to erode self-respect—need their rage in order to retain and rebuild that self-respect urgently needed to reconstitute their shattered lives. Any well-meaning person who, on Christian principles, would counsel "forgiveness" as a remedy to "their rage" would, in effect, be inadvertently collaborating with the rapist or with the torturer by eroding the divinely given instinct of rage. In the face of such crimes, one must allow that even God feels a sense of rage and joins in solidarity with the victims.

In this regard, the traditional theology of Jesus' atoning suffering and death upon the cross is subversive of the necessity of rage for the victims of heinous crimes and entirely undercuts the ability of Christians to show solidarity with the victims of such crimes. According to this theology, Jesus willingly submitted to the suffering and death of a Roman execution in order to merit the forgiveness of the sins of all humankind. Where there should be outrage at the suffering of the innocent, therefore, the theology of atonement has turned the image of a Jesus being tortured to death into a glorious act necessary for our redemption (see #16h).

In closing, let me again return to Luke's Gospel, which was cited initially as presenting a message against judging and in favor of forgiving:

> Be on your guard! If another disciple sins, you must rebuke the offender, and if there is repentance, you must forgive. And if the same person sins against you seven times a day, and turns back to you seven times and says, "I repent," you must forgive. (Lk 17:3f.)

Here the context becomes clear. One can oppose judging and condemning a disciple (esp. in their absence), because, in fact, the way of Jesus was directed toward taking action and bringing the offense to the attention of the offender. Then, "if there is repentance, you must forgive" (Lk 17:3). Well and good. Repentance means that the offender has repudiated his/her own actions and, this being done, both the victim and the perpetrator join together in lamenting the crime done. Repentance begins with an altered state of mind and leads directly to action: (a) the earnest endeavor to undo (to the degree possible) the harm inflicted and (b) submission to a just penalty imposed by competent authority advised by the victim. When such a repentance is not forthcoming, then the rage for justice continues and no forgiveness can or ought to be given. Even God cannot forgive the unrepentant sinner. Hence, when the *Didache* and Matthew come down hard on the action to be taken by the victim and the response to be made by the victimizer, this and not some lopsided plea for forgiving our enemies is to be considered as the Christian message.

In light of the above, it can also be seen that the *Didache*'s mandate to "love the ones hating you" (*Did.* 1:3) has nothing to do with advising the victims of rape or torture or racial-hatred. The abuses named in *Did.* 1:4 represent only the routine expressions of futility that parents and relatives impose upon children who are abandoning their family gods in favor of accepting those of unknown power associated with a despised people. In this context, one must also note that "love" does not mean self-surrender. Rather, the blow on the right cheek is delivered by a father precisely because his son refuses to surrender his religious convictions. "Love" can only mean "not speaking badly" (1:3) and not doing those things "you might wish not to happen to you" (1:2). Should an enraged father endeavor to crush his son's foot or to choke him to death, however, one can expect that the son would ward off this attack with all his might. Not everything is permissible, and not everything is forgiven—either in this world or in the next.

Theissen's Mistaken Association of Jesus with Nonviolent Resistance

Theissen and others (e.g., Wengst 1987: 68–72; Wink 1991: 7–24, 1992: 175–89) have made many of us comfortable with the idea that Jesus was proposing some form of nonviolent resistance when he spoke of "not resisting the evildoer." Here, too, there are soft spots:

1. Theissen appears to be personally influenced by the tradition of non-violent resistance that finds in the sayings of Jesus now under consideration a theologically and pragmatically sound formula for dealing with both the benign and the ruthless violence of Roman occupation during the first century. My reason for saying this is that Theissen brings forward two isolated events in the whole first century in which the success of nonviolent resistance of the weak against the powerful can be demonstrated.

The first event, which took place in 261 C.E. and which might be expected to be known by Jesus and his Jewish audience (Theissen 1992: 152), involves the tense situation when Pilate, immediately after taking up his new post as governor of Judea, made plans to introduce images of the emperor into Jerusalem. Josephus records how Jews, upon hearing of this intended sacrilege, surrounded Pilate's palace in Caesarea and knelt outside for five days and five nights. When given a personal audience, Pilate had the delegation surrounded by armed soldiers three ranks deep. During the tense exchange, Pilate had the soldiers draw their swords:

> But the Jews threw themselves down on the ground (as they had previously agreed to do), stretched out their necks to the swords, and cried that they would die rather than disobey the laws given to them by their fathers. Profoundly astonished by the fervor of their piety, Pilate ordered that the standards [with the images] should at once be removed from Jerusalem. (Josephus, *J.W.* 2.174)

Right after describing this case and citing the very text reproduced here, Theissen goes on to imagine the following application:

> The Jews' nonviolent resistance was successful. Even the powerful Romans showed that they were vulnerable. That must have made a tremendous impression on contemporaries, and it was at that very time (or shortly afterwards) that Jesus began his public ministry and taught: "Voluntarily offer your enemy your cheek when he strikes you!" How would people at the time have interpreted this saying? It must surely have been taken to mean that this formulated the principle of behavior also underlying the demonstration against Pilate. . . . (Theissen 1992: 151)

Theissen later steps back and cautiously acknowledges that it is "no doubt within the bounds of possibility, but it cannot be proved" (Theissen 1992: 152) that Jesus was influenced by this event in the formulation of his principle. More positively, "what can surely be maintained, however, is that

Jesus' contemporaries were not bound to reject as ridiculous from the outset the notion that the enemy could be 'disarmed' by demonstrative non-resistance" (ibid.).

2. While I personally believe that nonviolent protest can and ought to be included as a theologically sound and pragmatically viable mode of Christian resistance (especially in view of the mystique of the violence of the righteous that predominates in our culture), I am hesitant to imagine that Jesus' mandate to "turn the other cheek" was understood in the first century to formulate such a program. My reasons are as follows:

(a) As noted above, the situations envisioned by either Mt 5:38–48 or Lk 6:27–38 are devoid of any life-threatening intent.

(b) Beyond this, while the Gospels present Jesus as quite aware of the threat to his own life posed by the Jerusalem authorities, they fail to present him as doing anything in order to prepare his disciples to counter his arrest by some sort of nonviolent resistance parallel to the case cited in Josephus.

(c) More importantly, one fails to find a single instance of nonviolent resistance played out in the early church that explicitly appeals to Jesus' training of "turning the other cheek."

In sum, given the absence of any supportive clues from the Synoptics themselves, the appeal to the instance in Josephus appears to be well-intentioned but more along the line of a pious projection. Even the Jews who had been there and "offered their necks to the sword" (*J.W.* 2.196) would hardly have imagined that what they had done could be described as "turning the other cheek."

3. The mandate to "love your neighbor and hate your enemy" (Mt 5:43) could be construed, within Jewish circles, as calling for loving Jews and hating non-Jews (as Theissen implies). Yet it must be acknowledged that the Jewish Torah never uses this phrase at all, and, as a consequence, it is hazardous to interpret it outside of any context. In fact, the only safe context is that of Mt 5:45–48. Here again, the internal logic is that the standard of love to be employed by the disciples of Jesus has to exceed merely "loving those who love you"—conduct associated with tax collectors or "greeting only your brothers and sisters"—conduct associated with gentiles. The mention of "tax collectors" and "gentiles" in this context is not to offer these groups as the recipients of "love." There will be other points in the Gospel wherein Jesus will be presented as having favorable regard for and good working relations with both tax collectors and gentiles. Rather, tax collectors and gentiles enter into this context as exhibiting norms of reciprocal honor and care that stand to shame the disciple who can go no higher. Finally, when the benign character of Mt 5:40–42 is taken into account, it would appear impossible to decide how the mandate to "love your enemies" would apply to the disciple who was held up by highway robbers or who fell into the hands of menacing drunk soldiers.

4. Theissen links the "peacemakers" of Mt 5:9 with the issue of nonresistance to Roman occupation (Mt 5:41) by the common reference to "sons/children of God." Once the benign case of military conscription is seen for what it is, however, it is difficult any longer to imagine that "peacemaking" has any primary reference to military-civilian affairs. Nowhere in the Gospel is there the least interest in such matters. Even when Jesus has direct contact with a centurion, nothing of Roman–Jewish relations comes up, and the centurion ends up being praised for his faith (Mt 8:10) concerning the healing of his son (or servant) and not because he has adopted a benevolent attitude toward the Jews and their religion (only Lk 7:5 mentions this in passing).

The art of being a "peacemaker" (*eirēnopoios*), therefore, must be seen in ordinary circumstances in which quarrels and factions can occur in families, in synagogues, and even among Jesus' own disciples. With regard to the first arena, namely, the family, Matthew retains the tradition that Jesus "did not come to bring peace (*eirēnēn*) but a sword" (Mt 10:34):

> I have come to set a man against his father, and a daughter against her mother, and a daughter-in-law against her mother-in-law; and a man's foes (*echthroi*) will be those of his own household. He who loves father and mother more than me is not worthy of me; and he who loves son or daughter more than me is not worthy of me. (Mt 10:38)

How interesting that "Love your enemies (*echthrous*)" (Mt 5:44) makes use of this same term. "Peacemaking" and "enemies," as a consequence, might have very little to do with soldier–civilian affairs and much to do with the deep divisions in families occasioned not by war or by other factors in Jewish society but by the very promotion of the gospel. It is these family divisions that must now be investigated.

#12B FILIAL PIETY IN THE ANCIENT WORLD

While many scholars have noted that the Jesus tradition has some hard sayings regarding family ties, John Dominic Crossan characterizes the earliest layers of the Jesus tradition as portraying "an almost savage attack on family values" (1994: 58). This begins with the *Gospel of Thomas:*

> Jesus said: "Whoever does not hate father and mother cannot be a follower of me, and whoever does not hate brothers and sisters . . . will not be worthy of me." (*Gos. Thom.* 55)

The attack on family bonds continues in Mk 3:31–35, where Jesus receives word that "his mother and his brothers" are standing outside—they refuse to sit and to take their place among Jesus' disciples. As a result, Jesus shames and disowns his family by looking at those sitting around him and saying, "Here are my mother and brothers! Whoever does the will of God is my brother and sister and mother" (Mk 3:35). Why does Jesus treat his own family members so harshly? According to Mark's Gospel, his own family is not coming to hear God's word but "to seize him" because, in their judgment, "he has gone out of his mind" (Mk 3:21). This could mean that they judge that he has gone berserk and is an embarrassment to them; hence, they want to seize him, take him home, and keep him out of the public eye (as before). Crossan suggests that, more to the point, his family had expected to capitalize on his new popularity and to have him set up shop in Nazareth, where they could be his go-betweens (1994: 99–100). In either case, Mark shows that, even in the case of Jesus, he had to choose between his love for "his mother and his brothers" and his calling to live in conformity with the kingdom of God.

Anyone who would be his disciple also would have to make this same choice. A disciple said to him, "Lord, let me first go bury my father" (Mt 8:21). Here is an expression of filial piety at its best: the son wants to live in his father's house according to his father's traditions and then, after his father is dutifully buried (see, e.g., Gn 50:5–6; Tb 4:3; 6:14), he will come and follow Jesus. Jesus, far from praising his piety and saying he is not far from the kingdom of God, trashes his whole value system: "Follow me [now], and leave the dead to bury their dead" (Mt 8:22). Jesus is not speaking of zombies here. Rather he is implying that the way of his father is the way of death and, if he would live, he must break away from his father immediately and let those who are spiritually dead take care of their own (Gundry 1994: 153). Thus, when Matthew carries forward the tradition that Jesus said, "Call no man your father on earth" (Mt 23:9), he did so with the acute awareness that the "fathers" of many or most of his community did not approve of the way of Jesus and that they were forced to abdicate filial piety in favor of obeying their "one Father, who is in heaven" (Mt 23:9).

Going beyond this, A. D. Nock in his classic study of conversion in antiquity concluded that "our survey of paganism has given us little reason to expect that the adhesion of any individual to a cult would involve any marked spiritual reorientation, any recoil from his moral and religious past, any idea of starting a new life" (Nock: 138). Nock noted, however, a singular exception in the conversion of Lucius to the cult of Isis and Osiris as narrated in Apuleius's novel *Metamorphoses*. Other contemporary scholars have noted that conversion to the life of a wandering Cynic has marked parallels to the calling of Jesus to his disciples (Crossan 1994: 114–22;

Theissen 1992: 146–48; Downing: 115–68). In the case of conversion to Judaism, however, not only was a moral conversion required, but a sectarian resocialization and welcoming into a new community was also anticipated. Christianity maintained these same Jewish patterns when it preached the gospel to Jews and, in time, to gentiles as well—a profound sectarian resocialization was required in every instance.

Sectarian Resocialization in the Didache

The *Didache* provides a unique opportunity to examine the training program used by an essentially Jewish movement committed to Jesus for the resocialization of gentile recruits. Interestingly enough, this program of training moves from the general definition of the Way of Life to the specific character of dealing with enemies and suffering abusive treatment. If "loving your enemies" and "turning the other cheek" are to be understood as specifically formulated within this community as the first operative rules necessary for new recruits, then analysis might allow us to determine what social situation was envisioned that required such an orientation. To this, our attention now turns.

According to the rabbinic tradition, a gentile who comes forward asking for admittance into the community of Israel must be told: "Do you not know that Israel at the present time is persecuted and oppressed, despised, harassed, and overcome with afflictions?" (*b. Yebamot* 47a) Such an initial instruction was intended to signal to the would-be convert that becoming a Jew inevitably meant being despised and persecuted by gentiles—even including those who are presently regarded as family and friends.

The same thing holds true for the conversion to the life of a Cynic. When a sympathetic disciple came forward and inquired about the nature of the life of a Cynic, Epictetus's response had the character of warning him away. In the first instance, Epictetus replied that "he who attempts so great a matter without divine guidance" sets himself up for "divine wrath" and "public dishonor" (*Discourses* 3.22). Epictetus then made it abundantly clear that God "has a well-regulated household" and not just anyone can aspire to this or that position but, by implication, must wait to be assigned his role by the Lord. Having done this, Epictetus then launches into an unflattering description of the outward conduct of the Cynic:

> Deliberate carefully upon this undertaking; it is not what you think it [is]. [You may be thinking, for instance,] "I wear an old cloak now, and I shall have one then [i.e., after becoming a Cynic]. I sleep on the hard ground now, and I shall sleep so then. I will moreover take a wallet and a staff [on my travels], and go

about, and beg of those I meet, and begin by rebuking them. . . ." If you imagine this to be the whole thing, keep away; come not near it; it belongs not to you. (*Discourses* 3.22)

Then Epictetus begins to expose the inner transformation required of someone aspiring to be a Cynic:

> First, with regard to yourself; you must no longer, in any instance, appear as now. [How so?]
> [A] You must accuse neither God nor man [for what befalls you].
> [B] You must altogether control desire. . . .
> [C] You must have neither anger, nor resentment, nor envy, nor pity. (*Discourses* 3.22)

Relative to anger and resentment, Epictetus alerts the would-be disciple that a Cynic "must be beaten like an ass, and yet, when beaten, must love those who beat him as though he were the father, the brother of all" (*Discourses* 3.22). Here again, it can be seen that the abusive treatment received is not a direct threat to life and limb. What one has here is the mistreatment whereby those challenged, disturbed, and humiliated by the public discourse of the Cynic and unable to whip him by their words resort to stripes and blows. Meanwhile, the inner disposition of the Cynic has prepared for this eventuality by persuading him that such a beating is a tacit recognition of the truth of his words and that the abuse offers a precious moment to further advance in his quest for the perfection outlined above: [A] blaming neither God nor man for the beating; [B] controlling the desire either to be beaten or to avoid it; [C] having neither anger, nor resentment, nor envy, nor pity toward his antagonists.

Modern studies of cults demonstrate that hostility experienced by new recruits defending their new value system has the effect of providing a greater cohesion with group values and a greater dependence on group support. In the 1960s and 1970s, for instance, young recruits to the Unification Church who had received only two weekends of theological orientation were paired with an experienced member and sent out into the urban streets for the purpose of promoting their new beliefs and doing fund raising. This "was regularly punctuated by the derision and hostility of pedestrians" (Galanter: 139). Such abuse, however, is almost entirely negated by the expectation of its coming as well as by the discharging of the unpleasantness with a committed member after the event. In point of fact, some members report that their decision to request full membership in the Unification Church was consolidated during the time of their street corner and campus witnessing. One such case is as follows:

> I had just begun witnessing, and made the mistake of approaching a disagreeable, matronly woman who glared at me after I told

her why I was speaking with her. She said, "Get away from me, you little fool."

I was crushed by the thought that she could dismiss everything that I wanted to express without even listening, and with a feeling of hatred at that. But my mind flashed back right then to what the workshop leader had told us just before: that we had to expect people's anger, and that this was the beginning of a path that we'd follow in God's steps. I hadn't really understood that at that time, but suddenly I knew that it was literally true, and I felt warmed by an intense feeling of faith throughout my body. Suddenly I knew I was literally in the company of Jesus and Reverend Moon themselves, carrying God's mission forward. (Galanter: 143)

These two cases are limited because they provide details of experiences that cannot be shown to have any direct correlation to the lives of the members of the community of the *Didache*. Nonetheless, it is an amply attested fact that Christians were distrusted and ridiculed by large sectors of both the Jewish and gentile populations of the first century. In such an atmosphere, one can also surmise that certain persons resorted to taunting, ridiculing, and physically abusing members of this despised "third race." For the purpose of argument, let's assume that the details of *Did.* 1:4 are more than just the reproduction of an empty tradition and represent clues to the actual treatment that new recruits to the Jesus movement had to suffer.

How and by Whom New Recruits Were Abused

The first abusive behavior, "a blow on the right cheek" (*Did.* 1:4), has been widely accepted as designating an insult (see #12c). One might imagine that the "blow on the right cheek" would normally be expected as the outcome of an altercation between father and son. The father demands that his son withdraw any steps he might have taken relative to sympathizing with the Christians. The son, for his part, defends the Jesus movement and reveals to his father his determination to join them. The father first tries to dissuade his son using reasonable arguments. When these arguments repeatedly fail, the father feels (rightly) that his son's filial piety has been eroded by this "sect," he becomes totally frustrated, and, in exasperation, he backhands his son on the right cheek (to bring him to his senses). The son, prepared for this confrontation by prayer, might be expected to attempt to defuse the situation by reaffirming his love for his father while at the same time reaffirming his choice for the Christian way of life. "Turning the other cheek" should not be interpreted as a son bating his father "to strike him" in addition to insulting him. Rather, the sense is that the son ought not to defend himself or to retaliate. The son, it must be remembered, might in many instances be physically stronger than his father.

With regard to a daughter or a daughter-in-law, the father would not normally be expected to confront or strike a woman—even if she were his own daughter. Rather, one would expect that the mother or mother-in-law would be the natural person to direct or even to coerce the younger woman (see, e.g., Mt 10:35). When this failed, one could envision the older woman striking the younger.

#12c AN INSULTING BLOW ON THE RIGHT CHEEK

Walter Wink, who is solidly attentive to first-century traditions, expresses this as follows:

> A blow by the right fist [or open hand] in that right-handed world would land on the *left* cheek of the opponent. An open-handed slap would also strike the left cheek. To hit the right cheek with a fist would require using the left hand, but in that society the left hand was used only for unclean tasks [e.g., toilet cleansing]. . . . The only way one could naturally strike the right cheek with the right hand would be with the back of the hand. The intention is clearly not to injure but to humiliate, to put someone in his or her place. (Wink 1992: 176)

Wink further surmises that "one normally does not strike a peer thus" (Wink 1992: 176). The Mishnah, for instance, decrees that, if a man smacks an equal "with the back of his hand, he pays him four hundred zuz" (*m. Baba Qamma* 8:6). If a man so treats his slave, however, "slaves are not subject to compensation for indignity" (ibid., 8:3). Here the governing principle is: "Everything is in accord with one's station" (ibid., 8:6). Thus, masters backhanding slaves, husbands backhanding their wives, and parents backhanding their children—would seem to constitute "excusable conduct" in rabbinic circles.

Interesting enough, the cases of dyadic strife detailed in Mt 10:34–36 would all constitute instances in which backhanding by the second person in the dyad would be permitted:

> Do not think that I have come to bring peace on earth: I have not come to bring peace, but a sword. For I have come to set a man against his father, and a daughter against her mother, and a daughter-in-law against her mother-in-law; and a man's enemies will be those of his own household.

Note that the son-in-law is not mentioned relative to the father-in-law for the very reason that they do not live and work together. Nor is husband–wife, brother–brother, or sister–sister strife mentioned. Crossan is correct when he perceptively calls attention to the fact that all the divisions are cross-generational (Crossan 1994: 60):

> Jesus says that he will tear it [the nuclear extended family] apart. The usual explanation is that families will become divided as some accept and others refuse faith in Jesus. But notice where and how emphatically the axis of separation is located. *It is precisely between the generations.* (Crossan 1994: 60)

Luke has the same text as Matthew but adds the following words: "For henceforth in one house there will be five divided, three against two and two against three" (Lk 12:52). The classical Mediterranean family of "five" envisioned here would seemingly include father and mother, the firstborn son and his wife, and a fifth (a second son, an underage daughter, or a grandchild). If one allows that, in most circumstances, the older generation does not undertake new and untried religious commitments, one has to assume that it is the firstborn son and/or his wife who are the "converts." Since it would be rare for a young wife to undertake a commitment that set her against her husband, the division of "three against two" must imply that the younger parents attached themselves to Jesus and the other three (older couple and their second child) are against them. Alternately, the division of "two against three" might imply that the older parents are isolated as the antagonists. A grandchild might be expected to follow his parents; hence, some antagonism would be directed against him/her. If a younger son aligned himself with his older brother, this would pit the father against both of his sons. If an underage daughter aligned herself with her brother, this would mean that the mother would bring pressure on her daughter. The daughter, in this instance, would be the most vulnerable since her marriage prospects after an open dispute with her own parents would be greatly diminished.

Being "pressed into service" to go "one mile" has been widely interpreted, on purely linguistic grounds, as designating the right of Roman soldiers to commandeer pack animals or persons to carry their baggage. While there is an abundance of ancient testimony regarding this practice, there is not a single instance in which the "one mile" limit is spelled out (Wink 1992: 371 n. 17). Furthermore, there were so many other aspects of the Roman occupation (e.g., billeting soldiers in private homes, meeting them in the marketplace, undergoing searches and seizures) that are entirely passed over in silence. Why single this one out? Finally, neither here nor in Matthew or Luke does the text or context specifically draw attention to "Roman soldiers." Thus, while this rule might have been used as an illustrative case for nonresistance to the routine and non-death-dealing aspects of the Roman occupation, the suspicion might be that, just as in the first case, the language is symbolic and intended to give a practical orientation to new recruits in handling resistance at home to one's intended new way of life.

Going back to the case of a father who buffets his son in frustration, one must next ask whether the son, having been humiliated, should give his father the silent treatment or punish him, by running away, for example. To answer this, one might surmise from the first case that "turning the other cheek" may not be just a one-time event. How so? The *Didache* says, "turn to him the other, and you will be perfect" (1:4). Nothing in Judaism or in the *Didache* hints that perfection in terms of abstaining "from bodily and fleshly desires" (1:4) can be gained or illustrated in a never-to-be-repeated single moment. But, going beyond this, in most instances, a father and son are tied together in terms of a shared business (farming, fishing, basket-weaving). Thus the question remains whether they can work together once the humiliating back-hand is delivered.

Here again, the imagination must be used. Trust has broken down between father and son. The father, however, is still the senior and the boss in the family business. The same thing holds true when it comes to the mother and daughter-in-law regarding cooking, baking, sewing, etc. Since trust has broken down, however, the father might no longer treat his son as partner and as successor. Rather, he treats him in the fashion of Roman soldiers who press citizens into service for their own welfare. The mandate for the son, in this case, is not only to give in to this new attitude but to execute it such that the father, as in the case of the implied metaphorical soldier, will have no cause of complaint. Thus, the father is thrown off guard. In the domain of religion, his son stubbornly resists him. In the domain of the family business, his son is more compliant than ever before.

What is the strategy here? Does the son's excessive honoring of his father's wishes in one area negate his disobedience in another? Possibly. The immediate context, it must be remembered is that the son is learning what it means to "love the ones hating you" (*Did*. 1:3) which, in the long run, is directed to not having "any enemies" (1:3). More immediately, however, the goal appears to be to "abstain from fleshly and bodily desires" (1:4)—namely, anger, resentment, grumbling. Rather, as the novice will discover later, his goal will be to "become long-suffering and merciful and harmless and calm" (3:8). Then and only then will the general rule be put forward: "You will accept the experiences befalling you as good things, knowing that, apart from God, nothing happens" (3:10).

The metaphorical reading of this text also helps to resolve the issue as to why, despite the military language, the text does not read, "If a soldier should press you into service. . . ." Now the text would have too much definition and forfeit the intent of applying to the "enemies" in one's own household.

The third form of abuse refers to those who "take away your cloak" (*Did.* 1:4). The Matthean variant of this saying envisions a legal process ("if anyone wants to sue you") in which the plaintiff wants to "take your tunic" (Mt 5:40). This is confusing. In the Mediterranean world, the cloak (*himation*) was a woolen, wraparound constructed like a long cape. This cloak served not only to protect the wearer from the cold of winter or the chilly night air; it often served as a blanket, especially in the case of the poor. This is why, according to the Jewish Torah, "if you ever take your neighbor's cloak (*himation*) in pawn, you shall restore it before the sun goes down; for it may be your neighbor's only cloak (*himation*) to use as cover; in what else shall that person sleep?" (Ex 22:26 LXX; also Dt 24:10–13, 17). Thus, the implication is that someone might hand over his cloak to a moneylender as a pledge that he would repay. This might be extended to the case of someone being fined by a court who then would proceed to surrender his cloak to the plaintiff as a pledge that he intends to pay the fine levied against him. It is confusing, therefore, that Matthew envisions a court proceeding in which the intent of the antagonist is to seize one's tunic. The Jewish tradition could hardly allow that the plaintiff would shame all concerned by undressing. "Nakedness was taboo in Judaism, and shame fell less on the naked party than on the person viewing or causing the nakedness" (Wink, 1992: 179; Satlow: 431–40).

The *Didache*, in harmony with Luke, does not envision a legal process, yet it does envision that the one taking your cloak should be given "your tunic" (1:4) as well. Thus, one would be left stark naked (Wink 1992: 178; Beare: 159) or, minimally, have only a loincloth. What sense does this have?

F. W. Beare, following a traditional line of exegesis, suggests that one has here "another gigantic exaggeration by way of illustration of the principle that the disciple of Jesus must not stand upon his rights" (159). Wink, who regards nonviolent resistance as a key component of the gospel message, suggests that "the debtor parades his nakedness in prophetic protest against a system that has deliberately rendered him destitute" (Wink 1992: 179). This explanation seems farfetched, since undressing in public could hardly be suggested or practiced without bringing shame on the Jesus movement. Captives in war were sometimes humiliated by being stripped naked (Is 20:4; 47:1–3). Romans stripped men and women whom they were preparing to crucify as a way of adding public shame to public torture (Hengel 1977: 87). Slaves might occasionally be paraded nude in public at the time of a public auction or as part of a public festival. Free persons, however, would be ashamed to be treated in this way. This would be doubly true in Jewish society (Satlow: 451–53). As a result, it would seem very unlikely that a follower of Jesus would strip naked if someone seized his/her cloak. If this were to be done in the context of "appearing before a social superior," it would here be "seen not as a sign, as we might expect, of vulnerability and submission, but of insult" (Satlow: 440), which could have disastrous consequences (Satlow: 453). And even if some few men would be willing to do this, such immodesty would have been entirely unthinkable for women.

Theissen, and others with him (e.g., Fitzmyer 1979: 639; Gundry 1994: 95), propose that Luke did not envision a legal process but the act of a thief (Theissen 1992: 140 n. 48). The problem with this construction has already been considered. Moreover, this reconstruction fails to account for why a new recruit has to be prepared for highway robbers.

Let's go back to imagining the probable case of the split household. The parents have tried to argue, to coerce, to bully their children. The insulting slap does not sober them up. Nor do the demands that they serve them in the business and the home as Jews were required to serve their Roman overlords. Yet still they don't come around. What to do? Desperate parents, at that moment, would undoubtedly try to prevent any further contact with the despised Christians who are brainwashing their children. How do they do this? They begin by making Christians unwelcome in their home. Yet, before work begins in the morning, or after work ends at night, their children are off praying and meeting with the Christians. The parents then order them to stop seeing these people. Their children explain that they cannot. In fact, there are hints in the *Didache* that new recruits will begin spending almost all their free time with their personal one-on-one trainer ("the one speaking to you the word of God" [4:1]) and with "the saints" (4:1). So, they seize their cloaks—thereby hindering them from going outside at the times of their reunions. "Seize my cloak," responds a son or daughter, "and I will have to give you my tunic as well." Now the father or mother is shamed—embarrassed at the impending or actual nakedness of his adult son or daughter in the home. Since one is not dealing here with public nudity, one might expect that the average recruit, whether a woman or a man, could bring this off.

Eusebius recounts how the desire for martyrdom had so powerfully seized the soul of Origen that, when his father was arrested, he had determined to join him and, if need be, to die with him. Origen's mother then "implored and entreated him" and, when this failed, "concealed his clothes in order to compel him to remain at home" (Eusebius, *Church History* 6.2). Antiquity, therefore, offers us at least one specific instance in which a parent might resort to seizing clothing in order to compel a child to remain at home.

The fourth form of abuse prepares the new recruit for when "anyone should take from you [what is] yours" (1:4). At first glance, it might appear that this rule is simply a generalization of the one that went before. If the reconstruction above is correct, however, it is decidedly not so. The ploy of surrendering one's tunic is directed toward shaming one's parents to return one's cloak and to desist from trying to inhibit their going out to be with Christians. In fact, the first three cases all suggest what the recruit *must do* when abused. The fourth, in contrast, specifies what the recruit *must not do* and *cannot do*. The result, unlike what went before, is that the recruit irreversibly loses what the "enemy" takes from him or her.

If one is dealing here with inter-family conflict, then one must ask why, at this point, parents would begin seizing the goods of their offspring. My hunch is that this is intimately connected with the next rule: "To everyone asking you for anything give it" (1:5). Linguistically the structure has changed. The first four rules all begin with the conditional "if anyone (*ean tis*) . . ." thereby implying that these things might not and need not take place. In our reconstruction, therefore, one can easily envision cases in which parents support the new commitments of their children or cases in which the new recruit has, for various reasons, relocated to a city where he does not live with members of his own family. The fifth rule, however, has no conditional. The implication is that the unspecified but implied "requests" for money and assistance will inevitably come—and not from members of one's own family, who *seize* what they get.

What the fourth rule begins to envision is the realization, on the part of parents, that their children have become very liberal in their giving. One can imagine a son canceling a business loan for someone unable to pay or giving away produce from the family fields to beggars in the street. This follows the rule of the *Didache* that says: "To everyone asking you for anything, give [it to him/her] and do not ask for it back" (1:5). Now this rule of life might not immediately arouse too much alarm until the parents discover that, after becoming full members in this despised group, they fully intend to "share all" (4:8) with their new "brothers and sisters." Further details on how the giving to outsiders (1:5) was the necessary training ground for sharing with insiders is taken up in chapter 2 and will not be developed here. In any case, sharing within the extended family would have been ordinary and expected in traditional families. Yet, when this sharing was extended to "despised outsiders," concerned parents would be expected to step in.

What would parents be expected to do? In all probability, they would begin treating their own children as "outsiders" and seize all properties and assets which, given their seeming disregard for the present and future needs of their biological family, they seem intent upon giving away to "strangers." The rule given to new recruits, namely, "If anyone should take from you what is yours, do not ask for it back, for you are not even able to do so" (1:4), would appear to anticipate such frantic seizures on the part of parents and in-laws. Going even further, the new recruit is ready to be dispossessed and maybe even disowned and disinherited as well. Some may even be driven out of their own paternal homes with only the clothes on their back.

The curious addition of "for you are not even able [to ask for it back]" (1:4) has long puzzled scholars who commented on the *Didache*. Does this inability arise from the training received or from the powerlessness of the one who has been dispossessed? Neither of these explanations fits. Theissen imagines that the *Didache* is dealing here with "repayment of a loan" and that the Christian also is "powerless to pay back what is required" (Theissen 1992: 124). This makes no sense to me. How can the *Didache* be talking about Christians having their goods seized because they cannot pay their debts and then turn around and hear that Christians are asked to give "to everyone asking you for anything" (1:5)? If the ones seizing one's goods, however, are indeed members of one's own family who are disinheriting their children, then it makes sense that they "are not even able" (1:4) to ask for these things back. Why? No reason is given. If one looks just below the surface, however, a possible explanation is forthcoming. The message of Jesus is depriving parents of their own children and grandchildren—those who were to be their joy and support in their old age. It is fitting, therefore, that the children should not try to take anything of their parents' resources with them. Rob them of their company and support, yes. Rob them of their ancestral property and wealth, never.

Conclusion

In the course of this study, I concluded that Theissen's reconstruction of the social setting of "turning the other cheek" would have been entirely inappropriate for dealing with the death-dealing threats posed either by marauding soldiers or by highway bandits. Clearly the forms of harassment implied in *Did.* 1:4 (and parallels) were not life-threatening. Alternatively, therefore, I suggested that Matthew's identification of "enemies" as members of "ones own household" (Mt 10:36) offers a better point of departure for reconstructing the social setting of these texts. Using this possibility to good purpose, the opening rules of the Way of Life (*Did.* 1:3–5a) were examined in order to bring to the surface those measures whereby new recruits were prepared for the escalating harassment that their conversions would have occasioned in their families.

The Jesus movement threatened family unity. Parents, frustrated at their inability to verbally persuade their children of the folly and shame of their new commitments, finally lashed out at them—striking them on the left cheek. Work relationships associated with the family trade or business also deteriorated. Parents, forgetting that their children had once been partners, began to relate to them in the workplace in the same calloused way that Roman soldiers secured transport for their baggage. To prevent their children from meeting with the despised Christians, parents "took their cloaks"—but to no avail—for they shamed them by offering to give them their tunics as well. Finally, when parents discovered that their children had become recklessly generous to beggars and eventually planned to share everything they had with outsiders, parents resorted to seizing their goods so they would not squander family resources on outsiders who were regarded as inconsequential to the family welfare. Each of these steps, however, only served to alienate their sons and daughters further and to push them into the care and protection of those "brothers and sisters" ready to receive them.

In the end, Theissen has strong grounds for suggesting that the wandering charismatics originally spoke of "loving one's enemies" and "turning the other cheek" as reflecting the opposition that they often received from disgruntled hearers in the towns through which they passed. When these sayings were later adapted and used by householders, however, the evidence of the *Didache* clearly signals that new recruits to the Jesus movement had to anticipate various forms of abuse as originating not from strangers in the marketplace but from members of their own household. In view of Theissen's weakness in reconstructing the social setting of these texts in the Gospels of Matthew and of Luke, therefore, serious attention must be given to the possibility that the *Didache* carries clues as to the primary use of these texts within the social setting of householders.

13

WHETHER FINAL PERFECTION
REQUIRES OBSERVANCE
OF THE TORAH

Contents

Background Discussion Found in Boxes

Jonathan Draper has given considerable time and energy to sorting out troublesome areas in the *Didache*. I have gained important insights from his work and have enjoyed his company on numerous occasions. Draper is a penetrating and original thinker worthy of close attention. In a 1991 study, however, he championed the position that "the *Didache* allows the proselyte flexibility about the timetable, but at the end of the day, it is required of him/her that he/she become a full Jew in order to attain salvation" (1991: 368). While Draper is very persuasive and very keen to exploit every clue available to support this position, I believe he is fundamentally mistaken and risks misinterpreting a foundational issue, namely, the character of the perfection required of gentile proselytes in preparation for the coming of the Lord (*Did.* 16:2). Given the key importance of this issue and given the forceful apologetic supporting his position, this chapter is devoted to examining his position.

To my knowledge, Draper is the first person systematically to advocate that the Way of Life training for gentiles was merely the first step toward full compliance with the Mosaic Torah. In 1987, David Flusser argued that those preparing for baptism were told to observe as much of the Torah as possible, including food regulations, "in order to strengthen the ties of gentile Christian believers with Jews believing in Christ who were 'all zealous of the Law [Torah]' (Acts 21:20)" (86). Flusser's study, however, went unnoticed by Draper and by most other scholars as well. Clayton Jefford, in 1989, proposed that the Didachist "did not seek to replace the 'yoke of the Torah' with the 'yoke of Jesus' (cf. *Did.* 6:2) but instead . . . , was anxious to weld the two yokes into a single system" (1989a: 102). The details of Jefford's thesis were largely undeveloped, however, and in 1991 Draper effectively worked out his own understanding of the character of perfection in the *Didache*. Draper's thesis was enthusiastically received in some circles (e.g., Mitchell: 231–32).

#13A WHETHER MATTHEW'S GOSPEL CAN HELP INTERPRET THE *DIDACHE*

Draper repeatedly relies on the hypothesis that the *Didache* "draws on the same traditions as does Matthew" (1991: 354). In the course of his 1991 study, Draper accordingly discovers, again and again, that the Gospel of Matthew harmonizes with and illuminates obscure segments of the *Didache*. In the end, Draper even contends that they share a "common theological and structural conception" (1991: 372) that demonstrates that they originated in the same community:

That they originate in the same community is hard to deny; they breathe the same air and reflect the same historical development. What must remain a matter of debate is the question of priority. Our contention here is that the *Didache* is the community rule of the Matthean community, constantly in process of development. Naturally, if this is so, some of its parts will reflect a situation presupposed by Matthew's gospel, other parts may reflect a situation after its composition. (1991: 372; also 1996: 18–19)

On the basis of the studies undergirding chapter 11, my starting point is diametrically opposed to that of Draper. In part, my conclusions at the end of chapter 11 were as follows:

To establish dependence, one has to explore, even in cases of close or exact verbal agreement, to what degree the contexts and meanings overlap. Furthermore, one has to explore to what degree shared issues (fasting, praying, almsgiving, correcting, shunning) are defined and resolved along parallel lines. When these investigations were undertaken, however, they progressively revealed areas of wholesale divergence between Matthew and the *Didache*. In the end, consequently, this present study concludes that Matthew's Gospel and the *Didache* reveal independent religious systems reflecting two different modes of community existence. While they occasionally made use of parallel material in defining themselves, they shaped this in contexts that served their own distinctive ends. Hence, in the end, diversity marks even their common heritage. (ch. 11)

Should my conclusions be correct, it would be illegitimate to use Matthew's Gospel in order to clarify or illuminate obscure dimensions in the *Didache*. Should Draper's conclusions be correct, it would be a lost opportunity not to use Matthew's Gospel in this way. Thus, in the body of this chapter, it will be my task to explore whether Draper was ensnared into misinterpreting the meaning of "perfection" according to the *Didache* precisely because Matthew's interpretation distracted him from correctly hearing the internal evidence of the *Didache*.

The "Yoke of the Lord" Understood as Torah Observance

Draper aptly identifies the source of his fresh vision as follows: "The close connection between *Did*. 16 and *Did*. 6:2 and 11:1 has not been noticed before" (1991: 369). The entire synthesis of Draper emerges out of the intimate connection among these three texts. Draper's interpretation of *Did.* 6:2 is pivotal. He reads 6:2 as a sobering reminder to gentile initiates that the Way of Life just explained to them, combined with the prohibition against "food sacrificed to idols" (6:3), constitutes the bare *minimum requirements* necessary for baptism and table fellowship (7:1; 9:5). To be "perfected," much more is required, namely, "to bear the whole yoke of the Lord" (6:2a)—a phrase that Draper takes great pains to interpret (1991: 363–65) in the light of the use of *zygos* ("yoke") in the Christian Scriptures (Acts 15:10; Gal 5:1; Mt 11:29–30) and the church fathers (1991: 365). Draper concludes that "the 'yoke of the Lord' in the *Didache* refers to the Torah, as maintained and interpreted in the Christian community" (1991: 365).

Draper sees an exact parallel between how the Jewish rabbis welcomed gentile "godfearers" into their synagogues with only minimal requirements and how the Didache community opened up its eucharist to gentiles following minimal training and baptism. With regard to gentile godfearers in the synagogues, Draper notes the following:

> He/She must keep a minimum ritual purity, particularly with regard to the food laws. The Law [Torah] was given to Israel, and only Israelites were obliged to keep it; the moral law was sufficient for God-fearing gentiles who wished to attend the worship of the community, but the hope was that eventually the gentile would become a Jew. (1991: 368)

Gentiles admitted into the assemblies of the Didache communities form a parallel case:

> The food laws were the minimum legal requirement to ensure table fellowship between the "perfect" and the uncircumcised gentiles. The community of the *Didache* remains within the ambit of faithful Torah-observant Jewish Christianity, but takes an understanding line on the problems of Gentile believers, who are not excluded from the Christian community, just relegated to the status of second-class Christians [until they are circumcised]. (1991: 367)

In sum, Draper reconstructs *Did.* 6:2 as defining "perfection" to mean keeping the whole of the Torah as practiced by the Jewish disciples of Jesus. The gentiles coming for baptism "are not able" (6:2) to do this; hence, they are told: "that which you are able, do this" (6:2b)—namely, keep the food law of *Did.* 6:3 and walk in the Way of Life.

Given this reading of *Did.* 6:2, Draper then notes that the final chapter of the *Didache* supports this view. *Did.* 16 offers an apocalyptic exhortation in which neither "the way of life" nor "faith" is seen to suffice in the face of the Lord's coming: "if . . . you should not have been perfected" (16:2). The "perfection" required in the end times, Draper argues, must be the same perfection argued for in *Did.* 6:2, namely, "final acceptance of the Torah by gentiles" (1991: 368). Thus, "the *Didache* allows the proselyte flexibility about the timetable, but at the end of the day [when the Lord comes], it is required of him/her that he/she become a full Jew in order to attain salvation" (1991: 368).

The Lawless Wandering Apostles as Pauline Christians

Draper then surmises that *Did.* 11:1–6 refers to certain "apostles" coming with the intention of "tearing down" (11:2) the tradition of perfection set out in the *Didache*. Draper surmises that "the false apostle who advocates abolition of Torah is Paul" (1991: 372; also Flusser 1987: 71–90). Since the apostle Paul is the unnamed enemy of "perfection" designated by the *Didache*, it follows that the "lawlessness" (*Did.* 16:4 *anomos*) that will characterize "false prophets and corrupters" (*Did.* 16:3) just prior to the Lord's coming, can be identified with the message of Paul that the gentiles are saved in Christ without observing Torah (1991: 370)!

Soft Spots in Draper's Identification of "Yoke of the Lord" as Torah

Nearly everything in Draper's reconstruction stands or falls based on whether or not "the whole yoke of the Lord" (*Did.* 6:2) refers to the Torah. Draper reviews the use of *zygos* ("yoke") in the Christian Scriptures and in the church fathers (1991: 363–65) and concludes that, save for cases in which a literal yoke is meant, the consistent metaphorical usage "seems to confirm the supposition that the 'yoke of the Lord' in the *Didache* refers to the Torah, as maintained and interpreted in the Christian community" (1991: 365).

Methodologically, some caution is in order here. Three points:

1. A problematic phrase can be clarified by making reference to its meaning in other contexts only when it can be shown that the *Didache* knew of these other sources or emerged out of a tradition that shaped these sources. Draper, needless to say, concludes that the *Didache* and the Gospel of Matthew "originate out of the same community" (1991: 372) because they betray "a common theological and structural conception" (ibid.) regarding "perfection." The danger here is that of circular reason-

ing. By rights, Draper must first demonstrate dependence and then use the Gospel of Matthew to interpret *Did.* 6:2. Otherwise, as shown in chapter 11, he risks transposing meanings from Matthew that find no place in the context of the *Didache*.

2. At least one troubling spot is the fact that the *Didache* apparently refers to the "yoke of the Lord God" (*Did.* 6:2) (see #10n) while Matthew has Jesus speak of "my yoke" (Mt 11:29, 30). If this is the case, then Matthew's reference to Jesus speaking of "my yoke" would be out of place in the *Didache*, where Jesus was celebrated as "the servant" (*Did.* 9:2, 3; 10:2, 3) who reveals the life and knowledge of the Father. Going further, the *Didache* refers to "bear[ing] the whole yoke of the Lord" (6:2) so as to define how the novice "will be perfect." In Matthew, the contrast is between "the light yoke" of Jesus and "the heavy yoke" of the scribes and Pharisees.

> But in what does the easiness of the yoke Jesus imposes and the lightness of the load consist? In an interpretation of the law [Torah] less stringent than that of the scribes and Pharisees? Far from it! According to the Sermon on the Mount, Jesus teaches a more stringent law. . . . The heaviness of the burdens loaded by the scribes and Pharisees on their admirers (23:4) consists in demands that those admirers fawn on them in ways that feed their pride. "They do all their deeds to be noticed by men . . . and they love the place of honor at banquets . . . (23:6–7; see also 6:1–6, 16–18). Correspondingly, the lightness of the burden Jesus imposes consists in his meekness and humility of heart. . . . As counterparts to the scribes and Pharisees, the church leaders who lord it over "the little ones" are lurking in the shadows of Matthew's text. (Gundry 1994: 219–20)

The context of Matthew, consequently, clearly stands apart from the context of the *Didache*. It may be hazardous, therefore, to try to clarify what the author of the *Didache* had in mind in his context by referring to what Matthew had in mind by "yoke" in a foreign context.

3. Draper notes that the phrase "yoke of the Lord" does not appear in the rabbinic material. While "yoke of the Torah" is used, Draper cites its usage in a text that also uses "yoke of the [Roman] kingdom" and "yoke of worldly care" (*m. Avot* 3:5). This demonstrates that, in the early third century, "yoke" was a far-reaching metaphor that found applications to areas of existence apart from Torah (1991: 364). Even if "yoke of the Lord" had some consistent use in both the Christian Scriptures and the rabbinic sources, however, it would still have to be examined whether the internal rhetoric and logic of the *Didache* support the meaning determined by reference to these foreign contexts.

Examining the Rhetoric
and Logic of Did. 6:2

When the rhetoric and logic of *Did.* 6:2 are reexamined in their proper context, they reveal a coherence that weakens Draper's thesis. Seven points will be developed:

1. *Didache* 6:2 closes off the Two Ways section of the *Didache*. In this section, the Way of Life is defined (1:2), the training necessary to achieve it is systematically spelled out (1:3–4:14), and the Way of Death is defined (5:1f.). The "way" or "path of life" finds occasional use in Jewish literature (e.g., Dt 31:15–20; Jer 21:8; Prv 4:18f.; *Testament of Asher* 1:6–8), but there is nothing to suggest that this phrase is ever used to define "minimum requirements" or "propaedeutic material" undertaken by gentiles bent on eventually fulfilling the whole Torah. On the contrary, the negative golden rule that serves to define the Way of Life may be seen as an echo of Rabbi Hillel's response to a certain gentile who welcomed conversion "on the stipulation that you teach me the entire Torah while I am standing on one foot" (*b. Shabbat* 31a). If Hillel regarded the negative golden rule as "the entirety of the Torah" and considered everything else "as commentary" (*b. Shabbat* 31a), then it might follow that *Did.* 1:2 is the whole of the Way of Life and that 1:3–4:14 constitutes its commentary. The internal logic of the text suggests, therefore, that the Way of Life and its commentary present "the whole yoke of the Lord" (*Did.* 6:2).

2. The very contents of the Way of Life strongly suggest that one is dealing not with an elliptical presentation of the Mosaic Torah but with a deliberately contrived adaptation. *Did.* 2:2, for example, clearly spells out ten infractions using the same repetitive Greek construction (*ou/ouch* followed by a simple future verb, second person singular) that characterizes the Decalogue in the Septuagint (Ex 20:1–17; Dt 5:6–21). Some significant commandments are entirely omitted, however, while new ones are added:

> The decalogues of the *Didache* conspicuously omit any mention of "honoring parents," "discarding idols," or "keeping the Sabbath." These omissions are not accidental. Only when Christianity became the dominant culture could it afford to emphasize "honoring parents." When it was a minority religion that was forced to recruit members by dividing sons from fathers and daughters from mothers, it was impossible to imagine that "honoring parents" was required of God. Meanwhile, within a gentile milieu, how could an initiate be required to "discard idols" when, in the everyday management of his household, he had to continue to use and to receive Roman coins that bore pagan images?

Or, again, how could a gentile convert hope to "keep the Sab-bath" when the Roman calendar governing public life was orga-nized in such a way as to make absolutely no provision for a cessation of work every seventh day? On the other hand, among those offenses specifically enumerated within the decalogues [of *Did.* 2:1–2], there are many that found some degree of sanction within the Empire: pederasty, magic, sorcery, abortion, exposure of the newborn. In short, it appears that the decalogues of the *Didache* were intentionally redesigned to address the situation of a gentile within his or her milieu. (Milavec 1989a: 108–9; also see ch. 1)

In view of this intentional restructuring of the Decalogue, it seems difficult to understand how one decalogue would be presented to novices *prior to baptism* while another (the Mosaic Decalogue) would be made to replace it as the goal to be strived for *after baptism*. Such a change would run contrary to sound pastoral practice and would create cognitive dissonance. It would seem doubtful, therefore, that the Way of Life presented to novices can be anything less than the whole way of perfection to which their entire life will be dedicated.

3. If there were "more" rules or "different" rules to be presented later, this would have to be made absolutely clear from the very beginning. Draper, of course, argues that *Did.* 6:2 does make this clear. In interpret-ing this text, however, he overlooks the force of 4:13f. that stands as a stern warning at the end of the training in the Way of Life:

[1] You will not at all leave behind the rules of the Lord, but you will guard the things you have received neither adding anything nor taking away.
[2] In the church, you will confess your failings, and you will not go to your prayer in an evil conscience. (*Did.* 4:13–14)

The first admonition clearly warns the novice that what has been received is so complete and perfect that nothing may be added or deleted there-from. Such an admonition would be out of place if, at a subsequent moment, the novice would be told that he/she would be expected "to bear the whole yoke of the Lord," as something *more* and *less* than "the rules of the Lord" (*Did.* 4:13) already given. Draper's interpretation of *Did.* 6:2 thus runs headlong into the plain meaning of 4:13.

The second admonition brings the novice to consider the confession of failings, which, as one finds only later in the *Didache*, precedes each eucharist on the Lord's day (*Did.* 14:1). While many scholars have wanted to reduce this "confession" to a general acknowledgment of sinfulness (Rordorf 1978a: 68; Poschmann: 23), the text appears to support, in its context, holding the novice accountable to confessing any failings against "the rules of the Lord" to which he/she has just been told to cling. If Draper were correct, it would seem that such a practice would have the effect of enforcing the "status of second class Christians" (1991: 367) while neglecting the observance of the Torah for which the Lord would hold them accountable on the last day. Even more seriously, if Draper were correct, this would mean that the community maintenance procedures would be out of sync with the Lord's own final norms.

In sum, the closing admonitions of *Did.* 4:13–14 erode Draper's interpretation of a double standard and, on the contrary, enforce the notion that there is only one set of "rules of the Lord" that are referred to as either "the Way of Life" or "the yoke of the Lord."

4. The Way of Life ends with admonitions to conserve "the rules of the Lord" as they stand (*Did.* 4:13–14); similarly, the entire training program ends with a parallel admonition directed toward conserving "this way of training":

> Look out, lest anyone make you wander from this way of training, since without God he trains you.
> [1] For if, on the one hand, you are able to bear the whole yoke of the Lord, you will be perfect;
> [2] but if, on the other hand, you are not able [to bear. . .], that which you are able, do this. (*Did.* 6:1–2)

Draper's initial observation is correct: "[the] *Didache* takes a harsh line with those who oppose this instruction: anyone who teaches differently is teaching contrary to God himself!" (1991: 367). But then he goes wrong by seeing that the *gar*-clause defines what is being opposed, namely, "people who teach that one can be 'perfect' without taking up the whole yoke [of the Torah]" (ibid.). Rather, "*this* way of training" in the first line points to what began as "the training" (*didachē*) in *Did.* 1:3 and has just come to an end with a final appeal at the end of 5:2. The *gar*-clause in Greek ordinarily offers additional material serving to explain what has gone before. In this case, two conditional clauses are linked by *men-de*. Why, therefore, is the way of training to be safeguarded? For the good reason that those able to bear it will be perfected while those who are unable to bear it begin by doing what they can and, by and by, they gradually become capable of bearing the whole yoke.

On what grounds does the author of the *Didache* show himself to be uncompromising on some points and lenient on others? When it comes to defining what constitutes "the rules of the Lord" (4:13) and "the way of training" (6:1), there is no room for half measures. When it comes to applying these things to individual persons, however, allowance is made for failure and for gradualism. Thus, the intent of *Did.* 6:1 is to define and to conserve the Lord's standards of excellence *even if and when* it is evident that not every novice has been able perfectly to meet these standards.

In addition, *Did.* 16:1 seems to presuppose that some mentors have added to or taken away from what has been set down. Yet the pastoral genius behind the confession of failings is that the one who has failed clearly acknowledges the "rules of the Lord" as normative even though, for the moment, he/she has been unable to keep them. Similarly, through the maintenance of the whole way of training, the one who is seeking admission clearly acknowledges the whole of the yoke required by the Lord even though, for the moment, he/she may be able to bear only a portion of what is expected. This is part of the pastoral genius of the *Didache*, namely, being firm when it comes to defining the standards of the Lord while being lenient when it comes to persons who fail as long as they acknowledge those standards.

In sum, when *Did.* 6:2 is read as a *gar*-clause attached to 6:1, then the "whole yoke of the Lord" (6:2) looks back to "this way of training" (6:1). When read in context, therefore, the "whole yoke of the Lord" is found in "this way" and not in a hypothetical second training and second initiation as Draper implies.

5. In accordance with the above, a contextualized reading of *Did.* 11:1–2 is also called for. The prophet or teacher who would "train you in all the things said beforehand, receive him as the Lord" (*Did.* 11:1). So far so good. Prophets, however, were not expected to be mere repeaters; rather, they acted and spoke by virtue of their divine inspiration (see ch. 6 above). Even in these cases, however, the *Didache* was prepared to subjugate the prophets to certain boundary conditions enforced by the community at large (11:3–11:12). Thus, the general rule was that those making innovations "for the tearing down" of *Did.* 1–10 were to be responded to by nonreception while those making innovations "for the building up of righteousness and knowledge of the Lord" were to be received "as the Lord" (11:2).

Under this rubric, anyone who wanted to practice the whole Torah as a personal discipline would be admired; however, anyone who wanted to train novices in the Mosaic Decalogue as opposed to the modified decalogue of *Did.* 2:2 would be ignored. Why? Because this would be "for the tearing down" of what the *Didache* has set out as the Way of Life which "you will guard. . . neither adding anything nor taking away" (*Did.* 4:13).

Draper argues that the term *katalyein* ("to tear down/to destroy utterly") is "uncommon" and "seems to have the technical reference to undermining Torah" (1991: 357). Granted, in Mt 5:17 and elsewhere, the metaphor does function in this sense. Here, however, the term has to be interpreted in its immediate context:

> [A] Whoever, then, trains you in all these things said beforehand, receive him. [B] But if the one training, himself having been turned around, should train you in another tradition
>> [1] for the *tearing down,* do not listen to him;
>> [2] but if it is for the building up of justice and knowledge of [the] Lord, receive him as the Lord. (*Did.* 11:1–2)

Here now the sense of "tearing down" is clear. The object is the conservation of "all these things said beforehand." Anyone training in this mode is received. Anyone turning away from this way of training to "another tradition" has to be judged on the basis of its effects. If this other tradition effectively destroys and nullifies *Did.* 1–10, then such a one is not to be listened to. Draper makes the mistake of projecting onto this "tearing down" the meaning it has in other contexts. In the *Didache,* however, anyone coming from the outside, prophets included (12:1), was to be judged according to whether they build up or tear down what the *Didache* sets out as the tradition of the Lord. The *Didache,* as far as I can tell, shows no awareness of Paul or his writings and, accordingly, the "tearing down" has no reference whatsoever to his training of gentiles.

6. The *Didache* ends with an eschatological scenario that is well integrated with what has gone before (see ch. 10 above). Draper rightly notes that, in the last days, "the whole time of the proselyte's life will not avail unless he/she be found 'perfect' or 'perfects him/herself' (*teleiōthētē*)" (1991: 368). Draper continues:

> The connection of the noun *teleios* with Torah, which has been examined above, seems to indicate that final acceptance of the Torah by gentiles is at issue here, as the final mark of initiation. (1991: 368)

Thus Draper acknowledges that *Did.* 16:2 offers no independent confirmation of his thesis but takes its meaning from his interpretation of "yoke of the Lord" and "perfection" in *Did.* 6:2. When this earlier interpretation is corrected, then the final perfection required is nothing more nor less than the Way of Life that was defined and whose training was spelled out in *Did.* 1–5.

7. Draper puzzles over *Did.* 16:5. The troublesome last line has traditionally been rendered as "saved by him, the accursed" (*hyp' autou tou katathematos*) and perceived as having a veiled reference to Christ "becoming a curse (*katara*) for us" (Gal 3:13) (e.g., Harris: 62–69; Niederwimmer 1998: 264–65; Rordorf 1978a: 197–98). Draper, for his part, focuses on what comes before, namely, that "Christ redeemed us from the curse (*ek tēs kataras*) of the law" (Gal 3:13). Thus, despite the linguistic differences between *katathematos* and *katara,* and despite the total lack of any

demonstrated dependence of the *Didache* upon Paul, Draper suggests that "the accursed [thing]" is not "Christ crucified" but "the Torah." It then follows:

> The instruction in the *Didache* would then remind the community that they are saved by the very thing which they find brings a curse on them, namely the Torah. It is to this that they must hold fast if they are to be perfected on the last day. (1991: 371)

The term *katathema* ("the accursed") is very rare. It occurs in *Did.* 16:5 and only once in the entire Christian Scriptures in Rv 22:3. When the context of Rv 22:3 is examined, it quickly appears that *katathema* in this context can refer neither to "Christ crucified" nor to "Torah." According to Rv 22:2, the fruits of "the tree of life" are going to serve "for the healing of the nations" (Rv 22:2). Chapter 15 explores the possibility that "the accursed [thing]" refers to the "burning process of testing" referred to earlier (*Did.* 16:5a). This need not detain us here. In any case, the use of Paul to interpret an obscure passage in the *Didache* is like fishing in the dark—nothing can come of taking a related word in a totally foreign context and presuming that it provides light for understanding the *Didache*.

Conclusion

In retrospect, I am indebted to Draper for his imaginative reconstruction of *Did.* 6:2 in the direction of naming full incorporation into Judaism and being yoked to Torah as the source and meaning of "perfection" as understood by the Didache communities. If his thesis had been upheld by the rhetoric and logic of the text itself, it would have forced us to perceive the *Didache* as being in all ways an integral branch of Judaism. The failure of his thesis, however, leaves us with the vision that the Way of Life specified by the *Didache* was to be identified as the complete and entire "yoke of the Lord" bringing gentiles to the perfection required of them in the last days. As Paula Fredriksen (see #1o) puts it, the scandal of the gentile mission is that the Lord had made provisions for the *salvation of the gentiles in the end times without requiring them to become Jews:* "Gentiles are saved as gentiles: they do not, eschatologically, become Jews" (547).

The *Didache* proposed and vigorously defended a Way of Life revealed by the Father through his servant Jesus (9:3) for the sanctification of his name among the gentiles. That these "rules of the Lord" (4:13) should be understood as the "yoke of the Lord" signifies that the Jewish framer(s) of the *Didache* were able to regard the way of perfection attained by gentiles walking in the Way of Life as having a status in the eyes of the Lord equal to what Jews had attained through bearing the "yoke of Torah" revealed on Mount Sinai. This is a revolutionary step, for both gentiles and Jews in the Didache communities drank from the common cup while giving thanks "for the holy vine of your servant David" (9:2). Together they ate the broken loaf assuring both gentiles and Jews that they would someday be "gathered together . . . from the ends of the earth into your kingdom" (9:4). Until then, the Way of Life functioned for gentiles in the same way that the "yoke of Torah" functioned for the people of the covenant.

14

WHETHER THE "HYPOCRITES" WERE PROMOTERS OF TEMPLE SACRIFICE

Contents

Background Discussion Found in Boxes

The *Didache* does not offer any reason why those fasting on the second and the fifth day can be judged to be "hypocrites" (*Did.* 8:2f.; see #4b). Nor does the *Didache* offer any reason why the prayer used three times each day by the "hypocrites" was objectionable and needed to be replaced by the Lord's Prayer. In order to understand why the framers of the *Didache* were bent on resisting the "hypocrites" and removing the community from all solidarity with them, the indirect evidence of the *Didache* and the social and historical context in which it was formulated have to be considered.

Willy Rordorf, after carefully setting aside misleading evidence from Matthew, conjectures that the *Didache*'s "hypocrites" were a group of Judaizing Christians pressing gentile converts "to return to Jewish observances" (1978b: 37). The *Didache*, on the other hand, shows little hesitation in allowing the "Jewish observances" of semiweekly fasting or praying three times daily. Thus, this explanation has not found much acceptance (Draper 1996: 233). Most scholars have retained the notion that "hypocrites" refers to pious Jews generally who have refused to accept the gospel (Audet 1958: 367f.; Harnack 1884: 24f.; Niederwimmer 1998: 166 n. 4). Others, citing the evidence that the semiweekly fasting and praying three times each day was not characteristic of all Jews, believe that "hypocrites" must "more likely to refer to Pharisees in particular" (Draper 1996: 233). Neither of these suggestions, however, takes note of the fact that the *Didache* nowhere shows any sharp differentiation from, much less hostility toward the Jews in general or toward the Pharisees in particular (see #4e). All of these conjectures, therefore, fall flat.

Dissatisfied, I began to grope around for a better solution to the identity of the "hypocrites." After discarding many alternatives, a plausible alternative presented itself. This alternative took shape when I noted that the framers of the *Didache* purposely guided gentile Christians away from the divinely authorized temple cult. They accomplished this by systematically replacing the temple cult with the eucharist (*Did.* 14:1–3) and by denying that the temple sacrifices or the city of Jerusalem were to be given any role in God's plan for the future (*Did.* 16:3–8). Furthermore, Roman–Jewish relations were sharply deteriorating during the formative period of the *Didache*, and the framers of the *Didache* would have had solid reasons from removing gentiles both from the seemingly harmless mystique of temple sacrifices and from the potentially dangerous alliance of radical Jews who regarded the temple cult as the rallying point for Jewish independence from Roman control. Putting both the internal and external factors together, I conjecture that the "hypocrites" named by the *Didache* were those Jews (including many Jewish Christians) who innocently, or not so innocently, advocated temple piety for gentiles converts.

The Internal Evidence—Resistance and Replacement of Temple Functions

In the ancient world, the sight of priests offering animal sacrifices in a temple was entirely commonplace (see #8c). "Sacrifice permeated the ancient world, and it was a fact of life" (Stevenson: 11); hence, both Jews and gentiles stood in a cultural milieu in which such things were divinely sanctioned and routinely practiced. It is significant that the internal clues found in the *Didache* demonstrate a systematic attempt to demote and to displace the temple cult venerated by many first-century Jews. This can be seen at five crucial points:

1. *Did*. 4:6 had the effect of giving ordinary members of the community a way to effect the "ransoming of your sins" without any priesthood, without any temple, without any animal sacrifice.

2. *Did*. 8:2 had the effect of redefining the expectation of the kingdom using the Lord's Prayer. Three times each day, small groups of community members boldly addressed the Lord as "Father" and offered him their praise and petitions. They were persuaded that God received their prayers even though they were not priests and they ignored the temple cult. Their kingdom prayer, moreover, included no petition for the rebuilding of Jerusalem or for the reestablishment of the temple cult.

3. *Did*. 14:1–3 had the effect of establishing the eucharist as the "pure sacrifice" which, according to Mal 1:11, took place "in every place and time" and "among the gentiles" (ch. 8 above). Thus, by implication, the temple sacrifices in Jerusalem were entirely unnecessary and perhaps even contrary to "the divinely instituted rule of the Lord" (*Did*. 14:1; see #8a). Ordinary meals ritually served without any priests or a temple were thus understood as offering an acceptable communion sacrifice (see "The Language of Sacrifice" in ch. 8).

4. *Did*. 13:3 had the effect of establishing that "first fruits" were to be presented "to the prophets for they themselves are your high priests." This rule effectively bypassed the priests of the temple, who, according to divine decree, were elected to receive first fruits (Lv 23:10–14; Dt 26:1–11).

5. *Did*. 16:3–8 had the effect of recasting the end-time expectations such that Jerusalem and the temple had no role to play whatsoever—neither in the apostasy prior to the end nor in the coming of the Lord God at the end. Thus the end-times scenario of the *Didache* distinguishes itself from other Jewish prophetic and apocalyptic writings by affirming that the Lord will come to gather his elect without designating Jerusalem as the place (see #10q).

In and of itself, the spiritualization of the temple cult was not uncommon (see "Spiritualization of Sacrifice in Judaism" in ch. 8). Robert Daly, in his study entitled *The Origins of the Christian Doctrine of Sacrifice,* carefully shows how the spiritualization of sacrifice afoot in Jewish circles two centuries prior to Christianity found a strong resonance in early Christian sources. While the Christian church and the Jewish synagogue had their difference, they both shared a marked ambivalence to the temple cult and a ready ability to claim the interpretation of Torah and the conduct of worship in the home as a replacement for priestly interpretation and priestly sacrifices (see #14a). When Jesus was portrayed as citing the prophet Malachi as saying in the name of the Lord, "I want mercy and not sacrifices" (Mt 9:13; 12:7), this would have caught the enthusiasm of the Pharisees of his day as well. In an earlier period, the prophets of Israel had caustically critiqued the temple sacrifices because of the priests' neglect to offer proper animals (Mal 1:6–11) or because of the inappropriate conduct of those offering sacrifice (Is 1:11–20). The prophets, however, never anticipated a time or a place in which the temple cult would not be the center of Jewish piety. The Pharisees and the Jewish Christians, each in their own way, took the prophetic trajectory to its logical conclusion and found ways to be authentically Jewish without concerning themselves with animal sacrifices and with priestly power.

#14A THE IMPACT OF THE PHARISAIC REVOLUTION

The Jesus movement emerged out of the Pharisaic revolution that had transformed Jewish identity. Many Christians will find this strange. After all, don't the Synoptic Gospels portray the Pharisees as the enemies and rivals of the Jesus movement? Precisely. Yet it was because the church emerged out of the synagogue (and not out of the temple) that it inherited a system of thought liberated from the temple cult as defining worship and from the Aaronide priesthood as defining conduct. Ellis Rivkin in his fascinating book *The Shaping of Jewish History,* offers the following portrait of how the Pharisees turned temple Judaism on its head:

1. Instead of relying on the temple cult managed by the priests to define worship, the Pharisees gave every Jew the right and the obligation to address God. Thus, daily prayers and simple rituals conducted by ordinary individuals served "to bring the individual into direct communion with God" (Rivkin 1971: 58). Furthermore, these prayers and rites were performed not in the divinely ordained holy temple but in the ordinary places of their home and their synagogue.

This was a truly revolutionary step, for nowhere in the Pentateuch is prayer obligatory. Although prayer may indeed have been as old as Israel, it had never been required by law. The Pharisees were

therefore once again going off on a highly original tack when they
made mandatory the saying of the *Shema*—"Hear O Israel, the
Lord is our God, the Lord is one"—in the morning and evening,
and when they introduced the recitation of the prayer now called
the *Amidah* or *Shemoneh Esreh* as the prayer par excellence; when
they required each individual to utter benedictions before meals,
after meals, and on other occasions; and when they established
fixed readings from the Pentateuch and the prophets on the Sabbath. And although the synagogue may at first have been a place
where Scripture was read and only later a house of prayer, the
Pharisees were its creators. (Rivkin 1971: 58f.)

Furthermore, when it came to Jewish holidays, the Pharisees enabled ordinary Jews to celebrate these holidays in their homes thereby making their
homes a "sacred place." The mother and father officiated at simple rites
within their family without any need to be a priest or to call upon a priest.
This transformation paved the way for Jews to live out their entire lives
independent of the temple cult—a situation that became a permanent reality following the Roman destruction of the temple in 70 C.E.

2. Instead of having the priests direct the reading and the interpretation
of Torah (Rivkin 1971: 32–41), the Pharisees gave every male Jew the
right and the obligation to read and to interpret the Torah for himself
guided by the oral traditions handed down by the rabbis. The assertion
that there was a binding oral tradition alongside the binding written scroll
separated the Pharisees from the Aaronide priesthood. By taking charge of
their own interpretation, the Pharisees declared their intellectual and spiritual independence from the priests.

The Pharisees even went so far as to allow discussion, debate, and
even alternate renderings of the Law [Torah]. This too was revolutionary innovation; the oral laws had the status of divine revelation, yet they were thrown open to scholarly debate. What was
immutable was not the laws themselves, but the authority of the
Pharisees over the laws. Thus the controversial discussion of laws
came to be [sanctioned by] a divine mandate. (Rivkin 1971: 60)

The Pharisees made it possible for living oral traditions to expand and contract their sense of what God would have them be and do—something
which, according to the priests, was frozen in the Scriptures. When it came
to the discussions and debates with Jesus and his disciples, the Pharisees
sometimes took issue with their understanding and application of the
Scriptures, yet they never contested the right of non-priests to read and to
interpret Torah as such. This was their shared heritage.

3. Instead of allowing the centralized and centralizing temple to dominate Jewish religious existence, the Pharisaic revolution generated pinpoints of light throughout the Roman world. In local synagogues (which were frequently in private homes or in open spaces), ordinary Jews experienced greater responsibility and involvement in the shape and the shaping of their way of life.

> The Diaspora was overshadowed by Jerusalem, with its temple cult, even though large and significant settlements emerged during the Hellenistic period in Alexandria and Antioch. The Hellenistic forms of Judaism emerging in the Diaspora were not taken as models for the Judaism of Palestine. . . . (Rivkin 1971: 85)

In contrast to the centrist policies of the Jewish priesthood,

> . . . the triumph of the Pharisees was the triumph of universalism. Now the vital issue was salvation, not the land and the cult. . . . The Pharisaic revolution thus made it possible for the Diaspora to become a generating force free of the dependence on the land of Israel. . . . The obligations of the Jewish peasant in Palestine had been a vital concern of the Pharisees and continued to be one. But Pharisaism primarily appealed to Diaspora Jews as a form of Judaism addressed to the individual. It gave him the links with the land even as it freed him from the land. The idea that resurrection and eternal life were attainable even without a visit to Jerusalem or the offer[ing] of a personal sacrifice [in the temple] was exhilarating. Diaspora Jews also found appealing the Pharisees' effort to win proselytes from among the pagans; indeed some outstanding Pharisee leaders were reputed themselves to be of proselyte descent. (Rivkin 1971: 85f.)

In sum, when these three aspects of the Pharisaic revolution are taken together, they provide insights as to how the hellenized Jews in the Jesus movement were the first to gainsay the centrality of the temple and the first to extend the way of Jesus to outsiders (see Acts 6:8–8:8). All in all, therefore, the Pharisaic revolution served as the springboard for both rabbinic Judaism and the Jesus movement.

The External Evidence—Growing Conflict Centered on the Temple

Over and beyond the spiritualization of sacrifices and the replacement program of the *Didache*, however, one can discover political and social reasons why, at the very time that many Jews (including Jewish Christians) were becoming increasingly enamored of the temple cult, others were moving as far away from this cult as possible. To understand this, one has to review the political situation in the 40s. James D. G. Dunn summarizes this period as exemplifying the deterioration of the Roman–Jewish relations:

> Bear in mind the deteriorating political situation in Judaea during this period, not least the crisis caused by Emperor Caligula's attempt to have a statue of himself set up in the Jerusalem temple (40 C.E.), a threat every bit as serious as that which occasioned the Maccabean revolt. The death of King Agrippa (44) was probably a blow to more moderate hopes (given Agrippa's friendship with Emperor Claudius, and therefore potential for securing favorable treatment for his people). The succeeding Roman procurators [replacing Agrippa and his sons as rulers of Judea] were weak and heavy handed. Cuspius Fadus (44–46?) demanded that the vestments of the High Priest be returned to the Romans for safe-keeping. . . . (1991: 127)

The Jerusalem temple, it must be remembered, was the focal point of Jewish political, economic, social, and religious aspirations for a large number of Jews. Increasingly the Roman procurators realized that they had to retain a firm control over the priests of the temple if they were going to pacify the Jewish populations effectively. Not only did the Roman procurators have a direct hand in appointing high priests who were favorable to Roman policy, but Cuspius Fadus went so far as to retain the vestments of the high priest. This was done, not for "safe-keeping" as Dunn proposes but in order to ensure that those priests with political aspirations were continually aware that the temple cult was tolerated only because of Roman approval and that, should any unwelcome disruption occur, the cult could be brought to a grinding halt.

Josephus details confrontation after confrontation between Romans and Jews. Illustrative was the affair when Cumanus, Roman procurator from 48 to 52 C.E., caused ten thousand Jews to die in the temple courts. As Josephus reports it, the whole affair began during the Passover when a Roman soldier, after discreetly defecating, decided to moon the Jewish pilgrims using "such words as you might expect upon such a posture" (Josephus, *J. W.* 2.224). Thus, it would appear that a Roman soldier surprised at being spotted relieving himself tried to turn his embarrassment around by mooning the crowd while shouting something like, "Kiss my butt." Since an offense of honor had transpired, a Jewish delegation approached the procurator asking that the soldier be punished. Cumanus hesitated. Hotheaded Jewish youths, meanwhile, began to throw stones at Roman soldiers, who were quite numerous in and around the temple during the time of the feast (*J. W.* 2.224). In a show of force, Cumanus sent his troops into the crowded temple courts with orders to beat the pilgrims gathered there. In their panic, the pilgrims charged for the exits: "the violence with which they crowded to get out was so great, that they trod upon each other and squeezed one another till ten thousand of them were killed" (*J. W.* 2.227). Josephus may be inflating the numbers. Nonetheless, Josephus was quite correct in showing how the temple had become both a rallying point and a tinder box. Every so many years, open violence broke out. After recounting the Roman–Jewish conflicts of the late 50s, Josephus summarizes as follows: "The flame [of open conflict] was every day more and more blown up, till it came to direct war [in 66 C.E.]" (*J. W.* 2.265).

Jesus' Resistance to the Temple Cult

E. P. Sanders undertook an enormous study in order to sift through all the available evidence for "a convincing historical depiction of Jesus . . . which explains his execution, and which explains why his followers formed a persecuted messianic sect" (1985: 5) while studiously refraining from feeding popular resentment of Roman domination. In part, Sanders concludes:

> Jesus saw himself as God's last messenger before the establishment of the kingdom. He looked for a new order, created by a mighty act of God. In the new order the twelve tribes would be reassembled, there would be a new temple, force of arms would not be needed . . . and Jesus and his disciples—the poor, meek, and lowly—would have the leading role. (1985: 319)

So, if Jesus expected the Lord God to restore Israel and cautioned his disciples against taking up arms against Rome, what did he do or say that got him crucified at the hands of the Romans? After considering many possible alternatives, Sanders hits upon this solution:

> The one point that will not go away is the attack (both by word and deed) against the temple. The threat to destroy the temple is swept under the rug by Matthew and Mark in the trial scene, and Luke [entirely] omits it. It crops up, however, later (Mt 27:40//Mk 15:29; cf. Acts 6:14). Mark links the decisive plot to kill Jesus to the action (not the saying) (Mk 11:18). There is no reason to suppose that he here had access to the thinking of the Jewish leaders, but this time (unlike Mk 3:6), he seems to have hit it right. As we shall see more fully below, the temple scene is

the last public event in Jesus' life: he lived long enough for it, but not much longer. (1985: 301f.)

Thus, following Sanders for the moment, we have the following: (a) Jesus is never presented as offering sacrifices in the temple or encouraging his followers to do so; (b) When Jesus does finally arrive in Jerusalem, he disrupts the temple operations rather than contributing to them. The chief priests, who understood this rightly as a would-be prophetic act striking at their centrality in the scheme of things, accordingly took steps to have Jesus handed over and killed by the Romans as an insurrectionist (a charge the Romans would understand only too well) (see #14d). Thus, he was crucified as "King of the Jews"—a sober warning mocking any other Jews who might entertain self-rule in the face of the massive fact of Roman imperial rule.

John Dominic Crossan, seemingly working independently of Sanders and employing a much more narrow window for verisimilitude, surprisingly comes to much the same conclusion in his own critical study *Who Killed Jesus?*

> Cleansing or purification are . . . very misleading terms for what Jesus was doing, namely, an attack on the temple's very existence, a destruction—symbolic, to be sure but nonetheless dangerous for that. . . . My best historical reconstruction concludes that what led immediately to Jesus' arrest and execution in Jerusalem at Passover was that act of symbolic destruction, in deed and in word, against the temple. (1995: 64, 65)

Whatever the character of Jesus' conflict with the Pharisees in Galilee, one can conclude that it was not death-dealing. Thus, during the entire period of Jesus' operations in Galilee, he was never menaced nor, for that matter, even excluded from teaching in the synagogues. When Jesus elected to come to Jerusalem, however, and deliberately meddled with the smooth operation of the temple sacrifices (see #14b), he was doomed not to survive to the end of the week. The temple priests, unlike the Pharisees, knew how to wield ruthless power and did not hesitate to do so against someone who prophetically and symbolically heralded the destruction of the temple and the end of temple sacrifice (see #14d).

#14B CHRISTIAN AMBIGUITY REGARDING THE TEMPLE

Gerd Theissen and Annette Metz conclude that the Christian sources portray both a positive and negative assessment of temple sacrifice and that

Jesus, near the end of his life, deliberately created a rite to displace such sacrifices.

On the positive side, Theissen and Metz note that Jesus recognized "the holiness of the temple and priestly control in the case of the healing of lepers . . . and of the payment of the temple tax by his followers [Mk 1:44f and par.; Mt 17:24–27, 23:16–22, 23:35f/Lk 11:50f]" (1998: 602).

> The nucleus of these traditions will be historical, for unless Jesus had such an attitude it would be impossible to understand why the first Christian community had an important center in Jerusalem and continued to take part in the temple cult [Acts 2:46–3:1]. (1998: 602)

On the negative side, Theissen and Metz note that significant sayings of Jesus indicate a critical attitude toward the temple cult:

> Here the tendency is always to set the moral above the cultic: care of parents has priority over assigning goods to the temple (Mk 7:6ff.); tithing cooking herbs is not on the same level as a concern for law, mercy and faith (Mt 23:23f.); love of God and neighbor are more important than sacrifice (Mk 12:32–34 — this conclusion is drawn by a scribe and Jesus acknowledges it in 12:35); and a sacrifice is worthless unless it has been preceded by reconciliation between the parties in a dispute (Mt 5:23f.). (1998: 602)

It is no coincidence, therefore, that Jesus appealed to Hos 6:6 ("For I desire steadfast love and not sacrifice"), which is one of the rare prophetic sayings presenting God as positively declaring "this and not that."

Jesus' deeds go even further. According to Theissen and Metz, Jesus ignored the purification rites necessary for those entering the temple (see Nm 9:9; Jn 13:10; 18:28; P.Oxy. 840; Gospel of the Ebionites, frag. 6) (1996: 432). Added to this, Jesus anticipated the destruction of the temple with the understanding that "God will erect another in its place" (ibid.). Finally, one has Jesus' intention to create a provisional substitute to the temple cult at his last supper:

> Jesus offers the disciples a replacement for the official cult in which they could either no longer take part, or which would not bring them salvation—until a new temple came. This "substitute" is a simple meal. By a new interpretation, the last supper becomes a substitute for the temple cult—a pledge of the eating

and drinking in the kingdom of God which is soon to dawn. . . .
Perhaps Jesus only said, "This is the body for you," meaning by
that: this bread now replaces for you the sacrificial food which is
otherwise consumed in the temple. . . . And over the cup he
added: "This cup which we drink together (i.e., which is passed
around) is the new covenant"—namely a covenant without sacrifice which according to Jer 31:31–33 consists in the will of God
being put in human hearts and God forgiving them their sins.
(1998: 434)

In coming to this stark conclusion as part of Jesus' self-understanding, I
personally find Theissen and Metz to be overreaching the evidence and
ignoring historical development between the acts/words of Jesus and the
crafting of the Gospels. If their interpretation were correct, however, it
would follow that Jesus' separation from the temple cult was radically complete and that the Lord's Supper or eucharist had a sacrificial character
from its very origins. Thus, Theissen and Metz understand Jesus to have
deliberately provided his disciples with an alternative sacrificial cult
designed to serve them until the Lord came to rebuild the temple and to
establish his kingdom. "The Lord's supper is *de facto* a ritual which is a
substitute for the sacrificial cult" (1998: 436).

Resistance to Temple Piety in Acts

James D. G. Dunn, in turning his attention to when and how there was
a parting of the ways between Christianity and Judaism, took as his starting point the curious fact that, according to Acts, the Jerusalem church of
the 30s "remained very focused on the temple" (1991: 57). Stephen, a
leader of the hellenized Jews in the Jesus movement, however, disturbed
this status quo by speaking out against the temple (Acts 6:11, 14). If Acts
7 can be taken as representing his views, it is understandable how his out-
spoken views might have been so inflammatory as to trigger a "lynch
mob," which resulted in a general persecution (Acts 8:1). Ernst Haenchen
rightly notes that Luke-Acts fails to distinguish between the Peter Christians, who routinely prayed and preached in the temple, and those, like
Stephen, with anti-temple perspectives, who were singled out for persecution (Haenchen:297). Furthermore, it is possible that Luke's portrait of
Jesus in his Gospel deliberately downplays any antagonism toward the
temple, knowing that this antagonism began among the hellenized Jews in
the early church (Dunn 1991: 73). As a result, Dunn concludes that
"Stephen marks the beginning of a radical critique of the temple on the
part of the infant Christian movement" (1991: 67). From there, "the free

and unhindered acceptance of Samaritans [which follows in Acts 8] by the sect of the Nazarene [the Jesus movement] would have been seen as a sign of disregard for, even of disloyalty to the Jerusalem temple" (1991: 71). Thus, Dunn discerns a split within the early Jesus movement itself regarding the centrality of the temple. Over against the pro-temple stance of the Peter Christians, the Stephen Christians hammered out a self-definition that excluded both the temple and its sacrificial system. Since this was the group primarily responsible for the outreach to gentiles, it is no mystery that, once this branch of the Jesus movement predominated, Christians favoring an amalgamation of Jesus' message with traditional temple piety were in the minority. This is probably the minority that the *Didache* branded as "hypocrites" and with whom they broke solidarity.

In sum, Sanders, Crossan, and Dunn demonstrate that those who represented the historical Jesus and the Jerusalem church in the 60s and 70s presented the temple as being the burning point of contention. Sanders and Crossan conclude that this opposition to the temple is rooted in Jesus' prophetic and symbolic actions and words against the temple. Dunn, following Luke, roots this opposition in Hellenistic Jews like Stephen, who downplayed the importance of the temple and demeaned its sacrificial system without any reference to what Jesus did or said. In any case, each of these sources traces an anti-temple platform back to the early church. While circumcision, Sabbath, and food regulations played their part in dividing the church and in the breaking off of the gentile churches from Judaism, all three studies affirm that the first and most divisive issue coalesces around the role of the temple cult, both in the present and in the end times.

The Role of the Temple in God's Future Kingdom

The future expectation of Israel repeatedly embraced the theme of the restoration and/or enlarging of the Jerusalem temple. This is not to say that the expectation was uniform. E. P. Sanders summarizes his own study of the relevant texts as follows:

> This rapid survey of passages does not lead to the conclusion that all Jews everywhere, when thinking of the future hope of Israel, put foremost the building of a new temple. Further, when the temple is explicitly mentioned, it is not depicted in a uniform manner. To be more precise, sometimes is not *depicted* at all (2 Mc 2:7; *Jub.* 1:17, 27; *11QTemple* 29:8–10), and sometimes it appears that the present second temple [destroyed in 70 C.E.] is in mind (*1 Enoch* 25:5; 2 Mc 2:7). Sometimes the new temple is modestly expected only to be larger and grander than the present

temple (Tb 14:5, "glorious"; *1 Enoch* 90:28f., "greater and loftier"; *Testament of Benjamin* 9:2, "more glorious than the first"), in which case it will be built by human hands (see Tb 14:5); but sometimes the extravagant language of Micah 4 and Is 2 is recalled (*Pss. Sol.* 17:32; *Sib. Or.* 5:425). In some instances it is definitely said or clearly implied that God will build or provide a new temple (*1 Enoch* 90:28f.; *Jub.* 1:17; *11QTemple* 29:8–18 [also *4QFlorilegium*]), and in *Sib. Or.* 5:425 the builder is a "blessed man from heaven." (1985: 86f.; see also #10q)

When one examines the whole of the Christian Scriptures and the *Didache*, one finds scant expectation of a restored or purified temple. The Lord's Prayer and the eschatological scenario of the *Didache* do not even mention such things. Even the Book of Revelation which champions the expectation of a new Jerusalem coming down from heaven, soberly notes: "I saw no temple in the city, for its temple is the Lord God the Almighty and the Lamb" (Rv 21:22)—a clear case of substitution and "a polemic against the normal expectation of Judaism" (Sanders 1985: 86).

Closely associated with the centrality of the temple is the theme of the ingathering of the scattered Jews into the temple. As an illustration, consider the records of the successful Maccabean revolt against the Persians (176–161 B.C.E.). The revolt of the Maccabeans, it will be remembered, culminated in the liberation of Jerusalem and the "purification of the temple" (2 Mc 2:16)—an event commemorated annually in the Jewish feast of Hanukkah. The idealized record of these events interprets the success of the revolt as "the Lord showing his favor" (2 Mc 2:22) and preparing the way for the restoration of Israel, which is described in these terms:

> It is God who has saved all his people, and has returned the inheritance to all, and the kingship and the priesthood and the consecration, as he promised through the law [Torah]. We have hope in God that he will soon have mercy on us and will gather us from everywhere under heaven into his holy place [the Jerusalem temple]. (2 Mc 2:17f.)

The ingathering of the Jews scattered among the nations thus centers on "the holy place" where God dwells. Note, in contrast, that when the *Didache* speaks of this same expectation of ingathering in the eucharistic prayers, those who are gathered are now those who are eating and drinking (gentiles and Jews together) and the place of meeting is deliberately left blank (not the temple). Those praying these prayers, therefore, clearly had expectations that openly clashed with the text of 2 Maccabees just cited.

One could argue that Sabbath observance, Jewish food regulations, and circumcision also formed lines of division in the early church and could have led to a separation from the "hypocrites" as specified by the *Didache*. None of these issues, however, appears to be a point of contention in the *Didache*. It is striking that the *Didache* is completely silent regarding Sabbath observance even though the Jewish calendar of weeks was imposed upon gentiles (see #4a). Likewise, circumcision is never discussed (see #3b), nor is there any attempt to spiritualize it or to replace it with baptism. Later, in Paul, Barnabas, and Justin Martyr, extensive attention will be given to these matters. As for food regulations, the *Didache* reduced these to a minimum (*Did.* 6:3; see #1o and #1y) and there was no attempt to explain this minimum or to justify it. When it came to the temple cult, however, multiple segments of the *Didache* were deliberately crafted to offer a systematic mode for silencing and replacing any present need or future hope centered on the Jerusalem temple. The hidden logic of the *Didache* is thus evident.

The Traditional Appeal of the Temple Cult

The radical nature of the *Didache*'s program of silence and substitution can only be appreciated when it is placed against the backdrop of the traditional appeal of the temple cult within Judaism. When one reads the Hebrew Scriptures, one finds massive evidence that God himself had ordained that a temple ought to be built in his name and that the sons of Aaron ought to function forever as the priests who alone were authorized to offer sacrifice to the living God of Israel. At the end of the Babylonian captivity (538 B.C.E.), priests became the national heroes, and the reconstruction of the temple received first priority. A dispirited people thus renewed their Jewish identity and Jewish hope by rebuilding the temple. Following the Maccabean revolt (166–164 B.C.E.), politics and piety worked together to make the temple the center of Jewish independence and ushered in a century of inter-Jewish strife. When Herod became king (37 B.C.E.), he used Roman troops to brutally suppress guerrilla factions and bandits throughout Judea. During the period of enforced peace that resulted, Herod courted the favor of Jews scattered throughout the empire by providing funds for building their synagogues, libraries, and baths and for providing for their widows and orphans. Then, "Herod decided to encourage this practice [of making pilgrimages to the Jerusalem temple three times each year] especially from the diaspora, by providing Jerusalem with all the facilities of a modern Romano-Greek city and above all by rebuilding the temple itself as a monument-spectacle worth coming to see" (P. Johnson: 114):

> In 22 B.C.E., he summoned a national assembly and announced his life-work: the rebuilding of the temple on a magnificent scale,

exceeding even the glory of Solomon's. The next two years were spent assembling and training a force of 10,000 workmen and 1,000 supervisory priests. . . . To achieve the grandiose effects he desired, Herod doubled the area of the temple mount by building huge supporting walls and filling in the gaps with rubble. Around the vast forecourt thus created, he erected porticos and linked it all to the upper city by bridges. . . . Cash was spent profusely on the exterior, gates, fittings, and decorations being covered in gold and silver plate. Josephus says the stone was 'exceptionally white,' and the glitter of the stone and the gleam of the gold—reflected many miles away in the bright sun—was what made the temple so striking to travelers seeing it from afar for the first time. (P. Johnson: 114, 115)

For many Jews living in the first century, therefore, personal piety and national identity came together harmoniously in the divinely authorized temple cult.

Herod's temple was world-famous and greatly esteemed . . . and important gentiles [in addition to ordinary Jews] offered sacrifices, for pious reasons as well as to conciliate Jewish opinion. In 15 B.C.E., for instance, Herod's friend Marcus Agrippa [grandfather of Emperor Caligula] made the grand gesture of offering a hecatomb (100 beasts). . . . Foreign kings and statesmen from Artaxerxes to the Emperor Augustus presented it with vast quantities of gold vessels. . . . Jews from all over the diaspora poured money and plate into it, rather as they now contribute to [the State of] Israel. (P. Johnson: 117)

Various expression of Judaism in favor of the temple cult can be found scattered throughout its literature. An illustrative expression from Psalms is the following:

If I forget you, O Jerusalem, let my right hand wither!
Let my tongue cleave to the roof of my mouth,
        if I do not remember you [in prayer and in song],
        if I do not set Jerusalem above my highest joy! (Ps 137:4–6)

In rabbinic literature, the Mishnah asserts that "the land of Israel is holier than all lands" and that "the temple mount is more holy than it" (*m. Kelim* 1:6, 8). Even in Luke's Gospel, one finds the opening chapters espousing the romantic notion that the parents of John and of Jesus were firmly attached to the temple cult. One might even suspect that the reader of Luke's Gospel was expected to envy Anna, who "never left the temple but worshiped there with fasting and prayer night and day" (Lk 2:37).

Philo of Alexandria romanticized the temple in Jerusalem, even though many Jews in Alexandria may never have visited it. When it came to describing the "first fruits," for example, Philo asserts that those Jews living in Palestine "contribute their payments to the priests with joy and cheerfulness, anticipating the collectors . . . , thinking that they are themselves receiving rather than giving" (*Special Laws* 1.143)—clearly an idealized notion of things written by someone in the Diaspora who was exempt from such giving. Philo, after describing for gentiles how Jews were devoted to all their ancestor customs, then goes on to make the sweeping remark that "above all other observances, their zeal for their holy temple is the most predominant and vehement and universal feeling throughout the whole nation" (*Embassy to Gaius* 212). Thus, when it came time to explain the Jewish traditions, Philo delighted in explaining all the minute details of what sacrifice was suited for what occasion—a topic that consumes 22 percent of the *Special Laws* 1.66–298—and how everything was divinely ordained through "oracles directly given to them by God himself" (*Embassy to Gaius* 210).

Philo, being zealous for the temple, was quick to remind gentiles that great persons among them had found great consolation and beauty in their pilgrimages to the Jerusalem temple:

> Marcus Agrippa [grandfather of Emperor Caligula] . . . when he had beheld the temple and the decorations of the priests and the piety and holiness of the people of the country, he marveled, looking upon the whole matter as one of great solemnity and entitled to great respect and thinking that he had beheld what was too magnificent to be described [adequately in words]. And he could talk of nothing else to his companions but the magnificence of the temple and every thing connected with it. Therefore, every day . . . he went to the sacred place, being delighted with the spectacle of the building and of the sacrifices and all the ceremonies connected with the worship of God. . . . And after he had adorned the temple with all the offerings in his power to contribute and conferred many benefits on the inhabitants [of Jerusalem] . . . , he was conducted back again to the sea coast. (*Embassy to Gaius* 295f.)

Philo also narrates in great detail the heroic attachment to the purity of the temple which prompted hundreds of Jews in 40 C.E. to spontaneously surround the governor, who was charged with preparing and transporting a great statue of the emperor Caligula for erection in the holy of holies of the Jerusalem temple. These Jews promised to give all their possessions, their families, and their very lives so that this might not be done:

> We only ask one thing . . . , namely, that no innovations may take place in respect of our temple. . . . And if we cannot prevail with you in this, then we offer up ourselves for destruction, that we may not live to behold a calamity more terrible and grievous than death. (*Embassy to Gaius* 232f.)

In sum, given the abundant divine sanctions and given the glorious role played by the temple in garnishing the esteem of gentiles everywhere, it would have been entirely natural for many Jews in the Jesus movement to be zealous for the temple. Mark's Gospel even records that a disciple of Jesus drew his attention to the magnificence of Herod's temple, saying, "Look, Teacher, what large stones and what large buildings!" (Mk 13:2). Against this backdrop, one can imagine that those Jewish Christians zealous for the temple would have invited sympathetic gentiles and, more especially, the newly baptized (a) to pray and fast for the temple, (b) to make a contribution to the holy and pleasing sacrifices, and (c) to anticipate the great blessings that might come to them should they make a pilgrimage to this holy place. When faced with this, the framers of the *Didache* (as shown above) would have said, "We will have none of this among us!" And, to enforce this, they systematically designed many "fences" (see #1v) to remove Christians from the hypocrisy surrounding the temple cult.

Vices Associated with "Hypocrites" in the Didache

The word translated as "hypocrite" (*hypokritēs*) has a variety of meanings in Greek. The term can refer to an "interpreter" or "expounder," yet most often it refers to an "actor" on stage who makes his audience believe he is someone else, namely, the character he is portraying in the drama. The term "hypocrite," therefore, can have positive connotations. Among Greek-speaking Jews, however, the term took on strong negative connotations and pointed to someone pretending to be what he is not. In Matthew's Gospel, for example, this term is repeatedly used to characterize the false piety of the Pharisees (see #4d). For reasons already detailed in chapter 4, however, these "hypocrites" in Matthew's Gospel cannot be used as models for the "hypocrites" in the *Didache*.

The *Didache* made clear that the daily prayers and semiweekly fasts of the elect were not to coincide "with the hypocrites" (8:1f.). In the case of fasting, it sufficed merely to change the days of fasting. Presumably, the mode of fasting remained what it had been and was shared by the "hypocrites." In the case of praying, however, an alternate prayer (the Lord's Prayer) was given. This alternate prayer petitions the Lord to establish his kingdom without making any mention of the Jerusalem temple. Hence, if the Eighteen Benedictions did at this time include a petition for the temple or for Jerusalem (see #4f), then it might be understood why the Lord's Prayer separated the members of the Didache communities from the "hypocrites" zealous for the Jerusalem temple (as suggested above). This, however, cannot be demonstrated, since the sources that have come down to us do not preserve the form(s) of daily prayers used in the mid-first century (see #4h). The considerations noted above about the key importance of temple piety for most Jews in the first century, however, might incline one to believe that daily prayers frequently included a petition for the holy temple or voiced an expectation that the Lord would occupy the temple when he came. This, however, cannot be shown.

Sometimes, however, verbal associations show up in a text that can reveal something of how the framers of the *Didache* regarded the term "hypocrite." Consider the following two lists in this light:

Didache 2:6	*Didache* 5:1
[C1] You will not be covetous,	[A9] sorceries,
[C2] (and) not greedy,	[A10] perjuries,
[C3] (and) not a hypocrite,	[A11] hypocrisies,
[C4] (and) not malicious,	[A12] double-heartedness,
	[A13] trickery,
[C5] (and) not arrogant.	[A14] arrogance,
	[A15] malice,
	[A16] stubbornness,
	[A17] greed,
	[A18] foul-speech,

In the first list, the first two dispositions [C1 and C2] are associated—both pertain to an inordinate attachment to goods. Then the term "hypocrite" appears [C3], and this is immediately associated with one who is "bad-mannered/malicious/crafty" [C4] and "arrogant" [C5]. When the Way of Death (*Did.* 5:1) is described, the term "hypocrisies" [A11] shows up. Here again the term is loosely associated with "arrogance" [A14]. In *Did.* 5:1, "hypocrisies" is also associated with "double-heartedness" and "trickery."

Following up on the discussion above, it would make sense that those who relished the temple and saw it as the center and source of Jewish resistance to Roman tyranny would have been inclined to be religiously arrogant. The temple, after all, was built under divine direction, and God himself resided there. In the clash that was sure to come, therefore, many Jews must have felt that God would come down to fight on the side of those Jews who attached themselves to the Lord in his holy temple (see, e.g., Is 33:1–11; 34:1–8). Thus, in the end, zeal for the temple and zeal for Jewish independence were closely linked (as Josephus makes clear).

This, quite possibly, was the hypocrisy that the *Didache* opposed. The

Didache provided a program in holiness which opposed being "arrogant" (2:6) and proposed, in its stead, being "gentle . . . long-suffering, merciful" (3:8), "not exalt[ing] yourself" (3:9), and, more especially, acting in the world such that "you will not hate any person" (2:7)—Romans included. The *Didache* provided a prayer that waited for God to bring the kingdom upon the face of the earth. During this waiting, there was no expectation that the city of Jerusalem or its temple would be the center of God's future. By rejecting all reliance on priests (13:3) and by confessing their failings so as to offer "in every place and time" to God "a pure sacrifice" (14:1–3), the Didache community effectively established its alternative to the Jerusalem temple. Thus, the framers of the *Didache* thoroughly opposed the "hypocrites," who, in their eyes, had slipped into "double-mindedness," "trickery," and "arrogance."

One could always argue that the term "hypocrisy" could apply to many forms of conduct and that the vices associated with "hypocrites" in the *Didache* could also be interpreted to apply to alternative kinds of opponents. This, of course, is true. In the end, therefore, one can only make an educated guess based on the circumstantial evidence of the text regarding "hypocrites" and upon the systematic replacement motifs which flow throughout the *Didache*. When this is read against the background of the Pharisaic revolution and within the context of deteriorating Roman–Jewish relations in the 40s and 50s, one discovers the possibility of integrating many threads into a single fabric. However, in the end, it must be acknowledged that, from beginning to end, we have been working with indirect clues (internal and external) which appear to form a coherent picture. Since the text does not overtly define the way of the hypocrites, our hypothetical integration of these clues may be flawed. Until a more satisfying proposal is forthcoming, therefore, I will rest content with trying out and stretching the proposed hypothesis. The help of others in this endeavor will be deeply appreciated.

Conclusion

The Didache community took its stand within the Pharisaic revolution. In so doing, ordinary Jews and gentiles were given access to the Father through daily prayers and eucharistic meals. In these acts of worship, no special class of persons ("priests") was needed or desired in order to coordinate and authorize them. The Way of Life, meanwhile, was interpreted by teachers/mentors who (without having any special racial or family lineage) passed on "the life and knowledge" revealed by the Father through his "servant Jesus" (9:3). Finally, the *Didache* entirely passed over in silence the sacrifices, the first fruits, the festivals associated with the temple and, significantly, provided for alternatives whereby ordinary people could accomplish these things in their own homes and neighborhoods. Instead of vigorously faulting the temple cult, therefore, the *Didache* settled for systematically replacing its major functions.

How a community prays reveals how a community anticipates God to act in their behalf. Accordingly, instead of the prayer of the "hypocrites," the Didache community prayed the Lord's Prayer, which envisioned God coming to vindicate his holy name by bringing his will, once and for all, to bear upon all aspects of human existence. With regard to his coming, however, the framers of the *Didache* entirely left aside the destruction of the gentiles and the establishment of the Jerusalem temple as the center of God's dominion. Neither the Lord's Prayer (8:2) nor the end-times scenario (16:3–8) embraces either of these elements. The "hypocrites," on the contrary, probably prayed and acted to favor these things. Based on the "life and knowledge . . . revealed to us" (9:2f.), the framers of the *Didache* reacted vigorously by refusing to fast and pray "with these hypocrites" (8:1f.).

Nothing important is achieved with unanimous consent. The pastoral genius of the *Didache*, therefore, is manifested in the way it framed a Way of Life based on a revealed plan of holiness which was open to both Jews and gentiles. From our own perspective, the framers of the *Didache* might seem excessive when they resorted to a tough act of nonsolidarity with the "hypocrites." Even the term "hypocrite" may be seen as provocative name calling. In ordinary times, this could be faulted, yet in times of great danger this might be the necessary safeguard which a community stretches out to its beloved members.

In the end, the framers of the *Didache* made a passionate commitment in favor of a God bent on ushering the elect into a kingdom free of any temple cult and anti-gentile rhetoric. Their position, needless to say, did not attract and convert all Jews living either then or now. As in all great endeavors, they failed in some things in order to succeed in others.

> Nothing that results from human [or religious] progress is achieved with unanimous consent, and those that are enlightened before the others are condemned to pursue that light in spite of the others. (Christopher Columbus)

#14c TEMPLE DISPLACEMENT IN THE LETTER TO THE HEBREWS

The *Didache* represents one way in which some early Christians turned the religious attachment to temple sacrifice into alternative channels (see ch. 8 above). The Letter to the Hebrews represents quite another.

Hebrews is widely recognized as a theological treatise from an anonymous author. It contains neither the theology nor the influence of Paul. Taking up the Jewish concern with temple and priesthood as its central theme, the so-called Letter to the Hebrews stands as the only book in the Christian Scriptures which focuses on Jesus as "high priest."

At no time do the Christian Scriptures designate as "priest" any minister within the Jesus movement. The four Gospels and Acts use the terms *hiereus* ("priest") and *archiereus* ("high priest") frequently (121x), but, in every instance, these terms refer to Jewish or pagan priests. The reason for this is that the early churches shared the Jewish perspective that (a) only "sons of Aaron" were entitled to act as priests and (b) these priests were universally regarded as occupied with the worship of God in the context of the Jerusalem temple. Neither Jesus nor the Twelve were either "sons of Aaron" or occupied with temple worship. Hence, no one within or outside of the Jesus movement would have imagined that either Jesus or his disciples were "priests."

The Letter to the Hebrews constitutes a singular exception. Hebrews is a theological treatise which, in part, argues that God appointed Jesus as the eternal high priest who offers the perfect sacrifice in the heavenly sanctuary. In order to sustain this claim, Hebrews had to acknowledge (a) that on earth Jesus was not a priest and (b) that the sacrifice made by Jesus had nothing to do with the burnt offerings and sin offerings of the temple.

Hebrews promotes the prophetic critique of temple sacrifice. According to the "new covenant" (9:15) envisioned by Hebrews, Jesus' heartfelt fidelity to God—"Lo, I have come to do your will, O God" (10:7, 9, 16)—is specified as the only acceptable sacrifice that serves to blot out sins. Furthermore, this fidelity is not a given in the case of Jesus. It is something he came to after being tempted and made to suffer (2:18; 5:8; 12:4). Hebrews presents God's choice of Jesus (whom God has raised) as akin to God's earlier unpredictable choice of Melchizedek, the "king of righteousness" (7:2).

While the Letter to the Hebrews argued that Jesus was appointed high priest, his priesthood was understood as beginning not on earth (8:4) but only when he had entered into the heavenly sanctuary following his resurrection. According to Hebrews, the earthly sanctuary (in Jerusalem) was a mere "sketch and shadow of the heavenly one" (8:5; 9:24); hence, the new covenant is sealed by a new priesthood in the heavenly sanctuary where God continually dwells—"the greater and more perfect tent (not made with hands, that is, not of this creation)" (9:11).

In short, the *reality* of access to God [4:16; 7:25; 10:22; 11:6; 12:22], of a conscience cleansed from sin, of Christ's continuing priestly role, *has made the Jewish cult wholly redundant. . . .* Who

remains satisfied with the shadow when the substance is present?
The message surely was clear enough: there is no further need of
tabernacle or temple, no need of sacrifice or priesthood [outside
of Christ]; to go back to that as some of his readers seem to have
wanted was to go back to the shadow, the inferior copy. (Dunn
1991: 89)

Unlike the case of the *Didache,* in which the eucharist is regarded as the
pure and acceptable sacrifice offered "in every place and time" (Mal 1:11
cited in *Did.* 14:1–3), Hebrews has no investment in regarding the Last
Supper of Jesus or the eucharist of Christians as a "sacrifice." Hebrews, it
will be remembered, took the stand that "if he [Jesus] were on earth, he
would not be a priest at all" (9:4). Thus, Hebrews never had any reason to
associate the Lord's Supper with the priesthood of Jesus. Furthermore,
since Hebrews argues that "Jesus holds his priesthood permanently
because he continues forever" (7:24), he has no need of a successor; and
since his priestly functions are in heaven, no one on earth is able to assist
him. In sum, therefore, since Hebrews works against any notion that a
priesthood need function within the Jewish community, this argument also
works against any notion that some or all Christians need to function as
priests.

Hebrews closed with the exhortation that Christians "not neglect to do
good and to share what you have, for such sacrifices are pleasing to God"
(13:16). Thus, even Hebrews would seem to envision that Christians offer
to God a pleasing "sacrifice" when they share their resources. Beyond this,
Hebrews also exhorted Christians to "continually offer a sacrifice of praise
to God" (13:15). With the passage of time, it would become commonplace for Christians to regard the eucharist as a "sacrifice of praise." The
framer of Hebrews, however, seemed to have had no reason to anticipate
or to sanction such an identification.

Hebrews does not directly disclose why it is impelled to avoid relying
on the Jewish temple and its priesthood. Quite possibly, Hebrews was written after the destruction of the temple by the Romans. The reflection that
members of the community "had compassion on the prisoners" and "joy-
fully accepted the plundering of your property" (10:34) might point to the
conditions suffered during or after the siege. In any case, during the
decades after the destruction of the temple, there was a manifest wave of
hope that the temple would soon be rebuilt:

Most Jews of the time would probably assume or hope that the
temple would soon be rebuilt again (as it had after the exile in
Babylon); such a hope is probably implicit in the choice of
"Ezra" and "Baruch" as pseudonyms in the two main Jewish

apocalyptic writings of the period between the Jewish revolts
(*4 Ezra* and *2 Baruch*). And it is notable that the rabbis continued
to give rulings relating to the temple cult after 70, presumably on
the same assumption. (Dunn 1991: 87)

In sharp contrast, Hebrews places its hope in "the heavenly sanctuary"
(8:5) and "the heavenly Jerusalem" (12:22):

> The final consummation is yet to come. Christ will appear a sec-
> ond time to save those waiting for him (9:28; cf. 10:36–39).
> Christians seek the city which is to come (13:14). God will shake
> heaven and earth one more time so that the eternal kingdom
> might appear (12:26–28). The expectation of a future action of
> God is such a common element in the thought of the author and
> the recipients that it can be referred to by the simple Old Testa-
> ment term "day": " . . . encouraging one another, and all the
> more as you see the day drawing near" (10:25). (R. Johnson: 83)

All in all, the agenda of Hebrews served to dissuade Jewish Christians
from placing their hope in the rebuilding of the Jerusalem temple
destroyed by the Romans (68–70 C.E.). What need would there be for an
earthly temple when Jesus was already functioning as the *superior priest* in
the *superior place* according to a *superior covenant*? In brief, Hebrews took
the position that those who rely on Jesus have no need to anticipate a
renewed temple "made by hands" (9:11), for their hope is in "the heavenly sanctuary" (8:5) and "the heavenly Jerusalem" (12:22) which God
will bring with his kingdom.

The *Didache*, in contrast, was dealing with a temple still functioning.
Those who put their faith in this temple, however, were bound to become
embroiled in the impending Roman–Jewish conflict which was sure to
come. The framers of the *Didache*, accordingly, provided both Jews and
gentiles with an alternative for offering sacrifice to God (the eucharist) and
for giving the first fruits to the priests (the prophets), which entirely
bypassed the institutional modes then existing. Thus, for different reasons
at different times, both the framers of the *Didache* and the framer of
Hebrews provided alternative systems for distancing the minds and hearts
of their adherents from the Jerusalem temple.

#14D POLITICAL AND ECONOMIC ASPECTS
OF TEMPLE WORSHIP

During the first century, when Judea was subjugated by the Romans,
the chief priests and the Sanhedrin (supreme council/court) constituted

the official authorities responsible for maintaining law and order. In this scheme of things, James D. G. Dunn rightly notes that, for most Jews, the temple served as the religious, economic, and political center of Judaism:

> Judaea was technically a temple state or temple land. That is to say, that Jerusalem temple provided the rationale for Judaea's existence as a separate entity within the Hellenistic and Roman empires. According to the same rationale, the territory attached to the temple was the amount of land needed to provide the resources (wood, animals for sacrifice, etc.) for the temple cult. . . .
>
> Since Israel was a religious state, its religious law was also its state and civil law. Consequently also its chief court, the Sanhedrin, was the chief instrument of a wide range of legislative and executive power, much wider under Roman rule. . . . The temple was also an economic center. It needs to be recalled that the economic rationale for the location of Jerusalem was exceedingly weak. The city did not sit on any trade route, or river crossing, nor was it a port. The only reason for its continued existence, the only reason why people came to it was the temple, directly or indirectly. The temple was undoubtedly Jerusalem's main source of revenue. . . . The pilgrim traffic for the three main pilgrim feasts . . . must have been immense. . . . Every devout Jew was obligated to spend one-tenth of the produce of his land in Jerusalem (the so-called "second tithe"). The trade and business which this generated and supported must have been enormous. (Dunn 1991: 31–32)

From this vantage point, it no longer appears abnormal that *because of Jesus' one-time disruption of the temple operations,* he was arrested by the temple police sent into action by the chief priests (e.g., Mt 26:47). Nor does it appear abnormal that, after being tried or given a hearing by the priests (e.g., Mt 26:57), he was condemned and handed over to Pilate, the Roman procurator. John's Gospel presents Pilate as saying to the priests, "Take him yourselves and judge him by your law" (Jn 18:31). They responded: "It is not lawful for us to put any man to death" (Jn 18:32). The temple priests, therefore, were acting lawfully and responsibly when they tried Jesus and handed him over to Pilate with the hopes that Rome would second their judgment against Jesus.

Anyone challenging or disrupting the temple operations was seen as a threat to the continued economic, political, and religious well-being of temple-centered Judaism. The death of Jesus, the stoning of Stephen (Acts 7:58), the arrest of the apostles (Acts 5:17f.), and the persecution by Paul (Acts 9:1f.) all stemmed directly from a priestly aristocracy anxious to preserve their tenuous hold on power in a complex and changing world. Undoubtedly most priests saw the continuation of the status quo as the single most important ingredient to preserving Jewish identity during the Roman occupation. Other Jews, needless to say, strongly disagreed. Any disagreement with priestly power or any disruption of the temple cult, however, carried with it the threat to the whole economic, political, and religious status quo. The temple cult was never purely a religious matter.

15
Whether the "Burning-Process of Testing" (*Did.* 16:5) Offers Evidence for the Dual Functioning of Eschatological Fire

Contents

Background Discussion Found in Boxes

The purpose of this chapter is to reexamine the long-standing practice of finding in *Did*. 16:5 an implicit reference to the saving activity of the crucified Christ. Earlier segments of this volume have already shown that the saving activity of the Father envisioned by the Didache communities was principally eschatological and entirely silent respecting any Pauline theology of the cross. Once Pauline interpretations are viewed as foreign to the internal logic of the text itself, *Did*. 16:5 can then be reconstructed within an alternative horizon of understanding. Accordingly, this chapter will explore the dual functioning of eschatological fire within Jewish prophetic writings and early Christian apocalyptic literature as providing a way to recover an authentic voice for a *Didache* freed from the Pauline overlays.

The exposition will proceed in three phases. First, the narrative flow and linguistic structure of the apocalyptic ending of the *Didache* will be examined. Second, the traditional interpretation of *Did*. 16:5 will be critiqued. Third, the dual function of eschatological fire will be illustrated from select prophetic and apocalyptic texts by way of exploring a fresh understanding of *Did*. 16:5.

#15A THE STATE OF THE QUESTION

The Christian Scriptures take for granted that God's final judgment will be like a terrible fire consuming evil. Jesus' parables, more especially, make use of this metaphor when they depict "the bad trees" and "the weeds" being separated from the good in order to be "thrown on the fire" (Mt 7:20; 13:30; 13:50; 25:40). Fire, in these contexts, is the preferred metaphor presenting how God's final judgment will utterly destroy evil on the face of the earth. Even in the realm of metaphors, however, there is nothing in Jesus' parables that suggests a fire that is "purgatorial," that is, functioning to purify the elect of their minor sins and imperfections prior to their entrance into the world to come.

The Catholic doctrine of purgatory was defined by the two medieval councils (Lyons in 1274 and Ferrara-Florence in 1439), which tried to bring about a reunion with the Byzantine churches. While the Orthodox shared with the West the practice of interceding for the dead by prayer, alms, good works, and especially the eucharist, Eastern Christians were hesitant to accept the notion that punishment and atonement were to be associated with purgatorial fire in the afterlife. The Reformers, in the next century, formulated a doctrine of atonement that was entirely opposed to both the practice and the theology of requiem masses, because this appeared to be a vain superstition opposed to the complete sufficiency of

Christ's atoning work on the cross. During this period of open debate and fierce conflict, Catholics claimed that the doctrine of purgatory was clearly attested in Sacred Scripture and by the persistent tradition of the Catholic Church.

With the advent of critical biblical scholarship, it has become common to find Catholic scholars taking a much more circumspect view of proof texts and allowing that Catholic tradition was gradually shaped under the influence of the Holy Spirit. Within this rubric, the doctrine of purgatory need not appear full blown in the first century but, from obscure beginnings, might have developed when and where social conditions and the Spirit made ready. Accordingly, J. F. X. Cevetello, after reviewing the biblical warrants for purgatory (esp. 2 Mc 12:43–46 and 1 Cor 3:13–15), concluded that "in the final analysis, the Catholic doctrine of purgatory is based on tradition, not Sacred Scriptures" (1034; also Küng 1991: 137). Even Joseph Ratzinger, in his published university lectures on eschatology, was careful to allow that "the New Testament left open the question of the 'intermediate state' between death and the general resurrection" that only became "clarified by the gradual unfolding of Christian anthropology and its relationship to Christology" (1988: 219). Ratzinger stands firmly within the bounds of critical Catholic exegesis when he acknowledges the elusiveness of the biblical evidence at the same time that he allows that "the roots of the doctrine of Purgatory, like those of the intermediate state in general, lie deeply embedded in early Judaism" (1988: 220).

The most complete scholarly account of these "roots" can be found in the masterful study of Jacques Le Goff, which is appropriately entitled *The Birth of Purgatory* (1981). Le Goff summarizes his nearly exhaustive study of the primary sources as follows:

> When, between the second and the fourth centuries, Christianity set itself to thinking about the situation in which souls find themselves between the death of the individual and the Last Judgment, and when, in the fourth century, the greatest Fathers of the Church conceived of the idea (shared, with minor differences as we shall see, by Ambrose, Jerome, and Augustine) that certain sinners might be saved, most probably by being subjected to a trial of some sort, a new belief was born, a belief that gradually matured until in the twelfth century it became the belief in Purgatory; but the place where these souls were to reside and where this trial was to take place was not yet specified. Until the end of the twelfth century the noun *purgatorium* did not exist: *the* Purgatory had not yet been born. (3)

While Le Goff reserves the "birth of purgatory" for the closing decades of the twelfth century, when sufficient "spatialization of thought" (4) existed to transform maps of this world and of the world to come, he does not thereby wish to imply that the many small steps that led up to this achievement are of no account. When it comes to the story of origins, therefore, Le Goff traces those ideas associated with purgatory within primitive expressions of Indo-European folklore, but he specifically names Clement of Alexandria (d. 215) and Origen (d. 254) as "the two Greek inventors of Purgatory" (52). These two church fathers deserve this title insofar as they were the first to introduce the notion that the eschatological fire released at the time of the final judgment would serve to punish and destroy the wicked while, as far as the elect were concerned, it would serve to educate and purify:

> Those tainted by the flesh simply "pass through" the "spirit of judgment," which lasts only an instant. Those besmirched by sin, on the other hand, remain for a more or less extended period in the "spirit of combustion." Though horribly painful, this punishment is not incompatible with Origen's optimism: the more drastic the punishment, the more certain the salvation. (Le Goff: 55)

Having briefly examined the state of the question, our attention can now be directed to the *Didache* in order to discover to what degree it anticipates the dual functioning of eschatological fire found in Clement and Origen.

An Overview of the
End-Time Scenario of the Didache

The *Didache* closes with a terse end-time scenario that seems designed to reaffirm the grave importance of being "watchful" (16:1) and being "frequently gathered together" (16:2) in expectation of the Lord's coming "in the last days" (16:3). According to the *Didache*, the end time would begin when "the false prophets and the corrupters will be multiplied" (16:3). These are the very classes of persons that the body of the *Didache* regards as endangering the way of life defined therein (11:1–12). Now, however, they will succeed: "The sheep will be turned into wolves, and the love will be turned into hate" (16:3). The religious pretensions of the "world-deceiver" will then appear cloaked "as a son of God" (16:4) and will serve to enlarge the internal breakdown within the community of saints into a worldwide lawlessness. Faced with this triumph of evil, those trusting in the way of the Lord anticipate (1) judgment by the burning-process of testing, (2) the selective resurrection of the saints, and (3) the coming of the Lord God.

PART I: THE LINGUISTIC STRUCTURE
OF *DID.* 16:5

The ending of *Did.* 16:5 declares that those having remained firm in their faith will be saved "by the curse itself (*hyp' autou tou katathematos*)." This is one of the most obscure phrases in the *Didache*. To discern its meaning, one has to examine the linguistic clues and endeavor to access what range of meanings would be plausible (even demanded) by the internal logic of the text itself.

Beginning with the word *katathema,* Nancy Pardee provides the following apt summary of the difficulties and meanings associated with this word in the context of literature from the same period:

> This rare term seems to be found exclusively within Jewish and, more often, Christian writings, but seldom before the patristic era. It appears to be a later, modified form of *anathema* a word which in secular texts almost always has the broader meaning "something devoted," but which in Jewish and early Christian material often denotes "something condemned or accursed" or, metonymically, "ban" or "curse." The denominative verb *anathematizō* is also attested, but seems to reflect solely the negative aspect of the noun ("to curse"). From its contexts it is clear that *katathema* (verb *katathematizō*) shares these adverse senses and came into use perhaps as a way of making explicit the negative meanings of *anathema.* Yet the infrequency of the word, compounded by the obscure character of the *Didache* in this passage, has made it difficult to pinpoint the precise meaning intended by the author. (private communication; see Pardee 1995: 158–59)

Katathematos is a neuter noun, and the pronoun *autou* agrees with it. Given the position of *autou,* one would normally classify it as an intensive adjective pronoun that can be rendered into English as "by agency of the curse *itself.*" On the other hand, *autou* could be construed as a masculine or neuter third person singular pronoun. As such, the phrase could be rendered as "by agency of *him/it,* the curse." In this latter case, however, one should expect to find a masculine or neuter noun to which *autou* refers. The likely candidates are eliminated since *ktisis* ("creation"), *pyrōsis* ("burning process"), and *pistis* ("faith") are feminine nouns. Given the absence of any ready referent, one is forced back to the first option wherein *autou* is regarded as an intensive adjective pronoun.

This option, however, is problematic insofar as the text does not make clear what constitutes "the curse" that will save the elect. Historically, the overwhelming judgment of scholars has been that "the curse" is a veiled reference to Christ. In a moment, the emergence of this opinion and its assessment will be undertaken. At this point, however, some of the paths not taken need to be reviewed:

1. The "world-deceiver" (16:4) could be regarded as "the curse." When the logic of the text is examined, however, one discovers that the *Didache* clearly intends to vilify the world-deceiver and thereby seemingly to exclude him from any saving activity.

2. A more proximate referent would be the "burning-process of testing" (*tēn pyrōsin tēs dokimasias*) (16:5). While the "burning-process" may be understood as "the curse," it is not evident how such burning could be the agent saving the elect. Moreover, the verb *sōzō* followed by *hypo* normally looks to a personal agent. At first glance, therefore, the "burning-process" seems to be an unlikely referent. In just a moment, however, a case will be made for this very option.

3. The internal logic of the *Didache* does not favor regarding "faith" itself as the agent of salvation. Earlier in the apocalyptic section of the *Didache*, those following the Way of Life were told that "the whole time of your faith *will not be of use to you* if in the end time you should not have been perfected" (16:2). This coincides with what novices are told at the end of their training prior to baptism, namely, that "if you are able to bear the whole yoke of the Lord, you will be perfect" (6:2). Within the internal logic of the *Didache*, therefore, one has no notion of "saving faith"; hence, this option does not offer much promise. Furthermore, the acceptance of such an option would have to explain how it is that "faith" could be understood as "cursed."

The Linguistic Parallelism of Did. 16:5

The first piece of evidence that makes it difficult to set aside the "burning-process" as being the agent of salvation in the last days is the linguistic parallelism found in *Did.* 16:5. The term *pyrōsis* ("burning-process") is a derivative of *pyr* ("fire") and is found only once in the Christian Scriptures (1 Pt 4:12). *Dokimasia* (verb *dokimazein*) has the sense of "testing," normally with the prospect of approving something, e.g., a team of oxen, a piece of gold, a true prophet (C. Brown: 3.808f.; also *Did.* 11:11). The phrase, *eis tēn pyrōsin tēs dokimasias* ("through the burning process of testing"), therefore, aptly signals that both positive and negative results could be anticipated. In *Did.* 16:5, accordingly, two divergent results are indeed forthcoming:

A. Negative results of the burning
    For whom?   "many" (unspecified; includes false
                                     prophets, the world-deceiver, etc.)
    Effect?   *"entrapped and destroyed by the burning"*
B. Positive results of the burning
    For whom?   "the faithful" (those not corrupted
                                       or deceived as explained in *Did.* 16:4)
    Effect?   *"saved by the burning = by the curse"*

The negative results are named first: "Many will be entrapped and will be destroyed [by the burning-process]." The verb form (*apollymi* being an emphatic form of *ollymi*) stresses utter destruction and leaves little room for the medieval notion of the prolonged punitive torture of the damned. In this case, the "burning-process of testing" would be the implied agent that actively entraps and destroys "the many." The general term "the many" must minimally include the false prophets, the corrupters, the world-deceiver—and all those corrupted by them. Then the positive results are named: "The ones having remained firm in their faith will be saved by the curse itself." The elect pass through the "burning-process of testing"— but with quite different results. The "burning-process" clearly has the effect of approving them and maybe even of purifying them (as will be seen shortly).

The parallel construction following upon *eis tēn pyrōsin tēs dokimasias* would seemingly imply that the "burning-process of testing" is the implied agent in both the negative and positive results. Moreover the closing phrase, *hyp' autou tou katathematos* ("by agency of the curse itself), could be applied to both results as well. Those entrapped and destroyed would certainly regard the "burning-process" as a "curse" for them since they are utterly destroyed by it. The elect, however, find that this "curse" functions as the agent of their salvation.

How does this "burning-process" function to save the faithful? Here the text offers us only clues. When these clues are carefully weighed, however, I believe that their implied sense (which will become clear later) can be deciphered against the horizon of Jewish apocalyptic metaphors. Herein "fire" represents the preferred metaphor for that terrible eschatological judgment of God. According to the *Didache*, this "fire" will be experienced in two distinct ways: (1) those following "the way of death" (as defined in *Did.* 5:1–2 and 16:3–4) will be entrapped and destroyed by God's judgment; (2) those following "the Way of Life" (as defined in *Did.* 1:2–4:14) faithfully to the end will be approved and saved by God's judgment. Moreover, since the *Didache* makes it quite clear that God is "the Father" (*Did.* 8:2; 9:2, 3; 10:2) who reveals "through his Son" (9:3; 10:2) the "life and knowledge" (9:3) for obtaining "perfection" (esp. 6:2 and 16:2), this final passage through fire might also have been understood as having the effect of burning away any impurities that remain in the faithful, so that they can assume their places among the "holy ones" (16:7).

At first glance, this meaning might seem improbable for two reasons: (1) The scholarly consensus built up over the last hundred years has favored an alternative interpretation whereby *katathema* is understood as referring to Jesus, who, because of the manner of his death, was regarded as "the accursed" (e.g., Gal 3:13). (2) If Le Goff is to be credited when he judges that the dual effects of the eschatological fire (destroying and saving/purifying) took theological shape only in the third century, then it would be hazardous to interpret the first-century *Didache* against this backdrop. The linguistic analysis proposed above, therefore, can hardly be allowed to stand as long as these two considerations impede its acceptance. Accordingly, each of these difficulties must be examined in turn.

PART II: THE OBSCURING ALTERNATIVE

In life, as in scholarship, certain habitual ways of seeing things become established and positively impede that puzzlement that is the necessary prelude to discovering alternative ways of seeing. As a consequence, once "saved by the curse itself" (*Did.* 16:5) became established as a veiled reference to Christ, it became nearly impossible to search for and to accredit alternate explanations. Hence, the emergence and acceptance of this pattern of interpretation blocked the search for alternatives.

When the first English translation of the *Didache*, prepared by Roswell D. Hitchcock and Francis Brown, was released on 20 March 1884, five thousand copies were sold on the first day. Within three years, C. Taylor and J. Rendel Harris published extended commentaries. Both were persuaded that the obscure ending of *Did.* 16:5 contained a veiled reference to Christ under the metaphor of "the cursed." Both gave great weight to the notion of paradox:

> The woman, if she continue in faith, shall be saved through that which was her curse [viz., childbearing (1 Tm 2:15)]. To Israel in the wilderness the serpent was both plague and antidote. Through death the Lord destroys him that hath the power of death. (C. Taylor: 100)

Beyond this, both authors gave more attention to Justin Martyr's reflections on Christ as "the accursed" rather than the Pauline texts. Harris was convinced that, at certain points, the very language of Justin Martyr was "sufficient to show his use of the Teaching [i.e., the *Didache*]" (68–69):

> Our suffering and crucified Christ was not cursed by the law [Torah]; but he was only demonstrating that he would save those who did not depart from their faith. (*Dial.* 111)

Justin Martyr says this in the context of his argument that the actions of Joshua foreshadowed those of Jesus: Joshua held out the hands of Moses so as to secure victory over the enemies of Israel; Jesus (whose name is equivalent to "Joshua" in Hebrew) held out his hands so as to secure victory over death and sin. Harris, presuming that the *Didache* was known and cited by Justin Martyr, was prompted to find in Justin what he regarded as "a popular interpretation of the sentence [*Did.* 16:5] in the Teaching" (69).

On German soil, Harnack provided the first German translation and commentaries on the *Didache* (1884, 1886). As in the case of the early English-language commentaries, Harnack recognized that those who "*gerettet werden von dem Verfluchten selbst*" ("would be saved by the damned-one himself")(*Did.* 16:5) could only be understood as referring to Jesus Christ as "the one cursed" (1886: 62). Harnack, however, made no reference to Justin Martyr but took his departure from 1 Cor 12:3, which he regarded as early testimony that unbelieving Jews were already saying, *anathema Iēsous* ("a curse [is] Jesus"). To this he added various other texts (Pliny, *Letter to Trajan* 10.96; *Martyrdom of Polycarp* 9.3, etc.) that supported the notion that Christ was regarded as "*katathema = anathema*" (1886: 62) prior to the period 120–165 C.E., wherein Harnack presupposed that the *Didache* originated.

Franz Xavier Funk, in 1887, produced a Latin translation and commentary in which he tried to revive the original suggestion of Bryennios (dismissed by Harnack) that a scribal error caused *hyp'* instead of the intended *an'* to be written (1887: 48). Accordingly, he proposed that the troublesome text should be read as "*salvabuntur ex maledicto ipso*" ("they will be saved *from* the curse itself") where "the curse," Funk surmised, referred either to the Anti-Christ himself or to the curse that proceeded from the Anti-Christ. This alternative rendering of the text, however, gained no substantial hearing within German scholarship, and the most recent German commentaries produced by Wengst (1984: 99), Schöllgen (1991: 78–79), and Niederwimmer (1998: 221–22) all agree in passing over Funk in silence and upholding the position originally taken by Harnack a hundred years ago.

French scholarship took a parallel course. Paul Sabatier produced the first translation and commentary of the *Didache* in 1885. Sabatier was the first scholar to suggest that the *Didache* was composed as early as the mid-first century "before the missionary journeys of Paul" (165). Given this early dating, Sabatier therefore surmised that the *Didache* had no reliance on any written Gospel but made use of "the precepts of the Gospel circulating mouth to mouth" (152). Sabatier, influenced by this notion of the literary independence of the *Didache*, was inclined to follow neither Harnack nor Harris. He translated the troublesome text of *Did.* 16:5 as "*sauvé de cette malédiction*" ("saved from this curse" [66]) and wanted his readers to understand that the *Didache* assured the faithful that the world would be purged of evil by a supreme test that they would survive. A. Jacquier, writing six years later, notes the lack of agreement on this passage and simply presents the Sabatier/Funk position alongside the Harnack/Harris position (1891: 144–45). Since his own translation reads "*par l'athème lui-même*" ("by the anathema itself"), however, one can surmise that he was avoiding Sabatier's position. Recent French scholars such as Giet (1970: 252) and Rordorf (1978a: 198) have, in contrast, entirely returned to the mainstream tradition of finding in *Did.* 16:5 an implicit reference to the saving activity of Christ.

Deficiencies of the Prevailing Opinion

Faced with this nearly unanimous judgment, no place can be made for entertaining an alternative explanation as long as the intellectual satisfaction associated with the present consensus is nearly overwhelming. Our attention, therefore, must turn to deficiencies in this prevailing opinion. Three deficiencies can be discerned:

1. First, an interpretation based on an extraneous text is always hazardous unless there is sufficient evidence that the *Didache* was directly or indirectly influenced by such a text. In particular, resolving the obscure meaning of *Did.* 16:5 by an appeal to Paul (e.g., Gal 3:13; 1 Cor 12:3) is considerably weakened when one notes that the *Didache* exhibits no dependence on Pauline theology or Pauline letters. While space limitations do not allow a review of the arguments on both sides of this weighty issue, it does appear to me that the strongest argument against any Pauline influence is the fact that the *Didache* betrays none of the major themes evident in the Pauline letters. This will be considered shortly.

Niederwimmer brings to mind the dangers of making extraneous appeals, noting that the term *katathema* ("curse") appears in a well-known apocalypse, namely, Rv 22:3 (1998: 221). In this context, however, it is the leaves of the "tree of life" that will be used "for the healing of the nations" (22:2) while "every curse (*katathema*) will be no longer" (22:3 lit.). Needless to say, no one has suggested that "the curse" here is a veiled reference to the crucified Christ.

2. Even when direct or indirect textual dependence is not maintained, caution must be exercised against presuming that any given soteriological schema was so universally accepted as to offer a secure means for the interpretation of an obscure passage in the *Didache*. Early Christianity was theologically and organizationally diverse; hence, it seems hazardous for Rordorf, for example, to allow for the absence of any textual dependence on Paul, but then to turn around and allow that early texts such as Gal 3:13 and 1 Cor 12:3 serve to demonstrate that "the notion of curse was there-

fore so widely dispersed in the early church that one will not be surprised that the noun *katathema* might here designate Christ-himself" (1978a: 198). Rordorf was admittedly more tentative than his predecessors, yet in the end, he seems to presume too much.

It is a momentous jump, for instance, from the position that Jesus, because of his execution as a criminal, was considered "cursed" (according to Dt 21:23) to the position that "Christ redeemed us from the curse of the law [Torah], having become a curse for us" (Gal 3:13). This theological jump was not made everywhere, and modern scholarship makes it clear that the canonical Gospels and the non-Pauline letters do not understand the death of Christ in this mode even though they were written decades after Paul's letters. The earlier position (based on Dt 21:23), meanwhile, does not provide a sufficient interpretation of the text, since it fails to account for how or why Jesus, the one who suffered a "cursed" death on the cross, could or should have a saving efficacy at the time of the final judgment. Hence, when *Did.* 16:5 is read as referring to Jesus in this context, it must necessarily point toward some soteriological perspective based on Jesus' death. But which? For there are many. And why this one and not another? In this, of course, the internal evidence of the *Didache* must be given first place of importance, thereby leading to the last principle.

3. The interpretation of a troublesome text must first and foremost be negotiated by consulting the internal evidence of the text itself. When this is done, three things become evident:

(a) The text suggests that both the damned and the elect pass through the same "burning process of testing" (*Did.* 16:5). When "saved by the curse itself" is unraveled as pointing to Jesus, it is puzzling that *no explanation is forthcoming as to how or why the elect* are made to pass through "the burning process of testing." My suspicion is that most scholars have read the text as suggesting that "the burning process of testing" applies *only* to those doomed to destruction, while the elect are saved (i.e., dispensed) from this testing by the crucified Christ. This solution overlooks the linguistic clues examined above wherein *dokimasia* suggests "testing" with the prospect of approving, and the parallel construction suggests that the burning-process has both negative and positive results.

(b) If Christ is presumed to be the referent for "the accursed" (*Did.* 16:5), then it must be allowed that this saving activity is specifically designated as happening "in the last days" (16:3) and has little to do with freedom "from the curse of the law" (Gal 3:13) at the present time, as Paul would have it.

(c) Finally, when the *Didache* is read with integrity and allowed to speak for itself, one discovers that a soteriology based on the cross or on Christ as "accursed" is seemingly absent from the entire theological horizon of the *Didache*. Issues regarding the confession of transgressions (4:14; 14:1) and the forgiveness of sins (4:6; 8:2) are amply addressed and dealt with, but entirely outside the context of any appeal to the death of Jesus or his status as "accursed." Even the eucharistic prayers (*Did.* 9–10) have their own internal logic and symbolism without in the slightest way making any Pauline appeal to "covenant," "remembrance," or "the Lord's death" (1 Cor 11:25f.).

In sum, the theological integrity of the *Didache* inclines one to assign no special significance to the cross or to the crucifixion as a way of resolving any significant issue within the *Didache*. It remains problematic, therefore, to break the silence of the *Didache* on this score by supposing that a dubious reference in one of its closing lines can or ought to be clarified by such an appeal. One risks projecting an idea foreign to the original mindset of the author.

Part III: Exploring the Metaphor of Fire

Now that certain difficulties with the prevailing tradition of interpretation have been presented, the time is ripe to begin to reconstruct the Jewish horizon of understanding regarding eschatological fire. The image of fire is frequently used in both Testaments to evoke God's terrifying and mysterious presence (*TDNT* 6:928–53). More especially, fire functions as the preferred metaphor for evoking the fearsome and consuming judgment of the Lord.

> Certain formal expressions are used for Yahweh's intervention in judgment: "There went out fire from Yahweh" (Lv 10:2), "there came down fire from heaven" (2 Kgs 1:10), "the fire of Yahweh burnt among them" (Nm 11:1). In the prophets fire is one of the most common means of divine judgment. It smites both the vainglorious enemies of Israel (Am 1:4, 7, 10, 12, 14; 2:2; Jer 43:12; Na 3:13 etc.) and also the disobedient people of Israel itself (Am 2:5; Hos 8:14; Jer 11:16; 17:27; 21:14; 22:7; Ez 15:7; 16:41; 24:9 etc.). (*TDNT* 6:935).

Dual Function of Fire in the Prophetic Literature

In the Jewish prophetic tradition, alongside the metaphor of destructive fire as portraying God's judgment, one also finds intimations of those who pass through or near this fire unharmed. The earliest instance of this appears to be in Isaiah 33. In this apocalypse, we first see the Lord rising up and taking the field in response to the earlier (Is 33:2) prayer of those inhabitants of Jerusalem who find themselves completely surrounded by their enemy. As God's terrible judgment and fire blaze forth and consume the enemy "like thorns . . . burnt in the fire" (Is 33:12), the "sinners in Zion" witness this horrendous spectacle and they themselves begin to tremble because they are aware that they too deserve the fiery wrath of their God who is coming to dwell among them as fire (cf. Dt 4:24; 9:3; Ps 50:3; Ex 19:18; 1 Kgs 19:12). To their near-despairing question, "Which of us can live with this devouring fire?" (Is 33:14) some basis for hope is given: those who follow the torah (as defined by Is 33:15–16) will not be consumed by God's judgment. Such righteous ones "can exist in everlasting flames" (Is 33:14).

In this apocalyptic scenario, nothing yet appears regarding the approving or purifying effect of fire. Nonetheless, what one does find is the certainty that when the Lord comes both his enemies and friends (the righteous in Zion) will experience him as a blazing fire. One also finds anticipated certain dual effects of the Lord's fiery presence: (1) the enemies are utterly destroyed but (2) the righteous appear to be able to survive safely therein. Earlier in Isaiah, there was a passing reference to the Lord promising to "smelt away your [Zion's] dross in the furnace" (Is 1:25), but this theme does not seem to invade the apocalyptic of Is 33. One has to wait for the subsequent prophetic writing of Ezekiel and Malachi for a full development of this theme of purifying fire.

According to Ezekiel, Yahweh will collect his people inside Jerusalem and judge them:

> As men gather silver and bronze and iron and lead and tin into a furnace, to blow the fire upon it in order to melt it; so I will gather you in my anger and in my wrath. (Ez 22:20)

The process here is commonly known as "smelting"—ore-bearing rocks are pulverized and then fired in a furnace so as to allow the pure metal to be melted and thereby separated out from the rocks to which it adheres. Later one finds a variant image wherein a cooking pot is heated red-hot on the coals "that its filthiness may be melted in it, its rust consumed" (Ez 24:11). This image of God's judgment as the process whereby metals are purified by melting them down in a furnace (also Is 1:25–26; Jer 6:29; Zec 13:9; Mal 3:2–3; Sir 2:5; Prv 17:3) provides an opening in the direction of allowing that God's elect will be purified and saved (rather than destroyed) when they pass through the fiery judgment of his wrath.

Malachi takes these same images and refines them so as to present the clearest prophetic images of the dual functioning of fire within an apocalyptic scenario. "The day of his coming," we are told, will be like a "refiner's fire," and "he will purify the sons of Levi and refine them like gold and silver" (Mal 3:2–3). In contrast, when it comes to "the arrogant and all evildoers" among God's people, "the day that comes shall burn them up" (4:1) like straw in an oven. Hence, the terrifying fire of the final judgment will serve to purify some of God's people and to consume others. At this point the duality of the burning process is complete and the climate is set for a new understanding of *Did.* 16:5.

Dual Function of Fire
in Early Christian Literature

The Christian Scriptures provide nearly fifty instances of eschatological fire. Fire, in these contexts, functions predominantly to destroy. In two places, however, one finds obscure texts suggesting that fire might play a role in saving the elect: 1 Cor 3:13–15 and 1 Pt 1:5–7; 4:12–13:

1. The first text clearly speaks of the final judgment as "the fire which will test what sort of work each one has done" (1 Cor 3:13). Even in the case of those whose works are destroyed by this fire, however, it would seem that they would be capable of being personally saved "but only as through fire (*hōs dia pyros*)" (1 Cor 3:15). One might be tempted to interpret this as an allusion to the approving and purifying functions of the eschatological fire; however, lacking further particulars, Paul's precise meaning here must remain obscure (Conzelmann: 76–77; Fee: 144; Ratzinger 1988: 229).

2. The texts from 1 Peter are even more obscure and seemingly imply that "the burning-process for your testing" (1 Pt 4:12) takes place prior to the return of Christ and is to be identified with "the many kinds of trials you suffer" (1 Pt 1:6) and with being "reproached for the name of Christ" (1 Pt 4:14) (Arichea: 142–47; Best: 162–63). How this present testing by fire is related to the eschatological testing is unclear. Furthermore, since "the burning-process for your testing" (1 Pt 4:12) is seemingly provoked by the enemies of Christ, this cannot be equated with the prophetic images considered above or with "the burning process of testing" in the *Didache*, which has, as its first function, to halt the reign of evil under the direction of the "world-deceiver" (*Did.* 16:4).

In the Christian apocalyptic literature of the second century, the eschatological fire was sometimes portrayed as having a dual function. Two instances will be considered:

1. The *Shepherd of Hermas* (variously dated from the late first to mid-second century) concerns itself with the necessity of repentance for those saints who have sinned following baptism. To effect this repentance, God, at one point, is presented as sending "the angel of punishment" to seek out backsliders so as to punish them with "various tortures belonging to the present life" (Hermas *Sim.* 6.3). Those who submit to this present purification appear to be promised a certain immunity from the "impending

tribulation" (Hermas *Vis.* 4.2). This end-time tribulation is imaged as an attack of a great beast that has four colors on its head: "[first it was] black, then fiery and blood-red, then gold, then white" (*Vis.* 4.1.10).

The significance of these successive colors is explained as defining four stages or elements within the end-time scenario:

[1] The black is this world in which you dwell;
[2] (and) the fiery and blood-red [is next]
    because it is necessary that this world
    perish by blood and fire (*pyros*);
[3] (and) the golden part [are then] you
    who have escaped from this [perishing] world;
        for just as gold is tested (*dokimazetai*)
        through fire and becomes of good use,
    thus you also are being tested in yourselves.
Now the ones having remained [firm] (*meinantes*)
and having passed through the fire (*pyrōthentes*)
    will be purified by it (*hyp' autou katharisthēsesthe*).
Just as gold casts off its dross,
    thus [by this means]
    (a) you will cast off all sorrow and tribulation
    (b) and you will be purified (*katharisthēsesthe*)
    (c) and shall be useful for the building of the tower
    [which is a symbol for the perfected church].
[4] (And) the white portion is the coming age,
    in which the chosen of God will dwell,
    because the ones having been chosen by God
        will be spotless and pure (*katharoi*)
        in everlasting life. (Hermas *Vis.* 4.3.2–5)

What this symbolic language makes clear is that the elect will become spotless and pure only by having passed through the purifying fire—the same fire, it would appear, that has the effect of destroying this world. What is clear from both the larger context (esp. *Vis.* 4.1.8) and from this explanation is that Christians are encouraged to surrender themselves to the impending tribulation and to the purifying fire. It is difficult to decide, however, whether this therapeutic fire is associated with the end-time tribulation that is already begun or whether this fire is of a decidedly different and entirely future order. In any case, Hermas provides a clear instance of apocalyptic imagery wherein fire functions with a dual purpose: (1) the "black" world is destroyed while (2) those "who remain steadfast . . . pass through the fire" in order to be "purified by it" (*Vis.* 4.3.4).

2. The Christian *Sibyllines* (second century) are preoccupied with pre-

senting sobering visions of the end times as a stimulus to repentance and perseverance. In the apocalyptic scenario of book 2, the angels gather all mortals before God's judgment seat (2.237). Meanwhile, Christ returns on a cloud "with his blameless angels" (2.242) to judge with the Almighty. The judgment is tersely described as follows:

> And then shall all pass through the burning river
> And unquenchable flame; and the righteous
> Shall all be saved, but the impious shall perish. (2.252–54)

This text makes clear that the same fire is experienced by both the impious and the righteous but with two diametrically opposed results. The novelty introduced in the *Sibyllines* consists in having angels of the Lord functioning within the fire in two distinct ways: (1) the impious are bound and scourged by angels, while (2) those "who took thought for justice and noble works" (2.313) are rescued by angels and brought to the promised land. The following texts illustrate this:

> The angels of the immortal, everlasting God
> Shall punish fearfully with flaming whips,
> Binding them [the impious] tightly about with fiery chains.
>   (2.286–89)

> Angels shall bear them [the righteous] through the burning
>   river
> And bring them to light and to a carefree life,
> Where runs the immortal path of [our] great God. (2.315–17)

The *Sibyllines* purport to portray a God who says, "I bring all persons to proof by fire" (8.411), yet in practice, fire functions here quite differently than it did in Hermas: (a) Relative to the enemies of God, the metaphor of fire is here seen to be moving away from a destroying to a punishing function; and (b) relative to the elect, rather than being purified by the fire, now they are seemingly only rescued from it. This becomes more evident when the text notes that "to the pious, when they ask eternal God, he will grant them to save men out of the devouring fire and from everlasting torments" (2.331–33). Thus, the *Sibyllines*, while they portray a final judgment in which both the righteous and the impious pass through fire, the saving power of the fire is lost sight of in favor of emphasizing the power of fire to torment the wicked.

All of this indicates that the dual functioning of the eschatological fire was the preferred metaphor for God's final judgment long before Clement of Alexandria and Origen gave it theological precision within the Christian message (see #15a). In Hermas, more importantly, one finds the clearest instance of continuity with the purifying eschatological fire found in the prophetic literature. Paradoxically, one also finds herein the closest parallel to the troublesome text of *Did.* 16:5b, including a specific reference to "the ones having remained firm" (*hoi meinantes* instead of *hypomeinantes*) as looking forward to being purified *hyp' antou* ("by it [the fire]"). The agent of purification (which is a metaphor for salvation) here is clearly the fire (*pyr*). While it cannot be shown that this is the meaning intended by *Did.* 16:5b, Hermas does at least testify that the eschatological fire could be understood in some circles as destroying or as purifying.

The Christian *Sibyllines,* on the other hand, illustrate that the theme of a universal passing through fire with dualistic effects could be used in a setting in which the purifying effect of fire was entirely displaced by the punitive effect (see #15b). The fact that *Did.* 16:5 allows for the "destruction" of the unjust would seemingly indicate that the *Didache* did not follow that route. Nonetheless, the *Sibyllines* do show that alternate schemes were being worked out whereby angels were assigned the role of saving the elect as they pass through the river of fire.

#15b Purifying Fire According to Lactantius

Lucius Lactantius, following his conversion to Christianity in 300 C.E., wrote the *Divine Institutes* for the purpose of explaining the merits of his new way of life. The seventh book of this treatise is devoted to an exposition of the end time. Herein, the *Sibylline Oracles* are approvingly cited 50 percent more frequently than the Hebrew Scriptures (McGinn: 22). Overall, this treatise exhibits interesting parallels with the *Didache.*

According to Lactantius, the "Great King" will arrive from heaven accompanied by angels and preceded by an "inextinguishable fire" (7.17). This fire, like that of the *Didache*, will have a dual function: to torment the wicked and to prove the elect. In relating both functions, Lactantius offers these details:

1. "The divine fire will both burn and renew the wicked by one and the same force and power" (7.21). Those who have sinned in their bodies, therefore, will be horribly burnt by the fire: "It will burn and cause pain with no loss to the bodies that are being restored" (7.21)—thereby ensuring that there will be no end to their torments.

2. For the elect, their worth will be proved by this same fire:

When God has judged the just he will also prove them with fire.
[a] Those whose sins have greater weight or number shall be

scorched with fire and burnt; [b] those who have been dyed in the fullness of justice and the maturity of virtue [however] will not feel the flame, because they will have something divine in them that will repel and reject it. Such is the power of innocence that the fire will leave it unharmed because God has given this fire the ability to burn the wicked but to spare the just. (7.21)

Thus Lactantius presents the eschatological fire as having a dual function somewhat parallel to that of the *Didache*. While the just are proven by fire, however, Lactantius does not expressly say that they will be purified or saved by the burning-process. Rather, the elect pass through the fire unharmed thereby proving their worth, for their virtue repels and rejects the flame. The wicked, by contrast, are scorched and burnt by this same fire (see #15a).

According to Lactantius, the arrival of the "Great King" will be preceded by the appearance of "a king born of an evil spirit" (7.17) who will deceive many:

He will set himself up and call himself God and will command that he be worshipped as the son of God. He will be given the power to do signs and wonders. . . . By these miracles he will even attract many of the wise to himself. Then he will try to destroy the temple of God and will persecute the just people; there will be affliction and sorrow such as has never been from the beginning of the world. (7.17)

The linguistic development here is remarkably parallel to what one finds in *Did.* 16:4b, even though the details vary throughout.

Following the testing by fire, Lactantius advocated a selective resurrection: "Those whose sins and crimes are found out will not rise [from the dead] but will be buried with the wicked" (7.21). Unlike the *Didache*, however, this resurrection is followed by the thousand-year reign of Christ (7.24). At the end of these thousand years, "the final wrath of God [in the form of fire] will come upon the nations" (7.26) and they shall be utterly destroyed. Then the resurrection of the wicked will take place: "Because of their sins, the whole host of the wicked will be burned by eternal fire . . ." (7.26). Of these latter things, the *Didache* is entirely silent.

In one last arena, Lactantius finds a resonance with the *Didache*, namely, in his presentation of Jesus as the servant of the Father revealing "the path of justice" (7:27). At the end of his treatise, Lactantius writes as follows:

All ought to make an effort either to put themselves on the right path as quickly as possible. . . . Our Father and Lord, who founded heaven and made it firm . . . , and who created whatever exists in this world from nothing, saw the errors of men and sent a leader to open up for us a path of justice. Let us all follow him and pay heed to him. . . . He not only showed the way, but he also walked it before us so that no one would shrink from the path of virtue because of its difficulty. Let us abandon, if possible, the path of destruction and fraud in which death lies hidden. . . . (7.27)

Thus, Lactantius abandons the contrast between true and false religion at the end of his treatise and reverts back to an older Hebraic notion of distinguishing two paths. Readers are urged to assiduously place themselves on the path of truth, of justice, and of virtue which Jesus revealed. The path of destruction, of fraud, of death is, accordingly, to be avoided.

In the end, the reader can glimpse that the treatise of Lactantius retains elements of the tradition that found expression in the *Didache*. The possibility is then open that both works were influenced by the *Sibylline Oracles*. Further study is merited on this point. For the moment, however, it suffices to note that Lactantius clearly developed a variant notion of the dual process of testing by fire so as to portray the final judgment. The *Didache* and the *Divine Institutes* thus share parallel metaphors for describing the eschatological fire that will proceed the Lord when he comes.

Whether the Didache *Had a Lost Ending*

One final difficulty has to be treated. According to the end-time scenario of the *Didache*, the destruction of the lawless, the purification of the faithful, and the selective resurrection of the just take place prior to the Lord's coming. Robert Kraft reflected upon this as follows:

> In fact, in may be that 16:5 is intended as a reference to the judgment taking place *before* the Lord's return (but then, what does "the world" mean in 16:8a?), and that the Didache should end as in manuscript H, without further reference to judgment. The resurrection of 16:6–7, in any case, is only for "the saints," as a reward for endurance and a sign of triumph. (1965b: 176)

Kraft might also have noted that the resurrection of the saints also represents an effective presence of the Lord prior to his triumphal coming atop the clouds. This is very normal in apocalyptic literature. In the Book of Revelation, for instance, Satan's armies are storming the camp of the saints and then "fire came down from heaven and consumed them" (Rv 20:9). This metaphor represents God's judgment upon the living *even before his arrival*. In the next moment, the dead are raised, and "the dead are judged according to their works, as recorded in the books [of God's judgment]" (Rv 20:12). Here, again, God's activity is represented *even before his final arrival*. Then, and only then, does one have the triumphal advent of "the new Jerusalem coming down out of heaven from God, prepared as a bride adorned for her husband" (Rv 21:10). In this city, God dwells, and "he will wipe every tear from their eyes" (Rv 21:4). Thus the Book of Revelation offers this progression: (a) fiery judgment of the living, (b) resurrection and judgment of the dead, (c) triumphal descent of the new Jerusalem where God dwells among his people.

The unfolding of events in the *Didache* follows a parallel track: (a) fiery judgment of the living—some utterly destroyed, some purified (16:5); (b) resurrection of the holy ones only (*Did.* 16:7), (c) triumphal descent of the Lord God (16:8). The *Didache* envisions only the selective resurrection of the holy ones; hence, no explicit judgment is required at this phase since the principal of selection already implies God's judgment. In the final phase, God alone comes in triumph—Jerusalem is deliberately left out (see ch. 14 above). The "holy ones" form his entourage. The faithful, meanwhile, have already been gathered by the unfurling banner (Draper 1993: 1–21) and the sound of the trumpet (as also in 1 Thes 4:16; 1 Cor 15:52; Rv 8:6, 7, 8 10, 12, 13; 10:7; 11:15) so as to receive him and enter into his kingdom. Thus, judgment is neither needed nor implied at this point.

If one consults Zec 14, one can pick out the same development. The decisive battle and destruction of the wicked take place prior to Zec 14:5b. Immediately thereafter the perfection of the everlasting kingdom of the Lord is described (Zec 14:6–11). The "coming" heralded in Zec 14:5, therefore, is the coming in triumph: "And the Lord will become king over all the earth" (Zec 14:9). Here, again, therefore, the final coming is triumphant. The destruction by fire (Zec 12:6) and the purification by fire (Zec 13:9) took place earlier. Thus, in this and in other instances, judgment is neither needed nor implied at the time of the Lord's triumphal arrival from heaven.

#15C RESURRECTION AND ZECHARIAH 14:5

Jonathan Draper prepared an article in 1997 that supports the thesis that the fire in *Did.* 16:5 has a dual function and that "saved by the curse itself" (*Did.* 16b) refers to this fire "so that what was a curse to the wicked was understood as salvific for the righteous" (1997a: 155). In the course of the article, Draper gives special attention to Zec 14:5:

The use of Zechariah 14:5 as a proof text for the limited resurrection of the righteous in the *Didache*, without further explanation, is interesting. It is not an obvious choice of proof text,
however, and this raises the question as to whether such an interpretation was *sui generis* or whether it was commonly understood. . . . This paper will explore remnants of such an
interpretation in the New Testament, Patristic and Rabbinic exegesis to see whether the citation in the *Didache* represents a deep
rooted pattern of exegesis or an eccentric aberration. (1997a:
160)

In the rabbinic material, Draper finds only three uses of Zec 14:5, all in
the *Midrash Rabbah*. In these instances, the "holy ones" refers to those
prophets whose names or whose words have been lost (*Ru* 5; *Eccl* 1.11.1).
Zec 14:5 is used to sustain the assurance that they and their words will be
restored when the Lord comes. Draper makes use of a study by J. S. Pobee
to make the point that prophets were initially seen as "prototype martyrs"
and then later "martyrdom became a *sine qua non* of the prophetic vocation and, therefore, every prophet was regarded as having undergone a
martyr's death" (Pobee: 28). From this, Draper goes on to conclude that
Zec 14:5 was understood by the rabbis "as a proof-text for the resurrection of the martyrs" (1997a: 164) and that, in the *Midrash Rabbah*, this
text was used to argue that those prophets whose names or whose words
have been lost will be restored.

Draper has a very pointed agenda in his interpretation of the *Didache* in
discovering that "holy ones" refers to "the martyrs":

We may conclude this brief survey of interpretations of Zechariah
14:5 in Rabbinic and Christian exegesis by suggesting that it was
something of a proof text for the theology of martyrdom. . . . It
is only those who endure [the fiery ordeal of *Did.* 16:5a], even
to the point of martyrdom, who will experience the resurrection.
So the nature of "salvation by the curse itself" is highlighted by
a promise and a warning. (1997a: 178)

Draper, as usual, brings a fresh interpretation to the *Didache*. At first
glace, however, it would seem unusual that a cult of martyrdom would
show itself in the final lines of the *Didache* when there is no hint of this earlier. Moreover, what would one say of those who were perfected in the Way
of Life and died a peaceful death in the arms of those who loved them?
Must resurrection be denied them because they did not have the opportunity to prove themselves by passing through the fiery ordeal of the end
time?

Draper, it seems to me, takes a wrong turn when he interprets the rabbinic use of Zec 14:5. The rabbis did not intend that the "holy ones" referred only to the prophets (or, as Draper argues, to the martyred prophets). Here is the first text that Draper examines which makes reference to "the brotherhood of prophets":

> The verse says "prophets" which signifies a minimum number of two. For what reasons were their prophecies not made public? [Response:] Because they had no permanent value for future generations. Deduce from this that a prophecy of which there is no need for [future] generations is not published. But in the time to come the Holy One, blessed be he, will come and bring them with him and their prophecies will be published. That is the meaning of, *And the Lord my God shall come, and all the holy ones with you* (Zec 14:5). (*Midrash Rabbah, Ruth* 5)

The text hovers around the issue of the unnamed and unpublished prophets named in 2 Kgs 2:3. The commentary makes the point that they have been silently passed over "because they had no permanent value." In the world to come, however, the Lord will come and "bring them with him and their prophecies will be published." How can this be shown? Zec 14:5 says "all the holy ones" will come with him.

The use of Zec 14:5 by the rabbis has nothing to do with defining the "holy ones" as the prophets or with limiting the resurrection of the dead to the martyred prophets, as Draper suggests. Zec 14:5 is seized upon because it makes the point that "all the holy ones" will accompany the Lord and that this will include the unnamed and unknown prophets. This same understanding can be applied to the other texts that Draper finds as well. Draper even cites a reconstruction of Hippolytus that makes this point:

> Zechariah teaches that the righteous will be raised first: "The Lord will come and all the saints with him" (Zec 14:5). . . . And finally John has said that the martyrs will rise first on the glorious day. (1997a: 174f.)

Even supposing that Draper identified a tradition in which Zec 14:5 was used to support the selective resurrection of martyrs, it would also have to be shown that the framers of the *Didache* embraced this tradition. Consider two points. If *Did.* 16:7 puts forward "the theology of martyrdom" as Draper suggests, then it becomes very puzzling why the framers of the *Didache* would have emphasized how "they [Christians] will hate each other and they will persecute each other" (16:4) and passed over in silence persecution of the saints by the "world-deceiver" (16:4b). Second, if a "theology of martyrdom" was a requirement for salvation and/or resurrection, then it remains puzzling why the framers of the *Didache* would have made this point explicitly, for example, by saying something like the following: "The whole time of your faith will not be of use to you if in the last time you should not have suffered and died for your faith." All in all, therefore, the theology of martyrdom does not show up in the *Didache*, and this considerably weakens Draper's thesis.

Draper also has two additional soft spots regarding the last judgment:

1. At the beginning of his article, Draper presented his conviction that "the fire of testing" (16:5) signals that "what was a curse to the wicked was understood as salvific for the righteous" (1997a: 155):

> The fire would be purgative as in Malachi 3:2–4 and as in a number of Christian texts, especially Hermas, *Visions* 4.3, 4 and 1 Peter 4:12. . . . Aaron Milavec has made a strong case for the same understanding. (1997a: 156)

Right at this point a problem results. Draper never makes clear who is responsible for the "fire" in *Did.* 16:5. If "the fire of testing" is a metaphor for the tribulations caused by the "world-deceiver" or by evil persons in general, then it remains puzzling how this would be "a curse to the wicked." If "the fire of testing" is the metaphor for God's judgment, as I contend, then what Draper cites of my work would seem vindicated:

> According to the *Didache*, this "fire" will be experienced in two distinct ways: 1) those who follow the Way of Death (as defined in 5:1–2 and 16:3–4) will be entrapped and destroyed by God's judgment; and 2) those who follow the Way of Life (as defined in 1:2–4:14) faithfully to the end will be approved and saved by God's judgment. (Milavec 1995b: 174)

2. Once the dual effects of the burning-process are accepted, then it seems redundant for Draper to suggest that the coming of the Lord in *Did.* 16:8 is for judgment. Draper explains himself saying that "it is not judgment of the resurrected departed . . . who have already been proved by their suffering, perseverance and/or martyrdom . . . " or "[judgment of] the righteous living who are proved by their endurance in the suffering"; rather, "the judgment will be only of the living wicked, who will be rooted out and destroyed without a remnant or a trace" (1997a: 178).

Here, again, it is clear that Draper cites my work but overlooks what I had to say. If "those who follow the Way of Death . . . will be entrapped and destroyed by God's judgment" (cited above), then it follows that, when the Lord comes there will be no "living wicked" for the Lord to judge. The logic of the *Didache*'s end-time scenario does not support or need the additional judgment as Draper contends.

In the end, it seems clear that Draper has established that the rabbis used Zec 14:5 to develop a theology of the resurrection of the unknown prophets and martyrs. What is not evident, however, is that this late rabbinic tradition was embraced by the framers of the *Didache*. In fact, when the clues of the text are carefully examined, they point elsewhere.

Most scholars, however, have held out for the final judgment taking place after *Did.* 16:8 on the basis of the supposed "lost ending" of the *Didache* (e.g., Wengst 1984: 20, 90). The original Bryennios manuscript, which was copied by a scribe in 1056 C.E., has a space of seven blank lines (2.5 inches) at the end of 16:8. In no other text that he copied did the scribe leave such a large space at the end. On the other hand, the next leaf of velum begins the first of thirteen Ignatian epistles. It is possible, consequently, that the scribe preferred to start the Ignatian letters on a fresh page. The same can be said to hold true for the second volume of Pseudo-Chrysostom which also begins at the top of a fresh page (van de Sandt: 22). On the other hand, given the fact that the scribe did not generally leave spaces before beginning other works, it could be surmised that the end of the scroll that he was copying had broken off or had been effaced; hence, the space could be a clue to a "lost ending."

We do possess two later editions of the *Didache* that have longer endings: the Gregorian version (available only in rough translation and of doubtful authenticity) and the *Apostolic Constitutions*. The seventh book of the *Apostolic Constitutions* is especially valuable because it represents a moderately edited version of the *Didache* included in a larger church manual compiled around 380 C.E. The longer ending found therein has been widely accepted as providing "a very loose reproduction" (Niederwimmer 1998: 227) of the "lost ending" of the *Didache*. The *Apostolic Constitutions* reads as follows:

> Then the Lord and the holy ones will come with him
> in a commotion above the clouds with his force of angels
> [he being] on the throne of the kingdom
>   [a] to judge the world-deceiver, [the] devil,
>   [b] and to repay each one according to his deed.
> Then, on the one hand, the evil ones will go into eternal
>   punishment,
> but, on the other hand, the holy ones will go into eternal life
>   inheriting those things which eye did not see
>   and ear did not hear. . . . (7.32.4)

There are three reasons why this could not represent the "lost ending" of the *Didache*. These are as follows:

1. The *Apostolic Constitutions* has the Lord coming to judge the world-deceiver at this point precisely because the entire section respecting "the burning-process of testing" (namely, *Did.* 16:5) has been dropped. Since the power of the world-deceiver is unchecked at the time of the Lord's coming, it is imperative that he come "with his force of angels" to check these hostile powers. Moreover, at this point, the world-deceiver is identified as "the devil"—something that runs counter to the earlier orientation of the *Didache* (Rordorf 1998: 244).

2. The *Apostolic Constitutions* has the Lord repaying "each one according to his deed" at this point because, unlike the case of the *Didache*, both the good and the wicked are raised from the dead (7.32.3). When the selective resurrection is removed, then it follows that judgment is necessary in order to reward or punish those raised to life. Here, again, therefore, the *Apostolic Constitutions* requires a judgment after the Lord's coming, whereas the *Didache* does not.

3. The *Apostolic Constitutions* supports an anthropology in which "eternal punishment" is the fate of the unrighteous. In contrast, for the *Didache*, the world-deceiver and his lot are utterly destroyed—not punished. As for the wicked who are dead, the *Didache*, taking a consistent position, prefers to envision them as forever dead—not forever punished. Death, therefore, is the fate of the wicked; life in the kingdom is the fate of the saints.

In sum, the "lost ending" of the *Didache*, if indeed there was ever any "lost ending," would thus certainly not be the longer ending found in the *Apostolic Constitutions*.

#15D EXAMINING RORDORF'S RECONSTRUCTION OF THE "LOST ENDING"

Rordorf's colleague André Tuilier favored using the *Apostolic Constitutions* to gain "an idea of the conclusion of the *Didache*" (Rordorf 1978a: 199 n. 3). In his revised edition, however, Rordorf, for multiple reasons, found this unsatisfactory (Rordorf 1998: 243). Absolutely convinced, nonetheless, that there was a "lost ending," Rordorf conjectured that it would be "relatively easy to reconstitute" (ibid.) since we can rely on the Matthean tradition used by the Didachist, namely, Mt 24:30–31.

Earlier in this volume, the independence of *Did.* 16 from Mt 24 was established. As a result, Rordorf's initial assumption is dubious (see ch. 11 above). Without raising this issue here, however, it can still be demonstrated that Mt 24:30–31 does not provide a suitable ending for the *Didache*. First, we examine the text itself:

> Then the sign of the Son of Man will appear in heaven, and then all the tribes of the earth will mourn, and they will see "the Son of Man coming on the clouds of heaven" with power and great glory. And he will send out his angels with a loud trumpet call, and they will gather his elect from the four winds, from one end of heaven to the other. (Mt 24:30–31)

When examined closely, Mt 24:30–31 diverges strongly from the perspective guiding the eschatological scenario of the *Didache*. Consider the following three points:

1. The "sign" of the Son of Man in Matthew's Gospel (borrowed from Dan 7:13–14) is directed toward alerting his readers as to when and how Jesus will return (Mt 24:3). In the case of the *Didache*, on the other hand, the Lord God is expected (see #10m).

2. Matthew and the *Didache* also diverge respecting the function and the mood surrounding the one coming. The "Son of Man" anticipated by Matthew, scholars agree (e.g., Gundry 1994: 488), is Jesus coming to judge the nations. At his coming, "all the tribes of the earth will mourn" (Mt 24:30)—and "the context in Matthew favors a mourning of despair" (Gundry 1994: 488). In the case of the *Didache*, it is not Jesus but the Lord God who is anticipated "atop the clouds" (*Did.* 16:8). This Lord comes to bring the promised kingdom (*Did.* 8:2; 9:4; 10:5) to his elect who have assembled to meet him. The mood surrounding his coming is therefore triumphal and filled with unmitigated expectation.

3. The "coming on the clouds" and the "trumpet call" are reversed in the *Didache* and for good reasons. According to the *Didache*, "the burning-process of testing" will destroy the wicked and purify "the ones having remained firm in their faith" (*Did.* 16:5). The unfurling banner and trumpet call thus serve to assemble the purified elect and the resurrected saints who, together, form an entourage to welcome the Lord when he comes atop the clouds (16:8). No further separation or judgment is necessary.

According to Matthew, on the other hand, the one coming as the "Son of Man" is the one who "sits on his glorious throne" (Mt 25:31) for the purpose of judging. This is signaled by the phrase: "and then all the tribes of the world will mourn" (Mt 24:30; Gundry 1994: 488–89). The angels, therefore, along with the trumpet call come into play at this point for the purpose of gathering the elect on his right hand and, by implication, gathering those to be consigned to "the eternal fire" (Mt 25:41) on his left. Consequently, the ordering of the "coming on the clouds" and the "trumpet call" are distinctly different in Matthew and in the *Didache* because they hold different views on the resurrection and on the function of the one coming.

In sum, neither the ending found in the *Apostolic Constitutions* nor the one found in Matthew 24 provide a suitable fit for the *Didache*. With Niederwimmer, "I shall not be bold enough to attempt to reconstitute the lost conclusion of the *Didache* by conjecture" (1998: 227). Rather, I propose that *Did*. 16:8 forms a suitable and harmonious ending. The seven blank lines provided by the copyist, it will be remembered, might simply mean that he preferred to begin the letters of Ignatius on a fresh side of velum (van de Sandt: 22f.). Or, like scholars today, he might have been uneasy with the abrupt ending of the original and surmised (incorrectly) that "the reader expects a depiction of the judgment of the world" (Niederwimmer 1998: 226). But this final judgment, which the *Apostolic Constitutions* so readily adds and which is so evident in Matthew 24, is already there in the *Didache* for those who have ears to hear. It is found precisely (a) in the dual effects of the burning-process of testing as far as the living are concerned and (b) in the selective resurrection of the holy ones as far as the dead are concerned.

In the end, therefore, when the clues of the *Didache* are relied on, one discovers an internal logic that forces the *Didache* to stand alone as an independent religious system. Mt 24:30–31, therefore, cannot form the supposed "lost ending."

The Rule of Praying as the Rule of Believing

Stepping back from the entire discussion, it can now be appreciated how the end-time scenario of *Did*. 16 is entirely synchronous with the progressive eschatological unfolding implied in the close of the eucharistic prayers:

Remember, Lord, your church,
    to save her from every evil   → evil "utterly destroyed" (16:5a)
and to perfect her in your love → faithful purified by fire (16:5b)
and to gather her together
        from the four winds → banner/trumpet/resurrection (16:6)
as the sanctified
        into your kingdom   → Lord comes with holy ones (16:8)
which you have prepared for her,
because yours is the power
and the glory forever (*Did*. 10:5).

The rule of prayer is the rule of believing (*Lex orandi lex credendi*). The saving and the perfecting take place prior to the ingathering so that "the sanctified/the holy one" welcomes the kingdom that the Lord brings. This symmetry provides a clear indication that *Did*. 10 and *Did*. 16 were created out of the same piece of cloth. Since *Did*. 10 represents only a synopsis, the prayer leader would have been expected to elaborate spontaneously in the act of praying. What one finds in *Did.* 16, consequently, may have been the fruit of such praying.

The eucharistic prayers and the end-time scenario are not intent upon the coming of the Son of Man or the return of Jesus but await the "God of David" (*Did.* 10:6). Given all the failures of fleshly kings, the Didache communities wait for God to come and rule the world himself. The closing lines of the *Didache* return to this same expectation when citing Zec 14:7: "On that day . . . the Lord will become king over all the earth" (Zec 14:6, 9). Here again, John Meier's explanation of the second petition of the Lord's Prayer must again be brought to mind (see ch. 4 above). The daily calling upon the Father to have his kingdom come is tantamount to petitioning God to come himself to reckon with evil, to purify the elect, to gather the exiles, and to rule the earth:

> It does indeed sound strange to speak of a kingdom or kingly rule coming. It makes perfect sense [on the other hand]—given the OT prophecies and eschatological expectations of first-century Judaism—to speak of God coming or, as in the case here, to pray that he comes. That God *comes* to save is a common affirmation in the OT, and . . . it carries special weight in eschatological prophecy. For example, Is 35:4 proclaims: "Say to the faint-hearted, 'Be strong, fear not; behold, your God will come with vengeance and his own recompense; he will come and save you.' . . ." Zec 14:5–9 is of special interest, since there the promise that Yahweh will *come* is closely connected with the eschatological battle. . . . After winning the battle, "Yahweh will become king over all the earth." (Meier 1994: 298)

Conclusion

The investigation of this chapter was undertaken in order to provide an improved reading of *Did.* 16:5. Up to this point, the majority of scholars have explained the puzzling phrase "saved by the curse itself" as a veiled reference to the crucified Christ who "became a curse for us" (Gal 3:13). This solution, however, patently risks transposing into the *Didache* a horizon of understanding that is foreign to the internal logic of the text itself.

When the text is allowed to speak in its own voice, the term *dokimasia* ("testing") aptly prepared the hearer for the positive and negative results anticipated. Furthermore, the evocative metaphor of fire, when investigated in the prophetic and apocalyptic literature, supplies multiple instances supporting the *Didache*'s notion that a dual effect was being assigned to the eschatological fire. Then, by examining the linguistic parallelism in the text, therefore, the possibility remains that the *Didache* had in mind the utter destruction of those opposed to God and the purification of those "having remained firm in their faith" (16:5). The seemingly obscure ending of *Did.* 16:5 now becomes apparent—the elect "will be saved by the accursed [burning-process] itself."

How this salvation was to be effected by fire the *Didache* does not expressly say. One can surmise, however, that the prophetic tradition so respected by the *Didache* provided the necessary background for answering this question. The Jewish prophets investigated in this chapter looked forward to God coming and destroying the enemies of Israel with his burning judgment. These same prophets also knew that God's own people required purifying: "Which of us can live with this devouring fire?" (Is 33:14). Out of this tradition came the response that the same fire that destroyed their enemies "like cut thorns" (Is 33:12) would serve to purify the elect like a smelter: "I [the Lord] will smelt away your dross in the furnace" (Is 1:25). Here then one finds a satisfying and internally consistent horizon of understanding for interpreting *Did.* 16:5.

Epilogue
THE SPIRITUALITY OF THE *DIDACHE:* MODERN REFLECTIONS

Contents

U p to this point, the chapters in this volume have endeavored to unravel, section by section, the clues of the *Didache*. By interpreting these clues within a social context, each chapter raised pressing problems and concerns that the framers of the *Didache* attempted to satisfy by putting forward ways of being, ways of acting, and ways of believing. Now that we have passed through the entire matrix of the *Didache*, the opportunity is ripe to surface the spirituality of the Didache communities. This chapter, accordingly, will view the outline of the forest after stepping back from the clumps of trees. Those who have passed through the voyage of discovery will find in this chapter a synthesis of everything that has passed before, not so much in their particulars, but in their general tendencies and deep instincts.

While most will read this as their last chapter, I would not fault those who want to read this chapter first. Some of my readers will naturally want to get the big picture first and then dip in and explore the fine structure that takes shape around particular ways of being, ways of acting, and ways of believing. For those who come early to the theater and relish watching the end of the film first and then waiting during the intermission in order to see the film from the very beginning, this chapter ought to be read first. In this way, of course, much of what is said here will not make sense, yet as one goes back and reads the previous chapters, the story line will gradually fill in and a more and more satisfying synthesis will take place at every turn.

The spirituality of the *Didache* has to do with how actual persons were stretched, were overjoyed, were pained by their lived faith experiences. Quite often, I will marvel at how different the *Didache*'s Christians are from those whom I have known and loved and identified as Christians (myself included). From time to time, my aim will be to sharply cut these "differences" in order to allow that the believers of the *Didache* inhabited a time and a culture significantly different from my own. I may overdo these contrasts from time to time. Yet I ask the reader to indulge these efforts in view of the fact that they are deliberately drawn so as to clearly define what is not "ours" and what is not "us." The same holds true on the other side. At times, by virtue of leaps of the imagination, I will suggest striking parallels that place contemporary Christians in a situation only marginally removed from those encountered by the Didache communities. Here again I beg indulgence. I may overdo these parallels and project some of them quite uncritically, yet in every case it is in order to find a sharper outline whereby my contemporary readers might find the familiar joy and the familiar pain in the heart of the first-century believer.

#16A THE MEANING OF SPIRITUALITY

Catholics routinely speak of Franciscan spirituality, Benedictine spirituality, and Jesuit spirituality in order to describe that ethos that surrounds various religious orders that exist under the Catholic umbrella. This language of "spirituality" has been extended in an ecumenical era to enable one to speak of Anglican spirituality, Lutheran spirituality, Quaker spirituality, and, going even further, of Muslim, Buddhist, and Native American spirituality. Along these lines, Paulist Press, beginning in 1978, began publishing a sixty-volume set under the series title "The Classics of Western Spirituality." In this series, not only are Catholic and Protestant texts made available, but Jewish, Orthodox, Muslim, and Native American traditions are represented as well. Every religious tradition, consequently, can be understood as fostering a "spirituality" or "spiritualities."

Sandra Schneiders made a study of the history of the term "spirituality" and concluded that the term has always referred to some aspect of the "spiritual person" as contrasted with the "natural person" (1 Cor 2:14–15). In the fourth century, "spirituality" was sometimes used to refer to the extraordinary "penetration of scriptures and the capacity to search and guide the human heart" (258) exhibited by some of the desert fathers and mothers. In the eighteenth century, "spirituality" referred to "the pursuit of perfection in the interior life through spiritual exercises and the practice of virtue above and beyond what is required by the commandments" (259). Adolphe Tanquerey, in his systematic treatise *The Spiritual Life* (1930) described "ascetical and mystical theology" as those branches of theology that explore the interface of the dogmatic and practical principles that are conducive to perfection in the Christian life. In the second half of the twentieth century, Protestants and Jews began to become comfortable with using the Catholic term "spirituality" to refer to the practical pursuit of perfection practiced by their communities.

One can study the classical texts, the catechisms, and the rites of an unfamiliar religious tradition without coming to any adequate sense of how the practitioners of the religion pursue their religious goals on a day-to-day basis. The term "spirituality," on the other hand, emphasizes how scriptures, beliefs, and rites function to promote the distinctive form of perfection that adherents of a particular religious tradition cultivate in response to their divine calling. Thus, the study of the "spirituality" of a religious tradition is a secure way to come to grasp the distinctive religious identity of "the other"—to see them as they see themselves. Spirituality reveals the stubborn patterns of perception and habits of judgment that distinguish the "soul" of a movement. Likewise, spirituality touches upon the feeling tones evoked by particular beliefs and practices—what causes them suffering, what gives them satisfaction, what makes them anxious.

Jacob Neusner gave a presentation on Jewish-Christian dialogue at Xavier University in the fall of 1991. He effectively said that true dialogue had never yet begun. Up to this time, the dialogue partners had maintained a polite presence, had shared something of their particular religious feasts, had spoken of how they were committed to God and had postured to make a contribution or a change within society, yet "no one has yet asked me what makes me, as a Jew, suffer?" This I would understand as a charged and sensitive opening to explore the spirituality of Jews. All in all, it is very "safe" for Christians to inquire objectively as to what Jews believe, what Jews do (*halakhah*), what Jews celebrate (feasts). When one begins to explore the pains and the joys Jews experience when believing, doing, and celebrating, then one can say that one has been touched by the lived experience of being Jewish (Schneiders: 264–68).

Only the deliberative cultivation of empathy that follows upon a spontaneous admiration can open up and reveal the interiority of "the other." Mutual trust is the required foundation. Thus dialogue between Christians and Jews at first will generally touch upon safe neutral elements of dogma, practice, and celebration, but, as mutual trust and mutual empathy develop, the feeling tones and the habits of judgment associated with each of these things will progressively be revealed and shared. In the end, therefore, Neusner's fond wish to share his suffering as a Jew will have its rightful place.

In like fashion, when Neusner addresses himself to the task of discovering the "religious system" that stands behind a text, a rite, a movement, he is speaking of what, for him, is a close relative to "spirituality":

> It seems to me the simplest fact of all religions, hence of religion, is that religion is something people do together, something they do to accomplish shared goals. Hence religion is a social fact, and the artifacts of religion, texts, drawings, dances, music, for example, form components of a shared, therefore social, system. Religion encompasses a shared world view, explains a shared way of life, identifies the social entity of those that realize the one and live by the other. . . . (1988c: 9)

In order to describe a particular religious system, Neusner proceeds as follows:

> I ask three simple questions: what is the world view of the religion? what is the way of life of a religion? And what is the social entity to that the world view is addressed . . . ? The answers to

these questions in hand, I can describe a religious system. (1988c: 9)

In this chapter, I will offer my answer to these foundational questions for the members of the Didache communities. Having done so, I will provide the outline of the religious system of the *Didache* and thus expose some of the key traits that define "Didache spirituality."

What Was the All-Encompassing Question That the Didache Answered?

As might be expected, the *Didache* has no preface or introduction that explains the purpose and the use of what is to follow. In this, it is like the Mishnah or the *Derek Erez Zuta,* which simply begin treating the first topic. Everyone knew its purpose—no need to state it. We, however, receive the *Didache* without being able to see it in use. The *Didache,* consequently, is the answer to a pressing question that it remains for us to determine. Only at the end of a systematic investigation of the entire document, therefore, can this question be securely stated.

The pressing question that the *Didache* answers is this: *What is the order of training for reorienting gentiles so that they can fully participate in the promises made to Israel and be gathered among the elect when the Lord comes?*

The *Didache* has frequently been called a "church order" or a "manual for ordering church life." This is partially true and partially misleading. The *Didache* details the ordering of church life—this is true—but only in a carefully circumscribed situation: the *Didache* tracks the training of a gentile who has come forward seeking the truth and the knowledge of the Lord. All in all, therefore, the *Didache* traces the divinely sanctioned and pastorally refined route (see #16b) whereby gentiles might be progressively transformed for inclusion among the saints when the Lord comes on the last day. More than a "church order," the *Didache* is a "practical guide for spiritual mentors" who undertake the progressive reorientation of gentiles.

#16B A SYNOPSIS OF THE ORDERING OF TOPICS IN THE *DIDACHE*

Earlier chapters have shown that the *Didache* was not a randomly assembled collage of borrowed materials. Rather, from beginning to end, the framers of the *Didache* laid out the time-tested ordering of topics used by seasoned mentors training new members. At key points, the progression of topics was deliberately designed to address the felt needs of the candidate and/or to ready the candidate for new experiences that would follow shortly. All in all, the pastoral genius of the *Didache* was that it ensured a systematic, user-friendly guide for mentors that enabled them to profit from the skills and experience of the seasoned mentors who went before them.

Needless to say, while the *Didache* was an oral template memorized by mentors (and, with the unfolding of the training, by their candidates as well), no one ought to imagine that training consisted of merely repeating the words of the masters. On the contrary, each mentor was expected to illustrate, inquire, question, listen to, and challenge his/her candidate such that not only the words but also the deep meanings of the Way of Life were being suitably assimilated and applied at every step of the way. As in the case of every wise "father" or "mother," the mentor was expected to use the oral template as a reliable guide but to present it in such a way as to take into account the particular circumstances, particular strengths and weaknesses, and particular fears exhibited by the candidate.

The *Didache* begins immediately by offering the gentile candidate the key orientation that characterizes the Way of Life, namely, loving God and loving one's neighbor (1:2). Everything that follows is commentary designed to reveal the substance of "these words" (1:3) and to orient a gentile for full participation in the community of the saints. At every step, the order of topics follows the needs of the candidate: (a) Initially, the pressing concern is preparing the candidate for abusive treatment at home (1:3–5). (b) Midway, the language of "my child" predominates, signaling the deepening of the "father-son" or "mother-daughter" relationship (3:1ff.). (c) Near the end, the future tense is used to prepare the candidate for the community living that he/she has not yet known (3:9ff.). Baptism is the rite of passage (7:1–3). Just prior to baptism, the rule of eating is given (6:3). As the candidate is fasting (purging his/her body of food sacrificed to idols), he/she is being prepared to live the rest of his/her life (a) eating the safe food of the community table and (b) abstaining from food twice each week (8:1). At the close of the baptism, the newly baptized pray the Lord's Prayer with the community for the first time (8:2) and anticipate doing the same three times each day for the rest of their lives (8:3). All then join in the festive first eucharist (9–10). Given the festive character of new members being welcomed by their "family," the confession of failings normally used prior to the eucharist is deliberately suppressed and described later (14:1–3). At the eucharist the newly baptized encounter prophets for the first time (10:7), and the extended instruction on prophets and other visitors (11:1–13:2) is given following the first eucharist. Following this, the rules for first fruits are explained and the prophets are singled out as the ones who can best be counted on to offer up a rich, spontaneous prayer of gratitude to the Lord (13:3). Finally, the newly baptized (a) are prepared to participate in the confession of failings at their second and subsequent eucharists (14:1-3), (b) are alerted to the special honor due to bishops and deacons (15:1-2), something missed in the excitement of the first eucharist, and (c) are taught the rules for reproving and shunning. Participation at multiple eucharists undoubtedly stimulates a deep concern for the eschatological hope of the community. Thus, at some teachable moment, the final formal task of the mentor is to explain in detail the solemn warnings (16:1-2) and the sequence of events that will culminate in the Lord's coming to establish the kingdom (16:8).

Upon inspection, therefore, the *Didache* exhibits a remarkable unity and purpose. The *Didache* opens by offering the candidate the key orientation toward love of God and love of neighbor that characterize the Way of Life. The *Didache* closes by evoking the expectation of that glorious day when the Lord God will come atop the clouds of heaven (16:8) and gather into the kingdom those whose lives have exhibited this orientation. Thus, the *Didache* traces how the humble beginnings anticipate an exalted and transcendent end.

THE GENIUS OF MENTORING

The Pivotal Category and Relationship

Becoming a Christian in the first century was not like joining the cult of another deity, A. D. Noch informs us, for conversion to Christianity required the "the reorientation of the soul of an individual" (7). Accordingly, it is no surprise that the pivotal category of the *Didache* is training! Its title, consequently, even if it is not the original, aptly reveals the central category that unifies and defines the *Didache*. Gentiles could not be expected to have a father and mother who brought them into the ways of God by virtue of growing up in their household. Neither could gentiles be expected to invent the Way of Life nor to design rites and practices necessary for sustaining its practice. Jews, on the other hand, understood who they were by virtue of the grace of election. Accordingly, the role of Christians was not to noisily organize slick membership drives or even to quietly cultivate new members among their friends. Rather, the first order of the day was to wait and see whom the Lord would call to him/herself. This "calling" undoubtedly came in the form of a compelling admiration for particular Christians and was accompanied with an impulse to embrace their God and their spirituality, in a word, to become one of them. Thus, devoid of any recruitment techniques, those "whom the Spirit has made ready" (*Did.* 4:10) came forward and were assigned a suitable mentor for their age, sex, disposition, and station of life.

Just as grace and nature came together in the initial calling, so too, it proceeded throughout the training period. The assigned mentor did not imagine that the training of the candidate should be left entirely in God's hands or that the training should consist of special acts of piety. This would be a quietism that smacks of magic or superstition. Rather, once one was called, the mentor systematically proceeded to apprentice the candidate such that his/her habits of judgment and patterns of feeling regarding the expectations of God and the future of the elect would be progressively assimilated under the watchful, discerning, and loving direction of a "spiritual parent." Since gentiles could not be assumed to have been brought up in the ways of God, the pastoral genius of the *Didache* was to supply what was wanting.

The pivotal relationship that makes spiritual transformation possible is the father–son or mother–daughter relationship. Children assimilate for themselves the religious and cultural instincts of their parents. They do this progressively over a period of time as a result of the sheer satisfaction of mimicking and imitating what their parents do, say, and think. Those who embark on an apprenticeship later in life do so because they are first of all captivated by the allure of another person. One has here not so much a religious formation as a religious transformation. The religious orientation gained from one's biological parents was regarded as deeply flawed and unsatisfactory. Meanwhile, the religious orientation of the assigned mentor was perceived as true and fulfilling. Hence, spiritual mentors supplied, for gentile adults, that familiar and bonded introduction to the devout life that their own biological parents were unable to supply.

#16c THE MODEL OF TRANSFORMATION IMPLIED BY GRACED MENTORING

When one examines the model of transformation undergirding most traditional theologies of baptism, one quickly discovers that, beneath the outward appearances, a Cinderella-like transformation was taking place. The *Universal Catechism of the Catholic Church* (1989), for example, lists the wondrous effects of both infant and adult baptism as follows:

> By baptism, *all sins* are forgiven, original sin and all personal sins, as well as all punishment for sin. . . . Baptism not only purifies

from all sins, but also makes the neophyte "a new creature," an adapted son of God. . . . The Most Holy Trinity gives the baptized sanctifying grace, the grace of *justification:* enabling them to believe in God, to hope in him, and to love him through the theological virtues. . . . (sec. 1263, 1265f.)

My own parents were committed to this extraordinary power of the rite of baptism. Within a month of my birth, they accordingly took me to Holy Cross Parish Church and presented me to Father McMonigle for baptism. They stood by helplessly as the priest conducted his sacred rites on behalf of their firstborn son. These rites, in their understanding, operated much like a "fairy godmother" working a "Cinderella-like" transformation upon my soul—a mysterious and wonderful thing that they themselves were entirely incapable of effecting much less of understanding. After my baptism, however, they felt a sigh of relief: my soul was now purified of original sin. Now, if I should die a crib death, they felt sure I would go directly to heaven for I was a "son of God" and had the supernatural gift of faith required for salvation.

As I gradually learned to speak, it never occurred to them that I said nothing about and took no notice of "God." Even when I attended church with them every Sunday, I was oblivious to God. I didn't have the least sense of "God" being in church or being anywhere, for that matter. What I did notice, however, was that my dad and mom were strangely quiet. The tradition at Holy Cross Church, it is important to understand, was that no one spoke except in hushed whispers as soon as they entered the church. Then, on one particular Sunday, I remember something like the following exchange taking place:

Aaron: "Mama, why are the people not talking?"
Mom: "Shhhh! People come here not to talk but to listen to God!"
Aaron: "But I don't hear anything."
Mom: "Look at that gold box [tabernacle] on the table."
(*She points to the altar.*)
Aaron: "I see it. It's shiny."
Mom: "God lives in that little box. People come here to talk to God who lives there. And God silently talks back to them."

This was my first remembered introduction to "God." My parents never spoke of God in any setting that made an impression on me prior to that moment. Now, for the first time, I felt that my parents sensed the presence of something or someone that I had overlooked. This was not a first-order sensory impression like the kind offered by the cans of food that I rolled on the kitchen floor or by the cockroaches that sometimes came out from under the icebox. Nonetheless, the clues were present. The collective silence and the gold box pointed to some unseen and unheard "presence." As in the case of "germs" that Mom said made me sick or as in the case of the "tooth fairy," who left nickels under my pillow, I now took "God" into account as the "person hidden in the gold box who silently talks to my parents." I was impressed.

As this took place, my parents were undoubtedly thinking that the effects of baptism were taking place. In the official theology of the Catholic Church at that time, Thomas Aquinas was accepted as ensuring that all the marvelous things mentioned above had taken place during my baptism but that they were in a "sleeping" phase waiting to "awaken" as I matured (*Summa Theologica* 3.69). Had I been left to my own devices and those of my parents, I would have grown up thinking that "God" appears only in churches, where people keep silent in order to "hear" him. My father, however, wisely enrolled me in Holy Cross Grade School when I was seven. Here, under the gentle care of the Ursuline Sisters, I quickly came to understand and to experience "God" as having many more effects in the world than those of which my own parents were aware. In school, I enjoyed both the study and the practice of religion—although it was painful for me to be admonished to kneel up straight during mass (the eucharist).

In due course, "God" became very real for me. I too developed the practice of silently speaking to "God" in the gold box on the altar, and I "heard" him speak back to me in the quiet recesses of my heart. The tacit skills exemplified by my parents and by my teachers, therefore, gradually became my very own.

In the end, my parents were thinking that the instantaneous Cinderella transformation effected at my baptism was the means whereby I began to take notice of and to depend on "God." Other Catholic parents, however, might have seen my religious development as more akin to a Liza Doolittle transformation.

Liza Doolittle, it will be remembered, was the flower girl in *My Fair Lady*. Professor Higgins, a professional linguist, took her under his wing and gradually trained her to speak "correctly" and to act like a cultivated lady. During her training, the sheer effort and repetition demanded by a sometimes impatient Professor Higgins often led Liza to the point of despair. Her faith in his method and her hope in the kind of person she wanted to be, however, held up. In the end, the two of them working together succeeded. The confirmation of their success, as in the case of the legend of Cinderella, took place during a ball. A Rumanian count carefully observed the mysterious stranger at the ball and, near its end, proudly declared, despite the professor's complete silence on the subject, "She is a princess!" Liza thus becomes a "princess" not by catching the eye of the prince who desires to marry her but by puzzling the Rumanian count who feels he can correctly identify her. Higgins, gloating over *his* success, promptly ignores Liza. A verbal fight ensues. Liza rightly declares that it was *her efforts* that pulled the whole thing off. Furthermore, she claims that, now that she intimately understands the professor's techniques by virtue of having undergone an apprenticeship, she could go and find another flower girl and effect for her the same marvelous transformation that she herself experienced. Unlike her counterpart, the fabled Cinderella, Liza realizes all too well that her expanded powers of speaking, moving, and being in the world are the result of prolonged efforts under the direction of a capable master and that she has nothing to fear when the clock strikes midnight or when Higgins arrogantly imagined that her transformation was "his" success.

Thus, two models for accounting for religious transformation are evident: the Cinderella model and the Liza Doolittle model. The traditional theology of baptism, for a complex set of reasons, chose to downplay human agency and to overplay supernatural agency, thereby giving us a good illustration of the Cinderella model. On the basis of Michael Polanyi's analysis of parenting and of apprenticing, however, it might be expected that behind every Cinderella transformation, one can expect to find a Liza Doolittle story unobtrusively operating in the background (Milavec 1997). More importantly, however, it can be appreciated that the one-sided supernatural claims made by the traditional theology of the baptism hold up *only because* these claims were being silently supplemented and corrected by efficacious human agency

Given the growth of secularism in modern society, the Catholic Church, following on the decisions of Vatican II, revamped its practice of baptism:

1. For infants, the church has insisted that they "cannot have or profess personal faith" (Rites: 188), and, thus, in baptism, "this faith is proclaimed for them by their parents and godparents" (Rites: 188). Infant baptism, consequently, is the beginning of a spiritual journey (technically a "catechumenate"): "children must later be formed in the faith in which they have been baptized" (Rites: 188). When this formation is effective, those baptized as infants can be expected to live and profess a mature faith at the time of their confirmation. During this period of fifteen to eighteen years of "Christian initiation," parents are actively trained to recognize their essential role in manifesting their Christian way of life before their children and initiating them, using methods appropriate to their age, into a mature and living faith (Rites: 189–90; see esp. Humbrecht: 32–37, 124–30).

2. For adults, the church has insisted that the extended period of formation (technically known as "the catechumenate for adults" in the fourth century) should be suitably reinstated (Rites: 19). Prior to adult baptism,

therefore, at least a year is devoted to a maturation process in which conversion of life is fostered by doctrinal and pastoral formation suffused with a strong liturgical methodology. Aidan Kavanagh, the foremost expositor of these rites for the English-speaking Catholic Church, says this:

> Catechumens [those being initiated] are to be formed by living closely with others who know well the demands and advantages of a Christian way of life. The exemplary role of sponsors, godparents, and the whole local community of faith is paramount in this mode of formation. One learns how to fast, pray, repent, celebrate, and serve the good of one's neighbor less by being lectured on these matters than by close association with people who do these things with regular ease and flair. (122)

Without in any way disturbing or reexamining the Cinderella model presupposed in its theology, the Catholic Church has, nonetheless, undergone "a radical redefinition and refurbishing" (Kavanagh 1976: 119) of the human factors underpinning the sacramental rite. Infants are initiated principally by their parents into a way of life during the fourteen to eighteen years following infant baptism. Adults, on the other hand, are apprenticed by qualified mentors prior to receiving baptism. Thus, in a society where people no longer can be expected "to become Christian by cultural osmosis" (Keifer: 143), a pragmatic Doolittle model of transformation has been resurrected from the past in order to shore up the Cinderella claims made by a traditional theology.

When I visited mainland China, I was surprised to find a highly committed and active Catholic community in Beijing that celebrated the eucharist in Latin using the rite that was familiar to me from my youth. The bishops of China were prohibited from attending the Second Vatican Council. Nor did they think it wise to put into effect the changes in the liturgy that marked the aftermath of the council. However, given the fact that societal norms in modern China militate against a faith commitment, especially in the case of the youth, the Catholic Church decided to suspend the practice of infant baptism. I was initially astonished by this change. When I inquired why this was done, I was told the following: "We discovered that parents could no longer ensure that children baptized during their infancy would adhere to their religious faith. Given the current climate of antagonism toward 'foreign religions,' would-be Christians have to profess the faith for themselves and demonstrate their readiness to be baptized as adults."

As I thought about it, this response gradually made complete sense. As the schools and the youth movements openly despised "foreign ways" and "foreign culture" (Christianity included), the claims made by traditional theology concerning the supernatural effects of baptism were exposed as being either "magical" or "superstitious." Sensitive Chinese pastors had to alter their practice in order to safeguard the sanctity and the integrity of the rite itself. Pragmatic effects, therefore, sometimes do provide a corrective to the exaggerated aspects of traditional theology.

At this juncture, the practice of the church fathers is revealing. By the third century, the norm for admitting new converts was the intensive training (the adult catechumenate) that extended for two to three years prior to baptism. A well-defined and progressive transformation of life was presupposed by the instruction, the exorcisms, the examination of life in the training period. The church fathers had no illusions that a mere profession of faith would suffice to render a person fit for baptism or that a short-lived religious enthusiasm would suffice to sustain a lifelong Christian commitment. Contrary to the medieval theologians who transposed into infant baptism the real effects of patristic baptisms, the church fathers had no Pollyanna confidence in the waters of baptism. Cyril of Jerusalem (d. C.E. 386), for example, emphasized that it was fatal to imagine that the efforts of the catechumens could be curtailed in view of some irresistible grace inherent in the baptismal waters. Cyril then proceeded to name persons who had been baptized but not transformed. Gregory of Nyssa (d. C.E. 394), his contemporary, even went so far as providing a pragmatic test:

> If the washing [of baptism] has only affected the body . . . , and the life after the initiation is identical with that before . . . , I will say without shrinking that in such a case the water is only water, and the gift of the Holy Spirit is nowhere evident. (*Oratio catechetica magna* 40)

Far from pressing forward scriptural warrants or exalting the supernatural agency of the rite itself (as the medieval Catholic notion of *ex opere operato* was inclined to do), one can glimpse that Cyril and Gregory were constrained, by virtue of their pastoral experiences of the "failure" of the rite, to take a much more nuanced and existential approach to the efficacy of baptism.

The upshot of this whole discussion is that mentoring can be seen as the central work horse and transformative process dominating the whole of the *Didache*. While baptism was practiced as a kind of "rite of passage" in the mentoring process (to be considered below), there was no temptation on the part of the Didache communities to assign the rite itself any mysterious and unseen powers that would warrant extending baptism to infants or admitting untrained adults to the rite. In truth, the framers of the *Didache* did not even designate baptism as a "sacrament" or insist that it was "instituted by Christ." All of these things would come in due time

(Martos: 40–45). For the moment, however, the framers of the *Didache* knew themselves to be on solid ground when they embraced their effective pastoral practice of initiating gentiles and presupposed that the grace of human transformation took place prior to the rite itself.

Even in the Baptist tradition where only adults who have received saving grace, repentance, and the Holy Spirit with manifest signs are welcome to be baptized, there is still the tendency to downplay or even to deny outright the efficacy of parental upbringing and of role models in the church. While Baptists refuse to practice infant baptism and abhor the Catholic insistence that a rite confers "supernatural grace," this does not necessarily mean that Baptist reliance on a Cinderella model of human transformation is not present. Accordingly, traditional Baptist theology tends to emphasize that God gratuitously imparts "saving grace" prior to the rite such that the rite itself serves only to confirm what God has already done in advance to the one being baptized.

Time and space do not allow an extension of this horizon of understanding across the spectrum of rites and practices functioning in the *Didache*. My earlier analysis of Synoptic exorcisms and ordination rites, and of Pentecostal speaking in tongues (Milavec 1982: 18–36) might serve as a point of departure; however, I will leave this task to others. Suffice it to note that the framers of the *Didache* respected the mystery of the inscrutable calling of God (*Did.* 4:10). Once one was called, however, the *Didache* understood that face-to-face mentoring was the divinely ordained process whereby human transformation took place. Accordingly, "the one speaking to you the word of God" was to be remembered "night and day" and honored "as the Lord" (*Did.* 4:1). In contrast, the *Didache* was never tempted to encourage members to remember their baptism and to regard it as the moment when they "received the grace of the Lord." No! The framers of the *Didache* knew and celebrated grace-filled relationships and had little inclination to speak of grace-filled rites.

Any modern Christian who would fail to take this into account would be hindered from coming to a correct assessment of the self-understanding of the members of the Didache communities. In saying this, I am asserting that the framers of the *Didache* were different from us and that we ought not to project what is ours back upon them. In so doing, we do not idealize the framers of the *Didache* or imagine that we, in our time and our situation, ought to replicate them. Rather, the past lives within us and an appropriate study of the past should allow us, on the one hand, to retrace some of our roots and, on the other hand, to reexamine and to reimagine where we ought to be in fidelity to our own times and in fidelity to God's future.

As a footnote, I would like to draw attention to the fact that Jews have never been tempted to elaborate any mysterious Cinderella transformation associated with circumcision. This may be due to the historical and existential fact that circumcision did not apply to women; hence, the absence of circumcision for women prevented even the most imaginative men from claiming any mysterious or divine transformation connected with an essentially male rite. Imagine, for a moment, what would have happened in Christian theology if half the members of the Christian community were routinely denied baptism yet fully functioning as Christians. Under these circumstances, there would have been little impulse to claim supernatural interior transformations as marvelously taking place as the water was poured since comparable transformations would have been evident in the lives of those never baptized. The baptism of the *Didache*, consequently, might rightly be envisioned as being framed within a Jewish mind-set.

A Spirituality at Variance with My Own

The *Didache* is shot through with a spirituality that, in many ways, is so entirely different from the spirituality given to me in my youth:

1. *Sober view of Jesus.* The *Didache* did not offer a romantic view of Jesus. Members were not told that he is the Lord of Lords, the King of Kings, the Savior of the World. No one would have been tempted to imagine that Jesus had special divine powers that allowed him to read the secret thoughts of everyone he met and to know their past and future lives. No one, likewise, would have been tempted to imagine that Jesus healed the sick and drove out demons with a power that no one had exercised since the beginning of the world. Finally, no one would have imagined that the salvation of every individual from the beginning of the world to the end was absolutely dependent on the grace merited for them by Jesus.

On the contrary, the *Didache* presented Jesus first and foremost as the "servant" of the Father. Called by the Spirit (4:10), the members of the community were taught to embrace God and the Way of Life as "servants" of the Father. Novices were initially taught that they would use and distribute even their possessions as "the Father wishes" (1:5). They will enter into the family of the elect and live quiet and productive lives until, in the end, the Father gathers his sons and daughters into the kingdom which he has prepared for them. All of these things applied to Jesus as well as to every member of the Didache communities. Jesus may have been the "servant" who pioneered the Way of Life and revealed it to his companions; nonetheless, as in the case of the novice who responds to beggars, Jesus did not somehow feel superior to those whom he helped, nor were they somehow eternally indebted to him. Jesus simply gave to those who asked of him "for, to all, the Father wishes to give these things from his own free gifts" (1:5).

2. *Sober view of the church.* The *Didache* did not offer a romantic view of the church. Members were not told that their church is the one, true church and that its doctrines and rites are somehow entirely in harmony with God's will and entirely free from error because they conform to inerrant, inspired scriptures and/or were taught by an infallible, Spirit-led hierarchy. Likewise, members were not told that their church had a divine origin because it was instituted by the direct intention and will of the divine Savior, Jesus Christ.

On the contrary, the *Didache* offered a view of the church from God's side. Those in the church were those called out by the Spirit. Since they were the children of election, however, the Father expected more of them. Thus, in the end time, membership in the church or regular participation in its rites was not put forward as the guarantee of salvation. Rather, members experienced "the Lord" addressing them in their mentors (4:1) and found "rest" for their souls in "the presence of the saints" (4:2). Although the professed members were regarded as "the holy ones," they were not exempted from "confessing their failings" (14:1) or from being "reproved" (4:3, 15:3f.). One might even expect that the bishops and deacons welcomed the opportunity to make their confession and to receive the reproof of others because they knew that these things worked for their perfection.

3. *More is not better.* Sometimes Christians are tempted to imagine that spiritual practices good in themselves ought to be extended or increased in frequency. For example, if a short prayer three times each day is considered valuable, some might imagine that progress might be boosted by doubling or tripling the time spent in prayer. Similarly, others might imagine that, when spinning yarn or preparing clay for throwing, it might be good to pray while working. Likewise, if one was to be better than "the hypocrites," then those zealous for God might want to increase the rigor of the fast or multiply the number of fast days.

On the contrary, the *Didache* does not associate the quantity of time spent in prayer or its quality with spiritual progress. A spiritual master might be inclined to suggest that, even in the case of a human father, a daughter could only serve to irritate a loving father should she talk to him too much. The *Didache* seemed to understand that too much of any spiritual practice would only lead to frivolous repetition or to strained exhaustion.

On the other hand, it should never be imagined that one should strive at "being better" than someone else or that one could attain the status of "being better" by somehow doing more. Often one was better by doing less. Loving God and loving one's neighbor were not captured so much in "doing" as in "being." Thus, if one is sometimes uplifted or inspired in prayer, this is not "better" prayer than in those moments when one feels nothing at all. As in the love between a father and a child, there is no need to generate certain moods or feelings. Every prayer under every condition is an act of love.

4. *Progress and patience.* In Western society, our appreciation of progress has infused every aspect of our private and social existence. We are constantly confronted with faster and better modems, with faster and better ways to learn, with faster and better ways of preparing balanced meals for our family. Oftentimes this pushes beginners to want, for themselves, more progress in prayer, more progress in devotion, more progress in perfection. Meanwhile, these same Christians feel guilty about their lack of progress in these same areas.

The *Didache*, for its part, did not suppose that one could or ought to strive for faster or better progress in the spiritual life. To begin with, one only came to the community if and when the Spirit made a person "ready" (4:10). Even when members of the community were living in the expectation of the coming of the Lord at an hour unknown to them (16:1), there was no impulse to speed up recruitment or to speed up the training program in order that more persons could be baptized prior to this event. Thus, in the *Didache*, urgency was salted with patience. Even at the end of the training, the novice was told that "if you are not able [to do/bear everything], that which you are able, do this" (6:2). Thus, novices were effectively trained not to fret with their lack of progress nor to revel in what they had accomplished. At the weekly confession of failings, no one was applauded because they had nothing to confess nor shamed because they were burdened by many things. For one and for the other, the act of confessing sufficed. Even "in the last days," when massive defections were expected, members were not pushed to heroic efforts or heroic practices—faster and better ways to anticipate the Lord. Rather, they were told "frequently be gathered together seeking the things pertaining to your souls" (16:2). In a word, hold on to each other. Be content that you have come this far, and be assured that the Lord will take care of the rest 3:10; 16:5).

5. *No to regimentation.* Some may think that the spiritual life demands doing certain things at certain hours. In my youth, for instance, I was told that "eating meat on Fridays" or "skipping mass on Sundays" was a "mortal sin" (i.e., a sin that, if done deliberately with full knowledge of its seriousness, merited an eternity in hellfire). A cursory reading of the *Didache* might leave this understanding. Fasting takes place on certain days; confession of failings on another. Praying takes place at preordained times three times each day.

In reality, however, nothing in the *Didache* suggests that regimentation was necessary and that one had to maintain a spiritual routine even if and when it became nothing more than a grim duty. Regarding foods, the new member was trained to "bear that which you are able" (6:3)—something that the individual had to decide and, given the seasons of a person's life, this was something that changed. Regarding water used for baptism, alternatives are given depending upon what was available (7:2f.). Regarding the fast prior to baptism, those fast who "have the strength" to do so (7:4)— a clue that some could elect, for reasons of health, not to fast. From this point, one could continue on and on. One must suspect that every spiritual practice in the *Didache* was given for the benefit of the user and no banal regimentation was ever called for.

6. *Yes to joy and gratitude.* So often Christianity is a joyless affair. Some are uptight that the grace that brought them to the Lord might be withdrawn and they will fall, like a spider on a thread, into the pit of hell. Still others are anxious that certain sins may not have been adequately repented for and that they face the wrath of the Lord on the last days. Finally, there are those who feel that their perfection consists in being close to the Lord and that it is only their contact with real people that derails their spiritual progress.

The *Didache* says nothing about "joy" as such. Those who would walk in the Way of Life were simply told that this consisted in loving God and loving your neighbor—a condition that was bound to bring simple joys. Meanwhile, nothing enemies did could derail you (1:4). The saints, on the other hand, provided a deep rest and satisfaction for the soul (4:2). All "the experiences befalling you" were to be accepted as "good things, knowing that, apart from God, nothing happens" (3:10). All in all, therefore, those elected by the Lord for inclusion in the kingdom lived productive, harmless, and joyful lives in the expectation of things to come. Nothing could tear them from the hands and the heart of the Lord!

Finally, the *Didache* gave special attention to gratitude—gratitude for being chosen, being led, being gathered into the kingdom. This is what the eucharistic prayers were about (*Did.* 9–10)—giving thanks. This is what the first fruits were about—gratitude for the simple things that sustained life and that were the work of one's hands (*Did.* 13). There was also gratitude for life itself, which came from the "God who made you" (1:2). The *Didache* thus held the mystery of life and its goodness with gentleness and gave thanks to the unseen author of life. Even the events in life (good and evil, joy and suffering) were seen as coming from the hand of God and deserving gratitude (3:10). Life was accepted with a sense of gratitude. The members of the Didache community did not complain against God (3:6) about being too rich or too poor, too handsome or too plain, too intelligent or too learning-impaired, too healthy or too sickly. This is why there was no room in the *Didache* for general prayers for peace, for happiness, for health, etc. Only the kingdom prayer. If God stands behind everything, then whatever happens calls forth gratitude.

A Person-to-Person Oral Spirituality

Many times throughout this book, the oral character of the *Didache* has been spelled out. Already in the preface, we examined the clues in the text that indicate an oral enactment. At various other times, the transition from topic to topic as well as the development of a given topic was seen as having an oral character. This being done, it might now be possible to step back and to designate the abyss that exists between spiritualities built on orality and those built on textuality.

First, an oral gospel must be heard from a specific living person. Thus, upon first hearing, the gospel has a face, a life, a personality that is met and trusted as one hears and responds to the gospel. A written gospel, in contrast, can remain silent on the shelf. The reader who wants to hear it must take it down and sound the words (verbally or, in modern times, mentally). The written gospel is one step removed from the personal performance of the oral gospel. The reader hears the gospel at his/her discretion—when and where he/she pleases. The reader is left to interpret what is read within his/her own horizon of understanding. An oral gospel always remains attached to a living person who, in their life, gives meaning and content to the gospel.

> While there is no such thing as a face-to-face encounter with a text, the mouth-to-heart engagement in oral communication fosters personal and intimate relations. The spoken word, emanating from interiority and entering another interiority, creates a deep-set bonding of speaker with auditor. (Kelber: 146)

This "bonding," of course, only comes when the hearer respects and admires the speaker and endeavors empathetically to enter into his/her way of being in the world. In rabbinic Judaism, consequently, the master is always, first and foremost, living Torah. The words of a worthy rabbi come out of his practice, and his practice gives meaning to his words. In the case of texts, on the other hand, it becomes possible to cultivate an abstract loyalty to ideas, to doctrines, to practices without any intimate association with people.

Thus, the spirituality of the *Didache* is resistant to becoming an ideology. Nor can the one who embraces the *Didache* ever fall into any pseudo-conflict of conceptualizing the Way of Life as a written law that then allows for an open conflict between the letter and the spirit of this law. The Way of Life is always humanized by the interpersonal encounters between the mentor and the novice. The very meaning of fasting, of praying, of being "long-suffering" is suffused with the way of fasting, praying, and of being long-suffering, which the novice learns by empathetically entering into the practice of his/her mentor. Loyalty emerges not as faith in an abstract system but as an attachment to a living person who captivates the heart and transforms the interiority of the one seeking God.

> Oral synthesis creates a tense world of personal loyalties and betrayals. Not only is the message inseparable from the speaker, but the speaker is as important to the recipients as the message. . . . (Kelber: 147)

This is why, in rabbinic Judaism, the rule was to have only one master and to live with him until one had mastered the whole of his torah. Jacob Neusner, in reflecting upon what it meant for the disciples of Yohanan ben Zakkai (C.E. 1–80) to be attached to their master, has this to say:

> Disciples were not merely students who came to a master to learn facts or holy traditions. They came to study the master as much as what he said. "Torah" was revealed in traditions handed on orally as in writing. Just as one studied what was written, so he had to imitate what was not written but living in the master himself. A living Torah, his every gesture must have some basis in the ancient traditions. The disciples lived with the master because daily life, like classroom discourse, was a school for Torah. (1970: 97)

The framers of the *Didache*, accordingly, assigned one mentor/master to each novice. As shown in chapter 1, this relationship developed into a trusting and loving bond akin to that of parents caring for their children. Likewise, the novice was told, both night and day, to contemplate "the one speaking to you the word of God" (4:1). Thus, it was the person of the one mentoring and not his principles or rules that was of primary importance. Only someone who has been enlarged and nurtured into a godly way of life by someone older and wiser than him/herself could truly "honor him/her as the Lord" (4:1). A pedantic, a menacing, or a neglectful mentor could not be worthy of such honor. Thus, the spirituality of the *Didache* began and lived itself out based on personal attachments. The Way of Life could never be an abstract attachment to a set of rules.

Within such a religious system, "faith" is first and foremost a confidence in persons and is lived out by "doing faith." Only when religion has become an esoteric position of privilege does "faith" get reinterpreted as "knowing with certitude things that cannot be discovered by reason alone." In such a system, "faith" is a way of seeing the world and is divorced from a way of being and relating in the world.

Sometimes it is imagined that reading the holy books of the Bible produces "faith" in the hearts of the readers. Nothing could be further from the truth. The sacred texts of India, for instance, were routinely translated and studied by Western experts for over a hundred years without producing a single convert. As soon as gurus began to arrive in the West and set up ashrams, however, a significant number of converts came forward. One can remember, for example, the rather spectacular conversion of the Beatles in the late 1960s and their insistence that the doctrine and practices of the Maharishi made more sense to them than Christianity. I recently visited the Hare Krishna center known as New Vrindabad (near Wheeling, West Virginia) and discovered that, after a period of decline in the 1980s and early 1990s, a revival has set in which has reaped many new recruits. A young devotee in his late twenties spoke with pride of how chanting the names of Krishna and becoming completely vegetarian allowed him to regain a "spiritual intensity" that had been impossible earlier because of his constant accumulation of bad karma. Sacred texts, therefore, can be studied and dissected with relish but have little power to convert lives unless they are linked to spiritual masters who offer a humanized and attractive version of what these texts mean in their lives and in their words.

In the *Didache*, accordingly, one came to the movement because one was attracted by the ordinary living in an extraordinary way that characterized one or more members of the community. The training necessary to become one of them was offered in a one-on-one situation wherein the mentor became "a parent" who retrains "a child" in much the same way that a young person adopted by a foreign family is prepared to live and to flourish under a new set of values, rites, way of living. The novice was never told to study the scriptures or to believe a creed. Rather, the novice was told, "night and day, you will remember the one speaking to you the word of God" (4:1). In good and bad times, the novice was also told to "seek every day the presence of the saints" (4:2; 16:2). Attachment to special people was thus the preferred route to holiness. Everything else was secondary.

#16D THE POWER OF BEING GATHERED TOGETHER

In the late 1960s, I participated in my first Encounter Group in Berkeley, California, where I was a graduate student. Eight strangers came together and committed themselves to listening and to talking for three hours every Sunday evening for eight weeks. During the first hour, each person introduced him/herself by telling something significant that happened during the week. We were then told that, from this point onward, there was no agenda, no structure, and just a few rules: (1) Listen deeply. Help the one speaking to explore and to cherish his/her own experience. (2) Don't interrupt. Don't give advice. (3) Make space, from time to time, for quiet members to speak.

I was very nervous at the start. I considered myself to be a very private person. I had to develop a trust level with someone before I felt comfortable sharing the deeper currents in my life. Thus, I was mildly skeptical that trust could be established within a group so quickly that they could speak meaningfully about their lives.

By the end of eight weeks, I found myself deeply caring about the members of my group. They had demonstrated a certain vulnerability. They had shared something of the turbulence in their lives. Within the exchange, they had discovered inner resources and lived values that guided and sustained them in rough waters. A few even had their lives profoundly changed. I, for one, surprised myself. I discovered that I was capable of entrusting myself to a group. I also discovered that, within a group, there was enough shared wisdom to prevent the destructive and misguided behavior of a few from dominating or wrecking the whole. One of the men in the group, for example, admitted near the end that his initial reason for coming was to make out with the women in the group. In the fifth session, this young man did a complete turnaround and publicly wrestled with his felt need to be caught up in a seemingly unending string of short-term relationships with women.

Three years later, this same level of sharing was taking place in the religious community to which I then belonged. Wednesday evenings were set aside for ourselves. Each evening began with a eucharist celebrated informally in our living room. This was followed by a better-than-average community meal. Then three hours were devoted to listening to each other. Traditionally, we began with each of us reviewing the successes and trials experienced during the past week. Then the floor was thrown open. The revelations and exchanges had the effect of bonding each of us to the other even when, at times, we did not entirely agree with each other. All in all, as the weeks progressed, I felt that the others knew me deeply and cared about me. The others felt the same way.

David Bohm, in his own study of the innate capacity for collective intelligence, wrote of a tribe that did something of what I have known:

> From time to time, (the) tribe (gathered) in a circle. They just talked and talked and talked, apparently to no purpose. They made no decisions. There was no leader. And everyone could participate. There may have been wise men or wise women who

were listened to a bit more—the older ones—but everyone could talk. The meeting went on, until it finally seemed to stop for no reason at all and the group dispersed. Yet after that, everybody seemed to know what to do, because they understood each other so well. (cited from *On Dialogue* in Jaworski: 109)

In my Encounter Group, my religious community, and, later, my men's group, this same pattern prevailed. The participants talked openly and frankly because they wanted to understand themselves and the social environment in which they were living. No one ever said, "You can't think this," or "You can't do this"—because the very purpose was to push beyond social conventions and community rules to discover the roots of a wisdom for living that rang true in the collective life experience. In each instance, persons exposed their experience in order to discover what moved and guided them. To be sure, those who spoke from time-honored experiences were given special respect, not as authorities who set down rules but as persons who had explored life and had found a way of life that fitted them.

Applying this to the Didache community, it seems that something like the above lies behind the admonition "frequently be gathered together" (16:2). The advice for facing the end time is expressly not to pray more, to fast more, to confess more—the kind of advice that modern-day ministers sometimes give to troubled souls. Even novices were told of the special regard due to their mentor (4:1) and then immediately attention was given to "seek[ing] every day the presence of the saints in order that you may rest upon their words" (4:2). Here again, the way to peace, contentment, and holiness was not secured by directing the novice to pray more, to fast more, to confess more. The tacit presupposition was that being with and talking with "the saints" had the effect of enabling and empowering persons to deepen their chosen way of life. One must suspect, therefore, that conversation among the saints was not just casual talk about the weather, sports, and work; rather, one must suspect free-flowing conversations about the experience of living and finding "rest" in the Way of Life.

One can also note that conversation with "the saints" does not imply that the community has a subset of individuals who are routinely called "saints." The term "saints" here honors and upholds the efforts of every individual striving toward holiness of life and not just a few superstars. Note also that no special mention is made of the apostle-prophets or the bishops and deacons. The apostle-prophets, as was discovered earlier, were given over to tiptoe expectation and to heroic forms of sanctity (see #10b and the end of ch. 6). The *Didache* had no cause to dub this group "the saints," regarding whom members might "rest upon their words" (4:2).

The same holds for the bishops and deacons, who were known for their *leitourgia* ("unpaid public service") and not especially for their sanctity. In the end, therefore, the *Didache* implies the following:

1. The *Didache* had no superstars or divinely sanctioned leaders who were designated in advance and were to be sought out for their special wisdom, special holiness, and special guidance. The practice of one-on-one personal apprenticeship by mentors meant that wisdom was localized in the group.

2. The *Didache* has no mystique surrounding either baptism or eucharist that would allow its framers to promote indiscriminatingly something like worthy reception of these rites. Neither does the *Didache* give to formal preaching (which is nowhere mentioned) any special character as being the familiar vehicle for grace and conversion of life.

3. While the Didache communities had a routine of rites, prayers, confessions, and fasts, the framers of the *Didache* trusted instinctively in the exchange of "words" (4:1, 2) and in the "gathering together" (16:1). This people-to-people connection and the free flow of dialogue were acknowledged as safeguards in adversity and abundant sources of peace, rest, and satisfaction in ordinary times.

The Genius of Ordinariness

The Didache *as Favoring Ordinary Holiness*

In the first-century world of conflicting spiritualities, the *Didache* affirmed the everyday holiness practiced by householders while resisting the eschatological extremes practiced by those charismatic wanderers who had lost jobs, homes, and families in order to promote the Gospel. The pastoral genius of the *Didache* is that it knew how to honor the heroic virtue and charismatic gifts of the prophets without imagining that perfection consisted in doing what they did (11:11). The *Didache* celebrated the love of God and neighbor (1:2) in the daily little things: in short prayers (8:2), in sharing resources (4:8), in reconciling those fighting (4:3). Prolonged prayers, selling all one has in order to give it to the poor, and reconciling the whole world to Christ were left to others—the few and not the many. Here, then, in the moderate and delicate wisdom of the *Didache*, the unadorned attraction of ordinary holiness supplanted and tamed the excesses of the wandering apostle-prophets.

The *Didache* defined a Way of Life that enabled its adherents to attain that "perfection" that would be expected of them by the Lord on the last day (6:2; 16:2). By gathering together "frequently" (16:2) and maintaining a community rhythm of daily prayer (8:2–3), semiweekly fasting (8:1), and the weekly confession of failings followed by the eucharist (4:14; 14:1), the adherents of this community found "rest/refreshment" for their souls (4:2; 16:2). The emphasis here is clearly on a moderate middle way that the whole community could practice together. Continuous or prolonged fasting was not encouraged. At no point were special religious experiences, such as mystical visions or speaking in tongues, either referred to or prized. Working at a trade was commended to everyone (12:3); hence, no one would have been inclined to imagine that they ought to set aside the ordinary events attached to earning a livelihood in favor of accomplishing some heroic deeds. Some provision was made for prophets and teachers to be the exceptions, yet at no time did the framers of the *Didache* hold up their gifts as superior to all others or advocate that these persons somehow had gained a greater holiness. Quite to the contrary, the framers of the *Didache* were only too aware that prophets sometimes acted inappropriately and had to be checked (11:4–12:1). Furthermore, in the last days, the framers of the *Didache* imagined that the prophets would not be the saviors and sustainers but rather joined with the "corruptors" (16:3). At every point, therefore, the spirituality of everyday holiness was secured against heroic measures, extremes of piety, and apocalyptic fever.

The Spirituality of Living in the Presence of God

The spirituality of the *Didache* hinged upon God's presence in the world. God was not far off in his heavens such that, after death, those who were loyal to him might expect to be with him. No. God comes to us. His presence in the world was not limited or even expected in spiritual experiences. Rather, God was present in those events that he shaped.

What events? The God the novice met first was not the God of Genesis or the God of Exodus, but, on a much more personal note, the mystery of one's own formation in the womb of one's mother. Here the novice felt the "God who made you" (*Did.* 1:2). The implied theology here followed from the Jewish understanding that the biological father implants the seed (*semen* in Latin) in the fertile womb of the mother, but then he goes away in ignorance while God takes over and sees to its growth and development:

> For it was you [O Lord] who formed my inward parts;
>   you knit me together in my mother's womb.
> I praise you, for I am fearfully and wonderfully made. . . .
> My [skeletal] frame was not hidden from you
>   when I was being made in secret, intricately woven. . . .
> Your eyes beheld my unformed [embryonic] substance.
>   (Ps 139:13–16)

The notion that DNA molecules contain the entire blueprint of the living being was entirely unknown to the ancient Hebrews. If the seed grew into an embryo, it was molded by the Lord God, who worked unobtrusively and secretly within the human womb (Jer 31:7–9; Is 44:1–3, 21–24; 66:5–13; Job 31:15; Wis 7:1f.; Sir 1:15; Gal 1:15). In the face of this mysterious and majestic activity during nine months, a spontaneous response was forthcoming: "I praise you, for I am fearfully and wonderfully made" (Ps 139:14). As a pragmatic theology, therefore, the framers of the *Didache* identified "the God who made you" as the one "you will love" (1:2). The love of God, by implication, emerges out of a sense of gratitude and awe for having been so marvelously fashioned in the womb.

Once formed in the womb, God's work was not finished. The novice was keenly aware that, as in the case of Abraham, the Lord called the novice (*Did.* 4:10) to leave his/her pagan family and friends and to follow him to a new place. Just as the Israelites were led out of the land of slavery and, only then, did God reveal to them his Torah on Mount Sinai, so too gentiles meet the Lord in the words revealed by their mentors (*Did.* 4:1) as they exit from their own families. The mentor revealed "the life and knowledge" which Jesus brought from the Father. The *Didache* described the novice as becoming one "trembling continually at the words that you have heard" (3:8). Here again, the internal clues of the *Didache* demonstrate that the Way of Life was not received coolly as mere information. Having been set upon the path of life by "the God who made you" (1:2), the novice trembled with excited anticipation and reverential fear. This is the way that Israel originally experienced the word of the Lord from Mt. Sinai (Ex 19:16) and the way that others after them came to discover the transforming power of God's word (e.g., Ezra 9:4, Is 66:2, Hab 3:16).

Many of us today might be tempted to reduce this "trembling" to a pious metaphor rather than the lived experience of novices whose lives were blessed and transformed by a spiritual master in the Didache community. The very use of this term in the *Didache*, however, would have been a source of embarrassment if novices never experienced anything resembling trembling. Minimally, the *Didache* was signaling that novices were not receiving a philosophical rule of life that merited quiet contemplation. Maximally, the *Didache* was expressing that the deepest longings of the human heart were being addressed and that trembling was the most common and most appropriate existential response in the face of such experience. William James, in his *Varieties of Religious Experience,* provides numerous instances of "trembling" in the face of felt religious experience.

The Jewish tradition of the seventh century thought of each Jew as being called and trained individually by the Lord:

> Said Rabbi Levi, "The Holy One, blessed be he, had appeared to them like an icon that has faces in all directions, so that if a thou-

sand people look at it, it appears to look at them as well. So too when the Holy One, blessed be he, when he was speaking, each and every Israelite would say, 'With me in particular the Word speaks.' What is written here is not, I am the Lord your [second person plural] God, but rather, I am the Lord your [second person singular] God who brought you out of the land of Egypt [Ex 20:2]." (*Pesiqta of Rab Kahana* 12.25.2)

The *Didache* nowhere expressly parallels the calling one by one of each Israelite out of Egypt with the calling of each novice out of idolatry. Nonetheless, the notion that each Jew is called and addressed personally finds a strong parallel in the one-to-one meeting of the novice with a mentor in the *Didache*. Thus the novice in the *Didache* also understood the Lord to say: "I am the Lord your God who brought you out of the land of idolatry" (see *Did.* 4:10).

Having heard the life-giving wisdom of the Lord, the child of God trusts that his/her Father will act so that "the experiences befalling you" are "good things," for "apart from God, nothing happens" (*Did.* 3:10). Here again, the history of Israel was not examined, and the novice was not brought to admire how the Lord acted on behalf of an entire people. If that had been the case, then the *Didache* would have used words parallel to those found in a kindred Jewish document created during the same period:

God has created all the nations on the earth, and he has created us: he has foreseen what will happen to both them and us from the beginning of creation of the earth to the end of the age; and nothing has been overlooked by him, not even the smallest detail, but he has foreseen everything and brought everything about. (*Apocalypse of Moses* 12:4)

Nor, for that matter, did the *Didache* place the novice before the awesome providence exercised in the whole cosmos—how God guides the course of all the heavenly bodies and changes the season on earth with faithful regularity. For that matter, the *Didache* did not follow the course of Jesus in Q (Lk 12:22–31; Mt 6:25–34) where reflection on how the Father fed the ravens who "neither sow nor reap" (Lk 12:24) and clothed the lilies in a grandeur exceeding that of "Solomon in all his glory" (Lk 12:27) was used as the point of departure to instill a confidence in providence. No. The *Didache* chose to stay close to the seemingly insignificant yet personal "experiences befalling you" (3:10). The discovery of God's providence opened up when both mentor and novice begin reciting how their personal histories were peppered with events that happened because of the care of the Lord. Just as the God sought in the *Didache* was first and foremost the God close at hand, "the God who made you" (1:2), so too now the care of this God was found in the fabric of life into which each one was embedded.

The presence of God begins in the personal realm—formation in the womb, election, training, providential care—but it did not stop there. This was the spirituality of the neophytes. Later, in the eucharist, it is evident that the novices would be led into a larger world so that they would be able to comprehend "the vine of David" (9:2). Even here, however, it is quite conceivable that the narratives of the Father's raising up David to be king over against the objection of family, elders, and Saul might have been a natural starting point for understanding how Jesus brought "the life and knowledge" of the Father to the gentiles so that they might be grafted onto the history of God's chosen ones. So, too, with time, the neophytes would be prepared for that presence of God expected in the end time. The eucharistic prayers of the presider and of the prophets were filled with the message of expectation of the ingathering of the elect. God's will was not yet being done on earth; hence, God intended to come and establish his presence among humans as a permanent guarantee that evil would be no more and that every tear would be wiped away. The spirituality of the *Didache*, therefore, was poised on the brink of great expectations!

What to Do Until the Lord Comes

The *Didache* did not offer any plan for world transformation. Not even on the local level did the members of the Didache communities imagine that they would improve the economy, wage a war on poverty, prevent the abuse of the weak (slaves, women, children). The pathos of the *Didache* entered the pathos of God—these things were to be longed for—yet the members of the Didache communities had no mandate and no power to change the society in which they lived (see final box). The time was too short. The members were too weak. The society was too out-of-step with their ambitions. All they could do was take care of each other, work at their trades, and celebrate their daily lives until the Lord comes.

The pathos of God extended to all who suffered. In the ancient world, there were no enlightened social and governmental programs that cared for the crippled, the orphaned, the unemployed, the sick, the insane. People in bad situations had to find help from their own families and, when this was not forthcoming, from strangers. Thus, the new spiritual family closed around new members offering them nourishing food, simple lodging, and meaningful work.

Meanwhile, the quality of pathos was developed by asking the novice to give to everyone asking you for anything, "for, to all, the Father wishes that there be given [these things] from his own free gifts" (1:5). Perhaps, like most, the novice had been trained by his parents to avoid and to ignore the beggars on the streets. One has only to travel to a country without social welfare to discover what must have been the everyday reality of the disadvantaged. A widowed mother nursing a sickly child covered with scabs begs to be able to feed her two boys and hopes to save enough to buy medicine to treat her infant's disease. A former soldier with one leg removed because of injury in war begs to be able to keep his family intact in their rented flat. A group of orphaned children dressed in rags beg to forestall being sent to bed without supper or, worse, being beaten by their caretakers. The novice, perhaps for the first time, was forced to take notice and to give "for, to all, the Father wishes to give from his own free gifts" (1:5). Perhaps, in addition to reenvisioning themselves as stewards of God's resources, novices were also learning that these miserable beggars in the street did not represent what God had in mind. Thus, while encountering the castoffs of society, novices were perhaps being prepared to ask questions about why some are so superfluously rich while others are so miserably poor. Surely the Father did not design a world in which some exist in unbridled luxury while others suffer from chronic hunger. Giving cultivated the pathos of God and enlarged the expectation of the time when his will would be done on earth (8:1).

#16E REFLECTIONS ON THE CHRISTIAN MOTIVE FOR CHARITY

The practical directives of the *Didache* regarding the sharing of resources are significantly different from the impulse normally governing Christian charity. Charity has traditionally been upheld as a Christian duty and, in the face of gross inequities and exploitation of workers in the early part of the twentieth century, the public libraries and public parks created out of the fortunes of the American industrial magnates also served to atone for their sins against the working classes (*Did.* 4:6). Above all, however, charity has been tied in with the prospect of gaining leverage with the Lord in the life to come. For this, of course, Jesus' parable of the final judgment (Mt 25:31–46) is normally cited for support.

The problem with this parable is that it seemingly invites good Christians to "make believe" that they are serving Christ when they feed the hungry, clothe the naked, visit the sick. Mother Teresa was a fervent proponent of this kind of charity:

> God wanted me to be poor and to love him in the distressing disguise of the poor. (Mother Teresa cited in Hurley: 48)

> The poor who continue to suffer the sorrows of his passion, . . . we cannot offer them anything but our testimony of love, seeing Christ himself in each one of them. . . . (Mother Teresa cited in Benenate: 164)

Seemingly there would not be sufficient inherent worth in doing these things because the one hungry, naked, or sick is just an ordinary human being (as the *Didache* would have it). Hence, one has to imagine Christ being fed, Christ being clothed, Christ being comforted.

If one listens to Matthew's parable of the final judgment, one notices that both the just and the unjust are initially surprised and confused at the terms of the Lord's judgment. Many good Christians, however, imagine that they will *not be surprised* at the final judgment since they know in advance what the terms of the final judgment will be. The moment they claim this privileged insight, however, they fail to see *that this parable does not belong to them*. They have merely found a way to claim from God a reward for their own merits. Those in the parable are genuinely surprised and confused at the terms of the Lord's judgment precisely *because they did these things without any pretending*—that is, for ordinary, suffering human beings—and without any thought of a heavenly reward. The surprise in Matthew's parable is that, at the final judgment, it is the Son of Man who will do the pretending. He will say, in effect, "I was so moved by what you did 'to the least of these who are members of my family' (Mt 25:40) that I regarded it as though 'you did it for me'" (Mt 25:40). One has to be a sensitive parent to understand these words. Once understood, they dispel any notion of gaining leverage with God in the face of the final judgment.

The practice of sharing resources in the *Didache* has no affinity with the doctrine of prosperity (Robertson: 86f.), which is fashionable in most fundamentalist Christian circles today. The formula for prosperity, when all the pious layers are scraped away, amounts to this: "You give generously to God, and God will give generously to you." This "generosity to God" begins with but does not end with the collection plate; hence, it cannot be dismissed out of hand as entirely self-serving. What is new about this doctrine is that it is impatient with the traditional Christian doctrine that the unseen and unnoticed giving will be rewarded when the Lord comes (Mt 6:3–4) and insists, to the contrary, that "the man of faith will prosper now." Thus something like "tithing" (giving one-tenth of one's income to God) or "sacrificial giving" to one's church is no longer regarded as a suitable way to enable gifted servants of the community to do the work of the gospel, for now it becomes a sign made in faith that, once God takes notice of it, the giver will prosper (i.e., receive a better job, or better pay, or enjoy better health). This prospering, it should be noted, is not measure for measure but overflowing and superabundant—in a word, graced.

Pat Robertson is a fervent advocate of tithing and sacrificial giving. He tells the story of how a poor peasant congregation in Chile was reluctantly asked by their pastor to tithe (118f.). When a drought came into the area, however, the following happened:

> Crops failed; buildings deteriorated; gloom covered everything. But, miraculously, this was not so with the members of that little church [that tithed]. Their crops flourished as though supernaturally watered. But more than that, the yields were extraordinary, bounteous, healthy, flavorful. Their fields were green, while those around were withered. (120)

Robertson then goes on to explain, using Mal 3:7–10, that the ten-percent tithe is just the "expected minimal amount" (121). Those who wish to prosper give more:

> Many people ignore any ten percent cutoff and give out of the abundance of their provision. I know one New Jersey florist who had been thoroughly blessed by the Lord as he exercised the principles we are exploring in this book, and he frequently gave 90 percent of his annual income to the service of God. And the prosperity simply mounted. He was not able to outgive the Lord. (121)

I can appreciate the fact that many small congregations require tithing in order to keep the church operations and ministries afloat. The doctrine of prosperity, however, appears to offer the giver a route to bribe God for his blessings. While some Protestant fundamentalists have been particularly harsh in their judgment of Catholics for all their schemes to win heaven on their own merits, it is disturbing that their "doctrine of prosperity" is not submitted to this same scrutiny. It is also disturbing that this doctrine appears to have so many scriptural warrants that it can entirely turn a blind eye to those words attributed to Jesus that categorically condemn the prosperous (e.g., Lk 6:20–26). The *Didache*, needless to say, has no doctrine of prosperity.

The *Didache*, for its part, while it did not know of the theology of Mother Teresa or that of Pat Robertson, was seemingly not able to retain a pure notion of giving and taking and responsive stewardship without giving a nod to self-interest. Thus, the *Didache* does sanction giving motivated "for the ransoming of your sins," "for you will know the Lord God who will be giving back excellent recompense when he comes" (4:7). Thus, in the *Didache* itself there are inconsistencies that demonstrate that it was responsive to diverse opinions that held sway. All in all, however, the primary motive for giving is that the one giving acts as the agent of the Father who "wishes to give these things from his own free gifts" (1:5) to those who ask (see #2d).

THE GENIUS OF FAMILY WORKSHOPS

Theology of Work According to the Didache

The *Didache* had no knowledge of modern sweatshops, of mechanized production in which humans are forced to keep pace with machines, of enterprising entrepreneurs bent on extracting as much work as possible for the lowest pay. Yet, as detailed in chapter 2, the first century witnessed the outbreak of large commercial farms and tax-free workshops wherein slaves labored from dawn to dusk to make products that flooded the markets and threatened the viability of the modest family-owned and family-run enterprises. In response, the *Didache* put forward an alternative economic worldview. As a silent rebuke to the leisure class with inherited wealth and to the new managerial class who oversaw the work of slaves or indentured workers, the *Didache* put forward the notion that working with one's hands was normal and expected (12:3–5). In order to sever the nerve that allowed individuals to take pride in the illusion of their "private wealth," the *Didache* required novices to give "to everyone asking you for anything" (1:5) with the understanding that they were thereby acting as faithful stewards or brokers who dispensed the Father's resources to those making their requests known. The *Didache* also groomed its members to set aside the first fruits for the prophets or the beggars (13:3–4), so that those prospering in their trade or business were given to thanking the Father for what they had received. One has here, in germ, the cutting of the mainspring of the prevailing doctrine of private greed. According to the *Didache*, those who amass riches (whether by inheritance, by luck, or by personal ingenuity) were merely richer in the resources of their common Father and were thereby all the more capable and obliged to function as worthy entrepreneurs in the Father's business of ensuring that his blessings were available to all.

Individuals, according to the *Didache*, were to reenvision themselves as agents of God actively functioning with his care and concern for all. Even when giving, they were retrained to acknowledge that they dispersed "his own free gifts" and thus did not force the one receiving to be humiliated or beholden to them. Giving, therefore, was a lifelong orientation, and the members of the Didache communities continually offered the first fruits of all their enterprises in order to acknowledge that they were only faithful stewards of God's gifts to them (13:3–7).

Candidates were forewarned that they "will not be joined with the lofty but with the just and the lowly" (3:9). Their economic vulnerability, consequently, was enlarged by virtue of their Way of Life. Yet the framers of the *Didache* were acutely aware that, collectively, the ravages of economic competition could be contained by a program of sharing resources. The Way of Life, accordingly, proposed that reciprocal receiving and giving (4:5) formed the mainspring of a divinely instituted economic program that would exist in this world and would be perfected in the world to come. Among the saints, therefore, there was no option but to "partner together . . . sharing all things . . . for, if you are partners in the immortal things, by how much more are you partners in the mortal things?" (4:8) In a world without fair labor laws, without unemployment compensation, without sick pay, without social security, members of the family were for the most part forced to cultivate a protective regard for the weak, for the disadvantaged, for the sick, and for the aged. Since most members who joined the movement were uprooted out of their biological families, the genius of the *Didache* substituted the notion that God's family embraced them all so that every man in the movement had to be related to as a brother and every woman as a sister. No one, therefore, was expendable or sold into debt bondage—and it was the Lord's doing!

The Didache's *Opposition to Entrepreneurial Zeal*

Finally, the *Didache* provided an orientation that was decidedly bad for succeeding in business. The entrepreneurial experts and their Christian imitators today all agree that the successful entrepreneur must be aggressive, innovative, assertive, self-assured, and daring. Merril Lynch managing director Martin S. Fridson in his new book *How to Be a Billionaire* mined the financial wisdom of self-made billionaires such as Richard Branson, Bill Gates, Wayne Huizenga and concluded that most people, however greedy, are not capable of doing the dirty work that must be done to "vanquish the mighty economic and social forces that conspire against your rise to massive wealth." To illustrate this, Fridson explained how Wayne Huizenga used a "good-cop/bad-cop" tactic to get little video rental stores to sell out to Blockbuster. "If the [local] chain's owner did not sell out, Blockbuster might open additional stores in the region and become a greater threat [to their survival]." Thus, *only someone ruthless enough to dominate the market, outmanage the competition, and resist the unions is capable of becoming a billionaire.*

In contrast to this, the *Didache* advocated dispositions designed for entrepreneurial losers:

> [A] Become long-suffering
> > and merciful
> > and harmless
> > and calm
> > and good
> > and trembling through all time at the words
> > > that you have heard.

> [B] You will not exalt yourself,
> > (and) you will not give boldness to your soul.
> > Your soul will not be joined with the lofty,
> > but with the just and the lowly you will dwell.

> [C] You will accept the experiences befalling you as good things,
> > knowing that, apart from God, nothing happens.
> > (3:8–10)

When one examines the probable background for these lists (see ch. 2 above), it probably comes from those whose livelihood and standard of living had been curtailed or jeopardized owing to the "bigger is better" mentality that promoted huge managed farms and workshops. These enterprises competed unfavorably with local family-owned and family-operated farms and workshops that had been the order of the day. The ruthless "bigger is better" mentality that netted huge wealth for the few and huge suffering for the many finds its resonance in the characteristics of the Way of Death (*Did.* 5:2).

#16F THE RUTHLESS CHARACTER
OF AGRIBUSINESS

Each year hundreds of family farmers are forced to sell out in my own home state of Ohio. From the vantage point of agribusiness, these family-owned and family-run farms are seen to be "inefficient" and doomed to extinction. Now, as the latest threat to the existence of the remaining family farms, mammoth hog farms financed by entrepreneurial experts are being established throughout the state. These farms are being promoted by big business as bringing more employment and needed income to idle farm hands. In effect, however, the extra cash family farmers came to depend on by raising half a dozen hogs has completely disappeared because these new hog farms (raising two to twelve thousand hogs under a single roof) offer slaughter houses lower prices and an assured steady supply of hogs. Most of us have been led to believe that "mass production" serves to lower consumer prices. Not in this case. Following the introduction of these mammoth hog farms, the price for hogs ready for slaughter has fallen, while the price of pork at the checkout counters has remained surprisingly stable. The extra profits have gone into the pockets of the middlemen, especially the out-of-state investors bent on making hog farming the up-and-coming agribusiness in Ohio. Thus, while a small minority of farmers employed in this new agribusiness have received some benefit, their neighbors have suffered yet another beating from our laissez-faire economy.

In Third World countries, the plight of small, independent farmers verges on the catastrophic. In these countries, agribusiness zealously favors production for export and the lowering of trade barriers. Brazil, for instance, cuts down its rain forests at an alarming rate in order to raise grain for feed cattle, which are butchered and prepared for export to the tables of the comparatively rich meat-eaters of the United States and western Europe. Meanwhile, since more and more acreage has been removed from the production of beans and rice, the cost of these staples for the indigenous poor has drastically risen out of proportion with the general economy. Mexico, meanwhile, thanks to NAFTA (North American Free Trade Agreement), finds itself inundated with cheap U.S. corn (a staple in the Mexican diet) that is having the effect of driving hundreds of thousands of family farms out of business and dooming the people to relocate to overcrowded cities in search of jobs while living in squalid and overpriced rental units:

> Until Carlos Salinas de Gortari became president in 1988, Mexico attempted to protect its corn production system from artificially cheap U.S. corn. Corn is the Mexican food staple and is produced by 2.5 million small farmers, mostly of indigenous decent. Half of the land under cultivation in Mexico is dedicated to corn, which is as important culturally as it is economically. NAFTA's Congressional Budget Office Report on Agriculture stated that Mexico's corn program had been a "*de facto* rural employment and anti-poverty program." But to insure the passage of NAFTA, Mexico promulgated a series of reforms in the agricultural sector, including the breakup of the cooperative farms (*ejidos*) and signed away its right to protect [its homegrown] corn in NAFTA. As a result, economists predicted that as

few as seven hundred thousand and as many as ten million farmers could be displaced during the decade after NAFTA took
effect. (Lehman: 126)

Once Mexico had signed NAFTA and was admitted to the Organization for Economic Cooperation and Development, the twenty-five-mem-
ber club of industrialized nations, fresh capital investment was expected to
pour into Mexico creating new jobs and new opportunities. In effect, however, while the number of foreign-owned factories did increase, the influx
of inexpensive goods swamped the market and closed down many locally
owned factories. Carlos Heredia summarized the impact of NAFTA as
follows:

Signing NAFTA [in January 1994] has had similar [bad] results.
One year afterward, unemployment rates were on the rise, and
small and medium-sized factories were closing down. The 1995
crisis of the peso and the massive bailout has totally shattered
NAFTA's promise of prosperity for everyone. (279; see also
Chomsky 1999: 102–12)

Meanwhile the World Bank and the IMF (International Monetary Fund)
have required that the Mexican government institute austerity measures in
order to bring inflation under control (Heredia: 276–82; Chomsky 1999:
122f.). These measures (1980–1992) partially succeeded but left behind a
tripled rate of infant deaths due to malnutrition, a reduction in educational
spending by over 50 percent ($45 per person annually compared to
$1,400 in the U.S.) and an ever-increasing burden on the poor: "From the
initialization of the pact [to control prices and wages] in December 1987
until May 1, 1994, the minimum wage had increased 136 percent, while
the cost of the Basket of Basic Goods had gone up 371 percent" (Heredia:
281, citing a study of the Faculty of Economics of the National
Autonomous University of Mexico; Chomsky 1999: 126f.). Here, then,
are the economic conditions that lie behind the headlines regarding widespread social unrest in Mexico (Chomsky 1999: 121–28).

I take time to cite these things because they enable one to understand,
in terms of what is happening today in the global marketplace, what was
happening in the Roman Empire when huge agricultural estates put the
squeeze on family-owned and family-operated farms and when factories
mass-producing glassware, cloth, and pottery put the squeeze on the family-owned and family-operated workshops. True, the big-business mentality served the immediate needs of the expanding body of citizens living in
urban splendor (Karliner: 21). At the same time, however, the number of
those falling through the cracks, the number of those being sold into debt-

servitude, and the number of those being backed into banditry and revolution increased. Rome's "economic miracle," consequently, worked in
ways remarkably parallel to the last forty years of the so-called "alliance for
progress." Foreign aid and foreign investment were offered to the countries south of our border with the expectation that they would create a
level of prosperity akin to that seen on our soap operas. The reality, however, has been a nightmare for the poorer classes (Heredia: 284; Karliner:
21–29; Chomsky 1999: 25–40).

#16G EXPLOITATION OF CHILDREN IN DEVELOPING ECONOMIES

At the height of the Industrial Revolution, it was commonplace to find
children working from sunrise to sunset in the sweltering heat of the cotton factories or in the cold chill of the mine shafts. With time, however, the
industrialized nations increasingly limited through legislation the role children were permitted to play in the workplace. In the blossoming Third
World economies, however, such restrictions are not in place. As a result,
it is commonplace for parents to be forced to hire out or even to sell their
children to entrepreneurs.

On the Internet I discovered a group of grade-school children raising
the issue with their peers. A girl of twelve writes as follows:

> Recently your Mom or Dad bought you a new soccer ball. There
> is a good chance that the ball was made by someone younger
> than yourself. Fully half of the soccer balls sold in the United
> States are made in Pakistan, and every one of those soccer balls
> had an assist from a child under 14 who toils 10 hours a day in
> subhuman sweatshops, stitching the ball or cutting material used
> to make it.
>
> This is not an isolated problem. More than 200 million chil-
> dren worldwide, some as young as four and five years old, are
> slaves to the production line. Most of these children work in Asia,
> especially the nations of India, Pakistan, Bangladesh and Indone-
> sia, but Latin America is guilty of this human rights abuse as well.
> India alone employs 50 million children between the ages of 10
> and 14. . . .
>
> Indian and Pakistani rug makers love child workers so much
> that they buy them. That's right, children are bought and sold
> for cash or for the settlement of a debt. Iqbal Masih was sold into
> slavery when he was only four years old. His Pakistani parents,
> desperate for money, sold their young son for less than $16. For

six years he was shackled to a carpet-weaving loom most of the time, tying tiny knots 10 hours a day.

Carpetmakers like the young weavers because their tiny fingers can make very tight knots, and also because they are cheap to own and maintain. Masih was a free person by the age of 12 and crusaded against the horrors of child labor. In November 1994 Iqbal spoke out on the abysmal conditions in the sweat shops of Pakistan at the international labor conference in Stockholm, Sweden. The next month, he was given a Youth Action award in Boston. Shockingly, in March 1995 he was shot and killed in his village in Pakistan while riding his bicycle. Eshan Khan, chairman of the Bonded Labor Front, a group fighting child labor, said, "We know his death was a conspiracy by the carpet mafia." (www. madeuse.org/cause.html#child)

Thus, the so-called developing countries have reinstated practices that prevailed during the first century and that threatened the well-being of the Didache communities.

Exploitation, of course, is not limited to children. Consider, for example, the letter delivered to Phillip Knight, Nike's CEO, at Nike's annual shareholders' meeting on 22 September 1999. It was signed by forty-five human rights organizations, unions, and academic researchers from fifteen countries. The letter began as follows:

Almost a year and a half ago you made a speech to the US National Press Club announcing a series of measures to improve conditions in your suppliers' factories. Many of us concerned about these issues hoped that this announcement might signal a change in Nike's corporate heart. We hoped that the attitude to the human rights of workers who make your products might have moved from cynicism, denial and concealment towards a commitment to respect, openness and accountability.

Seventeen months later these hopes have proved false. Workers in your suppliers' factories continue to be overworked and subject to abusive management practices. Workers who tell journalists the truth about conditions in their factories or try to organize unions to defend their rights continue to be systematically humiliated and then dismissed.

Wages in Nike's suppliers' factories remain inconsciensably low. In Indonesia employees of your clothing suppliers are being expected to work in excess of 65 hours a week and yet are struggling to survive on less than $US1 a day. Research by the Interfaith Center for Corporate Responsibility last year indicated that a worker earning the minimum wage in a Nike factory in Vietnam must work for ten hours just to earn enough to buy one kilogram of chicken. . . .

Nike remains complicit in this exploitation. Your company continues to source products from totalitarian states where workers' human rights, including their right to form unions, are brutally repressed. If corporations choose to source their products from such places they have a huge responsibility to work actively to promote positive change. Instead Nike refuses even to make public statements calling for greater respect for human rights in these countries.

Worse, Nike turns its back on workers who are punished or dismissed for speaking out about the conditions in their factories. This not only punishes those workers, it sends a clear message to others that they must keep silent or else lose their jobs. It is hard to avoid the conclusion that Nike is determined to do all it can to conceal conditions in its suppliers' factories and to maintain the status quo in which workers producing Nike's products are powerless to assert their rights and afraid to reveal the conditions under which they work. (caa.org.au/campaigns/nike/index. html)

The remaining pages of the letter detail particular abuses that have taken place and that need rectification. Nike, in response to this letter, made efforts to address the complaints given. When the complaints touched upon wages and workers' rights to organize, however, nothing was done because, to do so would have made Nike less competitive in the world market. Nike directors had no interest in guaranteeing fair labor practices if this would result in higher costs of production and lower profits for their shareholders. Thus, in the end, only superficial changes were made in an attempt to placate the signers of the letter.

For every instance like Nike, there are hundreds of multinational corporations that escape public scrutiny. Thus, the Way of Death continues unimpeded by "those weighing down with toil the oppressed, those advocates of the rich, those lawless judges of the poor" (*Did.* 5:2). The prevalence of these practices today in our new global economy offers a vivid portrait of parallel practices that operated with even greater impunity in the economies of the first century. The owners and managers, both then and now, are not heartless and uncaring people; rather, the very conditions of competitive business make it advantageous to exploit the poor and the powerless as the sure route to becoming rich and powerful. In this arena, the late twentieth century reverted to the same Way of Death as in the first century.

The well-recognized financier George Soros is alarmed that the gap between the so-called "haves" and the "have-nots" has grown appreciably everywhere, including in the United States. Without any mechanism for rectifying this trend, "inequities can become intolerable." The *Investor's Business Daily* summarized Soros's fears as follows:

> Soros claims that many defenders of free markets espouse a sort of social Darwinism, and he says that this emphasis on the survival of the fittest is wrong. "The main point I want to make is that cooperation is as much a part of the system as competition," he wrote.
>
> Soros fears that market values may be displacing other values. "Unsure of what they stand for, people increasingly rely on money as the criterion of value," he wrote. "The cult of success has replaced a belief in principles. Society has lost its anchor." (14:111 [September 17, 1997] 12)

The character of the *Didache*, accordingly, was not born in anything like small-town or suburban America; rather it was born in places much more akin to the poor barrios scattered across the face of Mexico, where cheap U.S. corn, tools, and clothes are destroying the indigenous economy (see #16f). The *Didache* was born in the determination of local artisans and merchants to maintain their dignity of person and their quality of life through a system of partnering that increased their economic viability in the face of what the Roman Caesars regarded as the "economic miracle." The birth of the *Didache*, therefore, took place in the midst of those who had tasted economic suffering. When virtues are listed, consequently, "long-suffering" heads the list (*Did.* 3:8). And just prior to this the solemn promise for the eschatological future was sounded: "But be gentle, since the gentle will inherit the earth" (3:7).

Meanwhile, outside the safety net of the *Didache*, wealth and luxury were enjoyed by the privileged few—those with property, power, and multitudes of managers ensuring that each of their investments (mines, farms, factories) produced an ample profit. These sorts of persons get a scathing overview of their activities in the Way of Death:

[B09] those loving frivolous things,
[B10] those pursuing recompense,

[B11] those not showing mercy to the poor,
[B12] those not toiling for the one weighed down by toil,
[B13] those not knowing the one having made them,
[B14] those murderers of children,
[B15] those corrupters of God's workmanship,
[B16] those turning away the needy,
[B17] those weighing down with toil the oppressed,
[B18] those advocates of the rich,
[B19] those lawless judges of the poor
[B20] those totally sinful. (*Did.* 5:2)

One can note here that the framers of the *Didache* were content with honestly characterizing the economic exploiters they had known. Three reflections:

1. The framers of the *Didache* did not waste their breath threatening the hardhearted exploiters with the fire to come (16:5). Nor did they mobilize in order to try to close down their operations. On the other hand, they were quite sure that the future would hold no place for them and that God would utterly destroy them in his good time. At the same time, however, they created a safe haven whereby their loved ones would be preserved from the ravages of those living the Way of Death.

2. Neusner noted above (see #16a) that genuine dialogue does not take place until one knows what makes Jews suffer. In this list, accordingly, one finds the framers of the *Didache* exposing what has made their members suffer. Murders and adulteries are named first (*Did.* 5:1). One can surmise that these are rare events that are listed first because it was standard practice to do so. When one gets to acts of "trickery, arrogance, malice, self-pleasing, and greed" (*Did.* 5:1 [A13–17]), one is getting closer to the spontaneous deeds of the rich and powerful that caused widespread suffering. Finally, the end of the list [B9–20] reveals the kind of persons who have inflicted untold sufferings upon members of the Didache communities: "those loving frivolous things, those pursuing recompense, those not showing mercy to the poor, those not toiling for the one weighed down by toil, etc." Here again, most of the suffering hinted results from various aspects of economic exploitation.

3. Granted that the *Didache* had no explicit notion of sustainable development or of replenishing natural resources, yet one can surmise that it did voice a resounding "No" to exploitative business relations and did establish economic cooperatives that favored the well-being of all rather than the luxury of the few. Thus, while the *Didache* could not do away with the suffering caused by the rich and powerful, it could protect its own (as detailed in ch. 2) from the ravages of the Way of Death.

The Genius of Solidarity with Victims

The Limits of Forgiveness

It must also be noted that the *Didache* names those who have been a scourge to the vulnerable (5:2) without calling upon God or upon their victims to forgive their perpetrators. Forgiveness, according to the *Didache*, was not to be given out willy-nilly to just anyone. Even in the case of insiders, someone who was unwilling or unable to stop hurting others was given the cold shoulder and deliberately ostracized by the community (15:3). They acted, in other words, to protect the victims, even if this meant bringing pain and anguish upon the victimizers. Likewise, during the burning-process of testing, the members of the Didache community surely did not imagine that "those turning away the needy" and "those lawless judges of the poor" (*Did.* 5:2) would somehow be preserved from the flames by some last-minute act of divine forgiveness. Should the hundreds of young women humiliated, raped, and savagely murdered in the Jewish wars or in the recent wars in Bosnia be told that they must learn to kiss and embrace their perpetrators when the new age dawns? Should the young men cut down in wars and who died crying in pain as they slowly suffocated in their own blood be told again at the resurrection that all wars were good and all wars were justified because everyone fought for what seemed to them a just cause and everyone was expected to follow orders? Should those who spent their lives "weighing down with toil the oppressed" (5:2) and those who served as "advocates of the rich" (5:2) be granted equal and ready forgiveness along with their victims? The members of the Didache community would not have thought so.

Fyodor Dostoevsky, in his *Brothers Karamazov,* tested his own objections to the fanciful preaching that Jesus "can forgive everyone for everything because he himself shed his innocent blood for everyone and for everything" (300) in the character of Ivan. Faced with the innocent suffering of children, Ivan objects to the notion that Jesus (or anyone else for that matter) had the right to forgive, either now or at the final judgment, the torture inflicted on children. Ivan provides Alyosha, his brother, many graphic examples culled from the daily newspaper. One such tale he narrates is the following:

> A little girl of five was abused by her parents, "decent and most respectable people, well educated and cultured. . . ." Those educated parents subjected that poor little five-year-old to every conceivable torture. They beat her, whipped her, kicked her till she

was black and blue, all for no reason. Finally, they thought of the ultimate punishment; they shut her up all night in the outside privy, in the cold and the frost, because she wet herself at night (as if a five-year-old, sleeping soundly like an angel, could excuse herself in time)—for this, they smeared her face with her excrement and forced her to eat it, and it was her mother, her mother who did this to her! And that mother slept unconcernedly at night, oblivious to the sobs of the poor child shut up in that foul place! Can you understand such a thing: that small child, unable even to comprehend what is being done to her, in the dark and the cold of that foul place, beating her little panting breast with her tiny fists, sobbing, weeping humble tears of bloodstained innocence, praying to "Dear Father God" to protect her. . . . (2.5.4)

Only a pious, romanticized Christianity that mindlessly rhapsodizes about the unbounded love of God but has never felt the broken bodies and broken lives of the innocent victims of torture, of racial degradation, of systemic injustice would propose that everyone, no matter how heinous their crimes, need merely cry out for mercy in the face of the divine fire threatening to utterly destroy them and expect to be saved.

The survivors of the Shoah are much more on target when it comes to the issue of forgiveness: (a) No one can forgive on behalf of another. (b) No one ought to forgive unless there is *teshuvah* ("turning around" and repudiation of past crimes). (c) Finally, even when forgiveness comes, there is an obligation never to forget the past lest such crimes be repeated. The survivors of rape, incest, torture, spousal abuse, and of systemic injustice are likewise today wisely counseled to hold on to their rage since only by embracing it to its depth can they be healed of their victimization (see #12a). Yes, there is a moment of forgiveness, but it cannot come too early or too late, neither can it be given too promiscuously or too parsimoniously—otherwise the very justice of God is mocked. If God is not committed to bring justice and to ensure that "the gentle . . . inherit the earth" (*Did.* 3:7), then the entire community of the *Didache* would have to become a subversive organization bent on devising means to bring justice in the face of a God unwilling or unable to protect the victims of this world from the exploiters and abusers. In a word, when the victims of the Shoah are raised from the dead and called by the Father into the kingdom, they will never go in if their Nazi guards are handing out the invitations and ready to usher them in. Accordingly it might rightly be said that only someone who has been victimized or has been touched by loved ones who are victimized is able to read the thin raw echo of victimization that runs through the *Didache*.

#16H JESUS' ATONING DEATH AND SOLIDARITY WITH VICTIMS

More than one scholar has noted that the *Didache* makes no reference to the role or efficacy of Jesus' death in God's plan of salvation. For that matter, the *Didache* likewise refrains from casting any positive light upon suffering as such. This may strike many Christians as curious, since most Christians have become accustomed to accepting the efficacy of Jesus' suffering as imbued with God's mysterious plan of salvation. Hence the issue deserves some consideration. I frame my considerations under two test cases: (a) the suffering-death of my own mother; (b) the suffering death of a million Jewish mothers.

The Suffering Death of My Mother

By way of beginning, consider the following reflections upon suffering that I discover in my own mother's prayer book. I specifically chose her prayer book because she frequently read from this book while she suffered a prolonged and painful death as her body was being eaten away by an inoperable breast cancer during the second half of 1946.

> "Blessed are they that mourn, for they shall be comforted. . . ." (Mt 5:5, 10–12).
>
> By sufferings we become like to Christ and His blessed Mother, our Lady of Sorrows. Suffering was the lot of all the saints. Suffering is very meritorious. Suffering intensifies our love of God. Suffering has a refining influence upon our character. . . .
>
> Suffering is conducive to sanctity, for every sorrow, every trial, can be turned into a blessing. . . . St. Ignatius Loyola says: "If the Lord send you great tribulations, it is an evidence that he has great designs upon you, and that he wills that you become a saint. . . ."
>
> "The Son of God," says St. Theresa, "has accomplished our salvation by the means of sufferings; He would by this teach us that there is no means more proper to glorify God and to sanctify our souls than to suffer." (Lasance: 84–88)

Recently some Christians have become alarmed by the distortion present in such an image of suffering. Joanne Carlson Brown and Rebecca Parker, for instance, have stepped back from sentiments such as those found in my mother's prayer book and have concluded that "Christianity is an abusive theology that glorifies suffering" (cited in Heyward: 384). They accordingly end up asking a hard question:

> Is it any wonder that there is so much abuse in modern society when the predominant image or theology of the culture is of "divine child abuse"—God the Father demanding and carrying out the suffering and death of his own son? (cited in Heyward: 384)

Struggling to retain their faith in God and their solidarity with victims, Brown and Parker end up affirming categorically that "suffering is never redemptive and suffering cannot be redeemed" (cited in Heyward: 384).

At the time of my mother's death, a pious aunt tried to console me by saying, "God loved your mother so much that he took her early to be with him in heaven." I should have responded, "In that case, God must not love me very much because I need a mother and I don't see that God really cares much about either of us considering the way my mother died." As a boy of eight, I was too polite and too confused. But I remembered the shocking effect of my aunt's remark, and only many years later did I realize how sensitive and thoughtful Christians can sometimes say dreadfully silly things when faced with the enormity of the loss experienced by survivors.

A Million Jewish Mothers Die

Just to see how far some Christians have gone in order to extend the mystique of suffering, consider the responses made by highly educated Catholics to the extermination of the six million Jews during the Shoah (also referred to as the Holocaust). Cardinal John O'Connor, acting as the Catholic archbishop of New York, had this to say as part of his reflections upon visiting Yad Vashem, the Holocaust Museum in Israel:

> The crucifixion and its enormous power continue mystically and spiritually in this world in our day and will continue to the end of time. Christ . . . continues to suffer in his Body, the Church. . . . And this suffering has a purpose and an effect, as does ours if we conjoin it with his, if we "offer it up". . . . [Consequently] if the suffering of the crucifixion was infinitely redemptive, the suffering of the Holocaust, potentially conjoined with it, is incalculably redemptive. (47–48)

Archbishop O'Connor, mesmerized by the infinite redemptive suffering of Christ, undoubtedly thought he was honoring the dead Jews of the concentration camps when he associated their sufferings as being redemptive in a way analogous to those of Jesus. Many survivors of the death camps and their relatives (see Jacobs: 52–55) were neither flattered nor consoled by the archbishop's crude attempt to extend a Christian atonement theology to cover the enormity of evil involved in their loss.

Sorry to say, even Pope John Paul II has flirted with applying a mystique of suffering to the Shoah. When addressing the Jews of Warsaw on 14 June 1987, he spoke as follows:

> We believe in the purifying power of suffering. The more atrocious the suffering, the greater the purification. The more painful the experiences, the greater the hope. . . . (cited in Jacobs: 53)

A year later, while visiting Mauthausen Concentration Camp, the pope further observed that "the Jews [killed here] enriched the world by their suffering, and their death was like a grain that must fall into the earth in order to bear fruit, in the words of Jesus who brings salvation" (cited in Jacobs: 53).

Such language is confusing if not blasphemous in the ears of most Jews. Does a Jewish father whose daughter has been conscripted to provide sexual favors to the German troops on the front lines tell his daughter that her suffering will purify her love, purify her body, purify anything? Does a Jewish mother tell her little son who is about to be separated from her to die a slow starvation in the transport trains that the more painful the experience, the greater hope he ought to have? Hope for what? Even popes, one can see, sometimes make silly and injurious remarks when they are blinded by an unexamined and unreflective doctrine of the sufferings of Christ.

The truth is that Golgotha and Auschwitz do have a common thread of interpretation but this has nothing to do with a distorted mysticism of suffering or with the forgiveness of the guilty due to the death of the innocent. The common thread is that any system or person systematically dehumanizing others and using prolonged torture and slow starvation to make his/her point is acting cruelly and inhumanely. Inflicting torture cannot be sugarcoated. The screaming victims cannot be imagined as gaining for themselves or for others some mysterious benefit in this world or in the next. One can only say that the torture should never have happened and that the survivors stand as witnesses to the depth of sin in the world. As for God, we should never even hint that God would encourage, allow, or make use of torture (more on this later). Rather, we can only say that this kind of stuff makes God cringe and to avert his eyes such that the torture victims themselves cry out, "My God, my God, why have you forsaken me?"

Edward Schillebeeckx, in his two-volume work on Christology, came to this same conclusion after investigating the whole gamut of biblical references pertaining to the suffering and death of Jesus. He wrote:

God and suffering are diametrically opposed. . . . We can accept that there are certain forms of suffering that enrich our humanity. . . . However, there is an *excess* of suffering and evil in our history. . . . There is too much *unmerited* and *senseless* suffering. . . . But in that case we cannot look for a divine *reason* for the death of Jesus either. Therefore, first of all, we have to say that we are not redeemed *thanks to* the death of Jesus but *despite* it. (1980: 695, 724f., 729)

There is neither the time nor the space in this book to develop how Schillebeeckx moves through the familiar Hebrew and Christian Scriptures in order to arrive at this conclusion. It suffices for our purpose here to note that the *Didache* deliberately refrains from making any positive gesture toward the crucifixion of Jesus. My hunch is that the framers of the *Didache*, like contemporary Jews and like the young boy who lost his only mother, are repulsed by any notion of God that glosses over and makes torture acceptable. Whether it is Jews being tortured by medical experiments in the camps, or Jesus tortured on a Roman cross deliberately designed to humiliate and prolong death, or the case of a young mother tortured by the cancer eating her body—there is no divine reason for any of these. God cries out with the victim and tears his garments in grief as he does so. Any other God cannot be said to be in solidarity with victims.

#161 GOD TEARS HIS GARMENTS AND CRIES OUT FOR JESUS' DEATH

The more closely one examines the passion narratives, the more remote the Christian theology of atonement becomes. According to this theology, Jesus' death on the cross is the brightest moment in salvation history. According to the Synoptics, however, it is the darkest: "From the sixth hour, there was darkness over all the land until the ninth hour" (Mt 27:45 and par.). At the moment of Jesus' death, my childhood catechism presents the imagined image of the gates of heaven being thrown open after having been locked ever since the sin of Adam and Eve. According to the Synoptics, however, it is the temple veil that is rent in two "from top to bottom" (Mt 27:51 and par.). In most instances, this rending of the veil has been interpreted as a signal that the crime of the priests is so grievous that God abandons the holy of holies—tearing through the temple veil as he exits. Such an interpretation fails to take into account that the disciples of Jesus in Jerusalem went to the temple daily to pray and to teach (Acts 2:46; 3:1; 5:42). Other scholars have suggested that this tearing "originally represented Jesus' death" and later became a "supernatural portent of Jesus' deity" (Gundry 1994: 575). But why represent Jesus' death symbolically when, in actual fact, the event itself was narrated? Hebrews makes an oblique reference to "the new and living way that he opened for us through the [temple] curtain" (Heb 10:20), but it would be risky to transpose the theology of Hebrews back into the Synoptics. Following a suggestion of David Daube (23–26), a Jewish scholar, here is an interpretation that Christians have tended to overlook:

One has to be aware of the modes of expressing grief then current among the Jewish people. When a father of Jesus' day would hear of the death of a son, he would invariably rend his garment by grabbing it at the neck and tearing it from top to bottom [see, e.g., Gn 27:34; Jb 1:20; *b. Moed Qatan* 25a; *b. Menahot* 48a]. This is precisely the gesture suggested by the particulars of Matthew's text: "The veil of the Temple is torn in two from top to bottom" (27:51). In truth, God is Spirit. Symbolically, however, the presence of God within the holy of holies was rendered secure from prying eyes by the veil that surrounded that place. As such, the veil conceals the "nakedness" of God. It is this "garment" that grief-stricken Father of Jesus tears from top to bottom when he hears the final death-cry of his beloved son. Even for the Father, therefore, the death of Jesus is bitter tragedy and heartfelt grief (Milavec 1982: 57).

This should provide my readers with a point of departure for reeducating ourselves how to distinguish various kinds of suffering, how to recapture our rage and indignation at the suffering of the innocent, and how to wrest the message of Jesus from being a soft-headed plea for submitting to evil and forgiving enemies under any and all circumstances.

The Spirituality of Baptism and Eucharist

When approaching a foreign spirituality, the danger of reducing what we do not understand and what we do not participate in to manageable features that we do understand and in which we do participate is always present. One may be tempted to conclude, for example, that the framers of the *Didache* envisioned two key sacramental rites, baptism and eucharist, "just as we do today." Such a parallelism, however, is hazardous, for a cultural, historic, and religious chasm separates us from our spiritual ancestors, and two thousand years of development cannot simply be dismissed or overlooked. They may have done some of the same things, but, on the surface of it, there is no evidence that they took to these rites any of the emotional and perceptual habits of mind that govern contemporary church practice. Young boys play war games, yet how far removed this is from the actual experience of war that shatters the lives of even hardened men. Young girls play kissing games, yet how far removed this is from the passionate embraces of those who have become soul mates.

Baptism in the *Didache* has nothing to do with the mystique surrounding infant baptism in traditional theology (see #16c). Rather, it functions as a rite of passage. Prior to baptism, the novice was alienated from former gods, former kin, former friends. After the baptism, the novice was embraced by a new God, a new family, and (by anticipation) new friends. All in all, the transformative power of the rite evolved within very human terms. It began with an individual becoming enamored of the "difference" exhibited by a Christian. It ended with that same individual embracing the Way of Life and, in doing so, cutting him/herself off from all attachments and alliances that were incompatible with that Way of Life. Baptism was the turning point. The novice was told: "You will seek every day the presence of the saints in order that you may rest upon their words" (*Did.* 4:2). The newly baptized were alienated from all others, and these words describe the peace and security that they were bound to feel in the presence of those "saints" who shared their Way of Life. Baptism, consequently, was the gate to true companionship—"some you will love more than your soul" (2:7).

A teenage acquaintance of mine was attracted by the animal rights movement represented by the magazine *PETA* (*People for the Ethical Treatment of Animals*). His manner of life gradually changed in accordance with his new way of seeing animals. He instinctively began by refusing to eat meat or to use animal products. Thus, even while he remained within his family circle, a certain strain and mild alienation appeared with the assertion of his distinctive diet. With time, he came to recognize that members of his own family didn't have the courage or conviction to become "true believers." Gradually, he linked up with a small band of true believers and spent more and more time meeting and sharing his secret thoughts with them. Together, they decided to take action by passing out flyers that gave voice to the "unheard protests" on behalf of those animals raised in unnatural isolation in cramped cages and later killed in order to satisfy the "unnatural urge" of humans for the luxurious fur coats sold at a fashionable urban store. This was his rite of passage. The distribution of flyers resulted in arrests on the charges of "unlawful trespassing" and "disturbing the peace." These true believers were sentenced to serve six-month jail terms. Now his "brothers" and "sisters" were bound together not only by their beliefs and hopes but by their shared suffering. In jail they refused to eat. The magistrate ordered that they be "force fed." Thus a further humiliation and alienation occurred. In jail he read and discussed *Ishmael* (Quinn 1992) and *The Story of B* (Quinn 1996) and became all the more persuaded that the dominant culture of "takers" was bent on manipulating, destroying, and polluting the whole natural order of this world as they pursue the Way of Death. After his release, he told me that his vision of another world order is all the stronger and his time in prison galvanized his determination to live his way of life with his "new family."

I find in this young man's experience factors that correctly serve to highlight the rite of passage found in baptism. Training in the Way of Life was not just a spiritual exercise or a trendy adventure in personal growth; it was the truth that had been lost and was now recently revealed. Alienated by the old values, those who embraced their "new family" of true believers set themselves upon a course that consumed the whole of their lives. The local church was not "a temporary and part-time associational structure" or "a spiritual feeding station" (Keifer: 142). Rather, it was the eschatological community living and celebrating the mysterious designs of God for a whole new world order. Popular culture, for the most part, was the Way of Death.

It is difficult to know precisely how the newly baptized responded to their first eucharist. Many, in the process of embracing the Way of Life, created enemies among those who regarded them as shamelessly abandoning all piety—piety to the gods, piety to their father, piety to their ancestral "way of life." Having lost fathers and mothers, brothers and sisters, houses and workshops, the newly baptized were now embraced by a new family that restored fathers and mothers, brothers and sisters, houses and workshops twenty- or fiftyfold. For many, it must have been as though their whole lives were pointed in this direction: finding brothers and sisters with whom they would share everything—without jealously, without competition—with gentleness and truth. The mere act of eating together foreshadowed the rest of their lives, for here were the faces of their true family sharing, in the name of the Father of all, the wine and bread that were the substance of their lives, their labors, their hopes.

The consecrated cup evoked the holy vine of David; the consecrated broken loaf evoked the life and knowledge of the Father. The former indicated that the Father had elected Israel and established a kingdom of promise through David, his servant. The gentiles did not know what marvelous things the Father did for David and his contemporaries. Jesus revealed them. Drinking the cup of the holy vine, therefore, allowed newly baptized gentiles to feel their divine calling and to join in fellowship with Israel and to share her eschatological expectations. Yet the promises were not enough. The Lord required fidelity to the Way of Life that he revealed to the Israelites through Moses. In the case of the gentiles, however, they received the bread of God's Torah—the Way of Life and knowledge of the Father—through Jesus, his servant. The newly baptized undoubtedly felt a great sense of gratitude for Jesus and for their "father" or "mother," who, being God's chosen servants, had personally revealed these things to them. Very fittingly, therefore, their "father" or "mother" extended to them the cup of election and the bread of life during the eucharist.

Above all, the eucharist of the *Didache* was profoundly forward looking: Those whose lives were nourished on the broken loaf were set aside for the final ingathering—for just as the grains that form the loaf were once "scattered over the hills" (9:4) and, only later, kneaded and baked in one loaf, so too, those who ate of fragments of this consecrated loaf knew that the Father would one day harvest them "from the ends of the earth" so as to gather them into his kingdom on earth. Those who ate, therefore, tasted the future and collective promise that the "one loaf" signified. It is difficult to know precisely how much the newly baptized had already tasted of the future promises of God. The Way of Life is silent regarding these things. One can imagine, however, that every spiritual mentor was so filled with these things by virtue of their lives being nourished on the daily prayers and the weekly eucharist that they could hardly have stopped themselves from blurting out these things during the training sessions.

After the dishes and the tables were taken away, the prayers after the meal began. Now the newly baptized encounters the "holy name" of the "holy Father" that "you tabernacle in our hearts" (10:2). Then themes of creation and redemption were recounted (10:3). Then, "Remember, Lord, your church [assembly], to save her from every evil, to perfect her in your love, to gather her together from the four winds, sanctified, into your kingdom . . . (10:5). These words might have given voice to the deepest sentiments of the newly baptized. This new family, this wonderful family, may the God who created all things save her . . . , protect her . . . , gather her. Indeed, this was the greatest joy and the greatest expectation of the members of the Didache communities.

THE GENIUS OF VULNERABILITY

The Way of Vulnerability

At no point did the *Didache* give the least hint that its members would somehow acquire power to change or to improve the world. There was not even a hint that members would somehow be empowered to change or to improve themselves. The novices were not told that the Way of Life would bring them happiness, surround them with faithful friends, improve their love life. On the contrary, in the beginning, it was just the reverse. The novice was prepared to lose lifelong friends, to be opposed by lovers, to abandon the happiness of the status quo. The novices were prepared to face opposition from those who would speak badly of them, who would oppose them, who would even persecute them (1:3). Far from changing and improving the world, the neighborhood, or the family, the very act of joining the movement had the effect of bringing more strife into human relations. Far from making the world a better and kinder place, the novice, just by virtue of altering his/her commitments, unleashed an extra quotient of pettiness, of grief, of misunderstanding into the world.

The novice was not equipped with means to convert his opponents— not even the "enemies" within his own family. The novices were not told, for example, that the Way of Life would make them more charitable, more virtuous, more intelligent. Nor could novices presuppose that members of the movement might somehow be tolerated or even prized because the products coming out of their collective workshops were somehow superior in quality or lower in price than those of their competitors. The novice could not boast that members were more industrious, more honest, more generous and, as a consequence, deserved to be welcomed and cherished wherever they went.

This powerlessness to convert the world would not even change at the end of this age. The end-times scenario (*Did.* 16), consequently, did not present truth as marvelously succeeding in vanquishing error. Far from having the masses joining the movement, the end time was expected to produce defections even from among those already committed. As the end time approached, therefore, the powerlessness of the members of the Didache communities increased.

Even within the movement, therefore, there was no notion that members had joined the one true church and that, in the end, everyone would have their eyes open and be clamoring for a place therein. There were not even claims that their religion was the "one way" and that no one could come to know and serve the Father "outside the church." In the end, "the church" was simply gathered from the four winds and from the ends of the earth into the kingdom. Thus, the church as church ceased to exist. Those who had ministries in the church did not expect to continue these ministries in the kingdom. Nor did the *Didache*, at any point, presuppose that church members would have better places (or even exclusive places) in the world to come. The church, therefore, was also part of the mystique of powerlessness.

Faced with the powerlessness to convert or to change the world, novices could only diminish the aggression unleashed. How so? When being insulted by a blow on the right cheek, one did not defend oneself, demand justice, assert one's rights; rather, one turned the other cheek (*Did.* 1:4). By submitting gladly to insults and the like, the novice was not told that "this strategy will win over your opponents" or "you are superior to your opponent since you keep your cool." No. Such strategies would risk plunging the novice back into a position of imagined power—the power to accomplish one's ends despite the opposition, the power to feel "superior" in truth, in self-restraint, in goodness. Rather, the novice was trained to give in to the aggression of opponents with the assurance that "you will be perfect" (1:4[A]). What was this perfection? Surely it was not the perfection of being "able to bear the whole yoke of the Lord" (6:2) nor was it the perfection required of members "in the last time" (16:2). Quite simply, the novice knew nothing, at this point, of the yoke of the Lord or of the last days. For the moment, the novice was simply being trained to offer a "perfect surrender" to mild acts of aggression. Nothing more. Immediately thereafter, the novice would be trained in a "perfect surrender" to "everyone asking for anything" (1:5). Thus, as seen in chapter 1, there was a progression in the training in the Way of Life—what went before prepared for what was to come. The learning of perfection was thus a graded affair in which each successive step built upon the skills gained earlier.

In the first instance, for example, the novice was told that the Way of Life consisted in loving "your neighbor as yourself" (1:2). Immediately thereafter, however, the neighbor (family and kin as shown in ch. 12) turned out to be, more often than not, an "enemy" to the conversion anticipated by the new recruit. Thus, novices were trained to "love the ones hating you" (1:3). How so? By giving in to their petty acts of aggression (see ch. 12). Why so? Only so "you will not have an enemy" (1:3). Here again, it would be misleading to imagine that submitting to blows and other minor abuses serves somehow to convert the "enemy" into a "friend." This would be to slip back into the spirituality of power. To be consistent, therefore, one has to imagine that, only from the vantage point of the novice, did "the enemy" not exist. How so? Not by pretending that one's oppressor was somehow "still a beloved child of God" or doing some mysterious service, such as "perfecting the novice through suffering." The *Didache* presupposed that the victim felt pain, misunderstanding, insult— all these were normal and healthy responses in the face of evil. The *Didache* only supposed that novices wouldn't retaliate (1:2b; 2:6b; 3:9). Given the pragmatic character of the *Didache*, not having "an enemy" meant not singling anyone out for curses, backbiting (2:3), grudges (2:3), or plots (2:6b).

No Vengeance Even in the World to Come

The novices did not even have the comfort of knowing that, when the Lord came, he would extract vengeance on behalf of the victims of violence. How could the spirituality of powerlessness prevail as the Way of Life revealed by the Father, if the Father himself operated by some different rule—the rule of vengeance. So often the eschatology of Christians accepts the notion that evil persons will suffer eternal torments in hellfire (Gehenna). Punishment in hellfire has thus assured the servants of God that, even though they were powerless, the Lord would exact vengeance in their names in the world to come. While vengeance was prohibited to them and while the victims were asked (even required) to forgive their tormentors, God was not allowed either to forget or to forgive. God must wreak holy vengeance on the last day. In some cases, this vengeance was seen as required by a law of justice that binds even God. At other times, this vengeance was required in order to allow a portion of comfort to the former victims—they could relinquish the desire for vengeance in the firm knowledge that God would someday ruthlessly pursue the torturer, the thief, the rapist beyond the grave.

The *Didache* had no interest in punishing the wicked (either wicked nations or wicked individuals). Even the corrupting prophets who were singled out as particularly troublesome along with the world-deceiver were not set up for some special retribution or punishment. They were simply "utterly destroyed" in the burning-process of testing, so that the elect could remain unmolested when they would be raised from the dead (*Did.* 16:5–7). The spirituality of weakness, therefore, is amply demonstrated insofar as those persecuted did not gain, in either this world or the next, any satisfaction that their "enemies" were being duly punished for the pain they caused. In fact, according to the *Didache*, by surrendering to mistreatment and not plotting any revenge, one effectively had no "enemy" (1:3). The Way of Life made this clear: "You will not hate any person" (2:7).

#16J JUDGMENT, VENGEANCE, AND TORTURE IN AN ESCHATOLOGICAL SETTING

The *Didache* championed an end-times scenario in which evildoers living in the final generation would be utterly destroyed (16:5), while dead evildoers simply remained dead and were exempt from eternal punishments. The exceptional nature of the *Didache*'s omission of divine vengeance needs to be understood against the backdrop of the alternatives that were popular at the time.

In some eschatologies, it is true, the punishment of the wicked was very reserved. For example, in the *Syriac Apocalypse of Baruch* (100 C.E.), the elect are raised first, evildoers last:

> Then all who have died and have set their hopes on him [the Messiah of God] will rise. . . . Those who are first will rejoice, and those who are last will not be cast down. For each of them will know that the predetermined end of the times has come. But the souls of the wicked when they see all this, will be the more discomforted. For they will know that their torment is upon them and that their perdition has arrived. (30:2–3)

While this end-times scenario relates that those who have abandoned the covenant will likewise be abandoned by God, it also relates that "those who started in ignorance but afterwards found the secret of life, and joined the people set apart from other people—their former manner of life will count for nothing [against them]" (42:5). All in all, therefore, the entire book remains quite consistent in its purpose of sustaining those who are suffering because they are faithful to the way of God. With the glory of the future set before them, the writer asks, "Why concern yourselves about the downfall of your enemies?" (52:6). Hence, little is said of the plight of those to be damned.

In 2 Esdras (90–100 C.E.), more attention is focused upon the downfall of Israel's enemies. When "the Most High shall be revealed on the seat of judgment" (7:33), his first thought is not to comfort and wipe away the tears of the innocent who have suffered at the hands of their enemies; rather, his first act is to put the tormentors in their place:

> The pit of torments shall appear, and opposite it shall be the place of rest; and the furnace of hell [Gehenna] shall be disclosed, and opposite it the paradise of delight. Then the Most High will say to the nations that have been raised from the dead, "Look now and understand whom you have denied, whom you have not served, whose commands you have despised. . . ." (7:36f.)

Absolute power finally puts mortal power in its rightful place. In the two chapters appended to the original, even this restrained attention to punishment gives way to a wholehearted celebration of the terrible retribution that will fall upon Babylon-Rome. Here is a sample:

> "As you will do to my chosen people," says the Lord, "so God will do to you. . . ." Your children shall die of hunger, and you shall fall by the sword, your cities shall be wiped out. . . . Those who are in the mountains and in the highlands shall perish of hunger, and they shall eat their own flesh in hunger for bread and drink their own blood for thirst of water. (2 Esdras 15:56–58)

In later apocalyptic works, attention shifts from the temporal punishment of the wicked when the Lord comes (as illustrated above) to the eternal punishment in hellfire. The *Apocalypse of Peter* (early second century) illustrates this well. This eschatological work begins by asking about "signs of the Parousia [the return of Jesus] and the end of the world" (v. 1) but, after briefly recounting the events leading to the last judgment, the entire middle half of the book (vv. 7–14) narrates the eternal torments of the damned in the various pits of hellfire. An illustration:

> And again two women: they are hung up by their neck and by their hair and are cast into the pit [of fire]. These are they who plaited their hair, not to create beauty, but to turn to fornication, and that they might ensnare the souls of men to destruction. And the men who lay with them in fornications are hung by their thighs in that burning place, and they say to one another, "We did not know that we would come into everlasting torture." (v. 7)

The shift away from the last chapters of 2 Esdras is striking: (a) Temporal torments give way to eternal torments. (b) Punishment of wicked nations gives way to individual retribution. (c) Punishment for the mistreatment of Israel gives way to punishment for individual sins against the commands of God. In great and unrelenting anguish, the tormented call out to God, "Have mercy upon us!" (v. 13) The angels in response increase their torments telling them "there is no more time for repentance" (v. 13). The sinners respond: "Righteous is the judgment of God . . . since we are punished according to our deeds" (v. 13). Thus, it would appear that even some Christians were uneasy in the face of God's torture chambers and had to be reassured that the damned saw their torments as befitting their crimes. In later apocalyptic works, even this restraint will be lost. Thus, it would appear that the evocative power of the torments of the damned eventually overcame the original anticipation of the gathering of the elect into the kingdom.

Needless to say, there was not one neat trajectory from the *Syriac Apocalypse of Baruch* to the *Apocalypse of Peter*. These snapshots, however, allow those unfamiliar with the broader trajectories in the early centuries to glimpse the broad lines of eschatological development so as to better understand the uniqueness of the *Didache*'s complete omission of torments for the damned.

Spiritual Vulnerability in the Face of God

The novice cultivated religious vulnerability even in the face of God. Just as the novice was trained to be vulnerable to the request of beggars (*Did.* 1:5), in like fashion, the novice learned to be vulnerable in the face of "the experiences befalling you . . . knowing that, apart from God, nothing happens" (3:10). This, needless to say, included both good and bad things happening. On the positive side, for instance, the novice was embraced by a community of like-minded individuals. On the negative side, relatives and friends vented their anger and seized the assets of would-be joiners of this movement. Thus, even this vulnerability to one's "enemies" was received as a "good thing" allowed by God (3:10). The way of weakness and vulnerability went hand in hand.

Religious vulnerability also shows up in the renouncing of divination. The diviner, enchanter, and astrologer (3:4) employed means to gain power over spiritual forces. Minimally, they divined the future before it unfolded. The novice, on the other hand, was trained to keep far away from these spiritual power games: he/she was not even to "wish to see these things" (3:4b).

Community members remained vulnerable in the face of the last days. No one could claim that their sins were completely forgiven and that God could therefore not exclude them from his kingdom. The confession of failings, it will be remembered, had nothing to do with securing the forgiveness of sins (ch. 8 above). Rather, it emphasized the fact that one remained, for the whole of one's life, vulnerable to God's judgment. All in all, therefore, no one was told that by virtue of belonging to this movement, by virtue of their true doctrine, or by virtue of their devout life they were assured of a place in the kingdom to come. No one, moreover, was offered the prospect of being raptured in order to escape the burning-process of testing (*Did.* 16:5). In fact, one must suspect that members looked forward to this final process of purification (see ch. 15), since, by their own efforts, they had fallen short of attaining the perfection necessary (16:2). Therefore, it must be allowed that everyone anticipated the burning process, knowing that even here, "apart from God, nothing happens" (3:10).

Only one means was given for "ransoming" sins—that of sharing/giving those things one had accumulated "through the work of your hands" (4:6). Increased vulnerability in the face of one's neighbor's needs, therefore, paradoxically decreased vulnerability in the face of the final judgment. The *Didache* knew nothing of "being washed in the blood of the Lamb" or of being granted the assurances that one's sins were forgiven because of some private rite of penance or some official Sacrament of Reconciliation. In brief, the Christian life did not do away with vulnerability; it paradoxically increased it.

Of what good was vulnerability? The *Didache* responds: "The gentle will inherit the earth" (3:7). Daily members stand before the true God and Father and petition: "Your name be made holy; your kingdom come" (8:2). At the eucharist, members receive "Spirit-sent food and drink for life forever" (10:3). Even here, however, there were no guarantees, since it was the Lord who would do the saving, perfecting, and gathering of his elect into his kingdom (10:5). This was grace! This was the final redemption! This was the hope they lived for!

THE FUTURE DIDACHE COMMUNITIES

Living on the Threshold of the Lord's Coming

Just as the message of the *Didache* continued the message of Jesus of Nazareth, so too, the eucharist of the *Didache* perpetuated the proleptic anticipation of the kingdom that marked the table fellowship of Jesus. Fed on the eucharist, therefore, those who shared the Way of Life of the Father were nourished in their altered social reality. They were not of this world. Each day of the week, they thought and acted in anticipation of the world that was to come. Brothers and sisters bound together under the direction of the same Father shared their resources, shared their Way of Life, shared their dreams. Each new eucharist, consequently, celebrated the group identity, the standards of excellence, and the habits of judgment that the community stood for in the name of the Lord. Together, then, these early Christians faced a world that, in so many ways, had betrayed their trust and shattered their hopes. With their eyes on the future, they altered long-standing social barriers between Jew and gentile, male and female, slave and free. In their personal commitment to the future of God, they fully expected that the Lord would honor their trust and fulfill their dreams. Clinging to each other, they clung to the promises of God, and, in Jewish fashion (Vööbus 1968: 164–68), they prayed: "Come Lord [*marana tha*]!" (*Did.* 10:6).

The weekly eucharist was not envisioned as an unbloody reenactment of the sacrifice of Calvary. Nor were members of the Didache communities focused on applying the infinite merits of a suffering Redeemer. These things would all come much later. Redemption, for the members of the Didache communities, was principally a future expectation bound up with the coming of the Lord God at the end of time. Thus, participants at the eucharistic meal would have had little inclination to speculate regarding some form of bodily or sacramental presence of Jesus. Their focus was elsewhere. For them, *the Father was the unseen but very much present host at every eucharistic meal.* The drink and food served were provided by him (*Did.* 10:3; 1:5). His "holy name" was dwelling in their "hearts" (10:2). The prayers addressed to this "holy Father" (10:2) were directly and immediately received by him. But, above all, it was this "almighty Master" (10:3) who was poised "to save . . . to protect . . . and to gather" his entire church into "the kingdom . . . prepared for her" (10:5). In their way of experiencing things, consequently, they looked to the Father for their redemption—just as his "servant Jesus" (9:3; 10:3) had done before them.

The same thing holds for the Lord's Prayer, which provides the template structuring the daily prayers of the community. Reading between the lines, one discovers how their prayers reflected their dissatisfaction with the way things were. They were the malcontents who did not trust in the lords of this world and the lords of the pagan pantheon to give them a fair shake. As a result, they took as their own the prayer delivered over to them by a malcontent Jew ("the servant" who revealed the Way of the Father) who was crucified as a Roman insurrectionist. With Jesus, therefore, they took their stand in the Way of Life with the understanding that, when the Father came to gather the elect, his Way would finally succeed in ushering in a new order of justice and prosperity for those who were, for the time being, systematically excluded from both justice and prosperity. The rulers of this world, it will be remembered from chapter 2, were busy advancing their own economic and political interests, and the weak and powerless were being exploited and crushed in the process (see #16k).

#16K ESCHATOLOGY AND LIBERATION THEOLOGY IN LATIN AMERICA

Middle-class Americans find it difficult to understand how the expectation of the end time could be anything but piety gone awry. When listening to pastors and lay leaders of base Christian communities in Latin America, however, one discovers a different reality. Listen, for example, to the experience of Marcelo Barros:

> The poor have a special love of apocalyptic literature and read it "from their sufferings and struggles." Generally speaking, images of the end of the world and the coming of the Lord frighten those who lead peaceful and secure lives in society. These same images inspire and strengthen persons and groups who are already suffering as much or more than the afflictions described in the Apocalypse [= Rv]. On the peripheries of Latin American cities, a family can go to sleep without knowing if its members will wake up alive or whether they will fall victim to the gangs that roam the *barrios*. A mother never knows if she will be the next in her alley to mourn the death of a child. Every day the poor go to work in insecurity and in fear of being sacked. In this context, the promises of the Apocalypse are liberating, even if, as in all wars, there is danger for everyone. . . . People longing for God's intervention read the Apocalypse as applying directly to them[selves], since they have nothing to hope for from their actual situation. (102f.)

If this is true today, this might well have been the case two thousand years ago when men and women were being crushed by the social, political, and economic oppression of the Roman Empire. Those driven into greater debt and those who feared continually for their children would have welcomed the end-time hope as relief for their hopelessness. Those who ended up losing everything might indeed have ended up fleeing their creditors in order to roam the small towns and villages willing to give them limited hospitality in exchange for their harrowing stories and riveting prayers calling upon the Lord God to come and come soon!

In Latin America, fewer than ten percent of believers belong to base Christian communities. In these small groups, lay leaders assemble their neighbors, talk about their distress, and read the Bible in order to discover how the Lord regards their present situation. In this way, they bring to the text their distress and read the text as if the Lord was responding to their distress. The witness of Marcelo Barros continues:

> Once in Itacatiara, in Amazonia, a base community leader
> explained the unrolling of the seven seals [Rv 6:1–8:1] by count-
> ing the stages through that the industrial ships had invaded their
> lakes and swamps and little by little, with industrial fishing equip-
> ment and huge refrigerators, had taken all the fish from the poor
> people who lived on the banks by fishing. This injustice left them
> gazing for a long time at the little fish floating dead on the now
> polluted waters that had been caught up in the nets and thrown
> back as of no interest to the commercial fishermen. Interpreting
> this story from the Apocalypse helped the community to orga-
> nize the small fishermen to fight for their rights and to defend
> their waters. (103f.)

Scholars, of course, would find it difficult, if not impossible, to accept such
a reading of the narrative of the seven seals. Yet the poor are not impeded
by the need to read the Book of Revelation by unpacking the images
against the backdrop of the social and cultural world of first-century Jews
and Christians. For the poor, it suffices to notice that those being
addressed were distressed by their suffering; hence, the suffering of those
poor fishermen was sufficient background to bring forward their reading
of the text. The Franciscan Spirituals did much the same thing in order to
defend themselves in their era (McGinn: 203–21).

Awaiting the coming of the Lord can be a total capitulation born out of
total despair. Indeed, many who are crushed by poverty and oppression
arrive at this point. Not so, however, for those who banded together in the
Didache communities and the base Christian communities. Again, borrowing from the insights of Marcelo Barros:

> There is a profound difference between how the base church
> communities . . . who have a presence in the encampments and
> settlements of landless peasants, read and interpret the Apoca-
> lypse and how groups and movements waiting for the end of the
> world do. The difference is that engaged communities enjoy the
> promises of the Apocalypse, feel stimulated by its words, and
> nourish an eschatological vision of faith, but without divorcing
> this from a critical reading of history and of the responsibility
> Christians have for the here and now. . . . Even if the brothers and
> sisters of these communities believe that it may be mainly in
> God's hands, we too have to act and work. This means that in
> interpreting history they link faith with politics, avoiding an
> ingenuous or fanatical hope. (Barros:104)

As noted in the specific case above, poor fishermen seeing their way of life
wiped out by commercialization began to organize to defend their rights.
So, too, in the Didache communities, one can read between the lines and

note how the demand that all able-bodied persons work and share their resources points to a community bent on preserving the well-being of its members right now. Neither of these groups would be ready to go out into the desert in order to pressure the Lord to come now by refusing to eat and drink until he did so. Nor would the members of these groups be tempted to formulate a suicide pact in order to preserve their faith against unwelcome outsiders. All in all, therefore, the eschatology and hope, faith and action that bind together members of the base Christian communities of Latin America have much to say regarding their counterparts in the Didache communities of the mid-first century.

Daniel Quinn's Analysis of Our Culture of Death

A dozen persons have changed my life. And only a few books. *The Story of B* by Daniel Quinn (1996) is surely the most significant among the latter. This book is deceptive. On the surface, it appears to be a fictional story about a priest who has been sent to modern-day Germany to discover whether the man known as "B" is the Anti-Christ. Just below the surface, however, one is gently pushed into a seductive rehearing of the story of Cain and Abel, which reveals the hypocrisy of Western civilization: "You are captives of a civilization system that more or less compels you to go on destroying the world in order to live." This book, along with the author's earlier *Ishmael* (1992) and *My Ishmael* (1997), have become book-circle classics. For our purposes here, however, Quinn's book provides the background for reflecting on how Didache communities will emerge as the eschatological disaster suffocates the face of the earth.

The message of B to his audiences is very simple and very complex. I will endeavor to give a brief synopsis of it here in order to set the stage for revealing how the *Didache* will go on to address this situation in the future.

According to B, the origins of Western culture rest not in agriculture but in a peculiar form of "totalitarian agriculture" (Quinn 1996: 151–55) that was never practiced from the beginning of the world save by one culture, our own. According to totalitarian agriculture, the food produced is not only set aside as "off limits" to all others, but we actively destroy every species of animal, bird, or insect that persists in trying to forage in our fields. Since this totalitarian form of agriculture produced predictable food surpluses, the society practicing it grew in numbers and in strength. Agricultural domination thus necessitated territorial expansion, which, in turn, justified wars of domination and the enslavement of "weaker" cultures in order to promote the expansion of aggressive agriculture. The "stronger" culture, that of the Takers, thus survived and flourished while the "weaker" cultures of the Leavers were swept away by the territorial and cultural expansion of emerging Western culture. From the vantage point of the winners, every other culture was made to appear "primitive" and "localized"—terms deliberately crafted to suggest how "expendable" and "vulnerable" aboriginal tribes were when they came up against Western culture.

The expansion of Western culture has continued unabated for nearly ten thousand years. As a result, the Takers have extended totalitarian agriculture into every sector of life. Even the notions of "divine election" and "missionary zeal for the salvation of the whole world" so prevalent in Christianity and in Islam have been infected with the disease of Western culture. The agricultural revolution, the scientific revolution, and the Industrial Revolution, which moved forward by leaps and bounds during the nineteenth century, were also manifestations of aggressive agriculture extended to new arenas of application. In Western culture, meanwhile, the rich were naturally rewarded for exploiting the poor; the powerful were naturally rewarded for exploiting the weak. At the same time, the excess populations no longer needed by the agricultural-industrial-military complex at home poured out into the colonies, where they sought to prosper by extending the practice of Western culture in new worlds. Any tribal culture hindering this process of "manifest destiny," was either pacified, converted, or eliminated. Thus, in the course of only six generations, the cultural mythology of Western civilization came to dominate all the best portions of agricultural land and mineral deposits on the face of the inhabitable world.

One would have thought that the systematic destruction of primitive cultures by disrupting their way of life would have caused moral outrage during the period of colonial expansion. But no! If Buffalo Bill Cody obliterated hundreds of buffalo each week, so much the better. Their hides were in demand. No one seemed to care that thousands of pounds of meat were left rotting on the plains. For a brief span of twenty years, therefore, the buffalo hunters used their Yankee ingenuity and made windfall profits selling their hides. No one seemed to care that the "red savages" of the plains had been selectively harvesting buffalo and wisely feeding, clothing, and housing their families on this principal resource for untold generations. Too bad. If the dumb savages didn't have the savvy to make a fast buck by killing the buffalo, then leave it to the Americans to show them how. This same story, in its multiple forms, has affected the way that Western culture greedily grasps and uses up any and every natural resource on the face of the earth.

Then again, one might have thought that there would have been an overwhelming moral outrage at the unsanitary conditions, the unfair wages, and the extended use of child labor when the cotton mills were first introduced. But no! Allowing young girls to work ten to twelve hours each day was a blessing to their families, who could barely survive in the new urban economies. Allowing their fathers to work in the mines was a sign of progress and a way to let them build the future. Most of the miners and mill workers had been forced to sell their family farms because they were structurally inefficient, and the price of grain was falling as a result of the mechanization on larger farms. Here again, no one seemed to care that a way of life was being destroyed. Those who suffered, after all, were not the "savages" any longer. Give them charity, yes, but every form of inefficiency had to be punished by the market forces that favored progressive new means of production. One can't hold back progress. The same story was repeated over and over again as "bigger is better" became the order of the day.

Thus, it was only when Western culture was at its best that the cracks in our cultural mythology began to appear. According to B, this took place during the time of the postwar boom:

> In the late forties and fifties, the people of our culture . . . were still confident that a glorious future lay just ahead of us. All we had to do was to hold on to the vision and keep doing all the things that got us here. . . . In 1950 there wasn't the slightest whisper of a doubt about this anywhere in our culture, East or West, capitalist or communist. In 1950 this was something everyone could agree on: Exploiting the world was our God-given right. The world was *created* for us to exploit. Exploiting the world actually *improved* it! There was no limit to what we could do. Cut as much down as you like, dig up as much as you like. Scrape away the forests, fill in the wetlands, dam the rivers, dump poisons anywhere you want, as much as you want. None of this was regarded as wicked or dangerous. Good heavens, why would it be? The earth was created specifically to be used in this way. It was a limitless, indestructible playroom for humans. You simply didn't have to consider the possibility of running out of something or of damaging something. The earth was designed to take any punishment, to absorb and sweeten any toxin, in any quantity. (Quinn 1996: 278)

Then came the Great Awakening:

> I've said that this new era of the collapse of values began in 1960. Strictly speaking, it should be dated to 1962, the year of Rachel Carson's *Silent Spring,* the first substantive challenge ever issued to the motivating vision of our culture. The facts Carson brought forward to detail the devastating environmental effects of DDT and other pesticides were astounding: DDT didn't just do its intended job of killing unwanted insects; it had entered the avian food chain, disrupting reproductive processes and breaking down egg structures, with the result that many species had already been destroyed and many more were threatened, making it not unthinkable that the world might someday wake to a silent spring—a spring without birds. But *Silent Spring* wasn't just

another sensational exposé. . . . With a single powerful blow, it
shattered for all time a complex of fundamental articles of our
cultural faith: that the world was capable of repairing any damage
we might do to it; that the world was *designed* to do precisely this;
that the world was "on our side" in our aggrandizement . . . that
God himself had fashioned the world *specifically* to support our
efforts to conquer and to rule it. The facts in *Silent Spring* plainly
contradicted all these ideas. . . . The world was *not* supporting
our cultural vision. *God* was not supporting our cultural vision.
The world was *not* unequivocally on our side. *God* was not
unequivocally on our side. (Quinn 1996: 281f.)

So, in the end, when no one could say no to the steady march of Western
culture, God stepped in and said, "Enough." This, then, is the message of
B in Quinn's book.

Quinn does not go into detail regarding the report of the Club of
Rome, *The Limits to Growth* (1972), which generates various computer
models forecasting how natural resources, population, food production,
and pollution will interact during the next hundred years. Given the limited world reserves in key natural resources (coal, oil, iron, chromium,
etc.), each of the computer-generated models showed that the rise of population and of prosperity would continue unabated for one or two generations before experiencing a quick decline once the supply of readily
available resources began to taper off. Before every home had indoor
plumbing and long before even half of the world's inhabitants owned a car,
therefore, the supply of resources needed to pipe water and to manufacture
cars will have been stretched thin and the lakes, rivers, and atmosphere will
have become horribly polluted with industrial waste and toxic emissions.
The Report was widely criticized for being overly pessimistic and for not
giving due account to new sources of clean energy that have yet to be discovered (Körtner: 168f.).

The *Global 2000 Report* (1981) commissioned by President Carter, however, repeated most of the earlier warnings and extended them into areas
not even considered by the Club of Rome. The year after this report was
released, scientists became alarmed at the thinning of the ozone layer, which
shields the planet from dangerous forms of radiation, and the trend toward
climatic warming arising from the burning of fossil fuels and the continued
deforestation of the planet. The *Global Agenda for Change* (1987) produced by the World Commission on Environment and Development further consolidated all of the earlier data and showed that excessive
consumption by the developed countries along with rapid development by
the under-developed countries has created new pockets of poverty and of
environmental degradation. Meanwhile, the new global marketplace
wherein trade barriers have been vastly reduced or entirely disbanded has

led to the multiplication of multinational corporations, who seek to evade the strong ecological safeguards of the developed countries and to exploit the weak safeguards, weak safety standards, and weak unions of developing countries. Bent on creating products and creating a perceived need on the part of buyers to purchase their products rather than that of their competitors, multinational corporations have no special interest in harmonizing their operations with a local culture or a local economy save to the degree that it contributes to their annual profits (Chomsky 1999: 25–40; Mander: 319, 329). While transnational corporations sometimes devote large amounts of their advertising dollars to persuading the public that they have humanitarian aims and that the future of the planet is a precious gift to be safeguarded, the nature of economic competition ensures that the policy decisions that implement such laudable programs only go as far as economic advantage over their competitors (who may not be perceived as environmentally conscious) will allow (Mander: 316f.). Meanwhile the machinery of government in democratically elected countries has to continue to promise increased wealth, increased products, and increased opportunities for its citizens (Ewin: 26–33). No political lobby speaks for future generations of our children who are being impoverished today because the nonrenewable resources of the planet are being squandered by a few generations addicted to luxury and to license. In many respects, therefore, the recent reflections of the Club of Rome are sobering:

> Living as we do at the onset of the first global revolution, on a small planet that we seem hell-bent to destroy, beset with conflicts, in an ideological and political vacuum, faced with problems of global dimensions that the fading nation states are impotent to solve, with immense scientific and technological possibilities for the improvement of the human condition, rich in knowledge but poor in wisdom, we search for the keys to survival and sustainability. (King: 193)

The overall prospect for the planet is bleak. The prospect for our children's children is also bleak. As the readily available nonrenewable resources begin to give out, the cost of obtaining resources will increase in direct proportion to their scarcity. The increased cost of production will be passed on to the consumer. Real wages will drop. The standard of living of all wage earners will drop. Social unrest will occur. Persons who have been led to believe in progress and to demand more and better products will be reluctant to accept less and less. The powerful industrial nations and the large transnational corporations (Karliner: 5–7) will promote binding trade agreements to ensure a steady supply of raw materials for their industrial development while denying it to others. Raw power and military intervention will then be used in order to ensure that the economic and social elites do not have to suffer from the growing menace of scarcity. But this is just to delay the end; for, as nonrenewable natural resources become scarcer and growing numbers fall below the poverty line, even the industrialized nations will feel pressure to reduce their measures to control pollution. In so doing, peoples everywhere will suffer a decline in their prospects of good health, a decline in their experience of clear water and clean air, a decline in their standard of living. Meanwhile, accelerated depletion of the ozone layer and buildup of carbon dioxide will stunt many agricultural areas causing massive scarcity, starvation, and social unrest.

> Given the current corporate practices, not one wildlife reserve, wilderness, or indigenous culture will survive the global economy. We know that every natural system on the planet is disintegrating. The land, water, air, and sea have been functionally transformed from life-supporting systems into repositories for waste. There is no polite way to say that business is destroying the world. (Paul Hawkins as cited in Karliner: 13; also Ewin; Hynes; Tim Johnson)

Meanwhile, as the whole world is suffering signs of collapse, middle-class American teenagers still aspire, by and large, to own their own cars by the time they graduate from high school, and their proud parents want to save and scrimp to help make this possible for them. After all, owning one's own car was the status symbol that gave these parents an enormous sense of emotional well-being in their youth, and they want their children "to enjoy the best things life has to offer." They want still to believe, after all that has happened, that America is "the land of opportunity" and, accordingly, they naturally want to secure their share of the good life before all the oil wells run dry. Thus corporate greed will be matched, in the end time, by family pride in providing children with the best that life has to offer. As for their grandchildren, who knows? There may be no tomorrow for them!

Let us say, for the sake of discussion, that this represents the end-time scenario that more and more people see as inevitable. What will result? Many, of course, will make their fortunes producing newly invented water purifying systems and automobile engines capable of squeezing fifty miles out of each gallon. Many others, however, will curse their government, their scientists, and their God when they contract new diseases or suffer new forms of repression necessitated by scarcity. Others will vigorously organize so as to pressure the world governments to curtail their current wasteful policies, to stop squandering resources on instruments of war, to prohibit the manufacture of goods that cannot be recycled. All these measures, however, will only slow down the inevitable: increased scarcity, doing without, suffering deprivation.

As Western culture begins to deliver less and less of what it promised, some few will discover that the whole system of totalitarian agriculture and aggressive industrialization was riddled with the Way of Death from the very beginning. Yet it had to succeed massively in order to discover that it was massively doomed to fail (Körtner: 171; Quinn 1996: 268–75, 278–82). And this took some time to realize.

Then prophets will appear proclaiming that Western culture has been the "world-deceiver" that has produced the "signs and wonders" of aggressive industrialization and technology for a dozen generations but at a horrendous price—"the earth" was "betrayed into his hands" and he has done "unlawful things that never happened from the beginning of time" (*Did.* 16:4b). Still others will search back into the old ways and old cultures that were "inefficient" and that were overrun by booming populations espousing aggressive agriculture some ten thousand years ago. The lost wisdom of "primitive" cultures will be revived. Leaders will rise up who will invite people to abandon the Way of Death and to yield to the old tried and true Way of Life that was abandoned. Many of these leaders will attract followers who will form movements endeavoring to develop ways of being in the world that will incarnate the Way of Life.

Then Communities Like the Didache Will Reemerge

At just this point, communities like the Didache community will reemerge. These communities will be formed by those who are persuaded that the Way of Death is hollow and deceptive and that they need to get back to a simpler, saner, and sounder way of life. As such, the Way of Life will again be hailed as "the life and knowledge" of the Mother who made the heavens and the earth. Loving "the God who made you" (*Did.* 1:2) will mean accepting human existence as part of the great mystery of life that pulses in the fish of the sea, in the birds of the air, and in the land animals as well in humans. The norm, "You will not exalt yourself" (*Did.* 3:9), will then be understood as renouncing aggressive agriculture and commerce. It will also be understood as renouncing the so-called essential superiority of human life and acknowledging that the fish, the birds, the animals also have "their home" here and deserve to be allowed to prosper as their Lord wishes "from her own free gifts" (1:5). The "dominion theory" will thus fall out completely. "The gentle will inherit the earth" (3:7).

The members of the reconstituted Didache communities will live as they believe. As in the case of their first-century forebears, they will band together in hope; they will celebrate simple rites; and, above all, they will ground their everyday work in life-giving praxis. Because of their beliefs, they will suffer much from traditional Christians (see, e.g., Barros: 99), who will trot out the standard proofs for the immortality of the human soul and the standard explanations of the Lord's command to "fill the earth and subdue it" (Gn 1:28). Thus, "in the last days, the false prophets and the corrupters will be multiplied, and the sheep will turn into wolves, and the love will be turned into hate" (*Did.* 16:3) (Körtner: 173f.). But this is only the beginning. For "the creation of humans will come into the burning-process of testing, and many will be entrapped and will be utterly destroyed, the ones having remained firm in their faith, on the other hand, will be saved by the accursed burning-process itself" (16:5). Then the signs of truth will appear. . . .

This, then, is the truth presented by B:

> The people of our culture are used to bad news and are fully pre-pared for bad news, and no one would think for a moment of denouncing me if I stood up and proclaimed that we're all doomed and damned. It's precisely because I do not proclaim this that I'm denounced. Before attempting to articulate the good news I bring, let me first make crystal clear the bad news people are always prepared to hear.
>
> > Man is the scourge of the planet, and he was BORN a scourge, just a few thousand years ago.
>
> Believe me, I can win applause all over the world by pronounc-ing these words. But the news I'm here to bring you is much dif-ferent:
>
> > Man [Woman] was born MILLIONS of years ago, and he was no more a scourge than hawks or lions or squids. He lived AT PEACE with the world . . . for MILLIONS of years.
>
> This doesn't mean he was a saint. This doesn't mean he walked the earth like a Buddha. It means he lived as harmlessly as a hyena or a shark or a rattlesnake.
>
> > It's not MAN who is the scourge of the world, it's a single cul-ture. One culture out of hundreds of thousands of cultures, OUR culture.
>
> And here is the best of the news I have to bring:
>
> > We don't have to change HUMANKIND in order to survive.
> > We only have to change a single culture.
>
> I don't mean to suggest that this is an easy task. But at least it's not an *impossible* one. (Quinn 1996: 254f.)

"Then the world will see the Lord coming atop the clouds of heaven" (*Did.* 16:8).

When the Lord God comes, should we actually believe that he will pro-vide everyone with a new suburban home complete with a washer and dryer in every basement and a brand new fuel-efficient automobile in every garage? Should we actually believe that God will miraculously fill thou-sands of dry oil wells so that these engines can burn gasoline for another hundred years? What? If God has already said a resounding no to Western culture and its notion of development and well-being, will he/she suddenly change his mind on the last day. More importantly, however, even supposing that God did (for some crazy reason) decide to play Sugar Daddy, how would the Lord teach ecological responsibility if he/she used miraculous powers to overcome the results of our greed and waste? The same thing, of course, can be said of modern-day parents who lavish so many clothes and toys upon their children that they promote their thoughtless use and the throwaway mentality that goes with it. Will God, in the world to come, then have continually to save us from our garbage?

But, then, it must be remembered that God will come with his "holy ones" (*Did.* 16:7). Who will these holy ones be who have been raised from the dead at the Lord's coming? Surely the members of the Didache communities would not expect that the holy ones would be the architects of totalitarian agriculture and the designers of aggressive industrialization. Nor would they expect the masters of those multinationals, who quickened the pace of destroying the planet in the name of prosperity and of the annual profits declared to shareholders. Surely it would not be the generals and the torturers who pacified the poor masses in developing countries when they complained that their children were dying from the polluted waters resulting from the runoff of paper mills and petrochemical plants making products designed for export to the prosperous nations. Nor would the holy ones be those who discovered new oil wells and clear-cut forests but never stepped back in wonder and gratitude so as to offer first fruits to the Lord who provided these things. Reading the Way of Death (*Did.* 5:1f.) makes it quite evident that the members of the Didache communities would not expect the holy ones to be such as these.

There is not the least indication in the *Didache* that its members would be looking for holy ones from among those who destroyed their body's normal appetites through rigorous asceticism. Nor would they be looking for mystics and visionaries. Surely they would not expect the holy ones to be those stigmatics whose hands and feet have bled in imitation of Jesus' hands and feet. Nor would it be those who believe in the cosmic mystery of the pyramids or those who foresaw the future by contacting the spirits of the dead. The holy ones recognized by the Didache communities would not even be those who promoted rosary crusades or distributed papal encyclicals.

If not these, who then?

LIST OF ABBREVIATIONS

ABD   *Anchor Bible Dictionary*

2 Apoc. Bar.   *Syriac Apocalypse of Baruch* or *The Book of the Revelation of Baruch* (or *2 Baruch*) (100–120 C.E.). "A gifted Jew, using old traditions . . . , struggled to assert that Judaism is a religion based on Torah—Law—and that the loss of the temple was due to the failure of the chosen nation to be obedient" (*ABD* 1:620e). English translation by R. H. Charles as found in H. F. D. Sparks.

Apoc. Pet.   *Apocalypse of Peter.* This book was "probably composed around 135 C.E. since the activity of the Jewish messianic claimant, Bar Kokhba is indirectly portrayed as the eschatological crisis" (*ABD* 1:291d). In this book, "Jesus is the mediator of heavenly revelation . . . , of the signs and events of the end and visions of the places of reward and punishment" (ibid.). English translation by C. Maurer as found in Hennecke.

Apoc. Sed.   *Apocalypse of Sedrach.* In this Jewish book (150–500 C.E.), reworked by a Christian editor (1000 C.E.), Sedrach (not one of Daniel's companions but a corruption of Esdras) "stands before the Lord and questions him" (*ABD* 5:1066e). As in 2 Esdras, "the theme is God's compassion for the sinner" (*ABD* 5:1066). English translation by R. J. H. Shutt as found in H. F. D. Sparks.

Apoc. Thom.   *Apocalypse of Thomas* (fifth century). The shorter and older version describes the signs of the end times in terms of eight days. English translation by A. de Santos Otero as found in Hennecke.

Apos. Trad.   *Apostolic Tradition* (220 C.E.). Church order attributed to Hippolytus of Rome

ARN   *Avot de Rabbi Nathan* (fourth century). This rabbinic treatise is an expansion of *m. Avot.*

Asc. Isa.   *Ascension of Isaiah* or *Martyrdom of Isaiah.* "Most scholars agree that the *Martyrdom of Isaiah* (chapters 1–5) was composed by a Jew in Palestine no later than the second century" (*ABD* 3:507). An insert into this narrative known as the testament of Hezekiah (3:13–4:22) is of Christian origin and narrates the coming of the Lord and the final judgment. English translation by R. H. Charles as found in H. F. D. Sparks.

As. Mos.	*Assumption of Moses.* Only an incomplete Latin version has come down to us of this testament offered by Moses to Joshua prior to his death. The work is of Jewish origin written between 3 B.C.E. and 30 C.E. (Sparks: 603). The work recounts the suffering of the Jews due to their sins and holds out before them the hope that God will rise from his heavenly throne and come down to punish the gentiles. English translation by R. H. Charles as found in H. F. D. Sparks.
ATR	*Anglican Theological Review*
b.	*Bavli* or *Babylonian Talmud* (600 C.E.). See *m.* below. In this volume, English translations are taken from Neusner (1995), unless otherwise noted.
Barn.	*Epistle of Barnabas*
BTB	*Biblical Theology Bulletin*
CBQ	*Catholic Biblical Quarterly*
1 Clem.	*First Epistle of Clement*
2 Clem.	*Second Epistle of Clement*
DER	*Derek Erez Rabbah* (third century). See *DEZ* below.
DEZ	*Derek Erez Zuta* (third century). The term *Derek Erez* signifies "correct behavior." Since two such anonymous manuals treating *Derek Erez* have come down to us, one is called *Rabbah* ("the large"), and this present one is called *Zuta* ("the small"). "The first four chapters . . . may have been an independent collection already in existence in the time of the *Tannaim* [rabbinic sages of the first two centuries]" (Ginsberg: v).
Epictetus, *Discourses.*	In Arrian, *Epicteti Dissertationes* (first century). Epictetus of Hierapoli (50 B.C.E.–30 C.E.) was brought up as a slave in a Roman household and preached his Stoic philosophy to those who would hear him. The young Marcus Aurelius was his most capable and most distinguished disciple. Arrian, in his introduction, admits to having heard the moral discourses of Epictetus and having set them down in writing. In this volume, the English translation is taken from Higginson.
Ep. Arist.	*Epistle of Aristeas*
2 Esdras	Apocalypse of Ezra (4 Ezra in Vulgate) (90–100 C.E.). "Written a generation after the destruction of the temple, it is dominated by this catastrophe" (*ABD* 2:612c). 2 Esdras 3–14 was written by "an unknown Palestinian Jew who probably wrote in Hebrew or Aramaic near the close of the first century" (Metzger: 300). According to the manuscript, the prophet Ezra receives seven revelations from the angel Uriel concerning the future God has in store for those few who faithfully observe his commandments, especially, "the downfall of the Roman Empire and of the wicked nations together with the coming of the redeemer" (*ABD* 2:612c). Ezra was historically "the priest and scribe of the law [Torah]" (Ezra 7:12) active in the reconstruction period following the Babylonian deportation. English translation by R. J. H. Shutt as found in H. F. D. Sparks.
ETL	*Ephemerides theologicae lovanienses*
Gen. Rab.	*Genesis Rabbah*

Gos. Thom.   *Gospel of Thomas* (late first century). This listing of 108 sayings of Jesus was found in the Nag Hammadi Library. The term "gospel" in never used in the original text and was assigned on the basis of its first line: "These are the secret sayings which the living Jesus spoke and which Didymus Judas Thomas wrote down."

Hermas or the Shepherd of Hermas

Man.	*Mandates*
Sim.	*Similitudes*
Vis.	*Visions*
HTR	*Harvard Theological Review*
JAAR	*Journal of the American Academy of Religion*
JBL	*Journal of Biblical Literature*
JEH	*Journal of Ecclesiastical History*

Josephus (35–100 C.E.). "Flavius Josephus, or Joseph ben Matthias, is certainly the single most important source for the history of the Jewish people during the first century C.E. His lifetime spanned the turbulent years leading up to the revolt of the Jews against Rome, the period of the war itself, and the years immediately following, when Judaism was in the process of reconstituting itself on a new basis" (H. W. Attridge cited in Stone 1984: 185).

Ant.	*Antiquities of the Jews* (94 C.E.)
Ag. Ap.	*Against Apion* (95 C.E.)
J.W.	*Jewish Wars* or *The Wars of the Jews* (75–79 C.E.)
JQR	*Jewish Quarterly Review*
JSNT	*Journal for the Study of the New Testament*
JTS	*Journal of Theological Studies*
Jub.	*Jubilees* (100 B.C.E.). English translation by R. H. Charles as found in H. F. D. Sparks.

Justin Martyr (100–165 C.E.)

1 Apol.	*First Apology*
2 Apol.	*Second Apology*
Dial.	*Dialogue with Trypho*
LXX	Septuagint, the Greek translation of the Hebrew Scriptures
Lv. Rab.	*Leviticus Rabbah*
Nm. Rab.	*Numbers Rabbah*
NT	New Testament or, more appropriately, the Christian Scriptures
NTS	*New Testament Studies*
m.	Mishnah (200 C.E.). The Mishnah literally means "teaching" and represents the first written collection of oral traditions attributed to the rabbinic sages of the first two centuries. The Mishnah was compiled by R. Judah the Prince at Yavneh (in Palestine). "The Mishnah has been and is now memorized in the circle of all those who participate in . . . [rabbinic] Judaism. Of still greater weight, the two great documents formed around the Mishnah and so shaped as to serve, in part, as commentaries to the Mishnah, namely, the Babylonian Talmud [see *b.*] and the Palestinian Talmud [see *y.*], form the center of the curriculum of [modern] Judaism as a living religion" (Neusner 1988e: xv). In this volume, the English translation is taken from Neusner (1988e).

Odes. Sol.   *Odes of Solomon* (first or second century)

OT   Old Testament or, more appropriately, the Hebrew Scriptures (*Tanakh*)

Philo of Alexandria (20 B.C.E.–50 C.E.): "Philo was born . . . in a Hellenized Jewish family of Alexandria. His education followed the patterns of Greek schooling. . . . Philo had an excellent command of the Greek language . . ." (Koester 1995: 266). His extensive writings offer a wide range of information reflecting Hellenistic Judaism during the first century. "He restated the moral and legal content of the Pentateuch in Greek categories, thus perfecting what Jewish wisdom theology wanted to accomplish" (Koester 1995: 271).

Cherubim	*De Cherubim*
Contemplative Life	*De Vita Contemplativa*
Decalogue	*De Decalogo*
Embassy to Gaius	*De Legatione Ad Gaium*
Flight	*De Fuga et Inventione*
Life of Moses	*De Vita Mosis*
Mating	*De Congressu Quaerendae Eruditionis Studies*
Migration	*De Migratione Abrahami*
Providence	*De Providentia*
Special Laws	*De Specialibus Legibus*

Ps.-Phocy.   *Sentences of Phocylides* (or *Pseudo-Phocylides*) (first century B.C.E.). "While the purpose of this document is debated, it is best understood as [Jewish] moral teaching directed to the Greek world" (Koester 1995: 263).

Pss. Sol.   *Psalms of Solomon*

RHR   *Revue de l'histoire des religions*

Rites   *The Rites of the Catholic Church as Revised by Decree of the Second Vatican Ecumenical Council.* New York: Pueblo Publishing Co., 1976.

Sib. Or.   *Sibylline Oracles* (100 B.C.E.–150 C.E.). In this volume, the English translation is taken from Hennecke. The standard collection of the Sibylline oracles consists of twelve books. "It is difficult to distinguish between Jewish and Christian adaptations and earlier pagan materials, because much of the eschatological imagery was common" (Koester 1995: 254).

SJT   *Scottish Journal of Theology*

T. 12 Patr.   *Testaments of the Twelve Patriarchs* (100 C.E.). "The Testaments, as we know them, are a collection of the 'last words' of the twelve sons of Jacob" (H. F. D. Sparks: 505). Each of the twelve testaments has a uniform style and promotes fidelity to the Torah with an emphasis on a particular virtue and the admonition to avoid its corresponding vice. In this volume, the English translation is taken from H. F. D. Sparks.

TS   *Theological Studies*

Qumran   The term refers to the geographical location (Khirbet Qumran) near the northwest bank of the Dead Sea, which is commonly understood as having been inhabited by a Jewish community that observed the *Manual of Discipline* or *Community Rule* while awaiting the end times (135 B.C.E.–70 C.E.). Since current scholarship is undecided as to whether the 870 Dead Sea Scrolls found between 1946 and 1948 in the caves near Qumran represent the library of the community located at Qumran or whether the scrolls were buried there by refugees from elsewhere, the use of this term in the text does not indicate a determination of this issue (see discussion in Wise: 20–35). If it would be shown that the scrolls were brought to the hills surrounding Qumran without at any time being used to define the existence of the inhabitants of Qumran, then the term "Qumran" as found in this volume would simply refer to those locations wherein the *Manual of Discipline* was observed. In any case, the scrolls make clear that whatever the relationship between the Dead Sea Scrolls and Qumran, the *Manual of Discipline* "does not merely reflect a small community living there" but "itself refers to various groups or chapters scattered throughout Palestine" (Wise: 123).

1QM	*Milḥāmāh* (*War Scroll*)
1QS	*Manual of Discipline* or *Community Rule* or *Charter of a Jewish Sectarian Association* (Wise: 123)
t.	*Tosephta* (250 C.E.). Tosephta literally means "Additions" and consists of an expansion/commentary on the Mishnah.
Test. Mos.	*Testament of Moses*
Tg. Lev.	*Targum Leviticus*
TDNT	*Theological Dictionary of the New Testament.* 9 vols. Edited by Gerhard Kittel. Translated by Geoffrey W. Bromiley. Grand Rapids: Eerdmans, 1964–68.
Tb	Book of Tobit (200 B.C.E.). "The purpose of the book appears to be a description of the education of the pious through suffering, demonstration that prayers are heard by God, admonition to preserve one's Jewish heritage undefiled in an unfriendly gentile context, and encouragement to constant praise of the merciful God" (Koester 1995: 260).
Torah	The Hebrew term *torah* refers to the practical wisdom and know-how that loving parents pass on to their children. Being created by God was a condition that all people enjoyed. Being "fathered" by God, being trained in his Torah, however, was quite another thing. It is this latter experience that allowed Israel to realize that collectively they were God's "beloved son" whom he had called out of Egypt and trained in the desert (Dt 8:2–6). This sense of being fathered by God has been distorted in English translations of the Bible because the Hebrew word *torah* and the Greek word *nomos* have almost always been rendered into English as "law" (always in the singular). The term "law" in English is bound up with our legal tradition and is entirely opaque to the process of parenting which dominates the use of *torah*. Hence, in this volume, the term "Torah" will be used instead of "Law." While "Torah" is sometimes used to designate the five books of Moses, this will not be done in this volume.

BIBLIOGRAPHY OF WORKS CONSULTED

Note: Foreign language citations within this volume have been translated by the author. Abbreviations within citations have been standardized. Archaic English spellings, pronouns, and punctuation have been revised in accordance with standard English usage.

Achtemeier, Paul J.
    1978   "An Imperfect Union: Reflections on Gerd Theissen, *Urchristliche Wundergeschichten.*" *Semeia* 11:49–68.
    1990   "*Omne verbum sonat:* The New Testament and the Oral Environment of Late Western Antiquity." *JBL* 109, no. 1:3–27.
Agnew, Francis H.
    1986   "The Origin of the NT Apostle-Concept." *JBL* 105, no. 1:75–96.
Agnoletto, Attilio
    1968   *La "Didaché": Lettura di un testo Christiano antico.* Milan: La Goliardica.
Aland, Kurt
    1963   *Did the Early Church Baptize Infants?* London: SCM.
Allison, Dale C.
    1994   "A Plea for Thoroughgoing Eschatology." *JBL* 113, no. 4:651–68.
    1998   *Jesus of Nazareth: Millenarian Prophet.* Minneapolis: Fortress.
Alon, Gedalyahu
    1977   *Jews, Judaism, and the Classical World: Studies in Jewish History in the Times of the Second Temple and Talmud.* Translated by I. Abrahams. Jerusalem: Magnes.
Anderson, Megory, and Philip Culbertson
    1986   "The Inadequacy of the Christian Doctrine of Atonement in Light of Levitical Sin Offering." *Anglican Theological Review* 68, no. 4:303–28.
Arichea, Daniel C., et. al.
    1980   *A Translator's Handbook on the First Letter from Peter.* New York: United Bible Societies.
Arranz, Miguel
    1973   "La liturgie pénitentielle juive après la destruction du temple." In *Liturgie et rémission des péchés,* edited by A. Pistoia et al., 39–55. Rome: Edizioni Liturgiche.

Ascough, Richard S.
 1994   "An Analysis of the Baptismal Ritual of the *Didache.*" *Studia Liturgica*
        24:201–13.
Audet, Jean-Paul
 1952   "Affinités littéraires et doctrinales du 'Manuel de Discipline.'" *Revue
        biblique* 59:219–38. Translated and reprinted as, "Literary and Doctri-
        nal Relationships of the 'Manual of Discipline,'" in *The Didache in Mod-
        ern Research,* edited by Jonathan A. Draper, 129–47. Leiden: E. J. Brill,
        1996.
 1958   *La Didache: Instructions des apôtres.* Paris: J. Gabalda.
Aune, David E.
 1983   *Prophecy in Early Christianity and the Ancient Mediterranean World.*
        Grand Rapids: Eerdmans.
Bacchiocchi, Samuele
 1977   *From Sabbath to Sunday.* Rome: Pontifical Gregorian University.
 1982   "The Rise of Sunday Observance in Early Christianity." In *The Sabbath
        in Scripture and History,* edited by Kenneth A. Strand, 132–50. Wash-
        ington, D.C.: Review and Herald.
 1998   *The Sabbath Under Crossfire: A Biblical Analysis of Recent Sabbath/
        Sunday Developments.* Berrien Springs, MI: Biblical Perspectives.
Bahr, Gordon J.
 1965   "The Use of the Lord's Prayer in the Primitive Church." *JBL*
        84:153–59.
Bailey, Kenneth E.
 1976   *Poet and Peasant: A Literary-Cultural Approach to the Parables of Luke.*
        Grand Rapids: Eerdmans.
Balabanski, Vicky
 1997   *Eschatology in the Making: Mark, Matthew and the Didache.* Cambridge:
        University Press.
Bammel, Ernst
 1996   "Pattern and Prototype of *Didache* 16." In *The Didache in Modern
        Research,* edited by Jonathan A. Draper, 364–72. Leiden: E. J. Brill.
Barnard, L. W.
 1966   "The Dead Sea Scrolls, Barnabas, the *Didache* and the Later History of
        the 'Two Ways,'" 87–109. In *Studies in the Apostolic Fathers and Their
        Background.* Oxford: Basil Blackwell.
 1967   *Justin Martyr: His Life and Thought.* Cambridge: University Press.
Barros, Marcelo
 1998   "The Birth Pains of the Kingdom of God: Apocalypses of the Poor in
        Latin America." *Concilium* 1998, no. 4:98–105.
Bartlet, J. V.
 1921   "The *Didache* Reconsidered." *JTS* 22:239–49.
Bartlet, J. V., et al.
 1905   "The *Didache.*" In *The New Testament in the Apostolic Fathers,* 24–36.
        Oxford: Clarendon.
Bauckham, Richard J.
 1977   "Synoptic Parousia Parables and the Apocalypse." *NTS* 23:162–76.

1982   "The Lord's Day." In *From Sabbath to Lord's Day,* edited by D. Carson,
        221–50. Grand Rapids: Zondervan.
Bauer, Walter
1979   *A Greek-English Lexicon of the New Testament and Other Early Christian
        Literature: A Translation and Adaptation of the Fourth Revised and
        Augmented Edition of Walter Bauer's Griechisch-Deutsches Wörterbuch.*
        Translated by William F. Arndt and F. Wilbur Gingrich from the
        1949–52 German orig. Chicago: University of Chicago Press.
Baum, Gregory
1973   "Eschatology." In *An American Catechism. Chicago Studies* 12, no.
        3:304–11.
Barr, David L.
1986   "The Apocalypse of John as Oral Enactment." *Interpretation* 40, no.
        3:243–56.
Beare, Francis W.
1981   *The Gospel According to Matthew.* Peabody, Mass.: Hendrickson.
Beckwith, Roger T.
1984   "The Daily and Weekly Worship of the Primitive Church in Relation to
        its Jewish Antecedents." *Evangelical Quarterly* 56, no. 2:65–80.
Beers, William
1992   *Women and Sacrifice: Male Narcissism and the Psychology of Religion.*
        Detroit: Wayne State University Press.
Bell, Catherine
1992   *Ritual Theory, Ritual Practice.* New York: Oxford University Press.
Bellah, Robert
1975   *The Broken Covenant: American Civil Religion in a Time of Trial.* New
        York: Seabury.
Benenate, Becky, et al.
1989   *No Greater Love: Mother Teresa.* Novato, CA: New World Library.
Benjamin, Don C.
1991   "An Anthropology of Prophecy," *BTB* 21, no. 4:135–44.
Benoit, A.
1953   *Le baptême chrétien au second siècle.* Paris: Presses Universitaires de
        France.
Berger, Peter L., and Thomas Luckmann
1966   *The Social Construction of Reality.* Garden City, N.Y.: Doubleday.
Bernstein, Alan E.
1993   *The Formation of Hell: Death and Retribution in the Ancient and Early
        Christian Worlds.* Ithaca, N.Y.: Cornell University Press.
Berryman, Phillip
1987   *Liberation Theology: Essential Facts About the Revolutionary Religous
        Movement in the Latin America and Beyond.* Philadelphia: Temple Uni-
        versity Press.
Best, Ernest
1971   *I Peter.* London: Oliphants.
Betz, O.
1964   Review of Willy Rordorf, *Sunday. JBL* 83:81–83.

1996   "The Eucharist in the *Didache*." In *The Didache in Modern Research*, edited by Jonathan A. Draper, 2, 244–75. Leiden: E. J. Brill. Translated and reprinted as, "Die Eucharistie in der *Didache*." *Archiv für Liturgie-wissenschaft* 11 (1969): 10–39.

Bigg, C.
1904   "Notes on the *Didache*." *JTS* 5:579–89.
1905   "Notes on the *Didache*." *JTS* 6:411–15.
1922   *The Doctrine of the Twelve Apostles*. Translation and notes. London: S.P.C.K.

Bihlmeyer, Karl
1970   *Die Apostolischen Väter.* Tübingen: Mohr.

Blidstein, Gerald J.
1975   *Honor Thy Father and Mother: Filial Piety in Jewish Law and Ethics.* New York: Ktav.

Borg, Marcus
1984   *Conflict, Holiness & Politics in the Teachings of Jesus.* Studies in the Bible and Early Christianity 5. New York: Edwin Mellen Press.
1986   "A Temperate Case for a Non-Eschatological Jesus." *Forum* 2, no. 3:81–102.
1987   "An Orthodoxy Reconsidered: The End-of-the-World Jesus." In *The Glory of Christ in the New Testament: Studies in Christology in Memory of George Bradford Caird*, edited by L. D. Hurst et al., 207–17. Oxford: Oxford University Press.
1991   *Jesus: A New Vision: Spirit, Culture, and the Life of Holiness.* San Francisco: Harper & Row.

Boring, M. Eugene
1976   "The Unforgivable Sin Logion Mark III 28–29/ Matt XII 31–32/Luke XII 10: Formal Analysis and History of the Tradition." *TOA* 18, no. 4: 258–79.

Bousset, W.
1896   *The Antichrist Legend: A Chapter in Christian and Jewish Folklore.* London: Hutchinson.

Bowman, John
1983–84 "Metaphorically Eating and Drinking the Body and Blood." *Abr-Nahrain* 22:1–5.

Bradley, Keith
1986   "Wet-nursing at Rome: A Study in Social Relations." In *The Family in Ancient Rome: New Perspectives*, edited by B. Rawson, 201–29. Ithaca, N.Y.: Cornell University Press.
1998   "The Roman Family at Dinner." In *Meals in a Social Context: Aspects of the Communal Meal in the Hellenistic and Roman World*, 36–55. Aarhus: Aarhus University Press.

Bradshaw, Paul F.
1982   *Daily Prayer in the Early Church: The Study of the Origin and Early Development of the Divine Office.* New York: Oxford University Press.
1992   *The Search for the Origins of Christian Worship.* New York: Oxford University Press.

1993   "'Diem Baptismo Sollemniorem': Initiation and Easter in Christian Antiquity." In *Eulogēma,* edited by Ephrem Carr et al., 41–69. Rome: Ugo Detti.

Brawley, Robert L.
1990   "Anamnesis and Absence in the Lord's Supper." *BTB* 20, no. 4:139–46.

Bregman, Lucy
1986   "The Death of Everyone: Robert Lifton, Christian Theology, and Apocalyptic Imagery." *Horizons* 13, no. 2:306–20.

Brooks, Roger
1983   *Support for the Poor in the Mishnaic Law of Agriculture: Tractate Peah.* Brown Judaic Studies 43. Chico, Calif.: Scholars Press.

Brown, Colin, ed.
1978   *The New International Dictionary of New Testament Theology.* Grand Rapids: Zondervan.

Brown, Peter
1988   *The Body and Society: Men, Women, and Sexual Renunciation in Early Christianity.* New York: Columbia University Press.
1992   *Power and Persuasion in Late Antiquity: Towards a Christian Empire.* Madison: University of Wisconsin Press.

Brown, Raymond E.
1961   "The Pater Noster as an Eschatological Prayer." *TS* 22:175–208.
1967   *Jesus: God and Man.* Milwaukee: Bruce.
1970   *Priest and Bishop: Biblical Reflections.* New York: Paulist.
1980   "*Episkopē* and *Episkopos:* The New Testament Evidence." *TS* 41:322–38. Reprinted in R. Brown 1981: 96–106.
1981   *The Critical Meaning of the Bible.* New York: Paulist.
1984   *The Churches the Apostles Left Behind.* New York: Paulist.
1985   *Biblical Exegesis and Church Doctrine.* New York: Paulist.
1990   *Responses to 101 Questions on the Bible.* New York: Paulist.
1994   *An Introduction to New Testament Christology.* New York: Paulist.

Bruce, F. F.
1980   *Peter, Stephen, James, and John: Studies in Early Non-Pauline Christianity.* Grand Rapids: Eerdmans.

Büchler, Adolph
1967   *Studies in Sin and Atonement in the Rabbinic Literature of the First Century.* New York: Ktav.

Burford, Alison
1972   *Craftsmen in Greek and Roman Society.* Ithaca, N.Y.: Cornell University Press.

Burkitt, G. C.
1932   "Barnabas and the *Didache.*" *JTS* 33:25–27.

Burtchaell, James Tunstead
1992   *From Synagogue to Church: Public Services and Offices in the Earliest Christian Communities.* Cambridge: University Press.

Butler, B. C.
1960   "The Literary Relations of *Didache,* Ch. XVI." *JTS* 11:265–83.
1961   "The Two Ways in the *Didache.*" *JTS* 12:27–38.

Cadbury, H. J.
  1936 "The Epistle of Barnabas and the *Didache*." *JQR* 26:403–6.
Callan, Terrance
  1985 "Prophecy and Ecstasy in Greco-Roman Religion and in 1 Corinthians." *Novum Testamentum* 27, no. 2:125–40.
Campenhausen, Hans von
  1969 *Ecclesiastical Authority and Spiritual Power in the Church of the First Three Centuries.* Translated by J. A. Baker. Stanford, Calif.: Stanford University Press.
Capper, Brian
  1994 "The Palestinian Cultural Context of Earliest Christian Community of Goods." In *The Book of Acts in Its Graeco-Roman Setting,* edited by David W. J. Gill and Conrad Gempf, 323–56. Grand Rapids: Eerdmans.
Cardenal, Ernesto
  1978 *The Gospel in Solentiname.* Volume 2. Maryknoll, N.Y.: Orbis Books.
Case, Shirley Jackson
  1918 *The Millennial Hope: A Phase of War-Time Thinking.* Chicago: University of Chicago Press.
Celsus. *See* Hoffmann
Cerfaux, Lucien
  1959 "Le multiplication des pains dans la liturgie de la *Didache*: *Did* 9:4." *Biblica* 40, no. 3: 943–48.
Cevetello, J. F. X.
  1967 "Purgatory." In *New Catholic Encyclopedia*, edited by the editorial staff of the Catholic University of America, 11:1034–39. New York: McGraw Hill.
Chapman, John
  1908 "*Didache*." In *The Catholic Encyclopedia,* edited by Charles Herbermann et al., 4:779–81. New York: Robert Appleton.
Chilton, Bruce
  1994 *A Feast of Meanings: Eucharistic Theologies from Jesus through Johannine Circles.* Leiden: E. J. Brill.
  1996 *Pure Kingdom: Jesus' Vision of God.* Grand Rapids: Eerdmans.
Chomsky, Noam
  1985 *Turning the Tide: U.S. Intervention in Central America and the Struggle for Peace.* Boston: South End Press.
  1999 *Profit Over People: Neoliberalism and Global Order.* New York: Seven Stories Press.
Clegg, Claude Andrew, III
  1997 *An Original Man: The Life and Times of Elijah Muhammad.* New York: St. Martin's Press.
Cody, Aelred
  1995 "The *Didache*: An English Translation." In *The Didache in Context: Essays on Its Text, History and Transmission,* edited by Clayton N. Jefford, 3–14. Leiden: E. J. Brill.

Collins, John J.
   1974   "The Place of the Fourth Sibyl in the Development of the Jewish Sibyl-
           lina." *Journal of Jewish Studies* 25:365–80.
   1985   "A Symbol of Otherness: Circumcision and Salvation in the First Cen-
           tury." In *"To See Ourselves As Others See Us,"* edited by Jacob Neusner et
           al. Chico, Calif.: Scholars Press.
   1989   *The Apocalyptic Imagination: An Introduction to the Jewish Matrix of
           Christianity.* New York: Crossroad.
Cone, James H.
   1991   *Martin & Malcolm & America: A Dream or a Nightmare.* Maryknoll,
           N.Y.: Orbis Books.
Connolly, R. H.
   1923   "The Use of the *Didache* in the *Didascalia.*" *JTS* 24:147–57.
   1924   "Fragments of the *Didache.*" *JTS* 25:151–53.
   1932   "The *Didache* in Relations to the Epistle of Barnabas." *JTS* 33:237–53.
   1937a   "Agape and Eucharist in the *Didache.*" *Downside Review* 55:477–89.
   1937b   "Barnabas and the *Didache.*" *JTS* 38:165–67.
   1937c   "Canon Streeter on the *Didache.*" *JTS* 38: 364–78.
   1937d   "The *Didache* and Montanism." *Downside Review* 55:339–47.
Conzelmann, Hans
   1975   *A Commentary on the First Epistle to the Corinthians.* Translated by
           James W. Leitch. Philadelphia: Fortress.
Cooke, Bernard
   1976   *Ministry to Word and Sacraments.* Philadelphia: Fortress.
Cooke, S. M.
   1922   "Purification (Hebrew)." In *Encyclopedia of Religion and Ethics,* edited
           by James Hastings, 10:489–90. Edinburgh: T & T Clark.
Corley, Kathleen E.
   1993   *Private Women; Public Meals: Social Conflict in the Synoptic Tradition.*
           Peabody, Mass.: Hendrickson.
Countryman, L. William
   1988   *Dirt, Greed & Sex: Sexual Ethics in the New Testament and Their Impli-
           cations for Today.* Philadelphia: Fortress.
Court, John M.
   1981   "The *Didache* and St. Matthew's Gospel." *SJT* 34, no. 2:109–20.
   1985   "Right and Left: The Implications for Matthew 25:31–46." *NTS*
           31:223–33.
Crawford, Barry S.
   1982   "Near Expectation in the Sayings of Jesus." *JBL* 101, no. 2:225–44.
Creed, J. M.
   1938   "The *Didache.*" *JTS* 39:370–87.
Crockett, Candace
   1977   *The Complete Spinning Book.* New York: Watson-Guptill Publications.
Crossan, John Dominic
   1978   "A Form for Absence: The Markan Creation of Gospel." *Semeia*
           12:41–55.

1993   "Jesus in Gospel: From the Historical Jesus to the Canonical Gospels."
         The Rev. William Copley Winslow Lectures. Evanston: Seabury-West-
         ern Theological Seminary.
1994   *Jesus: A Revolutionary Biography.* San Francisco: Harper.
1995   *Who Killed Jesus?* San Francisco: HarperSanFrancisco.
1998   *The Birth of Christianity: Discovering What Happened in the Years
         Immediately after the Execution of Jesus.* San Francisco: HarperSanFran-
         cisco.

Cullmann, Oscar
1950   *Baptism in the New Testament.* London: SCM Press.

Cutrone, Emmanuel J.
1993   "The Lord's Prayer and the Eucharist: The Syrian Tradition." In
         Eulogēma, edited by Ephrem Carr et al., 93–106. Rome: Ugo Detti.

Dalmais, Irénée Henri
1984   "Themes biblique dans les anaphores eucharistiques de langue
         grecque." In *Le monde grec ancien et la bible,* edited by C. Mondésert,
         95–106. Paris: Beauchesne.

Daly, Robert J.
1978   *The Origins of the Christian Doctrine of Sacrifice.* Philadelphia: Fortress.

D'Angelo, Mary Rose
1992   "*Abba* and 'Father': Imperial Theology and the Jesus Traditions." *JBL*
         111:611–30.

Daube, David
1956   *The New Testament and Rabbinic Judaism.* London: Athone Press.

Davies, W. D.
1966   *The Setting of the Sermon on the Mount.* Cambridge: University Press.

Davis, Cyprian
1995   "The *Didache* and Early Monasticism in the East and West." In *The
         Didache in Context: Essays on Its Text, History and Transmission,* edited
         by Clayton N. Jefford, 352–67. Leiden: E. J. Brill.

de Halleux, Andre
1980   "Les ministères dans le *Didache.*" *Irénikon* 53, no. 1:5–29. Translated
         and reprinted as "Ministers in the *Didache,*" in *The Didache in Modern
         Research,* edited by Jonathan A. Draper (Leiden: E. J. Brill, 1996),
         300–320.

Dehandschutter, Bordewijn
1995   "The Text of the *Didache*: Some Comments on the Edition of Klaus
         Wengst." In *The Didache in Context: Essays on Its Text, History and
         Transmission,* edited by Clayton N. Jefford, 37–46. Leiden: E. J. Brill.

Demand, Nancy
1994   *Birth, Death, and Motherhood in Classical Greece.* Baltimore: Johns
         Hopkins University Press.

DeMaris, Richard E.
1995   "Corinthian Religion and Baptism for the Dead: Insights from Archae-
         ology and Anthropology." *JBL* 114, no. 4:61–82.

de Sainte Croix, G. E. M.
1981   *The Class Struggle in the Ancient Greek World from the Archaic Age to the
         Arab Conquests.* Ithaca, N.Y.: Cornell University Press.

Deterding, Paul E.
  1979   "Eschatological and Eucharistic Motifs in Luke 12:35–40." *Concordia Journal* 5, no. 3: 85–94.
Deutsch, Celia
  1987   *Hidden Wisdom and the Easy Yoke: Wisdom Torah and Discipleship in Matthew 11.25–30.* Journal for the Study of the New Testament Supplement Series 18. Sheffield: JSOT Press.
Dibelius, Martin
  1938   "Die Mahl-Gebete der *Didache*," *ZNW* 37:32–41.
Dickerson, John
  1974   *Pottery Making: A Complete Guide.* New York: Viking Press.
Dinkler, Erich
  1964   *Das Apsismosaik von S. Apollinare in Classe.* Wissenschaftliche Abhandlungen der Arbeitsgemeinschaft für Forschung des Landes Nordrhein-Westfalen 49. Cologne/Opladen: Westdeutscher Verlag.
Dix, Gregory
  1933   "*Didache* and Diatessaron." *JTS* 34:242–50.
  1938   "Primitive Consecration Prayers." *JTS* 37:261–83.
  1948   "'The Seal' in the Second Century." *Theology* 51:9ff.
Dixon, Suzanne
  1992   *The Roman Family.* Baltimore: Johns Hopkins University Press.
Dodd, C. H.
  1959   *The Primitive Catechism and the Sayings of Jesus.* Pp. 106–18.
Dölger, F. J.
  *1936   "Nilwasser und Taufwasser." In *Antike und Christentum: Kultur und religionsgeschichtliche Studien* 5:173–87.
Dollen, Charles J., et al.
  1979   *The Catholic Tradition: Mass and the Sacraments.* Volume 1. Wilmington, N.C.: McGrath. Pp. 1–7 presents translation of D7–16 with introduction.
Doran, Robert
  1995   *Birth of a Worldview: Early Christianity in its Jewish and Pagan Context.* Boulder, Colo.: Westview Press.
Dostoevsky, Fyodor
  1994   *The Karamazov Brothers.* Translated with introduction by Ignat Avsey of the 1880 Russian original. Oxford: Oxford University Press.
Douglas, Mary
  1966   *Purity and Danger: An Analysis of the Concepts of Pollution and Taboo.* London: Routledge.
Downing, F. Gerald
  1992   *Cynics and Christian Origins.* Edinburgh: T & T Clark.
Draper, Jonathan A.
  1983   "A Commentary on the *Didache* in the Light of the Dead Sea Scrolls and related Documents." Doctoral dissertation, St. John's College, Cambridge.
  1984   "The Jesus Tradition in the *Didache*." In *The Jesus Tradition Outside the Gospels,* edited by D. Wenham. Sheffield: JSOT Press.
  1989   "Lactantius and the Jesus Tradition in the *Didache*." *JTS* 40:112–16.

1991   "Torah and Troublesome Apostles in the Didache Community."
        Novum Testamentum 33, no. 4:347–72.

1993   "The Development of 'The Sign of the Son of Man' in the Jesus Tradi-
        tion." *NTS* 39:1–21.

1995a   "Social Ambiguity and the Production of Text: Prophets, Teachers,
        Bishops, and Deacons and the Development of the Jesus Tradition in
        the Community of the *Didache*." In *The Didache in Context: Essays on
        Its Text, History and Transmission*, edited by Clayton N. Jefford,
        284–312. Leiden: E. J. Brill.

1995b   "Barnabas and the Riddle of the *Didache* Revisited." *JSNT* 58:89–113.

1996a   "The *Didache* in Modern Research." In *The Didache in Modern
        Research*, edited by Jonathan A. Draper, 1–42. Leiden: E. J. Brill.

1996b   "The Jesus Tradition in the *Didache*." In *The Didache in Modern
        Research*, edited by Jonathan A. Draper, 72–91. Leiden: E. J. Brill.

1996c   "Christian Self-definition against the 'Hypocrites' in *Didache* 8." In *The
        Didache in Modern Research*, edited by Jonathan A. Draper, 223–43.
        Leiden: E. J. Brill.

1996d   "Torah and Troublesome Apostles in the Didache Community." In *The
        Didache in Modern Research*, edited by Jonathan A. Draper, 340–63.
        Leiden: E. J. Brill.

1996e   "Confessional Western Text-Centred Biblical Interpretation and an
        Oral or Residual-Oral Context." *Semeia* 73:61–80.

1997a   "Resurrection and the Cult of Martyrdom in the *Didache* Apocalypse."
        Journal of Early Christian Studies 5, no. 2:155–79.

1997b   "The Role of Ritual in the Alternation of Social Universe: Jewish-Chris-
        tian Initiation of Gentiles in the *Didache*." *Listening* 32:48–67.

1998   "Weber, Theissen, and 'Wandering Charismatics' in the *Didache*." *Jour-
        nal of Early Christian Studies* 6, no. 4:541–76.

2000   "Ritual Process and Ritual Symbol in *Didache* 7–10." *Vigiliae Chris-
        tianae* 54:121–58.

Dugmore, C. W.

1962   "Lord's Day and Easter." In *Neotestamentica et Patristica: Festschrift for
        Oscar Cullmann*. Supplement to *Novum Testamentum* 6, 272–81.
        Leiden: E. J. Brill.

Dujarier, Michel

1962   *Le Parrainage des Adults aux trois premiers siècles de l'Eglise*. Paris: Cerf.

Dulles, Avery

1992   *The Craft of Theology: From Symbol to System*. New York: Crossroad.

Dunn, James D. G.

1970   *Baptism in the Holy Spirit*. London: SCM Press.

1972   "Spirit-and-Fire Baptism." *Novum Testamentum* 14:81–92.

1977   *Unity and Diversity in the New Testament: An Inquiry into the Charac-
        ter of Earliest Christianity*. Philadelphia: Westminster.

1990   *Jesus, Paul, and the Law: Studies in Mark and Galatians*. Louisville:
        Westminster/John Knox.

1991   *The Partings of the Ways Between Christianity and Judaism and Their
        Significance for the Character of Christianity*. London: SCM Press;
        Philadelphia: Trinity Press International.

Edwards, Douglas R.
1996   *Religion & Power: Pagans, Jews, and Christians in the Greek East.*
        Oxford: Oxford University Press.
Eisenman, Robert, and Michael Wise
1992   *Dead Sea Scrolls Uncovered.* New York: Penguin Books.
Emmet, D.
1986   "Truth and the Fiduciary Mode in Michael Polanyi's Personal Knowl-
        edge." *Convivium* 23:4–8 and *Tradition and Discovery* 14, no. 1:32–
        36.
Enelow, H. G.
1956   *A Jewish View of Jesus.* New York: Macmillan.
Ewin, Alexander
1999   "Consensus Denied." *Native Americas* 16, nos. 3–4:26–33.
Fackenheim, Emil L.
1970   *God's Presence in History: Jewish Affirmations and Philosophical Reflec-
        tions.* New York: Harper Torchbooks.
Faivre, Alexandre
1980   "La documentation canonico-liturgique de l'église ancienne." *Revue des
        sciences religieuses* 54:273–97.
Falk, Daniel K.
1995   "Jewish Prayer Literature and the Jerusalem Church in Acts." In *The
        Book of Acts in Its Palestinian Setting,* edited by Richard Bauckham,
        237–301. Grand Rapids: Eerdmans.
Fant, Maureen B., ed.
1992   *Women's Life in Greece and Rome.* 2nd ed. Baltimore: Johns Hopkins
        University Press.
Farnell, Lewis R.
1922   "Purification (Greek)." In *Encyclopedia of Religion and Ethics,* edited by
        James Hastings, 10:482–88. Edinburgh: T & T Clark.
Fee, Gordon F.
1987   *The First Epistle to the Corinthians.* Grand Rapids: Eerdmans.
Feeley-Harnik, Gillian
1994   *The Lord's Table: The Meaning of Food in Early Judaism and Christian-
        ity.* Washington: Smithsonian Institution Press.
Fiensy, D. A.
1985   *Prayers Alleged to Be Jewish: An Examination of the Constitutiones Apo-
        stolorum.* Chico, Calif.: Scholars Press.
Figueras, Pau
1977   "Baptism." *Christian News from Israel* 26, no. 2:75–77.
Finkel, Asher
1981   "The Prayer of Jesus in Matthew." In *Standing Before God,* edited by A.
        Finkel et al., 131–70. New York: Ktav.
Finkelstein, Louis
1928   "The Birkat Ha-Mazon." *JQR* 19:211–64.
Finn, Thomas M.
1997   *From Death to Rebirth: Ritual and Conversion in Antiquity.* New York:
        Paulist.

Fiorenza, Elisabeth Schüssler
    1984   *In Memory of Her: A Feminist Theological Reconstruction of Christian Origins.* New York: Crossroad.
    1993   *Discipleship of Equals: A Critical Feminist Ekklesia-logy of Liberation.* New York: Crossroad.
Fiorenza, Francis Schüssler
    1984   *Foundational Theology: Jesus and the Church.* New York: Crossroad.
Fisher, Eugene
    1989   "Mysterium Tremendum: Catholic Grapplings with the Holocaust and its Theological Implications." *SIDIC* 22, nos. 1 and 2.
Fitzmyer, Joseph
    1979   *The Gospel According to Luke.* Anchor Bible 28 and 28A (1983). Garden City, N.Y.: Doubleday.
Flusser, David
    1987   "Paul's Jewish-Christian Opponents in the *Didache.*" In *Gigul,* edited by S. Shaked et al., 71–90. Leiden: E. J. Brill. Reprinted in *The Didache in Modern Research,* edited by Jonathan A. Draper (Leiden: E. J. Brill, 1996), 195–211.
    1988   "A Rabbinic Parallel to the Sermon on the Mount [and *Did.* 3]." In *Judaism and the Origins of Christianity,* 494–508. Jerusalem: Magnes.
Foss, Pedar W.
    1994   "Kitchens and Dining Rooms at Pompeii: The Spacial and Social Relationships of Cooking to Eating in the Roman Household." Ph.D. Thesis, University of Michigan.
Fox, Robin Lane
    1987   *Pagans and Christians.* New York: Alfred A. Knopf.
Fredriksen, Paula
    1991   "Judaism, the Circumcision of Gentiles, and Apocalyptic Hope: Another Look at Galatians 1 and 2." *JTS* 42:532–64.
Frend, W. H. C.
    1984   *The Rise of Christianity.* Philadelphia: Fortress.
Fridson, Martin S.
    2000   *How to Be a Billionaire: Proven Strategies from the Titans of Wealth.* New York: John Wiley & Sons.
Funk, Franz Xavier
    1913   *Patres apostolici.* Vol. 2. Tübingen: Laupp.
Funk, Robert
    1996   *Honest to Jesus: Jesus for a New Millennium.* New York: Macmillan.
Gager, John G.
    1983   *The Origins of Anti-Semitism: Attitudes Toward Judaism in Pagan and Christian Antiquity.* Oxford: Oxford University Press.
Gaier, Deborah Rose
    1996   "The *Didache*: A Community of Equals." Paper presented in the "Women and the Historical Jesus" section of the Society of Biblical Literature's 1996 Annual Meeting. Summarized in Crossan 1998: 369–73.
Galanter, Marc
    1989   *Cults: Faith, Healing, and Coercion.* Oxford: Oxford University Press.

Geertz, C.
   1973   *The Interpretation of Cultures.* New York: Basic Books.
Geraty, Lawrence T.
   1965   "The Pascha and the Origin of Sunday Observance." *Andrews University Seminary Studies* 3:85–96.
Gero, Stephen
   1977   "The So-called Ointment Prayer in the Coptic Version of the *Didache*: A Re-evaluation." *HTR* 70:67–84.
Gibbins, H. J.
   1935   "The Problem of the Liturgical Section of the *Didache*." *JTS* 36:373–86.
Giet, Stanislas
   1966   "Coutume, evolution, droit canon: A propos de deux passages de la *Didache*." *RDC* 16:118–32.
   1967   "La *Didache*: Enseignment des douze apôtres?" *Melto* 3:223–36.
   1970   *L'énigme de la Didache.* Publications de la Faculté des Lettres de l'Université de Strasbourg 149. Paris: Ophrys.
Ginsberg, M.
   1971a   "Derek Erez Rabbah: Large Tractate on Correct Behaviour." In *The Minor Tractates of the Talmud,* edited by A. Cohen, 529–66. London: Soncino Press.
   1971b   "Derek Erez Zuta: Short Tractate on Correct Behaviour." In *The Minor Tractates of the Talmud,* edited by A. Cohen, 567–96. London: Soncino Press.
Girard, René
   1986   "Generative Scapegoating." In *Violent Origins: Ritual Killing and Cultural Formation,* edited by Robert G. Hamerton-Kelly, 75–105. Stanford: University of California Press.
Glasson, Thomas Francis
   1947   *The Second Advent: The Origin of the New Testament Doctrine.* London: Epworth Press.
Glazier-McDonald, Beth
   1987   *Malachi: The Divine Messenger.* Atlanta: Scholars Press.
Glover, R.
   1958–59 "The *Didache*'s Quotations and the Synoptic Gospels." *NTS* 5:12–29.
Gold, Barbara K.
   1987   *Literary Patronage in Greece and Rome.* Chapel Hill: University of North Carolina Press.
Gonzalez, Justo L.
   1990   *Faith and Wealth: A History of Early Christian Ideas on the Origin, Significance, and Use of Money.* San Francisco: Harper & Row.
Goodman, Martin
   1994   *Mission and Conversion: Proselytizing in the Religious History of the Roman Empire.* Oxford: Clarendon Press.
Goodspeed, E. J.
   1945   "The *Didache*, Barnabas and the Doctrina." *ATR* 27:228–47.
Gordon, Robert P.
   1974   "Targumic Parallels to Acts XIII 18 and *Didache* XIV 3." *Novum Testamentum* 16, no. 4:285–89.

Gotthold, Zev
  1977   "Baptism." *Christian News from Israel* 26, no. 2:77–80.
Grant, Michael
  1974   *The Army of the Caesars.* London: Weidenfeld & Nicolson.
Greene, John T.
  1989   *The Role of the Messenger and Message in the Ancient Near East.* Brown Judaic Studies 169. Atlanta: Scholars Press.
Grimonprez-Damm, Benoit
  1990   "Le 'sacrifice' eucharistique dans la *Didache.*" *Revue des sciences religieuses* 64, no. 1:9–25.
Grubbs, Judith Evans
  1994   "'Pagan' and 'Christian' Marriage: The State of the Question." *Journal of Early Christian Studies* 2, no. 4:361–412.
Gundry, Robert H.
  1987   "The Hellenization of Dominical Traditon and Christianization of Jewish Tradition in the Eschatology of 1–2 Thessalonians." *NTS* 33:161–78.
  1993   *Mark: A Commentary on His Apology for the Cross.* Grand Rapids: Eerdmans.
  1994   *Matthew: A Commentary on His Handbook for a Mixed Church under Persecution.* 2nd ed. Grand Rapids: Eerdmans.
Haarbeck, H.
  1978   "*dokimos.*" In *The New International Dictionary of New Testament Theology,* edited by Colin Brown, 3:808–9. Grand Rapids: Zondervan.
Hadidian, Dikran Y.
  1982–83 "The Lord's Prayer and the Sacraments of Baptism and of the Lord's Supper in the Early Church." *Studia Liturgica* 15: 132–44.
Haenchen, Ernst
  1971   *The Acts of the Apostles: A Commentary.* Translated by Bernard Noble et al., from the 1965 German edition and brought up to date by R. McL. Wilson. Oxford: Basil Blackwell.
Hagner, Donald A.
  1984   *The Jewish Reclamation of Jesus.* Grand Rapids: Zondervan.
Hall, F. W.
  1922   "Adultery (Roman)." In *Encyclopedia of Religion and Ethics,* edited by James Hastings, 1:134f. Edinburgh: T & T Clark.
Hamel, Gildas
  1990   *Poverty and Charity in Roman Palestine, First Three Centuries CE.* Berkeley: University of California Press.
Hanson, K. C.
  1997   "The Galilean Fishing Economy and the Jesus Tradition." *BTB* 27, no. 3: 99–111.
Hanson, Paul D.
  1979   *The Dawn of Apocalyptic: The Historical and Sociological Roots of Jewish Apocalyptic Eschatology.* Philadelphia: Fortress.
Hanson, Richard P. C.
  1961   "The Liberty of the Bishop to Improvise Prayer in the Eucharist." *Vigiliae Christianae* 15:173–76.

Harnack, Adolf von
  1884   *Die Lehre der zwölf Apostel nebst Untersuchungen zur ältesten Geschichte der Kirchenverfassung und des Kirchenrechts.* Leipzig: Hinrichs.
  1886   *Die Lehre der Zwölf Apostel: Texte und Untersuchungen zur Geschichte der Altchristlichen Literatur.* Volume 2. Leipzig: Hinrichs. Pp. 1–70.
  1908   *The Mission and Expansion of Christianity in the First Three Centuries.* 2 volumes. Translated by J. Moffatt from the 1905 German orig. New York: G. P. Putnam's Sons.
Harris, J. Rendel
  1887   *The Teaching of the Apostles: Newly Edited, with Facsimile Text and a Commentary.* London: C. J. Clay.
Hastings, James, ed.
  1922   *Encyclopedia of Religion and Ethics.* Edinburgh: T & T Clark.
Heinemann, Joseph
  1977   *Prayers in the Talmud: Forms and Patterns.* Studia Judaica 9. Translated by Richard S. Sarasan from the 1966 Hebrew original. Berlin: Walter de Gruyter.
Henderson, Ian H.
  1992   "*Didache* and Orality in Synoptic Comparison." *JBL* 111:283–306.
  1995   "Style Switching in the *Didache*: Fingerprint or Argument." In *The Didache in Context: Essays on Its Text, History and Transmission,* edited by Clayton N. Jefford, 177–209. Leiden: E. J. Brill.
Hengel, Martin
  1974   *Judaism and Hellenism.* 2 volumes. Translated by John Bowden from the 1973 German orig. Philadelphia: Fortress.
  1977   *Crucifixion in the Ancient World and the Folly of the Message of the Cross.* Philadelphia: Fortress.
Hennecke, Edgar
  1965   *New Testament Apocrypha.* 2 vols. Edited by Wilhelm Schneemelcher. Translated by R. McL. Wilson from the 1959 German orig. Philadelphia: Westminster.
Heredia, Carlos, et al.
  1996   "Structural Adjustment and the Polarization of Mexican Society." In *The Case Against the Global Economy,* edited by Jerry Mander et al., 272–96. San Francisco: Sierra Club Books.
Heschel, Abraham J.
  1962   *The Prophets.* Part 2. New York: Harper & Row.
Heyward, Carter
  1989   "Suffering, Redemption, and Christ: Shifting the Grounds of Feminist Christology." *Christianity and Crisis* 49:381–86.
Higginson, Thomas Wentworth, trans.
  1944   *Epictetus: Discourses and Enchiridion.* Introduction by Irwin Edman. New York: Walter J. Black.
Hill, Julian
  1990   *Tradition and Composition in the Epistula Apostolorum.* Harvard Dissertations in Religion 24. Minneapolis: Fortress.

Hitchcock, Roswell D., and Francis Brown, eds.
  1884   *Teaching of the Twelve Apostles: Edited with a Translation, Introduction and Notes.* New York: Charles Scribner's Sons.
Hoffman, R. Joseph, trans.
  1987   *On the True Doctrine.* Translation by R. Joseph Hoffmann of the 180 C.E. Greek orig. as found in the extensive citations of Origen. Oxford: Oxford University Press.
Horner, G.
  1904   *The Statutes of the Apostles.* London: Williams & Norgate.
  1924   "A New Papyrus Fragment of the *Didache* in Coptic." *JTS* 25:225–31.
Horsley, Richard A.
  1989   *Sociology and the Jesus Movement.* New York: Crossroad.
  1991   "Ethics and Exegesis: 'Love Your Enemies' and the Doctrine of Non-violence." *JAAR* 54, no. 1:3–31. Reprinted in *The Love of Enemies and Retaliation in the New Testament,* edited by Willard M. Swartley (Louisville: Westminster/John Knox, 1992), 72–101.
Horsley, Richard A., with John S. Hanson
  1985   *Bandits, Prophets, and Messiahs: Popular Movements at the Time of Jesus.* San Francisco: Harper & Row.
Hruby, K.
  1972   "La 'Birkat Ha-Mazon.'" In *Mélanges liturgiques offerts au R.P. Dom Bernard Botte O.S.B,* edited by Ambroise Verheul, 205–22. Louvain: Abbaye du Mont César.
Humbrecht, Richard P., ed.
  1976   *Made, Not Born: New Pespectives on Christian Initiation and the Catechumenate.* From The Murphy Center for Liturgical Research. Notre Dame: University of Notre Dame Press.
Hurley, Joanna
  1992   *Mother Teresa: A Pictorial Biography.* Philadelphia: Courage Books.
Hynes, H. Patricia
  1989   *The Recurring Silent Spring.* New York: Paragon Press.
Idelsohn, A. Z.
  1967   *Jewish Liturgy and Its Development. 1932.* Reprint, New York: Schocken Books.
Jacobs, Steven L., ed.
  1993   *Contemporary Christian Religious Responses to the Shoah.* Studies in the Shoah 6. Lanham, Md.: University Press of America.
Jacquier, E.
  1891   *La doctrine des douze apôtres et ses enseignements.* Paris: Librairie Lethielleux.
James, William
  1958   *The Varieties of Religious Experience.* The Gifford Lectures, 1901–1902. New York: Mentor Books.
Jaspers, Karl
  1962   *Plato and Augustine.* Edited by Hannah Arendt. Translated by Ralph Manheim from the German orig. New York: Harcourt, Brace, & World.
Jaubert, Annie
  1960   "Jesus et le calendrier de Qumran." *NTS* 7:1–30.

Jaworski, Joseph
　　1998　*Synchronicity: The Inner Path of Leadership.* San Francisco: Berrett-Koehler Publisher.
Jay, Eric G.
　　1981　"From Presbyter-Bishops to Bishops and Presbyters." *The Second Century* 1:125–62
Jay, Nancy
　　1992　*Throughout Your Generations Forever: Sacrifice, Religion, and Paternity.* Chicago: University of Chicago Press.
Jefford, Clayton N.
　　1989a　*The Sayings of Jesus in the Teaching of the Twelve Apostles.* Supplements to *Vigiliae Christianae* 11. Leiden: E. J. Brill.
　　1989b　"Presbyters in the community of the *Didache.*" In *Studia Patristica* 21, edited by Elizabeth A. Livingstone, 122–28. Leuven: Peeters Press.
　　1989c　With Stephen J. Patterson. "A Note on *Didache* 12.2a (Coptic)." *The Second Century* 7, no. 2 (summer 1989–90): 65–75.
　　1990　"An Ancient Witness to the Apostolic Decree of Acts 15?" *Proceedings: Eastern Great Lakes and Midwest Biblical Societies* 10:204–13.
　　1992a　"Tradition and Witness in Antioch: Acts 15 and *Didache* 6." In *Perspectives on Contemporary New Testament Questions: Essays in Honor of T. C. Smith,* edited by Edgar V. McKnight, 75–89. North American Baptist Professors of Religion Festschriften Series 9. Lewiston: Edwin Mellen Press.
　　1992b　"Tradition and Witness in Antioch: Acts 15 and *Didache* 6." *Perspectives in Religious Studies* 19, no. 4:409–19.
　　1995a　"Did Ignatius of Antioch Know the *Didache*?" In *The Didache in Context: Essays on Its Text, History and Transmission,* edited by Clayton N. Jefford, 330–51. Leiden: E. J. Brill.
　　1995b　With Kenneth J. Harder. "A Bibliography of Literature on the *Didache.*" In *The Didache in Context: Essays on Its Text, History and Transmission,* edited by Clayton N. Jefford, 368–82. Leiden: E. J. Brill.
　　1997　"Household Codes and Conflict in the Early Church." *Studia Patristica* 31:121–27.
　　2001　"*Didache.*" In *Eerdmans Dictionary of the Bible,* edited by David Noel Freedman, 345a–46a. Grand Rapids: Eerdmans.
Jeremias, Joachim
　　1956　*Jesus' Promise to the Nations.* Translated by S. H. Hooke from the 1956 German orig. Philadelphia: Fortress.
　　1960　*Infant Baptism in the First Four Centuries.* London: SCM Press.
　　1963　*The Origins of Infant Baptism.* London: SCM Press.
　　1967　*The Prayers of Jesus.* London: SCM Press.
　　1971　*New Testament Theology: The Proclamation of Jesus.* Translated by John Bowden from the 1971 German orig. New York: Charles Scribner's Sons.
　　1972　*The Parables of Jesus.* 2nd rev. ed. Translated by S. H. Hooke from the 1970 German orig. New York: Charles Scribner's Sons.
　　1977　*The Eucharistic Words of Jesus.* Translated by Norman Perrin from the 1964 German original. New York: Charles Scribner's Sons.

Johnson, Paul
1987 *A History of the Jews.* New York: Harper & Row.

Johnson, Ricky L.
1989 "Heavenly Strength for an Earthly Journey: The System of Hebrews." In *Religious Writings and Religious Systems,* edited by Jacob Neusner et al., 2:75–88.

Johnson, Sherman Elbridge
1946 "A Subsidiary Motive for the Writing of the *Didache*." In *Munera Studiosa,* edited by S. E. Johnson et al., 107–22. Cambridge, Mass.: Episcopal Divinity School.

Jourjon, Maurice
1971 "Textes eucharistiques des pères ante-niceens." In *L'eucharistie: Le sens des sacraments,* edited and under the direction of R. Didier. Lyon: Faculté de théologie.

Johnson, Sonia
1981 *From Housewife to Heretic.* Garden City, N.Y.: Doubleday.

Johnson, Tim
1999 "World Out of Balance." *Native Americas* 16, nos. 3–4:8–25.

Jones, F. Stanley, and Paul A. Mirecki
1995 "Considerations on the Coptic Papyrus of the *Didache*." In *The Didache in Context: Essays on Its Text, History and Transmission,* edited by Clayton N. Jefford, 47–87. Leiden: E. J. Brill.

Karliner, Joshua
1997 *The Corporate Planet: Ecology and Politics in the Age of Globalization.* San Francisco: Sierra Club Books.

Kaufmann, Yehezkel
1988 *Christianity and Judaism: Two Covenants.* Translated from the Hebrew original by C. W. Efroymson. Jerusalem: Magnes Press.

Kavanaugh, Aidan
1976 "Christian Initiation of Adults: The Rites." In *Made, Not Born: New Pespectives on Christian Initiation and the Catechumenate,* edited by Richard P. Humbrecht, 118–37. Notre Dame, Ind.: University of Notre Dame Press.

1978 *The Shape of Baptism: The Rite of Christian Initiation.* New York: Pueblo.

Keifer, Ralph A.
1976 "Christian Initiation: The State of the Question." In *Made, Not Born: New Pespectives on Christian Initiation and the Catechumenate,* edited by Richard P. Humbrecht, 138–51. Notre Dame: University of Notre Dame Press.

Kelber, Werner H.
*1983 *The Oral and the Written Gospel.* Philadelphia: Fortress.

Kelly, Dean M.
1972 *Why Conservative Churches Are Growing.* New York: Harper & Row.

Kennedy, Teresa
1997 *Welcome to the End of the World: Prophecy, Rage, and the New Age.* New York: M. Evans.

Kenny, Anthony
  1986   *A Stylometric Study of the New Testament.* Oxford: Clarendon Press.
Kidd, Sue Monk
  1996   *The Dance of the Dissident Daughter: A Woman's Journey from Christian Tradition to the Sacred Feminine.* San Francisco: HarperSanFrancisco.
Kilmartin, Edward J.
  1965   *The Eucharist in the Primitive Church.* Englewood Cliffs, N.J.: Prentice-Hall.
  1974   "Sacrificium Laudis: Content and Function of Early Eucharistic Prayers." *TS* 35:268–87.
King, A., et al.
  1991   *The First Global Revolution: A Report by the Council of the Club of Rome.* London: Simon & Schuster.
Klauser, Th., ed.
  1946   *Reallexikon für Antike und Christentum.* Stuttgart: Hiersemann.
Klein, Terrance W.
  1993   "Institutional Narratives at the Crossroads." *Worship* 67, no. 5:407–18.
Kleist, James A.
  1961   *The Didache, The Epistle of Barnabas, et al., Newly Translated and Annotated,* 3–25. Westminster, Md.: Newman.
Klijn, A. F. J.
  1963   "An Ancient Syriac Baptismal Liturgy in the Syriac Acts of John." *Novum Testamentum* 6:216–28.
Kloppenborg, John S.
  1979   "*Didache* 16:6–8 and Special Matthaean Tradition." *Zeitschrift für die Neutestamentliche Wissenschaft* 70:54–67.
  1987a *The Formation of Q: Trajectories in Ancient Wisdom Collections.* Studies in Antiquity and Christianity. Philadelphia: Fortress.
  1987b "Symbolic Eschatology and the Apocalypticism of Q." *HTR* 80:287–306.
  1993   "Edwin Hatch, Churches and *Collegia.*" *Origins and Method: Toward a New Understanding of Judaism and Christianity.* Edited by Bradley H. McLean. Journal for the Study of the New Testament Supplement Series 86. Sheffield: JSOT Press.
  1995   "The Transformation of Moral Exhortation in *Didache* 1–5." In *The Didache in Context: Essays on Its Text, History and Transmission,* edited by Clayton N. Jefford, 88–109. Leiden: E. J. Brill.
Knox, W. L.
  1939   "*Perikathairōn (Didache* iii 4)." *JTS* 40:146–49.
Koch, Klaus
  1983   *The Prophets of the Assyrian Period.* Philadelphia: Fortress.
Koester, Helmut
  1990   *Ancient Christian Gospels: Their History and Development.* Harrisburg, Pa.: Trinity Press International.
  1992   "Jesus the Victim." *JBL* 111, no. 1:3–15.
  1994   "Written Gospels or Oral Traditions?" *JBL* 113, no. 2:293–97.
  1995   *History, Culture, and Religion of the Hellenistic Age: Introduction to the New Testament.* Volume 1. 2nd ed. Berlin: Walter de Gruyter.

Kohlenberger, John R., III, ed.

1984   *The Expanded Vine's Expository Dictionary of New Testament Words.* Minneapolis: Bethany House.

Kolbenschlag, Madonna

1981   *Kiss Sleeping Beauty Goodby: Breaking the Spell of Feminine Myths and Models.* Toronto: Bantam Book.

Körtner, Ulrich H. J.

1995   *The End of the World: A Theological Interpretation.* Louisville: Westminster John Knox Press.

Kraft, Robert A.

1965a   *Barnabas and the Didache.* New York: Thomas Nelson & Sons.

1965b   *The Apostolic Fathers: A New Translation and Commentary,* 1–16, 57–178. Toronto: Thomas Nelson.

Kuhn, Thomas S.

1963   "The Function of Dogma in Scientific Research." In *Scientific Change,* edited by A. C. Combie. London: Heinemann.

1970   *The Structure of Scientific Revolutions.* 2nd enlarged ed. Chicago: University of Chicago Press.

Küng, Hans

1991   *Eternal Life? Life After Death as a Medical, Philosophical, and Theological Problem.* Translated by Edward Quinn from the 1982 German orig. New York: Doubleday.

Krawutzeky, Adam

1882   "Über des altkirchliche Unterrichtsbuch: Die Zwei Wege oder dei Entscheidung des Petrus." *Theologische Quartalschrift* 3:359–445.

Ladd, George Eldon

1949   "The Eschatology of the *Didache.*" Doctoral disseration. Harvard University.

LaHaye, Tim, et al.

1995   *Left Behind: A Novel of the Earth's Last Days.* Wheaton, Ill.: Tyndale House Publishers.

Lake, K.

1912   "The *Didache.*" In *The Apostolic Fathers.* Loeb Classical Library. New York: Macmillan.

Lamy, Philip

1996   *Millennium Rage.* New York: Plenum Press.

Lanoir, Corinne

1982a   "Présentation de la '*Didachè.*'" *Foi et Vie* 81:48–61.

1982b   "Un exemple d'ensignement sans passion: La *Didache.*" *Foi et Vie* 81:55–61.

Lathrop, Gordon W.

1990   "Justin, Eucharist, and 'Sacrifice': A Case Metaphor." *Worship* 64, no. 1:30–48.

1994   "The Origins and Early Meanings of Baptism: A Proposal." *Worship* 68:504–22.

Layton, B.

1968   "The Sources, Date and Transmission of *Didache* 1.3b-2.1." *HTR* 61:343–83.

Leaney, A. R. C.
  1966   *The Rule of Qumran and its Meaning.* Philadelphia: Westminster. See esp. study of "The Two Spirits." pp. 37–56.
Lefort, L.-Th.
  1952   *Les Pères apostolique en copte.* 2 volumes. Louvain: L. Durbecq.
Le Goff, Jacques
  1981   *The Birth of Purgatory.* Translated by Arthur Goldhammer. Chicago: University of Chicago Press.
Lenski, Gerhard
  1966   *Power and Privilege: A Theory of Social Stratification.* New York: McGraw-Hill.
  1970   *Human Societies: A Marcolevel Introduction to Sociology.* New York: McGraw-Hill.
L'Eplattenier, Charles
  1982   "Présentation de la '*Didachè.*'" *Foi et Vie* 81:48–54.
Lernoux, Penny
  1982   *Cry of the People: The Struggle for Human Rights in Latin America.* New York: Penguin Books.
Levenson, Jon D.
  1993   *The Death and Resurrection of the Beloved Son: The Transformation of Sacrifice in Judaism and Christianity.* New Haven: Yale University Press.
Lewis, Jack P.
  1983   "Baptismal Practices of the 2nd and 3rd Century Church." *Restoration Quarterly* 26:1–17.
Liébaert, J.
  1970   *Les enseignements moraux des pères apostoliques,* 99–124. Gembloux: Duculot.
Lietzmann, Hans
  1979   *Mass and Lord's Supper: A Study in the History of the Liturgy.* Translated by Dorothea H. G. Reeve from the 1926 German orig. Leiden: E. J. Brill.
Lightfoot, J. B.
  1912   *The Apostolic Fathers: Revised Texts with Short Introductions and English Translations,* 215–35. London: Macmillan.
Lindblom, Johannes
  1962   *Prophecy in Ancient Israel.* Philadelphia: Fortress.
Lindsay, Norman, trans.
  1932   *The Complete Works of Gaius Petronius.* Translated and one hundred illustrations by Norman Lindsay. New York: Rarity Press.
Lindsey, Hal
  1970   *The Late Great Planet Earth.* New York: Bantam Books.
  1994   *Planet Earth—2000 A.D.* Palos Verdes, Calif.: Western Front.
Loisy, A.
  1921   "La *Didache* et les lettres des Pères Apostoliques." *RHL* 7:433–81.
Madden, John
  1996   "Slavery in the Roman Empire: Numbers and Origins." *Classics Ireland* 3. http://www.ucd.ie/~classics/ClassicsIreland.html

Magne, Jean
  1909   "Klasma, sperma, poimnion: Le voeu pour le rassemblement de *Didache*
          IX, 4." In *Melange d'histoire des religions*. By A. Bareau et al.
Malcolm X
  1965   *The Autobiography of Malcolm X*, as told by Alex Haley. New York: Bal-
          lentine Books.
Malina, Bruce J.
  1991   "Honor and Shame in Luke-Acts: Pivotal Values of the Mediterranean
          World." In *The Social World of Luke-Acts*, edited and co-authored by
          Jerome H. Neyrey, 25–65. Peabody, Mass.: Hendrickson.
  1995   *The New Testament World: Insights from Cultural Anthropology*. Rev. ed.
          Louisville: Westminster/John Knox Press.
  1996   "Mediterranean Sacrifice: Dimensions of Domestic and Political Reli-
          gion." *BTB* 26, no. 1:26–44.
Mander, Jerry, et al., eds.
  1996   *The Case Against the Global Economy*. San Francisco: Sierra Club Books.
Manson, T. W.
  1956   "The Lord's Prayer." *Bulletin of the John Rylands Library* 38:99–113,
          436–48.
Marrow, Stanley B.
  1999   "*ATHANASIA/ANASTASIS:* The Road Not Taken." *NTS* 45:571–
          86.
Martos, Joseph
  1981   *Doors to the Sacred: A Historical Introduction to Sacraments in the
          Catholic Church*. New York: Doubleday & Co.
Massaux, Edouard
  1949   "L'influence litteraire de l'evangile de saint Matthieu sur la *Didache*."
          ETL 25:5–41.
  1950   "Le problème de la *Didachè*." In *Influence de l'Evangile de saint
          Matthieu sur la littérature chrétienne avant saint Irénée*, 3–6, 604–46.
          Louvain. Translated and republished in *The Influence of the Gospel of
          Saint Matthew on Christian Literature before Saint Irenaeus* (Macon,
          Ga.: Mercer University Press, 1993), 3:167–73.
Mazza, Enrico
  1995   *The Origins of the Eucharistic Prayer*. Collegeville, Minn.: Liturgical
          Press.
  1996   "Elements of a Eucharistic Interpretation." In *The Didache in Modern
          Research,* edited by Jonathan A. Draper, 276–99. Leiden: E. J. Brill.
          Translated and reprinted as "*Didaché IX-X:* Elementi per una interpre-
          tazione Eucaristica." *Ephemerides Liturgicae* 92 (1979): 393–419.
McBrien, Richard P.
  1994   *Catholicism*. San Francisco: HarperSanFrancisco.
McGinn, Bernard
  1979   *Visions of the End: Apocalyptic Traditons in the Middle Ages*. New York:
          Columbia University Press.
McGowan, Andrew
  1995   "First Regarding the Cup. . ." *JTS* 46, no. 2:551–55.

Meadows, Donella H., et al.
  1972   *The Limits to Growth: A Report for the Club of Rome's Project on the Predicament of Mankind.* New York: Universe Books.
Meeks, Wayne
  1986   *The Moral World of the First Christians.* Philadelphia: Westminster.
Meier, John P.
  1994   *A Marginal Jew: Rethinking the Historical Jesus.* Volume 2. New York: Doubleday.
  1997   "The Circle of the Twelve." *JBL* 116, no. 4:635–72.
Meissner, W. W.
  2000   *The Cultic Origins of Christianity: The Dynamics of Religious Development.* Collegeville, Minn.: Liturgical Press.
Metzger, Marcel
  1976   "La Didascalie et les Constitutions Apostoliques." In *L'eucharistie des premiers Chrétiens,* edited by W. Rordorf et al. Paris: Beauchesne.
Meyers, Carol L., et al.
  1993   *Zechariah 9–14.* Anchor Bible 25C. New York: Doubleday.
Middleton, R. D.
  1935   "The Eucharistic Prayers of the *Didache.*" *JTS* 36:259–67.
Milavec, Aaron
  1978   "Matthew's Integration of Sexual and Divine Begetting." *BTB* 36:108–16.
  1982   *To Empower as Jesus Did: Acquiring Spiritual Power Through Apprenticeship.* Lewiston: Edwin Mellen Press.
  1984   "Jesus as Homeowner: Matthew's Perspective." In *New Testament Perspectives,* edited by William P. Frost, 46–60. Dayton: College Press. Also published in *Explorations* 1, no. 3 (1983): 11–20.
  1986   "Polanyi's Understanding of Religion Reconsidered." *Convivium* 22:1–14.
  1989a "The Pastoral Genius of the Didache." In *Religious Writings and Religious Systems,* edited by Jacob Neusner et al., 2:89–125. Brown Studies in Religion 2. Atlanta: Scholars Press.
  1989b "Mark's Parable of the Wicked Husbandman as Reaffirming God's Predilection for Israel." *Journal of Ecumenical Studies* 26, no. 2:289–312.
  1989c "The Heuristic Circularity of Commitment and the Experience of Discovery: A Polanyian Critique of Thomas Kuhn's *Structure of Scientific Revolutions,*" *Tradition and Discovery* 16, no. 2:4–19.
  1990   "The Identity of 'the Son' and 'the Others': Mark's Parable of the Wicked Husbandmen Reconsidered." *BTB* 20, no. 1:30–37.
  1992   "The Birth of Purgatory: Evidence of the *Didache.*" *Proceedings of the Eastern Great Lakes Biblical Society* 12:91–104.
  1993   "If I Join Forces with Mr. Kuhn": Polanyi and Kuhn as Mutually Supportive and Corrective." *Polanyiana* [Budapest] 2, no. 4 & 3, no. 1: 56–74. Reprinted in *From Polanyi to the 21st Century,* edited by Richard Gelwick (Proceedings of a Centennial Conference, Kent, Oh.: Kent State University, 1997), 224–59.

1994a   *Exploring Scriptural Sources: Rediscovering Discipleship.* Kansas City: Sheed & Ward.

1994b   "Distinguishing True and False Prophets: The Protective Wisdom of the *Didache.*" *Journal of Early Christian Studies* 2, no. 2:117–36.

1995a   "The Social Setting of 'Turning the Other Cheek' and 'Loving One's Enemies' in Light of the *Didache.*" *BTB* 25, no. 2:131–43.

1995b   "Saving Efficacy of the Burning Process in *Didache* 16.5." In *The Didache in Context: Essays on Its Text, History and Transmission,* edited by Clayton N. Jefford, 131–55. Leiden: E. J. Brill.

1996a   *Scripture Sleuth: Rediscovering the Early Church.* Interactive software version of 1994a. Liguori, Mo.: Liguori Faithware. Distributed by Easy-Greek Software, 329 W. Greene St.; Piqua, OH 45356 (937-778-1447).

1996b   "The Economic Safety Net in the *Didache.*" *Proceedings of the Eastern Great Lakes Biblical Society* 16:73–84.

1997   "Religious Pedagogy from Tender to Twilight Years: Parenting, Mentoring, and Pioneering Discoveries by Religious Masters as Viewed from within Polanyi's Sociology and Epistemology of Science." *Tradition and Discovery* 23, no. 2:15–36.

1999   "How the *Didache* Attracted, Cooled Down, and Quenched Prophetic Fire." *Proceedings of the Eastern Great Lakes & Midwest Biblical Society* 19:103–17.

2003   "The Purifying Confession of Failings Required by the *Didache*'s Eucharistic Sacrifice." *BTB* 33, no. 3:64–76.

2004a   "Synoptic Tradition in the *Didache* Revisited." *Journal of Early Christian Studies* 12, no. 1 (forthcoming).

2004b   *The Didache: With Commentary and Flowcharts.* Collegeville, Minn.: Liturgical Press (forthcoming).

Millgram, Abraham E.

1971   *Jewish Worship.* Philadelphia: Jewish Publication Society of America.

Mills, Watson E., general editor

1990   *Mercer Dictionary of the Bible.* Macon, Ga.: Mercer University Press.

Mitchell, Nathan

1995   "Baptism in the *Didache.*" In *The Didache in Context: Essays on Its Text, History and Transmission,* edited by Clayton N. Jefford, 226–55. Leiden: E. J. Brill.

Molland, E.

1955   "La circoncision, le baptême et l'autorité du décret apostolique dans le milieux Pseudo-Clémentines." *Studia Theologica* [Lund] 9:1–39.

Moran, Gabriel

1963   *Scripture and Tradition: A Survey of the Controversy.* New York: Herder & Herder.

Moule, C. F. D.

1955   "A Note on *Didache* IX. 4." *NTS* 6:240–43.

1960   "A Reconsideration of the Context of Maranatha." *NTS* 6:307–10

Moy, Arthur C.

1980   "Assertive Behavior in the New Testament Prespective." *Journal of Psychology and Theology* 8, no. 4:288–92.

Muilenburg, J.
  1929   "The Literary Relations of the Epistle of Barnabas and the Teaching of
          the Twelve Apostles." Doctoral dissertation, Yale University.
Murphy, Jeffrie G., et al.
  1990   *Forgiveness and Mercy.* Cambridge Studies in Philosophy and Law. Cam-
          bridge: University Press.
Myers, Ched
  1988   *Binding the Strong Man: A Political Reading of Mark's Story of Jesus.*
          Maryknoll, N.Y.: Orbis.
Myers, Jacob M.
  1974   *I and II Esdras: Introduction, Translation, and Commentary.* Anchor
          Bible 42. Garden City, N.Y.: Doubleday.
Nardo, Don
  1998   *Life of a Roman Slave.* San Diego: Lucent Books.
Nautin, Pierre
  1959a   "La composition de la '*Didache*' et son titre." *RHR* 155:191–214.
  1959b   "Notes critiques sur la *Didache* [11:3–5]." *Vigilae Christianae* 13:118–
          20.
Neusner, Jacob
  1970   *A Life of Yohanan ben Zakkai.* Leiden: E. J. Brill.
  1983   *Pirke Avot: Torah from our Sages.* Dallas: Rossel Books.
  1984   *Messiah in Context: Israel's History and Destiny in Formative Judaism.*
          Philadelphia: Fortress.
  1986   "The Jewish-Christian Argument in the First Century: Different People
          Talking About Different Things to Different People." *Religious Studies
          and Theology* 6, nos. 1–2:8–19.
  1988a   *Judaism: The Evidence of the Mishnah.* Brown Judaic Studies 129.
          Atlanta: Scholars Press.
  1988b   *The Systemic Analysis of Judaism.* Brown Judaic Studies 137. Atlanta:
          Scholars Press.
  1988c   *Wrong Ways and Right Ways in the Study of Formative Judaism: Critical
          Method and Literature, History and the History of Religion.* Brown
          Judaic Studies 145. Atlanta: Scholars Press.
  1988d   *The Incarnation of God: The Character of Divinity in Formative
          Judaism.* Philadelphia: Fortress.
  1988e   *The Mishnah: A New Translation.* New Haven: Yale University Press.
  1988f   *Why No Gospels in Talmudic Judaism?* Atlanta: Scholars Press.
  1994   *Rabbinic Literature & the New Testament: What We Cannot Show, We
          Do Not Know.* Valley Forge, Pa.: Trinity Press International.
  1995   *The Talmud of Babylonia: An Academic Commentary.* 36 vols. USF Aca-
          demic Commentary Series. Atlanta: Scholars Press.
Neusner, Jacob, et al., eds.
  1989   *Religious Writings and Religious Systems: Systematic Analysis of Holy
          Books in Christianity, Islam, Buddhism, Greco-Roman Religions, Ancient
          Israel, and Judaism.* Volume 2. Brown Studies in Religion 2. Atlanta:
          Scholars Press.
Newman, John Henry
  1974   *An Essay on the Development of Christian Doctrine.* Baltimore: Penguin
          Books. Orig., 1845.

Neyrey, Jerome H.
1991   "Ceremonies in Luke-Acts: The Case of Meals and Table Fellowship."
        The Social World of Luke-Acts, edited by Jerome H. Neyrey, 361–87.
        Peabody, Mass.: Hendrickson.

Nickelsburg, George W. E., Jr.
1972   *Resurrection, Immortality, and Eternal Life in Interestamental Judaism.*
        Cambridge, Mass.: Harvard University Press.

Niederwimmer, Kurt
1982   "Textprobleme der *Didache." Wiener Studien* 16:114–30.
1995   "Der Didachist und seine Quellen." In *The Didache in Context: Essays
        on Its Text, History and Transmission,* edited by Clayton N. Jefford,
        15–36. Leiden: E. J. Brill.
1996   "An Examination of the Development of Itinerant Radicalism in the
        Environment and Tradition in the *Didache."* In *The Didache in Modern
        Research,* edited by Jonathan A. Draper, 321–39. Leiden: E. J. Brill.
        Reprint and translation of "Zur Entwicklungsgeschichte des Wander-
        radikalismus im Traditionsbereich des *Didache." Wiener Studien* 11
        (1977): 145–67.
1998   *The Didache.* Translated by Linda M. Maloney from the 1989 German
        orig. Minneapolis: Fortress.

Nielson, Hanne Sigismund
1998   "Roman Children at Mealtimes." In *Meals in a Social Context: Aspects
        of the Communal Meal in the Hellenistic and Roman World,* 56–66.
        Aarhus: Aarhus University Press.

Nock, A. D.
1933   *Conversion: The Old and New in Religion from Alexander the Great to
        Augustine of Hippo.* Oxford: Oxford University Press.

Noll, Ray Robert.
1970   *Recherches sur les origines du sacerdoce ministériel chez les Pères apo-
        stoliques.* Strassburg. Pp. 215–272.
1993   *Christian Ministerial Priesthood: A Search for Its Beginnings in the Pri-
        mary Documents of the Apostolic Fathers.* San Francisco: Catholic Schol-
        ars Pess.

Noonan, J. T.
1965   *Contraception.* Cambridge: Harvard University Press.

Novak, David
1983   *The Image of the Non-Jew in Judaism: An Historical and Constructive
        Study of the Noahide Laws.* Lewiston: Edwin Mellen Press.
1989   *Jewish-Christian Dialogue: A Jewish Justification.* Oxford: Oxford Uni-
        versity Press.

Oakman, Douglas E.
1991   "The Countryside in Luke-Acts." In *The Social World of Luke-Acts,*
        edited by Jerome H. Neyrey, 151–79. Peabody, Mass.: Hendrickson.

O'Collins, Gerald
1993   *Retrieving Fundamental Theology: Three Styles of Contemporary Theol-
        ogy.* New York: Paulist.

O'Connor, John Cardinal
1988   "Yad Vashem Revisited." *Face to Face* 14:47–48.

Ong, Walter J.
  1967   *The Presence of the Word: Some Prolegomena for Cultural and Religious History.* Minneapolis: University of Minnesota Press.
  1982   *Orality and Literacy.* New York: Methuen.

Orr, David W.
  1992   *Ecological Literacy: Education and the Transition to a Postmodern World.* Albany: State University of New York Press.

Osborne, Kenan B.
  1988   *Priesthood: A History of the Ordained Ministry in the Roman Catholic Church.* New York: Paulist.
  1993   *Ministry: Lay Ministry in the Roman Catholic Church.* New York: Paulist.

Osiek, Carolyn
  1983   *Rich and Poor in the Shepherd of Hermas: An Exegetical-Social Investigation.* Catholic Biblical Quarterly Monograph Series 15. Washington: Catholic Biblical Association of America.

Oulton, J. E. L.
  1940   "Clement of Alexandria and the *Didache.*" *JTS* 41:177–79.

Overholt, Thomas W.
  1986   *Prophecy in Cross-Cultural Perspective: A Sourcebook for Biblical Researchers.* Atlanta: Scholars Press.
  1989   *Channels of Prophecy: The Social Dynamics of Prophetic Activity.* Minneapolis: Fortress.

Pardee, Nancy
  1989   "A Generic Uniderstanding of the *Didache.*" Draft of doctoral dissertation in preparation at the University of Chicago slated for completion in 2001.
  1995   "The Curse that Saves (*Didache* 16.5)." In *The Didache in Context: Essays on Its Text, History and Transmission,* edited by Clayton N. Jefford, 156–76. Leiden: E. J. Brill.
  2000   Review of Kurt Niederwimmer, *The Didache. Journal of Religion* 80, no. 3: 503–4.

Patterson, Stephen J.
  1995   "Didache 11–13: The Legacy of Radical Itineracy in Early Christianity." In *The Didache in Context: Essays on Its Text, History and Transmission,* edited by Clayton N. Jefford, 313–29. Leiden: E. J. Brill.

Payne, J. Barton
  1973   *Encyclopedia of Biblical Prophecy.* London: Hodder & Stoughton.

Peck, Scott
  1983   *People of the Lie.* New York: Simon & Schuster.

Peerbolte, L. J. Lietaert
  1996   *The Antecedents of Antichrist: A Traditio-Historical Study of the Earlier Christian Views on Eschatological Opponents.* Supplements to the Journal for the Study of Judaism 49. Leiden: E. J. Brill.

Peet, John
  1992   *Energy and the Ecological Economics of Sustainability.* Washington, D.C.: Island Press.

Perrin, Norman
  1967   *Rediscovering the Teaching of Jesus.* New York: Harper & Row.

Perrot, Charles, et al.

1983 *Le retour du Christ*. Brussels: Publications des Facultés universitaires Saint-Louis.

Peterson, E.

1944 "*Didache* cap. 9 e. 10." *Ephemerides Liturgicae* 58:3–13.

1959 "Über einige Probleme der *Didache*-Überlieferung." In *Frühkirche, Judentum und Gnosis*. Rome: Herder.

Petronius. *See* Lindsay.

Petuchowski, Jacob J.

1964 "Halakhah in the Church Fathers." In *Essays in Honor of Solomon B. Freehof,* edited by F.C. Schwartz et al., 257–74. Pittsburgh: Rodef Shalom Congregation.

1972 *Understanding Jewish Prayer.* New York: Ktav.

Piper, John

1979 *"Love your enemies": Jesus' Love Command in the Synoptic Gospels and in the Early Christian Paraenesis.* Cambridge: Cambridge University Press.

Pistoia, A., et al.

1975 *Liturgie et rémission des peches.* Rome: Edizioni Liturgiche.

Pitt-Rivers, Julian A.

1977 *The Fate of Shechem or the Politics of Sex: Essays in the Anthropology of the Mediterranean*. Cambridge Studies in Social Anthropology. Cambridge: University Press.

Pobee, John S.

1985 *Persecution and Martyrdom in the Theology of Paul.* Sheffield: JSOT Press.

Polanyi, Michael

1958 *Personal Knowledge: Towards a Post-Critical Philosophy.* London: Routledge and K. Paul.

1959 *The Study of Man*. The Lindsay Memorial Lectures of 1958. Chicago: University of Chicago Press.

1961 "Faith and Reason." *Journal of Religion* 41, no. 4:238–47.

1962 "The Unaccountable Element in Science." *Philosophy* 27:1–14.

1963a "Science and Religion: Separate Dimensions or Common Ground?" *Philosophy Today* 7:4–14.

1963b Comments on Thomas Kuhn's "The Function of Dogma in Scientific Research." In *Scientific Change,* edited by A. C. Combie, 375–80. New York: Basic Books.

1964 *Personal Knowledge*. 1958, Reprint, New York: Harper Torchbooks.

1966 *Tacit Dimension*. Garden City, N.Y.: Doubleday.

1967 "Science and Reality." *British Journal of the Philosophy of Science* 18:177–96.

1968 "Logic and Psychology." *American Psychologist* 12:27–43.

Polo, Marco

1984 *The Travels of Marco Polo.* Translated by Teresa Waugh from the Italian orig. New York: Facts On File.

Pomeroy, Sarah B.

1990 *Women in Hellenistic Egypt from Alexander to Cleopatra*. Reprint of the 1984 orig., with a new foreword. Detrtoit: Wayne State University Press.

1995   *Goddesses, Whores, Wives, and Slaves: Women in Classical Antiquity.* New
        York: Schocken.
Ponthot, Joseph
1959   "La signification religieuse du 'nom' chez Clement de Rome et dans la
        Didache." *ETL* 35:339–61.
Poschmann, B.
1940   *Paenitentia secunda.* Bonn: Hanstein.
Power, David N.
1987   *The Sacrifice We Offer.* New York: Crossroad.
Prusak, Bernard P.
1975   "Heaven and Hell: Eschatological Symbols of Existential Protest." *Cross
        Currents* 2, no. 19:475–91.
Quasten, Johannes
1975   *Patrology.* 1950. Reprint, Utrecht: Spectrum.
Quinn, Daniel
1992   *Ishmael: An Adventure of the Mind and Spirit.* New York: Bantam/
        Turner Books.
1996   *The Story of B: An Adventure of the Mind and Spirit.* New York: Bantam.
Rahner, Karl
1966   "The Hermeneutics of Eschatological Assertions." In *Theological Inves-
        tigations,* 4:323–46. Baltimore: Helicon Press.
1982   *Foundations of Chistian Faith.* New York: Crossroad.
Rambo, Lewis R.
1993   *Understanding Religious Conversion.* New Haven: Yale University Press.
Randi, James
1987   *The Faith Healers.* Buffalo: Prometheus Books.
Ratzinger, Joseph
1987   *Principles of Catholic Theology: Building Stones for a Fundamental The-
        ology.* San Francisco: Ignatius Press.
1988   *Eschatology: Death and Eternal Life.* Translated by Michael Waldstein
        from the 1977 German orig. Dogmatic Theology 9. Washington, D.C.:
        Catholic University of America.
Reed, Jonathan
1995   "The Hebrew Epic and the *Didache.*" In *The Didache in Context: Essays
        on Its Text, History and Transmission,* edited by Clayton N. Jefford,
        213–25. Leiden: E. J. Brill.
Reid, J. S.
1922   "Purification (Roman)," & "Charity, Almsgiving (Roman)." In *Ency-
        clopedia of Religion and Ethics,* edited by James Hastings, 10:500–503,
        3:391f. Edinburgh: T & T Clark.
Reiling, J.
1973   *Hermas and Christian Prophecy: A Study of the Eleventh Mandate.* Lei-
        den: E. J. Brill.
Reimer, Ivoni Richter
1995   *Women in the Acts of the Apostles.* Translated by Linda M. Maloney from
        the 1993 German orig. Minneapolis: Fortress.
Richardson, Cyril C., ed. and trans.
1953   *Early Christian Fathers: Newly Translated and Edited,* 167–79.
        Philadelphia: Westminster.

Richardson, Robert D.
1949   "Eastern and Western Liturgies: The Primitive Basis of Their Later Differences." *HTR* 42, no. 2: 125–48.
1957   "The Lord's Prayer as an Early Eucharistia." *ATR* 39:123–30.

Riesenfeld, Harald
1970   "The Sabbath and the Lord's Day in Judaism, the Preaching of Jesus and Early Christianity." In *The Gospel Tradition*, 111–38. Philadelphia: Westminster.

Riggs, John W.
1984   "From Gracious Table to Sacramental Elements: The Tradition-History of *Didache* 9 and 10." *The Second Century* 4, no. 2: 83–101.
1995   "The Sacred Food of *Didache* 9–10 and Second-Century Ecclesiologies." In *The Didache in Context: Essays on Its Text, History and Transmission*, edited by Clayton N. Jefford, 256–83. Leiden: E. J. Brill.

Rivkin, Ellis
1971   *The Shaping of Jewish History.* New York: Charles Scribner's Sons.
1984   *What Crucified Jesus? The Political Execution of a Charismatic.* Nashville: Abingdon Press.

Robeck, Cecil M., Jr.
1992   *Prophecy in Carthage: Perpetua, Tertullian, and Cyprian.* Cleveland: Pilgrim Press.

Roberts, Richard
1972   *Fisher/Spassky: The New York Times Report on the Chess Match of the Century.* New York: Bantam Books.

Robertson, Pat
1992   *The Secret Kingdom: Your Path to Peace, Love, and Financial Security.* Dallas: Word.

Robinson, J. Armitage
1920   *Barnabas, Hermas and the Didache.* London.
1934   "The Epistle of Barnabas and the *Didache.*" *JTS* 35:113–46, 225–48.

Robinson, John A. T.
1956   "The Most Primitive Christology of All?" *JTS* 7:177–89.
1979   *Jesus and His Coming.* 2nd ed. of 1957 orig. Philadelphia: Westminster.

Robock, Alan
1989   "New Models Confirm Nuclear Winter." *Bulletin of Atomic Scientists* 45, no. 17:32–35.

Romm, Joseph J., et al.
1996   "Mideast Oil Forever?" *Atlantic Monthly* 277, no. 4:57–74.

Roniger, Luis
1990   *Hierarchy and Trust in Modern Mexico and Brazil.* New York: Praeger.

Rordorf, Willy
1968   *Sunday: The History of the Day of Rest and Worship.* Philadelphia: Westminster.
1969   "Le sacrifice eucharistique." *Theologische Zeitschrift* 25:335–53. Reprinted in Rordorf 1986: 73–91.
1970   "Eglise de l'attente." *Communion* 95:86–96.
1971   "La vigne et le vin dans la tradition juive et chrétienne." *Université de Neuchatel, Annales 1969–1970*, pp. 131–46. Reprinted in *Liturgie, foi et vie des premiers chrétiens.* Paris: Beauchesne, 1986, pp. 493–508.

1972a   "Le baptême selon la *Didaché*." In *Mélanges liturgiques offerts au R.P. Dom Bernard Botte O.S.B.*, 499–509. Louvain. Reprinted in Rordorf 1986: 175–85. Translated and reprinted as "Baptism according to the *Didache*," in *The Didache in Modern Research*, edited by Jonathan A. Draper (Leiden: E. J. Brill, 1996), 212–22.

1972b   "Un chapitre d'ethique judéo-chrétienne: les deux voies." *Recherches de science religieuse* 60:109–28. Translated and reprinted as "An Aspect of the Judeo-Christian Ethic: The Two Ways," in *The Didache in Modern Research*, edited by Jonathan A. Draper (Leiden: E. J. Brill, 1996), 148–64.

1973   "La rémission des péchés selon la *Didache*." *Irénikon* 46:283–97. Reprinted in *Liturgie et rémission des péchés*, edited by A. Pistoia et al., (Rome: Edizioni Liturgiche), 225–38. Reprinted in Rordorf 1986: 209–23.

1975   "Une nouvelle edition de la *Didache*." *Studia Patristica* 15, no. 1:26–36.

1978a   *La doctrine des douze apôtres*. Translation of Greek and critical notes by A. Tuilier. Paris: Cerf.

1978b   "The *Didache*." In *The Eucharist of the Early Christians*, edited by Willy Rordorf et al., 1–23. Translated by M. J. O'Connell from the 1976 French orig. New York: Pueblo. French orig. reprinted in Rordorf 1986: 187–207

1980   "The Lord's Prayer in the Light of its Liturgical Use in the Early Church." *Studia Liturgica* 14:1–19.

1981   "Le problème de la transmission textuelle de *Didache* 1,3b–2,1." *Überlieferungsgeschichtliche Untersuchungen*, 139–53. Reprinted in Rordorf 1986: 499–513.

1986   *Liturgie, foi et vie des premiers chrétiens: Etudes patristiques* Paris: Beauchesne.

1991   "Does the *Didache* Contain Jesus Tradition Independently of the Synoptic Gospels?" In *Jesus and the Oral Synoptic Tradition*, edited by Henry Wansbrough, 394–423. Sheffield: Sheffield Academic Press. Reprinted in Rordorf 1993: 330–59.

1993   *Lex orandi lex credendi*. Publications de la Faculté de Théologie de l'Université de Neuchâtel 11. Freiburg, Schweiz: Unitersitätsverlag.

1997   "Die Mahlgebete in *Didache* Kap. 9–10." *Vigiliae Christianae* 51, no. 3:229–46.

1998   *La doctrine des douze apôtres*. 1978a edition (above) republished with an appendix comprising an updated bibliography (pp. 211–20) and extended notes revising and completing the earlier edition (pp. 221–46). Paris: Cerf.

1999   "'Ta hagia tois hagiois,'" *Irénikon* 72, nos. 3–4:346–64.

2000   "L'histoire du salut entre le 'milieu du temps' et l'eschatologie ou lat dynamique du 'déjà' et du 'pas encore.'" *Positions Luthéiennes* 48:123–43.

Ross, H. J.

1922   "Divination." In *Encyclopedia of Religion and Ethics*, edited by James Hastings, 5:759–71. Edinburgh: T & T Clark.

Rousselle, Aline
1988   *Porneia: On Desire and the Body in Antiquity.* Translated by Felicia
        Pheasant from the 1983 French orig. Oxford: Basil Blackwell.
Russell, D. S.
1964   *The Method and Message of Jewish Apocalyptic.* Philadelphia: Westmin-
        ster.
Russell, Jeffrey Burton
1997   *A History of Heaven: The Singing Silence.* Princeton: Princeton Univer-
        sity Press.
Sabatier, Paul
1885   *La Didachè or L'enseignement des douze apôtres.* Paris: Librairie Fis-
        chbacher.
Saldarini, Anthony J.
1994   *Matthew's Christian-Jewish Community.* Chicago: University of
        Chicago Press.
Sanders, E. P.
1977   *Paul and Palestinian Judaism.* Philadelphia: Fortress.
1985   *Jesus and Judaism.* Philadelphia: Fortress.
1990   *Jewish Law from Jesus to Mishnah.* London: SCM Press.
1992   *Judaism: Practice & Belief 63 BCE – 66 CE.* London: SCM Press.
Satlow, Michael L.
1997   "Jewish Constructions of Nakedness in Late Antiquity." *JBL* 116, no.
        3:429–54.
Schaff, P.
*1885   *The Oldest Church Manual Called the Teaching of the Twelve Apostles.*
        Edinburgh: Clark.
Schermann, Theodor
1914   *Die allgemeine Kirchenordnung, frühchristliche Liturgien und kirchliche
        Überlieferung.* Heft 1–3. Paderborn: Ferdinand Schöningh.
Schieber, David A.
1986   *Contagious Elements of the Early Christian Church and How They Have
        Been Appropriated at a New Church Development.* Louisville: Presbyte-
        rian Theologial Seminary.
Schillebeeckx, Edward
1969   "The Catholic Understanding of Office in the Church." *TS* 30:567–87.
1980   *Christ: The Experience of Jesus as Lord.* New York: Seabury Press.
1981   *Ministry: Leadership in the Community of Jesus Christ.* New York: Cross-
        road.
1985   *The Church with a Human Face.* New York: Crossroad.
Schmidt C.
1925   "Das Koptische *Didache*-Fragment des British Museum." *ZNW*
        24:81–99.
Schnackenburg, Rudolph
1963   *God's Rule and Kingdom.* Translated by J. Murray from 1959 German
        orig. New York: Herder & Herder.
Schneemelcher. *See* Hennecke.
Schneiders, Sandra M.
1986   "Theology and Spirituality: Strangers, Rivals, or Partners?" *Horizons*
        13, no. 2:253–74.

Schöllgen, Georg
1991   *Didache: Zwölf-Apostel-Lehre.* Fontes Christiani 1. Freiburg: Herder.
1996   "The *Didache* as a Church Order: An Examnation of the Purpose for the Composition of the *Didache* and its Consequences for its Interpretation." In *The Didache in Modern Research,* edited by Jonathan A. Draper, 43–71. Leiden: E. J. Brill.

Schottroff, Luise
1995   *Lydia's Impatient Sisters: A Feminist Social History of Early Christianity.* Translated by Barbara and Martin Rumscheidt from the 1994 German orig. Louisville, Ky.: Westminster John Knox.

Schürer, Emil
1986   *A History of the Jewish People in the Age of Jesus Christ.* 3 volumes. Translated and revised by Geza Vermes et al. Edinburgh: T & T Clark.

Schüssler Fiorenza, Elisabeth
1984   *In Memory of Her: A Feminist Theological Reconstruction of Christian Origins.* New York: Crossroad.
1993   *Discipleship of Equals: A Critical Feminist Ekklēsia-logy of Liberation.* New York: Crossroad.

Schwartz, Daniel R.
1983   "Two Pauline Allusions to the Redemptive Mechanism of the Crucifixion." *JBL* 102, no. 2:259–79.

Schweitzer, Eduard
1961   *Church Order in the New Testament.* Translated by Frank Clarke from the 1959 German orig. London: SCM Press.

Scott, R. B. Y.
1958–59
        "'Behold He Cometh with Clouds.'" *NTS* 5:127–32.

Seeliger, Hans Reinhard
1989   "Erwägungen zu Hintergrund und Zweck des apokalyptischen Schlusskapitels der *Didache.*" *Studia Patristica* 21:185–92.
1996   "Considerations on the Background and Purpose of the Apocalyptic Final Chapter of the *Didache.*" In *The Didache in Modern Research,* edited by Jonathan A. Draper, 373–82. Leiden: E. J. Brill.

Sered, Susan Starr
1994   *Priestess, Mother, Sacred Sister: Religions Dominated by Women.* Oxford: Oxford University Press.

Simoons, Frederick J.
1994   *Eat Not This Flesh: Food Avoidances from Prehistory to the Present.* Madison: University of Wisconsin Press.

Skarsaune, Oskar
1987   *The Proof from Prophecy.* Leiden: E. J. Brill.

Skehan, Patrick William
1963   "*Didache* 1,6 and Sirach 12,1." *Biblica* 44:533–36.

Slusser, Michael
1992   "Reading Silently in Antiquity." *JBL* 111, no. 3:499.

Smith, M. A.
1966   "Did Justin know the *Didache?*" *Studia Patristica* 7:287–90.

Sparks, H. F. D., ed.
1989   *The Apocryphal Old Testament.* Oxford: Clarendon Press.

Sparks, Jack N., ed. and trans.
1978   "The Teaching of the Twelve Apostles." In *The Apostolic Fathers.*
        Nashville: Thomas Nelson.
Stambaugh, John E.
1988   *The Ancient Roman City.* Baltimore: Johns Hopkins University Press.
Stanley, David M.
1955   "The *Didache* as a Constitutive Element of the Gospel-Form." *CBQ*
        17:336–48.
Stark, Rodney
1996   *The Rise of Christianity: A Sociologist Reconsiders History.* Princeton:
        Princeton University Press.
Steingraber, Sandra
1997   *Living Downstream: An Ecologist Looks at Cancer and the Environment.*
        Reading, Mass.: Addison-Wesley.
Steinhauser, Kenneth B.
1984   "Authority in the Primitive Church." *Patristic and Byzantine Review* 3,
        nos. 1–2:89–100.
Stevenson, Kenneth
1986   *Eucharist and Offering.* New York: Pueblo.
Stone, Michael E.
1976   "List of Revealed Things in the Apocalyptic Literature." In *Magnalia
        Dei: The Mighty Acts of God,* edited by Frank Moore Cross, 414–52.
        Garden City, N.Y.: Doubleday.
Stone, Michael E., ed.
1984   *Jewish Writings of the Second Temple Period.* Philadelphia: Fortress.
Stott, Wilfrid
1965–66
        "A Note on the Word *kyriakē* in Rev. I. 10." *NTS* 12:70–75.
Strand, Kenneth A.
1966–67
        "Another Look at 'Lord's Day' in the Early Church and in Rev. I. 10."
        NTS 13:74–181.
1982a   "The 'Lord's Day' in the Second Century." In *The Sabbath in Scripture
        and History,* edited by Kenneth A. Strand, 346–51. Washington, D.C.:
        Review and Herald.
1982b   "The Sabbath and Sunday from the Second Through the Fifth Cen-
        turies." In *The Sabbath in Scripture and History,* edited by Kenneth A.
        Strand, 323–32. Washington, D.C.: Review and Herald.
Streeter, H.
1936   "The Much-belaboured *Didache*." *JTS* 37: 369–74. → Connolly
Stuhlmueller, Carroll
1988   *Rebuilding with Hope: A Commentary on the Books of Haggai and
        Zechariah.* Grand Rapids: Eerdmans.
Suggs, M. J.
1972   "The Christian Two-Way Tradition." In *Studies in the New Testament
        and Early Christian Literature,* 60–74. Leiden, E. J. Brill.
Swidler, Leonard
1976   *Women in Judaism: The Status of Women in Formative Judaism.*
        Metuchen, N.J.: Scarecrow Press.

Talley, Thomas J.
  1976 "From Berakah to Eucharistia: A Reopened Question." *Worship* 50:115–37.
  1982 "The Eucharistic Prayer: Tradition and Development." In *Liturgy Reshaped,* edited by K. Stevenson. London: SPCK.
  1984 "The Literary Structure of the Eucharistic Prayer." *Worship* 58:404–20.
  1993 "Word and Sacrament in the Primitive Eucharist." In *Eulogēma,* edited by Ephrem Carr et al., 497–510. Rome: Ugo Detti.

Tarnas, Richard
  1991 *The Passion of the Western Mind.* New York: Harmony Books.

Taussig, Hal
  1992 Review of *Ursprung und Gestalten der frühchristlichen Mahlfeier* by Bernd Kollmann (Göttingen: Vandenhoeck & Ruprecht, 1990). *JBL* 111, no. 4:733–35.

Taylor, C.
  1886 *The Teaching of the Twelve Apostles with Illustrations from the Talmud.* Cambridge: Deighton Bell.

Taylor, Nicholas H.
  1995 "The Social Nature of Conversion in the Early Christian World." In *Modelling Early Christianity: Social-scientific Studies of the New Testament in its Context,* edited by Philip F. Esler. London: Routledge.

Telfer, W.
  1939 "The *Didache* and the Apostolic Synod of Antioch." *JTS* 40:133–46, 258–71.
  1944 "The 'Plot' of the *Didache*." *JTS* 45:141–51.

Theissen, Gerd
  1977 *Sociology of Early Palestinian Christianity.* Translated by John Bowden from 1977 German orig. Philadelphia: Fortress.
  1982 *The Social Setting of Pauline Christianity.* Translated by John H. Schütz from German articles published in 1974–1975. Philadelphia: Fortress.
  1992 "Nonviolence and Love of Our Enemies." In *Social Reality and the Early Christians,* 115–56. Minneapolis: Fortress.

Theissen, Gerd, and Annette Metz
  1998 *The Historical Jesus: A Comprehensive Guide.* Translated by John Bowden from 1996 German orig. Minneapolis: Fortress.

Tillich, Paul
  1955 *Biblical Religion and the Search for Ultimate Reality.* Chicago: University of Chicago Press.

Torjesen, Karen Jo
  1989 "Tertullian's 'Political Ecclesiology' and Women's Leadership." In *Studia Patristica,* volume 21, edited by Elizabeth A. Livingstone. Leuven: Peeters Press.

Trevett, Christine
  1983 "Prophecy and Anti-Episcopal Activity: A Third Error Combatted by Ignatius?" *JEH* 34:1–18.

Tsirpanlis, Constantine N.
  1982 "The Structure of the Church in the Liturgical Tradition of the First Three Centuries." *Patristic and Byzantine Review* 1, no. 1:44–62.

Tuckett, C. M.
　　1982　"The Sabbath, Sunday, and the Law in Luke/Acts." In *From Sabbath to Lord's Day: A Biblical, Historical, and Theological Investigation,* edited by D. A. Carson. Grand Rapids: Zondervan.
　　1989　"Synoptic Tradition in the *Didache.*" In *The New Testament in Early Christianity,* edited by Jean-Marie Sevrin, 197–230. Leuven: University Press. Reprinted in *The Didache in Modern Research,* edited by Jonathan A. Draper (Leiden: E.J. Brill, 1996), 92–128.

Tuilier, André
　　1962　*Evangélisation et catéchèse aux deux premiers siècles.* Paris.
　　1984　"Une nouvelle edition de la *Didache.*" *Studia Patristica* 15, no. 1:31–36.
　　1995　"La *Didache* et le probleme synoptique." In *The Didache in Context: Essays on Its Text, History and Transmission,* edited by Clayton N. Jefford, 110–30. Leiden: E. J. Brill.

Turner, M. Max B.
　　1982　"The Sabbath, Sunday, and the Law in Luke/Acts." In *From Sabbath to Lord's Day,* edited by D. Carson, 100–157. Grand Rapids: Zondervan.

Turner, Max
　　1992　"The Spirit of Prophecy and the Power of Authoritive Preaching in Luke-Acts: A Question of Origins." *NTS* 38:66–88.

Turner, Victor
　　1977　"Sacrifice as a Quintessential Process: Prophylaxis or Abandonment?" *History of Religions* 16:189–215.

Tyler, Alice Felt
　　????　"Millennial Madness." Waiting. (incomplete reference)

van de Sandt, Huub, and David Flusser
　　2002　*The Didache: Its Jewish Sources and Its Place in Early Judaism and Christianity.* Assen: Van Gorcum; Minneapolis: Fortress.

Vatican
　　1994　*Catechism of the Catholic Church.* Vatican City: Libraria Editrice Vaticana.

Vermès, Géza
　　1958　*Discovery in the Judean Desert.* New York: Desclee.

Viviano, Benedict T., and Justin Taylor, S.M.
　　1992　"Sadducees, Angels, and Resurrection (Acts 23:8–9)." *JBL* 111, no. 3:496–98.

Vokes, F. E.
　　1938　*The Riddle of the Didache: Fact or Fiction, Heresy or Catholicism?* London: SPCK.
　　1964　"The *Didache* and the Canon of the New Testament." *Studia Evangelica* 3:427–36.
　　1970　"The *Didache* — Still Debated." *Church Quarterly* 3:57–62.

Vööbus, A.
　　1968　*Liturgical Traditions in the Didache.* Stockholm: Estonian Theological Society in Exile.
　　1969　"Regarding the Background of the Liturgical Traditions in the *Didache.*" *Vigiliae Christianae* 23:81–87.

Vriezen, Theodorus C.
1975   "How to Understand Malachi 1:11." In *Grace Upon Grace,* edited by J.
        Cook. Grand Rapids: Eerdmans.
Waetjen, Herman C.
1976   *The Origins and the Destiny of Humanness: An Interpretation of the
        Gospel of Matthew.* Corte Madera, Calif.: Omega Books.
Wahlberg, R. C.
1975   *Jesus According to a Woman.* New York: Paulist.
Walker, Joan Hazelden
1962   "Terce, Sext and None: An Apostolic Custom?" *Studia Patristica*
        5:206–12.
1978   "A pre-Marcan Dating for the *Didache*: Further Thoughts of a Litur-
        gist." *Studia Biblica* 3:403–11.
Waterhouse, S. Douglas
1982   "The Planetary Week in the Roman West." In *The Sabbath in Scripture
        and History,* edited by Kenneth A. Strand, 308–22. Washington, D.C.:
        Review and Herald.
Watts, John D. W.
1985   *Isaiah 1–33.* Word Biblical Commentary 24. Waco, Tex.: Word Books.
Weeden, Theodore J., Sr.
1971   *Mark—Traditions in Conflict.* Philadelphia: Fortress.
Weinfeld, Moshe
1992   "Grace After Meals in Qumran." *JBL* 111, no. 3:427–40.
Weiss, Johannes
1971   *Jesus' Proclamation of the Kingdom of God.* Introduction (pp. 1–54) and
        translation by Richard Hyde Hiers and David Harrimore Holland from
        the 1892 German orig. Philadelphia: Fortress.
Wengst, Klaus
1984   *Didache (Apostellehre), Barnabasbrief, Zweiter Klemensbrief, Schrift an
        Diognet.* Darmstadt: Wissenschaftliche Buchgesellschaft.
1987   *Pax Romana and the Peace of Jesus Christ.* Translated by John Bowden
        from the 1986 German orig. Philadelphia: Fortress.
Wernberg-Möller, P.
1957   *The Manual of Discipline:* Translated and annotated with an introduc-
        tion. Leiden: E. J. Brill.
White, Joel R.
1997   "'Baptized on account of the Dead': The Meaning of 1 Corinthians
        15:29 in its Context." *JBL* 116, no. 3:487–99.
White, L. Michael
1998   "Regulating Fellowship in the Communal Meal: Early Jewish and
        Christian Evidence." In *Meals in a Social Context: Aspects of the Com-
        munal Meal in the Hellenistic and Roman World,* 177–205. Aarhus:
        Aarhus University Press.
Wilken, Robert
1971   *The Myth of Christian Beginnings.* Notre Dame, Ind.: University of
        Notre Dame Press.
Williams, James G.
1989   "Neither Here nor There: Between Wisdom and Apocalyptic in Jesus'
        Kingdom Sayings." *Forum* 5:7–30.

1991   *The Bible, Violence, and the Sacred: Liberation From the Myth of Sanctioned Violence.* San Francisco: Harper.

Williams, Sam K.

1975   *Jesus' Death as Saving Event: The Background and Origin of a Concept.* Harvard Dissertations in Religion 2. Missoula, Mont.: Scholars Press.

Willis, Wendell Lee

1985   *Idol Meat in Corinth: The Pauline Argument in 1 Corinthians 8 and 10.* SBL Dissertation Series 68. Chico, Calif.: Scholars Press.

Wilson, Luke P.

1996   "Does the Bible Teach Baptism for the Dead?" Institute for Religious Research. http://www.irr.org/mit/baptdead.html

Wilson, R.

1979   "Prophecy and Ecstasy: A Reexamination." *JBL* 98:321–37.

Wink, Walter

1991   "Neither Passivity nor Violence: Jesus' Third Way." *Forum* 7, nos. 1–2:5–28. Reprinted in *The Love of Enemies and Retaliation in the New Testament,* edited by Willard M. Swartley (Louisville: Westminster/ John Knox, 1992), 102–25.

1992   *Engaging the Powers: Discernment and Resistance in a World of Domination.* Minneapolis: Fortress.

Winkler, Gabriele

1976   "The History of the Syriac Prebaptismal Anointing in the Light of the Earliest Armenian Sources." *Symposium Syriacum* 317–24.

1978   "The Original Meaning of the Prebaptismal Anointing and its Implications." *Worship* 52:36ff.

Wise, Michael, et al.

1996   *The Dead Sea Scrolls: A New Translation.* San Francisco: HarperSanFrancisco.

World Council of Churches (WCC)

1977   *One Baptism, One Eucharist, and a Mutually Recognized Ministry.* Faith and Order Paper No. 73. Geneva: World Council of Churches.

Young, Brad

1984   *The Jewish Background to the Lord's Prayer.* Austin: Center for Jewish-Christian Studies.

1989   *Jesus and His Jewish Parables.* New York: Paulist.

Zizioulas, John D.

1983   "Episkope et épiskopos dans l'église primitive: Bref inventaire de la documentation." *Irénikon* 56, no. 4:484–502.

Zumstein, Jean

1982   "Matthieu à la croisée des traditions syro-palestiniennes." *Foi et Vie* 81:3–11.

Index of *Didache* References

Index of Subjects

menstrual uncleanness, 134, 170

mentor: honored as the Lord, 148; the model of transformation implied by graced mentoring, 848; one assigned to each novice, 76; remembered night and day, 103, 147, 359, 664; as spiritual parent, 147

mentoring. *See* training.

messianic age, 339, 367, 663, 678, 680

Midrash Rabbah, 830, 831

Miller, William, 628, 629, 632

Mishnah, 66, 113, 148, 186, 261, 293, 294, 296, 298–303, 310, 311, 314, 334, 335, 344, 360, 364, 407, 420, 437, 447, 455, 498, 502, 511–13, 557–60, 761, 798, 845; *Abot/Avot*, 664, 776; *Baba Mesia*, 148; *Baba Qamma*, 113, 761; *Berakhot*, 310, 314, 334, 335, 338, 342,

Index of Authors

Electronic Aids for the Study of the Didache

1. **Audio Cassette** — When I orally enact the *Didache*, the flow and unity of the production become aurally evident. Accordingly, *EasyGreek Software* has recorded my oral presentation (25 min.) and, on the reverse side, has recorded the feminist adaptation by Deb Rose-Milavec. By listening to this cassette as you travel back and forth to class, you will make discoveries and develop insights for yourself. Portions of this cassette can also be played in the classroom. A CD version is anticipated.

2. **Interactive Software** — Most people like to discover things for themselves and not simply be told. Accordingly, I have pioneered an electronic case study investigation of the *Didache* that allows you to take charge of your own learning. By unpacking the mysteries of the Didache communities for yourself, you will learn more easily, more enjoyably, and more deeply.

- *Didache Explorations* is an interactive electronic Case Study that enables you to conduct hands-on explorations of the *Didache*. Resources at your fingertips open up the cultural and religious milieu in which it was framed.
- The Warm Up perks your interest, the Sleuthing empowers you to make hunches, the Debriefing consolidates and verifies your results.
- A Guardian Angel (consisting of hidden subroutines) watches over your progress and, in unexpected moments, offers encouragement and advice in response to your input.
- You type in your hunches as you go, keep electronic journals, and engage in a debriefing interchange with your Guardian Angel.
- Software arrives on a 3.5" HD diskette, loads effortlessly into any version of MS Windows, and offers soothing colors, relaxing animations, and self-selected mood music. An enhanced CD-ROM version ($18 each) is also available.

3. **Web Sites** — For articles, exchanges, feedback, go to *www.Didache.info* and *www.JesusWomen.com*.

Order Form

Please rush me [   ] copy of the **audio cassette** ($12 each) and [   ] copy of the **interactive software** ($15 each) described above. I enclose a check or money order made out to "Aaron Milavec" for the amount of $_____. Ohio residents add 7% sales tax. After April 2004, see website for price changes.

Select one: {   } Send to the address on my check; {   ] Use the address label I have enclosed with this order. I understand that satisfaction is guaranteed and shipping costs ($5) are waived within the USA.

EasyGreek Software
attn: Dr. Aaron Milavec
P.O. Box 247
Piqua, OH 45356